International Labor and Employment Laws

Volume II

Second Edition

BNA Books Authored by the ABA Section of Labor and Employment Law

Covenants Not to Compete: A State-by-State Survey

The Developing Labor Law

Discipline and Discharge in Arbitration

Elkouri & Elkouri: How Arbitration Works

Employee Benefits Law

Employee Duty of Loyalty: A State-by-State Survey

Employment Discrimination Law

Employment Termination: Rights and Remedies, 2003 Supplement

Equal Employment Law Update

The Fair Labor Standards Act

How ADR Works

How to Take a Case Before the NLRB

International Labor and Employment Laws

Labor Arbitration: A Practical Guide for Advocates

Labor Arbitration: Cases and Materials for Advocates

Labor Arbitrator Development: A Handbook

Labor Union Law and Regulation

Occupational Safety and Health Law

The Railway Labor Act

Tortious Interference in the Employment Context: A State-by-State Survey

Trade Secrets: A State-by-State Survey

Wage and Hour Laws: A State-by-State Survey

International Labor and Employment Laws

Volume II

Second Edition

Editors-in-Chief

William L. Keller
Hunton & Williams
Dallas, Texas

Timothy J. Darby
The Bureau of National Affairs, Inc.
Washington, D.C.

Senior Editors

Carl Bevernage
Loyens
Brussels, Belgium

Renee S. Brown
The Bureau of National Affairs, Inc.
Washington, D.C.

Donald C. Dowling, Jr.
Proskauer Rose LLP
New York, New York

Matthew W. Finkin
University of Illinois College of Law
Champaign, Illinois

Roy L. Heenan
Heenan Blaikie
Montreal, Quebec, Canada

Jorge F. Perez-Lopez
U.S. Department of Labor
Washington, D.C.

Patrick M. Scanlon
Communications Workers of America
Washington, D.C.

International Labor Law Committee
Section of Labor and Employment Law
American Bar Association

The Bureau of National Affairs, Inc., Washington, D.C.

Library of Congress Cataloging-in-Publication Data

International labor and employment laws / editors-in-chief, William L. Keller, Timothy J. Darby ; senior editors, Carl Bevernage ... [et al.] ; International Labor Law Committee, Section of Labor and Employment Law, American Bar Association.-- 2nd ed.
p. cm.
Includes bibliographical references.
ISBN 1-57018-451-8
1. Labor laws and legislation. 2. Labor laws and legislation, International. I. Keller, William L., 1926- II. Darby, Timothy J. III. American Bar Association. International Labor Law Committee.

K1705.I58 2004
341.01--dc22

2003065337

Published by BNA Books
1231 25th Street, N.W., Washington, D.C. 20037
http://www.bnabooks.com

International Standard Book Number 1-57018-451-8
Printed in Canada

BOARD OF EDITORS

Australia
JORDAN W. COWMAN
Akin Gump Strauss Hauer & Feld LLP
Dallas, Texas
KIMBERLY F. RICH
Baker & McKenzie
Dallas, Texas
IAN M. DIXON
Baker & McKenzie
Melbourne, Australia
TIM DIXON
Baker & McKenzie
Sydney, Australia

Bulgaria
ASSEN A. DJINGOV
Djingov, Gouginski, Kyutchukov and Velichkov
Sofia, Bulgaria

Chile
LAURENCE E. STUART
Legge, Farrow, Kimmitt, McGrath & Brown L.L.P.
Houston, Texas
IGNACIO P. GARCÍA
DIEGO FERRADA
Cruzat, Ortucar & MacKenna Ltd.
Members of Baker & McKenzie
Santiago, Chile

Czech Republic
LUBOŠ TICHÝ
ROSTISLAV PEKAŘ
Squire, Sanders & Dempsey, v.o.s.
Prague, Czech Rupublic

Hungary
KATALIN HOLLÓ
Squire, Sanders & Dempsey L.L.P.
Budapest, Hungary
DAVID J. MILLSTONE
Squire, Sanders & Dempsey L.L.P
Cleveland, Ohio

India
RAVI SINGHANIA
Singhania & Partners
New Delhi, India

Ireland
PAUL GLENFIELD
BRIAN BUGGY
TONY WALSH
Matheson Ormsby Prentice
Dublin, Ireland

Israel
FRANCES RADAY
The Hebrew University
Jerusalem, Israel

The Netherlands
E. GRACE VAN ARKEL
CEES J. LOONSTRA
Erasmus University
Rotterdam, The Netherlands

Poland
ANDRZEJ CZOPSKI
Miller, Canfield, W. Babicki i Wspólnicy Sp. k.
Gdynia, Poland

Russia
Evgeny A. Danilov
Pepeliaev, Goltsblat & Partners
Moscow, Russia
Scott T. Adams
Restructuring Associates Inc.
Washington, DC

Saudi Arabia
Douglas M. Nabhan
Williams, Mullen, Clark & Dobbins
Richmond, Virginia

Singapore
Cheong Min Lee
Rodyk & Davidson
Singapore

South Korea
C. W. Hyun
J.C. Jung
Hye C. Yu
Kim & Chang
Seoul, South Korea

Sweden
Reinhold Fahlbeck
Lund University
Lund, Sweden

Taiwan
Baldwin J. Lee
Allen Matkins Leck Gamble & Mallory LLP
San Francisco, California
Joseph S. Lee
Institute of Knowledge-Based Economy and Management
Taipei, Taiwan

Turkey
Noyan Turunç
Turunç and Savasçin
Istanbul, Turkey
Melda Sur
Dokuz Eylül University Faculty of Law
Izmir, Turkey

Ukraine
Helen Kryshtalowych
Squire, Sanders & Dempsey L.L.P.
Ludmila Pavlenko
The Silecky Firm, PC, affiliated with Squire, Sanders & Dempsey L.L.P.
Kyiv, Ukraine

Venezuela
Miguel A. Zaldivar, Jr.
Hogan & Hartson L.L.P.
Miami, Florida
Ramón A. Azpúrua
Steel Hector & Davis, S.C.
Caracas, Venezuela

FOREWORD

Since 1945 the ABA Section of Labor and Employment Law has expanded its stated purposes in response to the evolution of the field. Currently, they include the following: (a) to study and report upon continuing developments in the field of labor and employment law; (b) to provide a forum for members of the Association interested in the field of labor and employment law to meet and confer; (c) to assist the professional growth and development of practitioners in the field of labor and employment law; (d) to establish and maintain working liaison with state, federal, and, where applicable, multi-national agencies having jurisdiction over matters affecting labor and employment law toward achieving procedural reform and administrative due process; (e) to study and report upon proposed and necessary legislation and rule making within the field encompassed by the jurisdiction of this Section; (f) to promote justice, human welfare, industrial peace, and the recognition of the supremacy of law in labor-management relations and the employment relationship; and (g) to establish, moderate, and sponsor seminars, workshops, forums, and other programs promoting the advancement of knowledge and practice in the field of labor and employment law.

Through the publication of books such as *International Labor and Employment Laws* and through annual and committee meeting programs designed to provide a forum for the exchange of ideas, the Section has pursued these stated goals. Gradually, the Section has built a library of comprehensive legal works intended for the use of the Section membership as well as the bar generally.

The Section of Labor and Employment Law is pleased to provide this Second Edition of Volume II of the treatise on international labor and employment laws as part of its library of books published by BNA Books, a Division of The Bureau of National Affairs, Inc. The combined efforts of many individual authors recruited by the International Labor Law Committee of the Section are reflected in this work.

The Section wishes to express its appreciation to the committee, and in particular to the editors-in-chief, William L. Keller and Timothy J. Darby; to the senior editors, and to the chapter authors. This group has tried to accomplish two primary objectives: (1) to be equally balanced and nonpartisan in its viewpoints, and (2) to ensure the book is of significant value to the practitioner, student, and sophisticated nonlawyer. The views expressed herein do not necessarily represent the views of the American Bar Association, or its Section of Labor and Employment Law, or any other organization, but are simply the collective, but not necessarily the individual, views of the authors. Information on the affiliation of government employees who contributed to this work is for informational purposes and does not constitute any official endorsement of the information provided herein.

HOWARD SHAPIRO
Chair
CHARLES A. WERNER
Chair-Elect
Section of Labor
and Employment Law
American Bar Association

October 2004

PREFACE

As we observed in the First Edition, the expansion of international trade, investment, and business operations to a worldwide arena has brought considerable changes in the labor and employment law systems in place in many countries. As these changes continue to rapidly occur, there is an increasing need for attorneys in one country to communicate on an informed basis—and act as liaisons—with clients both in their own country and in foreign countries, and with attorneys in other countries (who are appropriately the experts concerning their countries' systems of law).

Thus, the time seemed right for a First Edition of a concise Treatise setting forth the content and differences in the highly diverse international labor and employment law systems in place, furnishing the reader with basic research materials needed to understand the system in a particular country, or to compare the systems of two or more countries. This judgment proved correct; the initial Volume of this work was well received, and the Treatise has now grown into two Volumes, with additional country chapters in preparation. Two of those new chapters, on labor and employment law in India and Russia, are included in this second edition of Volume II. In addition, the chapter on Turkey is completely revised following the introduction of a new labor code in that country. This Volume covers developments through 2003, with a few updates into 2004.

The purpose of the Volumes is not to present an exhaustive discussion of the different systems of law, but rather to provide basic knowledge of the statutory and regulatory systems of the countries covered. The authors have attempted to describe the most prominent features in each country covered, in straightforward, understandable language. The complete outline sent to the author contributors is reproduced below, in the hope that it will give readers a meaningful overview of the broad subject matter approach that has been taken in preparing the work.

This Treatise remains a work in progress. Both Volumes I and II will continue to be supplemented periodically, and from time to time chapters on additional countries will be added, as was done in this Volume. Firms that have expertise in the labor and employment law systems of one or more countries not covered in these Volumes, and who have an interest in writing a chapter for publication, are requested to contact William L. Keller.

Deepest thanks are given to the members of the Senior Editorial Board, Carl Bevernage, Renee S. Brown, Donald C. Dowling, Jr., Matthew W. Finkin, Roy L. Heenan, Jorge F. Perez-Lopez, and Patrick M. Scanlon; and to the author contributors of the chapters, all of whom are fully identified herein. Without their strong commitment, many talents, expertise, and tireless work this publication would never have been possible.

WILLIAM L. KELLER
TIMOTHY J. DARBY
Editors-in-Chief

Dallas, Texas
Washington, D.C.
October 2004

Outline of Topics

The chapters were written following the basic outline shown below. Where the authors deviated from that outline, it was in the interest of giving a better, more understandable explanation of the law. They have, however, tried to at least cover, in some way, the points listed if relevant to the country they were writing about.

INTRODUCTION

A. Basic makeup of the government (legislative, executive, judicial?)
B. General sources of labor/employment law—domestic, international (membership in ILO, European Union?)
C. Division of responsibility for labor/employment law between federal and state or provincial and local governments
D. Major administrative bodies responsible for overseeing labor/ employment law regulatory system (with cross-references to later, more detailed discussions in the chapter)
E. Structure of judicial/dispute resolution system for labor law, including appeals system

I. INDIVIDUAL EMPLOYMENT

A. Individual Contract of Employment
    1. Historical Background
    2. Summary of main legal instruments regulating the individual contract of employment
    3. What forms of atypical employment are not covered by these laws (e.g., part-timers)?
B. Statutory Regulation of Employment
    1. Must an employer list job vacancies with the regional labor bureau?
C. Substance of the Individual Contract of Employment
    1. Mandatory terms in the contract
    2. Notice Periods
    3. Presumption of Term (indefinite or employee at will)
    4. Incorporation of terms in a collective agreement
D. Employee Dismissal
    1. Can the employer dismiss an employee for cause without warning or notice?
    2. Can the employer dismiss an employee without the union's or works council's approval?
    3. What employee conduct justifies dismissal? Is this set down in statutes or case law?
    4. How can the employee protest this dismissal?
5. Is there a government tribunal or other body that reviews complaints of unfair dismissal?

E. Privacy
  1. What laws if any govern this area in the employment context?
F. Employee Duty of Loyalty, Trade Secrets, Covenants Not to Compete
  1. What laws if any govern this area?

II. COLLECTIVE BARGAINING

A. Introduction
  1. Historical Background
  2. Summary of main legal instruments regulating collective bargaining
B. Union Recognition
  1. The Union Recognition Process
    a. How does a union become recognized for bargaining? Are there elections? Do workers indicate in some manner that the union is their representative?
    b. If workers elect a union as representative, describe the law regarding this process.
  2. Inter-union disputes. Does it happen that more than one union seeks to represent the same group of workers? If yes, how is this matter settled?
  3. Union Membership
    a. Aside from collective bargaining, do workers have a right to belong to a union? If yes, what is the source of this right?
    b. If there is a right to belong to a union, does this right extend to all workers, both public and private sector, and at all levels (including managers, high executives)?
    c. Does the employer have a right to know if a worker belongs to a union?
    d. Is a worker protected against discrimination in employment on the basis of union membership?
C. Level of Bargaining
  1. Summary of structure of bargaining
    a. Where does most bargaining take place—at plant, company, or industry level?
    b. Is bargaining local, regional, or national?
  2. Identity of the Signatory Parties
    a. Employers: Do employers negotiate through employers associations or individually?
    b. Unions: What level of the union is responsible for negotiating and signing the agreement?
    c. Does a central union federation coordinate bargaining?
D. Effect of the Agreement
  1. Is the collective agreement legally binding?
  2. If it is not legally binding, are its terms enforceable through the individual contract of employment?

3. Is the collective agreement binding on nonsignatory employers? If yes, how is the extension of the terms of the agreement accomplished (e.g., by ministerial decree, ministry regulations)?

E. Duration of the Collective Agreement
   1. Are collective agreements concluded for specific terms?
   2. If the agreement does not have a specific duration, does custom dictate when a new agreement is negotiated (e.g., the concept of the annual wage round, the Spring Wage Offensive, etc.)?
   3. When a collective agreement is deemed to have expired, do its terms survive in the individual contracts of employment? Can the employer unilaterally change the terms and conditions of employment?

F. Scope of the Collective Agreement
   1. Subjects of Bargaining. Must the parties, by law, bargain over certain subjects? If yes, list the subjects.
   2. Terms governing the employer-union relationship

G. Strikes and Other Industrial Action
   1. Strikes
   2. Lockouts
   3. Picketing
   4. Handbilling
   5. Slowdowns, sit-ins
   6. Secondary Action

H. Third Party Resolution of Disputes
   1. Are nongovernmental dispute resolution mechanisms used? If yes, how is the arbitrator or mediator elected?
   2. Is arbitration used? If yes, is the result binding on the parties?
   3. Is there a distinction between interest and rights disputes? If yes, are either or both types resolved through arbitration? What types of issues go to arbitration? Is arbitration used frequently?
   4. Is there judicial review of private arbitration awards?
   5. Is mediation or conciliation used?

I. Union Security
   1. Do employees have a right not to belong to a union?
   2. Does the union receive membership fees from workers? Can the union compel payment of such fees?
   3. Is the union obliged to represent non-members?
   4. Do all the terms of the collective agreement extend to non-members of the union?
   5. Does the union have the right to an office on company premises? If yes, who pays for this?
   6. Do union officers have the right to time off for duties connected to the collective agreement? If yes, is this paid time off? If yes, who pays for this?
   7. Do union officers have the right to time off for union training courses? If yes, is this paid time off? If yes, who pays for this?

III. Representation by Entities Other Than Unions

A. Introduction
   1. Historical Background
   2. Summary of main legal instruments regulating this other channel of employee representation
   3. Employer initiated forms of employee representation (e.g., consultation committees)

B. Establishment of the Works Council
   1. Must a works council exist in a company of a certain size or is it a voluntary option?
   2. How is a works council formed? Are there elections? If yes, describe any laws or regulations controlling this process.
   3. Are all employees represented by the works council or only certain classes of employees?

C. Scope of the Works Council's Powers
   1. Information Rights
   2. Consultation Rights
   3. Co-determination Rights
   4. Relationship between the works council and issues determined in the collective agreement

IV. Redundancy and Transfers of Undertakings

A. Redundancy
   1. Can an employer terminate employees for redundancy without warning or notice?
      a. Can the employer dismiss an employee without the union's or works council's approval?
      b. Must the labor ministry be notified? If yes, must it approve the redundancies before they can be carried out?
   2. What constitutes redundancy? Is this set down in statutes, regulations, or case law?
   3. If the employees disagree that a redundancy situation exists, what complaint mechanism is there?
   4. Must a redundancy payment be made by the employer? If yes, is there a mandatory formula for calculating the amount? If yes, is the actual amount paid often higher than that required by law?
   5. Is this subject covered in collective agreements?

B. Transfers of Undertakings
   1. Does a change in the ownership of an undertaking affect the employee's status especially in regard to the amount of service the employee has for purposes of the redundancy calculation?
   2. Which employer, the seller or the buyer, is responsible for making the redundancy payments to workers?

3. Must the new owner abide by the terms of the collective agreement that is in effect?
4. Must the new owner abide by the terms in the individual contracts of employment?

V. WAGES, HOURS, AND LEAVE

A. Wages
   1. Is there a minimum wage? If yes, what categories of workers does it cover?
   2. Overtime Pay
   3. Taxes (including Social Security)

B. Hours
   1. List any laws or regulations concerning
      a. The maximum length of the work day
      b. The maximum number of hours in a work week
      c. Restrictions on night work
      d. Restrictions on Sunday work
   2. Do any laws or regulations specify the payment of premium pay for work deemed to be in excess of a normal workday or work week?

C. Leave
   1. Do any laws or regulations mandate a specific amount of annual leave (vacation)? If yes, is this paid leave?
   2. Do any laws or regulations mandate the granting of time off for holidays? If yes, is this paid time off?
   3. Do any laws or regulations mandate pregnancy, childbirth, and/or family leave?
   4 Do any laws or regulations mandate time off for military service?

VI. ANTIDISCRIMINATION

A. Introduction
   1. Historical Background
   2. Summary of the main legal instruments regarding equality of treatment in employment

B. Protected Groups
   1. List the basis for protection (e.g., race, sex, religion, age)
   2. If handicap (disability) is not covered in an antidiscrimination statute, explain what laws relate to the employment of persons with disabilities.
   3. If pregnancy or maternity is not covered in an antidiscrimination statute, explain what laws and regulations relate to the employment of pregnant women or new mothers.
   4. Is there a mandatory maternity leave? If yes, what is the duration? If such a leave is paid, who pays for the leave?

SUMMARY CONTENTS

Part 2. NAFTA/NAALC and Member Countries

Part 3. Miscellaneous Countries*

*Countries organized by continent/region.

Part 4. International Organizations

Part 5. Multinational Corporations

DETAILED CONTENTS

Bulgaria—contd.

Bulgaria—contd.

Czech Republic—contd.

Czech Republic—contd.

Hungary—contd.

Hungary—contd.

Ireland—contd.

Ireland—contd.

Ireland—contd.

The Netherlands—contd.

The Netherlands—contd.

The Netherlands—contd.

The Netherlands—contd.

Poland—contd.

Sweden—contd.

Turkey—contd.

Turkey—contd.

Turkey—contd.

Part 2. NAFTA/NAALC and Member Countries

Member Countries

Part 3. Miscellaneous Countries*

Africa

Asia

*Countries organized by continent/region.

India—contd.

India—contd.

Singapore—contd.

South Korea—contd.

South Korea—contd.

South Korea—contd.

Taiwan—contd.

Taiwan—contd.

Taiwan—contd.

Russia—contd.

Ukraine—contd.

Israel—contd.

Israel—contd.

Saudi Arabia—contd.

Saudi Arabia—contd.

Oceania

Australia—contd.

Australia—contd.

Argentina—contd.

Chile—contd.

Chile—contd.

Chile—contd.

Venezuela—contd.

Venezuela—contd.

Venezuela—contd.

Part 4. International Organizations

Part 5. Multinational Corporations

PART 1

The European Union and Selected Member and Applicant Countries

BULGARIA*

INTRODUCTION

The Republic of Bulgaria is situated on the west coast of the Black Sea, with Romania to the north, Greece and Turkey to the south, and the former Yugoslavia to the west. It has a population of approximately eight million, placing it in the same category as Hungary, Austria, Belgium, and Sweden in terms of population size. After World War II, state industrialization policy promoted the growth of urban centers; however, over one-third of the population continues to live in rural areas.

Bulgaria had a communist form of government with only one legal political party, the Communist Party, from 1946 to 1990. As discussed below, a new Bulgarian Constitution was adopted early in 1990 to allow a multi-party political system.

Bulgaria has concentrated its resources on the development of certain industries, such as the production of mechanical handling equipment, pharmaceuticals, electrical engineering products, and electronics. Bulgaria's initial efforts to make the transition to a market economy were slow to take effect, so state-dominated industry continued to be the driving force of the national economy, accounting for about two-thirds of its economic output and employing nearly 40 percent of the working population, in the late 1990s. By 2001, Bulgaria's continuing efforts to make the transition to a market economy were more successful. As a result of the ongoing privatization process, state-dominated industrial enterprises are no longer the driving force of the national economy, although they continue to employ a significant number of individuals.

---

*Assen A. Djingov, Kalina Tchakarova, Djingov, Gouginski, Kyutchukov and Velichkov, Sofia, Bulgaria.

The 2002 Regular Report of the European Union (EU) on Bulgaria's progress toward meeting the criteria for membership stated that Bulgaria had made good further progress toward meeting the accession criteria. It also advised that while negotiations on Bulgaria's implementation of the EU social policy and employment chapter have been provisionally closed, Bulgaria should focus further efforts on continuing implementation of the *acquis communitaire* (i.e., the EU legislation, policies, and institutions) in the employment sector, particularly in the areas of antidiscrimination, equal opportunities for men and women, labor law, and occupational safety and health.

A. Constitutional Reform

The new Constitution of the Republic of Bulgaria, adopted on July 13, 1991,[1] reflects the aspiration to move from totalitarian political and economic control to a democratic free market society. The Constitution transformed the state into a parliamentary republic with plural political power and an economy based on free-market economic initiative. The new tripartite form of government in Bulgaria established by the Constitution consists of a legislative, executive, and judicial branch, each with its powers checked by the Constitutional Court.[2]

Under the new Constitution, the protection of investments and economic activities of Bulgarian and foreign, natural, and legal persons is declared to be a fundamental principle of law.[3] The Constitution expressly states that the national economy is based on free economic initiative and guarantees equal rights for all citizens and legal entities to engage in economic activities.[4] The Constitution further declares that private property rights are "inviolable and guaranteed by law."[5] As the basic law of the country, the new Constitution allows a greater degree of democracy, freedom,

---

[1]Constitution of the Republic of Bulgaria of 1991 (CONSTITUTION), published in *Darjaven Vestnik* (DV) No. 56 (1992).

[2]G. CURTIS, BULGARIA: A COUNTRY STUDY 2 (1993).

[3]CONSTITUTION art. 19(3).

[4]*Id.* art. 19(1).

[5]*Id.* art. 17(1), (3). The Constitution imposes restrictions on the private acquisition of land by foreigners, however. *Id.* art. 22(1).

autonomy, and creativity than existed under the prior constitution.[6] The new Constitution also fosters the progressive development of Bulgarian labor legislation.

1. *Form of Government*

The Constitution provides for a republican form of government led by a President directly elected by universal suffrage for a five-year term. The Bulgarian legislature, the National Assembly, is a unicameral body consisting of 240 elected numbers. The National Assembly elects the Council of Ministers, the highest administrative body in the government.

2. *The Courts*

The Constitution also establishes an independent judiciary and a Constitutional Court. The Supreme Court is located in the capital, Sofia. Trial courts are sited on a town or city basis, and appellate courts on a regional (county) basis. Special courts are established for the military.

Justice in the Republic of Bulgaria is administered by the Supreme Court of Appeals, the Supreme Administrative Court, the District Court of Appeal (regional and military), and the appellate and trial courts.[7] The Supreme Court of Appeals provides ultimate judicial supervision over the accurate and equal application of the laws of all courts.[8] The Supreme Administrative Court provides ultimate judicial supervision over the accurate and equal application of the law in the administrative justice system. This includes, for example, the authority to rule on disputes concerning the legality of acts promulgated by the Council of Ministers and individual ministers.[9]

As a general rule, the trial courts have original jurisdiction, and their decisions may be appealed to the District Court of Appeal and the Supreme Court. This is the so-called "full tier system": the trial court, District Court of Appeal, and Supreme Court.

---

[6] V. MRACHKOV, BULGARIA LABOR LAW 40 (1995).
[7] CONSTITUTION art. 119.
[8] *Id.* art. 124.
[9] *Id.* art. 125(1), (2).

The "two-tier system" refers to cases in which the District Court of Appeal decision is final and not appealable to the Supreme Court.

The Constitutional Court interprets the Constitution and rules on requests to decide the constitutionality of any law or legal act passed by the National Assembly or the President. Should a discrepancy between a law and the Constitution be found, the Supreme Court of Appeals or the Supreme Administrative Court will submit the matter to the Constitutional Court.[10] In addition, the Constitutional Court (1) settles disputes over the respective jurisdiction of the National Assembly, the President, and the Council of Ministers, and disputes between local self-governments and central executive bodies; (2) rules on the constitutionality of international treaties signed by the Republic of Bulgaria (prior to ratification); (3) determines the consistency between Bulgarian laws, universally accepted standards of international law, and the international treaties to which Bulgaria is a signatory; (4) issues opinions on disputes concerning the constitutionality of political parties and associations, the legality of elections of the President, the Vice-President, and national representatives; and (5) issues rulings on charges formulated in the National Assembly against the President or the Vice-President.[11]

B. Sources of Labor Law

1. *National Sources*

In addition to the Constitution, Bulgarian labor law is contained in a variety of normative acts issued by different state institutions and agencies. These acts can be categorized as follows:

- Laws of the National Assembly (the legislative body);
- Decrees adopted by the former State Council (which controlled until April 1990);
- Regulations and Ordinances promulgated by the Council of Ministers; and
- Instructions issued by the Council of Ministers.

---

[10] *Id.* art. 150(2).

[11] *Id.* art. 149.

a. Traditional Bulgarian Labor Law

Employment and labor relations in Bulgaria traditionally have been dominated by the central government, with the rights and obligations of individual employees, organized labor, and management established by statute. The traditional Bulgarian system that prevailed during the communist era allowed some involvement of employees in governing their relationship with employers, but strong national labor federations dominated collective representation.

The last major revision of the Bulgarian Labor Code to take place before the post-communist reform movement that began in 1989 was the 1986 Labor Code,[12] regulating both individual and collective labor contracts.

b. Recent Labor Law Reforms

Recent changes in Bulgarian labor law have occurred in the following areas:

- regulation of unemployment benefits,
- settlement of collective labor disputes, and
- amendments to the 1986 Labor Code.[13]

Labor Code amendments adopted during thc 1990s introduced new concepts and substantially changed the nature of Bulgarian labor law, reflecting the ongoing transition to a more democratic and decentralized social system and market economy.[14] With these amendments, the current labor law can be characterized as a mixture of traditional conservative norms, combined with a modest attempt to free the system from the existing bureaucracy and centralized governmental control. The reform process has been very tentative, however, and the Bulgarian Labor Code likely will need a more thorough revision in the near future to respond to changed economic and political conditions in the country.

---

[12]DV Nos. 26, 27 (1986), amended by DV No. 6 (1988), Nos. 21, 30, and 94 (1990), Nos. 27, 32, and 104 (1991), Nos. 23, 26, 88, and 100 (1992), Nos. 69, 87 (1995), and Nos. 2, 12, ad 28 (1996).

[13]MRACHKOV, *supra* note 6, at 39.

[14]*Id.* at 42.

One of the principal purposes of the labor laws is to set minimum standards for labor protection from which the parties to individual and collective labor contacts may deviate by mutual agreement. To this extent, the labor law permits freedom of contract. Despite the democratic trend reflected in the latest amendments to the Labor Code, however, there remain certain imperative legal norms that are not subject to negotiation by the parties in either individual or collective labor contracts. Examples include provisions on termination of the employment relationship, workers' disciplinary responsibility, and financial liability of the employee and the employer.[15]

Over the past few years, Bulgarian social policy and employment law have gradually been developing toward conformity with internationally accepted standards and the European Union's requirements. In 2001, 2002, and 2003, the following changes were made in Bulgarian labor law:

- Amendments to the Labor Code went into effect on March 31, 2001;[16]
- Amendments to the Labor Code entered into force on November 11, 2002, and January 2, 2003;[17]
- Provisions of the Law on Protection Against Unemployment and Encouragement of Employment (1997 Employment Law)[18] were replaced by a new Law on Encouragement of Employment, effective January 1, 2002 (2002 Employment Law),[19] and the 1997 Employment Law was abolished by the Law for Amendment of the Code on Social Security;[20]
- Amendments to the Labor Code were adopted February 25, 2003, September 30, 2003 (the latter entered into force on January 1, 2004), and October 28, 2003;[21]

---

[15]Termination is discussed below at I.E., discipline at I.D., and financial liability of employees at I.D.8.

[16]*See* 25 STATE GAZETTE (Mar. 16, 2001). See the discussion in the Introduction, at B.1.c., below.

[17]*See* 105 STATE GAZETTE (Nov. 8, 2002); 120 STATE GAZETTE (Dec. 29, 2002).

[18]See the Introduction, at B.1.d., below.

[19]*See* 112 STATE GAZETTE (Dec. 29, 2001).

[20]*See* 67 STATE GAZETTE (July 29, 2003).

[21]*See* 18 STATE GAZETTE (Feb. 25, 2003); 86 STATE GAZETTE (Sept. 30, 2003); 95 STATE GAZETTE (Oct. 28, 2003).

- Amendments to the Law on Encouragement of Employment;[22] and
- Adoption of a new Law on Protection Against Discrimination.[23]

The changes in Bulgarian labor legislation in 2001 and 2002 were aimed at the development of a more precise legal framework for collective bargaining and a more strict regulatory policy of the labor market. The 2003 amendments were initiated to further harmonize Bulgarian labor legislation with the *acquis communautaire*.

c. *The Labor Code*

Article 1, paragraph 3, of the Labor Code, regarding the protective purpose and function of Bulgarian labor legislation, was replaced by a more detailed provision, which reads as follows: "This Code guarantees the freedom and protection of labor and fair labor conditions, as well as the social dialogue between the state, employees and workers, employers and their organizations in the process of regulation of labor and directly related to labor relations." Recent amendments to the Labor Code are discussed below in chronological order.

i. *1990 revision*

In response to the massive strike movement that rapidly grew in early 1990, the Council of Ministers adopted the new Law on the Settlement of Collective Labor Disputes.[24] This was the first time in the history of Bulgarian labor legislation that the right to strike had been expressly recognized and a procedure for settlement of collective labor disputes was established.[25]

ii. *1992 revision*

The Labor Code amendment of November 1992 reflected the country's effort to move to a market economy and a more decen-

---

[22]*See* 26 STATE GAZETTE (Mar. 21, 2003); 86 STATE GAZETTE (Sept. 30, 2003); 114 STATE GAZETTE (Dec. 30, 2003).

[23]*See* 86 STATE GAZETTE (Sept.30, 2003), in force as of Jan. 1, 2004.

[24]DV No. 21 (1990), amended by DV No. 27 (1991).

[25]MRACHKOV, *supra* note 6, at 40. See also II.B., below.

tralized model of regulation. For the first time, the amended Labor Code legalized and established by law a system of tripartite participation among the government, the national representative organization of employers, and the national representative organizations of employees.[26]

iii. 1996 revision

Until 1996, collective bargaining in Bulgaria was within the exclusive province of large trade unions.[27] The significant changes effected by the 1996 revision of the Labor Code established a more flexible, decentralized approach in government regulation of labor relations.[28] This is consistent with the overall trend to a less centralized economic system as part of the national effort to promote political stability and economic growth.

iv. 2001 revision

The 2001 Labor Code amendments were initiated by the Association of Bulgarian Employers. The amendments were intended to harmonize Bulgarian labor legislation with EU standards and reflected the ongoing trend toward liberalization of the labor market. The amendments affected many Labor Code provisions, including those regulating collective bargaining, annual paid leaves, working time, termination of employment, and fixed-term labor contracts.

v. 2002 revision

The 2002 amendments to the Labor Code, as detailed by the newly issued Regulation No. 5 on the Contents and the Procedure for Delivery of the Notification under Article 62, paragraph 4 of the Labor Code, introduced new requirements to be followed by employers regarding the execution, amendment, and termination of employment agreements. Pursuant to these, employers are obliged to inform the Bulgarian National Social Security Institute

---

[26]MRACHKOV, *supra* note 6, at 29.

[27]*Id.* at 28. Collective bargaining is discussed at II., below.

[28]A significant change was made to ch. 9 of the Labor Code dealing with employee discipline. See I.D.1., below.

(NSSI) of the execution and termination of labor contracts, as well as about certain amendments thereto. The information is to be provided in a standard form notification letter in a relatively short period of time. This reporting is intended to increase the regulatory effect of the state over labor relations and to lower the size of the "grey economy" (underground economy) in the employment sector. These amendments are discussed in the appropriate locations below.

vi. 2003 revision

The 2003 amendments to the Labor Code imposed restrictions on the possibilities for becoming a civil servant.[29] The criteria cover conflict of interests arising from the family, business, professional, social, or political activities the potential employee is engaged in that might influence potential labor contract performance. The employee has to give due notice in such circumstances. If the civil servant fails to comply with the notification obligation imposed, the employer has the right to terminate the employment contract without prior notification.

The amendments to the Labor Code also focus on the conditions and procedure for obtaining labor permission by minors. These issues are to be addressed in a regulation issued by both the Minister of Labor and Social Policy and the Minister of Public Healthcare.[30]

d. Employment Laws

i. 1997 Employment Law

The Law on Protection Against Unemployment and the Encouragement of Employment[31] (1997 Employment Law) was promulgated by the 38th National Assembly in 1997. The 1997 Employment Law regulates the administration of social assistance provided to the unemployed, and also contains provisions on the encouragement and support of employment, professional qualifications, and regulations and procedures relating to the employ-

---

[29]In effect as of Jan. 1, 2004.

[30]These amendments are discussed at VI.A., below.

[31]DV No. 120 (1997), in effect as of Jan. 1, 1998.

ment of Bulgarian citizens abroad and the employment of foreigners in Bulgaria.[32] Effective January 1, 2002, provisions of the 1997 Employment Law regarding measures for encouraging employment were replaced by the new 2002 Employment Law. Additionally, the obligatory unemployment insurance regime is no longer subject to regulation by the specific legislation, but instead became part of the general social security regime, namely, the Code on Obligatory Social Insurance.[33] Voluntary unemployment and vocational qualification benefit contributions remain covered by the 1997 Employment Law (which was not renamed, even though it no longer governs the encouragement of employment).

ii. 2002 Employment Law

The 2002 Employment Law was promulgated by the National Assembly at the end of 2001 and became effective as of January 1, 2002.[34] The 2002 Law is aimed at the encouragement and support of employment, vocational counseling, training and retraining, coordination of employment information, and the employment of Bulgarian citizens abroad and foreign citizens within the Republic of Bulgaria. The 2002 Employment Law did not affect basic principles, but introduced more comprehensive and detailed regulations. Among the significant changes made by the 2002 amendments was the establishment of a new Employment Agency within the Ministry of Labor and Social Policy (and territorial divisions thereof).[35] The 2002 amendments also changed the definition of "collective dismissal" and the procedures for effecting collective dismissals.[36]

iii. 2003 revision of the 2002 Employment Law

The 2003 amendments[37] clarified the "collective dismissal" definition. The rights and obligations of persons actively looking

---

[32]1997 Employment Law art. 1. See also IX., below.

[33]Initially promulgated in 110 STATE GAZETTE (Dec. 17, 1999), last amended in 45 STATE GAZETTE (Apr. 30, 2002), in effect as of the promulgation date.

[34]*See* 112 STATE GAZETTE (Dec. 29, 2001).

[35]See the Introduction, at C., below.

[36]See IV.A., below.

[37]*See* 26 STATE GAZETTE (Mar. 21, 2003).

for a job previously enjoyed by refugees also are presently granted to persons with humanitarian status. The newly adopted Regulation for Implementation of the 2002 Employment Law[38] further developed more comprehensive and detailed rules regarding the status and functions of the employment bodies, procedures for adoption of a National Action Plan for Employment, funding and active labor policies, and rights and obligations of employers and persons actively looking for a job.

e. Ordinances and Regulations

The Council of Ministers adopted Ordinance No. 57[39] in 1989 in response to the rising unemployment rate, brought on by the widespread condition of economic disaster in Bulgaria. Ordinance No. 57 established regulations regarding unemployment benefits, vocational training, retraining of unemployment workers, and related matters.[40]

Other ordinances regulating labor relations include the following:

- Ordinance No. 4 of the Ministry of Labor and Social Policies for the Necessary Documents for the Conclusion of an Employment Contract;[41]
- Ordinance on the Negotiation of the Work Salary;[42]
- Ordinance on Additional and Other Work Remunerations;[43]
- Ordinance on Working Time, Rest Periods and Leaves;[44]
- Ordinance on Reduced Working Time;[45]
- Ordinance on the Hazardous and Heavy Working Conditions Prohibited for Women;[46]

---

[38]Promulgated in 58 STATE GAZETTE (June 27, 2003), in effect as of the promulgation date.

[39]*See* DV No. 96 (1989).

[40]MRACHKOV, *supra* note 6, at 40.

[41]*See* 44 STATE GAZETTE (May 25, 1993).

[42]*See* 55 STATE GAZETTE (July 12, 1991).

[43]*See* 67 STATE GAZETTE (Aug. 6, 1993).

[44]*See* 6 STATE GAZETTE (Jan. 23, 1987).

[45]*See* 59 STATE GAZETTE (July 19, 1993).

[46]*See* 58 STATE GAZETTE (July 6, 1993).

- Ordinance on the Registration of Data for Safe and Healthy Working Conditions;[47] and
- Ordinance No. 3 on the Procedure for Determining the Right to Additional Paid Leave for Work Under Harmful-to-the-Health Work Conditions or Work Under Special Conditions.[48]

In 1998, Ordinance No. 57 of 1989 was abolished by Ordinance No. 152, which simultaneously adopted the Regulation on Application of the Law on Protection Against Unemployment and Encouragement of Employment, providing for detailed regulation of the basic principles and rules set forth in the 1997 Employment Law. In 2002, by virtue of Ordinance No. 57,[49] the Regulation on Application of the Law on Protection Against Unemployment and Encouragement of Employment was abolished, and a new Regulation on Application of the 2002 Employment Law was adopted.

On April 19, 2001, a new Regulation No. 3 on the Minimum Requirements for Safe Working Environments and Protection of Employees' Health by Use of Personal Means of Protection was issued by the Minister of Labor and Social Policy and the Minister of Public Healthcare.[50]

In 2002, the Council of Ministers adopted several ordinances regulating labor relations, including:

- Ordinance on the Terms and Procedure for Issuance, Refusal and Withdrawal of Work Permits to Foreigners in the Republic of Bulgaria;[51] and
- Ordinance on the Terms and Procedure for Admission of Expatriates in the Republic of Bulgaria for Provision of Services.[52]

---

[47] *See* 32 STATE GAZETTE (1987).
[48] *See* 44 STATE GAZETTE (May 25, 1993).
[49] *See* 28 STATE GAZETTE (Mar. 19, 2002).
[50] See VII.A.2.a., below.
[51] *See* 39 STATE GAZETTE (Apr. 16, 2002), effective June 17, 2002.
[52] *See* 68 STATE GAZETTE (July 16, 2002), effective Sept. 17, 2002.

The legal framework for healthy and safe working conditions[53] was further detailed by two Regulations issued jointly by the Minister of Labor and Social Policy and the Minister of Public Healthcare, namely:

- Regulation No. 3 on the Minimum Requirements for Provision of Healthy and Safe Working Conditions in the Event of Operation with Video-displays,[54] abolishing Regulation No. 8 on the Sanitary Requirements to the Working Places for Operation with Video-displays; and
- Regulation No. 4 on the Protection of Employees from Risks Arising While Working with or Being Exposed to Biological Agents.[55]

In 2003, additional new regulations were adopted, namely:

- Regulation on the Conduct of Recruitment and Employment Agencies;[56]
- Regulation on the Protection of Workers from the Risks Related to Exposure to Asbestos at Work;[57]
- Regulation on the Protection of Workers from the Risks Related to Exposure to Noise at Work;[58]
- Regulation on the Protection of Workers from the Risks Related to Exposure to Chemical Agents at Work;[59] and
- Regulation on the Protection of Workers from the Risks Related to Exposure to Carcinogens and Mutagens.[60]

2. *International Sources*

International agreements and treaties to which Bulgaria is a party supersede domestic law. As discussed below, Bulgaria is a

[53]See VII.A. below.

[54]*See* 95 STATE GAZETTE (Oct. 8, 2002).

[55]*See* 105 STATE GAZETTE (Nov. 8, 2002), effective Feb. 9, 2003.

[56]*See* 49 STATE GAZETTE (May 27, 2003), in effect as of the promulgation date.

[57]*See* 32 STATE GAZETTE (Apr. 8, 2003), effective July 9, 2003.

[58]*Id.*

[59]*See* 8 STATE GAZETTE (Jan. 30, 2004), effective Jan. 31, 2005.

[60]Initially promulgated in 94 STATE GAZETTE (Oct. 24, 2003), last amended in 8 STATE GAZETTE (Jan. 30, 2004), in effect as of Jan. 31, 2005.

member of or seeking membership in a number of international organizations affecting labor and employment law.

a. European Union Membership

Bulgaria has actively pursued membership in the European Union (EU) and has achieved associate membership status under an agreement that calls for a reduction in trade restrictions, improved investment rules, and promotion of a closer political dialogue.[61]

In December 1997, Bulgaria was given pre-candidate status by the EU, rather than being invited to begin membership negotiations in March 1998 as were the Czech Republic and other Central European nations. The negotiations between the EU and Bulgaria opened in February 2000 and all 30 *acquis* chapters have been opened, 26 of which have been provisionally closed. The Copenhagen European Council stated that following the conclusion of the European Council in Brussels and depending on the further progress in complying with the membership criteria, the objective will be to welcome Bulgaria as a member of the European Union in 2007.

b. International Labor Organization

Bulgaria has ratified certain International Labor Organization (ILO) conventions, including those on Freedom of Association and Protection of the Right to Organize[62] and the Right to Organize and Collective Bargaining.[63] In 2002, Bulgaria ratified Convention No. 183 of the International Labor Organization, on the Protection of Maternity, and in 2003 it ratified Convention No. 180 of the International Labor Organization, on the Seafarer's Hours of Work and Manning of Ships Convention, 1996.[64]

---

[61] 2 E. EUR. REP. (BNA) 278. For a detailed discussion of the EU, see the chapter on the European Union in Volume I, Part 1.

[62] International Labor Organization Convention on Freedom of Association and Protection of the Right to Organize, 1948 (No. 87). For a detailed discussion of ILO conventions, see the chapter on the ILO in Volume I, Part 4.

[63] International Labor Organization Convention on the Right to Organize and Collective Bargaining, 1948 (No. 98).

[64] *See* 87 STATE GAZETTE (Oct. 3, 2003), effective Aug. 24, 2003.

c. Bilateral Treaties

In recent years the Bulgarian government has entered into a number of bilateral agreements with other countries with respect to employment relationships, particularly regarding employment of citizens of one country within the other based on the principle of reciprocity. These bilateral treaties govern, among other things, the competence for performance of intermediary activities vested in the Employment Agency of the Republic of Bulgaria. The Employment Agency is a specialized body within the Ministry of Labor and Social Policy.

C. Administration of the Labor Laws

The Ministry of Labor and Social Policies promulgates rules and regulations for the implementation of the labor laws, develops government policies on unemployment and employment matters, and protects the national employment market. It also issues ordinances and exercises overall supervision and control with respect to compliance with labor and employment laws.

Administration of labor laws is the responsibility of the General Labor Inspectorate, which is under the Ministry of Labor and Social Policies. The trade unions also have some oversight functions, although their role in this regard is significantly limited.

By virtue of the 2002 Employment Law, a new Employment Agency was established within the Ministry of Labor and Social Policy for implementation of state policies on encouragement of employment and protection of the labor market, for providing vocational information and counseling, and for coordinating employment information and recruitment. The Employment Agency has been constituted as a legal successor of the National Employment Office.

D. Resolution of Labor Disputes

Articles 357 to 363 of the Labor Code deal with disputes between employees and employers over the creation, existence, implementation, and termination of the employment relationship.[65] This

---

[65]Labor Code art. 357.

portion of the Code deals with rights under both individual employment contracts[66] and collective labor contracts.[67]

1. *Jurisdiction*

The 2002 amendments to the Labor Code introduced changes in the legal framework relating to the system of appeal for labor disputes resolution, as discussed below.[68]

a. *Trial Courts*

Unless a special act confers jurisdiction on another institution, all labor disputes are within the jurisdiction of the trial courts and are conducted pursuant to the rules of the Code of Civil Procedure.[69] The following individual grievances and labor disputes are not within the jurisdiction of the trial courts:

- dismissal of elected employees in state representative organizations, public organizations, or political parties and movements; and
- dismissal of high level state officials in the Council of Ministers, in the ministries, committees, agencies, and other central departments, in sections under the control of Ministries, county managers, and assistant county managers, and board directors in the county administration.[70]

Disputes as to the legality of elections[71] are heard by the district trial court.[72]

The 2001 Labor Code amendments clarified the categories of officials who are not subject to the jurisdiction of the trial courts in the event of dismissal.[73] This amendment aims to avoid the possibility of an incorrect interpretation of the term "high level state officials," by adding a reference to Article 28, paragraph 2 of the

---

[66]See I.A., below.
[67]See II.A., below.
[68]See the Introduction, at D.1.b., below.
[69]Labor Code art. 360.
[70]*Id.* art. 360(2), subs. 1–2.
[71]See I.A.7., below.
[72]Labor Code art. 87.
[73]*Id.* art. 360(2).

Law on State Administration, which enumerates the positions that meet this definition.

b. Appeals

Trial court decisions are appealable to the District Court of Appeal under the regular procedure and rules of the Code of Civil Procedure, except as excluded by special laws.

The 2002 Labor Code amendments abrogated Article 363 dealing with the appeals of court decisions on labor disputes. Corresponding amendments to the Code of Civil Procedure[74] introduced a one-tier appeals system for both individual and collective labor disputes, allowing appeals only to courts of second instance and not generally to courts of third instance as had been allowed pursuant to 2001 Labor Code amendments. However, a cassation appeal before the courts of third instance is possible by way of exception, for labor disputes related to (1) recognition of a dismissal as illegal, (2) reinstatement of the dismissed employee to his or her previous position, (3) payment of compensation for the period of unemployment due to illegal dismissal, and (4) payment of labor remuneration and compensation exceeding the amount of Bulgarian Leva (BGL) 5,000.

c. Foreign Nationals and Bulgarian Employees Working Abroad

Labor disputes between employees who are foreign citizens and employers who are foreign nationals or joint ventures with a domicile in the Republic of Bulgaria are under the jurisdiction of the Bulgarian courts, unless otherwise agreed to by the parties.[75] Labor disputes between Bulgarian employees working abroad and their employers are under the mandatory jurisdiction of Bulgarian courts and the jurisdiction cannot be modified by agreement.[76]

---

[74] *See* 105 STATE GAZETTE (Nov. 8, 2002).

[75] Labor Code art. 361.

[76] *Id.* art. 362.

2. Procedures

The prosecution of a labor case is free of charge for the employee,[77] who is exempt from paying court costs or taxes, or any fees for the taking of depositions of experts or witnesses.

3. Statute of Limitations

Article 358 of the Labor Code imposes certain definite periods within which a labor dispute may be brought before the courts. These periods are:

- one month for disputes involving limited financial liability and to repeal a disciplinary penalty of a "reprimand";
- two months for labor disputes to repeal a warning of dismissal, to appeal a modification in the place of work or employment assignment, or to challenge a termination of employment; and
- three years for all other disputes.[78]

The running of these special statute of limitations periods commences with the act of charging an employer with financial liability or imposing a disciplinary sanction on an employee.[79]

I. INDIVIDUAL EMPLOYMENT

At the conclusion of a collective labor contract,[80] an affected employee and employer are free to negotiate more favorable employment conditions under an individual employment contract. The collective labor contract and the labor law and regulations provide the basic legal structure on which an individual employment contract should be negotiated. If the individual employment contract provides less favorable employment conditions for the worker than those provided in the collective labor contract or under the labor

---

[77]*Id.* art. 359.
[78]*Id.* art. 358(1).
[79]*Id.* art. 358(2).
[80]See II.A.5., below.

laws, the individual employment contract is thereby rendered null and void.[81]

A. Formation of the Employment Relationship

The Labor Code provides that an employment relationship may be established by the following means:

- an employment contract,
- an election,[82] or
- a competitive examination.

The employment relationship also may be established by government act, judicial decision, or appointment by government officials.

1. Capacity of the Worker

Both the individual worker and the employer must possess contractual capacity to enter into an employment relationship. Individuals are competent to contract when they reach 16 years of age. However, the law does recognize limitations on the employment capacity of certain categories of citizens, including, for example, the following:

- convicted criminals may not occupy certain state or public positions and may not be appointed to jobs involving accounting or financial responsibility;
- professional drivers who have had their driving licenses temporarily suspended are subject to limitations on their employment; and
- professional drivers, pilots, and engine drivers who have caused an intentional accident are deprived of the right to practice their profession for an indefinite period.

---

[81] Labor Code art. 74(1).

[82] See I.A.7., below.

2. *Capacity of the Employer*

Whether the employer is a natural or legal person, it must have the legal capacity to enter into an employment relationship. If the employer is a natural person, this requires mental capacity and attainment of legal age. If the employer is a corporate entity, it must satisfy the requirements of a juridical person (i.e., registration, minimum number of employees, and minimum amount of capital).

With regard to the capacity of an employer that is a legal entity, Bulgarian law does not require a minimum number of employees. Upon registration in the Commercial Registry of the District Court where the company has its principal place of business, it may employ individuals without any numerical limitations

3. *Form of the Employment Contract*

An employment contract is a written agreement[83] that is concluded between the employee and the employer.[84] The Labor Code does not provide a legal definition of the term "employment contract," but certain essential requirements are stated in the Code. Specifically, the contract must contain the following elements:

- parties,[85]
- time of conclusion and execution,[86] and
- place of performance of the labor duties;[87] and
- position of the employee.[88]

The employment contract may be signed by a group of persons, in which case the employer and each member of the group have the same rights and obligations as if the contract had been signed by each person separately.[89]

The 2002 Labor Code amendments abolished the exception to a requirement for a written agreement that previously was al-

---

[83]Labor Code art. 62.
[84]*Id.* art. 61.
[85]*Id.* art. 66.
[86]*Id.* art. 63.
[87]*Id.* art. 66(1).
[88]*Id.* art. 66(1).
[89]*Id.* art. 61(3).

lowed when an employer accepts an employee and the employee begins performance. As of January 2, 2003, employers are obliged to inform the Bulgarian National Social Security Institute (NSSI) about the execution of employment agreements and are prohibited from allowing the employee to commence the performance before the employer has furnished the employee with a certified copy of the notification filed with the NSSI.[90]

4. *Content of the Employment Contract*

The employment contract aggregates a variety of rights and obligations of the participating parties. Article 66(1) of the Labor Code specifies that in order to conclude an employment contract, both parties must have reached an agreement on three central issues: (1) the workplace, (2) the nature of the work, and (3) the amount of compensation.[91] These three elements constitute the core of the labor contract and are of great significance to both parties.

The "workplace" is the designation of the employee's work territory within the employing entity. It usually is stated as the enterprise's place of business, unless another meaning is specified in the labor contract.

The employer determines the "nature of the work" assigned to the employee, which includes the requirements for quality and quantity of the work expected. The employer is required to submit these requirements to the worker in a written job description.[92]

The "amount of compensation" specified in the contract includes both the employee's basic wages and any additional remuneration. Additional compensation may be determined according to "the quantity and quality of the work performed by the employee."[93]

An employment contract may expressly contain statements of other benefits in addition to the employee's compensation. Such

---

[90]Regulation No. 5 on the Contents and the Procedure for Delivery of the Notification under Art. 62 para. 4 of the Labor Code. *See* 1 STATE GAZETTE (Jan. 3, 2003), effective Jan. 2, 2003.

[91]Labor Code art. 66.

[92]*Id.* art. 62(3).

[93]*Id.* art. 247(1). Labor Code provisions regarding compensation are discussed at V.A., below.

additions may include housing, educational courses for professional development, and other provisions that are "more favorable to the employee than those provided for in the collective labor agreement."[94] As noted above, individual employment contract terms that are less favorable to the worker than those provided in the collective labor agreement or under labor laws are void.

5. *Job Applications*

The filing of a written job application and the issuance of a written order for employment are not obligatory. The parties to a future individual labor relationship are free to meet and discuss the parameters of their relationship orally and, as a result of such discussion, enter into an employment contract. However, the contract must be in writing.[95] In cases where the employer issues a written order of employment, the order does not have the effect of unilaterally determining the employee's remuneration. Because it is necessary to obtain the employee's agreement to the amount of remuneration, it is more precise to say that the written order is an acceptance of the employee's offer of employment and an offer by the employer regarding the amount of remuneration.

A job applicant must submit a written application, which constitutes an offer to contract. The applicant is required to attach to the job application his or her passport, education certificate, workbook, medical certificate, and, in the case of applicants younger than the age of 16, the applicant's special work authorization.[96]

If the employer accepts the offer, it issues a written order for the applicant's appointment to the position. The written order proves the existence of the employment contract and establishes clarity in the relations between the parties regarding the content of the employment contract and the moment of its conclusion.

---

[94]Labor Code art. 66(2).

[95]See I.A.3., above.

[96]Ordinance No. 4 of the Ministry of Labor and Social Policies for the Necessary Documents for the Conclusion of an Employment Contract, DV No. 44 (1993). See also VI.A., below.

6. *Time of Conclusion and Execution of the Employment Contract*

As of January 2, 2003, employers are prohibited from allowing employees to perform their obligations under their labor contracts unless the employer has furnished them with copies of their written labor contracts and certified copies of the standard form notifications sent to the NSSI. In the event of the employer's failure to observe any of these requirements to execute a labor agreement in writing, or to communicate the required information to the NSSI within the specified deadlines, or to present the employee with original copies of the executed employment agreement and the notification form certified by the NSSI, the employer could be subject to a pecuniary sanction amounting to BGL 1,000 for each particular event of default, i.e., for each particular employee not furnished with original copies of the executed employment agreement and the notification form certified by the NSSI, for each failure to communicate the required information to the NSSI within the specified deadlines, etc.[97]

According to Articles 13 and 14 of the Law on Obligations and Contracts,[98] the employment contract is concluded when the worker receives a written order for his or her appointment to the job, signed by the employer. Article 63 of the Labor Code provides a one-week time limit within which the worker must commence work. Failure of the worker to assume job responsibilities within this period will result in dissolution of the contract. The execution of the contract begins when the employee begins work, an act that is verified in writing.[99]

---

[97]Regulation No. 5 on the Contents and the Procedure for Delivery of the Notification under Art. 62 para. 4 of the Labor Code. *See* 1 STATE GAZETTE (Jan. 3, 2003), in effect as of Jan. 2, 2003.

[98]DV No. 275 (1950), amended by DV No. 69 (1951), DV No. 92 (1952), DV No. 85 (1963), DV No. 27 (1973), DV No. 16 (1977), DV No. 56 (1993), DV No. 104 (1996), DV No. 83 (1999), and DV No. 103 (1999).

[99]Labor Code art. 63(2).

7. *Employment by Election*

An employment relationship can be created based on an election. The list of elected employment positions is determined and periodically updated by act of the Council of Ministers, or by other laws.[100] An example of an elected employment position is director of an enterprise.

B. Types of Employment Contracts

Article 67 of the Labor Code provides that employment contracts may be for an indefinite duration or for a fixed term. Contracts are deemed to be concluded for an indefinite duration if no fixed term is specified.[101]

1. *Indefinite-Duration Contracts*

The contract for an indefinite duration is the most commonly used type of employment agreement. Such contracts provide stability in the employment relationship and guarantee a longer term of job security than do fixed-term contracts.

2. *Fixed-Term Contracts*

Contracts with a fixed term are also widely used. Article 68 of the Labor Code establishes four kinds of fixed-term employment contracts:

- contracts with a fixed date of termination;[102]
- contracts that expire upon completion of a given task;[103]
- contracts for the employment of substitutes;[104] and
- contracts for the completion of a job that will be occupied by a nominee selected by competitive examination.[105]

---

[100] *Id.* art. 83.
[101] *Id.* art. 67(2).
[102] *Id.* art. 68(1).
[103] *Id.* art. 68(2).
[104] *Id.* art. 68(3).
[105] *Id.* art. 68(4).

The duration of these contracts may range from one day to several years. Termination of the fixed-term contract occurs upon expiration of the term stated in the contract.

Because fixed-term contracts do not guarantee continuous employment, workers are inclined to avoid them whenever possible. Nevertheless, fixed-term contracts provide a convenient tool for employers who require workers on a temporary or seasonal basis. Under the economic conditions that prevailed in Bulgaria in the mid to late 1990s, including the significant decline in employment opportunities, many employers preferred the fixed-duration contracts because of the simplicity of termination. The contract simply expires without notice.[106]

The 2001 Labor Code amendments placed new restrictions on fixed-term contracts that are concluded for periods of three years or fewer. If a fixed-term contract is concluded in violation of the statutory limitations, then the contract is considered to be an employment contract for an indefinite term.

As a general rule, a fixed-term contract for a period not exceeding three years may be concluded for performance of work that is temporary, seasonal, or short-term in character, or with employees who are hired by companies in bankruptcy or liquidation proceedings. The Labor Code recognizes that fixed-term contracts may be concluded in other "exceptional cases," although the minimum duration of such a contract should be one year. The one-year limit applies only to fixed-term contracts that are concluded in exceptional cases for performance of works that do not qualify as temporary, seasonal, or short-term. Upon written request of the employee, a fixed-term contract may be of shorter duration, but, in any case, a fixed-term contract with a single employee for a single position may be renewed only once, and the duration of the renewed contract must be at least one year.

An exceptional case for purposes of executing a fixed-term contract is one involving, at the moment of execution, technological, financial, marketing, or other circumstances out of the control of the employer that require a fixed-term contract, rather than a contract for an indefinite term. Although the legislature attempted

---

[106]V. MRACHKOV, BULGARIA LABOR LAW 67 (1995).

to limit the availability of fixed-term contracts, this definition of the term "exceptional cases" is so vague and broadly formulated that it makes it quite easy for employers to circumvent the new restrictions.

3. *Transformation of Fixed-Term Contract to Indefinite-Duration Contract*

A fixed-term contract can, by the conduct of the parties, be converted into a contract for an indefinite duration. If the worker continues to work in the enterprise for five or more days after the expiration of the fixed-term contract without written objection by the employer, the fixed-term contract is thereby transformed under Bulgarian law into a contract of indefinite duration.[107]

The same rules of transformation apply to a contract for a temporary internal substitute for an absent worker if the contract with the absent worker is terminated during the period of substitution.[108]

4. *Probationary Contracts*

Another type of employment contract in common use is the probationary contract. Under the terms of this type of agreement, an employer has up to six months to offer a temporary prospective employee a permanent labor contract.[109] This enables the employer to observe and assess the qualifications and skills of the worker before entering into a permanent employment relationship. Under the probationary contract, the employer decides whether to offer another contract to the worker after the expiration of the probationary period. The employer's determination must be based on the worker's fitness and qualification for the job. The employer's decision is discretionary and not subject to any control.[110]

Theoretically, at least, a probationary contract of employment may be desirable for the employee in some cases, because the employer's decision whether to continue the employment relation-

---

[107]Labor Code art. 69(1).

[108]*Id.* art. 69(2).

[109]*Id.* art. 70(1).

[110]MRACHKOV, *supra* note 106, at 71.

ship will depend on the employee's evaluation of the desirability of the job and his or her own fitness and qualification. In reality, however, this type of employment contract is rarely desirable for an employee, particularly during periods of widespread unemployment.

The 2001 Labor Code amendments introduced new paragraphs to Article 70, providing that the probationary contract should specify for whose benefit the probationary term is agreed. The party benefited is able to terminate the contract within the probationary term with immediate effect and without stating any motives for termination. If the contract does not specify for whose benefit the probation was agreed, it is considered to be for the benefit of both parties.

In addition, as a result of the 2001 amendments, the execution of a second probationary contract between the same employer and the same employee for the same job is explicitly prohibited.

C. Mutual Rights and Obligations

The employment relationship is a combination of diverse corresponding duties and obligations. Chapter Six of the Labor Code defines the general rights and duties of the employee and the employer. For example, the employee must perform his or her work obligations and observe the requirements of labor discipline, while the employer must provide employees with normal work conditions and pay for the work performed. The rights and obligations of the parties are specified in greater detail in various specialized acts and regulations.

1. Rights and Obligations of Workers

Article 124 of the Labor Code states that employees have a basic right to do the work and the right to be paid for the work performed. Other more specific employee entitlements include the following:

- payment according to the duration and results of the work performed;[111]

---

[111]Labor Code art. 247(1).

- statutory fixed working time,[112] rest,[113] and leave;[114]
- safe and healthy working conditions;[115] and
- professional training.[116]

Under Article 126 of the Labor Code, the employee has a basic obligation to do the following:

- perform work obligations in good faith;[117]
- strictly comply with established technical and technological rules;[118]
- maintain quantity and quality performance of entrusted tasks;[119]
- strictly observe health and safety rules;[120]
- appear at work ready and able to perform;[121]
- comply with established working hours;[122]
- carry out the lawful instructions of the employer;[123]
- observe the internal rules and regulations of the enterprise;[124]
- take care of the property entrusted to him or her in the course of performing job duties;[125] and
- act loyally and not disclose information of a confidential character, and protect the image of the employer's enterprise.[126]

The employee's duties, recited above, may be viewed as expectations to which the employer is entitled.

---

[112]Labor Code art. 136. See V.B., below regarding hours of work..
[113]Labor Code art. 151. See V.B.7., below regarding periods of rest.
[114]Labor Code art. 155. See V.C., below regarding leave.
[115]Labor Code art. 275. See VII.A., below.
[116]Labor Code arts. 229–241.
[117]*Id.* art. 126.
[118]*Id.* art. 126(5).
[119]*Id.* art. 126(4).
[120]*Id.* art. 126(6).
[121]*Id.* art. 126(2).
[122]*Id.* art. 126(1), (3).
[123]*Id.* art. 126(7).
[124]*Id.* art. 126(10).
[125]*Id.* art. 126(8).
[126]*Id.* art. 126(9).

2. *Rights and Obligations of Employers*

Articles 127 to 129 of the Labor Code state the obligations of the employer in the labor relationship. The first and most important obligation of the employer is to provide the worker with normal and adequate working conditions.[127] This is a complex obligation, requiring the employer to undertake the following:

- provide work that conforms to the labor contract;[128]
- provide a workplace and adequate working conditions;[129]
- provide a safe and healthy working environment;[130]
- inform the worker of his or her labor obligations, the required manner of performance, the internal rules and regulations of the enterprise, and the health and safety rules;[131]
- pay the worker the agreed remuneration for the work done within the time periods established under the contract (biweekly or monthly);[132]
- make social security contributions to protect the worker against certain risks (e.g., illness, occupational diseases, accidents at work, pregnancy, maternity, childcare, unemployment, retirement, and death);[133]
- provide employees with a short description of the work to be performed or a job description;[134] and
- respect the employees' dignity during the performance of their employment.[135]

D. Discipline

1. *Internal Rules of the Enterprise*

The 1996 amendments to the Labor Code changed most of the provisions in Chapter Nine dealing with labor discipline. How-

---

[127] *Id.* art. 127.
[128] *Id.* art. 127(1), subs. 1.
[129] *Id.* art. 127(1), subs. 2.
[130] *Id.* art. 127(1), subs. 3.
[131] *Id.* art. 127(1), subs. 5.
[132] *Id.* art. 128.
[133] *Id.* art. 129.
[134] *See id.* art. 127(1), subs. 4.
[135] *See id.* art. 127(2).

ever, one of the main provisions from the former law remaining in effect provides for the promulgation of internal disciplinary regulations within the enterprise.[136] Article 181 states that "every employer shall have its own internal regulations" by which the employer determines the rights and obligations of the employees. Employer discretion to create internal regulations is not as broad as it might appear, largely because strict compliance is required with the minimum requirements of the national labor laws and with provisions of the applicable collective labor contract.

2. *Breaches of Labor Discipline*

A breach of labor discipline is defined in Article 186 of the Labor Code as an intentional failure to perform work obligations. The penalties that may be imposed on the offending worker are expressly listed,[137] along with the different kinds of violations.[138] The penalties are imposed irrespective of any additional financial or legal liabilities that may be assessed against a worker by the employer.[139] Article 187 enumerates the following violations of labor discipline:

- failure to report for work on time;[140]
- departure before the end of the work day;[141]
- waste of working time;[142]
- failure to complete the assigned job;[143]
- nonobservance of technical or technological specifications;[144]
- nonobservance of the rules for safe and healthy working conditions;[145]

---

[136] *Id.* art. 181.
[137] *Id.* art. 188.
[138] *Id.* art. 187.
[139] *Id.* art. 186.
[140] *Id.* art. 187, subs. 1.
[141] *Id.*
[142] *Id.*
[143] *Id.* art. 187, subs. 3.
[144] *Id.*
[145] *Id.* art. 187, subs. 5.

- failure to carry out legitimate orders and decisions of management;[146] and
- failure to meet other labor obligations specified by law, by the internal regulations of the enterprise or by the collective labor contract, or arising from the employment relationship.[147]

The list of labor discipline violations is not exhaustive and may be supplemented by the employer's internal regulations.

3. *Disciplinary Penalties*

The following disciplinary penalties are listed in Article 188 of the Labor Code:

- reprimand,[148]
- warning of possible dismissal,[149] and
- dismissal.[150]

Unlike the listing of labor discipline violations, the statutory list of disciplinary penalties is exclusive and exhaustive. Under the law, there are no other disciplinary penalties that an employer legally may impose on a worker, except that a reprimand may be combined with certain financial penalties.[151] These additional financial penalties may include the reduction of the employee's monthly salary by withholding the employee's entitlement to additional compensation for lengthy service.[152]

The second disciplinary penalty (warning of possible dismissal) is administered without any financial consequences for the worker. Dismissal is the final disciplinary measure, resulting in complete termination of the employment contract. An important financial consequence of the dismissal penalty is that the employee

---

[146]*Id.* art. 187, subs. 7.
[147]*Id.* art. 187, subs. 10.
[148]*Id.* art. 188, subs. 1.
[149]*Id.* art. 188, subs. 2.
[150]*Id.* art. 188, subs. 3.
[151]*Id.* arts. 203–212.
[152]See V.A.4., below.

loses accumulated additional compensation for lengthy service, potentially up to six months.[153]

The Labor Code does not provide that financial penalties may be imposed as a means of discipline. In this regard, a distinction must be made between disciplinary penalties, such as a reprimand, and financial liability for damage caused by the employee's negligence.[154] Similarly, an employee's salary may not be reduced as a disciplinary sanction; a reduction in the monthly salary is a means of recouping damages[155] and, even then, is available only in the circumstances explicitly provided for by law and up to a certain amount.

4. *Disciplinary Procedures*

Disciplinary penalties normally are imposed by the director of the enterprise, although other managerial officials also may be vested with limited disciplinary authority.[156] Disciplinary penalties are implemented by a written order from the employer.[157] The order is delivered to the worker and signed and dated by the offending employee.[158] Disciplinary penalties may be imposed only after a written explanation is given and the offending employee receives a hearing.[159] The purpose of this provision is to ensure that evidence is collected and presented, as well as to ensure that management will make a fair and informed decision. The failure of management to comply with this provision (without fault on the worker's part)[160] will result in reversal of the dismissal by the courts.[161]

---

[153]Ordinance on Additional and Other Work Remunerations, approved by the Council of Ministers by Decree No. 133, DV No. 67 (1993).

[154]For a discussion of financial liability, see I.D.8., below.

[155]See I.D.9., below.

[156]Labor Code art. 192(1).

[157]*Id.* art. 195(1).

[158]*Id.* art. 195(2).

[159]*Id.* art. 193.

[160]*Id.* art. 193(3).

[161]*Id.* art. 193(2).

5. *Statute of Limitations*

The statute of limitations for the imposition of disciplinary penalties is one year from the date on which the violation was committed, but no later than two months after its discovery.[162] The statute of limitations is tolled under two circumstances:

- during a worker's lawful leave of absence;[163] and
- during the period of a strike in which a worker participates, regardless of the legality or illegality of the strike.[164]

6. *Deletion of Disciplinary Penalties*

All disciplinary penalties are considered "deleted" one year from the date they are imposed,[165] but these penalties may be deleted within a shorter period by written order[166] of the employer.[167] Deletion of a dismissal action, however, does not constitute grounds for reinstatement of the worker.[168]

7. *Appeals*

Disciplinary penalties are appealable to the courts.[169] The statute of limitations for an appeal from disciplinary action is one month for a reprimand.[170] In the event that a worker receives a written order for the imposition of either a warning concerning possible dismissal or a dismissal,[171] the appeal may be taken within two months from the date of receipt of the written order.[172]

8. *Financial Liability*

Limited financial liability may be imposed on an employee for damage caused in the performance of his or her assigned du-

[162] *Id.* art. 194(1).
[163] *Id.* art. 194(3).
[164] *Id.*
[165] *Id.* art. 197(1).
[166] *Id.* art. 198(2).
[167] *Id.* art. 198(1).
[168] *Id.* art. 197(2).
[169] *Id.* art. 360(1). See the Introduction, at D., above.
[170] Labor Code art. 358(1), subs. 1.
[171] *Id.* art. 358(1), subs. 2.
[172] *Id.* art. 358(2), subs. 1.

ties.[173] The imposition of financial responsibility is based on the existence of actual damage negligently caused by the worker as a result of unlawful conduct.[174] In these cases, the employee's financial liability is determined in accordance with civil law.[175]

The offending employee may be held liable only for damage actually caused, and not for any resulting lost benefits to the company.[176] The damage must have been discovered within a year after its occurrence for the employer to hold an employee accountable.[177] The Labor Code does not impose financial liability for damage due to normal risks of the production process or so-called "economic risks."[178]

Employee liability is "limited" to the extent that the Labor Code places a cap on liability, which is determined by the amount of the employee's monthly compensation.[179] Thus, the employee may be held responsible only for the amount of damage not exceeding the amount of one month's salary.[180] If the damage is caused by a manager, his or her financial responsibility may not exceed an amount equal to three months' salary.[181]

Increased financial liability is imposed on employees whose duties involve the safeguarding of and accounting for the employer's property.[182] For these employees, if the damages are assessable, liability may be as much as three months' salary[183] and is based on the full value of the damage plus interest from the date of causation or discovery of the loss.[184] If damages are not assessable, the liability is for the so-called "financial deficit."[185]

---

[173] *Id.* art. 203(1).
[174] *Id.* arts. 203(1), 205(1).
[175] *Id.* art. 203(2).
[176] *Id.* art. 205(1).
[177] *Id.* art. 210(2).
[178] *Id.* art. 204.
[179] *Id.* art. 206(1).
[180] *Id.*
[181] *Id.* art. 206(2).
[182] *Id.* art. 207.
[183] *Id.* art. 207(1), subs. 1.
[184] *Id.* art. 207(1), subs. 2.
[185] V. MRACHKOV, BULGARIA LABOR LAW 82 (1995).

9. *Procedure for Recoupment of Damages*

The procedure for recouping damages caused by an employee under the limited financial liability rules is established in Article 210 of the Labor Code. If the loss is caused by a worker, an order for deduction is issued by the employer. If the loss is caused by an executive or a manager,[186] an order by the superior administrative body or the collective managing body is required.

The deductions must be made within one month from the date the loss is discovered, but no later than a year from the date of occurrence.[187] Before making any deduction from the worker's salary, the employer must notify the worker regarding the deductions and allow an opportunity to contest the validity of the deductions. If the worker objects within 30 days of notification, the employer may refer the dispute to a court.[188] Deductions are made in accordance with the Code of Civil Procedure if no objection is filed within the 30-day period.[189]

The limited financial liability obligation may be enforced by writ of execution even after the contract of the responsible employee is terminated.[190] This writ is issued pursuant to the Code of Civil Procedure.[191]

In cases where the damage results from intentional, criminal acts of the worker, or occurs under circumstances outside the scope of the worker's employment obligations, the worker's liability is determined by the civil law,[192] which generally means that the worker must assume full responsibility to the enterprise for restitution of the damage caused. The enforcement of full financial liability is implemented by the courts[193] and is based on a civil claim made in accordance with the Code of Civil Procedure.

---

[186] Labor Code art. 210(1).
[187] *Id.* art. 210(2).
[188] *Id.* art. 210(3).
[189] *Id.* art. 210(4).
[190] *Id.* art. 210(5).
[191] *Id.*
[192] *Id.* art. 203(2).
[193] *Id.* art. 211.

E. Termination

1. *Automatic Termination*

The Labor Code states that a contract for employment may be terminated without advance notice in the following cases:[194]

- upon expiration of the contractual term;[195]
- upon completion of a definite amount of work;[196]
- upon the return of a substituted employee;[197]
- when a position is listed to be filled by a pregnant employee, or an employee reassigned for rehabilitation,[198] and a candidate entitled to that position appears;[199]
- upon the inability of the employee to perform the assigned job because of illness;[200]
- upon the death of the person with whom the employee has concluded the contract of employment;[201] and
- upon the death of the employee.[202]

The rule for automatic termination upon expiration of the contractual term is not absolute. A fixed-term employment contract automatically converts to a contract for an indefinite period if the employee continues to perform his or her duties for five business days after expiration of the contractual term, and the employer fails to object.[203]

2. *Termination by Employee With Notice*

An employee has the right to terminate his or her employment contract by giving 30-days' advance notice, unless the parties negotiate a longer notice period in the agreement.[204] The La-

---

[194] *Id.* art. 325.
[195] *Id.* art. 325, subs. 3.
[196] *Id.* art. 325, subs. 4.
[197] *Id.* art. 325, subs. 5.
[198] See VI.B. and VII.B., below.
[199] Labor Code art. 325(6).
[200] *Id.* art. 325, subs. 9.
[201] *Id.* art. 325, subs. 10.
[202] *Id.* art. 325, subs. 11.
[203] See I.B.3., above.
[204] *Id.* art. 326(1), (2).

bor Code provides for a longer notice period for certain categories of workers.[205]

During the notice period, the employment contract continues in force and the employee giving the notice must fulfill all of his or her work obligations. The notice period begins on the day following receipt of the notice,[206] and the employment contract is considered terminated on the last day of the notice period.

Articles 325 to 328 of the Labor Code provide different criteria for termination of employment contracts with indefinite and definite duration.[207] The length of the notice due by the worker under an indefinite labor contract is 30 days, while the required notice for a contract with a definite duration is three months.[208]

3. *Termination by Employee Without Notice*

The employee has the right to terminate the employment contract without advance notice in the following cases:

- the employee is unable to perform the assigned job because of illness and the enterprise fails to provide the employee with suitable work;[209]
- the employer fails to pay or delays payment to the employee;[210]
- the employer changes the place or character of work or the amount of agreed upon compensation;[211]
- the employee assumes a paid elected position or enters regular military service;[212]
- the employee continues his or her education as a regular student;[213]
- the employee was employed as a substitute for an absent employee, and the absent employee returns;[214] and

---

[205]*Id.* art. 326(3).
[206]*Id.* art. 326(4).
[207]See I.B., above.
[208]Labor Code art. 326(2).
[209]*Id.* art. 327(1), subs. 1.
[210]*Id.* art. 327(1), subs. 2.
[211]*Id.* art. 327(1), subs. 3.
[212]*Id.* art. 327(1), subs. 4, 5.
[213]*Id.* art. 327(1), subs. 6.
[214]*Id.* art. 327(1), subs. 7.

- the employee is being reinstated upon a finding that his or her dismissal was unlawful.[215]

4. *Termination by Employer With Notice*

An employer may terminate an employment contract with due notice under any of the following circumstances:

- total or partial liquidation of the enterprise;[216]
- reduction in the level of business activities within the enterprise;[217]
- personnel layoffs for economic reasons;[218]
- suspension of the work process for more than 15 days due to reasons such as strikes, economic slowdowns, or acts of God;[219]
- the employee does not satisfy the educational requirements for the particular job;[220]
- the employee refuses to transfer to another area where the enterprise is relocated;[221]
- the position must be vacated in order to reinstate an unlawfully dismissed employee to his or her previous position;[222]
- the position must be vacated for a person returning from military service;[223]
- an employee has become eligible for a retirement pension based on length of service and age;[224]
- the requirements for the job have changed, and the employee is no longer qualified for the position;[225] or
- it is objectively impossible to implement the contract of employment.[226]

---

[215] *Id.* art. 327(1), subs. 8.
[216] *Id.* art. 328(1), subs. 1, 2.
[217] *Id.* art. 328(1), subs. 3.
[218] *Id.* art. 328(1), subs. 2.
[219] *Id.* art. 328(1), subs. 4.
[220] *Id.* art. 328(1), subs. 6.
[221] *Id.* art. 328(1), subs. 7.
[222] *Id.* art. 328(1), subs. 8.
[223] *Id.* art. 328(1), subs. 9.
[224] *Id.* art. 328(1), subs. 10.
[225] *Id.* art. 328(1), subs. 11.
[226] *Id.* art. 328(1), subs. 12.

Amendments also have been made to the right of the employer to terminate employment agreements with managerial personnel in the event that the employer enters into a management agreement, i.e., in case of a change in the general manager(s) of the company.[227] The deadline for exercising this right is nine months from the initial date of performance under the management agreement.

The 2001 amendments also introduced a new provision, allowing the employer to offer an employee termination of the employment contract in exchange for payment of compensation amounting to four times the employee's gross monthly remuneration.[228] The employee has seven days to accept or reject such an offer. The employee's silence regarding the offer is considered a rejection. If the offer is accepted, the compensation must be paid within one month of the contract termination date. Failure of the employer to pay the compensation due invalidates the termination.

The 2003 amendments[229] introduced new requirements and conditions regarding a civil servant's employment contract. The employer is in a position to terminate the employment contract if the employee fails to comply with the requirement to give due notice with respect to the employee's incompatibility with the employment contract because of social, business, or personal position.

5. *Termination by Employer Without Notice*

An employee may be terminated without notice if he or she is detained by government authorities.[230] An employee must be terminated without notice if any of the following circumstances apply:

- the employee is disbarred by the competent authority and does not have the right or license to practice his or her profession;[231]

---

[227] *Id.* art. 328(2).
[228] *Id.* art. 331.
[229] *See id.* art. 303(2), subs. 7 and 8.
[230] *Id.* art. 330(1).
[231] *Id.* art. 330(2), subs. 1.

- compulsory transfer of the employee to another city upon conviction;[232]
- a disabled employee refuses to accept an offer of placement;[233] or
- the employee has committed a disciplinary offense.[234]

6. *Special Protections Against Nondisciplinary Termination*

Certain categories of employees are protected from nondisciplinary termination of the employment relationship. This protection is based on the employee's health, family status, occupied position, and other related factors. Protection against termination serves a social function by creating relative job security for certain categories of workers, such as:

- pregnant women, mothers of children who are 3 years old or younger, and mothers whose spouses are in the military;[235]
- disabled workers;[236]
- workers with an illness listed in a Ministry of Health Ordinance;[237]
- workers on paid leave; and[238]
- union leaders.[239]

In order to dismiss a protected employee, the employer must obtain advance authorization from the General Inspectorate of Labor, the Ministry of Labor and Social Policies, and the relevant trade union. If the employer violates this special procedure and dismisses a protected worker without the required permission, the employee is entitled to challenge the dismissal.[240]

Prior to the 2001 Labor Code amendments, the dismissal of a protected employee by prior notice was subject to the prior writ-

[232] *Id.* art. 330(2), subs. 3.
[233] *Id.* art. 330(2), subs. 4.
[234] *Id.* art. 330(2), subs. 5. See I.D., above.
[235] Labor Code art. 333(1), subs. 1.
[236] *Id.* art. 330(1), subs. 2.
[237] *Id.* art. 330(1), subs. 3.
[238] *Id.* art. 330(1), subs. 4.
[239] *Id.* art. 330(3).
[240] *Id.* art. 344(1).

ten authorization of the Labor Inspectorate, where the employee was being dismissed for nondisciplinary grounds such as the partial closing of the business, a decrease in the volume of work, or a lack of ability for effective performance of the employee's obligations. With the 2001 amendments, a dismissal for reasons that render performance of the employment agreement "impossible"[241] no longer requires the prior written permission of the Labor Inspectorate. At the same time, the Labor Code amendments added a right to protection against dismissal due to disciplinary violations, thus preventing employers from dismissing protected employees even for disciplinary reasons, without the permission of the Labor Inspectorate.

7. *Termination of the Employment Relationship Established by an Election*

An employment relationship established by an election[242] may be terminated under the same circumstances as any other nondisciplinary termination. In cases involving a disciplinary offense,[243] the employment of an offending elected employee may be terminated only by recall action of the electorate body.[244]

8. *Protection Against Unlawful Dismissal*

The Labor Code contains various provisions that describe the circumstances under which an employer is deemed to have made an unlawful dismissal:

- the employer failed to obtain the required permission of the General Labor Inspectorate or trade union to terminate a protected employee;[245]
- the employer violated the required criteria for imposition of the disciplinary sanction of termination;[246]

---

[241]*See id.* art. 328(1), subs. 12.
[242]See I.A.7., above.
[243]Labor Code art. 339(1).
[244]*Id.* art. 339(2).
[245]*Id.* art. 344(3).
[246]*Id.* art. 189(1), (2). See I.D.4., above.

- the employer violated the established periods for imposing sanctions;[247] and
- the employer failed to obtain written explanations from the sanctioned worker.[248]

A former employee who claims that he or she was unlawfully dismissed may file a petition with the court within six months from the date of receiving the order of dismissal.[249] The court will reaffirm the dismissal if it is found to be lawful. If the employee's challenge is successful, and the dismissal is found to be unlawful, remedies include the following:

- repeal of the dismissal;[250]
- reinstatement to the previous position;[251]
- compensation for the period of unemployment;[252] and/or
- revision of the grounds for dismissal in the employee's service record from a disciplinary termination to one of the nondisciplinary grounds allowed under the employment agreement.[253]

The employer may, on its own initiative, cancel the dismissal before a court action is instituted by the dismissed employee. In cases that require the prior consent of the Labor Inspectorate or a trade union as a prerequisite to dismissal, and the employer has failed to obtain consent, the court will adjudicate the order of dismissal as unlawful on this procedural ground alone, without considering the merits of the labor dispute.

An employer that wrongfully refuses reinstatement of an employee upon order of the court will be held administratively liable,[254] and a criminal penalty may be imposed under Article 172 of the Penal Code as well.

---

[247]Labor Code art. 194(1). See I.D.5., above.
[248]Labor Code art. 193(2), (3). See I.D.4., above.
[249]Labor Code art. 344.
[250]*Id.* art. 344(1), subs. 1.
[251]*Id.* art. 344(1), subs. 2.
[252]*Id.* art. 344(1), subs. 3.
[253]*Id.* art. 344(1), subs. 4.
[254]*Id.* art. 414.

F. Privacy

Privacy in the employment relationship relates to protection of personal data as regulated by the Personal Data Protection Act.[255] Data privacy protections are required by the EU Data Privacy Directive.[256] Under the law, "personal data" is defined as any data disclosing the physical, psychological, mental, family, economic, cultural, or social identity of an individual. As of January 1, 2002, any person, including employers, who is collecting, recording, organizing, or storing such data shall, prior to any event of such processing, notify the Commission for Personal Data Protection by filing an application and sample documents approved by the Commission. Further, employers are obliged to inform their employees regarding the purpose of collecting or otherwise processing such data and whether the provision is mandatory or voluntary. In addition, employers may not collect, store, or otherwise process such data without obtaining the explicit written consent of the employees to that effect. Such consent is not required where processing is needed by operation of the law (e.g., for the purpose of executing an employment agreement),[257] or in order to protect the life or health of the employees or other individuals.

The restrictions apply only where individually identified records are transferred or accessed or otherwise processed. Statistical reporting relying on aggregate employment data and/or the use of data not disclosing the identity of the employee does not give rise to any privacy concerns.

In addition, Regulation No. 14 on the Medical Service[258] issued by the Minister of Health regulates use of personal data related to the health status of employees. Any results from medical screening and testing of the employee may be disclosed to third parties other than physicians only with the prior written consent of the employee.

---

[255] *See* 1 STATE GAZETTE (Jan. 4, 2002), effective Jan. 1, 2002.

[256] For a detailed discussion of this directive, see I.C. in the chapter on the European Union in Volume I.

[257] *See* Regulation No. 4 dated May 11, 1993, on the Documentation to be Provided in View of the Execution of an Employment Agreement, promulgated in 44 STATE GAZETTE (May 25, 1993).

[258] *See* 95 STATE GAZETTE (Aug. 14, 1998).

G. Employee Duty of Loyalty, Trade Secrets, Covenants Not to Compete

1. *Employee Duty of Loyalty*

Under the Bulgarian Labor Code,[259] the duty of loyalty relates to the employee's obligations to refrain from abusing in any way the employer's confidence and to refrain from disclosing information of a confidential nature. Bulgarian legal theory further interprets the concept of loyalty by adding to employee's duties the obligation to protect the employer's interests and good will. The performance of activities inimical to the best interests of the employer is prohibited. This obligation refers to, *inter alia*, not joining companies performing competitive activities and not performing other activities that might qualify as unfair competition.

Failure of the employee to abide to the prohibitions enumerated above represents a material breach of workplace rules and serves as grounds for disciplinary dismissal.

2. *Trade Secrets*

Under Bulgarian law, any willful or negligent disclosure of confidential information by the employee constitutes a breach of the workplace rules and entitles the employer to dismiss the employee. Any information considered as confidential shall be outlined in the individual employment agreement, because the court will not enforce such an agreement if the employee can demonstrate that he or she has not been informed by the employer that the information must be considered as confidential.

In addition to the disciplinary sanctions that could be imposed for disclosure of confidential information, the employer is entitled to claim damages under general tort rules.

3. *Covenants Not to Compete*

Generally, covenants not to compete are contractual agreements between employees and employers whereby the employee undertakes not to compete with the employer for a specific period

---

[259] *See* Labor Code art. 126, subs. 9.

of time and/or within a particular geographic area, in the course of the employment relationship and following its termination.

As regards competition during employment, Article 111 of the Labor Code provides that the employee may enter into an employment contract with another (second) employer in the course of his or her primary employment unless otherwise provided in the respective employment agreement with the first employer. Therefore, the employer is entitled to ban the employee from entering into an additional employment contract in the course of the main employment relationship, notwithstanding whether the additional work with another employer qualifies as activities competitive with the activities performed by the employer.

As regards competition after employment, Bulgarian labor legislation does not specifically provide for a noncompetition arrangement in employment relationships after their termination. Yet no explicit prohibition against its use exists either. Therefore, a clause providing for an obligation of an individual not to accept employment in a company or organization performing activities that compete with those performed by his or her ex-employer for a certain period of time following the termination of the existing employment relationship, constitutes a valid and binding obligation. Further, since such an obligation is not classified as a labor provision, in the event of failure to observe the terms and conditions of the noncompetition agreement, the individual will be held liable for breach of contract under the general rules for contractual liability.

II. Collective Bargaining

A. Unions

Workers' and employers' unions have their own bylaws that regulate their internal structure and functions.[260] The government and employers are obligated to help unions by providing buildings, equipment, and other types of subsidies to support their activities.[261]

---

[260] *Id.* art. 33.
[261] *Id.* art. 46.

Union representatives have the right to participate in the preparation of a company's bylaws and regulations,[262] and in the discussion of labor and social security issues concerning employment issues.[263] Unions are authorized to represent workers in court in labor disputes, but they cannot settle, dismiss, or amend workers' claims unless expressly authorized.[264]

All employees, including managers and supervisors (as long as they are not employers), are eligible to join workers' unions. Employers' organizations are formed in ways similar to workers' unions, with equally representative and functional authority and independence.[265] Workers' and employers' unions have been granted significant freedom and independence, including the right to enact their own bylaws and other internal rules and regulations, to elect their representatives and representative bodies, and to determine independently their functions.[266] The only functional distinction between workers' and employers' unions is that workers' unions participate in the preparation of all internal company rules concerning employment relationships, over which the employer has final approval authority.[267]

In 2003, a new Regulation on the Trade Unions and Employers Organizations Recognition Criteria was adopted.[268] The Council of Ministers is competent to resolve whether a trade union or employers' organization is eligible to represent its members at the national level.

B. The Collective Labor Contract

1. Subjects of Bargaining

The collective labor contract occupies an important place in the regulation of the employment relationship in Bulgaria due to

[262] *Id.* art. 37.
[263] *Id.* art. 42.
[264] *Id.* art. 45.
[265] *Id.* art. 5.
[266] *Id.* art. 33(1), (2).
[267] *Id.* art. 37.
[268] Initially promulgated in 64 STATE GAZETTE (July 18, 2003), amended Oct. 15, 2003, in force as of Oct. 21, 2003.

the special social functions assigned to it. The Labor Code states that the collective labor contract is used to settle matters of labor relations "not settled by the mandatory stipulations of the Labor Code" or by other related labor regulations.[269] The subject matter of the collective labor contract consists of a variety of social security and labor issues, such as remuneration, working conditions, rest periods, leave, insurance, social security benefits, work time, and related matters.

2. *Superiority of the Labor Code*

The Labor Code states that the collective labor contract may not restrict the rights and privileges granted to workers under the Code. Furthermore, an employment contract, whether collective or individual, may not create less favorable benefits for employees than those existing under the current labor laws.[270] Thus, provisions of the collective labor contract must not fall below the minimum standards established by law. In case of a conflict with legal standards, the collective agreement is rendered null and void.[271]

3. *Relationship to Individual Contracts*

After conclusion of the collective labor contract, the affected employee and employer are free to negotiate more favorable employment conditions under an individual employment contract.[272] Taken together, the collective labor contract and the labor law and regulations provide the basic legal structure upon which individual employment contracts should be negotiated. If the individual employment contract provides less favorable employment conditions for the worker than those provided in the collective labor contract or under the labor laws, the individual employment contract is thereby rendered null and void.[273] In such cases, where particular terms of an individual employment contract are invalidated, the

---

[269]Labor Code art. 50(1).
[270]*Id.* art. 50(2).
[271]*Id.* art. 74(1).
[272]See I.A., above.
[273]Labor Code art. 74(1).

invalid terms are then replaced by the applicable statutory provisions or the provisions of the collective labor contract.

4. *Parties and Representation*

A collective labor contract is concluded between the relevant trade union and employer.[274] The Labor Code states that the collective labor contract is the product of collective negotiations between the parties, which may include the trade union organizations or their association on the one side, and a single employer, group of employers, or their respective organizations on the other.[275] Only one collective agreement may be concluded with an individual employer, employer's representative, or employer's association.[276] The trade union initiates the negotiation and seeks the conclusion of a collective labor contract.

The employer's representative must participate in and present information necessary for the bargaining process, including, for example, data on the economic situation of the enterprise, its marketing, profits and losses, organization of work, and related matters.[277] An employer that violates this bargaining obligation is subject to civil liability according to Article 52(2) of the Labor Code. The employer must inform the employees of the terms of the collective bargaining contract upon its conclusion, and make the contract available to all employees.[278]

With regard to the employer's obligation to provide information regarding the economic and financial status of the company, a new protection was added by the 2001 Labor Code amendments. Under the new provisions, if the information is considered to be of a confidential nature, i.e., its disclosure could cause damage to the company, then the employer may refuse to provide it or may condition release of the information on certain nondisclosure obligations.[279]

---

[274] *Id.* art. 51(2).

[275] *Id.*

[276] *Id.*

[277] V. MRACHKOV, BULGARIA LABOR LAW 194 (1995).

[278] Labor Code art. 58.

[279] *Id.* art. 52(1), subs. 2, pt. b.

In addition, a new provision was introduced, providing that upon the employer's request, made before commencement of the negotiation process, the trade union organizations are obliged to provide information about the actual number of their members.[280]

5. *Conclusion and Registration*

The resulting agreement must be in writing and signed by the parties, or by their designated representatives.[281] Article 53(3) requires that the collective labor contract be registered with the local Labor Inspectorate with jurisdiction over the enterprise's place of business. The procedure for registration is established in Article 53(4). This registration requirement does not affect the legality of the collective labor agreement, which is considered concluded from the date of signing, unless provided otherwise.

If the collective labor contract is concluded with a number of employers that have different places of business, then the contract may be registered with any Labor Inspectorates having jurisdiction over the company's place of business. According to the 2001 Labor Code amendments, collective labor contracts concluded on an industrial sector level or national level must be registered with the Central Labor Inspectorate.[282]

6. *Duration*

As noted immediately above, the collective labor contract takes effect from the date of its signing.[283] The contract duration is defined by the Labor Code as one year, unless otherwise agreed by the parties.[284] The Code provides for the extension and amendment of the contract.[285] The collective labor contract may be amended, partially or in its entirety, provided all parties agree to the proposed amendment.[286]

---

[280]*Id.* art. 52(4).
[281]*Id.* art. 53(1).
[282]*Id.* art. 53(3).
[283]*Id.*
[284]*Id.* art. 54(2).
[285]*Id.* arts. 55, 56.
[286]*Id.* art. 56(1).

As a result of the ongoing privatization process in Bulgaria and the need for ensuring that the new owners of state enterprises will be given the opportunity to renegotiate existing collective labor agreements, the 2001 Labor Code amendments changed the provision regarding the duration of collective labor contracts. While the parties still may agree to a contract term beyond the statutory one-year period, the Labor Code now provides that the duration of a contract may not exceed two years. In addition, the parties are given the right to agree on a shorter duration for separate clauses within the contract. The Labor Code also was amended to provide that negotiations for a new collective contract should commence no later than three months prior to the expiration date of the existing contract.[287]

7. *Coverage*

As a general rule, the collective labor contract applies to all employees who are members of the trade union that signed the contract.[288] The law, however, attempts to equalize the effect of the collective contract for all workers by providing them with uniform contractual benefits and work conditions. The Labor Code provides an opportunity for those employees who are not members of the trade union to join employees covered by the collective agreement upon submitting a written application for acceptance to the employer, or to the leadership of the trade union,[289] in accordance with the acceptance procedure determined by the parties to the collective contract.[290]

The 2001 Labor Code amendments also require that the acceptance procedure may not conflict with statutory requirements, aim at the achievement of illegal results through legal means, or violate the public order. This amendment does not appear to effect a significant change in the procedural requirements for acceptance; however, under the new provisions, the acceptance may not be conditioned on the payment of a fee.

---

[287] *Id.* art. 54(3).
[288] *Id.* art. 57(1).
[289] *Id.*
[290] *Id.* art. 57(2).

8. *Effect of Employer Noncompliance*

An employer may be held liable for noncompliance with the terms of the collective contract in an action brought in a civil court by the trade union or an aggrieved employee.[291]

C. Dispute Settlement

In addition to court actions, collective labor disputes may be settled by negotiation, voluntary arbitration, or strikes.[292] The Law on the Settlement of Collective Labor Disputes (Collective Disputes Law)[293] establishes procedures for the settlement of labor disputes through negotiation or arbitration and provides legal recognition of the right to strike.[294] New amendments to the law that became effective on March 31, 2001,[295] established a new National Institute for Arbitration and Reconciliation for the purpose of assisting in the amicable settlement of collective labor disputes between employees and employers. The National Institute is a legal entity with its principal place of business in Sofia.

The managing entities of the Institute for Arbitration and Reconciliation are the Supervisory Board and the Director. The Supervisory Board consists of two representatives of employee organizations, two employer representatives, and two representatives of the State. The members of the Supervisory Board serve for a one-year term. The Director of the Institute is a member of the Supervisory Board by virtue of his or her position.

The Supervisory Board adopts rules for the conduct of mediation and arbitration and criteria for nomination of mediators and arbitrators, and approves the list of mediators and arbitrators proposed by the organizations of employees, employers, or the State. The Director of the Institute is appointed by the Minister of Labor and Social Policy after consultation with the Supervisory Board. The activities of the Institute are financed with funds

---

[291] *Id.* art. 59.
[292] *Id.* art. 3.
[293] DV No. 21 (1990), amended by DV No. 27 (1991) (Collective Disputes Law).
[294] V. MRACHKOV, BULGARIA LABOR LAW 207 (1995).
[295] *See* 25 STATE GAZETTE (Mar.16, 2001).

from the state budget. Dispute settlement before the Institute is an alternative to settlement through negotiations and voluntary arbitration.

1. Negotiation

Employers and employees may participate in settlement negotiations through their representatives. The procedure is commenced upon submission of a written request by the affected employees that includes information regarding the representatives who will participate in the negotiations.[296]

The law states that the procedure is to be "freely decided" by the participating parties.[297] Both parties present arguments during the negotiations to justify their positions, and compromise generally is necessary in order to reach a final agreement. Negotiations may last up to 14 days, or longer if agreed to by the parties. In the event a disagreement persists, the superior body of the employer's organization and the trade union must become involved, and may reach an agreement to resolve the matter.

2. Arbitration

A collective labor dispute may be referred to an individual arbitrator or an arbitration panel upon written agreement of the parties.[298] The panel may consist of one or three arbitrators who are chosen by the parties from a list. Following the 2001 amendments to the Collective Disputes Law, the list of arbitrators must be approved by the Supervisory Board of the National Institute for Arbitration and Reconciliation and must be published in the *State Gazette*.[299] The arbitration procedure contemplates a hearing on the disputed issues, with the presentation of evidence and testimony of experts. The arbitration decision is binding and subject to immediate enforcement.[300]

---

[296]Collective Disputes Law art. 3(2).
[297]*Id.* art. 1(1).
[298]*Id.* art. 5(1).
[299]*Id.* art. 4a(7)(5) and (6).
[300]Collective Disputes Law, Supplementary and Final Provisions §1(1).

3. Strikes

The right to strike is a fundamental right of Bulgarian citizens guaranteed by the Constitution.[301] The Collective Disputes Law regulates in detail the right of Bulgarian employees to strike in an effort to solve their *collective* labor disputes.[302] In contrast, strikes are not allowed to settle *individual* labor disputes and grievances,[303] which must be resolved under the procedures established in Chapter 18 of the Labor Code.[304]

If a collective dispute cannot be settled by negotiation, or if the employer fails to perform its obligations, employees may strike by temporarily suspending work.[305] Employees also may announce a symbolic strike, without interruption of work, by carrying and placing appropriate signs, posters, or other symbols.[306] The decision to strike is made by a majority of the employees in the enterprise or branch.[307]

Seven days before commencement of a strike, the employees and their representative must inform the employer in writing about the strike, its duration, and the designated body that will lead the strike.[308] However, employees may conduct a warning strike for less than an hour without a preliminary warning.[309]

At least three days before the commencement of a strike, the employer and the employees should reach a written agreement to allow the normal, continuous operation of any activities that, if interrupted or suspended, might have the following effects:

- disruption of public utility services and transportation services or TV and radio communications;
- irreparable damage to public or private property or the environment; or
- endangering the public peace.

[301]CONSTITUTION art. 50.
[302]Collective Disputes Law arts. 10–19.
[303]*Id.* art. 16(5).
[304]See I.D. and I.E., above.
[305]Collective Disputes Law art. 11(1).
[306]*Id.* art. 10.
[307]*Id.* art. 11(2).
[308]*Id.* art. 11(3).
[309]*Id.* art. 11(5).

If the parties are unable to reach agreement on these issues, the dispute is referred to arbitration.[310]

Participation in a strike is voluntary. No one may be forced to participate or not participate.[311] Furthermore, strikers are not permitted to create obstacles or make it more difficult for employees who are not participating to continue to perform their work duties.[312] During a strike, the parties make efforts to settle their dispute through negotiations, mediation, or by any other appropriate means.[313]

Strikes are not allowed under the following circumstances:

- if the employees' claims are against the Constitution;
- in case of noncompliance with the requirements of negotiation, majority employee decision, employer notice, or an agreement to protect public services, etc.;
- on questions previously settled by agreement or arbitration decision;
- during a natural disaster and any related urgent and immediate rescue and restoration activities;
- in the fields of electrical production, distribution and supply, media, or the medical services;
- for settlement of individual labor disputes;
- within the Ministry of Defense, Ministry of Internal Affairs, armies of other institutions, or judicial, prosecutorial, and investigators' bodies;[314] or
- to assert political demands.[315]

The employer and the employees not participating in the strike may bring an action to declare the illegality of an announced, ongoing, or completed strike.[316]

---

[310]*Id.* art. 14.

[311]*Id.* art. 13(1).

[312]*Id.* art. 13(2).

[313]*Id.* art. 15.

[314]The former restriction on strikes within the Builders' Army no longer applies. Pursuant to the requirements of the North Atlantic Treaty Organization (NATO), the Builders' Army was transformed into a state-owned company, and the Collective Disputes Law was amended in 2000 to reflect this change.

[315]Collective Disputes Law art. 16.

[316]*Id.* art. 17.

Employees are not compensated by the employer for the time spent participating in a strike. However, they may be compensated from a special strike fund on the employees' own initiative with their personal or professional organizations' funds.[317] Time spent participating in a strike is considered as length of service for purposes of entitlement to pensions.[318] An employee who does not participate in a strike, but who is unable to work because of the strike of other employees, is entitled to receive compensation.[319]

Employees may not be disciplined or held financially liable for participation in a legal strike. However, discipline and financial liability may be imposed on employees who participate in an illegal strike.[320]

4. *Lockouts*

An employer may suspend work and announce a lockout to stop a legal strike, or to frustrate satisfaction of the employees' demands.[321] During a legal strike the employer is not allowed to hire new employees to replace those participating in the strike, except under the following circumstances:

- to guarantee the provision of public utility services;
- to assure normal TV and radio communications; or
- to prevent irreparable damage to public or private property or the environment.

Even in such cases, the hires must be temporary and only for the duration of the strike.[322]

III. REPRESENTATION BY ENTITIES OTHER THAN UNIONS

The Labor Code permits employee participation in the management of the enterprise through their trade union representative

[317] *Id.* art. 18(1).
[318] *Id.* art. 18(4).
[319] *Id.* art. 18(5).
[320] *Id.* art. 19.
[321] *Id.* art. 20.
[322] *Id.* art. 21.

on questions regarding professional qualifications, increases or decreases in production, expansion or reduction of personnel, improvement of work conditions, and worker layoffs.

Under Bulgarian law, only trade unions have the right to represent employees. Work councils are not recognized.

In certain cases provided by law, employees are entitled to participate in discussions related to the management of the enterprise through their elected representatives, whether or not the employees are represented by a trade union. For example, in the event of a transfer in company ownership, the employer is obligated to consult with the employees if, as a result of the transfer, it intends to take certain measures affecting employment.[323] If no trade union is present within the company, the general meeting of the employees may elect representatives for the purpose of conducting the consultations.[324]

IV. REDUNDANCY AND TRANSFERS OF UNDERTAKINGS

A. Redundancy

The 2002 Employment Law redefined the term "collective dismissal" to refer to a dismissal carried out by an employer for one or more reasons not related to performance of the affected employees, provided that within a period of 30 days, the employer has terminated the following numbers of employees:

- at least 10 employees, where the total number of employees in the particular enterprise is between 20 and 100;
- at least 10 percent of the total number of the employees, where the total number of employees in the enterprise is not less than 100, but does not exceed 300; or
- at least 30 employees, where the total number of the employees is 300 or more.

[323]Labor Code art. 123. See IV.B., below.

[324]*See* Labor Code art. 7(2) (providing that the general meeting of the employees may elect representatives to represent their mutual interests in regard to labor and social security issues before the employer or the state authorities).

The 2001 Labor Code amendments abolished provisions relating to selection criteria applicable to cases of dismissal. As a result, priority is no longer given to employees with family or health problems or to employees who are the sole support of their families.

The 2003 amendments further clarified the "collective dismissal" definition, limiting the grounds for dismissal carried out by the employer to those listed in the Labor Code,[325] namely:

- closing down of the enterprise;
- partial closing down of the enterprise or staff cuts;
- reduction of the volume of work; and
- work stoppage for more than 15 working days.

Regarding a planned mass dismissal, it is the obligation of the employer to notify in writing the Employment Agency division and the workers' and employees' representatives. It is the Employment Agency that is obliged to inform the other interested parties, namely the municipal administration, the territorial division of the National Insurance Institute, and the General Labor Inspectorate - Executive Agency. The notification must contain all necessary information regarding the planned mass dismissal—including the reasons for the planned dismissal, the number and category of workers and employees, the period during which the dismissal must be carried out, and the stipulated selection criteria as it relates to preliminary consultations with representatives of the workers and employees.

B. Transfers of Undertakings

Article 123 of the Labor Code states that the employment relationship with the employee is not terminated "in the event of a merger of enterprises, or a transfer of a part of one enterprise to another enterprise, or distribution of the operations of one enterprise among several enterprises." Liability for obligations to em-

---

[325] *Id.* art. 328(1), subs. 1–4.

ployees created before the merger, transfer, restructuring, or leasing of the business are apportioned as follows:[326]

1. in case of merger of enterprises—on the new enterprise;
2. in case of transfer of a part of one enterprise to another—on both enterprises jointly and severally;
3. in case of distribution of the operations of one enterprise between several enterprises—on the enterprises taking the operations over jointly and severally; or
4. the employment relationship with the employee shall not be terminated in the event of a change of the enterprise owner or a leasing out. In this case, the new owner, [or] the lessee respectively, shall be the employer.[327]

Article 123 of the Labor Code was amended in 2001 in view of Bulgaria's pending admission to the European Union and the necessity for adhering to European employment regulations. After the amendments, Article 123 enumerates more cases where the employment relationship passes to the new owner of an enterprise.[328] In the event of a proposed transfer, Article 123 also requires the employer to provide information to the employees or their representatives regarding the following:

- the type of transfer and the date of its implementation;
- the reasons for the transfer;
- the possible legal, economic, and social consequences of the transfer; and
- the measures intended to be undertaken with respect to the employees.

The required information must be provided at least two months before the consequences of the transfer are set to occur.

The Labor Code amendments also provide that the employer must consult with the employee representatives if it intends to undertake certain employment measures, such as dismissals. These

---

[326] *Id.* art. 123(2), subs. 1, 2, 3.
[327] *Id.* art. 123(3).
[328] *See id.* art. 123(1).

consultations must be conducted prior to the time that the employer provides employees with information regarding the transfer.

The consultations are not subject to any procedural requirements. The employer and the employees' representatives are free to agree on the procedure. The main aim of the consultations is to obtain the opinion of the employees' representatives regarding the transfer and, to the extent possible, to modify the parameters of the transfer to avoid any employment-related complications.

Bulgarian law does not include any specific legal consequences for noncompliance with the statutory requirements for informing and consulting with employees regarding a transfer. Therefore, noncompliance should be subject to the general administrative sanctions for breach of statutory labor obligations.[329] These sanctions are imposed by the competent Labor Inspectorate and are in the form of fines, varying from BGL 250[330] to BGL 1,000, or, in the case of a second violation, from BGL 500 to BGL 2,000.

V. WAGES, HOURS, AND LEAVE

A. Wages

1. *Mandatory Compensation*

Chapter Twelve of the Labor Code establishes detailed rules on employee compensation. The Code states the general rule that all work performed under an employment contract must be monetarily[331] compensated.[332] Parties may not avoid this provision by negotiating some other form of remuneration or for work to be performed without compensation.[333]

The 2001 Labor Code amendments explicitly prohibit discrimination in the compensation of men and women performing

---

[329] *Id.* art. 414.

[330] At the current exchange rate in effect in August 2004, 1 BGL was equal to approximately U.S. $1.60.

[331] Labor Code art. 269(1).

[332] *Id.* art. 242.

[333] *Id.* art. 74(1).

the same or equivalent work.[334] Accordingly, men and women performing the same or equivalent work are entitled to equal remuneration.

2. *Role of Trade Unions*

The role of the trade unions in the determination and negotiation of employee compensation has increased significantly under the 1996 amendments to the Labor Code. Trade union representatives participate actively in determining compensation under both individual and collective employment contracts.[335]

Trade unions may play a role in determining salaries to the extent that minimum salary amounts can be negotiated in a collective labor contract. However, they may not influence salaries that are established in an individual employment agreement.

3. *Minimum Wages*

A Bulgarian worker is entitled to basic compensation for the fulfillment of a given type of work under normal conditions and within legally established working hours. The amount of the basic remuneration is determined by mutual agreement of the parties under the individual employee's contract or under the collective labor agreement. Compensation also is based on the level of a worker's professional qualifications, experience, and skills.

The minimum monthly wage is determined by an ordinance of the Council of Ministers from time to time upon its own discretion. The ordinance is subject to promulgation in the *State Gazette*. Collective labor contracts and their provisions are not relevant to determination of the national minimum monthly wage.

According to the provisions of the Additional Remuneration Regulation,[336] additional work remuneration[337] usually is determined as a percentage of the basic salary under the labor contract,

[334] *Id.* art. 243.

[335] V. MRACHKOV, BULGARIA LABOR LAW 105 (1995).

[336] Regulation on Additional and Other Work Remunerations, approved by the Council of Ministers by Ordinance No. 133, 67 STATE GAZETTE (Aug. 8, 1993), as last amended in 25 STATE GAZETTE (March 19, 1999).

[337] See V.A.4., below.

and not on the basis of the national minimum monthly wage.

The minimum monthly salary is uniform throughout the country and is the basic salary upon which any additional labor remuneration is based. Any employment contract that attempts to provide for a monthly compensation below the established minimum limit is illegal.[338]

4. *Additional Work Remuneration*

Additional remuneration may be added to the basic compensation in recognition of additional requirements for the quantity and quality of the work performed, or to compensate employees for specific conditions under which their work is performed.[339]

The Council of Ministers is empowered to establish the different kinds and minimum amounts of additional compensation.[340] The Council of Ministers also prescribes the system and rate of labor remuneration for various industries and occupations.[341] The different types of additional work remuneration and their minimum rates are set by ordinance.[342] The most important types of work for which additional remuneration is provided include the following:

- internal replacement for an absent employee, [343]
- night work,[344]
- overtime work,[345]
- holiday work,[346] and
- long service.[347]

---

[338]MRACHKOV, *supra* note 330, at 108.

[339]Labor Code art. 260.

[340]*Id.* art. 244.

[341]*Id.* art. 244, subs. 2.

[342]Ordinance on Additional and Other Work Remunerations, approved by the Council of Ministers by Decree No. 133, DV No. 67 (1993) (Additional Remuneration Ordinance).

[343]Labor Code art. 259(1).

[344]*Id.* art. 261. See also V.B.6., below.

[345]Labor Code art. 262. See also V.B.2., below.

[346]Labor Code art. 264. See also V.B.8., below.

[347]Additional Remuneration Ordinance art. 3.

5. *Pay Reductions*

The Labor Code also provides specific rules for determining an employee's compensation in the event of failure to fulfill work quotas,[348] during a work stoppage or a transfer of work assignments,[349] or for poor quality of output due to fault or no fault of the worker.[350] These rules are summarized as follows:

- For failure to fulfill quotas where the employee is not at fault, the employee receives remuneration according to the output, but no less than the agreed remuneration for full output.[351]
- For failure to fulfill quotas where the employee is at fault, the employee receives remuneration according to the output.[352]
- For a work stoppage, an employee receives his or her gross remuneration when the stoppage is not the employee's fault and no remuneration if the stoppage is the employee's fault.[353]
- For performing work other than that regularly assigned to the employee, he or she receives the remuneration for the work done, but no less than the employee's regular gross remuneration.[354]
- For unfit products, an employee receives the remuneration for fit products when the unfitness is not the employee's fault, or no remuneration if the unfitness is the employee's fault.[355]
- For products that only partially meet quality standards, the employee's remuneration is reduced in proportion to the waste when the partial unfitness is the employee's fault.[356]

[348] Labor Code art. 266.
[349] *Id.* art. 267.
[350] *Id.* art. 268.
[351] *Id.* art. 266(1).
[352] *Id.* art. 266(2).
[353] *Id.* art. 267.
[354] *Id.* art. 267(3).
[355] *Id.* art. 268(1), (3).
[356] *Id.* art. 268(2).

6. *Methods of Computing Wages*

The manner of determining wage rates is based on a "time-work" (the length of working time) and/or a "piece-work" (work results) basis.[357] The time-work system of compensation is applied in cases where productivity cannot be measured by the quantity of work performed and where great accuracy and high quality work performance is needed. The piece-work system may be applied where productivity and performance can be precisely measured, evaluated, and controlled. Under this system, the compensation actually due is determined in proportion to the work done, which in turn is measured by the output produced.

7. *Form of Payment*

Bulgarian workers are paid in Bulgarian Leva, or in the corresponding national currency for workers abroad. The Council of Ministers, the collective agreement, or the labor contract may permit payment in kind (e.g., food, clothing, etc.), but only for the additional remuneration part of a worker's pay, not for the basic compensation.[358]

Following 1999 amendments to the Law on Obligations and Contracts,[359] which resulted from changes in foreign currency regulations, contractors may negotiate the price of a contract in foreign currency and make payments in the agreed currency. This rule extends to the payment of labor compensation.

8. *Place and Time of Payment*

Article 270 of the Labor Code provides that compensation should be paid to a worker at the place of business where the work is performed.[360] It should be paid in person or, upon signed authorization by the worker, to his or her relatives or to other authorized persons.[361] An employee's compensation may be paid either in advance or after the work is performed, twice every month.[362]

---

[357] *Id.* art. 247(1).
[358] *Id.* art. 269(2).
[359] Law on Obligations and Contracts art. 10(1).
[360] Labor Code art. 270(1).
[361] *Id.* art. 270(3).
[362] *Id.* art. 270(2).

9. Withholding of Compensation

Two provisions in the Labor Code provide employees with legal protection against the recovery or withholding of compensation by an employer. First, the Code provides that any remuneration received by a worker in good faith is not reimbursable.[363] Second, deductions from a worker's remuneration may be made only for certain specified reasons, as follows:

- to repay compensation advanced to the employee;[364]
- to repay compensation paid to the employee above the amount due as a result of a technical error;[365]
- for authorized taxes;[366]
- for insurance premiums;[367]
- pursuant to attachments authorized in accordance with established legal procedures;[368] or
- to satisfy the limited financial responsibility for losses caused by the employee.[369]

10. Tax Exemptions on Income

The Law on Taxation of Income of Individuals, which became effective on January 1, 1998,[370] abolished the Law on Income Tax of 1950. However, the principles of the 1950 Law relating to taxable income and exemptions remained unchanged to a great extent.

Under the 2002 amendments to the Law on Taxation of Income of Individuals,[371] income from investment of the amounts of contributions payable to the voluntary social security funds is not subject to taxation. Pursuant to the Law on Additional Voluntary

[363] *Id.* art. 271(1).
[364] *Id.* art. 272(1), subs. 1.
[365] *Id.* art. 272(1), subs. 2.
[366] *Id.* art. 272(1), subs. 3.
[367] *Id.* art. 272(1), subs. 4.
[368] *Id.* art. 272(1), subs. 5.
[369] *Id.* arts. 210(4), 272(2), subs. 6. See also I.D.8., above.
[370] 118 STATE GAZETTE (Dec. 11, 1997).
[371] *See* Law on Taxation of Income of Individuals, art. 12, para. 1, item 3, 118 STATE GAZETTE, effective Jan. 1, 2003.

Pension Security[372] at least 90 percent of the income realized by voluntary pension insurance companies through investment must be distributed among the people who voluntarily contributed the funds to obtain an additional pension, on a *pro rata* basis proportional to their participation in the funds of the pension company. Said personal income is exempt from taxation. The insured person is entitled to dispose at any time of the amounts so accumulated.

The regime established by the Law on Additional Voluntary Pension Security was abolished with the amendments to the Code on Social Security.[373] The new legislation stipulates that additional voluntary pension security is effected by a contract concluded with a licensed pension insurance company. Contracts with such pension insurance companies can be concluded either with the insured person or with the employer whenever it is an insurer.

B. Hours

1. Normal Working Time

The regular time for performance of the work entrusted to a worker is defined in Article 136 of the Labor Code as "working time." The legal workweek is a 40-hour, five-day week.[374] The workday must be a maximum of 8 hours per day.[375]

2. Overtime Hours

The Labor Code defines overtime work as "work performed by the employee over and above his agreed working hours under the order of, or with the knowledge of and with no objection from, the employer or the respective superior."[376]

As a general principle, overtime work is prohibited.[377] The Labor Code allows certain exceptions, however, including the following:

---

[372]*See* 65 State Gazette (July 20, 1997).
[373]*See* 67 State Gazette (July 29, 2003).
[374]Labor Code art. 136(1).
[375]*Id.* art. 136(3).
[376]*Id.* art. 143(1).
[377]*Id.* art. 143(2).

- work that is related to the national defense;[378]
- work performed in cases of natural and social disasters;[379]
- work that is necessary to restore water and electrical supply, heating, sewage, transport, and communication, and for medical assistance;[380]
- emergency repairs on the work premises;[381]
- work that cannot be performed during regular working hours for safety or health reasons;[382] and
- intensive seasonal work.[383]

An employee has the right to refuse to perform overtime work if it is in violation of the law or the collective agreement.[384]

The Labor Code expressly prohibits compensatory time off in lieu of overtime pay.[385] The employer and employee may agree on the rate of premium pay for overtime, subject to the following minimum statutory premiums based on the employee's regular wage rate:

- 50 percent for every additional overtime hour;[386]
- 75 percent for overtime during the weekly rest period;[387] and
- 100 percent for every overtime hour during official holidays.[388]

The Labor Code places strict maximum amounts on the duration of overtime work, allowing no more than the following:

- 30 hours of day work, or 20 hours of night work, to be performed within one calendar month;[389]

---

[378] *Id.* art. 144(1).
[379] *Id.* art. 144(2).
[380] *Id.* art. 144(3).
[381] *Id.* art. 144(4).
[382] *Id.* art. 144(5).
[383] *Id.* art. 144(6).
[384] *Id.* art. 148.
[385] *Id.* art. 150(2).
[386] *Id.* art. 262(1), subs. 1.
[387] *Id.* art. 262(1), subs. 2.
[388] *Id.* art. 262(1), subs. 3.
[389] *Id.* art. 146(2), subs. 1.

- six hours of day work, or four hours of night work, to be performed in one calendar week;[390]
- three hours of day work, or two hours of night work, to be performed in two consecutive working days.[391]

An annual cap of 150 hours is placed on accumulated overtime work.[392] However, these restrictions do not apply in cases of (1) national defense, (2) natural and social disasters, or (3) urgent public needs for the restoration of the water or electrical supply.[393]

The following categories of persons are prohibited from working overtime:

- employees younger than18 years of age,[394]
- pregnant employees,[395] and
- mothers of children younger than 3 years of age.[396]

Employers are prohibited from requiring overtime work by the following types of employees, unless the employee consents to the assignment:

- mothers of handicapped children regardless of the child's age;[397]
- workers who have been reassigned due to medical disability, but only if medical authorities determine that it will not be detrimental to their health;[398] and
- employees who are continuing their education while employed.[399]

Overtime work also is prohibited for workers whose working time has been reduced due to hazardous working conditions, with ex-

---

[390]*Id.* art. 146(2), subs. 2.
[391]*Id.* art. 146(2), subs. 3.
[392]*Id.* art. 146(1).
[393]*Id.* art. 146(3).
[394]*Id.* art. 147(1), subs. 1.
[395]*Id.* art. 147(1), subs. 2.
[396]*Id.*
[397]*Id.* art. 147(1), subs. 3.
[398]*Id.* art. 147(1), subs. 4.
[399]*Id.* art. 147(1), subs. 5.

ceptions allowed for work in (1) national defense, (2) natural and social disasters or dangers, and (3) public works sectors when urgently necessary.[400]

A number of special ordinances have been promulgated by the Council of Ministers, Ministry of Labor and Social Policies, and Ministry of Health to implement the Labor Code provisions on hours of work.[401]

The 2001 amendments also added a new Article 136a, which provides that employers may extend business hours for reasons related to the production process. In order to exercise this right, the employer must, in advance of the extension, consult the employees' representatives, unless otherwise agreed in the collective bargaining agreement, and must notify the Labor Inspectorate. When extended, business hours may not exceed 10 business hours per day. In addition, extended business hours may not exceed more than 20 consecutive days or more than 60 days annually.

Extension of the business day should be compensated within four months by a reduction in the number of business hours on other days, and these reductions in the normal duration of the business day should be recorded by the employer in a specially designated book. If the employer fails to compensate employees within the four-month period, then each employee may choose at his or her own discretion the moment to exercise the right of compensation by providing two weeks' advance notice to the employer. If the employee terminates employment before receiving reduced-hour compensation, monetary compensation equal to that payable for overtime work must be paid to the employee for the additional hours of work.

---

[400] *Id.* art. 147(2).

[401] Ordinance for Reduced Working Time, DV No. 59 (1993); Ordinance No. 7 by the Ministry of Labor and Social Policies and Ministry of Health for Determination of Dangerous and Hazardous Working Conditions for the Health of Women, DV No. 58 (1993); Ordinance No. 3 on the Requirements for the Determination of Additional Annual Paid Leaves Due to Work Under Dangerous and Hazardous Work Conditions, DV No. 44 (1993); Instruction No. 10 by the Ministry of Labor and Social Policies and by the Ministry of Health on the Implementation of Ordinance No. 3, DV No. 44 (1993); Ordinance for Working Time, Rest Periods and Leaves, DV No. 6 (1987), amended by DV Nos. 31, 55, and 59 (1991), Nos. 59 and 67 (1993), and No. 38 (1994).

3. *Reduced Work Hours*

Article 137 of the Labor Code provides for reduced working hours based on the nature of the working conditions and the age and health of the worker. The reduced workday is designed to protect workers from the dangerous impact of the work environment by reducing the length of time they are exposed to such conditions.

The amount of reduction in the workday depends on the degree of the danger posed to the employee.[402] The determination of reduced working time is based on the opinions of medical and technical experts and is regulated by numerous acts of the Council of Ministers. Regulation of work time is subject to change following the introduction of new technology and equipment that significantly improves the work environment.[403]

For employees entitled to reduced working time, the 2001 Labor Code amendments explicitly prohibit a reduction in remuneration or other benefits, such as the right to a paid annual leave. In addition, the 2001 amendments introduced the possibility of a reduction in work hours for employees working in harmful conditions for more than four hours per day.

4. *Part-Time Work*

The Labor Code contains a somewhat ill-defined distinction between full-time (normal) and part-time work.[404] The distinction is based on the length of daily working hours compared with the legally established normal duration of the workday. Part-time work is shorter in duration than the normal workday.[405] The parties are free to negotiate the duration and allocation of any part-time work assignment.[406]

---

[402] Ordinance of the Ministry of Labor and Social Policies and Ministry of Health Providing Free Food to Employees Working in Conditions Dangerous to Their Health, DV No. 58 (1993).

[403] Ordinance for Reduced Working Time, DV No. 59 (1993).

[404] *Compare* Labor Code art. 136 *with* Labor Code art. 138.

[405] Labor Code art. 138.

[406] *Id.*

The 2001 Labor Code amendments provide that an employer may introduce part-time work for all or some of its employees, for a term of not more than three months per year and conditioned on a reduction in the volume of work.[407] The introduction of part-time work must be agreed to in advance with the employees' representatives. Where a part-time work arrangement is implemented, working time should not be reduced to less than one-half of the normal working time, as reflected in the parties' employment contract.

5. *Stand-By Duty*

Certain categories of employees may be required to be on duty or on stand-by status during specified hours in a 24-hour period. The categories of employees, maximum duration of hours, and accounting procedures for stand-by duty are determined by the Minister of Labor and Social Policies.[408]

6. *Night Work*

According to Article 140 of the Labor Code, any work performed between the hours of 10:00 p.m. and 6:00 a.m. is considered night work[409] and is subject to strict limitations. The normal duration of a night shift is seven hours for employees on a five-day workweek.[410]

The law provides for increased compensation for night work, largely because it is considered hazardous to the worker's health. Based on this consideration, the law prohibits the assignment of the following workers to night work:

- employees younger than age 18 (for whom work performed between 8:00 p.m. and 6:00 a.m. is considered to be night work);[411] and
- pregnant women.[412]

---

[407] *Id.* art. 138(2)–(3).
[408] *Id.* art. 139(5).
[409] *Id.* art. 140(2).
[410] *Id.* art. 140(1).
[411] *Id.* art. 140(4), subs. 1.
[412] *Id.* art. 140(4), subs. 2.

The prohibition also applies to the following employees, but exceptions are allowed with the employee's consent:

- mothers of children younger than age six,[413]
- mothers taking care of handicapped children,[414]
- employees with disabilities,[415] and
- employees continuing their education.[416]

Night work rates may be negotiated between the parties under the employment contract, but strict compliance with the minimum rate as determined by the Council of Ministers is required.[417]

The Labor Code also requires that an employer provide hot food, refreshments, and facilities to night shift workers.[418] This provision reflects the legislative finding that night work is considered "harmful to the worker's well being because of the changes in the normal cycle of the physiological functions in the human body."[419]

7. *Rest Periods*

Article 153 of the Labor Code provides for a weekly rest period equal to an uninterrupted 48-hour period or two consecutive days, one of which is to be a Sunday.[420] The weekly rest period may be reduced under ccrtain circumstances, e.g., where the employer has a six-day workweek, but must be at least 24 consecutive hours in duration.[421]

The Code further guarantees an employee one or several rest periods that are not included in the calculation of daily working hours. For example, an employee working in an enterprise with continuous production is entitled to a paid rest period for one meal

---

[413] *Id.* art. 140(4), subs. 3.
[414] *Id.*
[415] *Id.* art. 140(4), subs. 4.
[416] *Id.* art. 140(4), subs. 5.
[417] *Id.* art. 261; Additional Remuneration Ordinance art. 7.
[418] Labor Code art. 140(3).
[419] V. MRACHKOV, BULGARIA LABOR LAW 94 (1995).
[420] Labor Code art. 153(1).
[421] *Id.* art. 153(2).

during each workday.[422] Employees also are entitled to at least 12 hours rest between two working days.[423]

The law does allow some exceptions to these rest period requirements. For example, the weekly rest period may be reduced to 24 hours in certain industries that have continuous production processes and therefore require the uninterrupted use of the work force through shift work.[424]

8. *Legal Holidays*

Official Bulgarian national public holidays, listed in Article 154(1) of the Labor Code, are as follows:

January 1	New Year
March 3	National Day
May 1	Labor Day
May 6	St. Georgie's Day
May 24	Education and Culture and Slavonic Alphabet Day
September 6	Reunion Day
September 22	Independence Day
November 1	National Revival Day
December 24	Christmas Eve
December 25 and 26	Christmas
Easter Sunday and Monday (two days)	Easter

Days classified as official holidays constitute paid days off for all employees. In the event that an employee voluntarily works on an official holiday, his or her compensation for that day is doubled.[425]

---

[422] *Id.* art. 151(3).
[423] *Id.* art. 152.
[424] *Id.* art. 153(2).
[425] *Id.* art. 262(1), subs. 3.

C. Leave

1. *Paid Annual Leave*

A worker's basic right to paid annual leave is guaranteed by Article 48(5) of the Constitution, and implemented by Articles 155 to 178 of the Labor Code. This right vests after eight months of service,[426] regardless of whether the service was acquired while employed by a different enterprise or was interrupted.[427] This eight-month qualifying period of service is necessary only for the initial acquisition of the right to annual leave.[428]

a. *Leave Accrual*

Under the 2001 Labor Code amendments, the length of paid annual leave no longer depends on the total length of an employee's service. Instead, a uniform requirement for at least 20 business days of annual paid leave was introduced, notwithstanding the employee's age or duration of employment.[429]

b. *Extended Annual Leave*

Extended annual leave is provided for certain categories of workers (e.g., teachers, professors, pilots, scientists, etc.), depending on the nature of their activities and the extent of their responsibilities.[430] These categories are expressly enumerated in an ordinance approved by the Council of Ministers.[431]

c. *Additional Paid Annual Leave*

Additional paid annual leave may be awarded for hazardous work and irregular work schedules imposed by the needs of the enterprises.[432] Under the 1996 amendments to the Labor Code, an

---

[426] *Id.* art. 155(1).

[427] V. MRACHKOV, BULGARIA LABOR LAW 99 (1995). The former requirement that the eight months' service should be uninterrupted and under the same employer was abandoned in the 1986 Labor Code.

[428] *Id.*

[429] Labor Code art. 155(2).

[430] *Id.* art. 155(3).

[431] Working Time Ordinance art. 22.

[432] Labor Code art. 156.

employer and employee may agree on a longer duration of leave and may include the agreement in either the individual or collective labor contract.[433]

d. Use of Annual Leave

As a general rule, annual leave should be used during the calendar year in which it is accrued. However, the 2001 Labor Code amendments changed the statutory requirement to provide that employees must use at least one-half of their annual leave during the year of accrual.

The employer is obliged to permit an employee to take paid annual leave by the end of the year in which it is accrued, unless use of the leave has been postponed. Annual leave may be postponed in the following cases:

- by the employer, because of material reasons related to its business;
- by the employee, if he or she is using another type of leave;
- upon agreement of the employer and the employee, if the employee requests postponement.

If the employee, after an offer by the employer, has failed to request the use of paid annual leave by the end of the year, or if use of the leave has not been postponed in the ways described above, the employer is obliged to procure its use within six months following the end of the year to which the leave pertains. If the employer fails to perform this obligation, the employee is entitled to determine the period during which he or she will take annual leave, by notifying the employer in writing at least two weeks in advance.

Annual paid leave also may be ordered by the employer, without the employee's request or consent, in the event of a business closing of more than five business days' duration, where paid annual leave is used by all the employees during the same period of time.

---

[433] *Id.* art. 156(a).

e. Rate of Compensation

The amount of compensation received when annual leave is taken is based on the remuneration received by the employee during the month preceding the leave.[434] The Labor Code prohibits payment of cash compensation in lieu of annual leave except in the case of termination of the employment contract,[435] when the worker is entitled to monetary compensation for the unused portion of his or her annual leave. This figure is determined in accordance with Article 224(1) of the Labor Code and the Ordinance on Working Time, Rest Periods, and Leave.[436]

2. *Other Types of Paid Leave*

The Labor Code provides additional leave for the following purposes:

- performance of public duties;[437]
- military training;[438]
- trade union activities;[439]
- accomplishment of important tasks of public significance, or creative tasks;[440]
- temporary disability;[441]
- pregnancy and maternity leave, or the adoption of a child;[442]
- raising a child;[443]
- nursing a child;[444]
- death or severe illness of a parent;[445]
- childcare (mothers of two or more children);[446]

---

[434] *Id.* art. 177.
[435] *Id.* art. 178.
[436] Working Time Ordinance art. 44.
[437] Labor Code art. 157.
[438] *Id.* art. 158.
[439] *Id.* art. 159.
[440] *Id.* art. 161.
[441] *Id.* art. 162.
[442] *Id.* art. 163.
[443] *Id.* art. 164.
[444] *Id.* art. 166.
[445] *Id.* art. 167.
[446] *Id.* art. 168.

- educational purposes;[447] and
- preparation for an examination for admission to a higher educational institution.[448]

The above types of leave are all paid by the employer.[449] Payment is made under the same rules and rates established for paid annual leave, and is based on the average wage received during the month preceding the leave.[450]

The 2001 Labor Code amendments did not change the types of paid leave available to employees, but they did make certain changes in leave duration. The annual paid leave was increased to 20 business days and no longer depends on the duration of employees' employment on record. Further, unified duration of pregnancy, birth, and adoption leave was introduced—135 calendar days per child. The 2001 Labor Code amendments also introduced unified duration of the paid leave extended to employees who are studying in secondary or higher educational institutions. The duration of the leave is 25 business days per year of education and does not depend on the time when the educational activities take place (weekends, evenings, and the like).

3. *Unpaid Leave*

Upon request by an employee, an enterprise may permit the employee unpaid annual leave for up to 30 working days, which will be considered as service time for purposes of retirement service requirements.[451] Any unpaid leave in excess of 30 working days will be considered as service time only if expressly provided by law.[452] Other types of unpaid leaves recognized in the Labor Code include:

---

[447] *Id.* art. 169.

[448] *Id.* art. 170.

[449] Additional regulations on the above types of paid leave are found in the Working Time Ordinance.

[450] Labor Code art. 177.

[451] *Id.* art. 160.

[452] *Id.* art. 160(2).

- leave for child rearing;[453]
- leave for working students;[454] and
- leave for preparation of a thesis or dissertation, or for other educational or professional requirements.[455]

There is an obvious overlap between the entitlements to paid leave and unpaid leave, and the Labor Code does not provide adequate guidance as to how the two may be reconciled.

VI. ANTIDISCRIMINATION

In the 2001 Labor Code amendments, the legislature tried to distinguish between direct and indirect discrimination. Both direct and indirect discrimination, resulting in the grant of privileges or the imposition of limitations, based on race, nationality, origin, sex, age, color, political or religious beliefs, membership in a trade union or other public organization, or family, public, or financial status, or health conditions were prohibited.[456]

In addition, the term "indirect discrimination" was defined to mean discrimination that occurs where ostensibly legal means are used to carry out employment rights and obligations but are applied in a way that actually places some employees in less favorable or more privileged positions as compared to others.[457]

Discrimination is not prohibited where it is based on the qualification requirements for performing a particular job, or where it is a means of carrying out the special legal protections accorded to certain employees, such as minors, pregnant women and mothers of young children, or the disabled.

The antidiscrimination provision of the 1997 Employment Law previously in effect and discussed in the First Edition was a specific provision prohibiting discrimination as far as the rights and obligations under that law were concerned, whereas the anti-

[453] *Id.* art. 165.
[454] *Id.* art. 171.
[455] *Id.* art. 161(1).
[456] Labor Code art. 8(3).
[457] *Id.* Concluding Provisions, para. 7.

discrimination provision of the Labor Code prohibits discrimination in cases where labor rights and obligations are exercised.[458] The antidiscrimination provision of the 1997 Employment Law was abolished by the new Law on Encouragement of Employment, which also prohibits discrimination.

A new Law on Protection Against Discrimination[459] was adopted in 2003. The legislation further develops the principles laid down in the Labor Code and the 2002 Employment Law. The law stipulates that introduction of requirements for minimum age, professional experience or length of service for recruitment or for access to certain advantages linked to employment, the special protection measures benefiting pregnant women and mothers, requirements for age and length of service provided for purposes of retirement, and the measures provided for under the Employment Law shall not constitute discrimination. Occupational activities for which gender is an essential and determining professional requirement are to be defined in ordinances issued by the Minister of Labor and Social Policy in coordination with the Minister of Internal Affairs and also by the Minister of Defense regarding professional military service. An independent specialized state agency was established for the prevention of and protection against discrimination and for the safeguarding of equal opportunities. Obligations with respect to announcing vacancies, employment refusal, equal remuneration and equal training opportunities, as well as with respect to taking effective measures to prevent all forms of discrimination, are imposed on the employer.

A. Protection of Minors

The special protection accorded to minors under Bulgarian law is based on consideration of their age, health, and their need for special care. The Labor Code requires that all workers be at least 16 years of age.[460] Exceptions are provided for light work not performed under dangerous or harmful conditions.[461]

---

[458] Labor Code art. 8(3).

[459] *See* 86 STATE GAZETTE (Sept. 30, 2003), in force as of Jan. 1, 2004.

[460] Labor Code art. 301(1).

[461] *Id.* art. 301(2).

The Ministry of Labor and the Ministry of Public Health are empowered to prohibit minors (children younger than age 16) from working in certain designated industries.[462] The employment of persons younger than age 15 is allowed only for film and theatrical work, circus performances, and related work.[463] The terms of such employment are determined by the Council of Ministers.[464]

The Labor Code further requires that minors undergo a mandatory medical examination before the commencement of employment.[465] Special preemployment authorization by the Labor Inspectorate is required for persons younger than age 16.[466] An employment contract concluded with a minor in violation of these requirements is considered null and void.[467]

The 2001 Labor Code amendments provide that persons younger than age 18 are prohibited from performing the following:

- activities that are unsuited to their physical or mental capacity;
- activities that involve exposure to harmful physical, biological, or chemical effects, especially toxic agents, carcinogens, or agents causing genetic or intrauterine damage;
- activities that involve harmful conditions that, in any way whatsoever, have unfavorable effects on the employee's health;
- activities that involve conditions of radiation;
- activities subject to exceptionally low or high temperatures, noise, or vibrations;
- activities presenting a risk of labor accidents, which may not be realized or avoided by a minor due to his or her physical or mental immaturity.[468]

---

[462] V. MRACHKOV, BULGARIA LABOR LAW 160 (1995).
[463] Labor Code art. 301(3).
[464] *Id.*
[465] *Id.* art. 302(1).
[466] *Id.* art. 302(2).
[467] *Id.* art. 74(2).
[468] *Id.* art. 304.

The list of activities that may be performed by minors, as well as the activities that, as an exception, may be performed by persons between 15 and 16 years of age, will be issued by the Minister of Labor and Social Policy and the Minister of Health.[469]

Under the 2001 amendments, the employer is obliged to inform employees younger than age 18, as well as their parents or guardians, about risks related to their work and about the measures taken for procuring safe and healthy work conditions.[470] In addition, minor employees are permitted to work only 35 hours per week, 7 hours per day.[471]

The 2003 amendments to the Labor Code[472] provide that the conditions and procedure for obtaining permission to work for employees younger than age 16 are to be further regulated with a bylaw issued by both the Minister of Labor and Social Policy and the Minister of Public Healthcare.

B. Protection of Women

Female workers are given increased protection under Bulgarian law from hazardous conditions that might prove to be harmful to their health. For example, the law requires that pregnant women and mothers of children younger than age three be placed in a "more suitable" position with appropriate compensation.[473] If the compensation in the more suitable position is less than in the woman's previous position, Bulgaria's social security system will pay the difference.[474]

Prior to the 2001 Labor Code amendments, employers were prohibited from sending on a business trip pregnant female employees or mothers of children younger than age three. Under the amended provisions of the Labor Code, employers now are allowed to send mothers of children younger than age three on business trips, with the mother's written consent.[475]

---

[469] *Id.* art. 304(2).
[470] *Id.* art. 305.
[471] *Id.* art. 305(3).
[472] *See id.* art. 303(4).
[473] *Id.* art. 309(1).
[474] *Id.* art. 309(3).
[475] *Id.* art. 310(2)

Pregnant employees may not be assigned to overtime or night work.[476] Overtime and night work restrictions also apply to mothers with young or handicapped children.[477]

Additionally, female workers are entitled to paid leave for pregnancy, maternity, adoption of a child, and childcare.[478] During the paid pregnancy and maternity leave, the mother is entitled to receive compensation in the same amount as her monthly salary preceding the commencement of the leave.[479]

The amount of paid maternity leave granted is 135 calendar days, regardless of the number of other children in the family.[480] Of this leave, 45 days represents maternity leave that is taken before the child is born.

The amount of paid leave for adoption of a child is equal to the amount of maternity leave granted according to the number of children minus the age of the child.[481]

Maternity leave can be used by the father of a newborn instead of the mother with the mother's consent.[482]

Additional paid leave is allowed until the child reaches two years of age. This optional leave can begin after the expiration of the ordinary paid maternity leave. It can be taken by anyone, for any length of time up to the full two years. Compensation for this leave is the amount of the nation's minimum salary.[483]

When a child is attending a childcare institution, a working mother is entitled to additional compensation (added to her monthly salary) in the amount of 50 percent of the nation's minimum salary.[484]

C. Protection of Persons With Reduced Work Capacity

Articles 314 to 320 of the Labor Code contain regulations protecting "persons with reduced work capacity" by providing them

---

[476] *Id.* art. 147(1), subs. 2. See V.B.2. and V.B.6., above.

[477] Labor Code arts. 147(1), 149(4). See V.B.2. and V.B.6., above.

[478] Labor Code arts. 163–166. See also V.C.2., above.

[479] Labor Code art. 156(2).

[480] *See* 1 STATE GAZETTE (Jan. 3, 2003), effective Jan. 2, 2003.

[481] Labor Code art. 163(6).

[482] *Id.* art. 164(3).

[483] *Id.* art. 164(1), subs. 4.

[484] *Id.* art. 164(5).

with more suitable working conditions and an opportunity to remain with the same employer. An employer with more than 50 employees must designate 4 to 10 percent of the total number of jobs, depending on the economic sector, for workers with diminished work capacity.[485] The 2001 Labor Code amendments require employers with more than 300 employees to establish workshops for employees with reduced work capacity.[486]

Overall, the recent legislative changes are aimed at ensuring a higher level of protection, including higher compensation, to persons with reduced working capacity. This higher compensation is a percentage of the minimum amount of social pensions and this increase is a result of the increase in such minimum amounts.

VII. OCCUPATIONAL SAFETY AND HEALTH AND WORKERS' COMPENSATION

A. Safety and Health Protections

1. Constitutional Protections

Article 48(5) of the Bulgarian Constitution guarantees all employees the right to safe and healthy working conditions. Safety and health rules must be uniformly applied regardless of the type and duration of the employment relationship. The state's goal is to guarantee a healthy and safe working environment for the entire working population.

2. Labor Code Rules

The general rules applicable in all economic sectors are contained in the Labor Code and in the implementing legislative acts. Additionally, special rules are established for different sectors of the economy.

---

[485]*Id.* art. 315(1). See also VII.B., below.
[486]Labor Code art. 316(1).

The rules regulating worker health and safety are designed to protect all workers from the harmful effect of hazardous substances, noise, vibrations, high temperature, extreme moisture, and other dangerous conditions. These conditions are taken into consideration by a special state commission, with the participation of government controlling bodies, before any plan for construction, reconstruction, or modernization is approved.[487]

Under Article 219 of the Labor Code, an employee has the right to refuse or to stop working because of a legitimate, serious, and direct threat to his or her life and health. An employee has a right to compensation in cases of lawful refusals to perform the job under existing conditions.[488]

The 2001 Labor Code amendments require that all employees must be instructed and trained on safe methods of work. No person without the knowledge and skills necessary to maintain healthy and safe work conditions may be admitted to work in the enterprise.[489]

a. Provision and Use of Protective Clothing and Equipment

Employers are obliged to provide workers with protective clothing and equipment such as gloves, goggles, masks, etc.[490] Such protective gear is required by law in situations where the production process involves the operation of dangerous machinery.[491] Workers involved in these occupations have a legally imposed duty to use the protective clothing and equipment during the performance of work assignments.[492]

Regulation No. 3 on the Minimum Requirements for Safe Working Environments and Protection of Employees' Health by Use of Personal Means of Protection was issued on April 19, 2001, by the Minister of Labor and Social Policy and the Minister of Public Healthcare. Regulation No. 3 provides a list of activities that entitle employees to use personal protective means and iden-

---

[487] *Id.* arts. 278, 280.
[488] *Id.* art. 219(1), (2).
[489] *Id.* art. 281.
[490] *Id.* art. 284.
[491] *Id.*
[492] *Id.* art. 284(2).

tifies personal protective means and parts of the human body that are at risk. Regulation No. 3 replaced Regulation No. 11 on Protective Working Uniforms and Personal Means of Protection, which granted employers the right to determine the types of risky activities.

b. *Production of Hazardous Materials*

Workers engaged in the production of hazardous and toxic substances are entitled to a free meal, and if necessary, to antitoxins to neutralize the harmful effects of the work environment.[493]

In 2003, the following new regulations were adopted, focusing on protection of workers from the risks related to exposure to asbestos, noise, chemical agents, carcinogens, and mutagens at work:

- Regulation on the protection of workers from the risks related to exposure to asbestos at work;
- Regulation on the protection of workers from the risks related to exposure to noise at work;
- Regulation on the protection of workers from the risks related to exposure to chemical agents at work; and
- Regulation on the protection of workers from the risks related to exposure to carcinogens and mutagens.

The potential risks related to the working environment are dealt with in a similar way in all of these regulations, which provide for regular assessment of risk, special training for employees, and planning measures to limit the dangerous impact on people in contact with the hazardous substances. The employer is obliged to keep workers and their representative bodies informed of the risk levels and to further exercise all steps available to reduce exposure to the lowest level reasonably practicable.

c. *Physical Examinations*

Mandatory periodic medical checkups are required for every worker.[494] The frequency of these checkups is determined by the

---

[493] *Id.* art. 285(1).
[494] *Id.* art. 287.

Minister of Health, based on the characteristics of the particular work environment.[495] The 2001 Labor Code amendments imposed certain statutory obligations on employers with respect to the provision of medical services to their employees.[496]

Detailed regulation of healthy and safe conditions is provided by the Law on Safe and Healthy Working Conditions.[497] Articles 24 and 25 of the Law on Safe and Healthy Working Conditions require the employer to appoint one or more employees to monitor safe and healthy working conditions or, alternatively, to establish a specialized department within the enterprise to deal with such conditions, as well as to establish a medical services department within the enterprise or assign the provision of medical services to qualified outside contractors. The activities of outside medical services contractors and the requirements applicable to their activities are governed by the Regulation on Medical Services Providers of 1998, issued by the Minister of Public Healthcare.[498]

d. Recordkeeping and Reporting Requirements

Employers must record and report all occupational injuries and registered occupational illnesses as part of a prevention plan for labor-related accidents.[499] The procedure for registration of incidents of occupational illnesses is governed by a special law,[500] the Ordinance on Registration and Accounting of Occupational Illness.[501]

B. Reassignment and Compensation of Workers Following Illness or Injury

Following a worker's illness or injury, the employer must comply with recommendations for reassignment given by the health authority and with the requirements established in the 1987 Ordi-

---

[495] *Id.*
[496] *Id.* art. 287.
[497] 124 STATE GAZETTE (Dec. 23, 1997).
[498] 95 STATE GAZETTE (Aug. 14, 1998).
[499] Labor Code art. 289(2).
[500] *Id.* art. 290.
[501] DV No. 5 (1985), amended by DV Nos. 34 and 87 (1994).

nance on the Reassignment of Persons with Reduced Work Capacity.[502] If the compensation of the reassigned worker is less than that earned by the worker in his or her previous assignment, the social security system compensates the worker for the difference.[503] Terminating the employment relationship of a reassigned worker is allowed only upon consent of the General Labor Inspectorate.[504]

Workers who are totally disabled due to a job-related illness or injury are categorized into levels by the Central Labor Expert Physician Commission according to the extent of their disability.[505] They are eligible to be placed in specialized companies employing persons with disabilities, with remuneration equal to that paid to healthy workers, plus additional compensation in the following amounts:

- workers categorized in the "50 or more than 50 percent reduction in working ability"[506] receive an additional 40 to 60 percent of their regular monthly salary;
- workers categorized in the second level of disability receive an additional 30 to 50 percent of their regular monthly salary; and
- workers categorized in the third level of disability receive up to 3 percent of their regular monthly salary.

With the 2003 amendments to the Code on Social Security,[507] compensation following work-related illness or injury is due both to workers covered by social security, even in cases when they have fewer than six months of service, and to workers younger than age 18. Compensation for the first working day of illness or injury and up to 15 working days in a calendar year is paid by the insurers.

---

[502]DV No. 52, amended by DV No. 58 (1993). See also VI.C., above.

[503]Labor Code art. 320(2).

[504]*Id.* art. 333(1), subs. 2.

[505]Ordinance on the Reassignment of Persons with Reduced Work Capacity art. 1(3).

[506]Labor Code arts. 319, 320(2).

[507]112 STATE GAZETTE (Dec. 23, 2003).

VIII. PENSIONS AND BENEFITS

Bulgarian workers have participated in public programs providing pensions, recreational facilities, and welfare benefits since 1957. In 2001 and 2002, the system of social security, health security, and unemployment benefit contributions was changed by the Code on Obligatory Social Security,[508] the Law on the Budget of the Social Security Fund,[509] and the Law on Additional Voluntary Pensions Assurance.[510]

A. Social Security Contributions

The monthly social security contribution rates for employees hired for eight hours per day are 36.7 percent of gross monthly remuneration for employees born before January 1, 1960, and 34.7 percent for employees born after December 31, 1959. These contributions are distributed as follows:

- 29 percent to the Pensions Assurance Fund, for employees born before January 1, 1960, and 27 percent for employees born after December 31, 1959;
- 3 percent to the Maternity Leave and General Disease Fund;
- 0.7 percent to the Labor Accident and Occupational Disease Fund; and
- 4 percent to the Unemployment Benefit Fund.

Contributions to the Pensions Assurance Fund and the Maternity Leave and General Disease Fund are divided between the employer and the employee, with 75 percent payable by the employer, and 25 percent payable by the employee. The payment levy will change gradually during the following years in such a way that in 2007 it will be equally divided between the employer and employee, at a ratio of 50 to 50 percent. Contributions to the Labor Accident and Occupational Disease Fund and the Unemployment Benefit Fund are paid entirely by the employer.

---

[508]110 STATE GAZETTE (Dec. 17, 1999), effective Jan. 1, 2001.

[509]The referenced law is adopted on an annual basis. The law valid for the year 2003 was promulgated in 119 STATE GAZETTE (Dec. 27, 2002).

[510]The reference law was abolished. *See* 67 STATE GAZETTE (Jul. 29, 2003).

According to the 2003 amendments[511] to the Code on Social Security,[512] contributions to the Pensions Assurance Fund and the Maternity Leave and General Disease Fund are still payable by and divided between the employer and the employee, however, with a changed ratio, e.g., in 2007 it will be 60 percent/40percent. Equal division of contributions (50 percent/50 percent) gradually will be reached by 2009.

B. Health Security Contributions

Contributions are payable to the National Health Security Fund by all Bulgarian citizens who are not, at the same time, citizens of other countries. The amount of the health security contribution is 6 percent of the employee's taxable income, determined according to the provisions of the Law on Taxation of Incomes of Individuals. The total contribution amount is divided between the employer and the employee, at a ratio of 75 percent to 25 percent, respectively. The payment levy will change the same way as in the case of social security contributions.

C. Pensions

In 1999, the Law on Pensions was replaced by the Code on Obligatory Social Security. Under the 1999 Social Security Code, the rules governing pension eligibility remain unchanged. The right to a pension on retirement is still acquired depending on the age of the individual and the years of social security contributions on record, and the amount of the pension is still based on the worker's particular category. Thus, for the year 2003, 57 years of age and 33 years of social security contributions on record are required in order for women to be eligible to pension, whereas the right to retirement pension for men is acquired subject to reaching 62 years of age and 38 years of social security contributions on record.

The 1999 Code on Obligatory Social Security also established a system of additional pension security for all individuals born

---

[511] 112 STATE GAZETTE (Dec. 23, 2003).

[512] *See* 67 STATE GAZETTE (Jul. 29, 2003) (where the name of the Act was changed).

after December 31, 1959, who are covered by the state social security system. The additional pension security contributions are made on monthly basis. For 2003, the monthly contribution rate is 2 percent of social security income, and is payable by both the employer and employee, at a ratio of 75 percent to 25 percent, respectively. The additional pension security contributions are accumulated in a personal account maintained for each covered individual by the private security fund designated by the employee.

D. Unemployment Benefits

Unemployment benefit contributions are no longer governed by the Law on Protection Against Unemployment and Encouragement of Employment, but are now regulated by the Code on Obligatory Social Security (discussed immediately above). Except for this change in the governing law, the system of unemployment benefits remains unchanged.

Currently, employees eligible to receive unemployment compensation are those who have been obligatorily insured against any and all insured social risks for a period of at least 9 months during the last 15 months prior to the suspension of the insurance. The period of payment of unemployment compensation depends on the years of participation in the social security system noted in the employee's records, but in no event may the period of unemployment compensation exceed 12 months.

The unemployment benefit contributions are payable toward a fund for unemployment and professional qualification and amount to 4 percent of employee's salary.[513] The payment levy is distributed between the employer and the employee in the following proportions: 80 percent employer/20 percent employee for the years 2000 and 2001 75 percent employer/25 percent employee for the year 2003; 65 percent employer/35 percent employee for the year 2004; 60 percent employer/40 percent employee for the year 2005; 55 percent employer/45 percent employee for the year 2006; and 50/50 for the following years.[514]

---

[513] *Id.* art. 20.
[514] *Id.* art. 20(2).

There are several forms of unemployment benefits, including:

- financial assistance in the amount of the nation's minimum salary for no more than five months;[515]
- free professional qualification;[516]
- use of employment agencies;[517] and
- financial incentives for employers who hire unemployed persons in the amount of up to six times the minimum monthly salary for each unemployed person hired.[518]

E. Welfare Benefits

The welfare program is supported by contributions from employers, and the welfare fund is budgeted in the national budget. Parents with children younger than age 16 are entitled to modest monthly allowances from the government. The Ministry of Public Health has jurisdiction over matters of health and medicine, and health services are provided free to all.

In 2002, a new Law on Family Support for Children was adopted,[519] superseding the Encouragement of Maternity Act. Except for this legislative change, the system of welfare benefits in its entirety remains principally unchanged, though additional detail on the system has been provided. In the event of the birth of a child, parents are still entitled to a one-time monthly allowance payment payable upon request filed by the parent within three years of the month of birth, funded from the national budget. In addition, parents with children up to 18 years of age are entitled to monthly allowances provided that their family income falls under BGL 200 per month.

---

[515] *Id.* art. 53(1).
[516] *Id.* art. 53(2).
[517] *Id.* art. 48.
[518] *Id.* art. 60(2).
[519] *See* 32 STATE GAZETTE (Mar. 29, 2002), effective Apr. 1, 2002.

IX. IMMIGRATION

Article 26 of the Constitution proclaims that "foreigners who reside in the Republic of Bulgaria have all the rights and obligations guaranteed by this Constitution, excepting those rights and obligations for which the Constitution and the laws require Bulgarian citizenship."[520]

As of January 1, 2002, the employment of foreign nationals is regulated by the 2002 Employment Law.[521] From a substantive standpoint, the rules for obtaining authorization to work in Bulgaria have not changed substantially, but they have become more precise. The legal framework was further detailed by the Ordinance on the Terms and Procedure for Issuance, Refusal, and Withdrawal of Work Permits to Foreigners in the Republic of Bulgaria[522] and the Ordinance on the Terms and Procedure for Admission of Expatriates in the Republic of Bulgaria for Provision of Services.[523]

According to the 2003 amendments[524] to the Ordinance on the Terms and Procedure for Issuance, Refusal, and Withdrawal of Work Permits to Foreigners in the Republic of Bulgaria, a foreigner who has been commissioned in the Republic of Bulgaria by a foreign employer for a term of up to 3 months may perform concrete assignments without a Work Permit, within 12 months after registration at the Employment Agency, in the following cases:

- performance of installation and warranty repair of machines and equipment shipped from abroad;
- training on maintenance, or acceptance of ordered equipment, machines, or other articles;
- attendance of a course within the framework of an export delivery contract or a licensing agreement; and
- control and coordination for implementation of a contract for tourist services between a foreign tour operator and a

---

[520] CONSTITUTION art. 26(2).

[521] See the Introduction, at B.1.d., above.

[522] *See* 39 STATE GAZETTE (Apr. 16, 2002), effective June 17, 2002.

[523] *See* 68 STATE GAZETTE (July 16, 2002), effective Sept. 17, 2002.

[524] *See* 53 STATE GAZETTE (June 10, 2003).

Bulgarian tour operator or hotel operator, under the terms and procedures of the Law on Tourism.

The registration shall be done before the foreigner enters the territory of the country except in case of a provision of an international agreement signed by the Republic of Bulgaria.

THE CZECH REPUBLIC*

INTRODUCTION

The Czech Republic is a parliamentary democracy. Legislative power is exercised by a two-chamber parliament. The lower chamber, the House of Deputies, makes laws and has the power to vote no-confidence in the government. The upper chamber, the Senate, is elected by majority vote and approves laws passed by the House of Deputies. Together, the House of Deputies and the Senate elect the President of the Republic and approve appointments of Constitutional Court Justices. The government is appointed by the President and is responsible to Parliament. The government is one of the entities that may introduce bills; in practice, it introduces most bills. The President of the Republic is not responsible to Parliament. The President can decline to sign a law (*ratihabitio*), is the supreme commander of the armed forces, and represents the country abroad.

The Czech Republic was created as an independent state on January 1, 1993, by the division of the Czechoslovak Republic. The Czechoslovak Republic came into being as a federation in 1969, from what had been the integral state of Czechoslovakia. In the Czechoslovak Republic, labor legislation was a matter for the state, not for the constituent republics.

The people of the Czech Republic have witnessed fundamental changes in basic labor law concepts within a relatively short time. The last century saw an increase in employee rights due to the workers' movement and trade union development, the implementation of these rights during a democratic period of the 1920s and 1930s, restriction during the German occupation and then a short

---

*Luboš Tichý and Rostislav Pekař, Squire, Sanders & Dempsey, v.o.s., Prague, Czech Republic.

flourishing immediately after World War II, and oppression again due to political changes instituted by the authoritarian regime of the following four decades. Today, labor law in the Czech Republic is an outcome of recent strides in liberal democratic principles and the legacy of the past. The development of labor law in the lands of Bohemia and Moravia has been particularly interesting; in the space of a few decades, there have been a number of fundamental conceptual changes.

A. Historical Development of Labor and Employment Law

Historically, labor laws in the territory of the current Republic fell into two basic groups: first, regulations on the hiring of employees (governing the minimum age for entering into employment, work contracts, and the like); and, second, regulations on the manner of using wage labor in the production process (governing working hours, health and safety, etc.). During the 19th century, contracts for services and contracts for work were regulated mainly by chapter XXVI of the general Civil Code of 1811. The applicable regulations contained nonmandatory provisions that left some scope to the contracting parties. The general Mining Code of 1854 and the Trades License Code of 1859 included certain provisions relating to the protection of employees. In 1916, the Civil Code was amended to add mandatory requirements on employee protection. In 1914, additional legislation was enacted to regulate the employment of state officials and state servants. In 1932, collective agreement was defined, although by then collective agreements already were being concluded and conditions for collective representation were being created. While clear improvements in the labor laws were evident, Czechoslovakia's coalition government debated for years over the drafting of a law on mediating work, which was not enacted until 1936.

After the Communist coup of 1948, labor law was adapted to suit the economic, social, and ideological requirements of the state. Employees entered a production process through a workers' collective and, in return for their work, received a portion of the product. Thus, labor law became an instrument for making the population submit to the Communist Party regime and an expression of the obligation of all citizens to work for the benefit of the whole. In the 1950s labor law was unified, making it largely the same for all types of employees. Working hours were adjusted, and regulations concerning vacation leave, occupational safety and health, and enterprise responsibility for work injuries and occupational illnesses were made more uniform. In 1965, a Labor Code[1] was adopted, which is still valid today, although amended 40 times.

Following the so-called Velvet Revolution of 1989, labor law reform began in December 1990 with the passage of laws abolishing the previous system of administrative regulation of employment and setting up the legal prerequisites to development of a labor market as an integral part of a market economy.[2] One of these laws, the Act on Employment,[3] specified rules regarding the right of people to find a job, job placement, worker requalification, obligation of employers for equal selection of employees, right of disabled employees, and financial support to unemployed. The Act on Collective Bargaining[4] created a structure for autonomous collective bargaining by addressing the whole process of concluding collective agreements, including dispute resolution procedures. In addition, changes to the Labor Code made a number of its mandatory provisions relatively mandatory or optional. Certain principles, such as disciplinary accountability and arbitration, were deleted altogether.

Since 1990, the Labor Code has been amended almost 30 times, reflecting the effort to change from a centrally planned to a market economy. As discussed below,[5] one of the most extensive Labor Code amendments was enacted effective January 1, 2001, for the purpose of harmonizing the laws of the Czech Republic with those of the European Union.

B. Sources of Czech Labor Law

1. *National Sources of Law*

The Czech Constitution[6] and the Bill of Fundamental Rights and Freedoms[7] are the main sources of Czech labor law. For indi-

[1]Act No. 65/1965 Coll.
[2]Act No. 1/1991 Coll.; Act No. 2/1991 Coll.; Act No. 9/1991 Coll.
[3]Act No. 1/1991 Coll.
[4]Act No. 2/1991 Coll.
[5]See the Introduction, at B.2.b., below.
[6]Constitutional Act. No. 1/1993 Coll.
[7]Constitutional Act No. 2/1993 Coll.

vidual employment matters, the Labor Code is of key importance. The Labor Code is implemented (made specific) through other regulations, such as the Act on Wages, Remuneration for Work Standby and on Average Earnings,[8] the Order on the Minimum Wage,[9] the Act on Travel Allowances,[10] the Act on Pay and Remuneration for Work Standby in Budgetary and Certain Other Organizations and Bodies,[11] the Act on Collective Bargaining,[12] and the Act on Employment.[13] Specific matters pertaining to the civil service are regulated by the Act on Civil Service.[14]

a. Applicability of the Labor Code

The basic source of legal regulation of labor relationships in the Czech Republic is the Labor Code of June 16, 1965, as amended. The current Labor Code is based on the absolute independence of labor law from civil law; the Civil Code, as the basic source of private law, may not be applied to a labor relationship, not even in a subsidiary manner. The Labor Code defines a labor relationship as that between employers and employees, including those relationships that arise from the assertion of claims for compensation if an employee dies as a result of an occupational injury or illness.

b. Public Office

The Labor Code affects labor relationships ensuing from the exercise of public office only where the Code or special regulations explicitly provide. Existing labor regulations in the Czech Republic do not specifically define the term "public office." However, public offices are considered to include only the offices of members of the House of Deputies, members of a municipal council, and judges. The definition of public office thus does not include positions in the civil service, which is defined as service provided to the public by the administrative offices of the state.[15]

---

[8]Act No. 1/1992 Coll. See V.A.2., below.
[9]Order No. 303/1995 Coll. See V.A.1., below.
[10]Act No. 119/1992.
[11]Act No. 143/1992 Coll. See V.A.2., below.
[12]Act No. 2/1991 Coll. See II., below.
[13]Act No. 1/1991 Coll. See VI.C. and IX., below.
[14]Act No. 218/2002 Coll.
[15]*See* Act No. 218/2002 Coll., §1.

c. Conflicts of Laws

Labor relationships generally are governed by the laws of the place where the work is performed, unless the parties choose a different governing law. The parties are free to designate any law to govern their relationship, whether or not it has any relation to the place where the work is performed.[16]

2. International Sources of Law

a. International Labor Organization

As a member of the International Labor Organization (ILO), the Czech Republic is obliged to respect ILO Conventions and Guidelines[17] (e.g., the provisions of the Labor Code on statutory workweek and workweek distribution are in full compliance with ILO Convention No. 1 on Hours of Work (Industry)).

b. European Union

Since 1993, the Czech Republic has been bound by the association agreement signed with the European Union (EU) and the individual Member States of the EU (the European Agreement).[18] The European Agreement obligates the Czech Republic to harmonize its labor law to that of the EU. In accordance with this obligation, an extensive amendment to the Labor Code was adopted, effective January 1, 2001. This amendment reflects several European Union Directives (e.g., Directives Nos. 75/117/EEC,[19] 76/207/EEC,[20] 97/80/EC,[21] 77/187/EEC,[22] and 93/104/EC[23]).

---

[16]*See* Act No. 97/1963 Coll., §16.

[17]For additional discussion of ILO Conventions, see the chapter on the International Labor Organization, in Part 4 of Volume I.

[18]See the chapter on the European Union, in Part 1 of Volume I.

[19]Equal Pay Directive, Council Directive 75/111/EEC, 1975 O.J. (L 45) 19.

[20]Equal Treatment Directive, Council Directive 76/207/EEC, 1976 O.J. (L 39) 40.

[21]Burden of Proof Directive, Council Directive 97/80/EC, 1998 O.J. (L 14) 6.

[22]Transfers of Undertakings Directive, Council Directive 77/187/EEC, 1977 O.J. (L 61) 26.

[23]Working Time Directive, Council Directive 93/104/EC, 1993 O.J. (L 307) 18.

On May 1, 2004, the Czech Republic became a full member of the EU. The Czech Republic's accession triggered the effectiveness of various partial amendments to Czech labor law aiming at further harmonization of Czech labor law with European labor law, e.g., the implementation of the principle of free movement of labor within the EU.

C. Unemployment and Labor Market Policy

The state's power in labor law is greatest in the areas of unemployment and organizing the labor market. The state's unemployment policy includes, in particular, the following aspects:

- evaluation of the state of the labor market,
- policy planning,
- free-of-charge provision of information,
- consulting and job placement,
- creation of socially beneficial jobs,
- worker re-qualification, and
- the provision of employment to the disabled.

The two types of state bodies engaged in these activities are the Ministry of Labor and Social Affairs, and the labor offices located in each of the Czech Republic's 72 districts. Labor offices provide placement services for job-seekers and work with organizations to requalify and retrain disabled citizens. The Labor Ministry, together with the labor offices, also procures requalification for job-seekers through various programs.

The Labor Ministry and the district labor offices have a supervisory role, with the power to enter onto employers' premises and request employers to submit necessary documentation, reports, and explanations. These state bodies also have the power to impose penalties, usually in the form of fines.

D. Labor Matters and the Justice System

The Czech Republic has no special courts for labor matters. Labor matters are handled by regular district courts, with appeals to regional courts. Disputes over entitlement to social security and sickness benefits and for declaration of an unlawful strike or lockout are brought in regional courts, with appeals to the superior court. In specific circumstances, an extraordinary appeal to the Supreme Court is possible against the decisions on ordinary appeals by the regional or superior courts. If fundamental human rights are involved, the dispute may be referred to the Constitutional Court.

I. INDIVIDUAL EMPLOYMENT

A. Creation of the Labor Relationship

For activities performed within a labor relationship, it is characteristic that the employee performs the work in a manner subordinate to the employer and according to the latter's instructions, and that the employer, not the employee, has the right of ownership with respect to the results of the work.

Creation of the labor relationship is regulated entirely by the Labor Code. Labor relationships are created in one of the following ways:

- by a contract entered into by the employer and employee;
- by election in cases specified in special regulations or statutes or in the bylaws of a cooperative or association of citizens; or
- by appointment, in the case of managing employees.[24]

Each of these methods is discussed in further detail below.

1. Creation of a Labor Relationship Based on Contract

The majority of labor relationships are based on employment contracts. The employer is responsible for an employment contract to be in writing. The absence of a written agreement or an inadequate writing does not vitiate the contract, but will expose the employer to a fine for violating the Labor Code. The contract does not have to be in writing only if it is concluded for a definite

[24]*See* Act No. 65/1965 Coll., §27.

period of less than one month and the employee does not request to conclude the contract in writing.[25]

The Labor Code imposes on employers the obligation to inform future employees, before signing an employment contract, of the rights and obligations that may ensue from the contract and of the terms and conditions of work and payment. In addition, in cases specified by state health administration bodies, employers must ensure that new employees have a physical examination before taking up employment.[26]

a. Required Terms

An employment contract must include the following terms:

- the type of work to be performed,
- the location of work (the community and organizational unit [branch] or other stipulated place), and
- the commencement date.[27]

No special form is necessary to create a valid employment contract. The legal relationship need not be called an employment contract. The critical point is that the agreement contains the terms required of an employment contract. Without agreement on the required terms, an employment contract is not valid. The employee is not required to perform work other than that described in the agreement, and the employer does not have the right to assign work different from the job description in the employment contract, except in specific situations stipulated by law.

The law does not explicitly state how detailed the description of the work must be in the employment contract. In this respect, the contracting parties have some freedom.

An accurate definition of the location where the work is to be performed is essential, because Czech law limits an employer's right to transfer the employee to another location or even to send the employee on a business trip. Where the employer intends that the job be performed in various locations, it must define a corre-

[25] *Id.* §32.
[26] *Id.* §28.
[27] *Id.* §29.

spondingly large geographic area in the employment contract. Similarly, where the employer intends that the job performance include business trips, such condition must be specified in the employment contract.[28]

The date of commencement of employment may be identified either by specifying the exact date or by reference to another circumstance, such as a certain time after termination of previous employment.

If an employment contract does not specify the rights and obligations ensuing from the employment, the employer must provide the employee with a written statement containing this information within one month from the creation of the labor relationship. The same obligation applies when work conditions change. The written statement must include the following specific information:

- identification of the employer,
- specification of the type and place of work,
- the right to annual leave,
- information on the notice period in case of employment termination,
- wage specification, and
- weekly working time and its distribution.

Information regarding annual leave, termination notice, and weekly working time may be provided in a reference to Labor Code regulations, a collective agreement, or the employer's internal regulations. The obligation to provide this written statement does not apply if the employment period does not exceed one month.[29]

b. Other Terms

In addition to the required terms, the employment contract may include other terms agreed upon by the employer and the employee. These other terms are severable; if any such term is contrary to the mandatory provisions of Czech law, it is deemed

---

[28]*Id.* §38.
[29]*Id.* §32.

null and void, but the remaining terms of the employment contract remain enforceable.

c. *Restrictive Covenants*

An employer and an employee may agree in writing on a restrictive covenant regarding activities that correspond to or are competitive with the activities that constitute the employer's scope of business.[30] In a restrictive covenant, the employee agrees, under a reasonable penalty, not to perform such activities, whether for another employer or as an independent entrepreneur, for a time period following the termination of the labor relationship. The time period cannot exceed one year, and the restrictive covenant can be agreed upon only if the circumstances justify such a restriction. A restrictive covenant that does not comply with the above conditions is deemed null and void.[31]

The reference to circumstances justifying such a restriction provides the employee with the ability to challenge a restrictive covenant in court, which will assess the validity of a covenant on a case-by-case basis. The courts usually will focus mainly on the employee's position in the firm (manager or other key employee) and the duration of the restriction.

2. *Creation of a Labor Relationship by Election or Appointment*

The Labor Code states that, unless otherwise provided, the same regulations apply to labor relationships based on election or

---

[30] *Id.* §29.

[31] Under a recent amendment to the Labor Code that became effective March 1, 2004, the rules regarding restrictive covenants substantially changed. Most important, the employer will have to pay a special monthly compensation that cannot be less than the employee's average monthly wage. The employer will have to pay such compensation for each month following the termination of the labor relationship when the restrictive covenant applies; the employer thus will have to pay a total compensation of not less than the employee's yearly salary if the covenant is applicable for the maximum 12-month period. The covenant will terminate whenever such monthly compensation is past-due for more than 15 days. Furthermore, the employer and the employee will not be able to agree on a restrictive covenant while the employee is in a trial period (see I.C., below). If the employer and the employee agree on a trial period, they will be able to agree on a restrictive covenant only when the trial period is over. This new regulation of restrictive covenants, however, will not apply to restrictive covenants agreed prior to March 1, 2004.

appointment as to those based on an employment contract. Neither election nor appointment affects the rights and obligations of the employee and employer under an existing labor relationship, unless otherwise agreed.

A labor relationship created by election or appointment begins on the date that is specified as the commencement date.

a. Election or Appointment to Management Positions

Employment is by "election" in situations set out by law, including but not limited to situations specified in bylaws of the statutory organs of cooperatives and other entities. "Appointment" is used for top officials in, *inter alia*, public service (i.e., working for the state or municipalities).

For members of higher levels of management appointed to a post by special regulations or by the employer, the labor relationship is established by appointment. The appointment is made by the employer's governing body if the employer is a legal person or by the employer if the employer is a physical person. The power to appoint and recall employees may not be transferred to another entity.

b. Severance Payments

In the case of appointed or elected managing employees, the employer and the employee may agree on a severance payment if the managing employee is recalled before the term for which he or she was appointed or elected.[32] However, such a provision is valid only if the employer and employee have agreed on a restrictive covenant.[33]

3. Secondary Labor Relationship

If the employee is performing work under an existing employment agreement with a statutory workweek,[34] this becomes

---

[32]*See* Act No. 65/1965 Coll., §29.

[33]*See* I.A.1.c., above. Under a recent amendment to the Labor Code that became effective March 1, 2004, the opportunity to agree on a severance payment is not tied to a restrictive covenant, nor is it limited to appointed or elected employees.

[34]*See* V.B.1., below.

the principal labor relationship, and any new labor relationship created on the basis of election or appointment is secondary.[35] This means that a new relationship may not be concluded for the statutory workweek, but only for a shorter period.

B. Duration of the Labor Relationship

The guiding principle regarding the duration of a labor relationship is that the term of the employment relationship is deemed indefinite unless the employment contract expressly provides for a fixed term.[36] A fixed term maybe expressed either in years, months, weeks or days, or by reference to other circumstances, such as the period of a certain campaign or season, or the maternity leave or other leave of another employee.

Renewable fixed-term contracts are valid and enforceable. However, in the event that a contractual term setting a definite period is deemed invalid, the duration of the labor relationship will be deemed indefinite. Unless the employee specifically requests to enter into a fixed-term employment contract, an employment contract for a definite period is invalid if the employee belongs to one of the protected groups:

- juveniles aged 15 to 18;
- employees designated by a collective bargaining agreement;
- partially disabled persons; or
- graduates of secondary schools, post-secondary schools, and other specialized educational establishments being hired for jobs that correspond to their qualifications within two years from their graduation.[37]

---

[35]*See* Act No. 65/1965 Coll., §70.

[36]*Id.* §30.

[37]Under a recent amendment to the Labor Code that became effective March 1, 2004, the rules regarding fixed-term contracts changed substantially. First, the duration of a fixed-term contract is limited to two years, in principle. The same two-year limit applies to the total duration of a renewed fixed-term contract or a series of consecutive fixed-term contracts, unless the fixed-term labor relationship has been interrupted for at least six months. If the fixed-term labor relationship lasts beyond the two-year limit, the employee has the option to convert it into an indefinite-term labor relationship by informing the employer in writing before the end of the agreed fixed term that the employee wishes that the labor relationship continue. Second, fixed-term con-

C. Trial Period (Probation)

The Labor Code allows for the negotiation of a trial period in an employment contract.[38] No trial period may be arranged for employees whose labor relationship arises as a result of election or appointment because no employment contract is entered into in such cases.

Agreements on trial periods must be in writing, the length of a trial period cannot exceed three months, and it may not be extended. Any provision regulating a trial period violating the above rules is deemed invalid. Obstacles preventing the employee from working during the trial period may extend the trial period up to a maximum of 10 days.

D. Withdrawal From the Employment Contract

In certain narrowly defined circumstances, both the employer and the employee may unilaterally withdraw from the employment contract.[39] Withdrawal, a unilateral legal act, nullifies the agreement *ab initio*, that is, from the very beginning. Withdrawal thus differs fundamentally from termination of the labor relationship.[40]

Either party to an employment contract may withdraw from the employment contract if the party entered into the employment contract because it acted in a substantial error that must have been known to the other party. An error is deemed substantial if the party that acted in error would not have entered into the employment contract in the absence of such error. Before the employee starts to work, the employer or the employee may withdraw from the employment contract also for reasons that the employer and employee have negotiated in the employment contract.[41] Finally,

---

tracts with graduates, the partially disabled, and juveniles are not contingent on their specific request. The only protected group are the employees designated in a collective bargaining agreement. Their protection is absolute, i.e., such employees no longer have the option to enter into a fixed-term contract upon their specific request.

[38]*See* Act No. 65/1965 Coll., §31.

[39]*Id.* § 245.

[40]See I.G., below.

[41]*See* Act No. 65/1965 Coll., §245.

the employer may withdraw from the contract if the employee has failed to appear for work on the commencement day, and if there were no obstacles preventing the employee from working or if the employee has not informed the employer of the existence of such obstacles within a week.[42]

E. Obligations Ensuing From the Labor Relationship

The Labor Code prescribes the following employer obligations:

- to assign the employee work in accordance with the employment contract;
- to pay the employee a wage for the work performed;
- to create conditions conducive to successful performance of work by the employee;
- to adhere to applicable legal regulations, collective bargaining agreements, or individual employment contracts;
- to adequately inform the employee at the time he or she begins work of the work rules in effect at the employer's location of operation and of the legal and other regulations regarding workplace safety and health that the employee must obey; and
- to properly inform the employee of the collective bargaining agreement and of the employer's internal regulations.[43]

The Labor Code prescribes the following employee obligations:

- to perform the work in accordance with the employer's instructions, in person and in accordance with the employment contract;
- to perform the specified work in the specified working period;
- to maintain work discipline;
- to work conscientiously and properly in accordance with his or her own strengths, knowledge, and abilities;

---

[42] *Id.* §33.
[43] *Id.* §35.

- to fulfill the lawful instructions of his or her superiors;
- to cooperate with other employees;
- to make full use of the work period and means of production to carry out the assigned work;
- to fulfill work tasks at a high level of quality, economically and on time;
- to adhere to all applicable legal regulations, provided that the employee has been properly informed of them;
- to properly manage funds entrusted by the employer;
- to guard and protect the employer's property against damage, loss, destruction, or misuse; and
- not to act in conflict with the legitimate interests of the employer.[44]

F. Changes in Negotiated Working Conditions

1. *Amendments to the Employment Contract*

In principle, any amendment to an employment agreement requires the employer's and the employee's mutual consent. The employer is responsible to put in writing an amendment to an employment contract. The absence of written form does not vitiate the amendment, but it exposes the employer to a fine for violating the Labor Code.[45]

2. *Reassignment to a Different Type of Work*

A basic principle of the Labor Code is that an employee is required to perform only the type of work provided for in the employment agreement. Consequently, changes in the type of work require the employee's consent. If the employer reassigns the employee to a different type of work without the employee's consent, the reassignment is valid, but the employee does not have the obligation to perform the work although he or she is still entitled to receive his or her original wage. The employee only must express his or her non-consent unambiguously. The law, however, defines

---

[44] *Id.* §73.
[45] *Id.* §36.

a few circumstances where the employee's consent to the reassignment is not required. These circumstances are as follows:

- the employer has terminated the employment relationship by notice:[46]
  - due to the fact the employee has not satisfied, over the long-term, the prerequisites specified in legal regulations for the performance of the agreed-upon work or does not meet the requirements established by the employer for the proper performance of the work, without the employer being at fault;
  - for reasons that would authorize the employer to immediately terminate the labor relationship, i.e., if the employee has been sentenced to an imprisonment exceeding one year for an intentional criminal offense, or an imprisonment of at least six months for an intentional criminal offense committed during the performance of the employee's work tasks or in direct connection therewith, or if the employee has particularly seriously violated work discipline; or
  - for serious violation of work discipline or for minor violations of work discipline that continued even though the employer alerted the employee in writing in the last six months that such minor violation would lead to the termination of the employment relationship;
- criminal proceedings have been brought against the employee because the employee is suspected of intentional criminal activities committed during the performance of the employee's work tasks or in direct connection therewith that resulted in a damage to the employer's property—in this event, the assignment is possible only until the final conclusion of legal proceedings; or
- the employee has lost, temporarily, the qualifications specified by legal regulations for the performance of the agreed-

[46]In the event of termination by notice, the notice period is, in principle, two months. The reassignment of the employee to a different work thus applies for the duration of the notice period. See I.G., below, for more details regarding termination by notice.

upon work. In this event, the reassignment cannot exceed 30 workdays in a calendar year.

Even in the circumstances specified above, the employer may reassign the employee to a different type of work only if a reassignment to a different position corresponding to the agreed type of work would compromise the purpose of the reassignment.

In addition, the employer is entitled to reassign an employee to a different type of work if the employee cannot perform the agreed type of work due to a stoppage or interruption of work caused by unfavorable weather conditions, or if such reassignment is necessary to avert catastrophic events or other threatening accidents or to mitigate their immediate consequences.

In certain situations, however, the employer has the obligation to reassign an employee to another type of work. These situations are as follows:

- the employee has lost the capacity, due to health, to carry out his or her existing work over the long term, or is unable to perform existing work on account of an occupational illness or the risk of such illness;
- a public health office has declared that the employee has reached the maximum permissible exposure level at his or her workplace;
- a pregnant woman, a breastfeeding mother, or a mother of a child younger than nine months of age is assigned to work that such women are not permitted to perform or that poses a threat to the woman's pregnancy or to motherhood;
- upon a doctor's judgment or a decision of a state health administration office, a specific employee must be reassigned to protect the health of other persons from infectious diseases;
- the reassignment is necessary to enforce a court decision;
- a doctor has judged an employee assigned to night shifts unfit for night work; or
- a pregnant woman or the mother of a child younger than nine months of age requests a reassignment from night work.

Whenever the employer reassigns an employee to a different type of work, the employer must also ensure that the substitute work is appropriate for the employee in light of his or her health condition and abilities and, if possible, in light of the employee's qualifications. The reassignment to a different type of work is invalid if it is inappropriate in light of the employee's health condition or if the employee is incapable of performing such work. The employer must inform the employee in advance of any reassignment and must discuss the reasons for the reassignment and its duration.[47] If the employer reassigns the employee without his or her consent and the period of reassignment exceeds 22 workdays in a calendar year, the employer must discuss the reassignment with the relevant trade union body.[48] The reassignment, however, is valid even if the employer does not comply with this requirement.[49]

3. *Changes in Location of Work*

The principle of the employee's consent also governs changes in the location of work. Unlike reassignment to a different type of work, the transfer to a different location of work is not subject to any exceptions that would allow for a transfer without such consent. Indeed, the employee must specifically agree to any transfer to a different location, and transfer is permitted only when it is essential to satisfy the employer's operational needs. The employee's consent is required even for business trips; the law only permits that the employee provide consent regarding the employer's right to send him or her on business trips generally in the employment contract. The employer, however, can send the employee on a business trip only for the period of actual need.[50]

4. *Substitutions*

The employer may agree in writing with an employee that the latter will be substituted to work temporarily for another legal or natural person. The written agreement always must contain the name of the legal person or the name and surname of the natural

[47]*See* Act No. 65/1965 Coll., §37.
[48]*Id.* §41.
[49]*Id.* §242.
[50]*Id.* §38.

person for whom the employee is to be substituted, as well as the starting date of the transfer, the type of work, the location of work, and the period for which the transfer has been agreed.[51]

5. *Changes at the Employee's Request*

The Labor Code allows an employee to request transfer to another type of work or another workplace (at the same or another location) if, according to a medical statement, it is not suitable for the employee to continue in the current type of work or at the current workplace. The employee has the same right to request transfer if he or she has other serious grounds for transfer. The Code provides that the employer must grant the employee's request as soon as operational possibilities permit.[52]

G. Termination of a Labor Relationship

The most common methods of termination of the labor relationship are as follows:

- agreement,
- notice,
- immediate termination, and
- termination during the trial period.

Each of these methods is discussed in greater detail below. In addition to the above-mentioned methods, the Labor Code expressly states that:

- employment always ends on the employee's death;
- employment contractually agreed for a certain definite term ends on the expiration of the agreed term; and
- employment of foreign citizens ends on their expulsion from Czech territory or on the legal force of a decision canceling their residency permit.[53]

---

[51] *Id.* §37.
[52] *Id.* §40.
[53] *Id.* §42.

1. *Termination by Agreement*

The employer and the employee may terminate employment by a written agreement at any time during the duration of an employment contract for any reason. The agreement does not have to indicate the reasons unless upon the employee's request.[54]

2. *Termination by Notice*

Either the employer or the employee may terminate employment by a written notice, delivered in accordance with the provisions of the Labor Code.

a. *Delivery of Notice*

In order to be valid, notice must be in writing and delivered to the other party.[55] The employer's notice must be delivered to the employee's hands.[56] The employer delivers the notice to the employee's work address, home address, or wherever else the employer may reach the employee.[57]

The employer also may send the notice by registered mail to the employee's home address. If the employee expressly refuses the delivery or if the employee deliberately fails to pick up the registered mail with the notice at the local Post Office, the notice is deemed served as of the day when the employee expressly refused its delivery or as of the 10th day after the Post Office informed the employee that the employee has a registered mail at the local Post Office branch.[58]

Once the notice has been delivered, it may be cancelled only with the consent of the party that delivered it. Cancellation of the notice and consent to cancellation must be in writing.[59]

---

[54] *Id.* §43.

[55] *Id.* §44.

[56] The same requirement applies to any notice regarding the beginning and the end of the labor relationship, its amendments, and the cessation of obligations ensuing from the employment contract.

[57] *See* Act No. 65/1965 Coll., §266a.

[58] *Id.* §266a.

[59] *Id.* §44.

b. Notice Period

Once notice has been delivered, the labor relationship ends with the expiration of the notice period. The notice period is two months, with the following exceptions:[60]

- the notice period is 15 days if the terminated labor relationship is secondary;[61] or
- the notice period is three months if the notice is served by the employer and if the employer serves the notice for the following reasons:
  - the employer is winding up its business or relocating, in full or in part; or
  - the employee becomes redundant owing to a decision by the employer or an authority to change the employer's function or technical equipment, reduce the workforce to increase efficiency, or make other operational changes.[62]

The notice period starts on the first day of the calendar month following delivery of the notice and ends on the last day of the relevant calendar month with the following exceptions:

- an employer giving notice must find suitable alternative employment for certain protected employees;[63]
- the period of notice does not include the protective period[64]—the labor relationship therefore concludes on the expiration of the remaining portion of the notice period after the end of the protective period, unless the employee declares that he or she does not insist on the extension of the labor relationship;
- if the employer serves notice in circumstances that would justify immediate termination and the employee is about to begin a maternity or parent leave, so that the notice period

[60]*Id.* §45.
[61]*Id.* §70b.
[62]*Id.* §45.
[63]See I.G.2.d.iv., below.
[64]See I.G.2.d.v., below.

would end during the maternity or parent leave, the notice period is extended and ends only upon the end of the planned maternity or parent leave;[65] or
- the notice period starts on the day when the notice is delivered or deemed delivered if the terminated labor relationship is secondary.[66]

c. Notice Given by the Employee

The employee has the right to give notice for any reason, or even without stating any reason, at any time.[67]

d. Notice Served by the Employer

i. Reasons for serving notice

The Labor Code protects employees by limiting the number of reasons for which employers may serve a termination notice. Employers cannot serve a termination notice for other reasons than those expressly permitted in the Labor Code. The permitted reasons are as follows:[68]

- winding-up or relocation of the employer's business, in full or in part;
- the employee's redundancy[69] by reason of a decision by the employer or a relevant authority to change the employer's function or technical equipment, reduce the workforce to increase efficiency, or make other organizational changes;
- the employee's health condition when the employee becomes unfit to perform work on a long-term basis or is not permitted to work by reason of occupational illness or the risk of contracting an occupational illness, or when a public health office declares that the employee has reached the maximum permissible exposure level at his or her workplace;

---

[65]*See* Act No. 65/1965 Coll., §45.
[66]*Id.* §70b.
[67]*Id.* §44.
[68]*Id.* §46.
[69]See IV.A., below.

- the employee's failure to meet the legal prerequisites for performance of the type of work stipulated in the employment contract;
- the employee's failure to meet the requirements established by the employer for due performance of the work, without the employer's being at fault[70]—where the employee's failure consists of unsatisfactory quality of work, termination by notice is permitted only if the employee was asked in writing in the last 12 months to improve the quality of his or her work, but failed to comply within an adequate time period;
- serious violation of work discipline by the employee;[71]
- minor violations of work discipline by the employee that have continued even though the employer has alerted the employee in writing in the last six months that such minor violations would lead to the termination of the employment relationship; or
- reasons that would justify an immediate termination.[72]

ii. Offering a modified employment contract

The employer's ability to serve notice for reasons other than those that involve a violation of work discipline or that would justify an immediate termination (i.e., for the reasons other than those stated in the last three bullet points above) is further limited. The employer may serve a termination notice for such reasons only if:

- the employer is unable to continue employing the employee at the location of work stipulated in the employment contract, or at the location of the employee's residence even after preparatory training; or

[70]The employer would be at fault especially if it did not provide the employee with adequate work conditions, including appropriate equipment or training, or if its requirements were unreasonable, unjustified, or abusive, etc.

[71]A violation of work discipline includes an intentional violation of the obligations imposed on the employee by law, the employer's own internal regulations, and the binding directions of superior employees.

[72]See I.G.3., below.

- the employee is not willing to accept a suitable type of work that the employer has offered to the employee at the location of work stipulated in the employment contract, or at the location of the employee's residence, or the employee refuses to receive preparatory training needed for the type of work.[73]

The employer is thus able to serve a termination notice for these reasons only if the employer cannot continue to employ the employee in a different work position or at a different location, or if the employee does not accept such modified terms of employment or refuses to receive training needed to perform the new type of work.

iii. Deadlines for serving notice

The deadline for serving a termination notice for reasons that involve a violation of work discipline or that would justify an immediate termination is two months from the day when the employer learned about the existence of such reason. In the event of a violation of work discipline that occurs abroad, the deadline is two months from the day when the employee returned to the Czech Republic. The employer, however, cannot serve a termination notice later than one year after the occurrence of the employee's conduct that constitutes the reason for serving notice.

If another authority (e.g., the police) starts to investigate the employee's conduct in the course of the two-month period, the employer may serve a termination notice within two months from the day when the employer learns about the results of such investigation.

If the termination by notice is subject to approval by a state administration authority,[74] the two-month period does not include the time between the employer's filing for the approval and the approval's entering into legal force.[75]

---

[73]*See* Act No. 65/1965 Coll., §46.
[74]See I.G.2.d.vi., below.
[75]*See* Act No. 65/1965 Coll., §46.

iv. Securing alternative employment

The employers must cooperate with the relevant state administration authority in finding suitable alternative employment with another employer for employees whose employment is terminated for reasons consisting of:

- winding-up or relocation of the employer's business, in full or in part;
- the employee's redundancy[76] by reason of a decision by the employer or a relevant authority to change the employer's function or technical equipment, reduce the workforce to increase efficiency, or make other organizational changes; or
- the employee's health condition when the employee becomes unfit to perform work on a long-term basis or is not permitted to work by reason of occupational illness or the risk of contracting an occupational illness, or when a public health office declares that the employee has reached the maximum permissible exposure level at his or her workplace.

The employer's obligation to secure an alternative employment is increased in cases of certain protected employees. The employer must secure a suitable alternative employment for:

- single employees bringing up a child younger than age 15 whose employment is terminated for redundancy;
- partially disabled employees without a pension whose employment is terminated for redundancy; and
- all employees whose employment is terminated for risk of contracting an occupational illness, or because they have reached the maximum permissible exposure level at their workplace.

In these cases, the notice period ends only when the employer finds such alternative employment unless the employee and the employer agree otherwise.

---

[76]See IV.A., below.

Such alternative employment should correspond to the employee's health condition, taking into account the employee's age, qualifications, and abilities, the length of prior employment, and accommodation opportunities. In principle, the decisive criteria are the employee's health condition and qualification (including potential additional training); the other criteria are more conditional on the actual situation of the labor market.

The employer does not have the obligation to effectively aid the employee in finding new employment or to provide alternative employment if the employee has refused to modify the employment contract with the employer and perform suitable work of another type even though the employer offered such modification prior to giving a termination notice. The employer's obligation ends also if the employee refuses, without serious reason, a suitable alternative employment with another employer.[77]

v. Protective periods

The employer may not terminate the employment when the employee is in a protective period. Where the employer served a termination notice before the employee entered into a protective period, the notice period is interrupted and continues to run only when the protected period is over. Protective periods are defined as periods:

- when the employee is temporarily unable to work due to illness or injury, unless he or she incurred the illness or injury intentionally or caused it while inebriated;
- from submission of a proposal for an institutional medical treatment or from approval for spa treatment until the day of the treatment's conclusion; in cases of tuberculosis, this protective period is extended by another six months after release from institutional treatment;
- from the date when an employee receives an order to perform military or civilian service, or when such order is published by a decree, until two weeks after the employee's release from such service;

[77]*See* Act No. 65/1965 Coll., §47.

- covered by a long-term release to carry out public office;
- when a female employee is pregnant or on maternity leave, or when an employee is in charge of a child younger than three years of age; or
- when an employee working at night has been confirmed on the basis of a doctor's decision to be temporarily incapable of night work.

The employer may, however, serve a termination notice during a protective period if the termination notice is given for:

- winding-up or relocation of the employer's business, in full or in part;
- reasons that would justify an immediate termination,[78] unless the employee is on a maternity or parental leave; if the employee was given such notice before the beginning of her maternity or his parental leave, the notice period will end on the same day as his or her leave; or
- serious violation or continuing minor violations of work discipline by the employee unless the employee is a pregnant woman or is in charge of a child younger than three years of age.[79]

vi. Notice to disabled employees

Disabled employees may be given notice of termination only with the prior consent of the appropriate state administrative body, i.e., the relevant labor office.[80] Exceptions to this rule are as follows:

- the notice is given to an employee who is older than 65 years of age;
- the notice is given due to organizational changes in which the employer's business is winding up or relocating in full or in part;

---

[78]See I.G.3.b., below.

[79]*See* Act No. 65/1965 Coll., §48.

[80]According to a recent amendment to the Labor Code, the obligation to obtain consent of the relevant labor office was abolished as of March 1, 2004.

- the employee has given reason for the employer to immediately terminate the labor relationship;
- the employee seriously violates employee discipline; or
- the employee consistently commits minor violations of employee discipline.

As defined by the Act on Employment, disabled employees ("employees with modified work capacity") include those whose long-term poor health fundamentally limits their ability to work or to prepare for work, or who are receiving a pension conditioned on long-term poor health.[81]

3. *Immediate Termination*

In certain situations, the employer or the employee may terminate the labor relationship immediately. The immediate termination is valid only if it is done in writing and clearly states the reason for termination.[82] Furthermore, the immediate termination is valid only if it is delivered to the other party within one month from the date that the terminating party learned about the reason for immediate termination, but no later than one year from the date that the reason arose.[83] This deadline is extended if the employer decides immediately to terminate the labor relationship for a violation of work discipline that happens while the employee is abroad; the one-month period then starts only upon the employee's return to the Czech Republic. The deadline is also extended if, in the course of the one-month period, another authority starts to investigate the conduct of the employee in question; the deadline is then extended until one month after the employer learns about the results of the investigation.

a. *Immediate Termination by the Employee*

The employee is entitled to terminate the labor relationship immediately if any of the following situations occur:

---

[81] *See* Act No. 1/1991 Coll., §21. See also VI.C., below.
[82] *See* Act No. 65/1965 Coll., §55.
[83] *Id.* §§53, 54.

- the employee, according to medical opinion, is not able to continue working without seriously endangering his or her health, and the employer has not, within a period of 15 days of submission of this opinion, transferred the employee to alternative suitable work; or
- the employer fails to pay the employee wages or other compensation for wages within 15 days of the date it is due.[84]

The employee may terminate immediately for health reasons if, in addition to the health condition, the medical opinion clearly states his or her incapacity to carry out the current job duties without serious risk to the employee's health. The Labor Code provides that the employee may not terminate a labor relationship immediately until 15 days have elapsed from receipt of the medical opinion by the employer. However, this does not mean that the employee is obligated to carry out his or her current work until such time. Upon receipt of the medical opinion, the employer is obligated to transfer the employee to alternative work. If the employer fails to do so, then the employer is considered to have imposed an obstacle to the employee's work.

An employee who immediately terminates a labor relationship has the right to compensation for wages in the amount of his or her average earnings during the normal period of notice.[85]

b. Immediate Termination by the Employer

The Labor Code considers the immediate termination of the labor relationship by the employer as an exceptional method of ending the relationship and, therefore, allows the employer to exercise this prerogative only under the following circumstances:

- the employee has been legally convicted of intentionally committing a criminal act and sentenced to an unconditional term of imprisonment for longer than one year;
- the employee has been legally convicted for intentional commission of a criminal act committed in the course of

---

[84] *Id.* §54.

[85] See I.G.2.b., above.

carrying out his or her work duties, or in direct connection with them, and sentenced to an unconditional term of imprisonment for a period of at least six months; or
- the employee violates employee discipline in an especially gross manner.[86]

The Labor Code does not directly define what it is to violate employee discipline "in an especially gross manner." Therefore, it is necessary to look at the particular violation, the period of time and the situation under which it was committed, and the character of the employee.

The employer cannot immediately terminate the employment of pregnant employees, or employees in charge of a child younger than three years of age. However, the employer is entitled to terminate a labor relationship with these employees by notice unless the employee is on maternity or parental leave; while on such leave, the employee may not be terminated even by serving notice.[87]

4. *Termination During the Trial Period*

Either the employer or the employee may terminate the labor relationship during the trial period in writing for any reason and even without giving reasons. The employer should give the other party a written notice at least three days prior to the date that the labor relationship is to end; failure to deliver such notice, however, does not invalidate the termination.[88]

H. Privacy

The right to privacy is one of the fundamental rights covered by the Bill of Fundamental Rights and Freedoms.[89] In addition to the right to privacy, the Bill of Rights sets forth the rights to protection against violations of privacy and interference with family life and the right to protection against collection, publication, and misuse of personal data.[90]

---

[86] *See* Act No. 65/1965 Coll., §53.
[87] *Id.*
[88] *See* Act No. 65/1965 Coll., §58.
[89] Act No. 2/1993 Coll., §7(1).
[90] *Id.* §§10(2) and (3).

The question of the right to privacy in the labor relationship arises with respect to processing of employees' personal data. This area of law is covered by the Act on Protection of Personal Data.[91] Personal data processing means any operation or a set of operations that is being systematically executed by a company that processes the personal data or by a processor with the personal data in an automatic or other manner. It includes without limitation, collection of the data, storage thereof on information carriers, disclosure, modification or alteration, search, use, transfer, distribution, publishing, saving, exchanging, sorting or combining thereof, blocking access, and deletion.[92]

Unless an employee provides his or her written consent, the employer cannot process an employee's personal data, except where the law requires the processing of an employee's personal data (e.g., for social care, health care, or tax purposes).[93] In case of violations of an employee's rights, the employee has the right to request restraint of such illegal action, changes to or updating of the personal data, blocking access to or deletion of the personal data, and compensation for damage suffered, if any.[94]

Moreover, whoever intends to process personal data is obligated to notify the Office for Personal Data Protection of this fact prior to commencement of processing of personal data.[95] However, the notification obligation does not apply to the processing of personal data which is (1) a part of a publicly available record; or (2) required by law (e.g., processing of the company's employees' personal data for social care, health care, or tax purposes).[96]

I. Employee Duty of Loyalty, Trade Secrets, Covenants Not to Compete

1. *Employee Duty of Loyalty*

Unless the employer grants prior written consent, the employee is not allowed to engage in any business activity that has a

---

[91]Act No. 101/2000 Coll.

[92]*Id.* §4(e).

[93]*Id.* §5(2)(a).

[94]*Id.* §21(2).

[95]*Id.* §16.

[96]*Id.* §18.

competitive character as regards to the scope of the employer's business.[97] Where the employer has granted prior written consent, it can revoke such consent at any time upon providing a reason for doing so. After such a revocation, the employee must terminate the competitive business activity.[98]

2. *Trade Secrets*

The Commercial Code[99] sets forth the general rules for protection of trade secrets. Pursuant to the Commercial Code, a trade secret is anything connected to the enterprise of an entrepreneur that (1) has a real or potential value, (2) is not regularly accessible in the relevant business, (3) the entrepreneur treats as a trade secret, confidentially, and (4) the entrepreneur protects as a trade secret.[100] In case of violation of the right to maintain a trade secret, the entrepreneur can request retention of the trade secret, restoration of the trade secret, and compensation for damages from the violator.[101]

In addition to general protection of employer's trade secrets, the employer and employee may agree on a specific confidentiality obligation in the employment contract. Such obligation can apply during the term of the labor relationship as well as afterwards.

3. *Covenants Not to Compete*

See the discussion on restrictive covenants in I.A.1.c., above.

II. COLLECTIVE BARGAINING

The law of collective bargaining has undergone a major turnabout and notable changes since 1989. While there existed in the earlier democratic Czechoslovakia, especially during the period

---

[97]*See* Act No. 65/1965 Coll., §75(1).
[98]*Id.* §75(2).
[99]Act No. 513/1991 Coll.
[100]*Id.* §17.
[101]*Id.* §53.

between the two World Wars, a labor union structure that was advanced for its time and that asserted the collective interests of its members, the Communist regime dismantled this area of labor law completely. To the Communist leaders, labor unions were a "school of Communism," the regime's long arm. Although Czechoslovakia acceded to world instruments issued by the ILO and signed the United Nations' Human Rights Convention, strikes and other forms of collective action were relegated to illegality. Strikes were not expressly banned, but a strike was interpreted as a threat to the power of the Communist Party, and the leaders of a strike could be tried for a criminal offense.

This position changed significantly after 1989, when laws were passed to reflect the international commitment of Czechoslovakia, and later the Czech Republic, in the area of collective bargaining.

The Constitution's Bill of Fundamental Rights and Freedoms, among other things, guarantees the right to strike and to bargain collectively. The legal bases for collective bargaining also are provided by the Act on Association by Citizens, which regulates the process for establishing a labor organization; Act No. 120/1990, which addresses certain relationships between labor unions and employers; and the Act on Collective Bargaining, which addresses the basic forms of bargaining and related proceedings. In addition, a 1991 decree of the Ministry of Labor and Social Affairs addresses the status of mediators and arbitrators and the manner of concluding collective agreements.

A. Union Structure and Status

1. *Historical Background*

Union activity in what is now the Czech Republic dates back to the year 1867, when employees were given the right to associate and assemble. At first, Czech unions established themselves as part of Austrian unions, but by January 1897, an independent Czech national union federation had been set up under the name of Czechoslovak Labor Association, which included 18 labor unions. Later, the Czech Workman's Community was born, associating 30 labor unions. In Moravia, strong Catholic unions, related to the Christian-Democratic Party, were active. Relationships between unions were marked by conflict between partisan unions on the one side and the nationalist-oriented union confederation on the other. The unions were unable to achieve supranational cooperation within the Austro-Hungarian Empire, and managed joint action in only a few cases, such as a general strike for universal voting rights in 1905. On a more limited basis, in what is now the Czech Republic, a series of strikes was undertaken for higher wages, observation of collective agreements, and an eight-hour workday around the beginning of the century.

After the birth of Czechoslovakia in 1918, union activity grew strong. Unions were recognized as parties to negotiations with private employers and the state. Nonetheless, they remained politically and nationally divided. By 1937, the democratically aligned unions of the time had 1.65 million members, divided up among numerous union federations, such as the Czechoslovak Labor Association (over 500,000 members), the Czechoslovak Workman's Community (366,000 members), and the German Labor League (206,000 members). During the German occupation, the collaborating National Employees' Labor Central (NOUZ) was created. Other unions were banned, as were strikes, collective bargaining, and elections to works councils. After 1945, Czechoslovak unions were integrated into the Revolutionary Labor Movement (ROH), which was active until 1990. These unions were controlled fully by the Communists, who made them an instrument toward the 1948 coup.

During the 1968 Prague Spring, unions underwent reform, which included the formation of 57 free unions. After the anti-Communist Velvet Revolution in 1989, the existing strike committees were transformed into a new, democratic trade-union confederation. In 1990, an all-union assembly ended the existence of the ROH and created a new, all-union confederation named the Czechoslovak Confederation of Labor Unions. After the breakup of the Czechoslovak Federation, this organization, under the new name of the Czech-Moravian Confederation of Trade Unions (CMKOS), became the main union confederation in the Czech Republic.

2. *Union Organization*

Unions now are politically and financially independent and democratic. Unions also have an exclusive position, which means that they associate employees in a single sector of the economy. Hence, all employees in a particular sector have only one labor union. As a general rule, this leads to unions being organized into associations of labor unions, which essentially duplicate the structure of the economy.

As discussed above, the main union confederation in the Czech Republic is CMKOS, with 34 member unions and some 833,000 members. The supreme decisionmaking body of CMKOS is the general assembly, a gathering of delegations of each member union, which is held yearly; between general assemblies the decisionmaking body is the assembly, which has about 130 members. At the assembly, individual unions are represented according to size, but even the smallest union is entitled to send at least one member. Assemblies meet at least once every three months. The executive body is the board, with 19 members. Its chairman is elected by the general assembly.

In addition to CMKOS, there are several other labor union associations, such as the Confederation of Art and Culture, which groups union confederations of employees in those fields. Another organization is the Labor Association of Bohemia, Moravia, and Silesia, which was created in 1991 as an alternative, leftist confederation. The Christian Labor Coalition was created in 1990 as an indcpendent association, espousing the Christian world view. There also exists an association of independent unions, created in 1995, which includes a union of employees in the agriculture and food industry, with 140,000 members.

Apart from the labor union associations, there are several independent labor unions, which are a reflection of the need of certain professions to maintain their independence and exclusivity. These have arisen mainly in the railway industry and in health care.

3. Employee Representation

Czech law recognizes unions as representatives of employees for purposes of collective bargaining. In most respects, individual labor unions operating at an employer's business act for the particular employees who are their members. However, in some ways unions represent even nonmember employees. For example, in negotiating collective agreements, individual unions operating at a single employer's business must act on behalf of, and represent, all employees jointly and in mutual accord.

Employees may be represented by a union or the council of employees[102] in their demands vis-à-vis the employer or the labor office. Only a union may represent an employee in case of a court dispute, provided that the employee is member of the union. No other form of representation is possible.

As discussed at various points in this chapter, Czech law requires that certain actions by the employer require union consent or consultation. In those instances where several unions operate independently of each other at the employer's business, the employer must, in cases involving all or the majority of employees, carry out its consent and consultation obligations vis-à-vis the respective bodies of all participating unions unless the unions and the employer agree otherwise. In cases of a plurality of union organizations at a single employer, the individual unions represent their respective members in individual matters. If the matter relates to a nonmember employee, his or her rights are exercised by the union organization that has the greatest number of members. However, the nonmember employee may stipulate otherwise.

B. The Bargaining Process

The goal of collective bargaining is a collective agreement. Thus, the principal parties to bargaining are labor unions and employers. Under certain conditions, the intercession of the state is permitted. In this case, the three parties are referred to collectively as "The Tripartite."

A representative of the union body may act in the name of employees. His or her authority to represent is based on the union's statutes or internal regulations. An employer is represented by its head or other authorized representative. Where an organization of employers is negotiating, the organization is represented by a person or persons with authority to conclude collective agreements pursuant to the employer organization's internal regulations.

---

[102]See III., below.

The law provides a specific procedure for collective bargaining. Under this procedure, collective bargaining commences upon the submission by one party to the other of a written proposal to conclude a collective agreement. The other party is obligated to respond without undue delay and to comment on those parts of the proposal that are not accepted. Both parties are obligated to negotiate and cooperate.

Sixty days prior to the expiration of an existing collective agreement, the contracting parties must commence the negotiation of a new collective agreement. The parties must file the concluded collective agreement with the Ministry of Labor and Social Affairs and the filing must be announced in the collection of laws. The respective union also must inform the employees of the content of the collective agreement no later than 15 days following its conclusion.

C. Collective Agreements

The substance of collective agreements consists of the regulation of individual and collective affairs between the employer and employees and the right and obligations of the contracting parties.

Union bodies on the one hand, and employers on the other, are the parties to collective agreements.

In terms of scope and effect, a distinction must be made between corporate collective agreements and superior collective agreements. Corporate collective agreements are concluded between union bodies and individual employers. Superior collective agreements are concluded between union bodies and employers' organizations.

Collective agreements must be in writing and are binding unless they are in conflict with law. Corporate collective agreements are not binding if the entitlements of the employees they regulate are less advantageous than the entitlements regulated in the superior collective agreement. The same applies to any part of a collective agreement that is in excess of the allowable wage entitlements permitted employees by a superior collective agreement.

A collective agreement is concluded for the term expressly stated in the agreement. The law does not specify either a maximum or a minimum term. If the term is not stated in the agreement, then it is assumed that the term is one year.

D. Bargaining Disputes

A bargaining, or collective, dispute is a dispute concerning the conclusion of a collective agreement or the performance of obligations thereunder unless these matters relate to individual employees only. Collective disputes must be resolved in the manner provided by law.

1. Mediation and Arbitration

If the parties to collective bargaining fail to reach agreement, then the dispute must be submitted to a mediator. The parties may agree on the mediator. If they fail to do so, a mediator will be designated, upon request of either party, by the Ministry of Labor and Social Affairs. Any individual or legal person may be a mediator. However, a mediator designated by the Labor Ministry must be recorded on the Ministry's list of mediators. A proceeding before a mediator is deemed unsuccessful if the dispute is not resolved within 30 days, unless the parties agree on another period.

If the mediation is unsuccessful, then the dispute may be submitted to an arbitrator. The arbitrator may be appointed by the parties. If the parties fail to agree on an arbitrator, or if the dispute in question involves a situation where a strike is prohibited, or if the dispute relates to the performance of an obligation under a collective agreement, then the Labor Ministry must appoint an arbitrator from the list of arbitrators. The arbitrator is obligated to decide the dispute. In a dispute concerning the conclusion of a collective agreement, the resolution of the arbitrator is substituted for the consensus of the parties.

The resolution of an arbitrator regarding the performance of obligations under a collective agreement may be challenged in court, based on a petition of a contracting party, where the arbitrator's resolution is in violation of a legal regulation or the collective agreement. A conclusive resolution of an arbitrator regarding the performance of an obligation under a collective agreement also may be enforced by the court.

2. Strikes

In the event that no collective agreement is concluded in a proceeding before a mediator, and the contracting parties fail to apply for an arbitrator's decision on their dispute, a strike may be announced. This clearly implies that a proceeding before an arbitrator is not mandatory. However, it is prohibited to commence a strike after the arbitrator has issued his or her decision.

The law defines a strike as a partial or full stoppage of work by employees.[103] A strike may be commenced as an extreme method of resolving a dispute over the conclusion of a collective agreement. Another type of strike, which is known as a solidarity strike, is a strike in support of the claims of employees in a dispute regarding the conclusion of a separate collective agreement.

In a dispute regarding the conclusion of a collective agreement, a strike may be declared by the appropriate union body, provided that at least one-half of the employees who are affected by the agreement agree with the strike. If a superior collective agreement[104] is involved, the strike must be declared by a superior union body. The decision to strike with respect to a superior collective agreement is made under conditions similar to those referred to above.

The union body must notify the employer, at least three days in advance, of the commencement of the strike, the reason and goals of the strike, and a list of names of the union representatives who are authorized to represent the participants in the strike. Preventing an employee from taking part in a strike is prohibited. However, no employee may be forced to participate in a strike. The representative of the union body that represents the participants must secure reasonable and safe access to the employer's workplace and may not prevent employees who want to work from entering or leaving the workplace.

The law defines an unlawful strike as a strike that was not preceded by a proceeding before a mediator, a strike that was declared and continues after a proceeding before a mediator com-

---

[103] *See* Act No. 2/1991 Coll., §16.

[104] See II.C., above.

menced, or a strike that was not declared or commenced on the terms specified by law. Also unlawful is a strike declared or commenced for reasons other than those permitted by law. A solidarity strike is unlawful if it cannot affect the course or result of a strike of employees in support of whom it is declared. Other examples of unlawful strikes are as follows:

- strikes declared during the state's military standby and during periods of extraordinary measures;
- strikes by employees who are not allowed to strike, such as employees in the health-care sector or establishments of social care, if the strike could endanger the life or health of the populace;
- strikes at nuclear power plants, nuclear fission facilities, and at oil-pipeline or gas-pipeline facilities;
- strikes of judges, procurators, members of the armed forces and armed corps during the controlling and securing of air traffic; and
- strikes of firefighters, forest firefighting units, rescue squad members, and employees working in areas affected by natural disasters.

A court may rule on the unlawfulness of a strike in a suit brought by an employer, an organization of employers, or a state attorney.

During a strike, the participants are not entitled to wages. Liability for damage caused by an event that occurs during a strike attaches to strike participants vis-à-vis the employer, or the employer vis-à-vis the participant, pursuant to the Civil Code. However, a participant may not be held be liable to the employer, nor may the employer be held liable to a participant, for damage caused exclusively by work stoppage during a strike.

An employer may not hire other individuals to substitute for strike participants in their respective jobs.

A strike is terminated on the decision of the union body that declared the strike or decided on the commencement of the strike.

3. *Lockouts*

If no collective agreement is signed after a proceeding before a mediator, and the contractual parties fail to request an arbitrator to resolve their dispute, then a lockout may be used by the employer as an extreme method of resolving a dispute regarding the conclusion of a collective agreement. The law defines a lockout as partial or full stoppage of work by the employer. The employer must notify the appropriate union body at least three days in advance of the commencement of the lockout, its scope, reasons, and objectives, and a list of the names of employees to whom the lockout applies.

A lockout is unlawful if it is not preceded by mediation, if it is declared or continued after a proceeding before an arbitrator commences, where the lockout is not declared by the employer for reasons or on the terms specified in the law,[105] or for other reasons similar to those making a strike unlawful. A court may be requested to declare a lockout unlawful.

In a lockout, employees are entitled to one-half of their average wage. A lockout is terminated by a decision of the employer.

III. REPRESENTATION BY ENTITIES OTHER THAN UNIONS

A. Council of Employees and Councils for Safety and Protection of Health at Work

The Council of Employees is an association of employees that may be elected within a company having at least 25 employees in labor relationships. The Councils for Safety and Protection of Health at Work may be elected within a company having at least 10 employees in labor relationships. As with unions, these bodies represent employees' rights and interests.

B. Employee Representatives on the Supervisory Board

In a joint-stock company with more than a certain number of employees, the law requires employee representation on the supervisory board. Employee representatives are selected not by the labor union or other body, but by direct employee ballot. This form of employee participation in supervising and managing the com-

[105]*See* Act No. 2/1991 Coll., §27.

pany (in some cases, the supervisory board can possess the authority of the board of directors) is completely separate from the unions.

IV. Redundancy and Transfers of Undertakings

A. Redundancy

1. Notice Requirements

As discussed above,[106] the Labor Code provides that an employer may serve a termination notice if an employee becomes redundant by reason of a decision on the part of the employer or an authority to change the employer's function or technical equipment, reduce the workforce to increase efficiency, or make other organizational changes.

The first prerequisite for a notice based on employee redundancy is a decision to make a specified organizational change, such as a change in technical equipment or a reduction in the workforce to increase efficiency. The second prerequisite is a causal connection between this decision and the employee's redundancy. Therefore, the notice may be given only after the decision on the organizational change.

If the employer decides to reduce the number of its employees for redundancy, the employer is free to decide which of the employees are to be terminated. However, the union body must be consulted.

In addition, an employer that decides to serve notice by reason of employee redundancy has an obligation to cooperate with the relevant labor office in finding suitable alternative employment for affected employees, or, in cases of single parents who have custody of a child younger than 15 years of age or disabled employees who do not receive a pension, to actually provide the employees with suitable alternative employment.[107]

---

[106]See I.G.2.d.i., above.

[107]See I.G.2.d.iv., above.

The content and form requirements for a notice based on redundancy must be carefully observed. Courts are strict in this area, and they have developed extensive case law.

2. Mass Layoffs

The Labor Code defines mass layoffs as situations where the total number of employees terminated by the employer for reasons of winding up, relocation, or redundancy exceeds the following 30-day limits:

- 10 or more employees laid off by an employer employing from 20 to 100 employees;
- 10 percent or more of the total number of employees laid off by an employer employing from 100 to 300 employees; or
- 30 or more employees laid off by an employer employing more than 300 employees.

These limits include employees who terminate their labor relationship by agreement for the reasons of winding up, relocation, or redundancy, provided that there are at least five employees terminated by the employer.

The employer must inform the appropriate union body or the council of employees at least 30 days before serving notices. The employer must discuss with the union body or the council of employees measures to prevent or limit the mass layoffs, primarily the possibility to assign the employees affected by the layoff to another appropriate work.

At the same time, the employer must inform the local labor office of the following:

- reasons for the mass layoff,
- number of employees concerned,
- their age and professional structure,
- timing of the layoffs,
- criteria for selecting employees to be laid off, and
- start of negotiations with the union body or council of employees.

The employer also must provide the local labor office with a written report on the layoff, the results of its discussions with the union body or council of employees, and information about the total number of employees concerned, their age, and professional structure. The employer must deliver a copy of this report to the union body or council of employees, which may express their views to the labor office. An employer in bankruptcy must deliver this report only if requested by the labor office.

If there is no union body or council of employees representing the employer's employees, then the employer must fulfill its information obligations with respect to each affected employee.

The labor relationship of the affected employees may not end sooner than 30 days after the report on the mass layoff is delivered to the labor office, unless the employee expressly waives his or her right to this extension period.[108]

B. Transfers of Undertakings

Czech law protects employees during transfers, mergers, acquisitions, and other organizational changes. In the event of these business changes, the Labor Code and, in some instances, the Commercial Code[109] expressly regulate the assignment of rights and obligations ensuing from a labor relationship.

If an enterprise is dissolved through merger or consolidation, the Labor Code generally requires the successor enterprise to assume the labor-law rights and obligations without restriction as to scope. In the division (splitting up) of an enterprise, the rights and obligations are assumed by the new employer. The body that decided on the division determines which of the new employers are to assume the dissolved employer's labor-law rights and obligations.

Where a part of an enterprise is transferred to another employer, the labor-law rights and obligations vis-à-vis the employees of the part transferred are assumed by the employer to whom the part is transferred. The rights and obligations ensuing from

[108] *See* Act No. 65/1965 Coll., §52.
[109] Act No. 513/1991 Coll.

labor relationships that ended before the transfer remain with the original employer.

The original and the new employer must inform the appropriate union body or the council of employees of a transfer and must discuss the proposed date of transfer, the reasons for the transfer, the legal, economic, and social consequences of the transfer, and potential measures vis-à-vis the employees. In the absence of either a representative union body or a council of employees, the employers must discuss the above with each of the affected employees.

Where an enterprise is winding up, the body ruling on the wind-up decides which employer is to satisfy the employees' rights and obligations.

Contracts on sale of an enterprise are regulated by the Commercial Code, which contains mandatory provisions specifying that the rights and obligations of employees of the enterprise pass from the seller to the buyer. The parties may not diverge from these provisions.

V. Wages, Hours, and Leave

A. Wages

1. Minimum Wage

The minimum wage is the lowest amount that an employer may pay an employee for work. The employer must always pay at least the minimum wage to an employee who has worked the number of hours specified for the statutory workweek.[110] Lower rates are set for youth employees and for those receiving full or partial disability pensions.[111]

The Labor Code provides that wages may not be lower than the minimum wage set by government order.[112] A collective agreement may provide for a minimum wage higher than that specified by the government.[113]

---

[110]See V.B.1., below.

[111]*See* Order No. 303/1995 Coll., §2.

[112]Order No. 303/1995 Coll.

[113]*See* Act No. 65/1965 Coll., §111.

2. *Remuneration for Employment Contract Work*

Remuneration for work under an employment contract is regulated comprehensively in the Act on Wages, Remuneration for Work Standby and on Average Earnings,[114] and the Act on Pay and Remuneration for Work Standby in Budgetary and Certain Other Organizations and Bodies.[115]

3. *Overtime Work*

For overtime work, employees are entitled to the wage earned increased by at least 25 percent of average earnings. The employer and employee may agree that the employee will receive compensatory time off instead of the increased wage. The increased wage and compensatory time off do not apply if an individual employment agreement or a collective agreement provide that the agreed wage was determined, taking into account potential overtime work.[116]

4. *Holiday Compensation*

When an employee works on a holiday, he or she is entitled to the usual wage earned plus compensatory time off. The employee must be given the time off by the end of the third calendar month following the month in which he or she worked on the holiday. The employee is entitled to substitute a wage equal to his or her average earnings for this compensatory time off. Alternatively, the employee may agree to receive an extra average daily earning instead of compensatory time off.

When the holiday falls on a normal workday and the employee does not work during this holiday, the employee is entitled to wages in the amount of his or her average earnings.[117]

5. *Taxes*

Employee income is subject to tax. The tax rate varies progressively with the amount of the income, ranging from 15 per-

---

[114]Act No. 1/1992 Coll.

[115]Act No. 143/1992 Coll.

[116]*See* Act No. 1/1992 Coll., §5.

[117]*Id.*

cent to 32 percent. Both employers and employees contribute to social security, unemployment insurance, and sickness funds and to the state's universal health insurance plan at rates set by law.

6. *Protection Against Employer's Insolvency*

Pursuant to the Act on the Protection of Employees Against Employer's Insolvency,[118] an employee is entitled to claim before a labor office wages unpaid by his or her insolvent employer. The employee's claim may be extended for a period of three months preceding the filing of a petition seeking a declaration of the employer's insolvency.

The Ministry of Labor specifies the maximum amount that may be claimed by an employee. An employee may seek compensation related to a certain employer only once within a three-year period.

The employer is obliged to pay back to the labor office any and all amounts, with accrued interest, extended to employees due to the employer's insolvency.

B. Hours

1. *Statutory Workweek*

The maximum allowable workweek ("statutory workweek") is 40 hours, not including any overtime. Employees younger than age 16 may not work more than 30 hours per week and 6 hours per day.[119]

a. *Shortened Workweek*

The Labor Code distinguishes between a shortened workweek without a reduced wage and a shortened workweek for which the wage is proportionally reduced. The workweek is shortened without a reduction of wages as follows:

- 37.5 hours per week for those who work underground and those in continuous and three-shift operations; or

[118] Act No. 118/2000 Coll.
[119] *See* Act No. 65/1965 Coll., §83a.

- 38.75 hours per week for those who work in two-shift operations.

A shortened workweek without reduced wages also may be instituted for health reasons under permit from the Ministry of Labor and Social Affairs after consultation with the Health Ministry and discussion with the central body of labor unions and the appropriate organization of employers. The workweek also may be shortened without reduced wages through a collective agreement or an internal regulation of the employer conducting business activities. No minimum length of a shortened workweek is specified by law; hence, it depends on the contract, collective agreement, or internal decision by the employer.[120]

Alternatively, the employer and employee may agree in an employment contract on a reduced-wage and shorter workweek for operational reasons. The employer also may agree to or permit a shorter workweek with reduced wages for health or other serious reasons on the employee's part, where the employer's operation permits.[121]

b. *Workweek Distribution*

Distribution of the workweek can be uniform, non-uniform, or flexible. A uniform workweek means one in which the workweek does not vary more than three hours per week and the workday is no longer than nine hours. Furthermore, the average workweek over a certain period, generally four weeks, may not exceed the statutory workweek.[122]

A non-uniform workweek is one in which the work period is not uniform over a number of weeks, with the difference being greater than three hours, but where the average workweek over a certain period, up to one year, equals the statutory workweek. In the case of a non-uniform workweek, a single shift may not exceed 12 hours. A non-uniform workweek is permitted only for a period agreed to in a collective agreement or in an agreement be-

---

[120] *Id.*

[121] *Id.* §86.

[122] *Id.* §84. As of March 1, 2004, the only requirement regarding uniform workweek distribution is that the workday be no longer than nine hours.

tween the employer and the employee. The employer must prepare a schedule of the non-uniform work time and provide it to the affected employees no later than two weeks prior to the beginning of the scheduled period.[123]

A flexible workweek enables employees to decide on the beginning and the end of their workdays. The employer's internal regulations set the basic work time of at least five hours per day at fixed hours, and two daily limits for the remaining, optional work time at the beginning and the end of the workday. The optional work time at the beginning of each workday may not be shorter than one hour. In case of a shortened workweek, the five-hour and one-hour periods are proportionally adjusted.[124]

The flexible work time may have the following forms:

- *Flexible workday*—the employee chooses the beginning and the end of the workday, but not the agreed length of the workday (usually eight hours);
- *Flexible workweek*—the employee chooses the beginning and the end of each workday and the length of each workday, so that the weekly total equals the agreed length of a workweek (usually 40 hours); or
- *Flexible four-week period*—the employee chooses the beginning and the end of each workday and the length of each workday so that the four-week total equals the agreed length of the four-week period (usually 160 hours).[125]

2. *Shift Work*

When assigning employees to shifts, the employer must take into account the needs of women caring for children and the prohibition of certain types of work by women and juvenile employees.[126]

---

[123]*See* Act No. 65/1965 Coll., §85.
[124]*Id.* §85a.
[125]*Id.* §85b.
[126]See VI., below.

3. *Overtime*

The Labor Code defines overtime as work carried out in excess of the statutory workweek and outside of scheduled work shifts. The employer must consent to or order overtime work. The employer cannot order more than 8 hours of overtime per week and 150 hours per calendar year. These limits do not include overtime work for which the employee receives compensatory time off.[127]

The 150-hour limit may be exceeded only if the employee agrees; however, in this event, the average overtime may not exceed eight hours per week. A collective agreement may provide for a shorter limit.[128]

4. *Night Work*

Night work is work conducted between 10 p.m. and 6 a.m. The Labor Code specifies certain terms for night work, including a maximum work schedule of 8 hours for each 24 hours, and obligates the employer to provide a medical examination for the employee prior to assigning night work, to provide for refreshment, and to ensure work safety.[129]

5. *Rest and Standby Periods*

The Labor Code sets out rules for minimum continuous rest periods between two shifts, the length of continuous rest periods during the week, and work standby periods.

C. Leave

1. *Vacation*

Minimum annual leave (vacation) is four weeks. Employees of non-business employers are entitled to an additional week. Teaching and other academic employees of universities are en-

---

[127] *See* Act No. 65/1965 Coll., §§83, 96.
[128] *Id.* §96.
[129] *Id.* §99.

titled to a total of eight weeks per year.[130] Certain dangerous and difficult professions are entitled to an additional one-week leave.[131]

The employee is entitled to annual leave in a calendar year whenever he or she has worked in continuous employment for a given employer for at least 60 days in the calendar year. An employee who has not worked the requisite 60 days in continuous employment is entitled to annual leave on a pro-rata basis, with the pro-rata entitlement for each continuous month of employment equal to 1/12 of the specified annual leave. An employee who is not entitled to all or a pro-rata portion of an annual leave is entitled to leave equal to 1/12 of the specified annual leave for every 22 days worked in the calendar year.[132]

The date of an employee's leave is set exclusively by the employer. In scheduling leave, the employer must take into consideration not only its business tasks but also the rightful interests of the employee. The employer must give the employee notice of the leave date at least 14 days prior to its start. If the leave is given in parts, one part must be at least two weeks long, unless the employee agrees otherwise. The employee must be permitted to use his or her unused leave for a calendar year by the end of the following calendar year. The employer must enable the employee to take at least four weeks of leave, if the labor relationship lasted for the whole calendar year, provided that the employee is entitled to such leave. This means that the employer must allow the time off and may not substitute pay, unless conditions specified by the labor code are fulfilled.[133]

The employee's vacation may not be scheduled during the period when the employee is on military duty or during illness, maternity, or parental leave. If an employee requests the employer to schedule his or her vacation to immediately follow maternity or parental leave, then the employer must agree.[134]

Annual leave is paid. The employee is entitled to substitute wages during the annual leave period in the amount of his or her

[130] *Id.* §102.
[131] *Id.* §105.
[132] *Id.* §§101, 104.
[133] *Id.* §108.
[134] *Id.* §108.

average earnings and any benefits in kind if conditions specified by law are fulfilled. If the employee is unable to use his or her annual leave by the end of the subsequent calendar year because the employer failed to or incorrectly set the leave date, because a barrier to employment on the employee's part arose, and/or because the labor relationship has ended, the employee must be provided substitute wages for any unused leave.[135]

Annual leave is interrupted automatically if the employee begins military or alternative service, becomes incapacitated for work due to illness or injury, is caring for a family member during illness, or begins maternity or parental leave.[136]

2. *Sick Leave*

The employer must excuse the employee's absence from work during periods of incapacity for a number of reasons, the most important being illness, injury, health spa care, maternity leave, and care for a family member during illness. Wages are not paid during these periods; support is provided by the state and regulated by sickness insurance laws.

Employee benefits during illness, governed by Act No. 54/1956 Coll., as amended, are paid out starting on the first calendar day of illness and for up to one year. Where the incapacity for work due to illness lasts longer than one year, the individual must apply for a partial or full disability pension. Sickness benefits are 69 percent of the daily assessment base, but only 25 percent of the daily base during the first three days of illness.[137] During the first 15 days of sickness, the daily base is equal to 90 percent of the employee's gross earnings, up to CZK 480,[138] plus 60 percent of the amount between CZK 480 and 690, with earnings exceeding CZK 690 being disregarded. After the first 15 days of sickness,

---

[135] *Id.* §109.

[136] *Id.* §108.

[137] *See* Act No. 54/1956 Coll., §17.

[138] At current exchange rates, the Czech Republic Koruna (CZK) is equal to approximately US$0.037.

the amount up to CZK 480 counts in full, the amount between CZK 480 and 690 counts by 60 percent, and the amount exceeding CZK 690 is disregarded.[139]

Support to an employee caring for a family member is calculated in the same way as sickness benefits. The support is available for a maximum of nine calendar days. An exception for a single parent continually caring for at least one child of school age provides benefits for up to 16 calendar days.[140]

The universal health insurance premium is 13.5 percent of the employee's work income, paid 1/3 by the employee and 2/3 by the employer, and is a state-budget revenue item.

3. *Maternity Leave and Parental Leave*

For the birth and care of a child, women are entitled to maternity leave of 28 weeks; in the case of multiple births and single mothers, the period is 37 weeks.[141] In addition to maternity leave, the employer must provide parental leave to a woman, upon her request, until her child reaches age three. A man is entitled to the parental leave from the moment of his child's birth until the child reaches age three. A man or woman may request a shorter parental leave.[142] The employee need not apply specially for maternity or parental leave; as with incapacity for work due to illness, the employee need only notify his or her employer of the leave starting date on the applicable form with certification by the doctor. After maternity leave, the employer must return the mother to the same work and workplace; after parental leave, the employer must find work for the mother or father in accordance with that specified in his or her employment contract.[143]

Maternity leave is unpaid; financial support comes from the state as social insurance sickness benefits paid out for 28 weeks, starting from the sixth week before the expected birth date, unless the mother is gainfully active or is collecting sickness benefits. If the mother uses fewer than six weeks of her pre-childbirth mater-

[139] *See* Act No. 54/1956 Coll., §18.
[140] *Id.* §25.
[141] *See* Act No. 65/1965 Coll., §157.
[142] *Id.*, §158.
[143] *Id.* §147.

nity leave for a reason other than the fact that the birth occurred earlier than forecast by the doctor, maternity benefits are provided only to the 22nd week (or 31st week for multiple births and single mothers) from birth.[144] Maternity benefits are calculated in the same manner as sickness benefits after 15 days of sickness. In order to be eligible for maternity benefits, the party must have paid into the universal health insurance system[145] for at least 270 days over the preceding two years.[146]

If another woman takes on care of a newborn child because of the death of the mother or under a judicial decision, maternity leave is available, but is shortened by six weeks, i.e., by the expected benefit period prior to birth. A man who cares for a newborn child where, for example, the mother is unable to because of long-term illness certified by a doctor, also is entitled to the maternity benefit.

4. *Military Service*

Employees are entitled to leave during their military service. The leave depends on the type of service and is unpaid, except for average wages paid out during the first two weeks of service. The amount is the same for all types of service, including service during military exercises, and is reimbursed to the employer by the military or state administration body, but only up to the amount provided by law. Any additional amounts provided per collective agreements or internal regulations are borne by the employer.

Every employee called up for any type of military service is entitled to one day of paid leave for arranging administrative and personal matters and enlisting.

The employee must return to work no later than the third day after the end of service and receives no wages for the two days not worked. The employee is entitled to wages starting on the first day of his return to work.[147]

---

[144] *See* Act No. 88/1968 Coll., §7.

[145] See V.C.2., above.

[146] *See* Act No. 88/1968 Coll., §6.

[147] *See* Act No. 65/1965 Coll., §125.

5. *Election to Public Office*

When an employee is elected to public office, the employer, at the time the employee is elected, is required to permit the employee to assume public office and grant him or her unpaid leave for the time necessary.[148]

VI. ANTIDISCRIMINATION

The Czech Constitution, Bill of Rights, the Labor Code, and the Act on Employment all guarantee fundamental rights and freedom, regardless of sex, race, color of skin, language, faith and religion, political or other views, national or social background, membership in a national or ethnic minority, property, descent, or other status. The Bill of Rights partially addresses economic, social, and cultural rights as well, providing that every person is entitled to choose one's occupation and education and to conduct business or other economic activity. Terms and conditions for conducting certain occupations or activities may only be set by statute. The Bill of Rights also ensures increased protection of health at work and special conditions for women, juveniles, and the disabled, as discussed below.

The Labor Code sets forth a principle of equal treatment for all employees in the process of hiring, work duties, compensation, and professional training. Any discrimination for reasons of sex, race, color of skin, language, faith and religion, political or other views, national or social background, membership in a national or ethnic minority, property, descent, or other status is strictly prohibited by the Labor Code.

A. Women

The Labor Code assumes that women, because of their role of motherhood and physiological differences, cannot perform all types of work. Hence, women are prohibited from performing certain work that would subject them to increased risk of injury or

[148] *Id.* §124.

permanently reduce fertility. Certain prohibitions apply to all women; other prohibitions apply specifically to pregnant women, breastfeeding women, and mothers up to the ninth month after birth.

The employer must reassign pregnant women, breastfeeding women, and mothers of children younger than nine months of age from prohibited or hazardous work to more suitable work and, if the woman requests, from night work to a day shift. In addition, a pregnant woman or one caring for children of up to eight years of age may be sent on a business trip or reassigned to another workplace only with her permission.[149]

The employer may terminate the employment of a mother who is pregnant or continually caring for children younger than three years of age only in exceptional cases specified by law. Additionally, the employer must consider the woman's interest when setting the work period if she is caring for a child younger than 15 years and requests a shorter work period or other appropriate modification of the workweek.[150]

B. Juveniles

A juvenile employee is an employee younger than 18 years of age. Generally, juveniles may work starting from age 15, but not earlier than the final day of the obligatory school attendance period, which is nine years. Juveniles are entitled to increased health protection at work and to special working conditions. An employee younger than 16 years of age may not work more than 30 hours per week. Juveniles may not work overtime, underground in mining or tunneling, and may not perform work that is unreasonable, dangerous, or unhealthy, or that involves increased risk of injury. Juveniles younger than 16 must not work at night, while those 16 or older may do so under certain exceptional conditions.

C. Employees With Modified Work Capacity

The Act on Employment provides that a person with modified work capacity is one who, due to long-term unfavorable con-

---

[149]See I.F.2., above.
[150]See I.G.2.d., above.

ditions of health, has a significantly reduced opportunity for employment or preparation for employment, or who is receiving a pension conditioned on long-term unfavorable health status.[151] Based on this definition, those who receive a pension conditioned on long-term poor health are considered to have a modified work capacity, even if their remaining work ability allows them to work or to prepare for work. Employees with modified work capacity also include those who, due to long-term poor health, only are capable of carrying out work quite incomparable to their previous abilities and the social importance of their previous employment, and who receive a partial disability pension or who have been recognized as partially disabled even if they are not entitled to a partial disability pension.

The Labor Code establishes a framework of obligations for employers of those with modified work capacity. Details are contained in the Act on Employment, Government Ordinance No. 228/2000 Coll., specifying the obligatory proportion of citizens with modified work capacity to all employees, and Decree No. 115/1992 Coll., on providing work rehabilitation for citizens with modified work capacity.

The obligatory proportion of citizens with modified work capacity to all employees is 4 percent and applies to employers with more than 25 employees. The employer must, up to the obligatory percentage, hire such persons who have been recommended for employment by the applicable labor office for vacant positions, or purchase certain volume of goods or services from entities where more than 50 percent of employees have modified work capacity, or pay a special contribution to the state budget.[152]

Employees with modified work capacity may be terminated only with the previous approval of the relevant labor office,[153] unless:

- notice is given to an employee who is older than 65 years of age;

[151]*See* Act No. 1/1991 Coll., §21.
[152]*Id.* §24.
[153]This previous approval is not required as of March 1, 2004.

- notice is given due to organizational changes in which the employer's business is winding up or relocating in full or in part;
- the employee has given reason for the employer to immediately terminate the labor relationship;
- the employee seriously violates employee discipline; or
- the employee consistently commits minor violations of employee discipline.

VII. OCCUPATIONAL SAFETY AND HEALTH AND WORKERS' COMPENSATION

A. Occupational Safety and Health

Legal provisions for occupational safety and health are set forth in the Labor Code and in numerous other acts and regulations. The provisions in the Code are often very paternalistic—a holdover from the socialist period prior to 1989. In 1994, the Code was amended in order to adapt its protection in this area to the needs and requirements of the International Labor Organization and the directives of the European Union and to consolidate employers' obligations in a statute, rather than in sub-legislative regulations, a structure that violated the Bill of Rights and the Czech Constitution. Current law in the area of occupational safety and health emphasizes the employer's obligation to reduce risks at work and employees' obligations to be concerned for their own safety at work.

Labor unions have the right to supervise the status of occupational safety and health. Measures taken by a labor union may be reviewed by the state body for professional supervision of occupational safety and health, which is regulated by Act No. 174/1968 Coll., and a number of other acts concerning mining, defense, the interior, transportation, etc. The state body may levy fines on both employees and employers for violations of regulations.

B. Workers' Compensation

The Labor Code differentiates between the following types of employer liability to employees:

- general liability for employee losses,
- liability for work-related injury and occupational illness,
- liability for damage to checked goods, and
- liability for losses incurred by an employee in the process of averting a loss.

The employer's general liability is broad. The employer may not waive such liability, but only limit it where it has been proved that the employee contributed to the loss suffered.

For losses due to occupational injury and illness, the liability is objective, i.e., it is irrelevant that the employee may have breached a duty or may otherwise be at fault. An employee's injury suffered on the way to or from work is not considered occupational. In certain cases specified by law, the employer may partially or completely waive liability for an occupational injury or illness. Justifications for waiver include violation by the employee of a regulation or instruction ensuring safety or health protection at work, drunkenness and other forms of intoxication, and negligent conduct.

To the extent of its liability, the employer must provide compensation to the employee for lost earnings, pain, stricken social application, medical treatment costs, and for specific material losses.

VIII. PENSIONS AND BENEFITS

A. Pensions

The pension insurance system is regulated by Act No. 155/1995 Coll. on Pension Insurance (Pension Act). Individuals in a labor relationship as well as the self-employed must participate in the pension system.

The pension insurance system provides pensions termed old-age, full and partial disability, widow and widower, and orphan. The Pension Act increases the base retirement age for men from 60 years to 62 years by the year 2007, gradually in two-month intervals. For women, the age will gradually increase to between 57 and 61 years, depending on the number of children raised. (Prior to amendment in 1995, the retirement age of women was determined as follows: 53 years with five or more children raised; 54 years with three or four children; 55 years with two children; 56 years with one child; and 57 years for childless women.)

The employee may receive pension benefits prior to reaching retirement age provided that he or she has participated in the pension insurance system for at least 25 years, has been listed as unemployed at a labor office for at least 80 days, and is no more than two years away from retirement age.

Pension insurance is one component of the social security premium and the state unemployment policy contribution, both of which are paid by both employer and employee. The employer's social security and unemployment policy premium is equal to 26 percent of the base, of which 3.3 percent is for sickness insurance, 19.5 percent is for pension insurance, and 3.2 percent is for the state unemployment policy. The employee's total contribution is 8 percent of base: 1.1 percent for sickness insurance, 6.5 percent for pension insurance, and 0.4 percent for the state unemployment policy. The basis is calculated under the rules specified in the Pension Act. These contributions are in addition to the amounts paid for universal health insurance.

The pension insurance premiums are a state-budget revenue item, accounted for separately. The Act on State Budget for the appropriate calendar year listed these premiums as a separate state budget revenue item.

Private insurers offer voluntary supplemental pension plans. In addition to employee contributions, the employer may contribute as well.

IX. IMMIGRATION

Pursuant to the Act on Employment, foreign nationals and persons without citizenship (collectively referred to as foreign nationals) have the same legal status as Czech citizens, provided that they are employed under Czech law. Foreign nationals only may be employed, however, if they have received a residency permit pursuant to Act No. 326/1999 Coll., on the Stay of Foreigners in the Territory of the Czech Republic, and an employment permit pursuant to Act No. 9/1991 Coll. Foreign nationals who, inter alia, have been granted refugee status, and who have either been in the

Czech Republic for five years, have married a Czech citizen, or have at least one child of Czech citizenship need not obtain an employment permit. As of May 1, 2004, EU citizens will no longer need a work permit, and they will obtain a residency permit upon simple request.

Where no Czech citizens, particularly job-seekers, are available for a vacant job position, the appropriate labor office may permit a foreign national to be employed. Decisions to permit or withdraw permission for employment of a foreign national and permission to hire a foreign national for a vacant job position are made by the labor office pursuant to section 12(2) of Act No. 9/1991 Coll.[154]

A foreign national found to be gainfully occupied without the proper residency permit and employment permit, or to have violated any other obligation imposed by law, may be forbidden from staying in the Czech Republic and may be deported. Pursuant to section 123 of Act No. 326/1999 Coll., any deportation costs are borne by the deportee or the person who unlawfully employed the deportee.[155]

---

[154] As of May 1, 2004, these special rules do not apply to EU citizens.

[155] As of May 1, 2004, these special rules do not apply to EU citizens.

HUNGARY*

INTRODUCTION

Hungary covers a territory of 93,032 square kilometers in the center of Europe and is bordered by Austria, Croatia, Romania, Serbia, Slovakia, Slovenia, and Ukraine. Due to its geographical location, Hungary constitutes a link between the East and the West. At present, the country has a population of 10 million people. The Constitution acknowledges 13 nationalities. About three to four million Hungarians live outside Hungary's borders, most of them in neighboring countries.

The state of Hungary originally was founded by Szent István (St. Steven), who was crowned on January 1, 1001. Although the country was alternately ravaged and occupied by the Turkish, Austrian, German, and Soviet armies during the centuries, most of her conquerors more or less acknowledged her independence. The third independent and free republic was declared on October 23, 1989.

Legislative powers in Hungary are exercised by a single-chamber Parliament. There are 386 members of Parliament, each elected for a term of four years, partly directly and partly by their respective parties. Some members are elected directly, where the voter votes for an individual candidate (so it can be an independent candidate). Other members are elected through slates of candidates offered by the party, where the voters vote for the party's list of candidates. Parliament elects the President of the Republic, the Prime Minister, the members of the Constitutional Court, the President of the Supreme Court, and the Attorney General. It also exercises control over the executive bodies (the governmental ministries and other governmental authorities), and possesses several other rights and obligations prescribed in the Constitution.

---

*David J. Millstone, Squire, Sanders & Dempsey, L.L.P., Cleveland, Ohio; Katalin Holló, Squire, Sanders & Dempsey, L.L.P., Budapest, Hungary.

The President of the Republic is elected by Parliament for a term of five years and may be re-elected once. The President represents the unity of the nation and safeguards the democratic operation of the organization of the state. The President is chief commander of the armed forces and represents the Hungarian state in its international relations. He appoints the ministers (nominated by the Prime Minister) and the President of the National Bank of Hungary (nominated by Parliament). He also sets the time for general and local government elections.

All judicial power resides in the courts. Decisions are announced in the name of the Republic. The President of the Supreme Court is elected by Parliament and nominated by the President of the Republic. The President of the Supreme Court then may nominate the deputies to be appointed by the President of the Republic. Judges also are appointed by the President of the Republic.

The Constitutional Court has 11 members elected by Parliament. Its function is to examine whether legal regulations comply with the Constitution. The Constitutional Court has the right to repeal any piece of legislation or government regulation determined to be in conflict with the provisions of the Constitution.

The Labor Courts hear legal disputes arising out of or relating to employment. The Labor Courts belong to the County Courts. All the counties and the capital have Labor Courts that have jurisdiction within the competent county. Appeals are heard at the Supreme Court of the Republic of Hungary.

A. Sources of Labor Law

1. Domestic Sources

a. Constitution

The highest source of domestic labor law is the Constitution of the Republic of Hungary.[1] Chapter XII of the Constitution declares several rights pertaining to work, including the right to work, the right of free choice of work, the right of recreation (free time),

---

[1]Act XX of 1949, as amended.

the right to strike, and the right of association. The Constitution also guarantees entitlement to various social welfare benefits and services, e.g., old age pensions, disability pensions, unemployment benefits, and health care services.[2] The Constitution also sets forth the obligations of workers.[3]

b. *National Legislation*

i. *Labor Code*

Although general rights and duties are stipulated and guaranteed by the Constitution, specific legal requirements are set forth in the Labor Code,[4] which is the main legislation governing employment. The Labor Code contains all laws relevant to the relationship between employers and employees. Its provisions cover trade unions, collective contracts, employment contracts, ordinary and extraordinary termination of employment, performance of work, working hours and leisure time, legal disputes and their settlement, the employment status of women and minors, and other aspects of the employment relationship.

Amendments to the Labor Code effective in July 2001 and September 2003 added provisions relating to foreign employees working in Hungary within the framework of posting, temporary assignment, or hiring-out of workers; employees working under a lease agreement; and the working time leave allowance for men after the birth of a child. The Labor Code now excludes from its scope the employment of foreign employees who perform work in Hungary for a non-Hungarian employer pursuant to a posting arrangement or secondment, temporary assignment, or labor force lease. The Labor Code has been extended to certain relationships under the Civil Code to performance of work by workers younger than 18 years of age by means other than employment contracts, and to employment contracts between an employment-business employer (lessor) and the user of the employee's services (lessee). The various requirements are discussed in more detail in later sections of this chapter.

---

[2]*See id.* §§70/B, 70/C, and 70/E.

[3]*See id.* §70/I.

[4]Act XXII of 1992 [hereinafter Labor Code].

In addition to the Labor Code, other pieces of legislation contain regulations on work and employment, e.g., the Act on Public Employees,[5] the Act on the Legal Status of Public Officers,[6] the Act on Strikes,[7] the Act on the Social Welfare Provisions for the Unemployed,[8] and related governmental and ministerial decrees.

Under Hungarian law, legal rights and duties differ depending on whether the employer is private sector or public sector. Public sector employment presents two kinds of legal relations: those of public employees and those of public officers. Legislation governing each type of public employment is discussed below.

ii. Act on Public Employees

The legal relationships of public employees are regulated by the Act on Public Employees (Public Employees Act).[9] Unless otherwise provided by law, the Public Employees Act applies to the legal relationship of those employed by budgetary organizations of the central and local governments or for the purpose of performing public services falling within the jurisdiction of the local governments (the employer). Those employed by local governments under communal work projects are not subject to the Public Employees Act. Additionally, the Public Employees Act is not applicable to legal relationships regulated by other legislation in a different manner (e.g., public officers).[10]

The Labor Code is subject to exceptions provided for in the Public Employees Act. At the end of each chapter, the Public Employees Act lists the regulations of the Labor Code that are not applicable to public employees.[11] Although the Labor Code allows the parties to determine the terms of employment in their employment or collective contract, the Public Employees Act contains its own detailed standards. This deviation ensures stability in the legal status of public employees.

---

[5]Act XXXIII of 1992.
[6]Act XXIII of 1992.
[7]Act VII of 1989.
[8]Act IV of 1991.
[9]Act XXXIII of 1992.
[10]*See id.* §1.
[11]*See id.* §2(3).

The public employee legal relationship is established by appointment. Once accepted, it is for an indefinite time period. The legal relationship also may be created for a definite term, but only for the purpose of substitution or for the performance of a specific job or task.[12] After lapse of the defined term, withdrawal of the assignment, or resignation from the assignment, the public employee must continue to be employed in his or her original job, or, if this is not feasible, in a job suiting the employee's education and qualifications. Should a court ascertain that withdrawal of an assignment was unlawful, the public employee—upon request—must be reinstated in his or her original higher-level executive position, or be employed in an executive position. In addition, the employee is entitled to the amount of supplementary pay received by executives during the period concerned.

Based upon the level of education and qualifications required for performance, the jobs of public employees are classified into four categories. These categories are divided into various payment brackets, which are further subdivided into different classes. After the lapse of a three-year waiting period following appointment, a public employee's salary increases to the next salary class, and the waiting period is started again. In the event of an outstanding accomplishment or permanently high standard performance, this waiting period may be shortened.[13]

Public employees are entitled to supplementary pay, a 13th month salary, and other benefits.[14] Public employees also are entitled to additional paid leave beyond their ordinary leave, the extent of which is established according to their salary brackets and positions.[15]

iii. Act on the Legal Status of Public Officers

The Act on the Legal Status of Public Officers (Public Officers Act)[16] was amended, effective September 1, 2003, to limit its

---

[12]*See id.* §21.
[13]*See id.* §§60–65.
[14]*See id.* §§67–68.
[15]*See id.* §57.
[16]Act XXIII of 1992.

coverage to public officers of the Prime Minister's Office, which includes ministries and organizations with national scope of authority, their local territorial organizations, the county and capital administrative offices, the offices of the representatives of local governments, administrative associations of authorities, and the offices of district notaries. The amendment also extended coverage to the Secretariat of the Hungarian Academy of Sciences. Administrators and physical employees are no longer subject to the Act. Under the law, managers and officials with decisionmaking powers are public officers, administrative employees perform administrative tasks, and all other employees are considered physical workers. Unless otherwise provided by law, the Public Officers Act also is applicable to public officers of the office of the President of the Republic, the office of the Parliament, the office of the Constitutional Court, the office of the Ombudsman, the State Audit Office, the Council of Public Procurements, the office of the National Radio and Television Authority, and the Competition Office. With respect to certain organizations (police, fire department, border guards, etc.), however, the Public Officers Act applies only as expressly provided in the specific laws pertaining to these bodies.[17]

Under the Public Officers Act, employers' rights are exercised by the head of the work organization of the public administrative body, or the body itself.[18] In the case of local governments, the employer's rights over the public officers of the representative body are exercised by the notary, who, nonetheless, requires the consent of the mayor before making certain decisions (appointment, assignment of a manager, withdrawal of an assignment, dismissal).[19]

The Public Officers Act projects a long-term career for specialists; therefore, it stipulates strict conditions for their employment. As a general requirement, they must have a clean criminal record, disposing capacity (legal competency), and Hungarian citi-

---

[17] *See id.* §§1, 2.
[18] *See id.* §6.
[19] Act LXV of 1990.

zenship. Pursuant to the provisions on qualifications, they are required to have at least a secondary school diploma, and executives must have a university or college degree.[20]

As a general rule, public officer applicants must declare in writing that they meet the secondary school diploma requirement. Only those applicants who fulfill the necessary "security" conditions for ensuring the legal mechanism of the state and who agree that the competent national security office controls the content of their declaration can be employed in important and confidential positions. In accordance with Section 1 of Act LXXXV of 1995 on the national security offices (the "NSO Act"), national security offices include the following: (1) Information Office, (2) National Security Office, (3) Military Reconnaissance Office, (4) Military Security Office, and (5) National Security Special Service. Pursuant to Section 8(f) of the NSO Act, the National Security Special Service is responsible for control of the persons under its purview.

Public officers are employed for an indefinite term. The employment relationship is established through a written appointment and its acceptance by the nominee. As with public employees, public officers may be employed for a definite term only for the purpose of substitution or the performance of a specific task. Public officers must take an oath upon their appointment.[21]

In order to ensure the economic and political independence of public officers, the Public Officers Act provides detailed regulations on the issue of conflict of interests.[22] Specifically, the Public Officers Act prohibits public officers from establishing any relationship that results in the management, control, supervision of or by, or any financial transactions with, their relatives. The existence of these conditions disqualifies the nominee from being appointed a public officer. To guarantee enforcement of basic rights and obligations, to ensure morality in public service, and to prevent corruption, most public officers are obliged to make a declaration of their assets.

[20]Act XXIII of 1992, §7.

[21]*See id.* §§11, 12.

[22]*See id.* §21.

During their employment, public officers may not be representatives of the local government or the municipality of the ethnic minority where their employer's public administrative body has jurisdiction. Minoritites in Hungary may establish their own local or national municipality.

In certain cases, the Public Officers Act permits outside employment provided it is approved by the party exercising the employer's rights; in other cases, outside employment is prohibited. However, the prohibition against outside employment does not apply to scientific, educational, or artistic activities; or proofreading, editing, or other intellectual activities protected by copyright.

Public officers are further prohibited from pursuing any activities that would hurt their reputation or that would endanger their impartiality and freedom from influence or prejudice. In addition, public officers may not accept any office in a political party or make any public appearance on behalf of, or in the interest of, any political party. This prohibition does not apply when public officers participate in parliamentary or local government elections as candidates. Thus, for the period of their candidacy, this provision of the conflict of interest rules is suspended.[23] The cause of any conflict of interest must be eliminated by the public officer. Should the officer not be willing to do so, after the lapse of a period defined by law, employment as a public officer will be terminated.

The Public Officers Act contains a hierarchy based on merits, i.e., a system of careers in public administration. This means public officers, like public employees, have a vested right to promotion. Officers may rise in the hierarchy simply due to lapse of time, although they also may be promoted upon the fulfillment of certain conditions.[24]

The remuneration of public officers consists of a basic salary, but occasionally they receive supplementary pay. Public officers are entitled to receive supplementary pay, including payment for education and training, social support (e.g., funeral aid, mailing costs, and/or holidays at reduced tariffs, and supplemen-

---

[23] *See id.* §§9, 21.
[24] *See id.* §§23, 25.

tary pay for pensioners), and financial assistance for the purchase of a home. Public officers also have a vested right to the 13th month of salary.[25] A public officer is entitled to severance pay when relieved from duty.

Public officers have 25 business days of basic paid leave annually, which may increase by a supplementary leave of 2 to 10 business days (depending on the employee's classification), or, in the case of executives, by 15 business days.[26] In addition to their annual basic leave, public officers are entitled to a recreation leave, which consists of an uninterrupted six-month period of paid leave after every ten years spent as a public officer.

Public officers are liable to pay indemnification for any damage caused by the reprehensible violation of obligations arising from their employment. In the event of damage due to negligence, the indemnification amounts to up to three-months' salary; damage caused willfully must be compensated in full.

iv. Civil Code

Although the provisions of the Labor Code pertain to employment, performance of work in a wider sense (e.g., under an entrepreneurial contract or letter of assignment) is regulated by the Civil Code.[27] Among other provisions, the Civil Code contains regulations concerning the rights and obligations of contracting parties, the establishment and the extent of their liability, the performance of their payment obligations, and the conditions for termination, taking into consideration the nature and specific features of the contract.

2. *International Sources*

In accordance with the European Union (EU) meeting held in Brussels in November 2000, Hungary became a full member of the EU on May 1, 2004. The harmonization of Hungary's laws to EU directives has been taking place since 1991, the year Hungary ratified the partnership agreement. At that time, Act XXII of 1992,

---

[25] *See id.* §§42, 49.

[26] *See id.* §41.

[27] Act IV of 1959, as amended. For a discussion of entrepreneurial relationships and assignments, see I.A., below.

the Labor Code, already met the expectations of the EU labor law standards. All past and present amendments of the Labor Code reflect the latest developments of EU labor directives.

Hungary is a member of the International Labor Organization (ILO). Therefore, it is bound by the guidelines and principles of that organization, as well as the conventions it has signed (e.g., Government Decree on the Promulgation of the Agreement Concerning the Establishment of the Budapest Office of the Eastern and Central European Multidisciplinary Task Force of the ILO).[28]

Furthermore, bilateral treaties, such as the Government Decree on the Promulgation of the Agreement Concerning the Legal Status, Privileges, and Exemptions of the International Organization of Migration in Hungary,[29] also play a significant role. In this regard, for example, the Hungarian government executed an agreement with the Republic of Germany with the aim of promoting the employment of those wishing to undertake a job for the purpose of improving their professional and language skills.[30]

3. *Conflicts of Laws*

If employment involves a foreign country, as a general rule, the legal relationship is governed by the law of the country where the work is to be performed.[31] However, due to the special nature of this relationship, various other regulations may be applicable. In the event of an employment established by way of appointment or election, the personal law of the appointing authority or the electing body is applied. If the employer is a foreign state or public administrative body, or if a foreign citizen is working in Hungary as a diplomat or enjoys immunity from the jurisdiction of Hungarian authorities for other reasons, and the contracting parties have identical personal laws, the employment is governed by the parties' law. In the event that performance of the work is not confined to the territory of a single country, the personal law of

[28]Government Decree No. 171/1993 (Dec. 8). For information on the ILO, see the chapter on the ILO in Volume I, Part 4.

[29]Government Decree No. 44/1993 (Mar. 12).

[30]Decree of the Council of Ministers No. 55/1990, ch. III §23; Decree of the Council of Ministers No. 54/1990 (Mar. 23).

[31]Law-Decree No. 13 of 1979 on International Private Law, §§51–53.

the employer is applicable. If an employee of a Hungarian employer performs work abroad (either in the form of a business trip or as a permanent mission abroad), the employment is governed by Hungarian law.

The 2001 Labor Code amendment describes the circumstances in which Hungarian labor law will apply to employment relationships with employees from European Union (EU)-Member countries and identifies certain terms that had to be harmonized prior to Hungary's entry into the EU.

Regulations pertaining to the employment of the cargo crews of water or air carriers also diverge from the general rule. In these cases, the law of the country of the flag or other official markings under which the carrier operates is applicable. For employees of other carriers, the personal law of the carrier will apply.

B. Employment Rights and Obligations

The Labor Code contains detailed regulations regarding the rights and obligations of employers and employees with respect to performance of work. The most important of these are summarized below.

1. Employer Obligations

The employer must employ the employee in accordance with the regulations pertaining to employment contracts,[32] employment relationships, and the provisions of other legal regulations.[33] The employer also must ensure safe and healthy labor conditions.[34] In addition, the employer must do the following:

- organize the work in such a way that employees may exercise their rights and fulfill their obligations arising from employment;
- provide employees with the information and guidance required for carrying out their work;

[32]For a discussion of employment contracts, see I.B., below.
[33]Labor Code §102. For a discussion of collective contracts, see II.B., below.
[34]See VII., below.

- ensure the acquisition of knowledge required for performing work; and
- pay remuneration in compliance with the regulations pertaining to employment and the provisions of the employment and/or collective contract.[35]

Finally, the employer must ensure the material conditions for the performance of work, i.e., premises, equipment, tools, raw materials, etc.

2. *Employee Obligations*

In addition to working, employees have several other obligations to ensure the efficient and safe performance of work. Specifically, employees must do the following:

- appear at the prescribed place and time in a condition fit for work, spend their working time at work, and, during this time, be at the employer's disposal for the purpose of performing work;
- perform their work with the expected professional expertise and diligence in accordance with applicable regulations, requirements, and instructions;
- cooperate with their co-workers and perform and behave in a way that, generally speaking, will not endanger the health and physical safety of others, disturb their work, cause damage to them, or elicit their disapproval;
- fulfill their work duties personally;
- keep confidential industrial (business) secrets that they learn in the course of their work, as well as information of fundamental importance pertaining to the employer or the employer's activities;[36] and
- attend training and educational courses chosen by the employer and pass the related exams, unless attendance would have a disproportionate adverse effect on the employee's personal or family status.

---

[35]Labor Code §102. For a discussion of employee remuneration, see V.A., below.
[36]Labor Code §103.

The employer has the power to decide the scope of business secrets. Data, documents, know-how, and business plans or ideas generally may be classified as business secrets, sometimes with the addition of a time frame.

3. *Employees' Obligation to Obey Instructions*

Employees must perform their work in accordance with the instructions of the employer. As a rule, the party entitled to exercise the employer's rights is not the same as the party entitled to give instructions; the former usually delegates the right to give instructions to the employee's immediate supervisor, although reserving the right, for example, to terminate employment.

In certain cases, the employee may, and in other cases must, refuse to obey an instruction. The latter applies if fulfilling the instruction would directly and seriously endanger another person's life, physical safety, or health.[37]

4. *Obligation to Cooperate*

Employers, factory councils, and employees are required by law to cooperate during the course of exercising their rights and fulfilling their obligations. Additionally, trade unions have an obligation to cooperate and the cooperation must be bona fide and respectful. All parties have the obligation to inform each other about any relevant circumstances or changes that might affect the exercise of employment rights and obligations. The employer's obligation in this respect applies even prior to the conclusion of an employment contract.

5. *Proper Exercise of Rights*

The rights and duties prescribed in the Labor Code must be exercised in accordance with their intended purpose. The exercise of rights is improper if its intent is to, or it results in, injury to the rightful interests of others, restrictions on the assertion of others' interests, harassment, or the suppression of others' opinions. Appropriate remedies are provided for any detrimental consequences resulting from the improper exercise of rights.

---

[37]*See id.* §104.

6. *Protection of Employee Data*

An employer may not request information concerning an employee or potential employee that is not directly related to employment. Employers may disclose facts, data, and opinions concerning an employee to third persons only as specified by law or with the employee's consent. Information and data pertaining to employees may be used for statistical purposes and may be disclosed for statistical use in a manner that precludes identification of individual employees.

7. *Protection of the Employer's Business Interests*

While in an employment relationship, employees may not act in a manner that poses a threat to the rightful business interests of the employer, unless authorized by law. Employees remain subject to this obligation following termination of the employment relationship only if they are subject to an agreement that meets the following criteria:

- the agreement is concluded for such purpose;
- the agreement is supported by appropriate consideration; and
- the agreement has a term of no more than three years.

Civil law governs such agreements.

8. *Grant of Mandatory Priority*

With respect to a specific group of employees, employment-related regulations may stipulate the obligation of priority under identical conditions in connection with an employment relationship.

C. Administration of the Labor Laws

1. *Major Administrative Bodies*

a. *Ministry of Labor or Ministry of Social and Family Affairs*

In 1998, the names of some ministries changed. Where the Ministry of Labor or Minister of Labor is mentioned, the Ministry of Social and Family Affairs or Minister of Social and Family Affairs should now be understood.[38]

The Ministry of Social and Family Affairs manages:

- the National Labor Research and Methodology Center,
- the labor development and training centers (training centers), and
- the county (metropolitan) labor centers.

The professional management organization of the labor safety and labor management supervisions operating within the labor centers is the National Occupational Safety and Labor Administration (abbreviated OMMF in Hungarian, NOSLA in English).

In its management capacity, the Minister of Social and Family Affairs:

- establishes the principles and main contents of the mandatory internal rules of institutions that form a part of the labor force organization and approves the organizational and operational rules of such institutions;
- determines requirements in relation to the tasks of the National Labor Research and Methodology Center with respect to the methodology of labor force services, information technology (IT) and computer systems, and the data content of central data collections as well as information and forecasts; and
- determines the range of training conducted by training centers that are acknowledged by the state, and the requirements of labor force and educational services provided and data collections performed, and approves the training center's annual educational material development and educational plan.[39]

The government has the duty of instituting the framework for labor safety by way of supervising relevant procedures through designated regulatory agencies. Within the framework of labor

[38]Act XXXVI of 1998.

[39]Decree of the Ministry of Labor No. 9/1996 (Dec. 20).

safety administration, the government must attend to the following duties:

- establishment of a national labor safety program;
- determination of the fundamental requirements for occupational safety and health, along with the associated rights and obligations;
- establishment of a curriculum related to general personal safety and to occupational safety and health regulations, for the purposes of general education and vocational training; and
- review of the labor safety situation within the national economy on an annual basis and disclosure of the results of such review, as well as establishment and operation of the labor safety information network.

Within its regulatory activities and administration proceedings, the government must

- promote and supervise the enforcement of labor safety regulations, and
- attend to the licensing and registration functions.

b. Agencies Responsible for the Execution of State Duties

The Parliament, the government, the Ministers of Social and Family Affairs, and the National Occupational Safety and Labor Administration (NOSLA) have jurisdiction to attend to the duties related to the enforcement of labor safety at the level of national economy.

NOSLA is an independent central office established for the initiation, preparation, and promotion of labor safety-related state administration duties and the exercise of general regulatory competencies related to occupational safety and health. The chief officer of NOSLA is its President. Under its competence as the authority of the first instance, NOSLA carries out licensing procedures regarding the operation of labor safety experts and maintains the register of such licenses in accordance with the decree of the Minister of Social and Family Affairs.

Inspectors of the county (Budapest) occupational safety and labor boards are entitled, as authorities of the first instance, to:

- hold inspections at all workplaces within their fields of competence, without a special permit;
- investigate industrial accidents, with the exception of those related to public roads and air transport, without prejudice to the employers' responsibility;
- instruct employers to satisfy the requirements of occupational safety and health;
- oblige employers to eliminate any deficiencies that are determined, within the deadline specified; and
- prohibit employees from working under conditions that are in grave violation of the regulations pertaining to occupational safety and health.

2. *National Labor Council*

On matters of national significance involving labor relations and employment, the government must cooperate with the organizations that represent employers' and employees' interests in the National Labor Council.

With the consent of the National Labor Council, the government must determine the regulations that depart from provisions of the Civil Code with regard to mass staff reductions,[40] make decisions regarding the statutory minimum wage[41] and the supervision of labor relations, and develop proposals for determining the maximum duration of daily work time and the number of public holidays.[42]

The government initiates national wage negotiations with the National Labor Council. The Minister of Social and Family Affairs, on the recommendation of the National Labor Council, then promulgates the agreement in the form of a legal regulation. The Minister of Social and Family Affairs—in agreement with the National Labor Council—also may determine the system of labor qualification.

---

[40]See IV.A., below.
[41]See V.A.1.b., below.
[42]See V.B., below.

D. Dispute Resolution

1. Legal Disputes

To be considered a legal dispute, the dispute must arise from, or be in connection with, employment and must involve a legal issue. In general, a legal action may be initiated against the employer in the following circumstances:

- due to an action or omission by the employer in violation of the regulations pertaining to employment;
- to assert a legal claim of the employee arising in connection with employment; or
- to assert a legal claim of the trade union, factory council, or factory representative arising in connection with the collective contract.

A legal action also may be initiated against a decision adopted by an employer within its own scope of authority, on the ground that the employer has violated standard regulations in the course of making its decision.[43]

An employer also may initiate a legal action against an employee for the purpose of asserting a legal claim in connection with employment.

Although the parties are not obliged to hold conciliatory negotiations prior to submitting the case to the court, in case of legal disputes, the collective contract or the agreement between the parties may stipulate that they will request the participation of a mediator.[44] In this case, the mediator must document any agreement that is reached in the course of conciliation. If the negotiations fail, the parties may turn to the labor court within the time of the applicable statute of limitations.

2. Labor Disputes

Any dispute arising in connection with employment between the employer (or an organization representing the employer's in-

[43]Labor Code §199.
[44]*See id.* §199/A.

terests) and the trade union or factory council may be considered a labor dispute, provided that it does not qualify as a legal dispute. A labor dispute can be settled in two ways: by involving a mediator, who is an independent third party, or by an arbitrator, whose decision is binding if the parties have accepted his or her exclusive jurisdiction.[45]

I. INDIVIDUAL EMPLOYMENT

A. The Employment Relationship

Hungarian law recognizes various forms of legal relationships intended for performing work, including:

- the employment relationship,
- entrepreneurial relationships, and
- assignments.

In an employment relationship, the employee agrees to perform the specified activity or work for and under the control of the employer, during a specified work time.

In an entrepreneurial relationship, the contractor is obliged to design or prepare an object or render a service; that is, to achieve a specific result through work and for which the customer is obliged to pay remuneration.

Assignments are given for the performance of management activities according to the instructions of, and in the interests of, the assignor. The person assigned undertakes an obligation to accomplish a certain objective, but without promising any specific results—only due diligence in performing his or her tasks. It is more difficult to make a distinction between an employment relationship and an assignment.

In both an entrepreneurial contract and the letter of assignment, the object of the service is defined. Consequently, in the course of performance, the customer (principal) cannot obtain a dominating position over the entrepreneur (person assigned). Thus,

---

[45]For more details, see II.C., below.

entrepreneurial contracts and letters of assignment are based on the mutual agreement of two independent parties, while in the case of an employment relationship, the employee has no role in the exchange of goods or services other than his or her own labor.

The terms used in an employment relationship do not apply to entrepreneurial or assignment relationships. In the civil law, for example, the terms "obligation to be available," "workplace" (place of performance), and "working hours" (period required for performance due), are unknown. Also, based on the principle of freedom of contract, the civil law allows the parties to freely establish the content of their contract, as well as to diverge therefrom upon mutual agreement. The Labor Code, however, limits the parties' freedom of contract. Although parties may freely decide whether they wish to enter into an employment relationship or create another type of relationship, if they decide on the former, they must enter into a contract with a content meeting the criteria set forth in the Labor Code.

Other types of relationships established with the objective of performing work include public employment, the employment-type or entrepreneurial-type legal relationship of members of a co-operative, outworkers' contracts (outworkers do not have an employment relationship with the employer, but perform specified work for the employer according to an entreprenurial contract), the legal relationship of members of business associations regarding their personal participation in the operation of the company, and the performance of a supplementary service by way of work.

1. Leased Employees

A temporary employment company or a placement agency may lease an employee with whom it has an employment relationship under contract to a user enterprise for work. The placement agency exercises the employer's rights and obligations jointly with the user enterprise as agreed. The agreement between the placement agency and the user enterprise must not contain any clause that restricts or excludes the rights to which the employee is entitled pursuant to the Labor Code and other legal regulations. Leased employees must follow the rules of the user enterprise in terms of work schedule, working time, and resting time. A placement agency must be a limited liability business association that is domiciled in Hungary, or a cooperative with respect to employees other than its members, and it must be registered by the local employment center.

A leased employee may not be employed (1) for any unlawful work, or (2) at any place of business of the user enterprise where there is a strike in progress, from the time when prestrike negotiations are initiated until the strike is called off. The user enterprise may not order a leased employee to work for another employer.

An agreement between the employee and the placement agency will be null and void if it contains the following:

- a clause to ban or restrict any relationship with the user enterprise following termination of the employment relationship on any grounds; or
- a clause to stipulate the payment of a fee by the employee to the placement agency (placement fee) if the employee wishes to enter into an employment relationship with the user enterprise.

Employment may be terminated only by the placement agency. The employee is required to communicate in writing his or her intention to terminate the employment relationship with the placement agency.

All obligations related to tax returns, data disclosure, deductions, and payments in connection with an employment relationship are the responsibility of the placement agency.

a. *Relationship Between the Placement Agency and the User Enterprise*

The agreement between the placement agency and the user enterprise must be made in writing, and it must contain at a minimum:

- the duration of placement,
- the place of employment, and
- the nature of work involved.

In addition to the contents of the agreement, the user enterprise must inform the placement agency in writing about:

- its normal course of work,
- the name of the person in charge of exercising employer's rights,
- the manner and the timeframe within which to supply the information necessary for the payment of wages,
- the employment conditions pertaining to the work in question, and
- all aspects that are considered significant in terms of the employment of the worker in question.

Unless otherwise agreed, the placement agency is required to cover all employment-related expenses specified by legal regulation, such as the employee's commuting expenses and the costs of a medical examination if such is required for employment.

Unless there is an agreement to the contrary, the user enterprise shall supply all information to the placement agency by the fifth day of the month following the subject month so that wages may be paid by the tenth day of the month following the subject month. If employment is terminated during the month, the user enterprise shall convey the above-specified information to the placement agency within three working days of the last day of employment.

For the duration of placement, the user enterprise will be the employer in terms of the regulations on:

- occupational safety;
- the employment of women, young people, and workers with any degree of incapacity;
- nondiscrimination;
- working conditions;
- job transfer; and
- working time and resting time;
- and any recordkeeping related to all of the conditions listed above.

b. Relationship Between the Placement Agency and the Employee

In the employment contract the parties must stipulate:

- that the employment contract is entered into for the purpose of placement,
- the employee's personal base wage, and
- a brief specification or description of the work.

The employment contract must contain the names of the parties, the placement agency's file number, and relevant data of the employee and the placement agency.

If the employment contract does not contain the information specified below, the employer must provide this information to the employee within two weeks of the date of signing the employment contract:

- the place of work,
- the normal course of work at the user enterprise,
- other components of remuneration,
- the date of payment of wages,
- the date when employment is to commence,
- the amount of paid leave and the procedures for allocating and determining such leave,
- provisions on the termination of employment,
- the rules that determine the period of notice to be observed by the placement agency and the employee,
- the rules of communication of the statement for termination of the employment relationship, and
- whether the placement agency is subject to any collective agreement.

In addition to the requirements listed above, prior to the commencement of employment the placement agency must inform the employee in writing of the following:

- the name, registered address, place of business, and corporate registration number of the user enterprise;

- the name of the department or person of the user enterprise designated to exercise the employer's rights;
- aspects of commuting, accommodation, and meals;
- the rules concerning the normal course of work, working time, and resting time; and
- the employment conditions pertaining to the work in question.

If, for the duration of employment, the placement agency is unable to arrange continuous work for the employee, at least 48 hours prior to the commencement of the next work assignment, the employee—unless otherwise agreed—must be informed of the following:

- the place of next employment,
- the date of commencement and its projected duration, and
- the employee's obligations concerning reporting to work.

With respect to employment abroad, all permits required by the law of the country of employment must be obtained before departure.

c. Assignment Agreements

From the standpoint of the Hungarian Tax Authority, an employment contract generally is more favorable than an assignment agreement. However, the Tax Authority has no independent right to reinterpret the nature of a contract but, in each case, must contest the validity of an assignment agreement by initiating a court procedure and arguing that the assignment was concluded with a "hidden" purpose of concealing an employment relationship. As a result of these efforts by the Tax Authority, Hungarian courts have begun to scrutinize assignment agreements in a more careful and precise manner. In certain instances, the courts will find an assignment agreement null and void because the elements and the real nature of the relationship prove that the agreement reflects an employment relationship rather than an assignment.

B. The Employment Contract

Unless provided otherwise by law, employment is created by way of an employment contract. In special cases, employment may be established through an appointment or election, e.g., the election of an executive officer of a business association, or the appointment of the manager of a state-held company under the supervision of a public administrative body.

1. Legal Capacity

The parties to an employment relationship are the employer and the employee. All employers must have legal capacity to contract.

Generally, all employees must be at least 16 years of age. While minors under the age of 16 generally may enter into an employment relationship only with the consent of their legal guardian, the Labor Code provides some flexibility in cases where the employment relates to particular sporting, artistic, modeling, or advertising activities, which are regulated by separate legislation. However, a person of 15 years of age pursuing elementary school, vocational school, or secondary school on a full-time basis may enter into an employment relationship during the summer vacation period. Persons of diminished capacity may enter into an employment relationship without the permission of their legal guardians.

2. Contract Requirements

An employment contract may not be in conflict with legal regulations or the provisions of an applicable collective bargaining agreement, unless it provides more favorable terms for the employee. Employment contracts must be in writing.

The employment contract must specify the employee's official duties, personal basic salary, and place of work. The parties may agree on other issues as well.[46] The obligation to agree on official duties means that the parties must specify the job to be permanently and regularly performed by the employee after the commencement of employment. The job may be described by indicating the occupation, referring to the nature of the tasks, defining the nature of the work to be performed, or listing the main tasks and responsibilities falling within the scope of the job.

---

[46]Labor Code §76.

Unless otherwise agreed, the employee is entitled to a salary corresponding to the personal basic salary specified in the employment contract.[47] Depending on the agreement between the parties, this may be established as an hourly wage, a performance wage (shift wage), or a monthly salary for employees employed by the hour, by the day, or by the month, respectively. No other benefits may be regarded as a basic salary (except the supplements classified as being salary-type pays, which are paid for night work, extraordinary work, etc.).[48]

The place of work may be defined as a permanent workplace in a single geographical location, but it also may be variable, comprising several geographical locations (town/city-district, street and number). In the latter case, the employer is entitled to define one of its contractual workplaces as the actual workplace and give unilateral instruction for the transfer of the employee from one place to the other. The workplace also may cover a larger geographical territory.

The 2001 Labor Code amendment imposes certain additional requirements in connection with entering into an employment contract. Specifically, the contract now must identify the parties and must set forth any information that is relevant to the employment. In addition, the employer must provide the employee, in writing, within 30 days from the date of agreement for the employment contract, the following information:

- the employee's working hours and schedule,
- any salary supplements to which the employee is entitled,
- the day on which the employee's salary will be paid,
- the date on which the employment commenced or will commence,
- the calculation and scheduling of basic annual leave,
- rules applicable to determining the period of ordinary notice of termination for both parties, and
- whether the employment is subject to a collective bargaining agreement.

---

[47]See V.A.1.a., below.

[48]Labor Division of the Supreme Court, Decision No. 83.

Also, as a result of implementing rules for work performed outside Hungary, the Labor Code requires that additional information be provided to employees posted abroad, including the following:

- the place and period of foreign employment,
- pecuniary and nonpecuniary supplements,
- the currency of remuneration, and
- rules in connection with the return home.

Certain of the information listed above may be provided by referring to the relevant provisions of the applicable law. In the event that any change occurs in the above-listed information or in any information relating to the employer, it must be communicated to the employee, in writing, within 30 days of the change.

For an employee who generally performs work outside any of the employer's facilities, the place of work designated in the employment contract must be the facility from which the employee is supervised. For employees who perform work at various employer sites, the designated place of work must be that where the employee is initially scheduled to work.

Employment contracts shall be concluded in writing, which shall be provided for by the employer. Invalidity on the grounds of failure to set the contract in writing may only be cited by the employee within a period of 30 days from the first day on which he commences work.

When employment is subject to official approval, the employment contract may be concluded only in possession of such authorization.

The type of employment contract shall be chosen with a view not to restrict or violate the employee's rightful interests. The parties shall choose that type of contract, irrespective of the name, which is the most applicable to their circumstances, such as:

- the parties' prior negotiations and their statements made at the time of contracting or during the performance of work,
- the nature of the work to be performed, and
- the rights and obligations of the parties.

Only one employment relationship may be created between a given employer and employee. However, the employee of a particular employer may undertake the performance of certain tasks under a separate contract not qualifying as an employment contract.

3. *Contract Term*

In the absence of an agreement to the contrary, all employment relations are concluded for full-time employment. In the case of part-time employment, all payment made to the employee in exchange for work, whether in money or in kind and whether directly or indirectly, must be provided in accordance with the length of time work is performed if remuneration is contingent upon the amount of working time.[49]

If an employment relationship is subject to official approval, it may only be for the duration specified in the authorization.

The parties may expressly agree that employment is established for a definite or indefinite term. Unless agreed otherwise, the term of employment is indefinite.[50] The definite-term employment relation may not exceed five years, including the duration of an extended relation and that of another definite-term employment relation created within six months of the termination of the previous definite-term employment relation. By way of derogation from the above, if the authorization is extended, the duration of the new definite-term employment relation may exceed five years together with the previous employment relation.

In case employment for a definite period is renewed or extended between the same parties without any rightful interest of the employer and the conclusion of the contract is aimed at infringing on the rightful interests of the employee, the employment shall be deemed to be established for an indefinite term.

Employment for a definite period changes into one of indefinite term, if, following expiration of the term, the employee works for at least one working day with the knowledge of his or her immediate supervisor. Employment established for 30 days or fewer,

---

[49]Labor Code §79.

[50]*See id.*

however, may not be altered to an indefinite term by additional work following the expiration of the original term; it can only be extended for the period of the original term. (This regulation does not apply to employment relationships established by way of election.)

4. *Trial Period*

A 30-day trial period may be stipulated when employment is established. A collective contract or the parties themselves may determine a shorter or longer trial period with a maximum duration of three months. The trial period may not be extended, and no valid departure from this provision is allowed. During the trial period, either of the parties may terminate the employment with immediate effect, without providing any reason.[51]

5. *Modification*

The parties may modify an employment contract only with mutual consent and only in writing. A collective contract may not modify the terms and conditions of an employment contract to the disadvantage of the employee, although it can modify the terms of an employment contract to the benefit of the employee.

In certain cases, the Labor Code prescribes modification of the employment contract in the interest of the employee. Thus, for example, pregnant women and employees with changed working abilities must be provided with working conditions suiting their state of health,[52] and the personal basic salary of employees returning from unpaid leave granted for nursing or family care, or those returning from military service, must be adjusted according to the increments given to other employees in similar positions while they were on leave.

Where an employee wishes to modify the employment contract in connection with

(1) full or part-time employment, or
(2) the indefinite-term of employment,

---

[51]*See id.* §81.
[52]See VI.B., below.

the employer shall, at its own discretion, determine whether to accept the proposal for modification in light of work scheduling, feasibility, and filling the position in question. The employer shall notify the employee within 15 days concerning its decision. The employer shall inform the employee in the most appropriate manner and in due time concerning the positions for which requests for modification of the employment contract under (1) and (2) above can be accommodated.[53]

An employer shall be deemed dissolved and a new entity established—the successor employer—when:

(1) the succession takes place by virtue of legal regulation, and
(2) an independent unit (such as a strategic business unit, plant, shop, division, workplace, or any section of these) or the material and nonmaterial assets of the employer are transferred by agreement to an organization or person falling within the scope of the Labor Code for further operation or for restarting operations, if such transfer takes place within the framework of sale, exchange, lease, leasehold, or capital contribution for a business association.

The rights and obligations of the predecessor employer concerning employment relations existing at the time of succession shall be transferred to the successor at the time of succession, and the predecessor employer shall inform the successor employer regarding these rights and obligations. Failure to supply this information shall have no effect concerning any legal consequences arising from the succession or on the employees' rightful claims. The predecessor and the successor employer shall be subject to joint and several liability for liabilities incurred prior to legal succession if such claims are enforced within one year of the legal succession.

If an employee is terminated by the legal successor employer within one year of the date of legal succession (1) by ordinary dismissal for reasons in connection with the employer's operations, or (2) by unilateral agreement, the legal predecessor em-

[53]Labor Code §84/A.

ployer shall, as a surety, be liable for the employee's compensation and benefits due upon the termination of employment.

The surety liability applies if (1) the predecessor employer, (2) the company controlled by the predecessor employer, (3) the majority owner of the predecessor employer, or (4) the company in which the majority owner is an organization referred to in item (3) holds more than 50 percent of the votes in the supreme body of the successor employer.

In the case of legal succession, the predecessor and the successor employer shall, no later than 15 days prior to the date of succession, inform the local trade union branch or, if there is no trade union, the workers council or, if there is no workers council, the committee formed from the representatives of non-union employees concerning (1) the schedule or proposed date of legal succession, (2) the reasons, and (3) the legal, economic, and social consequences affecting the employees, and the predecessor and successor employer shall initiate talks concerning other proposed actions that affect the employees. The talks shall cover the principles of the actions, the ways and means of avoiding detrimental consequences, and the means for mitigating such consequences.

Where legal succession is decided by the organization or person who controls the predecessor employer, it shall have no effect concerning the predecessor and successor employers' obligation to supply information and hold talks as specified above. The predecessor and the successor employer shall not be excused for failure to satisfy the obligation to supply information and hold talks on the grounds that the controlling organization or person did not inform them about its decision for succession.

If an employer is dissolved without succession, the obligations regarding legal succession shall be honored by the liquidator or receiver. If an employer violates the rights of the workers council or the trade union, the affected workers council or the trade union may seek a remedy in court.

If there is any change in an employee's place of work due to a change in the employer's domicile or place of business, the employment contract must be amended if:

- on account of the change, the time of daily commute to and from work between the employee's place of residence and workplace—traveling by public transportation—has increased by one-and-a-half hours or more, or by one hour if the employee is a woman raising a child under ten years of age or is a single man raising a child under ten years of age, or is a worker with any degree of incapacity using other means of transportation; or

- it constitutes unreasonable or substantial detriment to the employee with respect to his or her personal, family, or other conditions, in particular the conditions of work and/or the duration and costs of commuting to work.

The amendment of the contract of the employment based on the above grounds must include an agreement between the employer and employee concerning any extra costs of travel.[54]

An employee who is ordered to work in a position other than his or her original position for a lower salary than before shall be entitled to receive his or her average earnings instead of the lower pay.[55]

Employees who are ordered to perform work in addition to their regular duties during specific and identifiable periods of their work hours are entitled to remuneration commensurate with the work actually performed. If the duration of additional work performed by an employee cannot be determined separately, the employee is entitled to receive extra remuneration apart from his or her regular wages (substitute pay). The amount of the substitute pay is determined based on the remuneration that is due for work performed under transfer.[56]

C. Cessation and Termination of Employment

The Labor Code distinguishes between the cessation of employment (requiring no action by the parties) and its termination by way of an act. In the first case, employment ceases to exist with immediate effect, due to and upon the occurrence of an objective condition, without a separate statement by either the employer or the employee. In the second case, employment is terminated by

---

[54] Act XIX of 2002.

[55] *Id.*

[56] *Id.*

the mutual consent of the employer and the employee, or upon the unilateral statement of either party. In the case of termination, employment terminates with immediate effect, at the point of time defined by the parties or after lapse of the notice period.

1. Cessation of Employment

Employment ceases upon the following occurrences:

- the death of the employee;
- the cessation, without legal successor, of the employer (in case of legal entities);
- the expiration of the term designated;[57] and
- the transfer of an employer under the scope of the Labor Code to an employer falling outside the scope of the Labor Code and covered by another law.[58]

In the event of an employee's death, his or her heirs will be entitled to those material-type benefits to which the employee has acquired a vested right.[59]

The cessation of the employer without a legal successor is based upon the decision of the founder, but only the Company Registration Court is entitled to delete the company from the register of companies. A company is considered to be ceased by the deletion from the register by the court. Upon cessation of the employer, employment ceases to exist, even if the employee is protected by law from termination of employment or the employment was established for a definite term. However, the employee is entitled to the amount of his or her average salary for the period of exemption that otherwise would apply in the event of a termination with ordinary notice.[60] Employees are not entitled to their average salary if they would not otherwise be eligible for a salary during the period of exemption.

---

[57]Labor Code §86.

[58]Amendments to the Labor Code, effective September 1, 2003, created a new form of cessation based on the transfer of employer status.

[59]See VIII.A.1.b., below.

[60]See II.C.2.a.i., below.

Employment established for a definite period ceases upon expiration of the designated term. However, in order to avoid an unintended extension of the term, the employer can notify the employee of the termination. This notice has no requirements; it is an informal notice and there is no notice period. However, an employment relationship established for a period of 30 days or fewer shall be extended by only the amount of time for which it was originally established. To avoid such an unintended extension, notice is recommended.

Amendments to the Labor Code effective September 1, 2003, created a new form of cessation. Where an employer that falls within the scope of the Labor Code changes its status because the employer is transferred in whole or in part (strategic business unit, specific material or non-material assets, or specific duties and competencies)—by decision of the founder or the employer—to an employer that falls within the scope of the Act on the Legal Status of Public Servants or the Act on the Legal Status of Civil Servants, the organizational unit that is transferred and the employment relationship of its employees terminates at the time of transfer.

The transferring and receiving employer shall, no later than 30 days prior to the date of transfer, inform the employees, the local trade union branch, and the workers council concerning (1) the date of transfer, (2) the reasons, and (3) the legal, economic, and social consequences affecting the employees, and shall initiate talks with the trade union and the workers council concerning other proposed actions that will affect the employees. These talks shall cover the principles of the actions, the ways and means of avoiding detrimental consequences, and the means for mitigating such consequences.

Simultaneously with the information supplied, the transferring and receiving employers shall inform the affected employees as to whether their new employment will be continued in public service or civil service. The information also must include a proposal pertaining to the content of appointments for further employment and shall address the obligations that the employees must fulfill once the legal relation has been created in order to be promoted and to maintain the legal relationship.

If the receiving employer has not yet been established, the obligations conferred upon the receiving employer must be fulfilled by the founder of the receiving employer (a state administration body) or by the organization acting in the name of and on behalf of the founder.

Within 15 days of receiving the information, the employee must notify the transferring employer in writing of his or her decision as to whether he or she will continue employment at the receiving employer. The employee's failure to convey such decision within the specified deadline shall be construed as consent by the employee to discontinue employment.

If the employee does not wish to continue employment at the receiving employer, the transferring employer must notify the employee of the termination of his or her employment relationship prior to date of transfer and must pay the employee a severance pay or the average wage in connection with definite-term employment.

If an employee affected by the transfer is not eligible to enter into a public-servant or civil-servant relationship with the receiving employer by virtue of the Act on the Legal Status of Public Servants or the Act on the Legal Status of Civil Servants, the employee's employment relationship shall be terminated.[61]

If the employee wishes to continue employment at the receiving employer, the receiving employer shall give an appointment to the employee in order to establish a public-servant or civil-servant relationship. In connection with the appointment, the receiving employer shall be bound by the information supplied previously; any deviation from this information may be permitted only upon the express consent of the employee. The transferring employer shall notify the employee in writing concerning the termination of the employment effective as of the day of transfer.

The employee shall be classified according to the provisions governing public-service and civil-service relations, as appropriate. In the case of public-service relations, the combined total of the salary and bonuses established on the basis of the appointment cannot be less than the personal base wage the employee received immediately preceding the transfer. In the case of civil service, if the personal base wage the employee received immediately preceding the transfer is higher than the combined total of the basic salary, extra pay, and executive bonuses payable on the basis of

[61]Labor Code §86/B.

legal regulation, the basic salary shall be increased to make up the difference, not to exceed 20 percent of the amount that is in excess of the basic salary.

Employment concluded for an indefinite-term shall continue as a public-service or civil-service relationship for an indefinite-term at the receiving employer, unless otherwise prescribed by statutory provision. Full-time employment shall continue as full-time employment at the receiving employer. The receiving employer shall not make the public-service or civil-service relationship conditional upon a trial period.

The public-service and civil-service relations established with the receiving employer are governed, respectively, by the provisions of the Act on the Legal Status of Public Servants and the Act on the Legal Status of Civil Servants, with the exception that the employee's employment at the transferring employer shall be treated as if it had been spent as employment at the receiving employer.

If, upon the termination of a public-service or civil-service relationship that was established by appointment, the employee in question is entitled to a notice period or severance pay, the extent of such shall be determined on the basis of the combined duration of employment spent at the transferring and at the receiving employers in accordance with the rules pertaining to public-service and civil-service relations. By way of derogation, the extent of the notice period and the severance pay shall be determined on the basis of the combined duration of employment spent at the transferring and receiving employers effective on the day of transfer if it is more beneficial for the employee.

If a workers council was functioning at the transferring employer up to the date of transfer, the right of participation of the employees of the transferred organizational unit shall be ensured at the receiving employer unless the Act on the Legal Status of Civil Servants permits a workers council for the employees in question.[62]

When the employer is transferred wholly or partially to an employer that falls within the scope of the Act on the Legal Status

[62]*See id.* §86/C.

of Civil Servants, the provisions of the Labor Code shall apply to the employees of such employer.

The employment relationship terminates at the time of transfer if an employer that falls within the scope of the Act on the Legal Status of Civil Servants is not permitted to enter into an employment contract with the employee in question by virtue of the Labor Code. In this case, the transferring and receiving employers are required to inform the employee of the above circumstance. The transferring employer must notify the employee by the date of transfer concerning the termination of his or her employment and must pay the employee a severance pay or, in the event of definite-term employment, the average wage.[63]

2. *Termination of Employment*

a. *Employment for an Indefinite Term*

Employment established for an indefinite term may be terminated by the following means:

- by the mutual consent of the employer and the employee,
- by ordinary notice,
- by extraordinary notice, or
- with immediate effect during the trial period.

The agreement or notice to terminate employment must be in writing.

i. *Ordinary notice*

Employment established for an indefinite period may be terminated by either the employee or the employer by ordinary notice; no valid departure may be made from this provision. The employee need not justify the termination of employment. The employer, however, is obliged to clearly indicate the reasons for termination (unless the employee is eligible for an old-age pension or receives an early retirement pension or service pension).

---

[63]*See id.* §86/D.

Although the Labor Code does not provide a detailed list of reasons for termination, it does provide that the reason for notice must be a cause connected with one of the following:

- the employee's ability;
- the employee's behavior in relation to the employment (e.g., unsuitability for the job, absence without justification); or
- the employer's operations (e.g., reorganization, staff reduction, etc.).

In the event of a dispute, the employer must substantiate the veracity and cause of the reason for notice. The cause for notice must already exist at the time of notice; the employer may not try to prove a cause that is not included in the written justification.

The period of notice is at least 30 days, but may not exceed one year. No valid departure may be made from this provision. The period of notice increases pro-rata according to the period spent in employment. The 30-day notice period is extended by five days after three years, and by as much as 60 days after 20 years of employment with the same employer.[64] Time spent at the legal predecessor must be taken into account in determining the duration of employment. Furthermore, if the employment was established by transfer prior to the enactment of the Labor Code, time elapsed prior to the transfer also is included. Special notice rules apply in the case of a mass staff reduction.[65]

In the case of ordinary notice, the employer must exempt the employee from his or her duties for at least one-half the notice period. During this exemption period, the employee nonetheless is entitled to his or her average salary (except for any period during which the employee would not have been entitled to a salary for independent reasons).

The Labor Code specifies certain prohibitions and restrictions on the employer's right to terminate employment by ordinary notice. In this regard, the employer may not terminate by ordinary notice under the following circumstances:

---

[64] *See id.* §92.

[65] See IV.A., below.

- due to the employee's inability to work because of illness for a maximum period of one year following the exhaustion of the employee's sick leave;
- during sick leave for the purpose of nursing sick children;
- during pregnancy, for three months after giving birth, and during maternity leave;
- during unpaid leave granted for nursing or taking care of children or a close relative; or
- during regular or reserve military service, from the date of receipt of the enlistment order or the appeal pertaining to the fulfillment of civilian service.[66]

Additionally, legal succession, in itself, may not serve as a basis for terminating employment by ordinary notice.[67] The above prohibitions do not apply to employees eligible for old-age pensions or those receiving disability pensions.

The prohibition against termination means that during the period specified by law, or, if this period exceeds 15 days, within 30 days thereafter, the employer may not terminate employment with ordinary notice. In calculating the prohibition period, the date of the announcement of termination, or if earlier the date of commencement of the notice period, must be taken into consideration.

Restrictions on the employer's right to terminate do not prohibit termination; they only make it subject to certain conditions. For example, an employer may terminate employment within five years of an employee's becoming eligible for an old-age pension only for especially justified reasons.[68]

ii. Extraordinary notice

Extraordinary notice is a unilateral legal statement of one of the parties—always in writing—indicating the reasons for the termination. Termination with extraordinary notice may occur if employment is established for a definite or indefinite term and may be carried out by either the employer or the employee. Ex-

[66]Labor Code §90.
[67]See IV.B., below.
[68]Labor Code §89.

traordinary notice announced orally, in the absence of a written statement, is invalid.

Resort to termination by extraordinary notice is allowed only in special cases. Although the Labor Code does not specify the causes supporting extraordinary notice termination, it provides general contours for the circumstances under which a party may exercise this right. Under these provisions, extraordinary termination may take place in two cases:

- if the other party, intentionally or via grievous negligence, violates substantial obligations arising from the employment; or
- if the other party otherwise demonstrates a behavior that makes continuance of employment impossible.[69]

An employment contract or collective contract may define the causes that will support extraordinary notice. If, at the time of entering into these contracts, the parties include provisions relating to extraordinary notice, they also may stipulate causes reflecting the specific conditions and interests related either to the employer's operation or the employee's job.

The cause of extraordinary notice is always a condition that makes the continuation of employment impossible or especially difficult. When such conditions occur, they require prompt measures. For this reason, extraordinary notice takes effect immediately, and there is a time frame for exercising this right. Specifically, extraordinary notice must be given within 15 days of gaining knowledge of the cause, but no later than one year from the occurrence of the cause. When an extraordinary notice provision is included in a collective contract, the time period is also one year, but, in the event of a criminal offense, it is extended until the expiration of the statute of limitations.[70] In the case of a criminal offense, the deadlines are calculated from the date of effect of the court verdict thereon. The six-month, one-year, and statute of limitations periods are objective deadlines; that is, after their expiration, the right of termination by extraordinary notice is forfeited.

---

[69] *See id.* §96.
[70] *Id.*

When the employer terminates employment by extraordinary notice, the notice must state the cause of termination. In addition, prior to the notice, the employer must allow the employee an opportunity to learn about the cause for termination and submit arguments in his or her own defense, unless this cannot be expected of the employer due to the circumstances of the case. If the extraordinary notice of the employer is lawfully served, the employee may not claim any severance or other allowance.

When employment is terminated by the employee by extraordinary notice—prompted by the employer's substantial breach of its obligations—the employer must pay the employee his or her average salary for the period of time that would be applicable in the case of an ordinary notice. If the employment has existed for the time specified by law, the employee also will be entitled to severance pay according to the rules of ordinary notice.[71] Furthermore, the employee may claim indemnification for any damage incurred.

iii. Severance pay

Employees are entitled to severance pay if their employment ceases as a result of ordinary notice by the employer or the employer's cessation without legal successor.[72]

The amount of severance pay depends on the period spent in employment. The minimum period required for eligibility is three years. In that case, severance pay is equal to one month's average salary. After 25 years, the employee is entitled to his or her average salary for six months.

The amount of severance pay increases by three months' average salary if employment is terminated by ordinary notice of the employer or cessation of the employer without legal successor within five years of an employee's eligibility for an old-age pension. This special provision is due to the fact that it is more difficult for older people to find a job. In the employment or collective contract, the parties may—to the advantage of the employee—diverge from this provision. This provision also is applicable as regards an old-age pension with age allowance, i.e., a partial old-

[71] *Id.*
[72] *See id.* §95.

age pension. An employee who previously received extra severance pay is not entitled to additional increments in severance pay under this provision.[73]

b. Employment for a Definite Term

Employment established for a definite term may be terminated in only three situations:

- by mutual consent,
- by extraordinary notice, or
- with immediate notice during the trial period.

In certain cases, the employer may terminate the employment with advance payment of one year's average salary, or the average salary for the period remaining if such period is less than one year.[74]

If the employer terminates a definite-term employment relationship in a manner other than those specified above, the employee is entitled to his or her average salary for one year, or, if the time remaining in the term is less than one year, to the average salary for the balance of the contract period.[75]

c. Employment Certificate

Upon cessation or termination of employment, employees must be paid their salary and other benefits on the last day spent in work. They also must be provided a certificate as prescribed by law. The certificate must contain the following information:

- the duration of employment;
- the amount, if any, to be deducted from the employee's salary due to an enforceable ruling or a rule of law;
- a statement that the employee has no debts owed to the company;
- the duration of any sick leave taken in the year of the termination; and

---

[73]*Id.*
[74]*See id.* §87.
[75]*See id.* §88.

- the name, address, and bank account number of the private pension fund chosen by the employee, or, if no pension fund was chosen, an indication of this fact.

At the request of the employee, a work certificate of operation may be issued with the content specified by law, upon or within one year from the termination of employment.

d. Unlawful Termination and Its Legal Consequences

i. Termination by the employer

Whether a termination is unlawful may only be ascertained by a court. If the court determines that the employer has terminated an employee's employment unlawfully, the employee, upon request, must be reinstated to his or her original position. If the employer cannot be expected to continue to employ the employee, the employer may request the court to waive the above obligation. However, the employer may not submit a waiver request to the court, if its action violates any of the following:

- the proper execution of the law,
- a prohibition against employment discrimination,
- restrictions on termination, or
- certain special rules applicable to elected trade union representatives.

If, at the request of either party, the employee is not reinstated, the court may require the employer—after considering all the circumstances of the unlawful action—to pay the employee an amount equal to at least two, but not more than 12, months' average salary. In such cases, the employment relationship will be deemed terminated on the day the decision declaring the legal violation takes effect.

In the event of an unlawful termination, the employee must be reimbursed for any unpaid salary, together with other benefits and the amount of damage incurred, less any portion of the salary that was compensated from another source.[76] This provision must

[76]*See id.* §100.

be applied in all cases in which the employer's unilateral termination is subsequently deemed unlawful. If the employer terminates employment in a way other than ordinary notice, the employee is entitled to average pay for the notice period, as well as severance pay.

The same rules apply to termination of employment established for a definite period. However, if the remaining time period is shorter than the notice period, the employer must pay the employee only the salary due for the remaining contract period.

ii. Termination by the employee

An employee also may terminate employment unlawfully—whether established for a definite or indefinite term. Examples of unlawful termination of employment by the employee include situations where the employee stops coming to work without any prior notice, the employee stops coming to work prior to the end of the termination period, or the employee submits an immediate termination notice without any proper grounds. An employee who causes damage by terminating employment unlawfully must pay compensation therefor.

Employees who terminate an indefinite term employment relationship in violation of the Labor Code are liable to pay the employer an amount equal to their average earnings payable for the notice period. Employers are entitled to demand payment for damages in excess of this amount. However, the amount of compensation may not exceed the employee's average salary for one and one-half months. A collective contract may modify the extent of compensation, up to three months' average salary.

D. Liability for Damages Caused in Connection With Employment

1. Employee Liability

Employees are liable for damages caused by violation of their employment obligations.[77] Employers are required to prove the liability of employees, including the occurrence, the amount of damage, and the causal correlation.

---

[77] *See id.* §166.

Generally, an employee who causes damage by negligence is liable for no more than 50 percent of the employee's average monthly wage. An employment contract may increase liability up to a maximum of one and one-half months' average salary; a collective contract may increase maximum liability up to six months' average wages. No further deviation from this provision will be considered valid. Financial institution tellers and supervisors also are subject to full liability for damages caused by negligence in the course of accounting or by omission or incomplete fulfillment of related inspections. Additionally, employees are subject to full liability for damages caused willfully.

Full liability also may be imposed on an employee irrespective of culpability, for the loss of objects received under a duty to be returned or accounted for, and that are permanently safeguarded and exclusively used or handled by the employee, if the object (tool, product, commodity, material, etc.) is received with a list or receipt attached. The employee will be relieved of liability if able to prove that the loss was caused by an unavoidable reason beyond his or her control, or that the employer failed to provide the conditions necessary for safeguarding. Notwithstanding the foregoing, cashiers and handlers of money and valuables are liable for the money, securities, and other valuables that they handle.

An employee subject to an agreement on inventory liability is liable for all shortages regardless of any misconduct. The agreement must be in writing and must specify the scope of stock for which the employee is responsible.

When several persons together cause damage, liability is borne by each person according to the degree of their involvement, or in proportion to their wages with respect to the disappearance of objects received for safeguarding. The liability for damages caused willfully by several persons is joint and several.

2. *Employer Liability*

Employers generally are subject to full liability for damages caused to employees in connection with their employment, regardless of culpability.[78] An employer is relieved from liability if able to prove that the damage was caused by an unavoidable event out-

[78] *See id.* §174.

side its control or solely by the unavoidable conduct of the aggrieved party. No liability applies to the portion of damage caused by the employee's negligence. A private individual employer of ten or fewer full-time employees is only liable for damages to an employee if the damages are attributable to the employer's negligence.

Employers are liable for damages caused to possessions of employees brought to the workplace. Employers may require things brought to the place of employment to be deposited in a safe place (dressing room) or to have them reported. Employers may prohibit, restrict, or impose certain conditions regarding carrying things not required for commuting to work or for the performance of work. If the employee violates the prescribed regulation, the employer shall be liable only for damages caused willfully.

Where liability is established, employers must reimburse employees for the loss of income, material damages, and justified expenses incurred in connection with the damage and its prevention. Employees also are entitled to compensation for noneconomic damages.

E. Confidentiality of Information

Employees shall not convey to unauthorized persons any data obtained in connection with their activities that, if revealed, would result in detrimental consequences for the employer or other persons. The requirement of confidentiality shall not apply to any information that is declared by specific other legislation to be information of public interest or public information and as such is rendered subject to disclosure.[79]

F. Employee Duty of Loyalty, Trade Secrets, Covenants Not to Compete

1. *Employee Duty of Loyalty*

See the Introduction, at B.3.and B.7., above.

[79] *Id.* §103. See the Introduction, at B.6., above.

2. *Trade Secrets*

See the Introduction, at B.2.and B.7., above.

3. *Covenants Not to Compete*

See the Introduction, at B.7., above.

II. COLLECTIVE BARGAINING

A. Trade Unions

1. *The Right of Association*

Trade unions and other trade associations safeguard and represent the interests of employees, members of co-operatives, and entrepreneurs.[80] In the Republic of Hungary, everyone is allowed to establish or join associations founded for lawful purposes.[81]

A society association is a voluntarily established, self-governing organization that is founded for the purpose set forth in its deed of foundation, has a registered membership, and organizes the activities of its members in order to accomplish its purpose.[82] In order to found a society association—including a trade union—at least 10 founding members must declare its establishment, draw up its deed of foundation, and elect its administrative and representative bodies.

2. *Establishment of a Trade Union*

For purposes of the Labor Code, a trade union is an employee organization whose primary objective is the promotion and protection of the interests of employees concerning employment.[83] Trade unions are deemed to be established when they register with either the court of the competent county or the Metropolitan Court. Their operation is supervised by the Attorney General, who may seek court intervention to restore lawful order.

---

[80] Act XX of 1949, §4.
[81] *See id.* §63.
[82] Act II of 1989.
[83] Labor Code §18.

3. *Trade Union Membership*

Only private individuals may join a trade union. An employer may not demand a statement from employees concerning trade union membership. The employee's employment may not be made dependent on or terminated due to his or her membership in a trade union. Furthermore, an employer may not cause any disadvantage to the employee due to his or her trade union membership or trade union activity.[84]

4. *Trade Union Rights*

It is the trade union's duty to inform its members of their rights and obligations concerning their material, social, cultural, living, and working conditions; to represent them against the employer on matters concerning labor relations and employment; and to represent them before courts and other authorities and bodies.[85] The trade union also is entitled to enter into a collective agreement.[86]

Trade unions are entitled to request information from the employer on all issues related to the economic and social welfare interests of employees. The employer may not refuse to provide this information. Trade unions also are entitled to request information and inspect compliance with regulations pertaining to working conditions.[87] The trade union may draw the attention of the competent authority to mistakes or omissions observed during an inspection, and, if the authorities fail to take the necessary measures, the trade union may institute the appropriate procedure.

Government offices, local governments, and employers are obliged to cooperate with trade unions and to facilitate their activities of safeguarding employee interests by providing the information they request. The employer must inform the trade union's representative at the workplace prior to taking a measure directly affecting the following groups of employees:[88]

---

[84] *See id.* §26.
[85] *See id.* §19.
[86] *See id.* §20.
[87] *See id.* §22.
[88] *See id.* §21.

- at least 10 persons, when employing more than 20, but fewer than 100 employees;
- ten percent of the employees, when employing 100 or more, but fewer than 300 employees; or
- at least 30 persons, when employing 300 or more employees.

The employer must ensure an opportunity for the trade union to make information, announcements, and data public at the workplace. Under an agreement with the employer, the trade union is entitled to use the employer's premises after or during working hours for the purpose of conducting its activities.[89]

Employers must consult the local trade union branch prior to passing a decision relating to any plans for actions affecting a large group of employees, in particular related to proposals for the employer's reorganization or transformation, or the conversion, privatization, or modernization of a strategic unit into an independent organization.[90]

5. *Benefits of Union Officers and Members*

The employer shall grant each trade union official two hours of worktime allowance monthly for every three trade union members in the company's employ. The trade union shall determine the appropriation of the worktime allowance. The period of time spent on negotiations with the employer is not included in this reduction. Absence from work for any reason, including negotiation, must be reported in advance; for the time of the absence, a trade union official is entitled to remuneration.

The trade union may request reimbursement for the unused portion of the reduced working hour entitlement, up to a maximum of half of the total worktime allowance, and must use this sum for purposes related to its interest representation activities.[91] The amount of reimbursement must be determined based on the

---

[89] *See id.* §24.

[90] Act XIX of 2002.

[91] Labor Code §25.

average earnings during the previous calendar year of the trade union officials affected, and must be paid in gross amount to the trade union on a monthly basis.

The employer must grant each employee one day of extraordinary paid leave annually for every 10 trade union members in the company's employ. The employer must be notified as to the use of this leave at least 30 days in advance.

An employer may not transfer an elected trade union official and may not terminate a trade union official's employment by ordinary notice without prior consent of the immediate superior trade union body. Likewise, prior to termination by extraordinary notice, the opinion of the appropriate trade union body must be requested.[92]

An employer may not temporarily appoint an elected trade union official, send him or her on an assignment for more than 15 working days, transfer him or her to another employer, redeploy him or her if such redeployment involves transfer to another workplace or termination of his or her employment by ordinary dismissal, without prior written consent of the immediate superior trade union body. Likewise, prior to termination by extraordinary notice, the opinion of the appropriate trade union body must be requested.

Officials are entitled to the protections set forth above—in the case of succession of the employer as well—for the duration of their term and for a period of one year following expiration of such term, provided that the trade union official held the office for at least six months.[93]

B. The Collective Bargaining Contract

The collective contract may regulate any issues pertaining to the employment relationship. This includes rights and obligations arising from employment, the mode of exercising and fulfilling those rights and obligations, the procedural rules related thereto, and the relations between the contracting parties.[94] However, the

[92]*See id.* §28.
[93]*See id.* §28(1).
[94]*See id.* §30.

terms of a collective contract may not violate a legal regulation and may modify the provisions of the Labor Code only to the advantage of the employee.

1. Parties

A collective contract may be concluded by one employer, an organization representing the employer's interests, or several employers, on the one hand, and by one or more trade unions, on the other.[95] An organization representing the employer's interests is entitled to conclude a collective contract only if it is authorized to do so by its members.[96] A collective contract also must be concluded by a party that is independent from the other party with respect to the representation of interests. This provision—which accords with ILO Convention No. 98—prevents the execution of a collective contract between subordinated organizations.

Only one collective contract may be concluded with a single employer.[97] This provision prevents the possibility of a conflict between several collective contracts executed at the same workplace.

2. Scope

A collective contract extends to the employer that concluded it or was a member of the organization representing the employer's interests at the time the collective contract was concluded (in which case the contract must define the scope of employers to which its provisions apply). A collective contract also may be extended to an employer that joins an employer organization after the contract was concluded, although this requires the consent of the employer's trade union representative. The collective contract is applied to all employees of the employer, including those who are not members of the trade union concluding the contract.[98] However, a collective contract may not apply to employees holding executive offices.[99]

---

[95]*See id.* §31.
[96]*See id.* §32.
[97]*See id.* §33.
[98]*See id.* §36.
[99]*See id.* §189.

Upon the joint request of the contracting parties, the effect of a collective contract may be extended to an entire sector by the Minister of Social and Family Affairs, provided that the organizations concluding the contract qualify as representative of the sector (i.e., they must be the main representative organization in the particular sector on the basis of their membership, economic weight, supporters, etc.).[100]

3. *Negotiations*

All trade unions represented at an employer may attend negotiations aimed at concluding a collective contract.[101] This provision implies that all trade unions having a representative at the employer should participate in the talks and act jointly.

A proposal for the conclusion of a collective contract may not be rejected by either party, provided that the proposal is made by a party entitled to conclude the contract. In the event of any dispute concerning entitlement, the court, at the request of the party, will settle this issue in out-of-court proceedings.

The employer, in addition to providing the necessary data, must annually propose to the trade unions entitled to conclude the collective contract the rules pertaining to remuneration for work within the framework of the collective contract.[102]

4. *Registration and Publication*

Within 30 days following its execution, a collective contract must be reported to the Ministry of Social and Family Affairs, which will then register it.[103] An originally signed copy of the contract executed by the employer interest representative also must be sent to the Ministry.

The Ministry of Social and Family Affairs maintains a publicly available computer database containing the registration number of each collective contract, general data about the contracting parties, and the term of the contract. Employers and trade unions operating in a given sector of the economy have the right to in-

---

[100]*See id.* §34.
[101]*See id.* §33.
[102]*See id.* §37.
[103]Decree of the Ministry of Labor No. 19/1997 (Dec. 18).

spect the Ministry's copy of the collective contract. Otherwise, the registration form and the Ministry's copy of the contract may be used only for statistical purposes.

5. *Term*

Unless otherwise agreed by the parties, a collective contract enters into effect upon its promulgation.[104] In the absence of an agreement to the contrary, either party may terminate the contract with three months' notice. This right, however, may not be exercised within six months of the conclusion of the contract.[105]

In the event that the employer or the trade union ceases operation without a legal successor, the collective contract loses effect. If the contract is concluded by several employers or trade unions, the collective contract loses its validity only in the event of the cessation of all the employers and trade unions without legal successors.[106]

The cessation of the contracting parties with a legal successor does not affect the validity of a collective contract.

C. Settlement of Collective Labor Disputes

1. *Labor Disputes*

Any dispute arising in connection with employment between the employer (or an organization representing the employer's interests) and the trade union or factory council[107] may be considered a labor dispute, provided that it does not qualify as a legal dispute. Legal disputes concern the assertion of a claim arising from the employment or a dispute related to the violation of law or the collective contract.[108]

The parties to a labor dispute must engage in reconciliatory negotiations. These negotiations commence upon the submission of the initiating party's written position to the other party. During the period of conciliation—a maximum of seven days—the action

---

[104] Labor Code §38.
[105] *See id.* §39.
[106] *See id.* §40.
[107] For a discussion of factory councils, see III., below.
[108] See the Introduction, at D.1., above.

serving as the basis of the dispute my not be executed. The parties also must refrain from all acts that might endanger their agreement.[109]

The parties may apply one of two methods for the settlement of their dispute: (1) they may either employ a mediator, who will try to reconcile the parties' positions, or (2) they may turn to an arbitrator. Both procedures are considered as an agreement on the collective contract. In the course of mediation and arbitration, by agreement of the parties, experts or witnesses may be consulted.[110]

2. *Mediation*

The parties may jointly request the participation of an independent mediator who is not involved in the conflict. As a rule, the participation of a mediator accelerates the settlement of a dispute. The mediator does not make a substantive decision in the dispute but only tries to resolve the conflict and reconcile the positions of the parties.

With a view to resolving the conflict, the mediator is entitled to request data and information from the parties. Upon completion of mediation, the mediator must clearly document the parties' positions and the results (whether positive or negative) of the mediation and deliver this document to the parties.[111]

3. *Arbitration*

The parties, on the basis of a mutual agreement thereto, may avail themselves of an arbitrator to settle a labor dispute. The decision of the arbitrator will be binding if the parties have, in advance, submitted themselves to binding arbitration in a written statement.

The arbitrator may set up a conciliation committee, to which the parties each delegate an equal number of representatives.

Arbitration is compulsory in the event of certain types of disputes, including disputes arising out of the following circumstances:[112]

---

[109]Labor Code §194.
[110]*See id.* §198.
[111]*See id.* §195.
[112]*See id.* §196.

- Employer's obligation to ensure the opportunity for trade unions to publish the information and announcements they regard as necessary, along with the data related to their activities, in a manner customary with the employer or in any other way deemed appropriate.
- Trade unions' right to use the employer's premises after or during working hours, as agreed with the employer, for the purposes of interest representation activities.
- Employer's obligation to cover the justified and necessary costs of election and operation of the works council, the extent of such shall be determined jointly by the employer and the works council.
- Works council's right of codetermination with regard to the appropriation of welfare funds specified in the collective bargaining agreement and with regard to the utilization of institutions and property of such nature.

D. Strikes

1. Lawful Strikes

Pursuant to the provisions of the Constitution,[113] the right to strike may be exercised within the limits of the rules of law regulating strikes. Employees' right to strike is intended as a means to protect their economic and social welfare interests. In this context, the right to strike may be exercised only in the following cases:

- the conciliatory procedure relating to the dispute fails to bring any results within seven days, or
- the conciliatory procedure fails due to reasons not attributable to the party initiating the strike.[114]

A strike may be held once during the conciliatory procedure, but may not last longer than two hours.

Employees also have the right to a solidarity strike (sympathy strike). However, because this type of strike may affect employers that are unable to meet the demands of the strike, a soli-

---

[113] See the Introduction, at A.1.a., above.

[114] Act VII of 1989 on Strikes (Act on Strikes) §2.

darity strike may be initiated only by the trade union. In the case of an ordinary economic strike, the strike may be initiated by groups of employees without the sanction of the trade union.

During a strike, the parties must cooperate. The parties must continue conciliatory negotiations during a strike and must ensure the protection of persons and assets.[115] Participation in a strike is strictly voluntary: no one may be forced either to participate in or stay away from a strike. No coercive measures may be taken in order to have the strike ended.

Employees of judicial bodies, the armed forces, police forces, and civil national security bodies have no right to strike. Employees whose work substantially affects the general public (such as public transportation, electric power, water, gas, and energy supply) may strike only in a way that does not prevent the delivery of sufficient services. The scope and conditions of such a strike must be negotiated during the preliminary conciliatory talks.[116] In addition, the right to strike may not be exercised if it would pose serious and direct danger to life, health, or the environment, or would impede efforts to deal with a natural disaster.[117]

Lockouts are not regulated in the present Act on Strikes.

2. *Unlawful Strikes*

Any strike not conducted in compliance with the regulations described above is unlawful. Similarly, if the objective of a strike violates the Constitution, the strike will be considered unlawful. A strike also is unlawful if initiated against a specific act or omission of the employer that may be changed only by a court, or during the term of the collective contract for the purpose of amending the terms of the agreement.[118]

Establishment of the lawfulness or unlawfulness of a strike may be requested by the party having an interest in the ascertainment of this fact. This issue falls within the jurisdiction of the labor court, which makes its decision within five days in the course of nonlitigious proceedings.

---

[115] *See id.* §4.
[116] *Id.*
[117] *See id.* §3.
[118] *Id.*

3. *The Rights of Strikers*

Neither initiation of, nor participation in, a lawful strike has an adverse effect on the obligations arising from employment; therefore, no adverse action may be taken against an employee on these grounds.

For working time lost due to a strike, an employee is not entitled either to a salary, or to other benefits that otherwise would be due for the performance of work. However, the employee is entitled to other rights arising from his or her employment. For purposes of social security,[119] the time of a lawful strike must be included in the period of employment.[120]

III. Representation by Entities Other Than Unions

While the trade union performs tasks related to the protection of employees' interests, the participation of employees in the management of the employer is secured through the factory council. Thus, the trade union and the factory council are not competitors, but bodies representing employees' interests in different ways.

A. Election of the Factory Council

A factory council must be elected at all employers or at all employer sites where the number of employees exceeds 50 persons. At an employer or employer site where the number of employees is fewer than 51, but more than 15, a factory representative must be elected. In the case of a newly established employer, the factory council must be elected within three months.[121] Both the factory council and the factory representative are elected for a term of three years.

The number of factory council members depends on the number of employees. For a workforce of fewer than 100, three members may form a factory council; proportionate to the increase in staff, the number of members increases up to 13 in the case of a workforce exceeding 2,000.

---

[119]See VIII.A., below.
[120]Act on Strikes §6.
[121]Labor Code §43.

Employees who are physically able and who have been in the employer's employ for at least six months may be elected factory council members. This regulation does not apply to newly established employers.[122]

Factory council candidates may be nominated by at least 10 percent of the employees eligible to vote or at least 50 employees eligible to vote, whichever is fewer. A trade union represented at the employer may independently nominate a candidate from among its members. The candidates must declare in writing that they accept the nomination.[123]

Provided that the nomination of candidates is valid, a list of candidates is published. The nomination of candidates is valid if the number of candidates corresponds to at least the number of members that can be elected to the factory council. In the event of invalid nomination, the nomination period must be extended.

Members of the factory council are elected by secret and direct ballot. The elected members of the factory council are those who obtain the most valid votes cast and at least 30 percent of the votes. In the event of a tie vote, the length of employment with the particular employer must be taken into consideration. A candidate obtaining at least 20 percent of the valid votes is regarded as an alternate member. This rule does not apply to the election of factory representatives.[124]

The election must be announced as unsuccessful if the number of candidates elected does not reach the number of members to be elected to the factory council. In this case, any candidate obtaining at least 30 percent of the votes is deemed elected, and a new election must be held for the remaining members within 30 days. At the repeat election, new candidates also may be nominated.

The election is valid if more than one-half of those eligible to vote participate. For purposes of this calculation, no consideration is made for eligible employees who at the time of the election were subject to the following conditions, unless they actually participate in the election:

---

[122]*See id.* §46.
[123]*See id.* §49.
[124]*See id.* §51.

- employees who are unable to work because of illness;
- employees on maternity leave or on unpaid leave to take care of a sick child or construct their home;
- employees performing regular or reserve army or civilian service;
- employees on a duty assignment (working abroad on behalf of the employer) of more than one week.

In the event of an invalid election, the election must be repeated within 30 to 90 days.[125] The repeat election is valid if more than one-third of those eligible to vote participate, but in this case, the factory council is elected for only two years.

The reasonable and justified costs of the election and operation of the council are borne by the employer. If a dispute arises in connection with the nomination, the election, or its results, conciliatory negotiations may be initiated within five days. A request for negotiations may be made by the employer, an employee, the trade union represented at the employer, or the election committee organized to carry out the election. Upon the failure of the negotiations, or in the event of an appeal against the agreement made at the negotiations, the parties may turn to the court. The court must issue its decision within 15 days, in noncontentious proceedings.

B. Operation of the Factory Council

The factory council must convene within 15 days from its election and elect a chairperson from among its members. The factory council may hold meetings as often as the need arises. It must always be convened if requested by a member or an employee indicating the reason therefor. The factory council is convened by the chairperson. It has a quorum if at least one-half the members are present. Members must attend the factory council meetings in person. The factory council defines its own rules of procedure. Resolutions are adopted with a simple majority of votes.

Issues related to the exercise of certain rights by the council and its relationship with the employer may be defined in the factory agreement. The employer must ensure the opportunity for the

---

[125] *See id.* §51/A.

factory council to publish the information and announcements of the council. Members of the factory council are entitled to reduced working hours. Members of the factory council are entitled to an allowance of 10 percent of their monthly work time, while the chairperson of a factory council is entitled to 15 percent. A plant agreement may establish the appropriation of the total time allowance for factory council members and the chairperson in deviation from the provisions of the Labor Code. Even in such case, the time allowance granted may not exceed half of the members' or chairperson's work time. Absentee pay shall be paid for the duration of the work time allowance.

The factory council has the right of joint decision in regard to the utilization of welfare funds specified in the collective contract and to the utilization of institutions and property of this nature. Welfare funds must be determined in the collective contract and these funds include things like a fund established for workers' holiday, and a fund established for support of workers' expenditures, e.g., marriage, birth, funeral, etc. In addition, the employer must seek the factory council's opinion prior to making decisions concerning the following:

- measures affecting a large group of employees,[126]
- plans related to employee training or early retirement schemes,
- measures pertaining to the rehabilitation of employees with changed working abilities, and
- plans for distributing annual leave, etc.

The employer also must inform the council on basic issues concerning its financial standing, on any plan to significantly modify its scope of activities, on changes in wages and salaries,

[126]For this purpose, a large-scale dismissal occurs when an employer, due to reasons in connection with its operations and based on the average statistical work force for the preceding six-month period, or for the number of months of the employer's existence if the employer was established fewer than six months before, intends to terminate the employment relationship of: at least 10 persons, when employing more than 20 and fewer than 100 employees; 10% of the employees, when employing 100 or more, but fewer than 300 employees; or at least 30 persons, when employing 300 or more employees. Such termination is done with a 30-day notice by regular dismissal.

on the utilization of working time, and on any other terms of employment or working conditions. The factory council must communicate its opinion on planned employer measures within 15 days. Failure to meet this deadline may be deemed consent.

The difference between the factory council and the trade union can best be highlighted by their conduct during a strike. In the event of a strike, the factory council must remain unbiased; it may not organize, support, or prevent a strike. However, the mandate of a factory council member participating in the strike is suspended for the period of his or her participation.[127]

C. Cessation of the Council and Its Members

1. Cessation

The factory council ceases to exist under the following circumstances:

- if the employer ceases operation without a legal successor;
- if its mandate expires;
- if it is removed;
- if its membership, for any reason, decreases by more than one-third;
- if the number of employees falls below 50 or by a minimum of two-thirds;
- if, due to the consolidation of several employers or sites, more than one factory council would operate at the same employer; or
- upon the de-merger of an employer or site.

The mandate of a factory representative ceases only in the first three cases listed above or if the representative is prevented from performing his or her duties for a period exceeding three months. The representative's mandate also ceases if the number of employees remains below 15 for a period of at least six months.

The mandate of a factory council member ceases under the following circumstances:

---

[127]Labor Code §70.

- if the member resigns;
- if the member is removed;
- if the member loses his or her disposing capacity (legal capacity);
- if the member is entitled to exercise employer's rights for more than six months (this occurs when some of the employer's right is delegated to an employee by the employer);
- if the member becomes a close relative of the employer or the employer's executive managers;
- if the factory council ceases to exist; or
- if the member's employment is terminated.

2. *Removal*

A vote must be held on the removal of the factory council or factory representative at the request of at least 30 percent of the employees eligible to vote. Removal requires two-thirds of the valid votes.

D. European Works Council

The 2001 Labor Code amendment introduced the institution of the European Works Council and procedures relating to communication and consultation with employees working within the EU.

IV. REDUNDANCY AND TRANSFERS OF UNDERTAKINGS

A. Redundancy

The regulations pertaining to mass staff reductions are different from the general rules governing employment termination.[128] The 2001 Labor Code amendment changed the definition of mass staff reduction and provided more detailed regulations in connection with the required notice to employees. As amended, the regulations relating to a mass staff reduction must be applied where

---

[128] See I.C., above.

the employer, for reasons related to its operations, intends to terminate employment with ordinary notice, within a 30-day period, of the following numbers of employees:

- at least 10 workers, where the total number of employees is more than 20 but less than 100;
- 10 percent of the employees, where the total number of employees is 100 or more but less than 300; or
- at least 30 employees, where the total number of employees is 300 or more.

The most important change made in this area by the 2001 amendment is that the regulations relating to mass staff reductions now must be applied in mutual termination cases. Prior to the amendment, some employers tried to avoid application of the mass staff reduction rules by negotiating a mutual termination with employees.

In the event of a planned mass staff reduction, the employer must advise both the employees and the competent labor center in writing before serving the notice. The date of the preliminary notification will be determinative in applying the rules governing termination. Ordinary notice served in violation of the regulations concerning mass staff reduction is deemed ineffective.

1. Competent Labor Centers

The labor market organization is composed of the following organs:

- National Employment Center (NEC),
- the county (Budapest) employment centers, and
- employee development and training centers.

County (Budapest) employment centers (employment centers) are central budgetary organs with legal personalities, managing their own financial affairs as authorities independent of the county (Budapest) local governments.

The employment center is composed of central organizational units and branch offices. Upon recommendation of the state secretary for public administration of the Ministry of Social and Family Affairs, the directors of employment centers are appointed and recalled by the Minister of Social and Family Affairs, for which he or she is to obtain the preliminary opinion of the competent labor council. Other employers' rights over such directors shall be exercised by the deputy state secretary appointed by the Minister of Social and Family Affairs. The directors of employment centers are public officers in the position of ministerial department managers.

Through its central organizational units, the employment center must:

- perform duties relative to the operation of financial assets of the Labor Market Fund within the county;
- perform duties relative to permits for foreign nationals seeking employment in Hungary and to civil service tasks;
- execute the secretarial duties of the labor council;
- supervise its branch offices;
- collect and provide information on county (Budapest) labor market trends and situations, and prepare projections on the expected changes;
- orient school administration bodies for determining the education structure and the extent of enrollment;
- form and operate a rehabilitation working group for the promotion of employment rehabilitation of partially disabled workers;
- assist in finding solutions for employment policy–related problems caused by collective redundancies;
- attend to official supervision of the appropriation of subsidies granted from the Labor Market Fund;
- direct the activities of county (Budapest) employment centers related to occupational rehabilitation; and
- perform the other tasks assigned to its authority by law.[129]

2. *Procedures for Large-Scale Dismissals*

Prior to the decision for large-scale dismissals, employers must initiate talks with the works council or, if no works council exists, with the committee formed by the local trade union branches and/or by the representatives of non-union employees (representatives of employees). Such discussions must address the principles of

[129]Act IV of 1991 on Job Assistance and Unemployment Benefits.

the large-scale dismissal, possible ways and means of avoiding dismissals and of reducing the number of employees affected, and means of alleviating the consequences. At least seven days before the discussions, the employer must inform the representatives of employees in writing regarding:

- the reasons for the planned work force reduction;
- the number of employees to be dismissed broken down per job category;
- the number of employees employed prior to the decision, based on the average statistical work force for six months prior to the decision; and
- the proposed schedule and aspects of the execution of the dismissal.

Discussions must commence at least 15 days prior to the decision for a large-scale dismissal.

Employers must notify in writing the employees concerned and the competent local employment center, according to the employer's registered office or the premises in question, regarding the decision for large-scale dismissals at least 30 days prior to the announcement of the regular dismissal.

The provisions also must apply if an employer proceeds to terminate the employment relationship of fewer employees than initially planned, but at least five, as a result of the discussions with the work council, etc., by regular dismissal due to reasons in connection with its operations.

The obligation to conduct discussions and notification also applies to the employers being dissolved without legal succession or to parties handling the liquidation or voluntary dissolution of such employers.

A regular dismissal notice announced in violation of the provision of notification is unlawful.

In the event that an employer violates the rights of the works council and the trade union in the course of its actions in connection with collective redundancy, the works council and the trade union may file for court action for the establishment of such violation.[130]

---

[130]Labor Code §94/A.

B. Transfers of Undertakings

A change of employer due to legal succession does not affect the employment relationship or the validity of a collective contract. Thus, employment established with a legal predecessor remains in effect without any changes with the legal successor. In particular, this means that the aggregate period in employment must be taken into consideration when calculating the notice period and severance pay.[131] The legal successor is liable for all obligations of the prior employer, including those involving severance pay. The 2001 Labor Code amendment expanded the definition of legal successor. As amended, the transfer of a business, in whole or in part (division, store, business premises, place of employment), on the basis of an agreement such as a sale, exchange, lease, usufruct lease, and merger with a business association by way of contribution of assets, including continuous employment of the employee(s), is construed as a change of employer by legal succession.

V. WAGES, HOURS, AND LEAVE

A. Remuneration for Work

Employees are entitled to a wage from the employer; any agreement departing from this rule is void.[132] The Labor Code does not regulate the elements of the salary (e.g., bonus, premium) that may be subject to the terms of an employment contract or collective contract. The Labor Code regulates only certain elements of the salary when social reasons make it necessary, e.g., extra salary for night work.

The 2001 Labor Code amendment introduced the principle of equal pay and treatment.[133] It provides that with respect to the remuneration of employees who perform the same work or work to which equal value is attributed, no discrimination is allowed on

[131]Labor Division of the Supreme Court, Decision No. 154.
[132]Labor Code §141.
[133]See also VI.A., below.

any ground. Similarly, the treatment of employees must be based on the nature of work, its quality and quantity, working conditions, vocational training, physical and intellectual effort, experience, and responsibilities.

The wage payable to an employee shall be established on the basis of time or performance, or a combination of the two. The personal base wage shall be specified on the basis of time. Performance requirements shall be determined by the employer on the basis of preliminary and objective surveys and calculations covering the potential to perform 100 percent of such requirements during regular work hours. Performance requirements—such as the objective requirements relating to the performance of work, work organization, and the technology employed—are to be established in a manner consistent with the employer's operating conditions. The employees concerned must be given written notice of performance requirements and performance-based wage factors in advance. Publishing the relevant information in the manner customary at the employer shall be construed as written notice.

In the event of any dispute concerning performance requirements, the employer must prove that the procedure did not violate the above provisions and that it was performed in good faith and fairness.

If the fulfillment of the performance requirement, for the most part, is not dependent on the employee, a guaranteed salary shall also be established.[134]

1. *Types of Remuneration*

a. *Personal Basic Salary*

In the absence of an agreement otherwise, the employee is entitled to remuneration corresponding to the personal basic salary specified in the employment contract.

Hungarian law distinguishes between two types of salary systems: time wage, established on the basis of time spent at work, and performance wage, depending on work efficiency. The personal basic salary must be specified as a time wage.[135]

---

[134]Labor Code 143(2)–(5).

[135]*See id.* §143.

b. Minimum Wage

The mandatory minimum wage is established by the government, with the consent of the Interest Reconciliation Council, and is promulgated in the form of a decree.[136] The mandatory minimum wage is reviewed regularly. The minimum wage applicable for 2004 for a full-time employee is Hungarian Forint (HUF) 53,000 per month. If wages are calculated on an hourly basis, the minimum is HUF 305.[137] (The average exchange rate in 2004 is approximately 210 HUF/1USD.)

c. In-Kind Wage

Employment regulations may establish a wage in-kind in the form of a commodity or service that contributes to meeting the needs of employees and their family members.[138] However, the in-kind wage may not exceed 20 percent of the wage specified in cash.

d. Average Wage

Employment regulations provide when the employee is entitled to his or her average salary. Average salary is due in certain circumstances under the Labor Code, for example, during the termination period.

Although the calculation of the exact amount of the average wage is very complicated, it usually does not differ much from the monthly salary. The average wage is calculated on the basis of the wages paid for the last four calendar quarters. If the period of an employee's employment is less than four calendar quarters, the average wage of such employee is calculated on the basis of the wages paid for the relevant calendar quarter(s), or for the last calendar month(s), as appropriate.

If an employment-related provision prescribes the application of monthly average wages for the establishment of payment

---

[136]See the Introduction, at C.2., above.

[137]Government Decree 210 of 2003 (XII.10) on the Minimum Wage.

[138]The wage in-kind can either be granted through the collective contract or through various regulations, such as the Decree of the Ministry of Factories and Commerce No. 1/1990 (Aug. 21), which gives permission for in-kind wage for workers in mining.

obligations, one day's average wage multiplied by 22 shall be applied as the employee's monthly average wage. With respect to hourly wages, the average wage for a day shall be calculated by multiplying the average established for one hour by the employee's full daily work time.[139]

If an employee has been employed for a period of less than one calendar month, the average wage of such employee shall be the same as the absentee pay.

e. Salary Supplements

The Labor Code enumerates the cases when an employee may be entitled to a salary supplement. Unless otherwise agreed by the parties, this supplement is calculated on the basis of the personal basic salary of the employee.

Supplements are due for night work, multi-shift work, and extraordinary work. An employment or collective contract may diverge from the salary supplement provisions of the Labor Code to the benefit of the employee.

Employees shall be paid a 50-percent wage supplement for working on Sundays—with the exception of employees working in continuous shifts or working in a position or with an employer who regularly operates on Sundays by the nature of its business, and seasonal workers—if such work is performed

- in three or more shifts, or
- during normal work hours as defined in the employee's work schedule.[140]

With respect to standby duty and emergency duty, a wage corresponding to 20 percent and 40 percent, respectively, of the personal base wage shall be paid.

An employee on emergency or standby duty who is ordered to work shall be paid a flat-rate payment, which is to include the standby fee and the remuneration as defined below:

---

[139]Labor Code §152.

[140]Act XIX of 2002.

- employees shall be entitled to a 50-percent wage supplement for work performed in excess of the daily working time cycle or over and above the weekly or monthly working time;
- employment-related provisions or an agreement between the parties may stipulate the provision of time off in lieu of a wage supplement, where the time off shall not be less than the duration of the work performed;
- the rate of wage supplement for work on a resting day (resting period) shall be 100 percent, where the rate of a wage supplement shall be 50 percent if another resting day (resting period) is provided;
- the time off and the resting day (resting period) defined above shall be allocated at the latest in the month following the month in which the special work was performed; when working time is specified in cycles, the time off, or the resting day (resting period) shall be allocated before the end of the given working time cycle; and
- flat rate compensation also may be provided for special work duty in addition to the regular wages due.[141]

f. Absentee Salary

If an employee is unable to perform work for a reason within the employer's control, the employee is entitled to pay for the time lost. Similarly, if an employee is exempted from working with the employer's permission, remuneration is due in accordance with the parties' agreement. Under the law, absentee salary also is paid for work time lost due to a public holiday, leave, etc.

If an employment regulation so provides, the employee's remuneration must be supplemented to his absentee salary. Otherwise, the employee must be paid the absentee salary. The absentee salary also must be paid if employment regulations prescribe the payment of a salary for time not worked, without specifying the actual sum due.

---

[141]Labor Code §126.

g. *Other Employer Support*

The employer may support the fulfillment of employees' cultural, welfare, and health care needs, as well as the improvement of their living conditions. The scope and extent of such benefits are determined by collective contract, but the employer may render support even beyond this.

h. *Employee Expenses*

The employer must reimburse the employee for the justified and reasonable costs incurred in the course of fulfilling obligations related to work.

Expenses incurred in connection with delegation, a foreign mission, or commuting to work are reimbursed in accordance with a separate rule of law.[142]

2. *Salary Payment and Deductions*

Salary must be determined and paid in official Hungarian legal tender. Unless employment regulations or the agreement of the parties provide otherwise, salary due to the employee must be accounted for and paid on a single occasion, not later than the 10th day of the month following the month in which it was earned. In the event of a delayed payment, the employee is entitled to the interest specified in the civil law for the period of delay.

Employees must be provided with a detailed written statement on the accounting of their salary. The statement must be prepared in a way that allows employees to check the correctness of the calculations, as well as the grounds and amount of deductions.

Deductions from salary may be made only on the basis of the rule of law, an enforceable ruling, or the employee's approval. The employer may deduct any debt arising from a salary advance provided to the employee. In other respects, deductions are governed by rules of law pertaining to enforcement by court order.

Salary paid without a legal basis may be reclaimed from the employee in writing within 60 days. After the lapse of this deadline, salary paid without a legal basis may be reclaimed only within

---

[142]Decree of the Council of Ministries No. 23/1989 (Mar. 12); Government Decree No. 168/1995 (Dec. 27); Government Decree No. 78/1993 (May 2).

the general statutory limitations, provided that the employee should have realized the absence of the legal basis for the payment, or the payment was induced by the employee.

B. Working Hours and Time-Off

1. Working Hours

The total working day is eight hours. Employment regulations or the agreement of the parties may establish working hours that are shorter (e.g., at locations exposed to radioactivity). Longer hours also may be established in the case of positions requiring partial or full readiness (e.g., receptionist, night watch, etc.), up to a maximum of 12 hours per day or 60 hours weekly.[143] If someone is required to spend less than the full number of working hours at work, it is considered part-time work and not shortened working hours.

Although the Labor Code sets a daily limit for working time, the limit also may be expressed in terms of weeks or even longer (several weeks, several months, or annual) periods. Even in such cases, however, the daily working hours may not exceed 12. The framework for working time is established by the collective contract or, in its absence, by the employer.

The distribution of working hours (work order) also is established by the collective contract or, in its absence, by the employer. Working time may be distributed unevenly over the work days. The collective contract or the agreement of the parties also may prescribe divided daily working time. The employer must inform employees about the work order at least one week in advance. Upon failure to receive timely notice, employees are not obliged to obey an instruction concerning a new work order, but may perform their duties according to the previous order.

Collective agreements for (1) employees working as navigators, flight attendants and aviation engineers or engaged in the operation and control of ground equipment serving aircraft; (2) employees working in travel-intensive jobs in domestic or international carriage of passengers and goods by road; (3) carriers

---

[143]Labor Code §126.

and traffic controllers working in an urban mass transportation system; and (4) travelers and traffic controllers working in international carriage of passengers by rail and in domestic and international carriage of goods by rail, may contain derogations from the provisions pertaining to the limitation of daily working time, breaks, daily leisure time, weekly rest time and rest period, working Sundays and public holidays, and the annual limit on work done outside of regularly scheduled hours. Moreover, they may establish a maximum one-year or 52-week working timeframe.

For healthcare employees working standby or emergency duty, as defined in specific other legislation pertaining to healthcare service, the collective agreement may

- stipulate a maximum six-month or twenty-six-week working timeframe,
- determine the average duration of emergency duty on the basis of the length of time usually spent on emergency duty,
- prescribe a compulsory eight-hour daily leisure time,
- determine the average duration of standby duty on the basis of the length of time usually spent on standby, or
- determine the average duration of emergency duty on the basis of the length of time usually spent on emergency duty.

If, in connection with an industry or subsector, any trade regulations particular to that industry or subsector are prescribed by an act, the provisions of the Labor Code on working time and rest periods shall apply in addition to and along with the different provisions stipulated in such trade regulations unless it is precluded by the trade regulations.[144]

2. *Night Work*

Night work refers to work performed between the hours of 10:00 p.m. and 6:00 a.m. Work carried out between the hours of 2 p.m. and 10 p.m. qualifies as the afternoon shift. The afternoon shift supplement is 15 percent and the night shift supplement is 30 percent.

---

[144] *See id.* §117/A.

Employees working varying shifts or according to a nonstop work schedule are entitled to an afternoon or night shift supplement. Employees working according to a nonstop work schedule are entitled to an additional 5 percent shift supplement for afternoon shifts, and an additional 10 percent shift supplement for night shifts.

Night work may not be assigned to pregnant women, women with children younger than one year of age, or to employees younger than the age of 18.[145]

3. *Extraordinary Work*

The employer may, in an exceptional case, require an employee to perform work outside the official working hours. Overtime, work performed on a rest day or public holiday, or readiness at a specified time and place qualifies as extraordinary work duty. If provided by the collective contract or if the employee so requests, notification of extraordinary work must be made in writing. As a general rule, assigning extraordinary work may not endanger employees' physical safety or health; nor may it represent a disproportionate burden in regard to their personal, family, or other circumstances. The Labor Code specifies the minimum pay for extraordinary work; these statutory amounts may be increased by the collective contract or the agreement of the parties.

An employee may be required to perform standby (emergency) duty at a place and for a duration specified by the employer or at a location specified by the employee that can be reached from the place of work:

- for the uninterrupted provision of basic services for the general public;
- to prevent or mitigate any imminent danger of accident, natural disaster, or serious damage as well as any danger to life, limb, health, or physical integrity; and
- for the proper maintenance and safe operation of technological equipment.

---

[145]See VI.B., below.

Employees on emergency or standby duty are obliged to remain on call and ready to work.

Unless otherwise prescribed in the collective agreement, the maximum duration of standby duty an employee may be ordered to perform in a month or in a four-week period is 168 hours. For employees working in a working timeframe, the length of standby duty to be performed in a month or in a four-week period shall be determined in the average of the working timeframe.

Unless otherwise prescribed in the collective agreement, an employee may not be ordered to stand by during the weekly rest day or weekly rest period if he has been on standby duty on his weekly rest day or during his weekly rest period during the preceding 168-hour period.

Emergency and standby duty shall be scheduled one month ahead and the actual time shall be communicated one week in advance. The employer shall be entitled to deviate from this provision under extraordinary circumstances, during which time the safety and health requirements must be observed. Different rules for ordering emergency and standby duty may be stipulated in the collective agreement.

With respect to employees working in the medical profession, the law governing the healthcare sector may deviate from the above provisions.[146]

a. Overtime

Overtime is work carried out by an employee beyond his or her regular daily working hours. If working time is not divided into work days in advance, work carried out over and above the established working timeframe qualifies as overtime. No valid departure may be made from this provision. The upper limit of assignable overtime on four consecutive days is a total of eight hours, or a total of 144 hours per year. A collective contract may increase this annual maximum to 200 hours, or in the case of a collective contract extending to several employers, to 300 hours. Work carried out on a rest day or a public holiday is subject to the same total limit as overtime.[147]

---

[146] Labor Code §129.

[147] *See id.* §127.

For overtime work, employees are entitled to a 50 percent salary supplement on the basis of individual accounting, or, as a flat rate, in addition to their regular salary. On the basis of employment regulations or the agreement of the parties, employees also may be entitled to time-off in consideration for overtime, but, in this case, the duration of the time-off may not be less that that of the overtime worked.

Overtime may not be assigned to pregnant women, women with children younger than one year of age, employees who are younger than age 18, or employees who work in positions that are hazardous to their health.[148] Single parent employees may be assigned overtime only with their consent until the time their child reaches four years of age.

b. Work on Rest Days or Public Holidays

An employee obliged to work on the weekly rest day is entitled to at least a 50 percent salary supplement in addition to the salary for the work carried out. In addition, another rest day must be granted to the employee by the end of the month subsequent to performance of the work. In the absence of an alternative rest day, the employee is entitled to at least a 100 percent salary supplement.

An employee obliged to perform work on a public holiday is entitled to his or her average pay in addition to the salary due to the employee for that day's work.

c. Readiness Duty

For readiness duty, employees are entitled to a salary corresponding to 25 percent of their personal basic salary. If the employee performs work during readiness duty, he or she is entitled to remuneration for this time in accordance with the regulations pertaining to overtime. Alternatively, remuneration that includes both a readiness fee and remuneration for overtime may be established (e.g., remuneration for being on duty).

---

[148] See VI.B., below.

4. *Time-Off*

Time-off is the period of time during which the employee may relax and need not work, while the employer is not obliged to give work. Types of time-off include breaks, daily leisure time, weekly rest time, and public holidays.

a. *Breaks*

All jobs must provide a break during working hours when the daily work is more than six hours.[149] The Labor Code specifies only the lower limit of breaks: 20 minutes. The collective contract may regulate the length and the method of providing the break, with the exception of the cases specified by law, when it is compulsory to provide a break during working hours (e.g., positions of readiness character, jobs where eating meals also can be ensured within working hours).

b. *Daily Leisure Time*

Employees must be granted at least 11 hours of leisure time between completion of their daily work and the commencement of the next day's work.[150] Although the collective contract or the agreement of the parties may depart from this requirement, even in these cases, at least eight hours of leisure time must be ensured. The employer must ensure that leisure time is taken without interruption, even in the case of overtime work. The requirement for uninterrupted leisure time may be overruled by the collective contract only in the case of jobs of a readiness nature, where the contract may prescribe that following the alert period, the employee will be entitled to leisure time.

c. *Weekly Rest Time*

Employees are entitled to two rest days per week; one of these must fall on Sunday.[151] A rest day is 24 hours in length, but it is not regulated to begin and end at a specific time. The provision for weekly rest time is intended to ensure that working time, as a rule,

---

[149]Labor Code §122.
[150]*See id.* §123.
[151]*See id.* §124.

is distributed for five days a week. Employees working under an uneven work order are entitled to an uninterrupted rest time of at least 42 hours weekly. This time must include Sunday or, if the work by its nature is performed on Sunday, another full calendar day. With the exception of a position that is hazardous to employees' health, rest time may be established by agreement of the parties, or may be allocated bi-weekly or monthly under a collective contract, provided that one rest day falls on Sunday.[152]

An amendment to the Labor Code[153] established that employees working in a working time cycle[154] may be provided a minimum weekly resting period of 48 consecutive hours, which is to include a Sunday, in lieu of the resting days provided based on the work schedule, if

- working in standby duty,
- working in continuous shifts,
- working in three or more shifts, or
- working as a seasonal worker, where it is to include a Sunday at least once a month.

An employee is entitled to have Sunday off, if working in a position or with an employer who regularly operates on Sundays, even if it would be a working day according to his or her work schedule.

For employees working in a working time cycle in lieu of the resting days specified above, based on the work schedule, an employee may be provided a minimum weekly resting period of 40 consecutive hours, that is to include one full calendar day and a Sunday at least once a month. Where the weekly working period is at least 40 hours, the employee must receive a resting time of at least 48 hours on the average of the working time cycle.

The resting days may be carried forward and allocated—in part or in full—bi-weekly or monthly, if so stipulated by the collective agreement or the parties. One resting day must be provided

---

[152]*Id.*

[153]Act XIX of 2002.

[154]A "working time cycle" means that working time is not established daily, but rather in an 8-week or 12-week long period.

after six days of work, unless otherwise provided in the collective agreement in the case of employees working in alternating shifts or in continuous shifts, and in the case of seasonal workers.[155]

d. Public Holidays

Employees may not perform work on the days declared public holidays by law. On public holidays, an employee may be given work regularly only by an employer that operates without interruption. The length of the public holidays is identical to that of the weekly rest day, that is, it begins and ends at midnight.

Public holidays currently include the following:

- January l,
- March 15,
- Easter Monday,
- May 1,
- Whitsun Monday,
- August 20,
- October 23,
- November 1, and
- December 25 and 26.

The Minister of Social and Family Affairs regulates annual changes in the work schedule that are necessitated by public holidays. In the course of these changes, however, no Sunday may be declared a working day.

C. Leave

The objective of ordinary leave is to allow a longer time period for employees—in addition to daily and weekly leisure time—for recreation and relaxation. Employees are entitled to ordinary leave for every calendar year spent in employment. Employees are entitled to ordinary leave even though they are not full-time employees (e.g., they work only four to six hours per day). The right to ordinary leave is a vested right; therefore, employees may

[155]Labor Code §129.

not validly waive their claim to it. The only condition of entitlement is that the employee must actually perform work.

While the employment relationship is suspended, the employee is entitled to additional ordinary annual leave for the following:[156]

- the duration of illness causing an inability to work;
- the duration of maternity leave;[157]
- the first year of unpaid leave to care for or nurse a child younger than 10 years of age;
- the duration of unpaid leave that does not exceed 30 days;
- the duration of reserve military service; and
- all time not spent in work, for which the employee receives his or her average salary.

Employees also are entitled to basic annual leave on the basis of their additional employment.[158] In these cases, the extent of the leave to be granted to the employee is determined separately in each employment relationship. The length of the period of leave is not determined by the length of employment; instead, the age of the employee determines the amount of leave granted. Part-time workers are entitled to the same amount of leave as full-time workers.[159]

1. *Basic Annual Leave*

Employees are entitled to a basic annual leave. Basic annual leave is 20 work days, which increases between the ages of 25 and 45. After age 45, all employees are entitled to 30 work days of basic annual leave.

It is the employer's obligation to allow employees to take their leave. Leave generally must be taken in the year in which it is due. If justified by exceptionally important economic interests, the employee may take the leave the following year, but not later than

---

[156]*See id.* §130.
[157]See VI.B.1.e., below.
[158]Labor Division of the Supreme Court, Decision No. 18.
[159]Labor Division of the Supreme Court, Decision No. 19.

June 30, or, if the collective contract allows, not later than December 31. If the leave cannot be taken by the employee due to illness or other conditions beyond his or her control, the leave may be taken within 30 days after the cessation of such obstacles.

One-fourth of the leave must be scheduled according to the employee's request. Leave may be taken in more than two installments only upon the employee's request. In scheduling leave, the employee's regular work days must be taken into consideration. In the event of a work schedule ensuring more than two rest days weekly, every day of the week counts as a work day from the viewpoint of scheduling leave, except for the employee's two rest days and public holidays. (Thus, if the employee works three days a week and wishes to have a whole week off, he or she is considered to have taken leave for five work days.)

2. *Supplementary Leave*

Supplementary leave is specified in the Labor Code for employees younger than age 18,[160] employees rearing one or more children younger than age 16, employees with disability (e.g., blindness), and those working in hazardous jobs (e.g., underground workplaces, radiation exposure).

In the collective contract or the agreement of the parties, other forms of supplementary leave also may be specified for certain employees or employee groups.

3. *Sick Leave*

Sick leave shall be determined according to the number of workdays stipulated in the work schedule. Public holidays when the employee is not required to work shall be treated as working days.

Employees are entitled to 15 days of sick leave annually for the time they are unable to work because of illness. During this period, they are entitled to 70 percent of the absentee salary.

The employee's inability to work must be certified by the physician who treats the employee. Any part of the sick leave not used during the calendar year may not be carried over.

---

[160]See VI.B.2.d., below.

Where the weekly work schedule contains two rest days, the above shall be applied with the exception that all days of the week shall be treated as working days exclusive of the employee's two rest days.[161]

4. *Conditional Leaves*

The Labor Code specifies when an employee must be granted certain mandatory leaves, and when an employee may be granted other discretionary work time concessions. For example, employees may be granted leave for the following purposes:

- maternity leave;[162]
- breastfeeding;
- unpaid child-care leave up to the time a child reaches the age of three, or the age of 14 in the case of a chronically ill or seriously disabled child;
- unpaid leave for taking care of an ill child (for the duration of the child's illness, up to the time the child reaches the age of 12); and
- unpaid leave to take care of a close relative or to construct a home with the employee's own resources.

These are conditional leaves that must be applied for and granted subject to the existence of required legal conditions. Although the Labor Code does not specify other grounds for unpaid leave, the employer may, at the employee's request, grant leave based on an individual evaluation of the circumstances (e.g., a trip abroad, study trips).

Employers shall keep records of the employees'

- regular and special work hours, emergency and standby duty,
- vacation time, and
- other worktime allowances.[163]

---

[161]Labor Code §137(6)–(7).

[162]See VI.B.1.e., below.

[163]Labor Code §140/A.

VI. ANTIDISCRIMINATION

A. Prohibition of Discrimination

The 2001 Labor Code amendment extended protection against employment discrimination to include marital or family status and disability.

The amendment also introduced the concept of collective discrimination, where discrimination is directed against a particular group of employees.

The Labor Code's antidiscrimination provisions are applicable not only during the employment relationship, but also in circumstances relating to the establishment of employment, i.e., the hiring and application process.

1. *Domestic Law*

Hungarian law prohibits employment discrimination against employees directly or indirectly on the grounds of sex, age, marital or family status, handicap, motherhood, nationality, race, ethnic origin, religion, political affiliation, or membership in workers representation organizations or activities connected therewith, on the grounds of being employed part-time or for a fixed period of time, or on the basis of any other circumstance not related to employment.[164] Discrimination following unequivocally from the character or nature of the work does not qualify as unlawful discrimination.

Indirect discrimination is also prohibited where—on the basis of the characteristics defined above—an employment-related provision, criterion, condition, or practice that is apparently neutral or that affords the same rights to all disadvantages a substantially higher proportion of the members of a particular group of employees, unless that provision, criterion, condition, or practice is appropriate and necessary and can be justified by objective factors. Any provision, criterion, condition, or practice in connection with the hiring process is also employment-related.

---

[164] *See id.* §5.

Employers must provide employees with the opportunity for advancement and promotion without discrimination, solely on the basis of professional skills, experience, and performance, and on circumstances deemed substantive for the employee's position. Any differentiation clearly and directly required by the character or nature of the work shall not be construed as discrimination.

Any consequences of discrimination must be properly remedied. The legal remedy afforded to an employee discriminated against must not result in any violation of or harm to the rights of another worker.

In the event of any dispute in connection with the employer's actions, the employer is required to prove that its actions did not violate the provisions for the prohibition of discrimination.[165]

2. *The New York Treaty*

Hungary is party to the 1979 New York Treaty on the Elimination of all Types of Discrimination against Women.[166] Under the terms of the treaty, signatory countries commit to take all measures required to eliminate any and all discrimination against women in the field of employment and to ensure equal employment rights for men and women, with special regard to the following:

- the right to work, which is an inalienable universal right;
- the right to equal employment conditions, including the application of equal criteria for recruitment with regard to the same job;
- the right to enter into employment at one's own choice and the right to freely choose one's profession;
- the right to promotion, safe labor conditions, and all benefits and allowances, including the right to vocational training and re-training (among others, vocational training of apprentices, higher level vocational training, and continuous education);

---

[165]*See id.* §5(1).

[166]Law-Decree No. 10 of 1982.

- the right to equal pay, including premiums, as well as the right to equal treatment for work of equal value and in the evaluation of performance;
- the right to social security benefits, especially in the cases of retirement, unemployment, illness, disability, old age, and other causes preventing employment, and the right to paid leave; and
- the right to protect one's health, and the right to safe labor conditions, including the right to relax.

In order to prevent discrimination against women due to marriage or motherhood, and to ensure their right to work, the member countries also commit to the following measures:

- to prohibit by sanctions the dismissal of women during pregnancy or maternity leave and any discrimination on the basis of marital status;
- to introduce maternity leave with entitlement to a salary or other social benefits, without loss of employment, classification, or social benefits;
- to promote the provision of auxiliary services allowing parents to reconcile their obligations toward their families and employment as well as their participation in public life, with special regard to the establishment and development of child-care institutions; and
- to ensure special protection for women during their pregnancy in jobs harmful to their health.

B. Regulations on the Employment of Women, Minors, Persons of Changed Working Abilities, and Men

1. *Women*

a. Conditions of Employment

A woman may not perform work that may endanger her physical constitution or its development.

b. Transfer

A woman must be placed temporarily in a position appropriate to her condition from a medical viewpoint, or the working conditions in her existing position must be appropriately modified, from the time her pregnancy is established until her child reaches one year of age. This transfer or modification must be based on a medical opinion pertaining to her suitability for the position. If the employer is unable to ensure a position suited to the woman's medical condition, she must be relieved of work, and for this period of time, must be paid the salary due for idle time.

The designation of a new position requires the employee's approval. Likewise, pregnant women may be transferred to a new position only with their approval.

The salary of a woman temporarily transferred to a different position, or employed under modified work conditions without being transferred, may not be less than her previous average earnings. Women temporarily transferred to a different position are entitled to their average salary in their previous position, even if the transfer results in a reduction of their working time or the cessation of working at night or on a particular shift.

In the case of an adoption, the rights of childbearing women inure to the benefit of the adoptive mother.[167]

c. *Night Work*

No woman may be assigned night work (work performed between 10:00 p.m. and 6:00 a.m.) from the time her pregnancy is determined until the time her child reaches one year of age.

d. *Overtime*

No overtime may be assigned to a woman from the time her pregnancy is determined until her child reaches one year of age.

e. *Maternity, Nursing, and Child-Care Leave*

A woman who is pregnant or has given birth is entitled to 24 weeks of paid maternity leave. Preferably, this leave should be allocated in a way that four weeks is taken prior to the expected date of birth.

---

[167]Labor Division of the Supreme Court, Resolution No. 57.

During the first six months of nursing, a woman is entitled to two hours time-off each day, and thereafter one hour daily, up to the end of the ninth month. In the case of multiple births, the time-off for nursing is commensurate with the number of births.

The employee also may take unpaid leave as follows:

- to care for a child until the child reaches the age of three;
- if the employee receives child care benefits for the purpose of taking care of an ill child, until the child reaches the age of 14; and
- for the purpose of taking care of an ill child at home, if the employee does not receive child care benefits, until the child reaches the age of 12.

2. *Minors*

a. *Conditions of Employment*

Minors (employees younger than age 18) may not perform work that endangers their physical constitution or its development.[168]

b. *Night Work and Overtime*

The working time of minors may not exceed eight hours daily or 40 hours weekly.[169] In the event that working hours are determined in weekly schedules, the schedule may not cover a period longer than one week. In addition, minors may not be assigned night work, overtime, or standby duty.[170]

c. *Compensation*

Compensation for minor employees must be reviewed when they turn 18, or upon the lapse of one year subsequent to their completion of studies pursued to acquire vocational qualifications. Thereafter, compensation is determined in accordance with their qualifications and ability to work.

---

[168]Labor Code §72.

[169]For a general discussion of working hours, see V.B.1., above.

[170]For a discussion of extraordinary work, see V.B.3., above.

d. Supplementary Leave

An employee younger than age 18 is entitled to five days supplementary leave annually through the year in which they turn 18.

e. Time-Off

Any minor whose working hours are greater than four and one-half hours on a daily basis is entitled to a break of at least 30 minutes. Any collective bargaining provision regulating the time or methods of employee work breaks is not applicable to the breaks of minors unless the break-related provisions would be more favorable to the minor employee.[171]

For minors, the daily leisure period, between the end of one working day and the commencement of the next, must be at least 12 hours.[172]

3. Persons With Changed Working Abilities

The employer must continue to employ an employee whose working ability has changed in the course of employment in a position suited to his or her condition.[173]

4. Supervision

Pursuant to the Act on the Supervision of Labor Relations,[174] supervision by NOSLA and the occupational safety and labor boards also extends to the enforcement of legal regulations pertaining to the prohibition of discrimination and the employment of women, minors, and people with changed working abilities.[175] Among its powers, NOSLA and the occupational safety and labor boards can fine an employer for violating the rules regarding anti-discrimination.

---

[171]For a general discussion of employee breaks, see V.B.4.a., above.

[172]For a general discussion of daily leisure time, see V.B.4.b., above.

[173]*See, e.g.*, Joint Decree of the Ministry of Health and Ministry of Finance No. 8/1983 (June 29) (regarding employment and social benefits of persons with changed working abilities).

[174]Act LXXV of 1996.

[175]*See id.* §39.

5. *Men*

Within two months from the birth of his child, a man is entitled to five days of working time leave allowance—even if the child has died.[176]

C. Disabled Employees

A separate law regulates the rights of the disabled and ensures their equal treatment.[177] According to this law, disabled workers must be integrated into the organization or, if this is not feasible, must be employed under protection. The employer must ensure that work tools and furnishings are adjusted to the special needs of the disabled. Upon the application of the employer, these adjustment costs may be reimbursed from a budgetary appropriation.[178]

If disabled employees cannot be employed in an integrated way, a special workplace must be created for them. When creating jobs for handicapped or disabled people, the physical environment must be adjusted to take into account their needs. Special workplaces receive a normative subsidy from the central budget. The conditions for special workplaces must be established gradually, but not later than January 1, 2005.

Any person discriminated against due to his or her disability has all rights applicable to the violation of personal rights.[179] Under civil law, a person whose personal rights have been violated may, depending on the circumstances of the case, do the following:

- demand a court declaration of the occurrence of the infringement;
- demand to have the infringement discontinued and the perpetrator restrained from further infringement;
- demand that the perpetrator make restitution in a statement or by some other suitable means and, if necessary, that the

---

[176]Act XIX of 2002.
[177]Act XXVI of 1998.
[178]*See id.* §15.
[179]*See id.* §27.

perpetrator, at his own expense, make an appropriate public disclosure for restitution;

- demand the termination of the injurious situation and the restoration of the previous state by and at the expense of the perpetrator and, furthermore, to have the effects of the infringement nullified or deprived of their injurious nature; or
- file charges for punitive damages in accordance with the liability regulations under civil law.

If the amount of punitive damages that can be imposed is insufficient to mitigate the gravity of the actionable conduct, the court shall also be entitled to penalize the perpetrator by ordering him to pay a fine to be used for public purposes.

VII. OCCUPATIONAL SAFETY AND HEALTH AND WORKERS' COMPENSATION

A. Occupational Safety and Health

1. Labor Conditions

Every person working in the Republic of Hungary is entitled to work in healthy and safe labor conditions. Healthy and safe labor conditions are principally specified in the Act on Labor Protection (Labor Protection Act).[180] Pursuant to the authorization of the Labor Protection Act, detailed regulations, with special regard to the activities of the different industrial branches, are promulgated by various government and ministerial decrees. The Labor Protection Act is applicable to all types of work performed in an organized way, regardless of the organizational structure or the type of ownership. In a decree regulating work to be performed under extraordinary circumstances (e.g., aversion of a catastrophe), by armed forces, public security forces, or law enforcement authorities, the appropriate minister may deviate from the provisions of the Labor Protection Act.

---

[180]Act XCIII of 1993 (Labor Protection Act).

2. *Employer Obligations*

According to the Labor Code, it is the responsibility of the employer to ensure healthy and safe working conditions, in compliance with applicable regulations.[181] The Labor Protection Act contains the same provision: "It is the employer's responsibility—taking also into consideration employee liability in this respect—to ensure that the working conditions are safe and not harmful to health."[182]

Employees may be employed to perform a job only under the following conditions:

- their physiological characteristics suit the job;
- their employment does not have an adverse effect on their health, physical safety, and—in the case of minors—their healthy development;
- their employment poses no danger to their offspring; and
- the work does not pose a danger to the health and physical safety of others and the employee is qualified for the job (as specified in a separate piece of legislation).[183]

Physical suitability may be verified on the basis of a preliminary and, in jobs specified by law, periodic medical examination.[184] Those jobs that require periodic medical examinations include those in the maternity ward of a hospital, restaurants, mines, etc.[185]

Employers must ensure that the number and qualifications of employees are adequate for performance of the task. Dangerous work may not be performed by a single employee. If two or more employees perform the same task simultaneously, in order to ensure safe performance, one of them must be designated to be in charge of the work, and the others must be informed of this designation.[186]

---

[181]Labor Code §102(2).

[182]Labor Protection Act §2(2).

[183]Decree of the Ministry of Labor No. 6/1994 (Aug. 31) on the requirements for job qualification.

[184]Labor Protection Act §49.

[185]Decree of the Ministry of Welfare No. 33/1998 (June 24).

[186]Labor Protection Act §51.

Each employee must be provided with drinking water of an appropriate amount and quality, and facilities as required by the nature of the work (change room, shower, toilet, and/or a room where the employees can eat, relax, and warm up).

Work rules must be worded in such a way to ensure the safety of employees, others within the range of the workplace, and those using the service.

An employer may not give the employee monetary or other compensation as a substitute for providing healthy and safe working conditions. Retaliation against an employee for demanding appropriate working conditions is prohibited.

3. *Employee Rights and Obligations*

An employee may request the employer to ensure safe and healthy labor conditions, to provide training on labor safety, and to provide the required protective clothing and equipment.

In order to ensure that working conditions are safe and not harmful to their health, employees are expected, to a reasonable extent, to examine the condition of provided tools and equipment, and use them according to the employer's instructions. Employees also are expected to wear appropriate clothing, maintain order and discipline at the workplace, learn and adhere to safety regulations, take part in compulsory medical examinations, and report any irregularity, malfunctioning, accident, injury, or sickness without delay.[187]

An employee may refuse compliance with an instruction if it poses a direct or serious threat to his or her own life, physical safety, or health, and must refuse the instruction if it poses the same threat to the life, safety, or health of others.[188]

4. *Labor Safety Supervision and Enforcement*

a. *Labor Safety Regulations*

At the national level, labor safety regulations fall within the authority of Parliament, the government, the Minister of Social

[187] *See id.* §60.
[188] *See id.* §63.

and Family Affairs, the Minister of Health, the Minister of Economic Affairs, the respective central public administrative bodies operating under the supervision thereof, as well as the National Labor Safety and Employment Supervision, the National Public Service, and the Hungarian Mining Supervision.

Minimum health and safety standards for work tools are determined by the Minister of Social and Family Affairs, in agreement with the Minister of Health.[189]

b. Safety Representatives

In order to represent their occupational safety and health interests, employees may elect one or more safety representatives from among themselves, if the number of employees at the particular workplace exceeds 10, or in the case of employers whose exclusive or primary activity is of a nonphysical nature, if the number of employees exceeds 20. Labor Code provisions governing the factory council and factory representatives[190] are applicable to the number, election, removal, and authority of safety representatives.[191]

It is the employer's obligation to ensure the conditions necessary for the labor safety representatives to exercise their rights, especially the following:

- free time required for justified proceedings, with pay based on the employee's average salary;
- the required tools; and
- participation, in each election cycle, in a minimum of 32 hours' training (or, if the representative has labor safety qualifications, eight hours' training) within one year from the representative's election.

The costs of the above must be borne by the employer.[192]

---

[189]The current standards are specified in the Decree of the Ministry of Labor No. 8/1998 (Mar. 31).

[190]See III., above.

[191]Labor Protection Act §70.

[192]*See id.* §75.

c. *Reconciliation of Interests*

National reconciliation of interests is performed by the interest representative organizations of employees and employers and the Labor Safety Commission, consisting of the representatives of the government and acting in accordance with its own rules of procedures.

d. *Labor Safety Enforcement*

Compliance with labor safety regulations is facilitated and supervised by the following agencies:

- the municipal (Budapest) labor safety and employment agencies having the legal status and scope of authority stipulated in the Labor Protection Act and a separate rule of law;[193]
- the National Labor Safety and Employment Organization (*OMMF*, under its Hungarian acronym);
- the head and local offices of the National Public Health Service (*ÁNTSZ*, under its Hungarian acronym); and
- the Hungarian Mining Supervision.

In order to eliminate deficiencies revealed during their inspections, the enforcement agencies are entitled to take the measures and impose the fines specified in this Labor Protection Act and a separate rule of law.[194]

The enforcement agencies may impose labor safety fines on employers that fail to meet the requirements pertaining to the provision of a healthy and safe work environment, and thus, severely endanger the life, physical safety, or health of their employees. The amount of these fines may range between HUF 50,000 and HUF 3,000,000.[195]

---

[193]Decree of the Ministry of Labor No. 9/1996 (Dec. 20); Act IV of 1991.

[194]Labor Protection Act §82; Act LXIX of 1999 on Minor Offences.

[195]Labor Protection Act §82.

B. Workers' Compensation

Employees who suffer an employment-related accident or an occupational illness are eligible to receive the following benefits:[196]

- health care services,
- sick pay,
- accident allowance, and/or
- disability pension.

If an employee dies due to an employment-related accident or occupational illness, retirement benefits also are available to the surviving dependents.

VIII. PENSIONS AND BENEFITS

A. Social Security Benefits

1. Retirement Pensions

a. Social Security Pension

A social security pension consists of benefits paid to the employee after the accumulation of a defined service time. This category includes old-age pensions, disability pensions, and accident-related disability pensions.

i. Old-age pension

Old-age pensions are payable to employees after reaching a certain age and accumulating a certain service time. The conditions of entitlement to an old-age pension differ depending on whether the entitlement is established between December 31, 1997, and January 1, 2009, or after January 1, 2009.

Between December 31, 1997, and January 1, 2009, entitlement is established on the basis of the following conditions:

[196]For a complete discussion of accident-related benefits, see VIII.A.3., below.

- A *full old-age pension* is payable to any woman or man who, prior to January 1991, reached the age of 55 or 60, respectively, and had accumulated 10 years of service. Alternatively, a full old-age pension is payable to any person who, prior to January 1991, had accumulated at least 20 years of service, and—as the second condition of entitlement—in the case of women, had reached age 55 to 61, or in the case of men, had reached age 60 or 61 (based on the year of birth; persons born earlier are eligible at a younger age than those born later).
- A *partial old-age pension* is payable to any man or woman who, between January 1, 1991, and July 1, 1993, reached the age of 55 or 60, respectively, and had accumulated at least 10 years, but fewer than 20 years' service time. A partial old-age pension also is available to those who, between July 1, 1993, and January 1, 2009, reach the relevant retirement age and accumulate 15 years' service.

As of 2009, only those who have reached the age of 62 and have accumulated at least 20 years' service will be entitled to an old-age pension. From that year on, partial old-age pensions will cease to exist.

The amount of an old-age pension depends on the accumulated service time and the average gross monthly earnings that can be taken into account. This calculation determines the amount of old age-pension to be disbursed during the period between December 31, 1997, and January 1, 2013. For a worker with 10 years' service, the amount is 33 percent of average earnings; this amount increases proportionately with the time of service, up to a maximum of 80 percent of average earnings for a worker with 40 years' service.

If the worker pays pension contributions not only to the social security pension fund, but also to a private pension fund, but subsequently requests the amount in the private fund to be transferred to the social security pension fund, the amount of old-age pension is determined according to the general rules set forth above.[197] However, if the private pension account is not transferred

[197]See VIII.B., below, for a discussion of private pensions.

to the social security pension fund, the amount of old age pension due from the social security (i.e., the state) fund is 75 percent of the pension payable under the general rules.

ii. Disability pension

Disability pensions are payable to employees who have lost at least 67 percent of their working abilities due to the deterioration of their state of health or physical and mental faculties, and for whom no improvement is expected for at least one year. In addition, to be eligible for a disability pension, employees must have acquired the necessary service time, and they may not work on a regular basis or their income must be significantly lower than that received before becoming disabled.

iii. Accident-related disability pension

Accident-related disability pensions are available to employees who have suffered an employment-related accident, or who have incurred an occupational illness.[198]

b. Retirement Benefits for Dependents

Upon the death of a worker, the surviving dependents specified by law are entitled to a retirement benefit. The following types of retirement benefits are available:

- widow's pension,
- orphan's allowance,
- parental pension, and
- accident-related benefits for surviving dependents.

2. *Health Insurance Benefits*

a. In-Kind Services Provided by the Health Insurance Fund

The basic principle of providing in-kind health insurance services is that they may be used by employees to the extent justified by their state of health. Health care benefits are available to de-

[198]See VIII.A.3., below.

pendents if they are insured. The types of in-kind services are as follows:

- health care services rendered free of charge (e.g., x-rays, examinations, medical care, medical aid to outpatients and those confined to bed);
- subsidized health care services (medicines, therapeutic equipment); and
- partially subsidized health care services (e.g., dental care).

b. Health Insurance Benefits Paid in Cash

Monetary health insurance benefits consist of maternity and confinement allowance, and sick pay. These benefits are paid to employees who have obtained a right thereto by meeting their personal contribution payment obligations. The extent of the benefit is proportionate to the amount of the contributions.

3. Accident-Related Benefits

Accident-related benefits and pensions are granted to employees and their surviving dependents if the employee has an employment-related accident (whether or not the employee survives), or if the employee has an occupational illness. Accident-related benefits include the following:

- accident-related health care service,
- accident-related sick pay,
- accident-related allowance, and
- accident-related disability pension.

Accident-related retirement benefits are granted to dependents if the worker dies due to an employment-related accident or occupational illness. Surviving dependants are eligible for accident-related retirement benefits even if the employee already has received an accident-related disability pension and then dies for reasons unrelated to the employment-related accident. The surviving dependents of the worker may receive the following types of retirement benefits:

- temporary widow's pension,

- widow's pension,
- orphan's allowance, or
- parental pension.

4. Social Security Contributions

Employees' eligibility for social security benefits is subject to meeting their social security payment obligations. Both employers and employees must pay pension and health insurance contributions. If employees are members of a private pension fund that they joined either voluntarily or pursuant to law, they also must pay the required membership fees in addition to their social security contributions.

The amount of the social security contribution varied annually between January 1, 1998 and January 1, 2000. However, the trend was a decrease in the contribution paid by the employer and an increase in that paid by employees. In 1998 and 1999, employees had to pay 10 percent and 11 percent of the contribution, respectively. Of this, the pension contribution for employees having no private pension insurance amounted to 7 percent of income (salary paid by the employer) from January 1, 1998, 8 percent from January 1, 1999, and 9 percent from January 1, 2000.

If the employee is a member of a private pension fund, the pension contribution payable to the social security fund was 1 percent of income in 1998, and increased in 1999 to 2 percent, and in 2004 decreased to 0.5 percent. The membership fee payable to the private pension fund amounted to 6 percent from January 1, 1998, 7 percent from January 1, 1999, 8 percent from January 1, 2000, 8.5 percent from January 2003, and currently remains at that rate. The employee's health insurance contribution is 4 percent of the income subject to social security contribution.

Effective January 1, 2002, the employer's social security contribution is 29 percent of the income subject to contribution. Of this total, 18 percent is the pension contribution, and 11 percent is the health insurance contribution.

As of January 1, 1999, employers also are obligated to pay health care contributions (*EHO*, under their Hungarian acronym), in order to ensure the financial coverage of the health care services system. There are two types of *EHO*: the income-proportionate *EHO* and the itemized *EHO*.

Income-proportionate *EHO*—which usually amounts to 11 percent—is paid on income or income parts that are not otherwise subject to social security contribution payment, but only to personal income tax payment.

Itemized *EHO*, which is a determined amount based on month or calendar day, applies to legal relationships with defined individuals. The payor of the income has an itemized contribution obligation. This contribution is paid for employees, public employees, and the professional staff of bodies of public interest, the courts, public prosecutors' offices, armed forces and law enforcement organizations, as well as on almost all forms of memberships.

5. *Employer Recordkeeping*

With respect to social security contributions, the employer must maintain records as specified by law and must supply data thereon.

a. Requirements

The employer must establish and maintain a registration file for each employee in a way that allows collection of the data specified by law from the time employment commences. The registration file maintained by the employer must contain the name and personal information about the employee, his or her social security identification number, data relating to the employer, data on the length of insurance and service, the basis and amount deducted from the employee's income, and the amount of any itemized *EHO* paid on behalf of the employee (or other worker).

By January 31 of each year, the employer must issue a certificate (attached to the certificate on income) to the employee, containing all data kept in the registration file with regard to contributions deducted during the preceding year and income from which the contributions were deducted. If the employment relation is terminated during the year, the certificate must be issued without delay.

The employer must close the registration files and place them in archives at the end of each year and must file a report thereon with the Tax Authority by February 20.

The Tax Authority provides employers with the software and instructions necessary to comply with the registration requirements. For employers that maintain paper-based records, the Tax Authority issues the necessary printed forms as specified by government decree. Registration may be kept on electronic or optical media as well, if the system ensures that all data in the register may be generated without delay and retrieved at any time and excludes the possibility of subsequent modification.

Upon the request of the pension insurance Tax Authority, the employer must furnish information within 15 days. However, the Tax Authority may not repeatedly request information that already has been provided in the reports or statement of the employer. This exception is not applicable to data requested by the Tax Authority on the income of the party obliged to pay the contribution or membership fee.

b. Employees Working in Other Countries

Employers have social security recording obligations with respect to Hungarian employees living in neighboring countries.[199] Ethnic Hungarians working in Hungary—with a work permit—must pay pension contributions and health insurance contributions in accordance with the Hungarian legal regulations, and they are entitled to thc same pension and health insurance services as the Hungarian citizens. Ethnic Hungarians living and working in neighboring countries are not obliged to pay pension contributions and health insurance contributions, but if they would like to use the Hungarian pension and health services they are entitled to apply for them at the public organization established for this purpose. Ethnic Hungarians living and working in neighboring countries are entitled to emergency health service under bilateral social security (social policy) treaties.

Act LXII of 2001 on Hungarians living in neighboring countries applies only to ethnic Hungarians who live in the Croatian Republic, Yugoslav Republic, Romania, Slovenian Republic, Slovakian Republic, or in Ukraine, but who are not Hungarian citizens. Consequently, these regulations do not apply to Hungar-

---

[199] Act LXII of 2001.

ian citizens working abroad or to non–Hungarian citizens working in Hungary, although non–Hungarian citizens may work in Hungary with a work permit and those who are ethnic Hungarians under the Act can apply for a work permit in an accelerated process.[200]

c. Leased Employees

An employer must establish and maintain records for leased employees as a result of the 2001 amendments to the Labor Code.[201] The employer of the leased employee is the lessor, and thus the lessor is obliged to keep the employer's records and do the reporting.[202]

d. Electronic Filing

Certain reporting obligations under the Social Security Act now may be fulfilled electronically. Any information provided electronically is subject to the Act on Electronic Signatures,[203] which entered into force on September 1, 2001. The Act on Electronic Signatures is a major step toward the subject of legal recognition of the electronic signature in Hungary, and it aims to establish the preconditions for reliable and trusted electronic commerce services. Almost all official institutions are required to accept e-signatures as readily as paper versions unless otherwise provided by a separate statute, e.g., in judicial, municipal, or administrative proceedings.[204] Electronic signatures can be used in the public sector within administrations and in communications between such administrations, with citizens and economic operators, etc. For example, the public procurement, taxation, social security, health, and justice systems; passport requests; land registration; banking; and telephone and electricity bills are only a few of the processes that will become e-compatible.

---

[200]See IX.B., below.

[201]See I.A., above.

[202]Act LXXX of 1997 on Social Security, §4(a), point 7.

[203]Act XXXV of 2001.

[204]*See id.* §3.

B. Private Pensions and Private Pension Funds

Effective September 1, 1997, a new pension scheme was introduced in Hungary[205] with the aim of maintaining the statutory social security pension, while supplementing it with certain privately financed forms. This pension legislation authorized private pensions operating on a capital adequacy (fully funded) basis and regulated the organizational structure and the operation of private pension funds. Private pensions are also based on statutory participation, but only for employees who started working after June 30, 1998, and who are younger than the age of 42.

Private and social security pension schemes are interrelated at several points, primarily through the collection of contributions and registration systems.[206] In addition, under the statutory pension scheme, employees may receive both a social security pension (from the social security fund) and a supplementary pension (from the private pension fund). With the exception of those starting their careers, Hungarian citizens were free to decide whether they wished to join the mixed scheme, provided they made their decision prior to September 1, 1999. Employees who chose the mixed scheme voluntarily could change their minds and return to the social security pension scheme until December 31, 2000. In this case, the entire amount of the membership fee paid to the employee's account at the private pension fund must have been transferred to the social security fund, from which the employee thereafter will be entitled to receive a full old-age social security pension.

The mixed scheme of social security and private pensions is supplemented with the establishment of voluntary mutual pension insurance funds. Under the latter scheme, the employer can provide a special form of pension to employees and their beneficiaries as a fringe benefit. In addition, individual citizens may join a private pension insurance fund, in order to ensure their future income.

Those becoming a member of a private pension fund (operating on the basis of capital adequacy—fully funded) pay a mem-

---

[205] Act LXXXII of 1997.

[206] See VIII.A.4., above.

bership fee in the amount specified by law. The employer may pay fully or in part the membership fee of the private pension fund for its employees.[207] This membership fee may be used by the pension fund as capital to guarantee coverage for performance of its pension payment obligations. The fund keeps the payments made by its members on the member's individual account; the amount paid and its yields serve as coverage for the benefit chosen by the member. When the member reaches the age of retirement, the pension is paid by the private pension fund in a manner requested by the member. This type of pension is not linked to the central budget and must finance its income and expenses itself.

Statutory pension funds, which are private funds authorized by statute, are autonomous bodies operating on the principle of self-government and are supervised by the state via the National Supervision of Funds.

C. Unemployment Benefits

1. Benefits

The unemployed are entitled to unemployment benefits, pre-pension unemployment benefits, and certain cost reimbursements (e.g., justified public transportation expenses).[208]

2. Contributions

Employers must pay a contribution amounting to 3 percent of the taxes paid by the employer to the state on employees' gross salary, wages, income, severance pay, anniversary awards, pay during sick leave, as well as in-kind allowances, meal contributions, and holiday contributions, plus 3 percent of the 25 percent tax paid on a company car (provided the latter four are subject to personal income tax).[209]

Employees pay 1.5 percent of the gross salary or income received from their employer. This contribution requirement is not applicable to those receiving or obtaining eligibility for old age, disability, or accident-related pension benefits.

---

[207] Act XIX of 2002.

[208] Act IV of 1991, §24.

[209] *See id.* §40.

D. Rehabilitation Contribution

In order to promote the rehabilitation of people with changed working abilities, employers of more than 20 employees must pay a rehabilitation contribution if less than 5 percent of their workforce consists of employees with changed working abilities. The contribution amount is 3 percent of the national annual average income in the second year preceding the year in reference, as published by the Central Statistical Office.

IX. IMMIGRATION

A. Governing Law

Unless a legal rule provides otherwise, the law of the country in which work is to be performed applies to employment.[210] The law of the appointing authority or electoral body applies to employment arising from appointment or election.

Foreign nationals who perform work in Hungary within the framework of an employment relationship or other legal relationship aimed at work, as well as employers that employ foreign nationals, generally are governed by the provisions of the Labor Code, as well as the Decree of the Minister of Social and Family Affairs on Permitting Foreigners to Take Up Work in Hungary.[211]

B. Work Permits

As prescribed by the Minister of Social and Family Affairs, foreign nationals may perform work in Hungary only with a proper permit. Likewise, the employer may establish an employment (or other working) relationship only with a foreigner who is in possession of both a work permit and a visa issued for taking up work or residence.

Work permits are issued by the Labor Exchange Center. An employer must maintain an authentic copy of the work permit, the

---

[210]Decree No. 13 of 1979 on International Private Law.

[211]Decree of the Ministry of Social and Family Affairs No. 8/1999 (Nov. 10).

visa issued for performing work, and the residence permit, and must present them to the proper authorities upon request.

Legislation enacted on January 1, 2002,[212] allows Hungarian nationals living abroad to apply for work in Hungary without first obtaining a work permit and to receive certain social benefits, such as access to Hungarian culture, science, libraries, museums, and public transportation at reduced tariffs, and they may be enrolled in Hungarian schools, colleges, and universities as Hungarian citizens and also are entitled to student cards, scholarships, and honors. Scientists who are Hungarian nationals can be members of the Hungarian Academy of Science. Hungarian nationals also are entitled to certain accelerated administrative procedures, e.g., those related to acquiring a work permit in Hungary.

Based on an agreement between the Hungarian and the Romanian governments, signed on May 9, 2000, in Budapest and enacted by Government Decree 246 of 2001, Romanians are now entitled to work in Hungary for a limited period of time without a work permit.

1. Individual Permit

An individual permit is issued if the employer meets the following manpower criteria:

- prior to submission of the application, the employer is in possession of a valid manpower claim in connection with the work to be performed by the foreign national; or
- after submission of the application, no Hungarian manpower is available that is suitable for the employment criteria as described in the applicable laws and in the employer's manpower claim.

A valid manpower claim is one that the employer submits according to the following timetable:

- at least 30 days, but not more than 60 days, prior to submission of the application; or

[212]Act LXII of 2001.

- more than 60 days prior, but renewed every 60 days with the last renewal not more than 60 days before submission of the application.

If the employer wants to employ the foreign national at company sites in different counties, the manpower criteria necessary for issuance of the permit must be met in the county of the employer's registered site. At other company sites, no Hungarian manpower can be available that is suitable for the employment criteria described in the applicable laws and in the employer's manpower claim. If the work will be performed in more than one county, the manpower criteria must be met in the county where the work is to be commenced.

An application for an individual permit will be dismissed under the following circumstances:

- the necessary manpower criteria are not satisfied;
- the employer does not wish to start working with the foreign national within 120 days from submission of the permit;
- Hungarian manpower suitable for the employment criteria described in the applicable laws and in the employer's manpower claim was sent to the vacancy, but the employment failed due to reasons within the employers' control;
- the foreign national works for an employer different from the one that submits the application;
- the labor relationship is not formed between the foreign national and the employer that submits the application;
- the exclusive subject of the employment is the permanent assignment of the foreign national pursuant to a private legal contract concluded between the foreign national and the employer; or
- pursuant to reciprocity agreements between Hungary and other countries.

For purposes of the above, reasons within the employer's control would include cases where the employer lists employment criteria in its claim that are unnecessary to performance of the work, or the employer does not want to employ a Hungarian national who was suitable for the work.

An individual permit will be issued without regard to manpower criteria in the following cases (among others):

- if annually (according to December 31 data of the previous year), no more than 2 percent of all the employees at the company are foreign nationals, and the majority owners of the company are foreign nationals;
- for the employment of close relatives of the foreign national if the foreign national has worked continuously in Hungary for at least eight years and has lived together continuously in Hungary with the close relative in question for at least five years; or
- for the employment of the spouse of the foreign national if they have lived together continuously for at least one year in Hungary.

Even in these cases, the work permit is not issued automatically because the foreign national must meet the employment criteria specified in applicable laws and must have a certificate of medical fitness for the job (if a certificate is issued abroad, a certified copy of it, as well as its authenticated Hungarian translation, are required).

In certain cases, no permit is required for foreign nationals to work in Hungary. These cases are as follows:

- pursuant to an inter-state or inter-governmental agreement, or an international treaty;
- for the foreign personnel of a diplomatic (consular) mission or other body of a foreign state functioning in Hungary, or an international organization or body set up jointly through an inter-state agreement;
- for activities connected with putting into operation equipment, guarantees, servicing, or warranty under a contract concluded with a foreign supplier (on an occasional basis, for not longer than 15 continuous days);
- for work performed by the senior official of an economic association with foreign participation;
- for work performed by members of the supervisory board of economic associations with majority foreign ownership;

- for educational, scientific, or artistic activities of internationally recognized foreign personalities who are invited by higher educational institutions, scientific research institutes, or public cultural institutions, for not longer than five working days;
- for a foreign national winning a tender for post-doctorate employment, or for work performed as part of the tender or scholarship program under the János Bolyai Research Scholarship;
- for the employment of the foreign student of a foreign institution of higher education as part of an apprentice training program arranged by an international student organization;
- for work performed by foreign nationals who maintain a full-time student relationship with a vocational school, secondary school, elementary school, educational institution for the arts, or an institution of higher education;
- for foreign nationals who perform work within the framework of building camps organized pursuant to the conditions defined in a separate legal rule;[213]
- for the activities of foreign church personnel who perform work in a church registered in Hungary, or in an institution thereof;
- for work performed by foreign nationals who enjoy temporary refuge within the territory of Hungary for performing work in connection with applicants for refugee status;
- for work performed by a senior official of the branch office or agency of an economic association with a foreign registered seat;
- for work performed as a member of an international organization or a joint organization established by an international agreement; or
- for employment in Hungary of refugees with identification papers granting permanent residency, asylum-seekers with documents granting temporary residency, and immigrants.

---

[213]Decree of Government No. 63/1997 (Apr. 18) on Voluntary Youth Building Camps.

The employer, the sphere of activity, the working hours, and the employee's status at the company must be set forth in the individual permit. Individual permits are issued for a maximum period of one year, but may be extended. For extensions, the same rules as for issuing the permit are applicable.

An employer that employs a foreign national without a work permit must pay into the employment segment of the Labor Market Fund[214] double the salary or wages paid to the foreign national from the commencement of employment until the illicit nature of the employment is established. If the offense of illegal employment is repeated within three years, the penalty payable by the employer is five times the amount of salary paid to the foreign national from the commencement of continuous employment until the offense of illegal employment is reestablished. The employer's penalty for illegal employment may not be less than five times the compulsory minimum wage in effect at the time of inspection for the first offense, or not less than 10 times the minimum wage for the second and any subsequent offenses. This provision also applies if the amount paid to the foreign national cannot be determined. An employer is subject to penalty for each person employed without a permit, and as many times as the offense of illegal employment is established.

---

[214]The Labor Market Fund is a special state fund created by the consolidation of the Unemployment Solidarity Fund, the Employment Fund, the Vocational Education Fund, the Rehabilitation Fund, and the Wage Guarantee Fund. The liabilities and receivables of these consolidated funds are settled and collected by the Labor Market Fund. The Labor Market Fund is under the control of the Minister of Social and Family Affairs.

By concentrating and uniformly managing funds related to job assistance, unemployment, and vocational training, the objectives of the Labor Market Fund are to: provide assistance to the unemployed; support the unemployed in finding jobs and facilitate adjustments in the work force; promote the social security of employees of business organizations under liquidation; support the improvement of vocational training programs; increase the job opportunities available to persons with reduced capacity to work; assist in the partial financing of early retirement pension benefits; provide funding for expenses related to the provision of subsidies and benefits financed by the basic segments; and contribute to the financing of operation and development costs of the labor market organization.

2. *General Group Permit*

The employer may submit an application for a general group permit to the Labor Exchange if employment in Hungary of several foreign nationals is justified by a civil law contract to be concluded on the basis of competitive bidding. The application for a general group permit may be submitted prior to concluding the civil law contract. The number and qualifications of the foreign nationals intended to be employed, and the activity for which they would be employed, must be designated in the application.

The general permit remains in force until fulfillment of the civil law contract.

Individual workers may not be be employed exclusively on the basis of the general group permit, but are required to obtain individual permits. During the term of a valid group permit, individual permits will be issued to foreign nationals according to the number, qualifications, and activity designated in the group permit application.

C. Visas

The issuance of visas falls within the jurisdiction of the following authorities:

- the Ministry of Foreign Welfare,
- national police headquarters,
- regional police headquarters,
- the Border Guard Directorate and its regional branches, and
- authorized foreign representatives.

Visa applications must be submitted in person at the Hungarian consulate office corresponding to the permanent or usual place of residence of the foreign national. Under special circumstances, an application may be submitted to one of the other authorities listed immediately above, and the authority may grant an exemption from requiring the application to be submitted in person.

Applications must be submitted along with a valid passport and three passport photos. The fee specified is due at the time the application is submitted.

If no factors for disqualification apply regarding a foreign national lawfully staying in Hungary, the Hungarian consular office corresponding to the permanent or usual place of residence of the foreign national will issue the visa together with the temporary residence permit if the foreign national's planned stay does not exceed one year; if the foreign national's planned stay exceeds one year, the national police headquarters will issue an extended residence permit. Applications for extension of the period of stay specified in the permit must be submitted to the competent immigration office of the Ministry of Domestic Affairs.[215]

Residence permits for members of diplomatic missions and consular offices in Hungary are issued and extended by the Ministry of Foreign Affairs.

[215]Act XXXIX of 2001.

IRELAND*

INTRODUCTION

A. Political System

Until 1922, the 26 counties of Ireland that make up the Irish Republic formed part of the United Kingdom (UK), so that the Irish legal and judicial system closely mirrored that which existed in the UK. Until 1948, what then was known as the Irish Free State remained a member of the British Commonwealth, with the British monarch as its titular head of state. Following Ireland's declaration of a Republic, a new constitution, *Bunreacht na hEireann* (Constitution) was introduced.

The Irish governmental system is based on a democratic model of an interactive legislature and executive. The legislature is composed of two houses: the *Seanad*, the lower house; and the *Dáil*, the upper house. Government members invariably are chosen from the upper house, the members of which all are elected, usually every four years, by general plebiscite.

The Irish judicial system sits alongside, but wholly independent of, the government. The interrelationship of the executive, the legislature, and the judiciary is based on the French political model of the separation of powers, with each arm of the state providing a system of checks and balances over the other.

In 1973, Ireland, accompanied by the UK and Denmark, became a member of the European Economic Community, which is now the European Union (EU), and since then Ireland has looked increasingly to the EU, and less to the UK, for its legislative and economic development.[1] Ireland arguably has been much more

---

*Paul Glenfield, Brian Buggy, and Tony Walsh, Matheson Ormsby Prentice, Dublin, Ireland.

[1]For a discussion of the EU, see the chapter on the EU in Volume I, Part 1.

enthusiastic than the UK in embracing Europe and European integration. Ireland has joined the European Monetary Union and has been within the euro currency zone since its launch. Within the EU, Ireland long has been perceived as an ideal location for inward investment because of its place in the political and economic structure of Europe: a young, well-educated, English-speaking population, a favorable tax regime, and a good industrial relations climate supported by collective bargaining at the national level.

B. General Sources of Labor and Employment Law

Labor and employment law in Ireland derives from a number of different sources, including rights that derive from the Constitution, common law principles, and statutory provisions.[2]

1. Constitutional Rights

Ireland's Constitution affords rights to employees in three distinct areas. First, the Constitution guarantees the right to earn a livelihood. This right has not been interpreted to provide employees either substantive private rights to sue an employer for loss of employment or a prospective employer for failure to give employment, or any public law entitlement against the government of Ireland for failure to provide employment or adoption of policies that fail to promote employment.

Second, Irish employees have the right to join or not to join a trade union as they see fit.[3]

Third, the Constitution has given rise to the concept of what is known as constitutional or, perhaps more appropriately, natural justice, which will apply whenever an employee faces accusations of wrongdoing. In this event, the employee will be entitled to fair procedures, which involve two core principles: first, knowing the allegations to be answered, and, second, being given a fair opportunity to refute those allegations without having the matter pre-

---

[2]*See generally* ANTHONY KERR, IRISH EMPLOYMENT LEGISLATION (Sweet & Maxwell 1999); FRANCES MEENAN, WORKING WITHIN THE LAW (Oak Tree Press 2d ed. 1999).

[3]See II.D., below.

judged before being given an opportunity to respond (known as the *audi alteram partem* rule).

2. *Common Law Principles and Statutes*

With respect to common law principles, Irish labor and employment laws bear marked similarities to the principles that apply in the UK. Indeed, in the absence of any Irish judicial authority on a particular point, the Irish courts will look to the UK and other common law jurisdictions for precedent authority and frequently will find such authorities persuasive. Due to its common law origins, Irish labor and employment law differs significantly from the civil code models operated throughout most of the rest of the EU.

3. *International Sources*

Ireland is a member of the EU, and consequently has had to harmonize a large part of its laws with EU law by incorporating EU directives and regulations into domestic legislation, and by complying with the provisions of the Treaty of Rome (and subsequent EU treaties) and the decisions of the European Court of Justice. EU law has had a huge impact on Irish employment law since 1973. In comparison with the approach of the UK, Ireland has tended to adopt a more straightforward transposition of EU Directives into domestic legislation.

Ireland is a member of the International Labor Organization (ILO).[4] Therefore, internationally it is bound by the guidelines and principles of that organization, as well as the conventions it has signed.

Ireland is also a signatory to the European Convention for the Protection of Human Rights and Fundamental Freedoms 1950 and Associated Protocols. All of the provisions of the European Convention of Human Rights Act 2003 (ECHR) became effective in Ireland on December 31, 2003.[5] The ECHR gives further effect

---

[4]For additional information on the ILO, see the chapter on the ILO in Volume I, Part 4.

[5]European Convention on Human Rights Act 2003 (Commencement) Order 2003, S.I. 483/2003.

(subject to Constitutional provisions) to the European Convention on Human Rights and Fundamental Freedoms together with associated Protocols. Unlike EU law, which is given ultimate precedence over Irish constitutional law, the Convention is subject to Irish constitutional law.

The ECHR seeks to ensure that the courts, in interpreting and applying any statutory provision or rule of law, shall, as far as possible, do so in a manner that is compatible with the obligations of the state under the Convention and its Protocols. The ECHR also imposes on all government departments and state agencies a requirement to perform functions in a manner compatible with the obligations under the Convention.

The rights protected under the ECHR will only be enforceable by individuals where they are bringing an action directly against a particular contracting state. These rights cannot give rise to a direct cause of action against a private individual or employer. Therefore, any cause of action that is brought under the ECHR or before the European Court of Human Rights can only be brought against a contracting state or a public body employer representing that state.

However, it should not be presumed that private sector employers are therefore immune from the ECHR. The ECHR requires that all Irish legislation and rules of law must be interpreted in accordance with the ECHR (subject to the overriding provisions of the Constitution). It is therefore very probable that in the course of an individual action against a private employer, an employee can still rely on the ECHR. This is because the Employment Appeals Tribunal, the Labor Court, and civil courts, as public bodies, will be required to uphold the provisions of the ECHR in their determinations. While private sector employees will not have a direct cause of action under the ECHR, this manner of interpretation will nonetheless allow employees to indirectly rely on the ECHR in actions against their employer. Therefore, when considering complaints relating to unfair dismissal, wrongful dismissal and discrimination, the courts, Labor Court, and Employment Appeals Tribunal must consider the ECHR rights, and they must provide a fair hearing in compliance with Article 6.

Finally, the Convention does allow, subject to certain conditions, for a remedy in damages if there is a contravention of the

Convention's provisions. In the recent decision of the European Court of Human Rights in *Doran v. Ireland*,[6] the plaintiff complained to the Court that they had been denied a right to a hearing within a reasonable time (contrary to article 6 of the Convention), and that Irish domestic law either conferred no such right, or if it did confer such a right, Irish law did not provide any effective remedy for its breach (contrary to article 13). The Court agreed and awarded the frustrated buyers €25,000 for nonfinancial damage. Significantly, no appropriate right was available to the litigants under present constitutional law in Ireland.

C. Administration of the Labor and Employment Laws

The State of Ireland is divided into four provinces—Leinster, Munster, Connaught, and Ulster, which together contain 26 counties. However, for purposes of the labor and employment laws, Ireland can be treated as one jurisdiction, with no differences on a provincial or county level. The government department that has the most responsibility for employment and labor-related issues is the Department of Enterprise, Trade, and Employment.

D. Dispute Resolution System

Irish employment law rights fall into three distinct categories: constitutional, statutory, and contractual. The way in which these rights are enforced involves a complex interweaving between labor and employment-related tribunals and the civil courts.

Generally speaking, contractual and constitutional claims are dealt with in the civil courts, whereas statutory claims are dealt with by bodies or tribunals such as the Rights Commissioner Service, the Labor Court, and the Employment Appeals Tribunal (EAT), though usually with a right of appeal to the civil courts.

1. Courts

The civil judicial system in Ireland follows a tiered jurisdiction, based on monetary levels. At the lowest level, the district

[6](50389/99) [2003] ECHR 417 (31 July 2003).

court deals with claims not exceeding €6348.69 (IR£5,000) and is very rarely used in employment or labor-related matters.

The next level is the Circuit Court, whose jurisdiction generally is limited to awards up to €38092.14 (IR£30,000), although in certain specified areas it can make awards in excess of that amount. For example, in appeals from determinations of the EAT, the Circuit Court has jurisdiction to make awards up to the jurisdictional level of the tribunal, i.e., two years' gross remuneration. The Circuit Court also may have original jurisdiction, for example, in claims for sexual harassment under the Employment Equality Act, 1998.[7]

Where the sums involved in a contractual claim exceed €38092.14 (IR£30,000), the action must be brought in the High Court, which has unlimited jurisdiction. Both the High Court and the Circuit Courts can exercise equitable jurisdiction and grant injunctive relief that, in the case of the High Court, is a remedy used frequently by Irish employment law practitioners.[8]

The Courts and Court Officers Act, 2002, which contains provisions to increase limits of the district, circuit, and high courts, came into effect on April 10, 2002, although the relevant provisions have not yet been enacted by the Minister for Enterprise, Trade, and Employment (ETE Minister).[9]

2. *Tribunals and Industrial Relations Bodies*

The primary bodies responsible for dealing with statutory labor and employment rights are the Labor Relations Commission, the Rights Commissioner Service, the Labor Court, the EAT, and the Equality Authority and Director of Equality Investigations.[10]

---

[7]For a discussion of the Employment Equality Act, 1998, see VI.A.3., below.

[8]See I.C.2., below.

[9]The monetary limits mentioned above will be increased to €20,000 (IR£5,750) for the District Court, and €100,000 (IR£78,750) for the Circuit Court, when the Courts and Court Officers Act provisions are enacted.

[10]For a discussion of the Equality Authority and Director of Equality Investigations, see VI.F., below.

a. Labor Relations Commission

The Labor Relations Commission (LRC) was established under the Industrial Relations Act, 1990, and is a body consisting of employer, trade union, and independent representatives. Its primary functions are to promote good industrial relations, provide conciliation and advisory services, and prepare and offer codes of best practice. The conciliation service assists employers and trade unions in resolving disputes where direct negotiations have failed.[11]

b. Rights Commissioner Service

The Rights Commissioner Service forms a part of the LRC. Although Rights Commissioners are appointed by the ETE Minister, they are independent in their investigative functions. Rights Commissioners may hear individual grievances or complaints pursuant to various employment legislation,[12] with their determination binding on the parties. They also are empowered to investigate industrial disputes, other than disputes relating to pay, hours or times of work, or annual holidays of a body of workers.

c. Labor Court

The Labor Court was established under the Industrial Relations Act, 1946, and provides the machinery for formal investigation of industrial disputes. The Labor Court is a 12-member body made up of a chairperson, a deputy chairperson, and representatives of employers and employees, all of whom are appointed by the ETE Minister. The primary functions of the Labor Court are as follows:

- to investigate industrial disputes and issue recommendations for settlement;[13]
- to establish and service joint labor committees and ratify, by means of employment regulation orders, minimum wages

[11]For a detailed discussion of Labor Relations Commission (LRC) functions, see II.H., below.

[12]*See, e.g.*, Organization of Working Time Act, 1997 (OWTA). For a discussion of the OWTA, see V.C., below.

[13]See II.H., below.

and conditions of employment proposed by the committees;[14]

- to register and vary certain employment (collective) agreements relating to the pay and conditions of employment of certain groups of workers;[15]
- to register and service Joint Industrial Councils;[16] and
- to decide on appeals from the recommendations of Rights Commissioners or Equality Officers.

The Labor Court is not a court in the strict sense of the word. Procedures are informal and flexible, hearings usually are in private, and members of the court need not have any legal qualifications. The Labor Court can, however, summons witnesses, order the production of documents, and hear evidence under oath. Recommendations of the Labor Court under its authority to investigate industrial disputes previously were not legally binding on the parties. In recent years, the jurisdiction of the Labor Court has expanded considerably, particularly in the area of individual employment rights.[17] Enactment of the Industrial Relations (Amendment) Act, 2001, provides for circumstances in which a determination by the Labor Court concerning terms and conditions of employment may be legally binding on the parties to a dispute.[18] However, the number of legally binding determinations is still very low.

Under the Sustaining Progress Social Partnership Agreement, where the parties cannot reach agreement through negotiations on any matters covered by this Agreement, most of which deal with pay increases over the next three years, they will be referred to the Labor Relations Commission (LRC) and, if unresolved, shall jointly be referred to the Labor Court or, where appropriate, to other agreed

[14]See V.A.1., below.

[15]See II.F.2., below.

[16]See V.A.1., below.

[17]*See, e.g.*, National Minimum Wage Act, 2000 (discussed at V.A.1., below); Organization of Working Time Act, 1997 (discussed at V.C., below); Parental Leave Act, 1998 (discussed at V.D.4., below); Employment Equality Act, 1998 (discussed at VI.A.3., below).

[18]See II.A. and B., below.

machinery. This is a further example of the Labor Court's ever-increasing function in Irish industrial relations.

d. Employment Appeals Tribunal

The EAT was set up under the Redundancy Payments Act, 1967, to hear and make binding recommendations with respect to claims by employees for lump-sum redundancy payments.[19] The jurisdiction of the EAT gradually has been increased and expanded, so that now it is the primary forum for bringing statutory claims to enforce individual employment rights.[20]

e. Personal Injuries Assessment Board

The Personal Injuries Assessment Board Act, 2003 (PIAB Act), was signed into law on December 28, 2003, and provides for the establishment of the Personal Injuries Assessment Board (PIAB) as a statutory body. The PIAB aims to provide a less costly and speedier means of finalizing personal injury claims than exists within the current court based system. The PIAB Act has not yet come into operation and requires commencement orders to be made before personal injuries claims can be submitted to the PIAB.

The PIAB initially will deal only with employment liability cases. However, in due course it is intended that the PIAB also will deal with road traffic and public liability cases, and eventually with all civil personal injury actions. Medical negligence claims are excluded from its ambit. The PIAB has no role in assessing liability (i.e., fault, such as negligence or contributory negligence), which remains a matter for the courts. However, no claim for personal injuries that would otherwise be within the jurisdiction of the PIAB may be litigated in the courts unless PIAB has first authorized that litigation.

Although every qualifying claim for personal injuries must be submitted to PIAB, the PIAB has jurisdiction to deal with a claim only if the party against whom the claim is made (the respondent) consents to that jurisdiction by conceding liability. However, even if a respondent consents to the PIAB procedure, he or

---

[19]See IV.A.2.a., below.

[20]*See, e.g.*, Unfair Dismissals Act, 1977 and 1993 (discussed at I.C.2.c., below).

she may dispute liability at a later stage if the PIAB permits the matter to proceed to litigation. In cases that must be submitted to the PIAB, the limitation period within which litigation must normally be commenced is suspended from the date the application is made to the PIAB until six months after the PIAB has authorized litigation.

The PIAB will authorize litigation in a number of different situations. First, if the respondent does not consent to PIAB dealing with the case (in a qualifying case, the claimant has no choice but to bring his or her claim to PIAB); second, if the PIAB makes an assessment and it is rejected by either the claimant or the respondent; and, finally, if the PIAB decides in its discretion that it should not make an assessment, due to the particular complexity of the case or for any other reason set out in law, e.g., if the claimant in good faith seeks aggravated damages.

Although no time limit for doing so is yet stipulated, the legislation proposes that third parties must be notified of claims within two months of the date of the incident giving rise to the claim. Upon receipt of an application from a claimant, the PIAB will notify the respondent of the application. If the respondent does not consent to the PIAB dealing with the case, the PIAB must permit the matter to proceed to litigation, in which case the claimant will have to commence proceedings in the normal way to pursue his or her claim. However, if the respondent consents to the PIAB having jurisdiction, the PIAB will proceed to make an assessment of damages based on the book of quantum.

The approach of the PIAB assessors is inquisitorial rather than adversarial. There is no oral testimony and the investigation is conducted and the assessment made on the basis of documents only. The claimant is responsible for furnishing all relevant documentation to the PIAB, including experts' reports. The PIAB then notifies its assessment to the parties.

The assessment process is subject to certain time limits. The PIAB must notify the parties of its assessment within nine months from the date on which it receives the respondent's consent to the assessment procedure, although that period may be extended by a maximum of six months. If at the end of that maximum period of 15 months the PIAB has not made an assessment, then it must approve the matter proceeding to litigation. The claimant has 28 days from the date of service of the notice of the assessment to inform the PIAB whether the amount of the assessment is being accepted or rejected. If the claimant fails to respond, he or she will be deemed not to have accepted the assessment, and litigation will be authorized. The respondent has only 21 days from the date of service of the notice of the assessment to inform PIAB whether the assessment is being accepted or rejected. If the respondent fails to respond, he or she is deemed to have accepted the assessment. If the assessment is rejected by either party, the PIAB must permit the parties to proceed to litigation.

Assessment of damages for pain and suffering is based primarily on medical reports from the claimant's treating doctor, although the claimant may also be examined by a member of PIAB's independent medical panel. The PIAB is compiling a "book of quantum" and will publish it as a guideline to general damages. The level of general damages is expected to be comparable to those awarded by the courts or achieved in settlement negotiations prior to the establishment of the PIAB. The PIAB may at its discretion compensate a claimant for out-of-pocket expenses such as wage loss, calculated by PIAB assessors.

The PIAB has discretion to reimburse a claimant in respect of his or her outlay (including the cost of medical reports); it will not make any award for the costs incurred by a claimant in obtaining legal advice. However, the PIAB must ensure that a "vulnerable" claimant receives assistance and it has the discretion to make an award in respect of legal expenses of such a claimant. Claimants pay a small (refundable) administrative fee that must accompany their application to the PIAB, and respondents are subject to a levy calculated on a case-by-case basis. Parties to a claim before the PIAB are entitled to seek independent legal advice from a solicitor, although the PIAB will not award legal costs for or against any party in respect of that legal advice, except in relation to vulnerable persons. The PIAB communicates directly with the parties and it will not normally copy correspondence to their solicitors. Nonetheless, a solicitor is in the best position to advise the parties on procedures for dealing with the PIAB. For example, a solicitor can advise on the important decisions relating to the drafting of submissions and medical and other expert evidence, and whether to accept or reject an assessment made by the PIAB.

3. Appeals

The appeals structure can be quite complicated depending on which statute and tribunal is involved. For example, under the Unfair Dismissals Act, 1977 and 1993,[21] if both parties consent, a claim initially may be brought before a Rights Commissioner, whose determination may be appealed, with a full rehearing, to the EAT. Alternatively, if either party objects, the claim first is heard by the EAT. An appeal, in the form of a full rehearing, then will lie from the EAT to the Circuit Court. Even though the legislation does not provide for an appeal from the Circuit Court, except on a point of law, the High Court has held that a full appeal may be brought to the High Court from the Circuit Court's decision. From the High Court, an appeal to the Supreme Court is allowed on a point of law. Thus, it may be possible in an unfair dismissal case to have four full hearings, with one additional appeal on a point of law to the Supreme Court.

In contract-related matters, an appeal will lie from the Circuit Court to the High Court and from the High Court to the Supreme Court on a point of law only.

Appeals from determinations of the Labor Court under the Organization of Working Time Act, 1997,[22] and the Employment Equality Act, 1998,[23] lie with the Circuit Court.

It is possible for a reference to be made to the European Court of Justice (ECJ) on a relevant point of EU law at any stage.

I. INDIVIDUAL EMPLOYMENT

A. Employment Status

A great deal of employment, tax, and social welfare legislation in Ireland depends on the existence of an employment contract. Thus, it is central to the application of employment rights and obligations that an individual work under such a contract or

---

[21]See I.C.2.c., below.
[22]See V.C., below.
[23]See VI.A.3., below.

otherwise be deemed an employee. Unfortunately, there is no general statutory definition of an employee in Irish employment law, although there are definitions specific to particular pieces of legislation.[24]

Originally, the Irish law of employment contracts was based on traditional concepts of master and servant developed under British common law. Over time, the common law developed a variety of tests to determine an individual's employment status. The definitive test in Irish law[25] now combines "the control requirement"[26] and the "in business on one's own account" test.[27] Thus, an employee is an individual who carries out services for another, rather than for him- or herself, and who is subject to some degree of control from the other person. Alternatively, a person is deemed to be self-employed, or working under a contract for services, where that person provides his or her own premises, equipment, or investment, employs others to assist, and does not receive a predetermined salary.

Any clause in an employment contract identifying a worker as self-employed is not conclusive, but instead will be considered as only one factor in determining the nature of the relationship.

B. Individual Employment Contracts

1. *Terms and Conditions*

a. *Formalities*

An employment contract may be entered into either orally or in writing, and its terms may be agreed expressly between the parties or implied, either at common law or by statute. Under Irish law, there is no obligation for an employer and an employee to

---

[24]*See, e.g.*, Organization of Working Time Act, 1997 (defining "employee" to mean "a person of any age, who has entered into or works under (or, where the employment has ceased, entered into or worked under), a contract of employment").

[25]*See* Henry Denny & Sons v. Minister for Social Welfare, [1998] I.R. 34 (Ir. S. Ct., Keane, J.).

[26]Yewen v. Noakes, 6 Q.B.D. 530 (1880).

[27]Ready Mixed Concrete South East Ltd. v. Minister for Pensions and Nat'l Ins., [1968] 1 All E.R. 433 (Q.B.) (adopting into UK law a standard established in *United States v. Silke*, 331 U.S. 704 (1946)).

enter into a formal written contract of employment or service agreement. Indeed, the increasing amount of legislation regulating the employment relationship lessens the necessity for a written contract.

The Terms of Employment (Information) Act, 1994 (Employment Information Act), does require that certain core terms of the employment relationship be set out in what is described as a Statement of Terms and Conditions (Statement).[28] The Statement must be furnished to the employee within two months after starting employment and must contain the following particulars:[29]

- the identity of the employer and the employee;
- the address of the employer's principal place of business or registered office in the state;
- the place of work;
- the job title/description;
- the date of commencement of employment;
- in the case of a temporary employment contract, its expected duration, or, if the contract is for a fixed term, the date on which the contract expires;
- notice entitlement in the event of dismissal;
- any collective agreements that directly affect the terms and conditions of the employee's employment;
- the rate or method of pay calculation, the intervals at which the employee is paid, and the pay reference period;[30]
- hours of work (including overtime);
- rest periods and breaks;[31]
- paid leave (other than paid sick leave); and
- any terms or conditions relating to sickness and paid sick leave and pensions.

---

[28]Terms of Employment (Information) Act, 1994 (Employment Information Act), §3. The Employment Information Act implements the provisions of EU Directive 91/533/EEC, 1991 O.J. (L 288) 32, relating to an employer's obligation to inform employees of the conditions applicable to the contract or employment relationship.

[29]Employment Information Act §3.

[30]For an explanation of the pay reference period, see V.A.1., below.

[31]Terms of Employment (Additional Information) Order, Statutory Instrument (S.I.) 49 (1998).

The Statement itself is not a contract of employment, but merely sets out certain of the key terms. If the specified information already is contained in a formal written employment contract, that will satisfy the requirements of the Employment Information Act.

When an employee is required to work outside the state for a continuous period greater than one month, the employer must provide the employee with the following information:[32]

- the period of employment outside the state;
- the currency in which the employee is to be paid;
- any benefits in cash or in kind; and
- the terms and conditions governing repatriation.

If there is any change in any of the particulars required by the Employment Information Act, the employer must, within one month after the change, provide the employee with an additional written statement setting out the changes.

The Unfair Dismissals Act, 1977, requires the employer, not later than 28 days from the commencement of employment, to give the employee a written copy of the procedure that the employer must follow if the employee is going to be dismissed. The procedure should follow the Code of Practice on Grievance and Disciplinary Procedures published by the Department of Enterprise, Trade, and Employment.[33]

Under the Payment of Wages Act, 1991, all employees are entitled to a written statement, showing the gross wages payable and the nature and amount of any deductions, at the time of payment, or as soon as possible after a credit transfer.[34]

Employees or their representatives also are entitled to information where collective redundancies are proposed,[35] where there is a transfer of an undertaking,[36] and pursuant to health and safety legislation.[37]

---

[32]Employment Information Act §4.

[33]Industrial Relations Act, 1990 (Code of Practice on Grievance and Disciplinary Procedures) (Declaration) Order, S.I. 146 (2000).

[34]See V.A.2.c., below.

[35]See IV.A.1.c.i., below.

[36]See IV.B.3., below.

[37]See VII.A.3.c., below.

b. Implied Terms

Certain terms automatically are implied into all contracts of employment, whether the contract is in writing or otherwise. For example, under the Employment Equality Act, 1998, all contracts of employment contain implied equal pay and nondiscrimination clauses.[38]

c. Contract Changes

A distinction must be drawn between provisions that constitute terms and conditions, as opposed to work practices or procedures. Although the former may not be changed without the employee's consent, the latter may. However, the distinction between the two in certain cases can be very blurred, particularly where a collective agreement deals with a whole range of issues, including working practices.

Neither party to the employment contract may vary the terms and conditions, even by consent, if the variation is by virtue of a transfer within the meaning of the EU Transfer of Undertaking Regulations.[39]

2. Incorporation of Terms in a Collective Agreement[40]

The terms of a collective agreement, either in whole or in part, can, in certain circumstances, be incorporated into an individual contract of employment. The terms can be incorporated expressly, either by virtue of a written employment contract between the employer and the employee, or on the basis that the parties to a collective agreement intended the whole or part of the individual contract to be legally binding, and the union side concluded the agreement with the authority of its affected members (so as to comply with the principles of agency).

Contract terms also can be incorporated by implication. Of significance in determining incorporation is the nature of the terms,

---

[38]See VI.A.3., below.

[39]Wilson v. St. Helens Borough Council, [1996] I.R.L.R. 320; Meade v. British Fuels Ltd., [1997] I.R.L.R. 505 (C.A. H.L.). For a discussion of the EU Transfer of Undertakings Regulations, see IV.B., below.

[40]*See generally* Kevin Costello BL, Sources of the Contract of Employment, Lecture at University College, Dublin (Oct. 1999).

such that terms that normally are regarded as fundamental in the individual employment contract, such as hours of work, sick leave pay, etc., are incorporated more readily than those that simply deal with work practices or procedures, or that go solely to regulating the relationship between the employer and the trade union. Implied incorporation occurs where it is shown that there is a custom or practice to incorporate the terms of the collective agreement into the individual contract or where incorporation is necessary to give efficacy to the individual contract.

In general contract law, the principle of privity prevents a contract between two parties from binding a third party. Based on this principle, a collective agreement made between an employer and a trade union should not be incorporated automatically into individual employment contracts. In fact, in Irish labor law, it is well established that a trade union is not per se the agent of its employee members,[41] and, therefore, collective agreements do not become part of the employment contract automatically. Nonetheless, the terms of a collective agreement may become part of an individual employment contract where the union is expressly authorized to act as the negotiating agent of its members. In these cases, it has been held that the particular terms agreed to by the employer and the union should be incorporated into the employment contracts because they were negotiated by the employees' agents.[42] Similarly, a collective agreement negotiated by a union may form part of the employees' terms by operation of an estoppel or ratification.

One other approach favored by some employers is to insert a clause in the individual contract whereby the employee accepts any collective agreement as being part of the employment contract.[43] Often, an employer may include in the written employment Statement[44] a provision that all collective agreements will

---

[41]*See* Goulding Chems. Ltd. v. Bolger, [1977] I.R. 211, 231 (Ir. H. Ct., O'Higgins, C.J.) (membership in an association like a union should not bind all members individually to the terms of a collective agreement merely because the agreement was made by the union).

[42]O'Rourke v. Talbot Motors Ltd., [1984] I.L.R.M. 587 (Ir. H. Ct.).

[43]*See* NCB v. Galley, [1958] 1 W.L.R. 16 (Ir. H. Ct.) (employee deemed to have given advance consent was bound by whatever terms the employer would negotiate with employees' union).

[44]See I.B.1.a., above.

form part of the contract; in the absence of an immediate objection from the employee, the collective agreement generally will become binding.[45] Clearly, this approach would avoid any privity issue. Other collective agreements simply may formalize a custom and practice within the particular occupation or industry and so become a term of the contract.[46]

Conversely, if the employer is a limited company, in certain circumstances a collective agreement may not be legally binding on the employer and so will not be incorporated into employees' individual employment contracts. For example, where the subject of the collective agreement goes beyond the purposes or objects of the company, it will be deemed ultra vires and unenforceable under company law. Similarly, any agreement negotiated in breach of the employer company's articles of association will be unenforceable.[47] In these cases, even where the union may be authorized to contract for the employees, the violation of company law requirements would render the terms nonbinding.

C. Employee Dismissal[48]

1. Notice Periods

If an employer or employee wishes to end the employment contract, the party must give notice, unless the employer is entitled to dismiss the employee summarily for gross misconduct, or the employee is entitled to act as constructively dismissed.

At common law, in the absence of an express provision dealing with notice, there is an implied term in every contract of employment that it can be terminated by giving reasonable notice, unless there are grounds justifying summary termination. What is reasonable notice depends on the circumstances of the case. An

---

[45]*See* Camden Exhibition Ltd. v. Lynott, [1966] 1 Q.B. 55 (considering a UK equivalent of an Employment Information Act provision).

[46]Edwards v. Skyways Ltd., [1964] 1 All E.R. 494 (Eng. H. Ct.).

[47]*See* Kenny v. An Post, [1988] I.R. 285 (Ir. H. Ct.) (holding certain agreed terms on rest periods unenforceable on grounds that the personnel manager who negotiated the terms had not been authorized to bind company to the agreement).

[48]*See generally* ANTHONY KERR, TERMINATION OF EMPLOYMENT STATUTES (Sweet & Maxwell 1995).

employee who is paid weekly may be entitled to only a week's notice, while an employee who is paid monthly may be entitled to at least a month's notice, although the payment interval will be only one factor. Some employees may be entitled to notice of three months', six months', or even longer, depending on seniority, length of service, and other factors. The High Court has, on occasion, held that 12 months' notice was appropriate.[49]

Currently, the minimum periods of employer and employee notice are set out by statute in the Minimum Notice and Terms of Employment Act, 1973 (Minimum Notice Act). The requirements of the Minimum Notice Act do not apply either to full-time or part-time employees who have been in continuous service for fewer than 13 weeks prior to termination.

a. Employer Notice

The statutory minimum periods of notice that must be given by an employer are based on the employee's length of continuous service. These periods are as follows:

Continuous Service	*Minimum Notice*
13 weeks–2 years	1 week
2–5 years	2 weeks
5–10 years	4 weeks
10–15 years	6 weeks
15 years or more	8 weeks

The law provides that an employee is entitled to the longer of contractual notice or statutory minimum notice as set out in the Minimum Notice Act. On termination of employment, an employee may waive his or her right to notice and accept payment in lieu of notice. Failing that, unless the employment contract expressly allows the employer to make a payment in lieu of notice, or to put

[49]Carvill v. Irish Indus. Bank Ltd., [1968] I.R. 325 (Ir. H. Ct.) (managing director of bank); *see also* Lyons v. M F Kent & Co., [1996] E.L.R. 103 (Ir. H. Ct.) (12-months' notice necessary based on plaintiff's status, level of responsibility, professional qualifications, and requirement that he work abroad).

the employee on "garden leave"[50] during the notice period, the employee is entitled to stay on and be paid during the notice period, even if there is no work for the employee to do. In addition, during the notice period, the employee is entitled to normal pay and other rights, such as sick leave, pension contributions, or use of a company car, on the basis that the employee is available and willing to work, even though work may not be provided.

b. Employee Notice

An employee is obliged by the Minimum Notice Act to give the employer only one week's notice, irrespective of the length of the employee's service.

c. Exceptions to Notice Requirement

In Irish employment law, an employee may be dismissed summarily if the employee is found guilty of such serious misconduct so as to constitute a repudiation of the contract at common law. In order for a summary dismissal to be upheld, either in court or by the EAT, the employer must satisfy a very high burden of proof, as well as show that the dismissal was carried out in accordance with the terms of the contract. Typical examples of gross misconduct that would provide for summary dismissal under a contract of employment would include dishonesty, fraud, or theft; being under the influence of alcohol or illegal substances during work hours; conviction of a criminal offense (although this usually excludes offenses under the Road Traffic Acts); misuse of company property or confidential information, etc. In one EAT decision, a summary dismissal arising out of a drug-related offense was justified on the grounds that the relationship of trust and confidence had clearly broken down between the parties.[51] In another case,[52] the managing director of a bank had a new carpet installed in his home

---

[50]Whereas an employer normally is obliged to provide an employee with work, a "garden leave" clause exempts the employer from this obligation. It usually is put into effect during an employee's notice period as a means of delaying the employee's departure to a competitor, while at the same time preventing the employee from using his or her position to gather confidential information and such from the original employer.

[51]Owen v. Superquinn Ltd. (1982), UD932/1982.

[52]Carvill v. Irish Indus. Bank, [1968] I.R. 325 (Ir. S.C., O'Keeffe, J.).

at the company's expense. He was dismissed without notice and claimed wrongful dismissal and payment of his notice. The court stated that certain breaches of contract are so serious that they inherently repudiate the contract. In such circumstances, it is the employee who ends the contract and precipitates such summary dismissal. However, in that case, the court held that the misuse of company expenses was not sufficient to justify summary dismissal, and a 12-month notice period was awarded.

In a similar case,[53] the plaintiff director had been working with a competitor, a fact that he did not disclose to his employer. He also had work done for his own benefit through the company, for which he made no payment. The plaintiff's contract defined misconduct as "conduct so serious as to damage the interests of the company." The court ruled that, on the facts, the plaintiff's conduct did not represent such conduct as to seriously damage the company. The court thus felt that, although the conduct was misconduct in the general sense, it was not such as to justify summary dismissal under the contract.

2. *Wrongful and Unfair Dismissal*[54]

Termination of the employment relationship may give rise to a civil court action where there has been a breach of contract or a violation of the principles of natural or constitutional justice. Alternatively, a dismissed employee may have a statutory claim under the Unfair Dismissals Act, 1977 and 1993, the Employment Equality Act, 1998,[55] or, in the case of a dismissal by reason of redundancy, the Redundancy Payments Acts, 1967 to 1991.[56]

It is important to distinguish wrongful dismissal from unfair dismissal. Wrongful dismissal essentially is an action for breach of contract. Unfair dismissal is a statutory remedy that exists notwithstanding provisions of the contract. Thus, even where the employee has no claim for wrongful dismissal, a claim for unfair dismissal still may arise. Both are discussed in greater detail below.

---

[53]Glover v. BLN, [1973] I.R. 389 (Ir. H. Ct., Kenny, J.).

[54]*See generally* MARY REDMOND, DISMISSAL LAW IN IRELAND (Butterworths 1998).

[55]See VI.A.3., below.

[56]See IV.A.2.a., below.

Contractual rights are governed by the terms and conditions contained in the contract of employment where such terms and conditions are express (written or oral), or implied. The fact that there is no written employment contract, or even any statement of terms and conditions of employment as required by the Employment Information Act,[57] does not mean that no contract of employment exists. Common law rights arising from the employment contract are enforceable in proceedings claiming wrongful dismissal (where the primary claim of the employee will be for damages) or seeking a declaration that termination of the employment contract is null and void, either as a breach of contract, or for some fundamental procedural irregularity that violates the terms of an express disciplinary procedure or the principles of natural or constitutional justice.

Although the Irish courts, in a similar fashion to their UK counterparts, will not grant an order for specific performance of a contract of service, they are much more amenable to granting interlocutory injunctive relief either to restrain an employer from proceeding with a dismissal or to require the employer to continue paying the employee's normal remuneration until the matter can be heard.[58]

For higher paid executives, High Court proceedings for wrongful dismissal are more common than claims for unfair dismissal before the EAT.[59] This occurs because executives may be entitled to lengthy contractual notice periods involving potentially substantial damages, or, perhaps more importantly, the use of an interlocutory injunction application may be used as a tactic to persuade the employer to more quickly negotiate a much higher level of compensation than might be the case if the matter went to the EAT.

A further distinction concerns time limits. An employee must present an unfair dismissal claim within six months of the date of termination. However, a claim for wrongful dismissal may be

---

[57]See I.B.1.a., above.

[58]This type of interlocutory injunction commonly is known as a *Fennelly* Order, following the leading Irish decision in this area. See I.C.2.b., below.

[59]See the Introduction, at D.2.d., above.

brought within six years, which is the normal limitation period in a breach of contract claim. The EAT normally will hear a case within three months of referral (although it may take another three months before its determination issues), whereas claims in the High Court may take anywhere from six months to two years to go to trial, depending on the urgency of the case and whether an interlocutory order has been made.

a. Wrongful Dismissal

Where an employee dismissal is in breach of contract, for example, because the employer does not give the appropriate notice or does not follow fair procedures in effecting the dismissal, it is known as a wrongful dismissal. The majority of employment contracts are of indefinite duration, terminable by either party on giving either the notice expressly provided for in the contract or, in the absence of an express notice provision, the reasonable notice period implied by the court. Once notice, either express or implied, is given, the contract has been honored, and no breach of contract or wrongful dismissal claim should arise.

Alternatively, an employee could bring a wrongful dismissal claim on the basis of a constructive dismissal. If an employer behaves in a manner that clearly evidences an intent not to be bound by one or more fundamental terms of the contract, then the employee is entitled to accept that repudiatory breach, resign, and claim constructive dismissal. Likewise, as with any contract, an employment contract only may be varied with both parties' consent. If the employer attempts to impose unilaterally a variation of a fundamental term of the contract, this would entitle the employee to resign and claim constructive dismissal. Finally, if the employer behaves so unreasonably toward the employee that no reasonable employee would be expected to continue the employment relationship, and in those circumstances resigns, then again, a claim for constructive dismissal would lie.

The employee's normal remedy for the employer's breach of contract is to sue for damages, usually in either the Circuit Court or the High Court, depending on the level of damages claimed.[60]

---

[60]See the Introduction, at D.1., above.

Damages are calculated so as to put the employee in the position he or she would have been in had the contract been properly performed.[61] Usually, this will involve assessing the employee's loss over a period equal to the required notice period. Where a contract is for a fixed term and is terminated unlawfully prior to expiration, damages would represent the salary and benefits the employee would have earned up to the expiration date. Under common law, an employee is under a duty to mitigate and, therefore, must take reasonable steps to seek alternative employment.

b. Interlocutory Injunctions

In Irish employment law, it is established that a court will refuse to order specific performance of personal service contracts, which long have been regarded as possessing fundamentally different characteristics from commercial "arms length" contracts.[62] One of the factors that distinguishes employment contracts is the requirement that mutual trust and confidence must exist between the parties for the relationship to continue. In circumstances where either the employee or employer no longer wishes to maintain the relationship, a court is unlikely to compel them to stay together. However, this rule is not absolute.[63] An application for an interlocutory injunction of this nature will only be allowed in dismissal-related claims that are brought before either the Circuit Court or, more frequently, the High Court. An employee's right to claim unfair dismissal derives from statute;[64] accordingly, this common law interlocutory remedy is not available from the Employment Appeals Tribunal.

In order to secure an interlocutory injunction in any cause of action, a plaintiff must show the following:

---

[61]However, see *Phelan v. BIC (Ireland) Ltd.*, [1997] E.L.R. 208 (Ir. H. Ct., Costello, J.), in which the court considered that Mr. Phelan, in an interlocutory application for an injunction to restrain his dismissal, had made out a prima facie case for exemplary damages, which have not normally been awarded in dismissal cases.

[62]*See* Yeates v. Minister for Posts and Telegraphs, [1978] I.L.R.M. 22 (Ir. H. Ct.).

[63]In *Hill v. C.A. Parsons & Co. Ltd.*, [1972] Ch. 305, 314, the English Court of Appeal (Lord Denning) stated that "the rule is not inflexible. It permits of exceptions. The court can, in a proper case, grant a declaration that the relationship still subsists and an injunction to stop the master treating it as at an end," and further, "it may be said that, by granting an injunction in such a case, the court is indirectly enforcing specifically a contract for personal services. So be it."

[64]See I.C.2.c., below.

- that he has a stateable case, and there is a serious issue to be tried;
- that the balance of convenience favors the granting of an injunction; and
- that the case is one where damages would not be an adequate remedy.[65]

The most important Irish High Court decision in the area of employment-related injunctions is *Fennelly v. Assicurazioni Generali S.P.A.*[66] In *Fennelly*, the defendant employer purported to dismiss the plaintiff by reason of redundancy. The plaintiff claimed that he was employed under a fixed-term contract for a period of 12 years and that the defendant was not entitled to terminate the contract any earlier. The High Court held that there was a fair question for trial. On the issue of the balance of convenience, the court held that "the plaintiff (would) be left without a salary and nothing to live on," that the balance of convenience was in the plaintiff's favor, and that it would be unjust to leave him in a situation where he would "be virtually destitute with only a prospect of damages" pending the trial of the action. In view of these "very special circumstances," the court ordered the defendant to pay the plaintiff's salary and bonus until the trial of the action.[67]

---

[65]Campus Oil Ltd. v. Minister for Energy, [1983] I.R. 88 (Ir. H. Ct.); American Cyanamid Ltd. v. Ethicon Ltd., [1975] A.C. 396, 408 (C.A.).

[66][1985] 3 I.L.T.R. 73 (Ir. H. Ct., Costello, J.).

[67]*Id.* at 74. In his decision, Mr. Justice Costello stated:

> I accept that the court should not require an employer to take on an employee where serious difficulties have arisen between them or where there is no work for the employee but in this case the parties have obviously the highest regard for one another. I will take an undertaking that the plaintiff will be prepared to carry out such duties as the defendant will ask of him until the trial. If they would make use of him until the trial of the action, the plaintiff should attend and carry out such duties as they give him. They might prefer not to give him any duties and put him on leave of absence. That is for the defendant but they must continue to pay his salary until the trial.

Id. This decision was followed in *Shortt v. Data Packaging Ltd.*, [1994] E.L.R. 251 (Ir. H. Ct.), and in *Phelan v. BIC (Ireland) Ltd.*, [1997] E.L.R. 208 (Ir. H. Ct.). *See also* Harte v. Kelly, [1997] E.L.R. 125 (Ir. H. Ct.); Boland v. Phoenix Shannon Plc., [1997] E.L.R. 113 (Ir. H. Ct.); Courtenay v. Radio 2000 Ltd. (Ir. H. Ct., July 2, 1997) (unreported decision); Doyle v. Grangeford Precast Concrete Ltd., [1997] E.L.R. 260 (Ir. H. Ct.).

c. *Unfair Dismissal*[68]

The Unfair Dismissals Act, 1977 and 1993 (UDA), vests in all employees to which it applies an entitlement to redress for unfair dismissal in the form of compensation, reinstatement, or re-engagement unless the employer can establish that the dismissal was not unfair.

In general, the UDA applies to all persons engaged under a valid employment contract or apprenticeship, who have more than one year of continuous service with the employer,[69] who have not reached the normal retirement age (66 years) or the contractual retirement age, and who work more than eight hours per week.

A dismissal within the meaning of the UDA occurs in the following circumstances:

> (i) on the termination by the employer of the employee's contract of employment, whether prior notice was or was not given, and
>
> (ii) on the termination by the employee of his contract of employment, whether prior notice was or was not given to the employer, in circumstances in which, because of the conduct of the employer, the employee was or would have been entitled, or it was, or would have been, reasonable for the employee to terminate the contract of employment without prior notice of the termination to the employer.[70]

An employee claiming unfair dismissal must refer the claim within six months of the date of the purported dismissal either to a Rights Commissioner or the EAT.[71] There is a discretion to extend the notice period for up to 12 months from the date of the dismissal, if the EAT is satisfied that "exceptional circumstances prevented the giving of the notice" within the six-month period.

Although the onus is on the employee to establish a dismissal within the meaning of the UDA, once dismissal is established, the employer, in order to escape liability, must show that there were

---

[68] *See generally* DECLAN MADDEN & ANTHONY KERR, UNFAIR DISMISSAL, CASES AND COMMENTARY (Irish Bus. & Employers Confederation 2d ed. 1998).

[69] Certain discriminatory dismissals are excepted from this one-year requirement. *See* Unfair Dismissals (Amendment) Act, 1993, §14.

[70] S.I. 1977 Act.

[71] See the Introduction, at D.2., above.

substantial grounds justifying the dismissal, or that the dismissal resulted wholly or mainly from one or more of the following factors:

- the capability, competence, or qualifications of the employee for performing work of the kind for which he was employed by the employer;
- the conduct of the employee (e.g., refusal to follow reasonable instructions, unjustified absence from work, a breach of the employer's rules, unauthorized use of property, non-cooperation with the reasonable reorganization plans of the employer, etc.);
- redundancy; or
- the employment having been prohibited by statute.

Dismissals for any of the following reasons automatically are deemed to be unfair:

- membership or proposed membership in a trade union, or activities on behalf of a trade union;
- religious or political beliefs;
- involvement in civil or criminal proceedings against the employer, whether as a claimant or witness;
- race or color;
- pregnancy, unless the employee thereby is precluded from adequately performing her usual work function and there is no available suitable alternative work function for her;
- selection for redundancy for one of the reasons specified immediately above, or selection in contravention of an agreed selection procedure or a procedure established by custom and practice, where there are no special reasons justifying departure from the agreed or established procedure;
- sexual orientation;
- age; or
- membership in the "traveling community."[72]

[72]The "traveling community" is not defined in legislation, but it is a term that refers to a distinct group of non-settled Irish people who lead an itinerant lifestyle.

In all circumstances, employees are entitled to constitutional due process and procedural fairness. The principles of natural justice must be observed.[73] Accordingly, reasonable procedures must be adopted, such as the giving of warnings, an opportunity for the employee to present his or her case, and a proper and fair investigation into the circumstances leading to the dismissal.

The UDA provides the following alternative remedies to employees who have been unfairly dismissed:

- *Reinstatement*: the re-employment of the employee in the same position as if no dismissal had taken place, with compensation for lost benefits, no loss of rights, and identical terms and conditions of employment;
- *Re-engagement*: the re-employment of the employee, with no compensation for loss of benefits, although not necessarily in the same position or on identical terms; or
- *Compensation*: limited to an amount not exceeding 104 weeks' gross remuneration, including overtime and all benefits in-kind.

A provision in an agreement that purports to exclude or limit the application of, or is inconsistent with, any provision of the UDA is void and unenforceable. The provisions of the UDA may apply notwithstanding the choice of a foreign governing law clause in an employment contract, where the employee is domiciled, resident, or the ordinary place of employment is in Ireland.

D. Atypical Workers

1. Young Persons

The Protection of Young Persons (Employment) Act, 1996 (PYPEA), incorporates the provisions of the 1994 EU Directive concerning the protection of young people at work (Young Persons Directive).[74] The Young Persons Directive covers two classes of individuals: children and young persons.

---

[73]See the Introduction, at B.1., above.

[74]Council Directive 94/33/EC, 1994 O.J. (L 216) 12.

a. Children

A child for the purposes of the PYPEA means a person who is younger than 16 years of age or the school leaving age, whichever is higher. The school leaving age is the minimum age at which compulsory full-time schooling ends, which currently is age 16, under the Education (Welfare) Act, 2000.

The PYPEA prohibits an employer from employing a child, except in certain circumstances. For example, the ETE Minister may, by license, authorize in individual cases the employment of a child in what is described by the PYPEA as "cultural, artistic, sports or advertising activities which are not likely to be harmful to the safety, health or development of the child and which are not likely to interfere with the child's attendance at school, vocational guidance or training programmes or capacity to benefit from the instructions received."[75]

Exceptions also are made for children older than age 14 to do light work outside the school term or for those older than age 15 to do light work during the school term. Additional exceptions are recognized for the employment of a child older than 14 years of age who is a full-time student in an institute of secondary education, where the employment is part of a program of work experience or education. An employer also may employ a child older than age 15 to participate in a training or work experience program, as approved by the Minister or FAS[76] (the state training and employment agency).

b. Young Persons[77]

The PYPEA prohibits the employment of a young person to perform any work, except under certain specified conditions.[78]

---

[75]Protection of Young Persons (Employment) Act, 1996 (PYPEA), §3(2). The PYPEA also places hours and rest period restrictions on the employment of children. For a summary of these restrictions, see V.C.6., below.

[76]Foras Aiseanna Saothair, a Gaelic language abbreviation.

[77]For the purposes of the PYPEA, a "young person" is defined as a "person who has reached 16 years of age or the school leaving age (whichever is higher) but is less than 18 years of age." 1996 S.I. (I). At present, the school leaving age is 16.

[78]See V.C.6., below.

2. *Part-Time Workers*

The Protection of Employees (Part-Time Work) Act, 2001 (PTWA), which implements the provisions of the EU Part-Time Work Directive,[79] set out below, went into effect on December 20, 2001. The PTWA provides that part-time employees[80] may not be treated less favorably than comparable full-time employees with respect to their conditions of employment, unless objective grounds exist to justify the difference in treatment. A "part-time employee" is defined by the PTWA as "an employee whose normal hours of work are less than the normal hours of work of an employee who is a comparable employee in relation to him or her."[81] Casual workers are included as part-time workers under the PTWA.

Objective grounds that will justify less favorable treatment under the PTWA must be based on a consideration other than the part-time nature of the employment and must be intended to achieve a legitimate objective of the employer and be necessary for that purpose.[82] With respect to casual workers, it is acknowledged that there may be objective reasons for treating them differently from regular full-time workers. Therefore, a ground that may not justify different treatment of regular part-time workers may, nonetheless, be considered an objective ground justifying different treatment of casual workers.[83]

The PTWA abolishes the previous minimum threshold of eight hours per week that had to be satisfied before part-time employees could rely on many of the provisions of protective employment legislation. Under the new legislation, a part-time employee will now enjoy the right to claim unfair dismissal, and receive the benefit of statutory redundancy payments and statutory minimum notice, irrespective of what hours they work each week. However, the PTWA does not apply to pension rights of employees whose normal hours of work constitute less than 20 percent of the normal

---

[79]Council Directive 97/81/EC, 1998 O.J. (L 14) 9.

[80]The Part-Time Work Act applies to posted workers and to other employees working within Ireland, regardless of their nationality or place of residence. See IX.B., below.

[81]Protection of Employees (Part-Time Work) Act, 2001, §7(1).

[82]*Id.* §12(1).

[83]*Id.* §12(2).

hours of work for a comparable full-time employee. If the full-time and part-time employees are involved in similar work such that they are deemed "comparable" for the purposes of the legislation, the employer will not be obliged to provide pension scheme membership or contributions to such part-time employees if they work less than 20 percent of the hours of the comparable full-time employee. The distinction is not 20 percent of the normal working hours for the organization, but 20 percent of the normal working hours of the comparable full-time employee.

The Part-Time Work Directive applies to part-time employees engaged in atypical work. Atypical work in this context includes part-time workers, agency workers, job sharers, fixed-term contracts, etc. Part-time employees are defined as those whose hours (calculated on an average over a one-year period) are less than those of a comparable full-time employee. Although this definition is quite broad, it is limited by reference to a comparable full-time employee. For this purpose, "comparable" means the full-time employee is engaged in similar work, with similar seniority, qualifications, and skills. Part-time workers within the meaning of the Part-Time Work Directive do not include casual employees. However, the exclusion of casual employees must be reviewed periodically by the ETE Minister to establish that there are objective reasons to justify their continued exclusion.

The purpose of the Part-Time Work Directive is to prohibit discrimination against part-time employees. In implementing this objective, the Part-Time Work Directive places one clear, definitive obligation on employers: that a worker's refusal to transfer from full-time to part-time work or vice-versa may not be used, in and of itself, as a valid reason for termination of employment. Additional employer obligations are somewhat more limited. For example, the Part-Time Work Directive provides that part-time workers should not be treated in a less favorable manner than comparable full-time workers solely because they work part-time, unless different treatment is justified on objective grounds. Also, access to particular conditions of employment may be made subject to a period of service, time worked, or earnings qualification, where justified by objective reasons.

Under the provisions of the Part-Time Work Directive, employers also should give consideration to the following:

- requests by workers to transfer from full-time to part-time work, and vice versa;
- providing information on the availability of part-time and full-time positions in the establishment, so as to facilitate transfers from full-time to part-time work;
- facilitating access of part-time workers to skilled and managerial positions and to vocational training to enhance career opportunities; and
- providing appropriate information to employee representatives about part-time work in the enterprise.

3. *Agency Workers*

An agency worker is one who agrees with an employment agency to do work or carry out a service for a third person (the hiring company). Generally, agency workers are not regarded as employees of the hiring company and, accordingly, have very few statutory employment rights directly against the hiring company. However, any employer doing business in Ireland that wishes to use the services of an employment agency should be aware that the use of agency workers may not relieve it of all the normal statutory obligations that employers have to employees, particularly where the agency worker is paid directly by the company (the so-called deemed employee).

a. *Employment Agencies*

Employment agencies in Ireland must comply with the provisions of the Employment Agency Act, 1971 (Employment Agency Act), and the regulations prescribed thereunder. The Employment Agency Act defines the business of an employment agency as "the business of seeking, whether for reward or otherwise, on behalf of others, persons who will give or accept employment, and includes the obtaining or supplying for reward of persons who will accept employment from or render services to others."[84]

---

[84]Employment Agency Act, 1971, §27.

The Employment Agency Act prohibits any person from carrying on the business of an employment agency unless they have a license under the Act.

b. Unfair Dismissal

The Unfair Dismissals (Amendment) Act, 1993, allows agency workers to bring unfair dismissal claims against the hiring company. Under section 13 of the 1993 Act, persons who are employed through the medium of an employment agency (within the meaning of the Employment Agency Act) are deemed to be employees of the hiring company for purposes of a dismissal occurring after the commencement of work.[85] Therefore, any redress awarded to the worker under the UDA will be awarded against the hiring company whether or not the hiring company is a party to the contract between the employment agency and the worker, and whether or not the hiring company pays the wages or salary of the worker. The UDA generally will apply, however, only where the worker has been in the service of the hiring company for longer than one year.

c. Payment of Wages

In the event that the hiring company pays the wages of the agency worker (as opposed to paying a fee to the employment agency for the worker's services), certain other important statutory provisions will apply. The first is the Payment of Wages Act, 1991 (PWA),[86] which, for purposes of the PWA, defines a "contract of employment" as follows:

(a) a contract of service or apprenticeship; and

(b) any other contract whereby an individual agrees with another person to do or perform personally any work or service for a third

---

[85]Because §13 applies to persons employed through the medium of an employment agency within the meaning of the Employment Agency Act, its scope extends beyond what probably was intended to include workers supplied by companies that are not licensed employment agencies. *See* Bourton v. Narcea Ltd., U.D. 186/94 (EAT).

[86]For additional discussion of the Payment of Wages Act, 1991 (PWA), see V.A.2., below.

> person (whether or not the third person is a party to the contract) whose status by virtue of the contract is not that of a client or a customer of any profession or business undertaking carried on by the individual, the person who is liable to pay the wages of the individual in respect of the work or service shall be deemed for the purposes of this Act to be his employer, whether the contract is express or implied and if express, whether it is oral or in writing.

Based on this definition, if the "third person" (hiring company) proposes to pay the agency worker directly, it will be the employer for purposes of the PWA. Three main consequences arise from this relationship:

- the mode of payment of wages must comply with section 2 of the PWA;
- the hiring company must provide to the worker concerned a statement of wages and deductions from wages, as required by section 4 of the PWA; and
- no deductions may be made from wages except under the circumstances specified in section 5 of the PWA.

d. Maternity Protection

The second area of legislation that potentially could apply to agency workers is the Maternity Protection Act, 1994 (the MPA),[87] which defines a contract of employment in a fashion similar to that found in the PWA. The employer for purposes of the MPA again is deemed to be the person who is liable to pay the employee's wages. A hiring company that falls within the statutory definition would have to comply with all provisions of the MPA, as if it were the employer. This would mean, for example, that a female employee would be entitled to be paid for absences from work due to pre- or postnatal care. In addition, if a female worker were entitled to health and safety leave, the hiring company would be obligated to pay her for the first three weeks of this leave.

Following on the recommendations of the Working Group on the Review and Improvement of Maternity Protection Legisla-

---

[87]For a complete discussion of the Maternity Protection Act, 1994 (MPA), see V.D.3., below.

tion, the Maternity Protection (Amendment) Bill, 2003, has been published. The bill proposes a number of changes to existing arrangements for prenatal, maternity, and postnatal needs.[88]

e. Additional Employer Obligations

The Organization of Working Time Act, 1997 (OWTA),[89] defines a contract of employment in a manner similar to that in the PWA and the MPA. Thus, the party that is liable to pay the wages of the worker with respect to the particular work or service will be deemed to be the employer and, therefore, will have to comply with all obligations set out in the OWTA. Similar provisions are contained in the Employment Equality Act, 1998.[90]

f. Agency Obligations

The Terms of Employment (Information) Act, 1994, requires the employment agency to furnish agency workers with a statement of particulars containing specified terms and conditions of employment.[91]

4. Fixed-Term Workers

The Protection of Employees (Fixed-Term Work) Act 2003 (FTWA) provides that a fixed-term employee cannot be treated in a less favorable manner than a comparable permanent employee in relation to conditions of employment, unless such treatment can be justified on objective grounds. This can be seen in the area of pensions, as the FTWA specifically states that a fixed-term employee may be treated less favorably than a comparable permanent employee in relation to any pension scheme or arrangement when his or her normal work hours constitute less than 20 percent of the normal work hours of the comparable permanent employee. This provision does not prevent an employer and a fixed-term employee from entering into an agreement whereby the employee

---

[88]See V.D.3.a., below.

[89]For a complete discussion of the Organization of Working Time Act, 1997 (OWTA), see V.C., below.

[90]See VI.A.3., below.

[91]See I.B.1.a., above.

may receive the same pension benefits as a comparable permanent employee.

In general, the FTWA applies to any fixed-term employee working under a contract of employment or apprenticeship. The FTWA does not apply to agency workers placed by an employment agency at the disposition of a user enterprise, but does apply to agency workers employed directly by an employment agency. The term fixed-term employee means a person who has entered into a contract of employment with an employer where the end of the contract is determined by an objective condition, such as arriving at a specific date, completing a specific task, or the occurrence of a specific event. The FTWA provides that a fixed-term employee shall be informed in writing by the employer as soon as practicable of the objective condition determining the contract.

Equally, the FTWA provides that where an employer proposes to renew a fixed-term contract the employee shall be informed in writing, not later than the date of renewal, of the objective grounds justifying the renewal of the fixed-term contract and the reason why a contract of indefinite duration is not being offered. The FTWA further provides that the written statements referred to in this paragraph are admissible as evidence in any proceedings under the Act. The FTWA also provides that a Rights Commissioner or the Labor Court may draw any inference considered just and equitable if it appears that (1) an employer failed to provide a written statement, or (2) a written statement is evasive or equivocal.

Once a fixed-term contract employee completes or has completed three years of continuous employment with his or her employer or associated employer on the expiration of such contract, the employer may renew the contract for a fixed term on one further occasion only, and that renewal may be for a period of no longer than one year. Where such an employee is employed by the employer or associated employer on two or more continuous fixed-term contracts, the aggregate duration of those contracts combined may not exceed four years. However, it appears from the legislation, though not specifically expressed, that it is still permissible for an employee to be retained on one single contract for a fixed term in excess of four years, provided it is the first such contract. Where a term of an employment contract purports to limit the term of the employment contract of either category of employee mentioned above, in contravention of the above rules, that term shall be void and of no effect and the contract concerned shall be deemed to be one of indefinite duration, i.e., a permanent contract. The above-mentioned rules do not apply where there are objective grounds justifying the renewal of a contract of employment for a fixed term only. However, in practice this may be difficult to establish, and in the absence of any judicial consideration of this requirement at this point, it is difficult to assess just how flexible this exception is.

The FTWA provides that in order for a fixed-term employee to have the same opportunity as other employees to secure a permanent position, an employer shall inform the employee about relevant vacancies that occur in the undertaking. This information may be provided by means of a general announcement at a suitable place in the employee's place of employment. However, as regards access by a fixed-term employee to appropriate training opportunities, the FTWA provides that such access shall be provided by an employer as far as practicable.

E. Privacy

In Ireland, as in many nations, the sources of the right to privacy, and more specifically the right to workplace privacy, are subtle but numerous. However, when these sources are aggregated, there is no doubt that excessive or unreasonable invasions of workplace privacy constitute a legal wrong under Irish law.

1. *Sources*

a. Fundamental Rights

An individual's right to privacy is recognized in the European Convention for the Protection of Human Rights and Fundamental Freedoms (ECHR).[92] Specifically, Article 8 of the ECHR provides for an individual's "right to respect for his private and

---

[92]See I.C. in the chapter on the European Union in Part 1 of Volume I.

family life, his home and his correspondence." Notably, this provision does not grant a right to privacy, but a right to respect for privacy. Also, the right to privacy under the ECHR is not absolute and may be restricted in order to protect other parties' interests and rights.

Ireland has now implemented the ECHR.[93] In addition, Ireland has established a Human Rights Commission to provide further protection for human rights. The Commission was created by the Human Rights Commission Act, 2000, in part, for the purpose of protecting certain of the rights established under the Belfast Agreement.[94]

b. The Constitution

The Irish Constitution has been interpreted as recognizing an implied right to privacy in Article 40.3.1. This general right to privacy was successfully invoked before the High Court in *Kennedy and Arnold v. Ireland*,[95] where the plaintiffs complained that the state had tapped their telephones without justification and sought damages for this alleged breach of privacy. The Court, finding in favor of the plaintiffs, held that the right to privacy is a fundamental personal right. However, the Court recognized that the right to privacy may be qualified by the constitutional rights of others and the requirements of the common good, and is subject to the requirements of public order and morality. Thus, in any particular case, the courts will seek to balance any interference with the right to privacy against other rights and interests.

The Irish High Court previously has ruled that individuals have a constitutional right not to have private information about them disclosed.[96] Therefore, an employer that seeks information

---

[93]European Convention on Human Rights Act, 2003.

[94]The Belfast Agreement, which was signed on April 10, 1998 (a Good Friday), sets up a system of governance within Northern Ireland and addresses the relationship between the Republic of Ireland and Northern Ireland, as well as the relationship between both parts of Ireland and the United Kingdom. Among other things, the Belfast Agreement recognizes principles of equality and human rights, including the right of free political thought, the right to freedom of religion, the right to equal opportunity in all social and economic activity, the right to freedom from harassment, and the right of women to full and equal political participation.

[95]Kennedy v. Ireland, [1987] I.R. 576.

[96]Murphy v. PMPA, [1978] I.L.R.M. 25.

about a prospective employee risks infringing the prospective employee's constitutional right to privacy.

The issue of whether the constitutional right of privacy will permit surveillance of employees in the workplace has yet to come before the Irish courts. Conceivably, the Irish courts will hold that employees' right to privacy is subordinate to the rights and interests of their employer where it is shown that a legitimate purpose requires certain degrees of monitoring. In this context, a legitimate purpose might be the exercise of reasonable control and supervision over employees and their use of business resources. However, the measures invoked would have to be proportionate and, therefore, an effective way of achieving the employer's legitimate objective in the least intrusive way. A claimed breach of employee privacy also may require consideration of other, competing constitutional rights, such as the employer's right to protect its property.

c. *Data Protection*

The Data Protection Acts, 1988 and 2003 (collectively, the DPA), are the main piece of Irish legislation dealing with privacy. The DPA implement the provisions of the 1995 EU Data Protection Directive.[97] Employees may be considered "data subjects" within the meaning of the DPA and, thereby, can avail themselves of the statutory protection.

The DPA only apply to "personal data," which is defined as data (in turn, defined as information in a form that can be processed) relating to a living individual who can be identified either from the data or from the data in conjunction with other information in the possession of the data controller. The DPA extend data protection to include certain types of "manual data," which means data that, although it is not processed by computer or other automated equipment, forms part of a filing system that is structured by reference to particular individuals or criteria relating to those individuals in such a way that specific information relating to a particular individual is readily accessible.

---

[97]Council Directive 95/46/EC, 1995 O.J. (L 281) 31, discussed in I.C.1. in the chapter on the European Union in Part 1 of Volume I.

The DPA regulate the collection, processing, keeping, use, and disclosure of certain information relating to individuals that is processed both automatically and manually. This is achieved through a regulatory framework involving the following:

- adherence to certain principles in the collection, processing, keeping, use, and disclosure of personal data (Data Protection Principles);
- a requirement that any processing must come within one of a limited number of specified grounds (limited processing);
- restrictions on the use of automated decisionmaking processes that impact on data subjects;
- restrictions on employers requiring employees, employee candidates, or persons who provided contracted services to make data subject access requests or to supply information relations to such persons received as a result of such a request (this provision has yet to come into force);
- establishment of individual legal rights with respect to processing personal data, including establishing the existence of accessing and correcting such personal data, objecting to processing, making complaints regarding personal data, and having one's name removed from mailing lists;
- a requirement to take "appropriate security measures" when processing personal data;
- imposition of specific requirements when data controllers engage data processors;
- restrictions on the transfer of personal data outside Ireland;
- establishment of a duty of care owed by data controllers and data processors toward the data subject;
- an obligation to register with the Data Protection Commissioner;
- establishment of enforcement procedures; and
- creation of certain offenses.

The issue of monitoring employee e-mails and web browsing in the context of the right to privacy was considered by the Irish Data Protection Commissioner in his 1999 Annual Report. The report concluded that employers are entitled to exercise reasonable control and supervision over employees and their use of business resources. Employers also are entitled to promulgate policies to protect their property and good name and to ensure that they do not become inadvertently liable for the misbehavior of their employees. However, the report reminds employers that employees retain privacy and data protection rights that must be respected by an employer.

The Commissioner's report recognized that the scope of e-mail and Internet privacy will depend largely on the culture of the particular employment. If a culture has developed that is consistent with the use by employees of e-mail as a personal resource, then this may well circumscribe the freedom of action available to an employer that wishes to monitor employee e-mail. This would apply particularly where employees use company e-mail systems for personal correspondence with the tacit agreement of the employer. In any event, it is important that employers have a clear statement of company policy in regard to the use and confidentiality of e-mail and the Internet. If an employer wishes to monitor, then employees should be fully apprised of this, particularly if the employer wishes to change from a "relaxed" regime, in which e-mail for personal purposes was permitted, to a more restrictive regime.

These comments of the Data Protection Commissioner should be read in the context of a later Opinion of the Article 29 Working Party on the Processing of Personal Data in the Employment Context,[98] which was adopted on September 13, 2001, and on the later Working Document adopted on May 29, 2002, by the Working Party on the Surveillance of Electronic Communications on the Work Place. Both of these documents indicate that the circumstances in which employers may monitor e-mail and Internet usage may be more restrictive than was previously considered to be the case.

In his 2001 Annual Report and 2002 Annual Report, the Commissioner drew attention to the work of the Article 29 Working Party. He emphasized that the legitimate interests of the employer to process personal data that are necessary for the normal development of the employment relationship and of the business operation justify certain limitations to the privacy of individuals at the

---

[98]Opinion 8/2001.

workplace, but that no business interest may ever prevail over the principles of transparency, lawful processing, legitimization, proportionality, necessity and others contained in data protection laws. An employee can always object to the processing when it is susceptible to unjustifiably overriding his or her fundamental rights and freedoms. Any monitoring or surveillance (whether in terms of e-mail use, internet use, video cameras, or location data) must be a proportionate response by an employer to the risk it faces, taking into account the legitimate privacy and other interests of workers, and should be carried out in the least intrusive way possible. At a very minimum, staff need to know what personal data the employer is collecting about them. The staff in charge of, or with responsibility for, processing personal data of other employees needs to be aware of requirements for data protection and needs to be adequately trained.

One significant potential limitation is that if data processing, such as monitoring or surveillance, is necessary as a result of the employment relationship, it is misleading to seek to legitimize this processing through consent. Reliance on consent should be confined to cases where the employee has a genuine free choice and is subsequently able to withdraw the consent without detriment.

One of the main recommendations or the Article 29 Working Party is that prevention is more important than detection, and that the interests of the employer are better served in preventing Internet misuse through technical means rather than in expending resources in detecting misuse. Thus, the recommendation is that employers should try to rely on technical means to restrict access, e.g., by having some sites blocked or installing automatic access warnings rather than on monitoring behavior.

F. Employee Duty of Loyalty, Trade Secrets, Covenants Not to Compete

1. *Employee Duty of Loyalty*

The common law courts will imply a duty of loyalty in all contracts of employment. The duty is one of the most basic elements of the employment relationship. Thus, if an employee comes into possession of information that may assist the employer's business, such information should be imparted to the employer and should not be used to further the employee's own interests or sold to a third party. This duty also clearly includes a duty not to compete with the employer while in its employment.[99] While the duty clearly applies to the normal hours of work, a question arises in relation to activities outside the workplace not during work hours. In other words, what limits, if any, does this duty of loyalty place on the ability of an employee to work for a competitor in the employee's free time. In *Hivac Ltd v. Park Royal Scientific Instruments*,[100] the employer succeeded in preventing competing activity during the employee's free time because, the court ruled, the employer was entitled to have its confidential information protected. In *Preece v. Irish Helicopters Limited*,[101] the EAT commented that

> An employer is entitled to insist that an employee does not interest himself in a company which will compete with the business of the employer. Failure of the claimant to commit himself not to do anything while in the respondent's employment in pursuit of his own interest which might conflict with the interest of his employer was reasonably construed as a breach of duty or loyalty.

When the contract comes to an end, the duty also comes to an end unless the contract contains a specific provision whereby the parties agree that the restriction will continue to apply.[102] That is not the case as is detailed immediately below, where the employer is seeking to protect trade secrets.

2. *Trade Secrets*

It is well established that trade secrets of the employer will be protected even after termination of employment and even though there is no express covenant relating to such information.[103] What an employer cannot prevent, however, even with the use of an express covenant, is employees using their general skills and knowl-

[99]Permissible methods of post-employment restraint of competition are discussed in I.F.3. below.

[100][1948] 1 Ch.169.

[101]UD 236/84.

[102]See the discussion in I.F.3. below.

[103]*See* MICHAEL FORDE, EMPLOYMENT LAW 96 (Round Hall Ltd. 2001).

edge pertaining to their job or career, even if those skills and knowledge were obtained in the course of their employment.

The crucial questions are, of course, what constitutes confidential information and how does one distinguish between each of these three categories: highly confidential information (trade secrets), mere confidential information, and general skill and knowledge. While the courts have laid down certain general guidelines, it really depends on the facts of each individual case whether the information the employer is seeking to keep confidential falls within one of these categories.

What constitutes confidential information was considered by the High Court in the case of *House of Spring Gardens Limited & Others v. Point Blank Limited & Other.*[104] The High Court stated:

> If the information has been compiled by the expenditure of skill, time and labour by the informant, then although he has obtained it from sources which are public (in the sense that any member of the public with the same skills could obtain it had he acted like the compiler of the information) the information may still, because of its value, be regarded, as "confidential" information and subject to an obligation of confidence.

While the *Point Blank* decision was not directly concerned with employment contracts, the subsequent decision of the English High Court in the case of *Faccenda Chicken Ltd. v. Fowler*[105] did lay down some useful guidelines in this area. The court classified confidential information in the field of employment contracts as falling into two categories (as the court did not regard general skill and knowledge as being confidential information in any event), namely information which:

(a) the employee must treat as confidential (either because he or she is told it is confidential or because from its character it is obviously so) but which once learnt necessarily remains in the employee's head and becomes part of his or her own skill and knowledge applied in the

---

[104][1984] I.R. 611.

[105][1987] Ch. 117; Lancashire Fires Limited v. S.A. Lyons & Co. Ltd., [1997] IRLR 113.

course of his master's business. So long as the employment lasts, he or she cannot otherwise use or disclose such information without it being a breach of duty of good faith or fidelity. However, when he or she leaves his or her employment he or she may use his or her full skill and knowledge for his or her own benefit in competition with his or her ex-employer. If an employer wants to protect information of this kind, it may be able to do so by express covenant restraining the employee from competing with the employer (within reasonable limits of time and space). Examples of this category are manufacturing processes and list of customers. This information is proprietary in character, in that it relates to the particular employer's business and not to general skill or knowledge of the employee acquired in the course of the employment. An employee could not after termination of his or her employment be prevented from using general skill or knowledge except indirectly by way of a non-competition clause or to a lesser extent by a non-solicitation clause.

(b) amounts to trade secrets that even though they have been learnt by heart, may not, even after termination of the employment contract, be used to anyone's benefit except that of the ex-employer, e.g., secret processes.

In *Faccenda*, after resigning from the company, Mr. Fowler set up a similar competing business with eight ex-employees of Faccenda. None of the contracts of employment contained express covenants against the use of confidential information or trade secrets gained by the employees while in the employ of Faccenda. The High Court refused to grant an injunction regarding the information being used in that case (names of customers, the prices they were paying for product), since it fell within the category of "mere confidential information" that was automatically protected by the implied duty of fidelity during employment, but not thereafter in the absence of express covenants.

While the distinction between trade secret and confidential information often is difficult to draw in practice, the distinction is fundamental given the differing rights that an employer will have.

At the end of the day, except at the extremes, the principal difference between the two categories of confidential information outlined above appears to be a matter of degree. An employer who wishes to allege that its information amounts to a trade secret and is not merely confidential must, even in obvious cases, provide the court with sufficient details justifying this higher categorization.

The distinction between general skill and knowledge and confidential information or trade secrets can be even more difficult to draw and often lies at the heart of disputes relating to confidential information. In particular, it is often extremely difficult to say whether a specific item of information forms part of the employee's skill and knowledge and is therefore "mere confidential" information or amounts to special knowledge of the employer's business, or highly confidential amounting to a trade secret. However, the mere fact that the ex-employee has retained information in his or her memory (even though the employee did not deliberately memorize it to compete with the former employer after termination of employment) does not mean that this information is not secret. That which is not confidential, the employee is free to use.

Employers must try to define with sufficient precision the confidential information that they wish to protect as against ex-employees. Part of the rationale for the requirement of particularity in defining exactly what information the employer is trying to protect, is that an injunction must be framed with sufficient precision to enable the person enjoined to know what it is he or she is prevented from doing.

Finally, a third party, such as a new employer, who knowingly receives confidential information may be restrained from using it. The third party also will be liable to account for profits derived from using the information, or for damages.

3. *Covenants Not to Compete*

a. *Common Law*

At common law there is no implied restriction on an employee competing with his or her ex-employer, in the absence of a specific restriction in the contract of employment. Even where there is a specific restriction, covenants restricting the freedom of an employee to compete with the ex-employer after the end of the employment may be held void for being contrary to public policy on the basis of the restraint of trade doctrine. In general, while post-employment restraint-of-trade clauses can be deemed unenforceable if thought to be overly restrictive or in restraint of trade, they will be upheld if the ex-employer can show that the covenants are designed to protect its legitimate interests and extend no further than is reasonably necessary to protect those interests.[106] If, however, the protection provided in a contract is found to be unduly onerous or unreasonable compared with the interest being protected, the clause—and in certain circumstances the contract—will be held unenforceable. In essence, case law states that to be enforceable a clause must be reasonable as to duration and geographical extent and relate to the business the employer is engaged in. With regard to duration, the factor generally considered is the length of time it will take the employer to take the necessary steps to protect the goodwill of its business,[107] while with regard to geographical extent, it is the area where the employer operates that is relevant.[108]

b. Competition Act 2002

In addition to the common law position, employment contracts in Ireland must be considered in the light of the Competition Act 2002 (CA 2002) (which repealed the CAs of 1991 and 1996), which contain a comprehensive prohibition-based system of competition law based on European law.[109] Section 4(1) of the CA 2002 prohibits and renders void all agreements between undertakings which have as their object or effect the prevention, restriction, or distortion of competition in trade in any goods or services in the state. Under the 1991 and 1996 Acts, the Competition Authority

---

[106]Vescom B.V. v. John Orr [[1986] 1 EHC1 (Ir. H. Ct.); International Consulting Servs. (UK) Limited v. Hart, [2000] I.R.L.R. 227.

[107]Cantor Fitzgerald UK Ltd. v. Wallace, [1992] I.R.L.R. 215 (Queen's Bench Division).

[108]Commercial Plastics Ltd. v. Vincent, [1965] 1 Q.B. 623 (Court of Appeal); Marley Tile Co. v. Johnson, [1982] I.R.L.R. 75 (Court of Appeal); Spencer v. Marchington, [1988] I.R.L.R. 392. (Chancery Division).

[109]EC Treaty, arts. 81, 82.

(Authority) had the sole jurisdiction to either (1) certify that an agreement did not fall within the prohibition in section 4(1), or (2) license the agreement, where it fulfilled certain criteria such that the anticompetitive effect was outweighed by specified benefits, without eliminating competition. The CA 2002 eliminated the Authority's approval function; parties to an agreement now are responsible for self-assessment of the agreements. Any agreement that breaches competition law may be challenged in court either by an aggrieved party (e.g., the employee) or by the Authority.

In its 1992 notice on employment agreements, the then Authority noted that in general employees are not deemed to be undertakings within the meaning of the Competition Act and that therefore agreements between an employer and employee do not fall within the ambit of section 4(1). However, if an employee leaves an employer and establishes his or her own business, the Authority regards the former employee as an undertaking and in such circumstances the clause will fall within the ambit of section 4(1) and as such cannot be overly restrictive.

The leading decision in this area is *Apex Fire Protection Ltd. v. Murtagh.*[110] In this case an interlocutory injunction was sought to stop a former employee, who had set up a similar business to that of his employer, from breaching a two-year non-solicitation-of-customers clause. The court heard a defense based on Section 4, and granted an injunction to the employer. Prior to the hearing of the court case, the employment agreement had been "notified" to the Authority, with a request for a certificate or license under the now-defunct procedure described above. Because the ex-employee was deemed to be an undertaking, since he now owned and controlled his own business, the agreement could be considered by the Authority under section 4(1). The Authority gave its decision[111] on the agreement after the hearing of the court case, but refused either a license or a certificate. As for the non-solicitation clause, it was found by the Authority to be in breach of section 4 for several reasons. First, the clause went beyond what was neces-

[110]Unreported, Jan. 25 1993.

[111]Competition Authority Decision No. 2, June 10, 1993.

sary to protect the employer's customer list in that it prevented solicitation not only of existing customers at the time the ex-employee left the company, but also of those who had ceased to be customers in the previous two years. Secondly, the clause prohibited solicitation for two years, which was deemed unnecessarily long by the Authority, taking into account the fact that fire equipment must be serviced once a year. Thus, in the Authority's opinion, a year could allow the company to confirm its business connections and goodwill. Furthermore, as most of the goodwill remained with the company when an employee left, protection for one year was adequate. The effect of the Authority's decision was that the two-year non-solicitation clause was void and could not be enforced against the ex-employee. As noted above, the Authority no longer certifies or licenses agreements, as a result of the introduction of the CA 2002. However, former decisions of the Authority remain instructive for the self-assessment now required to be undertaken by an employer. When assessing restrictive covenants in an employment contract under the CA 2002, it is therefore necessary to bear in mind that the employee may become an undertaking in the future. At that point in time, the restriction will only be valid if it can be shown to give rise to improvements in production or distribution or technical or economical progress, without eliminating competition. Although there has as yet been no case law on the subject under the CA 2002, if the duration, scope and geographic extent are restricted to what is objectively necessary to protect the employer's interest, the clause is likely to be enforceable.

II. COLLECTIVE BARGAINING

A. Introduction

One of the most marked features of Irish industrial relations and collective bargaining law[112] is the general absence of statutory

---

[112]*See generally* ANTHONY KERR, THE TRADE UNION AND INDUSTRIAL RELATIONS ACTS OF IRELAND (Sweet & Maxwell 1991); MICHAEL FORDE, INDUSTRIAL RELATIONS LAW (Round Hall Press 1991); TONY KERR & GERRY WHYTE, IRISH TRADE UNION LAW (Butterworths 1985).

regulation. For a long time, no definite framework existed to regulate collective bargaining; instead, employers and employees entered into bargaining voluntarily. This system, which has been referred to as "voluntarism,"[113] allowed all parties greater freedom to regulate their own collective bargaining procedures. Article 40.6.1 of the Constitution guarantees an employee's right to join a trade union, but does not provide for a right to strike. Similarly, the employer is under no legal obligation to negotiate with its employees' trade union,[114] even where the union holds a negotiating license. Voluntarism was, therefore, a necessary process. What little law that did develop to govern collective bargaining was introduced piecemeal in response to difficulties existing at a particular time.

The common law traditionally regarded trade union involvement in collective agreements as illegal, on the ground that intervention was contrary to the doctrine of privity of contract. Similarly, any form of industrial action was actionable as a breach of contract or as an industrial tort, such as inducement to breach of contract, intimidation, conspiracy, or trespass.

The Trade Union Act, 1871, and the Trade Dispute Act, 1906, recognized, for the first time, the legal status of trade unions and industrial action in certain circumstances. Trade unions were exempted from liability for industrial torts, if carried out in contemplation or furtherance of a trade dispute, although liability still could attach to members and officials in their personal capacity. This saw the creation of a free collective bargaining system.

Today, statutory provisions on collective bargaining are found in the Industrial Relations Acts, 1946 to 1990. The Industrial Relations Act, 1946 (1946 Act), introduced a formal dispute resolution framework, which maintained the voluntary element of collective bargaining. The Labor Court was set up under the 1946 Act to assist in the settlement of trade disputes, although it is not a court of law and its recommendations are not always binding.[115]

---

[113]For a discussion of the voluntarist system of collective bargaining, see II. in the chapter on the UK in Part 1 of Volume I.

[114]Association of General Practitioners Ltd. v. Minister for Health, 10 J.I.S.L.L. (1994); Abbot and Whelan v. ITGWU, 1 J.I.S.L.L. 56 (1982) (Ir. H. Ct.).

[115]See also the Introduction, at D.2.c., above.

The 1946 Act also created a two-tiered structure for negotiations. Conciliation Officers or Industrial Relations Officers were appointed to conciliate between negotiating parties. Where this failed, the parties referred their dispute to the Labor Court for resolution.

Although the 1946 Act was instrumental in promoting collective bargaining, the system was not without problems. This period was marked by industrial action across a broad section of industry, with frequent disruptions of public and private services and production. The Labor Court became inundated with individual employee claims, and, at the same time, a disproportionate number of disputes were bypassing the conciliation process and going straight to the Labor Court for resolution. Passage of the Industrial Relations Act, 1969 (1969 Act), sought to address this backlog by creating the Rights Commissioner Service to deal with individual employee rights matters.[116]

By 1981, with continued industrial unrest and the more interventionist approach of EU law, the Minister for Labor conceded that voluntary collective bargaining was no longer suited to resolving industrial disputes.[117] While industrial relations improved during the 1980s, the 1987 Programme for National Recovery[118] brought the government into discussion with the social partners (comprised mainly of the Irish Congress of Trade Unions (ICTU) and the Irish Business and Employers Confederation (IBEC)), with a view to formulating "a better framework for collective bargaining and dispute settlement."[119] This eventually manifested itself in the Industrial Relations Act, 1990 (1990 Act).

The 1990 Act introduced a whole new dispute resolution framework via the Labor Relations Commission (LRC).[120] The LRC includes a conciliation process, and the Rights Commissioner Service and (until recently) Equality Officers.[121] The LRC can investigate and conciliate in any dispute referred to it, and only if the

---

[116]See the Introduction, at D.2.b., above.

[117]This conclusion followed a three-year Commission of Inquiry on Industrial Relations, regarding the relationship between a legislative and a voluntary approach.

[118]See II.E., below.

[119]See II.E., below.

[120]See also the Introduction, at D.2.a., above.

[121]See VI.F., below.

LRC is unable to resolve the dispute will it be referred to the Labor Court. The LRC also may issue Codes of Practice to address disputes in certain industries. The 1990 Act also repealed a great deal of previous industrial relations legislation, in particular, the Trade Disputes Act, 1906.

Since the mid-1980s, local collective bargaining, particularly in relation to pay, has been taken over by centralized national bargaining.[122] As the law now stands, interventionism has replaced voluntarism. In effect, before any collective negotiations even begin, the employee already has the benefit of a number of statutory rights that provide for basic minimum entitlements. This now represents the framework for collective bargaining.

The Industrial Relations (Amendment) Bill, 2003, proposes to amend the earlier Industrial Relations Act 2001 and proposes the introduction of an amended code of practice on voluntary dispute resolution and a new code of practice on victimization. The bill gives a number of new powers to the Labour Court, including the power to investigate cases where the specific time-frames, to be set out in the new Code of Practice on Voluntary Dispute Resolution, have been breached or exhausted or where the Labour Relations Commission have indicated that no further efforts on their part will advance the resolution of the dispute. It also provides for a prohibition on victimization arising from an employee's membership or activity on behalf of a trade union, a manager discharging his or her managerial functions, or other employees arising from disputes relating to trade union recognition. No further action has been taken to implement the bill.

B. Union Recognition

At present, Irish labor law does not require an employer to recognize any one trade union for purposes of collective bargaining.[123] This principle first was established in *Abbot v. Irish Trans-*

---

[122]See II.E., below.

[123]Limited statutory exceptions to this rule can be found in the Protection of Employment Act, 1977 (duty to consult with trade unions on collective redundancies), and in the European Communities (Safeguarding of Employees' Rights on the Transfer of Undertakings) Regulations, 1980 (duty to consult on measures envisaged on transfer of employment and to abide by any pre-transfer collective agreements). See IV.A.1., below.

port and General Workers Union (ITGWU),[124] in which Mr. Justice MacWilliam stated: "[T]here is no duty placed on the employer to negotiate with any particular citizen or body of citizens . . . the plaintiffs have no constitutional right to compel the [employer] to engage in negotiations either with them or with their union." This decision was followed by *Abbot and Whelan v. ITGWU*,[125] where the same judge ruled that "outside the terms of the contract of employment, employers are not bound to take part in any particular form of negotiation."

The issue of trade union recognition recently has been reviewed, primarily at the behest of the ICTU in response to falling trade union membership and what is perceived as an anti-trade union stance adopted by new employers investing in the Irish economy. A group of senior individuals from varying sides involved in any one area under review (in this case the Social Partners, being IBEC, ICTU, and the government), established in part to secure a new national pay agreement, examined and reported on the issue of trade union recognition and the right to bargain and put forward proposals to deal with the issue. These proposals resulted in the 2001 Industrial Relations Act.

The Industrial Relations (Amendment) Act, 2001, was passed into law on May 31, 2001. The Act does not impose obligatory trade union recognition on employers, but, nonetheless, vests the Labor Court with authority to issue binding determinations in trade disputes arising out of terms and conditions of employment.[126] Trade unions can therefore influence terms and conditions for their members, even where the employer refuses recognition.

The 2001 Industrial Relations Act arose from an attempt to increase the ability of trade unions to negotiate with employers, without introducing compulsory trade union recognition. The Act arguably gives trade unions an even stronger legal right than obligatory recognition. If compulsory trade union recognition had been introduced, it is likely that the only obligation would have been to consult and negotiate, not to actually reach agreement on anything.

---

[124]Unreported decision (Ir. H. Ct., MacWilliam, J., Dec. 2, 1980).

[125]1 J.I.S.L.L. 56 (Ir. H. Ct., MacWilliam, J., 1982).

[126]The specific procedures for resolving trade disputes following enactment of the 2001 Industrial Relations Act are discussed at II.H., below.

In contrast, the mechanisms introduced by the 2001 Industrial Relations Act allow trade unions to make application for a binding determination in regard to employees' pay and working conditions, something arguably more significant.

C. Inter-Union Disputes and Recognition

Most Irish trade unions are members of the ICTU. Clause 47 of ICTU's constitution[127] regulates inter-union disputes and multiplicity of union issues. Clause 47 provides that where a union representing a majority or substantial proportion of workers in any one establishment is involved in a collective bargaining process with the employer, no other union may represent those members without the original union's consent. This provision, although not legally binding, is enforced by the ICTU's Disputes Committee. In the absence of the original union's consent to a transfer of membership, the right guaranteed by the Irish Constitution to join a trade union effectively does not extend to a right to join a union of one's choice. The operation of clause 47 therefore prevents a situation arising in which two unions could claim to represent the same group of workers.[128]

In certain circumstances, a number of unions may seek to represent different groups within the same workforce. The Labor Court has devised guidelines to be applied in this event.[129] Ideally, the Labor Court always will try to deal with one negotiating union. However, a second union will be recognized where it represents a considerable number of employees. The rationale for this position is that any collective agreement that ignores the interests of a large part of the workers clearly will be unworkable. The second union will be admitted only where its participation will not render the negotiating process impractical or unduly onerous for the management negotiators.

---

[127]Clause 47 mirrors the Bridlington Principles regulating inter-union disputes in UK trade union law. See II.B.5. in the chapter on the UK in Part 1 of Volume I.

[128]*See* Murphy v. Stewart, [1973] I.R. 97 (Ir. S.C.) (deciding on the constitutionality of refusal to consent under clause 47).

[129]Royal Liver Friendly Soc'y v. Irish Liver Assurance Employers Union, 2 J.I.S.L.L. (Lab. Ct. 1983); Hospital Trust Ltd. v. Workers Trade Union (Lab. Ct. 1982).

D. Union Membership[130]

Article 40.6.1.iii. of the Constitution guarantees the right to form associations and trade unions, subject to the proviso that suitable legislation may be enacted to regulate and control the exercise of this right. Similarly, article 2 of ILO Convention No. 87[131] guarantees workers the right to establish and join organizations of their own choosing, subject only to the rules of the organization concerned. As discussed above, this is a right to join *a* union, not necessarily the union of one's choice. The right to join is limited by the eligibility requirements of the union, as well as by clause 47 of ICTU's constitution.

1. Waiver

It is possible that the right to join a trade union may be waived by the employee. In the case of *G. v. An Bord Uachtala*,[132] a majority of the Supreme Court decided that it could be permissible to waive one's constitutional right. By extension, where an employment contract requires an employee to waive his or her right to join a trade union, and the employee accepts this clause,[133] then the right may not be available to the employee thereafter in that employment. The waiver must be "a free consent . . . given in the full knowledge of the consequences which follow."[134] Similarly, even without a written contract, an employee arguably might forfeit the right to join a trade union by conduct or by accepting a trade practice. To have this effect, the conduct would have to be clear and unambiguous, so as to infer a clear intent to surrender the right to trade union membership. However, this argument does not rest easy against constitutional public policy in the area of trade union law, so considerable doubt about its viability must remain.

---

[130]*See generally* CATHY MAGUIRE, TRADE UNION MEMBERSHIP AND THE LAW (Sweet & Maxwell 1999).

[131]For a general discussion of ILO Conventions, see the chapter on the ILO in Volume I, Part 4.

[132][1980] I.R. 32 (Ir. S.C.) (deciding whether a mother could forfeit her constitutional right to custody of her child).

[133]An agreement of this type, whereby an employee undertakes to his or her employer never to become part of a union, often is referred to as a "yellow dog contract."

[134]G. v. An Bord Uachtala, [1980] I.R. 32, 57 (Ir. S. Ct., O'Higgins, C.J.).

2. *Public Sector Employees*

In order to preserve public order, as well as many essential public services, public service industrial action must be curtailed. For this reason, *gardai* (police officers) and members of the armed forces are prevented by statute from joining trade unions whose purpose is to negotiate on pay, pensions, or other conditions of employment.[135] In addition, the regulatory framework created under the Industrial Relations Acts, 1946 to 1990, excludes a large proportion of public sector employees in certain circumstances, including anyone employed by or under the state, school teachers, and local authority officers.

3. *Employer Knowledge of Union Membership*

Under Irish law, employers have no specific right to know whether an employee is a trade union member or not. Because all employees (with the limited exception of certain public sector employees) have a constitutional right to join a trade union, the employer can at least presume that its employees may be union members. In reality, the employer invariably will know.

First, if union membership dues are deducted from an employee's wages directly, the employee must authorize this deduction.[136] Similarly, the trade union is obliged to provide the employer with notice of this deduction and the amount due. Thus, the employer not only will know that the employee is a trade union member, but also will know to which union the employee belongs.

Second, the Trade Union Act, 1941, requires all registered trade unions to maintain a register of their members. This membership register may be inspected at any reasonable time by any interested party, defined for these purposes as any person so authorized by the Minister for Labour (now the Minister for Enterprise, Trade, and Employment).[137] Employers also may use this inspection mechanism.

---

[135]Garda Siochana Act, 1924, §13.3; Defense Amendment Act, 1990, §2.4.

[136]See V.A.2.d., below.

[137]Trade Union Act, 1941, §12(4).

4. *Protection Against Discrimination Based on Trade Union Membership and Activities*

No employee may be dismissed under Irish law because of trade union membership or activities arising out of such membership. However, this protection applies only to activities that take place outside normal working hours or permitted work hours.[138] Section 6(2) of the Unfair Dismissals Act, 1977, automatically deems such a dismissal to be unfair. In addition, if the employee can show union membership or protected activities to be the reason for dismissal, he or she will be eligible to claim unfair dismissal even without one year of continuous service.[139] Case law of the EAT on this point shows a definite policy toward upholding the employee's right to trade union membership.[140] However, in these cases, the onus is on the employee to prove the reason for the dismissal.

The Code of Practice on the Duties and Responsibilities of Employee Representatives and the Protection and Facilities to be Afforded to Them[141] provides that union members should not suffer any unfavorable change in their conditions of employment, or suffer any action prejudicial to their employment, as a result of their union duties.

E. Level of Bargaining

Collective bargaining, as generally defined under Irish labor law, is a process leading to "an agreement relating to terms and conditions of employment made between parties who are or represent employers and parties who are or represent employees."[142] Within this relatively loose framework, the structure for collective bargaining can depend on industry or company practice, as agreed between the employer and the employees' union. From 1970 to 1982, wage negotiations, in particular, were addressed by central-

---

[138]Wixted v. Slang Mann, [1991] E.L.R. 208 (EAT).

[139]See I.C.2.c., above.

[140]White v. Betson, U.D. 99/92 (EAT). Indeed, dismissal due to trade union membership is automatically an unfair dismissal under §6(2)(a) of the 1977 Act.

[141]*See* S.I. 169 (1993).

[142]Anti-Discrimination (Pay) Act, 1974.

ized bargaining in national wage agreements, known as the "pay rounds." This gave way to the National Understandings for Economic and Social Development negotiated between the government, ICTU, and the employers' representative bodies (primarily IBEC). These agreements also dealt with issues such as employment legislation, taxation, and health and safety in the workplace. In effect, they were collective agreements bargained at national level, which then were implemented at industry, company, and plant levels.

Employees and employers remain free to negotiate among themselves at whatever level they wish, be it local, regional, or national. However, the aim of recent governments has been to encourage more centralized bargaining. Since 1987, this approach has resulted in the development of various national "Programmes." Currently, the Sustaining Progress Partnership Agreement will run from 2003–2006.[143] These Programmes can be treated as national collective agreements, negotiated between the "social partners," comprised of the government, ICTU, IBEC, and other parties representative of interest groups such as the unemployed.

F. Collective Agreements

1. Legal Effect

There is no uniform legal definition of a collective agreement. A definition contained in the Organization of Working Time Act, 1997, provides for an agreement by or on behalf of an employer, on the one hand, and by or on behalf of a body or body's representative of the employees to whom the agreement relates, on the other hand.[144] A slightly different definition is contained in the Protection of Young Persons (Employment) Act, 1996, which defines a collective agreement as one "by or on behalf of an employer on the one hand and by or on behalf of a trade union or a

---

[143]Prior Programmes have included the Programme for National Recovery (PNR), the Programme for Competitiveness and Work (PCW), the Programme for Economic and Social Progress (PESP), and Partnership 2000, and the Programme for Prosperity and Fairness (PPF).

[144]Organization of Working Time Act, 1997, §2(I).

trade union representative of the employees to whom the agreement relates on the other hand."[145]

In essence, a collective agreement is any agreement that is entered into between an employer and a trade union or staff association acting on behalf of employees. Subject to what is set out below and to the registration process discussed in the next section, collective agreements generally are not legally enforceable contracts per se, but are regarded as contracts of honor.

The provisions of a collective agreement do not automatically become part of the terms of the employment contract for employees covered by the agreement. However, the terms of a collective agreement may be incorporated into a contract of employment. Statements of particulars provided to employees under the Terms of Employment (Information) Act, 1994,[146] must refer to any collective agreements that apply to the employee's employment and, except where the worker promptly objects, it generally is accepted that he or she is then bound. An employer also may be obliged to abide by the terms of a collective agreement until it either expires or is lawfully terminated, pursuant to the EU Transfer of Undertakings Regulations.[147]

Whether collective agreements are legally enforceable between the parties to the agreement, i.e., the employer and the trade union, is a gray area. The law recognizes a presumption, rebuttable by evidence to the contrary, that the parties generally do not intend collective agreements to be legally binding. However, where the parties clearly intend that an agreement shall be enforceable between them, then, in principle, it is legally enforceable, except to the extent that it contains illegal or impossible terms or there exists an explicit statutory prohibition against the enforcement of such an agreement.

If the parties to a collective agreement expressly agree that it is to be legally binding, either in whole or in part, this can take two forms. First, the parties may agree that it is legally binding as between the employer and the trade union or trade unions who are parties to the agreement. Alternatively, the parties may agree on a

---

[145]Protection of Young Persons (Employment) Act, 1996, §1(1).

[146]See I.B.1.a., above.

[147]See IV.B., below.

binding effect as between the employer and the individual employees who are represented by the trade union.

The leading cases in this area are *Goulding Chemicals Ltd. v. Bulger*,[148] and *O'Rourke v. Talbot*.[149] In *Goulding*, the Supreme Court considered a situation where an agreement was reached between the company and representative trade unions as to the manner in which a plant would be closed and the amount of redundancy payments the employees were to receive. A significant minority of the trade union members voted against the deal. The Court analyzed the nature of the agreement and concluded that it was a "business like document and had all the appearances of being intended to create legal relations."[150] In his decision, Mr. Justice Kenny stated: "An agreement between parties is enforceable by the law unless the agreement itself or the surrounding circumstances show that the parties did not intend to enter into legal relations," and further, "it seems to me that the six point agreement was intended to create legal relations and was intended to be a contract between the plaintiffs and the unions engaged in the negotiations—when an apparent agreement in relation to business relations is entered into the onus on the party who *asserts* that it was not intended to have legal effect is a heavy one."[151]

In *Talbot*, the plaintiffs, through their trade union, initially had received a written assurance from the company that compulsory redundancies would not be introduced. This was followed by a written guarantee that no compulsory redundancies would be implemented before a certain date. The High Court held that collective agreements similar to the first agreement, which contained the assurance that there would be no compulsory redundancies, were agreements of the sort that "did not contemplate legal relations, at any rate so far as all their clauses were concerned but were meant to be binding in honour only on the management and trade union."[152] However, in relation to the guarantee, the court held that it was "satisfied that not only were the men looking for

---

[148] [1977] I.R. 211 (Ir. S.C., Kenny, J.).
[149] [1984] I.L.R.M. 587 (Ir. H. Ct.).
[150] [1977] I.R. at 231.
[151] *Id.* at 236.
[152] [1984] I.L.R.M. at 590.

something which was legally binding but the management knew this" and the second commitment was therefore legally binding.[153]

However, a recent UK decision[154] shows that a collective agreement will not be readily incorporated into the individual employees' contract of employment. The employees' union had negotiated a collective agreement that reduced pay rates and was accepted by a majority of the affected staff. A small number of the staff rejected the agreement and ultimately brought proceedings claiming unlawful deduction from wages. An employment tribunal acknowledged that there had been a history of collective bargaining between the employer and its unions. However, the tribunal, and subsequently on appeal the EAT, held that this was insufficient to establish that it was a custom and practice that would support such fundamental changes being automatically incorporated directly into the individual contracts of employment. The EAT specifically ruled that for terms to be incorporated from a collective agreement by way of custom and practice, such custom and practice must be reasonable, certain, and notorious. Nonetheless, the EAT did find that incorporation could not be undermined simply by showing that certain individuals did not know of the practice or intend it to apply.

2. *Registered Agreements*

The Industrial Relations Act, 1946 (as amended by the Industrial Relations Act, 1990), allows for the registration of a collective agreement with the Labor Court, making it legally binding on the parties. The effect of registration is to extend the agreement to workers and employees in the industry sector, to which the agreement applies, who were not themselves party to the negotiations. Before an agreement may be registered, the Labor Court must be satisfied that the parties to the agreement are substantially representative of the industry sector to be covered by the agreement. The agreement will not be registered if it has the intent of restricting employment or causing unduly expensive work practices.

---

[153] *Id.* at 591.

[154] Henry v. London & Gen. Transp. Servs., [2001] I.R.L.R. 132 (Queen's Bench Division).

The terms of a registered agreement must provide that, if there is a trade dispute, a strike or lockout will not occur until the dispute resolution provisions in the agreement have been exhausted. The contents of a registered agreement become contractual provisions of the employment contract. If a sum is due to a worker pursuant to a registered agreement, or if there is a breach of such an agreement, a Labor Court inspector can institute proceedings for recovery of the sum or enforcement of the condition on behalf of the worker. This course is in addition to the worker's right to initiate proceedings on his or her own behalf.

3. *Duration of a Collective Agreement*

There is no requirement for a collective agreement to be for a specific term. However, as collective agreements relate to such variables as salaries, realistically, they are not intended to last indefinitely. If negotiated locally, company or industry practice may dictate when they are to be reviewed. Alternatively, they may apply indefinitely until either of the parties terminates the agreement by notice and re-engages the collective bargaining process. In the case of centralized agreements, these typically provide for a review date. More specific rules apply to collective agreements registered under the Industrial Relations Act, 1946, as discussed in 2., above. Nonetheless, the parties may provide for such term of duration and review date as they wish.

Once an unregistered fixed-term collective agreement expires, its terms no longer apply unless continued by a subsequent agreement. If a registered agreement provides for a specific term and, following expiration of the term, neither party has given notice to terminate the agreement, it remains in force until the registration is cancelled by either party.[155] On the transfer of ownership of an undertaking, any existing collective agreements will continue to apply as if they had been negotiated between the employees and the new employer. Any failure to honor the terms of a pre-existing collective agreement in these circumstances would violate the EU Transfer of Undertakings Regulations.[156]

---

[155]Industrial Relations Act, 1946 (1946 Act), §29(4)a.

[156]See IV.B., below.

Where a registered collective agreement contains a variation clause, either party may apply to the Labor Court, on notice, for it to be varied at any time without the other party's consent.[157]

Where a collective agreement regulates what could be described as certain core terms and conditions of employment, such as rates of pay, overtime, annual leave entitlements, etc., all of which would form part of an employee's employment contract in the absence of a collective agreement, those terms and conditions continue to apply to the individual employment contracts, even after expiration or termination of the collective agreement.

G. Strikes and Other Industrial Action

1. Strikes

Irish law does not recognize a right to strike. Instead, a system of immunities exists that protect trade unions from liability that they otherwise would incur at common law. The Industrial Relations Act, 1990 (1990 Act), is the principal legislation regulating trade disputes in Ireland.

If a trade union wishes to engage in industrial action, it must obtain a secret ballot of its members who will be affected by the action. If a majority of members vote in favor of industrial action, the union management committee may, at its discretion, sanction a strike. The management committee may not sanction an official strike if it is against the wishes of the majority of the members. The 1990 Act provides for a minimum of one week's notice of intended industrial action to be given to the employer following a secret ballot.

So long as the industrial action is in contemplation or furtherance of a trade dispute, the trade union will be immune from liability in tort. Furthermore, provided that a secret ballot is held and the relevant notice is given under the 1990 Act,[158] the employer cannot obtain an ex parte injunction to prevent a strike. In order to seek an injunction to prevent a strike or other form of industrial action, the employer must give appropriate notice to the

[157] 1946 Act §28.

[158] Industrial Relations Act, 1990 (1990 Act), §17(1).

trade union. However, if the trade union can establish that it is acting in contemplation or furtherance of a trade dispute, the court cannot enjoin the action.[159]

Theoretically, an employer could sue a striking employee for breach of contract; however, in practice this is never done. The employer also might terminate an employment contract because of strike action, although selective terminations in this situation are prohibited by the Unfair Dismissals Act, 1977.[160]

2. *Lockouts*

The employer's right to enforce a lockout has been viewed as corresponding to the employee's right to strike. Where, in the case of a strike, the employee refuses to work for the employer, in a lockout, the employer refuses to employ the employee. As such, the right to lock out has been upheld under the common law. Similarly, there is no legislative restriction of this right under Irish law. It is thought likely that any attempt to restrict this right would be unconstitutional, as it would severely limit the employer's right to take counteractive industrial action.

From an international law perspective, ILO Convention No. 87 restricts national governments from imposing strict limits on employee strike action without alternative guarantees. As the right to lock out is an equal but opposite right, it arguably would be entitled to the same protection under international law as the right to strike.

If during a lockout an employee is refused entry to work, but on ending the lockout is offered reinstatement or reengagement,[161] no dismissal will be deemed to have occurred under the Unfair Dismissals Act.[162]

3. *Picketing*

Industrial disputes in Ireland often result in picketing of a target employer's premises. Picketing is not, in itself, unlawful

---

[159] *Id.* §17(2).

[160] See I.C.2.c., above.

[161] For definitions of reinstatement and reengagement under the Unfair Dismissals Act, see I.C.2.c., above.

[162] Unfair Dismissals Act, 1977, §5(1).

under the common law, and is protected under certain conditions under the Industrial Relations Act, 1990, as discussed below.[163] This practice also may be protected under the Irish Constitution's guarantees of freedom of expression, peaceful assembly, and equality. In practice, however, picketing frequently is viewed as unlawful because, as normally conducted, it gives rise to certain common law torts, particularly nuisance.[164] If picketing is deemed unlawful, an injunction then may be granted to prevent its continuation.

A picket may be regarded as a private nuisance where it unlawfully interferes with persons' ordinary use or enjoyment of their land, including the right to be left alone without such unreasonable interference. As stated by the court in *Educational Co. of Ireland Ltd. v. Fitzpatrick (No. 2)*: "The inevitable effect of a picket causes such a conditioned effect in all trade unionists as inevitably to interfere with the business of the party picketed and with the ordinary user and enjoyment of his property."[165]

A picket also may be a public nuisance by interfering with the rights of a section of the community, as where, for example, the picket assembles in large numbers outside a premises. In *Hubbard v. Pitt*,[166] a relatively discreet picket of 8 to 12 persons outside an employer's office was deemed an obstruction of the public highway and, thus, was unlawful.

Picketing also may constitute an indirect inducement of a breach of contract, where the object is to frustrate the completion of a contract or order. Certain forms of picketing, depending on the size and atmosphere, may even be unlawful as harassment. This theory first was accepted at the height of the UK miners' strike in the mid-1980s as a means of enjoining mass picketing of premises where employees were continuing to work.[167]

---

[163] Ward Lock & Co. v. Operative Printers' Assistants' Soc'y, 22 T.L.R. 327 (1906).

[164] Educational Co. of Ireland Ltd. v. Fitzpatrick (No. 2), [1961] I.R. 345, 391 (Ir. H. Ct., Kinsmill-Moore, J.) ("Picketing as ordinarily conducted . . . interferes very seriously with the user and enjoyment of the premises picketed and amounts to a common law nuisance.").

[165] *Id.* at 391.

[166] [1976] Q.B. 142.

[167] *See* Thomas v. National Union of Mineworkers, [1985] 2 W.L.R. 1081 (U.K. H. Ct.) (relying on the tort of unreasonable harassment in the absence of assault or private nuisance).

In certain circumstances, picketing may be permitted. Section 11 of the Industrial Relations Act, 1990, provides that "it shall be lawful for one or more persons, acting on their own behalf or on behalf of a trade union, in contemplation of a trade dispute, to attend at, or where that is not practicable, at the approaches to a place where an employer works or carries on business." Where this section applies, an employer may not take any action against the picketers on the basis of the common law torts. Section 11 immunity has a number of preconditions. First, the immunity only applies to authorized trade union members and officials acting on their own behalf. Therefore, picketers who are not union members,[168] or whose own personal interests are not affected, will be acting unlawfully. Second, immunity is restricted to peaceful picketing; physical violence, abusive language,[169] and even excessive numbers[170] all will put a picket beyond the protection of section 11. Third, a lawful picket may be held only *at* a targeted employer's place of business; a picket *in* or *on* the premises is immediately unlawful.[171] Fourth, the object of the picket must be to distribute information or to persuade employees not to attend work; any purpose beyond this will render the picket unlawful. This condition is focused particularly at the practice of persuading customers or suppliers not to carry on business with the employer.

Finally, any single worker dispute must exhaust all internal grievance procedures before resorting to industrial action, including picketing. Considering the serious impact of a picket on an employer's rights, section 11 immunity is applied only where these preconditions have been met. In all other circumstances, picketing will have no such immunity and likely will be treated as unlawful.

---

[168]*See* Penny's Ltd. v. Kerrigan (unreported decision) (Ir. H. Ct., Feb. 7, 1977) (dismissed employee's father and sister-in-law removed from picket as non-union members).

[169]EI Co., Ltd. v. Kennedy, [1969] I.R. 69 (Ir. H. Ct.).

[170]Brendan Dunne Ltd. v. Fitzpatrick, [1958] I.R. 29 (Ir. H. Ct.) (holding that a large number of even peaceful picketers may make picket intrinsically intimidating).

[171]Ryanair v. Members of SIPTU Irish Times (unreported decision) (Ir. H. Ct., Mar. 12, 1998).

4. Handbilling

Handbilling in the course of an industrial action is not, in itself, inherently unlawful under the common law and may even have a constitutional basis as an exercise of the rights to freedom of association and expression. However, the action of handbilling may be rendered unlawful based on the subject material being distributed or the persons to whom it is given. Section 11 immunity applies to picketers peacefully communicating information to employees or trying to persuade them not to work. Where handbilling goes beyond these objectives, it becomes unlawful. Therefore, if handbilling is being used as a means to encourage customers or suppliers not to carry on business with the target employer, it will go beyond the permitted objects of the section 11 immunity.[172]

In certain industries where information is of a commercially sensitive nature, individual employment contracts may contain strict confidentiality clauses. Handbilling often may involve the disclosure of information employees would not know except for their position within the particular company. As such, the dissemination of confidential information may be deemed a serious breach of the employment contract, justifying dismissal and/or injunctive relief and damages.

Handbilling also may result in the tort of defamation if the information being communicated is untrue, defamatory, or made with malicious intent. The fact that the allegation is made maliciously means that it is not afforded the qualified privilege that normally would apply where the persons communicating and receiving the information have an interest in the communication.

5. Slowdowns and Sit-ins[173]

All employment contracts contain an implied term that normal working duties will be performed at the pace set by custom or practice. As with all contractual terms, any variation of the implied term as to speed of work requires the consent of the em-

---

[172] *See* Newbridge Indus. v. Bateson (unreported decision) (Ir. H. Ct., July 15, 1978); Cooke v. Ryan, [1938] I.R. 512 (Ir. H. Ct.).

[173] *See* MICHAEL FORDE, INDUSTRIAL RELATIONS LAW 109 (Round Hall Press 1991).

ployer. Moreover, employees are under an implied contractual obligation to obey their employer's reasonable instructions. A slowdown constitutes a breach of the employee's contract on both grounds. In such circumstances, the employer has a right to refuse to pay the employee. However, in order to withhold pay, the employer must give the employee advance warning of this right.

A series of English decisions have ruled that part performance indicates that employees are unwilling to perform the duties they were employed to do, and because this constitutes a breach of contract, they are not entitled to any remuneration.[174] Because a slowdown involves a refusal to honor certain implied contractual terms, these cases would support the employer's right to refuse employees' pay.

Sit-ins or occupation of the employer's premises are, by their very nature, a breach of both the common law and statute. As discussed above, the section 11 immunity afforded to picketers applies only where the picket takes place *at* the workplace, not *in* or *on* the premises. In the case of *Ryanair v. Members of SIPTU*,[175] union members occupied a runway on the employer's premises; this action was held to be beyond the protection of section 11. Even if the occupation is peaceful, and no damage is caused to the employer's equipment or premises, a sit-in is an unlicensed interference with the employer's property rights and constitutes the tort of trespass. In addition, there is a view that those involved in sit-ins may be guilty of criminal offenses.[176]

6. *Secondary Action*

The process of secondary action in Irish industrial disputes focuses on pressuring third parties with a view to creating an adverse impact on the target employer. Typically, this takes the form of encouraging an employer's main customers or suppliers (and their employees) to cease doing business with the target employer

---

[174]Wiluszynski v. Tower Hamlets London Borough Council, [1989] I.C.R. 493 (U.K. C.A.); Miles v. Wakefield Metro. Dist. Council, [1987] A.C. 529 (H.L.). These decisions were accepted in Irish law in *Maher v. AIB Plc.* 1998 ELR 204 (Ir. Dist. Ct., May 22, 1997) (concerning action taken in the course of a bank employees' dispute).

[175]Unreported decision (Ir. H. Ct., Mar. 12, 1998) (published in *Irish Times*).

[176]Prohibition of Forcible Entry and Occupation Act, 1971, §§2, 3.

while the dispute continues. Where this succeeds, it can greatly increase the union's bargaining power and can have severe economic consequences for both the employer and the third party.

Normally, secondary action will give rise to one of the industrial torts, although immunities to such torts are in effect in certain circumstances, as discussed below. Where a union encourages a third party's employees to go on strike, the striking employees will be breaching their contracts. Thus, the union causes a direct inducement of a breach of contract, actionable at common law.[177] Similarly, where the union persuades a customer or supplier not to deal with the target employer, the union induces a breach of the purchase or supply contract.

Secondary action that induces a breach of contract may be actionable under Irish law even if the inducement is indirect.[178] However, indirect inducement is a little more difficult to prove, as it requires the use of unlawful means, knowledge of the contract on the defendant's part, and the intent to frustrate the secondary contract. Secondary industrial action also can give rise to a claim for inducing a breach of statutory duty,[179] or the tort of intentionally interfering with trade by unlawful means.[180]

In certain very limited circumstances, secondary picketing may be protected by the 1990 Act. Section 11(2) of the 1990 Act provides that where the picketers reasonably believe that the target has assisted their employer in the course of a trade dispute to frustrate the strike or action, secondary picketing is lawful. However, to remain within the protection of section 11(2), the picketing should not go beyond obtaining or communicating information. Also, it is essential that the picketers believe that the secondary target's intention was to undermine their action, not that the secondary target simply is carrying out orders for their employer in the normal course of business. Section 11(2) immunity does not apply to essential public utilities and services.

Another source of statutory protection for secondary action is section 13 of the 1990 Act, which grants immunity to trade unions

---

[177]Temperton v. Russell, [1893] 1 Q.B. 715.

[178]Sherrif v. McMullen, [1952] I.R. 236 (Ir. H. Ct.).

[179]*See* Meade v. Haringey LBC, [1979] I.C.R. 494 (H.L.).

[180]*See* Hadmor Prods. v. Hamilton, [1982] I.R.L.R. 103.

for otherwise tortious acts committed in connection with a trade dispute. Section 13 immunity requires very strict compliance with the definition of a trade dispute, which means "any dispute between employers and workers which is connected with the employment, or non-employment, or terms or conditions of, or affecting the employment, of any person." Where a trade dispute exists, section 13 protects the trade union from liability with the following provision:

> [A]n action against a trade union whether of workers or employees or its trustees or against any members or officials thereof on behalf of themselves and all other members of the trade union in respect of a tortious act committed by or on behalf of the trade union in contemplation or furtherance of a trade dispute shall not be entertained in any court.

In addition, section 12 of the 1990 Act grants specific immunity to trade unions with respect to a direct inducement of a breach of contract, if done in contemplation or furtherance of a trade dispute. The effect of these provisions is to limit any legal action to suits against individual workers or union officials in their personal capacity, neither of whom will have sufficient funds to meet any losses.

H. Third Party Resolution of Disputes

In the course of collective bargaining, parties frequently will reach an impasse that, if allowed to continue, may develop into industrial action. The existence of a third party dispute resolution procedure helps to mediate between the parties with a view to resolving the issue at hand and, thus, avoiding an unnecessary trade dispute. The combined resolution procedure of the LRC and the Labor Court represents this third party in Irish law.[181]

Trade disputes initially are referred to the LRC. Referral to the LRC may be provided as a matter of industry practice, in a collective agreement, or on the suggestion of either party to the dispute. Alternatively, where the Minister for Enterprise, Trade,

---

[181]For additional discussion of the LRC and the Labor Court, see the Introduction, at D.2.a. and D.2.c., above.

and Employment (ETE Minister) decides that a particular dispute is of special importance or affects the public interest, he or she may refer the matter to the LRC.[182] Also, to qualify for statutory immunity for industrial action, an individual employee grievance first must exhaust the LRC resolution procedure.[183]

LRC members all are appointed by the ETE Minister, in consultation with the employer and employee organizations. The precise function of the LRC is to provide a conciliation and industrial relations advisory service to help resolve trade disputes.[184] The conciliator acts as a go-between, discussing various proposals and counterproposals with each of the parties. The Labor Court may step in only after the LRC has waived its conciliation function, or has investigated the matter fully and reported to the Labor Court that it cannot advance the matter to resolution.

Once the matter is referred to the Labor Court, the LRC no longer has jurisdiction. The members of the Labor Court are selected from employer and employee representative bodies or unions in order to give a balanced expertise. The Labor Court has a number of functions, all of which work toward promoting harmonious industrial relations by resolving and preventing disputes in the collective bargaining process. More specifically, the Labor Court's function relates to investigating and arbitrating in trade disputes and eventually issuing its recommendations. This investigative procedure[185] may, in effect, amount to arbitration where both parties to the dispute request the Labor Court to investigate the matter and undertake to be bound by its recommendations.

Although the LRC/Labor Court procedure operates within a statutory framework and is, therefore, government sponsored, nothing prevents the parties from using nongovernmental dispute resolution mechanisms. These can be either specifically provided for in the collective agreement or can be agreed to in the event of a specific dispute. Likewise, the parties can agree in advance whether they are prepared to be bound by the recommendations of a third party, particularly where an arbitrator is appointed.

---

[182] 1990 Act §38.
[183] *Id.* §9(4).
[184] *Id.* §25.
[185] *Id.* §20(2).

The Industrial Relations (Amendment) Act, 2001, provides the Labor Court with authority to issue binding determinations in trade disputes concerning terms and conditions of employment. The 2001 Industrial Relations Act exists in conjunction with the Industrial Relations Act, (1990) (Code of Practice on Voluntary Dispute Resolution) (Declaration) Order, 2000 (VDR Code),[186] and the Industrial Relations Act, (1990) (Code of Practice on Grievance and Discipline) (Declaration) Order 2000.[187] These two Codes of Practice represent a voluntary framework within which the parties can resolve disputes, whereas the 2001 Industrial Relations Act creates a mechanism for a trade union to bring a dispute before the Labor Court for a binding determination where the employer refuses to engage in collective bargaining or voluntary dispute resolution.

The purpose of the VDR Code is to introduce a recognized and established framework for addressing disputes where negotiating arrangements are not already in place between the employer and any representative trade union. The Code is not legally binding and does not place any obligation on an employer to engage in voluntary dispute resolution with a trade union.

The procedure under the VDR Code begins when a dispute is referred to the Labor Relations Commission (LRC). Upon referral, an officer is appointed from the LRC Advisory Service to assess the issues in dispute. Before any dispute or issue can be processed under the VDR Code, the parties (in practice, this is the trade union), must show that no negotiating arrangements are in place or that collective bargaining has failed to take place. The LRC officer works with the parties to resolve the issues in dispute. If the dispute is not resolved at this point, an agreed "cooling off" period is put in place. During this period, the LRC Advisory Service will continue to work with the parties in an attempt to resolve the outstanding issues. If, after the cooling off period, all issues have been resolved, the LRC may, at its discretion, make further proposals for the parties to ensure that there is no recurrence of the issues giving rise to the dispute. In the event that the matter re-

---

[186]S.I. 145 (2000).
[187]S.I. 146 (2000).

mains unresolved after the cooling off period, the LRC will provide a written report to the Labor Court, which then must issue recommendations on outstanding matters. These recommendations are not binding on the parties.

If no collective bargaining takes place and the employer refuses to engage in the voluntary dispute resolution process, or does so in bad faith, a trade union or excepted body[188] may refer the dispute to the Labor Court, pursuant to the 2001 Industrial Relations Act, provided that the following requirements are satisfied:

- the employer does not have a practice of engaging in collective bargaining negotiations with the trade union, and all internal dispute resolution procedures, if any (apart from the VDR Code procedures), normally used by the parties have failed to resolve the dispute;
- the employer has failed to observe a provision of the VDR Code or has failed to observe such provision in "good faith";
- the trade union, excepted body, or the employees have not acted in a manner that frustrated the employer's capacity to observe the VDR Code; and
- the trade union, the excepted body, or the employees have not engaged in any industrial action after the dispute was referred to the LRC pursuant to the VDR Code.[189]

The Labor Court may hold a preliminary hearing[190] to determine whether these statutory requirements have been met. Once the requirements are satisfied, the Labor Court begins an investigation of the dispute. Following this investigation, the Labor Court may make a recommendation and, if necessary, suggest a course of action that should be taken with regard to the terms and conditions of employment. A recommendation may not impose any arrangements for collective bargaining between the parties.[191]

---

[188]An excepted body means an excepted body within the meaning of section 6 of the Trade Union Act 1941, as amended by the Trade Union Act, 1942, and is defined as "an employee grouping which represents employees in only one employment."

[189]Industrial Relations (Amendment Act), 2001, §2.

[190]*Id.* §3.

[191]*Id.*

Where a dispute continues even after a recommendation has been made, the Labor Court may, at the request of a trade union or excepted body, make a determination. The determination may relate to terms and conditions of employment, as well as the dispute resolution and disciplinary procedures that exist in the employment.[192] In a new departure for the Labor Court, its written determinations now must include a full statement of the reasons for the decision.

Either party may appeal a Labor Court determination to the High Court, but only on a point of law. Either party also may apply to the Labor Court for review of its determination. An application for review may be made only after three months, but not later than 12 months, after the determination has been issued. Following review, the Labor Court may do any of the following:

- vacate the determination, if the dispute has been resolved;
- affirm the determination, if the dispute has not been resolved; or
- vary the terms of the determination.[193]

Where an employer fails to comply with the terms of the determination within one year of the time it is issued, or within six weeks of the time it is reviewed, then the trade union or excepted body may apply to the Circuit Court for an order directing the employer to carry out the determination. This application may be made without the need to hear the employer or any other additional evidence.

In the course of its investigation, the Labor Court is entitled to examine and consider the employer's labor relations practices, not only in the particular employment at issue, but in any other employment in which the employer or an associated employer is involved, both in and outside the state.

The Labor Court may suspend any investigation or review, or withdraw any recommendation already made, if it is satisfied that industrial action has taken place in regard to the dispute. However, an industrial dispute is not fatal to Labor Court jurisdiction;

---

[192]*Id.* §6.
[193]*Id.* §9.

if the Court is satisfied that it is reasonable to proceed with an investigation or review, it will do so.[194] While it is not apparent from the Act itself, it appears from the *Dáil* debates[195] that the purpose of this exception is to allow the Labor Court to continue its investigation where there are valid reasons for the industrial action. For example, if the employer behaves in such a manner so as to intentionally provoke employees into industrial action, the employer otherwise would be able to restrict the employees from having the matter referred to the Labor Court. In such circumstances, the Labor Court would be entitled to exercise its discretion and continue its investigation.[196]

I. Union Security

1. *Employees' Right Not to Belong to a Union*

The corollary of employees' constitutional right to form associations and unions is the right to disassociate, or not join a trade union. In *Educational Co. of Ireland Ltd. v. Fitzpatrick*,[197] the Supreme Court held that the right to form associations or unions only was intelligible where there was an implicit right to abstain from joining associations or unions. Thus, in this particular instance, a strike and picket of the plaintiff's premises, in an attempt to coerce non-union employees to join the union, was unlawful. Post-entry (i.e., post-hire) closed shops, therefore, were adjudged to be unlawful.

The *Fitzpatrick* decision was followed in the case of *Meskill v. Coras Iompair Eireann*.[198] In the *Meskill* case, the company dismissed all its employees and offered them immediate re-employment on the same terms and conditions as before, provided they joined a specified union, in an attempt to ensure that all employees would become a member of one of four recognized trade unions. The High Court held that the imposition of such an obligation in-

---

[194] *Id.* §8.

[195] The *Dáil* is the upper house in the Irish Legislature. See the Introduction, at A., above.

[196] See II.A., above.

[197] [1961] I.R. 345 (Ir. S.C.).

[198] [1973] I.R. 121 (Ir. H. Ct.).

fringed the plaintiff's right to disassociate, which was protected by Article 40.6.l.iii. of the Constitution.

Although the case law makes clear the right of existing employees to refuse to join a trade union, it is less clear whether employers may request prospective employees to join a trade union, i.e., whether the pre-entry closed shop is lawful. The issue is whether an employee, in effect, waives his or her constitutional right not to join a trade union by signing a contract of employment that requires trade union membership. If the employee can waive the right not to join a trade union in the circumstances, but then subsequently repudiates membership in the union, that could be treated by the employer as a breach of contract and, following adequate warnings and fair procedures, could result in dismissal. In fact, it is almost inevitable that if such a circumstance arose, the trade union and its members would insist that the employer dismiss the employee for breach of contract based on a refusal to maintain union membership.

In two early decisions, the Irish courts upheld the validity of pre-entry closed shop agreements.[199] However, there have been no recent Irish decisions in relation to pre-entry closed shops, making it difficult to assess the continuing legality of such agreements.

A pre-entry closed shop agreement may be unlawful if it operates to provide a trade union with an effective monopoly in a particular area of work or excludes protected categories of workers from employment without an objective justification for the exclusion.[200]

The pending incorporation by Ireland of the European Convention for the Protection of Human Rights and Fundamental Freedoms 1950 (European Convention on Human Rights)[201] could impact significantly this area. The European Court of Human Rights has taken the view that compulsion to join a particular trade union amounts to a violation of the right "to form and to join trade unions"

---

[199]Buckley v. Rooney, [1950] Ir. Jur. Rep. 5 (Ir. Cir. Ct., O'Connor, J.) (commenting, without elaboration, that closed shop agreement did not violate article 40 of the Constitution); Hynes v. Conlon, [1939] Ir. Jur. Rep. 49.

[200]Nathan v. Bailey Gibson Ltd., [1993] E.L.R. 106 (Ir. H. Ct.).

[201]For a discussion of the European Convention on Human Rights, see the Introduction, at E., in the chapter on the EU in Part 1 of Volume I.

within the meaning of article 11 of the Convention.[202] Once the terms of the European Convention on Human Rights are incorporated into domestic law, decisions by the European Court of Human Rights will have greater authority in Irish law. Thus, it may be that the issue of pre-contract closed shop agreements will have to be revisited following incorporation.

In the meantime, unless a pre-employment closed shop agreement is discriminatory or prevents an individual from earning a livelihood, contrary to his or her constitutional right, the agreement arguably would be lawful under Irish law. That position, however, is not particularly strong, and it may be that it simply will take one case to come before the High Court or the Supreme Court to render such agreements unlawful.

2. *Union Membership Fees*

Most, if not all, unions rely on membership subscription fees for their income. The level and variation of membership fees is provided for in the union's "rule book." In one sense, the rule book is the member-union contract. Although it may not be strictly enforceable, it will be persuasive in court action. Thus, rule book provisions on union membership fees may be relied on to compel a member to pay fees. Typically, rule books will provide that where a member's fees are in arrears for a specified period of time, membership will lapse automatically. This practice has been upheld as a means of compelling payment of fees.[203]

3. *Obligation to Represent Non-Members*

Irish labor law does not require unions to represent non-union members in collective bargaining. To do so would undermine the entire trade union movement because employees would receive the benefits of negotiated collective agreements whether or not they were union members. Furthermore, it would deprive the unions

---

[202]Young v. UK, 5 E.H.R.R. 201 (Eur. Ct. H.R. 1981). Although not commenting specifically on closed-shop arrangements, the court concluded that an individual does not enjoy the right of freedom of association if, in reality, the freedom of action or choice that remains available is either non-existent or so reduced as to be of no practical value.

[203]Moran v. Rooney, [1943] I.R. 485 (Ir. S.C.).

of their right to receive membership fees because the threat of automatic membership lapse would be an empty one.

As discussed above, the Industrial Relations Act, 1946, does provide a voluntary scheme for registering collective agreements with the Labor Court.[204] The main advantage of registering an agreement is that its terms and conditions will be extended to employers and employees in the particular sector who may not have been represented in the negotiations.

4. Union Rights in the Workplace

As discussed above, Irish labor law does not require the employer to recognize the employee's union.[205] Therefore, Irish trade unions do not enjoy a right to an office on company premises or to any time off, paid or otherwise, for union-related activities. Where an employer does choose to recognize its employee's union, the relationship should be regulated by the Code of Practice on the Duties and Responsibilities of Employee Representatives and the Protection and Facilities to be Afforded Them by their Employer (Code of Practice).[206] Under the Code of Practice, there should be an agreement between management and the employees' representatives as to the provision of reasonable facilities to assist them in their union duties. The facilities granted should enable the representatives to carry out their role effectively and efficiently, having regard to the size of the union membership. Thus, it is conceivable that where a union representative acts on behalf of an extremely large staff, the representative may be given an office. The representative should be granted access to all work areas in order to meet with members. The arrangements also should allow for reasonable time off where there is prior permission for union duties and training courses. Whether this will be paid time off is left to the agreement of the parties.

---

[204]See II.F.2., above.

[205]See II.B., above.

[206]S.I. 169 (1993); *see* FRANCES MEENAN, WORKING WITHIN THE LAW 154–56 (Oak Tree Press 2d ed. 1999).

III. REPRESENTATION BY ENTITIES OTHER THAN UNIONS

Since Ireland joined the EU in 1973, a certain number of legislative measures have addressed the matter of employee participation in management. This concept first was introduced in the Worker Participation (State Enterprises) Act, 1977, which permitted employees to take part in the decisionmaking process of certain state-owned entities. The Protection of Employment Act, 1977, granted certain information and consultation rights to employees where large-scale redundancies were being considered.[207] Similarly, the European Communities (Safeguarding of Employees Rights on Transfer of Undertakings) Regulations, 1980 (Transfer of Undertakings Regulations), oblige the transferor-employer and the transferee-employer to provide certain specified information to, and consult with, their respective employees' representatives on any measures envisaged.[208]

By the late 1980s, a commitment to employee participation was set out in the EU's new Charter of Fundamental Social Rights.[209] In 1994, the EU adopted the Works Council Directive, under which employees of certain large multinational companies are entitled to a whole range of management information relating to developments within the company.[210] For Ireland, this represented a significant expansion of employees rights' to information. The Works Council Directive was implemented in Irish law as the Transnational Information and Consultation of Employees Act, 1996.

The EU Directive on Employee Information and Consultation,[211] which was adopted on March 11, 2002, is to be transposed

---

[207]See IV.A.1.c., below.

[208]For a discussion of the Transfer of Undertakings Regulations, see IV., below. These Regulations have now since been extended to include representation by a nominated employee of any unrepresented employees within the undertaking.

[209]For a detailed discussion of the Charter of Fundamental Social Rights, see the Introduction, at E., in the chapter on the EU in Part 1 of Volume I.

[210]Council Directive 94/45/EC, 1994 O.J. (L 254) 64. For a detailed discussion of the European Works Council Directive, see III.B.2. in the chapter on the EU in Volume I, Part 1.

[211]Parliament and Council Directive 2002/14/EC, 2002 O.J. (L 80) 29. For a detailed discussion of this Directive, see III. in the chapter on the EU in Part 1 of Volume I.

into national law no later than three years after its adoption, which means that Member States will have until early 2005 to implement its provisions.

It is expected that the Employee Information and Consultation Directive will have major implications for industrial relations practice in Ireland by setting out minimum requirements for the right to information and consultation of employees in particular circumstances. These rights will cover the following:

- information on recent and probable developments of the business or the establishment's activities and economic situation;
- information and consultation on the situation, structure, and probable development of employment within the business and on any anticipatory measures envisaged, in particular those that threaten employment.

The Directive leaves it to Member States to implement the practical arrangements for information and consultation with employees, in line with each state's own legislative framework and industrial relations practice. The Directive, will, at the option of Member States, apply to all undertakings employing at least 50 employees or, alternatively, to all establishments employing at least 20 employees. Information must be given at such time, in such fashion, and with such content as is appropriate to enable, in particular, employees' representatives to conduct an adequate study and, where necessary, prepare for consultation.

Interested parties in Ireland were given an opportunity to influence the form of the Irish legislation implementing the Consultation Directive by making submissions to the Department of Enterprise, Trade, and Employment in response to a consultation paper published in July 2003. While the deadline for receipt of submissions on the legislation implementing the Consultation Directive has passed, it is likely, given the significance of the legislation for Irish industrial relations, that a process of dialogue with social partners will continue prior to the publication of the legislation. The draft bill is due for publication in the summer of 2004, with a view to being introduced on a phased basis between March 2005 and March 2008 and will (depending on the submissions received) apply either to "undertakings" (meaning companies, partnerships, or co-operatives) having 50 or more employees or to "establishments" (meaning a branch or business unit) having 20 or more employees.

Considering the provisions in the Directive for the interim transition period, it is expected that the application of the Employee Information and Consultation Directive in Ireland will be staggered. Beginning in 2005 or when the Directive is implemented locally, the Directive will apply to undertakings with more than 150 employees or establishments with more than 100 employees; in 2007, it will apply to undertakings with more than 100 employees or establishments with more than 50 employees; and finally, in 2008, it will apply to all undertakings with more than 50 employees or establishments with at least 20 employees. No decision has been taken as to which level the ETE Department will opt for in the implementing legislation. There is no existing equivalent to these provisions in Irish law. Indeed the Directive will, for the first time, oblige Irish employers to develop structures for informing and consulting with employees (other than in the limited context of transfers of undertakings, collective redundancies, and health and safety, where information and consultation obligations already exist).

IV. REDUNDANCY AND TRANSFERS OF UNDERTAKINGS

A. Redundancy

1. Termination by Reason of Redundancy

Employers may not terminate employees by reason of redundancy without warning or notice. To do so would amount to a breach of contract or a violation of statute and would give rise to a claim for wrongful or unfair dismissal.[212]

Even apart from the issue of notice, an employee terminated for redundancy may be entitled to bring a claim for unfair dismissal. Although redundancy normally is regarded as an absolute defense to a claim for unfair dismissal, an employee, nevertheless,

[212]See I.C.2., above.

may succeed with a claim if it is established that the employee was selected unfairly for redundancy or that the employer acted unreasonably. This is discussed in greater detail below.

The EAT[213] long has held that a dismissal by reason of redundancy should be the last option for an employer, not the first. For this reason, the EAT will seek evidence from an employer to establish what alternatives were considered before a decision was taken to dismiss an employee by reason of redundancy. The EAT will expect the employer to have consulted with the employee and his or her trade union representatives with a view to seeing whether there were viable alternatives to redundancy, in particular, relocation within the employer's organization. Only following such consultation and consideration of any proposals offered by the employee and/or his or her representatives should the employer make a decision to dismiss. Furthermore, in circumstances where there is a collective redundancy, the provisions of the Protection of Employment Act, 1977, will apply.

a. Fair Selection

The Unfair Dismissals Act, 1977–2001 (UDA), provides that the dismissal of an employee will not be deemed to be an unfair dismissal if it results wholly or mainly from, inter alia, the redundancy of the employee. However, a dismissal due to redundancy may be deemed an unfair dismissal if the circumstances constituting the redundancy apply equally to one or more other employees, in similar employment, with the same employer, who are not dismissed, and if either of the following circumstances apply:

- The selection of the employee for dismissal resulted wholly or mainly from one or more of the following matters:
  - membership in a trade union or engaging in trade union activity;
  - religious or political opinions;
  - civil proceedings, whether actual or threatened, against the employer, to which an employee is a party or is likely to be a witness;

---

[213] See the Introduction, at D.2.d., above.

- criminal proceedings against the employer, in which the employee has made a complaint or statement to the prosecuting authority or in which the employee is likely to be a witness;
- the exercise of the employee's right to parental or *force majeure* leave under the Parental Leave Act, 1998;[214]
- pregnancy or exercise by the employee of rights under the Maternity Protection Act, 1994, or Adoptive Leave Act, 1995;[215]
- age;
- membership in the traveling community; or
- another matter that would not be a ground justifying dismissal; or

• The employee was selected for dismissal in contravention of an agreed procedure (one that has been agreed between the employer and the employee or a trade union or that has been established by the custom and practice of the employer relating to redundancy), and there are no special reasons justifying a departure from that procedure.

Hence, where two or more employees are engaged in similar employment, the employer is obliged, in the absence of criteria specifically agreed to with a trade union, to adopt some sort of objective criteria for differentiating between one employee and another. In theory, nothing prevents employers from using any of a wide range of objective criteria such as ability, attendance record, disciplinary record, skill levels, etc. All other things being equal, and with no objective criteria to select between one employee and another, an employer will be expected to resort to the "last-in, first out" rule.

In the case of *Dawson v. Eir Imports Ltd.*,[216] an employee was selected for dismissal based on a determination that she was not as competent as other members of staff. The EAT laid down the following principle:

[214]See V.D.4., below.
[215]See V.D.3.a., below.
[216]U.D. 616/93 (EAT).

Following an assessment of the comparative performance of all similar staff the claimant was selected. The respondent retained the employees who he thought could best contribute to the company. The claimant's performance was judged to be weakest. The criteria used in the absence of any other procedures was appropriate in the circumstances. The respondent was competent to make the assessment having regard to the small number of staff and his close contact with them. The principles of natural justice did not require the respondent to give the claimant (employee) details of this assessment and his not doing so resulted in no injustice.

b. Redundancy Procedure

An employer that wishes to dismiss an employee for reason of redundancy must give the employee at least two-weeks' notice, in writing. This usually is achieved by giving the employee a completed redundancy notice form (RP1). The RP1 notice is separate from any notice required to be given by contract or by the Minimum Notice Act.[217] A copy of the RP1 must be sent to the ETE Minister. On the date of dismissal, the employer then must give the employee a completed redundancy certificate (RP2), together with any statutory lump sum payment to which the employee is entitled.[218] The employee signs this form as a receipt for his redundancy payment.

Provided that the procedures have been complied with fully, the ETE Minister may make a payment to the employer from the Social Insurance Fund amounting to 60 percent of the statutory lump sum paid to an employee. The claim form (RP3) must be sent to the Minister within six months of the date the redundancy lump sum payment is made.

c. Collective Redundancies

The Protection of Employment Act, 1977 (as amended) (Protection of Employment Act),[219] sets forth certain procedural re-

---

[217]See I.C.1., above.

[218]See IV.A.2., below.

[219]Protection of Employment Act, 1977, as amended by the Protection of Employment Order, 1996, S.I. 370 (1996), and as further amended by the European Communities (Protection of Employment) Regulations, 2000, S.I. 488 (2000).

quirements that an employer must follow in case of collective redundancies. Collective redundancies mean dismissals arising from redundancy during any period of 30 consecutive days, where the numbers being made redundant fall within the following categories:

- at least 5 in an establishment normally employing more than 20 and fewer than 50 employees;
- at least 10 in an establishment normally employing at least 50 but fewer than 100 employees;
- at least 10 percent of the number of employees in an establishment normally employing at least 100 but fewer than 300 employees; or
- at least 30 in an establishment normally employing 300 or more employees.

The Protection of Employment Act incorporates the two EU Collective Redundancies directives into Irish law.[220]

i. Notice to employee representatives

An employer proposing to make collective redundancies must initiate consultations with employee representatives[221] with a view to reaching an agreement as to the manner in which redundancies are to be implemented and whether they can be avoided, reduced, or their consequences mitigated. An employee representative means a trade union, staff association, or a person or persons chosen by

[220]Council Directive 75/129/EEC, 1975 O.J. (L 48) 29; Council Directive 92/56/EEC, 1992 O.J. (L 245) 3. The two directives were consolidated into Council Directive 98/59/EC, 1998 O.J. (L 225) 16. For additional information about these directives, see IV.A. in the chapter on the European Union in Part 1 of Volume I.

[221]The definition of employee representatives has been extended by the European Communities (Protection of Employment) Regulations, 2000, S.I. 488 (2000), to include "in the absence of a trade union, staff association or excepted body, a person or persons chosen (under an arrangement put in place by the employer) by such employees from amongst their number to represent them in negotiations with the employer."

the employees likely to be affected by the proposed redundancies to represent them. The consultation should take place at least 30 days before the first dismissal takes effect.

The employer is obliged to provide the employee representatives with full information, in writing, in relation to the proposed redundancies. The information must include the following specifics:

- the reasons for the proposed redundancies;
- the number and descriptions or categories of employees proposed to be made redundant;
- the number of employees and description of categories normally employed;
- the period in which it is proposed to effect the redundancies;
- the criteria proposed for the selection of the workers to be made redundant; and
- the method of calculating any *ex gratia* redundancy payments.[222]

ii. *Notice to Minister for Enterprise, Trade, and Employment*

The employer also is obligated to notify the ETE Minister of the proposed redundancies at the earliest opportunity, but at least 30 days before the first dismissal takes effect.[223] Collective redundancies may not take effect before expiration of the 30-day period beginning on the date of notification to the Minister. Given the wording of the relevant section of the legislation,[224] it is arguable that the ETE Minister, or an individual employee or group of employees, could apply to the courts for an injunction preventing the redundancies until the necessary notice had been provided.

---

[222]See IV.A.2.b., below.

[223]S.I. 140 (1977) sets out the particulars that must be included in notification to the Minister.

[224]Protection of Employment Act, 1977, §14.

The ETE Minister may request the employer to enter into consultations with an officer authorized by the Minister in order to seek solutions for the problems caused by the proposed redundancies. Authorized officers usually are civil servants of the Department of Enterprise, Trade, and Employment, and they have the power to enter an employer's premises and make inquiries to be satisfied that the Protection of Employment Act has been complied with.

Failure to comply with the above obligations is a criminal offense punishable by a maximum fine of IR£1,500. Where the failure relates to the non-observance of the 30-day time period, the fine is a maximum of €12,500 (IR£9,844.55), under the Protection of Employees (Part-Time Work) Act, 2001.[225] Although failure to comply with the Protection of Employment Act potentially is a serious matter, it is fair to say that prosecutions are rare.[226]

d. Union Agreement

Although the consultation obligations under both the Protection of Employment Act and the Transfer of Undertakings Regulations specify that consultation should be with a view to seeking agreement, there is no absolute obligation to reach an agreement and, therefore, no requirement in law for the approval of the union. However, in practice, it may well be that the orderly wind-down of an operation would require agreement on who is to be made redundant (or more particularly, the selection criteria to be used) and the formula to be used for calculating the redundant employees *ex gratia* termination payments.[227]

e. Consultation With European Works Council

There is no requirement for prior approval of redundancies by the European Works Council, even where the proposed redundancies have a cross-border effect. However, the failure to inform

---

[225]Protection of Employees (Part-Time Work) Act, 2001, §21.

[226]Failure to comply with the requirements of the Act, as now amended, will give employees who have been disadvantaged a right of action, among other remedies, to compensation not exceeding four weeks remuneration.

[227]See IV.A.2.b., below.

and consult with the Works Council in advance of implementing cross-border redundancies potentially could have serious consequences for the employer. This could include fines of up to IR£10,000 or even imprisonment for a period of up to three years for the individuals directly involved. In addition, breach of the constituent documentation of the Works Council may itself represent a breach of agreement between the employer and the employees that could result in industrial action. To date, there has been no judicial intervention in this regard in Ireland. However, in *Comite de Groupe Europenne Renault v. Renault Groupe*,[228] a French court granted an "ordonnance de référé" (equivalent to a common law injunction or interim order) to restrain the employer from closing its Belgian plant until all information and consultation obligations under national law and the individual Works Council Agreement had been complied with. Although this decision was made at the national level, it has significance for Irish employers in that the law ultimately derived from the Works Council Directive.

2. *Redundancy Payments*

a. *Statutory Redundancy Payments*

The primary legislation in this area of Irish employment law is the Redundancy Payments Act, 1967 to 2003 (RPA), which provides, inter alia, for payments from employers to employees in the event of redundancy. Redundancy is defined in the RPA as occurring in one of the following situations:

- the employer has ceased, or intends to cease, to carry on the business for the purposes for which, or in the place where, the employee was employed;
- the requirements of a particular business in a particular place for employees to carry out work of a particular kind have ceased or diminished or are expected to;
- the employer has decided to carry on the business with fewer or no employees, by requiring other employees to do the work for which the employee had been employed;

---

[228]This 1997 case is unreported.

- the employer has decided that, henceforth, the work should be done in a different manner for which the employee is not sufficiently qualified or trained; or
- the employer has decided that, henceforth, the work should be done by a person who also is capable of doing other work for which the employee is not sufficiently qualified or trained.

Redundancies also can occur in a layoff or short-time situation. A layoff occurs where an employee's employment ceases because the employer is unable to provide work, it is reasonable in the circumstances for the employer to believe that the cessation of employment will not be permanent, and the employer gives such notice to the employee prior to the cessation. A short-time situation arises where there is a decrease in the employee's work so that the employee's pay is less than 50 percent of normal weekly pay. If the employee has been laid off or kept on short-time for four or more consecutive weeks, or for a series of six or more weeks (of which not more than three are consecutive) within a period of 13 weeks, then the employee may be entitled to a redundancy payment. In a layoff or short-time situation, the onus is on the employee to claim a payment.

The employee must fulfill certain conditions in order to qualify for a statutory redundancy payment. Specifically, the employee must meet the following criteria:

- work or have worked under a contract of service, including, in a redundancy situation, a fixed-term expired contract, or under an apprenticeship or as an agency worker;
- have been in employment which was insurable for all social welfare benefits and have earned at least €31.75 (IR£25) per week;
- be between 16 and 66 years of age;
- normally have been expected to work at least eight hours per week (this includes regular part-time employees);
- have been continuously employed for 104 weeks between the ages of 16 and 66 years; and

- have been dismissed within the statutory definition of dismissal.[229]

An employee who fulfills the above conditions, and who has been dismissed by reason of redundancy, is entitled to a statutory redundancy payment, calculated as follows:

- two week's normal remuneration for each year of continuous and reckonable service between the ages of 16 and 66;[230] plus
- the equivalent of one week's normal weekly remuneration.

Various complex rules apply to the calculation of statutory redundancy payments to take account of commission and other varied payments. The weekly wage that is used for the calculation of statutory redundancy pay is the wage applying on the date that the employee is declared redundant, subject to a ceiling of €507.90 per week, or alternatively, €26,410.80 (IR£20,800) per year.[231]

In the event that an employee is offered suitable alternative employment by the employer, this may disqualify the employee from receiving a redundancy payment.

Statutory redundancy payments, i.e., that part of any severance package to which a redundant employee is entitled under the RPA, are tax free.

b. Ex Gratia *Termination Payments*

Given the relatively low level of statutory redundancy payments, employers often will provide employees with *ex gratia* termination pay, i.e., monies over and above the statutory minimum. Subject to the following comments, there normally is no legal obligation for employers to make *ex gratia* payments.

In unionized employment, there may be a written agreement dealing with the question of redundancy payments. If such an agreement exists, the employer will be bound by its terms if the parties

[229]See I.C.2.c., above.

[230]For a definition of "reckonable service," see V.A.1., below.

[231]Redundancy Payments (Lump Sum) Regulations, S.I. 41 (2000), applied these limits as of April 1, 2001.

intended the agreement to be legally binding[232] and, thus, will be obliged to pay the levels of redundancy payments set out in the agreement.

Even in the absence of a written agreement, if there is an oral agreement as to the level of redundancy payments that the employer will make, or if the employer previously has adopted a particular policy (albeit unwritten) in relation to the question of redundancy payments, then the employer may find itself bound by the oral agreement or previous policy. In the absence of any precedent binding the employer on the question of redundancies, it is likely that the expectation of employees, or a union acting on their behalf in any redundancy negotiations, will be based loosely around recent redundancy arrangements in comparable industries.

The employer always should be aware, when making redundancy payments in excess of the statutory minimum, of section 51 of the Redundancy Payments Act, 1967, which states that "any provision in an agreement (whether a contract of employment or not) shall be void insofar as it purports to exclude or limit the operation of a provision of this Act." Under section 51, it is valid for the employee to sign an agreement acknowledging receipt of the statutory lump sum and waiving any claim against the employer arising out of the redundancy. However, that agreement must be express and untainted by any hint of undue pressure. The employee also must be fully informed of the consequences of his or her decision. Oftentimes, it may be worthwhile for the employer to insist that the employee obtain independent legal advice on this matter. In any event, caution always must be exercised in redundancy settlements to ensure that either the statutory lump sum is paid separately, or to specify that amount separately in any agreement, so that the employee knows what the statutory payment is and cannot claim subsequently that it was not received.

In addition to the tax-free status applicable to statutory redundancy payments, the Finance Acts[233] provide certain additional allowances for employee termination payments. The Finance Act, 2001, provides that the first €10,160 of a termination payment,

---

[232]See II.F.1., above.

[233]The "Finance Acts" is the collective term used to refer to annual Finance Act introduced to implement the budgetary policies of the Government.

together with €765 for each complete year of service, may be paid tax free. On application to the Revenue Commissioners, an employee may receive an additional €10,000 tax free, provided that he or she has not availed of this exemption in the previous 10 years.

B. Transfers of Undertakings

1. Application

The European Communities (Protection of Employees on Transfer of Undertakings) Regulations, 2003 (the 2003 Regulations), implement the provisions of EU Council Directive 23/2001[234] and replace the 1980 Regulations previously in force. The new Directive was essentially an amalgamation of the Acquired Rights Directive[235] and principles of law that have been handed down on that Directive by the European Court of Justice (ECJ). As such, the Regulations do not substantially revise this area of the law; instead, the Regulations clarify it.

The Regulations apply to any transfer of an undertaking or business (or parts thereof) from one employer (transferor) to another employer (transferee) as a result of a legal transfer or merger. A legal transfer in this regard can include the assignment or forfeiture of a lease. A transfer is defined as the "transfer of an economic entity, i.e. an organized grouping of resources which has the objective of pursuing an economic activity, which retains its identity."

The basic provisions of the Regulations are:

- the right not to be dismissed for a transfer-connected reason;

[234] Council Directive 2001/23/EC, 2002 O.J. (L 82) 16. For a more detailed discussion of this Directive, see IV.B. in the chapter on the EU in Part 1 of Volume I, and I.C.1.a. in the chapter on Employment and Corporate Law Issues When Restructuring Companies in the EU, in Part 5 of Volume I.

[235] Council Directive 77/187/EEC on the approximation of the laws of the Member States relating to the safeguarding of employees' rights in the event of transfers of undertaking, businesses or parts of businesses, 1977 O.J. (L 61) 26.

- the right to have maintained by the transferee the employment rights and obligations previously owed by the transferor;
- existing terms and conditions of employment may not be made any less favorable, by reason of the transfer, even with the consent of the employees who are transferring;
- the transferee must continue to observe the terms and conditions of any collective agreement which applies to the employees, on the same terms previously applicable to the transferor;
- the transferor and the transferee must inform the representative(s) of their respective employees affected by the transfer, of the implications of the transfer (see below); and
- the transferor and transferee must consult with the representative(s) of their respective employees affected by the transfer on any measures envisaged in relation to the employees, with a view to reaching an agreement.

Therefore, all employees wholly or mainly engaged in the business transferring, are entitled to transfer automatically to the transferee on the same terms and conditions of employment, with their continuity of service intact.

The Regulations do not apply in relation to employees' rights to old age, invalidity, or survivor's benefits under company pension's schemes, which fall outside the scope of the Social Welfare Acts. However, if these benefits are provided for under a company pension scheme that is an occupational pension scheme within the meaning of the Pensions Act, 1990–2003, their accrued rights must be protected under those Acts. This is the responsibility of the transferee under the Regulations. However, recent interpretation of the initiating directive in the U.K. suggests that pension schemes intended to cover situations other than old age, invalidity, or death of a spouse may be covered, such that the Regulations could apply in the simple form to a scheme to provide a pension or similar payment in the event of redundancy. This issue is by no means conclusive.

The Regulations do not prohibit dismissals by reason of economic, technical, or organizational reasons entailing changes in the workforce (this has been broadly defined in relevant case-law as redundancy).

2. *Information and Consultation Obligations*

As before, transferor and transferee are obliged to inform the representatives of their respective employees affected by the transfer of:

- the date or proposed date of the transfer;
- the reasons for the transfer;
- the legal, social, and economic implications of the transfer for the employees; and
- any measures envisaged in relation to the employees.

However, the Regulations now give a specific time period in which this must be done, which did not exist previously. This information must be given to the employees' representatives where reasonably practicable, not later than 30 days before the transfer is carried out, otherwise in good time before the transfer is carried out.

Where there are any measures envisaged in relation to the employees, consultation must take place, in relation to any such measures, with a view to reaching an agreement. The time frame for such consultation period is, again, where reasonably practicable, not later than 30 days before the transfer is carried out, but, if not practicable, in good time before the transfer is carried out. Note that the Regulations do not specify that an agreement must be reached on all issues, but simply that the employer consult "with a view to reaching an agreement."

Employee representatives are defined in the Regulations as a "trade union, staff association or excepted body, with which it has been the practice of the employer to conduct collective bargaining negotiations." However, if none exists in the organization, the definition is extended to include persons elected under an arrangement put in place by the employer by the affected employees to represent them in consultations with the employer. If, therefore, the employees concerned do not have a trade union or employee representative body to represent them in the negotiation process, the transferor and transferee will be required to put in place a procedure under which their respective employees can elect one or more from among their number for the purpose of consultation.

In circumstances where there are still no representatives of the employees, written notification containing the above details must be given to all affected employees, within the same time frame as above.

3. Collective Agreements and Employee Representation

Where there are any collective agreements in force between the transferor and the employees, the transferee is obliged, under the Regulations, to continue to observe the terms and conditions agreed in that collective agreement, on the same terms as were applicable to the transferor, until the date of termination or expiration thereof, or until a new collective agreement comes into force.

Regulation 7 governs employee representation, and it states that where the business or undertaking (or parts thereof) that is transferring preserves its autonomy after the transfer, the status and function of employees' representatives affected by the transfer must be preserved by the transferee on the same terms and conditions as existed prior to transfer, whether by virtue of relevant legislation or a collective agreement. Further, where that business transferring does not preserve its autonomy, the transferee must arrange for the transferring employees, who were represented before the transfer, to elect person(s) from among their number to represent them during the period necessary for the reconstitution of their old representation or the reappointment of employee representatives.

4. Agreement to Limit or Waive Application of the Regulations

Regulation 9 provides that a provision in any agreement that purports to exclude or limit the application of any provision of the Regulations, or that is inconsistent with any of its provisions, will be void. Indeed, where a provision of such an agreement is or becomes less favorable in relation to an employee than his or her corresponding entitlement under the Regulations, that provision shall be deemed to be modified so as to conform to the entitlement conferred under the Regulations. Therefore, an employee cannot even agree to waive a benefit or entitlement that he or she previously enjoyed, even if paid compensation for such waiver, unless such compensation were of equal value or more favorable to the employee.

There is no prohibition on an employee agreeing to an entitlement or benefit that would be more favorable to them than their entitlement would be under the Regulations.

5. *Liability*

Either an employee or the employee's representative can bring a complaint to a Rights Commissioner stating that an employer has contravened any of the Regulations. The Rights Commissioner can require the employer to comply with the Regulations and to take a specified course of action, or can require the employer to compensate the employee in an amount not exceeding four weeks remuneration (in the case of breach of consultation and notification obligations) and not exceeding two years remuneration (in the case of contravention of any of the other provisions of the Regulations).

The decision of the Rights Commissioner can be appealed to the Employment Appeals Tribunal within six weeks of the date on which the decision was communicated to the parties. A further appeal from a determination of the Tribunal lies to the High Court on a point of law only. Where a Rights Commissioner or the Tribunal requires the employer to take a specified course of action and the employer fails to do so, the employee or his or her representative, or the Minister for Enterprise, Trade and Employment, may make an application to the Circuit Court, which, without hearing the employer's evidence, can make an order directing the employer to carry out the decision or determination in accordance with its terms.

If an employee is dismissed or resigns from a position following a variation on his or her terms and conditions of employment, that employee could claim unfair dismissal or constructive dismissal under the Unfair Dismissals Acts, 1977–2001, where the maximum compensation is two years gross remuneration. However, an employee cannot take a claim against an employer in respect of such dismissal under both the 2003 Regulations and the Unfair Dismissals legislation.

V. WAGES, HOURS, AND LEAVE

A. Wages

1. Minimum Wage

Until early 2000, there was no legislation fixing a national minimum wage in Ireland. Workers in certain industry sectors, such as contract cleaning, had minimum rates of pay (and other conditions of employment) set for them by employment regulation orders issued by Joint Labor Committees (JLCs). The JLCs are set up by the Labor Court pursuant to the Industrial Relations Act, 1946, and are composed of an equal number of employer and employee representatives. Similarly, minimum rates of pay applied where certain collective agreements were registered with the Labor Court.[236] These collective agreements are concluded by Joint Industrial Councils (JICs), which are voluntary negotiating bodies for a particular industry, representative of employers and trade unions within that industry.

The National Minimum Wage Act, 2000 (NMWA), came into force on April 4, 2000. The NMWA fixes a national minimum wage. As of October 2002, the minimum wage is €6.35 (IR£5.00) per hour. The NMWA applies to persons of any age who work under a contract of employment, including part-time employees. Any contractual provision that provides for a lower rate of pay than that to which an employee would be entitled under the NMWA is modified to the extent necessary to comply with the statutory minimum wage.

All employees older than age 18, with the exception of apprentices and employees who are close relatives of the employer, are entitled to the minimum hourly rate of pay, unless the employee falls into a category to which the sub-minimum rate applies. Sub-minimum rates apply to employees younger than age 18, job entrants who enter employment for the first time, and trainees. The sub-minimum rate varies from 70 percent to 90 percent of the national minimum hourly rate.

---

[236]See II.F.2., above.

In calculating the minimum hourly rate under the NMWA, "working hours" are defined in the alternative, according to which definition produces the greatest number of working hours in the particular case. These alternative definitions are as follows:

- the hours of work set out for the employee in the employment contract, any collective agreement (including a registered agreement), any employee regulation order, any statement of terms and conditions,[237] any notification to the employee under the OWTA,[238] or any other agreement that includes a provision in relation to hours of work; or
- the total hours worked by the employee at the place of employment, or the total hours that the employee is required by his or her employer to be available for work there and for which the employee is paid as if carrying out work.

Working hours include overtime, time spent traveling on business, and time spent on training or courses during normal working hours. Working hours do not include travel to and from work; time spent on annual, sick, protective, adoptive, or parental leave; periods of layoff, strike, or lockout; time for which an employee is paid in lieu of notice; or time spent on standby or on-call at a place other than a place of work.

Under the NMWA, reckonable pay includes basic salary, as well as any shift premium, service pay distributed through the payroll, piece and incentive rates, or commissions and bonuses that are productivity-related. However, service pay (if given directly to the employee, not distributed through the payroll), overtime, callout, public holiday, Saturday and Sunday premiums, any payment attributable to the employee's redundancy, pension contributions paid by the employer, and any payment in-kind or benefit in-kind (other than payment of board and lodgings), all constitute nonreckonable pay for purposes of the NMWA.

An employee's average hourly rate of pay is calculated over a specified pay reference period by dividing reckonable pay by the number of hours worked during such period. For this purpose, the

---

[237]See I.B.1.a., above.

[238]OWTA §§17, 18. See V.C.8., below.

maximum pay reference period is one calendar month. The hourly rate then is compared with the minimum hourly rate as prescribed by NMWA. In the event that the actual hourly rate of pay is less than the statutory rate, the underpayment must be paid to the employee.

2. *Payment of Wages*

The Payment of Wages Act, 1991 (PWA), confers three rights on employees, as follows:

- the right to a readily negotiable method of payment,[239]
- the right to a written statement of wages and deductions,[240] and
- protection against unlawful deductions from wages.[241]

Employers and employees may not, by contract, waive provisions of the PWA. The PWA covers all employees who are working under an employment contract or apprenticeship, who are employed through an employment agency or subcontractor, or who are employed in the service of the state.[242]

a. *Definition of Wages*

Wages for purposes of the PWA are defined to include normal basic pay, as well as any overtime; any fee, bonus, or commission; holiday, sick, or maternity pay or any other form of payment; or any sum payable to an employee in lieu of termination notice. In *Sullivan v. Department of Education*,[243] the EAT interpreted this definition to include a degree achievement allowance paid to a secondary school teacher.

Payments that are not regarded as wages include the following:

---

[239]Payment of Wages Act, 1991 (PWA), §2.
[240]*Id.* §4.
[241]*Id.* §5.
[242]*Id.* §4.
[243][1998] E.L.R. 217 (EAT).

- expense payments;
- any payment by way of pension, allowance, or gratuity in connection with the death, retirement, or resignation of the employee or compensation for loss of office;
- any payment relating to the employee's redundancy;
- any payment to the employee otherwise than in the employee's capacity as an employee;
- any payment in-kind or benefit in-kind; or
- any repayment of loans to employees as individuals, other than as benefits under a loan scheme.

b. *Modes or Methods of Payment*

Section 2(1) of the PWA lists the following permissible methods of payment of wages:

- check or bank draft drawn on any of the commercial banks or a trustee savings bank;
- payable order warrant issued by a government minister or a public authority;
- postal order, money order, or paying order warrant issued by or drawn on *An Post* (post office);
- credit transfer to an account specified by the employee;
- cash; or
- any other mode specified in regulations issued by the ETE Minister after consultation with the Minister for Finance.

The last method enables the ETE Minister to keep up to date with rapid developments and advances in electronic data processing. Employers are required to make alternative arrangements for wage payments where a strike or other industrial action affects banks or other financial institutions, so that cash is readily available to employees who are paid by a noncash method.

c. *Right to a Written Statement*

Section 4 of the PWA imposes an obligation on employers to give each employee a written statement indicating the gross amount payable, and the nature and amount of any deduction. The statement must be given to the employee at the time of wage payment, except in the case of payment by credit transfer, in which case the statement should be given as soon as possible thereafter. The employer is not under an obligation to treat all such information as confidential.

d. Deductions From Wages

i. Allowable deductions

Section 5 of the PWA sets out the deductions that employers are entitled to make from their employees' pay. In general terms, deductions may be made only where they are authorized or required to be made by or under statute, under a term of the employment contract, or pursuant to an advance written agreement from the employee.

Decisions of the EAT emphasize that there must be a document clearly stating that the deduction is to be made from the employee's wages. In *Murphy v. Ryanair*,[244] the employee was suspended without pay for one week. However, because there was no provision for the deduction in the employment contract or in a written statement prior to the suspension, the EAT held that the employee was entitled to pay for that week. In *Curust Hardware Ltd. v. Dalton*,[245] the employer deducted a sum corresponding to one month's pay plus a bonus because the employee failed to give termination notice as required by her employment contract. Although the contract provided for one month's notice, there was no express provision allowing a deduction in wages for failure to give notice. Accordingly, the EAT ruled that such a term could not be implied, and that the employee was entitled to the monies due for the period she worked.

An employer may not make a deduction from wages for any act or omission of the employee, or any goods or services supplied to the employee where they are necessary for the employment, unless the deduction or payment to the employer is provided for in the employment contract, and the amount of the deduction or payment is fair and reasonable. At some time prior to the act or omission or the provision of goods or services, written details of the

---

[244]P.W. 2/92 (EAT).
[245]P.W. 1/92 (EAT).

contract terms governing the deductions or payments must be provided to the employee.

ii. Deductions and payments outside the application of the PWA

The restrictions on deductions do not apply in certain circumstances, such as the following:

- statutory deductions (for example, PAYE and PRSI);[246]
- deductions for the overpayment of wages and expenses;
- deductions arising from a strike or industrial action in which the employee was involved; or
- deductions arising from certain court orders (e.g., an attachment of earnings order to pay spousal maintenance).

iii. Redress and complaints procedure

Employees who have been subject to unlawful deductions may complain to a Rights Commissioner[247] within six months of the alleged deduction. The claimant may be awarded the net amount of wages in the week preceding the deduction, or, if the amount of the deduction is greater than one week's wages, then twice the amount of the deduction.

An appeal may be made first to the EAT and then, on a point of law only, to the High Court. Decisions made by the Rights Commissioner or determinations of the EAT on appeal may be enforced as if they were an order of the circuit court in civil proceedings.

B. Taxes (Including Social Insurance)

1. Residence and Domicile

a. Residence

An individual's liability for taxation in Ireland is based on residence, not citizenship. An individual is regarded as resident in Ireland for a tax year if any of the following criteria are satisfied:

---

[246]See V.B.3., below.
[247]See the Introduction, at D.2.b., above.

- the individual has spent 183 days or more in Ireland in the tax year;
- in the current tax year and the preceding tax year, the individual has spent a total of 280 days or more in Ireland; or
- the individual elects to be treated as Irish resident for the tax year, provided that the individual satisfies the Revenue Commissioners that he or she is in Ireland with the intent of being a resident for the following tax year.

For purposes of the 183- and 280-day criteria, an individual will not be regarded as a resident for a tax year in which he or she does not spend 30 days in Ireland. For purposes of determining the number of days someone spends in Ireland in the tax year, the individual will be regarded as being present in Ireland for a particular day if he or she is in Ireland at the end of that day, i.e., at midnight.

As of January 1, 2001, the Irish tax year runs from January 1 to December 31.

b. Domicile

The concept of domicile is different from residence. Essentially, domicile means the place where one has a permanent home and roots, i.e., where one ultimately intends to live and be buried. Individuals acquire the domicile of their parents at birth (domicile of origin). Subsequently, an individual may change domicile and acquire a "domicile of choice." Generally, however, it is very difficult to change domicile. A corollary of this is that it is relatively easy to maintain a non-Irish domicile as long as one does not give any indication of an intent to reside in Ireland permanently.

Individuals who are non-Irish domiciled can take advantage of the remittance basis of taxation.[248]

c. Ordinarily Resident

An individual is regarded as ordinarily resident in Ireland for a tax year if he or she has been an Irish resident for each of the

---

[248]See V.B.2., below.

three preceding tax years. However, an individual will not cease to be ordinarily resident in Ireland for a tax year until he or she has not been resident in Ireland for each of the three preceding tax years.

d. Foreign Contract of Employment

In order to obtain the advantages of the remittance basis of assessment for employment income (discussed immediately below), it is necessary to have a foreign contract of employment (i.e., non-Irish or UK) and to be paid outside Ireland. Under Irish tax law, the source of employment income is not the place where the activities of employment are exercised, but is determined by the place where the employment contract is deemed to have a locality and where the payments for the employment are made. Therefore, to ensure that the employment contract is regarded as foreign, the following steps should be followed:

- the offer and acceptance of the employment contract should be made in the country where the contract is located;
- the contract should be governed by the particular law of the country where it is located, rather than the country in which the services are to be performed; and
- payments must be made into a bank account outside of Ireland and the UK.

(For purposes of Irish tax legislation, references to the UK do not include the Isle of Man or the Channel Islands.)

2. Remittance Basis of Assessment

The income of individuals who are resident in Ireland but not domiciled in Ireland and of Irish citizens who are not ordinarily resident in Ireland is taxed as set out below.

a. Income

Income from sources in Ireland and the UK is taxed in full in the year in which the income arises. Where the employment contract is a foreign contract of employment, as defined immediately above, employment income should be regarded as foreign source income and taxable only to the extent that the income is remitted to Ireland. Remittances may be either actual or constructive. The latter includes situations where a person in Ireland meets an expense on an employee's behalf, and the employee subsequently reimburses that person outside Ireland from unremitted (and therefore untaxed) income.

Where an individual is appointed a director of an Irish company, the remuneration received from the directorship is considered Irish source income and subject to Irish tax. Also, amounts paid by a company on an individual's behalf with respect to Irish tax liability are taxable as an additional benefit if the individual is resident in Ireland when this happens.

Benefits in-kind (e.g., cars, accommodation) provided in Ireland also are taxable in Ireland. Where a car is provided to an individual in Ireland, the individual is taxable on 30 percent of the original cost of the car, assuming that the company pays all motoring costs including private mileage. This figure can be reduced to the extent that the individual contributes in Ireland toward the cost of the benefit. The provision of accommodation by a company also is regarded as a benefit in-kind and normally is subject to tax on an amount equal to the rental payment made by the company.

As of January 1, 2004, the taxable benefits of most benefits in kind will be taxable under the Pay As You Earn (PAYE) system.[249] In general, the amount subject to tax is the higher of (1) the expense incurred by the employer in connection with the provision of the benefit to the employee, or (2) the value realizable by the employee for the benefit on money or in money's worth. In addition, specific statutory valuation rules apply regarding the private use of a company car and the provision of preferential loans.

For the tax year ending December 31, 2002, individuals are entitled to standard personal tax credits as set out in the following tables:

---

[249]See V.B.3.a., below, for a detailed discussion of the PAYE system.

INCOME TAX RATES AND CREDITS

Tax Year Ending December 31, 2003

TAXABLE INCOME

Single €	Married One Income (Joint Returns) €	Married Two Incomes (Joint Returns) €	One-Parent Families €	Marginal Tax Rates €
28,000	37,000	56,000*	32,000	20%
Balance	Balance	Balance	Balance	42%

*Transferable between two spouses up to a maximum of €37,000 for any one spouse.

CREDITS

	Single €	Married (Joint Returns) €
Personal Allowance	1520	3040
PAYE Allowance	800	800

Gains of individuals who are resident in Ireland but not domiciled in Ireland are taxed as set out below.[250]

b. Capital Gains

Capital gains derived from assets located in Ireland and the UK are subject to Irish capital gains tax. For an individual who is non-Irish domiciled, capital gains derived from assets located outside of Ireland and the UK are subject to Irish capital gains tax only to the extent that the proceeds of sale are remitted to Ireland. The current rate of Irish capital gains tax is 20 percent.

c. Remittances of Capital

Capital may be remitted to Ireland without incurring any liability for income tax. For this purpose, "capital" comprises any funds that are available at the date of taking up residence in Ireland and any subsequent acquisition of capital funds by way of gifts or sale of tax-exempt assets.

---

[250]Remittance basis for capital gains tax purposes does not apply to Irish citizens who are not ordinarily resident in Ireland.

Where, prior to taking up residence in Ireland, an individual has accumulated savings, these savings should be regarded as "capital." Provided that the savings are not tainted with subsequent income, they can be remitted to Ireland without incurring an Irish tax liability.

3. *Income Tax and Social Insurance Deductions*

a. *Pay-as-You-Earn System*

Every employer making any payment of employment income to an employee is obliged to deduct income tax from the payment. This system is referred to as the "pay-as-you-earn" (PAYE) system. The PAYE system has been designed to ensure, so far as possible, that the total income tax deducted from each employee's remuneration during the tax year approximates the income tax payable by the employee for that particular year. Historically, this was done through a system of tax free allowances, which spreads each employee's personal allowances and other deductions evenly through the year, and by the use of PAYE tax tables, under which tax was deducted from an employee's net taxable pay at the rate or rates applicable to his or her expected income level for the year. As of April 6, 2001, PAYE is operated using a tax credit system whereby credits are given against the individual's tax liability. The main features of the PAYE system are summarized below.

For an employee who has a foreign contract of employment,[251] the PAYE obligations do not apply. An employee who is on a temporary assignment in Ireland[252] is subject to the PAYE system only if the employee is working under an Irish contract of employment.

i. *Employer registration*

Every employer that pays remuneration at a rate exceeding €8 per week to one or more employees, whether employed on a permanent or temporary basis, is required to register as an employer with the Revenue Commissioners. Thereafter, the employer

[251] See V.B.1.d., above.
[252] See V.B.3.a.iii., below.

is required to implement the PAYE procedure with respect to all employee remuneration and to account monthly to the Collector-General for all tax deducted from employees. The employer also is required to prepare returns of employees and the tax deducted at the end of each year.

The employer is provided with a tax deduction card by the PAYE Inspector of Taxes for each employee liable for PAYE. The Inspector of Taxes advises the employer with respect to each employee of the tax credits, standard rate cut-off point, and rate of tax to use in calculating the tax for each payday. Employers that use a manual PAYE system receive this information in the tax deduction card for the employee. Employers that use their own system receive the information in a notice called a "Certificate of Tax Credits and the Standard Rate Cut-Off Point." Employers that are members of the Computer Media Exchange Scheme receive the information in electronic format. An employer that fails to deduct any required tax from an employee's pay may be held directly liable for the tax.

ii. Notice of determination of tax credits and standard rate cut-off point

The notice of determination of tax credits and standard rate cut-off point is issued by the PAYE Inspector of Taxes and contains details of the tax credits and standard rate cut-off point to which the employee is entitled for the tax year. An individual who commences employment for the first time, or who is assigned to work in Ireland for the first time, should apply for a notice of determination by completing a Form 12A. PAYE is applied to the new employee's pay in accordance with this notice of determination as soon as it is received by the employer.

iii. Employees on temporary assignment

An employee who is on temporary assignment in Ireland should qualify for the remittance basis of taxation.[253] However, where the employee has an Irish contract, he or she will come within the scope of the PAYE system.

[253]See V.B.2., above.

iv. Taxable pay

The employer deducts income tax computed at the appropriate PAYE tax rate from each employee's cumulative taxable pay at the time each payment is made. Taxable pay is gross pay less the amount of the employee's contributions (if any) to an exempt, approved pension plan or to a statutory plan. A benefit in-kind is not regarded as a payment for this purpose. Consequently, the amount taxable with respect to in-kind benefits is not included in gross pay or taxable pay, and tax is not deducted directly for such benefits. However, the PAYE Inspector seeks, where possible, to bring in-kind benefits indirectly within the PAYE system by deducting them from the individual's tax free credits.

v. Emergency card procedure

The PAYE System provides for the employer to deduct income tax through an emergency card procedure in cases where the necessary notice of determination of tax credits and standard rate cut-off point has not been received from the employee. The emergency card procedure allows the employee minimum tax credits for the first four weeks of a new employment, and no credits thereafter until the necessary certificate is received. It is very important for all employees to ensure that they comply with the necessary formalities so that they can obtain their proper credits as soon as possible. When the proper notice is obtained, the employee is entitled to be repaid any excess tax incurred through the emergency procedure.

b. Pay-Related Social Insurance

In addition to the deduction of taxes under the PAYE system, employers also are obliged to deduct Pay-Related Social Insurance (PRSI) on behalf of the Department of Social Welfare and pay the same to the Collector-General concurrently with the remittance of income tax deductible under the PAYE system. The employer is liable to pay to the Collector-General both the employee's and its own PRSI contributions with respect to the remuneration paid to the employee each month.

The employee's PRSI contribution is made up of two main components, as follows:

- *Social Insurance*: This varies according to the earnings of the employee and the benefits for which the person is insured. The rate at which PRSI is calculated is determined by the PRSI class of the individual employee.
- *Health Levy*: The current health levy rate is 2 percent.

The employer's PRSI contribution for each employed contributor also is made up of two parts, namely, the employer's contributions to the social insurance fund and the employer's contribution to the redundancy fund.

PRSI contribution rates for the tax year ending December 31, 2003, are set out in the table below.

PRSI CONTRIBUTIONS

Tax Year Ending December 31, 2003

SOCIAL INSURANCE	PERCENT	PAYABLE TO
Employer's Portion	10.75	Department of Social Welfare
Employee's Portion (first €127 of weekly earnings exempt) (up to a maximum of €40,420)	4	Department of Social Welfare

HEALTH LEVY	PERCENT	PAYABLE TO
Payable by Employee (total income)	2	Collector-General

Individuals working in Ireland under foreign contracts of employment[254] are regarded as being in insurable employment and, consequently, liable for PRSI contributions on employment income under a special collection system (whether remitted or not). However, individuals who are nationals of another EU Member State or of the United States may be exempted from PRSI for up to five years if they obtain a certificate of coverage from the social insurance authorities in their home country.

---

[254]See V.B.1.d., above.

c. P35 End-of-Year Return

The P35 is the annual return of PAYE/PRSI details that employers are obliged to complete and submit to the Collector-General at the end of each tax year. The purposes of the P35 are as follows:

- to provide details of pay, tax, and social insurance contributions for all employees (including directors) employed by an employer during the tax year or, in the event of cessation or insolvency, during the current tax year to cessation; and
- to provide a balancing statement with respect to tax and social insurance contributions deducted and paid to the Collector-General for the tax year.

Beginning with tax years ending December 31, 2001, a set of P35 returns and instructions is issued to each employer prior to the year end, with a date of February 15 by which they must be returned to the Employer's (P35) Unit.

4. Tax Payment

a. Payment Schedule

The Irish tax year now ends on December 31. In order to avoid interest penalties, individuals (excepting those whose tax liability has been satisfied through the PAYE system) are required to make a preliminary payment by October 31 of the tax year in an amount equal to 90 percent of the individual's final tax liability for the current year. This payment may be based on 100 percent of the individual's tax liability for the previous year. For the year 2002 only, preliminary tax is payable in an amount equal to 135 percent of the amount payable for the previous "short" tax year.

b. Filing of Returns

For each tax year of residence in Ireland, individuals are required to submit a return of income. With the move to a calendar tax year, individual tax returns now must be submitted before October 31 of the year following the end of the tax year. Once a return has been submitted, the Inspector of Taxes will send out a notice of assessment, and any balance of tax must be paid within one month of receipt.

C. Hours

The Organization of Working Time Act, 1997 (OWTA), implements into Irish law the provisions of the 1993 EU Directive, which establishes certain standards for working time (Working Time Directive).[255] The OWTA applies to employees, unless otherwise excluded or exempted by the statute or pursuant to regulations issued by the ETE Minister.

The OWTA includes agency workers, who are placed by an employment agency, within the meaning of the Employment Agency Act, 1971.[256] However, the obligations imposed on an employer under the OWTA apply to the party liable to pay the wages of the agency worker. Thus, if the worker's wages are paid by the agency, any obligations that arise under the OWTA are those of the agency and not the business for whom the worker is actually providing services.

The ETE Minister may by regulations exempt from the application of any part of the OWTA persons employed in an activity involving the transport of goods or persons, or in what are described as the "civil protection services." Such services include fire and ambulance services, coast guard, and mountain rescue services.

The European Commission has published a new Directive on certain aspects of the organization of working time.[257] The new Directive consolidates the provisions contained in a number of earlier Directives on the organization of working time including Directive 93/104/EC,[258] which was given effect in this jurisdiction by the Organization of Working Time Act, 1997, and Directive 2000/43/EC. The original 1993 Directive had introduced certain minimum safety and health requirements for the organization of

---

[255]Council Directive 93/104/EC, 1993 O.J. (L 307) 18, amended by Council Directive 2000/34/EC, 2000 O.J. (L 195) 41. For a discussion of the Working Time Directive, see V.B. in the chapter on the EU in Volume I, Part 1.

[256]See I.D.3., above.

[257]European Parliament and Council Directive 2003/88/EC, 2003 O.J. (L 299) 9.

[258]Council Directive 93/104/EC, 1993 O.J. (L 307) 18.

working time and set out minimum periods of daily rest, weekly rest, and annual leave, as well as provisions dealing with maximum weekly working time and certain aspects of night work, shift work, and patterns of work. It also provided for a substantial amount of derogations and exceptions, including those that may be agreed by collective agreements. The new consolidated Directive is deemed to enter into force on August 2, 2004.

1. Rest Periods

Employees are entitled to a 15-minute break after four and one-half hours of continuous work, and to a break of at least 30 minutes after six hours of work. If the 15-minute break is not provided, then it may be included as part of the 30-minute break. Thus, if the 15-minute break is not taken after four and one-half hours, then a break of at least 45 minutes must be allowed after six hours.

Employees are entitled to a daily rest period of at least 11 consecutive hours. In each period of seven days, they also are entitled to a rest period of at least 24 consecutive hours, which should be preceded immediately by the daily rest period. If the employer is unable to provide a day off during a particular week, the requirement is satisfied if, during the following week, two days off are granted. Once again, if the two days off are granted consecutively, they must be preceded by the daily rest period. If the two days are granted separately, each one must be preceded by the daily rest period. Unless otherwise provided in the employment contract, the weekly rest period must include a Sunday. Thus, if a day off is missed during one week, such that two days off must be granted the following week, one of those days must be a Sunday.

2. Sunday Work

An employee who is required to work on a Sunday must be compensated for having to do so, unless this otherwise has been taken into account in determining the employee's rate of pay. The OWTA allows compensation to be paid in the form of a reasonable "allowance," by increasing the rate of pay by a reasonable amount, by allowing paid time off work, or by a combination of two or more of these methods.

3. *Weekly Working Hours*

An employer may not permit an employee to work, in each period of seven days, more than an average of 48 hours, calculated over a four-month averaging period. Under the OWTA, "working time" is defined to include only that time that the employee is at work or at the employer's disposal and is actually working.[259] Thus, rest breaks are not included in the basic 48-hour calculation.

The four-month averaging period may be increased to six months where there is a need for continuity of service or production (e.g., hospitals, docks/airports, gas, water, and electricity production), or where there is a foreseeable surge of activity, particularly in agriculture, tourism, or postal services. Furthermore, where an employee's weekly working hours vary on a seasonal basis, or where it would not be practical for the employer concerned to comply with the four (or six) month period, because of "objective considerations of a technical nature or related to the conditions"[260] under which the work concerned is organized, then a collective agreement, approved by the Labor Court, may specify a longer averaging period of up to 12 months.

It is not possible for an employer to pay a premium to an employee for working in excess of the 48-hour week. Indeed, even if an employee wished to contract out of the prohibition on working in excess of 48 hours per week, they are not permitted to do so. However, apart from this, certain employees, by virtue of the seniority of their positions, can determine the duration of their own working hours. Such employees are *ab anitio* not covered by the requirements of the OWTA on the 48-hour week and, accordingly, are permitted to work in excess of this period.

4. *Night Time Working Hours*

An employer may not require a night worker to work more than an average of eight hours per night, calculated over a two-month reference period. As in the case of weekly working hours, the reference period may be extended by way of a collective agree-

---

[259]OWTA §2(1).
[260]*Id.* §15(5)(b).

ment approved by the Labor Court. The term "night time" is defined by the OWTA as the period between midnight and 7:00 a.m., and "night worker" is defined as an employee who normally works at least three hours during night time and at least 50 percent of his or her total working hours for that year during night time.

Special category night workers may not be required to work more than eight hours per night. No averaging is allowed. "Special category night worker" covers those workers whose work involves special hazards or heavy physical or mental strain, which would make it undesirable and unsafe for them to work more than a maximum of eight hours in any 24-hour period.

5. *Prohibition on Double Employment*

An employer may not employ someone who also is working for another employer if the double employment would result in a breach of the OWTA, because the aggregate of the periods of work exceed what is permitted.

6. *Children and Young Persons*

No child[261] may be employed between 8:00 p.m. on any one day and 8:00 a.m. the following day. Children also are entitled to minimum rest periods of 14 consecutive hours in each 24-hour period, and a minimum rest period of two days in any seven-day period. After every four hours of work, a child must be given a break of at least 30 minutes.

For young persons,[262] working time is subject to the following special restrictions:

- work is not permitted for more than 8 hours per day or 40 hours per week;
- work is not permitted between 10:00 p.m. and 6:00 a.m. or, in exceptional circumstances, between 11:00 p.m. and 7:00 a.m.;
- there must be a daily rest period of at least of 12 consecutive hours;

[261]For a definition of child worker, see I.D.1.a., above.

[262]For a definition of young persons, see I.D.1.b., above.

- there must be a weekly rest period of at least two days; and
- there must be a rest break of at least 30 minutes after four and one-half hours of work.

7. *Exemptions*

The provisions on minimum rest periods and working time do not apply to a person who determines the duration of his or her own working time. This exception applies even if the employer stipulates a minimum period of time that must be worked and does not stipulate what freedom an employee has to decide his or her working time. Hence, it generally is regarded that the rest period provisions do not apply to senior management of a company.

The daily/weekly rest requirements do not apply to a person employed in shift work, whenever the rest periods cannot be taken because of a change in the employee's shift. Likewise, the daily and weekly rest periods do not apply to someone whose work is spread out over the day. The daily/weekly rest and work breaks provisions also do not apply where they are excluded by virtue of a collective agreement approved by the Labor Court, a registered employment agreement,[263] or an employment regulation order.[264]

The ETE Minister can, by regulations, exempt certain activities from application of the daily and weekly rest period requirements, work break requirements, and night time working hours restrictions. Exemptions apply, for example, to activities that require a continuity of service or production or that involve a foreseeable surge in the level of activity.[265] In addition, an employer need not comply with the provisions for daily and weekly rest, work breaks, or night time working hours where, due to exceptional circumstances or an emergency (including an accident or the imminent risk of an accident), compliance would not be practicable.

---

[263]See II.F.2., above.

[264]*See* Industrial Relations Act, 1990, §48.

[265]*See* EU Working Time Directive, art. 17, para. 2, pt. 2.1; *see also* Organization of Working Time (General Exemption) Regulations, 1998; Organization of Working Time (Exemption of Civil Protection Services) Regulations, 1998; Organization of Working Time (Exemption of Transport Activities) Regulations, 1998.

As a condition of any of the above exemptions, the employer must ensure that employees have available compensatory rest periods, or, where this is not possible, the employer must make available compensatory arrangements that will afford appropriate protection to the employee. The LRC has issued a Code of Practice on Compensatory Rest.[266]

8. *Notice of Working Hours*

Where the employee's normal or regular starting and finishing times of work are not specified in an employment contract, employment regulation order, or collective agreement, the employer must notify the employee, at least 24 hours in advance of the first or only workday in each week, of the times the employee normally will be required to start and finish work each day and the day(s) required in each week. If the hours for which an employee is required to work include such hours as the employer may from time to time decide, notice of additional hours must be given at least 24 hours in advance of the first or only workday in that week.

9. *Recordkeeping*

Additional, and rather onerous, recordkeeping obligations have been placed on employers in accordance with the Organization of Working Time Act, 1997 (OWTA). Effective November 1, 2001, the Organization of Working Time Act (Records) (Prescribed Form and Exemptions) Regulations, 2001, require employers to maintain specified records, including the following:

- a record of the number of hours worked by employees on a daily and weekly basis (excluding meals and rest breaks);
- a record of leave granted to employees in each week by way of annual leave, or with respect to a public holiday, and payment made for that leave;
- where applicable, a weekly record of the notice given to employees of starting and finishing times.[267]

---

[266]Organization of Working Time (Code of Practice on Compensatory Rest and Related Matters) (Declaration) Order, 1998. A claim for compensatory rest breaks was made by crane drivers in Coastal Line Container Ltd. v. SIPTU, [1999] E.L.R. 209 (Lab. Ct.), [2000] E.L.R. 1 (Ir. H. Ct.).

[267]See V.C.8., above.

The OWTA Regulations also incorporate a new statutory form on which employers that do not have electronic means of recording must record the number of hours worked by employees on a daily and weekly basis. Employers also are obliged to keep a copy of the statement given to each employee under the provisions of the Terms of Employment (Information) Act 1994.[268] The OWTA Regulations provide for exemptions, subject to certain conditions, with regard to recordkeeping requirements for employee rest periods. These exemptions will apply to those employers who have electronic recordkeeping facilities in place or those employers that do not have clocking in facilities, but require the employees to fill in the statutory OWT1 form to record their working hours. These exemptions will only apply to the employer if the employer complies with further conditions requiring them to notify employees in writing of the rest periods to which they are entitled under the 1997 Act, the existence of a procedure whereby employees may notify their employer in writing of any rest period or break entitlement which they were not able to avail of (which notification should include the reason for not availing of such rest period or break), and requiring the employer to keep a record of having notified employees of their entitlements as outlined and to maintain a record of all such notifications.

An employer must keep records, which must be retained for at least three years, to evidence compliance with the OWTA.

10. Employee Complaints

An employer may not penalize an employee for having, in good faith, opposed any action of the employer that is unlawful under the OWTA. An employee, or any trade union with the consent of the employee, may present a complaint to a Rights Commissioner[269] alleging that the employer has violated the OWTA.

A decision of a Rights Commissioner may require the employer to comply with the OWTA or require the employer to pay the employee such compensation as is "just and equitable," up to two years' remuneration.[270] The Rights Commissioner's determi-

---

[268]See I.B.l.a., above.

[269]For a discussion of the Rights Commissioner Service, see Introduction, at D.2.b., above.

[270]OWTA, §27.3(c).

nation is binding. However, a decision of the Rights Commissioner can be appealed to the Labor Court.

An employee has six months from the time of the employer's violation within which to bring a complaint, although this period may be extended to 12 months if the Rights Commissioner is satisfied that the failure to present the complaint within that period was due to reasonable cause.

D. Leave

1. Annual Leave

Every employee is entitled to paid annual leave, equal to whichever of the following periods is greater:

- four working weeks for a leave year in which the employee works at least 1,365 hours (unless it is a leave year in which there is a change of employment);
- one-third of a working week for each month in the leave year in which the employee works at least 117 hours; or
- 8 percent of the hours the employee works in a leave year (subject to a maximum of four working weeks).

All employees, not just those who normally are expected to work more than eight hours per week, are entitled to annual leave. If an employee has worked eight or more months in a leave year, then leave normally must include an unbroken period of two working weeks.

The times at which annual leave may be taken must be decided by the employer, having regard to work requirements. However, the employer must take into account the need for the employee to reconcile work and any family responsibilities and the opportunities for rest and recreation available to the employee. The employer also is obliged to consult with the employee or his or her trade union not later than one month before the day on which the annual leave is to be taken.

Annual leave must be granted within the leave year to which it relates or, with the consent of the employee, within six months thereafter.

An employee is entitled to be paid in advance of taking annual leave, at the normal weekly rate.

2. *Public Holidays*

The following are statutory public holidays:

- January 1;
- St. Patrick's Day;
- Easter Monday;
- The first Mondays in May, June, and August, and the last Monday in October;
- Christmas Day; and
- St. Stephen's Day.[271]

For each public holiday, the employee is entitled to one of the following, at the employer's discretion:

- a paid day off on that day,
- a paid day off within a month of that day,
- an additional day of annual leave, or
- an additional day's pay.[272]

An employee may request the employer, not later than 21 days before the public holiday, to nominate which of the above options will apply. Where the employer fails to nominate within 14 days of the public holiday, the employee automatically is entitled to a paid day off on that day.

Part-time employees are not entitled to a public holiday unless they have worked for the employer for at least 40 hours during the five-week period ending on the day before the public holiday. In addition, an employee will not be entitled to a particular public holiday if he or she is absent from work immediately before that holiday in any of the cases set out in the Third Schedule to the OWTA. For example, an absence in excess of 52 consecutive weeks, due to an injury sustained by the employee in an occupational accident; an absence in excess of 26 consecutive weeks, due to an injury sustained by the employee in an accident other

---

[271]OWTA, Second Schedule.

[272]*See* Cadbury Ireland Ltd. v. SIPTU, [1999] E.L.R. 202 (Lab. Ct.); Oceanmanpower Ltd. v. Marine Porter and General Workers Union, [1998] E.L.R. 299 (Lab. Ct.).

than an occupational accident or as a result of any disease from which the employee suffers or suffered; an absence in excess of 13 weeks, caused by any reason not referred to in the previous three cases but being an absence authorized by the employer, including layoff; or, finally, an absence due to a strike in the business or industry in which the employee is employed.

3. *Maternity and Adoptive Leave*

Following the recommendations of the Working Group on the Review and Improvement of Maternity Protection Legislation, the Maternity Protection (Amendment) Bill, 2003, has been published. The bill proposes a number of changes to existing arrangements for prenatal, maternity, and postnatal needs.

The bill introduces a number of changes to arrangements for maternity leave in the event of sickness, hospitalization, or death of the child. In certain circumstances, related leave will be available to the father of the child. Among the specific provisions contained in the bill are:

- provision for expectant mothers to attend one set of prenatal classes without loss of pay;
- provision of a once-off right of fathers to paid time off to attend two prenatal classes immediately prior to the birth of the child;
- specific provisions for breastfeeding mothers in relation to working hours and breaks without loss of pay; and
- provision that an employee's absence from work on additional maternity leave will count for all employment rights associated with the employment (except remuneration and superannuation benefits), such as seniority and annual leave.

a. *Maternity Leave*

The Maternity Protection Act, 1994 (MPA), provides for the protection of pregnant workers and workers who recently have given birth or are breastfeeding. The MPA covers all employees, irrespective of length of service.

An employee is entitled to maternity leave of 18 consecutive weeks. The employer has no obligation to pay an employee when she is on maternity leave. However, provided that she has paid 26 weeks' PRSI contributions in the 12 months immediately preceding maternity leave, she is entitled to state social welfare payments at the rate of 70 percent of her reckonable earnings,[273] subject to a weekly ceiling.

Entitlement to the minimum period of maternity leave is subject to written notification provided by the employee of her intent to take leave. This notice should be given no later than four weeks before the commencement of maternity leave and must include a medical certificate confirming the pregnancy and specifying the expected week of confinement.

In addition to the basic 18-week leave period, an employee also is entitled to an additional eight weeks of unpaid maternity leave and to paid time off during normal working time for prenatal and postnatal medical checks. In addition, employees who have returned to the workplace before the full statutory entitlement of maternity leave has expired are entitled to paid time off for postnatal care during the 18-week period following the birth.

The employer may not treat maternity leave as sick leave. Maternity leave is regarded as continuous employment and reckonable for the purposes of calculating annual leave. An employee on maternity leave also retains full public holiday entitlements.

As a general rule, the employee has a right to return to the same job she held prior to maternity leave. If the employer cannot give the employee back her old job, then it must provide suitable alternative work.

Notice of employment termination given during maternity leave, to take effect either during or after the end of the leave period, is void, and the employee will remain in employment.

b. Adoptive Leave

The Adoptive Leave Act, 1995, entitles an employed adopting mother (or sole male adopter) to a period of 14-weeks' unpaid leave, commencing on the day of the child's placement. This entitlement is subject to the same notice requirement as that applicable under the MPA. As with maternity leave, the employee has a

[273]For a definition of reckonable earnings, see V.A.1., above.

general right to return to the same job or to one that is a suitable alternative.

4. Parental Leave

The Parental Leave Act, 1998 (PLA), gives effect to the 1996 EU Directive on parental leave.[274] Under the PLA, parents of children born on or after June 3, 1996, or adopted on or after that date, are entitled to unpaid parental leave. Each parent is entitled to 14-weeks parental leave for each qualifying child. Except in certain circumstances, the leave must be taken before the child reaches five years of age, and the employee must have at least one year of continuous service with the employer before he or she is entitled to take parental leave. However, where the child is approaching the age threshold, and the employee has more than three months, but less than one year's, service with the employer, he or she is entitled to leave on a pro-rated basis. In such a case, the employee is entitled to one week's leave for every complete month of continuous employment with the employer at the time the leave begins.

Parental leave may be taken as a continuous block of 14 weeks, or, by agreement between the employer and the employee, may be broken up over a period of time. The employee must give written notice to the employer of his or her intention to take parental leave, not later than six weeks before the proposed leave commencement date. The employer may require the employee to provide evidence of his or her entitlement to parental leave (for example, the child's date of birth, the date of the adoption order, or evidence of parentage).

The employer may decide to postpone the parental leave if granting the leave would have a substantial adverse effect on the operation of its business. The postponement may not exceed six months, to a date agreed on by both parties. The employer also may refuse, in writing, to grant parental leave if there are reasonable grounds to believe that the employee is not entitled to such leave. The reasons for such refusal must be specified.

[274]Council Directive 96/34/EC, 1994 O.J. (L 145) 4. For a discussion of the Parental Leave Directive, see V.C.2. in the chapter on the EU in Part 1 of Volume I.

During absence on parental leave, the employee is regarded as being in the employment of the employer and retains all employment rights (except the right to remuneration and superannuation benefits). Therefore, the absence will count as reckonable service for the purposes of annual leave, increments, seniority, etc. However, an employer may require that a period of probation, training, or apprenticeship be suspended while the employee is on parental leave.

Parental leave may not be treated as part of any other leave to which the employee is entitled (e.g., sick, maternity, adoptive, annual, or *force majeure* leave). Employees retain an entitlement to any public holidays that fall during a period of parental leave. The PLA requires that a corresponding number of days in lieu of public holidays be added to the end of the leave period. Annual leave that accrues during an absence on parental leave must be granted by the employer in accordance with the OWTA.[275]

An employee must use parental leave to take care of the child concerned. The employer may terminate the leave if there are good reasonable grounds to believe that the leave is being used for a purpose other than taking care of the child. If parental leave is terminated, the employee must return to work.

The employee is entitled to return to work at the end of the parental leave period to the job held immediately prior to the leave and under the same contract and terms and conditions of employment. If the business has changed ownership during the employee's absence, then the employee is entitled to work under an employment contract identical to the contract that existed with the former employer.

If it is not reasonably practicable for the employer to allow the employee to return to the job held immediately prior to the leave, then the employer must offer the employee suitable alternative employment under a new employment contract. The terms of the alternative employment must not be substantially less favorable to the employee than the terms of his or her former position.

The dismissal of an employee based on his or her exercise of the right to parental leave, or a refusal to allow the employee to

[275]For a discussion of annual leave accrual, see V.D.1., above.

return to work following parental leave, is regarded as an unfair dismissal for purposes of the Unfair Dismissals Act,[276] unless there are substantial grounds justifying the dismissal.

5. Force Majeure *Leave*

An employee is entitled to *force majeure* leave,[277] i.e., leave with pay for urgent family reasons, owing to the injury or illness of any of the following persons:

- a child or adoptive child of the employee;
- the spouse of the employee, or a person with whom the employee is living as husband and wife;
- a person to whom the employee is in *loco parentis*; or
- a brother, sister, parent, or grandparent of the employee.

An employee may not be absent on *force majeure* leave for more than three days in any 12 consecutive months, or five days in any 36 consecutive months.

Entitlement to *force majeure* leave is limited to circumstances where the immediate presence of the employee is indispensable. During an absence on *force majeure* leave, the employee is regarded as being in the employment of the employer and retains all of his or her employment rights. *Force majeure* leave is paid leave. It may not be treated as part of any other leave (e.g., sick, maternity, adoptive, annual, or parental leave) to which the employee is entitled.

As soon as reasonably practicable after return to work, the employee must confirm that he or she has taken *force majeure* leave.

The dismissal of an employee based on his or her exercise of the right to *force majeure* leave is regarded as an unfair dismissal for purposes of the Unfair Dismissals Act,[278] unless there are substantial grounds justifying the dismissal.

---

[276] See I.C.2.c., above.

[277] *See* Parental Leave (Notice of Force Majeure Leave) Regulations, S.I. 454 (1998).

[278] See I.C.2.c., above.

6. *Health and Safety Leave*

Health and safety leave is available to employees in the following situations:

- pregnant employees who have notified their employers of their condition;
- employees who have recently given birth, i.e., within 18 weeks after birth; and
- employees who are breastfeeding, for at least 26 weeks after birth.

Under the Safety, Health, and Welfare at Work (Pregnant Employees) Regulations, 1996, every employer must carry out a risk assessment of the health and safety of employees who are pregnant or breastfeeding. This assessment examines any activity at the workplace that is likely to involve a risk to pregnant or breastfeeding employees due to exposure to an agent, process, or other working conditions. Where the risk assessment reveals a risk to the employee's safety or health, and it is not practical to ensure the safety or health of the employee through a protective or preventive measure, then one of the following measures must be taken:

- the working conditions or hours should be adjusted to remove the risk; or, if this is not possible,
- the employee should be provided with other work; or, if this is not suitable or possible,
- the employee is entitled to health and safety leave.

Health and safety leave covers the whole of the employee's pregnancy, including the period of leave after birth and continues through the period necessary for breastfeeding. The employer must pay the employee only for the first 21 days of health and safety leave. For the balance of the leave period, the employee is entitled to social welfare payments.

7. *Carer's Leave*

The Carer's Leave Act, 2001, came into effect on July 2, 2001. This Act allows workers to take leave for a period of up to 65 weeks if they need to attend to someone requiring full-time care and attention. Eligibility for carer's leave requires 12-months' continuous service and a medical assessment that the care recipient is in need of full-time care and attention. The employee need not be related to the care recipient. At any one time, not more than one employee may take leave to care for the same care recipient. Carer's leave may be taken in a block of up to 65 weeks, or in a series of shorter periods not exceeding an aggregate of 65 weeks. This is a standard period of leave that will apply to all eligible employees, irrespective of their length of service.

Employers are not required to pay employees during the period of carer's leave but must hold the employee's job open for the duration of the leave. Employees who take carer's leave also retain all other employment rights, and the leave counts as reckonable service, except for purposes of superannuation (retirement) benefits and certain public holidays. In addition, employees may not be dismissed because they avail themselves of carer's leave.

An employee who wishes to take carer's leave is required to furnish written notification to the employer no later than six weeks prior to the proposed commencement of leave (unless notice of this length is not reasonably practicable). The Carer's Leave Act requires the employer to retain this notice, and the employer and employee must sign a confirmation document, at least two weeks prior to the beginning of leave, specifying the duration and form of the leave and when it is to commence.

In addition, the Carer's Leave Act specifically requires employers to keep and maintain a record of carer's leave, showing the period of employment for each employee and the dates and times during which carer's leave was taken. These records must be retained for a period of eight years. A failure to keep and maintain the required records may result in an employer being liable for a fine not exceeding €3,000 (IR£2,362.69).

VI. Antidiscrimination

A. Background

1. Early EU Framework

Irish antidiscrimination law only really started to develop after Ireland joined the EU in 1973. Article 119 of the Treaty of

Rome, which created the European Economic Community in 1957,[279] contains a prescription of equal pay for equal work: "Each Member State shall during the first stage ensure and subsequently maintain the application of the principle that men and women should receive equal pay for equal work." The word "pay" has been interpreted to mean ordinary, basic, or minimum wage, salary, or any other consideration, whether in cash or kind, which the worker receives directly or indirectly with respect to his or her employment.

Initially, article 119 was seen as aspirational, rather than conferring any individual rights on individuals. However, in 1976, in the case of *Defrenne v. Sabena*,[280] the European Court of Justice (ECJ) recognized the direct legal effect of article 119. In *Defrenne*, a female cabin crew member employed by the Belgian airline Sabena claimed pay equal to a male crew member, who received a higher rate of pay despite the fact that they performed the same work. The ECJ held that the female crew member was entitled to claim equal pay under article 119.

The 1975 EU Directive known as the Equal Pay Directive[281] clarified the right to equal pay under article 119 by guaranteeing equal pay for the same work or work of equal value. This was mirrored in domestic Irish legislation by the Anti-Discrimination (Pay) Act, 1974 (ADPA), which introduced the principle of equal pay for like work in compliance with article 119. Under the ADPA, a woman who worked in the same place as a man, and who performed like work, was entitled to the same rate of remuneration for that work as the man.

2. *1977 Employment Equality Act*

The 1976 EU Directive on equal treatment in working life (Equal Treatment Directive)[282] gave effect to the principle of equal

---

[279]For a discussion of the Treaty of Rome, see the Introduction to the chapter on the EU in Part 1 of Volume I.

[280][1976] E.C.R. 455 (ECJ). For a more detailed discussion of this case, see VI.A.1.a. in the chapter on the EU in Part 1 of Volume I.

[281]Council Directive 75/117/EEC, 1975 O.J. (L 45) 19. For a more detailed discussion of this directive, see VI.A.1. in the chapter on the EU in Part 1 of Volume I.

[282]Council Directive 76/207/EEC, 1975 O.J. (L 39) 40, amended by Council Directive 2002/73/EC, 2002 O.J. (L 269) 15. For a more detailed discussion of this directive, see VI.A.2.a. in the chapter on the EU in Part 1 of Volume I.

treatment on grounds of sex and marital status, in relation to employment access, vocational training, promotion, and working conditions. The provisions of the Equal Treatment Directive were implemented into Irish law by the Employment Equality Act, 1977 (1977 EEA), which prohibited direct and indirect discrimination in employment on grounds of a person's sex or marital status. The 1977 EEA provided for equal treatment in regard to employment access, conditions of employment (except remuneration and pension rights), training, and promotion. The 1977 EEA also made it unlawful for employment agencies to discriminate and prohibited discrimination in vocational training, advertisements, and access to employer and trade union organizations and professional bodies.

3. 1998 Employment Equality Act

The 1992 Maastricht Treaty Protocol and Agreement on Social Policy[283] made a specific commitment to improving employment equality throughout the EU Member States. In Irish labor law, this commitment eventually took form in the Employment Equality Act 1998 (EEA).[284] The EEA has two main aims: to implement new provisions in relation to discrimination and harassment, and to promote equality in the workplace.

Until the enactment of the EEA, Irish employment law only prohibited discrimination on the basis of sex or marital status. There now are nine grounds on which it is unlawful to discriminate against a person in employment: gender, marital status, family status, sexual orientation, religion, age, disability, race, and membership in the traveling community.

The EEA prohibits discrimination by employers against employees or future employees in relation to employment access, conditions of employment, training and promotion, and regrading and classification of posts. The EEA also prohibits discrimination in relation to terms and conditions in collective agreements, advertising, services of employment agencies, vocational training,

---

[283]For a complete discussion of the Maastricht Treaty, see the chapter on the EU in Part 1 of Volume I.

[284]The Employment Equality Act, 1998 (EEA), became effective on October 1, 1999, and repealed in their entirety the Anti-Discrimination (Pay) Act, 1974 (ADPA), and the Employment Equality Act, 1977 (1977 EEA).

and membership and access to benefits of a professional, trade, or employer/employee organization.

Protection from discrimination under the EEA will be required to be extended in a number of regards, in particular, protection from discrimination on the age ground will apply to persons over 65 years and, for the first time, self-employed people will be brought within the general scope of the Act. A number of other exclusions will have to be amended or removed and the duty on employers to adapt the workplace to facilitate employees with disabilities will be enhanced. The definition of indirect discrimination in both the Employment Equality Act and the Equal Status Act[285] is also being amended with the result that such claims will now be easier for employees to prove.

4. *Recent EU Directives*

Subsequent to the implementation of the EEA, an EU Directive was adopted on June 20, 2000, implementing the principle of equal treatment between persons irrespective of racial or ethnic origin, inter alia, in social policy, employment, and access to goods and services (Race Directive).[286] It is planned that in 2004, Ireland will implement EU Council Directive 2000/43/EC concerning the principle of equal treatment between persons irrespective of racial or ethnic origin, Council Directive 2000/78/EC establishing a general framework for equal treatment in employment,[287] and Directive 2002/73/EC of the European Parliament and of the Council on the implementation of the principle of equal treatment for men and women as regards access to employment, vocational training, and promotion and working conditions.[288]

The Directives require all EU Member States to prohibit direct discrimination, indirect discrimination, harassment and vic-

---

[285]See VI.B.6., below.

[286]Council Directive 2000/43/EC, 2000 O.J. (L 180) 22. For a more detailed discussion of this Directive, see VI.B.1. in the chapter on the EU in Part 1 of Volume I.

[287]Council Directive 2000/78/EC, 2000 O.J. (L 303) 16. For a more detailed discussion of this Directive, see VI.B.2. in the chapter on the EU in Part 1 of Volume I.

[288]Council Directive 2002/73/EC, 2002 O.J. (L 269) 15.

timization on grounds of gender, racial or ethnic origin, religion or belief, disability, age, or sexual orientation, in relation to employment, self-employment, and occupational and vocational training. In addition, the Race Directive prohibits such actions in relation to access to and the provision of goods and services. The ETE Minister noted that many of the provisions of these Directives are already in place as a result of Ireland's equality legislation. The main effect of the amendments would be to broaden the scope of the Acts.

B. Non-Gender Discrimination

As discussed above, EU law, as set forth in article 119 and the Equal Pay and Equal Treatment Directives, defines the prohibitions on gender discrimination. However, these provisions do not apply to the non-gender area, thereby giving Ireland greater discretion in drafting non-gender discrimination legislation.

In the EEA, gender and non-gender discrimination are set out separately, in Parts III and IV, respectively. In general, the EEA establishes similar protections against gender and non-gender discrimination with respect to pay and other work conditions. However, there are some differences, for example, with respect to the definition of indirect discrimination.[289]

Some of the EEA provisions relating to non-gender discrimination are discussed immediately below.

1. Family Status

The EEA prohibits discrimination against an employee based on his or her family status. For this purpose, family status is defined as responsibility as a parent, as a person in *loco parentis* in relation to a child younger than 18 years, or a resident primary care giver in relation to a person older than age 18 with "a disability" who requires ongoing support or care.[290]

---

[289]See VI.C., below.

[290]EEA §2(1).

2. *Sexual Orientation*

Sexual orientation is defined broadly in the EEA to mean heterosexual, bisexual, or homosexual orientation.

3. *Age*

It is unlawful to discriminate against a person older than age 18 but younger than age 65 on the basis of their age. However, the EEA allows employers, in setting an age for recruitment, to take into account that it may involve cost or time to train new employees before they become effective in their jobs. The EEA also allows employers to set different retirement ages for employees or any class of employees. Discrimination on the ground of age also is permitted where there is "clear actuarial or other evidence that 'significantly increased costs'" would result if the discrimination were not permitted.[291] Thus, discrimination can be justified on grounds of cost.

Case law now has developed in the area of age discrimination under the EEA. The first decision[292] involved a job advertisement that sought a "young dynamic" applicant. The Equality Officer rejected the employer's argument that "young" referred to a state of mind, rather than a chronological age, finding that, as normally understood, the ad precluded consideration of older applicants. The Equality Officer ruled that the word "young" imposed an age requirement in the employment advertisement, thereby constituting clear discrimination. A sum of €10,158 (IR£8,000) was awarded to the claimant. The employer also was ordered to publish a statement clearly stating that it was committed to an equal opportunity policy and to review its recruitment, selection, and promotion guidelines. Recent decisions have examined age discrimination in promotion. Each of the decisions has found in favor of the complainants.[293]

---

[291] *Id.* §34(3).

[292] Equality Auth. v. Ryanair, DEC–E2000-14.

[293] O'Mahony v. Revenue Comm'rs, DEC-2002-018 (Mar. 18, 2002); O'Byrne v. Department of Pub. Enters., DEC-E2002-040 (Sept. 4, 2002); Freeman v. Superquinn, DEC-E2002-013 (Mar. 5, 2002).

4. Disability

The EEA defines disability as follows:

> (a) the total or partial absence of a person's bodily or mental functions including the absence of a part of a persons body; or
> (b) the presence in the body of organisms causing, or likely to cause, chronic disease or illness; or
> (c) the malfunction, malformation or disfigurement of part of the person's body; or
> (d) a condition or malfunction which results in a person learning differently from a person without the condition or malfunction; or
> (e) a condition, illness or disease which affects a persons thought processes, perception of reality, emotions or judgement or which results in disturbed behaviour; and
>
> shall be taken to include a disability which exists at present or which previously existed but no longer exists or which may exist in the future or which is imputed to the person.[294]

This broad definition has been criticized for its concentration on purely medical criteria. By comparison, the UK definition of disability, contained in the Disability Discrimination Act, 1995, refers to the impact of a disabled person's disability on his or her ability to "carry out day to day activities." The Irish EEA definition requires no such assessment. Thc UK provisions also specifically exclude certain conditions such as addiction to alcohol, drugs, or nicotine. There are no such exclusions in the EEA definition and, arguably, alcoholism could constitute a disability "which affects a person's thought processes," within the meaning of the Irish statute.

An employer is not required to employ an individual who is either unwilling or incompetent and incapable to do the job. However, a person with a disability "shall not be regarded as other than fully competent to undertake, and fully capable of undertaking, any duties, if with the assistance of special treatment or facilities, such person would be fully competent to undertake, and be fully capable of undertaking, those duties."[295] In addition, employers

---

[294] EEA §2 Interpretation.
[295] EEA §16(3)a.

must "do all that is reasonable to accommodate the needs of a person who has a disability by providing special treatment or facilities . . . ."[296] However, a refusal or failure to provide for special treatment or facilities shall not be deemed reasonable unless such provision would give rise to a cost, other than a nominal cost, to the employer. The EEA does not define nominal cost, which would not appear to impose any significant burden on an employer. By comparison, the Employment Directive requires employers to accommodate the needs of employees unless such measures would "impose a disproportionate burden on the employer,"[297] which is arguably more onerous on employers than what is provided for under the EEA.

To date, there have been an increasing number of EEA decisions dealing with disability discrimination. In one of the most significant decisions in this area,[298] the claimant maintained that he had informed the employer at the interview stage that he was suffering from cerebral palsy. The employer disputed this, claiming that it only became aware of the claimant's disability when it realized he was having difficulty with his work performance. The claimant ultimately was dismissed, according to the employer, on grounds of his poor performance and not due to his disability. The Equality Officer found that the deterioration in the claimant's performance was the result of his disability, and so ruled that the employer had erred in failing to ensure that the claimant was given a medical examination, once it became aware of his disability, before dismissing him. Other decisions to date have dealt with reasonable accommodation and the nominal cost of adapting the workplace to an individual's disability to facilitate the individual taking up a position, statistical evidence in proving indirect disability discrimination, imputed disability, and victimization.[299]

[296]*Id.* §6(3)b.

[297]Council Directive 2000/78/EC, art. 5.

[298]Kehoe v. Convertec Ltd., DEC-E2001-034 (November 2001).

[299]An Employee and a Local Authority, DEC-2002-2004 (Feb. 4, 2002); A Complainant v. Civil Serv. Commiss'rs, DEC-E2002-015 (Mar. 13, 2002); A Complainant and a Department Store, DEC-2002-016 and DEC-2002-017 (Feb. 14, 2002); A Motor Co. v. a Worker, EED026.

5. *Race*

The EEA makes it unlawful to discriminate on grounds of someone's race, color, nationality, ethnicity, or national origin. This is a new ground of discrimination in Irish law, so no doubt much guidance on this issue will be sought from UK case law dealing with race discrimination.

The first case brought under the EEA on grounds of race was decided in December 2001.[300] In this case, the claimant, a Malaysian trainee doctor, alleged he was discriminated against on the basis of his race because he did not receive the remuneration provided to his Irish counterparts, who received a basic salary in what were known as funded posts. The respondent hospital claimed that Irish work permit regulations and principles of freedom of movement of labor within the EU meant that preference had to be given to European Economic Area nationals (the European Economic Area comprises the member states of the EU, Norway, Iceland, and Liechtenstein) over non–European Economic Area nationals. Therefore, the employer argued, its decision to award funded posts to European Economic Area nationals constituted a ground other than race. The Equality Officer disagreed, ruling that while the purpose of the EU was to ensure nondiscrimination among EU Member State nationals, that did not mean that employers were required to discriminate against non-EU nationals, where domestic law prohibited it. The claimant was awarded backpay for the period during which he had not been given a funded post. Since then, there have only been three further decisions on this ground, all of which have held against the applicant.[301]

6. *Status*

The Equal Status Act, 2000 (ESA), became effective on October 25, 2000. The ESA differs from the EEA in that it seeks to apply equality principles beyond the employment area and into the broader social environment. The ESA prohibits discrimination

---

[300]Dr. Bennett Heng Eng. v. St. James's Hosp., DEC-E2001-041.

[301]Sergides v. Feehily's Pub, DEC-E2002-022 (May 2, 2002); Fernandez v. Cable & Wireless DEC-E2002-052; Ann Martinez v. Network Catering, DEC-E/2001/004 (Jan. 16, 2001).

in the provision of goods and services, accommodation, and education and seeks to prevent sexual and other harassment in the public arena (including those places where such services are provided). The ESA also prohibits discrimination by registered clubs (i.e., clubs with a drinks license) against members or membership applicants.

Despite its broader ambit, the ESA may affect employers and their employees who are involved in any of the activities covered by the Act. An employer must act in a nondiscriminatory fashion when involved in covered activities and must ensure that all actions are based on nondiscriminatory grounds. Employers also are obliged to ensure that their employees act in accordance with the ESA. This is particularly significant because employers will be vicariously liable for acts of employees committed during the course of their employment, whether or not the employer had knowledge of the acts.[302]

The ESA prohibits both direct and indirect discrimination on the same grounds as those specified in the EEA: gender; marital status; family status; sexual orientation; religion; age; disability; race, color, nationality, and ethnic or national origin; and membership in the traveling community. In addition, the ESA prohibits discrimination for reasons that a person has exercised his or her rights under the Act, by, for example, filing a complaint, appearing as a witness, or opposing unlawful conduct.

The ESA also prohibits a form of discrimination not covered by the EEA, known as discrimination by association. This occurs where a person, who associates with a member of a protected group, is treated less favorably by virtue of that association. This is important for both employers and employees in that it extends the scope of the ESA beyond those in protected groups to those associated with them. Thus, employers will be required to exercise caution in supplying services to the public to ensure that they are not engaging in discrimination by association.

Issues of sexual harassment and harassment based on the other discriminatory grounds also are addressed in the ESA. The ESA, unlike the EEA, prohibits same-sex sexual harassment. Based on

[302]Equal Status Act, 2000, §42.

these provisions, employers providing a service have a responsibility to ensure that customers do not suffer harassment, either from another customer or an employee. An employer or its employee may, therefore, be obliged to ensure that customers are not harassed by fellow customers and take all reasonable steps to prevent such harassment.

C. Direct and Indirect Discrimination

Discriminatory behavior under both Irish and EU equality legislation is divided into two distinct forms: direct and indirect.

1. Direct Discrimination

The EEA defines direct discrimination as occurring "when on any of the (discriminatory grounds) one person is treated less favourably than another is, has been, or would be, treated."[303] This definition requires objectively less favorable treatment of an individual on the basis of one of the discriminatory grounds. The fact that the claimant thinks he or she has been treated less favorably is not enough. Instead, the claimant must show that it was reasonable for him or her to experience the treatment as less favorable.

A showing of direct discrimination requires a comparison of treatment given to individuals in similar or comparable circumstances. In gender discrimination cases, the comparison must be between a man and a woman. However, discrimination based on pregnancy is prima facie regarded as sex discrimination, and, consequently, no male comparison is required.[304] For religious discrimination, as another example, the comparison must be with a person of a different religious belief or no religious belief.

To succeed with a charge of direct discrimination, the claimant must be able to illustrate that "but for" the discriminatory characteristic, for example, race or sex, he or she would not have been treated in the same way. However, proof of intent or motive is not relevant in establishing direct discrimination. If direct discrimina-

---

[303]EEA §6(1).

[304]*See* Webb v. EMO Air Cargo (UK) Ltd., [1994] E.C.R. 1-3567 (ECJ); Dekker v. Stichting VSW Centum, [1990] E.C.R. 1-3941 (ECJ).

tion is proved, the treatment is deemed unlawful. There is no objective justification defense for direct discrimination.

2. *Indirect Discrimination*

Generally, indirect discrimination arises where conditions or practices appear neutral but are discriminatory in their impact in that they impact adversely on a particular group of people.

Unlike direct discrimination, indirect discrimination can be justified if the employer has objective reasons for the action or practice that do not relate to the prohibited ground for discrimination, e.g., race or sex. The general approach of the courts has been that if indirect discrimination is established, the burden of proof shifts to the employer to objectively justify the criteria and/or practice. If the discriminatory action or practice cannot be justified objectively by factors unrelated to any discrimination, it will be deemed unlawful.

The issue of indirect discrimination was before the ECJ, for example, in *Bilka Kaufhaus v. Weber Von Hartz*,[305] in which the court was asked to rule on the legality of excluding part-time workers from occupational pension plans. The ECJ held that a pension constituted pay for the purposes of article 119, so that if fewer women than men worked full time, the exclusion of part-time workers would be discriminatory. In considering the employer's defense, the court stated that it is not sufficient to show that the employer sought to achieve objectives other than discrimination against women where the pay practice, in fact, discriminates against women. Rather, in order to justify such a practice, the employer must put forward objective economic grounds relating to the management of the undertaking, as well as evidence to show that the pay practice is necessary and in proportion to the objectives pursued by the employer. In other words, the court must undertake a balancing exercise, taking into account all surrounding circumstances, and giving emphasis to the degree of discrimination caused in comparison to the objects or aims to be achieved.

[305] [1988] I.R.L.R. 317, [1987] I.C.R. 110 (ECJ).

A recent Irish example of this principle can be found in *Nathan v. Bailey Gibson Ltd.*,[306] where the Supreme Court set out what it described as the correct approach to indirect sex discrimination claims:

> It is sufficient to show that the practice complained of bore significantly more heavily on members of the complainant's sex than on members of the other sex. At that stage the complainant has established a prima facie case of discrimination and the onus of proof shifts to the employer to show that the practice complained of is based on objectively verifiable factors which have no relation to the claimant's sex.[307]

Under the EEA, there are different definitions for indirect discrimination based on gender[308] and indirect discrimination based on non-gender.[309] To successfully defend a claim of indirect discrimination on gender grounds, the employer must demonstrate "objective factors" for the discrimination not based on the person's sex. By comparison, a defense against a claim of indirect discrimination on a non-gender ground can be made out if the employer can show that the discriminatory actions were "reasonable in all the circumstances." This suggests that a lower standard of proof is required for a defense to a non-gender discrimination claim.

D. Affirmative Action

The EEA allows for affirmative action, or what otherwise is known as positive discrimination, in relation to the promotion of equal opportunities for men and women, workers older than age 50, the disabled, and members of the traveling community.

---

[306] [1998] E.L.R. 52 (Ir. S. Ct.).
[307] *Id.* at 178.
[308] EEA §22(1).
[309] *Id.* §31.

E. Harassment

The EEA defines sexual harassment and harassment for the first time under Irish law. Sexual harassment is defined as follows:

> (a) any act of physical intimacy by B towards A; or
> (b) requests for sexual favours; or
> (c) any other conduct by B (including, without prejudice to the generality, spoken words, gestures, or the production, display or circulation of written words, pictures or other material).[310]

Conduct will constitute sexual harassment if the action is unwelcome and it is reasonable for the employee affected to consider it offensive, humiliating, or intimidating.

Until the enactment of the EEA, the attitude of the Irish courts in evaluating whether conduct was offensive had been to view the conduct purely from the victim's standpoint. The EEA now requires the court to adopt a more objective test and consider whether it is reasonable for the victim to consider himself or herself as having been harassed. However, there is no requirement for a comparison as to how another person might feel if faced with the same conduct. This approach contrasts with the result in *Stewart v. Cleveland Guest (Engineering) Ltd.*,[311] an English case, in which the Industrial Tribunal held that a female claimant had not been subject to sexual harassment based on pornographic material displayed in a workplace because a man might have been equally distressed by the material.

The employer may be held vicariously liable for the action of its employees who harass another employee in the course of their employment. More controversially, an employer also may be liable for the actions of "a client, customer or other business contact."[312] However, defenses are available to the employer if it can be shown that it took such steps as were reasonably practicable to prevent the harassment and if, insofar as harassment occurred, it has taken steps to reverse its effects.

---

[310] *Id.* §23(3).
[311] [1994] I.R.L.R. 440.
[312] EEA §23(4).

The EEA covers not only events that happen in the workplace, but also outside events that occur in the course of the employee's employment. Thus, events such as training courses and conferences likely are covered.

The EEA does not expressly cover same-sex harassment, although the provisions relating to non-gender discrimination would appear to ensure that the harassment of a person is prohibited if based on a discriminatory ground prohibited by the Act, for example, marital status or sexual orientation.

F. Enforcement and Remedies

The Equality Authority has responsibility for promotion of the standards required by the EEA and for enforcement of its provisions, for example, by way of non-discrimination notices. The Equality Authority is entitled to invite particular businesses with more than 50 employees, or groups of such businesses or industry sector, to carry out equality audits and to prepare equality action plans. It also is entitled to carry out an audit and action plan itself and can require employers to supply it with information and documentation to assist in the preparation of the audit or plan. It can impose the findings of the audit or plan on employers.

The Office of the Director of Equality Investigations was established by the EEA. The Director and duly appointed Equality Officers are responsible for investigating discrimination claims and, if necessary, mediating or issuing decisions. Investigations are heard in private. If the Equality Director decides that the matter can be dealt with by way of mediation, then it can be referred to a mediation officer. However, if either party objects, the matter is dealt with by the Director or the Labor Court. Cases involving employment dismissal automatically are referred to the Labor Court for determination.

If the Equality Director finds that there has been discrimination, he or she may order one or more of the following forms of redress:

- an order for equal treatment;
- an order that a person take a specified course of action;
- an award for payment of wage arrears for a period not exceeding three years before the complaint was issued;

- an order for equal remuneration from the date the case was referred; or
- an order for compensation for the effects of discrimination/victimization that occurred within six years prior to the date of referral.

In cases involving employment dismissal, the Labor Court also can order reinstatement or re-engagement.[313]

The maximum level of compensation that can be awarded by the Equality Director or the Labor Court is 104 weeks times the claimant's weekly pay. Alternatively, in cases where the claimant is not an employee, the maximum award is €12,700 (IR£10,000). This would cover cases where someone was refused employment on one of the discriminatory grounds.

The EEA provides that complaints of discrimination must be referred within six months of the discrimination, or within six months of the most recent occurrence of the discrimination. In cases where discriminatory treatment is alleged, the time limit may be extended to 12 months in exceptional circumstances. There are no service requirements in order to invoke the protections of the EEA.

Perhaps one of the most radical advancements in the 1998 EEA is the provision that allows for a direct reference concerning discrimination on grounds of sex to the Circuit Court, thereby short circuiting the Labor Court and Equality Officers mechanisms. Such a referral is only available for a claim of discrimination on the grounds of sex under the EEA and does not extend to any of the other eight prohibited grounds. The Circuit Court is empowered to obtain a report from an Equality Officer on any question arising from the matter before it. The report then is entered as evidence in the Circuit Court action, with the possibility of the Equality Officer being called as a witness. Jurisdiction of the court to award damages is unlimited, coupled with the right to award costs to a successful party.

Since the EEA came into effect in October 1999, the Office of the Director of Equality Investigations has received just over

[313]See I.C.2.c., above.

700 claims and has issued more than 140 determinations. Claims have been submitted under each of the nine grounds recognized by the Act. The majority of claims to date have involved allegations of discrimination based on grounds of gender, disability, age, and race, in that order. The decisions have been evenly divided in favor of claimants and employers. The decisions also appear to be quite proactive, in that they have recommended such courses of action as making every effort to bring gender balance to future selection boards, advising employees of equal opportunity policies and bringing them to staff's attention, and requiring the transfer of a supervisor who sexually harassed a claimant and monitoring of his future behavior.

VII. OCCUPATIONAL SAFETY AND HEALTH AND WORKERS' COMPENSATION

A. Occupational Safety and Health[314]

1. Introduction

Article 45.4.2 of the Constitution sets out, as a basic principle of social policy, that "the State shall endeavour to ensure that the strength and health of workers, men and women and the tender age of children shall not be abused." Implementation of this principle took a big step forward with the passage of the Safety, Health, and Welfare at Work Act, 1989 (Safety Act), and the Safety, Health, and Welfare at Work (General Application) Regulations, 1993 (Safety Regulations).

Prior to the enactment of the Safety Act and the Safety Regulations, the law on safety, health, and welfare at work was piecemeal, diverse, technical, and largely inflexible and, it is estimated, covered only 20 percent of the working population. Although the legislature enacted provisions to deal with specific areas or as-

[314] *See generally* JOHN P.M. WHITE, CIVIL LIABILITY FOR INDUSTRIAL ACCIDENTS (Oak Tree Press 1993).

pects of workplace health and safety, it was left to the common law to lay down general principles that applied, and continue to apply, to all places of work. It is intended that the Safety Act, as the framework within which the whole legislative thrust in this area is to operate, gradually will replace and repeal earlier, piecemeal legislation. However, until that time, earlier statutes and regulations remain very relevant for employers.[315]

The Safety Act is under review, and draft revising legislation was introduced in 2004 providing for more extensive penalties for breach of the specific statutory obligations.

2. *Common Law Principles*

Common law principles, which have been developed by the courts independently of the legislature, impose duties and obligations on employers toward their employees or those who are on their premises or affected by their activities.

The duty of an employer toward an employee is to take reasonable care for the employee's safety in all the circumstances. The law does not require employers to ensure, in all possible circumstances, the safety of their workers. Rather, employers will have discharged their duty of care if they do what a reasonable and prudent employer would have done in the circumstances. In simple terms, liability is based on a negligence standard, i.e., did the employer do something that a reasonable and prudent employer would not do, or did the employer omit to do something that a reasonable and prudent employer would have done? Issues of negligence are concerned with the duty of care between a particular employer and a particular worker. That duty may vary with the worker's age, knowledge, and experience.

The courts, in applying the above general principles, have laid down a fourfold obligation on an employer, as follows:

- provision of competent staff,
- provision of proper equipment,

---

[315]*See, e.g.*, the Factories Act, 1955, as amended and extended by the Safety in Industry Act, 1980 (collectively, the Safety in Industry Acts, 1955 and 1980); the Mines and Quarries Act, 1965; the Office Premises Act, 1958; the Shops (Conditions of Employment) Act, 1938 and 1942; the Dangerous Substances Acts, 1972 and 1979.

- provision of a safe place of work, and
- provision of a safe system of work.

Before the employer will be held liable by the courts for having failed to provide competent staff, it must be shown that the employer had reason to be aware of the staff person(s)' incompetence. With respect to the duty to provide proper equipment, the employer has a duty to take reasonable care to provide proper appliances, to maintain them in a proper condition, and to carry on its operations so as not to subject those employed to unnecessary risk. The employer may be liable equally for failure to provide equipment essential to the safety of an employee, or for failure to maintain equipment in a safe condition.

As regards the employer's duty to provide a safe place of work, it is not a defense for the employer to establish that the employee was aware of the danger on the premises. The duty to provide a safe system of work was defined in the case of *Kinsella v. Hammond Lane Industries Ltd.*[316] as follows: "If an accident causes injury to a workman and the accident results from a risk of an unsafe system of work, against which the employer should have, but did not, take reasonable precautions to guard, then the employer is liable for damages."

The word "safe" has been defined to mean no more than "as safe as is reasonably possible in the circumstances." Thus, the degree of safety required would depend on the particular job and would vary between wide limits.

To succeed in a common law claim, it is not sufficient for an employee to establish that the employer has been negligent; it also is necessary to show that the negligence caused the employee's injury. In addition, an employee's failure to wear protective clothing or to comply with safety requirements of which the employee was aware, could result in a finding of contributory negligence. However, where a regular unsafe practice exists unchecked, it is difficult to ascribe contributory negligence to a worker who simply follows the particular practice.

---

[316] 96 I.L.T.R. 1, 4 (High Court).

3. *Safety Act*

The Safety Act is the most important piece of legislation in Ireland in the health, safety, and welfare at work area. It applies to employers, self-employed persons, manufacturers, suppliers, and importers.

a. *General Employer Duties*

The Safety Act imposes a series of general duties on employers. The overall duty is to ensure, so far as reasonably practicable, the safety, health, and welfare of all employees.[317] Specifically, the Safety Act imposes a duty on employers to do the following:

- design and maintain a safe place of work;
- provide safe means of access to and egress from the workplace;
- provide and maintain safe plant and equipment;
- provide and maintain safe systems of work;
- provide information, instruction, training, and supervision for safe and healthy working;
- in circumstances where it is not reasonably practical to control or eliminate workplace hazards, to provide and maintain suitable protective clothing or equipment;
- prepare adequate emergency plans;
- prevent risks to health and safety in relation to use of articles or substances;
- provide welfare facilities; and
- acquire, where necessary, the services of a competent person to ensure employees' safety and health at work (this duty arises where such competence is not available in-house).

b. *Employee Duties*

The Safety Act requires employees to take reasonable care for their own safety, health, and welfare and that of others who may be affected by their acts or omissions at work. Employees

[317]Safety, Health, and Welfare at Work Act, 1989 (Safety Act), §6(1).

also are under a duty to cooperate with their employer, use any of the protective equipment supplied, and report to their employer, without unreasonable delay, any defects in plant or equipment, place of work, or system of work, which might endanger their safety or welfare. In addition, employees must not intentionally or recklessly interfere with or misuse anything provided for safety, health, or welfare purposes.

c. Safety Statement

One of the most important requirements placed on employers by the Safety Act is to provide a safety statement, specifying the manner in which the safety, health, and welfare of employees will be secured at work.[318] The safety statement must be based on an identification of the hazards and an assessment of the risks to safety and health at the place of work to which the safety statement relates. Generally, the safety statement must specify the following:

- the arrangements made and resources provided for safeguarding the safety, health, and welfare of employees in the workplace;
- the cooperation required from employees as regards safety, health, and welfare; and
- the names, including the names of authorized deputies and job titles where applicable, of the persons responsible for the performance of tasks assigned to them by the statement.

For those companies subject to section 158 of the Companies Act, 1963, an annual evaluation of the statement must be provided with the annual accounts. This requirement effectively covers all incorporated bodies under Irish law.

d. Consultation and Safety Representatives

The employer is required to consult with employees for the purpose of making cooperative arrangements to promote and develop workplace health, safety, and welfare. Employees have the

---

[318] *Id.* §12.

right to make representations to their employer on any issues of safety, health, and welfare, and employers must, so far as reasonably practical, take account of such representations and act on them. In addition, employees may select a person to represent them on issues of safety, health, and welfare. The employees' safety representative has the right to information, insofar as reasonably practical to provide such information, to ensure employees' safety and health at the workplace.

e. National Authority for Occupational Safety and Health and Enforcement

The National Authority for Occupational Safety and Health and Enforcement (HSA) was set up under the Safety Act and took over the functions of the old Industrial Inspectorate of the Department of Labor. The HSA has wide-ranging powers of investigation and enforcement, including the power to issue improvement and prohibition notices and to apply to the High Court for orders restricting or prohibiting the use of a workplace.

4. Safety Regulations

The 1993 Safety Regulations establish general safety and health rules and impose a general duty on employers to take account of changing circumstances and the general principles specified in the First Schedule of the Regulations. The Regulations address avoidance of risk, evaluation of unavoidable risks, combating of risks at the source, adaptation of work to the individual, adaptation of the place of work to technical progress, replacement of dangerous articles, development of an adequate prevention policy, giving effect to collective protective measures, the priority of individual protective measures, and giving appropriate training and instruction to employees. The Safety Regulations also require employers to evaluate, from time to time, risks to workplace safety and health.

With respect to the safety statement required by the Safety Act, the Safety Regulations require the employer to include an assessment of the risks to safety and health at the workplace, and to identify any protective measures to be taken and, if necessary, protective equipment to be used.

The Safety Regulations also place an obligation on employers to provide information to their employees concerning issues of health, safety, and welfare at work, and to allow consultation and participation of employees. Employees, in turn, are required to make correct use of machinery, dangerous substances, etc., and to make full and proper use of personal protective equipment where it is provided.

The Safety Regulations provide greater detail regarding general obligations under the Safety Act and implement EU directives on health and safety.

More specific regulations deal with the workplace, use of work equipment, personal protective equipment, manual handling of loads, display screen equipment, electricity, first aid, and notification of accidents and dangerous occurrences. In addition, other regulations of general effect address safety, health, and welfare issues relating to children and young persons, night and shift work, pregnant employees, etc.[319]

B. Workers' Compensation

All occupational injuries potentially are actionable at common law under the tort of negligence or as a violation of statutory duty. Claims are brought before the civil courts.

The Personal Injuries Assessment Board Act 2003 (PIAB Act) was signed into law on December 28, 2003, and provides for the establishment of the Personal Injuries Assessment Board (PIAB) as a statutory body.[320] The PIAB aims to provide a less costly and speedier means of finalizing personal injury claims than exists within the current court-based system. The Board will deal initially with employment liability cases only.

---

[319] *See* Safety Health, and Welfare at Work (Children and Young Persons) Regulations, 1998; Safety, Health, and Welfare at Work (Night Work and Shift Work) Regulations, 1998; Safety, Health, and Welfare at Work (Signs) Regulations, 1995; Safety, Health, and Welfare at Work (Miscellaneous Welfare Provisions) Regulations, 1995; Safety, Health, and Welfare at Work (Construction) Regulations, 1995; Safety, Health, and Welfare at Work (Pregnant Employees, etc.) Regulations, 1994. *See also* European Communities (Protection of Workers) (Exposure to Noise) Regulations, 1990.

[320] For a more detailed discussion of the PIAB, see the Introduction, at D.2.e., above.

VIII. PENSIONS AND BENEFITS

A. Pensions[321]

The earliest regulation of pensions in Ireland can be found in the ancient Celtic legal system known as Brehon Law. Brehon Law imposed a legal responsibility on the kin group to take care of its members who were aged, blind, deaf, sick, or insane. Brehon Law gradually fell into disuse and, by the 1600s, largely was displaced by English Feudal Law. The earliest pension schemes in the modern sense were established in the public sector. The first such scheme was a fund established for customs and excise officers by treasury warrant in 1712, which was extended by the Superannuation Act, 1834. Gradually, a tax regime developed that nurtured the growth of private occupational pension plans.

1. Governing Legislation

The main pieces of legislation governing pensions in Ireland today are the Taxes Consolidation Act, 1997 (Taxes Consolidation Act), and the Pensions Acts, 1990-2003 (Pensions Act). Case law from the ECJ also has direct effect.

a. Taxes Consolidation Act

All occupational pension plans are subject to approval by the Revenue Commissioners under part 30, chapter 1, of the Taxes Consolidation Act. There are significant tax advantages in obtaining Revenue approval. First, any pension contributions paid by the employer into an approved plan are tax deductible and accrue as a tax-free benefit to the employee. Second, contributions by employees are tax deductible and exempt from employment levies and pay-related social insurance. Third, income and gains in the fund accrue tax free, thus allowing the fund to grow quickly. Finally, no tax is paid by the employee on receipt of any lump sum retirement benefit from an approved plan.

---

[321] *See generally* KEVIN FINUCANE & BRIAN BUGGY, IRISH PENSIONS LAW & PRACTICE (Oak Tree Press 1996).

The Finance Act, 2002, has changed the contribution levels that may be paid by an employee into an approved plan. Specifically, employees will have the option to increase their contributions over the amount previously allowed. This change has been made in an effort to increase savings and encourage future pension provision.

b. Pensions Act

The main provisions of the Pensions Act, the principal piece of legislation governing occupational pension plans in Ireland, are summarized below.

i. Establishment of the Pensions Board

The Pensions Board is the regulatory body for occupational pension plans in Ireland. Its principal functions are as follows:

- to monitor and supervise the operation of the Pensions Act and pension developments generally;
- to advise the Minister for Social, Community, and Family Affairs on all pension matters, as appropriate;
- to issue guidelines and codes of practice relating to the responsibilities and duties of pension plan trustees;
- to issue guidelines on the operation of the Pensions Act and other relevant legislation; and
- to encourage the provision of appropriate training for pension plan trustees.

ii. Preservation of benefits

Under the Pensions (Amendment) Act, 2002, if an employee has been a member of an occupational pension plan for two or more years, he or she may not withdraw contributions from the plan (unless transferring them to another approved fund) on leaving service. Instead, the contributions must be received in the form of a deferred pension benefit.

Effective September 15, 2003, any employer that does not provide an occupational pension scheme, or who operates an occupational pension scheme that limits eligibility for membership, or imposes a waiting period for membership that is greater than six months from the date of commencement of the member's employment, or that does not have a facility for additional voluntary contributions (AVCs) is obliged to provide access to at least one type of standard Personal Retirement Savings Account (PRSA).[322]

iii. Funding

The Pensions Act stipulates a minimum funding level for defined benefit plans. Additionally, the Pensions Act provides for the distribution of pension funds on the winding up of any occupational pension plan.

iv. Disclosure of information

The Pensions Act requires trustees of occupational pension plans to prepare and issue annual reports, actuarial valuations, and member explanatory documentation, as appropriate, at regular intervals.

v. Trustees

The Pensions Act outlines the general duties of trustees of occupational pension plans. Specific provisions apply to the appointment of member-nominated trustees.

vi. Equal treatment

The Pensions Act incorporates the principle of equal treatment with respect to occupational pension plans and sets out procedures for resolving disputes in this area. Currently, the provisions in the Pensions Act relating to equality of treatment differ significantly from those in the Employment Equality Act, 1998. It is envisaged that forthcoming legislation will specifically deal with this area, but such legislation has not yet been drafted

vii. Whistleblowing

The Pensions Act provides for compulsory and voluntary reporting to the Pensions Board (known as whistleblowing) in cases of suspected misappropriation of pension funds.

---

[322]For a more detailed discussion of PRSAs, see VIII.A.2.c., below.

viii. Personal retirement savings accounts

A new type of personal retirement savings arrangement has been introduced under Part 2 of the Pensions (Amendment) Act, 2002, which will be known as a Personal Retirement Savings Account (PRSA). PRSAs are available beginning from the first quarter of 2003, following finalization of the regulations governing their establishment. The arrangement is aimed at those persons who are not members of an occupational pension scheme and have no other type of pension plan. It is a contract-based arrangement between an individual and a PRSA provider. The PRSA provider would typically be a life assurance office or credit institution. All PRSA products must be approved by the Revenue Commissioners and the Pensions Board.

ix. Pension ombudsman

The Pensions Act provides for the establishment of the Office of Pension Ombudsman. The main functions of the Ombudsman include the power to investigate and make decisions concerning:

- complaints from actual or potential plan beneficiaries with respect to financial loss arising from maladministration on thc part of the person responsible for a plan's management; and
- any dispute of law or fact in relation to an act done by a person responsible for the management of a plan.

The Minister for Social & Family Affairs published Regulations in September 2003 establishing the Office of the Pensions Ombudsman as provided for under Part XI of the Pensions Acts 1990–2003 (the Act). The Pensions Ombudsman Regulations 2003 (Pension Regulations) set out matters relating to the operation and jurisdiction of the Office of the Pensions Ombudsman.

Section 131(6) of the Act provides that the Pensions Ombudsman does not have jurisdiction to consider a complaint unless the scheme's internal dispute resolution procedures have been employed. Article 5 of the Pension Regulations sets out the provisions in relation to the internal dispute resolution procedures that must be adopted. Certain time limits are specified (primarily that a complainant must receive a response in writing within three months from receipt of all relevant particulars concerning the complaint or dispute), as are certain matters that must be stated in the decision (including a restatement of the rule of a scheme or clause of a PRSA contract that has been relied upon in reaching the decision). The Office of the Pensions Ombudsman is now accepting complaints.

x. Remittance of contributions

The Pensions Act obliges employers to remit employee plan contributions, once deducted from employees' salaries, within 21 days of the end of the month in which the deduction is made. Also, employer contributions payable under a defined contribution plan in respect of an employee must be paid within 21 days of the end of the month in which they fall due. Additionally, trustees of plans are obliged to ensure that all contributions are properly invested in accordance with the rules of the pension plan within 10 days of the date by which those contributions should have been remitted or paid by the employer.

xi. Revision of funding standard

Trustees of defined benefit pension schemes are required under Part IV of the Act to certify at 3½-year intervals that the assets of the scheme would have been sufficient at a specified date to meet the liabilities of the scheme if the scheme had wound up at that date. If the assets would not have been sufficient, a funding proposal must be submitted to the Pensions Board.[323]

The trustees of a scheme must, when submitting a funding proposal to the Pensions Board, ensure that the proposal is designed to ensure that, in the opinion of the actuary, the scheme could reasonably be expected to satisfy the funding standard at the effective date of the next actuarial funding certificate (i.e., in 3½ years time).[324]

---

[323]Pensions Act §49.

[324]*Id.* §49(2)(a).

Section 49(3) (following amendment in the Social Welfare (Miscellaneous Provisions) Act, 2003) allows the Pensions Board, on application to it by the trustees, to specify a later date (not being more than 10 years after date of the certificate) than the effective date of the next actuarial funding certificate where certain specified conditions are met and in the circumstances and on the terms that the Pensions Board considers appropriate. These terms include a requirement for an opinion from the scheme actuary.

In August 2003, the Pensions Board set out the recommended guidelines to be followed when making applications under Section 49(3). These guidelines have now been amended by the Pensions Board with effect from December 5, 2003.

The most recent guidelines indicate that, while the Pensions Board's normal policy is to only consider extensions for up to 10 years, it may now consider applications for longer extensions in exceptional circumstances. As before, any extensions are confined to schemes whose funding difficulties relate wholly or mainly to investment market falls. It is clear that extensions will only be granted where a strong case can be made that any such extension is necessary or appropriate and not contrary to the interests of members. Each individual application received by the Pensions Board is considered on a case-by-case basis.

2. *Types of Plans*

Occupational pension plans are not compulsory in Ireland and there is no legal requirement on employers to provide them. However, under provisions introduced by the Pensions (Amendment) Act, 2002, employers are obliged to either provide to employees (within six months of an employee's joining service) membership in a pension plan or immediate access to Personal Retirement Savings Accounts (PRSAs). Access to PRSAs means, in summary, that an employer must, among other things, provide employees with reasonable periods of paid absence, make the necessary payroll deduction arrangements, and allow PRSA providers reasonable access to the workplace.

There are four separate categories of pension plans in operation, each of which is discussed below.

a. *State-Sponsored Pension*

The state-sponsored pension system covers almost all employed persons. The state-sponsored system is funded through pay-related social insurance (PRSI) deductions taken directly from employee salaries.[325] Employers also must pay PRSI for every employee. The state-sponsored system provides a flat-rate pension, with the same amount paid to a high earner as a low earner.

b. *Occupational Pension Plans*

An occupational pension plan may be structured either as a defined contribution plan or as a defined benefit plan and must be approved by the Revenue Commissioners. A defined contribution plan is one in which the employer, and usually the employee, make specified contributions to a fund, which then is used on retirement to fund a pension and/or lump sum retirement benefit. Although not compulsory, employers often match any contribution made by their employees. A defined benefit plan is one in which a specified benefit is promised on retirement to an employee, based on salary and length of service. The employee makes contributions throughout his or her years of service, with the balance of the benefit cost funded by the employer.

c. *Personal Pension Plans*

A personal pension plan may be established by a self-employed person or an employed person who is not a member of an occupational pension plan. Personal pension plans are set up under a policy of assurance effected with a life assurance office and approved by the Revenue Commissioners. An employed person or a self-employed person may establish a PRSA.[326]

---

[325]For a complete discussion of pay-related social insurance (PRSI), see V.B.3.b., above.

[326]PRSAs are described in detail under VIII.A.1.b.viii., above.

d. Personal Retirement Savings Accounts

This is a new type of retirement savings arrangement. It is described in VIII.A.1.b.viii., above.

B. Health and Disability Funds

1. Private Health Insurance

The principal legislation governing private health and disability funds is the Health Insurance Act, 1994 (Health Insurance Act). Prior to the enactment of the Health Insurance Act, the only body that provided private health insurance in Ireland was the Voluntary Health Insurance Board (VHI), which was established under the Voluntary Health Insurance Act, 1957. The VHI, in effect, had a monopoly in this area. In 1994, Ireland implemented the EU Third Non-Life Insurance Directive (Insurance Directive)[327] through the European Communities (Non-Life Insurance) Framework Regulations, 1994. The Insurance Directive provides that insurance undertakings are entitled to exercise freedom of establishment throughout the EU. The effect of the Insurance Directive on health insurance in Ireland was to eliminate the VHI monopoly.

Currently, only two insurers provide private health insurance in Ireland: the VHI and BUPA. The level of coverage is discretionary; employers have no obligation to provide private health insurance. To reduce premiums, employers may subscribe to group plans. Premiums paid by an employer to a private health insurance fund on behalf of an employee are taxed as a benefit in-kind to the employee.

2. Sick Pay and Disability Benefits

Under the Irish social welfare system, employees are entitled to certain state sickness and disability benefits. Employers have no legal obligation to pay sick pay. However, employers sometimes arrange to pay an amount in addition to state sickness benefits, for example, to bring employees up to their normal level of pay. Employers normally insure against payment of long-term sick

[327]Council Directive 92/49/EEC, 1992 O.J. (L 228) 1.

pay by effecting a disability insurance policy with a life assurance office.

3. *Death Benefits*

Most employers also extend life assurance coverage to provide a defined death-in-service benefit for employees (usually expressed as a multiple of salary). A plan of this kind generally is referred to as a group life plan and is operated in conjunction with an occupational pension plan.

C. Other Employee Benefit Arrangements

1. *Share Option Plans*

Under a share option plan, an employee is granted options to acquire shares in the employer company at a certain price, which can be at a discount to the market value of the shares on the date the options are granted. It is usual for an employee to pay a nominal amount of consideration (e.g., IR£10) for the grant of an option. Each employee to whom a share option has been granted is required to exercise the option within a specified period (typically seven years) from the date of the grant.

Share option plans have certain income and capital gains tax consequences. First, where an option is exercisable within three years of grant, no charge to income tax arises upon grant of the option. However, a charge to Irish income tax does arise on the exercise, assignment, or release of an option.

The income tax charge is calculated by reference to the gain realized on exercise or assignment. The gain realized on exercise of the option is the difference between the market value of the shares at the time of acquisition, and the aggregate amount or value of the consideration given for the shares and for the grant of the option. The gain realized on the assignment or release of an option is the difference between the amount or value of the consideration for the assignment or release and the amount or value of the consideration, if any, given for the grant of the option.

The Finance Act, 2000 (Finance Act), provides that income tax arising on the exercise of share options may be deferred by an appropriate election to the earlier of the following dates:

- November 1 of the tax year beginning seven years after the tax year in which the options were exercised; or
- November 1 of the tax year following the tax year in which the shares so acquired were sold.

Where an option is capable of being exercised later than seven years after it was obtained, the Finance Act permits income tax to be charged with respect to the grant of the option, as opposed to when the option is exercised. Any tax charged on the grant of the option under this rule is deductible from any tax that is chargeable to the gain resulting from the subsequent exercise, assignment, or release of the option.

A charge to Irish capital gains tax arises on the sale of shares obtained through the exercise of an option. The current rate of Irish capital gains tax is 20 percent. If shares are sold immediately on exercise, there are no capital gains. However, if the shares are retained and sold at a later date, there may be a liability for capital gains tax on the gain. The capital gains tax liability is based on the difference between the proceeds received from sale of the shares and the option price. A deduction is available for any amount chargeable to income tax on the exercise of the share option.

A deduction is available to the participant for any consideration paid for the acquisition of the shares and for the consideration, if any, paid for the granting of the option or right. This is in addition to any deduction referred to in the previous paragraph.

The preceding paragraphs address the principle taxation issues for share option plans which are not approved by the Revenue Commissioners. The Finance Act, 2002, which changed the tax treatment of a share option plan approved by the Revenue Commissioners, is summarized as follows:

- a share option plan that is Revenue approved will secure more favorable tax treatment;
- with respect to options granted under a Revenue approved plan, no income tax charge will arise on the exercise of the options, but a charge to capital gains tax (currently at a rate of 20 percent) will arise on the full gain (being the difference between the amount paid for the shares under the option and the amount received on disposal of the shares);

- in order to secure capital gains tax treatment, there must be a period of time of at least three years between the grant of the options and any subsequent sale of the shares acquired under the options; and
- in order to secure Revenue approval, plans will have to satisfy a number of conditions, including:
  - the plan must be open to all employees and employees must be able to participate in the plan under "similar terms";
  - under the "similar terms" provisions, options may be granted by reference to remuneration, length of service, or other similar factors, but the plan cannot contain features that would discourage qualifying employees from participating or effectively ensuring that the benefits arise mainly to selected higher-paid employees or executives;
  - the plan may contain a "key employee" element where options can be granted without the "similar terms" conditions, but in no case can more than 30 percent of the options granted in a particular year come under this key employee provision; and
  - shares granted under the plan must be free from restrictions that would not apply to other shares of the same class.

2. *Employee Share Ownership Trust*

An employer may, through the creation of a trust (commonly known as an ESOT), purchase company shares for the benefit of employees. The transfer of shares to employees renders them liable for income tax unless the trust qualifies as a profit-sharing plan. For this reason, an ESOT usually is established in conjunction with an approved profit-sharing plan. The ESOT can retain the shares for up to 20 years, thus enabling employees to buy and sell at beneficial times.

3. *Approved Profit-Sharing Plans*

Under an approved profit-sharing plan, it is possible to transfer up to €12,700 worth of ordinary shares in the employer company, or in a group company, per annum to each eligible employee free of income tax, provided that the plan complies with a number of prescribed conditions and has been approved by the Revenue Commissioners. A plan may be so structured as to allow employees to elect that bonus payments due from their employer be used by plan trustees to acquire shares in the employer company or a group company. Many Irish publicly quoted and private companies have profit-sharing plans in place. There is a dedicated section of the Revenue Commissioners, known as the Employee Share Schemes Section, dealing with profit-sharing plan applications.

Each participant in an approved profit-sharing plan must permit his or her shares to be held in the name of the trustees for a minimum period of two years. Where the trustees retain the shares for at least three years from the date the beneficial interest is appropriated to the participants, no income tax liability will arise. Where the period of the trustees' share retention is fewer than three years, an income tax liability based on 100 percent of the "locked in value" of the shares will arise. Where a participant has ceased to be an employee or director of the company or has reached pensionable age, he or she will be taxed on 50 percent of the locked-in value. The "locked in" value of the shares is their market value on the date they are appropriated to participants.

A participant is liable for income tax on any dividends received with respect to the shares after the date the beneficial interest in the shares is appropriated.

Capital gains tax is chargeable on gains in excess of the market value on allocation of the shares. The company must contribute funds to the trustees to purchase the shares. However, by concession, the Revenue Commissioners will permit employees to sacrifice up to 7.5 percent of their basic salary (including bonus) and treat this as the employer's contribution, provided that the amount contributed by way of an employee salary deduction does not exceed the balance of the employer's contribution.

4. Save-As-You-Earn Plans

A Save-As-You-Earn (SAYE) plan allows employees to save part of their after-tax salary—between €12 and €320 per month—over a stated period (usually three or five years) (the savings period). At the end of this period, the savings may be used by the employees to purchase shares in their employer's company. The savings accumulate free of income tax and deposit income retention tax (DIRT).

During the savings period, the employee may obtain share options exercisable at a discount of up to 25 percent of the market value of the shares. So long as the option is not exercised during the savings period, no charge to income tax arises on grant of the option. At the end of the savings period, the employee may take the accumulated savings tax free or use the cash to exercise the share options. No charge to income tax arises to the employee on the purchase of shares at the discounted price.

From an implementation perspective, there are two aspects to a SAYE plan: an approved savings-related share option plan and a certified contractual saving plan. The contractual saving plan is used to fund the purchase of shares allocated to employees under the option plan. Certain conditions must be complied with in order for a savings-related option plan to be approved by the Revenue Commissioners. These conditions govern the type of company, eligibility of employees, type of shares, and the share price. Contractual saving plans must operate in conjunction with qualifying savings institutions as listed in the relevant legislation.[328]

The cost of establishing a savings-related option plan is allowed as a deduction for corporation tax purposes.

IX. IMMIGRATION

A. Work Permits, Work Authorizations, and Visas

Nationals of Member States of the European Economic Area (EEA)[329] are automatically entitled to work in Ireland. Non-EEA nationals require differing types of permission work in Ireland depending on their circumstances. The two most common ways for employers to obtain permission to employ a non-EEA national, in Ireland, are to obtain a work permit or a work authorisation/working visa.

---

[328]Taxes Consolidation Act, 1997, Schedule 12A.

[329]All EU Member States (including those joining in 2004) and Norway, Iceland and Liechtenstein.

1. Work Permits

a. Requirement

Section 2 of the Employment Permits Act 2003 makes it an offense for a non-national to be employed in the State except in accordance with an employment permit granted by the ETE Minister. The Act provides for penalties for both the employee and employer in the event of non-compliance. Penalties range from a €3,000 fine or 12 months imprisonment, or both, on summary conviction and up to €250,000 or 10 years imprisonment, or both, if the employer is convicted on indictment. The 2003 Act remedies a defect in the pre-existing law whereby no penalties could be enforced against an employer for employing non-nationals without a work permit. It is a defense for employers charged with an offence under the Act to show that they took all such steps as were reasonably open to them to ensure compliance with the Act.

b. Application

Work Permits are issued by the Department of Enterprise, Trade and Employment ("DETE"). In accordance with the policy of the DETE that employers should seek to employ an Irish or EEA national before applying for a Work Permit, employers are required to advertise the position to be filled with FÁS, the national training and employment agency, for at least one month. In certain circumstances, it is possible to obtain an exemption from the advertising requirement with FÁS if it can be demonstrated that the intended recipient of the work permit is a "key employee". If FÁS considers that an application for a work permit is appropriate, on the basis of the responses to the vacancy listing, the employer may apply for a work permit to the Work Permits Section of the DETE. The authorisation from FÁS to apply for a work permit is only valid for three months, therefore, an application for a work permit must be submitted to the DETE within this period. The requirement to register with FÁS does not apply in respect of applications for professional medical personnel, and certain categories of sports professionals and entertainers.

The DETE, in conjunction with FÁS, publish, on a quarterly basis, a list of job sectors that are ineligible for work permits. Individuals employed in one of these sectors will not be granted a work permit.

The processing time of work permit applications may vary from 4 to 10 weeks. Work permits will issue for a maximum of 12 months but they can be renewed. A decision to refuse a work permit may be appealed in writing to the DETE. Work permits entitle the non-EEA national to work for the specific employer named, for a specific period of time, and are non-transferable.

In general, work permits will not be granted (however, there may be room for discretion in certain cases) if:

- the prospective employee is in the State illegally;
- the prospective employee has entered the State on the basis that they will not take up employment;
- the prospective employee has been deported or is in the process of being deported;
- the prospective employer is operating in the State without business permission from the Minister for Justice, Equality and Law Reform.

c. *Permit Exceptions*

i. List of Exceptions

Work permits are not required for the following:

1. A citizen of a Member State of the EEA, and where such a citizen is employed or self-employed within the State, his or her spouse and any of their children who are under the age of 21 years or are dependent on the EEA citizen. New arrangements are due to come into operation to exempt spouses of non-EEA nationals who are working in Ireland from the requirement to obtain a work permit.
2. Persons who have been granted refugee status by the Minister for Justice Equality and Law Reform.
3. Persons in the State on a Work Authorization/Working Visa.
4. Post graduate students where the work is an integral part of the course of study being undertaken. (A letter is required from the College stating that they are studying).

5. The European Court of Justice delivered a judgment on the *Van der Elst Case* on 9 August 1994. The Court ruled that in the case of non-EEA nationals legally employed in one Member State who are temporarily sent on a contract to another Member State, the employer does not need to apply for work permits in respect of the non-nationals for the period of the contract.
6. Persons who have been granted permission to remain in the State on one of the following grounds:
   a. Persons with permission to remain as spouse of an Irish national;
   b. Persons with permission to remain as the parent of an Irish citizen; and
   c. Persons who have been given temporary leave to remain in the State on humanitarian grounds, having been in the Asylum process.
7. Swiss nationals do not require work permits in accordance with the terms of the EC and Swiss Confederation Act, 2001 which came into operation on 1 June 2002.

ii. Intra-Company Transfer Scheme

An Intra-Company Transfer Scheme was introduced in 1999 as a facility whereby companies with a bona fide presence in Ireland and at least one other non-EEA country, could transfer employees to Ireland, without a work permit being necessary, for a period of up to four years. Those being transferred presented an appropriate letter from the headquarters of the company to immigration officers upon arrival. This concession was intended primarily to facilitate international companies who needed to relocate key personnel to Ireland for a limited time. The Scheme was suspended in October 2002 and is currently under review. At present the DETE is considering Intra-Company Transfer applications on an ad-hoc basis in respect of senior management positions that are occupied by key employees.

iii. Non-EEA Trainee Scheme

The Non-EEA Trainee Scheme was introduced in 1999 and permitted an Irish company to bring in non-EEA personnel for a period of up to three years for the purposes of training. This scheme was temporarily suspended in October 2002 and is currently under review. The DETE will consider applications on an ad-hoc basis if there is a genuine, urgent need to transfer key, skilled personnel to Ireland in the interim.

2. *Work Authorization and Visas*

The Working Visa/Work Authorization Scheme was introduced to facilitate the recruitment of suitably qualified people from non-EEA countries for designated sectors of the employment market where skill shortages are particularly acute. The designated sectors of employment cover information and computing technologies, construction professionals, and across a broad range of medical, health and social care professions (including medical practitioners, nurses, speech and language therapists, occupational therapists, radiographers, physiotherapists, social works and psychologists).

The distinction between the work authorization and the working visa is that non-EEA nationals who require a visa to enter Ireland apply for a working visa and non-EEA nationals who do not require a visa[330] apply for a work authorization. In either case, the applicant must have an offer of employment in Ireland in one of the designated categories of employment. Applications must normally be made through the Irish Embassy/Consulate in the applicant's country of permanent residence and applicants may be required to attend for personal interview.

---

[330] Holders of passports from the following Non-EEA countries are not required to have visas to travel to Ireland: Andorra, Antigua, Barbuda, Argentina, Australia, Bahamas, Barbados, Belize, Bolivia, Botswana, Brazil, Brunei, Canada, Chile, Costa Rica, Cyprus, Czech Republic, Dominica, El Salavador, Estonia, Fiji, Grenada, Guatemala, Guyana, Honduras, Hong Kong, Hungary, Israel, Japan, Kiribati, Korea, Latvia, Lesotho, Lithuania, Malawi, Malaysia, Malta, Mauritius, Mexico, Monaco, Nauru, New Zealand, Nicaragua, Macau, Maldives, Panama, Poland, Saint Kitts & Nevis, Saint Lucia, Saint Vincent & the Grenadines, San Marino, Seychelles, Singapore, Slovenia, Slovak Republic, Solomon Islands, South Africa, Swaziland, Switzerland, Tonga, Trinidad & Tobago, Tuvala, United States, Uruguay, Vanuata, Vatican City, Venezuela, Western Samoa.

Working visas/work authorizations are usually granted for two years and are transferable between employers within the same skills category after the holder's arrival in Ireland. The scheme does not replace but rather supplements the Work Permit Scheme.

A Working Visa or Work Authorization does not give the holder an automatic right to enter Ireland and immigration officers retain discretion, in specified circumstances, to refuse entry to any non-national at a port of entry. The following are the principal reasons for which an immigration officer may refuse a non-EEA national leave to enter Ireland:

- Insufficient funds;
- Criminal record in relation to an offence punishable by imprisonment for a period of at least one year;
- A deportation order or exclusion order is in force in relation to that person;
- No valid passport;
- National security or public policy grounds; or
- If the immigration officer has reason to believe that the person has come to Ireland for a purpose or purpose other than those expressed.

3. Registration

All non-EEA nationals intending to reside in Ireland for a period in excess of three months, including persons who are exempt from obtaining a work permit or work authorization/working visa, must present themselves for registration purposes to the local Garda station where they reside or if they reside in Dublin to the Garda National Immigration Bureau.

B. Workers Posted Abroad

Workers posted to work in Ireland from other EU Member country have the protection of all Irish employment legislation in the same way as employees who have an Irish contract of employment. This is by virtue of the Protection of Employees (Part-Time Work) Act 2001, section 20, which states that all employment legislation that confers rights or entitlements on an employee applies to a posted worker in the same way that it applies to any other employee and that a national of a EU Member country, irrespective of nationality or place of residence, who works in another Member country (e.g., Ireland) under a contract of employment, has the same rights under that country's employment protection legislation as do employees who are nationals of that country.

THE NETHERLANDS*

INTRODUCTION[1]

A. History of the Netherlands

The Netherlands has been a constitutional monarchy since 1814. Before that the Netherlands was a republic, established by the Treaty of Utrecht of 1579. Queen Beatrice of Oranje-Nassau is the present monarch.

Together with the Netherlands Antilles and Aruba, the Netherlands forms the Kingdom of the Netherlands. The Statute of the Kingdom of the Netherlands of 1954 regulates the relationship among the Netherlands, the Netherlands Antilles, Aruba, and Surinam. Surinam became independent in 1975; earlier, in 1949, Indonesia (previously a colony of the Netherlands) became independent. The Netherlands is divided into provinces, which again are divided into municipalities.

The population in the Netherlands amounts to more than 16 million people. About 750,000 are self-employed; the rest of the active and inactive workforce consists of about 7.5 million people: about 5.4 million people are employed by an employer in the private sector, about 1 million are employed by the government, and 1.1 million are unemployed (400,000) or (at least partly) disabled (700,000). The national language is Dutch.

---

*E. Grace van Arkel, Attorney at Law/Research Fellow, Employment and Labor Law, Erasmus University Rotterdam, the Netherlands; and Cees J. Loonstra, Professor, Employment and Labor Law, Erasmus University Rotterdam, the Netherlands.

[1]The chapter about the Netherlands is not meant as a legal treatise, but rather as an introduction to important topics in labor and employment law in the Netherlands. Where it refers to men, women are also meant. The chapter discusses the law and developments through January 2004.

Elections on January 22, 2003, resulted in a new Dutch government as of May 27, 2003. The government is formed by the *CDA* (*Christen-Democratisch Appel* or Christian Democratic Appeal (Catholics and Protestants)); the *VVD* (*Volkspartij voor Vrijheid en Democratie* or People's Party for Freedom and Democracy (Liberals)); and *D66* (*Democraten 66* or Democrats 66 (Democrats)). Other parties include the *PvdA (Partij van de Arbeid* or Labor Party (Social Democrats)); the *Christenunie* (Christian Union); the *SGP* (*Staatkundig Gereformeerde Partij* or Political Reformed Party (Religious and Conservatives)); *Groen Links* or Green Left (Socialists and Pacifists); and the *LPF* (*Lijst Pim Fortuyn* or List *Pim Fortuyn* (Ultra Progressive)).

The governmental structure of the Netherlands was influenced by the French Revolution of 1789 (i.e., the French Codes that were in force during the French occupation of the Netherlands (1795-1813) in particular). One of the characteristics of the Dutch governmental structure is the separation of legislative, executive, and judicial powers.

B. Separation of the Legislative, Executive, and Judicial Powers

1. *Legislative Powers*

Under the Dutch Constitution, legislative powers are vested in the government and the Parliament (*Staten-Generaal* or *Parlement*). The government is formed by the monarch and government ministers, also referred to as the crown.

The Parliament has a bicameral structure and consists of the Upper House or Senate (*Eerste Kamer*) and the Lower House (*Tweede Kamer*). The Upper House, composed of 75 members elected by the provincial councils for four-year terms, cannot initiate or amend legislation. The Lower House, consisting of 150 members directly elected for four-year terms, alone has the authority to amend bills.

The initiative for introducing bills can be taken by members of the government or the Lower House of the Parliament. Before a bill becomes law, it first needs the approval of the Lower House, followed by approval of the Upper House, and is finalized by the signature of the monarch and the appropriate minister. The law becomes enforceable through publication in the Statute Book (*Staatsblad*). These laws are known as statutes.

Under the Province Act (*Provinciewet*) and the Municipal Act (*Gemeentewet*), the highest authorities within a province and a municipality have legislative powers as well. The highest authorities within a province and a municipality, respectively, are the provincial council (*Provinciale Staten*), with the Queen's commissioner as the chairman, and the municipal council (*Gemeenteraad*), with the mayor as the chairman. Their laws are known as ordinances.

The hierarchy of legislative sources—from highest to lowest—is (1) treaties, (2) constitution, (3) statutes, and (4) ordinances. In general, case law has the same weight as the law it interprets.

2. *Executive Powers*

Under the Constitution, the executive powers are vested in the government. The monarch can do no wrong and the ministers are responsible for government acts. The people can show their influence through the Parliament, which has control over the executive power of government. Members of the Lower House, as well as the members of the provincial councils, are directly elected by the people. As noted above, members of the provincial councils choose the members of the Upper House.

The Parliament has been given the following rights as means of control over the executive branch:

- *the right of questioning*: a member of a chamber can question a minister via the chairman;
- *the right of interrogation*: at the request of the majority of the chamber, the chamber can ask a minister for information; and
- *the right of inquiry*: at the request of the majority of either chamber, the chamber can start an inquiry with regard to an act of a minister.

In a province or a municipality, the highest authorities also have executive powers, unless otherwise stated by the Province Act or the Municipal Act. In general, the county aldermen (*Gedeputeerde Staten*) in a province and the court of mayor and aldermen (*College van Burgemeester en Wethouders*) in a municipality have these executive powers.

3. *Judicial Powers*

The establishment, structure, and competence of the judicial branch are regulated by the Constitution and the Judiciary Act (*Wet op de rechterlijke organisatie*).

Under the Constitution, the members of the highest judicial body, the Supreme Court (*Hoge Raad*), are appointed for life by royal decree; however, they can be dismissed upon request. The members are chosen from a list of recommendations prepared by Parliament.

Under the Constitution and the Judiciary Act, the civil court system consists of, in order from lower to higher courts, 59 "district courts, cantonal sections," also referred to as cantonal judges (*Kantonrechters*); 19 district courts (*Rechtbanken*); five courts of appeal (*Gerechtshoven*); and one Supreme Court in the Hague.[2]

The Netherlands does not have a jury system. Court decisions, with some minor exceptions, are public. The structure of the judicial system for labor and employment law disputes is discussed under F., below.

C. General Sources of Labor and Employment Law

1. *Statutes*

a. *Book 7, Title 10 of the Civil Code*

The Dutch legislature has enacted a law that regulates the individual relationship between the private employer and employee. This law has been amended several times through the years (including in 1954, 1981, 1997, and 1999), and presently it is known as Book 7, Title 10 of the Civil Code (*Burgerlijk Wetboek*).

b. *Book 6 of the Civil Code*

In general, employment is considered a special contract to which primarily the special rules of Book 7, Title 10 of the Civil Code apply. When, however, special rules are lacking, the law of

---

[2]See C.2., below.

obligations that applies to contracts in general will apply to the employment agreement. The law referring to general rules for obligations (*verbintenissen*) can be found in Books 3 and 6 of the Civil Code.

c. *The Minimum Wage and Minimum Holiday Allowance Act*

The Minimum Wage and Minimum Holiday Allowance Act (*Wet minimumloon en minimumvakantiebijslag* or *WMM*) refers to minimum wages and holiday bonuses and is discussed further in V.A., below.

d. *The Working Time Act*

The Working Time Act, also referred to as Working Hours Act (*Arbeidstijdenwet* or *ATW*), refers to working hours and is discussed further in V.B.1., below.

e. *The Occupational Safety and Health Act*

The Occupational Safety and Health Act, also referred to as the Health and Safety at Work Act or Working Conditions Act (*Arbeidsomstandighedenwet* or *Arbowet*), refers to safety and health in the workplace and is discussed further in VII., below.

f. *The Works Councils Act*

The Works Councils Act (*Wet op de ondernemingsraden* or *WOR*) refers to the representation of employees through works councils and similar bodies within the enterprise and is discussed in III., below.

g. The Collective Labor Agreement Act (*Wet op de collectieve arbeidsovereenkomst* or *WCAO*) and the Act on Administrative Extension and Non-Extension of Collective Labor Agreements (*Wet op het algmeen verbindend en het onverbindend verklaren van bepalingen van collectieve arbeidsovereenkomsten* or *Wet AVV/OVV*)

Both these Acts refer to collective labor agreements, also referred to as collective bargaining agreements, and are discussed further in II., below.

2. *Case Law*

The Act on the New Civil Procedure (*Wetboek van Nieuw Burgerlijk Rechtsvordering*), which went into effect on January 1, 2002, changed the Dutch civil court system. As a result, the district court, cantonal section (*Rechtbank, Sectie Kanton*), also referred to as the cantonal judge (*Kantonrechter*), has exclusive authority to decide employment and labor cases. If the parties do not agree with the decision of this court, they can—unless restricted by law[3]—appeal to the court of appeal (*Gerechtshof*), and, ultimately, they can file for review with the Dutch Supreme Court (*Hoge Raad*). A review by the Dutch Supreme Court is possible only on limited grounds, and the facts cannot be reviewed. The Supreme Court can either reject or grant the review and, in the latter, either issue a new decision or refer the case to the appellate court, which then must issue a new decision that takes the decision of the Supreme Court into consideration.

The decisions of the Dutch Supreme Court are mandatory and binding on all courts. A significant number of decisions by the Supreme Court have even led to statutory changes. In practice, however, decisions in employment and labor cases from the cantonal judges are important sources of employment and labor law as well.

3. *Treaties*

a. *European Convention for the Protection of Human Rights and Fundamental Freedoms (EVRM)*

Before the establishment of the European Union (EU), there was already the Council of Europe (*Raad van Europa*). The Council of Ministers signed the European Convention for the Protection of Human Rights and Fundamental Freedoms, also referred to as the European Convention on Human Rights and Fundamental Freedoms (*Europees Verdrag tot Bescherming van de Rechten van de Mens en de Fundamentele Vrijheden* or *EVRM*), in 1950 to stimulate economic and social progress. The Convention is self-executing, which means that citizens of member countries of the Council of Europe—in general the same member countries that

---

[3]See I.4.a., below.

joined the European Union—can directly rely on provisions of the Convention. The freedoms of speech and association granted by the Convention directly involve employment and labor law.

b. Treaty of Rome of 1957

The European Economic Community was established by the Benelux countries (Belgium, the Netherlands, and Luxemburg), the Federal Republic of West Germany, France, and Italy through the signing of the Treaty of Rome in 1957.[4] Other countries have since joined this treaty. The Treaty of Rome[5] is not self-executing, with the exception of some of the rules. Article 141[6] (former Article 119), for example, is self-executing and has had an important impact on Dutch employment and labor law. This article requires equal pay for men and women doing the same work. It has led to case law and to the enactment of statutory provisions in Book 7, Title 10 of the Civil Code.

c. The European Social Charter

The Netherlands signed the European Social Charter (*Europees Sociaal Handvest* or *ESH*) in 1961. The treaty was ratified in 1978 and entered into force in 1980. The European Social Charter is not self-executing, with an exception held by the Dutch Supreme Court in the *NS* (*Nederlandse Spoorwegen* or *Dutch Railway*) case regarding the Article 6.4 right of private employees to engage in collective action, including the right to strike.

d. The Maastricht Treaty of 1993

The Maastricht Treaty, also referred to as European Union Treaty, introduced the European Union in 1993. One important aspect was the introduction of the social provisions. Among other

---

[4]For additional information about the establishment of the European Union, see the Introduction, at B., in the chapter on the EU in Volume I, Part 1.

[5]The Amsterdam Treaty led to a renumbering of the entire EU Treaty. The new numbers will be used in this chapter, with the numbers of the provisions being replaced shown in parentheses.

[6]For a discussion of Article 141 (Article 119), see VI.A. in the chapter on the European Union in Volume I, Part 1.

provisions, it contained rules relating to the establishment of the European Works Council and resulted in the EU Works Council Directive of September 22, 1994.[7] This directive has been incorporated into Dutch law by the European Works Councils Act (*De Wet op de Europese Ondernemingsraad*). For additional discussion of this Act, see III., below.

e. International Labor Organization Conventions

The International Labor Organization (ILO) was established in 1919.[8] As of 1946, the ILO has been a specialized agency of the United Nations. An important goal of the ILO is to achieve social justice.

The plenary legislative body of the ILO, the International Labor Conference, gathers every June in Geneva to make decisions concerning recommendations and conventions. Conventions are adopted with the goal that they will result in national legislation. Governments of member countries have a choice whether to ratify an accepted convention or not. If a member country ratifies a convention, that country must adjust its national laws to the convention. The Netherlands has ratified 104 conventions.

4. Case Law of the European Court of Justice

Under the Treaty of Rome, the European Court of Justice (ECJ) was given the authority to issue preliminary rulings (*prejudiciele beslissingen*). Preliminary rulings interpreting the provisions of EU treaties, ordinances, or directives may, and in some cases must, be requested by the courts of EU member countries. ECJ decisions are not subject to review and requesting courts must apply the law as interpreted by the ECJ without modification or distortion. With respect to self-executing provisions, generally in treaties, citizens of member countries can appeal to the ECJ themselves, but only if all national remedies have been exhausted.

---

[7]Council Directive 94/45/EC, 1994 O.J. (L 254) 64. See III.B.1. in the chapter on the European Union in Volume I.

[8]For additional information on the ILO, see the chapter on the ILO in Volume I, Part 4.

D. Division of Responsibility for Labor and Employment Law

1. Labor Law

In the Netherlands, the term, "social law" (*sociaal recht*) is used to refer to social security law (*socialezekerheidsrecht*) and employment law (*arbeidsrecht*).

In employment law, a distinction is made between workers' representation law (*medezeggenschapsrecht*), dismissal law (*ontslagrecht*); and collective bargaining law (*cao-recht*). The latter can be compared with labor law in the United States and refers to union-management relations and collective bargaining agreements.

a. Unions

The most important trade union federations with respect to union-management relations are:

- *Federatie Nederlandse Vakbeweging* (*FNV*);
- *Christelijk Nationaal Vakverbond* (*CNV*); and
- *Vakcentrale voor Middelbaar en Hoger Personeel* (*MHP*).

Individual trade unions are members of the aforementioned trade union federations. The trade unions negotiate collective bargaining agreements and decide whether or not to strike; the trade union federations have a coordinating and advisory task.

b. Employers' Associations

For the manufacturing, business, banking, and insurance industries, the major employers' associations are the *Verbond van Nederlandse Ondernemingen* (*VNO*) and the *Nederlands Christelijk Werkgeversverbond* (*NCW*), which have merged under the name *Vereniging VNO-NCW*.

For small- and medium-sized businesses, the major employers' association is the *Vakcentrale MKB Nederland*. For agricultural concerns, the major employers' association is the *Vereniging LTO Nederland*.

Individual employers are members of these employers' associations, which function in an advisory and coordinating capacity. The employers negotiate collective bargaining agreements, except for the *Vereniging LTO Nederland*, which conducts its own negotiations.

2. *Employment Law*

Employment law consists mainly of statutory law. Employment law statutes generally define to whom the statute applies. Overall, employment law statutes apply to an employer and employee working on the basis of an employment agreement as defined in Article 610, Book 7, Title 10 of the Civil Code.[9] If there is an employment agreement according to this article, all provisions of Book 7, Title 10 of the Civil Code apply to the relationship, as well as all other statutes using the same definition.

3. *Advisory Organizations Consisting of Employees and Employers*

Representatives of trade union federations and employers' associations are represented in two important organizations that advise the government: the Labour Foundation (*Stichting van de Arbeid* or *STAR*) and the Social and Economic Council of the Netherlands (*Sociaal-Economische Raad* or *SER*).

The *STAR* is a private organization consisting of an equal number of representatives of trade union federations and employers' associations. Upon request, the *STAR* advises the government on labor-related topics. At the same time it also provides a forum in which its members discuss relevant issues in the field of labor and industrial relations.

The *SER* is a public organization consisting of an equal number (11 each) of representatives of trade union federations, employers' associations, and members appointed by the crown. Upon request or at its own inititative, the *SER* advises the government regarding socio-economic policies.

---

[9]See I.A., below, for additional discussion of individual employment agreements.

E. The Labor Inspectorate

The most important body responsible for overseeing labor and employment law regulatory systems is the Labor Inspectorate (*Arbeidsinspectie* or *AI*). The *AI* is part of the Ministry of Social Affairs and Employment.

Under the Working Time Act (*Arbeidstijdenwet*) and the Occupational Safety and Health Act (*Arbeidsomstandighedenwet or Arbowet*), the *AI* has the authority to inspect all work places to see if employers and employees comply with these laws. The *AI* also has the authority to sanction employer violations.

In regard to collective bargaining agreements, the Central Office of the *AI* (*Centraal Kantoor van de Arbeidsinspectie*) also has an important role. Collective bargaining agreements that are new, altered, or terminated must be reported to the Central Office so that the government stays aware of the process with regard to collective bargaining agreements and can consider the existing collective bargaining agreements when forming its social policy.

F. Structure of the Judicial System for Labor and Employment Law

1. *Jurisdiction*

a. *Exclusive Jurisdiction*

As of January 1, 2002, the district court, cantonal section (*Rechtbank, Sectie Kanton*), also referred to as cantonal judge (*Kantonrechter*), has exclusive jurisdiction in employment and labor cases.[10] Thus, the private employer and employee or the contracting parties to a collective bargaining agreement must file their claims with the cantonal judge. The Court of Appeal is the appellate court for decisions of the cantonal judge.

A special judge of the district court—either of the cantonal or civil section—decides on injuctions (*Voorzieningenrechter*), with appeals also addressed to the Court of Appeal.

---

[10]See the Introduction, at C.2., above.

Parties do not need to be represented by an attorney when they appear before the cantonal judge. In case of a petition filed with district court, civil section, the plaintiff, however, needs to be represented. In case of appeals, all parties need to be represented by an attorney.

Other courts that are involved in labor and employment issues are the Central Appeal Tribunal (*Centrale Raad van Beroep*), with exclusive authority in disputes as regards social security laws and civil servants, and the Enterprise Section (also referred to as the Companies Bench) of the Amsterdam Court of Appeal (*Ondernemingskamer Gerechtshof Amsterdam*), to whom employers and employees must address disputes under the Works Councils Act (*Wet op de ondernemingsraden* or *WOR*).

b. Venue

Venue refers to the area within which a court exercises its jurisdiction. Under the new civil court system, which became effective on January 1, 2002, the area in which the district court, cantonal section (*Rechtbank, Sectie Kanton*), also referred to as cantonal judge, has jurisdiction will vary, based on the nature of the case.

- In cases that must be introduced by a subpoena (e.g., a claim based on manifestly unreasonable termination of employment),[11] the cantonal judge has jurisdiction in the area where the defendant lives or the place of employment.
- In cases that must be introduced by a request or petition (e.g., dissolution of the employment agreement based on urgent cause or change of circumstances),[12] the cantonal judge has jurisdiction in the area where the petitioner lives, the place of employment, or the area where the defendant lives.

2. *The Government Financial Legal Aid System*

The Dutch government has established a financial aid system by which any citizen is given the ability to hire a lawyer and get

[11] See I.C.3.b.v., below.
[12] See I.C.4.a., below.

access to the judicial system. An individual seeking such financial assistance must address the Legal Assistance Council (*Raad voor Rechtsbijstand*) through an attorney. The request will be granted (*toevoeging*) if the individual's income and assets stay within the bounds set by the government.

If the request is granted, the Legal Assistance Council will assess a contribution from the client based on the client's income, with the contribution generally ranging from approximately US $100 to about US $1,000. The client must pay this contribution to his or her lawyer. The lawyer then seeks the remainder of his or her fees from the Council for Legal Assistance.

Costs such as administrative fees, bailiff's costs, and litigation costs remain the responsibility of the client; the financial aid contribution only applies to attorneys' fees.

G. Structure of the Third Party Dispute Resolution System for Labor and Employment Law

1. *Arbitration*

Parties to a dispute can agree to arbitration instead of litigation. Parties electing to go into arbitration no longer have access to a civil court, with one exception: parties can petition the president of the district court if the urgency of the case requires a judicial decision on short notice.

If arbitration is agreed upon, Articles of the Code on Civil Procedure (*Wetboek van Burgerlijke Rechtsvordering*) apply. These rules include the requirement that an uneven number of arbitrators hear the case and that the arbiters' decision is enforceable after one of the parties obtains leave to enforce (*exequatur*) from a court.

2. *Enforceable Mediation*

Parties to a dispute can also agree to have the matter resolved by enforceable mediation. The mediation decision becomes part of the contract and therefore, a party must seek judicial intervention if the other party fails to comply with the enforceable mediation decision. This method of execution is in contrast to arbitration decisions, which are enforceable after one of the parties has obtained a judicial enforcement order.

I. INDIVIDUAL EMPLOYMENT

A. Individual Employment Agreements

Book 7, Title 10 of the Civil Code contains specific rules with regard to individual employment agreements. These rules are either:

- fully mandatory (*dwingend*)—allowing no deviation unless in favor of the employee;
- three-quarters mandatory (*driekwartdwingend*)—permitting deviation solely by collective bargaining agreement or public arrangement;
- five-eighths mandatory (*vijfachtste dwingend*)—permitting deviation solely by an (enterprise) agreement between the employer and the works council;
- semi-mandatory (*semidwingend*)—allowing deviation only when variations are recorded in writing; or
- supplementary (*aanvullend*)—regulating relationships between the parties in matters not covered by agreements.

This system of incorporating degrees of flexibility is unique in Dutch law and is probably considered unique in other countries as well.

1. Historical Background

The Employment Agreement Act (*Wet op de arbeidsovereenkomst*) was enacted in 1907, and became effective in 1909 as Title 7A, Book 7A of the Civil Code. This Act, which contained more than 80 articles, replaced three previous articles—deriving from the French Civil Code—in the Civil Code. The Employment Agreement Act regulated private employer–employee relationships. The majority of the rules were mandatory to protect employees from the economically stronger employers and to place employees on the same bargaining level as employers.

In 1954, Title 7A, Book 7A of the Civil Code, in which the Employment Agreement Act was laid down, was amended. Among the important changes brought about through these amendments, the 1954 amendments introduced the three-quarters mandatory rules discussed in A., above, allowing deviation through collective bargaining agreements. Further, it became illegal to terminate employees during the first two years of illness. In addition, an employee was allowed to bring an action based on "manifestly unreasonable dismissal". This meant that although the employer had terminated the employment agreement with permission of the *CWI* (*Centrum voor Werk en Inkomen* or Center for Work and Income) and with observance of the notice period, due to factors such as satisfactory performance and/or length of service, the employee could nevertheless ask for compensation.

In 1981, a major change occurred, when employees were given additional protections from dismissal after transfers of undertakings such as changes in ownership.

On April 1, 1997, in a technical revision, the provisions of the Employment Agreement Act were superseded by Book 7, Title 10 of the Civil Code.

On March 4, 1998, a new rule was introduced giving employers the right to change employment agreements unilaterally, provided it was done in writing, and provided the right was exercised only where employers had serious interests outweighing the interests of employees.[13] An employee thus can object to unilateral changes, based on the latter provision.

On January 1, 1999, the Flexibility and Security Act, also referred to as the Flexicurity Act (*Wet Flexibiliteit en zekerheid* or *Flexwet*), became effective. This Act thoroughly revised Book 7, Title 10 of the Civil Code. Among the important changes was the introduction of Article 668a, which allowed for continuing employment agreements for definite periods. The rule was revised as regards probationary periods (*proeftijden*). In order to be valid, the provision for probationary periods needed to be in writing. Prior law had allowed for oral agreements in this regard. In addition, the Flexicurity Act introduced rules concerning minimum pay for on-call workers[14] and rules concerning temporary workers.[15]

---

[13]Book 7, Title 10 of the Civil Code, art. 613.

[14]For further discussion of on-call workers, see I.B.2., below.

[15]For further discussion of temporary workers, see I.B.1., below.

Book 7, Title 10 of the Civil Code was amended again by the Vacation and Parental Leave Act (*Wet wijziging 7.10 BW met betrekking tot vakantie en ouderschapsverlof*), which went into effect on February 1, 2001.[16] The Act *WVP* (*Wet Verbetering Poortwachter* or Gatekeeper Improvement Act) also amended Book 7, Title 10 of the Civil Code by adding new Articles 658a and 660a. Articles 658a and 660a, which went into effect on April 1, 2002, affect the obligations of employers and employees with respect to short-term sickness benefits.[17]

2. *Substance of the Individual Employment Agreement*

The majority of the working people in the Netherlands work on the basis of individual employment agreements. In principle, the parties can agree upon any terms they like; however, where there is an employment agreement, the rules of Book 7, Title 10 of the Civil Code apply, most of which are mandatory to some degree. Also, the parties are limited as to the terms to which they can agree on when a collective bargaining agreement applies to the individual employment agreement. The provisions of the collective bargaining agreement prevail over the terms of the individual employment agreement.

a. *Statutory Regulation of Individual Employment Agreements*

Book 7, Title 10 of the Civil Code contains 11 major categories of rules applicable to individual employment contracts:

- general terms (610–615);
- wages (616–633);
- vacation and leave (634–645);
- equal treatment (646–648);
- special terms of the employment agreement (650–653);
- obligations of employers (654–658);
- obligations of employees (659–661);

---

[16]See V.C.1.a. and V.C.2.a., below.

[17]See I.C.3.a., I.C.3.b.i., I.C.4.a., and VIII., below.

- transfer of enterprises (662–666);
- termination of employment agreements (667–686);
- trade representatives (687–689); and
- temporary workers (690-691).

b. Definition

An employment agreement is defined as an agreement by which the employee, in exchange for payment, commits himself or herself to the service of the other party to work for a period of time.[18] This definition is further articulated by judicial opinions finding the existence of an employment agreement where the employee agrees to work for the employer, the employer agrees to pay the employee, the employer is entitled to give instructions to the employee, and the employee, in principle, does not have the liberty to have the job done by another.

c. Formation

Contract principles in Book 6 of the Civil Code apply to employment agreements. In general, if the employee accepts the offer of the employer, then there is an employment agreement. Oral and written employment agreements both are valid.

The existence or terms of oral employment agreements are more difficult to prove when there is a conflict. More importantly, certain terms are null and void if not agreed upon in writing. The probationary period (*proeftijd*), for example, must be agreed upon in writing to be valid and therefore enforceable.

Whether the employment agreement has been agreed upon verbally or in writing, employers have a fully mandatory duty to inform employees in writing about certain terms of the employment agreement, including the amount of wages and period of service.[19]

d. Duration

An employment agreement can be agreed upon for a definite or an indefinite period. An employment agreement for a definite period can be agreed upon for a certain time or for a certain project.

---

[18]Book 7, Title 10 of the Civil Code, art. 610.

[19]*Id.* art. 655.

An employment agreement for a definite period ends automatically after expiration of the period or project.[20] If parties have not agreed upon a new period and the employee continues employment after the expired period, there is an automatic renewal of the contract on the same terms as agreed upon with the first contract. Under Article 668a, such agreements end automatically after three successive expirations and automatic renewals, or not exceeding a maximum period of three years.[21] In case of a fourth contract, the third contract converts automatically into a contract for an indefinite period. Where the successive employment agreements for definite periods exceed the three-year maximum, the employment agreement converts automatically into an employment agreement for an indefinite period as well. A contract for a definite period between the same employer and employee that is formed and renewed within a three-month period is considered to be a successive employment agreement. Article 668a is a three-quarters mandatory rule; deviation is possible only by a collective bargaining agreement.

Whether the employment agreement is for a definite or indefinite period, the parties cannot, during the period of the employment agreement, terminate the agreement without the permission of the *CWI* (*Centrum voor Werk en Inkomen* or Center for Work and Income) or through the dissolution procedure (*ontbindingsprocedure*) with the district court, cantonal section (*Rechtbank, Sectie Kanton*), also referred to as the cantonal judge (*Kantonrechter*).[22]

The foregoing two-way system is called the dual dismissal system (*duaal ontslagstelsel*). The authority to grant permission for employment termination was previously held by the Regional Director of Labor Services (*Regionaal directeur van de arbeidsvoorzieningsorganisatie* or *RDA*), but this authority was transferred as of January 1, 2002, to a new institution, the *CWI* (*Centrum voor Werk en Inkomen* or Center for Work and Income), by the *Act SUWI* (*Wet Structuur uitvoeringsorganisatie werk en*

[20] *Id.* art. 667.
[21] *Id.* art. 668a.
[22] *Id.* art. 685.

inkomen or Act on the Implementation Structure for Work and Income).

In the case of employment agreements for a definite period, it is possible to terminate the employment agreement with permission of the *CWI* during the contract period only if this is explicitly agreed upon by the parties in writing. Otherwise, the agreement can only be terminated on the last day of the agreement period.

Permission of the *CWI* for termination is not required when the dismissal occurs during a probationary period, when there is urgent cause, and when the parties mutually have agreed upon termination. See C., below, for a further discussion of termination procedures.

e. *Collective Bargaining Agreements*

Collective bargaining agreements apply to individual employment agreements if:

- the employer and employee have mutually agreed upon applicability of the collective bargaining agreement;
- the employer and employee are both parties to the collective bargaining agreement;
- the employer is party to the collective bargaining agreement, but the employee is not; or
- the Minister of Social Affairs and Employment has declared the collective bargaining agreement generally binding.

If there is a collective bargaining agreement in place, the Collective Labor Agreement Act (*Wet op de collectieve arbeidsovereenkomst* or *WCAO*) provides that the terms of the collective agreement determine the effect of any individual employment agreement.[23]

B. Contingent Employment Arrangements

Most of the rules in Book 7, Title 10 of the Civil Code governing employment agreements are mandatory, leaving little room for deviation by the parties. As employers attempt to gain more

[23]See II.D.2.c., below.

flexibility, the Netherlands has experienced an increase in the use of contingent employment arrangements. The three most common contingent arrangements are temporary workers (*uitzendkracht*), on-call workers (*oproepkracht*), and independent contractors or freelancers. Each of these arrangements is discussed below.

1. *Temporary Workers*

In the case of temporary workers, three parties are involved in the employment relationship: the temporary agency, the temporary worker, and the principal (the client of the temporary agency).

On January 1, 1999, a new Section 11 of Book 7, Title 10 (adding Articles 690 and 691) went into effect. According to these rules the relationship between the temporary agency and the temporary worker is regarded as an employment agreement subject to Book 7, Title 10 of the Civil Code. However, on the other hand, it also permits employment agreements on a temporary basis more flexibility than standard employment agreements. One important exception in this respect created by this new section is that Article 668a, Book 7, Title 10, is not applicable during the first 26 weeks of temporary work, so the parties are free to agree in writing that the temporary employment agreement ends every time the job terminates. This means that a series of more than three successive contracts can be agreed on, with less than three months between each contract, without the last contract being automatically converted into a permanent employment agreement.

With the exceptions in Articles 690 and 691, all rules of Book 7, Title 10 of the Civil Code apply to the relationship between the temporary worker and the temporary agency.

2. *On-Call Workers*

Employers with varying workflows or seasonal tasks frequently use on-call workers. The relationship between employers and on-call workers depends on what they have agreed between themselves.

In some cases, employers and on-call workers agree upon the terms of employment that will apply if work becomes available. Such an agreement is called a pre-agreement (*voorovereenkomst*). In these cases, the employer is free to call on the worker and the worker is free to refuse when he or she is called upon. If the worker does appear on the job, however, there is an employment agreement.

In other cases the parties agree upon specific terms of employment except for working hours and working times; in such situations there is an employment agreement with a postponed duty to perform (*arbeidsovereenkomst met een uitgestelde prestatieplicht* or *mup*), which means that if work is available, then the employer is obligated to call on the worker. If the employer does not call on the worker, the employer is obligated to pay salary, regardless of whether there is work available, unless the parties have agreed upon "no work, no pay." The latter can only be agreed upon for a maximum period of six months, however, meaning that after expiration of this period the employer is again obligated to pay salary. There is no smaller pay for being on call than there is when there is actual work the worker does. The employer has an obligation to pay salary when there is no work available because the employee has no option to refuse an employer's call under this contract; thus, in effect, the employee is completely dependent on the employer.

On January 1, 1999, on-call workers with both types of arrangements discussed above were accorded a degree of income security with a rule requiring employers to pay a minimum of three hours' wages per call even if on-call workers work fewer than three hours. In case of a *mup*, the worker, however, in practice, will primarily ask for her or his full salary.

3. *Independent Contractors*

Employers sometimes seek to create greater flexibility for themselves by classifying relationships with some workers as independent contractor arrangements. Independent contractors, sometimes called freelancers, do not work as employees of a particular company, and may well work for more than one principal. There is no employment agreement between independent contractors and principals.

If a dispute arises, courts decide whether this classification is appropriate according to the facts and circumstances of each case. In general, courts will find workers to be freelancers if they do not meet the definition of an employment agreement under Article 610 of Book 7, Title 10 of the Civil Code.

Among the hallmarks that distinguish independent contractors are that they have different principals for whom they work, have the right to refuse assignments, are free to have another perform the job, pay their own taxes, and do not receive wages but invoice the principal for services rendered.

C. Termination of Employment

An individual employment agreement can terminate by mutual agreement, the death of the employee, unilateral termination or resignation, or through dissolution by the district court, cantonal section, also referred to as the cantonal judge. The rules governing each of these situations are discussed below.

1. Mutual Agreement

When employment agreements terminate by mutual agreement, neither the rules in Book 7, Title 10 of the Civil Code nor the rules of the 1945 Special Decree on Labor Relations (*Buitengewoon Besluit Arbeidsverhoudingen* or *BBA 1945*)[24] apply. Employees cannot obtain unemployment benefits if the employment agreement has been terminated by mutual agreement. In cases involving termination by mutual agreement, the employer must show that the employee has clearly and unambiguously agreed upon termination. If the statement of the employee is not clear and unambiguous, the employment agreement is still in place and thus the employee is entitled to a salary.

2. Death of the Employee

An employment agreement ends with the death of the employee and requires the employer to pay the employee's relatives (as defined in the article) a death benefit equivalent to approximately one month of the employee's salary.[25] The employment agreement does not end with the death of the employer.[26]

3. Unilateral Termination/Resignation

The two primary sources for the rules with regard to unilateral termination or employee resignation are found in the 1945

[24]See I.C.3.a., below.

[25]Book 7, Title 10 of the Civil Code, art. 674.

[26]*Id.* art. 675.

Special Decree on Labor Relations (*Buitengewoon Besluit Arbeidsverhoudingen* or *BBA 1945*) and Book 7, Title 10 of the Civil Code. Other laws that may be applicable in certain situations in which one party ends the employment agreement are discussed in IV., below.

a. 1945 Special Decree on Labor Relations

The 1945 Special Decree on Labor Relations applies to employees working on the basis of an employment agreement as defined in article 610, Book 7, Title 10 of the Civil Code. This Decree does not apply to public employees, teachers, housekeepers, clerical clerks, and managerial directors who have been appointed pursuant to the Articles of Incorporation (*statutair directeuren*).

As of January 1, 2002, pursuant to the Act on the Implementation Structure for Work and Income *(Wet Structuur uitvoeringsorganisatie werk en inkomen* or *Act SUWI*), an employer needs the permission of the Center for Work and Income (*Centrum voor Werk en Inkomen* or *CWI*)[27] to unilaterally terminate an employment agreement under the 1945 Special Decree on Labor Relations. Prior to the *Act SUWI*, employers needed permission from the Regional Director of the Labor Market Agency *(Regional Directeur Arbeidsvoorzieningsorganisatie* or *RDA*) to terminate an agreement. The *CWI* is bound by the Dismissal Decree (*Ontslagbesluit*), which provides that permission to unilaterally terminate an employment agreement may be granted only if it is socially or economically justified.

An important change was made to the Dismissal Decree as of April 1, 2002, under the Gatekeeper Improvement Act (*Wet Verbetering Poortwachter* or *Act WVP*). This change requires employers to make serious attempts to integrate sick employees back into the workplace and requires employees to cooperate with these attempts. If the employee does not cooperate with the employer's efforts, the employer may request permission to terminate the employment agreement from the *CWI*. Before granting permission, the *CWI* must ask for a so-called "second opinion" from the Institute for Employee Benefit Schemes (*Uitvoeringsinstituut Werknemers Verzekeringen* or *UWV*), a new institution that has replaced the National Institute for Social Security (*Landelijk Instituut voor Sociale Verzekeringen* or *LISV*).

---

[27]See I.A.2.d., above.

The Dismissal Decree (*Ontslagbesluit*) sets out the rule that when an employer is granted permission of the *CWI* to unilaterally terminate an employment agreement, the employer must apply the rule "last in, first out," unless the employer can prove that a particular employee is especially qualified for the job and should be retained. An exception has been made for cleaning personnel and temporary workers of temporary agencies.

b. Book 7, Title 10 of the Civil Code

Section 9 of Book 7, Title 10 of the Civil Code contains specific rules governing particular aspects of termination the employment agreement. These rules can be divided into the following five categories:

- prohibitions against termination;
- notice periods for termination;
- irregularity of termination;
- termination for urgent cause; and
- manifestly unreasonable termination of the employment agreement.

i. Prohibitions against termination

Prohibitions against termination can be found in the articles 646 to 649 in Book 7, Title 10 of the Civil Code. These articles include the prohibition against discrimination and in effect prohibit termination based on gender (7:646); the hours that an employee works (full-time or part-time); and the duration of the employment agreement (definite or indefinite).[28] As from December 1, 2003, the Act on Equal Treatment Based on A Handicap or Chronic Illness (*Wet gelijke behandeling op grond van handicap of chronische ziekte*) includes the prohibition against discrimination and in effect prohibits termination because of a handicap or chronic disease. The Bill on Equal Treatment Based on Age was still pending in Parliament in 2003.

In addition, the employer is prohibited from terminating the employment relationship because of:

---

[28]See VI.2.c.i-iii., below.

- employee illness, during the first two years of such illness (but see exception discussed below);
- pregnancy and/or maternity leave;
- military service or alternative compulsory service;
- membership in a works council or related committees;
- union membership or performance of union activities;
- political leave, i.e., performance of duties of elected office; or
- appeals for parental leave.[29]

While, as noted above, in general under Dutch Law an employer is not allowed to dismiss an employee during the first two years of illness, there are two exceptions to this rule.[30]

- As of April 1, 2002, the employer under the Gatekeeper Improvement Act (*Wet Verbetering Poortwachter* or *WVP*), has an obligation to reintegrate a sick employee.[31] As of January 1, 2003, this obligation has been strengthened for employees who became ill after January 1, 2003, such that when reintegration within the company of the employer is not possible, the employer has to look for possibilities outside the company. If, however, the employee does not cooperate with serious attempts on the part of the employer to integrate the sick employee back into the workplace (e.g., by refusing an employer's reasonable offer of another suitable job), the employer may request permission from the Center for Work and Income (*Centrum voor Werk en Inkomen* or *CWI*) to terminate the sick employee, in spite of the rule that an employer in principle is not allowed to dismiss an employee during the first two years of illness.[32]
- Moreover, under the Flexicurity Act (*Wet Flexibiliteit en Zekerheid* or *Flexwet*), which went into effect on January 1, 1999,[33] the rule that prohibits an employer from terminating an employee during the first two years of illness does

[29]Book 7, Title 10 of the Civil Code, art. 670.
[30]*Id.* art. 670.1.
[31]*Id.* art. 658a.
[32]*Id.* art. 670b.3.
[33]See I.A.1., above.

not apply if the employee becomes ill after the *CWI* has received an employer's request for its consent to dismiss the employee.

As of June 1, 2003, an employer is also prohibited from terminating the employment agreement with an employee who, within the margins of the Working Time Act (*Arbeidstijdenwet* or *ATW*), has refused to work on Sundays.[34]

In situations where there has been a termination in violation of one of these prohibitions, the employee has two months in which to seek to have the termination invalidated. If the employee fails to contest the termination within the two-month period, the termination becomes valid. If the employee contests the termination and the termination is found to be invalid, the employee may seek reinstatement and restoration of pay. Alternatively, the employee may choose not to be reinstated and instead can ask for damages, for example, based on manifestly unreasonable dismissal.[35]

ii. Notice periods for termination

There are required notice periods for the regular termination of the employment agreements by employers or resignation by employees.[36] In general, the notice period begins on the last day of the month; however, parties are permitted to agree otherwise, provided this agreement is in writing.

Employees can only unilaterally terminate their employment agreements if they give one month's notice. Parties are permitted to agree on other employee notice periods, provided (i) this agreement is in writing; (ii) the notice period of the employee does not exceed six months; and (iii) the notice period of the employer is at least twice as long as the notice period of the employee. (Deviation from iii is allowed by collective bargaining agreement only, under the condition that the notice period of the employer is at least as long as the notice period of the employee.)

[34]Book 7, Title 10 of the Civil Code, art. 670.9.
[35]*Id.* art. 681.
[36]*Id.* art. 672.

The notice requirements for employers as regards employees depend on the length of the employment agreement. Employers unilaterally terminating employment agreements for service of fewer than five years are required to give their employees, one month's notice; for agreements for 5 to 10 years, two months' notice; for agreements for 10 to 15 years, three months' notice; and for agreements of 15 years or more, four months' notice. Deviation from these requirements to the detriment of employees is possible by collective bargaining agreement; deviation in favor of employees is possible if agreed to in writing.

iii. Irregularity of termination

If an employment agreement is terminated without notice, such a termination is considered irregular.[37] Examples of irregular terminations would be when an employer terminates the employment agreement giving a one-week notice period, where the statutory requirement is for one month, or if the employer fires the employee for urgent cause but a court later finds that there was no urgent cause.

An employee who has been dismissed without proper notice has six months in which to contest the invalidity of the dismissal.[38] The employee may ask for either a fixed compensation of the wages that would have been paid if the notice period had been taken into account, a full compensation for the damages suffered as a result of the irregularity, or reinstatement of the employment agreement (*herstel van de arbeidsovereenkomst*).

iv. Termination for urgent cause

Both the employer and the employee can terminate the employment agreement for urgent cause.[39] If the employment agreement is terminated for urgent cause, the other party must be immediately informed of the basis for the termination. Conduct that justifies immediate termination of employment must be such as to

[37] *Id.* art. 677.

[38] *Id.* art. 683.

[39] Examples of urgent causes are enumerated in Book 7, Title 10 of the Civil Code, articles 678 and 679.

make continuation of the employment relationship unreasonable, i.e., impossible.

If an employer terminates an employment agreement on grounds of urgent cause, the employee's typical defense is that there is no urgent cause or that the cause is not severe enough to be urgent cause. In such a case, the employee will seek to invalidate the termination because the employer did not obtain permission of the Center for Work and Income (*Centrum voor Werk en Inkomen* or *CWI*) to terminate the employment agreement. Alternatively, the employee may choose not to be reinstated and instead can ask for damages because the termination was irregular since no notice was given[40] or it was without cause.[41]

The court decides whether urgent cause exists according to the circumstances of the case. If the court finds that there was urgent cause, then the employer can immediately terminate the employment agreement and the employee has no redress.[42]

v. Manifestly unreasonable termination

A unilateral termination, although valid and complying with notice requirements and with *CWI*'s consent to terminate the employment agreement, can be ruled manifestly unreasonable (*kennelijk onredelijk*) under certain circumstances.[43] The law provides examples of situations in which termination may be considered manifestly unreasonable, such as in the case of a constructive discharge or, for example, when an employee has worked for many years without any performance complaints and is fired at age 50 without severance pay.

Employees must contest the invalidity of the termination within six months.[44] The employee can seek compensatory damages or reinstatement of the employment agreement (*herstel van de arbeidsovereenkomst*).

[40]Book 7, Title 10 of the Civil Code, art. 677.
[41]*Id.* art. 681.
[42]*Id.* art. 677.
[43]*Id.* art. 681.
[44]*Id.* art. 683.

4. *Dissolution*

Employment agreements may only be dissolved by the cantonal judge through findings of either serious cause (*gewichtige redenen*)[45] or breach of contract (*wanprestatie*).[46]

a. *Serious Cause: Urgent Cause or Change of Circumstances (Article 7:685)*

Serious cause required for dissolution consists of either an urgent cause (e.g., gross misconduct) or a change of circumstances since the employment agreement was made.[47] After the request for dissolution is made by the employer or employee, the other party is allowed to provide a written response, and then a hearing takes place. Requests for dissolution are most frequently made by employers. The dissolution procedure generally takes about two months.

As of January 1, 2002, under the Act on the New Civil Procedure (*Wetboek van Nieuw Burgerlijk Rechtsvordering*),[48] parties must file a request for dissolution of the employment agreement (*ontbindingsprocedure*) with the district court, cantonal section (*Rechtbank, Sectie Kanton*), also referred to as the cantonal judge (*Kantonrechter*). The cantonal judge decides whether the circumstances either constitute an urgent cause or change of circumstances.

If the cantonal judge determines that urgent cause is the proper ground for dissolution, the employment agreement will be dissolved without severance pay. If change of circumstances is determined to be the grounds, then severance pay can be granted, although it is not mandatory. The amount of any severance pay granted is based on the so-called Cantonal Court Formula—also as of January 1, 2002 referred to as the District Court Formula (*Kantonsrechtersformule*)—which is discussed further under IV.A.2.a.i., below.

The decision itself provides the requesting party with the opportunity to withdraw the request. If the requesting party does

---

[45] *Id.* art. 685.

[46] *Id.* art. 686.

[47] *Id.* art. 685.

[48] See the Introduction, at C.2., above.

not withdraw the request, then the employment agreement will be dissolved as of the date stated on the decision.

The dissolution decision of the cantonal judge may only be appealed in very rare cases, e.g., if there was a violation of a fundamental principle such as the right to a fair trial.

As of April 1, 2002, under the Gatekeeper Improvement Act (*Wet Verbetering Poortwachter* or *Act WVP*),[49] an approved reintegration plan is no longer required. Previously, beginning in January 1, 1999, if an employee became sick before the employer filed a dissolution request, the employer was required to file a reintegration plan along with the dissolution request, and dissolution requests filed without reintegration plans were not considered. The employer's obligation to reintegrate a sick employee now is based instead on the new Article 658a in Book 7, Title 10 of the Civil Code, which has its own sanctions for noncompliance.

b. Breach of Contract (Article 7:686)

Dissolution of the employment agreement may also be based on the general contract rule regarding a breach of contract.[50] In this case, either the employee or the employer may seek dissolution on the ground that the other party is not honoring its obligations under the employment agreement and may request economic and non-economic damages. Dissolutions for breach of contract are rare, because limited damages are available. Employees for this reason prefer to use the special rule of Article 7:685 in Book 7 Title 10 of the Civil Code regarding dissolutions based on urgent cause or change of circumstance.

In contrast with decisions under Article 7:685, it is possible to appeal from a court decision rescinding an employment agreement for breach of contract based on Article 7:686.

D. Privacy

A specific clause concerning privacy is not included in Book 7, Title 10 of the Civil Code regulating the employment relationship between the private employer and employee. However, vari-

---

[49]See I.A.1., above.

[50]Book 7, Title 10 of the Civil Code, art. 686.

ous privacy protections in the workplace are derived from other sources of law, as discussed below.

The Dutch Constitution (*Grondwet* or *Gw*) grants citizens an explicit right to privacy. The most important article in this respect is Article 10, which states that everyone shall have the right to respect for his or her privacy. In general, privacy rights under the Constitution can only be limited by an Act of Parliament.

It should be noted, however, that these privacy rights under the Constitution are only applicable in the (vertical) relationship between the Dutch government and its citizens, and thus do not appear upon first inspection to apply to the (horizontal) relationship between employer and employee. There is debate, however, about this interpretation of the Dutch Constitution, as follows: based on Article 611 Book 7 Title 10 of the Civil Code, an employer is obligated to behave as a good employer, i.e., has a duty of good care toward the employee.[51] This duty of the employer arises out of a general duty under the Civil Code—Articles 2 and 648 Book 6—that people have to act in a reasonable and fair manner in their relationships with others. According to Article 12 Book 3 of the Civil Code, the question of what is reasonable and fair is partly determined again by principles of law, including those under the Articles 10 and 11 of the Dutch Constitution. Under this analysis, Articles 10 and 11 of the Dutch Constitution can thus indirectly be applicable in the relationship between an employer and an employee under the Articles 611 Book 7 Title 10 of the Civil Code and Article 12 Book 3 of the Civil Code. This expansive interpretation of obligations under the law has been upheld in case law as regards other rights established in the Dutch Constitution.

In addition to the foregoing, an employee can always directly base a cause of action on Article 8 of the European Convention on Human Rights (*Europees Verdrag tot bescherming van de rechten van de mens en de fundamentele vrijheden* or *EVRM*), which establishes a right to privacy as regards one's life.

Furthermore, the Personal Data Protection Law (*Wet Bescherming Persoonsgegevens* or *WBP*), which went into force September 1, 2001, directly applies to employers and employees.

---

[51]See discussion under I.D.3., below.

This Act is based on an EU Directive.[52] In general, the WBP regulates the right to privacy as regards information only, and with regard to an employer, specifies that the employer may only use such data about an employee as are needed to serve a legitimate purpose, for example, the date of birth to determine the wage scale. Also, the employer is not allowed to provide such data to third parties. Further, the employer cannot examine an employee's e-mail account at work unless the search serves a legitimate goal. An example of a legitimate goal would be to investigate an employee who uses the employer's Internet connection to access pornographic web sites and to download material from them.

E. Employee Duty of Loyalty, Trade Secrets, Covenants Not to Compete

1. Employee Duty of Loyalty

No specific clause is included in Book 7, Title 10 of the Civil Code with regard to the employee duty of loyalty. However, it does include a clause specifying that an employee must behave as a good employee and an employer as a good employer.[53] This clause, however, does not specifically point out what duties of a good employee are covered by the clause. From case law, however, it can be derived that the duty of loyalty is included in the duty to act as a good employee. The question is, to what extent is an employee obligated to be loyal to the employer? Some indications of the parameters of this obligation are noted in E.3., below. For example, with regard to a covenant not to compete, after termination of employment the employee still has to be loyal; even if the employee is not bound by a post-employment covenant, the employee nonetheless cannot act in a tortious manner as regards the former employer. Concerning the issue of whistleblowing, as indicated in E.2., below, an employee has to be loyal to the extent that the employee has to try to deal with the matter first internally.

---

[52]Council Directive 95/46/EC, 1995 O.J. (L 281) 31. See the discussion of the EU Data Privacy Directive in the chapter on the European Union in Volume I, at I.C.

[53]The duty to behave as a good employee is set forth in Book 7, Title 10 of the Civil Code, art. 611.

2. *Trade Secrets/Whistleblowing*

No specific clause is included in Book 7, Title 10 of the Civil Code with regard to trade secrets. The only article in which trade secrets are mentioned is the article dealing with termination for urgent cause.[54] Under this clause, one type of employee conduct that justifies immediate termination of employment by the employer without being liable, is an employee giving information to third parties about trade secrets of the employer. However, under the duty of an employee to act as a good employee,[55] an employee has the duty to be loyal to the employer and, thus, also has to keep trade secrets confidential. Of course, an employer and an employee can also agree voluntarily upon a covenant of secrecy, which usually is the case.

An issue that arises is what an employee has to do if the employee discovers that the employer is engaging in wrongdoing, e.g., is using defective parts in its production process. There is no law regarding whistleblowing that protects whistleblowers. Under case law, whistleblowers, who usually get fired by their employers for breach of the duty to act as good employees or breach of a covenant of secrecy, have minimal legal protection, particularly if, in the opinion of the court, they have revealed the problem to the press or other third party without first attempting to resolve the problem internally through discussions with representatives of the employer. Although an employer may consider filing suit against the employee based on contract or tort law, employers generally confine themselves to terminating the employment relationship.

3. *Covenants Not to Compete*

In Book 7, Title 10 of the Civil Code regulating the employment relationship between the private employer and employee, a specific clause is included with regard to covenants not to compete. According to this article, an employer and an employee can agree upon a covenant not to compete applicable during employment and after the employment agreement has come to an end.

[54]See I.C.3.b.iv., above.
[55]See I.E.3., below.

This covenant, however, is valid only if it is in writing and if the employee has at least reached the age of 16 years. In case of a valid covenant, an employee in general is bound to this covenant and thus is limited by the terms as mentioned in the covenant (i.e., duration, geographic area, range of work). Nevertheless, an employee can request a court to declare the covenant invalid, in whole or in part (e.g., the employee may ask for a limitation on the geographic area covered by the covenant). The court will compare the interests of the employer with those of the employee. If there is no longer an interest on the part of the employer, the court will declare the covenant invalid. In addition, if the employer has not respected the term of notice for termination of the employment agreement, the employee is not bound by the covenant. Under case law, finally, it has been decided that if during the employment relationship the employee is appointed to a totally different position with new responsibilities and tasks, an employer again has to agree with the employee on a new covenant not to compete.

If an employer and an employee have not agreed upon a covenant not to compete, or in case that the court has declared the covenant invalid, this does not mean that an employee can act wrongfully towards the employer, for example, by using trade secrets of the employer for his or her own company and by inviting the customers of the former employer to do business with the former employee. Under case law, the employer in such a case can state a cause of action based on a tort.

II. COLLECTIVE BARGAINING

A. Historical Background

In 1927, the law on collective bargaining agreements was enacted as the Collective Labor Agreement Act (*Wet op de Collectieve Arbeidsovereenkomst* or *WCAO*). The *WCAO* defines a collective labor agreement (also referred to as collective bargaining agreement) as an agreement concluded between one or more employers or employers' organizations and one or more trade unions that contains terms of employment that must be respected by the individual employer and employee. The *WCAO* also regulates to whom a collective bargaining agreement applies, and which rules apply in the event an individual employment agreement contains terms that conflict with the collective bargaining agreement.[56]

B. Union Recognition Process

The *WCAO* entitles trade unions and employers' organizations to negotiate only if both the union and the employers' organization are legally constituted organizations and their Articles of Association explicitly give them the right to conclude a collective bargaining agreement.

Trade unions do not have an automatic right to negotiate collective bargaining agreements. To negotiate on behalf of workers in a particular sector, trade unions must seek court authority to do so if they are refused access by the employer or the employer's organization involved in the collective bargaining negotiation. This authority is granted if the trade union can establish that it represents a high proportion of the employees involved (either in numbers or as a percentage compared with other unions), or that it represents employees with special interests who are inadequately represented by other unions.

Once authority to negotiate has been granted to a trade union, this does not mean that the employer or employers' organization must then conclude a collective bargaining agreement with the union; the employer's obligation is to bargain, but not necessarily to reach an agreement with the union.

Under the *WCAO*, only the parties who are signatories to a collective bargaining agreement are recognized as parties to the agreement.

C. Collective Bargaining Agreement Process

The *WCAO* does not describe the collective bargaining agreement process. An informal procedure is normally followed. Unions usually formulate a memorandum of conditions of employment for members' comments and then draw up an employees' list of demands that is sent to the relevant employers' organizations. The employers' organization then considers the demands in consulta-

---

[56]Collective Bargaining Act (*WCAO*), arts. 9, 12, 13, and 14.

tion with its members and formulates an employers' package of reactions that is sent to the unions involved. The first official meeting takes place after this exchange of packages.

An agreement regarding conditions of employment may be made within the Labor Foundation (*Stichting van de Arbeid* or *STAR*), the private organization that consists of representatives of trade union federations and employers' associations and advises the government on policy issues.[57] Agreements of this type are known as central agreements (*centraal akkoord*). Central agreements do not bind contracting parties. However, they do influence contracting parties in reaching agreement on the terms of a collective bargaining agreement.

The positions of both sides are subject to negotiation after they have been presented. If all parties agree unanimously and sign the contract, the collective bargaining agreement comes into existence.

Collective bargaining agreements can be either standard or minimum, a classification that is stated in the agreement itself. In a standard agreement, it is not possible to deviate from the agreement. With a minimum agreement, deviations in favor of the employee are possible. Most collective bargaining agreements are minimum agreements.

D. Scope and Effect of Agreements

1. *Effect*

Under the Act on Determining Wages and Salaries (*Wet op de Loonvorming*), the parties to a collective bargaining agreement must report the agreement to the Central Office of the Labor Inspectorate (*Arbeidsinspectie* or *AI*). On the day after the AI has acknowledged receipt of the collective bargaining agreement, the agreement will come into effect. As of this date, all terms of the agreement will have effect, including a term referring to the date the agreement will begin. If such a term was not provided in the agreement, the *WCAO* provides that the agreement shall be effective as of the 15th day after it was signed by the parties.

---

[57]See the Introduction, at.D.3., above.

2. *Scope*

A collective bargaining agreement can apply to an individual employment agreement under several different scenarios. When this does happen, not all of the terms of the collective bargaining agreement are incorporated into the individual employment agreement. Only normative provisions (provisions relating to hiring, termination, ages, working hours, etc.)[58] will be incorporated into the individual employment agreement.

a. *Situations When a Collective Bargaining Agreement Applies to an Individual Employment Agreement*

i. *Mutual agreement*

The parties can always mutually agree upon the applicability of a collective bargaining agreement, without there being any obligation to do so.

ii. *Employer and employee are both members of parties to the collective bargaining agreement*

If both the employer and the employee are members of the contracting parties to the collective bargaining agreement, then the individual employment agreement between them is regulated by that collective bargaining agreement.[59]

iii. *Employer is a member of a contracting party to the agreement but the employee is not*

If an employer is a member of a contracting party to the collective bargaining agreement, then the employer has a duty to apply the terms of the collective bargaining agreement also to the individual employment agreements of employees who are not members of parties to the agreement.[60] However, if an employer fails to do this, then the employee has no direct recourse against the employer. Only the contracting parties to the collective bargaining agreement can demand compliance with this obligation.

---

[58]See D.2.b.iii., below.
[59]*WCAO* art. 9.
[60]*Id.* art. 14.

iv. The collective bargaining agreement is declared generally binding

According to the Act on Administrative Extension and Non-Extension of Collective Labor Agreements (*Wet op het algmeen verbindend en het onverbindend verklaren van bepalingen van collectieve arbeidsovereenkomsten* or *Wet AVV/OVV*), the Minister of Social Affairs and Employment has the authority to declare certain terms of a collective bargaining agreement generally binding for a certain sector or industry for employers and employees other than those who are parties to the agreement. Such a declaration has been made frequently, but it can only take place upon the request of one or more of the contracting parties, and only if the collective bargaining agreement applies to at least 55 percent of the employees in the relevant industrial sector. In this circumstance, provisions in individual agreements that conflict with the generally binding provisions of a collective bargaining agreement are considered invalid.

The Minister can also declare terms of a collective bargaining agreement nonbinding. This declaration can be made at the Minister's own initiative, after hearing the view of the contracting parties. Nonbinding declarations are made very rarely.

b. Collective Bargaining Agreement Terms

There are three types of provisions in a collective bargaining agreement: compulsory, diagonal, and normative.

i. Compulsory provisions

Compulsory provisions are those that concern the rights and obligations of the contracting parties. Only the contracting parties may demand compliance with these provisions. Compulsory provisions may include an obligation to establish an arbitration committee, an obligation to promote compliance with the collective bargaining agreement, an obligation to make available to all members of the contracting parties a complete copy of the collective bargaining agreement, and an obligation to refrain from trying to settle conflicts by the exercise of economic power (e.g., strikes). This last obligation may be absolute, relating to all conflicts between the contracting parties, or relative, relating only to conflicts about issues covered in the collective bargaining agreement (the latter being the more common situation).

ii. Diagonal provisions

Diagonal provisions are obligations by parties to a collective bargaining agreement (employers and employees) toward their own contracting party and the other contracting party. Included in this category are fringe benefits, such as training opportunities for workers, or provisions by employers for special facilities for union activities.

iii. Normative provisions

Normative provisions are the only type of provision that can be incorporated into a collective bargaining agreement. Normative provisions include such elements as hiring, termination, wages, working hours, overtime, vacation, leave, etc. In principle, the individual employer and employee can insist on compliance with these conditions.

c. Conflicts Between Terms in Collective Bargaining Agreements and Individual Employment Agreements

In the event of conflicting terms between a collective bargaining agreement and an individual employment agreement, the conflicting term in the individual employment agreement is null and void and will be replaced by the term in the collective bargaining agreement.[61] Any conditions of employment not covered by the individual employment agreement are regulated by the collective bargaining agreement.[62]

E. Duration of Collective Bargaining Agreements

Collective bargaining agreements usually last for a period of one or two years. Under the *WCAO*, the maximum operational period for an agreement is five years, with a possibility of renewing the agreement for a maximum of five years.

---

[61]*Id.* art. 12.
[62]*Id.* art. 13.

In general, after a collective bargaining agreement has expired, the agreement's normative provisions applicable to individual employment agreements remain in effect for the contracting parties, unless they reach a new agreement.

F. Strikes and Other Industrial Actions

The European Social Charter (*Europees Sociaal Handvest* or *ESH*) recognizes the right to engage in collective action.[63] Unlike other provisions of the Charter, this right to engage in collective action is self-executing in the Netherlands, as a result of a decision of the Netherlands Supreme Court known as the *NS (Nederlandse Spoorwegen* or *Dutch Railway)* case. However, actions that are designed to put pressure on employers without the employees having to sacrifice all their pay (for example, selective strikes in specific locations) can be ruled wrongful.

1. Strikes

a. The Right to Strike

Under Dutch law, there is no statutory provision recognizing the right to strike. The Dutch legislature determined that such a provision was not necessary because the *ESH* explicitly recognizes the right to engage in collective action, including the right to strike. The Charter was ratified by the Netherlands in 1980.

Under the *ESH*, the right to strike may be limited by the legislatures of the member countries.[64] Case law determines issues such as when a strike is justified, and whether striking employees are entitled to receive a salary.

A strike is considered justified if the following characteristics are met:

- the parties have negotiated but have been unable to reach an agreement;
- the employer has been given the opportunity to meet the demands of the strikers voluntarily;

---

[63]European Social Charter, art. 6.4.

[64]*Id.* art. 31.

- the effects and goals of the strike are not disproportionate, e.g., if a strike will affect the entire Dutch economy it can be considered disproportional in reaching its goal; and
- the strike is being used as the last resort.

Employees who strike have no right to be paid. Similarly, those who want to work, but who are unable to do so because of a strike, have no right to be paid. The situation is different when the strike is of the "wildcat" variety (meaning that the strike is not supported by trade unions, but is organized by a minority of employees to protest a specific issue). Employees who can establish that they are willing to work and do not support the wildcat strike are entitled to be paid.

A temporary agency is not allowed to provide temporary workers during a strike. After a strike has ended, the striking employees are entitled to return to their jobs. An employer exposes itself to risk if it permanently replaces the striking employees, because the employer must obtain permission of the *CWI* to terminate the employment agreement with the former employee or must ask the cantonal judge to dissolve the employment agreement. Until the employment agreement with a former striker has been validly terminated, the employer must pay that employee his or her salary.

b. Types of Strikes

Several types of strikes have been used in the Netherlands.

- *Conventional strikes* occur when all employees of an enterprise stop work at the same time. This is the most common form of strike.
- *Protest strikes* occur when employees stop work for a brief period to register a protest or warn employers of the potential consequences of a particular action.
- *Selective strikes* occur when employees stop work at critical points in a plant, resulting in other employees being forced to stop work.
- *Expanding strikes* occur when employees in different parts of a company stop work gradually, so that in the end there is a complete work stoppage throughout the company.

- *Estafette (relay) strikes* involve different companies of an enterprise. Employees of one company strike for a limited period, at the end of which the employees of another company follow suit, and so on.

2. *Work-to-Rule or Slow-Down Actions*

An alternative to the total work stoppage is the work-to-rule or slow-down action. This involves all employees continuing to work, but observing work rules so meticulously or working so slowly that the workflow slows down.

3. *Employer Lockouts*

Lockouts by employers are very rare in the Netherlands, and for that reason there is no case law providing guidance on what are, and what are not, acceptable lockout activities.

4. *Disciplinary Sanctions*

Employers are not allowed to terminate an employment agreement solely on the basis of the employee's participation in a strike or other collective action. Less severe disciplinary sanctions against strike participation also are prohibited.

G. Governmental and Third-Party Resolution of Disputes

Most collective bargaining agreements include provisions for resolution of disputes by nonjudicial mechanisms. Frequently, provision is made for establishment of arbitration committees, dispute resolution by enforceable mediation, or settlement of issues through the use of an ad hoc committee that advises the parties to the dispute.

If a collective bargaining agreement does not provide for a system of third-party dispute resolution, the parties can file a claim with the cantonal judge who has exclusive jurisdiction over disputes between the contracting parties to a collective bargaining agreement. Only the contracting parties can file claims regarding compulsory and diagonal terms, whereas only the employer and employee can file claims regarding normative terms that have become part of their individual employment agreement.[65]

H . Union Security

An employer is barred from terminating an employment agreement solely because of an employee's union membership.[66] This protection extends to employees performing union activities, even if they are not union members.

Terms in collective bargaining agreements that impose a duty on an employer to hire employees of a certain race or religion, or requiring or forbidding the hiring of members of a particular organization, are null and void.[67]

III. Representation by Entities Other Than Unions

A. Historical Background

The Netherlands has a long history of labor participation in workplace management. Prior to 1950, the practice was for industrial plants to have so-called factory committees (*fabrieks-commissies*). In 1950, a statutory basis was established for employee participation, through the Works Councils Act (*Wet op de Ondernemingsraden* or *WOR*). This law required a works council to be established in companies with 100 or more employees. Works councils were chaired by a management representative.

In 1971, revisions to the *WOR* provided works councils with additional consultation rights and some new co-determination rights. The councils continued to be chaired by management representatives.

In 1979, major changes again were made to the *WOR*. The chairpersons of works councils were to be chosen from and by the council members.

---

[65]See discussion of compulsory, diagonal, and normative terms in II.D.2.b., above.
[66]Book 7, Title 10 of the Civil Code, art. 670.
[67]*WCAO* art. 1.3.

In 1981, the *WOR* was revised again. There were less stringent rules for companies with at least 35, but fewer than 100, employees.[68] In addition, a new meeting with employees (*personeelsvergadering*) was introduced for companies with between 10 and 35 employees.[69]

In 1990, amendments to the *WOR* changed procedural rules for resolution of disputes between works councils and management. In 1995, another amendment brought public servants (with some exceptions) within the scope of the *WOR*.

In 1998, as of March 4, additional changes were made to the *WOR*. The most important of these was that companies with 50 or more employees must establish works councils; companies with between 10 and 49 employees must establish an employee representative body (*personeelsvertegenwoordiging*) at the request of a majority of the employees, and if no such request is made, then the company must establish a meeting with employees; and companies with fewer than 10 employees may establish an employee representative body.

B. Establishment of a Works Council

1. Companies With 50 Employees or More

If a company has at least 50 employees, management must establish a works council.[70] The obligation to establish a works council also can derive from a collective bargaining agreement or through the voluntary decision of the employer.

In calculating the number of employees in a company, both full-time and part-time employees are counted. Employees who are considered to be working for a company are those:

- who work on the basis of an employment agreement or public assignment with the company;[71]
- who have an employment agreement or public assignment with the employer but work elsewhere;[72]

---

[68]Works Councils Act (*WOR*), art. 35a.
[69]*Id.* art. 35b.
[70]*Id.* art. 2.
[71]*Id.* art. 1.
[72]*Id.*

- who are temporary workers having an employment agreement with their principal and who have worked in the company for at least 24 months;[73] or
- who are identified as employees under article 6 of the *WOR*.

Members of the works council are chosen by and from the employees. Employees are eligible to serve on the works council after they have worked for the company for one year. Employees are eligible to vote in works council elections after they have been employed at the company for at least six months. Temporary workers are not eligible to serve on the works council or vote in works council elections until they have worked for the company for 24 months.

Elections of works council members take place through a vote by secret ballot.

The number of works council members is directly related to the number of employees working in the company. If there are fewer than 50 employees, the works council will have 3 members; if there are between 50 and 100 employees, the works council will have 5 members. This number can increase with the number of employees in a company, to a maximum of 25 members on a works council. The chairperson is chosen by the members of the works council.

2. *Companies With 10 to 49 Employees*

If there is no works council and a majority of employees votes for establishment of an employee representative body (*personeelsvertegenwoordiging*), the company must establish this body.[74] If there is no request for an employee representative body and no works council, the company must establish a meeting with employees (*personeelsvergadering*).[75]

3. *Companies With Fewer Than 10 Employees*

These companies are under no obligation to establish a works council, an employee representative body, or a meeting with em-

---

[73]*Id.*

[74]*Id.* art. 35c.

[75]*Id.* art 35b.

ployees. However, management may establish an employee representative body if it chooses.[76]

C. Works Council Powers

The Works Councils Act (*Wet op de ondernemingsraden* or *WOR*) enumerates the powers of the works council (*ondernemingsraad*), the employee representative body (*personeelsvertegenwoordiging*), and the meeting with employees (*personeelsvergadering*). In addition to those powers specifically enumerated in the *WOR*, these powers can be expanded by either the decision of the company, an (enterprise) agreement between the employer and the works council (*ondernemingsovereenkomst*), or a collective bargaining agreement.[77]

1. Companies With 50 Employees or More

a. Deliberation and Initiative Rights

After a request for a deliberation meeting (*overlegvergaderingen*) is made by either the company or the works council, the parties have a duty to gather within two weeks of the request.[78] In these deliberation meetings, any subject relating to the company can be brought forward by either the works council or the company.

The works council also can bring forward proposals or initiatives relating to the company, either inside or outside the deliberation meetings. If the company does not accept the proposal, it must explain its decision to the works council. However, the works council has no right to appeal this decision, because the works council is not considered to be a policymaker.

b. Consultation Rights

The *WOR* gives works councils the right to advise companies on a number of important business issues. Management must consult with works councils regarding:

---

[76] *Id.* art. 35d.
[77] *Id.* art. 32.
[78] *Id.* art. 23.

- changes in the ownership or control of the company, or parts of it, and changes in or terminations of enduring relationships with other companies;
- closing of the company, or an important part of it;
- major expansions, contractions, or changes in activities of the company;
- significant reorganizations within the company;
- changes in the location of company activities;
- hiring groups of employees;
- important company investments;
- decisions to seek major loans and other forms of credit for the company;
- decisions to extend major credit and/or provide security for major debts of another company, unless these actions are part of the normal course of business;
- introduction of major new technology, or a major modification of existing technology;
- major management decisions in regard to the environment;
- rulings concerning the Disability Insurance Act (*Wet op de arbeidsongeschiktheidsverzekering* or *WAO*); and
- seeking the services of external consultants for advice on any of the subjects mentioned above.

If the company fails to consult the works council about any of the items just listed, the works council can appeal to the Enterprise Section or Companies Bench of the Court of Appeal (*Ondernemingskamer Gerechtshof*) in Amsterdam.[79]

c. *Co-Determination Rights*

Works councils have the right to approve or reject management decisions (right of co-determination) in a number of matters listed in the *WOR*. Specifically, management is required to obtain works council approval for changes affecting pensions, profit-sharing, or savings plans; working hours and vacation; job rating sys-

[79]For a more detailed discussion of this appeals procedure, see III.D.2., below.

tems; workplace arrangements involving safety, health, or welfare; hiring, termination, and promotion policies; employee education; employee evaluations; use of social workers on the job; meetings; complaint procedures; privacy rights of employees concerning collection of employees' personal data; and management monitoring of employee attendance, performance, and behavior.[80]

Rights of co-determination do not apply to issues that are regulated in collective bargaining agreements.

If the company fails to ask the works council for permission about any of the subjects listed above, the works council can address to the cantonal judge. However, if the works council fails to grant permission to the employer, the latter can address to the cantonal judge and ask to grant the permission.

d. Information Rights

The WOR states that works councils are entitled to receive general information about the company to the extent necessary to function properly. They are also entitled to receive specific information relating to the operations of the business, and financial, economic, and social information.

2. Companies With 10 to 49 Employees

a. Meeting with employees (Personeelsvergadering)

The most important rights of the meeting with employees are:[81]

- deliberation and initiative rights like those of the works council;
- management is obliged to annually discuss the general state of affairs of the company, to provide information about the results for the past year and the current year, and to present and discuss the company's annual report;
- information rights regarding social strategy; and
- consultation rights concerning management decisions that can result in a loss of jobs or an important change in duties

---

[80] *WOR* art. 27.

[81] *Id.* art. 35b.

or working conditions for at least 25 percent of the employees working for the company.[82]

b. An employee representative body (Personeelsvertegenwoordiging)

The most important rights of an employee representative body are:[83]

- management is obliged to annually discuss the general state of affairs of the company, to provide information about the results for the past year and the current year, and to present and discuss the company's annual report;
- information rights regarding social strategy;
- consultation rights concerning management decisions that can result in a loss of jobs or an important change in duties or working conditions for at least 25 percent of the employees working for the company;[84] and
- co-determination rights concerning decisions management intends to make regarding working time, sick leave, or safety, health, and welfare on the job.

3. Companies With Fewer Than 10 Employees

The rights of an employee representative body are narrower than those for companies with 10 to 49 employees who have an employee representative body. The most important rights are:[85]

- management is obliged to annually discuss the general state of affairs of the company, to provide information about the results for the past year and the current year, and to present and discuss the company's annual report;
- information rights regarding social strategy; and

[82]These consultation rights do not exist if the subjects are covered by a collective bargaining agreement.

[83]*WOR* art. 35c.

[84]*Id.* art 2. These consultation rights do not exist if the subjects are covered by a collective bargaining agreement.

[85]WOR art. 35d.

• co-determination rights concerning decisions management intends to make regarding working time.

There are no consultation rights for an employee representative body in companies with fewer than 10 employees.

D. Procedures for Resolving Disputes Between the Works Council and the Employer

1. *Violations of the Works Councils Act (Wet op de ondernemingsraden* or *WOR)*

In a conflict deriving from a violation of any article of the WOR, parties must first ask for mediation and advice of a so-called Joint Industry Committee (*bedrijfscommissie*), which is installed by the Social and Economic Council of the Netherlands (*Sociaal Economische Raad* or *SER*). If the mediation by the enterprise committee does not lead to a solution, then the committee will issue a report that provides a possible solution.[86]

If the parties still cannot resolve their dispute, then they can file a claim with the district court, cantonal section.[87] The latter will dismiss a claim if the parties have already filed a claim on the grounds that the company failed to ask the works council for advice, or an order to comply has already been issued under the Occupational Safety and Health Act (*Arbeidsomstandighedenwet* or *Arbowet*) due to a failure to ask permission.

2. *Company Fails to Ask Works Council for Advice*

If the company fails to ask the works council for advice, or if management delays asking for advice until it is too late for the works council to influence any decision, then the works council can address to the Enterprise Section of the Amsterdam Court of Appeal. The works council must prove that the company could not have reached its decision reasonably. In such a case, the works council can request the Enterprise Section to issue an order stating that the company is not allowed to execute its decision.

---

[86] *Id.* art. 36.
[87] *Id.*

3. *Company Fails to Ask Works Council for Permission*

If the company fails to ask the works council for permission, then the works council must file a claim with the cantonal judge. The works council can ask the court to prevent any performance of the void decision. The decision is null and void if the works council contests the decision within a month after knowledge or performance of the decision.

4. *Works Council Fails to Grant Permission to the Company*

If the works council fails to grant permission to the company upon request, then the company can file a claim with the cantonal judge requesting that the court grant the permission instead of the works council. The cantonal judge will grant such a request if the works council is unreasonably withholding its permission or if important organization, economic, or social interests require that permission be granted.

E. Relationship Between Unions and Works Councils

In general, unions have the principal right to bargain over the primary terms of the employment agreement, such as wages and working hours. Consequently, co-determination of the works council is not required if the subject already has been addressed in a collective bargaining agreement. However, collective bargaining agreements frequently authorize works councils to bargain on certain subjects.

F. European Works Council

Under the Directive on European Works Councils of September 22, 1994,[88] a company with more than 1,000 employees, and that has at least two subsidiaries with at least 150 employees in different member states of the EU, must establish a European Works Council. This Directive has been incorporated in Netherlands law by the Act on European Works Councils (*De Wet op de Europese Ondernemingsraad*).

---

[88]Council Directive 94/45/EC, 1994 O.J. (L 254) 64.

The Act on European Works Councils requires a company's board of directors to meet at least once each year with the European Works Council. At these meetings, the board must submit a written report informing the European Works Council of the general condition of the company and of all decisions under board consideration that affect the interests of employees of the subsidiaries in EU member countries.

IV. REDUNDANCY AND TRANSFERS OF UNDERTAKINGS

A. Redundancy

1. Layoffs

a. Individual Terminations for Economic Reasons

If an employer wants to terminate an employment agreement for economic reasons, certain procedures must be followed. Depending on the circumstances of such a termination, the employee can file a request with either the Center for Work and Income (*Centrum voor Werk en Inkomen* or *CWI*) or the cantonal judge.[89]

i. CWI

An employer is prohibited from unilaterally terminating an employment agreement without the permission of the *CWI*.[90] If an employer wishes to terminate an employment agreement for economic reasons, then it can follow either the standard procedure[91] or the expedited procedure (*verkorte procedure*) under the Dismissal Decree (*Ontslagbesluit*).

[89]The Act on the New Civil Procedure (*Wetboek van Nieuw Burgerlijk Rechtsvordering*), which went into effect on Jan.1, 2002, transferred authority from the RDA to the newly created institution, the *CWI* (*Centrum voor Werk en Inkomen*).

[90]Article 6 of the 1945 Special Decree on Labor Relations established the prohibition against terminations. The *Act SUWI*, effective Jan. 1, 2002, transferred notification requirements to the *CWI*. See the Introduction, at C.2., above.

[91]For an explanation of the standard procedure, see the discussion in I.C.3., above.

Under the expedited procedure, the employee must sign a written statement (for which a special form has been created) indicating that he or she has no objection to the termination. The employer sends this statement to the *CWI* along with its request for permission to terminate the employment agreement. In these cases, the *CWI* can issue a decision shortly after receiving the request and its accompanying statement. The *CWI* is bound by the 1945 Special Decree on Labor Relations and the Dismissal Decree when making its decision.

When the *CWI* grants permission to terminate the employment agreement, it does not have any authority to grant severance pay. However, if the employee believes that the termination was manifestly unreasonable (*kennelijk onredelijk*), then he or she can file a claim with the cantonal judge and may be able to obtain severance pay through that forum.[92]

In terminations for economic reasons, the *CWI* in principle enforces a seniority principle, which, in general, means that "last in, first out" is the rule for each company and each employment category within the company, unless the employer can prove that a particular employee is especially qualified for the job and should be retained.

ii. District Court, Cantonal Section

An employer may request the district court, cantonal section (*Rechtbank, Sectie Kanton*), also referred to as cantonal judge (*Kantonrechter*), to dissolve an employment agreement because of a major change in circumstances, including economic conditions.[93] If the district court, cantonal section grants dissolution based on economic change of circumstances, then severance pay can be granted.[94]

---

[92]Book 7, Title 10 of the Civil Code, art. 681.

[93]*Id.* art. 685. For an additional discussion of this procedure, see I.C.4., above. For a discussion of the changes in the Dutch civil court system, see the Introduction, at C.2., above.

[94]See IV.A.2., below.

b. *Mass Layoffs (also referred to as Collective Dismissals)*

Under the Notification of Collective Dismissals Act (*Wet melding collectief ontslag* or *WMCO*), the employer must notify both the *CWI* and the unions of any mass layoffs before the *CWI* can consider the request. The goal of the *WMCO* is to prevent unemployment through the early involvement of third parties such as the *CWI* and the unions.[95]

The Works Councils Act (*Wet op de ondernemingsraden* or *WOR*) also imposes a duty on the employer to consult the works council.

Dismissals are considered to be mass layoffs if, over a three-month period, the employment agreements of 20 or more employees in the same *CWI* district are intended to be terminated. The requirement of 20 employees includes any requests for dissolution based on change of economic circumstances that are pending with the cantonal judge as well as any requests filed with the *CWI*.

A mass layoff usually is a consequence of cutbacks or a reorganization.

i. *Obligation to notify union*

The employer must notify the unions in writing about the mass layoff before the *CWI* can take into consideration any of the employer's requests to terminate the employment agreements.[96] The employer must inform the union about the criteria for dismissal and provide information about severance payments. The employer must invite the unions to discuss the mass layoff.

ii. *Obligation to report to CWI*

An employer who intends a mass layoff must report the mass layoff to the *CWI* before the *CWI* can consider the requests for termination of the employment agreement.[97] Failure to comply with this rule will lead to an administrative sanction; the employer will have to wait an extra month before the *CWI* will consider the request for permission to dismiss.

---

[95]The *WMCO* was a result of Council Directive 75/129/EEC, 1975 O.J. (L 48) 29.
[96]*WMCO* art. 3.
[97]*Id.*

iii. Obligation to seek advice of works council

The Works Councils Act (*Wet op de ondernemingsraden* or *WOR*) requires the employer to consult the works council if there are plans to lay off a significant number of employees.[98]

2. Severance Payments

Under Netherlands law, severance payments may be made under employer-employee arrangements. Severance pay also may be awarded by the cantonal judge as compensation for economic changes (*verandering van omstandigheden*) or as compensation for manifestly unreasonable termination (*kennelijk onredelijk ontslag*).

a. Individual Termination

In the termination procedure before the *CWI*, the employee cannot obtain a severance payment. The *CWI* does not have the authority to grant severance payments, it can only grant or deny the request for a permit to terminate the employment agreement.

In the procedure before the cantonal judge, an employee can ask for a severance payment if the dissolution is based on a change of economic circumstances[99] or if it is a case of a manifestly unreasonable dismissal.[100]

i. Compensation for job losses resulting from a change in economic circumstances

In the case of a dissolution of an employment agreement based on a change of economic circumstances, the cantonal judge can determine a severance payment that is fair and reasonable under the circumstances.

As of January 1, 1997, severance payments are determined by the so-called Cantonal Court Formula—also as of January 1, 2002, referred to as the District Court Formula

[98]See III.D.2., above, for a discussion of what happens if the employer does not consult the works council.

[99]Book 7, Title 10 of the Civil Code, art. 685.

[100]*Id.* art. 681.

(*kantonrechtersformule*)—which is N × W × C (*A* × *B* × *C*). In this formula, N = the number of years of service (*aantal dienstjaren*) modified depending on age as discussed below; W = wages (gross salary, including vacation bonuses) (*beloning*); and C = correction factor (*correctiefactor*).

N, the number of years of service, is also related to the age of the person. N = 1 for each year of service when the employee was younger than 40 years old; N = 1.5 for each year of service when the employee was between ages 40 through 49; and N = 2 for each year of service when the employee was age 50 and older.[101]

Normally, the correction factor is 1, which is called a neutral dissolution. A termination of the employment agreement for economic reasons is considered a neutral termination. The cantonal judge can grant a severance payment that is greater or less than the neutral amount. If the cantonal judge determines that the employee to a large degree is responsible for the termination of his or her employment, the cantonal judge can set the correction factor to be less than one, or even zero. If the cantonal judge determines that the employer is at fault, he or she can set the correction factor to be greater than one. A correction factor that is greater than three is exceptional.

ii. Compensation for unreasonable termination

In the case of a manifestly unreasonable termination (*kennelijk onredelijk ontslag*), the cantonal judge must determine a severance payment. The law does not indicate how to calculate this severance payment, nor does it state anything about the level of the payment. It only indicates that the severance payment must be fair and reasonable. An employee may appeal from this decision to the District Court.

Under case law, the severance payment is determined by the totality of the facts and circumstances (age of employee, years of service, economic circumstances, etc.). The actual level granted tends to conform to the Cantonal Formula.

---

[101]For example, if an employee is 48 years old and has 20 years of service, N will be (8 × 1.5) + (12 × 1) = 24.

b. Mass Layoffs (also referred to as Collective Dismissals)

i. Social plan

Many large companies, such as multinational corporations, have a social plan (*sociaal plan*) that provides for severance payments for employees in the event of mass layoffs.

The social plan can take various forms. It can be a declaration by the employer, an agreement between the employer and the employees, an agreement between an employer and the company's works council, or a provision in a collective bargaining agreement.

ii. Compensation for job losses resulting from a change in economic circumstances

If an employee has filed a claim with the cantonal judge based on a termination due to a change in economic circumstances, the employee can contest the level of severance pay that is granted under the social plan.

The cantonal judge generally will follow the payment level as determined by the social plan if the social plan has been agreed to by the employee's representative union. An exception will be made if following the plan for the employee in question leads to a result that appears to be unreasonable to any reasonable person. However, if the economic situation of the employer is such that higher severance payments are not possible, then the cantonal judge will set the correction factor at a maximum of one.

iii. Compensation for manifestly unreasonable termination

If an employee believes that his or her termination under the social plan is unfair in light of his or her individual circumstances, the employee can also file a claim under the manifestly unreasonable dismissal procedure.[102]

---

[102]For discussion of these procedures, see I.C.3.b.v. and IV.A.2.a.ii., above.

B. Transfers of Undertakings

1. *EC Directive on Transfers of Undertakings*

Transfers of business ownership, in whole or in part, are covered by the EC Directive on transfers of undertakings.[103] The Netherlands first incorporated Directive 77/187/EC into national law as of July 27, 1981.[104] The purposes of the EC Directive are to maintain the rights of employees and to protect employees against dismissal in situations where a business changes hands and to enable employees' representatives to participate through information and consultation rights before the transfer takes place. The Directive does not apply in cases of bankruptcies.[105]

2. *National Laws Regarding Business Transfers*

a. *Book 7, Title 10 of Civil Code*

EC Directives 77/187 and 98/50[106] are incorporated in Articles 662 through 666, Book 7, Title 10 of the Civil Code. These articles apply if the company or part of the company is transferred. Such a transfer must include employees, customers, performance of work, etc. A transfer of shares only is not a transfer for these purposes.[107]

The most important protections for employees resulting from these directives are that:

- all of the employee's existing rights and obligations (such as years of service, supplementary pension rights,[108] and

[103]Council Directive 2001/23/EC of 12 March 2001 that consolidates Council Directive 77/187/EC of 14 February 1977 and Council Directive 98/50 EC of 29 June 1998.

[104]Book 7, Title 10 of the Civil Code, arts. 662–666.

[105]*Id.* art. 666.

[106]Both consolidated in Council Directive 2001/23/EC of 12 March 2001.

[107]Book 7, Title 10 of the Civil Code, art. 662.

[108]Supplementary pension rights were added by the Act on Incorporation of EC Directive 98/50 (*Wet tot uitvoering van de Richtlijn 98/50/EG inzake behoud van rechten van werknemers bij overgang van ondernemingen*), amending article 664, effective July 1, 2002.

covenants not to compete) are transferred to the new employer if the employing company changes ownership; and
- for a period of one year after the transfer, the former employer remains responsible for all obligations that have arisen out of the employment agreement prior to the transfer.[109]

Articles 662 through 666 are mandatory; the employer cannot deviate from them. Any conflicting terms in any agreement are null and void.

The ECJ has held that dismissals because of a transfer violate the EC directive. However, terminations for economic, technical, or organizational reasons resulting from a transfer are possible. In such cases, the national rules regarding such terminations apply.

b. The Works Councils Act

The EC Directive 77/187 also imposes an obligation for management to consult with employees' representatives if a change in business ownership is contemplated. The Netherlands Works Councils Act (*Wet op de ondernemingsraden* or *WOR*) puts this provision into effect by requiring company management to consult with the works council regarding a transfer of an undertaking.[110]

c. Merger Code of 2000 (SER-besluit Fusiegedragsregels 2000)

A transfer is a merger under the Merger Code if one entity obtains control over the activities of part of the other entity.[111] The newly revised Merger Code 2000 that replaced Merger Code 1975 covers mergers involving a Dutch company with at least 50 employees. The Merger Code 2000 requires that the union, as well as the works council, must be informed about an employer's intent to merge. In addition, before the works council is asked for advice, it must be informed about the union's point of view with regard to the merger.

[109]Book 7, Title 10 of the Civil Code, art. 663.

[110]*WOR* art. 25. See III.C.1.b., above.

[111]1975 Merger Code, art. 14.

V. WAGES, HOURS, AND LEAVE

A. Wages

The Act on Minimum Wage and Minimum Holiday Allowance Act (*Wet minimumloon en minimumvakantiebijslag* or *WMM*) was passed in 1968, and became effective in 1969. Terms in collective bargaining agreements or individual employment agreements that conflict with the *WMM* are invalid.[112] The *WMM* does not apply to public employees; they are covered by the Civil Servants' Act (*Ambtenarenwet*).

1. Minimum Wages

Under the *WMM*, employees 23 to 65 years old are entitled to minimum wages.[113] Employees younger than 23 years of age are entitled to minimum youth wages. The level of the minimum youth wage is a certain percentage of the minimum wage.[114] Minimum wage rights apply to part-time as well as full-time workers.

As of July 1, 2003, the gross minimum monthly wage for employees 23 to 65 years of age was €1264.80. The gross minimum youth wage for employees 22 years of age is calculated at 85 percent of the adult minimum wage and for employees 15 years of age, 30 percent. These amounts are pro-rated for part-time workers.

2. Holiday Allowance

Every employee, regardless of age, has a right to a minimum holiday allowance equal to 8 percent of wages, including sickness or unemployment benefits. The holiday allowance is calculated annually, based on the period from June 1 to May 31, and is paid in June. It is also due, and must be paid, upon the termination of an employment agreement.

---

[112]Minimum Wage and Vacation Allowance Act (*WMM*), art. 19.
[113]*Id.* art. 7.
[114]*Id.* art. 8.

3. *Enforcement Mechanism*

The Labor Inspectorate of the Ministry of Social Affairs and Employment (*Arbeidsinspectie* or *AI*) enforces the *WMM*. The AI is authorized to investigate compliance with the law, on its own initiative or at the request of the union, works council, or individual employees. The *AI* has the authority to seek all information, including that contained in company documents, necessary to carry out its enforcement functions. If an employer fails to comply, the *AI* will first seek compliance through deliberations with the employer. If the employer refuses to cooperate, this is considered an offense (*economisch delict*) under the Economic Offenses Act (*Wet Economische Delicten* or *WED*).

The *AI* cannot consider back pay claims for an employee. Employees must file claims for back pay with the cantonal judge.

B. Hours

The Working Time Act of 1996 (*Arbeidstijdenwet* or *ATW*) that replaced the 1919 Labor Act (*Arbeidswet*) regulates working hours of both private and public sector employees. It applies to men and women 18 years or older.

The *ATW* includes (i) standard clauses (*standaardbepalingen*), which apply if parties have not made alternative arrangements through collective agreements; and (ii) deliberation clauses (*overlegbepalingen*), which allow the parties to deviate from the standard clauses through collective agreements. For purposes of the *ATW*, collective agreements include collective bargaining agreements as well as an (enterprise) agreement between the employer and the works council.

The Work and Care Act 2001 (*Algemene Wet Arbeid en Zorg* or *WAZ*) sets forth all rules concerning employment and care. The Act is in four parts.[115]

The first part, the Act on the Adjustment of Working Time (*Wet Aanpassing Arbeidsduur* or *WAA*), went into effect on July 1, 2000. The *WAA* provides employees with a right to ask for an adjustment of their working hours (for either more or fewer hours).

---

[115]The second and third parts are discussed at V.C., below. The fourth part, on long-term leaves, is in the process of lawmaking.

There are conditions that must be satisfied before the employee is entitled to an adjustment. The employee must work with the employer for at least one year, and the request must be filed in writing, at least four months before the requested adjustment. If the request is granted, the hours adjustment is made on a permanent basis. The employer may refuse an employee's request for an adjustment only where there are extraordinary grounds for doing so. If the employer refuses the employee's request, the employee may then go to the cantonal judge to challenge the refusal.

The *ATW*, aside from regulating duration of working hours and times of rest, also grants employees some limited control over their working hours. The latter has taken place through an amendment of the *ATW* as of June 1, 2003. Under the new articles, an employer needs to take into account private circumstances of the employee in determining working hours, and employees are not obligated to work on Sundays unless they consent to it.

1. Working Hours

Standard working hours under the Working Time Act of 1996 (*Arbeidstijdenwet* or *ATW)* are a maximum of nine hours per shift for a total of 45 hours per week, with an average of eight hours per shift for a total of 40 hours per week during a 13-week period. Deviation by collective agreement is possible but, in this event, the maximum is 10 hours per shift, and average hours worked must not exceed 50 hours per week during each four-week period and 45 hours per week during each 13-week period.

Under the *ATW*, an employer prior to February 21, 2003, had an obligation to offer employees age 18 years or older a rest time of at least 36 hours within a period of 7 times 24 hours, or at least 60 hours within a period of 9 times 24 hours. As of February 21, 2003, the possibility of 60 hours within a period of 9 times 24 hours no longer applies to office personnel, in conformity with ILO Convention 106.

2. Night Work

The period during which the night work rules apply is between midnight and 6:00 a.m. There is a maximum of eight hours per shift during these hours. A deviation by collective agreement is possible, to a maximum of nine hours per shift and an average of 40 hours per week during each 13-week period.

The standard number of night shifts allowed during each four-week period is 16 shifts before 2:00 a.m. and 10 shifts after 2:00 a.m., and during each 13-week period it increases to 25 shifts after 2:00 a.m.. A collective agreement may provide for a deviation from this standard, up to a maximum of 52 night shifts before 2:00 a.m. and 28 night shifts after 2:00 a.m. during each 13-week period.

3. *Overtime*

The standard overtime allowable is 11 hours per shift and 54 hours per week, with an average of 45 hours per week during each 13-week period. A deviation by collective agreement is possible to a maximum of 12 hours per shift and 60 hours per week, with an average of 48 hours per week during a 13-week period.

4. *Special Rules*

The *ATW* contains special rules for three categories of workers: children younger than age 15, youthful employees 16 or 17 years old, and pregnant women and women who have given birth within the past nine months.

a. *Children and Youthful Employees*

In general, children younger than age 16 are not permitted to work, but exceptions can be made. For example, the *ATW* allows a child of 15 to deliver newspapers in the morning, outside school hours. Also, the Labor Inspectorate (*Arbeidsinspectie* or *AI*) may grant exemptions for children to perform in fashion shows.

With regard to youthful employees who are ages 16 or 17, the rule is that they can work outside of school hours. However, they are not allowed to work at night or to work overtime.

b. *Pregnant Women and Recent Mothers*

The employer is obliged to ensure that pregnant women are not required to work during a period beginning four weeks before the probable delivery date and ending six weeks after childbirth.

For women who have given birth within the past nine months, the *ATW* gives breast-feeding mothers the right to feed their children for nine months after birth, with a maximum of one-quarter of working time per shift allowed for this purpose.

5. *Enforcement Mechanism*

The *AI* is the enforcement authority under the *ATW*. If an employer does not comply with the deliberation clauses, the *AI* can order the employer to immediately cease work. If the employer fails to comply with this order, this is considered an offense under the Economic Offenses Act (*Wet Economische Delicten* or *WED*).

If an employer disregards the standard provisions of the *ATW*, then employees must seek enforcement themselves by filing a lawsuit with the cantonal judge.

C. Leave

Netherlands law provides for paid leave for vacation, bank holidays, sickness, pregnancy, childbirth, and duties associated with works council membership. Unpaid leave is available for maternity leave and for political leave.

The Work and Care Act 2001 (*Algemene Wet Arbeid en Zorg* or *WAZ*), which went into effect on December 1, 2001, is composed of the second and third parts of the General Work and Care Act. Under the *WAZ*, the possibilities to take leave have been expanded, and existing possibilities to take leave have been made more flexible in order to optimize the combination of employment and family care.

1. *Paid Leave*

a. *Vacation*

Every employee is entitled to annual vacation of at least four times the number of days regularly worked per week.[116] Therefore, an employee who regularly works five days per week is entitled to at least 20 days or four weeks of paid annual vacation. Employees are entitled to receive their salary during these vacation days.[117]

---

[116]Book 7, Title 10 of the Civil Code, art. 634.

[117]*Id.* art. 639.

Under the Vacation and Parental Leave Act,[118] employees are allowed to make more flexible arrangements with regard to vacation days that exceed the annual minimum of four times the number of regular weekly workdays. With regard to the annual minimum, parties are not allowed to deviate from the rule that, during a call for military service, sickness, or pregnancy, the employee still builds up his or her right to vacation days. To the extent that this right exceeds the annual minimum, however, parties can deviate from this rule.

b. Bank Holidays

Every employee has a right to time off with pay during bank holidays.

c. Sick Leave

Employees who are unable to work as a result of sickness are entitled to paid sick leave for a maximum of 52 weeks at 70 percent of the wages he or she last earned (but not less than the minimum wage).[119] An upper limit on sick pay is set at 70 percent of the maximum daily pay (*dagloon*), which, as of July 1, 2003, was about €165 per day. As of January 1, 2004, the maximum of 52 weeks became 104 weeks.

As discussed above,[120] the Gatekeeper Improvement Act (*Wet Verbetering Poortwachter* or *WVP*)[121] requires an employer to make serious attempts to integrate sick employees back into the workforce. If the employer does not make serious attempts at integration, the legal obligation to pay a sick employee 70 percent of his or her wage during the first 52 weeks of illness can be lengthened to two years.

---

[118]The Act of November 30, 2000, on Vacation and Parental Leave (*Wet wijziging 7.10 BW met betrekking tot vakantie en ouderschapsverlof*), effective Feb. 1, 2001, changed the provisions concerning vacation in Book 7, Title 10 of the Civil Code.

[119]Book 7, Title 10 of the Civil Code, art. 629.

[120]See I.A.1. and I.C., above.

[121]The new law, effective Apr. 1, 2002, added Article 658a to Book 7, Title 10 of the Civil Code.

d. *Pregnancy and Childbirth*

Under the Sickness Benefits Act (*Ziektewet* or *ZW*), a woman has a right to pregnancy and childbirth leave of 16 weeks with full pay. The sick leave provisions noted above also apply, so that a woman is entitled to paid leave of up to 70 percent of her salary if she becomes sick during pregnancy or after childbirth.

Under the Working Time Act (*Arbeidstijdenwet* or *ATW*), for nine months after childbirth a breast-feeding mother has a right to feed her child during work with full pay, to a maximum of one-quarter of working time.[122]

Effective January 1, 2002, pursuant to changes made by the Act on the Implementation Structure for Work and Income (*Wet Structuur uitvoeringsorganisatie werk en inkomen* or *SUWI*), the National Institute for Social Security (*Landelijk Instituut voor Sociale Verzekeringen* or *LISV*) has been replaced by a new institution, the Institute for Employee Benefit Schemes (*Uitvoeringsinstituut Werknemers Verzekeringen* or *UWV*). Accordingly, salary payments made during pregnancy and childbirth leave are no longer made by the LISV, but by the *UWV*.

Under the 2001 Work and Care Act (*Wet Arbeid en Zorg* or *WAZ*), the partner of a female employee who has given birth is entitled to paid leave up to a maximum of two days, with payment of wages made by the employer.

e. *Works Council Membership*

Under the Works Councils Act (*Wet op de ondernemingsraden* or *WOR*), a works council member (or a member of a works council committee) has a right to conduct works council business during working time with full pay for a minimum of 60 hours per year. Works council members also have the right to attend training courses during work time, with a minimum of three days per year for committee members, five days per year for works council members, and eight days per year for employees who are both committee and works council members.

---

[122]See V.B.4.b., above.

f. Adoption and Fostering

The 2001 Work and Care Act (*Wet Arbeid en Zorg* or *WAZ*), creates a new leave entitlement for employees who adopt or foster a child. In these cases, the employee is entitled to a paid leave of up to four weeks' duration, with payment of wages made by the Institute for Employee Benefit Schemes (*Uitvoeringsinstituut Werknemers Verzekeringen* or *UWV*), not by the employer. This entitlement begins two weeks before the first day of the actual adoption.

g. Family Medical Leave

Under the 2001 Work and Care Act (*Wet Arbeid en Zorg* or *WAZ*), a paid leave, up to a maximum of 10 days in a 12-month period, is granted to an employee who wishes to care for a sick relative. In these cases, the employee is entitled to receive up to 70 percent of his or her salary, with the payment of wages made by the employer. The employee must inform the employer in advance that he or she will make use of this leave, stating the reason for the leave and its possible duration.

2. *Unpaid Leave*

a. Parental Leave

The Parental Leave Act of 1990 (*Wet op het Ouderschapsverlof*), incorporated in Article 644, Book 7, Title 10 of the Civil Code, is applicable to both private and public employees. It was revised as of July 1, 1997, and then amended through the Act on Flexibility and Security (*Wet Flexibiliteit en zekerheid* or *Flexwet*) as of January 1, 1999. As of February 1, 2001, it was revised again.

Under the Parental Leave Act, employees who are parents of (or who are raising a child as if they were the parents) or who adopt a child younger than eight years are entitled to unpaid parental leave, if they have been working for at least one year.[123] The

---

[123]The Act of November 30, 2000, on Vacation and Maternity Leave (*Wet wijziging 7.10 BW met betrekking tot vakantie en ouderschapsverlof*), effective Feb.1, 2001, changed the rules concerning maternity leave in Book 7, Title 10 of the Civil Code.

maximum annual amount of leave is 13 times the working hours per week, and may not exceed six months. For example, if an employee works 40 hours per week, the parental leave per child may not exceed 13 (weeks) × 40 (hours) = 520 hours per year.

The law makes no distinction between full-time employees and part-time employees.

The employee must make a written request for parental leave at least two months in advance. The request must indicate the period for which leave is sought, the number of hours, and the weekly schedule for the leave (to a maximum of 50 percent of the normal working hours per week). Employers in principle must grant parental leave, unless severe business reasons outweigh the interests of employees. For example, an employer may refuse requests for parental leave that would seriously disrupt the work of the organization.

b. *Political Leave*

Employees are entitled to leave, without pay, to exercise responsibilities connected with their membership in Parliament, regional assemblies, or other directly chosen political bodies.[124]

VI. ANTIDISCRIMINATION

Netherlands law protects against discrimination in recruitment and hiring practices, during the period of employment (e.g., in regard to terms of employment and promotion opportunities) and when employment is terminated.

A. Sources of Antidiscrimination Law

1. *Constitution*

The Dutch Constitution contains a general rule with regard to antidiscrimination, stating that all people living in the Netherlands shall be treated equally in similar situations, and that discrimina-

[124]Book 7, Title 10 the Civil Code, art. 643.

tion on the basis of religion, life principles, political affiliation, race, gender, or any other similar ground is prohibited.[125]

In the employment context, employees may not rely directly on the Constitution in pursuit of a claim of unfair discrimination. Instead, the claim must be based on article 611 Book 7 Title 10 of the Civil Code according to which an employer must act in a reasonable and fair manner toward the employee, and Article 12 Book 3 of the Civil Code that states that what is reasonable and fair is partly determined by principles of law, including those under the Articles of the Dutch Constitution. Under this analysis, Article 1 of the Dutch Constitution can thus indirectly be applicable in the relationship between an employer and an employee.[126]

2. *Statutory Provisions*

a. *Act on Equal Treatment of Men and Women of 1980*

In 1974, the European Union adopted a program based on several directives relating to the equal treatment of men and women. In the Netherlands, this program led to the Act on Equal Treatment of Men and Women (*Wet gelijke behandeling van mannen en vrouwen* or *WGB*), which became effective in 1980. This law superseded a similar 1975 law, the Equal Renumeration for Men and Women Act (*Wet gelijk loon voor vrouwen en mannen* or *WGL*).

The 1980 Act is broader than the 1975 law. For example, the *WGB* contains provisions prohibiting discrimination relating to wages for reasons other than just gender; it includes indirect discrimination, thus including instances of discrimination even when there was no discriminatory intent; and it applies to public employees as well as private sector employees.

Indirect discrimination can be permissible if it can be objectively justified. Direct discrimination can be permissible:

- if gender is determinative for the job (a bona fide occupational qualification (BFOQ));

[125] Constitution, art. 1.

[126] See I.D., above.

- to protect women during pregnancy; or
- to favor women through affirmative action programs to abolish inequalities.

Discriminatory discharges and provisions conflicting with the WGB are null and void.

b. Equal Treatment Act of 1994

The Equal Treatment Act (*Algemene Wet Gelijke Behandeling* or *AWGB*) of 1994 interprets Article 1 of the Constitution. It explicitly prohibits discrimination on the basis of religion, life principles, political affiliation, race, and gender. In addition, the AWGB also prohibits discrimination based on national origin, sexual orientation, and family status. It applies to both public and private sector employees.

Under the *AWGB*, indirect discrimination can be permissible if it can be objectively justified. Direct discrimination can be permissible:

- based on gender[127]
  - if gender is determinative for the job (a BFOQ),
  - to protect women during pregnancy, or
  - to favor women through affirmative action programs to abolish inequalities;
- based on race, if race is determinative for the job; or
- based on national origin, if national origin is determinative for the job.

Discriminatory discharges and provisions conflicting with the *AWGB* are null and void.

c. Book 7, Title 10 of the Civil Code

i. Articles 646 and 647

Articles 646 and 647, in Book 7, Title 10 of the Civil Code, address gender discrimination in private sector employment. Like

[127] AWGB art. 2.

the 1980 Equal Renumeration for Men and Women Act, Article 646 prohibits both direct and indirect discrimination with respect to employment conditions, employment agreement negotiations, on-the-job training, promotion, and termination. Deviation from these provisions is possible if gender is a BFOQ, to protect women during pregnancy, or to favor women through affirmative action programs. No other grounds for deviation are allowed, although indirect discrimination is permissible if it can be objectively justified.

Article 647 allows employees to file claims contesting terminations resulting from violations of or for exercising rights under the antidiscrimination provisions of Article 646. These employee claims, which must be initiated within two months after termination, can seek reinstatement and retroactive salary payments.

ii. Article 648

Article 648 Book 7 Title 10 of the Civil Code, which applies to private sector employment, prohibits employers from discriminating on the basis of the hours that employees work. Article 125g of the Civil Servants' Act (*Ambtenarenwet*) contains an identical prohibition applicable to the public sector. These statutes prohibit employer discrimination between part-time (mostly women) and full-time workers in regard to the terms, continuation, and termination of employment agreements. Employers can seek reinstatement and back pay for violations of these statutes by filing lawsuits within two months of their terminations.

iii. Article 649

Private employers are not allowed to treat employees who work under an employment agreement for an indefinite period more favorably than those working under an employment agreement for a definite period, unless objectively justified.[128]

---

[128]Book 7, Title 10 of the Civil Code, Article 649, effective Nov. 22, 2002.

d. Act on Equal Treatment Based on a Handicap or Chronic Illness of 2003

Based on EC Directive 2000/78,[129] this Act went into force December 1, 2003, and protects those with a handicap or chronic disease against discrimination and intimidation with respect to employment and occupation. It applies to the private and public sectors. It prohibits discrimination on these grounds when hiring, during employment, and when terminating the employment relationship. Indirect discrimination can be permissible if it can be objectively justified. Direct discrimination can be permissible, for example, when the safety of others is threatened. Discriminatory discharges and provisions conflicting with this Act are null and void.

The Bill on Equal Treatment Based on Age was still pending in Parliament in 2003.

e. *Collective Labor Agreement Act*

The Collective Labor Agreement Act *(Wet op de collectieve arbeidsovereenkomst* or *WCAO)* invalidates collective bargaining agreement provisions that would require an employer to hire or refrain from hiring individuals because they have a certain racial or religious background, or because they belong to a particular organization.[130]

3. Case Law

The fact that the legislature has not yet explicitly prohibited discrimination based on age (the bill was pending in Parliament 2003) does not mean that such discrimination is permissible. An employer at all times has to behave as a good employer based on Article 7:611 of the Civil Code.

B. Protected Groups

1. Gender

Discrimination on the basis of gender is prohibited by the 1980 Act on Equal Treatment of Men and Women (*Wet gelijke*

[129]Council Directive 2000/78/EC, 2000 O.J. (L 303) 16.
[130]*WCAO* art. 1.3. See II.H., above.

behandeling van mannen en vrouwen or *WGB*), the 1994 Equal Treatment Act (*AWGB*), and the Civil Code. All three statutes contain exceptions to prohibited gender discrimination if gender is a BFOQ, to protect pregnant women, or for affirmative action purposes.

2. *Family Status*

Discrimination on grounds of pregnancy, childbirth, or status as a parent is explicitly prohibited.[131] Discrimination on the ground of family status is explicitly identified as direct discrimination under the *WGB*.[132] This would include, for example, discrimination on the basis of marital status or being an adopted child.

3. *Religion*

Discrimination on the ground of religion is explicitly prohibited by the *AWGB*.[133] This includes, for example, discrimination on the basis of holding certain religious beliefs or following the practices of a specific religion.

4. *Race or National Origin*

Discrimination on grounds of race—which includes color or ethnic origin—as well as discrimination on grounds of national origin are explicitly prohibited by the *AWGB*.[134] However, exemptions contained in the Act provide that race or nationality may be taken into consideration where relevant to the job.[135]

5. *Sexual Orientation*

Discrimination on the ground of sexual orientation is explicitly prohibited by the *AWGB*.[136] This includes discrimination on the basis of homosexuality.

---

[131] *WGB* art. 1; Book 7, Title 10 of the Civil Code, art. 646.5.
[132] *WGB* art. 1.
[133] A*WGB* art. 1.
[134] *Id.*
[135] *Id.* art. 2.
[136] *Id.* art. 1.

6. *Working Hours*

Employers are prohibited from discriminating between full- and part-time employees, whether in the public or private sector.[137] Employers may not take hours worked into account when making hiring or firing decisions, or in the course of employment.[138] Exceptions are possible where an objective case can be made for variations.

7. *Disability*

Under the Act on Equal Renumeration for Handicapped Employees (*Wet Arbeid Gehandicapte Werknemers*), disabled employees are guaranteed equal payment as non-disabled employees. Additionally, if an employer directly discriminates against a disabled employee, although there is no statute explicitly prohibiting such discrimination, the disabled employee could file a claim against the employer for violating the duty of care (*goed werkgeverschap*) under the Civil Code.[139]

8. *Sexual Harassment*

Although the protections under the WGB and articles 646 and 647 of the Civil Code do not apply to sexual harassment,[140] sexual harassment is explicitly defined under the Occupational Safety and Health Act (*Arbeidsomstandighedenwet* or *Arbowet*). Under this Act, an employer must pursue a preventive sexual harassment policy within the company to promote the safety and health of the employees. In the event of a violation of this duty, an employee can file a claim against the employer for violating the duty of care under the Civil Code.[141]

9. *Age*

The Netherlands Supreme Court previously held that termination of an employment agreement because an employee reached

---

[137] See VI.A.2.c.ii., above.

[138] Book 7, Title 10 of the Civil Code, art. 648; Civil Service Act, art. 125g.

[139] Book 7, Title 10 of the Civil Code, art. 611.

[140] For a discussion of these protections, see VI.A.2.a. and VI.A.2.c.i., above.

[141] Book 7, Title 10 of the Civil Code, art. 611.

age 65 was not discriminatory, because several statutes indicated that this was an acceptable age for employees to stop working. In the future, the Supreme Court is unlikely to uphold such terminations, because there is currently a bill pending that will regulate discrimination on the basis of age.[142]

C. Enforcement Mechanisms

The Dutch Equal Treatment Commission (*Commissie gelijke behandeling* or *CGB*) is an independent organization that was established in 1994 to promote and monitor compliance with equal treatment laws. Anyone who feels that he or she has been discriminated against—for example, under the Equal Treatment of Men and Women Act (*Wet gelijke behandeling mannen en vrouwen* or *WGB*), the Equal Treatment Act (*Algemene Wet Gelijke Behandeling* or *AWGB*), Articles: 646 and 647 (gender: male/female); 648 (hours of work: part time/full time); or 649 (duration of employment: indefinite/definite) of Book 7 Title 10 of the Civil Code; or the Act on Equal Treatment Based on Handicap or Chronic Illness (*Wet gelijke behandeling op grond van handicap of chronische ziekte*)—can file a claim with the *CGB*. The employee, however, can also file a claim directly with the cantonal judge.

If the employee files a complaint with the *CGB*, the *CGB* will start an investigation and will question both parties and will then hold a hearing. After subsequent discussion in a closed meeting, the *CGB* generally decides within two months whether the equal treatment law has been violated. In some respects, the *CGB* is similar to a court, with the important difference being that decisions of the *CGB* are not legally enforceable. However decisions of the *CGB* can be influential in court proceedings in the following manner: If an employee wants to take the matter further, he or she can either file a claim with the cantonal judge or authorize the *CGB* to file a claim on his or her behalf. If the *CGB* files a claim, it can seek a court ruling that an equal treatment law had been violated. The court can be asked to prohibit future discriminatory action, or to issue an order requiring an employer to remedy the effects of discriminatory actions.

---

[142]Bill No. 26 880. This bill is likely to be adopted.

VII. OCCUPATIONAL SAFETY AND HEALTH AND WORKERS' COMPENSATION

A. Occupational Safety and Health

1. Historical Background

The first law regulating working conditions for employees in the private sector was the Safety Act of 1895 (*Veiligheidswet*). The miserable working conditions that resulted from the Industrial Revolution led to this law. The Safety Act imposed no general workplace safety obligations on employers and was confined to the protection of employees against health and safety hazards.

The Occupational Safety and Health Act of 1980 (*Arbeidsomstandighedenwet* or *Arbowet* or OSHA) replaced the Safety Act and promotes human working conditions in general. That is, the OSHA goes beyond specific rules and imposes general requirements on employers to protect workers' safety. The OSHA further applies to the public sector and to those who work outside the employers' premises.

2. Summary of Main Legal Provisions

Under the OSHA, every employer (public as well as private) must carry out a risk inventory and evaluation (*risico-inventarisatie en evaluatie* or *RIE*), in which the risks arising from machinery, tools, materials, production activities, and workplace organization must be identified. Based on the *RIE*, employers have a general obligation to ensure the highest possible safety standards at work and to make every possible effort to protect the health and welfare of workers.

Employers are also required to adopt an explicit policy regarding employee absences from work due to illness.

Employers also must create an Occupational Safety and Health Service (*Arbodienst*), with whom the employer must deliberate in matters such as employee absenteeism.

3. Enforcement Mechanisms

Enforcement of the OSHA is in the hands of the Labour Inspectorate of the Ministry of Social Affairs and Employment

(*Arbeidsinspectie* or *AI*). The *AI* has the authority to visit all workplaces, either on its own initiative, at the request of a company's works council, or because of employee complaints.

In most cases the *AI* tries to resolve problems by mediation or by issuing warnings. In a few cases, the *AI* may invoke statutory sanctions, which include orders directing compliance with workplace safety rules or penalties.

B. Workers' Compensation

1. Historical Background

Workers' compensation means compensation for individuals injured while at work. Injured employees may seek relief from their employers in the form of economic damages based on Article 658, Book 7, Title 10 of the Civil Code, and/or tort damages based on Article 162, Book 6 of the Civil Code. These provisions are discussed in more detail below.

2. Summary of Main Legal Provisions

a. Economic Damages

The employer is liable for the economic damages suffered by employees in the course of their work.[143] An employee is not required to prove that the employer did not comply with the law; instead, an employee needs to prove only that he or she suffered damages during work. The burden of proof is on employers, who will not be liable if they can prove that the legal provisions were observed. Employers are not liable if they can prove that injuries resulted from the employee's own intentional behavior (*opzet*) or deliberate recklessness (*bewuste roekeloosheid*).

b. Tort Damages

A person who commits a tort is liable for the resulting damages, unless a justification for the action can be established.[144] A

[143]Book 7, Title 10 of the Civil Code, art. 658.

[144]Book 6 of the Civil Code, art. 162.

tort (*onrechtmatige daad*) is defined as a violation of someone's rights or an action or omission that conflicts with a legal duty or with norms of behavior.[145] The burden of proof rests on an employee who charges that a tort has been committed in the workplace. Both economic and non-economic damages can be requested. The concept of punitive damages is not a feature of Netherlands tort law.

3. Enforcement Mechanisms

Claims based on Article 658, Book 7, Title 10 of the Civil Code must be taken up with the district court, cantonal section also referred to as cantonal judge. Employee *tort* claims for amounts up to €5,000 should be filed with the cantonal judge. However, tort claims for more must be pursued by the employee in the District Court.

VIII. PENSIONS AND BENEFITS

A. Social Security

The social security system (*Sociale Verzekeringen*) is intended to offer security of income to all residents of the Netherlands. The social security system consists of employee insurance schemes (*werknemersverzekeringen*), national insurance schemes (*volksverzekeringen*), and social assistance schemes (*sociale voorzieningen*). As will be discussed below, the distinction among these three schemes is that national insurance covers all inhabitants of the Netherlands, while employee insurance covers workers only, and social assistance provides a "safety net" if the other schemes prove to be insufficient.

Under the Act on the Implementation Structure for Work and Income (*Wet Structuur uitvoeringsorganisatie werk en inkomen* or *SUWI*), the National Institute for Social Security (*Landelijk Instituut voor Sociale Verzekeringen* or *LISV*) has been replaced

---

[145] *Id.* art. 162.2.

by a new institution, the Institute for Employee Benefit Schemes (*Uitvoeringsinstituut Werknemers Verzekeringen* or *UWV*). As a result, effective January 1, 2002, the *UWV* administers the benefits that previously were administered by the *LISV*.

Effective April 1, 2002, the Gatekeeper Improvement Act (*Wet Verbetering Poortwachter* or *WVP*) changed the law on short-term sickness benefits in an attempt to reduce the large number of employees on sick leave (estimated at one million). These changes obligate employers to make serious efforts to integrate sick employees back into the workforce, and obligate employees to cooperate with the employer's efforts.[146]

1. Employee Insurance Schemes

In general, employee insurance schemes cover only employees in the private sector.[147] The three most important employee insurance schemes are:

- short-term sickness benefit covering periods of illness of up to 52 (as from 2004: 104) weeks, provided by the Sickness Benefits Act (*Ziektewet* or *ZW*);
- disability benefit covering periods of illness of more than 52 (as from 2004: 104 weeks), provided by the Disablement Benefits Act (*Wet op de Arbeidsongeschiktheidsverzekering* or *WAO*); and
- unemployment insurance covering a varied period depending on the years of service and the age of the employee, provided by the Unemployment Insurance Benefits Act (*Werkloosheidswet* or *WW*).

Employers have to pay differentiated contributions under the Act known as *PEMBA* (Differentiation in Contribution Rates and Introduction of Market Incentives in Connection with the Disablements Benefits Scheme) that went into force as of January 1, 1998, and applies to all private sector employees; the higher the number of ill employees, the higher the contributions. As of January 1,

---

[146]See I.A.1. and I.C. above.

[147]A similar system has been introduced for public employees as well, as of Jan. 1, 2001 (Operation OOW).

2003, companies with 25 employees or fewer (average wage sum of €600,000) are exempted.

Employee insurance schemes are financed by employer and employee contributions, which are a specified percentage of the employee's gross salary. The level of contributions is set in the Coordination Social Insurances Act (*Coordinatiewet Sociale Verzekering* or *CSV*).

2. *National Insurance Programs*

National insurance programs are those that apply to all residents of the Netherlands. They include the following:

- general old age benefits for people age 65 or older, provided by the State Old Age Pensions Act (*Algemene Ouderdomswet* or *AOW*);
- disability benefits for independent contractors under the Self-employed Persons Disablement Benefits Act (*Wet arbeidsongeschiktheid Zelfstandigen* or *WAZ*); and
- disability benefits for young people under the Disablement Assistance Act for Handicapped Young Persons (*Wet arbeidsongeschiktheid Jongeren* or *Wajong*).

National insurance schemes are financed through contributions. Through income tax (*loonheffing*), employees pay wage taxes (*loonbelasting*) as well as contributions for national insurance programs. The level of contributions is set by the National Insurance Plans Financing Act (*Wet Financiering Volksverzekeringen*).

3. *Social Benefits Provisions*

In general, social benefits are available to residents of the Netherlands and are financed through taxes. Social benefits include the following:

- social minimum benefits, which ensure that a minimum standard of living is attained, provided by the National Assistance Act, also referred to as Social Assistance Act (*Algemene Bijstandswet* or *ABW*); and

- supplementary allowances to the social minimum benefits, provided by the Supplementary Benefits Act (*Toeslagenwet* or *TW*).

B. Pensions

1. State Old Age Pensions

Old age benefits are provided by the State Old Age Pensions Act (*Algemene Ouderdomswet* or *AOW*). All residents of the Netherlands who are 65 or older are entitled to old age pensions. The old age pension is tied to the minimum wage standard but can be supplemented through supplementary pensions.[148]

The pension benefit level depends on rights the person has built up between the ages of 15 and 65 and his or her family status. Eligibility for the maximum 100 percent pension is earned at an average rate of 2 percent per year from age 15 to 65 (2 percent annually × 50 years).

If a married couple, or the partners separately, apply for the old age pension, the couple in total receives a maximum of 100 percent of the basic minimum wage. If one of the partners is younger than 65, the couple's pension is 50 percent of the basic minimum wage, plus an additional amount up to 50 percent of the basic minimum wage, depending on the income of the younger partner. Thus, if the partner younger than age 65 has no income at all, the older partner will get a pension of 50 percent of the basic minimum wage, plus an extra allowance of 50 percent of the minimum wage, resulting in a total pension of 100 percent of the minimum wage.

If a parent in a single-parent family applies for an old age pension, the applicant receives a maximum of 90 percent of the basic minimum wage. If a single person applies for the pension, the applicant gets a maximum of 70 percent of the basic minimum wage.

---

[148]See VIII.B.2., below.

2. *Supplementary Pensions*

Because the old age pension establishes only a minimum standard of living, workers may use supplementary pensions as a means of retaining the same standard of living they had when they were working. The social security system does not offer supplementary pensions, nor are employers under any legal obligation to provide supplementary pensions for their employees. Supplementary pensions can be arranged in two different ways: through mandatory participation (occupational pensions), or voluntarily through a contract (private pensions).

a. *Types of Supplemental Pensions*

i. *Mandatory pension fund participation or occupational pensions*

The vast majority of those employed in the Netherlands participate in an occupational pension scheme. Occupational pensions are subject to negotiation between employers' associations and trade unions. Under the Mandatory Participation in a Sector Pension Fund Act (*Wet verplichte deelneming in een bedrijfspensioenfonds* or *BPF*), when these social partners reach a collective pension agreement in a specific industrial sector for all of their members, and if the representatives of organized businesses in this sector file a request, then the Minister of Social Affairs and Employment can declare the collective pension agreement binding for all other employers in that industrial sector.

ii. *Private pensions*

Supplementary pensions can be provided through various private arrangements. For example, an employer and employee can voluntarily agree to a supplementary pension for the employee. In this situation, the Pension and Savings Fund Act (*Pensioen-en Spaarfondsenwet* or *PSW*) regulates the agreement to require that the employer place the contributions paid in a special pension fund or with a certified insurer, to ensure that the funds result in a pension for the employee.

Alternatively, an employer can arrange for a private insurance company to provide pensions for all its employees. The *PSW* also governs this situation. Finally, an employee can make arrangements with a private insurance company for a supplementary pension, for example, through an annuity (*lijfrente*). Annuity arrangements typically provide for the individual to pay a specified amount to a private insurer, with the amount increasing over the years, and, from the age of 65, the private insurer will then pay the individual a monthly amount.

b. Level of Supplemental Pensions

Supplementary pensions can reach a level that is a maximum of either 70 percent of the employee's last earned salary (*eindloonsysteem*) or the average salary (*middelloonsysteem*), where the level of pension is related to the average salary the employee has earned over the years. The old age benefit provided by the *AOW* is included in the 70 percent under the last earned salary system.

Financing supplemental pensions based on the last earned salary method is more expensive that the average system, since salaries tend to increase over time. The higher the salary, the higher the premium. Therefore, the average salary system is more common because it is less expensive.

C. Benefits

1. Employees' Insurance Programs

a. Short-Term Sickness Benefits

The Institute for Employee Benefit Schemes (*Uitvoeringsinstituut Werknemers Verzekeringen* or *UWV*) enforces the law on short-term sickness benefits. Employers are required to pay the salaries of sick employees for a maximum period of 52 weeks.[149] Payment is at the rate of 70 percent of the wage the employee last earned, with a minimum of the minimum wage and a maximum of 70 percent of the daily pay (*dagloon*), which is about €165, as of July 1, 2003. In an effort to decrease the number of sick employees, the Civil Code makes employers responsible for the absenteeism of their employees.[150]

---

[149]Book 7, Title 10 of the Civil Code, art. 629. As from 2004, 104 weeks.
[150]*Id.*

For certain groups of employees, there are variations from the general rules. For example, under the Sickness Benefits Act (*Ziektewet*), pregnant women are entitled to short-term sickness benefits equal to 100 percent of their last earned salary, up to a maximum of 70 percent of the daily wage, for a maximum period of 16 weeks.

b. Disability Benefits

The National Institute for Social Security administers the Disablement Benefits Act (*Wet op de Arbeidsongeschiktheid* or *WAO*). The *WAO* offers disability benefits to employees who have not recovered after 52 weeks of illness. The *WAO* provides for salary-related benefits (*loondervingsuitkering*) and follow-up benefits (*vervolguitkering*).

The level of the salary-related benefits depends on the percentage of disability. For example, employees determined to be 15 to 25 percent disabled are entitled to disability benefits equivalent to 14 percent of their daily salaries; employees 80 percent or more disabled receive 70 percent of their wages. The duration of benefits depends on the age of the employee and ranges from six months to six years. Employees younger than age 33 are not entitled to these benefits; employees ages 33 to 38 may receive six months' benefits; ages 38 to 43, one year; and 58 and older, six years.

After the expiration of these periods, employees are entitled to a continuing disability benefit, which can extend until they have reached the age of 65. The amount of the continuing benefit is less than that of the salary-related disability benefit.

c. Unemployment Benefits

The Institute for Employee Benefit Schemes (*Uitvoeringsinstituut Werknemers Verzekeringen* or *UWV*) administers benefits under the Unemployment Insurance Benefits Act (*Werkloosheidswet* or *WW*). The *WW* provides for salary-related unemployment benefits and six-month unemployment benefits (*kortdurende uitkering*). In August 2003 the Government decided to abolish the follow-up benefits (*vervolguitkering*) to reduce the costs of the Unemployment Insurance Scheme. As of August 2003, those who are no longer entitled to this follow-up benefit may fall back on social assistance under the National Assistance Act, also referred to as the Social Assistance Act (*Algemene Bijstandswet* or *ABW*), provided they qualify under income and means tests.

To qualify for salary-related benefits, an employee must have lost at least five hours of work time, or half of the hours worked per week, as well as the income associated with the lost work time, and the employee must be available for work. In addition, an employee must have worked for at least 26 out of the last 39 weeks (although the time worked need only be one hour per week), and the employee must have earned income during at least 52 days per year during four of the five years preceding the period of unemployment. An unemployed worker who meets these conditions will receive a salary-related unemployment benefit of 70 percent of the daily wage for a period of six months to five years, depending on the employee's years of service (e.g., workers with four years of service are entitled to six months' benefits, while workers with 40 years of service are entitled to five years' benefits).

An employee is entitled to six-month unemployment benefits if he or she meets all the requirements for salary-related benefits except for earning an income for at least 52 days per year in four of the past five years. In such cases, the benefit is 70 percent of the minimum wage for a period of six months.

Those who do not meet the requirements for unemployment benefits under the *WW* can seek a social minimum benefit under the National Assistance Act, also referred to as the Social Assistance Act (*Algemene Bijstandswet* or *ABW*), mentioned above.

2. *Social Benefits*

a. *Social Minimum Benefits*

A social minimum benefit is provided under the National Assistance Act, also referred to as the Social Assistance Act (*Algemene Bijstandswet* or *ABW*), which is administered by the government. Every resident of the Netherlands can apply for a social minimum benefit to ensure that all residents attain a minimum standard of living. The benefit levels are 100 percent of the net minimum wage for a two-parent family and other equal partnerships, 70 percent of the net minimum wage for single-parent families, and 50 percent of the net minimum wage for single individuals.

b. Supplementary Allowances

The Institute for Employee Benefit Schemes (*Uitvoeringsinstituut Werknemers Verzekeringen* or *UWV*) under the Supplementary Benefits Act (*Toeslagenwet* or *TW*) administers a system of supplementary allowances designed to ensure that all residents of the Netherlands receive their legal entitlement of the social minimum benefit. Anyone whose total income is less than the social minimum, after receiving all benefits allowed under any other applicable acts, can apply for a supplementary allowance.

IX. IMMIGRATION

A. National Immigration Laws

1. Historical Background

In 1964, the Foreign Nationals Work Permit Act (*Wet Arbeidsvergunning Vreemdelingen*) replaced a 1934 immigration statute. The 1964 Act entered into force in 1969, when economic growth led to the creation of more jobs than Dutch employees could fill, and so immigration was increasing. This Act tried to regulate the immigration of foreigners and offer protection to foreigners working in the Netherlands.

A subsequent increase in immigration to the Netherlands led to a more restrictive immigration policy, embodied in the Foreign Employees Employment Act (*Wet Arbeid Buitenlandse Werknemers*) of 1978.

Netherlands immigration law was changed again in 1995, when the 1979 Act was replaced by the Foreign Nationals Employment Act of 1995 (*Wet Arbeid Vreemdelingen* or *WAV*). The *WAV* responded to further increases in immigration and increasing unemployment by imposing additional immigration restrictions.

2. Foreign Nationals Employment Act of 1995

The most important provisions in this Act are:

- employers are prohibited from hiring aliens without a work permit;[151]
- exceptions to this work permit rule exist, for example, citizens of EU member countries do not need work permits;[152]
- employers are required to ask for work permits;[153]
- work permits must be denied for certain enumerated reasons, for example, if the work could be done by unemployed Dutch citizens or citizens of other EU member countries;[154]
- work permits may be denied for certain enumerated reasons, for example, if Dutch citizens or citizens of other EU member countries are likely to become available;[155] and
- work permits may be issued only for limited periods, with maximums of three years for regular permits, one year for conditional permits, and 24 weeks for temporary employment, such as seasonal employment.[156]

B. International Law

1. Treaty of Rome of 1957

The Treaty of Rome prohibits any discrimination on the basis of nationality among citizens of EU member countries in regard to employment, remuneration, and other conditions of employment.[157]

2. EU Regulation 1612/68

The nationality antidiscrimination provision from the Treaty of Rome resulted in EU Regulation (*Verordening*) 1612/68.[158] This Regulation provides that every citizen of an EU member country

---

[151] 1995 Act on Employment of Foreign Nationals of 1995, art. 2.
[152] *Id.* arts. 3–4.
[153] *Id.* art. 6.
[154] *Id.* art. 8.
[155] *Id.* art. 9.
[156] *Id.* art. 11.
[157] Treaty of Rome, art. 39.
[158] Council Regulation 1612/68/EEC, 1968 O.J. (L 257) 475.

has the right to accept and perform paid work in another member country on the same terms as a national of the other member country, and it prohibits any discrimination on the ground of nationality between the employees of EU member countries in matters of remuneration and other terms and conditions of employment.

3. EU Posted Workers Directive

The EU Posting of Workers Directive of 1996[159] intends to offer equal protection to an EU-member state employee posted in another EU member state. In the Netherlands, the Terms of Employment Cross Border Work Act (*Wet Arbeidsvoorwaarden Grensoverschrijdende Arbeid* or *WAGA*) have come into force to fully implement the Directive. In sum, the *WAGA* offers foreigners from other EU countries working in the Netherlands on a temporary basis equal to what protection. Dutch employees enjoy under Dutch laws, for example, as regards minimum wages and equal treatment. It, however, is meant to serve as a minimum protection only. If foreign law is applicable as well and is more favorable for the foreign employee, such law will supersede the provisions of the *WAGA*.

POLAND*

INTRODUCTION

The turnover of political power in Poland in 1989 from the Communists to the democratic opposition led by Solidarity began the large-scale transformation of Poland's political, economic, and legal systems. At the present time, the Polish state is based on a tripartite form of government comprised of the following authorities: the Parliament (*Sejm*) and the Senate (*Senat*), as the legislative bodies; the Council of Ministers (*Rada Ministrów*) and the President (*Prezydent*), as the executive bodies; and the independent State Courts (*Sądy*) and the Tribunals (*Trybunały*), as the judicial bodies.

As of January 1, 1999, a long-awaited and wholesale governmental and administrative reform was implemented in Poland. Generally, the former administrative system suffered from a lack of political empowerment to manage local and regional problems independently. The new reforms established three levels of administrative units: provinces (*województwa*), which are the regional administrative units of the national government; communes or municipalities (*gminy*); and districts (*powiaty*). The fundamental purposes of this administrative reform were to create a clear division of responsibility between national and local authorities, and to provide regional authorities with the political and legal authority to resolve local problems and take responsibility for dealing with local issues, such as regional employment, unemployment, and social problems.

---

*Andrzej Czopski, legal advisor and associate with Miller, Canfield, W. Babicki i Wspólnicy Sp. k., Gdynia, Poland.

The development of a free market economy and Poland's reorientation of its foreign policy toward the goal of integration into the European Union (EU)—which was finally completed on May 1, 2004, with Poland's accession to the EU—has had had a significant impact on Polish labor law and employment relationships, as has the increased presence of foreign businesses in Poland. Labor law in Poland is an independent, codified branch of the Polish legal system. In general, the labor laws govern and control all labor relationships and other labor related issues. Primarily, the labor laws govern employment relationships that are based on the employment contract (*umowa o pracę*).[1] However, in certain cases specified by law,[2] the employment relationship also can be established on other bases, e.g., appointment (*powolanie*), election (*wybór*), nomination (*mianowanie*), and cooperative contract of employment (*spółdzielcza umowa o pracę*). These types of employment relationships apply to only certain groups of employees based on the type and character of the work performed (e.g., general directors of state-owned enterprises, members of trade union boards, certain officials of national and local government, teachers, and public service employees).

Polish labor law does not cover all types of relationships under which work may be performed. Most importantly, a labor law contract is distinguished from work rendered under other types of service contracts that are based on civil-law relationships. These include, for example: an agency contract (*umowa agencyjna*), entered into for either a limited purpose or an indefinite period (e.g., sales representation services); a contract for the performance of a specific job (*umowa o dzieło*) (e.g., to draft a legal document or provide financial expertise); and a mandate contract (*umowa zlecenia*) (e.g., to teach a foreign language or provide cleaning services). These relationships are governed by the Polish Civil Code

---

[1]See discussion at I.B., below.

[2]*E.g.*, Act on Employees of Local Government (Mar. 22, 1990), unified text published in Journal of Laws (*Dziennik Ustaw* (Dz.U.)) No. 142/01, item 1593, with subsequent amendments; Act on Employees of State Agencies (Sept. 16, 1982), unified text published in Dz.U. No. 86/01, item 953, with subsequent amendments; Act on State-Owned Enterprises (Sept. 25, 1981), unified text published in Dz.U. No. 112/02, item 981, with subsequent amendments; Trade Unions Act (May 23, 1991), unified text published in Dz.U. No. 79/01, item 854, with subsequent amendments.

(*Kodeks Cywilny*).[3] Individuals providing services under such arrangements generally are not regarded as employees but as independent contractors. As a result, they are not subject to protection under labor law.

An employment relationship based on a civil law contract may be considered a labor law relationship, regardless of its formal title or name, should the work performed fulfill all criteria and elements of the employment relationship as defined by provisions of the Labor Code.[4] This principle, however, does not automatically turn a civil law contract into an employment contract. Rather, it provides an employee, or a labor inspector acting *ex officio*, with the right to file a claim against the employer seeking a judicial ruling from the labor court that the contract under which work is or was performed is, in fact, an employment contract, no matter what it might be called by the parties.

Several fundamental principles of labor law are recognized by the Labor Code. These include, *inter alia*:

- the right to freely choose employment,
- the right to choose an employer,
- the right to create and participate in unions,
- the right to equal treatment and protection from discrimination in employment relationships,
- the right to fair remuneration,
- the right to paid holidays, and
- the right to healthy and safe working conditions.

In addition, the Labor Code provides for a general rule of automatism,[5] stating that the terms of employment contracts (or other actions creating an employment relationship) may not be less advantageous for the employee than those provided by general labor law. Thus, contract provisions that are less favorable are rendered null and void and replaced with relevant terms and provisions of the labor law.

---

[3]Dated Apr. 23, 1964, Dz.U. No. 16/64, item 93, with subsequent amendments.

[4]Labor Code, art. 22, §1[1] (June 26, 1974), unified text published in Dz.U. No. 21/98, item 94, with subsequent amendments. See discussion at I.A., below.

[5]Labor Code, art. 18.

A. Sources of Labor Law

1. National Sources

a. The Constitution

Following a long period of democratic change, the new Constitution of Poland became effective in July 1997.[6] The new Constitution is the supreme source of Polish law. It provides numerous fundamental guarantees regarding employee rights and social benefits, including: the right to equal treatment regarding employment and remuneration for work of the same value, irrespective of gender; the right to receive a minimum wage; the right to annual paid holidays; and the right to social security and social benefits. At the constitutional level, employees also are guaranteed the right to establish and participate in trade union organizations, the right to enter into collective labor agreements, and the right to strike. Under the new Constitution, the terms and conditions of work are subject to the supervision of the state.[7]

b. Legislation

Under the Polish legal system, the fundamental source of legislation is the acts (*ustawy*) introduced and adopted by the Polish legislative bodies and signed by the President. The Labor Code is one such act.

i. The Labor Code

The central legislative act governing employment relationships is the Polish Labor Code (*Kodeks Pracy*), which was introduced in 1975.[8] The first substantial amendment to the Labor Code reflecting new economic realities was introduced in 1996.[9] Fur-

---

[6]Constitution of the Republic of Poland (Apr. 2, 1997), Dz.U. No. 78/97, item 483 (July 16, 1997).

[7]See discussion in the Introduction, at C., below.

[8]Unified text of the Labor Code published in Dz.U. No. 21/98, item 94.

[9]Amendment published in Dz.U. No. 24/96, item 110.

ther significant changes in the regulations of the Labor Code resulted from the need to harmonize Polish employment laws with the EU law and employment standards; these were implemented from 2002 through 2004.

In its original form, before the political changes of 1989, the Labor Code distinguished between socialized and nonsocialized enterprises. Over time, however, this distinction became archaic and no longer reflected economic reality. Although numerous amendments were adopted between 1975 and 1996, most did not keep pace with the changes taking place in the economic transformation toward a free market system and the dynamic growth of private enterprises. With the 1996 amendments, the Labor Code finally provided a more flexible infrastructure to regulate employment relationships. Although providing stronger and more effective protection of employee rights, it also grants employers more flexibility in their dealings with employees. Amendments implemented in the recent years led to harmonization of Polish labor law with European Union legal requirements in this field, thus ensuring adjustment to and conformity with European standards.[10]

The Labor Code is divided into the following 15 major parts:

1. General Provisions (definitions, basic rules of labor law)
2. The Employment Relationship
3. Wages and Other Forms of Reimbursement
4. Duties of Employee and Employer
5. Material Responsibility of Employees
6. Working Time
7. Leaves
8. Employee Rights Related to Parenthood
9. Employment of Minors
10. Work Safety and Hygiene
11. Collective Labor Agreements
12. Resolution of Disputes Related to Claims Arising from Employment Relationships
13. Responsibility for Violation of Employee Rights
14. Claims Limitations
15. Final Provisions

---

[10]See the chapter on the European Union in Part I of Volume I.

ii. Other labor acts and regulations

The branch of law known as labor law includes other acts and regulations in addition to the Labor Code. These acts and regulations consist of (1) acts that may be considered redundant in that they govern the same types of matters covered by the Labor Code,[11] and (2) acts that address and regulate other issues, such as the following:

- employment measures and the prevention of unemployment,[12]
- trade unions,[13]
- employer organizations,[14]
- collective bargaining,[15]
- protection of employees' claims in case of employer insolvency,[16]
- employment of disabled persons,[17] and
- social assistance funds.[18]

[11] *E.g.*, Act on the Specific Principles of Dissolution of Contracts of Employment as a Result of Reasons Unrelated to Employees (Mar. 13, 2003), Dz.U. No. 90/03, item 844, with subsequent amendments; Act on Social Insurance of Accidents and Occupational Diseases (Oct. 30, 2002), Dz.U. No. 199/02, item 1673, with subsequent amendments; Act on Social Insurance Pecuniary Benefits in Case of Sickness and Maternity (June 25, 1999), Dz.U. No. 60/99 item 636, with subsequent amendments.

[12] Act on Promotion of Employment and Labor Market Institutions (Apr. 20, 2004), Dz.U. No. 99/04, item 1001.

[13] Trade Unions Act (May 23, 1991), unified text published in Dz.U. No. 79/01, item 854, with subsequent amendments.

[14] Employers' Organizations Act (May 23, 1991), Dz.U. No. 55/91, item 235, with subsequent amendments.

[15] Collective Bargaining Settlement Act (May 23, 1991), Dz.U. No. 55/91, item 236, with subsequent amendments.

[16] Act on Employees' Claims Protection in Case of Employer's Insolvency (Dec. 29, 1993), unified text published in Dz.U. No. 9/02, item 85, with subsequent amendments.

[17] Act on Employment and Rehabilitation of Disabled Individuals (Aug. 27, 1997), Dz.U. No. 123/97, item 776, with subsequent amendments.

[18] Enterprise Social Benefits Act (Mar. 4, 1994), unified text published in Dz.U. No. 70/96, item 335, with subsequent amendments.

This body of law, including the Labor Code, may be supplemented by ordinances issued by the Council of Ministers or ordinances issued by particular Ministers, most notably by the Minister of Economy and Labor. These supplementary ordinances are issued pursuant to specific authority granted in an act as legislative or administrative implementing and executive provisions. For instance, supplementary ordinances may pertain to occupational safety and health, protection of women and minors, specific rights of certain groups of employees, minimum wages, rights of employees transferred abroad, work certificates, leave for child care, work safety and hygiene, financial liability of employees for damage to the employer's property, and the calculation of remuneration and other benefits due to employees.

In addition, because of the civil nature of an employment relationship, the Labor Code states that provisions of the Civil Code will apply to any employment issues not covered by the labor laws, so long as such provisions do not contravene labor law principles.[19]

iii. Collective arrangements applying to the employment relationship

Beyond this official body of labor law, the employment relationship may be further defined by collective labor arrangements or internal labor rules specifying the rights and duties of the parties. In particular, these include: (1) collective labor agreements, which may apply to one or more enterprises, or to the employees of a particular branch of the economy, group, or profession;[20] and (2) an enterprise's internal labor bylaws and rules relating to organization and system of work, time of work, remuneration and benefits terms, etc. Internal labor bylaws covering these issues are compulsory in any enterprise employing at least twenty people, unless it is party to a collective bargaining agreement.

2. *EU and International Sources*

Poland acceded to the EU on May 1, 2004. As a result of accession, Poland became fully bound by all *acquis communautaire*

---

[19] Labor Code, art. 300.

[20] See II., below.

developed in the EU so far, which—pursuant to the principle of supremacy—has priority over Polish national law. Depending on the category of the EU sources of law, some of them are directly applicable in the Polish legal order, without the need for further implementation ("regulations"), others need to be implemented by acts of internal law to be applicable ("directives").[21]

Poland also is a member of the International Labor Organization (ILO). The various conventions of the ILO, as well as directives promulgated by the EU, have significantly influenced the recent amendments to the Labor Code. Poland has signed and ratified 81 ILO conventions, including those addressing working time, leaves, work safety and hygiene, freedom of association, protection of union rights, and elimination of discrimination.[22]

In addition, Poland is a party to several bilateral treaties on the employment of expatriates in Poland and on the employment of Polish citizens in other countries.[23]

B. Jurisdiction

As a rule, employment relationships applicable to work performed within the territory of Poland are subject to Polish law and the jurisdiction of Polish labor courts.[24] The jurisdiction of Polish law includes employment contracts with expatriates employed by Polish employers, unless international treaties provide otherwise or the parties choose other law (e.g., the national law of an expatriate). Jurisdictional disputes arising out of the employment relationship are always recognized and accepted for consideration by Polish labor courts.

---

[21]For information on EU labor and employment standards and related implementation procedures, see the chapter on the European Union in Volume I, Part 1.

[22]For information on ILO conventions, see the chapter on the ILO in Volume I, Part 4.

[23]These include treaties with Belgium, the Czech Republic, France, Germany, the Slovak Republic, and Switzerland, though the significance of such treaties has considerably diminished as a result of accession to the EU and in view of the fact that EU law covers issues relating to employment in the countries mentioned above.

[24]For a discussion of Polish labor courts, see the Introduction, at D.2., below.

C. Administration

Two separate networks of government agencies are responsible for supervising the labor and employment matters in Poland: the State Labor Inspection office (*Państwowa Inspekcja Pracy,* or *PIP*),[25] whose main competence is to supervise observation of labor law provisions, and the public employment services, responsible for unemployment issues and labor market policy.[26] Each has its own area of authority, and PIP is supplemented by a separate network of Voluntary Labor Inspections.[27] All three networks are discussed below.

1. PIP

PIP's purpose is to supervise the proper implementation of labor law provisions, mainly workplace safety and health regulations.[28] PIP is comprised of the General Labor Inspectorate and regional labor inspectorates. Regional inspectorates are established for one or more provinces (*voivodships*). The PIP inspectors have the authority to supervise the observance of labor law requirements, and to inspect enterprises and examine their conditions of employment (legal and physical), as well as the safety of the workplace. Should the inspectors notice any violations or infringement of employee rights, they have the authority to impose fines on the employer.

2. Voluntary Labor Inspection

The Voluntary Labor Inspection is comprised of inspectors who are elected by employees within a single enterprise, within particular departments of an enterprise, or within union groups.

---

[25]The organization and authority of the State Labor Inspection are regulated by the State Labor Inspection Act (Mar. 6, 1981), unified text published in Dz.U. No. 124/01, item 1362, with subsequent amendments.

[26]The organization and authority of the public employment services are regulated by the Act on Promotion of Employment and Labor Market Institutions (Apr. 20, 2004), Dz.U. No. 99/04, item 1001.

[27]The organization and responsibilities of the Voluntary Labor Inspection are regulated by the Voluntary Labor Inspection Act (June 24, 1983), Dz.U. No. 35/83, item 163, with subsequent amendments.

[28]See additional discussion at VII.D.1., below.

They operate only in enterprises where trade unions have been formed. The Voluntary Labor Inspection oversees workplace conditions and cooperates with the employer to prevent accidents and diseases.[29]

3. *Public Employment Services*

On the central governmental level, employment and labor policy issues are managed by the Minister of Economy and Labor, who provides general administration in this field. Locally, employment matters are handled by Labor Offices, either provincial (usually covering one province) or district (covering a district comprised of a single town or several local municipalities). Labor offices provide practical and individual assistance, e.g. they are responsible for job distribution and creation, as well as education and training projects for the unemployed. They also distribute unemployment compensation, can grant loans for the unemployed, and may also reimburse expenses (wages) incurred by an employer who employs the graduates directed to it by the labor office.

D. Dispute Resolution

1. *Conciliation Committees*

The Labor Code provides for the possibility of conciliation proceedings to resolve labor disputes.[30] Conciliation proceedings are conducted before a conciliation committee, a body appointed or elected for a specified term to resolve disputes within a particular enterprise. The creation and utilization of such conciliation committees is not compulsory. However, a committee may be created by the employer and the union acting within the enterprise, or, if there is no union, by the employer itself upon approval of the employees. If a conciliation committee has been established, the employee may voluntarily bring a dispute before the committee prior to commencing court litigation.

---

[29]See additional discussion at VII.D.2., below.

[30]Labor Code, arts. 242–258.

The purpose of conciliation proceedings is to settle disputes out of court. However, such settlements cannot be in contravention of compulsory labor laws or general principles of community life.[31] A settlement can be executed under the supervision of the labor court, in accordance with the provisions of the Code of Civil Procedure, if the employer does not execute it voluntarily.

Should conciliation proceedings not result in a settlement, upon demand by the employee the matter may be filed before the relevant labor court, subject to the conditions described below.

It should be noted that only a small percentage of labor disputes are resolved in the course of the conciliation proceedings, and the significance of that institution for effective resolution of labor matters is currently minimal in Poland.

2. *Labor Courts*

The courts having jurisdiction over labor law issues, i.e., the Labor Courts (*Sądy Pracy*), are part of the ordinary state judicial system. Generally, the Polish court system is based on three levels of courts, including the courts of the first instance, the courts of the second instance, and the Supreme Court. The structure of labor courts is parallel to and synchronized with the general court system, and includes:

General System	Labor Courts
District Courts	District Labor Courts
Provincial Courts	Provincial Labor and Social Insurance Courts
Courts of Appeal	Labor and Social Insurance Courts of Appeal
Supreme Court	Supreme Court—House of Administration, Labor, and Social Insurance

Labor court jurisdiction is based primarily on the type of employment matter involved.[32] The District Labor Courts, the

[31]Although Polish law does not provide an express definition of the term "general principles of community life," it is understood to mean commonly accepted customs and moral rules.

[32]Code of Civil Procedure arts. $461(1^1)$, 477^8.

courts of first instance, have jurisdiction over almost all typical employment matters, irrespective of the claim value. In addition, the District Labor Courts have been given jurisdiction over cases involving certain social insurance matters (e.g., social allowances, labor accidents, and occupational diseases). The Provincial Labor and Social Insurance Courts, as courts of first instance, determine specific employment matters involving amounts in excess of PLN 30,000, as well as matters involving social insurance claims (except for the types listed above).

Generally, the labor courts address disputes between individual employees and employers using a liberal procedure, commonly regarded as employee-oriented. This procedure, which covers disputes in labor and social insurance matters, is specifically regulated by the Code of Civil Procedure (*Kodeks Postępowania Cywilnego*, or *KPC*).[33] This procedure is guided by the following principles:

- *Special consideration for employee interests:* As a rule, the labor courts are obligated to consider the just interests of the employee and to support the employee as the less experienced and qualified party in the relationship. In particular, this rule applies to the situation where the employee is not represented by a qualified attorney. For example, the labor court has the power to act *ex officio* in order to demand information, inquiries, investigations, expert examinations, and other things with regard to the particular case. The court also may provide an employee with information as to applicable labor laws and regulations and legal steps that may be undertaken by the employee. The labor court, acting *ex officio*, also has the power to award more than the amount demanded in the employee's claim if such a ruling is justified by the status of the case. In addition, the court has the power to disagree with the terms of a proposed settlement if it determines that the settlement would not be in the employee's just interest.

---

[33]Dated Nov. 17, 1964, Dz.U. No. 43/64, item 296, with subsequent amendments.

- *Amicable settlements:* As a rule, the labor court should encourage amicable settlement between an employee and an employer at any stage of the proceedings, provided that such a settlement is not contrary to compulsory labor laws or general principles of community life.
- *Speedy proceedings:* The labor courts should consider cases promptly. Formally, the first hearing should be arranged no later than two weeks from the date the claim is submitted, unless extraordinary reasons for delay exist. The court is allowed to use any measures pertaining to formal notifications and deliveries in order to shorten the proceedings and avoid procedural delays.
- *Limited formalism:* As a rule, employees acting without the professional assistance of an attorney are allowed to submit their claims or appeals in any form, even orally. Generally, it is only the court, not the parties, that is bound by minimum procedural requirements.
- *Cost-free litigation:* Employees lodging their claims against employers are legally exempted from any court fees.[34] If the employee loses the case, he or she may be required by the labor court to reimburse certain costs related to the case (e.g., the cost of expert examination), but only in particularly justified cases. The exemption for court fees does not apply to employers; they are required to pay all fees incurred in the course of lodging a lawsuit against an employee.

An employee may submit a claim either to the labor court located in the jurisdiction that is the legal seat of the enterprise involved, or to the labor court located in the jurisdiction where the work is, was, or was supposed to be, performed.

Any judgment issued by the court of the first instance is immediately enforceable up to the amount of the employee's monthly pay, provided that the case involves the adjudication of wages or other employee compensation. If the claim involves reinstatement of employment, the employer may be obliged by virtue of the judg-

[34]Labor Code, art. 263; Code of Civil Procedure, art. 463.

ment issued by the court of the first instance to employ the employee until the case is validly and finally considered.

A judgment issued by the first instance court (District Labor Court or Provincial Labor and Social Insurance Court) is subject to appeal by either party to the second instance court. The second instance courts are as follows:

- the Provincial Labor and Social Insurance Court, for matters considered by the District Labor Courts in the first instance; and
- the Labor and Social Insurance Court of Appeal, for matters considered by the Provincial Labor and Social Insurance Court in the first instance.

A party generally may appeal a judgment of the second instance court to the Supreme Court. However, a Supreme Court appeal is not allowed in certain cases, e.g., if the value of the claim is less than PLN 10,000; for claims related to work certificates (issued by an employer upon termination of employment); or for claims pertaining to in-kind benefits due to an employee under a collective labor agreement. In appellate proceedings before the Supreme Court, unlike cases before the first and second instance courts, an employee must be represented by an attorney at law or other legal counsel.

I. INDIVIDUAL EMPLOYMENT

A. Employment Relationship

Under the Polish Labor Code,[35] the employment relationship is defined to include the following elements:

- personal performance of a specific type of work by the employee,
- performance of work for the benefit and risk of the employer,

[35]Labor Code, art. 22.

- performance of work under the supervision or authority of the employer,
- performance of work at the place and time specified by the employer, and
- compensation for work performed.

As a rule, work performed under the above conditions will be deemed an employment relationship regardless of the name or title given the relationship by the parties. Formally, the employment relationship is established between the employee and the employer. By law, any person who is older than age 18 and who has full legal capacity may become an employee. Minors older than age 16 and younger than age 18, as well as persons limited in capacity, may be employed under certain conditions specified by law.

An employer is defined in the Labor Code as "any organizational unit even if it has no legal personality, and any natural person, if they employ employees."[36]

B. Employment Contract

The individual employment contract is the primary form of employment relationship regulated by the Labor Code. An employment contract is to be concluded in writing and must specify the nature and essential elements of the contract, including the kind of work to be performed, the location in which the work is to be performed, remuneration, and working time.[37] Employment based on an oral agreement is valid and effective; it is the obligation of the employer to confirm to the employee in writing the conditions of the contract, at the latest on the day when the employee starts working.

In principle, the mutual duties and obligations of an employee and an employer are established by law. They also may be defined more specifically in the employment contract, to the extent not inconsistent with the labor laws. If a collective bargaining agreement or any internal bylaws (e.g., remuneration bylaws) take effect, they substitute for any individual employment contract made

---

[36] *Id.* art. 3.

[37] *Id.* art. 29.

with covered employees, except where provisions of the individual contract are more favorable to the employee.[38]

The Labor Code distinguishes several types of employment contracts. Specifically, a contract may be concluded: (1) for an indefinite period of time (a contract for an indefinite period); (2) for a specified period of time (a contract for a definite period); (3) for the time of performance of a specified task; or (4) for a trial period.[39] These various types are discussed in more detail below. As a rule, the parties are free to determine the type of employment contract that will govern their relationship. Importantly, certain employer responsibilities and obligations, as well as the procedures for terminating an employee's employment, depend on the type of employment contract existing between the employer and the employee.

1. *Employment Contract for an Indefinite Period*

This type is a typical employment contract and is common in Poland. An employment contract for an indefinite period has two distinctive features. First, the contract is made without any limitation as to time. Second, in case of termination with notice, the employer is required to specify just cause for the termination and to follow the termination procedures specified by law.[40]

In practice, such contracts are concluded with employees with whom the employer is interested in a long-term relationship. From the employee's standpoint, this type of contract offers greater protection and stability of employment than other types of employment contracts.

2. *Employment Contract for a Definite Period*

A second type of employment contract commonly used in Poland is a contract for a definite period. Under this type of contract, the parties specify the term of the contract and its termination date. An employment contract for a definite period may be

[38]*Id.* art. 9.
[39]*Id.* art. 25.
[40]See discussion at I.C.2., below.

concluded for any type of work and for any period of time, without any statutory limitations as to the minimum or maximum duration. However, given the purposes of such contracts, determination of their period of duration should be justified and connected to the real needs of the employer or the employee, in particular when an employment contract is to be concluded for a longer period of time (e.g. 3 to 5 years). Too long a term in an employment contract for a definite period of time, unrelated to objective and actual needs of the parties, may in the event of a dispute be considered by the labor court as an abuse of law and not subject to protection.

To prevent employers from concluding a continuous series of such definite contracts with their employees, the Labor Code provides that the third consecutive contract concluded between the same employee and the employer for a definite time will be deemed, by virtue of law, to be for an indefinite period.[41] This rule, however, is not applicable either to replacement contracts discussed in a. below, concluded in the event of justified absence of a regular employee, or to employment contracts covering seasonal or other irregular jobs or tasks performed periodically.

A contract for a definite period automatically terminates after the period of time for which it was concluded, without any need for notice. An employee employed under such a contract does not have the right to demand that the contract be renewed. However, the contract may be renewed upon the consent of both parties.

As discussed below, termination of a contract for a definite period longer than six months is free from certain procedural restrictions that normally must be followed in terminating contracts for an indefinite time.[42] For this reason, employers prefer contracts for a definite period.

a. Replacement Contracts

To the category of contracts concluded for a definite period also belong the so-called replacement contracts. Beginning No-

---

[41]Labor Code, art. 25^1.

[42]See I.C.2.b., below.

vember 29, 2002, the Labor Code expressly allows the employer to conclude an employment contract for a definite period where it is necessary to replace an employee during the employee's justified absence. The period of such an employment contract will normally equal that of the employee's absence. This regulation is primarily aimed at facilitating replacement of employees who are absent for a considerable period of time, i.e. due to a long-lasting disease or maternity leave. Such a replacement employment contract is governed by general provisions relating to contracts for a definite period, subject to a certain modification in relation to termination of such contracts.[43]

3. *Employment Contract for the Time of Performance of a Specified Task*

This type of employment contract is characterized by the absence of a strict period of duration. The contract specifies only the task to be performed (e.g., to construct a house or to carry out a function for a member of the Board of Directors) and the date of its commencement. This type of contract is automatically terminated upon completion of the specified task.

4. *Employment Contract for a Trial Period*

This type of contract may precede any other type of employment contract, i.e., a contract for an indefinite period, for a definite period, or for the performance of a specific task. In general, a contract for a trial period is concluded in order to give the employer an opportunity to assess the employee's usefulness.

A contract for a trial period may be concluded only once between the same employer and the employee. In addition, a contract of this type is limited to a maximum term of three months. This period may not be extended by the parties. A contract for a trial period in excess of three months must, in case of a dispute, be regarded as a contract for a definite period. Importantly, the employer has no obligation to offer the employee any other type of employment contract after expiration of the contract for a trial

[43]See I.C.2.b., below.

period, even if the employee has performed his or her duties perfectly.

C. Termination of Employment Contracts

The law provides certain requirements and formalities that must be observed in terminating employment contracts. Formally, an employment contract may be terminated: (1) by mutual agreement of the parties; (2) upon notice by one of the parties with observance of the appropriate notice (termination by notice); or (3) upon a declaration by one of the parties without observance of the notice period (termination without notice).[44]

As discussed above, the applicability of particular rules and procedures for termination depends mostly on the type of employment contract that exists between the parties. The procedures and requirements applicable to each method of termination are explained below.

1. Termination by Mutual Agreement

Each type of employment contract may be terminated by mutual consent of the employer and the employee. The law does not impose any restrictions concerning this method of termination. Thus, termination by mutual consent is free from any requirements relating to specification of cause or consultation with a trade union. By mutual consent, a contract of employment can be terminated at any time determined by the parties.

2. Termination by Notice

a. Contracts for an Indefinite Period

Under the Labor Code, an employment contract for an indefinite period may be terminated by the employer's notice only for just cause, i.e., a reason justifying termination of the contract. The Labor Code does not provide a definition of "just cause," nor any list of qualifying reasons. However, according to decisions of

---

[44]Labor Code, art. 30.

the Supreme Court, just cause means a reason that is true, real, and important enough to discontinue the employment relationship.[45] For example, the case law has accepted the following reasons, among others, as just cause for termination of employment:

- breach of the employee's duties,
- lack of required qualifications and skills,
- failure to perform a superior's orders,
- negligence and/or carelessness in the performance of the employee's duties,
- absence from work without leave,
- loss of confidence in the employee,
- violation of noncompetition obligations, and
- reasons provided under the Collective Dismissal Law.[46]

An employer's declaration (notice) of termination should be made in writing and must state the reason justifying termination. It also should include information regarding the employee's right to appeal the termination to the labor court.[47]

When terminating the employment contract by notice, the employer is required to satisfy a specified notice period. The notice period depends on the employee's period of employment with a given employer, as follows:[48]

- two weeks—if the employee has been employed for fewer than six months;
- one month—if the employee has been employed for at least six months; or
- three months—if the employee has been employed for at least three years.

In particular cases, the law allows the employer to shorten the statutory length of notice. However, only the three-month notice period may be shortened, and then only to at least one month.

---

[45]Resolution of the Supreme Court (June 27, 1985), III PZP 10/85.
[46]See IV.A.1., below.
[47]Labor Code, art. 30.
[48]*Id.* art. 36.

In such a case, the employer is obliged to compensate the employee at his or her regular pay rate for the remaining length of the three-month period.

The employer also is required to observe specified termination procedures if there are one or more trade unions operating at the employer's business. Namely, the employer is obliged to seek the representative trade union's opinion regarding the intention to terminate an employee's employment contract. This obligation applies to employees who are members of the company's trade union(s) or who are under the trade union's protection.[49] However, irrespective of the opinion of the union, the employer makes the final termination decision.[50]

Under the Labor Code, the employee is entitled to terminate a contract for an indefinite period by notice at any time, for any reason. However, the employee must satisfy the same notice periods specified above for the employer, depending on the length of the employee's service.

b. Fixed-Term Contracts

In the case of a contract for a definite period of six months or less, or a contract for performance of a specified task, the contract may not formally be terminated with notice by the employer prior to completion of the agreed term or task.

In the case of a contract for a definite period greater than six months, the contract may be terminated by either party upon two weeks' notice, provided that a termination clause permitting such termination is included in the contract. Formally, such a contract may be terminated at any time, without any specific cause for termination.[51]

In the case of a contract for a trial period, either party may terminate it by notice before the lapse of time for which the contract was concluded. The notice period ranges from three working days to two weeks depending on the duration of the trial period.[52]

---

[49]See II.A., below.

[50]Labor Code, art. 38.

[51]*Id.* art. 33.

[52]*Id.* art. 34.

For replacement contracts, the notice period is three working days.[53]

The employer has no duty to specify a reason or to consult with the trade union in terminating fixed-term contracts.

3. *Termination Without Notice*

The Labor Code provides for certain situations in which the employer is allowed to terminate the employment contract immediately, without notice.[54] First, termination without notice is permitted due to the fault of an employee who commits any of the following acts:

- a serious violation of basic employee duties, e.g., several unjustified absences from work, offenses against the property or economic interest of the employer, consuming alcohol during working hours, disclosure of confidential information or secrets of the employer, etc.;
- commission of an offense, either obvious or established by a court judgment, that renders further employment impossible (e.g., a larceny offense committed by a cashier); or
- loss of a license or other qualifications necessary for the performance of the employee's duties.

Termination of the employment contract without notice due to the employee's fault may not be effected later than one month after the employer becomes aware of the circumstances justifying termination.

The employer's intention to terminate due to the fault of the employee must be followed by consultation with the company's trade union, if one exists. As a rule, however, the final termination decision is made by the employer, no matter what the opinion of the trade union.

The employer also may terminate the employment contract without notice in case of the employee's incapacity to work by reason of illness for longer than the period covered by sickness

[53] *Id.* art. 33^1.

[54] *Id.* arts. 52, 53.

benefits,[55] or, in case of a justified absence from work, for a period longer than one month due to certain reasons other than illness (e.g., taking care of a child or other family member after lapse of the maximum leave period).[56]

D. Protection Against Termination of the Employment Contract

1. Prohibitions

The Labor Code and other applicable regulations prohibit the termination or dissolution of an employment contract with certain groups of protected employees, including those who fall into any of the following categories:

- a pregnant woman,
- an employee on maternity leave,
- an employee who will reach the required pension age in no more than four years,
- a board member of the trade union operating within the particular business, or
- an employee drafted for military service,
- a member of the employees' council, a voluntary labor inspector, a deputy to the local government council, a member of the Parliament, or a senator.

Irrespective of the above general rules, employment contracts with protected employees may be terminated under exceptional circumstances as specified in the applicable regulations (e.g., bankruptcy or liquidation of the enterprise, termination without notice due to the employee's fault).

2. Employee Rights in Case of Unjustified Termination

An employee may appeal a notice of termination to the labor court. In the case of a contract for an indefinite period, if it is established that the termination notice is unjustified or violates statu-

---

[55]See VIII.B.2.a., below.

[56]See V.C.3., below.

tory or contractual requirements for termination, then the court, upon the employee's claim, may:

- declare the termination notice to be ineffective (if the court's decision is made before the lapse of the notice period),
- order that the employee be reinstated in his or her job, or
- award monetary damages to the employee.

If the court finds that, despite an employer's violation of termination requirements, it would be impossible or without purpose to restore the employee to work, the court has the power to award money damages to the employee and reject the employee's request for reinstatement.[57] Money damages, in contrast, are always available in case of wrongful termination and may be demanded by the employee as an alternative to reinstatement. The amount of damages awarded is equal to the remuneration due the employee for a period ranging from two weeks to three months, but not less than the required period of notice.

In the case of fixed-term contracts, if a contract has been terminated in violation of termination requirements, the employee is entitled only to damages, and not reinstatement. In this case, the amount of damages is to equal the remuneration due the employee for the time period during which the contract would have been valid, though not longer than three months.

E. Privacy

The individual's right to privacy is recognized as one of the most important rights under the European Convention for Protection of Human Rights and Fundamental Freedoms, which Poland implemented in 1993. Accordingly, the Polish Constitution guarantees protection of privacy, family life, and dignity.

These general rules are reflected in the Polish Labor Code, which imposes an obligation on the employer to honor dignity and other personal rights of the employee, including the right to privacy.[58]

---

[57]Labor Code, art. 45.

[58]*Id.* art. 11^1.

Pursuant to the above, the employer must not interfere with the employee's private life outside work or with other aspects of life that are deemed to fall in the employee's sphere of privacy. Such conduct would amount to violation of the employee's right to privacy and thus be subject to challenge in courts.[59]

In addition, employees' personal information is subject to the Data Protection Act (DPA),[60] which deals with collection, storage, processing and deletion of personal data, and the employer is bound to observe conditions and requirement arising from the DPA.

However, the employee's right to privacy is not absolute and certain essential limitations to it are permissible.

First, the nature of the employment relationship is such that the employee works under supervision and for the benefit and risk of the employer. In order to protect its own interests, the employer has a right to control the employee in relation to performance of duties, quality, and quantity of work and the way the enterprise's property or its other resources are used. For that purpose, the employer is allowed to establish certain monitoring procedures, such as a check of the contents of e-mail and Internet accounts, duration of telephone calls, etc., provided that the employee has been notified about them. With these conditions fulfilled, the employer will not be considered to be violating the employer's privacy. However, any of the employee's actions in this respect should be the least intrusive possible and must not go further than it is essential to ensure adequate performance of work.

Second, the employee's right to privacy is limited where the applicable provisions of law directly authorize the employer to seek and keep certain personal information, such as name and given names, parents' names, date of birth, address of residence (correspondence address), certificates of education, and professional qualifications as well as information about previous employment. Apart from that, the employer is entitled to require only personal details that are necessary for performance of its contractual and statutory obligations arising from the employment contract (e.g.,

---

[59]The Supreme Court has recognized that unauthorized disclosure of information about remuneration may violate the employee's right to privacy. Resolution of the Supreme Court (June 16, 1993), I PZP 28/93.

[60]Dated Aug. 29, 1997, unified text published in Dz.U. No. 101/02, item 926.

social security or tax obligations) or related to performance of work by the employee. Information outside this scope will be deemed as falling in the sphere of the employee's privacy, and subject to protection, unless voluntarily provided by the employee. The employer also is entitled to request relevant documents confirming the information provided by the employee. As regards personal information not covered by the provisions discussed above, the DPA will be applicable. This means that if the employer wishes to obtain an employee's personal data that exceeds the permissible scope provided for in the Labor Code, the employer must observe all conditions and requirements flowing from the DPA, especially those relating to the voluntary manner of providing information and to the consent of the individual to processing of his or her personal details.

F. Employee Duty of Loyalty, Trade Secrets, Covenants Not to Compete

1. *Employee Duty of Loyalty*

The Labor Code does not expressly provide for the employee duty of loyalty. However, it may be inferred from a number of provisions relating to employees' duties in relation to the employer, such as the duty to show care for the interests of the employer, to keep certain information secret, or to perform the employer's orders.

The employee is obliged to perform work in a proper way, and may be required to undertake actions outside the scope of the employee's contractual obligations on the employee's own initiative if it is necessary to avert a threat of damage to the employer or try to reduce the amount of damage. Specifically, the employee is under a duty to protect the property of the employer from loss or damage.

The employee must obey orders from the employer in the course of performance of work, with the exception of orders that are illegal, contrary to the contents of the employment contract, or impossible to perform.

The employee duty of loyalty does not preclude the employee's right to make justified critical remarks in relation to the employing enterprise, especially on the organization of work.[61] Employee criticism should be expressed in an appropriate way, however, without using offensive words or slanderous allegations. On no account does the employee's critical attitude toward the employer release the employee from duties owed to the employer, including those which make up the duty of loyalty.

2. *Trade Secrets*

Under the provisions of the Labor Code, one of the basic duties of the employee is to show care for the interests of the employer and to keep secret any information of which disclosure could cause damage to the employer.[62] The duty of confidentiality does not relate to any information the employee has acquired in the course of work, but only that which, if disclosed, may negatively affect the employer, e.g., worsen its position in the market in relation to competitors. Violation of these duties may result in termination of the employment contract.

Under other regulations, such as the Competition Law,[63] the former employee is required not to disclose trade secrets of the employing enterprises, such as technical or organizational information as well as other information of economic value, in relation to which the enterprise has undertaken actions necessary to keep it confidential. Such a prohibition is in force for three years from termination of the employment relationship, subject to other agreement by the parties.

3. *Covenants Not to Compete*

Under the Labor Code, the employee is not under a general duty not to undertake any activity which might appear competitive in relation to that of the employer's. This applies also to employment with any entity conducting such competitive activity. Any employee's obligation in this respect must flow from an agree-

---

[61]Resolution of the Supreme Court, dated Sept. 7, 2000, I PKN 11/00.

[62]Labor Code, art. 100.

[63]Art. 11 of the Act on Suppressing Unfair Competition, (Apr. 16, 1993), unified text published in Dz.U. No. 153/03, item 1503 with subsequent amendments.

ment (i.e., a covenant not to compete) between employee and the employer.[64] If the employee should violate a covenant not to compete, causing the employer to incur loss, the employer is entitled to seek adequate compensation. Additionally, such violation may constitute grounds for termination of the contract of employment, including termination without notice.

Normally, the duration of a covenant not to compete would equal the period of the contract of employment. However, it is possible to extend it even after termination of the contract, subject to agreement of the parties, if the employee had access to particularly important information, disclosure of which could cause damage to the employer. There is no limit to the duration of an extended covenant not to compete. However, during the time that it is in force, the employer is under a duty to compensate the employee for not being able to undertake other competitive employment or activity. The amount of the compensation is agreed on by the parties, but it may not be lower than 25 percent of the employee's remuneration before termination of the contract of employment in a period equal to the duration of the covenant. The employee is discharged from the obligation not to compete upon expiration of the agreement, or on employer's default on payment of compensation, as well as when the grounds justifying the covenant have ceased to exist.

II. COLLECTIVE BARGAINING

A. Union Rights

Trade unions exist and operate under the Trade Union Act.[65] A trade union is a voluntary, self-governing organization of working people (employees, agency contractors, cooperative members), which is independent from employers, government agencies, local authorities, and other institutions. The existence of trade unions in Poland is based on the principle introduced by the Constitution

---

[64]Labor Code, arts. 101^1–101^4.

[65]Dated May 23, 1991, unified text published in Dz.U. No. 79/01, item 854, with subsequent amendments.

and the Labor Code,[66] which states that employees (and employers) are free to create their own organizations and representative bodies and to participate in trade unions.

A trade union may be created without permitting or licensing from any authority. There must be at least 10 members. Admission to and resignation from union membership is voluntary. Every union is registered by the relevant Provincial Court. The employer is obligated to allow the union to act freely within the enterprise. An employer violating this obligation may be fined.

Trade unions are to represent the interests of all employees, including those who are not members of the union. Unions are entitled to carry out collective negotiations, to represent employees throughout the collective bargaining process, and to organize strikes. Unions may protect individual employee rights, in addition to protecting employees' collective rights, examples of the latter being agreements concerning mass layoffs,[67] holiday schedules, and working time schedules.[68]

Multiple unions existing in one enterprise may act collectively and create a system of common representation for dealings with the employer. In a multiple union situation, each union represents all of the enterprise's employees with regard to collective rights and interests, while the individual interests of particular employees are represented by the specific union of which they are a member.

Pursuant to the Labor Code,[69] the employer must consult the trade union regarding an intention to terminate an employment contract concluded for an indefinite time.[70] The purpose of consulting the union is to obtain the union's opinion concerning the employee and the employer's intent. If there is more than one union in an enterprise, each union is to be consulted about the employment rights of its own members. Each union also may protect the employment rights of nonmember employees, but only upon the employee's request. Should no union choose to represent the non-

---

[66]Constitution, art. 59; Labor Code, art. 18^1.

[67]See IV.A., below.

[68]See V.B., below.

[69]Labor Code, art. 38.

[70]See discussion at I.C.2.a., above.

member, the employer is released from its duty to consult with the union about matters concerning that particular employee.

Union members and leaders are protected against discrimination by employers. Union leaders are released from their duties as employees to perform work and are protected from dismissals though the breadth of protection has been reduced in comparison to previous regulations, under which all union leaders were protected. As of July 1, 2003[71] the prohibition on dismissing employees performing such functions will refer only to those who have been specified by a special resolution of the trade union. The prohibition remains in force for a period stated in the resolution, plus an additional period not longer than one year.

B. Collective Bargaining

The collective bargaining process is regulated by the Collective Bargaining Settlement Act.[72] Matters subject to collective bargaining include working conditions, wages, social benefits, and other employee rights and freedoms. Existing collective bargaining agreements may be amended or new provisions adopted through bargaining. The bargaining procedure may not be used to protect the rights of an individual employee; instead, such matters must be resolved by the labor courts.[73]

During negotiations, employees always must be represented by a trade union or unions, either by one operating within the enterprise or by an outside organization. The employer may act for itself or be represented by a relevant employers' organization.

The collective bargaining process is a three-step procedure consisting of: (1) claim submission and negotiation, (2) mediation, and (3) arbitration. Each of these steps is discussed below.

1. Claim Submission and Negotiation

During this first step, the union representing the employees should submit specified claims to the employer and should indi-

---

[71]Act of Amendment of the Labor Code, dated July 26, 2002, effective July 1, 2003.

[72]Dated May 23, 1991, Dz.U. No. 55/91, item 236, with subsequent amendments.

[73]For a discussion of the labor courts, see the Introduction, at D.2., above.

cate a time limit for the employer to meet the employees' demands. However, if the claim submission refers to an existing collective bargaining agreement or other collective arrangements, it may not take place earlier than the termination date of the existing agreement. When submitting its claims, the union may set a deadline and declare that if its demands are not satisfied by that time, a strike shall be called (upon completion of the required procedures described below).

In the event that the employer does not meet the union's demands, the collective bargaining process commences. The employer is obligated to start negotiations with the trade union and must notify the District Labor Inspector (PIP)[74] about the dispute. If the negotiations are successful, the parties sign a "conciliation deed" to reflect their agreement. If the parties cannot reach a settlement, a "protocol of differences" is concluded.

2. *Mediation*

In the event that the employee and trade union cannot reach agreement, they jointly appoint a mediator to help them. If the parties cannot agree on a mediator, the mediator is appointed by the Minister of Labor and Social Policy. If the mediation process is successful, the parties sign a conciliation deed to reflect their agreement. Should mediation prove unsuccessful, another protocol of differences is signed, and the parties proceed to the next step. The union, however, is authorized to commence a strike following unsuccessful mediation.

3. *Arbitration*

The third stage of the collective bargaining process is arbitration. This stage is optional and may be initiated only by a union that does not exercise its right to strike. Arbitration proceedings are held before a social arbitration board established either at the Provincial Court or at the Supreme Court, depending on whether the dispute is within one enterprise or encompasses several enterprises. The arbitration board is comprised of a professional judge of the respective court, who acts as a presiding judge, and six arbi-

---

[74]See the Introduction, at C.3., above.

trators. Each party appoints three arbitrators. The judgment of the arbitration board is binding on the parties, unless otherwise declared by the parties prior to submission of their dispute to the board.

C. Strikes

The collective bargaining procedure described above may be followed by a strike. A strike may be declared only as follows:

- during mediation proceedings, in which case a single warning strike may last up to two hours; or
- after mediation is finished unsuccessfully, when the union decides not to pursue arbitration; or
- after arbitration proceedings that have proven to be unsuccessful, i.e., when the arbitration board issues a decision that is not accepted and implemented by the employer.

A strike is an ultimate measure and may not be declared without carrying out negotiations and mediation first; otherwise, it is illegal. Notwithstanding the above, a strike may be declared without prior mediation if the employer has unlawfully made it impossible to carry out negotiations or mediation.

Certain groups of public service employees are not granted the right to strike, e.g., police officers, members of the army or coast guard, intelligence employees, firefighters, judges, and prosecutors.

Employees are not required to go on strike; taking part in a strike is voluntary. A strike is deemed legal if a majority of the employees employed in an enterprise agree upon it, provided that 50 percent of the employees take part in the strike vote.

During a strike, employers (or managers) may not be limited or deprived of their rights and powers with regard to those employees not on strike. Strike organizers are obligated to cooperate with management in order to protect the fixed assets of the enterprise and the safety and health of the employees.

Throughout the strike period, striking employees are entitled to social insurance benefits,[75] but not remuneration. However, the employer may agree to pay wages. Those employees not participating in the strike retain their full benefits and remuneration.

A strike that does not comply with the above requirements is illegal. Those who organize an illegal strike may be fined. Employees who participate in an illegal strike are in breach of their basic duties, i.e., they are absent from work without a justified reason and eventually may be dismissed.

III. Representation by Entities Other Than Unions

Generally, it is the unions that protect and represent employees' rights and interests. Other entities have a limited authority to represent employees in certain areas; their competencies are advisory in nature, and their role is to communicate employees' needs to the employer. Such entities have no power to represent employees in collective bargaining. The specific non-union representatives recognized by the labor laws are discussed below.

A. The Staff Delegate (*Przedstawiciel Załogi*)

The staff delegate is a person elected by all employees to represent their interests in an enterprise where no union is operating. This person should be consulted by the employer when a mass layoff is intended within the enterprise. In addition, the staff delegate should be consulted when establishing and managing the social fund maintained by the employer. The terms of temporary suspension (for up to three years) of collective labor agreements or other labor arrangements, including the employees' terms of employment, have to be agreed upon with the staff delegate. As of January 1, 2004, an obligation has been imposed on the employer to consult with the employees or their representatives regarding

[75]See VIII.B., below.

all activities related to work safety and hygiene unless this obligation is discharged through the Work Safety and Hygiene Committee discussed in C. below.

B. Work Safety and Hygiene Service (*Służba Bezpieczeństwa i Higieny Pracy*)

The work safety and hygiene service is appointed by the employer in enterprises employing more than 100 people. This body has as its purpose to control and, if necessary, demand improvement of the working conditions within an enterprise, according to safety and hygiene regulations.[76]

C. Work Safety and Hygiene Committee (*Komisja Bezpieczeństwa i Higieny Pracy*)

The work safety committee is appointed, in addition to the work safety and hygiene service, in enterprises employing more than 250 people. This committee is authorized to prepare opinions and evaluations of an employer's actions in the fields of safety and hygiene.[77] In addition, the committee is obligated to cooperate with the employer to provide the best possible working conditions for the employees.

D. Employees Council (*Rada Pracownicza*)

The employees council functions only in state-owned enterprises. The council is an elected body with advisory and control authority, which is to be respected by management. In addition, the council participates in operating and managing certain areas of the enterprise.

E. European Works Council

European Works Councils have been introduced in Poland by the Act of European Works Council dated Apr. 5, 2002[78] in

---

[76]See additional discussion at VII.D.3., below.
[77]See additional discussion at VII.D.3., below.
[78]Dz.U. 62/02, item 556.

order to implement the European Union Directive of Establishment of a European Works Council or the Procedure of Informing and Consulting the Employees in Community-scale enterprises or groups of enterprises.[79] The Act imposes an obligation to establishment a European Works Council in enterprises where more than 1.000 employees from European Union members states are employed, including at least 150 employees from at least two such member states. The Act lays down the procedure aimed at reaching an agreement with the management board either to establish a European works council or on an official manner of informing and consulting the employees.

IV. Redundancy and Transfers of Undertakings

A. Redundancy

1. Collective Dismissals

As of January 1, 2004, issues related to collective dismissals are governed by the Act on Specific Principles of Dissolution of Employment Contracts for Reasons Unrelated to the Employees,[80] referred as the Collective Dismissal Law. The new Collective Dismissal Law, unlike the previous regulations, does not provide a specific list of reasons for dismissals. On the contrary, under the new collective dismissal regulations the employer is allowed to terminate any type of an employment contract for any reason, provided that it is unrelated to the employee. In practice these may include any reasons leading to reduction of employment: economic reasons; organizational, production, technological changes; limitation of the employer's scope of activities; or bankruptcy or liquidation of the enterprise.

The main goal of the Collective Dismissal Law is to make it easier for the employer to terminate employment contracts by establishing a specific procedure and rules on the one hand and by

---

[79]Directive 94/45/EC dated Sept. 22, 1994, published in the Official Journal of the EU, L 254 of Sept. 30, 1994. See the discussion in section III. of the chapter on the European Union in Part I of Volume I.

[80]Dated Mar. 13, 2003, published in Dz.U. No. 90/03, item 844.

ensuring certain benefits to the terminated employee on the other. Importantly, the Collective Dismissal Law also applies to individual employment terminations,[81] so long as the reasons unrelated to the employee are the only reasons for the dismissal. The Collective Dismissal Law also applies to workplaces that are subject to bankruptcy proceedings or liquidation.

In a termination notice based on the Collective Dismissal Law, the employer must state the particular reason for termination (e.g., liquidation of existing work places due to organizational changes). Under the general rules governing termination of an employment contract, the stated reason must be true and objective, and, in case of an employee's appeal, the employer is obliged to prove it before the labor court.[82]

For terminations effected pursuant to the Collective Dismissal Law, the special protection generally provided under the labor laws for certain groups of employees (e.g., pregnant women, workers who will reach the required pension age in fewer than four years, or members of the union's board[83]) is significantly reduced. Termination of employees within these groups is limited to cases of liquidation or bankruptcy. The employer also is allowed to change the protected employee's terms and conditions of employment (e.g., by lowering the number of working hours). However, if this results in decreasing the employee's pay, the employee is entitled to a compensation allowance for the entire period of protection.

An employee dismissed under the Collective Dismissal Law has a right to reemployment in the event that the employer subsequently hires employees of the same profession. In such a case, the employer should reemploy the former employee within 15 months from the date of the layoff, provided that the employee declares his or her availability to return to the workplace within one year of the date of the layoff.

---

[81]*I.e.*, where termination applies to one or more employees, but fewer than the limits quoted in IV.A.2., below.

[82]See I.C.2. and I.D.2., above.

[83]See I.D.1. and II.A., above, and VI.C., below.

2. *Procedure for Collective Dismissals*

The provisions of Collective Dismissal Law apply only to enterprises employing at least 20 employees and where, within 30 days period, the dismissals refer to:

- at least 10 employees in workplaces employing fewer than 100 employees; or
- at least 10 percent of the total number of employees in workplaces employing at least 100, but fewer than 300 employees; or
- at least 30 employees in workplaces employing 300 or more employees.

The collective dismissals must be effected by way of a termination notice in compliance with all labor law requirements relating to termination of employment contracts by notice, or by way of a mutual agreement.

Prior to dismissals, the employer must consult regarding its intention in this respect with trade unions operating within the enterprise or, where no union has been established, with the employee representatives. The employer must provide them with information on the reasons for collective dismissals, the number of employees to be dismissed, the period during which collective dismissals are to take place, and criteria governing selection of employees to be dismissed. The same information must be provided to the local labor office.

Within 20 days of notification, the union(s) and the employer must conclude an agreement stating particulars applicable to employees to be dismissed, i.e. rules of collective dismissals, the amount of severance pay or other benefits payable to the dismissed employees, and other employer obligations essential for the purposes of resolving labor matters related to the intended mass layoff. Where it is impossible to conclude an agreement in question, the employer will be authorised to establish the rules of collective dismissals individually in bylaws, taking into consideration any proposal present by the union on the course of negotiations. The possibility of determining the rules in bylaws also applies where there are no unions operating in the enterprise, but the employer nonetheless must consult with the employee representatives. The district labor office must be notified of the agreement or bylaws. Terminations under the collective dismissal procedure may not be effected earlier than 30 days after said notice is provided.

The above-described statutory procedure for collective dismissals does not apply in the event of individual termination, even if such termination is otherwise subject to the Collective Dismissal Law. In such a case, the employer need only comply with the general termination procedures laid down in the Labor Code.

3. Severance Pay

Employees whose employment relationships are terminated pursuant to the Collective Dismissals Law are entitled to severance pay. The amount of severance pay depends on the employee's period of employment with the employer who effects the dismissal. The severance pay will equal:

- one-month's pay—if the employee has been employed for less than two years;
- two-months' pay—if the employee has been employed for two or more years, but not more than eight years;
- three-months' pay—if the employee has been employed for more than eight years.

Notwithstanding the above, the amount of severance pay may not exceed 15 times the statutory minimum wage unless the parties agree otherwise

B. Transfers of Undertakings

1. Effects on Individual Contract Relationships

As a general rule, the Labor Code provides that where a business organization is transferred in whole or in part from one employer to another, the new (successor) employer, as a matter of law,[84] becomes party to the existing employment relationships with the employees of the business. In other words, the successor employer automatically becomes bound by the employment contracts

---

[84]Judgment of the Supreme Court (May 20, 1993), 1 PRN 40/93.

entered into by the previous employer.[85] A business transfer subject to this succession rule may result from a variety of legal acts, including acquisition of the enterprise, a merger or division of enterprises, transfer of fixed assets of an enterprise, or even the lease of an enterprise.[86]

Following a transfer, both parties—the new employer and the employees—are bound by all provisions of any pre-existing employment contracts. Thus, the successor employer does not have to execute new employment contracts with the employees,[87] although the parties are free to enter into new contracts by mutual consent. Otherwise, all existing individual employment contracts remain valid, and only may be changed or terminated pursuant to the general rules and procedures provided under the Labor Code.[88]

Any attempt to alter the succession rules by a contractual arrangement between the old employer and the new employer will be ineffective. The former employer and the successor may not decide on a different scheme as to the transfer of employees without the employees' consent.[89] It is always possible, however, to change the terms of existing employment contracts or to terminate existing employment relationships by mutual agreement of the successor employer and the affected employees.

In cases where only part of an enterprise is transferred, the successor employer and the former employer are jointly and severally liable for all obligations resulting from the employment relationships existing prior to the transfer. In cases where the whole enterprise is transferred, all liability for obligations resulting from existing employment relationships rests solely with the new employer.

As a formal requirement, both the existing and the future employer must notify trade unions operating in their enterprises of the transfer of undertakings, indicating the planned date of the transfer, the reasons for the transfer, and the transfer's legal, economic, and social effects for the employees. If there are no trade unions

---

[85]*See* Labor Code, art. 23^1.

[86]Judgment of the Supreme Court (Apr. 28, 1997), I PKN 122/97; Judgment of the Supreme Court (Sept. 29, 1995), I PRN 38/95.

[87]Judgment of the Supreme Court (Sept. 28, 1990), I PR 152/90.

[88]Labor Code, arts. 42, 43.

[89]Judgment of the Supreme Court (May 17, 1995), I PRN 9/95.

operating in the enterprise, the notification must be made to the employees directly. In both cases the notification must be made at least 30 days prior to the planned date of the transfer. The employees whose enterprise has been transferred may terminate the employment contract with the new employer upon seven-days' advance notice within two months of the transfer.

2. *Effects on Collective Agreements*

According to the Labor Code, when an enterprise is transferred in whole or in part, the provisions of any collective agreement then in force remain applicable for one year from the day of the transfer.[90] Although formally the successor employer does not become party to the existing collective agreement, the employer is bound by the agreement's terms and conditions and may not modify its provisions. Of course, the new employer may elect to apply terms that are more favorable than those set forth in the existing collective agreement.

Additionally, after the expiration of the collective agreement, the existing terms of employment legally remain in force until changed or terminated pursuant to the general rules provided by the Labor Code.[91]

V. WAGES, HOURS, AND LEAVE

A. Wages

1. *General Rules for Remuneration*

Polish labor law imposes few specific limits on the elements or amount of remuneration for work. One important restriction is that the employee's basic pay may not be lower than the minimum amount determined by the applicable regulations.[92] The law also guarantees extra pay for overtime and for work performed at night.[93]

---

[90]Labor Code, art. 241^8.

[91]*Id.* arts. 241^7, 241^9.

[92]The Minimum Wage Act, dated October 10, 2002, published in Dz.U. 200/02, item 1679. The current minimum wage for 2004 is 824 PLN.

[93]See V.B., below.

The general rule stated by the Labor Code is that remuneration for work is to correspond with the type of work performed and the qualifications or skills required for its performance.[94] Thus, there are no provisions linking pay raises to the rate of inflation or other index, except for some specific situations.[95]

Another general rule is that remuneration is due to the employee for work performed. For any period of nonperformance, the employee retains the right to remuneration only when provided by the labor laws or regulations.[96] The employee also is entitled to regular remuneration in cases where he or she was ready to perform, but was prevented from doing so by reasons attributable to the employer (e.g., a shutdown or other break in the work process). The employee is not entitled to remuneration for making defective products or for unsatisfactory performance.[97]

Employees generally are paid in cash and must receive regular pay at intervals of no more than one month, on the same day of the month, fixed in advance, except for those elements that are paid for a longer period.[98]

Any employer employing at least 20 employees is required to fix the conditions of remuneration and allocation of other work-related benefits in the form of the company's bylaws.

2. *Protection of Remuneration*

As a general rule, employees may not waive their right to remuneration or transfer such right to another person. Basic pay, along with all other elements of remuneration, is fully protected by law. As a result, apart from statutory deductions made for personal income tax and pension and health contributions, items (and their amounts) that may be deducted from remuneration without the employee's consent are strictly limited by law.[99]

---

[94]Labor Code, art. 78.

[95]Act on Determining the Amounts for Remuneration in the Public Sector (Dec. 23, 1999), Dz.U. No. 110/99, item 1255, with subsequent amendments.

[96]See V.C., below.

[97]Labor Code, arts. 80–82.

[98]*Id.* art. 85.

[99]*Id.* arts. 87–91.

B. Hours

1. *Working Time*

For most employees, rules regulating working time are set forth in Chapter VI of the Labor Code.[100] In principle, working time is based on a five-day workweek. The standard workweek may not exceed 40 hours per workweek and 8 hours per day, on average, within an account (clearing) period not exceeding four months, as adopted by the particular employer.

Weekly working time including overtime hours may not exceed 48 hours on average within an account period (clearing period) adopted by the employer. The employee is entitled in each week to a continuous rest break of 35 hours, covering at least 11 hours of continuous rest per each 24 hours. As a rule, the rest break should include Sunday.

Within a company, the specific time of work for employees, or for certain groups of employees, is flexible. The law provides various possibilities in this matter. For instance, if justified by the type of work or organization, e.g., health service, catering, or hotels, the daily working time may be extended up to 12 hours. However, even where the daily working time is extended, it is always required that within an account period, the employee's working time may not exceed the statutory standards noted above. As a result, extended working time is compensated by additional time off. So long as these rules are followed, work within the extended work limits is not considered as overtime work.

Employees may be employed on a full-time or part-time basis. The law does not provide specific restrictions in this respect.

If the daily working time is at least six hours, the employer is required to allow a break of at least 15 minutes. This break is counted as working time.[101] Additionally, the employer may introduce an additional break of up to 60 minutes for a meal or for an employee to deal with personal matters. This break may be introduced in the employment contract, a collective agreement, or the enterprise's other internal regulations. Unlike the 15-minute break,

---

[100] *Id.* arts. 128–151^{12}.

[101] Labor Code, art. 134.

which must be allowed if the daily working time exceeds six hours, the additional break is not to be counted as working time.[102]

2. *Overtime*

Work performed in excess of the standard working time constitutes overtime.[103] Formally, overtime is allowed only in case of (1) particular needs of the company (limited to 150 hours per year), or (2) the necessity of organizing a rescue group to save people's lives or health, or to protect the company's property by repairing a breakdown (not limited).

Effective as of January 1, 2004, the total working time per week, including overtime work, may not exceed 48 hours on average.[104] Given the standard workweek of 40 hours on average, this means that the maximum average amount of overtime hours per week should not exceed 8 hours. Additionally, the number of overtime hours worked per one calendar year may not exceed 150 although the Labor Code provides for a possibility of extending this limit in individual employment contracts, collective agreements, and/or the enterprise's other internal regulations.

In exchange for overtime work, an employee is entitled to additional pay at the following rates:

- *for work performed overtime on weekdays, Sundays, and holidays that are usually the employee's working days:* 50 percent of the employee's usual remuneration (based on the individual hourly or monthly rate);
- *for work performed overtime at night, on Sundays, and on holidays that are not working days for the employee, as well as for work on days off provided in exchange for work on Sundays or holidays which are working days for the employee:* 100 percent of the employee's remuneration (based on the individual hourly or monthly rate).

As compensation for overtime, the employer may, if the employee so requests, grant the employee time off for an equivalent number of hours. Also, the employer may solely decide (i.e. with-

[102] *Id.* art. 141.
[103] *Id.* arts. 151-151^{6}.
[104] *Id.* art. 131.

out the employee's request in the respect) to grant the employee time off for overtime work. In such a case, the amount of time off must be 50% greater than the number of overtime hours worked. In either case, the employee is not entitled to additional overtime pay.

Separate rules regarding overtime are provided for senior staff: employees holding managerial positions may, if needed, be required to work overtime. In principle, they are not entitled to separate wages and additional pay, except in the case of overtime work on Sundays and official holidays performed by managers of lower rank.[105]

Overtime work is forbidden for minors (employees younger than 18 years of age) and pregnant women. An employee taking care of a child younger than four years of age may be employed overtime only upon his or her consent.

3. *Work on Sundays and Official Holidays*

By statute, Sundays and official holidays are days free from work.[106] Performance of work on these days is permissible only in situations specified by the Labor Code. These situations include, *inter alia*:

- work in businesses that operate on a continuous basis;
- the performance of necessary repairs;
- the performance of necessary public services;
- transport and public transportation;
- work in the catering, hotel, and health service industries; and
- work in businesses providing cultural, educational, tourist, and recreational activities.

In exchange for work performed on Sunday or on official holidays, the employer must allow the employee another day off during the following week. The day should be granted:

---

[105] *Id.* art. 151^4.
[106] *Id.* arts. 151^9–151^{12}.

- for work performed on Sundays—within six calendar days preceding or following such Sundays; and
- for work performed on official holidays—until the end of the current clearing (account) period.

In companies where work regularly is performed on Sundays, the employee is entitled to have at least one Sunday off every four weeks. So long as the employee is allowed a day off, the law does not require extra pay for work performed on Sundays or official holidays, unless it is overtime work. Commonly, however, extra pay is provided for by collective agreements or in an employer's remuneration bylaws. If the employee is not provided with a day off, he or she is entitled to extra pay at the rate of 100 percent of regular wages.

4. *Night Work*

According to the Labor Code, night time means any eight-hour period between 9 p.m. and 7 a.m. These definitional parameters are obligatory, and an employer may not extend or reduce them. Within these parameters, the period of night work is determined by the employer's internal regulations (for example, from 10 p.m. to 6 a.m.) adopted upon consultation with trade unions or employee representatives.

The Labor Code[107] defines an employee working at night as one who works at least three hours during night time or at least one-quarter of whose working time is counted as night time. The total working time of such an employee may not exceed eight hours per day if the employee performs particularly dangerous work or work requiring considerable physical or mental effort. A list of such work is determined by the employer upon consultation with trade unions or employee representatives.

An employee who works at night is entitled to extra pay for each night time working hour, in the amount of 20 percent of the hourly wage established by the applicable regulations.[108] Fre-

[107]*Id.* art. 151^7.

[108]See V.A.1., above.

quently, however, higher pay for night work is provided by collective agreements or by remuneration bylaws.

Night work is forbidden for minors (employees younger than age 18) and pregnant women. An employee taking care of a child younger than four years of age may be employed at night only upon his or her consent.

C. Leave

1. Vacation Leave

Pursuant to the Labor Code each employee is entitled to annual, continuous paid vacation leave. The employer is under an obligation to grant the vacation leave to the employee in the calendar year in which the employee acquired the right to the vacation leave. Vacation leave that the employee has not used in a given calendar year should be granted until the end of the first quarter of the next calendar year at the latest. As a rule, the employee acquires the right to vacation leave in each calendar year (i.e. on January 1 each year).

The length of vacation leave is as follows:[109]

- if the employee's total length of employment is less than 10 years: 20 days; or
- if the employee's total length of employment equals at least 10 years: 26 days.

For the purposes of calculating vacation time, all of the employee's previous employment time (including employment with both present and former employers), as well as the period of his or her post-primary education, are included in the period of employment. For instance, an employee who graduates from an academic school is entitled to add 8 years of academic education to his or her total period of employment for the purposes of calculating the length of vacation leave. Neither interruptions in employment, nor the manner of termination of the employment relationship, have any negative effect on the employee's right to

[109]Labor Code, art. 154.

vacation. The leave should be granted on the employee's working days, depending on the individual working schedule. As a result, these may be weekdays as well as Sundays or even official holidays, as long as they are usual working days for a given employee. When the employee becomes entitled to vacation time, it does not mean that he or she may automatically take it; it is the employer who grants vacation. Formally, vacation time should be granted in a lump and vacation may be taken in parts only at the employee's request. However, even with the employee's request, one portion of the vacation time should last for an uninterrupted period of at least 14 days. The specific periods of vacation time in a given calendar year should be settled under a schedule worked out by the employer in consultation with the company's trade union(s) or through an agreement with the employee. Both the employee's request and the necessity to ensure normal process of work must be taken into consideration. However, the employee may also request leave without needing the employer's prior approval.[110] In such a case the employer is obliged to grant vacation time, but the duration of such leave is limited only to four days per calendar year.

In the event of termination of the employment contract, the employee has the right to receive vacation time only in proportion to the time the employee worked for the employer during the year of termination. This solution may work to the benefit of a new employer, i.e., in the event that a departing employee has taken vacation leave in excess of the proportional time worked for the former employer, the employee would be entitled to vacation leave from a new employer for a proportionately shorter time, and if the employee has already used the full yearly vacation allotment at the time of termination, he or she would not be entitled to any additional vacation leave from the subsequent employer during the same year.

During the notice period in a pending termination, the employee is obliged to take the vacation leave to which the employee is entitled if the employer grants such leave.[111] The employee cannot refuse to take the leave. When vacation leave cannot be taken

---

[110] *Id.* art. 167^2–167^3.

[111] Labor Code, art. 167^1.

in whole or in part due to termination of the employment relationship, the employee acquires the right to be compensated for the unused vacation time. The amount of compensation due is calculated on the basis of the employee's regular rate of remuneration.

2. *Maternity Leave*

Pursuant to the Labor Code, an employee is entitled to maternity leave due to the fact of childbirth.[112] The right to maternity leave may not be restricted based on the seniority of the employee, the type of employment relationship, or the type of work.

Under the Labor Code employees are entitled to 16 weeks of maternity leave for a single birth, 18 weeks of maternity leave for the birth of twins, or 26 weeks for the birth of triplets or other multiples.

In a case of adoption, the employee who takes care of the child and who applied to the court for the adoption is entitled to 16 weeks of maternity leave, although no longer than the time the child attains 12 months of age.

At least two weeks of maternity leave may be taken before the anticipated date of birth. The employee-mother, after taking at least 14 weeks of maternity leave, may forego the remainder of the leave. In such a case, an employee-father is entitled, upon a written request, to take the remaining portion of the maternity leave that has not been taken by the employee-mother.

For the period of maternity leave, the employee is entitled to a maternity benefit in the amount of 100 percent of the pay received at the time directly preceding the leave.[113] During the maternity leave, the employee is protected against an employer's notice of termination, except in specific situations of employer liquidation or bankruptcy.[114]

3. *Childcare Leave*

In addition to maternity leave, the employer is required, at the request of the employee, to grant an unpaid leave for personal

---

[112]*Id.* arts. 180–184.

[113]Act on Pecuniary Benefits in Case of Sickness and Maternity (June 25, 1999), published in Dz.U. No. 60/99, item 636, with subsequent amendments.

[114]Labor Code, art. 177.

childcare.[115] To qualify for this leave, the employee must be employed and his or her total period of employment, including all previous employment and any period of maternity leave, must be at least six months. Except for some specific situations,[116] the maximum duration of childcare leave is three years, and may last no longer than the time the child reaches age four.

During the period of childcare leave, the employer is not allowed to terminate the employee's employment contract. The only exceptions are liquidation or bankruptcy of the employer, or other reasons identified in the Collective Dismissal Law.[117] An employee returning from childcare leave is entitled to a job in the same position or—if that is impossible—in an equal position or in another position adequate to his or her skills, with a wage rate not lower than the rate scheduled for the position held immediately prior to the leave.

Depending on the family's financial situation, an employee may be eligible to receive a childcare allowance during the period of leave.[118]

4. *Other Leaves of Absence*

An employee is entitled to take time off work, with full pay, for important personal reasons recognized by the labor laws and regulations.[119] For instance, the employee is entitled to:

- two days for marriage;
- two days on the birth of his child;
- one day on the marriage of a child;
- two days for the death and funeral of his or her spouse, child, mother, or father; and

[115] *Id.* arts. 186–186[7].

[116] In cases where the child requires permanent personal care for health reasons, e.g., chronic disease or disability, the employee is entitled to additional leave for a maximum period of three years; however, the leave may be taken only until the child reaches age 18.

[117] See IV.A.1., above.

[118] See VIII.C., below.

[119] Ordinance of the Minister of Labor and Social Policy (May 15, 1996), Dz.U. No. 60/96, item 281.

- one day on the death and funeral of his or her sister, brother, mother-in-law, father-in-law, grandmother, grandfather, or any other person in the employee's care.

5. *Unpaid Leave*

Pursuant to the Labor Code,[120] on the written request of an employee, the employer may grant the employee unpaid leave. The period of such leave is not restricted by law. The employee is not required to justify his or her request for unpaid leave, although the decision whether to grant the unpaid leave is left to the employer's discretion. The period of any unpaid leave is not included in the period of employment on which employees' rights depend.

As a specific form of unpaid leave, the employer may, with the employee's consent, allow the employee unpaid leave to undertake work for another employer, pursuant to an arrangement made for this purpose between the two employers. In this case, the period of unpaid leave is included in the employment period that determines the employee's rights in relation to the current employer.[121]

In addition to the above, there are certain other situations in which the employer is required to grant unpaid leave to an employee, for example, to carry out his or her duties on a trade union board,[122] to participate in military training, or to serve as a congressman or senator.

VI. ANTIDISCRIMINATION

A. Introduction

The issue of discrimination based on specific characteristics, such as race, gender, age, or disability, is a constitutional matter in

---

[120]Labor Code, art. 174.

[121]*Id.* art. 174^1.

[122]Act on Trade Unions (May 23, 1991), Dz.U. No. 55/91, item 234, with subsequent amendments.

Poland. Chapter II of the Polish Constitution[123] sets forth a citizen's rights and duties, which include the right to equal treatment by public authorities. As a fundamental rule, no one may be discriminated against for any reason in political, social, or economic life.[124] The Constitution also establishes the right to equal remuneration for work of the same value, the right to social security, the right to hold the same positions and functions, and the right to receive public honors, irrespective of an employee's gender.[125]

The Labor Code follows the constitutional framework by specifically prohibiting any discrimination in employment relations because of gender, age, disability, race, religion, nationality, political views, trade union membership, ethnic background, religious beliefs, sexual orientation, or employment for a definite or an indefinite period, full-time or part-time.[126]

1. *Equal Treatment*

Under the Labor Code, all employees have the right to equal treatment with respect to conclusion and termination of the employment contract, employment conditions, and access to professional training. Equal treatment consists of non-discrimination on the grounds mentioned in the paragraph above. Discrimination may be direct if the employee was, is, or could be treated less advantageously in a comparable situation than another employee, or it may be indirect if, as a result of a seemingly neutral arrangement, criterion applied, or action undertaken, there is disproportion in employment conditions to the disadvantage of all or a considerable number of employees, where such disproportion may not be justified by other objective grounds.

The definition of discrimination also covers harassment (widely defined as any conduct that aims at or results in the violation of an employee's dignity, humiliation, or abasement of the employee), including sexual harassment, as well as conduct aimed at encouraging someone else to violate the equality of treatment.

---

[123]Constitution of the Republic of Poland (Apr. 2, 1997), Dz.U. No. 78/97, item 483 (July 16, 1997) (Constitution).

[124]*Id.* art. 32.

[125]*Id.* art. 33.

[126]*Id.* art. 11^3.

An employer's action resulting in differentiation of an employee's status as against other employees does not violate the rule of equal treatment as long as said action may be justified by objective reasons. The Labor Code provides certain specific exceptions in this respect, allowing the following situations:

- determination of conditions related to employment and remuneration and promotion of employees as well as access to professional training, based on their experience;
- differentiation of an employee's legal status for reasons related to parenthood (maternity) protection, age, or disability;
- alteration of employment conditions with respect to working time if such alteration is justified by reasons unrelated to employees; or
- non-employment of a person for reasons otherwise constituting discrimination if it is justified by the kind of work, conditions related to performance of such work, or professional requirements.

An employee affected by discrimination has the right to compensation in an amount not lower than one month's minimum wage,[127] while the maximum amount of compensation for discrimination is not limited in the Labor Code.

2. *Mobbing*

An employee should also be protected from mobbing at his or her place of work. The employer is required to prevent mobbing in the enterprise.[128] Mobbing is defined as actions or behavior relating to an employee or directed against the employee resulting in persistent harassment or intimidation of the employee, causing the employee to develop a low assessment of his or her professional capacities and resulting in or aimed at humiliating, ridiculing, isolating or eliminating the employee from the staff. The employer is under a duty to prevent such conduct in the

[127]Dated Oct. 10, 2002, published in Dz.U. No. 200/02, item 1679.

[128]Labor Code, art. 94^3.

enterprise's premises. An employee who falls victim to such conduct and suffers health problems as a consequence may sue the employer for compensation for harm sustained. Additionally, if mobbing led to termination of the employment contract by the employee, the employee may demand to be compensated by the employer in an amount no lower than one month's minimum wage.

B. Age

1. Minors

The Labor Code defines minors as persons between 16 and 18 years of age. Employment of a person younger than age 16 is prohibited, except for certain specific situations mentioned below. Minors may be employed only under certain conditions. Specifically, employers are allowed to employ only those minors who have completed their primary education, and who have submitted a medical certificate stating that the intended work will not be hazardous to their health. Also, a minor who is not certified to work in a particular occupation may be employed only for the purpose of occupational training.

The labor regulations also provide for specific situations in which a person who is not yet 16 years of age, and who has completed primary education, may be employed (mainly to do simple jobs), as well as those in which an employed minor may be exempt from the duty to attain further education.[129]

As a rule, minors may be employed to perform occupational training or for other limited purposes, i.e., light works. Terms and conditions of employment of minors to perform light work are fully adjusted to EU directives in that field.[130] Under the new regulations, light work performed by a minor may not be dangerous to the minor's life, health, or growth, and may not impose undue burdens on the minor's education. A minor in school may not be employed for more than 12 hours per week. During vacation periods, working time may be extended, but may not exceed seven

---

[129]Ordinance of the Minister of Labor and Social Policy (May 29, 1996), Dz.U. No. 62/96, item 291.

[130]Council Directive 94/33/EC of June 22, 1994, on the Protection of Young People at Work, 1994 O.J. (L 216) 12.

hours per day and 35 hours per week. A list of light-work occupations is established by the employer and is subject to approval by an occupational health doctor and the local labor inspector.

It is absolutely forbidden to employ minors at night or to work overtime. Minors also are prohibited from performing certain types of jobs. The Labor Code poses additional requirements with respect to the employment of minors, such as:

- an obligation to provide at least 48 hours per week time off (including Sunday), as needed for rest;
- a longer interval of night time work (at least 14 hours);[131]
- a shorter working day (limited to six or eight hours);
- longer vacation leave;[132] and
- a shorter entitlement period for the first annual vacation leave.

2. *Retired Workers*

As a rule, it is not forbidden to employ retired workers. Pursuant to general health and safety requirements,[133] they are subject to medical examination before being employed, and at the request of the employer, may be subject to periodic examinations during the course of their employment.

C. Gender and Pregnancy

Fundamental provisions of the Polish Constitution, as well as the Labor Code, mandate professional equality between men and women and prohibit discrimination based on gender or family status, unless expressly allowed by law.[134]

Under the provisions of the Labor Code,[135] women and men must be treated equally with respect to establishing or terminating the employment relationship, conditions of employment, career prospects, and access to training in order to improve professional

---

[131]See V.B.4., above.

[132]See V.C.1., above.

[133]See VII., below.

[134]Constitution, art. 33; Labor Code, arts. 11^2, 11^3.

[135]Labor Code arts. 18^{3a}–18^{3e}.

qualifications. The requirement for equal treatment of women and men also prohibits any types of gender discrimination whatsoever, direct or indirect.

As of January 1, 2004 the Labor Code contains express provisions regarding sexual harassment as a form of discrimination based on gender. Sexual harassment is defined as any unaccepted behavior of a sexual nature or relating to the employee's gender, the purposes or effect of which is abuse of dignity, humiliation, or abasement of the employee; such conduct may involve physical, verbal or other than verbal elements. An employee suffering sexual harassment is entitled to compensation in an amount not lower than one month's minimum wage, while the maximum amount of compensation for discrimination is not limited in the Labor Code.

Polish law sets forth certain restrictions on work that may be performed by women.[136] Women are particularly protected from having to perform certain types of physical work. They also are protected during pregnancy and maternity from performing certain types of jobs, night work, or overtime work. These provisions are discussed in greater detail below.

Pregnant women may not be employed to work overtime or at night. It is not permitted to assign a pregnant woman outside her normal place of work (i.e., as defined in her employment contract) without her consent. When she is taking care of her child younger than four years of age, her consent is necessary to employ her at night, for overtime, or outside the normal workplace. Also, the employer is obliged to transfer a pregnant employee to another job if her normal job is of a nature prohibited during pregnancy,[137] or upon presentation of a medical certificate prohibiting her from performing a particular job based on the individual course of her pregnancy. A pregnant woman is entitled to a supplementary allowance if her pay is lowered as a result of a necessary job transfer.

An employer also is required to give the pregnant employee time off from work to undergo medical tests and examinations

---

[136]Certain issues concerning the protection of women in the workforce are regulated by Chapter VIII of the Labor Code, arts. 176–189.

[137]*See* The List of Jobs Prohibited for Women, Ordinance of the Council of Ministers (Sept. 10, 1996), Dz.U. No. 114/96, item 545.

connected with the pregnancy if such medical exams cannot be performed outside working hours. For the time of such absence, the employee retains her right to remuneration.

Pregnant employees, as well as employees on maternity leave and childcare leave, are protected against dismissal. For a termination with notice, this protection applies during the length of the notice period, which becomes ineffective when a woman supplies a medical certificate of pregnancy. Termination of a contract of employment without notice, e.g., a disciplinary termination, requires consent of the company's trade union. If a contract of employment is one for a definite time and would terminate after the third month of pregnancy, the contract is automatically extended to the day of confinement. A declaration of insolvency or liquidation allows an employer to terminate an employment contract during pregnancy or maternity leave, although the specific termination date must be settled with the trade union.

D. Disability

Apart from the general constitutional and statutory prohibitions against discrimination discussed above, disabled workers are protected by specific labor law regulations.[138] In addition, the rights of disabled persons have been guaranteed and confirmed in the Polish Parliament's Resolution of August 1, 1997, entitled "The Charter of Rights of Disabled Persons."[139] These various regulations, all of which are based on and correspond to EU standards,[140] set forth antidiscrimination policies relating to the participation of disabled persons in public, social, economic, and cultural life. Among other things, these provisions guarantee the disabled the right to work according to their qualifications and possibilities. All of these provisions implement EU standards. Enforcement of

---

[138]Basic regulations are provided under the Act on Professional and Social Rehabilitation and on Employment of Disabled Individuals (Aug. 27, 1997), Dz.U. No. 123/97, item 776, with subsequent amendments.

[139]Published in *Monitor Polski* No. 5, item 475.

[140]*See* Compendium on Member States' Policies on Equality of Opportunity for People with Disabilities, European Commission Report (June 30, 1999), Directorate General V.

these rights is carried out by means of certain preferential rules. For example:

- working time may not exceed 8 hours daily and 40 hours weekly, and for persons disabled to a considerable or moderate extent, 7 and 35 hours, respectively;
- disabled workers may not be required to work at night or overtime;
- disabled workers are entitled to an additional 15-minute break, with pay, for rest or therapeutic exercise, to longer annual vacation leave, and to take paid time off for therapeutic trips of up to 21 days once per year;
- the employer of a certain number of disabled persons, or an employer that manages an enterprise qualified as a Disabled Persons Enterprise (*Zakład Pracy Chronionej*)[141] can receive a refund of costs connected with creating special work conditions for disabled employees;
- Disabled Persons Enterprises are allowed significant tax exemptions, provided they employ a certain number of disabled workers; and
- companies employing at least 25 workers are obliged to make monthly payments to the State Fund for the Rehabilitation of Disabled.

VII. OCCUPATIONAL SAFETY AND HEALTH

Article 15 of the Labor Code obligates employers to provide and maintain health and safety standards in the workplace. This general rule is elaborated on in Chapter X of the Labor Code (Work Safety and Hygiene) and other executive acts.[142] Generally, these

---

[141]To qualify as a Disabled Persons Enterprise, a company must employ at least 25 persons, at least 40% of whom must be disabled, and must be adapted for the special needs of disabled persons, especially with respect to the availability of various facilities. The status of Disabled Persons Enterprise is granted by an administrative decision issued by the relevant governor.

[142]*See, e.g.*, Ordinance of the Minister of Labor and Social Policy (Sept. 26, 1997), Dz.U. No. 129/97, item 844; Ordinance of the Council of Ministers (Sept. 2, 1997), Dz.U. No. 109/97, item 704; Ordinance of the Minister of Labor and Social Policy (May 28, 1996), Dz.U. No. 62/96, item 285.

regulations impose on both employers and employees many detailed duties and obligations with respect to health and safety at work, as summarized below.

A. Employer's Duties

A fundamental duty of the employer is to protect the health and life of employees, by ensuring safe and hygienic work conditions, through the appropriate use and application of science and technology. In particular, the employer is required to do the following:

- instruct and acquaint employees with the rules, requirements, and procedures relating to health and safety at work;
- inform workers about any risk connected with the performed work;
- limit harmful factors in all work facilities;
- perform, at the employer's cost, periodic examinations of harmful work environment factors;
- ensure observance of safety rules by giving instructions to stop any rule violations and by supervising the implementation of such instructions; and
- ensure execution of orders, decisions, and other regulations of a public labor inspector and of any other officials supervising working conditions.

Employees who are not acquainted with health and safety regulations at their workplace or who do not possess the necessary skills must not be allowed to perform work. In addition, employees should be provided with protective clothing and other essentials; the washing and cleaning of protective clothing is the employer's responsibility.

When an employer is setting up or reorganizing a business organization or when it is installing new machinery or technical facilities, health and safety requirements must be taken into consideration.

Employers also are obligated to provide medical care for employees, through medical examinations performed before employment and then periodically thereafter. The employer is required, when given a medical certificate stating that the employee has become unable to perform his or her job because of a work accident or occupational disease, to move that employee to another suitable post.

B. Employee's Duties

A basic duty of employees is to observe the provisions and rules of work safety and hygiene. In particular, employees are obligated to do the following:

- become familiar with safety regulations, attend safety training and teaching, and take any required test or examinations;
- ensure the proper condition of machines, facilities, tools, equipment, etc.;
- use the means of personal protection provided (clothes, shoes, etc.);
- undergo periodic tests and other medical examinations; and
- notify a supervisor of any accident or hazard to human life or health observed in the workplace.

The labor laws also impose specific duties on employees holding managerial positions who are in a position to be especially well acquainted with matters of health and safety.

C. Accidents at Work and Occupational Diseases

1. Covered Accidents and Diseases

The rules governing accidents at work and occupational diseases have changed considerably as a result of adoption of the Social Insurance of Accidents at Work and Occupational Diseases Act,[143] which became effective January 1, 2003. The Act partly abolished the employer's liability for such accidents and diseases, based on broad insurance risk principles, and introduced a scheme where all allowances and benefits due to the employee as a result of suffering an accident or a disease are financed from an Accident Fund within the Social Insurance Fund.[144]

---

[143]Dated Oct. 30, 2002, published in Dz.U. No. 199/02, item 1673.

[144]See VIII.B.2.c, below.

An accident at work is defined as a sudden event caused by external factors and taking place in connection with work.

To be considered work-related, an accident need not take place within the premises of the business for coverage to apply; the employee also is covered when at the employer's disposal in other circumstances, e.g., while on a business trip. The employer is under an obligation to comply with detailed rules of conduct governing the procedure for determination of the circumstances and causes of the accident at work as well as to maintain appropriate documentation and records. Each case of a fatal or severe accident at work or of an accident involving one or more employees must be reported without delay to the competent labor inspector and the public prosecutor.

An occupational disease usually appears as a consequence of a long-time exposure to harmful substances in connection with the work performed. Occupational diseases include only those diseases listed in the Annex to the Regulation by the Council of Ministers of July 20, 2002. [145] In addition, the disease must have occurred as a result of harmful factors existing in the work environment or in the manner of performing work.

2. *Employer Liability*

The scope of the employer's liability for consequences of an accident at work suffered by the employee has been reduced to resultant loss or damage to the employee's personal belongings or items indispensable for performance of work, except for mechanical vehicles and money. There are no exceptions to such liability; the employer will be liable irrespective of its own fault or lack thereof, even when the accident is solely the employee's fault.

Additionally, based on general principles of liability set forth in the Civil Code, the employer may be held liable for any damage or loss suffered by the employee or the employee's family members as a result of an accident at work or occupational disease, discussed above, that has not been covered by social insurance benefits and allowances.

---

[145] Dz.U. No. 132/02, item 1115.

3. *Indemnity*

Due to the limitation on the scope of employer's liability, an employee who has suffered an accident at work is entitled to receive compensation from the employer only for resultant loss or damage to his or her personal belongings or items indispensable for performance of work, except for mechanical vehicles and money. However, as discussed above, the employee or his or her family members also may try to seek indemnity pursuant to general liability principles set forth in the Civil Code.

D. Supervision and Enforcement

1. *State Labor Inspection (*Państwowa Inspekcja Pracy *or* PIP*)*

The supervision and enforcement of workplace safety and hygiene regulations is the main task of PIP, the State Labor Inspection.[146] PIP inspectors have authority to monitor and inspect all enterprises and other places of employment, and to examine working conditions and the safety of the workplace. If the inspectors find any violations of health and safety regulations, they have authority to:

- order the employer to eliminate the problems within a certain period of time;
- prohibit the business from continuing activities that pose a threat to life and health;
- prohibit the business from commencing an activity that would not conform to health and safety requirements; and
- impose fines on persons in charge where there is an evident violation of workplace safety and hygiene rules.

2. *Voluntary Labor Inspection*

In addition to PIP, Voluntary Labor Inspections operate in enterprises where trade unions have been formed.[147] These inspec-

---

[146]For a general discussion of PIP's organization and responsibilities, see the Introduction, at C.1., above.

[147]For a general discussion of the Voluntary Labor Inspection, see the Introduction, at C.2., above.

tions are comprised of voluntary inspectors elected by the employees within an enterprise, or within particular departments of an enterprise, or within union groups. The main task of the voluntary inspectors is to ensure observance of rules and requirements relating to workplace health and safety. The inspectors can control safety, hygiene, and technical conditions of work, and cooperate with the employer to prevent accidents and diseases. The difference between PIP and the Voluntary Labor Inspection is that the voluntary inspectors deal only with matters relating to a particular enterprise, in cooperation with the PIP inspectors.

3. *Work Safety and Hygiene Service and Commission*[148]

Under the Labor Code, every employer employing more than 100 employees is required to establish a Work Safety and Hygiene Service (*Służba Bezpieczeństwa i Higieny Pracy*) as a consulting, executive, and supervisory body to deal with workplace safety and hygiene. In companies employing up to 100 employees, the above tasks may be performed by any employee appointed by the employer and having or obtaining the appropriate qualifications in work safety and hygiene matters or by an outside specialist in this subject area. In very small companies, i.e., those employing up to 10—or, in certain situations, 20—employees, the tasks of the Work Safety and Hygiene Service may be performed directly by an employer who completes the required work safety and hygiene training program.

Every employer employing more than 250 employees is subject to an additional requirement to create a Work Safety and Hygiene Commission (*Komisja Bezpieczeństwa i Higieny Pracy*). The Commission consists of the members of the Work Safety and Hygiene Service, a doctor providing medical care to the employees, a voluntary labor inspector, and additional employee representatives. The Commission acts as an advisory and consulting body, and is charged with examining health and safety conditions in the workplace and evaluating the employer's efforts toward improving them.

---

[148]The organization and responsibilities of the Work Safety and Hygiene Service and the Work Safety and Hygiene Commission are regulated by Articles 237^{11}–237^{13a} of the Labor Code, and the Ordinance of the Council of Ministers (Sept. 2, 1997), Dz.U. No. 109, item 704. See also III.B. and III.C., above.

VIII. PENSIONS AND BENEFITS

As of January 1, 1999, the Polish government implemented a long awaited reform of the social insurance system, the integral and the most important part of which is the pension system. Reform of the Polish pension system is one of the biggest and most significant reforms in Poland since the 1989 elections. The reform is intended to secure fair maintenance for retired persons, decrease state spending on the social security system, and reduce employer expenditures. It also should create more self-responsibility among Polish workers for their own financial security. The reform is a great legislative challenge. New acts adopted by the Polish Parliament to implement this reform[149] introduced to the Polish legal system several new legal institutions and concepts, the full impact of which will only be possible to judge over the next few years. Acts of law constituting the basis of the new social insurance system have been amended on many occasions since 1999, which resulted from the need to modernize the scheme of pensions and benefits and adapt Polish regulations to the requirements of the European Union.

A. Pension System

The new pension reforms create a three-pillar system, based in general on the Latin American model. Each of the three pillars is discussed in detail below.

1. *First Pillar*

The first pillar is government administered by a reformed Social Insurance Office (ZUS under its Polish acronym). The purpose of this pillar is to secure a minimum pension level, protected from inflation. This first pillar is divided into the following funds:

---

[149] *See* Act on Pensions from Social Insurance Fund (Dec. 17, 1998), unified text published in Dz.U. No. 39/04, item 353; Act on Social Insurance System (Oct. 13, 1998), Dz.U. No. 137/98, item 887, with subsequent amendments; Act on Organization and Functioning of Retirement Pension Funds (Aug. 28, 1997), unified text published in Dz.U. No. 159/04, item 1667 with subsequent amendments; Act on Employees' Retirement Pension Plans (Apr. 20, 2004), Dz.U. No. 116/04, item 1207, with subsequent amendments.

- *Retirement Fund*: The contribution for retirement insurance amounts to 19.52 percent of the employee's full pay (subject to the maximum described below), and is paid in equal parts by the employer and the employee;
- *Disability Pension Fund*: The contribution for disability pension insurance amounts to 13 percent of full pay (subject to the maximum described below), and is paid in equal parts by the employer and the employee;
- *Sickness Fund*: The contribution for sickness insurance amounts to 2.45 percent of full pay, and is paid in total by the employee; and
- *Accident Fund*: The contribution for accident insurance differs for individual employers, depending on the level of occupational hazards and their effects in the particular enterprise. The contribution amounts range from 0.4 percent to 8.12 percent of full pay, and are paid in total by the employer.[150]

The contributions for retirement insurance and disability pension insurance are limited by a maximum amount per annum, equal to 30 times the average monthly remuneration predicted in the national economy for a given year. Once an employee's pay equals this limit, no insurance contributions are made for additional amounts earned by the employee during the calendar year.

Additionally, employers are required to make monthly payments equal to 2.45 percent of employees' monthly wages as a contribution to the Labor Fund,[151] and 0.15 percent of monthly

[150]Ordinance of the Minister of Labor on variation of rates of contribution to social insurance of accidents at work and occupational diseases (Nov. 29, 2002), Dz. U. 200/02, item 1692.

[151]Act on Promotion of Employment and Labor Market Institutions (Apr. 20, 2004), Dz. U. 99/04, item 1001. The basic function of this state fund is to finance unemployment prevention projects and allowances and benefits for unemployed persons.

wages as a contribution to the Employees' Security Benefits Guarantee Fund.[152]

2. *Second Pillar*

The second pillar is based on several open pension funds, managed commercially by strong financial institutions (Pension Societies). The purpose of the second pillar is to create secure, full pensions utilizing private fund management and employee-directed contributions. To accomplish this, a portion of the retirement insurance contribution designated for the first pillar (7.3 percent of the contribution amount) is directed to the open pension fund selected by the employee. The compulsory character of the second pillar contribution depends on the age of the employee. For young employees (born after December 31, 1968), this system is compulsory. For middle-aged employees (born after December 31, 1948, and before January 1, 1969), the system is voluntary. The oldest employees (born before January 1, 1949) are not allowed to participate in this program.

3. *Third Pillar*

The third pillar is voluntary in nature and is intended as a means to institutionalize pension plans offered by employers for their employees. Employers have the option to offer their employees the opportunity to participate, on a voluntary basis, in various forms of additional pension savings, e.g., employee pension funds, group life insurance policies, investment funds, etc. All forms utilize professional asset management, and are fully funded and without credit risk to the employer. Under this program, the employer withholds contributions for individual employee accounts from employees' net salaries.

---

[152]Act on Employees' Claims Protection in Case of Employer's Insolvency (Dec. 29, 1993), Dz.U. No. 9/02, item 85, with subsequent amendments. The basic function of this fund is to satisfy employees' claims in case of employer insolvency.

B. Social Insurance Benefits and Allowances

1. General

The Act on Social Insurance System,[153] which took effect on January 1, 1999, is pivotal in the reformed social insurance system. This law sets forth general principles of social insurance, the function and goals of institutions engaged in social insurance, the means of financing the social insurance system, and the amount and manner of collecting contributions. The fundamental feature of the national social insurance scheme is its obligatory character. As a result, by virtue of law, all employees are insured automatically at the moment of entering into an employment relation until the day of termination, irrespective of the ultimate reason for termination.

Each employee covered by the compulsory insurance system is subject to reporting requirements. As a rule, the obligation for reporting rests with the employer. Employers also are required to calculate the contributions due for social insurance for each of their employees, deduct the contributions from the employee's pay, and forward them to the Social Insurance Office (ZUS), along with the employer's required contribution.

ZUS is primarily responsible for administering the national social insurance program. Any disputes that may arise between ZUS and the employers or the employees are settled by the Provincial Labor and Social Insurance Court in the first instance and by the courts of appeal in the second instance.[154]

2. Benefits and Allowances

The social insurance program provides comprehensive social benefits and allowances to all employees and their beneficiaries, in situations specified by law. The social insurance program can be divided into the following three groups of benefits: (1) sick-

---

[153]Dated Oct. 13, 1998, Dz.U. No. 137/98, item 887, with subsequent amendments.

[154]For a description of the Polish court system, see the Introduction, at D.2., above.

ness and maternity benefits, (2) pension benefits, and (3) benefits in case of accidents at work and occupational diseases.

a. Sickness and Maternity Benefits

Sickness and maternity benefits include the following benefits and allowances, payable from the Sickness Fund within the Social Insurance Fund:[155]

- *Sickness Benefit*: The employee is entitled to receive a sickness benefit in an amount of 80 percent of remuneration if the period of incapacity to work due to illness lasts longer than 33 days per calendar year. This benefit is increased to 100 percent of remuneration in case of an accident on the way from or to work, disease during pregnancy, or illness lasting for a period of 90 days without interruption. The employee is entitled to this benefit for the period of incapacity, but no longer than six months. This period may be extended for a maximum of three months, provided that further treatment of the employee is likely to restore his or her capacity to work. If the incapacity is shorter than 33 days, the employee is entitled to receive 80 percent of the remuneration (increased to 100 percent in case of an accident on the way from or to work or disease during pregnancy), which is paid by the employer from its own funds.
- *Rehabilitation Benefit*: An employee who has exhausted his or her sickness benefit and is still unable to work is entitled to a rehabilitation allowance if further treatment is likely to restore his or her capacity to work. The rehabilitation allowance is payable for a maximum period of 12 months in an amount equal to 75% of an employee's remuneration.
- *Compensatory Allowance*: The compensatory allowance may be granted to an employee with diminished ability to work, whose pay has decreased as a result of participating in professional rehabilitation to adapt or train for a specific job. The compensatory allowance is payable throughout the rehabilitation period, up to a maximum of 24 months.

---

[155] Act on Pecuniary Benefits in Case of Sickness and Maternity (June 25, 1999), Dz.U. No. 60/99, item 636, with subsequent amendments.

- *Maternity Benefit*: For the period of maternity leave, an employee is entitled to a maternity benefit in an amount equal to 100 percent of her remuneration.
- *Care-taking Allowance*: This allowance may be paid to an employee who takes leave from work to provide necessary care to a child younger than age eight, to a sick child younger than age 14, or to another sick member of the family. The allowance is limited to a maximum of 60 days per calendar year if the care is provided for the employee's children, or 14 days per calendar year if the care is provided for other family members. The care-taking allowance amounts to 80 percent of the employee's remuneration.

b. Pension Benefits

The group of pension benefits[156] includes the following benefits and allowances:

- *Old Age Retirement Pension*: This pension is payable to employees who have retired from work. As a rule, for persons born after December 31, 1968, the retirement age is 60 years for women, and 65 years for men. The amount of an old age retirement pension is based on the total amount of contributions made to the individual employee's account, under the three-pillar system discussed immediately above.
- *Disability Pension*: This pension is payable to eligible employees who are unable to work as the result of a qualifying disability. To be eligible for a disability pension, employees must satisfy minimum service requirements (e.g., three years for employees who become incapacitated between ages 22 and 25). The determination of a qualifying disability is made by a medical commission appointed by the Social Insurance Office (ZUS) and charged with handling disability and employment matters. The amount of the pension depends on the percentage of disability, the age of the employee, and the length of covered employment.

[156]Act on Pensions from Social Insurance (Dec. 17, 1998), unified text published in Dz.U. No. 39-04, item 353.

- *Training Pension*: This pension is payable to employees who must change their skills as result of an incapacity to perform a previous job. Eligibility is determined by a medical commission appointed by ZUS. As a rule, this pension is paid for a six-month period, which may be extended up to 30 months. In comparison to the compensatory allowance payable from the Sickness Fund, this pension is used for training purposes only.
- *Family Pension*: This pension is payable to family members of an employee who dies. The death need not be work related. The amount of the pension depends on the number of eligible dependents: for one dependent, 85 percent of the remuneration previously paid to the deceased employee; for two dependents, 90 percent of remuneration; for three or more dependents, 95 percent of remuneration. Children of a deceased employee are eligible to receive the pension for the period of their education, up to age 25. The spouse and parents of a deceased employee may, if certain requirements are met, be eligible to receive the pension for life.
- *Funeral Allowance*: This allowance is paid to the person responsible for funeral expenses relating to the death of a covered employee, a person receiving an old age retirement pension or disability pension, or a member of the employee or pensioner's family. The amount of the allowance is 200 percent of the average monthly remuneration in Poland, as determined for purposes of the allowance.

c. *Benefits in Case of Accidents at Work and Occupational Diseases*

An employee who has suffered an accident at work or an occupational disease is entitled to the following benefits, payable from the Accident Fund within the Social Insurance Fund:[157]

[157]*See* Act on Social Insurance of Accidents at Work and Occupational Diseases (Oct. 30, 2002), Dz. U. 199/02, item 1673 with subsequent amendments. For a discussion of employer liability for work accidents and occupational diseases, see VII.C., above.

- *Single Indemnity*: The single indemnity is paid to (1) employees who suffer permanent or long-lasting damage to their health, or (2) family members of a deceased employee. Eligibility for a single indemnity is determined by a medical commission appointed by the Social Insurance Office (ZUS).
- *Disability Pension*: A disability pension is payable to employees whose disability is caused by an accident at work or an occupational disease. Disability is determined according to the principles and procedures described above in relation to the pension benefits scheme. The amount of the disability pension depends on the percentage of disability and the employee's remuneration prior to the accident or disease.
- *Training Pension*: This pension is payable to employees who are incapable of performing their previous job as a result of an occupational accident or disease, but who are not eligible for a disability pension. This allowance is determined according to the same rules applicable to the training pension described above as a pension benefit.
- *Family (Survivor's) Pension*: This allowance is payable to the family members of an employee who dies as a result of an occupational accident or disease. It is determined according to the principles described above for the family pension payable as a pension benefit, but the amount of this survivor's allowance may not be lower than 120 percent of the lowest family pension.
- *Sickness Benefit*: The sickness benefit is granted to employees for the period of inability to work resulting from an accident at work or an occupational disease. This benefit is equal to 100 percent of an employee's remuneration.
- *Rehabilitation Benefit:* An employee who has exhausted his or her sickness benefit granted as a result of an accident at work or an occupational disease and is still unable to work, is entitled to a rehabilitation allowance if further treatment is likely to restore the employee's capacity to work. The rehabilitation benefit is equal to 100 percent of the employee's remuneration.

- *Compensatory Allowance*: The compensatory allowance may be granted to an employee whose ability to work has diminished as a result of an accident at work or an occupational disease, leading to a decrease in remuneration. The allowance is payable during the period of rehabilitation aimed at adapting or training for a specific job, up to 24 months.
- *Payment for Lost or Damaged Items*: The employee is entitled to compensation for lost or damaged items from the employer irrespective of whether that employee is eligible for other allowances related to accidents at work.

C. Other Allowances

In addition to the benefits and allowances covered by the social insurance system, another group of allowances is financed from the state budget. In most cases, the right to these allowances depends on the financial situation of the family (based on the income of each family member in relation to a prescribed amount, as determined by the applicable regulations for purpose of a given allowance). The most important of these allowances are as follows:[158]

- *Family Allowance*: The purpose of this allowance is to support families whose income per family member does not exceed a limit of the prescribed amount mentioned above; the family allowance is supplemented by additional benefits, such as child-birth allowance or child-care allowance.
- *Nursing Allowance*: The following groups are eligible to receive this allowance: disabled children; persons older than age 16 with a medium rate disability; persons with a major rate (significant) disability; and persons older than age 75. The amount of the allowance is determined by the applicable regulations.
- *Care Allowance:* the purpose of this allowance is to support a person taking care of a disabled child.

---

[158]Act on Family Allowances (Nov. 28, 2003), published in Dz.U. No. 228/03, item 2255, with subsequent amendments.

D. Company's Social Assistance Fund

Pursuant to the Act on Company's Fund for Social Assistance,[159] all companies employing at least 20 employees are required to establish a company social fund. The purpose of this fund is to finance social activities of the company (e.g., recreational, sport, cultural, or educational activities; financial aid and in-kind assistance; and subsidies for children's holidays), and the maintenance of the company's social facilities. Detailed rules and procedures for granting social assistance are set forth in the social fund rules agreed to with the company's trade union, or with an employee representative in the case of a non-union business. The basic rule is that social aid should depend on the life, family, and financial situation of the particular employee or other person to benefit from the fund, such as pensioners or employees' families.

The social fund is created from an annual contribution equal to 37.5 percent of average monthly pay in the Polish economy, multiplied by the average number of employees employed in the particular company.

IX. IMMIGRATION

Polish immigration policy has undergone a major change in the past few years. Two factors have contributed to the adoption of a new immigration policy: first, the fact that Poland has become a transit and destination country for immigrants; and, second, Poland's accession to the European Union and the resulting need to harmonize Polish immigration laws and regulations with those of the EU.[160] In consequence, a new Foreigners Act was adopted in 2003, which established the principles of Polish immigration policy.[161] The Foreigners Act does not apply to European Union citizens and their families, whose immigration status in Poland is governed by the Treaty establishing the European Community and

---

[159]Dated Mar. 4, 1994, Dz.U. No. 70/1996, item 335, with subsequent amendments.

[160]See the chapter on the EU in Volume I, Part 1, for information on EU immigration policies.

[161]Foreigners Act (June 13, 2003), Dz.U. No. 128/03, item 1175.

by the Treaty of Accession as well as by a number of other acts of law, enacted both by the organs of the European Community and by Polish authorities.

Depending on the citizenship of a foreigner (i.e. whether the individual is a national of an EU member state or not), the foreigner's rights and obligations in relation to residence and employment in Poland will differ. Basically, employment of non-EU citizens in Poland is subject to legally imposed restrictions, which take the form of required permits to work and live in Poland. Such foreigners must obtain a work permit before their arrival if they intend to work in Poland.[162] Additionally, they are required to obtain a visa with a right to work or a temporary residence permit. As a rule, after becoming lawfully employed, they enjoy the same benefits as those granted Polish employees. As for EU citizens, the general principle is that they will be exempted from an obligation to obtain a work permit and the residence documents mentioned above. The applicable regulations are discussed below.

A. Work Permits

1. EU Citizens

Now that Poland has become a member of the European Union, EU citizens in principle will not be required to obtain a work permit to be able to legally take up employment in Poland. Theoretically, the same rule should apply to Polish nationals wishing to take up employment in an EU member state. This is a direct consequence of Article 39 of the European Community Treaty, establishing freedom of movement for workers within the Community. Article 39 of the European Community Treaty, establishing freedom of movement for workers within the Community. Article 39 is applicable without any limitations in relations between Poland and the new EU member states, which acceded the European Union alongside with Poland on May 1, 2004, meaning that citizens of such countries may take up employment in Poland without having to obtain a work permit first and vice versa. As the

---

[162]This obligations is provided under Article 87 of the Promotion of Employment and Labor Market Institutions Act (dated Apr. 20, 2004), published in Dz. U. 99/04, item 1001.

"old" member states, the Treaty of Accession provides them with a right to introduce transitional measures postponing full implementation of the free movement of workers between them and Poland. Accordingly, Poland may introduce its own measures of equivalent effect on a reciprocal basis in relation to those countries. As a result, almost all European Union countries (apart from Ireland, Great Britain and Sweden where Polish nationals may be employed without any restrictions) have decided to introduce such transitional measures, which limit free access of Polish employees to their labor markets. In response Poland has implemented corresponding provisions in this respect.[163] Restrictions applicable to particular EU member states vary depending on the scope and amount of limitations introduced by each of these countries in relation to Poland.

2. *Non-EU Citizens*

With regard to citizens of states outside the EU, foreign nationals who intend to work in Poland must obtain a work permit, except for certain situations as provided by law.[164] Under the applicable regulations, the concept of work is understood broadly to include any kind of professional activity performed individually by the foreign national in Poland, based either on an employment contract or any civil contract for profit. Also, effective January 1, 2002, foreign nationals holding positions on management boards of Polish companies (e.g., limited liability companies or joint stock companies) are required to obtain a work permit if the period of their work in Poland will exceed a cumulative total of 30 days in a calendar year. This new requirement applies to foreign executives even if they are not paid for their work by Polish companies.

An employer that wishes to employ a foreign national must apply for a work permit from the provincial governor. Work per-

---

[163]Ordinance of the Minister of Economy and Labor on restrictions applicable to employment of foreigners in the Republic of Poland (dated May 26, 2004), published in Dz. U. 123/04, item 1293.

[164]Promotion of Employment and Labor Market Institutions Act; Ordinance of the Minister of Labor and Social Policy (Dec. 19, 2001), Dz.U. No. 153/01, item 1765 (specifying situations when work permit is not required for employment of foreign nationals).

mits are obligatory, whether the employment is direct[165] (i.e., an individual employment contract or a civil contract made directly with a Polish company) or indirect[166] (i.e., the individual is assigned by his or her parent company to work in a Polish company).

The process of obtaining a work permit involves several steps. First, an employer that wishes to employ a foreign national must obtain a promise (*przyrzeczenie*), on the basis of which a foreign national will be able to apply for a visa with the right to work (D08) or a temporary residence permit. Once the employee has obtained a visa or a temporary residence permit, the employer may apply for a final work permit (*zezwolenie na pracę*) from the province Governor (*wojewoda*). Work permits are granted for each foreign worker, stating the period of work, the type of work, and the employer. A work permit may be issued only for the same period as the duration of the worker's visa or temporary residence card.

A foreign national working in Poland without a required work permit can be expelled from Poland and fined. As a rule, after becoming lawfully employed, a citizen of a foreign country enjoys the same benefits as Polish workers.

Foreigners holding a permanent residence permit are allowed to undertake work without the need to obtain a work permit.

B. Visas and residence permits

1. Non-EU Citizens

The Foreigners Act provides for one universal type of visa, which specifies the visitor's purpose of entry and stay in Poland. A residence visa may be issued as a short-term or as a long-term visa. A short-term visa gives the right to enter Poland and remain for an aggregate period of 3 months within a period of 6 months

---

[165]Ordinance of the Minister of Labor and Social Policy (Dec. 19, 2001), Dz.U. No. 153/01, item 1766 (specifying conditions for granting promises and work permits for foreign nationals).

[166]Ordinance of the Minister of Labor and Social Policy (Dec. 19, 2001), Dz.U. No. 153/01, item 1768 (specifying conditions for employing foreign citizens for realization of export services performed by foreign companies in Poland).

beginning the day of the first entry. A long-term visa gives the right to enter Poland and stay here for an aggregate period of one year during the validity period of the visa (which is not to exceed 5 years). A long-term visa may be issued if the duration of the foreigner's stay in Poland will exceed 3 months. A visa for the purposes of employment is issued for the period of the planned stay in Poland though for not longer than a year.

A foreigner may apply for a temporary residence permit if it is expected that his or her stay in Poland for the purposes of employment will exceed 3 months. A temporary residence permit is issued for a period of up to two years and may be extended for subsequent periods of up to two years. The total period of stay on the basis of such a permit is not limited. A temporary residence card is granted to an individual who has been granted a temporary residence permit.

A foreign national also may apply for a permanent residence permit, which is issued only if the foreigner demonstrates, among other things, that he or she has legally resided in Poland for a minimum of five years on the basis of visas and temporary residence permits, and the existence of permanent family or business ties in Poland. A foreign national who has received a permit for settlement is granted a permanent residence card and is allowed to undertake work without the need to obtain a work permit.

2. *EU Citizens*

Now that Poland has become a member of the European Union, EU citizens are no longer required to obtain a visa or a residence permit under the Foreigners Act. Instead, the Act on Conditions and Terms of Entry and Residence of EU Member States' Nationals and Members of their Families in Poland[167] will apply. In accordance with that Act, EU nationals have the right to stay in Poland for up three months for any purpose, including employment (with exceptions flowing from transitional measures applicable to citizens of certain EU member states, as discussed in IX.A.1 above), without having to go through any immigration formalities.

---

[167]Dated Jul. 27, 2002, published in Dz.U. No. 141/02, item 1180.

If the period of residence lasts longer than three months, an EU national is required to obtain a residence permit especially designed for EU citizens. This may be either a regular or a temporary residence permit, depending on whether the intended stay—respectively—exceeds 12 months or is between 3 and 12 months. However, residence permits will not be necessary even though EU nationals are employed in Poland for longer than three months if the EU nationals preserve their permanent residence in another EU member state, to which they return each day or at least once a week.

The regular residence permit is issued for five years on a renewable basis, whereas the term of the temporary residence permit depends on the period of intended employment. The application for a residence permit has to be accompanied by a certificate of engagement from the future employer or a certificate of employment. The residence permit in question will also refer to the EU nationals' family members. The residence permit may only be refused (or withdrawn if issued already) on the grounds of public policy, public security, or public health.

SWEDEN*

INTRODUCTION

Sweden is a parliamentary democracy. Its present constitution is quite new—the 1974 Instrument of Government—but constitutional traditions stretch back centuries.

The Head of State is the King who, however, plays a formal role only. Public power is divided between three independent branches: the executive (hereafter the government), headed by a Prime Minister, the legislature (the one-chamber *Riksdag* composed of 349 members), and the judiciary. Political representation is proportional, majority representation never having been part of the Swedish political system. Sweden is a unified country. Legislation is under the exclusive authority of the *Riksdag*. Thus, public provincial or local rulemaking of a general nature does not exist in the field of labor law.

The government enjoys a strong position vis-à-vis the legislature despite the fact—or perhaps because of the fact—that it must enjoy the support of a majority of the members of the *Riksdag*. The strong position of the government is demonstrated, *inter alia*, by the fact that it, rather than the legislature, is the main initiator and architect of new legislation. Adoption of government bills often involves little more than rubber-stamping.

The Swedish legal system belongs to the European civil law tradition. Codification of the law began in the twelfth century. Germany has been the main source of inspiration for legal reform throughout the centuries. Swedish jurists cherish the notion—or fiction, as some would say—that the 1734 Law of the Realm is

---

*Dr. Reinhold Fahlbeck, Lund University, Faculty of Law, Lund, Sweden. This text is current through January 1, 2004. It is based on REINHOLD FAHLBECK, LABOUR LAW IN SWEDEN (Acta Societis Juridicae Lundensis 2d ed. 1997), with permission of the copyright holders.

still in force, though virtually nothing remains from the original text. New issues, not dealt with in the 1734 Law, are mostly considered not to belong to the 1734 statute, however. Labor law belongs to this category, but there have been advocates of the idea to codify all labor and employment law into a Labor Code to become part of the 1734 Law of the Realm.[1]

There is no equivalent in Sweden to the U.S. National Labor Relations Board (NLRB), nor is there any state labor inspectorate. The role of government institutions in administering day-to-day labor relations is rather limited.

However, active labor market policies—e.g., policies to promote full employment, the creation of new jobs, employee retraining and mobility, and policies to mitigate the adverse effects of industrial restructuring—play a very important role in Sweden. These are administered by the Labor Market Board together with its provincial and local branches. Despite its name, the Board plays no role in administering labor and employment law or labor relations generally.

The Industrial Safety Board and its local branches are in charge of administering matters involving the Work Environment Agency and its local branches are in charge of administering matters involving the working environment.[2]

Sweden is a member of the European Union (EU) and is subject to EU law. Sweden is also a member of various other international bodies of interest in the labor field, including the Council of Europe and the International Labor Organization (ILO). Sweden is an ardent proponent of ILO conventions and recommendations. Their influence on Swedish labor and employment law is discussed below. In addition, the 1950 European Convention of Human Rights has played an important role in Sweden.

A. Characteristics of Swedish Labor and Employment Law

Under Swedish law, agreements to perform work fall into two major categories: employment work agreements and contract work agreements. Labor law is concerned with employment work agreements. The employment relationship under employment work

---

[1]See discussion in I., below.

[2]See VII., below.

agreements is covered by a vast body of law; there is, however, little concerning contract work agreements.

Typically, an agreement is considered to be an employment work agreement, as opposed to a contract work agreement, when the party performing the work becomes part of an organizational structure established by the other party. Generally speaking, the vast majority of the working population are employees and the employment work category has slowly but steadfastly gained ground compared with the contract work category. (A reverse trend might be at work at the present time but, if so, only marginally.) The distinction between the two is of great importance: labor law on the whole aims to protect one party to the contract, i.e., the employee (often referred to as the weaker party), and labor law is binding upon employers in the sense that provisions in employment contracts contrary to the rules in statutes or collective agreements are void. Law relating to contract work diverges from labor law in both these respects.

The line between employment work and contract work is decisive not only for the applicability of labor legislation but for legislation in many other areas as well, such as taxation and social security. Despite the importance of the distinction between them, Swedish law offers no definition of either. Rather, it is the task of the courts to establish the line of demarcation in the various legal areas when the need arises, and thus an important body of law has emerged. To distinguish between the two, one must look to the degree of independence of the party performing work for the opposite party—employees by and large being heavily dependent whereas contract workers are much less dependent (e.g., self-employed professionals, such as attorneys, dentists, or independent contractors and craftsmen).

Labor law is considered to be private rather than public law; thus, legal rights and obligations under that body of law are private, just as they are under individual employment law. In fact, there is no government agency to bring suit; sanctions are generally confined to awards of damages.[3]

---

[3]See the Introduction, at H., below.

1. *Employer Prerogatives*

The point of departure of Swedish labor law is a set of employer prerogatives established at the turn of the century. Referred to as "section 32 rights," these employer prerogatives were phrased in the following way:

The employer has the right

- to hire and fire at will and to employ workers whether unionized or not, and
- to direct and distribute the work.

These prerogatives are quite far-reaching indeed. They were accepted by the union movement in the epochal "compromise" between labor and management in 1906,[4] and upheld by the Labor Court as "generally prevailing principles of law" in the formative years of the court following its establishment in 1928.[5]

The twentieth century has seen a gradual and partial dismantling of these unilateral rights through legislation. Traditionally, the labor market parties, i.e., management and labor (sometimes referred to collectively as "labor market organizations"), opposed legislative intervention, the notion of "the freedom of the labor market parties" being cherished. Starting in the early 1970s, however, Sweden witnessed massive legislative activity in labor relations—changes both in substance and in procedure. Some rather far-reaching limitations on employer prerogatives have taken place since then, most notably the substitution of the "fire-at-will" doctrine by a *just cause* requirement and the introduction of equal opportunity and nondiscrimination legislation. Absent other rules, however, employers still enjoy their traditional prerogatives. Because most of those survived the legislative assault, employers by and large still command the terrain.

This, *inter alia*, means that there is no generally prevailing principle of objectivity[6] in employment law, except in the area of

---

[4]See the discussion in II.B.5., below.

[5]See the Introduction, at G.2., below.

[6]"No generally prevailing principle of objectivity" means that except for the legally verifiable standards of conduct encompassed in just cause and equal opportunity legislation, employers have discretionary decision-making power not subject to legal scrutiny.

employment protection law and equal opportunity. These two bodies of law have the potential to serve as a rationale for the introduction by case law of a generally prevailing standard of objectivity, but the Labor Court has so far firmly declined to initiate such a process. The EC directive 91/533,[7] mandating written notice to employees of the terms and conditions of employment, has similar potential but until now the directive has not produced any such result. Thus, although the trend is unmistakable, Swedish employment law presently is far from imposing a general norm of objectivity. In the absence of substantive rules on matters covered by their prerogatives, employers still enjoy their relatively unfettered traditional authority.

2. *Role of Legislation*

Legislation covers many aspects of working life, in particular the employer–union– employee relationship (i.e., what is termed labor law or collective bargaining law[8]). The law of contracts of hire and the relationship between an employer and an employee (individual employment law) is only partly covered by legislation, with case law providing the bulk of what legal regulation there is, but many gaps exist.[9] Legislation in the 1970s to some extent created a new balance between the actors in the labor market field and an intricate system has emerged.

- First, in most instances statutory regulation is very general and provides for general matters only, leaving detailed matters to be regulated by the labor market parties.
- Second, labor legislation, though binding upon individual employers and employees in most instances, can to a large extent be derogated from by the labor market parties by means of collective agreements. The most important provisions usually cannot, strictly speaking, be superseded as they reflect the political will of the legislature, but the imple-

---

[7]Council Directive 91/533/EEC of 14 October 1991 on an employer's obligation to inform employees of the conditions applicable to the contract or employment relationship, 1991 O.J. (L 288) 32.

[8]See II., below.

[9]See I., below.

mentation of these rules is often left to the labor market parties.

- Third, collective agreement regulation is more or less exclusive in vast areas concerning the individual employment relationship, e.g., most conspicuously regarding pay where no legislation exists in Sweden (not even regarding minimum wages[10]).

Thus, there is a close interplay between legislation and collective agreements. Case law also is of great importance. The Labor Court is the main actor here, and it has created a voluminous body of law.[11] Ironically, though the prime task for the Labor Court has been to adjudicate in collective labor law matters, it seems fair to say that its most crucial rulings deal with individual employment law because, as noted above, individual contracts of hire have received little attention as regards legislation, leaving this area of the law open to regulation by adjudication.

B. Coverage of Swedish Labor and Employment Law

Swedish labor and employment law covers virtually all employees, private as well as public, Swedish or foreign. Few categories of employees are excluded. Even employees representing management are covered with only very limited exceptions, such as a provision in the 1982 Employment Protection Act excluding top management. Management representatives are covered by collective bargaining legislation with few exceptions and subject to only few and insignificant qualifications. Senior management representatives in the private sector, however, tend not to belong to unions, though such individuals in the public sector often belong to unions.

Whether the legislation applies to public as well as private employees is sometimes expressly spelled out in the statute, but most statutes either simply state that they "apply to the relationship between employer and employee"[12] or ignore the issue com-

---

[10]See V.A., below.

[11]See the Introduction, at G.2., below.

[12]1976 Co-Determination Act, §1.

pletely by referring to employers and employees without further ado. Under either approach, the result is to make the legislation applicable in both the public and the private sectors. Because the public sector accounts for approximately 35 percent of total employment in Sweden, this principle of parallel treatment in the private and public sectors is of eminent importance.

On the whole, the idea of public employment as being something intrinsically different from private employment has been abandoned and the public sector has been "privatized" with regard to labor and employment matters. Existing exceptions are few and becoming fewer all the time. Those remaining primarily reflect concerns about maintaining the supremacy of political democracy over freedom of contract in employment matters and about maintaining the independence of the judiciary. Public employees, including judges and military personnel, have the right to bargain collectively, as will be discussed in greater detail in II., below.

C. Sources of Swedish Labor and Employment Law

1. *Hierarchy of Domestic Labor Law*

From a formal, juridical point of view, the hierarchy of domestic legal rules is as follows: constitution, statutes at large, case law, collective agreements, individual contracts of employment, and finally unilateral employer rulemaking. In reality, the reverse order would probably come closer to the hierarchy as it is experienced on the shop floor.

2. *Statutes*

The 1982 Employment Protection Act is one of the most important pieces of labor legislation to be enacted in Sweden. It, along with the 1976 Co-Determination Act and the 1977 Act on Working Environment, form the three pillars of Swedish statutory labor regulation. The 1982 Act is probably the single most important piece of labor legislation in Sweden, at least from the employee point of view. It completely outlaws dismissal at will and replaces it by a just cause requirement. The Act has a profound influence on conditions at workplaces and its consequences for personnel policy and personnel management are considerable. It applies to all employees alike—private or public, unionized or not, typical or atypical, Swedish citizens or foreign citizens (provided that their employment relationship is governed by Swedish law)—with only four minor exceptions. The primary exception to the just cause requirement applies in the case of managerial employees, but it is limited to those having truly managerial positions.[13]

The Act deals with some 10 related yet distinct matters:

- First are provisions outlining various categories of employment contracts.[14]
- Second are provisions on information about the employment relationship. These are a transposition of EC directive 91/533 on employee rights of information.
- Third come the most important provisions, i.e., those on just cause for dismissal (see below), including rules concerning procedures and formalities on the termination of employment contracts.[15]
- Fourth, the Act contains detailed provisions on ranking in redundancy dismissals.[16]
- Fifth, closely related to the redundancy provisions, are provisions on recall.
- Sixth are rules implementing EU directive 2001/23/EC[17] on transfers of undertakings.
- Seventh are provisions relating to preferential rights of part-time employees to additional working time.[18]
- Eighth, the Act contains provisions on payment during the period of notice and during layoff.[19]
- Ninth are procedural rules governing mandatory advance negotiations or consultation on matters covered by the Act.[20]

---

[13]The other exceptions to the just cause requirement apply to (1) employees who are members of the employer's family; (2) domestic helpers (where a separate statute applies (but there are virtually no domestic helpers working as employees of the family where they perform work)); and (3) employees performing work financed by public funds.

[14]See the Introduction, at A., above.

[15]See I.E., below.

[16]See IV., below, regarding redundancy, recall rights, and transfers of undertakings.

[17]Council Directive 2001/23/EC, 2001 O.J. (L 82) 16.

[18]See I.C.1., below.

[19]See IV.A.1., below.

[20]See IV.A., below.

- Tenth are dispute procedure provisions,[21] and, finally, rules on sanctions and remedies.[22]

These provisions are discussed in greater detail in the appropriate sections below.

In the field of collective bargaining, four key statutes rule:

- 1974 Act on Trade Union Representatives;
- 1976 Co-Determination Act[23] (alternatively, the Act on the Joint Regulation of Working Life);
- 1987 Act on Board Representation for Employees in Private Employment; and
- 1996 Act on European Works Councils.

All are discussed in detail below.

Other labor and employment statutes discussed in this chapter include:

- 1999 Act on Arbitration;
- 1999 Act Against Ethnic Discrimination;
- 1997 Unemployment Insurance Act;
- 1993 Act on Private Employment Exchange and Hiring Out of Manpower;
- 1991 Equal Opportunity Act;
- 1989 Act on Foreigners;
- 1976 Act on Workers' Compensation Insurance;
- 1974 Act on Litigation in Labor Disputes; and
- 1974 Employment Promotion Act.

---

[21]Disputes arising out of contested dismissals are discussed below at I.E.3. See also the Introduction, at G., below.

[22]See I.E.4., below. See also the Introduction, at H., below, discussing grievance handling and arbitration.

[23]This is probably the most accurate translation into English of the Swedish designation of this Act and it will be used here. A word of caveat is appropriate, however. The designation makes one think of the German type of co-determination, termed *Mitbestimmung*, discussed in Volume I in the chapter on Germany at III.A.2.d.i., which is misleading because Swedish co-determination differs sharply from German *Mitbestimmung* and does not involve representation by entities other than unions. The designation of the Swedish Act is a misnomer and the Act should rather have been entitled "Act on Collective Labor Relations and Employee Consultation." See II., below.

D. International Sources

1. *The "Social Dimension" of EU Law and Swedish Labor Law*

EU law towers above domestic law.

The "social dimension" of the EU is primarily an offspring of the desire to ensure the effectiveness of fair competition.[24] In the labor context, it is primarily concerned with rules relating to safety of work places and the working environment generally. Here the need to ensure neutrality in competition is most keenly felt. In addition, a total of some 15 directives apply to the individual employment relationship. With one limited exception (EU directive 94/45 on European Works Councils[25]), the collective labor law field has remained untrodden. To some extent it has even been explicitly excluded from the competence of the EU.[26]

As a member of the EU, Sweden is obliged to adopt the entire structure of legal regulation of the EU, and has done so through transposition of EU directives into national legislation. The process has not always been an easy one. Swedish labor market traditions of, on the one hand, employer discretion and, on the other, collectivization differ from much of what EU directives stand for. However, the process of transition is over now and Sweden has started living with these employment laws. Because, in actuality, they affect only a very small part of the total bulk of Swedish labor regulation, the EU rules are not too onerous. As a result of the revisions, however, there has been an important change toward a less collectivized way of looking upon employment matters, as well as an increased emphasis on employer objectivity in dealings with employees.[27]

---

[24]For a more detailed discussion, see the chapter on the European Union in Volume I.

[25]Council Directive 94/45/EC of 22 September 1994 on the establishment of a European Works Council or a procedure in Community-scale undertakings and Community-scale groups of undertakings for the purposes of informing and consulting employees, 1994 O.J. (L 254) 64, amended by Council Directive 97/74/EC, 1998 O.J. (L 10) 22.

[26]See, e.g., the Social Policy Agreement attached to the Maastricht Agreement, Article 2.6, explicitly excluding from EU oversight the right of association and industrial actions. Incidentally, pay is also excluded. *Id.* See also the European Union chapter at V., in Volume I.

[27]See the Introduction, at G.2., below.

The Social Policy Agreement attached to the Maastricht Treaty has been replaced by the social provisions of the Treaty Establishing the European Community (EC Treaty), as amended by the 1999 Treaty of Amsterdam and the 2000 Treaty of Nice. Article 137(5) of the EC Treaty restates the exclusion of matters such as the right of association and the right to strike from European Union (EU) oversight.[28]

2. *International Labor Organization*

Sweden has consistently played a very active role in the ILO,[29] vigorously promoting ILO rulemaking. Sweden has ratified most ILO conventions, in particular the core conventions. Sweden in several cases has taken a somewhat cavalier attitude toward ratification, in particular considering its vigorous support for ILO rulemaking. This pragmatic attitude is rooted in a (tacit) conviction that labor standards in Sweden are superior—or at least equivalent—to ILO standards, making it unnecessary for Sweden to promptly ratify every convention.

In 1992, Sweden denounced the 1949 ILO Convention No. 96 banning private employment agency systems. This paved the way for a sweeping reform of employment exchange and hiring out legislation, the 1993 Act on Private Employment Exchange and Hiring Out of Manpower.[30]

E. Employment Exchange and Hiring Out of Employees

The employment "exchange" (or the employment agency system) and concomitant information and promotion activities play crucial roles in labor market policies in Sweden. The labor market to a great extent is external (i.e., hiring from without) rather than internal (in the Japanese tradition of hiring from within the company) and thus relies on market mechanisms for the employment

---

[28]For a complete discussion of the EC Treaty, see the chapter on the European Union in Part 1 of Volume I.

[29]For more information on the ILO, see the chapter on the ILO in Part 4 of Volume I.

[30]In 1997, the 1949 Convention was revised and the Convention Concerning Employment Agencies was adopted.

"exchange" and for employment policies such as the promotion of full employment, job retraining, help for job seekers in finding suitable employment, and grants for relocating workers.

The government-run employment exchange system, administered by the Labor Market Board and its regional and local branches, enjoyed a virtual monopoly in the years between 1935 and 1993. In recent years, however, the law governing the employment exchange has changed completely. Deregulation was completed in 1993.

The 1993 Act on Private Employment Exchange and Hiring Out of Manpower is an archetypical example of deregulation. It marks the end of a regulatory regime that had existed for nearly 60 years.

The statute is also an archetypical example of the present international surge toward decentralization. The 1993 Act introduces a profit-making private employment exchange to the market and treats that exchange like any other business. There is only one restriction: the firm and uncompromising prohibition against charging employees and job seekers a fee of any kind. Indeed, it is a crime to do so. Only those recruiting manpower (i.e., employers) can be charged for the services of the private employment exchange firm.

With only few and insignificant restrictions, temporary hiring out of manpower (the use of "temps") also is permitted under the 1993 statute. In this respect as well, the 1993 statute represents a sharp shift from a previous strict ban. Because hiring out of employees had been forbidden prior to 1993, until then manpower policies of Swedish employers did not include temporary work arrangements. Hiring out has expanded very quickly since it became legal and temporary work firms have mushroomed, but the practice is still very much in its infancy and such arrangements account for only a tiny proportion of total employment. No official statistics exist so far, but information provided by private manpower organizations indicate that as of the end of 2003 approximately 1 percent of all those employed worked for hiring-out firms.[31]

---

[31]See I.C., below.

F. Promotion of Employment Act

Sweden is determined to keep down unemployment. To accomplish this goal, an extensive array of schemes aims at promoting employment. The 1974 Employment Promotion Act was enacted in tandem with the first Employment Protection Act.[32] To some extent the two Acts form a unity. Rules in the Employment Promotion Act call for advance notice to local branches of the Labor Market Board and subsequent discussions, if called for by the Board, concerning redundancy dismissals and layoffs involving 25 or more employees.[33] These rules are coordinated with similar rules in the 1982 Employment Protection Act.

The 1974 Employment Promotion Act is also concerned with employers' personnel policies. In this respect, the Act can be viewed as legislation on equal opportunity. It aims at promoting job opportunities for people with various labor market handicaps, whether social or physical.[34] The Act's approach is based on the idea that employers have a responsibility to employ less coveted and less "profitable" people. Another leading idea is that the workforce of an employer should represent a cross-section of the local population. If implemented, these ideas would have far-reaching consequences. So far implementation has been considerably less ambitious.

G. Grievance Handling and Litigation

Alleged infringements of labor and employment law can always be brought before a court for final adjustment. The 1974 Act on Litigation in Labor Disputes in most cases requires that the parties negotiate before going to court. As a consequence, most disputes concerning rights are submitted to a procedure consisting of two distinct stages: grievance negotiations and litigation. As noted in the Introduction, at G.3., below, arbitration is not widely used to resolve such disputes.

---

[32]See the discussion of the 1982 Employment Protection Act and its predecessor at I.E., below.

[33]Redundancy is discussed further in IV., below.

[34]See VI.C., below.

1. The Grievance Structure

The 1976 Co-Determination Act contains some provisions on grievance handling, and detailed rules on grievance negotiations are found in collective agreements. The epochal 1938 master agreement between the Swedish Employers Federation (SAF) and the Swedish Confederation of Trade Unions (known as LO after the abbreviation of its Swedish name) provides rules for grievance processing in the private sector blue-collar market but has also served as a model for the rest of the labor market.[35] Thanks partly to this agreement, the orderly and peaceful handling of grievances is a hallmark of Swedish labor relations. By and large a two-step grievance procedure prevails—local handling by the parties directly involved at the place of work where the dispute originated and central handling by representatives of the industrywide organizations on both sides. Unions represent their members but they have little discretion to process grievances as they see fit (much less discretion than have U.S. unions under the duty of fair representation doctrine).[36]

Nonunionized employees are entitled to take their grievance to court if they fail to persuade the employer to settle with them. Individual unionized employees have no standing in the grievance procedure. However, without exception, unionized employees are entitled to take their grievance to court in the event no amicable settlement is reached during grievance negotiations and the union declines to take the grievance to court.

2. The Labor Court

District courts try labor cases as a court of first instance in some situations, but the Labor Court dominates the field.

The Labor Court came into existence in 1928 and plays a central role in Swedish industrial relations. The Labor Court is a court of last instance; there are no appeals. The court was created primarily to be instrumental in promoting industrial peace—and it

---

[35]See II.B.5., below

[36]See also II.G., below.

certainly has done so—but its most prominent contribution has been in the area of individual employment law rather than in collective labor law. The reason for this is that the court has been called upon to rule on the scope of employer prerogatives. In doing so, the court originally accepted the *de facto* state of affairs in labor relations in 1928, and by so doing, profoundly influenced the balance of power between the labor market parties and the rulemaking structure. "Labor market parties" is a term that includes not only employer associations and unions, but also individual employers and employees.

The Labor Court is a tripartite body where members representing the two sides of the labor market always form the majority. The public is represented by professional judges and experts on labor market matters. The most senior of the professional judges serves as chairperson. The chairperson enjoys no particular statutory authority, but has a considerable *de facto* authority.

In most cases, the court is composed of seven members: three representing the public, two being professional judges and one a labor market expert; and four representing the labor market parties, two from each side. Decisions are made by simple majority. Thus, a majority of four members is needed if the court is split into two (or more) parties, something that is rather rare. More often than not the decision of the court is unanimous. Conceivably, the lay members could unite and overrule the professional members, but that has rarely happened.

Generally, the Labor Court acts as do other Swedish courts in administering justice, though it is heavily influenced by the views and philosophies of unions and employer associations.

Proceedings before the Labor Court are public. The rulings of the court are published.

3. *Arbitration*

Arbitration as a final and binding method for settling disputes is permitted in disputes concerning rights. The 1999 Act on Arbitration applies. Arbitration is not used often to settle disputes involving individual employers and employees, however. On the whole, it is confined to some few sectors of the labor market, e.g., banking, or to some specific issues, such as piece-rate disputes.

Interest arbitration is virtually nonexistent but may emerge in the future.[37]

Disputes between employer associations and unions, or between employer associations and their members or unions and their members, are commonly referred to arbitration but such disputes are rare, particularly disputes between the labor organizations and their members.

Certain disputes, such as those involving antidiscrimination legislation,[38] are not subject to arbitration.

Awards by arbitrators are not made public. There are no private publishers of awards of the kind found in the United States. Nor is there any professional association of labor arbitrators such as the National Academy of Arbitrators in the United States. There simply is no need for either.

H. Sanctions and Remedies

Labor and employment law generally is considered to be private law.[39] One consequence of this is that infringements are dealt with under private law with only few examples where resort is made to administrative or criminal law. Sanctions are primarily of a pecuniary nature, damages being the standard sanction. Punitive damages play an important role because all labor law statutes provide that "regard shall be paid to (the aggrieved) person's interest that statutory provisions or provisions in the collective agreement be observed and to factors other than factors of purely economic significance."[40] Awards are high in the Swedish legal context, but may look less fearful from a U.S. common law perspective. As of 2004, awards rarely have exceeded SEK 80,000 (about U.S. $10,000), even for serious infractions. Equitable remedies such as specific performance (e.g., the restoration of the *status quo ante*) exist. They are of some importance in collective bargaining law,

---

[37]See II.B.5., below, regarding the 1997 Labor Agreement.

[38]See VI., below.

[39]See the discussion on coverage and characteristics of Swedish labor and employment law above.

[40]1976 Co-Determination Act, §55.

such as in cases involving violations of basic trade union rights, but much less so in individual employment law, where, as noted below, the employer can always substitute payment of a sum of money for specific performance.[41] As in many other countries, however, contracts of employment cannot be specifically enforced against employees (e.g., wildcat strikers)[42] or employers (e.g., to reinstate an employee dismissed without cause).[43]

Employer discipline of employees is of marginal importance. Imposition of discipline is not part of management prerogatives.[44] Disciplinary dismissal is highly restricted and ruled by the 1982 Employment Protection Act.

"Contempt of court" is not known to Swedish law in its common law form. However, a somewhat similar enforcement mechanism exists in that courts and administrative agencies often have the power to issue an order of specific performance, including provisions for payment of a penalty in the event of noncompliance (i.e., default fine). Decrees of this kind often are used by agencies responsible for regulating the working environment, e.g., the Industrial Safety Board.

Criminal sanctions are common in statutes in the intersection between labor law and public law, e.g., occupational safety and health.

I. Individual Employment

Individual employment contracts generally co-exist with collective agreements, and typically refer to them in most regards. Various aspects of the individual relationship, however, are covered by legislation that applies to both types of contracts, as discussed here. Still, the individual employment relationship is only partly covered by legislation. There simply is no such thing as a comprehensive employment law code. Government proposals in 1910 and 1911 to introduce such legislation failed. The last at-

---

[41]See I.E.4., below.
[42]See II.F.10., below.
[43]See I.E.4., below, regarding sanctions and remedies.
[44]See I.F., below.

tempt was made in the mid-1930s. It also failed. In the past two decades, many have advocated that the numerous scattered statutes concerning the individual employment relationship be codified. A codification would be in perfect harmony with Swedish legislative traditions and add yet another code to the 15-odd already in force.[45] Nothing has come out of these proposals.

Though not a comprehensive codification, in recent years the 1982 Employment Protection Act has become *the* centerpiece of employment law. First enacted in 1974, this piece of legislation was one of the many scattered employment law statutes, though arguably the most important one. Originally, the statute was basically confined to issues concerning the termination of employment contracts. In recent years, however, the scope of the Act has widened considerably as a result of Sweden's joining the EU. Several EU directives have been transposed via provisions inserted into the 1982 Act.[46] Its central role has been greatly enhanced by these developments, but the Employment Protection Act is still far from a codification of employment law generally; rather, a number of specific matters are regulated separately.

Absent such statutory regulation, freedom of contract prevails, but numerous important principles have been laid down by the Labor Court, and labor market customs also play an important role. Collective agreements are of greater importance than individual employment agreements, which have little individual content. Indeed, collective agreement regulation is more or less exclusive in some areas concerning the individual relationship, e.g., most conspicuously regarding pay where no legislation at all exists in Sweden (not even on minimum wages). By and large, the individual employment agreements simply refer to the applicable collective agreement, where one exists. As a matter of actual practice, national or industrywide collective agreements often provide for binding minimum standards but allow improvements by col-

---

[45]Together with the Constitution and the 1734 Law of the Realm; see the Introduction.

[46]Council Directive 98/59/EC, of July 20, 1998, 1998 O.J. (L 225) 16, on collective dismissals; Council Directive 2001/23/EC, 2001 O.J. (L 82) 16, on transfers of undertakings (see IV.B., below); Council Directive 91/533/EEC, 1991 O.J. (L 288) 32, on employee rights of information. See the chapter on the European Union in Part 1 of Volume I, at IV.A.

lective agreements covering a specific workplace or individual contracts. Matters relating primarily to individual employees even under collective agreements are discussed here in Part I, with references to unions and to Part II as appropriate.

A. Contract Formation

The traditional employer freedom to hire at will still prevails. Union attempts to impose restrictions have met with very little success. However, beginning in the 1970s, statutory provisions have curbed employer freedom considerably, particularly in equal opportunity and antidiscrimination legislation.[47] In the public sector, particularly the state government sector, there is even less employer freedom.

Employers are under an obligation to report most job vacancies to the local branch of the Labor Market Board. This obligation does not in any way limit the employer's freedom to choose among applicants, nor does it mean that the employer must hire anyone who applies just because a vacancy was listed with the local labor bureau.

In the private sector, no rules of general applicability on formal, substantive, and procedural requirements exist. No statutory provisions on mandatory terms exist but collective agreements often contain provisions regarding both substantive and formal matters. In the absence of such provisions, freedom of contract prevails. Thus, to give just one example, oral agreements are binding. The decisive factor is whether the parties did in fact agree to enter into an employment relationship. EU directive 91/533 on employee rights of information, now part of the 1982 Employment Protection Act,[48] has not brought about any change in this respect. The information required under the directive must be in writing, but the information does not necessarily have to be part of the employment contract, separately provided information being perfectly permissible.

[47]See VI., below, regarding antidiscrimination measures.

[48]1982 Employment Protection Act, §6a.

B. Duration

The 1982 Employment Protection Act contains provisions on the duration of employment contracts. Indeed, they are among the most important and most contested provisions of the Act. A distinction is made between contracts for a limited period (fixed-term employment) and contracts for indefinite duration (permanent employment). Generally speaking, indefinite employment offers the employee considerably better legal protection. Because the aim of the Act is to protect employees, it is only natural that the Act favors indefinite employment by restricting employer freedom to contract for a limited period. Unless explicitly agreed upon, employment is for an indefinite period (i.e., permanent employment). Nonpermanent employment is allowed only under certain circumstances. The present 1982 statute is far less restrictive than its 1974 predecessor, however, particularly after its amendment in 1996.

A 2001 amendment to the 1982 Employment Protection Act has changed the situation for temporary replacement workers. Prior to the amendment, employment for temporary replacement could last "forever," with the replacement worker moving from one replacement position to another. The 2001 amendment ended this temporary replacement misery (as it was called in common parlance). If an individual has been employed by an employer as a temporary replacement worker for more than a total time of three years during the last five years, the employment is automatically transformed into employment for an indefinite period (i.e., permanent employment).

C. Atypical Employment

Various forms of what is termed "atypical employment" arrangements[49] (i.e., temporary work) have proliferated in recent years, primarily part-time and fixed-term employment. It is in fact anachronistic to refer to them as "atypical." They are so common that they are atypical only in the historical sense. They should be considered in the light of the trend in employment law toward

---

[49]See I.B. in the chapter on the European Union in Part 1 of Volume I.

increasing flexibility in working arrangements. An array of other kinds of arrangements entailing flexibility also exists, in particular distance work (telecommuting), flexible working time, and various forms of time off.[50]

1. Part-Time Employment

Widespread part-time employment is a recent phenomenon, dating back no later than the 1960s. It has grown very rapidly and is now quite common. Previous rapid increases in the number of part-timers abated toward the end of the 1980s and the absolute number has receded somewhat in recent years. Some 40 percent of employed women were part-timers in 2000, for example, and they account for some 85 to 90 percent of all part-timers. The trend today among part-timers is to increase their working hours, and many switch to full-time work. A 1996 amendment to the 1982 Employment Protection Act has given part-timers a strong position from which to push for an increase in their working hours, should they so wish.

To some extent, part-time employment has promoted disposition of working conditions by individual contract because one individual element is added to the employment contract, i.e., the number of working hours. Swedish law does not contain any mandatory rule on standard working hours for part-time work although collective agreements often specify a set number of hours to be worked.

2. Fixed-Term Employment

Paralleling the evolution and structure of part-time employment in many respects, fixed-term employment as a common phenomenon is relatively recent. It is much more common in the public sector and among women (though to a considerably lesser degree). In the 1990s, around 10 percent of all employees were employed on a fixed-term basis at any given time. The percentage has decreased slightly. Young workers are much overrepresented

[50]Various types of leave are discussed in V., below.

and account for around half of all employees with fixed-term contracts.

3. Distance Work

Few employees work full time away from the premises of their employer but an increasing, yet still small, number do so occasionally. Most statutory rules apply to distance work, so a 1997 government commission found only little need for additional statutory regulation.

4. Non-Discrimination of Part-Time and Fixed-Term Employees

The 2002 Act Prohibiting Discrimination Against Part-Time Employees and Fixed-Time Employees implements two EU directives, Directive 97/81/EC[51] concerning the Framework Agreement on part-time work concluded by ETUC, UNICE, and CEEP, and Directive 1999/70/EC[52] concerning the Framework Agreement on Fixed-Term Work, signed by ETUC, UNICE, and CEEP.[53] The Act protects part- and fixed-time workers from direct and indirect discrimination related to pay and other terms of employment. These concepts of direct and indirect discrimination conform to antidiscrimination legislation generally.[54] A part-time worker is defined as an employee who regularly or temporarily works fewer hours per week or other applicable periods than a comparable employee working full time as defined by the applicable collective agreement, custom within the industry or statute. Fixed-term employees are those holding a position that will come to an end at an objectively determinable time. Employees on probation fall within this category and so do temporary replacement employees.

Protection under the Act is limited to pay and other terms of employment. Unlike other antidiscrimination legislation,[55] the 2002 Act does not apply to (1) decisions concerning hiring, interviews of potential employees, or other actions during the hiring process;

---

[51]Council Directive 97/81/EC, 1998 O.J. (L 14) 9.

[52]Council Directive 99/70/EC, 1999 O.J. (L 175) 43.

[53]See the chapter on the European Union in Part I of Volume 1, at I.B.1 and 2.

[54]See VI., below.

[55]See, e.g., VI.B.2., below.

(2) decisions regarding promotion or selection for training in view of a future promotion; (3) decisions concerning the management and direction of work; (4) decisions that involve termination with notice, summary dismissal, or layoff, or that are otherwise of fundamental importance to an employee. The 2002 Act is limited to employees and excludes job applicants, unlike antidiscrimination labor legislation generally.

An employer who is found guilty of discrimination against an employee is liable for damages, financial (compensatory) and as well as non-financial (punitive). Discriminatory agreements and individual acts of discrimination are null and void.

D. Principal Obligations of Employers and Employees

1. *Employer Obligations*

Law on the internal relationship between employers and employees is based on the principle of freedom of contract. In reality, however, there are few contractual provisions, the field being ruled by generally prevailing principles of law with roots in the pre-industrialization master and servant regulation. That regulation gave rise to employer prerogatives to direct and distribute work.[56] Because these prerogatives are still in force, employers to a great extent decide the day-to-day duties of employees. Coupled with these employer prerogatives is the duty of employees to obey, discussed next (subject to some qualifications, e.g., reasonableness and the priority of interpretation rules, discussed in II.H.3., below).

Employers have far-reaching obligations as well. The principal duty is to provide paid work. If no work is provided, employers are obliged in most instances to provide pay nevertheless (even if employees are free to stay away from the workplace). The 1970 Act on Set-Off by Employers largely protects employee claims on the employer. Liability for damages to third parties (including fellow-workers and the employee himself or herself) as a result of employee negligence during work rests primarily with the employer. The 1972 Act on Damages exempts employees from li-

---

[56]See the Introduction, at A.1.

ability with the exception of situations involving very grave employee misconduct.

Personnel management must be carried out in accordance with "good labor market practice."

2. *Employee Obligations*

a. *Performing Assigned Tasks*

Employee obligations are of different kinds. Of particular importance is *what* employees can be ordered to do, i.e., what work tasks they can be assigned legally. Other aspects are *where, when,* and *how* the work is to be performed. As to *what* and *how* to perform, employees are subject to employer discretion, absent discrimination and unfairness. Far-reaching changes in work assignments sometimes require just cause, subject to court review, and in some instances even employee consent.[57] Excluding these rather exceptional instances, the general rule is that employees can be transferred from one job to another; in other words, job classifications do not restrict employer discretion.[58]

i *Individual employment contracts*

Freedom of contract is the point of departure in Swedish law concerning work tasks. If the employee is hired to perform a specific job spelled out in the employment contract, then that settles the issue of work tasks. Traditional contract interpretation will be used to resolve disputes concerning work tasks. Many employment contracts are of this kind, in particular in the public sector.

ii. *Collective agreements*

The overwhelming majority of employees, both in the private and the public sector, however, work under collective contracts, which are differently structured. It is a principle of long standing under Swedish law that collective agreements are based

---

[57]See discussion in the Introduction, at I.D.2.b., below.

[58]However, negotiations in advance with the employee's union often are required. See II.H.1., below.

on the principle that an employee is obliged to perform all tasks that meet two standards:

- first, the work must be part of the core work performed at the place of work, and
- second, the employee must be qualified to perform these tasks.

The principle holds that employees are obliged to perform all tasks that are covered by the applicable collective agreement.

Most collective agreements are of the industrywide type and cover all work tasks at the specific workplace. The basis for the doctrine is contractual but the contract here is not the individual contract of hire but the collective agreement. Unless the parties to the individual contract agree to something else, the principle of the applicable collective agreement prevails.

Swedish employers have been very careful not to allow employment contracts to limit the managerial freedom that the overriding collective agreement principle discussed above gives them. Indeed, the overriding principle mirrors the actual state of affairs in private industry at the time when collective agreement regulation came into existence nearly a century ago. As can easily be surmised, this principle is a manifestation of the managerial prerogatives discussed above in the Introduction. In one of its first rulings, the Labor Court accepted this state of affairs and confirmed it as a contractual principle.[59] Initially limited to the blue-collar sector, the principle now extends to virtually the entire labor market.

b. *Altering the Employee's Job Duties*

Recently, some important changes in this field have occurred as consequence of the just cause requirement for termination of employment contracts that was laid down in the Employment Protection Act. Although the reasoning springs from the individual contract agreement, the remedy involves the union where there is

[59]Nicknamed the "29:29-principles" after Labor Court ruling 1929 number 29, where it was laid down.

one, as discussed below. The reasoning is as follows: If important changes take place in the work situation of an employee, the employee might find himself or herself in a position that, from the employee point of view, means an entirely new job. That may or may not be the case from the point of view of what the law strictly is. If the employee's perspective is correct legally, then the employment contract has to be renegotiated, in accordance with generally prevailing principles of contract law (the *renegotiation* doctrine). The Employment Protection Act does not apply, as that statute is concerned with situations where the employer wants to terminate the employment relationship, not alter it.

If the alterations are within the boundaries of the employment contract, neither employee consent nor renegotiation is required. But the Labor Court has ruled that if alterations are such that, from an objectively justified point of view, the employee is justified in considering that he or she has a new job, then the employer is authorized to undertake such alterations only for just cause and after having negotiated with the union ("primary" negotiations[60]). Furthermore, an aggrieved employee can challenge the employer's decision before a court and the court can issue an order of specific performance, reinstating the employee to his or her former position.

This principle (nicknamed "the sauna bath" principle) represents one of the rare situations where the Labor Court has created new law. The court reasoned that the logic of the Employment Protection Act would best be served with a principle of this kind. The absence of such a principle would undermine the effectiveness of the Act and constitute an important loophole.[61]

---

[60]See II.H.1., below.

[61]The principle was established in Labor Court ruling 1978 number 89. In that case, the legality of an employer order to transfer an employee—who was discovered in the company sauna rather than at his work site—from a well-paid job involving a fair amount of independence and responsibility to a low-paid, dirty, and insignificant job was at issue. In line with Swedish traditions of compromise, the court found for the employer on matters of principle but for the employee in the case at hand.

c. When and Where: Transfers

In matters concerning *when* and *where* work is to be performed, employer discretion is less pronounced. Regulation of working hours is discussed in V.B., below.

As to *where* work is to be performed, the law is less clear but it seems fair to say that absent contractual provisions to the contrary, employees are not obliged to accept transfers implying geographical moves of any significant importance. A Japanese-type system of employee transfers from one location to another in the country is utterly alien to Swedish traditions.

d. Duty of Loyalty

Employees have a far-reaching duty to be loyal to their employer, including the duty to look after the employer's interests and to perform work in a careful and diligent way.

e. Duty of Confidentiality/Whistleblowing

Employees are under an obligation to keep secret confidential information obtained during work. The 1990 Act on the Protection of Trade Secrets is of general coverage but applies to the employment relationship as well. A conflict between freedom of speech and secrecy exists. Under both the statute and generally prevailing principles of employment law, employees are entitled to reveal illegal practices and, to some extent, also serious deficiencies at the workplace (*whistleblowing*). The employee takes a risk in engaging in whistleblowing, and miscalculations on his or her part as to whether there are actual illegalities or serious deficiencies can result in disciplinary dismissal.[62]

f. Duty Not to Compete

Employees are also under a far-reaching obligation to refrain from competing with the employer. Upon termination of employ-

---

[62]The Labor Court has usually found for the employer on matters of principle in this field but for the employee in the specific case; e.g., see preceding footnote. *See, e.g.*, Labor Court rulings 1994 number 79 (the "Väröbacka case") and 1997 number 57 (the "ambulance case").

ment, no ban on competition applies unless specifically contracted. However, Swedish law looks on restrictive covenants not to compete with a certain amount of suspicion and they can be partly or totally set aside by the courts.

g. Off-the-Job Conduct

Employees by and large spend their spare time as they see fit but case law nevertheless imposes several restrictions, e.g., anything that has an injurious effect on the employee's job performance is not permitted.[63]

h. Ownership of Work Product

The employee's work product belongs to the employer in most instances. This also applies in the intellectual property field, based on statutory and contractual provisions, e.g., the 1949 Act on Employee Inventions.

i. Privacy and Personal Data

Employee privacy is a field where legal regulation is emerging; Swedish law is still somewhat embryonic. Controls, e.g., drug testing, are sometimes allowed and have become quite prevalent in recent years. The Labor Court will accept mandatory controls in some instances where there is an objectively justified need and provided that employees are informed about the tests well in advance. Of particular importance is that controls are systematic and conducted in a reliable way. Close cooperation with the union is a factor of great importance as well.

The 1998 Personal Data Protection Act implements Directive 95/46/EC on Data Privacy.[64] Legislative history shows that the various statutory rules are intended to have the same meaning as the Directive. The Act aims to protect people from violation of privacy by means of processing of personal data, electronic or other. Processing is defined as any operation concerning personal data

[63]See the discussion on just cause in I.E.1., below.

[64]Council Directive 95/46/EC, 1995 O.J. (L 281) 31. See the chapter on the European Union in Part 1 of Volume I, at I.C.1., for a more detailed discussion of this directive.

that can be linked directly or indirectly to a specific living person, for example by collecting, storing or treating it. Central to the Act is a prohibition against processing sensitive personal data, such as, *inter alia*, race, ethnic origin, health, sexual orientation, and union membership. However, processing of such data is legitimate in specific situations, for example, when the person concerned, e.g., an employee, has given express consent. Another example is processing data that enables the data user to fulfill obligations and exercise rights under labor law. Such data can be legitimately disclosed to a third party but only if there is an obligation for the data user under labor law to do so lodged in legislation, a mandatory administrative decision, or a binding contract, collective or individual. Processing of sensitive data without consent is allowed for health and medical service purposes, when necessary, for example, for preventive health care at workplaces, company medical services, and work rehabilitation. This franchise also applies to data resulting from medical screening of employees and tests, e.g., drug tests, when necessary. Unions, when acting within the scope of their business, are entitled to process sensitive personal data concerning their members also without their consent. However, disclosure of such data to a third party, e.g., an employer, is permissible only upon express consent by the individual concerned. This, *inter alia*, means that union check-off depends on individual, express consent by every member.

j. Trade Secrets

The 1990 Trade Secrets Act strikes a delicate compromise between several competing interests: e.g., business secrecy versus freedom of information, employee interest in free agency versus employer interests to restrain former employees form competing, consumer interests that competition be free and fair versus business interests to limit competition, business interests to promote development of know-how for exclusive exploitation versus employee interests to be allowed to exploit their knowledge for private benefit.

The Act covers all information concerning the commercial and operational circumstances of an entrepreneur's business, which it keeps confidential or whose divulgement is liable to damage its competitiveness. The information concerned may be of any nature (technical, commercial, administrative, or any other) and need not have reached the actual exploitability that is often required to qualify for protection under intellectual property law. Information can remain protected even if shared between two or several employers, thus allowing for common R&D. Information on culpable activities or particularly serious infractions is not protected. Anyone, including an employee, who in an unauthorized way gains access to or handles a trade secret may be held liable for damages, including non-financial (punitive) damages, and in certain cases may incur criminal liability for industrial espionage.

Employees are subject to a comprehensive duty of confidentiality but as a general rule that obligation ends with the termination of the employment relationship. At that time employees are free, subject only to a minor limitation under the 1990 Act, to exploit all their knowledge, including knowledge of trade secrets of their former employer, for their own benefit and also to compete with their former employer. Restrictive clauses (covenants in restraint of competition) may limit that freedom but the legally permissive range of such clauses is circumscribed under the 1915 Contracts Act. Courts can set them aside if they go beyond what is deemed reasonable. In addition, a 1969 collective agreement covering virtually the entire private white-collar sector of the economy imposed strict limits. The principles laid down in the agreement have acquired the stature of general principles of law and are consequently applied also outside of the legal field of applicability of the agreement. Courts look restrictively upon clauses that go beyond the agreement. Under the agreement, restrictive clauses can be used only to protect know-how specific to the particular company concerned. Personal abilities, knowledge, and experience of employees are excluded, even when acquired at the company concerned. Covenants are normally allowed for a maximum period of 24 months and are not valid if the employee was dismissed, even for reasons of redundancy and for reasons of personal misconduct only if the employee is guilty of a breach of the employment contract. Breach of a covenant usually incurs liability to pay damages or pre-scheduled amount of money. The 1969 agreement states that damages corresponding to six months' pay should normally suffice. However, the Labor Court in one case accepted a sum that amounted to one year's pay. Very high sums can be adjusted under the 1915 Contracts Act.

E. Just Cause Termination—1982 Employment Protection Act

Under the law that emerged during the latter part of the nineteenth century, employment contracts in industry and commerce could be terminated without cause. The "right to fire at will" doctrine became virtually all-embracing in the private sector in the first part of the twentieth century and was part of the employer prerogatives, the so-called "section 32 rights."[65] Attempts by the union movement to restrict that freedom met with only limited success. As part of the legislative avalanche of the 1970s, legislation abolishing the "fire at will" doctrine was passed. The epochal 1974 Act was replaced in 1982 by the present Employment Protection Act. As noted in the Introduction, the 1982 Employment Protection Act completely outlaws dismissal at will and replaces it with a just cause requirement.

1. Just Cause for Dismissal

The just cause requirement primarily applies to employees hired for an indefinite period.[66] Those employed for a limited period can be dismissed only rarely, as discussed below in subsection 3. Dismissal is categorized as either with or without notice. The distinction is very important because dismissal without notice (summary firing) carries a strong stigma and severely blots the reputation of the employee. Consequently, dismissal without notice is permitted only in rare situations of truly egregious misconduct. Dismissal with notice for disciplinary reasons is a serious blot on the employee's reputation as well but far less so than dismissal without notice. The discussion to follow will be limited to dismissal with notice.

Dismissal is never dependent on approval by the union (or any other employee body). Employers may nonetheless be obliged under a collective agreement to negotiate with or consult the es-

---

[65]See the Introduction, at A.1., above.

[66]See I.B., above.

tablished union[67] in many instances. Authorization by a public agency is never needed but notification and subsequent discussions sometimes are required, e.g., in mass redundancy situations.

The Employment Protection Act does not define what "just cause" for dismissal means. The legislative history of the Act (and in particular its 1974 predecessor) elaborates extensively on the matter but the 1982 Act (as the 1974 predecessor) nevertheless leaves it to the courts to work out the exact meaning of the concept. The legislature wanted to avoid a static and rigid construction that would exclude modifications as attitudes in society and the labor market changed. The Act states, however, that there is no just cause for dismissal "where it is reasonable to require that the employer provides the employee with alternative work in his undertaking."[68] Based on legislative history, the courts have held this obligation to be far-reaching. Only if no alternative work is available or if the employer cannot reasonably be required to look for alternative work for the employee is there just cause for dismissal. If the employer has failed in this respect, there is no just cause for dismissal (even though the situation at hand might have justified dismissal if the employer had fulfilled its obligation to attempt to find alternative work and nonetheless was unable to do so).

The Act distinguishes between two major causes for dismissal with notice, i.e., dismissal for reasons relating to the employee personally and dismissal by reason of redundancy (economic reasons). The distinction is crucial because economic reasons always constitute just cause whereas protection against dismissal for personal reasons is very substantial. Reasons relating to the employee

---

[67]Unions that have concluded a collective agreement with the employer, or employer federation, on wages and general conditions of employment are termed "established unions" and are entitled to additional rights, e.g., the 1976 Co-Determination Act obliges employers to negotiate with established unions before making certain decisions and to provide established unions with information regarding production, personnel policies, and the financial status of the enterprise (see II.H.1. and 2., below); the 1987 Act on Board Representation for Employees in Private Employment entitles established unions in the private sector to elect members to boards of directors in corporations and cooperative associations having at least 25 employees (see II.I., below); the 1982 Employment Protection Act mandates advance negotiations in situations involving mass redundancies, under the rules spelled out in the 1976 Co-Determination Act, with established unions and to some extent with nonestablished unions.

[68]1982 Employment Protection Act, §7.

personally are those that take into consideration only the individual employee and his or her situation at the workplace. In most instances, dismissal for personal reasons is for misconduct, i.e., disciplinary dismissal, but shortcomings of some other kind may in special circumstances be invoked, e.g., physical or mental disability, prolonged sickness, or chronic (or pathological) alcoholism. Dismissal for personal reasons is discussed immediately below. Economic dismissal is discussed in IV., below.

2. *Dismissal for Personal Reasons*

As noted above, the Employment Protection Act takes a radically different approach to dismissal for personal reasons. Here employees enjoy considerable protection. Employers have a far-reaching duty to try to correct any improprieties or wrongs by pointing them out in advance to the employee, providing the employee a chance to remedy the situation, and assisting the employee in attempting to remedy the situation. Part of that obligation is to rehabilitate an employee suffering from any kind of physical or mental condition negatively affecting his or her job performance and job ability. Generally speaking, dismissal is justified only if these attempts fail and provided further that employee wrongs or shortcomings are serious. In many instances, employers have to accept conduct or job performance that is not exemplary. Employers also have to try to find alternative work for the employee.[69] Dismissal is considered as the last resort.

The Labor Court has developed a voluminous body of case law on dismissal for personal reasons. Fairly precise answers can be given to questions such as what type of conduct will make an employee liable to dismissal and whether there is just cause in a given situation. The boundaries are relatively wide, however, because the Labor Court has refused to lay down rigid standards applicable to specific types of conduct regardless of other factors. An assessment of the entire situation is made and several factors, primarily relating to the specific employer and the employee concerned, are taken into account. For this reason, it is impossible to state unequivocally, for example, how many days of nonexcused

---

[69] See I.D.2.b., above.

absence or how much money stolen from the employer can be tolerated before there is just cause. Difficulties for the employer are even more evident when the reason for dismissal is less tangible, e.g., incompetence.

When reviewing a dismissal, the courts make an overall assessment of all relevant factors, such as length of employment, previous conduct, prior warning(s), rehabilitation efforts, other efforts to solve the situation short of dismissal, and prospects for satisfactory employee performance in the future. Factors such as race, gender, nationality, social origin, and religious and political beliefs generally are not considered relevant (except in rare instances where such factors are truly relevant). Age, and in particular seniority, are relevant and so is previous behavior. Personal problems at the time of misconduct can be considered as mitigating, e.g., illness of the employee or in the employee's family, a divorce, or a death in the family. Prospects for the future are of utmost importance, in particular whether the employee can be expected to function well in the workplace, so a prognosis must be made (except in instances of gross misbehavior). Of very great importance is whether the employee has a position of trust and whether the conduct is intentional or unintentional, particularly in cases of theft, embezzlement, or violence.

Conduct outside the workplace is not totally exempted from consideration, depending on the circumstances. The controlling factor is whether private behavior is work-related in the sense that it affects legitimate employer expectations concerning employee job performance. The fornicating clergyman is in trouble as is the cashier embezzling the funds of his or her local football club. An employee competing with the employer is equally in trouble and so is the marijuana-smoking prison guard. The mere fact that an employee has been found guilty of some crime does not per se justify dismissal, not even if a prison sentence has been served.[70]

Factors relating to the employer can influence the outcome as well. For example, supervisory indulgence of similar misconduct in the past can render dismissal void until work rules are en-

[70]In one case the Labor Court refused to uphold the dismissal of an employee sentenced to one year in prison for a nonwork-related crime; Labor Court ruling 1986 number 21.

forced to the letter. The potentially damaging consequences of employee conduct to the employer is of great importance, e.g., whether customer (or government) trust in the employer has been undermined. Of prime importance is whether the employer has made the employee aware of the nonacceptable conduct—perhaps also reprimanded or warned the employee[71]—and made efforts to assist him or her in overcoming the problem.

As can be seen, the just cause requirement for disciplinary dismissal is very strong. Even what looks like Herculean efforts on the part of employers prior to dismissal to correct employee misconduct or to rehabilitate the employee and to assist in changing the work situation of the employee for the better are sometimes deemed insufficient by the Labor Court. Whether the strong requirements of the Employment Protection Act should be relaxed is a matter of some political concern but not very much. By and large Swedish employers manage to function under this strict regime.

3. Termination of Employment Contracts

The 1982 Employment Protection Act contains several provisions on termination of contracts of employment, i.e., notice, procedures, and formal requirements. One set of rules applies when an employer wants to terminate an employee and another when the employee wants to leave voluntarily. Rules are much stricter and more detailed in the first of these situations.

An employee holding a permanent position can be terminated with or without notice (summary dismissal). The Act spells out the period of notice, which depends on length of service and ranges from one month to six months (after 10 years of employment). Collective agreements often contain rules on longer periods of notice, sometimes up to one year. Age is no longer a special factor because of the 1997 repeal of prior provisions affording older employees longer periods of notice, in the interest of increased flexibility and also as a means to eliminate employer reluctance to hire the elderly. Dismissal must be in writing but oral dismissals are legally effective as well, although oral dismissals render the employer liable for damages.

---

[71]See the discussion in the next section.

Employees on probation can be terminated at any time, but the statutory maximum for probationary employment is six months. Derogation in collective agreements is legal and not uncommon.

Employees holding fixed-term positions are obligated to leave once the agreed-upon period is over but, in many instances, are entitled to a formal termination notice. They can be dismissed prior to the expiration of the agreed-upon period only in instances of truly grave misconduct (summary dismissal).

Permanent employees may leave on their own volition with or without notice. In most instances notice is required, the statutory period being one month, but longer periods are often required by the collective agreement. Termination without notice (immediate effect) is legal "where the employer has breached his obligations towards the employee to a significant extent,"[72] i.e., upon material breach by the employer.

The most important provision concerning disputes arising out of contested dismissals is one that entitles employees in most instances to continue to work during grievance negotiations and court proceedings. Employee interests not to have to suffer suspension for any period of time until the dispute has been finally settled prevail over employer interests to the contrary, even though the outcome of the dispute may be that there was just cause. Only where the court considers that there are special reasons for suspension or where dismissal is without notice can the employer have the employee cease work during the proceedings.

4. *Sanctions and Remedies*

Damages, compensatory and punitive, are the standard sanction for infringements of the many formal, procedural, and substantive provisions of the 1982 Employment Protection Act. Reinstatement is also a remedy under the Act. Dismissal found to be without cause is void. The invalidation order by the court is retroactive in most instances and the employment relationship is considered not to have terminated. As a consequence, there is no need for a reinstatement order. Employees rarely ask for invalidation or reinstatement, however, but generally opt for damages only. In

[72] 1982 Employment Protection Act, §18.

Sweden, human relations and employment relations are considered personal matters more than simply business matters. For that reason, few employees would even entertain the idea of returning because essential elements of the employment relationship, such as mutual trust and understanding, are gone.

Can a court order an employer to remove a reference to misconduct from personnel files? To the best of the author's knowledge, no court in Sweden has ever squarely faced this issue. The issue is not that sensitive because the impact of employee misconduct tends to fade away as time goes by.

The 1982 Act anticipates the possibility that an employer will simply refuse to obey an invalidation order or an order to reinstate. The position of the Act is that specific enforcement is out of the question because there can be no such thing as an enforceable obligation to provide (or perform) work in employment law. As a consequence, the employment relationship is considered to have been dissolved upon such a refusal, but it is a costly way to terminate it. The aggrieved employee then is entitled to damages ranging from 16 to 48 months' pay, depending on seniority and age. Because legal rights and obligations in labor law are considered private law, however, this blatant act of disobedience on the part of the employer will not result in fines or any contempt of court type sanction.[73]

F. Employee Discipline Short of Dismissal

The most severe form of discipline is dismissal (with or without notice).[74] Discipline in the employment context is dealt with in the 1976 Co-Determination Act. That Act frowns on discipline. The Minister of Labor, in discussing disciplinary measures in the proposed 1976 Act before Parliament, stated, "As a matter of principle it can be questioned if there is any justification at all for such measures."[75] The philosophy of the 1976 Act is that damages assessed against the employee by a court (under the Act itself) and

---

[73]See also the Introduction, at H., above.

[74]See I.E.1., above.

[75]Proposition 1975/76:105, appendix 1, p. 296 (author's translation of remarks of Minister of Labor).

dismissal (under the Employment Protection Act) are sufficient as punitive measures to correct employee misbehavior. Section 62.1 of the 1976 Act states that "no other sanction may be invoked against that employee unless provided for in a statute or in a collective agreement." This, *inter alia*, means that discipline is not within the unilateral employer prerogatives to direct and distribute work. Thus, with the exception of state government employees, few employees are subjected to statutory rules on discipline.

Discipline is thus a matter for regulation by collective agreements. As noted in the discussion below on collective bargaining, however, the typical collective agreement in the private sector does not contain any rules on discipline.

By and large employers do not press for rules on discipline to be placed in collective agreements. They seem to prefer unilaterally adopted rules of conduct, despite the fact that disobedience does not per se form the basis for any specific disciplinary measures. Such rules are in fact rather common. They are undoubtedly within the unilateral authority of employers, provided that they are in conformity with "good labor market practice."[76]

The statutory requirement in the 1976 Co-Determination Act that rules on discipline be rooted in statutes or collective agreements is confined to employees covered by a collective agreement. This means that disciplinary rules can be agreed upon in individual contracts of hire with nonunionized employees. By and large they are not, however.

Nondisciplinary corrective measures by the employer can be of a wide variety, ranging from rebukes to transfers and changes in assigned tasks. The borderline between discipline and personnel management is primarily one of employer purpose and, in cases in which the employee has been reprimanded, the circumstances surrounding the reprimand as well as its wording. Discipline is punishment for something that has happened; decisions that do not have this punitive character, purpose, or effect are expressions of personnel management. Nevertheless, corrections of a nondisciplinary nature (e.g., transfer) can be very hard on the em-

---

[76]"Good labor market practice" (*god arbetsmarknadssed*) is sometimes invoked by the Labor Court as an overriding principle of law. It resembles Anglo-Saxon common law in the sense that it is used to legitimize rules not previously known to exist.

ployee, much harder than one single instance of discipline (e.g., disciplinary warning) as punishment for the same conduct.

One may wonder how there can be rules of conduct in the absence of supporting rules of discipline. History provides an answer, at least partially. Before the advent of employment protection statutes (beginning in 1974), employers were at liberty to fire at will. Disobedience of rules of conduct made it less painful for employers to justify disciplinary dismissal, one must presume. Today, the rules still play an important role in personnel management, despite their lack of real clout, because of the characteristic feature of the Swedes, both as employer and employee: a desire to avoid conflicts and disagreement and to favor "soft" relations based on mutual accommodation, understanding, and compromise. Disobedience of company rules is also of great importance when assessing whether there is just cause for dismissal.[77]

Warnings can be used as disciplinary measures. Warnings as discipline are permitted only if supported by a statute or a collective agreement. The 1994 Act on Public Employment provides an example of the former. However, employers can use warnings in a nondisciplinary way as well, i.e., as admonitions to employees to cease some misbehavior or else risk disciplinary dismissal. This kind of warning is part of the employer prerogatives. Indeed, unless the employer had warned an employee, admonishing him or her to change his or her behavior, disciplinary dismissal is generally not accepted.

II. COLLECTIVE BARGAINING

The Swedish labor market is heavily organized. The overall rate of unionization is around or above 80 percent of the working population and the rate is increasing or at least stable.[78] As noted in I., most workers' individual contracts refer to the collective agree-

---

[77]See I.D.2. and I.E.2., above.

[78]A 1997 ILO report puts the overall unionization rate in Sweden in 1995 at 91% of the working population. That is somewhat higher than official statistics in Sweden. *See, e.g.*, Government White Paper, Ny anställningsskyddslag, SOU 1993:32 (ISBN 91-38-13332-6), ch. 5.

ment for content. Individual protections for employees covered by collective agreements, the Labor Court, and labor market customs were discussed in I., above.

Swedish employees are traditionally classified in three broad categories: "blue collar" (or "manual"), "white collar" (or "clerical"), and "professional" employees, depending on their education and consequent work tasks. The classification system plays an enormous role in the actual functioning of the labor market as the trade union structure mirrors it.[79] Collective agreements basically reflect this structure, which means that more often than not there are separate agreements for these different categories of employees at places of work. As noted in II.B.1., below, there is a strong trend toward cooperation across organizational divides. In a few sectors, the same collective agreement now covers all employees. Employers increasingly refer to all employees as "members" (or "participators"), regardless of their educational background.

In earlier times, "white" collar employees and professionals have enjoyed more favorable conditions under collective agreements than have "blue" collar workers, but by now differences have virtually disappeared. With very few exceptions, Swedish labor legislation makes no distinction between employees in terms of this classification. To some extent legislation instead has been used to overcome existing differences in collective agreements between employees of these different categories. Today there is in fact a strong trend toward union cooperation across the classification divide borderline and joint union action at the bargaining table.

A. Statutes

Four statutes rule this area:

- The 1974 Act on Trade Union Representatives;

[79]See II.B., below.

- The 1976 Co-Determination Act[80] (or, alternatively, the Act on the Joint Regulation of Working Life);
- The 1987 Act on Board Representation for Employees in Private Employment; and
- The 1996 Act on European Works Councils (implementing EC directive 94/45 on European Works Councils).

The 1976 Co-Determination Act is *the* focal piece of Swedish collective labor legislation. It replaced four previous statutes dating from 1920, 1928, and 1936, and added several provisions aimed at introducing employee participation in managerial decisionmaking. It governs virtually the entire area of collective bargaining and industrial relations. When introduced it was hailed as an epochal turning point in the running of private enterprises but experience has proved such rosy expectations to be wrong. The Act does introduce a scheme for consultation but final decisionmaking powers remain firmly in the hands of management.

B. Overview of Industrial Relations in Sweden

1. Unions

Union membership is fairly evenly distributed among the three main sectors of the labor market: private, local government, and state (central government).[81] The size of the company is not much

---

[80]This is probably the most accurate translation into English of the Swedish designation of this Act and it will be used here. A word of caveat is appropriate, however. The designation makes one think of German type *Mitbestimmung*, which is misleading because Swedish co-determination differs sharply from German *Mitbestimmung*. The designation of the Swedish Act is a misnomer and the Act should rather have been entitled "Act on Collective Labor Relations and Employee Consultation."

[81]As noted in I., above, public employees (including judges and military personnel) have the right to bargain collectively with their employers, i.e., public bodies of whatever kind, and to conclude collective agreements. They also have the right to go on strike in collective bargaining interest disputes concerning their own conditions of employment. They have done this frequently since they were given that right as of 1965. Correspondingly, with only limited exceptions, public sector bodies are equal to private sector employers when acting as employers.

of a factor in terms of unionization rates, nor is geographical location or branch of industry. Employee gender and age are also immaterial, women in fact being unionized to a slightly higher degree than men. The unionization rate among part-time and fixed-term employees is around the average.

Unionism is divided into three main federations, one for blue-collar employees, one for white-collar employees, and one for professionals. Today this division is largely an anachronistic remnant of a more class-oriented society.

- In the blue-collar sector, workers belong to some 15 industrywide unions, mainly of the industrial type, federated into the Swedish Confederation of Trade Unions (the LO). With a membership of about 1.9 million in 2004, the LO includes as members nearly 50 percent of all employees in Sweden, but total membership shows a slowly declining trend due to changes in the overall composition of the national labor force.
- White-collar employees are unionized to a great extent as well. Industrywide industrial unions, mainly belonging to the Central Organization of Salaried Employees (TCO), with some 1.3 million members in 2003, organize the bulk of them.
- Among professionals, the unionization rate is somewhat lower in the private sector than in public service, where it often reaches the 90 percent level. The majority of unionized professionals belong to national craft unions amalgamated into a central federation (SACO) with a membership of approximately 550,000 employees in 2004.

A strong trend among unions to cooperate across the traditional borderlines is noticeable.

2. *Employers*

Employers in the private sector are organized in much the same way and to the same extent. Most of them either belong to an industrywide organization of employers or sign a collective agreement of their own.

- In 2001, the Swedish Employers Federation (SAF) merged with the Federation of Swedish Industries to form a new association, the Confederation of Swedish Enterprise (*Svenskt Näringsliv*). The Confederation has taken over all of SAF's pre-existing obligations.
- In the public sector, agencies represent the state (central government) and the local governments for the purpose of collective bargaining and employment matters generally.

3. *Centralized System*

Collective bargaining in Sweden is very centralized. Few nations with a market economy and privately owned industry have equally centralized bargaining. Strong forces today advocate less centralization. To some extent that has already materialized. The process of decentralization will probably continue, but given the very centralized nature of Swedish society at large, it does not seem likely that the process will bring about a truly profound change. Traditionally, bargaining in the private sector has taken place at three levels:

- *national* between the Confederation of Swedish Enterprise (*Svenskt Näringsliv*) and the employee federations,
- *industrywide* between industrywide organizations on both sides, and
- *local* between the company and the local union.

The Confederation, however, does not take part in any wage bargaining so bargaining in the private sector at the national level has come to a virtual stop.

Legally binding agreements are concluded at all levels of bargaining. Due to limitations in their bylaws, the national federations are not authorized to enter into legally binding *collective* agreements but many agreements entered into by the federations assume that quality when ratified by member organizations. Traditionally, the industrywide level has been the focus of bargaining and there are industrywide collective agreements in every sector of the Swedish economy. Some agreements cover vast sections of the economy. For instance, one single agreement for blue-collar employees covers the core of the Swedish engineering industry and, though renegotiated at intervals, dates back to 1905.

The decisionmaking structure within labor unions and employer associations is also very centralized. Democracy in unions is predominantly indirect. Local officials are elected but officials higher up in the union hierarchy are nominated by elected representatives of members rather than by direct vote. Membership referenda and votes are rare. By and large, unions are democratic institutions of the one-party type in the sense that it is very uncommon for there to be two or more factions competing for leadership. The LO and its affiliated member unions have a strong political inclination. There is a socio-political concept of "the workers' movement." Its two most important manifestations are the political party known as the Social Democratic Workers Party (SAP) and the LO trade union movement. The TCO has no official political links but tends to lean toward social-democracy. The SACO is strictly neutral.

4. *Mutual Acceptance*

Strong elements of trust, cooperation, and mutual understanding between the employer and employee communities are further characteristics of the industrial relations system. A high degree of acceptance of employee trade unionism on the part of employers and of employer appreciation of trade union contribution to the day-to-day running of the business is coupled with a pragmatic acceptance on the part of the union movement of employer freedom to manage the business and of technological change. In most instances, the relationship between an employer (or an employer organization) and the union is firm and longstanding. The parties live in something of a "compulsory marriage" with no recourse to "divorce," as it were. Despite this somewhat cozy relationship there is little collusion between the parties and "featherbedding" is unknown to Swedish industrial relations. By and large, the parties proceed from opposing sides and keep their distance, dealing with each other at arms' length, while at the same time managing to maintain a "marriage of reason." Orderly and peaceful ways for the parties to meet, to bargain, and to (try to) settle disputes are at the heart of "the Swedish model" for industrial relations.[82]

---

[82]See the Introduction, at G., above, and II.F.11., below.

5. Continuity: The Evolution of Labor Agreements

Continuity is another characteristic of the Swedish industrial relations system. During the entire twentieth century, Sweden was spared wars and other upheavals so it was able to develop its system without interruptions. The long-term cooperative climate among labor market actors means that they have participated in a continuous process ever since their formation around the turn of the twentieth century. Epochal agreements in the labor market were concluded in the years 1906, 1938, 1946, 1982, and 1997, all between the LO and the SAF (now *Svenskt Näringsliv* or Confederation of Swedish Enterprise) (or, in the case of the 1997 agreements, between member organizations). The agreements are as follows:

- The 1906 agreement is the founding stone of Swedish industrial relations. In a way, the 1906 "compromise" is still in force. The employer community accepted employee unionism and the employee community accepted employer prerogatives.[83] As part of its commitment, the employer community also accepted collective bargaining and regulation of employment conditions by means of collective agreements.
- The Saltsjöbaden agreement was concluded in 1938. It is still in force. That agreement was reached to avert an impending intervention by the legislature to reduce the occurrence of industrial conflicts. The agreement contains rules to accomplish this reduction of industrial conflict, primarily by introducing mandatory procedures for bargaining prior to any industrial action, and rules to protect neutral third parties. It also introduced orderly procedures for individual grievance handling. Even more important than the formal rules of the agreement was the spirit of cooperation that it engendered. The 1938 agreement marked the coming of age of the Swedish model for industrial relations. One of the characteristics of that model has been the notion that the labor market parties share a common responsibility toward society to act in a balanced and responsible way, in particular in handling industrial conflicts.

[83]See the Introduction, at A.1., above.

- The 1964 agreement on shop floor committees first introduced procedures for information and consultation; it has been replaced by the 1976 Act on Co-Determination.[84]
- The 1982 agreement, entitled "The Development Agreement" (*Utvecklingsavtalet*), is a hymn in praise of cooperation, mutual understanding, and accommodation as well as in praise of business efficiency. It acknowledges in an optimistic way the need for continuous change. It stresses the need for business flexibility and the concomitant continuous process of adaptation, both for companies and for employees. It underlines the necessity of continuous learning and skill formation but at the same time acknowledges the legitimacy of employee expectations to experience a rewarding and fulfilling professional life. The agreement is miles away from looking at employees as an anonymous mass with uniform and limited horizons. On the contrary, in the agreement the employee is treated as an individual with legitimate personal expectations of his or her own.
- The ground-breaking 1997 agreement is concerned with collective bargaining; it builds on the 1938 agreement and tries to reinforce orderly procedures and safeguard industrial peace. It foresees a stronger role for neutral mediators or even arbitrators in interest disputes. Hailed as a "new Saltsjöbaden agreement," it has so far lived up to the realities of the labor market. It has proved to withstand the pressures very successfully.[85]

6. *Collectivization*

Coupled with the dominant position of established unions is another characteristic feature of modern Swedish labor regulation, namely that of collectivization. Up until the 1970s, the employer had the right to unilaterally decide in a number of matters that now have become subject to statutory regulation (e.g., the 1982 Employment Protection Act[86]) or employee participation by means of

---

[84]See III.A., below.

[85]See also II.F.11., below.

[86]See I.E., above.

bargaining (e.g., the 1976 Co-Determination Act[87]). In either case, established unions have far-reaching rights to enter into agreements of vital importance for the individual employee. Statutes fail to a large extent to provide employees with any "rights" that cannot be disposed of by the established union(s) together with the employer. The 1976 Act does not provide employees with any "rights" within the domain of joint regulation at all nor does it regulate employer freedom to direct and distribute work with any specific, detailed provisions regarding the direction and distribution of work. Instead, the Act invites established unions to participate at their own discretion in the dynamic process of directing and distributing work. The previous unilateral discretion of the employer has been partly replaced by bilateral discretion of the employer and the established union(s). The collective interest of the employee community prevails over the interest of the individual employee.

C. Freedom of Association

Employees and employers both enjoy full freedom of association, both in the private and in the public sector. Four separate elements of this freedom are specified in the 1976 Co-Determination Act, i.e., the right to:

- belong to a union or an employers' association,
- make use of the membership,
- work for the organization, and
- work to establish such an organization.

Any violation makes the malefactor liable for damages (compensatory as well as punitive). Improper acts are void. In other words, employees are protected against any kind of discrimination on the basis of union membership. Employers have no statutory right to know if a worker belongs to a union. There are no reported cases on this subject.

Unions and employer associations enjoy only indirect protection, through protections against violations of members' rights. Direct attacks on an organization—e.g., verbal attacks in the me-

[87]See III.A., below.

dia or a refusal to sign a collective agreement with it—do not constitute actionable infringements of any labor rights.

1. Organizational Structure

Unions (and employers' associations) are voluntary, nonprofit associations. There is no legislation of general application for such associations in Sweden, nor is there any specific regulation applying to unions. Some common law–type general principles of law apply, e.g., a principle of equal treatment of members, discussed below, but apart from those, unions enjoy far-reaching freedom of self-governance. Allegations of abuses of this freedom have been comparatively few and on the whole have not involved instances of truly serious misconduct or wrongs. Corruption or dictatorial practices are very rare. Calls for statutory regulation of unions have nevertheless been frequent, but unions have consistently and adamantly opposed them. Given the strong position of unions in Swedish political life and the fact that union conduct has never caused truly serious concern in society, whatever impetus there has been at any given time to regulate union self-governance has never gained any significant momentum.

One generally prevailing principle of law holds that voluntary, nonprofit organizations like unions are open to all who meet the membership requirements of the organization. Swedish case law reveals only one case involving a situation in which an employee who met the membership requirements was denied membership.[88] The court ruled in favor of the employee. In the same vein, members are protected against unjustified or discriminatory expulsion from their union. A few cases exist articulating this principle.[89]

2. Union Dues

Unions charge fees. Unions decide the amounts and, excepting instances of discrimination, the courts have no jurisdiction. No reported case on discriminatory fee structures exists. Failure to pay dues will result in expulsion from the union. Check-off ar-

[88]Supreme Court 1948 p. 513.

[89]Supreme Court 1945 p. 290 and 1946 p. 83; Supreme Court 1990 p. 386.

rangements are common in collective agreements but individual employee consent is required.

3. Interunion Disputes

Jurisdictional agreements between unions are common. Interunion disputes are rare. Still, instances of jurisdictional disputes are not unheard of and the main victim here usually is the employer, who is caught in the cross-fire between warring unions. Because actions of this kind have not haunted Sweden to any truly disquieting extent, calls for legislation to curb them have gone unheard. No public agency has authority to interfere with, much less to settle, a bargaining agent issue. (As noted in the Introduction, Sweden has no government agency equivalent to the NLRB in the United States that might resolve such matters.) Jurisdictional disputes are settled by the unions concerned and by the federations to which they belong (i.e., LO, TCO, and SACO). The Labor Court is sometimes called upon to decide whether specific work tasks are blue-collar or white-collar work, however. In deciding this, the Labor Court *de facto* decides union affiliation of the employees involved, but case law is far from voluminous on this issue.

4. Union Recognition

Union recognition is not much of an issue either because all unions enjoy basic representation rights as bargaining agents for their members by force of statutory fiat. No certification is needed. From a comparative law perspective, this is a rather startling phenomenon, but Sweden shares it with its fellow Nordic countries.

5. Union Rights

Labor unions all enjoy the same basic rights. Generally speaking, every union is the exclusive representative for its members, but only for its members—a principle of proportional representation. There is no equivalent to the principle of majority rule or exclusive representation that exists under U.S. labor law. The Swedish experience here probably mirrors its system for political representation as described in the Introduction. Representation elections to choose a bargaining agent do not occur. Employees express their preferences by joining the union of their choice. With few exceptions, employees have no real choice as regards which union to join because the unions each represent different kinds of employees.[90]

Some unions have additional rights. That is the case with unions (including all their local bodies) that have concluded a collective agreement with the employer (or the federation of employers) on wages and general conditions of employment. Generally speaking, such "established" unions, as they are called, organize the majority of employees in their sector of the labor market. Though Swedish law does not provide for exclusive representation, established unions *de facto* often speak for the entire employee community. The reason is that by and large only established unions take part in joint decisionmaking and other forms of statutorily imposed or encouraged cooperation between employers and employees.[91]

There is no legal obligation that established unions represent nonmembers but when labor-management discussions deal with matters that concern all employees, the established union *de facto* represents nonmembers as well. Labor organizations do not represent nonmembers on individual employment matters.

Traditionally, Swedish labor law has protected only the right to make use of the right of association (the *positive* side) but not the right to refrain from it (the *negative* side). Although voluntarism prevails and no one can be legally forced to enter a union (or an employer association), those who decide to remain outside may face reprobation by members and retaliation of a nonlegal nature. Pan-European law is changing the legal vista, in particular the 1950 European Convention on Human Rights, adopted by the Council of Europe. Case law developed under this convention protects the negative right of association and this case law is binding on Sweden both because Sweden has ratified the convention and because the convention was adopted as domestic Swedish statutory law in 1994. The reference for incorporation of the 1950 European Con-

---

[90]See discussion in II.B., above.

[91]See, e.g., II.H.1. and 2., below.

vention of Human Rights into EU law is Article 6 of the Treaty on European Union, popularly known as the Maastricht Treaty.[92]

6. *Union Security*

The closed shop or other union security clauses, e.g., union hiring halls, are legal per se but they are uncommon. Closed shop clauses are virtually nonexistent because employers have successfully resisted them. Employer freedom to hire employees regardless of union affiliation was part of the 1906 "compromise" discussed above and the agreement reached in 1906 has remained part of Swedish industrial relations ever since. At those rare places of work where a closed shop clause is in force, nonmembers cannot be dismissed for refusing to join the union but job applicants can legally be denied employment. Because of its extreme rarity and the 1906 "compromise," the closed shop is not much of an issue in Swedish industrial relations.

Unions are highly centralized and decisions are made by elected (or employed) officers rather than by membership votes.[93]

Union office-holders representing established unions are entitled to far-reaching privileges and benefits under the 1974 Act on Union Representatives. Apart from employment protection, they are entitled to fully paid time off for the purposes of trade union activities at the workplace,[94] provided that such time off is necessary for the union mandate and is of "reasonable" proportions. In addition, time off without pay is also part of the statutory scheme. The Act provides for time off for certain union training courses, sometimes with pay and sometimes without, but not for basic training. Regional union officers service small workplaces where no plant union exists. Under the Act, employers are expected to be supportive of union work. As a consequence, union representatives have a statutory right to an office on company premises. Further assistance, such as office equipment or secretarial help, falls outside the mandatory scope of the statute but many collective agreements provide for it.

---

[92]See the Introduction, at G.1., in the chapter on the European Union in Part 1 of Volume I.

[93]See discussion in II.B.1., above,

[94]1974 Act on Trade Union Representatives, §7.

Union officials enjoy no particular protection against dismissal for personal reasons.[95] If anything, the opposite is true as they are in a position of trust at the workplace. Union work is privileged in many respects and union officials enjoy ample protection when performing union work. Apart from that, they are not treated as a privileged group of employees.

D. The General Right of Negotiation

Swedish labor law recognizes three different types of collective negotiations:

- negotiations in general on the relationship between employers and employees represented by a union (general negotiations or collective bargaining in general);
- negotiations to give the employees a say in running the business (called "joint regulation" bargaining, "primary" negotiations, or decision bargaining); and
- grievance bargaining.

The aim of collective bargaining in general is to regulate matters concerning the relationship between the negotiating parties, generally (but not necessarily) by means of a collective agreement. The subject matter is the widest possible in that it covers all questions relating to the relationship between employers and employees (including unions). With some minor exceptions set out in Section 2 of the 1976 Co-Determination Act, there are no managerial exemptions. The duty to bargain is limited, however, in terms of what it entails. There is no obligation to sign a contract (even if agreement has been reached on all substantive matters) nor is there any obligation to compromise or even to show a willingness to compromise or to reach common ground. In other words, Swedish labor law does not recognize a good-faith bargaining requirement. Strength at the bargaining table thus does not stem from legal requirements on bargaining behavior; it stems from the willingness and ability on the part of unions to resort to industrial action. Given the cooperative and understanding attitudes of Swedish employ-

[95]See I.E.2., above.

ers toward unions, however, bargaining tends to produce a settlement short of industrial strife, in particular when established unions are involved.

Every labor union is entitled to bargain collectively with an employer employing at least one of its members. All such unions have a corresponding duty to bargain with the employer at its request. In other words, the right (and duty) to bargain is reciprocal. Bargaining rights extend to all levels of trade union hierarchy and the corresponding hierarchy on the employer side. This generally means that negotiations take place at two levels, local level (company or plant) and central level (industrywide).

Breach of the duty to bargain is sanctioned by damages (compensatory, if any, and punitive). Because the duty to bargain is so limited, damages on the whole are confined to situations where the employer has refused to appear at the bargaining table at all.

E. The Collective Agreement

Collective agreements are of paramount importance. Given the high unionization rate and the fact that most employees work for employers that are parties to collective agreements or members of organizations that have signed such agreements on their behalf, it follows that the overwhelming majority of Swedish employees are covered by collective agreements, including most employees in low- and middle-range managerial positions. Collective agreement regulation is more or less exclusive in some areas concerning the individual relationship, e.g., most conspicuously regarding pay where no legislation at all exists in Sweden (not even on minimum wages).[96]

1. Collective Agreement Defined

By definition a collective agreement is "an agreement in writing between an organization of employers or an employer and an organization of employees about conditions of employment or otherwise about the relationship between employers and employees."[97]

[96]Wages are discussed below in V.

[97]1976 Co-Determination Act, §23.

Thus, the subject matter of collective agreements is the widest possible, encompassing all matters subject to collective bargaining.[98] On the employee side, only an association can be a party to a collective agreement, not a group of employees even if they act concertedly unless their concert amounts to a union, which is conceivable under Swedish law as little is required for a voluntary association to come into existence. Such instances have nevertheless been very rare in the past 60-odd years.

2. *Binding Effect of Collective Agreements*

A collective agreement is legally binding upon the parties to the agreement as they do not act solely as agents for their members but for themselves as well. Unless otherwise stated in the agreement, it also is binding upon all members of the parties to the agreement. In case the agreement is industrywide, it binds all individual members and member-organizations on both sides. Because membership rates are very high and because there is an industrywide agreement in virtually every sector of the economy, it follows that the vast majority of employers and employees in any particular sector of the labor market are covered by such an agreement.

Collective agreements are mandatory for employers and employees covered by them.[99] Unless the collective agreement provides otherwise, the parties have no authority to agree on terms and conditions inconsistent with the collective agreement (the *normative* effect of collective agreements). In other words, the statutory rule leaves it to the parties to the collective agreement to decide the extent to which individual employers may contract with their employees (and, in the case of an industrywide collective agreement, the extent to which employers can contract with the local union). As a matter of actual practice, national or industrywide collective agreements often provide for binding minimum standards but allow improvements by collective agreements covering a specific workplace or individual contracts.

---

[98]See II.D., above.

[99]1976 Co-Determination Act, §27. Coverage includes nonmember employees, as discussed below in II.E.3.

3. *Extension of Agreement*

Swedish labor legislation does not contain any mechanism for the extension of collective agreements nor does it provide for an automatic *erga omnes* effect of agreements, but much the same result is obtained in other ways.

- First, although employees not members of the signatory union are never legally bound by the agreement, in most instances the agreement affects such employees nevertheless. One reason is that a collective agreement usually has an *erga omnes* effect in the sense that the parties to the agreement have an understanding that the employer must provide nonmember employees no less in wages and other benefits than the agreement provides for those directly covered by it.
- Second, a collective agreement very often affects employers not covered by it. It is often held by courts that industrywide agreements in any sector set standards that will be applicable at all workplaces in that sector unless there is an agreement to some other effect in force at the particular place of work.[100] Still, this means that implementation of EU directives cannot be made exclusively by means of collective agreements but require supplementary legislation to cover gaps in collective agreement coverage.[101]

4. *Duration*

Collective agreements are concluded for a specific time or until terminated after notice. Most collective agreements on pay and other conditions of work are concluded for a specific period of time, such as one or two years. Most master agreements on overriding matters, e.g., working environment, equal opportunity,

---

[100]See, e.g., V.A., below, discussing "reasonable" minimum levels of pay in an industry sector.

[101]EU directives must be implemented in such a way that all those concerned by them become legally entitled to the rights that the directives confer. Swedish collective agreements do not meet this standard because they do not necessarily provide all employees with legally protected rights.

or severance pay, are for an indefinite period of time (coupled with a termination procedure).

When a collective contract expires, its terms to some extent continue in force. This is particularly the case with terms that directly apply to the working conditions of employees, often referred to as "normative rules"; these are considered to have become part of the individual employment contract of the employee after expiration of the collective agreement. This obviously means that unilateral changes by the employer are out of the question. However, rules that concern the contracting parties, e.g., union security clauses, do not survive unless a new collective agreement is likely to be signed shortly after the expiration of the previous collective agreement. The same is true with many rules that apply to the running of the workplace, e.g., work schedules.

5. *Breach of the Agreement*

Anyone in breach of a collective agreement is liable for damages (compensatory and punitive). On the employee side, both the aggrieved employee and the union are entitled to damages. On the employer side, both the employer and the employer federation are entitled to damages, where applicable. Under the 1976 Act,[102] serious breach of the agreement entitles the aggrieved party to ask the Labor Court to annul the agreement in part or in whole, but so far the provision has been invoked only once since 1976, and a similar provision in the prior Act replaced in 1976 had not been used since 1935. Partial modification or complete annulment of a collective agreement by court order based on generally prevailing principles of equity in contractual relationships is possible under Section 36 of the Contracts Act. Case law offers only rare examples of actions under Section 36.

F. Industrial Actions

Statutory regulation of industrial actions covers employers and employees alike. The Swedish Constitution (the 1974 Instrument of Government), Chapter 2, article 17, states: "Any trade union or employer or association of employers shall be entitled to

[102] 1976 Co-Determination Act, §31.

strike or lock-out or resort to any similar measure unless otherwise provided by law or arising out of an agreement." Similarly, the 1976 Co-Determination Act deals with all industrial actions in the same context and the rules are basically identical, regardless of whether it is an employer or an employee action. The constitutional rule is of very recent origin. Prior to its enactment in 1974, no equivalent rule existed and there were no strong demands to have such a rule. Mirroring this somewhat off-handed attitude to the present constitutional rule, it should be noted that the rule is not of great significance as its actual scope depends not on constitutional regulation, but on statutes (or even rules in collective agreements). A joint committee of the Supreme Court and the Supreme Administrative Court stated, quite correctly in the author's opinion, that the constitutional rule is of "very limited reach."[103]

1. *The Right to Engage in Industrial Actions*

Industrial actions in Sweden are discussed in terms of a *right*—the right to strike—rather than a *freedom*. However, any distinction between *right* and *freedom* in this respect is alien to Swedish law. The reason is that Swedish law at an early stage in the industrialization process adopted the position that industrial actions are lawful unless specifically prohibited. Once this approach had been taken, there was no need for the distinction between a right versus a freedom in this area of the law.

In sum then, a basic principle in Swedish labor law, supported by the above-mentioned provision in the Constitution, is that industrial actions are lawful and that all industrial actions that are not specifically prohibited are permissible and legal. This has implications that at first may not be obvious.[104] No social justification is required, nor is there any generally applicable principle of proportionality, regarding an industrial action and the desired result.[105] There is no general requirement that industrial actions have

[103]The Law Council (*Lagrådet*) in a statement to the Labor Market Committee of the Swedish legislative body, the *Riksdag*; AU 1989/90:24 p. 12.

[104]See II.F.7., below.

[105]Under EU law a generally applicable principle of proportionality prevails. It is conceivable that the philosophy behind this principle will influence Swedish law. So far that has not happened as far as industrial action law is concerned.

to be effective in the sense that they will have, or at least will have some likelihood of, if not potential to, achieve the result wanted by the party undertaking the action. Indeed, many industrial actions in Sweden are ineffective in the sense of having a likelihood of success and become truly effective only when coupled with sympathy actions by some other union.

The premise underlying the Swedish approach to regulating (or, more accurately, not regulating) industrial actions is that the labor market parties have assumed certain responsibilities to use the industrial action weapon in a balanced and responsible way that will make statutory regulation on social justification or on effectiveness unnecessary. The idea is that the labor market parties will refrain from actions that are not socially justified or just ineffective. Signs that this voluntary social compact no longer holds in some sectors of the labor market have caused considerable strain in Swedish society in the last 15 to 20 years, and has resulted in calls for intervention by the legislature or for a renegotiated social compact. However, apart from a statutory ban on industrial actions by unions against one-man and family companies introduced in 2000, little has happened to change the legal vista in this respect.

As an exception to the above, generally speaking, industrial actions to promote political causes are not permissible.

2. *Mutual Rights and Obligations of the Parties*

One of the characteristics of Swedish law on industrial actions is the theory that there should be equality between employers and employees in the sense that each should have the same rights and obligations. The legislature is in fact aware of the reality of differences in the importance and function of industrial actions by the two sides. Nevertheless, Swedish law adheres as strictly as possible to the principle of "equality of arms." In other words, the government has refrained from actively promoting the interests of either side.

3. *Public and Private Sector Distinctions*

Another characteristic feature of Swedish law in this field is that virtually no distinctions are made between the private and the public sector. This is in accordance with the overriding tendency in Swedish labor and employment law regulation to eliminate differences between the two sectors of the labor market.[106] Although there are some statutory limitations in the public sector not imposed on the private sector, they are not that far-reaching, particularly in the local government (municipal) sector. In fact, statutory limitations are so negligible that master collective agreements have been concluded in the public sector as a way of achieving further restrictions in the absence of statutory limitations. The rationale for this approach is understandable when one is informed that industrial actions in the public sector have been rather common since 1965 and some of the most spectacular strikes have occurred there.[107]

4. *No Strikes During Life of Collective Agreement*

In most instances industrial actions are illegal during the lifetime of a collective agreement: the collective agreement is a "peace treaty." Exceptions are few and of limited range, with one notable reservation: sympathy strikes are permitted—i.e., strikes of a secondary nature to support a legal primary action by another union.[108]

5. *Who Can Strike*

Industrial actions (strikes) are firmly in the hands of unions. Most important, *no* concerted actions by individual employees are ever legal industrial actions; they are always illegal (wildcat) actions.[109] This is true regardless of whether or not the employees are members of a union and whether there is a collective agreement in force. Only actions authorized by a union are permissible, provided in addition that the decision has been duly taken in ac-

---

[106] See the Introduction, at B., above.

[107] On one most remarkable occasion, the Swedish government, acting as the employer, notified a majority of Swedish military officers that they were to be locked out. The impeding lockout was called off only at the last minute. Mass media from all over the world had rushed to Sweden to witness the closing down of military forces as officers left their posts.

[108] See II.F.7.c., below.

[109] Although the Labor Court is the prime creative force in shaping industrial action case law, the Supreme Court has played an important role, as well. In an epochal ruling, the Supreme Court in 1974 held that employee actions are lawful only if organized by a union.

cordance with the bylaws of the union. A corresponding principle applies for employers who are members of an employers' association. Nonorganized employers are the only individuals that can legally resort to industrial actions (lockouts) on their own volition without organizational fiat. Perhaps nothing better illustrates the weak role of individuals in Swedish labor law and its high degree of collectivization than this principle. Moreover, the bylaws of most unions vest the right to make decisions in this regard at a high level in the hierarchy. Votes by members are not required by law and rules requiring such votes are very rare indeed in union bylaws.

6. *Employee Rights During a Strike*

Employees do not have to give notice to terminate their employment contracts before going on strike. The employment contract continues to be in force during the strike, albeit suspended for the duration. The strikers remain employees. They are entitled, and obliged, to return once the strike is over. Refusal by the employer to take back returning strikers is tantamount to summarily firing without just cause in blatant violation of the 1982 Employment Protection Act. Such behavior has been unknown for the past several decades. Because the employer generally is blocked from hiring replacement workers during the conflict, though not actually prohibited from doing so,[110] a situation of the type found in the United States under the *Mackay* doctrine does not arise.[111] A refusal by striking employees to report back for work once the conflict is over amounts to voluntary termination of employment. There have been no reported instances of such refusals for decades.

Obviously, employees cannot be fired for taking part in a lawful strike. There is one exception. Industrial actions are supposed

---

[110]See II.F.7.b., below.

[111]The "*Mackay* doctrine" refers to a decision by the U.S. Supreme Court in 1937, NLRB v. Mackay Radio & Telegraph Co., 304 U.S. 333, 2 LRRM 610 (1938). Under *Mackay*, employers can hire permanent replacements during an economic (as opposed to an unfair labor practice) strike, thus effectively barring returning strikers from getting their jobs back. Though often criticized, *Mackay* remains in force. See the chapter on the United States at II.H.1. in Volume I. Swedish employees faced a similar situation in the past.

to last for only a relatively short period of time. If a strike goes on for a very long time, it can jeopardize the financial health of the company, indeed its ability to survive. If this is the case, it may sometimes be lawful to terminate the strikers. Just how long a strike must go on for this situation to materialize cannot be determined in the abstract, as that will depend on the financial health of the company.[112]

7. *Types of Industrial Actions*

The 1976 Act provides that "stoppage of work (lockout or strike), blockade, boycott, or other industrial action comparable therewith" are permissible.[113] These terms are discussed below. The Act does not elaborate on what "comparable" actions are, leaving that to the courts. One common "comparable" action by unions is the partial work stoppage, e.g., refusal to work overtime.

a. *Partial Actions*

Partial actions are very common. In addition to refusal to work overtime, case law offers a wide spectrum of other actions—employees may refuse to go on business trips, to drive cars or trucks during working time, to work on a particular day, e.g., Fridays (when demand perhaps peaks), or may refuse to work according to any work-schedule other than the one in force when the conflict started. Other examples are concerted refusals by train conductors to sell and to check passenger tickets and concerted refusals by flight controllers to handle the flights of a particular carrier. These and other similar forms of partial actions are lawful per se under the prevailing doctrine, discussed in II.F.1., above, that everything that is not specifically prohibited is lawful.

A characteristic feature of Swedish strike patterns is that strikes rarely are total in the sense that all employees are called out on strike. Unions prefer to call out only key employees, thereby, in many instances, effectively crippling the entire plant. Other employees (even those belonging to another union) are excused from performing the work of strikers by virtue of "neutrality provisions"

---

[112] Labor Court ruling 1983 number 65, *obiter dicta.*

[113] 1976 Co-Determination Act, §41.

in collective agreements exempting them from performing "smitten work."

b. Boycotts and Blockades

Boycotts and blockades are common. Distinctions between "strikes," "boycotts," and "blockades" are blurred. Many of the partial actions mentioned above are in fact called boycotts or blockades in Sweden, e.g., the refusal to work overtime is referred to as an "overtime blockade."

Blockades in the traditional sense of cutting off the opposite party from access to something also occur. A strike is routinely coupled with a blockade against the hiring of new employees. This action does not legally prevent employers from recruiting new employees but, under the 1997 Unemployment Insurance Act (and its predecessor), those who receive unemployment benefits are not obliged to accept employment at workplaces experiencing an industrial action. The blockade will, therefore, effectively cut employers off from this pool of otherwise available workers. Attempts by the employer to recruit other workers from any other source would cause an uproar.

Blockades against hiring new workers even when there is no strike are frequently used as independent actions by unions as well. A hiring blockade is an announcement by the union in a newspaper, coupled with information to the media and the government agencies concerned, stating that the union has imposed a hiring blockade because the employer mentioned in the announcement has turned down a union demand, usually to sign a collective agreement. Unions use them as an opening gambit together with an overtime blockade to show their seriousness of mind, hoping not to provoke any serious reprisal by the employer.

c. Secondary Actions

Sympathetic actions (secondary actions) are also permitted in many instances. They are common, particularly sympathetic blockades by truck drivers who refuse to handle any goods incoming or outgoing related to the stricken employer. The distinction between primary and secondary actions is not unknown to Swedish law but it is of little import and it works in ways that differ sharply from U.S. labor law. This means, *inter alia*, that actions against neutral, secondary parties on the opposite side—generally (but not necessarily) employers—by and large are legal.

d. Picketing and Handbilling

Picketing is uncommon in Sweden but not unlawful, provided that it is peaceful and does not involve occupation of employer property (or other forms of coercive hindrance of the employer's business). Sit-ins have not been part of the Swedish labor vista for decades. Scattered incidents where striking employees have tried to block the entrance or exit of their workplace have occurred, but only very rarely. Such behavior constitutes a criminal offense.[114]

Handbilling is not part of the Swedish experience. There is no need for it from a union point of view as employers by and large do not interfere with union membership solicitation.

e. Work-to-Rule Actions

Work-to-rule actions are quite uncommon, as are overt slowdowns. Slowdowns are never authorized by unions and work-to-rule actions are authorized only under exceptional circumstances. The lawfulness of such actions has not been put before the courts, but it seems reasonable to believe that they are lawful if overt. Because there is nothing unlawful per se about work-to-rule actions, the general principle of lawfulness should apply.[115]

f. Actions to Prevent Social Dumping

Under 1991 amendments to the 1976 Co-Determination Act, industrial actions to prevent what a union considers to be social dumping[116] by a foreign firm temporarily operating in Sweden are legal to a great extent. This is so even if the industrial action means substituting a Swedish collective agreement for a foreign collective agreement, thus disrupting a perfectly legal relationship be-

---

[114]See note 125, below.

[115]Work-to-rule situations have been before courts in some cases but their lawfulness has never been at issue; Supreme Court case NJA 1970 p. 216 and Labor Court case 1967 number 9.

[116]"Social dumping" means competition by an employer using substandard wages (and other work benefits).

tween the foreign employer and its employees. This state of the law partly reflects the fact that Swedish collective agreements cannot be extended and that there are no statutory rules on minimum wages in Sweden. Because there are no statutory rules on minimum wages, a foreign employer doing work in Sweden—e.g., construction work—can pay its employees wages that are far below generally prevailing levels in Sweden (but wages that are considered satisfactory in the country of origin of the foreign employer and its employees, e.g., Portugal). The EC directive 96/71[117] on temporary posting of workers has been transposed into Swedish law, but that did not lead to any alterations to the 1991 amendments (except, perhaps, as regards employers from other EU member states).[118]

g. *Other Concerted Actions*

Concerted quitting by employees, often coupled with ads in newspapers in the "jobs wanted" section, is not uncommon but never authorized by unions. The risk is great when the employees hand in termination notices to the employer because a termination notice (oral or in writing) is binding and cannot be unilaterally revoked and the employer might decide to accept the termination notices of its employees.

Concerted calling in to take sick leave is not uncommon either, but the lawfulness of such action is doubtful as it may involve insurance fraud. Unions never authorize this type of action, thus making it an illegal, or wildcat, action.[119]

8. *Lockouts and Blockades*

Under the prevailing principle of "equality of arms" in Swedish labor law, employer lockouts are legal. Furthermore, Swedish law makes no distinction between offensive and defensive lockouts. Both are lawful to the same degree and there is no social disapproval of lockouts per se. As unions are entitled to use the strike weapon offensively, so are employers allowed to use lockouts.

---

[117]Council Directive 96/71/EC, 1997 O.J. (L 18) 1.

[118]See IX.B. in the chapter on the European Union in Part 1 of Volume I.

[119]See II.F.5., above. Only unions are authorized to call for industrial action.

a. Choice of Partial or Total Lockouts

As noted earlier, because of prevailing strike patterns, most strikes in Sweden are partial, i.e., unions call out only a few key employees, thus effectively crippling the workplace. In defending itself, the employer has few choices. Some partial responses are available to employers to put pressure on the union, e.g., to cease collecting union dues, but these are not very effective as countermeasures. There are basically only two options, continued operations or a total lockout.

- If the employer decides to continue operations, it must operate as best it can, which in most instances is very poorly. The employer cannot hire replacement workers—less for legal than political reasons[120]—and nonstriking employees are excused from performing struck work under extensive "neutrality agreements in collective agreements." Nonunionized foremen and managerial employees might be willing to do struck work but they are few in number and perhaps not skilled in the tasks at hand. Because costs will remain more or less the same but output will be much reduced, this option is very expensive. In addition, customer satisfaction may decrease because of poor service, putting the employer's business at risk. The strike will hurt the employer considerably.
- If, however, the employer declares a total lockout of the employees of the attacking union, it will have to shut down the workplace completely. A complete shutdown may put the employer in a bad light, although fellow employers may be sympathetic. However, a lockout hurts the employees just as much as it hurts the employer, perhaps even more. The burden on union coffers is heavy and unions face the risk that members may become disgruntled with low strike benefits and with the need to replenish strike coffers once the conflict is over.

[120]See II.F.7.b., above.

Faced with this dilemma, employers often opt for the total lockout. Many of the most spectacular labor market conflicts in recent decades have started as partial strikes but escalated into all-out battles when employers responded with total lockout.

b. Employer Blockades

Blockades by employers are common as well. Employers usually do not hire employees who are on strike or are locked out. Blockades of this kind are not announced as industrial actions in most instances as employers are entitled to "hire at will" and also to refrain from hiring, and are considered to be exercising this prerogative by such a tack.

c. Suspension of Employer Obligations

By and large employers are relieved of their obligations toward employees for the duration of a strike. Thus, they have no obligation to pay employees any remuneration during a strike. Can employers lawfully respond to a strike by withholding payments due to employees at the outbreak of the strike, based on work performed prior to the strike? The Labor Court thought so and ruled for the employer, relying—quite correctly in the author's opinion—on the doctrine that everything that is not forbidden is lawful.[121] The ruling of the court, however, was overturned by the legislature by amending the 1976 Co-Determination Act to specifically outlaw such actions, whether offensive or defensive. Employers only pay what is due at the start of the conflict. No pay is accrued/earned by strikers (or people locked out) during the industrial action.

9. *Government Intervention*

Industrial actions threatening important societal interests are not per se illegal but can be enjoined by an act of Parliament. Provisions in some master agreements between major federations in the labor market, for example, the 1938 Saltsjöbaden Agreement discussed above,[122] aim at preventing such actions. Swedish toler-

---

[121]Labor Court 1980 number 94.

[122]See II.B.5., above.

ance levels are quite remarkable in this respect, however, so industrial actions will not be found to endanger important societal interests other than in the most outrageous situations. For example, early in 1990 industrial actions in the banking sector (a partial strike followed by a total lockout) led to a complete closure of *all* banks in the entire country for several weeks. No emergency was considered to exist.[123] The Swedish Parliament has intervened only once, in 1971, to end extensive industrial actions in the public sector. In other instances, the government has intervened unofficially by dealing directly with the disputing parties to bring about a settlement, using everything from appeals to threats and serious arm-twisting.[124]

10. Liability for Damages

Anyone in breach of the peace is liable for damages, compensatory as well as punitive. Individual employees are excused if the action was duly organized by their union. Wildcat strikers are also privileged because they cannot be ordered to pay full compensation to the injured employer. A previous rule limiting damages for breach of the peace to a mere SEK 200 (about $25) has been replaced by a rule carrying no maximum amount. Courts must adhere to statements made during the legislative history of the new rule to the effect that damages shall be reasonable, in most instances not in excess of SEK 2,000 (in 1991 dollars, about $250). In most instances, employees cannot be fired for taking part in an illegal industrial action. Participation is never a crime.[125] Employ-

[123]During this particular period, no cash could be withdrawn, many payments could not be made, and activities at the stock exchange came close to a standstill. People hoarded cash before the lockout became effective. During the closure, people were able to manage partly because shopkeepers found themselves loaded with cash that they could not deposit since bank deposit boxes were not operational; they willingly accepted personal checks in exchange for cash.

[124]This happened, e.g., in 1980 and 1985. Direct government interventions are questionable from a constitutional point of view as responsibility in this area rests exclusively with the legislative branch of government.

[125]Criminal acts in connection with industrial actions are very rare in Sweden. The police are virtually never needed to maintain or establish order. The last reported incidents where police were called in date back to 1980 and 1982 and those instances were the first of their kind for many years. The conflicts in both instances involved ports and longshoremen.

ees can be ordered to report back to work but, obviously, specific performance is unenforceable and no equivalent to an Anglo-Saxon contempt of court sanction exists in Sweden.[126] Repeated refusal by wildcat strikers to obey the order to return to work will either go unpunished or, ultimately, result in dismissal.

Injunctions to stop industrial actions are not part of the Swedish legal system nor have they been for a century.

11. Arbitration and Mediation

Compulsory arbitration does not exist in Swedish labor law.

Mediation in labor disputes is offered by mediators appointed by the state Mediation Authority. Swedish law makes no distinction between conciliation and mediation, the two being functionally identical. In most instances, mediation is at the request of either or both parties to a dispute, although the Mediation Authority may intervene at its own initiative as well.

It is not mandatory that the parties to a mediation reach agreement. The role of state mediators is rather limited and primarily confined to mediation (conciliation) proper. The parties to a dispute are not legally obliged to stop industrial actions pending mediation but the Mediation Authority can order a temporary two-week postponement (a "cooling-off" period). State mediators have no other power at their disposal than their own creativity, ingenuity, personal authority, and force of persuasion. Though admittedly not very potent per se, these techniques, coupled with the wish of the parties to reach an agreement, have proved sufficient in most instances. As a last resort, the government can—and does—engage in arm-twisting (albeit with dubious constitutional authority). Under amendments to the 1976 Co-Determination Act adopted in 2000, the role of government-operated mediation has been strengthened, e.g., the new authority to impose a "cooling off" period.

Private mediation arrangements, ruled by collective agreements, have been adopted in many sectors of the economy in the past few years. The most important agreement dates from 1997 and covers the private manufacturing industry. The agreements

---

[126]See the Introduction, at G., above.

confer considerably more authority on mediators than the statutory rules. Mandatory interest arbitration is foreseen in the 1997 agreement, but a decision by a mediator to submit issues to binding arbitration is based on consent by all parties to the negotiations.

G. Individual Employee Grievances

Employees are always entitled to take their grievance to court in the event no amicable settlement is reached during grievance negotiations and the union declines to take the grievance to court. Unions have little discretion to process grievances as they see fit.[127]

H. Direction and Distribution of Work

As was pointed out in the Introduction, employers traditionally enjoy far-reaching managerial prerogatives. Beginning in the early 1970s, however, legislation has changed that to some extent. The 1976 Co-Determination Act is the major piece of legislation in this regard. On the whole, the Act does not deprive employers of their traditional prerogatives; employers retain the right to decide unilaterally how to manage the business, but they are obliged to negotiate with the established union(s) before making a decision. The ideological underpinning of the Act that capital and labor have equal rights in making decisions at workplaces has been implemented to only a very limited extent. The rationale behind the Act is that negotiations will bring about joint decisions in most instances.[128]

1. "Primary" Negotiations (Decision Bargaining)

The 1976 Co-Determination Act imposes an obligation on employers to negotiate with the established union(s) before making certain decisions. The Act limits the scope of mandatory negotiations in advance to matters involving an "important alteration" of either the employer's "activity" or of "work or employment conditions for employees."[129] Other decisions are exempted from

---

[127] See also the Introduction, at G.1., above.

[128] See also the discussion in III., below.

[129] 1976 Co-Determination Act, §11.

negotiations in advance but may be submitted to negotiations at the request of the established union(s). The employer can excuse itself from awaiting the outcome of mandatory negotiations only if "urgent" reasons necessitate this and may excuse itself from union-initiated negotiations only for reasons involving "special" necessities. Because no managerial exemptions exist, the rules imply a virtually complete ban on unilateral employer decision-making procedures.

The significance of the rules is offset, however, by the limited obligations imposed on employers in terms of the activity required of the employer at the bargaining table. The duty means nothing more than the minimum activity required at collective bargaining in general. Statutory reason and logic might point at some kind of "good faith bargaining," but the Labor Court has refused to construe the Act in that way, so the rules carry little clout. In addition, there is no right to call an industrial action before, during, or after "primary" negotiations. Some EU directives specifically require employers to bargain "with a view to seeking agreement" (e.g., article 6.2, directive 77/187 on transfers of undertakings, discussed in IV.B., below), but the Swedish legislature has not considered it necessary to amend Swedish law in this regard.

Of major importance is the stage during the decisionmaking process at which negotiations must start. Clearly, the earlier negotiations start the better the prospects for meaningful employee participation and thus for chances to reach a joint decision. The 1976 Co-Determination Act acknowledges this by requiring the employer to initiate negotiations at a very early stage and to continue discussions throughout the entire decisionmaking process.

If a joint decision is reached, negotiations have fulfilled their most important aim. If no agreement is reached, the employer decides the issue unilaterally. (There is only one limited exception, applicable to the situation where the union has a priority of interpretation. See II.H., below.) The decision taken by the employer is final and binding. There is no appeal.

Nonestablished unions[130] have only limited rights to take part in negotiations in advance and nonorganized employees have no such rights.

---

[130]See II.C.5., above, regarding nonestablished unions.

2. Union Access to Information

A condition for joint regulation is that employees are adequately informed about the employer's business. The 1976 Co-Determination Act contains provisions aimed at bridging the gap in knowledge and information. The bulk of information is given during "primary" negotiations. In addition, the Act imposes an obligation on an employer to keep the established union(s) "continuously informed about how his activity is developing in respect of production and economically, and about guidelines for personnel policy." Also, the established union(s) has some right to "examine books, accounts, and other documents which concern (the employer's) activity."[131] Rules on confidentiality apply to protect sensitive information.

3. Union Priority of Interpretation (Rights Disputes)

Disputes over the proper meaning of agreements (disputes of rights), collective or individual, ultimately can be settled by courts. Because a court decision cannot be had immediately after a dispute has arisen, the problem is how the parties are to act in the meantime.

Historically, employees were under a far-reaching duty to obey orders by employers. Disgruntled employees were left with the option to contest the order subsequently. This body of law was referred to as the employer's priority of interpretation. That priority was not in accord with generally prevailing principles of contract law. Priority of interpretation is a power to decide *ad interim*, but in most instances where the priority right was invoked, the decision was final. It simply was not feasible in practice to contest every employer decision imposed on employees by means of the employer's priority power.

In the 1970s, a number of statutes shifted the priority right of interpretation to the employee side. The 1976 Co-Determination Act represents the most important switch. (It must be stressed that priority rights refer to matters of contractual (or statutory) interpretation only and not to matters of suitability. Here the employer retains sovereignty.)

---

[131] 1976 Co-Determination Act, §19.

Under the 1976 Co-Determination Act,[132] established unions have priority rights of interpretation in three situations. One is of considerable importance: disputes over a union member employee's contractual "duty, under an agreement, to perform work." The duty to perform work under the collective agreement or the individual employment agreement is far-reaching and includes a number of only loosely related matters. First and foremost comes matters concerning the work tasks proper, *what* to do. But other matters are also covered, such as *where* and *when* work is to be performed, many aspects concerning *how* it is to be performed, and the duty to *obey*. Employers can overrule union interpretations only in rare instances.

4. *Union Veto Rights*

Illegal practices exist in the labor market as elsewhere. To combat certain illegal employer employment practices, the legislature gave the unions veto rights under the 1976 Act. The legislation essentially represents a delegation of public authority to unions. The idea is to combat evils at the outset, before the illicit practice has been put into effect. Veto rights are concerned with contracts by employers "to allow anybody to perform certain work on his behalf or in his business without that person thereby being employed by him."[133] A veto can be imposed when "the arrangement proposed by the employer supposedly entails circumventing the law or a collective agreement for the work, or the arrangement is otherwise in violation of what is generally accepted by the parties concerned within their bargaining sector."[134] In other words, union veto rights are aimed at contracts circumventing prevailing rules in favor of some illegal manpower arrangement—"gray" or "black" market manpower, as it were.

However, the veto rules have a potential to lead to results that are questionable under antitrust legislation. Unions may (and sometimes do) use the rules (either explicitly or by hints that they might use them) to steer work to employers that the unions accept,

[132] *Id.* §§33, 34.
[133] *Id.* §38.
[134] *Id.* §39.

e.g., employers who sign collective agreements. Antitrust authorities have expressed serious concern about this practice.

In other words, the rules are very controversial. The employer community wants them repealed, as indeed they were temporarily in January 1993. However, when the Social Democratic Party was returned to power in 1994, so were the union veto rules.

5. *Collective Agreements on Co-Determination*

The 1976 Co-Determination Act does not introduce any true co-determination. The Act relies on the labor market parties to realize that goal voluntarily through collective agreement regulation. Section 32 of the Act invites, even urges, employers to enter into such agreements with unions but imposes no obligation to do so. With one exception,[135] the Act does not restrict traditional freedom of contract, including the freedom not to contract.

For the most part, the expectations of the legislature in 1976 have gone unfulfilled. Co-determination based on collective agreements remains more a dream than a reality. The resoluteness of unions in 1976 to obtain co-determination has not been matched by any pressure on their part to accomplish co-determination. However, the focal point of the 1982 master agreement between the major federations in the private sector (the SAF, LO, and TCO) was on cooperation, mutual understanding, and accommodation as well as on business efficiency.[136]

I. Board Representation for Employees

The 1987 Act on Board Representation for Employees in Private Employment (and its 1976 predecessor) entitles established unions in the private sector to elect members to boards of directors in limited companies and cooperative associations. A number of conditions must be met. One condition is that the association must have at least 25 employees. Unions are entitled to elect two (in some cases, one, and in others, three) members but employee representatives always remain in the minority. With few exceptions,

---

[135] *Id.* §44 (of no proven importance).

[136] See II.B.5., above.

employee board members have the same position in terms of status and responsibilities as those representing owners. They have no veto power; they cannot stop majority decisions taken against their wishes.

In the public sector, employee participation is much more limited. It is basically confined to a right to be present and to express opinions.

III. Representation by Entities Other Than Unions

A. Works Councils

Under the 1946 master agreement between the SAF (now *Svenskt Näringsliv* or Confederation of Swedish Enterprise) and the LO (amended in 1964), company (or shop floor) committees were set up. These were joint management-labor bodies for the purpose of information and consultation, with the ultimate aim of introducing a certain degree of industrial democracy. Proposals to that effect had been put forward after World War I but they came to nothing. Note that this was not a statutorily mandated action but one the parties agreed to by private negotiations. The 1946 agreement was hailed as an important turning point in labor-management relations; however, the initial enthusiasm on the employee side slowly turned into disappointment.

When preparations for legislation on consultation and employee involvement in business management began in the early 1970s, unions were not eager to try to build on the 1946 shop floor committee agreement but wanted to start from afresh. The resulting 1976 Co-Determination Act contains no provisions on joint committees of any kind, but relates to the role of unions. It aims at introducing joint decisionmaking and equality between capital and labor, but it prescribes no specific organizational structure. Its mechanisms are "primary" negotiations and access to information.[137] In other words, no equivalent to the French *comité d'entreprise* or the German *Betriebsrat* exists in Sweden.

---

[137]See II.H.1. and 2., above.

Few places of work in Sweden have works councils. Labor-management cooperation is less institutionalized, but no less intense, for that.

"Safety committees" dealing with working environment matters exist in all but the smallest places of work. These represent all employees whether unionized or not, and are not union bodies proper. Safety committees are discussed below in VII.

B. European Works Council

The 1996 Act on European Works Councils implements EC directive 94/45.[138] The statute closely follows the directive.

C. Safety Committees

See the discussion in VII.B., below.

IV. Redundancy and Transfers of Undertakings

A. Redundancy

"Shortage of work" (i.e., economic reasons) is the common denominator for all reasons for dismissal other than personal. Of course, the prime example is redundancy proper. However, all instances where the decisive considerations are of a purely business nature belong under the rubric of economic reasons. Such instances cover a wide spectrum of issues at the core of entrepreneurial control, which means that management enjoys considerable freedom to dismiss employees for business reasons. Examples include the decision to close down a business facility (regardless of whether it is profitable or not), the decision to downsize or to relocate a facility when there is a shortage of work, and the decision to introduce labor-saving technology, making certain employees redundant. Subcontracting also belongs in this category, as does the use of independent contractors or hired-in[139] employees. As these ex-

[138]Council Directive 94/45/EC, 1994 O.J. (L 254) 64. See III.B.2. in the chapter on the European Union in Volume I, Part 1.

[139]Hired-in employees are not necessarily temporary employees, because hiring in can legally go on indefinitely.

amples demonstrate, the employer can create a redundancy situation. The 1982 Employment Protection Act does not interfere with employer freedom to manage as it sees fit. Employees have no recourse to the courts as it is not the task of courts "to assess the merits from a business point of view of alterations in the running of the business[,]" for "in the final analysis employer assessment of the need to undertake a change in the mode of operating the business must prevail."[140] The Act tries to soften the harsh realities of a competitive market-economy in various ways.

- Dismissal must be with notice,
- Negotiations in advance with the established union(s) are mandatory, and
- Priority ranking must be made.

1. *Notice*

Periods of notice are often quite long in mass redundancy situations, sometimes as long as well over a year before the last employee leaves. It is never possible to close down immediately. Extensive negotiations with unions and the local branch of the Labor Market Board are required. Employees receive full pay during this period regardless of whether they perform work or not.

2. *Severance*

Employees are often entitled to severance pay under master agreements between the labor market parties. No statutory rules concerning severance pay exist. Severance pay is provided by an insurance system financed by the employer community collectively. Thus, the individual employer does not have to shoulder any burden in a given situation, but it is very common for employers to assist their redundant employees in various ways.

3. *Ranking*

In situations of redundancy, the problem arises as to *who* to dismiss. The Act contains detailed provisions in this regard. Rank-

[140]Government Bill 1973:129 at p. 123 (author's translation).

ing is based on length of service (*seniority* or *last-in-first-out*) and age. All employees working in the same production unit and covered by the same collective agreement are ranked together. The effect of the rules in this respect is to widen the group of employees to be ranked beyond the immediate locus of redundancy. As can be seen, the rules are based on notions of solidarity among employees and on assessments of what is best from the point of view of labor market policy generally rather than on business efficiency and employee ability and usefulness to the company. Collective agreements are allowed to contain different criteria, however, and ad hoc derogations agreed upon between the employer and the established union are permitted as well.

Net results of the statutory rules are that the average age of employees tends to become rather high, that transfers among the various sub-units within the production unit concerned become necessary in many instances, and that the competitive edge of the unit is jeopardized. For these and other reasons, the rules are under heavy attack from the employer community, which has called for total repeal of all statutory rules on termination ranking. Though derogation from the rules is permitted, as noted above, derogation is in fact controlled by unions as the only way to set aside statutory rules is by means of a collective agreement.

For ranking purposes, the production unit is the determining factor. The production unit is determined mainly in geographical terms, not functional terms. However, under a 2001 amendment to the 1982 Employment Protection Act, the Act now states that "the mere fact that an employee's workplace is in his or her home does not signify, in itself, that that workplace constitutes a separate production unit."

Under another amendment to the 1982 Employment Protection Act, the Act provides that, before drawing up an order of selection for redundancy, employers with no more than 10 employees may exempt a maximum of two employees, whom they consider to be of key importance for the continuation of the business.

4. *Recall*

Employees dismissed for reasons of redundancy enjoy a right to recall to their previous employment. Several conditions must be met, such as a nine-month maximum time limit for a right to recall after termination of employment. Ranking applies to recalls, which are in the inverted order to dismissal, i.e., last fired, first rehired.

5. *Blue-Collar Employees*

Under conditions laid down in case law, blue-collar employees can be laid-off during short periods of redundancy. The employment contract remains in force and the employer is obliged to recall employees as the shortage of work subsides. In most instances, such employees receive full pay.

B. Transfers of Undertakings

As a result of the implementation of EU directive 2001/23[141] (and its 1977 predecessor), the 1982 Employment Protection Act provides that "the transfer of an undertaking, a business or a part of the undertaking or business"[142] "shall not in itself constitute grounds for dismissal of an employee."[143] However, the exception is limited. First, EU Directive 2001/23 does not apply to stock transfers. Second, redundancy at the business of the buyer/transferee as a result of the transfer constitutes just cause.

V. WAGES, HOURS, AND LEAVE

A. Wages

Sweden has no legislation on minimum pay. Apart from some specific situations, there is no generally applicable legislation on any other aspect of pay for employment work. One example of a situation covered by legislation is pay during the period of notice before termination of employment. Other examples are pay during annual leave, lay off, and illness. Of great importance are the

---

[141] Council Directive 2001/23/EC, 2001 O.J. (L 82) 16.
[142] 1982 Employment Protection Act art. 6(b).
[143] *Id.* art. 7.3.

rules regarding equal pay for work considered to be of equal value.[144]

Thus, pay is more or less exclusively in the hands of the labor market parties. In the past, pay levels and pay structures have been highly collectivized in the sense that regulation in collective agreements has been dominant. Recently, individual bargaining has gained ground and the employer community is strongly advocating a much more decentralized and individualistic pay system.

Some generally prevailing principles of law exist in the area of pay. Foremost is the principle of premium pay for overtime work. The Labor Court, however, has not been called upon to develop any detailed rules on the matter. Another principle of general applicability is that remuneration for work must not be below what is "reasonable." To some extent, this principle limits freedom of contract, but courts will rule for the employee only if remuneration is considerably below what is "reasonable." The norm for reasonableness is usually the minimum level of pay established by the collective agreement in the industry.

The 1970 Act on Set-Off by Employers largely protects employee claims on the employer for unpaid wages.

The 1992 Act on Pay Guarantee protects employees against employer insolvency. The Act implements EU directive 80/987 (as amended by 2002/74).[145]

B. Hours

Traditional employer discretion to decide *when* work is to be performed, e.g., hours and schedules, is greatly restricted by provisions in the 1982 Act on Working Time and in collective agreements. Generally speaking, an eight-hour-day workweek, Monday through Friday, prevails. As a matter of actual practice, the average working hours have been reduced for most employees to around 37.5 hours per week. Because the total number of working hours is rather limited in Sweden, Swedish regulation of working

---

[144]These rules are discussed in VI., below.

[145]Council Directive 80/987/EEC, 1980 O.J. (L 283) 23, *amended by* Council Directive 2002/74/EC, 2002 O.J. (L 270) 10. See IV.C. in the chapter on the European Union in Part 1 of Volume I.

time allows for considerable flexibility. For example, no statutory maximum exists for daily or weekly working hours. Restrictions apply for night work and work during weekends, but they are not severe and collective agreement regulation trends in this respect favor increased flexibility. A new statute is under preparation to achieve final implementation of EU directive 93/104, amended by Council Directive 2000/34, on working time.[146] The proposed statute would strengthen employer prerogatives in unilaterally scheduling working hours and contribute to increased flexibility in some respects, but not in others.

C. Leave

Employees are entitled to time off for several purposes. In fact, the combined effect of all plans for time off is such that the annual work year in Sweden is among the shortest in the world, a total of only some 1,600 hours.

1. Parental Leave

Leave for childbirth and child care (parental leave) is the oldest plan for time off. The present 1995 Act on Parental Leave is not confined to mothers, and the government actively promotes paternal leave (though admittedly with very mixed results). EU directive 92/85[147] on safety and health of "pregnant workers or workers who have recently given birth or are breastfeeding" applies and has been transposed in to Swedish law.[148] A minimum period of 14 weeks of maternity leave applies. In addition, the 1995 Act on Parental Leave contains a spectrum of rules allowing for leave for considerable periods of time for other purposes. The statute does not provide for pay during such leave, but, under social security legislation, parents are entitled to compensation for lost income in many situations, the compensation level being around 80 percent of wages.

---

[146]Council Directive 93/104/EC, 1993 O.J. (L 307) 18, *amended by* Council Directive 2000/34/EC, 2000 O.J. (L 195) 41. See V.B. in the chapter on the European Union in Part 1 of Volume I.

[147]Council Directive 92/85/EEC, 1992 O.J. (L 348) 1.

[148]See V.C.1. in the chapter on the European Union in Part 1 of Volume I.

2. *Vacation Leave*

Leave for an annual paid vacation is the second oldest plan. The present 1977 Act on Vacation applies to the entire labor market, private as well as public. It entitles employees to a total of five weeks paid leave per annum. Payment equals earnings during a corresponding period of work, with a slight additional increase in compensation. Only those who have been employed during a 12-month period prior to the vacation year are entitled to full payment.

3. *Other Leave*

There are 12 holidays during the working year, coupled with a certain number of nonworking afternoons preceding them.

Numerous other schemes exist. There are provisions on time off to:

- study (statutes from 1974 and 1986),
- take care of sick relatives (1989 statute),
- job hunt (provisions in the 1982 Employment Protection Act),
- start a business (1997 statute),
- hold elected political office, and
- perform military service (or some nonmartial alternative).

In addition to statutory schemes, collective agreements often allow for leave in other instances, e.g., for personal or family matters.

VI. ANTIDISCRIMINATION

A. Overview and Framework Legislation on Discrimination

Virtually non-existent only 20 years ago, antidiscrimination legislation is now extensive. EU law has been the triggering factor. Some direct influence from U.S. law can also be detected, e.g., on disability legislation. All essential legislation is now in place. Legislators will need to continue to synchronize and simplify the various laws. The courts are increasingly being asked to rule on discrimination cases and a body of case law is emerging.

The 2003 Act Prohibiting Discrimination is the legislative centerpiece. It serves both as a framework for four specific labor law antidiscrimination statutes[149] and as a substantive piece of antidiscrimination legislation.

In its framework capacity, the 2003 Act Prohibiting Discrimination refers to (but does not supplement or otherwise interfere with) four specific antidiscrimination labor statutes:

- the 1991 Equal Opportunities Act;
- the 1999 Act Against Discrimination in Working Life for Reasons of Ethnic Belonging, Religion or Other Belief;
- the 1999 Act Prohibiting Discrimination Against Disabled Persons in Working Life; and
- the 1999 Act Prohibiting Discrimination in Working Life Based on Sexual Orientation.

The 2003 Act and these four statutes are closely linked. The same definitions apply to key concepts, such as direct and indirect discrimination, comparable situation, ethnic origin and belonging, sexual orientation, and disability. Rules on burden of proof are conforming. The statutes are all closely linked to EU antidiscrimination legislation and mostly implement various directives. Legislative history shows that the statutes shall be interpreted and applied in accordance with EU legislation. Despite their recent enactment, the four specific antidiscrimination statutes have been changed on several occasions and further changes are envisioned in the near future. An amalgamation of the existing four statutes and the framework statute is under consideration. In the same vein, an amalgamated antidiscrimination agency comprising all the present four *Ombudsmen*, one for each of the specific acts, is being considered. A government bill is expected in late 2004.

In its second capacity, the 2003 Act Prohibiting Discrimination also implements two EU directives: Directive 2000/43/EC implementing the principle of equal treatment between persons irrespective of racial or ethnic origin (*Equal Treatment Directive*)[150]

---

[149]The 2003 Act also is framework legislation for a fifth statute, the 2001 Act on Equal Treatment of University Students, but this 2001 Act falls outside the field of labor law and is not discussed here.

[150]Council Directive 2000/43/EC, 2000 O.J. (L 180) 22.

and Directive 2000/78/EC establishing a general framework for equal treatment in employment and occupation (*Labor Market Directive*).[151] In this respect, the 2003 Act prohibits discrimination outside the field of working life proper on the same grounds as the three 1999 specific antidiscrimination statutes listed above. Where applicable, the 2003 Act protects not only employees but also job applicants. Discrimination under the 2003 Act covers direct and indirect discrimination, harassment for any of the same grounds as prohibited by the three 1999 specific antidiscrimination statutes, and instructions by someone in a superior position to a subordinate to discriminate on any of these grounds. Discrimination in any of these ways is prohibited in several areas related to work, namely (1) employment policy measures such as employment exchange and job placement; (2) starting and conducting a business; (3) exercise of a profession; and (4) membership and participation in certain organizations, for example labor unions, business organizations, or professional societies. The 2003 Act is novel—in its inclusion of an antidiscrimination provision for group (4) above, organizations—in that it encroaches on the traditional self-governance of such organizations.[152] Discrimination is prohibited to some extent in other areas of human life as well, e.g., social security and unemployment insurance.

Anyone covered by the 2003 Act, for example, employees, job applicants, union members, and persons applying for membership, can sue under the Act and is entitled to non-financial (punitive) damages. Discriminatory agreements and individual acts of discrimination are null and void. No cases have been brought before the courts to date.

Reference should also be made to the 2002 Act Prohibiting Discrimination Against Part-Time Employees and Fixed-Time Employees.[153]

Finally, reference should be made to protection against discrimination as part of freedom of association.[154] To some extent

[151]Council Directive 2000/78/EC, 2000 O.J. (L 303) 16. See also the chapter on the European Union in Part 1 of in Volume I, at VI.B.2.a.

[152]See II.C.1., above.

[153]See I.C.4., above.

[154]See II.C., above.

this protection also carries with it protection for unionized employees against pay discrimination. However, there is no general legislation in this respect and no corresponding protection for non-unionized employees. These employees are often treated less favorably than unionized employees and by and large no legal redress is available to them.

B. Gender Discrimination

1. Constitutional Provision

The constitutional rule prohibiting gender discrimination states:

> No Act of law or other statutory instrument may entail discrimination against any citizen on grounds of sex, unless the relevant provision forms part of efforts to bring about equality between men and women or relates to compulsory military service or any corresponding compulsory national service.[155]

2. Statutory Requirements

The first gender antidiscrimination legislation was enacted in 1979. The present Equal Opportunity Act dates from 1991 but has been amended several times, most recently in 2000. It is drafted to conform to corresponding regulation in the EU.[156] Generally, the purpose of the Act is to rectify a labor market that still is segregated to a great extent along gender lines and where women are underrepresented in higher positions. In addition, jobs typically performed by women are less well paid than jobs typically performed by men, and women also earn less than men working in the same sector of the economy.

The Act aims to promote "equal rights for women and men with regard to employment, conditions of employment and other conditions of work as well as opportunities for personal develop-

---

[155]Ch. 2, art. 16 of the 1974 Instrument of Government.

[156]Council Directive 75/117/EEC, 1975 O.J (L 45) 19, on equal pay; Council Directive 76/207/EEC, 1976 O.J. (L 39) 40, *amended by* Council Directive 2002/73/EC, 2002 O.J. (L 269) 15, on equal treatment. See VI.A.1. and VI.A.2.a., in the chapter on the European Union in Part 1 of Volume I.

ment in employment."[157] The Act protects both men and women but it "aims at improving primarily women's conditions in working life."[158] The Act applies to employees and job applicants alike. It contains two sets of provisions, one on active measures to promote gender equality and one on prohibitions against gender discrimination in individual cases. Each set of provisions is discussed below. An Ombudsman for Equal Opportunity (*Jämställdhetsombudsmannen*), together with a Commission for Equal Opportunity (*Jämställdhetsnämnden*), initiates, directs, and supervises efforts to promote gender equality.

Active measures are designed to combat and abolish all gender-related differences in working life and to ultimately arrive at an equal, 50:50 distribution of jobs at all places of work. At present a 40:60 female/male distribution is considered acceptable. Employers are legally obliged to make systematic efforts to realize these goals. The government has assumed the responsibility to ensure that employers do so and collective agreement provisions no longer may deviate from the statute's requirements. As part of their statutory obligations, employers with 10 or more employees are to draw up an annual "equality plan," listing necessary measures and specific dates by which these measures are to be executed as well as an assessment of the extent to which measures listed in the previous annual plan have been accomplished. A similar obligation concerns the existence of differences in pay. Close cooperation between the employer and its employees as well as the established labor union(s)[159] is part of the statutory scheme in both these respects. Employers failing to comply with their statutory obligations can be ordered to comply on penalty of payment of a sum of money specified in the order.[160] The imposition of sanctions has been very rare, not so much because employer compliance has been scrupulous, but because enforcement has been relatively lenient. There is no right of individual redress nor is there any provision for class actions by individuals.

[157] Equal Opportunity Act §1.

[158] *Id.*

[159] See II.C.5., above.

[160] See the discussion in the Introduction, at G., above, regarding sanctions and remedies.

The other set of statutory provisions deals with discrimination in individual cases, direct or indirect, and with harassment because an employee has rejected sexual advances by the employer.

Generally, gender discrimination is considered to exist when someone is treated improperly and there is a direct or indirect connection between such improper treatment and the gender of that person. This means that discrimination under the Act is limited to situations involving people of different gender. The Act specifies five instances where improper treatment based on gender constitutes illegal discrimination: when an employer (1) makes a hiring decision, interviews a potential employee, or takes any other kind of action during the hiring process; (2) makes a decision regarding promotion or selects an employee for training in view of a future promotion; (3) applies conditions regarding pay or other employment matters to work that is equal or of equal value; (4) manages and directs work; and (5) makes a decision that involves termination with notice, summary dismissal, or layoff, or is otherwise of fundamental importance to an employee. To a great extent, these five instances substitute standards of objectivity for employer discretion in employment matters. However, similar to the other antidiscrimination statutes, the 1991 Act makes an exception for situations where an ideological, business-related, or other special interest is manifestly more important than protection against direct gender discrimination. The scope of such exception is very limited. An example is that gender can be decisive for certain professions such as those having roles such as theater actors, opera singers, and models.

3. *Hiring, Promotion, and Affirmative Action*

One provision against illegal discrimination deals with hiring of employees. It limits employer prerogatives to hire at will (and to promote and to select employees for the purpose of training to qualify for promotion), but only in the sense that a better qualified person of one gender has priority over a less qualified person of the opposite gender and never in the sense that a less qualified (or equally qualified) person of one gender has preference over persons of the opposite gender. Affirmative action to promote equality at work is permitted, provided, however, that it is done in a consistent and systematic way. The statutory provision here is rooted in the Constitution.[161] A 1995 ruling by the EU Court called into question whether affirmative action programs are compatible with EU law.[162] This ruling caused considerable consternation in Sweden. A subsequent amendment to the Rome Treaty[163] allows for affirmative action to some extent. The Swedish legislature has refrained from changing the Swedish statute. However, it is extremely unclear how far affirmative action can be pursued legally. In any case, mandatory quotas or the similar are non-existent in Sweden, although there is strong political pressure on employers to achieve equal representation, for example, in terms of numbers of each gender at every hierarchal level of enterprises and in all professions therein.

4. *Equal Pay*

Another provision in the Act deals with differences in pay or other conditions of employment for work that objectively is considered to be the same or of equal value. Such differences in pay are illegal unless the employer can demonstrate that the difference is not related directly or indirectly to the employee's gender.

5. *Sanctions*

An employer who is found guilty by a court of discrimination against an individual is liable to financial (compensatory) damages and in some instances punitive damages as well. In many instances, the discriminatory action by the employer can also be declared null and void but in other cases it will stand. The most important example of the latter is a discriminatory decision to hire one person in preference to another of the opposite gender. No order to vacate the decision and replace it by a nondiscriminatory one is possible under Swedish law so the person discriminated against cannot obtain the job, i.e., Swedish law does not allow for specific performance in such situations. No compensation for the

---

[161] See the Constitution as quoted in VI.B.1., above.

[162] Case C-450/93, Kalanke v. Bremen, 1995 E.C.R. I-3051. See the chapter on the European Union in Part 1 of Volume I, in the Introduction, at D.3.c.

[163] Amsterdam Treaty art. 141.4.

loss of employment other than financial (compensatory) damages is available.[164]

6. *Marriage and Maternity Leave Issues*

Legislation originally dating back to the 1930s protects women against dismissal because of engagement, marriage, pregnancy, childbirth, and maternity leave. Today protection is afforded by section 7 of the 1982 Employment Protection Act.[165] Where applicable, men also are protected.

C. National or Ethnic Origin, Race, Skin Color, Religion, or Other Belief

Chapter 2, article 15 of the 1974 constitution (the Instrument of Government) states:

> No Act of law or other statutory instrument may entail discrimination of any citizen because he belongs to a minority on grounds of race, skin color, or ethnic origin.

It was not until 1994 that Sweden enacted a statute of general scope on protection against discrimination due to race, color, or national or ethnic origin. The 1994 Act did not apply to religion or other belief, political creed, or union affiliation). It replaced a 1986 statute based on moral persuasion only. In turn, the 1999 Act Against Discrimination in Working Life for Reasons of Ethnic Belonging, Religion or Other Belief (as amended) has replaced the 1994 statute. The concept of "religion" was introduced only in 2003, prompted by Article 13 of the Rome Treaty (as amended by the Amsterdam Treaty). Ethnic origin is defined as national or ethnic origin, race, or skin color. Similar to the other antidiscrimination legislation, the 1999 Act contains mandatory rules on and mechanisms for coercive legal enforcement. The Ombudsman Against Ethnic Discrimination (*Diskrimineringsombudsmannen*) is charged with the task of supervising and enforcing the Act, together with a Commission (*Diskrimineringsnämnden*). In all other

[164]See I.E.4., above.
[165]See I.E., above.

aspects, the 1999 Act is parallel to the other antidiscrimination legislation.

Religious attire and accoutrements, such as the Christian cross, the Jewish kippa, the Muslim veil, and the Sikh turban, are rapidly becoming a controversial phenomenon in all fields of life. The factor here is freedom of religion, primarily the freedom to manifest religion (the positive side) and the freedom not to be exposed to manifestations of religion (the negative side). Article 9 of the 1950 Convention for the Protection of Human Rights and Fundamental Freedoms of the European Council provides the legislative basis.[166] Sweden is bound by the Convention under public international law but in 1994 also enacted it *verbatim* as domestic law. Case law under the Convention provides some guidance. No modern Swedish case law exists (an infamous 1986 ruling by the Labor Court being obsolete[167]) and neither the 1999 antidiscrimination act itself nor its legislative history provides any guidance. Legislation on this issue is not under consideration but administrative guidance has been provided to schools regarding student behavior.

D. Disability Discrimination

Replacing a 1994 statute, the 1999 Act Prohibiting Discrimination Against Disabled Persons in Working Life has introduced a legal regime that closely coincides with the other antidiscrimination statutes.[168] The Act is supervised by the Disabled Persons Ombudsman (*Handikappombudsmannen*).

Scattered provisions in other statutes protect the handicapped as well. Perhaps the most important rules are concerned with employment protection and employer obligations to try to rehabilitate the handicapped.[169] The 1974 Promotion of Employment Act is also of relevance.[170]

---

[166]See the discussion in the Chapter on the European Union in Part 1 of Volume I, in the Introduction, at E.

[167]Labor Court 1986 No. 11.

[168]See VI.A., above.

[169]See also the discussion in VII., below.

[170]See the Introduction, at F., above.

E. Sexual Orientation

The 1999 Act Prohibiting Discrimination in Working Life Based on Sexual Orientation is the first of its kind in Sweden. It is modeled on the three other antidiscrimination statutes.[171] No constitutional rule against discrimination based on sexual orientation exists. However, Article 13 of the EU Treaty (as amended by the Amsterdam Treaty), which provides the antidiscrimination framework of the Rome Treaty, includes sexual orientation. Sexual orientation under the Swedish statute refers to homosexual, heterosexual, and bisexual orientation. Sexual variances such as pedophilia, exhibitionism, or transsexualism fall outside the statute. Sexual orientation is normally considered irrelevant in working life so the Act takes the position that it must not be taken into account. However, in common with the other antidiscrimination statutes, the 1999 Act does make an exception for situations where an ideological, business-related, or other special interest is manifestly more important than protection against direct discrimination in this respect. The scope of such exception is limited.

Of the four antidiscrimination statutes, the 1999 sexual orientation act imposes the least extensive obligations in terms of active measures to promote equality. Except for the exemptions mentioned above, employers are obliged to refrain from attaching any importance to sexual orientation but that obligation is not enforceable per se. The only substantive employer obligation is to provide the relevant Ombudsman (*HomO*) with certain information. In common with the other antidiscrimination statutes, failure to do so is punishable by a fine. No such case has been recorded so far.

VII. OCCUPATIONAL SAFETY AND HEALTH AND WORKERS' COMPENSATION

Together with the 1976 Co-Determination Act and the 1982 Employment Protection Act, the 1977 Act on Working Environ-

[171]See VI.A., above.

ment can be said to be one of the three pillars of Swedish statutory labor regulation. To a considerable extent the three statutes form a unit, in particular the 1976 and 1977 acts, as they all adopt an overall perspective of working life—although from different angles—and overlap in many ways. The 1977 Act defines working environment in the widest possible way and encompasses all conditions at places of work. The Act applies to the physical health and safety of employees but also to mental and psychological conditions at workplaces generally. This in turn means that matters such as organization of work, work tasks of individual employees, pay systems, procedures and methods for directing and distributing work, job rotation, team work, and quality circles are within the ambit of the statute. As can be seen from the foregoing, the statute is very ambitious in scope.

A. The Four Cornerstones of the Act

The prime responsibility for working environment rests with employers. However, the Act considers industrial safety and working environment to be matters of concern for society and the employees as well. There are four policies that are cornerstones of the Act. They are:

- The three parties must cooperate.
- Efforts to provide a satisfactory working environment must be carried out in a systematic and orderly way. Administrative systems in conjunction with action plans are often required to achieve this goal. Follow-up procedures are equally important.
- Employers are responsible for rehabilitation of employees with medical or other problems and for continuous efforts to adjust work to the needs, prospects, and capabilities of employees.
- Efforts to promote a healthy environment should be future-oriented. Thus, prevention is considered a necessary and indispensable element in all planning at workplaces, in particular when new buildings and work sites are projected or when new technology is considered.

B. Safety Committees; Safety Delegates

Institutionalized cooperation between management and employees is obligatory. The Safety Committee is a joint body mandated by the Act at all places of work with 50 employees. Additional safety committees can be set up at larger workplaces. The committee plays a central role. Apart from representatives on the safety committee(s), the employees are represented by "Safety Delegates," generally (but not always) nominated by the established unions. Safety delegates are entitled to full pay during time off required for performing their duties. The Act does not prescribe the number of these, leaving that to the employee party, but the number must not exceed the needs. If the number is contested (which experience indicates virtually never to be the case), the Work Environment Agency (which replaced the Industrial Safety Board in 2001) decides what number is appropriate. One (or several) of the delegates will serve as Head Delegate(s). Regional (union) Safety Delegates attend to the smallest places of work where there is no delegate. Delegates take part in everything relating to the working environment.

If no remedy is obtained in discussions with the employer, delegates in some instances have the authority to order work to be stopped where there is imminent and serious danger. Employers are obliged to comply with such orders. In most instances, however, delegates and employee members on safety committees have primarily advisory roles.

C. Work Environment Agency

The Work Environment Agency replaced the Industrial Safety Board in 2001. The Work Environment Agency and its local branches play a focal role in promoting a better work environment. The Agency conducts extensive research on its own and cooperates with other scientific institutions. The local branches of the Agency inspect workplaces to verify compliance with specific safety standards and, in particular, to verify that administrative systems and action programs for working environment are satisfactory. The Agency is authorized to issue recommendations and adopt ordinances to implement the Act. The number of ordinances is very substantial. In recent years, a great many ordinances have been adopted or amended to bring Swedish regulation in line with EU regulation. Ordinances are binding on employers and failure to comply with them is a criminal offense in many instances. The Agency and its branches are authorized to impose injunctions and order specific performance. Noncompliance on the part of the employer is a crime or renders the employer liable to payment of a default fine.[172]

D. Workers' Compensation

Workers' compensation is governed by the 1976 Act on Workers' Compensation Insurance.

VIII. Pensions and Benefits

Retirement age under the 1982 Employment Protection Act is now 67. In 2001, the 67-year age limit replaced the previously prevailing age of 65. The increase in retirement age reflects the aging of the population and growing fears that the pension system will come under unbearable strain in the future. Collective agreements in force in 2001 or negotiated after 2001 specifying a lower mandatory retirement age are null and void.

While employees are entitled to retire on their own initiative with full pension rights at age 65, they are entitled, also on their own initiative, to continue to work until age 67. Under an individual agreement with their employer—or some other employer—an employee may choose to work beyond the age of 67. However, employees above age 67 enjoy only limited employment protection.

Employee retirement benefits were originally regarded as voluntary and gratuitous contributions by employers. Today, employee retirement benefits are considered to be delayed pay. In other words, such benefits are vested.

Most employees receive retirement benefits from at least three different sources—two under statutory pension plan legislation and one under a collective agreement. Many nonunionized employees

---

[172]For more information on sanctions, see the Introduction, at H., above.

are covered by such collective agreements as well because the parties to the agreement usually have an understanding that the employer must provide nonmembers no less in wages and other benefits than the agreement provides for those directly covered by it. Private benefit plans predate state benefit plans; private benefits are not insubstantial; however, they are lower than the statutory benefits.

A. Statutory Plans

The two statutory plans have different structures. The first and oldest of these provides an old age pension to every person with a close connection to Sweden (i.e., even foreigners in some circumstances), regardless of previous employment and individual contribution. The total amount is rather low, somewhat below the poverty level, but those who are entitled to no other retirement payments will receive additional benefits (discussed below) as part of the regular old age pension plan.

In addition to the old age pension, those who have been employed (including self-employed individuals) receive a pension based, somewhat loosely, on their previous earnings. This "additional pension" provides the bulk of retirement benefits for those who receive it. The "additional pension" is fully paid for by contributions from employers or individual payments by the self-employed. As of 2004, the fee amounted to 10.21 percent of total direct wage labor costs (or 11.91 percent, when the fee to cover pension payments to surviving kin is added). Full benefits amount to 60 percent of annual employee wage earnings in real terms during the employee's 15 best years. A ceiling limits benefits for those whose incomes have exceeded a specific level, and that ceiling is fairly low. The "additional pension" is fully portable. On principle, it is also vested.

A completely new system for the "additional pension" program has been adopted. It is being slowly phased in to replace the existing system. It will allow for more flexibility and will establish a closer link between contributions and benefits. It is based on employer contributions, but it will provide benefits in situations not covered by the present system, e.g., during parental leave. Benefits are based on lifetime earnings rather than on the 15 best years.

B. Private Pension Plans

Private pension plans are mostly based on collective agreements. A 1967 statute protects employee benefits under employer pension plans. Two master agreements cover virtually the entire private sector of the labor market, one for blue-collar employees and one for white-collar employees regardless of union membership. Benefits under these agreements are financed by employer contributions of somewhat more than 3 percent for blue-collar and 6 percent for white-collar workers. Benefits are portable and vested.

IX. IMMIGRATION

Sweden is a member state of the EU. One of the "freedoms" of the EU is free movement of workers. That freedom means a right to seek and accept work in any other member state of the union without having to obtain a residence or work permit. Work permits for employment in Sweden are not required of citizens from countries within the European Economic Area (EEA).[173]

The Nordic countries (i.e., Denmark, Finland, Iceland, Norway, and Sweden) also form a common labor market. The basic convention for this market dates from 1954.

With few exceptions, citizens from countries outside the EEA must obtain a work permit before being allowed to accept work in Sweden. On several occasions after World War II, Sweden has actively recruited manpower from other countries and a considerable immigration has taken place for that reason. Today the situation is completely different; with high unemployment in Sweden, it has become difficult for foreigners to obtain a work permit. The controlling statute in this area is the 1989 Act on Foreigners. The statute is administered by the Migration Agency.

Foreigners who do have a work permit are treated like any Swedish employee. Labor and employment statutes make no distinction based of nationality. In one respect foreigners are privileged. The 1986 Act on Time Off for Instruction in Swedish for

[173]The EEA includes the EU Member States, plus the three countries of the European Free Trade Association: Iceland, Liechtenstein, and Norway.

Foreigners are afforded time off to study Swedish. Time off is considered working time for the purpose of computing aggregated working time, but the employer is exempted from paying the employee for this time. Some public financial assistance is provided for this time off, however.

TURKEY*

INTRODUCTION

Turkey is a parliamentary republic with well-rooted democratic institutions. Separation of legislative, executive, and judiciary powers, as well as the rule of law, is the basic principle guiding the functioning of the state.

Turkish law is based on the Napoleonic legal system, where the role of written rules is predominant. The Civil Code and the Code of Obligations were translated from the Swiss laws and incorporated in 1926 into the Turkish legal framework. The Civil Code recently has been subject to a full-scale revision, and the Code of Obligations will be updated in the near future.

Turkey's administrative structure is centralized, which means that the sources of law are state-based. In addition to constitutional and statutory norms, collective labor agreements and individual employment contracts are the main sources of employment rights and conditions and worker benefits.

The Ottoman Empire that spread through three continents was transformed into the Republic of Turkey. In the 1920s, Turkey chose, under the leadership of Kemal Atatürk, to become a modern secular republic with democratic rules and institutions based on 600 years of tradition. It currently has a population of over 66 million with a considerable number of young citizens. A member of European organizations such as the Council of Europe, the Organization for Economic Cooperation and Development (OECD)[1] and NATO, Turkey has been an associate member of the European Union (EU) since 1963 and applied for full membership in 1987. Effective December 31, 1995, Turkey entered into a formal

---

*Noyan Turunç, Turunç & Savaşçın, Istanbul, Turkey; Melda Sur, Professor of Law, Dokuz Eylül University Faculty of Law, Izmir, Turkey.

[1]See the chapter on the OECD in Part 4 of Volume I.

customs union agreement with the EU,[2] which among other things, provides for the elimination of customs duties and quotas on industrial goods imported or exported between the parties.

A. Sources of Turkish Labor Law

The Constitution, the Code of Obligations, and the Labor Law govern individual labor relations, and special laws cover maritime and press workers. Two laws regulate collective relations: the Law on Unions and the Law on Collective Agreements, Strikes, and Lockouts. International treaties also are an important source of Turkish labor law.

1. The Constitution

The Constitution, adopted in 1982, sets forth the fundamental characteristics of the republic as "a democratic, secular and social state governed by the rule of law, safeguarding public peace, national solidarity and justice, respecting human rights."[3] In the social and economic fields, the state is obligated to fulfill its constitutional duties within the limits of its financial resources.[4]

Article 10 of the Constitution provides that: "all individuals are equal, without any discrimination before law, irrespective of language, race, color, sex, political opinion, philosophical belief, religion and sect, or any such considerations."

Among the fundamental rights and freedoms guaranteed by the Constitution, the prohibition against forced labor[5] and the freedom to work and conclude contracts[6] are closely related to labor life. Other provisions governing labor include the right and duty to work;[7] the right to suitable working conditions, rest, and leisure;[8] the right to organize labor unions;[9] the right to bargain col-

---

[2]*See* Decision 1/95 of the EC-Turkey-Association Council, 1996 O.J. (L 35) 1.

[3]CONST. OF THE REPUBLIC OF TURKEY, NO. 2709 (*TÜRKIYE CUMHURIYETI ANAYASASI*) art. 2.

[4]*Id.* art. 65.

[5]*Id.* art. 18.

[6]*Id.* art. 48.

[7]*Id.* art. 49.

[8]*Id.* art. 50.

[9]*Id.* art. 51.

lectively;[10] workers' right to strike and employers' recourse to the lockout;[11] the guarantee of a fair wage and the determination of a minimum wage;[12] and the right to social security.[13]

The Constitution also provides that the fundamental rights and freedoms of aliens may be restricted by law consistent with international law.[14]

2. *National Labor Legislation*

a. *Individual Relations*

Labor Law No. 4857 (the Labor Law or *İş Kanunu*), enacted in 2003, governs individual employment relations. However, the Labor Law does not apply to all workers; some categories of workers are subject to special laws. Except for loading and unloading operations to and from the coast, which remain within the scope of the Labor Law, sea transport work is covered by the Maritime Labor Law (*Deniz İş Kanunu*).[15] While manual press workers are covered by the Labor Law, press workers such as journalists and press photographers are subject to the more favorable provisions of the Press Labor Law (*Basın İş Kanunu*).[16]

Other categories of workers are excluded from the Labor Law and are covered under the general and relatively liberal provisions of the Code of Obligations (*Borçlar Kanunu*), which governs contracts of service.[17] These categories include: agricultural workers in workplaces where up to 50 workers are employed; laborers in small workplaces where up to three persons are employed; house porters and household service workers; individuals (i.e., members of a family or relatives) engaged in a handicrafts business at home; and professional athletes.

---

[10] *Id.* art. 53.
[11] *Id.* art. 54.
[12] *Id.* art. 55.
[13] *Id.* art. 60.
[14] *Id.* art. 16.
[15] Law No. 854, enacted 1966.
[16] Law No. 5953, enacted 1952, amended 1961.
[17] Law No. 818, enacted 1926, arts. 313–54.

b. Collective Relations

Two major laws govern collective labor relations. The Law on Unions[18] confirms the freedom of association of workers and employers and regulates the functioning and activities of unions. The Law on Collective Labor Agreements, Strikes, and Lockouts[19] (the Collective Labor Law) regulates collective bargaining and industrial action.

Both the Law on Unions and the Collective Labor Law are applicable, regardless of the activity or size of the workplace. Thus, the right to form and join unions, as well as the right of collective bargaining and the right to strike, apply in principle to all workers under private labor contracts, including such categories as agricultural, maritime, and press workers.

c. Social Security

Since 1945, a public social insurance system has been evolving by the state. The primary law in this area is the Social Insurance Law No. 506, enacted in 1964. With some exceptions, all workers under employment contract are covered by the official and mandatory social security system. Therefore, the Social Insurance Law covers a large part of the working population.

3. International Sources

Turkey has ratified numerous conventions of the International Labor Organization (ILO), including Convention No. 87 (Freedom of Association and Protection of the Right to Organize), No. 98 (Right to Organize and Collective Bargaining), No. 151 (Public Service Labor Relations), and No. 158 (Termination of Employment).[20] Turkey also is a party to the 1950 European Convention for the Protection of Human Rights and Fundamental Freedoms and the Council of Europe's 1961 European Social Charter.

---

[18]Law No. 2821, enacted in 1983.

[19]Law No. 2822, enacted in 1983.

[20]See the chapter on the ILO in Part 4 of Volume I.

B. Government Agencies

1. The Ministry of Labor and Social Security

a. Supervision and Inspection

The Ministry of Labor and Social Security (the Ministry of Labor) and its Regional Directorates are the government agencies responsible for labor issues. The Ministry of Labor and the Regional Directorates are entitled to examine the administration of the workplace and to inspect the books, records, and accounts, as well as the tools and materials required for work, when deemed necessary. Installations and arrangements may be observed and examined at any time.[21]

During an inspection, the employer, the employer's representative, employees, and all other persons are obliged to furnish any information requested, to deliver all relevant documents and records, and to assist authorities and officials. Each employer must keep a register in which results of inspections must be entered.

The Ministry of Labor and the Regional Directorates also administer, supervise, and inspect the application of labor legislation. They discharge this duty through labor inspectors who are attached to the Ministry of Labor. The labor inspectors are authorized to prevent labor law offenses, especially with respect to the health and security of workers.

Municipalities and other authorities that are authorized to permit the establishment and operation of a business will, before granting permission, check to see whether the necessary permit and license are available from the Ministry of Labor. These public institutions also report the results of their inspections to the Regional Directorate of Labor.

b. Exemption From Fees and Taxes

Written applications made to the Ministry of Labor by employees, employers, and by their professional organizations on

---

[21]Controls and inspections of military establishments and those manufacturing facilities necessary for the security of the country are carried out according to regulations drawn up jointly by the Ministry of National Defense and the Ministry of Labor.

matters related to employment, as well as any petitions, reports, documents, books, and transactions related to employment, are exempt from stamp tax and all other fees and taxes.

2. *Turkish Employment Agency*

The recruitment of workers is regulated by the state as a public service and is performed by the Turkish Employment Agency *(Türkiye İş Kurumu*, or *İŞKUR)*. The Employment Agency is attached to the Ministry of Labor but has autonomous financing and administration.

The Employment Agency provides the following services free of charge:

- collecting data regarding available employment in the industry;
- regulating and facilitating employment opportunities for both workers and employers;
- publishing charts listing employers and workers in different areas of industry;
- providing vocational guidance and training;
- undertaking measures necessary to improve workers' occupational qualifications and to develop qualified workers;
- acting as an intermediary in the conclusion of employment contracts;
- performing duties pertaining to private employment agencies (granting permits and controlling their activities);
- following up the EU and other intergovernmental organizations' decisions, executing international agreements to which Turkey is party; and
- conducting unemployment insurance services.

In addition, under certain conditions, the Employment Agency may authorize private employment offices to perform the duty of labor exchange. This permission is granted for three years and may be withdrawn in some cases.

3. *Social Security Institution*

The Social Security Institution *(Sosyal Sigortalar Kurumu)* is attached to the Ministry of Labor and Social Security, but it is a public corporate body with autonomous financing and administration. This institution provides social insurance aids and benefits to those who suffer hardships due to occupational accidents and illnesses, illness, motherhood, disability, and old age, under various conditions.

C. Labor Courts

Legal disputes arising from individual, as well as collective, employment relations fall under the jurisdiction of the Labor Courts *(İş Mahkemeleri)*. The Labor Courts have the same single-judge structure as Turkish civil courts, which handle labor disputes where no Labor Court is available.

The competent court will be, at the choice of the plaintiff, either the court where the defendant resides at the date the suit is filed or the place where the work is performed.[22] The Regional Directorates of Labor also may bring cases to the Labor Courts, if a dispute has not been resolved within 15 days after a complaint is submitted.

Labor Court litigation is ruled by "oral proceedings" system, where the judge first invites the parties to an amicable settlement, and then, if no settlement is reached, examines the case. In practice, despite legal efforts to shorten the process, labor litigation usually lasts years before reaching a final decision.

A judgment of the Labor Court may be appealed within eight days to the Supreme Court of Appeals (Court of Cassation, or *Yargıtay*). The 9th, 10th, and 21st Chambers of the Court of Cassation deal with labor and social security matters. A panel of the Court of Cassation examines the decisions of the Labor Court. If the Court of Cassation reverses a judgment, the Labor Court must re-examine the case. The Labor Court then either complies with the Court of Cassation's reversal decision or insists on its own view. If the Labor Court holds to its original decision, the Court of Cassation will re-examine the case. After re-examination, the decision of the Court of Cassation is final, and thus, the Labor Court will be bound.

---

[22]Law on Labor Courts No. 5521, enacted in 1950, art. 5.

I. INDIVIDUAL EMPLOYMENT

A. Individual Contract of Employment

1. Historical Background

Until the enactment of Labor Law No. 3008 in 1936, the more general and liberal provisions of the Code of Obligations governed employment contracts. The 1936 Labor Law was prepared and adopted after Turkey joined the International Labor Organization (ILO) in 1932. Modeled around ILO standards, the Labor Law brought about a certain social progress. However, the Law was limited essentially to manual (blue-collar) workers and, therefore, did not cover a large portion of the labor force. It was not until 1971 that the general legal framework, under Labor Law No. 1475 (*İş Kanunu*), encompassed both white-collar and blue-collar workers. In June 10, 2003, the new Labor Law No. 4857 entered into force governing individual labor relations.

2. Legislation Concerning Individual Employment

a. Basic Legislation

i. Turkish Constitution No. 2709 (Türkiye Cumhuriyeti Anayasası)

Chapter 3 of the Turkish Constitution, Social and Economic Rights and Obligations, in Articles 48 through 55 and 60 through 65, sets forth general rules and principles regarding employment and the fundamental rights and freedoms of workers and employers.

ii. Labor Law No. 4857 (İş Kanunu)

Labor Law No. 4857 (the Labor Law), enacted by the Turkish Parliament in 2003, regulates all individual employment between a worker and an employer at a workplace, regardless of the nature of the operation, with some exceptions for positions as in the maritime and press sectors.[23]

---

[23]Labor Law art. 4. See also I.A.3., below.

Under the Labor Law, "worker" means any person who works under a service contract at a job for a wage. "Employer" means any real or legal person or corporate institution or organization that employs workers. An "employer's representative" means any person who acts at a workplace on behalf of the employer and who is charged with the direction of the work and the workplace. The employer is responsible for the behavior of its representative and is bound by agreements made by the employer's representative in relation to other workers. The employer's representative also assumes the same obligations and responsibilities for which the employer is liable under the Labor Law. The status of the employer's representative does not affect the rights and obligations of the workers.

A "workplace" (*işyeri*) means the place where workers and material and immaterial elements are organized by the employer in order to produce goods and services. All premises used for the execution of the work, as well as vehicles and facilities such as restrooms, day nurseries, dining rooms, dormitories, bathrooms, rooms for medical examination and nursing, places for physical or vocational training, and courtyards are deemed to be part of the workplace; so that the workplace is an integrated complex consisting of those parts. Thus defined, the workplace may include places and offices that may be situated outside the location of the main establishment, but integrated in the same complex. Therefore, places such as service and liaison offices should not be considered as distinct or independent workplaces. In the event that a subcontractor operates exclusively in a specified section of a workplace or a subordinate facility, both the employer and the subcontractor are jointly responsible for the subcontractor's obligations under the Labor Law and the employment contracts, as well as collective labor agreements binding the subcontractor.

iii. Maritime Labor Law No. 854 (Deniz İş Kanunu)

Maritime Labor Law No. 854, effective April 29, 1967, covers employers whose employees work on ships of 100 gross tons or more that are sailing in seas, lakes, and rivers and are carrying the Turkish flag. However, work at sea for employers that produce water products does not fall within the scope of Maritime Labor Law, but is subject to the Labor Law.

*iv. Law Concerning the Relationship Between Workers and Employers at Press No. 5953 (*Press Labor Law, or Basın İş Kanunu*)*

The Press Labor Law No. 5953 covers those white-collar workers who contribute intellectual or artistic work at daily papers, or to other printed media, news, or photograph agencies, and who are outside the scope of the Labor Law.

v. Code of Obligations No. 818 (Borçlar Kanunu)

Articles 313 to 354 of the Code of Obligations are applicable in a large part to workers engaged in temporary employment, i.e., work that does not last for more than 30 workdays,[24] and to other categories of workers who do not fall within the Labor Law.[25]

b. Specific Legislation

i. Law on Rest at Noon No. 6301 (Öğle Dinlenmesi Kanunu)

The Law on Rest at Noon No. 6301[26] provides that workers are entitled to have a break of not less than one hour during the noontime.

ii. Law on Weekend Holiday No. 394 (Hafta Tatili Hakkında Kanun)

The Law on Weekend Holiday No. 394[27] provides that workers are entitled to one day off each week.

iii. Law on National Holiday and General Holidays No. 2429 (Ulusal Bayram ve Genel Tatiller Hakkında Kanun)

The Law on National Holiday and General Holidays No. 2429[28] establishes a number of public holidays. Under the Labor

---

[24]See I.A.3.b., below.

[25]Labor Law art. 4. See I.A.3.a., below.

[26]See V.B.1.e., below.

[27]See V.C.2.a., below.

[28]See V.C.2.b., below.

Law, workers are paid for these holidays if they do not work and receive premium pay if they do work.

iv. Law on Combat Against Terrorism No. 3713 (Terörle Mücadele Kanunu)

The Law on Combat Against Terrorism No. 3713[29] requires employers having a workforce of 50 or more to allocate 3 percent of their jobs for the employment of public servants or soldiers who became disabled due to terrorism, or for the employment of their families.

v. Law on General Health No. 1593 (Umumi Hıfzısıhha Kanunu)

Articles 155, 173 to 180, 282, and 295 of the Law on General Health No. 1593[30] regulate certain employment conditions, particularly health of and work safety for children and young workers. Those minimum standards were later improved by the labor legislation.[31]

vi. Law Allowing Foreigners of Turkish Origin to Freely Perform Their Professions in Turkey and to Work at Public and Private Undertakings No. 2527 (Türk Soylu Yabancıların Türkiye'de Meslek ve Sanatlarını Serbestçe Yapabilmelerine, Kamu, Özel Kuruluş veya İşyerlerinde Çalıştırılabilmelerine İlişkin Kanun)

The Law Allowing Foreigners of Turkish Origins to Freely Perform Their Professions in Turkey and to Work at Public and Private Undertakings No. 2527[32] permits covered individuals to work in Turkey on a temporary basis. The right to work under this law is conditioned on permission from the Ministry of Interior and is subject to certain exceptions.

---

[29]See VI.B.3., below.
[30]See VII.A.1., below.
[31]See VI.B., below.
[32]See IX., below.

c. Other Related Legislation

i. Labor Courts Law No. 5521 (İş Mahkemeleri Kanunu)

Labor Courts Law No. 5521 (*İş Mahkemeleri Kanunu*) sets forth provisions about the competent court for the resolution of disputes arising from individual, as well as from collective employment relations by Labor Courts (İş Mahkemeleri), proceedings and such, as specified therein.[33]

ii. Law on Associations No. 2908 (Dernekler Kanunu)

The Law on Associations No. 2908 (*Dernekler Kanunu*) sets out provisions on establishment, operation, organization, bodies of associations and their duties and powers, membership, rights and powers of members, and such. In exceptional cases, where some issues regarding unions are not regulated under the Law on Unions, relevant provisions of the Law on Associations apply.

iii. Apprenticeship and Occupational Training Law No. 3308 (Çıraklık ve Meslek Eğitimi Kanunu)

The Apprenticeship and Occupational Training Law No. 3308 establishes principles concerning the occupational training at schools and the education of apprentices and qualified and master workmen.

d. Regulations

Regulations on individual employment include the following:

- Regulation on Suspension of Work or Closing Down of Undertakings (*İşyerlerinde İşin Durdurulmasına veya İşyerlerinin Kapatılmasına Dair Yönetmelik*);
- Regulation on Minimum Wage (*Asgari Ücret Yönetmeliği*);
- Regulation on Working Time Related to the Labor Law (*İş Kanununa İlişkin Çalışma Süreleri Yönetmeliği*);

[33] Labor Law art. 4. See also I.A.3., below.

- Regulation on Tasks for Preparation, Completion, and Cleaning (*Hazırlama, Tamamlama, Temizleme İşleri Yönetmeliği*);
- Regulation on Overtime Work and Extra Hours Work Related to the Labor Law (*İş Kanununa İlişkin Fazla Çalışma ve Fazla Sürelerle Çalışma Yönetmeliği*);
- Regulation on Paid Annual Leave (*Yıllık Ücretli İzin Yönetmeliği*);
- Regulation on Employment of the Disabled, Ex-Convicts and Victims of Terrorism (*Özürlü, Eski Hükümlü ve Terör Mağduru İstihdamı Hakkında Yönetmelik*);
- Regulation on Work Health and Safety (*İş Sağlığı ve Güvenliği Yönetmeliği*);
- Regulation on Heavy and Dangerous Work (*Ağır ve Tehlikeli İşler Tüzüğü*);
- Regulation on Work Health and Safety Boards (*İş Sağlığı ve Güvenliği Kurulları Hakkında Yönetmelik*);
- Regulation on Health and Safety Precautions to Be Taken While Working with Means with Screens (*Ekranlı Araçlarla Çalışmalarda Sağlık ve Güvenlik Önlemleri Hakkında Yönetmelik*);
- Regulation on Noise (*Gürültü Yönetmeliği*);
- Regulation on Vibration (*Titreşim Yönetmeliği*);
- Regulation on Health and Work Safety at Construction Work (*Yapı İşlerinde Sağlık ve Güvenlik Yönetmeliği*);
- Regulation on Signs of Safety and Health (*Güvenlik ve Sağlık İşaretleri Yönetmeliği*);
- Regulation on Health and Safety Precautions to Be Taken While Working with Asbestos (*Asbestle Çalışmalarda Sağlık ve Güvenlik Önlemleri Hakkında Yönetmelik*);
- Regulation on Protecting Workers from Hazards of Explosive Conditions (*Patlayıcı Ortamların Tehlikelerinden Çalışanların Korunması Hakkında Yönetmelik*);
- Regulation on Health and Safety Precautions to Be Taken at Works with Carcinogen and Mutagenic Products (*Kanserojen ve Mutajen Maddelerle Çalışmalarda Sağlık ve Güvenlik Önlemleri Hakkında Yönetmelik*);
- Regulation on Health and Safety Precautions to Be Taken at Works with Chemical Products (*Kimyasal Maddelerle*

Çalışmalarda Sağlık ve Güvenlik Önlemleri Hakkında Yönetmelik);

- Regulation on Duties, Authority, and Responsibility and Working Procedures and Principles of Work Safety Engineers or Technical Personnel (*İş Güvenliği ile Görevli Mühendis ve Teknik Elemanların Görev, Yetki ve Sorumlulukları ile Çalışma Usul ev Esasları Hakkında Yönetmelik*);
- Regulation on Conditions of Health and Safety in Using Work Equipment (*İş Ekipmanlarının Kullanımında Sağlık ve Güvenlik Şartları Yönetmeliği*);
- Regulation on Health and Safety Precautions to Taken in the Premises of Work and its Annexes (*İşyeri Bina ve Eklentilerinde Alınacak Sağlık ve Güvenlik Önlemleri Hakkında Yönetmelik*);
- Regulation on Personal Protective Equipment (*Kişisel Koruyucu Donanım Yönetmeliği*);
- Regulation on Using Personal Protective Equipment and Products at Workplaces (*Kişisel Koruyucu Donanımların İşyerlerinde Kullanılması Hakkında Yönetmelik*);
- Regulation on Conditions of Health and Work Safety at Mines (*Yeraltı ve Yerüstü Maden İşletmelerinde Sağlık ve Güvenlik Şartları Yönetmeliği*);
- Regulation on Establishment and Working Principles of the Authorized Committee that Will Use the Fines that are Deducted from Wages of Workers (*İşçi Ücretlerinden Ceza Olarak Kesilen Paraları Kullanmaya Yetkili Kurulun Teşekkülü ve Çalışma Esasları Hakkında Yönetmelik*);
- Regulation on Distribution of Tips to Workers (*Yüzdelerden Toplanan Paraların İşçilere Dağıtılması Hakkında Yönetmelik*);
- Regulation on Janitors of Residential Buildings (*Konut Kapıcıları Yönetmeliği*);
- Regulation on Works Deemed as Industrial, Commercial, Agricultural, and Forestry Works (*Sanayi, Ticaret, Tarım ve Orman İşlerinden sayılan İşlere İlişkin Yönetmelik*);

- Regulation on Short Work and Short Work Payment *(Kısa Çalışma ve Kısa Çalışma Ödeneğine İlişkin Yönetmelik)*;
- Regulation on Procedures and Principles of Training of Work Health and Safety (*Çalışanların İş Sağlığı ve Güvenliği Eğitimlerinin Usul ve Esasları Hakkında Yönetmelik*);
- Regulation on Procedures and Principles of Employment of Children and Young Workers (*Çocuk ve Genç İşçilerin Çalıştırılma Usul ve Esasları Hakkında Yönetmelik*);
- Regulation on Work Health and Safety Boards (*İş Sağlığı ve Güvenliği Kurulları Hakkında Yönetmelik*);
- Regulation on Suspending Work at Workplaces or Closing of Workplaces (*İşyerlerinde İşin Durdurulması veya İşyerlerinin Kapatılmasına Dair Yönetmelik*);
- Regulation on Procedures and Principles of Working of Tripartite Consultancy Board (*Çalışma Hayatına İlişkin Üçlü Danışma Kurulunun Çalışma Usul ev Esasları Hakkında Yönetmelik*);
- Regulation on Working Periods that Cannot be Divided into Working Days of the Week (*Haftalık İş Günlerine Bölünemeyen Çalışma Süreleri Yönetmeliği*);
- Regulation on Working Conditions of Workers at Works Considered as Agricultural and Forestry (*Tarım ve Ormandan Sayılan İşlerde Çalışanların Çalışma Koşullarına İlişkin Yönetmelik*);
- Regulation on Special Procedures and Principles for Works Carried Out Through Shifts (*Postalar Halinde İşçi Çalıştırılarak Yürütülen İşlerde Çalışmalara İlişkin Özel Usul ve Esaslar Hakkında Yönetmelik*);
- Regulation on Works To Be Done Only Seven-and-a-half Hours or Less Per Day Due to Health Rules (*Sağlık Kuralları Bakımından Günde Ancak Yedibuçuk Saat veya Daha Az Çalışılması Gereken İşler Hakkında Yönetmelik*);
- Regulation on Working Conditions of Pregnant and Nursing Women, as well as Nursing Rooms and Child Care Houses (*Gebe veya Emziren Kadınların Çalıştırılma*

Şartlarıyla Emzirme Odaları ev Çocuk Bakım Yurtlarına Dair Yönetmelik);

- Regulation on Health Units at Workplaces and Duties and Working Procedures and Principles of Workplace Doctors (*İşyeri Sağlık Birimleri ve İşyeri Hekimlerinin Görevleri ile Çalışma Usul ev Esasları Hakkında Yönetmelik*);
- Regulation on Establishment and Working Principles and Procedures of the Commission that Will Use the Fines to be Collected from Employers Who Do Not Employ Disabled and Ex-convict Workers (*Özürlü ve Eski Hükümlü Çalıştırmayan İşverenlerden Ceza Olarak Kesilen Paraları Kullanmaya Yetkili Komisyonun Kuruluşu ile Çalışma Usul ve Esasları Hakkında Yönetmelik*); and
- Regulation on Work Health and Safety (*İş Sağlığı ve Güvenliği Yönetmeliği*);.

3. *Employment Not Covered Under the Labor Law*

a. *Excluded Categories*

The following categories of employment are not covered under the Labor Law:

- sea and air transport (except loading and unloading operations at ports and coastal points, and ground-staff activities in air transport);
- agriculture in workplaces where up to 50 workers are employed, including construction of forest roads (Agriculture is defined in the Labor Law. Crafts utilizing or processing agricultural products; employment in workshops and factories manufacturing implements, machinery, or spare parts for use in agricultural operations; and construction work in agricultural undertakings; as well as employment performed in public parks and gardens or those that are subsidiaries of any undertaking remain covered by the Labor Law.);
- housework by members of the family or near relations living in the home, without employing any outside help;
- household domestic services;
- workplaces employing up to three people, as defined in Article 2 of the Labor Law on Tradesmen and Artisans, that

are independent enterprises of a smaller scale whose operations are based on the small capital by self-employment of the principal, that are not covered under the Commercial Law, and have a maximum of three individuals who work in such workplaces;
- apprentices younger than 18 years of age;
- any construction work on farms that fall within the scope of the self-supporting family economy;
- professional athletes; and
- persons undergoing rehabilitation.

b. Transitory Employment

The Labor Law defines work that, by its nature, does not last for more than 30 workdays as "transitory employment." Certain provisions of the Labor Law do not apply to workers engaged in transitory employment.[34] With respect to issues that are not covered by the Labor Law, transitory workers are subject to provisions of the Code of Obligations.

B. Employer's Notice

Any employer that establishes or takes over an undertaking or completely or partly changes the nature of its business must

---

[34]Article 3 (Notification Regarding the Undertaking); Article 8 (Written Agreement); Article 12 (Labor Contract for a Definite Period); Article 13 (Part-Time Working Contract); Article 14 (Work on Call); Article 15 (Working Contract with a Trial Clause); Article 17 (Notice for Termination of the Contract); Article 23 (Responsibility of the New Employer); Article 24 (Right of the Worker to Terminate the Contract Without Advance Notice); Article 25 (Right of the Employer to Terminate the Contract Without Advance Notice); Article 26 (Period for Exercising the Right to Terminate a Contract); Article 27 (Leave of Absence to Seek a New Job); Article 28 (Certificate of Employment); Article 29 (Collective Dismissals); Article 30 (Obligation to Employ Disabled Persons, Ex-Convicts and Victims of Terror); Article 31 (Military Service and Statutory Labor Service); Article 34 (Non Payment of Wages in Due Time); Article 53 (Paid Annual Leave); Article 54 (Determination of the Right to Paid Annual Leave); Article 55 (Periods Considered as Though Worked); Article 56 (Limitation in Application of Paid Annual Leave); Article 57 (Leave Pay); Article 58 (Prohibition of Work During Paid Leave); Article 59 (Leave Pay in Case of Termination of Contract); Article 75 (File of the Worker); Article 80 (Workers' Health and Work Safety Board); and Article 14 of the former Labor Law No. 1475 regarding severance pay, still in force according to a transitional provision (Art. 6).

notify the Regional Directorate of Labor within one month of the transaction. The notification must include the name and the address of the undertaking, the number of workers, the type of business activity, the date of starting operations, the employer's name and address, and the names and addresses of the employer's representatives, if any. A subcontractor who establishes as such his own place is under the same obligation.

C. Individual Employment Contracts

1. Requirement of a Written Contract

Employment contracts for a period of one year or more with a definite term must be concluded in writing.[35] A written form also is required for "work on call" contracts,[36] "gang" contracts,[37] and "temporary employment" contracts where a worker works for another employer for a certain period of time.[38] Such contracts are exempt from all types of fees and taxes. If an employment contract is drawn up by a notary public, only notary fees are payable.

In the absence of a written contract, the employer is obligated to give the worker a certificate bearing the employer's signature and showing the general and special conditions of employment. Such certificates also are exempt from all fees and taxes.[39]

Employment contracts under Maritime Labor Law and Press Labor Law must be concluded in writing regardless of their duration.

2. Contract Terms

The Labor Law provides that, in order to meet their needs, parties are free to define the type and terms of their employment contracts. Nevertheless, those contracts must be drawn up in compliance with the limitations and prescriptions set forth by the Labor Law.[40]

---

[35]Labor Law art.11/1.
[36]*Id.* art. 14.
[37]*Id.* art. 16.
[38]*Id.* art. 7.
[39]*Id.* art. 8.
[40]*Id.* art. 9.

This provision, however, does not apply to contracts with a definite term up to one month.

No provisions may be inserted in an employment contract that would violate the rights granted to workers for weekly rest periods, national and general holidays, and paid annual leaves that would violate the worker's rights under the Labor Law. Conversely, more advantageous rights acquired by workers through contract or custom prevail over the provisions of the Labor Law concerning weekly rest, public holidays, paid annual leave, and rights based on a percentage.[41]

The parties are free to change the working conditions anytime by mutual consent. In case of a unilateral modification by the employer of the conditions set forth in the employment contract or other sources such as workplace practices, a written notice must be served to the worker. The worker may accept this modification in writing within six working days; otherwise, the change shall not bind the worker. However, if the employer indicates in writing a valid reason for the proposed change or another valid cause of termination, the employer may terminate the employment contract by giving a notice. In such cases, the worker can file a lawsuit under the provisions set out in Articles 17–21.[42]

3. *Probationary Period*

In cases where parties include a trial clause in the employment contract, the maximum probationary period is two months. However, this period may be extended to a maximum of four months by a collective agreement.[43]

4. *Gang Contracts*

A "gang contract" is defined as a contract concluded between an employer and a number of workers who are represented by a worker acting as a team leader. Gang contracts must be concluded in writing, irrespective of their term. When a worker named in the gang contract begins work, the contract is deemed to have been

[41]*Id.* art. 45.
[42]*Id.* art. 22.
[43]*Id.* art. 15.

concluded directly between the employer and the worker as of the time work begins.[44]

5. *Contracts for a Definite Term*

Articles 338, 339, and 343 of the Code of Obligations regulate employment contracts that are concluded for a definite period.

The duration of a fixed-term employment contract may either be specified or inferred from the purpose or nature of the work.[45] The maximum duration is 10 years.[46]

Contracts for a definite term are deemed to be renewed for the same period—but at most for one year—if the parties do not include an expiration date.[47]

An employment contract for a definite term ends automatically with the lapse of the term, and the worker is not entitled to severance compensation (*kıdem tazminatı*).[48] However, according to the rulings of the Court of Cassation, if an employer extends a contract for a definite term by way of renewals, such employment contracts are considered to be as one single contract for an indefinite term. In this event, the worker may claim notice compensation and severance pay if the contract is not renewed. Those Court rulings are reflected in the Labor Law, which specifies that, except when justified by an essential reason, an employment contract for a definite term must not be concluded more than once. Otherwise, the renewed contracts shall be deemed to have been made for an indefinite term as a single contract.[49]

To protect the rights of the workers, Articles 11–12 of the Labor Law set forth some limitations concerning employment contracts for a definite term. Workers on definite term contracts must be granted similar rights to those working for an indefinite term; prorated wages and other monetary benefits must be given according to seniority, i.e., the length of time they have worked. Except when different criteria due to seniority are justified by specific

---

[44]*Id.* art. 16.
[45]Code of Obligations art. 338.
[46]*Id.* art. 343.
[47]*Id.* art. 339.
[48]See I.D.7., below.
[49]Labor Law art.11.

reasons, other benefits that are based on seniority must be applied to workers on definite term contracts.

6. *Temporary Employment*

"Temporary employment" means a temporary transfer of a worker from one employer (Transferor Employer) to another (Transferee Employer). Such transfers may only be made between companies of a holding or a same group; otherwise, the work performed must be of a similar nature. In all cases the worker's written consent is required. The transfer is limited to six months. However, if required, the term may be renewed twice so that the total time can be extended to a maximum of 18 months.

In those cases, the employment relationship between employee and employer remains unchanged and the Transferor Employer continues to pay the wages. However, the Transferee Employer is liable together with the Transferor Employer to protect the worker and pay social security contributions. Both employers are jointly liable for the unpaid wages relating to the period spent under the service of the Transferee Employer.

The Labor Law specifies that, provided the Transferee Employer is a party to a collective agreement, a worker may not be engaged in work during a strike and lockout, except in cases of compulsory work under Article 39 of the Law No. 2822.

It is also specified that no temporary employment relationship may be engaged where a mass termination has taken place, during a period of six months following the mass termination.[50]

7. *Part-Time and Full-Time Employment Contracts*

Work is considered part time in cases where the weekly working time is substantially shorter than the regular weekly work. Part time may be defined as a term that is shorter by two-thirds than the regular full-time work.

The Labor Law protects against discriminatory treatment that would be due solely to the part-time nature of a job. Monetary benefits must be prorated by comparing the length of the working time to a worker doing a full-time job of the same nature.

---

[50] *Id.* art.7.

Vacancies for full time or part time should be announced in a timely manner. When a worker's qualifications fit the vacant positions, requests of the full-time workers to move into part- time jobs or part-time workers to full-time jobs must be taken into consideration.[51]

8. Work on Call

"Work on call" is a specific type of part-time job where the worker will be called to perform work on an as-needed basis.

Such work must have been agreed upon by a written contract. If the work time is not determined in the employment contract, it is accepted as 20 hours per week by law. Then the worker is entitled to wages, regardless of whether the work was performed during the determined time.

Unless decided otherwise, the call must be made at least four days in advance and the worker must work for a minimum of four consecutive hours per call.[52]

D. Worker Dismissal

1. Termination of a Probationary Worker

During the one-month probation or up to three months if extended by collective agreement,[53] either party may terminate the employment contract without giving notice or paying compensation. However, the worker is entitled to wages, other rights, and social insurance benefits for the time actually worked.[54]

2 Termination With Advance Notice

The rules concerning workers' dismissals were amended with the adoption of Law No. 4773 and Labor Law No. 4857. Such amendments were influenced by the ILO Convention No. 158 on the Termination of Employment, to which Turkey is a party. Workers' dismissals comply with a procedure allowing the workers to

[51] *Id.* art.13.
[52] *Id.* art.14.
[53] See I.C.3., above.
[54] Labor Law art. 15.

be informed of the causes of termination and furnishing them with the opportunity to challenge unjustified dismissals in the Labor Courts.

a. Termination Without Cause

In workplaces where there are 29 or fewer employees, employers are given wide latitude to dismiss workers. In those workplaces, either the employer or the worker may terminate a permanent employment contract made for an indefinite period without cause, by giving the other party written advance notice. Following the receipt of written notice by either party, the contract of a worker will terminate as follows:

- at the end of the second week, if the employment lasted less than six months;
- at the end of the fourth week, if the employment lasted more than six months but less than 1½ years;
- at the end of the sixth week, if the employment has lasted more than 1½ years but less than three years; or
- at the end of the eighth week, if the employment lasted three years or more.

The above periods are minimums and may be increased by individual employment contract or collective agreement. The employer, by making an advance payment corresponding to the required notice period, may terminate the contract immediately.

During the notice period, the employer must allow the employee to use working hours to seek new employment without any deduction from wages. The worker must be given at least two hours per day to seek new employment. However, at the worker's request, the hours may be aggregated and taken at one time. A worker who wishes to make aggregated use of hours must do so on the days immediately preceding the date of separation and must so inform the employer in advance.[55]

In the event of failure to comply with the notice requirements, the defaulting party is liable to pay a "notice compensation" (*ihbar*

[55]*Id.* art. 27.

tazminatı) to the other, equal to the wage corresponding to the required notice period.[56]

b. Termination in Accordance With Articles 18–21

The Labor Law No. 4857, effective June 2003, sets forth important dispositions protecting the job security of workers. Nevertheless, application of these provisions is not a general practice and only concerns workplaces of a certain scale.

Thus, under the Labor Law, in workplaces where there are 30 or more employees, any dismissal must be subject to a valid cause. A valid cause may be the requirements of the job or the workplace, or the capacities or behavior of the worker. However, the provision of Article 18 is applicable for those who have been employed for at least six months under an employment contract with a definite term.

The employer must issue a written notification where the cause of dismissal is clearly and precisely specified. If and when the cause is the capacity or behavior of the worker, a worker is given the opportunity to defend against the claim.[57]

The number of workers must be calculated by taking into consideration all workers employed in all workplaces belonging to the same employer. Similarly, the minimum six-month seniority of a worker must be calculated by taking into consideration his or her employment periods in all workplaces as a whole.

The same article enumerates some particular cases that will not constitute valid causes, such as union membership or union activities outside working hours; a suit or complaint by the worker against an employer concerning legal and contractual rights; reasons of race, color, gender, marital status and familial duties, pregnancy, religion, political belief, and ethnic or social origin; and illness or accident preventing the employee from performing work for a period not exceeding the time specified in Article 25(I)(b) of the Labor Law.

In cases where no valid cause is specified, or if the cause is not correct, the employee may bring suit within a month in the

---

[56] *Id.* art. 17.
[57] *Id.* art. 19.

Labor Courts. A private arbitrator also may be appointed by agreement of both parties. The burden of proof of the existence of a valid cause lies on the employer.[58]

If an employee obtains a favorable judgment from the Labor Court, the termination of the contract is invalid. Upon application by the ex-worker within 10 working days of the judgment, the employer must rehire the ex-worker within a month. If the employer fails to rehire the ex-worker, the employer will pay a compensation amounting to no less than four and no more than eight months' wages; the amount of this compensation will be determined by the Court in its judgment.

Up to four months' wages and other pecuniary rights also will be paid to the worker to cover the period beginning from the time of the termination until the final court decision. However, if any wage and severance compensation was paid before, such payment must be deducted from the compensation. If a term of notice had not been given nor advance notice pay paid, a compensation for the notice period can be claimed by the ex-worker not rehired.

The ex-worker must apply for his or her former job within 10 working days after the final judgment. Otherwise, the dismissal will become valid and the worker may only claim what is due in cases of termination in general (such as advance notice compensation, severance pay, and annual leave wages).[59]

The above provisions cannot be changed by way of agreement.

3. *Termination Due to Cause Without Advance Notice*

a. *Termination by the Employer*

The employer may immediately terminate a contract, whether for a fixed or an indefinite period, due to one of the just causes specified in Article 25 of the Labor Law. In those cases enumerated below, no severance pay and notice pay will be due.

---

[58] *Id.* art. 20.
[59] *Id.* art. 21.

i. Health reasons

The employer may terminate workers for health reasons if a worker has contracted a disease or suffered an injury due to his or her own deliberate act, loose living, or drunkenness and, as a result, are absent for three successive workdays or a total of more than five working days in one month.

Workers also may be terminated for health reasons if they suffer an incurable disease or when the disease is incompatible with the performance of their duties, as determined by the Health Committee.[60] In the case of an illness or accident that is not attributable to the worker's fault, or in cases of pregnancy or birth, the employer is entitled to terminate the contract without notice, provided that the employee is absent due to the illness or accident for more than six weeks beyond the ordinary notice periods (set forth above). In cases of pregnancy or birth, the allowable termination date is six weeks after the date of birth, plus the ordinary notice period, as set forth in Article 74 of the Labor Law.[61]

No wages are payable for the period when the worker fails to report to work.

ii. Grounds of bad faith, immorality, or other misconduct

Bad faith, immorality, or other misconduct sufficient to justify termination by the employer consists of the following:[62]

- at the time of the contract, the worker misled the employer by making false statements of his or her qualifications relating to an essential feature of the contract;
- the worker offends the honor or the dignity of the employer or a member of the employer's family, directly or indirectly, by word or deed or levels groundless accusations against the employer's honor or dignity;
- the worker sexually harasses another worker of the employer;

---

[60] *Id.* art. 25, para. I(b).

[61] See V.C.3.a., below.

[62] Labor Law art. 25, para. II.

- the worker assaults the employer, a member of the employer's family, or a fellow worker;
- the worker violates the prohibition against alcoholic drinks and narcotics in the workplace;[63]
- the worker commits a dishonest act against the employer, such as theft, breach of trust, or disclosure of the employer's trade secrets;
- the worker commits an offense within the premises of the undertaking that entails (or could entail) a sentence of seven days' imprisonment or more without probation;
- the worker, without the employer's permission and without good reason, is absent from work for two consecutive days, or twice in one month on the workday after a rest day, or on a total of three workdays in one month;
- the worker refuses, in spite of warning, to perform his or her duties; and
- the worker, willfully or through gross negligence, imperils workplace safety or damages machinery, equipment, or other articles or materials, whether these are the employer's property or not, and the cost of the damage cannot be offset by withholding 30 days' pay.

The contract may be terminated for cause by the employer, on grounds of bad faith, immorality, or other misconduct within six days following the date that the employer became aware of the specific ground for termination, but in any event, within a year after the cause arose. The employer's right to terminate ceases after six workdays from the time the employer became aware of the cause.[64] However, if the employer has extracted material gains from the concerned act, the one-year limitation does not apply.

iii. Force majeure

Workers may be terminated for cause if reasons of *force majeure* prevent them from performing their duties for more than one week.[65]

---

[63] *Id.* art. 89.
[64] *Id.* art. 26.
[65] *Id.* art. 25, para. III.

iv. Other causes

In cases where the worker is taken into custody or arrested, or the worker's absence from work exceeds the notice period set forth in Article 17, the contract may be terminated by the employer.

b. Termination by the Worker

The worker may terminate a contract, whether for a fixed or an indefinite period, for cause. The following are causes specified in Article 24 of the Labor Law that entitle workers to terminate a contract.

i. Health reasons

A worker may terminate a contract for health reasons if performing the work endangers the worker's health or life in a way that was impossible to foresee at the time of the contract or if the worker is constantly near or is frequently in direct contact with a person (e.g., the employer, the employer's representative, or another worker) who is suffering from a contagious disease.

ii. Grounds of bad faith, immorality, or other misconduct

Bad faith, immorality, or other misconduct sufficient to justify termination by the employee consists of the following:

- at the time of the contract, the employer misled the worker by stating the conditions incorrectly or by providing false information or making false statements concerning any essential point of the contract;
- the employer is guilty of any speech or action that constitutes an offense against the honor or reputation of the worker or a member of the worker's family, or if the worker is sexually harassed;
- the employer assaults or threatens the worker or a member of the worker's family or urges, instigates, or induces the worker or a family member to commit an illegal action, or commits an offense that entails (or could entail) imprisonment of the worker or a member of the worker's family; or

makes groundless accusations against the worker's honor and dignity;

- in cases where the worker was sexually harassed by another worker and the employer did not take appropriate measures in spite of knowing of the harassment;
- the employer fails to make out the wages account or to pay wages in conformity with the Labor Law or in accordance with the terms of the employment contract; or
- in cases where wages are payable an hourly rate basis or fixed-wage basis, the employer makes a reduction in payment for the reason that less work was assigned to the worker; and the employment conditions are not applied.

The contract may be terminated by the worker due to bad faith, immorality, or other misconduct within six days following the date that the worker became aware of the cause, but in any event, within a year after the cause arose. The right to terminate ceases after six workdays from the time the worker became aware of the cause.[66]

iii. Force majeure

A worker may terminate the contract when reasons of *force majeure* cause the suspension of work for more than one week in the workplace.[67]

4. *Mass Termination*

Employers may terminate more than one worker at a time. Mass termination due to economic, technological, structural, and similar reasons is at the discretion of the employer, who must comply with the notice periods provided in Article 17. If those terminations occur within a 30-day period whether on the same date or different dates, the law imposes obligations to the employer in cases where the number of workers dismissed reaches a certain

[66] *Id.* art. 28.

[67] *Id.* art. 24, para 3.

percentage of the total of workforce employed in the workplace, as defined below: [68]

- if 10 or more workers are terminated in a workforce of 20 to 100 employees;
- when the number of those dismissed is at least 10 percent of a workforce of 101 to 300 employees; or
- when a minimum of 30 workers are dismissed in a workplace of 301 or more employees.

The employer is obliged to give one-month's advance notice to the Employment Agency, union representatives, and the Regional Directorate of Labor. The notification must specify the causes of termination and the number and date of the dismissals. After this notification, workers' or union's representatives and the employer must meet in view to research ways of preventing a mass termination, or alleviating the adverse effects of such a measure.

The termination will become effective 30 days after its notification to the Regional Directorate. Otherwise, in cases of closing the workplace with a definitive cessation of activity, a posting of the announcement at the workplace and a notification to the Regional Directorate and to the Employment Agency is sufficient.

For seasonal and campaign work, in cases of termination due to the nature of the work, the above mentioned provisions shall not apply.

The law specifies that the employer cannot utilize the provisions regarding mass termination in order to avoid the application of Articles 18–21 of the Labor Law requiring valid causes of dismissal and providing a special procedure. Otherwise, the worker can file a lawsuit under these articles.

5. *Additional Employer Obligations*

Except in cases where a collective labor agreement contains provisions requiring a decision by a disciplinary body, the employer may dismiss a worker without the approval of the union or any other party.

---

[68] *Id.* art. 29. See also IV.A., below.

If employment is terminated, the employer must furnish the worker with a certificate stating the nature and duration of the employment. This certificate is exempt from all fees and taxes. If the employer refuses to furnish the certificate or makes any false statement, the worker or the new employer may file a claim with the Regional Directorate of Labor. In addition, either the worker or the new employer may file a claim against the former employer for recovery of any damages suffered.[69]

6. *Unjust Termination*

a. *By the Employer*

Even in workplaces where fewer than 30 workers are employed, a worker also may refer the matter to a Labor Court in some cases. If the dismissal is determined to be unjust or not in compliance with the rules set forth in the Labor Law or the employment contract, then the worker will be entitled to notice compensation as provided in Article 17[70] if those terms are not observed and also to compensation in the form of severance pay.[71]

If the employer's termination amounts to a manifest abuse of the right to terminate, such as a termination based on the worker's membership in a trade union or filing a grievance, then the employer will be liable to the worker for "bad faith compensation" (*kötüniyet tazminatı*), equal to three times the wage corresponding to the appropriate term of notice.

The Labor Court is the only body authorized to review a complaint of unfair dismissal.

In workplaces where 30 or more workers are employed, the procedure and provisions specified in Articles 18–21 shall apply.

b. *By the Worker*

If a worker leaves employment before the expiration of the contract or without giving due notice and a new employer hires

---

[69]Labor Law art. 28.
[70]See I.D.2., above
[71]See I.D.7., below.

the worker, the new employer will be liable for damages suffered by the former employer due to the unjust separation of the worker, in the following cases:

- the new employer caused the worker's conduct;
- the new employer knew or should have known the worker's conduct; or
- the new employer continues to employ the worker after becoming aware of the worker's conduct.[72]

7. *Severance Pay* (Kıdem Tazminatı)

Although the previous Labor Law No.1473 is no longer in force, its Article 14 concerning severance pay remains applicable. Cases of termination for which severance pay is due are strictly limited by the Labor Law.[73] Specifically, the employer is obligated to make severance payments where the employment contract is terminated for any of the following reasons:

- by the employer, for reasons other than bad faith, immorality, or misconduct;
- by the worker, for reasons of employer bad faith, immorality, or misconduct;
- by the worker, who is called for military service;
- by the worker, in order to receive an old age, retirement, or disability pension, or a lump sum payment from an organization or fund established by law, with which the worker is affiliated;
- by a female worker who terminates within one year of the date of her marriage; and
- in case of the worker's death.[74]

Unless an individual contract or collective agreement increases the amount, severance pay is equal to 30 days of the worker's latest wage and supplements, for each full year of service from the

[72]Labor Law art. 23.

[73]Labor Law No. 1475 art. 14.

[74]In the event of a worker's death, the severance payment is made to the worker's legal heirs.

commencement of the employment contract. For periods less than one year, payment must be prorated. However, there is a cap on the severance payment, as described below. Severance payments are free from income tax and subject only to stamp duty.

The above provisions are mandatory and, except for provisions relating to the 30-day wage, may not be modified by contract. In practice, provisions regarding severance payment, including the calculation and amount are covered at length under collective agreements.

Under the Labor Law, the calculation of severance payments is based on the worker's last wage.[75] If the last wage cannot be fixed, the severance payment is based on the average wage, calculated by dividing the total wage paid during the year by the number of days worked within the same year. If the worker's wage was raised during the year, the average wage is calculated by dividing the total wage paid after the wage increase until the termination by the number of days worked within the same period.

The length of a worker's service must take into account the whole period of employment with the same employer, whether the worker worked continuously or at intervals, or at one or more workplaces. Severance payments are not made more than once for the same period of service.

Severance payments are subject to a cap. Specifically, the severance payment for each year of service may not be more than the retirement bonus payable for each year of service to the highest ranking civil servant under the Civil Servant Law. However, in practice, particularly by multinationals, there is a tendency to pay over the cap as a sign of goodwill. Such an overpayment is not considered as a severance payment, but as part of the separation package that is subject to income tax.

The employer may not insure the liability arising from severance payment obligations with third parties or insurance companies.

If the employer fails to make severance payments in a timely manner, then it is obliged to pay interest at the highest rate paid for

[75]For purposes of calculating severance payments, the worker's wage is the wage defined in Article 32 of the Labor Law (see V.A.1., below), plus any and all legal and contractual interests such as social benefits, in cash or in kind.

deposits, for the period from the payment due date until the date of actual payment.

An administrative appeal procedure does not exist with respect to severance disputes. However, a worker may seek compensation by referring the matter to a Labor Court.

8. *Replacement and Re-employment*

Article 29 provides that after mass termination, during a six-month period, if the employer desires to employ workers at the workplace for the same kind of work, priority must be given to the terminated workers.

E. Privacy

The right to privacy for all individuals is recognized in Article 20 of the Turkish Constitution, which provides: "Everyone has the right to respect for his/her private and family life. Privacy of individual and family life cannot be violated." Further, Article 22 (Freedom of Communication) grants to everyone the right to freedom of communication and states that "secrecy of communication is fundamental."

For both liberties, interference by public authorities is authorized under certain conditions defined strictly by constitutional provisions, which correspond with terms analogous to those of Article 8 in the European Convention for the Protection of Human Rights and Fundamental Freedoms.

The issue of eventual incursions to privacy in the workplace has not been a topic much dealt with in practice and no specific legislation has been adopted on this matter.

F. Covenants Not to Compete, Trade Secrets, Employee Duty of Loyalty

1. *Covenants Not to Compete*

Taking into consideration the professional future of ex-workers, the Code of Obligations, in Articles 348 through 350, restricts such ex-workers from competing with the employer. However, such restriction is subject to limitation by law. Thus, the worker can, by written agreement with the employer, agree not to engage, after the end of the employment contract, in an activity that would compete with those of the former employer, either on the ex-worker's own account, as a partner, or as an employee in a competitor company. Such limitations are allowed only in cases where the worker had access to trade secrets or knowledge of the customers of the former workplace. These provisions are valid if the use of this knowledge would significantly harm the employer.

Additionally, Article 349 sets forth that undertaking by employees not to compete must not hinder or endanger the economic future of such workers and the undertaking should be limited in time, place, and kind of work; otherwise, those non-competing provisions shall be null and void.

Undertaking not to compete becomes more effective, in practice, when coupled with a contractual compensation *(cezaî şart).* However, excessive amounts of contractual compensation may be reduced by courts.[76]

2. *Trade Secrets*

Serious misconduct such as theft, disclosure of trade secrets, and disrespectful behavior is cause for immediate termination by the employer, without any severance or other payment. The employer can claim an appropriate compensation in case of damage.[77]

There is no other law specifically governing trade secrets.

3. *Employee Duty of Loyalty*

The employment contract contains a moral and personal aspect as well as a business aspect. Accordingly, employee's duty of loyalty is considered as one of the inherent and essential obligations in all employment contracts.

Under this obligation, employees must perform their work in manner to protect the honor, interests, and security of the employer and undertaking. The employee has the duty to take the necessary measures to prevent damage and risks, and inform the employer of any danger, theft, fraud, missing of things such as equipment, safety measures, etc., or disorder in the workplace.

---

[76]Code of Obligations art. 161, para. III.

[77]Labor Law art. 25, para. b, c, d, e, f.

There are numerous rulings of the Court of Cassation with respect to this topic that set precedent. For example, the Court has decided that employees who discredit the reputation of the employer are in breach of their work obligations. More precisely, such activities as putting the security of a military plant at risk by introducing unauthorized persons from outside the plant, accepting bribe or gifts exceeding the usual norms, working in another place while on sick leave, entering into competition with the employer, or engaging in business with the bank's customers are examples of breach of the duty of fidelity and are justified causes for immediate termination.

II. COLLECTIVE BARGAINING

A. Introduction

Some trade unions appeared during the late Ottoman period at the end of the 19th century. However, the country's economy preserved its essentially rural and agricultural character for a long time, and trade unions developed gradually. The industrialization efforts of the young republic gave fruit following the Second World War, and after the 1950s a genuine unionization took place in Turkey.

The first law on unions was enacted in 1947. Nevertheless, it was with the 1961 Constitution that the right to organize in trade unions, as well as the right of collective bargaining and the right to strike, were explicitly recognized and guaranteed. Thereafter, collective labor relations developed rapidly. In 1963, two laws were enacted to regulate collective labor relations: the Law on Unions No. 274 and the Law on Collective Labor Agreements Strikes and Lockouts No. 275. The enactment of these two laws was considered a turning point in Turkish labor-management relations, permitting collective action to spread and gain vigor.

After the brief period of military rule between 1980 and 1982, the present Constitution was adopted in 1982. Two laws governing collective bargaining rights were enacted in 1983: the Law on Unions No. 2821 (*Sendikalar Kanunu*); and the Law on Collective Labor Agreements, Strikes, and Lockouts No. 2822 (*Toplu İş Sözleşmesi, Grev ve Lokavt Kanunu*) (Collective Labor Law). These laws recognize and guarantee the right to form and join unions, the right of collective bargaining, and the right to strike. A set of detailed regulations also was issued, providing guidance for the implementation of the laws' provisions.

B. Union Organization

Under Turkish law, trade unions retain a monopoly for negotiating and concluding collective agreements on workers' behalf. In comparison, employers may be party to a collective bargaining agreement, if they are not members of an association. With this arrangement, trade unions are the principal legal actors in the context of collective labor relations in Turkey.

The basis of union formation is the industry sector (*işkolu*). The Law on Unions and the applicable regulations enumerate 28 sectors.[78] Thus, unions are formed on the basis of a defined sector and may not encompass more than a single sector of activity. An exception is provided for public employers' associations, which can cover different sectors of activity. This exception takes into account the reduced number of public enterprises in certain sectors and aims to permit public institutions to form their own organizations.

In a given workplace, workers join the union founded on the basis of the major activity of the workplace, regardless of any subsidiary works that are being performed.[79] A compulsory rule states that trade unions and employers' associations may not be formed on an occupational, establishment (workplace), or geographical basis. While unions may not be formed on a local or regional basis, they may create local branches. It is understood that these branches have no corporate personality and may not be party to a collective agreement, but they do provide a means for a union to be active throughout the entire country.

Upper-level union organizations may be constituted on a national level. A "confederation" is a higher organization formed by at least five unions from different sectors of industry. Three major

---

[78]Law on Unions art. 60; Regulation on Sectors of Industry No. 83/7376, Nov. 11, 1983 (*İşkollar1 Tüzüğü*).

[79]Law on Unions art. 60.

union confederations dominate the labor scene in Turkey: *Türk-İş*, which is the most representative organization; *DİSK*; and *Hak-İş*. On the employers' side, *TİSK* constitutes the sole upper organization. Confederations may not conclude collective labor agreements.

C. Union Recognition

1. Conditions for Recognition

To conclude a collective agreement, a union must fulfill certain conditions. First, the union must be recognized as the bargaining representative of workers (*yetkili sendika*) in a given undertaking or workplace. This means that the major activity of an undertaking or workplace must be within the same sector as the union. In addition, at the national level, the union must represent at least 10 percent of the workers in the sector.[80] Another, and most decisive, requirement is that more than one-half of the total number of the workers employed in the undertaking or workplace must be affiliated with the particular union. Given this requirement, at the beginning of some bargaining processes a very intense competition takes place between rival unions seeking new members.

2. Authorization (Yetki Belgesi)

The process of determining the most representative union may start within 120 days before the expiration of an existing collective labor agreement. An application to this end is made by the union to the Ministry of Labor. The Ministry first examines the capacity of the union as regards the sector of industry, then the percentage of members within the industry on a national level, according to the statistics established by the Ministry.

The statistics established by the Ministry of Labor and published in the Official Gazette each January and July remain valid until the publication of the following statistics. The accuracy of these statistics may be challenged by the interested parties within

[80]An exception is made for the agriculture, forestry, hunting, and fishing sectors, where this representation barrier is not required. This exception is based on the temporary and scattered character of labor in this field, and the feeble level of unionization among these workers.

15 days from the date of their publication, in an Ankara Labor Court, which then must render its decision within 15 days. The Labor Court's decision may be appealed to the Court of Cassation.[81]

The Ministry of Labor determines the representative union on the basis of each union's membership numbers. The date for which the memberships are taken into account is the date on which the union applies to the Ministry. If the Ministry of Labor determines that conditions of representation are met (representing at least 10 percent of the total number of workers in the industry and the majority of the workers in the undertaking or workplace), it will notify the applicant union and other unions organized in the same sector, as well as the employer's union.[82]

The decision of the Ministry of Labor defining the most representative union may be contested at the local Labor Court (*yetki itirazı*)[83] within six workdays after receipt of the Ministry notification. Before filing a complaint, the party concerned must register it at the Ministry or with the Regional Directorate of Labor. The appropriate Labor Court for challenging the representation decision is that located in the same area as the Regional Directorate of Labor to which the undertaking or workplace is attached. Where the collective agreement covers workplaces in different areas, the complaint must be filed with a Labor Court in Ankara.

Except for a claim based on errors of form or relating to the time of the application (which may not, as mentioned above, be made earlier than 120 days before the expiration date of the collective agreement), other complaints may, after being heard by the Labor Court, be appealed to the Court of Cassation. The decision of the Court of Cassation is final.

A shortcoming of this system is its length, despite the efforts of the legislature to simplify the process. This process, as well as the process for contesting the sector of plant activity,[84] is sometimes misused by rival unions.

---

[81]Collective Labor Law art. 12.

[82]If the Ministry determines that the applicant union has not met the required majority, notice is served only to the applicant.

[83]Collective Labor Law art. 15.

[84]*See* Law on Unions art. 4.

The authorization for representation granted by the Ministry of Labor gives the union the following rights:

- the exclusive right to negotiate and be a party to the collective labor agreement;
- the right to collect as "solidarity dues" (*dayanışma aidatı*) two-thirds of the regular membership dues from nonmember workers who wish to benefit from the provisions of the collective agreement;
- the right to collect membership fees and solidarity dues directly from the employer, through a deduction, or "check-off" from wages; and
- the exclusive right to designate union representatives in the workplace.

D. Levels of Bargaining

Collective labor agreements typically are negotiated and concluded either at the workplace or the undertaking level. However, the Collective Labor Law leaves to the parties the possibility of including several undertakings in a single bargaining process. In any event, a collective agreement may never exceed the boundaries of a defined industry sector.

1. Workplace Collective Agreement (İşyeri Toplu İş Sözleşmesi)

The basic level of bargaining is the workplace, although the Collective Labor Law does permit a collective labor agreement to encompass more than one workplace.

Provided that workplaces operate within the same industry sector, a "group collective agreement" (*grup toplu iş sözleşmesi*), that is, an agreement including several workplaces belonging to different employers, may be negotiated and concluded. In this case, the general rule governing union recognition is that the union must represent the majority of the workers in each separate workplace.

In practice, group collective agreements are often concluded, although the process of dispute resolution generally is conducted separately for each workplace.

2. Undertaking Collective Agreement (İşletme Toplu (İş) Sözleşmesi)

If separate workplaces within the same industry sector belong to the same real person or legal entity, then the Collective Labor Law requires bargaining to be conducted at the undertaking level.[85] In these cases, the conditions for representation, as well as the process for union recognition, also must be satisfied at the undertaking level.

In the private sector, an undertaking collective agreement may not encompass more than a single legal entity. The rule is different in public organizations and institutions, where distinct entities attached to a public institution must enter in the scope of a single "undertaking agreement" unit. This differentiation aims to preserve the unity of public enterprises and institutions.

E. Effect of the Agreement

1. Effect on the Parties

Collective agreements are legally binding on the trade union representing the workers and on the employer.

A change in the identity of the employer by sale of the undertaking or otherwise will not affect the collective agreement, which must remain in force in the workplace and bind the new owner.[86] Nor may the employer escape the binding effect of a collective agreement by quitting an employers' association. In either case, the collective labor agreement continues to govern working conditions at the workplace.

2. Effect on Employment Contracts

The effect of collective agreements on individual employment contracts is automatic and binding in the workers' favor. Any less favorable terms in individual contracts are replaced automatically by the provisions of the collective agreement.

---

[85] Collective Labor Law art. 3, para. 2.

[86] *Id.* art. 8.

The Turkish labor system promotes union membership. Thus, in principle, workers who are not members of the signatory union may not benefit from the provisions of a collective agreement relating to wages or other pecuniary benefits. However, by paying solidarity dues (two-thirds of regular membership dues) to the union, nonmembers may benefit from the pecuniary provisions of the collective agreement.

Non-pecuniary provisions, especially those regarding the organization of the workplace and conditions of work, generally are applicable to all workers in the workplace, whether or not they are union members. However, the provisions of a collective bargaining agreement do not apply to contract workers, i.e., workers of an employer that contracts with a signatory employer to perform a particular job.[87]

3. *Subjects of Bargaining*

The subjects of bargaining are not defined or limited by the Collective Labor Law or regulations. However, because a collective labor agreement is aimed at regulating economic and social matters and conditions of employment, by implication, the agreement must be limited to these issues.

From another perspective, collective agreements should not contain any provision contrary to the obligatory rules of law or any provision encouraging, supporting, or protecting crimes.

4. *Extension of Collective Labor Agreements*

Employers that are not parties to a collective agreement, but operate in the same industry sector, may come within the scope of the agreement through a decree of extension (*teşmil*) issued by the Council of Ministers.[88] In this event, the collective agreement will bind all employers within the sector covered by the decree. In practice, this authority is seldom used.

Article 11 of Collective Labor Law requires specific conditions for a decree of extension. The union that is party to the collective agreement must be the most representative union in the

[87] See Court of Cassation rulings on this issue since 1996.

[88] Collective Labor Law art. 11.

sector covered by the decree and must represent at least 10 percent of the workers within the sector at the time the decree is issued. No application for bargaining authorization must have been made in the undertakings and workplaces subject to the extension, and they should not be covered by an existing collective agreement. In any case, no more than one collective labor agreement may be concluded or applied at the same undertaking or workplace.

A decree of extension may be contested by the interested parties. If determined to be unlawful, it will be declared void by the Council of State (High Court of Administration, or *Danıştay*), which is the supreme court for administrative disputes and litigation in general. Annulments have occurred when the decree of extension covered a period of time prior to the date of the extension. A retroactive effect of this nature is not accepted with respect to administrative acts.

F. Duration of the Collective Labor Agreement

1. Duration and Expiration

As a general rule, collective labor agreements are concluded for a definite duration that may not be less than one year or more than three years. When the term has expired, the provisions of the agreement will continue to apply "as labor contract terms" until a new collective agreement is concluded.[89] This effect applies to the parties covered by the collective agreement. Thus, as terms of a labor contract, the parties to the agreement can always modify the provisions.

For projects shorter than one year, the collective agreement may have a shorter duration and will continue to apply until the end of the work, but can continue for no longer than one year.[90]

The length of a collective agreement may not be modified, either by shortening or prolonging it. However, the parties may, by protocol, amend other provisions such as wages and various pecuniary provisions. Amendments are not considered to be independent collective labor agreements, and they may be concluded only between the parties to the collective agreement by consen-

---

[89]*Id.* art. 6, para. 3.
[90]*Id.* art. 7, para. 2.

sus. As discussed immediately below, no collective dispute is allowed as long as the term of the collective agreement has not expired.

2. *Obligation of Peace*

The "obligation of peace" *(iş barışını koruma yükümlülüğü)* is a decisive principle of collective labor relations under Turkish Law. The principle implies an obligation not to engage in any collective action throughout the duration of a collective labor agreement for all workers and unions, parties or not to the collective agreement, regardless of the subject of the claims.

3. *Application of a Single Collective Labor Agreement*

According to both the Constitution and Collective Labor Law,[91] no more than one collective agreement may be concluded or put into effect at the same workplace for the same period. Thus, two collective agreements will never overlap. When a new collective agreement enters into force, it replaces the former agreement, which then ceases to exist.

G. Strikes and Other Industrial Action

1. *Conditions for a Legal Strike*

The right to strike is guaranteed by the Constitution[92] and is subject to a detailed set of legislative rules.

The legislature defines a strike as a concerted and complete cessation of work by some or all workers, aiming to halt or at least hinder significantly the activities of the workplace.[93] A strike is legal provided that it complies with the conditions set forth by the Collective Labor Law and other legislation. To begin with, a strike may be engaged in only during the collective bargaining process. More specifically, a decision to call a strike may be made only after having tried to settle the dispute by legal mediation. If the

---

[91]CONST. art. 53, para. 3; Collective Labor Law art. 3, para 4.
[92]CONST. art. 54.
[93]Collective Labor Law art. 25, para. 1.

parties fail to reach an agreement, the authorized trade union has the right to call a strike after six workdays from the time the parties receive a record from the mediator of the failure to reach agreement and within six workdays thereafter. Notice of the starting date must be provided to the employer by a notary, and the strike must begin within 60 days following notice of the decision to call the strike.[94] These provisions allow the employer to receive notice of a planned strike and to take certain mitigating measures in the workplace.

Although the decision to call a strike is a prerogative of the authorized union, a strike vote may be requested by at least one-fourth of the workers employed in the workplace. In this case, if the majority of the workers employed in the workplace vote against the strike, it may not be implemented. The union then has the choice either to reach an agreement or refer the matter to the High Arbitration Board.

2. *Rules Concerning the Conduct of Strikes and Lockouts*

a. *Safeguarding the Freedom to Work*

The legislature attaches great importance to the freedom to work, and a number of legal provisions aim to protect the liberty and free choice of workers.

With the beginning of a strike or lockout, the striking workers must leave the workplace and are required not to obstruct its entrance or exits. Those who refuse to join the strike or who decide to abandon the strike may, in no manner, be barred from working.[95] The entry of persons, materials, equipment, and tools, as well as the sale of goods produced by non-striking workers, must be secured without hindrance.

b. *Maintaining the Security of the Workplace*

To ensure the functioning of activities necessary for the security of the workplace and the preservation of equipment, raw materials, and products, those workers whose designation is regu-

---

[94] *Id.* arts. 27, 28, 37.
[95] *Id.* art. 38.

lated by law[96] must continue to work during the strike or lockout. Such work must not aim at production or sale.

c. Suspension of Work

The law grants the employer the right to suspend work temporarily, even for those who do not take part in the strike. In this case, the rights and obligations based on the workers' employment contract are suspended, and the employer is not required to pay wages.[97] In addition, the workers whose labor contract is suspended may not engage in other work during the strike.

It is evident that a work suspension by the employer would have socially adverse effects on the workers. This is a major reason that all workers typically join a strike, whether or not they are members of the union that called the strike.

d. Protecting the Rights of Strikers

The legislature gives the strike maximum effectiveness by providing that during a strike the employer must not recruit, employ, or assign anyone to perform the work normally done by those on strike or by the other workers whose labor contract is suspended. The Regional Directorate of Labor may control compliance with this restriction at the request of the strikers or the authorized union. Sanctions for violation of this provision are imposed by the Collective Labor Law as fines.[98]

3. Picketing and Handbilling

Strike picketing is regulated mainly by Article 48 of the Collective Labor Law and in a bylaw issued by the Ministry of Labor.[99] The legislature has established many rules aimed at protecting the freedom of those who are not taking part in the strike.

Strike pickets (*grev gözcüleri*) are assigned by the authorized trade union from among its member-workers, and their number is limited to four at each door of the workplace. They may not resort to force or threats or stop those entering and leaving the premises.

[96] *Id.* arts. 39–40.

[97] *Id.* art. 38, para. 2.

[98] *Id.* arts. 43, 78.

[99] *See* Official Gazette No. 19926, Sept. 11, 1988.

Except for a sign indicating "This Workplace Is on Strike," any type of sign, poster, or writing is prohibited.

4. *Prohibited Strikes and Lockouts*

The Collective Labor Law, as well as the Constitution, forbids political strikes, general strikes, solidarity strikes, the occupation of work premises, labor slowdowns, and other forms of obstruction.[100]

The Collective Labor Law also enumerates certain jobs and workplaces where strikes and lockouts are prohibited.[101] In these cases, after a mediation stage, either party may bring the dispute before the High Arbitration Board for final resolution. The jobs where industrial action is prohibited include: rescue work; production of lignite for use in thermal plants; water, electricity, and city gas; exploration, production, processing, and distribution of natural gas and petroleum; petrochemical work starting from naphtha and natural gas; banking and notary services; firefighting; and urban sea, land, and railway transportation services provided by the public sector.

Workplaces where industrial action is prohibited include: health centers and hospitals; vaccine and serum manufacturing institutions; pharmacies (except medicine manufacturers); education and teaching institutions; and establishments directly run by the Ministry of National Defense, the General Command of Gendarmerie, or the Coast Guard Command.

There also are temporary strike and lockout prohibitions concerning times of mobilization and natural disasters and in sea, air, and land transportation vehicles that have not completed the journey to their domestic terminal points.

5. *Postponement of Strikes and Lockouts*

A strike or lockout may be suspended by a Labor Court decision if the right is misused or when a strike or lockout becomes harmful to society or destroys national wealth.[102]

---

[100]CONST. art. 54, para. 7; Collective Labor Law art. 25, para. 3.
[101]Collective Labor Law arts. 29, 30.
[102]*Id.* art. 47.

The Council of Ministers, by a decree, also has the power to postpone a strike or lockout if these actions endanger the general health and national security. However, the Council of State may annul such decrees, and an injunction may be demanded during the process of the lawsuit.

If the parties do not reach an agreement during a postponement, the case must be referred to the High Arbitration Board.

6. *Slowdowns and Sit-Ins*

Slowdowns, as well as any other form of concerted action having an adverse effect on production, are prohibited[103] and are subject to the same civil sanctions as an illegal strike. The labor contracts of those who take part in such acts may be terminated without any period of notice or compensation. Penal sanctions also are provided in the Collective Labor Law.[104]

Sit-ins also are legally prohibited and sanctioned; at of the beginning of a strike, all workers who are on strike must leave the workplace.[105]

7. *Ending a Legal Strike*

A strike ends by decision of the authorized union. It also may end automatically if the union is barred from activity or dissolved, or by court decision in cases when at least three-fourths of the members resign from the union.

Recourse to private arbitration by mutual agreement also is possible at any stage of the dispute, although this method is not common. If the parties agree in writing to refer the dispute to arbitration, the provisions on mediation, strike, and lockout, as well as compulsory arbitration, do not apply. In this situation, an arbitration award has the force of a collective labor agreement.

8. *Consequences of Legal Strikes*

The rule protecting the exercise of the right to strike is that a worker who takes part in a strike may not be dismissed for having

---

[103] CONST. art. 54, para. 7; Collective Labor Law art. 25, para. 3.
[104] Collective Labor Law, *Fifth Section.*
[105] *Id.* art. 38.

participated in the decision to strike or the strike itself. Until the end of the strike, the obligation to work, and the obligation to pay wages and benefits corresponding to the duration of the strike, is suspended. However, the employer must pay wages and supplements earned before the strike, on the normal payday.

The period of a strike is not taken into account in the calculation of severance compensation, and no wage may be paid for the period of the strike. These rules are compulsory, so nothing to the contrary may be decided, even in collective labor agreements.[106]

Even if a strike is legal, the union that called for the strike may be liable for damages to the workplace caused by the actions of the striking workers.[107]

9. *Consequences of Illegal Strikes and Collective Actions*

The employer may terminate the labor contract of those who participate in the decision or the application of an illegal strike, without any period of notice or compensation.[108] Notification of the termination, according to court practice, must be within six working days from the day the employer becomes aware of the action.[109]

Damages resulting from an illegal strike are the responsibility of the union that called for the strike or the workers involved, if the strike was not decided by any workers' organization.

The Collective Labor Law also imposes penal sanctions for various categories of illegal strikes and other forms of illegal collective actions.

During a strike, any party may apply to a Labor Court to determine whether the strike or lockout is illegal.[110] The court's decision is binding on the parties and the members of the union and serves as absolute evidence before the criminal courts.

---

[106]*Id.* art. 42, para. 5.

[107]CONST. art. 54, para. 3; Collective Labor Law art. 47, para. 4.

[108]Collective Labor Law art. 45.

[109]Labor Law art. 26.

[110]Collective Labor Law art. 46.

10. Lockouts

A lockout typically is defensive in nature, although it gains an "offensive" character where it is used in workplaces for which a strike has not been called.[111] Under Turkish law, the initiative of collective action belongs to the workers' union. Thus, a lockout is legal when it intervenes after a decision to strike is made and notice is given to the employer by the authorized trade union. The employer may not legally decide to lock out employees when no strike has been called. However, the termination of a strike does not necessarily imply that the lockout will end at the same time.

The effect of a legal lockout is the suspension of the obligation to pay wages. An illegal lockout continues the obligation to pay wages and all other worker benefits, without any work being performed.

In other respects, the legislature has respected a certain symmetry between strikes and lockouts; the same prohibitions and limitations apply, and comparable, if not identical, civil and legal sanctions are provided.

H. Third-Party Resolution of Disputes

Turkish labor legislation contains a set of compulsory rules for different forms of peaceful dispute resolution.

1. Rights Disputes

A "rights dispute" is a dispute arising from the interpretation or application of existing legal norms or contracts. A basic principle prevailing in the Labor Law is that a rights dispute may never be subject to collective action, such as a strike or lockout. Instead, rights disputes must be resolved either by the courts or by arbitration, according to general rules.

2. Voluntary Arbitration

At any stage of a collective dispute, the parties may agree in writing to bring the case before an arbitrator or arbitration board

---

[111] *Id.* art. 27, para. 3.

of their own choosing. The High Arbitration Board also may be designated as a private arbitration institution. In all cases, recourse to voluntary arbitration will end the collective dispute, and the arbitration award will have the same effects as a collective labor agreement. As discussed above, voluntary arbitration is not often used in collective labor disputes.

3. *Mediation*

If the parties are not able to reach agreement within 60 days from the beginning of collective negotiations, a compulsory phase of mediation (*arabuluculuk*) is instituted, according to provisions of the Collective Labor Law.[112]

The Official Mediation Organization (*Resmî Arabuluculuk Teşkilatı*) attached to the Ministry of Labor provides mediation services. A list of the mediators who are independent from the parties and have certain qualifications is set by this organization.

The parties may choose a mediator from the official list after the lapse of 30 days from the commencement of negotiations. However, after the 60-day period, the competent court appoints a mediator from the official list.

The duration of mediation is 15 days, but, with the consent of both parties, this term may be extended by six workdays. The mediator expends all efforts to bring the parties to an agreement and to cause conclusion of a collective labor agreement. In the alternative, the mediator sets up a record of the disagreement, which must be submitted to the Regional Directorate of Labor and then forwarded to the parties.

It is only at this stage that a strike, and thereafter a lockout, may begin. In jobs or workplaces where strikes and lockouts are prohibited, the dispute may be brought by either party before the High Arbitration Board.

4. *The High Arbitration Board* (Yüksek Hakem Kurulu)

Arbitration becomes compulsory in cases where strikes and lockouts are prohibited, or in other situations such as the post-

---

[112]*Id.* arts. 21, 22.

ponement of a strike by the Council of Ministers, or when the majority of workers vote against the strike and the parties are not able to reach an agreement.

Except for the postponement of a strike, where the Minister of Labor must take the initiative, either party may refer a dispute to the High Arbitration Board. The difference from a voluntary arbitration is that either party may refer the matter to arbitration, and the agreement of both parties is not required.

The High Arbitration Board is an official institution organized by law.[113] Titles and qualifications of the members of the High Arbitration Board are defined in Article 53 of the Collective Labor Law.

An award by the High Arbitration Board is final and binding on the parties. The Board's decision has the power and effect of a collective labor agreement.

I. Union Security

1. Union Membership

a. Freedom to Organize and Join Unions

The Turkish Constitution grants the freedom to organize unions: "Working people and employers have the right to form labor unions and employers' associations and higher organizations, without prior permission, in order to safeguard and develop the economic and social rights and interests of their members in their labor relations, to join them and withdraw freely from such organizations."[114] This freedom is coupled with the provisions of the Law on Unions and accompanied by specific rules preventing any discrimination based on union membership or activity.[115]

---

[113]*See* Decree No. 84/8078, May 17, 1984. Decree No. 84/8078 puts into effect the Regulation on Arbitration and Official Mediation (*Hakeme ve Resmî Arabulucuya Başvurma Tüzüğü)*, Official Gazette No. 18433, June 16, 1984. This Regulation also contains some provisions concerning private arbitration of collective interest disputes.

[114]CONST. art. 51, para. 1.

[115]Law on Unions art. 31.

Unions are organized within their respective industries as corporate associations. Membership is fully voluntary. A worker and an employer may join only one union in a given sector. The Constitution and the Law on Unions prohibit concurrent memberships within the same industry sector.[116]

Any union member has the right to withdraw from the union. A withdrawal takes effect one month after an application to this effect to a notary public. If the resigned member joins another union during this one-month period, the new membership becomes effective at the end of the one-month period.[117] This rule is important with respect to the application of the collective labor agreement, because the agreement's financial terms apply only to those who are members of the union at the date the collective agreement is concluded, and application of the financial terms lasts as long as membership in the union is maintained.

Union members also may be expelled for reasons specified in the union's charter. The decision to expel a member belongs to the general assembly of the union and may be challenged within 30 days at the local Labor Court. In the event of a challenge, membership continues until the decision to expel becomes final.[118]

The employer is informed of union memberships at two different stages of the recognition process: when the union seeking authorization sends member registration forms to the Ministry of Labor and to the employer, and when the union gives a list of members to the employer for the purpose of deducting membership and solidarity dues from wages.

b. Membership Rights and Dues

Union members have an equal right to vote and be elected to different legal bodies of the unions. The principle of union democracy is emphasized in the Law on Unions, as well as in the Constitution: "The status, administration and functioning of the labor unions and their higher bodies should not be inconsistent with the characteristics of the Republic and democratic principles."[119]

---

[116] CONST. art. 51, para. 5; Law on Unions art. 22, para. 1.

[117] Law on Unions art. 25, para. 2.

[118] *Id.* art. 25, para. 3.

[119] CONST. art. 51, final para.

Union members also have obligations, such as the obligation to pay membership dues. The legislature has set some limits on membership dues by providing that the monthly dues may not exceed the daily basic wage of the worker.[120] As regards employers, monthly membership dues may not exceed the total amount of wages paid for a single day in the workplace. No other dues or additional fee may be required.

2. *Antidiscrimination*

Employment in a workplace may not be conditioned on membership or nonmembership in a labor union. Both the Constitution and the Law on Unions prohibit union security practices such as the closed shop and union shop.[121] Any such clause is considered null and void, and a penal sanction is provided. In practice, union security clauses and practices are unknown in Turkey.

The law also forbids any discrimination by the employer, including dismissal, based on union membership or activity. Article 31 of the Law on Unions provides that "no discrimination will be made between workers who are union members and those who are not, or those who are members of different unions with respect to recruitment, arrangement and distribution of work, promotion, wages, bonuses, gratuities, fringe benefits, application of disciplinary rules or provisions on other questions, including termination of employment."[122]

Union membership or participation in union activities outside working hours or with the consent of the employer within working hours cannot constitute a valid reason for dismissal.[123]

In case of discriminatory treatment or dismissal, in addition to the provisions of the Labor Law concerning unjustified termination,[124] workers are entitled to specific compensation, called in

---

[120]Law on Unions art. 23.

[121]CONST. art. 51; Law on Unions art. 31.

[122]Excepted are collective labor agreement clauses on wages and pecuniary matters, the benefits of which are reserved to workers who are members of the party union. See II.D.2., above.

[123]Labor Law art. 18(a).

[124]See I.D.2.b., above; Labor Law arts. 18–21.

practice "unionism compensation" (*sendikal tazminat*), amounting to no less than the worker's total annual wage.[125]

III. Representation of Workers

Under current Turkish law, since the enactment of the Law on Unions in 1963, union representatives are the sole legally provided form of worker representation in the workplace. Thus, union representation emphasizes the strength of the authorized union in the undertaking.

Up to eight union representatives are appointed by the authorized union, depending on the number of workers in the workplace.[126]

The role of union representatives, as set forth in Article 35 of the Law on Unions, is to promote and follow up the rights and interests of the workers, safeguard peace and harmony within the workplace, and help implement working conditions as provided by labor legislation and collective agreements. Representatives must perform their duties without either impairing the performance of the work or interfering with workplace discipline.

While Labor Law No. 4857 strengthened job security in general, the specific protection of workers' representatives has been diluted. In cases of discrimination against union members and representatives, compensation amounting to no less than a year's wage can be claimed. However, the Labor Law provides that being a union representative should never constitute a valid cause of dismissal.[127]

A protection that a union representative enjoys is the prevention of unilateral modifications by the employer of the working conditions: the representative's written consent is required before a transfer to another workplace or an essential modification of the conditions of work.[128]

---

125 Law on Unions art. 31. See also VI.B., below.

126 Law on Unions art. 34.

127 Labor Law art. 18 b.

128 Law on Unions art. 30.

IV. REDUNDANCY AND TRANSFERS OF UNDERTAKINGS

A. Redundancy

Mass terminations are justified by economic, technological, structural or similar reasons related to the undertaking or activity. Workers who are terminated for reasons of redundancy are entitled to advance notice, time-off to seek new employment, and severance pay. Upon termination, the employer must furnish the worker with a certificate stating the nature and duration of the employment.[129]

Employers may terminate more than one worker at a time, without the approval of the Employment Agency.[130]

B. Transfers of Undertakings

1. *New Owner's Duty to Abide by the Terms of the Collective Agreement*

In the event of a change in the ownership of an undertaking, the new owner must comply with the terms of the collective agreement then in effect because collective agreements are concluded by and between unions and employer entities, and not by the owners. The new owner normally knows or must know that a collective agreement is in effect at the time of the acquisition.[131]

The new owner also must comply with the terms of individual employment contracts that are in effect at the time of the ownership change.

2. *Effect of a Change in Ownership on Workers' Status and Benefits*

a. *Transfer of the Employment Contracts*

In case of transfer of the workplace or of one of its sections, the new owner also must abide by the terms of individual employment contracts that are in effect at the time of the ownership change.

---

[129] Labor Law art. 28. See also I.D.5., above.

[130] See I.D.4., above.

[131] Collective Labor Law art. 8.

Neither employer is authorized to terminate employment contracts solely because of the transfer. However, the labor contracts may be terminated if necessitated by economic, technological, or organizational changes, or in cases of just cause.

A change in the ownership of a workplace does not affect the worker's status, especially regarding the length of the worker's service.[132] The length of service is unaffected regardless of the reason for transfer, including sale, inheritance, or moving the workplace to another location. The acquisition of a workplace or any other change in ownership does not adversely affect, in any way, the rights of the workers to paid annual leave.[133] Even if there is an agreement to the contrary, the agreement would be invalid, and the remuneration of workers corresponding to periods of paid annual leave must be paid by the new owner.

The law provides a specific guarantee for the workers: In such cases of transfer due to a legal transaction, both employers (transferor and transferee) shall be jointly liable for the obligations due at the date of the transfer. However, the liability of the former owner is limited to a period of two years following the date of the transfer.[134]

However, these provisions on joint liability shall not apply in cases where the corporate personality of the undertaking ends as a result of merger and participation or transformation into another corporate type. More generally, the provisions of this article regarding transfers of the workplace are not applicable for transfers in cases of liquidation due to insolvency and bankruptcy of the employer.

b. Severance Payments

In the event of a change in ownership, both the old owner and the new owner (transferor and transferee) are responsible for accrued severance payments.[135] However, the liability of the transferor is limited to the wage of the worker at the time of transfer.

---

[132] Labor Law No. 1475 art. 14.

[133] For a discussion of paid annual leave, see V.C.1., below.

[134] Labor Law art. 6.

[135] For a discussion of severance payments, see I.D.7., above.

c. Annual Leave

The acquisition of a workplace or any other change in ownership does not adversely affect, in any way, the rights of the workers to paid annual leave.[136] Even if there is an agreement to the contrary, the agreement would be invalid, and the remuneration of workers corresponding to periods of paid annual leave must be paid by the new owner.[137]

V. WAGES, HOURS, AND LEAVE

A. Wages

1. Wage Payments

The wage is the amount of money paid in cash by the employer to the worker for work performed by the worker. In principle, wages are paid in Turkish Lira, at least once per month at the workplace or to the worker's bank account. However, if payment in a foreign currency is agreed upon, it may be paid in Turkish currency at the rate applicable on the payment date. Minimum weekly payments may be agreed to in individual employment contracts and collective agreements.

No reduction of any kind may be made from workers' wages on the grounds that the daily or weekly working hours have been reduced by law or because of a mandatory obligation placed on the employer under the provisions of the Labor Law.[138]

For each wage payment, the employer is obliged to issue each worker a slip bearing the employer's signature or the special emblem of the workplace and showing the wage calculation. Dates of payments, amounts of additions to the base wage such as overtime, weekend, national and general holiday pay, and deductions such as tax, insurance premium, advance payment, alimony, and attachments must be shown separately on the wage slip or book. Wage slips are exempt from stamp tax and all duties and charges.

---

[136]For a discussion of paid annual leave, see V.C.1., below.

[137]Labor Law art. 53.

[138]*Id.* art. 32.

A worker must be paid half wages for each day up to one week when reasons of *force majeure* cause the suspension of work or prevent a worker from performing his or her duties.

2. *Minimum Wage*

A minimum wage is applicable in Turkey. It covers all workers, including seamen and journalists employed under service contracts and falling within the scope of the Labor Law.

Minimum wages are determined by the Minimum Wage Board at the Ministry of Labor. The Minimum Wage Board is composed of the following directors or their deputies: the General Director of Labor and General Director of Workers' Health and Safety of the Ministry of Labor; the Director of Economic Statistics Office of the State Institute of Statistics; the Director of the Office of Conjuncture and Publications of the Ministry of Industry and Commerce; a representative of the Undersecretariat of Treasury, the Director of the relevant section of the State Planning Department, or a person authorized by the Director; five workers' representatives from the largest unions within the various branches of industry; and five employers' representatives from the employer organizations representing the majority of employers within the various branches of industry. The Minimum Wage Board requires that at least 10 members are present for its meetings. It makes its decisions by majority vote; in case of a tie, the Chairperson's side has the majority. Decisions of the Board are final and come into force upon publication in the Official Gazette.

The minimum wage must be determined at least once every two years. However, during recent years, there has been a tendency to determine the minimum wage at six-month intervals.

3. *Overtime and Extra Hours Pay*

a. *Overtime Work*

Workers are entitled to premium pay for working hours, in principle, in excess of the weekly maximum of 45 hours (overtime).[139] If 45 hours per week is exceeded, provided that it meets

[139] See V.B.1.a., below.

the rule of balancing according to Article 63 of the Labor Law (see V.B.1.a., below), no premium pay will be applicable. For the overtime work, the hourly premium is 50 percent above the normal hourly wage.[140] However, workers, at their discretion, instead of receiving premium pay may take one hour and thirty minutes of free time for every one hour of overtime worked.

b. Extra Hours Work

If the weekly work is determined for less than 45 hours, by contract, the work in excess of such predetermined weekly work but up to 45 hours per week is defined as the "extra hours work." Workers are entitled to premium pay for extra hours. For extra hours, the hourly premium is 25 percent above the normal hourly wage. However, workers, at their discretion, instead of receiving premium pay may take one hour and fifteen minutes of free time for every extra hour worked. Uninterrupted free time may be used within a six-month period without any reduction in wages.

Overtime and extra hours work are subject to the worker's consent and may not exceed 270 hours per annum.

4. Tip Income

In workplaces where tips are paid, such as hotels, restaurants, entertainment places, fast food restaurants, or stands serving alcoholic beverages, the employer must pay the workers for tips, in full, regardless or whether tips are included in the bill or are discretionary. The employer also is obliged to document that tips are distributed to workers.[141]

---

[140]Labor Law art. 41. See also V.B.2., below.
[141]Labor Law art. 51

B. Hours

1. *Arranging of Work*

a. Working Hours

As a general rule, the duration of the workweek may not exceed 45 hours.[142] If not agreed otherwise, the 45 hours of work per week must be distributed evenly over the working days of the week.

Subject to the agreement of the parties, the 45 hours of work per week may be distributed unevenly over the working days of the week, provided that it does not exceed 11 hours per day.

In such an event, however, even if in some weeks 45 hours of work are exceeded, within a two-month period the average of weekly work cannot exceed 45 hours (rule of balancing). Balancing may be made within a four-month period through collective labor agreements.

The weekly day of rest may be any day of the week, not necessarily Sunday. Workers may begin and stop work at different hours.

b. Work for Compensation

If work is suspended due to *force majeure*, workplace closings before or after a national or general holiday, reduced or stopped working hours, or if leave is granted upon request of a worker, the employer may request to compensate such lost time within two months thereafter by requiring an employee to work. Work for compensation shall not be deemed as overtime or excesstime work and may not exceed three hours a day, provided that maximum working hour per day is not exceeded. No work for compensation can be performed on holidays.[143]

---

[142]*See also* Regulation on Working Time Related to the Labor Law (*İş Kanununa İlişkin Çalışma Süreleri Yönetmeliği*); Regulation on Works To Be Done Only Seven-and-a-half Hours or Less Per Day Due to Health Rules (*Sağık Kuralları Bakımından Günde Ancak Yedibuçuk Saat veya Daha Az Çalışılması Gereken İşler Hakkında Yönetmelik*).

[143]Labor Law art. 64.

c. Short-Time Work and Payment for Short-Time Work

Due to general economic crisis or *force majeure*, an employer that reduces working hours substantially, or temporarily stops its operation in part or completely, must inform the Employment Agency and the union party to the collective labor agreement, if applicable.

Provided that work stops temporarily for at least four weeks or working time is reduced, and provided that workers are entitled to payment for such short-time work by means of their seniority and paid-up premium for the unemployment insurance, workers are paid for short-time work by the unemployment insurance for an amount equal to their entitlement under the unemployment coverage. Periods of short work cannot exceed three months.[144]

d. Periods Considered as Working Time

The following periods are considered as part of the statutory hours of work:

- time spent by workers in mines, stone quarries, or any other underground or underwater work to descend into the pit or workings or to the actual workplace and to return there from to the surface;
- time spent in travel to and from a workplace outside the undertaking by workers who were sent by the employer;
- time when a worker stays idle at the disposal of the employer;
- time spent by the worker without performing his or her duties due to instruction by the employer to do some other work, such as an errand for the employer or work at the employer's household;
- time allowed to nursing mothers for feeding their babies; and
- in works such as railway, road, and bridge construction and repair, where due to the nature of the work, the workers are carried together to and from the workplace, time spent on

[144] *Id.* art. 65.

the way from and to workplaces where the actual work takes place.[145]

Regular time spent on transportation to and from the workplace, which is financed by the employer solely as a form of social benefit, is not considered as part of the statutory hours of work and is not included in the calculation of working hours.

e. Regulation of Time and Rest Periods

The starting and closing hours of work and the hours of rest periods must be posted at the workplace.

The Law on Rest at Noon No. 6301 (*Öğle Dinlenmesi Kanunu*) provides that, in towns, workers are entitled to have a break of not less than one hour during the noontime. In addition, under the Labor Law,[146] workers must be allowed an uninterrupted rest period in the middle of the workday for a minimum period, as follows:

- 15 minutes when the work lasts four hours or less;
- one-half hour when the work lasts more than four hours but less than 7½ hours; or
- one hour when the work lasts 7½ hours or more.

These rest periods may be split up by collective agreement or by contract where the climate, season, custom, or nature of the work so require. Except as otherwise agreed in an individual employment contract or a collective agreement, rest periods may be allowed at the same or different times for work in the same part of the undertaking.

The rest periods described above are not considered as part of the statutory hours of work and are not included in the calculation of working hours.

f. Restrictions on Night Work

"Night work" (*gece çalışması*) means a part of the day beginning at or after 8:00 p.m., ending at or before 6:00 a.m., and lasting no more than 11 hours.[147]

---

[145]*Id.* art. 66.
[146]*Id.* art. 68.
[147]*Id.* art. 73.

As a general rule, persons younger than the age of 18 may not be employed in industrial work during the night. Women ages 18 or older can be employed on night shifts in operations under a regulation to be issued by the Ministry of Labor. A night-work shift may not exceed 7½ hours. Night-work shifts may last no more than one week, and workers on a night-work shift must change to day work during the following week.[148] However, shift changes every 15 days are allowed.

Before assigning an employee to a night shift, a report certifying his or her health must be obtained. Employers must require regular health inspections at two-year intervals.

The Ministry of Labor has issued two regulations covering night work,[149] which set forth provisions regarding the beginning of night work according to the nature and requirements of the work or the differences of climate and custom among the various regions of the country. The regulations also distinguish between summer time and winter time, establish the beginning and end of the period to be regarded as "night" for men, women, and children in different kinds of work, and set standards for the payment of extra wages for certain types of night work.

2. *Overtime Work*

a. Ordinary Overtime[150]

Under the Labor Law, overtime work is allowed for reasons of the public interest if the nature of the operation so requires, or to increase production.[151] Overtime is work that exceeds 45 hours per week. Overtime is subject to the following conditions:

---

[148] *Id.* art. 69.

[149] *See* Regulation on Special Procedures and Principles for Works Carried Out Through Shifts (*Postalar Halinde İşçi Çalıştırılarak Yürütülen İşlerde Çalışmalara İlişkin Özel Usul ve Esaslar Hakkında Yönetmelik*); Regulation on Conditions for Women Workers Working in Industrial Undertakings at Night Shifts No. 7/6909, July 27, 1973 (*Kadın İşçilerin Sanayie ait İşlerde Gece Postalarında Çalıştırılma Koşulları Hakkında Tüzük—Kadınların Gece Çalıştırılması Tüzüğü*).

[150] Labor Law art. 41.

[151] *Id. See also* Regulation on Overtime Work and Extra Hours Work Related to the Labor Law (*İş Kanununa İlişkin Fazla Çalışma ve Fazla Sürelerle Çalışma Yönetmeliği*. For a discussion of overtime pay, see V.A.3., above.

- the total working hours per day must not exceed eleven hours,
- the total number of days in which overtime is worked must not exceed 270 per year, and
- overtime work requires the worker's consent.

The hourly rate for overtime is 50 percent above the normal hourly wage.

b. Overtime in Case of Emergency

Some or all workers may be requested to work overtime in case of an emergency, to ensure normal operation of the undertaking. Emergencies may include an actual or threatened defect or failure, urgent work to be performed on machinery or tools or equipment, or because of *force majeure.*[152] For the overtime work, the premium is 50 percent above the normal hourly wage. However, workers, at their discretion, instead of receiving premium pay may take one-hour and thirty minutes of free time for every one hour of overtime work. For excess-time work, the hourly premium is 25 percent above the normal hourly wage. However, workers, at their discretion, instead of receiving premium may take one hour and fifteen minutes of free time for every one hour of overtime work. Free time can be used uninterrupted within a six-month period without any reduction in wages.

c. Overtime During Mobilization

The Council of Ministers may, during mobilization if it deems it necessary, extend daily working hours in undertakings serving the needs of national defense for a limited time.[153] Daily hours may be extended up to the workers' maximum capacity, according to the nature of the operation and the urgency of the need in question.

With respect to payments for overtime work and excesstime work, see the preceding paragraph (b) above.

[152]Labor Law art. 42.
[153]*Id.* art. 43.

C. Leave

1. Paid Annual Leave

a. Determination of the Right to Paid Annual Leave

Workers who have completed at least one year of service following the date of employment, including the probationary period, are entitled to annual leave with pay as follows:

- 14 workdays of leave for service of one year to five years;
- 20 workdays of leave for service of five years to 15 years; and
- 26 workdays of leave for service of 15 years or more.[154]

Paid annual leave for workers age 18 or younger and those ages 50 and older may not be less than 20 workdays. The leave periods listed above may be extended by individual employment contract or collective agreement. However, the right to paid annual leave may not be waived.

Paid annual leave does not apply to workers employed in seasonal jobs or in other jobs that, due to their nature, last less than one year.[155]

In calculating the length of service required to qualify for paid annual leave, the total period during which a worker has been employed at one or more workplaces of the employer is taken into consideration, regardless of whether the worker worked in a workplace not covered by the Labor Law.

For purposes of calculating paid annual leave, the periods listed below are considered as time worked:[156]

- days the worker failed to report to work, due to accident or illness;
- the eight-week periods before and after the birth of a child, when a female worker is not working;

---

[154] *Id.* art. 53.
[155] *Id.* art. 54.
[156] *Id.* art. 55.

- with the exception of compulsory military service, up to 90 days per year when a worker is unable to report to work because of being called up for military maneuvers or for the performance of a task under any law;
- during a suspension of work due to reasons of *force majeure*, up to a maximum of 15 workdays, provided that the worker reports to work thereafter;
- periods considered as statutory working time;[157]
- weekly days of rest, and national and public holidays;
- half-day leaves, in addition to Sundays, granted by law to workers working in radiology clinics;
- days when a worker is unable to report to work because of a need to attend meetings of conciliation or arbitration boards, or because of attendance at assemblies, boards, committees, or meetings organized under relevant labor legislation, or because of attendance at conventions, conferences, or committee meetings of international organizations as a worker or union representative;
- leave of up to three days due to a worker's marriage;
- leave of up to three days due to the death of a worker's father, mother, wife, sister, brother, or child; and
- other leaves granted by the employer.

Except as specified above, interruptions in a worker's service are not taken into consideration in calculating the amount of paid annual leave.

b. Implementation of Paid Annual Leave

Workers must use the paid annual leave to which they are entitled at the end of each full year of work, during the following year of employment.

As a general rule, paid annual leave must be given without interruption, and may not be split by the employer. However, provided that one part of the leave will not be less than 10 workdays, paid annual leave may be divided into three parts by mutual consent of the worker and the employer.

---

[157]See V.B.1.d., above.

In cases where a worker will spend his or her leave in a place other than the place of work, at the worker's request, the employer is obliged to grant the worker a leave without pay for up to four days to cover transportation time.

Other leaves granted by the employer, with or without pay, rest or sick leave days, weekly days of rest, and national and public holidays coinciding with the period of leave may not be deducted from the period of paid annual leave.[158]

The employer must make a leave payment, in advance, to a worker who is leaving the workplace for his or her paid annual leave. Remuneration for weekly days of rest and national and public holidays that coincide with the period of paid annual leave must be paid in addition. For workers who are paid other than a daily, monthly, or weekly wage (e.g., on a piece-rate, commission, or share-of-profit basis, or based on tips), annual leave remuneration is based on the worker's average daily earnings, which is calculated by dividing the total wages earned during the previous year by the number of days actually worked during the same year.[159]

The law prohibits working during paid annual leave. If it is ascertained that a worker who was on paid annual leave worked for consideration during the leave period, the employer may request reimbursement of the advance leave payment made to the worker.[160]

Upon termination of the employment contract by either party, the employer must pay the worker the wage corresponding to any leave to which the worker was entitled but did not use. Where the employment contract is terminated by the employer, any unused paid annual leave must be treated separately from the notice period granted to the worker by law or the leave granted to the worker by law to look for a new job.

Additional procedures and conditions regarding the application of annual leave are set forth by regulation.[161] Covered topics include the periods of the year during which paid annual leave

---

[158]Labor Law art. 56.

[159]*Id.* art. 57.

[160]*Id.* art. 58.

[161]Labor Law art. 60. *See* Regulation on Paid Annual Leave (*Yıllık Ücretli İzin Yönetmeliği*).

may be used based on the nature of the work performed, the scheduling of leave periods, and measures to be taken by the employer to achieve the most appropriate annual leave periods.

c. *Recordkeeping*

The employer must maintain records of paid annual leave for each worker.[162]

2. *Paid Time Off for Rest and Holidays*

a. *Weekly Rest Period*

Workers who have worked for six full working days must be paid wages for the seventh day of the week, equal to a full day of work, and are entitled to an uninterrupted rest during the seventh day.[163] The following are considered as days worked:

- the time in which actual work is not performed but is considered as statutory working time;
- paid or unpaid legal or contractual holidays,
- a leave of absence of up to three days in case of the worker's marriage;
- a leave of absence of up to three days in case of the death of the worker's mother, father, wife, husband, brother, sister, or child;
- other leave granted by the employer not to exceed one week; and
- sick leave or rest leave based on a doctor report.

In the event that the employer suspends operations for one or more days, those days are considered in the calculation of the six days required to qualify for the weekly paid rest period.

b. *Public Holidays*

The Law on National Holiday and General Holidays No. 2429 (*Ulusal Bayram ve Genel Tatiller Hakkında Kanun*) provides that

---

[162]Labor Law art. 60.
[163]*Id.* art. 46.

October 29, the day that the Republic was proclaimed, is the National Holiday. The National Holiday begins at 1:00 p.m. on October 28 and expires at 12:00 a.m. on October 29.

The Law on National and General Holidays also establishes the following general holidays.

- Official Holidays:
  - April 23, National Sovereignty and Children's Day;
  - May 19, Youth and Sport Day; and
  - August 30, Victory Day.
- Religious Holidays:
  - Feast of Ramadan, 3½ days, starting at 1:00 p.m. on the day before the holiday; and
  - Feast of Sacrifice, 4½ days, starting at 1:00 p.m. on the day before the holiday
- New Year Holiday:
  - January 1.

Workers must be paid full days' wages for days established as public holidays if they do not work on such days. If they do work on public holidays, they must be paid double the regular wage.[164] A worker's holiday pay is one day's proportionate share of earnings for the days worked. The holiday pay of a worker working on an hourly wage basis is 7½ times the hourly rate.

Individual employment contracts or collective agreements establish whether or not operations will be suspended on general holidays or on October 28 and 29 for the National Holiday.[165]

c. Common Provisions

For workers who are receiving temporary disability pay, payment for the weekly rest day and for public holidays is made by the institution or fund compensating the worker for the disability, in proportion to the rates applying to the degree of disability.[166]

---

[164] *Id.* art. 47.
[165] *Id.* art. 44.
[166] *Id.* art. 48.

The value of overtime wages and premiums, as well as the wages and benefits paid to workers for preparatory, completion, or cleaning work in workplaces, are not taken into consideration in calculating the payment due for the weekly rest day or for public holidays.[167] The preparatory, completion, and cleaning work is the work that is necessary in order to carry out the regular work at workplace, such as preparation and cleaning, and providing any missing tools and equipment.

3. *Other Leaves*

a. *Maternity and Family Leave*

Pregnant workers may not work during the eight-week period before birth or the eight-week period after birth.[168] Workers on mandatory maternity leave are paid by the Social Security Institution.[169] These eight-week leave periods are increased to ten weeks, in the event of pregnancy for multiple births. Subject to a doctor's report, these mandatory eight-week leave periods may be extended, depending on the health of the worker or the nature of the work. If she wishes so, the worker may continue to work until three weeks before the birth, and, corresponding to the period worked, she may use maternity leave after the birth. In such a case, a medical report on the fitness to work is required.

An employment contract may not be terminated because of health reasons or absence before the lapse of time corresponding to the ordinary notice period,[170] plus a six-week period beginning at the end of the eight-weeks' maternity leave.[171]

At the worker's request, an additional six-month unpaid family leave may be granted to the worker following the end of the mandatory maternity leave. Unpaid family leave may not be taken into consideration in computing the worker's paid annual leave.

---

[167] *Id.* art. 50.
[168] *Id.* art. 74.
[169] See the Introduction, at B.3., above, and VIII.B., below.
[170] See I.D.2.a., above.
[171] Labor Law art. 25.

b. Time Off for Military Service or Statutory Labor Service

Except for compulsory military service, a worker who is called up by the military or who leaves employment to perform statutory labor service is considered to be terminated after the lapse of two months from the date of separation. This disposition applies to a worker who has worked at the workplace for at least one year. For workers who have been employed for more than one year, the two-month period is extended for two additional days for each additional year of service. However, the total period of absence may not exceed 90 days. Priority in filling vacancies must be given to workers who left their employment to carry out military or statutory duties, and who make application within two months after completion of those duties.[172]

VI. ANTIDISCRIMINATION

A. The Principle of Equal Treatment

Turkish culture rejects discriminatory treatment in diverse fields, political as well as civil. This is especially true in labor matters, where a long tradition tends to ensure equal access to work and similar treatment for all persons of comparable qualifications and services.

As discussed above,[173] Article 10 of the Constitution establishes the principle of equality, irrespective of language, race, color, gender, political opinion, philosophical belief, or religion. Other constitutional provisions recognize fundamental rights and freedoms—such as the right to work and conclude contracts, the right to organize unions and bargain collectively, and the right to a fair wage—which are guaranteed to every person, without discrimination.

Some constitutional provisions aim to protect specific categories of individuals. For example, the state has a constitutional obligation to protect the disabled and secure their integration into

---

[172] *Id.* art. 31.

[173] See the Introduction, at A.1., above.

the community life.[174] Labor legislation adds special provisions aimed at preventing discriminatory treatment toward union members.[175]

The Labor Law, in a similar disposition, forbids not only all discrimination based on language, race, gender, political opinion, philosophical belief, religion, and sect or other similar reasons, but also provides that, unless essential reasons justify a different treatment, no discrimination must be made between full-time and part-time workers, or those working under contracts of either a definite duration or for an indefinite period.

In cases where the employer does not comply with these provisions regarding equal treatment in the execution or termination of the labor contract, compensation of no less than four months' wage plus other rights of which the worker has been deprived may be claimed.[176]

B. Specific Categories of Protection

1. Women

Article 5 of the Labor Law prohibits discrimination between men and women, by providing that except for biological reasons or reasons related to the nature of the job, no discrimination due to the employee's gender or maternity may be done directly or indirectly in the conclusion of the labor contract, as regarding the conditions, execution, and termination of the labor contract. No difference in wages may be based on gender for workers performing jobs of the same value.

Additional provisions regarding the employment of pregnant women and nursing mothers, including rooms for nursing, are set forth by regulation.[177]

---

[174]CONST. art. 61.

[175]Labor Law art. 26, para. IV; Law on Unions art. 31.

[176]Labor Law art. 5.

[177]*Id.* art. 88. *See also* Regulation on Working Conditions of Pregnant and Nursing Women, as well as Nursing Rooms and Children Care Houses (*Gebe veya Emziren Kadınların Çalıştırılma Şartlarıyla Emzirme Odaları ev Çocuk Bakım Yurtlarına Dair Yönetmelik*).

2. *Children*

The minimum working age is 15 years. However, children who are age 14 and have completed their primary education may be employed in light work, provided that this work is not of the nature to hinder the health, development, schooling or vocational training, or capacities of the child.[178] For those attending school, the work hours must be arranged in a way that does not interfere with school attendance. The time spent at school is considered to be part of the 7½-hour workday.

The minimum age for heavy and dangerous work is 16. The applicable regulation[179] specifies the types of work that fall within this category and the types of work that may be performed only by children who are age 16.

Before the employment of children between ages 14 and 18 (inclusively), the child must be examined by a physician. Employed children must be examined at least every six months until they are 18 years of age.[180]

3. *Disabled Persons, Ex-Convicts, and Victims of Terrorism*

The Labor Law as well as the Law on Combat Against Terrorism No. 3713 (*Terörle Mücadele Kanunu*) requires employers with a workforce of 50 or more workers to allocate a ratio of 6 percent of their workforce, which is to be defined each year by the Council of Ministers, to disabled persons, ex-convicts, and victims of terrorism. However, the ratio of the disabled shall never be less than half of the total ratio. For employers that operate more than one undertaking in the same province, the number the persons to be hired is based on the total number of workers. In computing the 3 percent requirement, fractions up to one-half are not taken into consideration; fractions of one-half or more are rounded up.

These workers must be assigned to work according to their occupational skills as well as their physical and mental capaci-

---

[178] Labor Law art. 71.

[179] Regulation on Heavy and Dangerous Works (*Ağır ve Tehlikeli İşler Tüzüğü*).

[180] Labor Law art. 87.

ties.[181] The employer is obliged to employ this category of workers through the Employment Agency.[182] In the employment of ex-convicts, special provisions apply with respect to public security. The qualifications of the persons to be employed and the employment conditions are determined by regulation.

Priority in hiring disabled persons for an undertaking must be given to those who became disabled during their previous employment with the same employer. If vacant positions are available and they wish to resume their old employment, the employer must give priority over other applicants to those persons who left the undertaking because of a disability and later recovered. If no vacant positions are available, disabled workers have the right to be employed, when vacancies occur at their previous jobs or at other comparable jobs, based on prevailing employment conditions. An employer who fails to comply with this obligation shall pay to the ex-worker compensation equal to six months' wages.

"Victims of terrorism" are the following: public servants or soldiers who became disabled due to terrorism; or spouses, or in the absence of a spouse, one of the children, or in the absence of a child, one of the brothers or sisters of public servants or soldiers who died or became disabled due to terrorism.

C. Union Membership and Activity

The Constitution, as well as the Law on Unions, contains important provisions aimed at safeguarding both the freedom to join a union and the freedom not to be a member of a union.[183] Any kind of discrimination based on union membership or activity is illegal.

Workers subject to discriminatory treatment are entitled to compensation amounting to no less than the worker's total annual wage. For the worker, the main difficulty in these cases is to prove discriminatory treatment, especially in times of economic crisis.

---

[181]*Id.* art. 30; Regulation on Employment of the Disabled, Ex-Convicts, and Victims of Terrorism (*Özürlü, Eski Hükümlü ve Terör Mağduru İstihdamı Hakkında Yönetmelik*).

[182]See the Introduction, at B.2., above.

[183]CONST. art. 51; Law on Unions art. 31. See also II.I.1.a., above.

However, in cases of dismissal, the burden of proof will lie upon the employer.[184] The Turkish courts take into consideration the circumstances and the stream of events, which in some cases render the discriminatory cause obvious.

VII. OCCUPATIONAL SAFETY AND HEALTH AND WORKERS' COMPENSATION

A. Safety and Health in the Workplace

1. Health and Safety Conditions

a. General Obligations

Every employer in Turkey is obliged to do the following with respect to workers' health and safety:

- take the necessary measures to protect workers' health;
- provide the conditions required for a safe operation at the workplace;
- make available all the equipment needed to protect the health of workers and secure a safe operation; and
- inform and give training with respect to health and safety.

Employers, through suitable means, also must warn workers of the danger arising from the utilization of machines in the workplace and the protective measures that might be taken in advance. In addition, employers are obliged to make a written report to the Regional Directorate of Labor of any accidents occurring in the workplace, no later than two days following the date of the accident.[185]

Workers are obliged to comply with the procedures and conditions relating to a healthy and safe operation.[186]

---

[184]*See* Law on Unions art 31, para. 7.
[185]Labor Law art. 77.
[186]*Id.* art. 77, para. 2.

Pursuant to Article 74 of the Labor Law, the Ministry of Labor and the Ministry of Health and Social Welfare jointly issued a set of regulations (Workers' Health and Safety Regulations).[187] The Workers' Health and Safety Regulations set forth provisions regarding the following:

- health (and hygiene) requirements in undertakings;
- workers' living quarters and other affiliated units;
- measures for prevention of accidents and occupational diseases that may arise from the use of tools, machinery, or raw materials;
- permits for establishing and/or operating an undertaking;
- the nature and characteristics of the work to be performed; and
- hazardous and dangerous work.

---

[187]Regulation on Work Health and Safety (*İş Sağlığı ve Güvenliği Yönetmeliği*); Regulation on Health Units at Workplaces and Duties and Working Procedures and Principles of Workplace Doctors (*İşyeri Sağlık Birimleri ve İşyeri Hekimlerinin Görevleri ile Çalışma Usul ev Esasları Hakkında Yönetmelik*); Regulation on Vibration (*Titreşim Yönetmeliği*); Regulation on Noise (*Gürültü Yönetmeliği*); Regulation on Health and Safety Precautions to Be Taken While Working with Means with Screens (*Ekranlı Araçlarla Çalışmalarda Sağlık ve Güvenlik Önlemleri Hakkında Yönetmelik*); Regulation on Signs of Safety and Health (*Güvenlik ve Sağlık İşaretleri Yönetmeliği*); Regulation on Health and Work Safety at Construction Work (*Yapı İşlerinde Sağlık ve Güvenlik Yönetmeliği)*; Regulation on Health and Safety Precautions to Be Taken While Working with Asbestos (*Asbestle Çalışmalarda Sağlık ve Güvenlik Önlemleri Hakkında Yönetmelik*; Regulation on Protecting Workers from Hazards of Explosive Conditions (*Patlayıcı Ortamların Tehlikelerinden Çalışanların Korunması Hakkında Yönetmelik*); Regulation on Health and Safety Precautions to be Taken at Works with Carcinogen and Mutagenic Products (*Kanserojen ve Mutajen Maddelerle Çalışmalarda Sağlık ve Güvenlik Önlemleri Hakkında Yönetmelik*); Regulation on Duties, Authority, and Responsibility and Working Procedures and Principles of Work Safety Engineers or Technical Personnel (*İş Güvenliği ile Görevli Mühendis ve Teknik Elemanların Görev, Yetki ve Sorumlulukları ile Çalışma Usul ve Esasları Hakkında Yönetmelik*); Regulation on Personal Protective Equipment and Products (*Kişisel Koruyucu Donanım Yönetmeliği*); Regulation on Health and Safety Precautions to Be Taken in the Premises of Work and its Annexes (*İşyeri Bina ve Eklentilerinde Alınacak Sağlık ve Güvenlik Önlemleri Hakkında Yönetmelik*); Regulation on Conditions of Health and Safety in Using Work Equipment (*İş Ekipmanlarının Kullanımında Sağlık ve Güvenlik Şartları Yönetmeliği*); Regulation on Using Personal Protective Equipment and Products at Workplaces (*Kişisel Koruyucu Donanımların İşyerlerinde Kullanılması Hakkında* Yönetmelik); Regulation on Conditions of Health and Work Safety at Mines (*Yeraltı ve Yerüstü Maden İşletmelerinde Sağlık ve Güvenlik Şartları Yönetmeliği*).

No permit for the establishment and operation of a workplace may prevent the application of the Workers' Health and Safety Regulations.

b. Workplace Doctors

Employers with a workforce of 50 or more permanent workers, depending on the number of employees and the risk factors involved, must employ one or more doctors and set up a health unit at the workplace to: protect the health of the employees; provide medical treatment for workers who fall outside those provided for by the Social Insurance Institution; take occupational health and safety measures; and provide first aid, urgent treatment, and preventive health services.[188]

c. Engineers and Technical Staff

Employers in industrial workplaces that employ 50 or more permanent workers and operate for more than a six-month period, depending on the number of employees and the risk factors involved, must employ one or more engineers or technical staff at the workplace to provide measures for safety at work, determine measures to prevent work accidents and occupational diseases, and monitor implementation of these measures.[189]

d. Rights of Employees

A worker who is threatened by an imminent, urgent danger that poses a health hazard or endangers bodily integrity may request the Occupational Health and Safety Board (Board) to determine the threat and take necessary measures. The Board shall decide on the same day and issue a written report. The worker will be informed in writing of the Board's decision. In the absence of the Board at the workplace, the application can be made to the employer or the employer's representative.

---

[188]Labor Law art. 81.

[189]*Id.* art. 82.

If the Board perceives a health threat in the workplace, a worker may refrain from working until the necessary occupational health and safety measure is taken. The worker's wages and other entitlements are reserved for the period the employee did not work.

At workplaces where the necessary measures are not taken, despite the decision of the Board, workers may terminate their employment contracts within the six working days as set out in Article 24(1) of the Labor Law.[190]

2. *Heavy and Dangerous Work*

For those who are engaged in heavy and dangerous work, a health certificate is required.[191] These health certificates are exempt from all fees and taxes.[192] Children younger than age 16 may not be employed in heavy or dangerous work.[193]

The Regulation on Heavy and Dangerous Works No. 7/6174, March 29, 1973 (*Ağır ve Tehlikeli İşler Tüzüğü*) sets forth provisions regarding the categories of work deemed to be heavy and dangerous, as well as working conditions in relation to heavy and dangerous work for children between 16 and 18 years of age and women.

3. *Enforcement Mechanisms*

a. *Suspension of Work and Workplace Closing*

In a workplace that has an operation license, if it is discovered that defects threatening the lives of the workers exist in its facilities or annexes, in the methods, processes, or conditions applicable at the workplace, or in the machinery or equipment, then operations may be stopped totally or partially until the threat is eliminated.[194]

---

[190] *Id.* art. 83.
[191] *Id.* art. 86.
[192] *Id.* arts. 86, 87.
[193] *Id.* art. 85.
[194] *Id.* art. 79.

The decision to stop work is made by a committee consisting of five members: the director of the Regional Directorate of Labor; two health and safety inspectors; one worker representative; and one employer representative. An appeal of the committee's decision may be lodged with a Labor Court within six workdays.

In a workplace that has no operation license, if it is discovered that there are defects threatening the lives of the workers, then the workplace will be barred from continuing its operations. The closed workplace may not be reopened without an operation license. An appeal of the decision to close down may be filed with a Labor Court within six workdays.

If a workplace is closed down because of the reasons described above, the employer is obliged either to pay workers their full wages or to employ them in other jobs related to their occupational skills or conditions without reducing their wages. However, employees whose age, sex, or health condition restricts them from working in an alternative workplace will not be permitted to work.

The Ministry of Labor issued the Regulation on Suspension of Works at Undertakings and Closing Down of a Workplace No. 87/11798, April 26, 1987 (*İşyerlerinde İşin Durdurulmasına veya İşyerlerinin Kapatılmasına Dair Tüzük—İşi Durdurma Tüzüğü*), which establishes procedures with respect to the following:

- preventing the operation of machinery, equipment, installations, or arrangements that are deemed to be dangerous for workers;
- a new permit for re-operation;
- the closing down and reopening of a workplace;
- stopping the work;
- precautions to be taken in urgent cases until a decision for closing down is rendered;
- qualifications of worker and employer representatives who are assigned to the workplace closing committee; and
- procedures for establishing the workplace closing committee, and election and functioning of workplace closing committees.

b. Workers' Health and Work Safety Boards

The Regulation on Work Health and Safety Boards (*İş Sağlığı ve Güvenliği Kurulları Hakkında Yönetmelik*), sets forth provisions regarding workers' health and job safety and identifies undertakings that must establish Work Health and Safety Boards, and the functions and powers of such boards.[195]

Employers that employ in an industrial workplace at least 50 workers for work lasting more than six months are obliged to establish a work health and safety board for each workplace.

The duties and powers of the work health and safety boards are to: protect workers' health and provide work safety; make recommendations to employers for establishment of systems to secure workers' health and work safety, in order to understand the cause for preventive reasons; conduct investigations in the event of occupational death; plan for educational seminars regarding workers' health and work safety; prepare annual reports; and provide other similar duties.

c. *Penalties Relating to Workers' Health and Safety*

The employer or the employer's representative is subject to fine for the following actions:[196]

- failure to take the necessary actions to protect the health of the workers;
- failure to provide the conditions required for a safe operation at the workplace;
- failure to make available all the equipment needed to protect the health of the workers and to secure a safe operation;
- opening a workplace without procuring an operation license; and
- violating the provisions of the Workers' Health and Safety Regulations.

Fines are assessed for each measure required to be taken for the workers' health and safety, at the then-current rate. If required measures are not taken, an additional fine is imposed for each successive month.

---

[195] *Id.* art. 80.
[196] *Id.* art. 105.

The employer or employer's representative also is subject to fine for continuing an operation without obtaining an approval or reopening a closed undertaking without permission.[197]

An employer that fails to form a Workers' Health and Safety Board when required by law to do so, or prevents the operation of a Workers' Health and Safety Board, also is subject to a fine.[198] If the violation is repeated, the fine is doubled.

B. Workers' Compensation

In the event of a work accident, the employer is obliged to make payment to the worker in support of the recovery until the Social Security Institution (SSI, or *Sosyal Sigortalar Kurumu*) takes charge of the case and the related expenses.[199] If a worker suffers damages because an employer failed to comply with its obligations regarding safety and health measures listed in Section A., above, then the employer will be liable to the SSI for the expenses incurred by this institution.

If a work accident or occupational illness is attributable to the employer, the employer is liable for damages suffered. In cases where a work accident or occupational illness is attributable to a third party, the third party is liable for damages. The worker or the SSI, as the case may be, has the right to seek compensation from the third party on a recourse basis.[200]

VIII. PENSIONS AND BENEFITS

A. Summary of Main Legal Instruments Regulating Social Insurance System

The Turkish social insurance system evolved gradually after World War II. Various categories of social security have been es-

[197] *Id.* art. 105.
[198] *Id.*
[199] Social Insurance Law art. 15.
[200] *Id.* art. 26.

tablished. At present, comprehensive social insurance coverage is provided by the state, including the recently established unemployment benefit.

Following is a list of some of the legislation relating to the social insurance system:

- Social Insurance Law No. 506 (*Sosyal Sigortalar Kanunu*);
- Social Security Law for Workers in Agriculture No. 2925 (*Tarım İşçileri Sosyal Sigortalar Kanunu*);
- Unemployment Insurance Law No. 4447 (*İşsizlik Sigortası Kanunu*);
- Law on Unification of Services Performed Under Different Social Security Coverages No. 2829 (*Sosyal Güvenlik Kurumlarına Tabi Olarak Geçen Hizmetlerin Birleştirilmesi Hakkında Kanun*);
- Law for Evaluation of Employment Terms of Turkish Citizens Working Abroad under Social Security Systems No. 3201 (*Yurt Dışında Bulunan Türk Vatandaşlarının Yurt Dışında Geçen Sürelerinin Sosyal Güvenlikleri Bakımından Değerlendirilmesi Hakkında Kanun*);
- Social Insurance Law for Tradesmen, Artisans and Other Independent Workers No. 1479 (*Esnaf ve Sanatkarlar ve Diğer Bağımsız Çalışanlar Sosyal Sigortalar Kurumu Kanunu – Bağkur Kanunu*); and
- Law on Individuals Working in Agriculture on Their Own Account No. 2926 (*Tarımda Kendi Adına ve Hesabına Çalışanlar Sosyal Sigortalar Kanunu*).

B. Social Insurance Benefits

1. *Coverage*

a. *Social Insurance Law*

Turkish workers are covered by a government-controlled social insurance system.[201] For many workers, this system is regulated by Social Insurance Law No. 506 (SIL). The SIL provides

---

[201]Labor Law art. 96.

for payments in case of accidents at work, occupational illness, sickness, maternity, disability, retirement, and death. The Social Security Institution (SSI) is the government agency responsible for implementing the SIL.

The SIL provides that any employee who begins work is automatically insured by law. Therefore, those who are working under employment contracts are deemed to be insured and covered under the SIL. Employers must inform the SSI before a worker begins employment, but this formality is not a prerequisite for coverage under the public social insurance aid and assistance.

With regard to foreign employment, SIL insurance applies to all foreign workers as of August 6, 2003, when Law No. 506 was modified.

b. *Other Social Security Coverage*

Social security for non-permanent agricultural workers is provided by the Social Security Law for Workers in Agriculture No. 2925.

The Law on Unification of Services Performed Under Different Social Security Coverages No. 2829, unifies services of employees who have been subject to different social insurance schemes such as the State Retirement Institution, the Social Insurance Institution, the Institution for Tradesmen, Artisans, and Other Independent Workers, and other retirement funds.

2. *Employer Contributions*

Employers are obliged to contribute toward worker social insurance benefits according to the provisions of the SIL.[202] Premium rates and employer contributions of the most general types of insurance are shown in the following table.

---

[202] *Id.* art. 73.

Coverage	Premium Rate	Employer Contribution
Accidents at Work/ Occupational Illness	1.5%–7%	1.5%–7%
Illness (Worker)	11% of wage	6%
Illness (Apprentice)	4% of wage	2%
Maternity	1% of wage	1%
Disability/Retirement/Death	20% of wage	11%
Disability/Retirement/Death (Mine and Underground Workers)	22% of wage	13%
Unemployment	7% of wage	3%

With regard to unemployment insurance, the employer's contribution is 3 percent.[203]

3. *Benefits*

The social security system provides free medical care in principle through its own public hospitals and centers, pharmaceutical aid, prosthesis, pensions, and benefits.

IX. IMMIGRATION

A. Work Permits

The previous legislation restricted work by non-citizens in some professions.[204] These restrictions were gradually diluted by recent laws and then abrogated in a large scale.[205]

[203]Unemployment Insurance Law art. 49.

[204]The Law on Professions and Services Reserved to Turkish Citizens No. 2007, 1932, has been abrogated by the Law No. 4817, enacted in 2003.

[205]*See* Law for the Promotion of Tourism Industry No. 6086; Law on Industrial and Insurance Companies No. 3293, 1938; Law on Petrol No. 6326, 1954; Law on Free Zones No. 3218, 1985.

Concerning permissions and formalities, under Law No. 4817 on Work Permits of Foreigners,[206] persons of foreign nationality who want to work on their own account, as well as workers, must have a residence permit and a work permit unless international agreements provide otherwise. Foreign nationals who want to engage in a self-employed profession in Turkey may obtain a work permit, provided they have been residing in Turkey legally and without interruption for at least five years. Upon their application, a work permit may be granted by the Ministry of Labor and Social Security.

Work permits for workers can be obtained by applying to the Ministry of Labor and Social Security. The Ministry will, in granting this permit, take into account the situation of the labor market, the developments in labor and employment, and variable changes in different sectors of the economy. The work permit is granted by taking into consideration the duration of the residence permit and an employment contract, for a maximum of one year. This permit will be limited to a defined workplace, undertaking, and profession and may be renewed within the same limits, up to three years and then again up to six years, for the same profession at the service of an employer of the worker's choice.

Unless the relevant international agreements provide otherwise, those who have been living with a valid residence permit and without interruption for at least eight years, or have worked with a valid work permit for six years, can be granted an unlimited work permit without taking into consideration the workplace, time, professional area, or the situation of the labor market.

Article 8 of the Law provides flexibility as to time limitations for different categories, for example, persons married to Turkish citizens, citizens of member states of the European Union, and persons who will be employed in key positions in public service institutions or by concession of a government contract. In those cases the restrictions concerning the duration of the work permit are not applicable. Except when international agreements provide

---

[206]Law No. 4817, Feb. 27, 2003, Official Gazette, Mar. 6, 2003. *See also* Regulation on the Application of the Law on Work Permits of Foreigners, Official Gazette, Aug. 29, 2003.

otherwise and taking into account reciprocal obligations of nations, temporary and limited restrictions may be imposed on permits because of the labor market situation and developments in labor and employment conditions.

For those residing abroad, applications may be addressed to the Turkish consulates, who will send these to the Ministry of Labor. The work permit is valid only if both the work visa and residence permit have been obtained. Those individuals who obtained work permits must apply within 90 days to obtain an entry visa and also must apply to the Ministry of the Interior within 30 days from the entrance date to obtain a residence permit.[207] The Ministry must respond within 90 days. Applications for work permits can be declined for reasons indicated in Article 14 of the Law No. 4817.

Self-employed professionals as well as those employing foreigners must, within 30 days from the date their work begins, and within 15 days from the end of their work, give notice to the Ministry of Labor.[208]

B. The Status of Foreign Workers

Turkish nationals enjoy broader organizing rights than foreign nationals in the field of collective labor legislation. Only Turkish citizens may establish unions and hold the offices of union representative and membership in some of the union's compulsory bodies (i.e., managing committee, disciplinary board, and auditing committee).[209]

Foreign citizens of Turkish origin enjoy the liberal provisions of the 1981 Law on the Free Exercise of Professions by Foreigners of Turkish Origin,[210] under which temporary work permission may be granted to such workers and professionals by the Ministry of the Interior, with the exception of work in the Turkish armed forces and security departments.

---

[207]Law No. 4817 on Work Permits of Foreigners, art. 12.

[208]*Id.* art. 18.

[209]Law on Unions arts. 5, 13, 34.

[210]Law No. 2527 (Sept. 25, 1981).

Part 2

NAFTA/NAALC and Member Countries

PART 3

Miscellaneous Countries

*Countries organized by continent/region.

South America

INDIA*

INTRODUCTION

India's government has a quasi-federal structure and a parliamentary system. Governing authority is divided between states and the union (central government).

Below the level of the central government, India is composed of 28 states plus seven union territories. A union territory is an administrative division of India. Unlike states, which have their own local governments, union territories are governed directly by the national government.

The 28 states are:

- Andhra Pradesh, Arunachal Pradesh, Assam, Bihar, Chhattisgarh, Goa, Gujarat, Haryana, Himachal Pradesh, Jammu & Kashmir, Jharkhand, Karnataka, Kerala, Madhya Pradesh, Maharashtra, Manipur, Meghalaya, Mizoram, Nagaland, Orissa, Punjab, Rajasthan, Sikkim, Tamil Nadu, Tripura, Uttar Pradesh, Uttaranchal, and West Bengal.

The seven union territories are:

- Andaman and Nicobar Islands, Chandigarh, Dadra and Nagar Haveli, Daman and Diu, Delhi, Lakshadweep, and Pondicherry.

Among the union territories, Delhi has been granted its own government with limited powers.

---

*Ravi Singhania, Singhania & Partners, New Delhi, India.

The Constitution of India is the supreme legal document. It was adopted by Constituent Assembly on November 26, 1949, and came into force on January 26, 1950.

The Constitution of India envisages a parliamentary form of government, which is federal in structure with unitary features—i.e., the Constitution provides that the central government has the exclusive power to legislate in areas specified in Schedule I of the Constitution, the state governments have exclusive power to legislate in other areas specified in the Constitution, and both the central government and the state governments may legislate in areas specified in a third list in the Constitution. Many labor law matters are on this third list (see the discussion under B.2. below).

A. Branches of Government

Governmental powers at the central and state government levels are divided into executive, legislative, and judicial as discussed below. A single judicial system resolves disputes involving both central government and State government laws, applying the appropriate level of government's body of law to each case, as also discussed below. The courts below the High Court level are part of each State's governmental system; the High Courts and Supreme Court are part of the central government system, with the Supreme Court having administrative control of all the High Courts in the country as well as taking appeals from decisions by the High Courts under appropriate circumstances.

1. Executive Branch

The President of India is the constitutional head of the executive branch of the union (i.e., the central government). Article 74(1) of the Constitution provides that there shall be a Council of Ministers with the Prime Minister as head to aid and advise the President, who shall act in accordance with such advice in the exercise of his functions. Real executive power thus vests in the Council of Ministers, which is collectively responsible to the lower house of the Indian Parliament, the House of the People (Lok Sabha), discussed below. Similarly, in the states, the Governor is head of the executive branch, but it is the Council of Ministers of each state that is collectively responsible to the Legislative Assembly of that state.

The Attorney General for India is appointed by the President under Article 76 of the Constitution. He or she must be qualified to be appointed as a judge of the Supreme Court. It is the duty of the Attorney General to advise the government on legal matters and to perform other legal duties that may be referred or assigned by the President. In the performance of his or her duties, the Attorney General has the right of audience in all courts in India as well as the right to take part in the proceedings of Parliament without the right to vote. The Attorney General is assisted by a Solicitor General and four additional Solicitors General.

In a parallel to the office of Attorney General for the central government, each state has an Advocate General appointed by the state Governor; each such Advocate General holds office at the pleasure of the Governor. An Advocate General must be qualified to be appointed as a judge of the High Court. His or her duty is to give advice to state governments on legal matters and to perform other legal duties referred or assigned by the Governor. The Advocate General has the right to speak and take part in the proceedings of the state legislature without the right to vote.

2. *Legislative Branch*

The Indian Parliament has two houses.

- The Lok Sabha is composed of representatives of the people chosen by direct election on the basis of adult suffrage. The maximum strength of the house envisaged by the Constitution is 552—up to 530 members representing the states and up to 20 representing the union territories, plus no more than two members of the Anglo-Indian community[1] to be nominated by the President, if, in his or her opinion, that community is not adequately represented in the Lok Sabha. The total elective membership is distributed among the states in proportion to each state's share of the population in the country as a whole. The Lok Sabha sits for a period of five years unless dissolved early by the President. After a disso-

[1]The community of individuals having both an English parent and an Indian parent.

lution, general elections are held for all seats in the Lok Sabha.

- The Rajya Sabha is the upper house of Parliament. It has no more than 250 members. Members of Rajya Sabha are not elected by the people directly, but indirectly by the legislative assemblies of the various states. Each state is allotted a certain number of members. No member can be under 30 years of age. Twelve members are nominated by the President from among those who have earned distinctions in the fields of literature, art, science, and social service. The Rajya Sabha is a permanent body that is not subject to dissolution, but one-third of its members retire every two years.

Indian law is founded in the Constitution. It is the supreme law on which all legislation is based. Even the personal (religious) laws—i.e., laws that apply to members of a particular religion, such as Hindus, as regards personal matters such as marriage and inheritance—are established in written legislation. The Constitution distributes legislative power between central and state legislatures and provides for the vesting of residual powers in the central government Parliament. Power to amend the Constitution also vests in Parliament. Article 246 and Schedule VII of the Constitution deal with the distribution of legislative powers between the union and the state legislatures. Under these articles, the law-making powers of the union (central government) and state bodies have been demarcated and divided into three "lists": the Union (List I), the State (List II), and Concurrent Lists (List III).

- The Union Parliament has full and exclusive powers to legislate on matters in Lists I.
- The state legislatures have exclusive power to legislate on matters in List II.
- Both the union and the states have powers to legislate on matters in List III (the Concurrent List), but if there is a conflict between a union law and one or more state laws, the union law prevails.

Legislation concerning labor and employment law falls on the Concurrent List, as discussed in B. below.

3. *The Judicial Branch*

One of the unique features of the Indian Constitution is that, despite the division of legislative powers between the central government and the state governments, there is a single integrated system of courts that reviews both central government and state government laws, whether cases involve civil or criminal laws. The court system, from the lowest level to the highest, has three components: subordinate courts, High Courts, and the Supreme Court.

Disputes involving labor and employment laws are considered by administrative bodies before entering the court system, and are often resolved at that level. Disputes are referred by the appropriate government, central or state. The central government has a system of "adjudicating bodies" (industrial tribunal-cum-labor courts) at the administrative level that consider many disputes in the first instance; these are established under the Ministry of Labour, as discussed in B.3.a.ii. below. Each labor statute specifies which administrative bodies (e.g., boards of conciliation) are charged to resolve disputes under the provisions of the act concerned. An appeal from the decision of such an administrative body will go to the proper court in the usual way. For instance, the Industrial Disputes Act, 1947 specifies which industrial disputes are under the jurisdiction of conciliation officers (who try to conciliate the dispute and get the parties to agree on a resolution), with appeals to the board of conciliation, and then to the tribunal or national tribunal, and subsequently to the courts as described below:

- Most industrial disputes are referred by the appropriate government (central or state) from the board of conciliation to the tribunal, with appeals going to the High Courts.
- Disputes of national importance are referred by the central government from the board of conciliation to the national tribunal, with appeals going to the Supreme Court.

In the case of individual disputes, if the employee is a regular worker (i.e., fits under the definition of a "workman"[2]) and the grievance is of common interest, then the matter would go to the labor courts. Employees with individual contracts would instead file a civil suit in the regular courts for enforcement of their rights based on the terms of their contract of employment.

The three levels of courts are discussed below, from lowest to highest.

a. Subordinate Courts

The Constitution provides for two categories of subordinate courts—a) district courts and b) other courts that are subordinate to district courts. All these courts apply central government law or state law, as appropriate.[3] At the lowest level, there are judicial first class magistrates and judges/chief judicial magistrates. At the highest level of the subordinate judiciary are the district/sessions judges. The same presiding officers while dealing with civil cases are called munsifs/sub judges/district judges, and while dealing

---

[2]Sec 2(s) of the Industrial Disputes Act defines "workman" as follows:

> any person (including an apprentice) employed in any industry to do any manual, unskilled, skilled, technical, operational, clerical or supervisory work for hire or reward, whether the terms of employment be express or implied, and for the purposes of any proceeding under this Act in relation to an industrial dispute, includes any such person who has been dismissed, discharged or retrenched in connection with, or as a consequence of, that dispute, or whose dismissal, discharge or retrenchment has led to that dispute, but does not include any such person -
>
> > (i) who is subject to the Air Force Act, 1950 (45 of 1950), or the Army Act, 1950 (46 of 1950), or the Navy Act, 1957 (62 of 1957); or (ii) who is employed in the police service or as an officer or other employee of a prison; or (iii) who is employed mainly in a managerial or administrative capacity; or (iv) who, being employed in a supervisory capacity, draws wages exceeding one thousand six hundred rupees per mensem or exercises, either by the nature of the duties attached to the office or by reason of the powers vested in him, functions mainly of a managerial nature.

Thus, an employee would have resort to the labor courts only if he or she falls under the definition of "workman"; employees who do not fall within this definition have the remedy of a civil suit based on their contract in the regular courts.

[3]See the discussion of the division of lawmaking authority between the central government and state governments in A.2., above.

with criminal matters are called first class magistrates/chief judicial magistrates/sessions judges. There also other courts and tribunals for specialized subjects, for example, the State Administrative Tribunal for hearing employment disputes involving state government employees and the Central Administrative Tribunal to hear cases involving employment disputes involving central government employees. Motor accident claims tribunals deal with motor accident cases, and family courts deal with matrimonial cases. There are also quasi-judicial bodies such as the Consumer Disputes Redressal Forums to deal with consumer disputes. The High Courts have supervisory powers over all of these bodies.

b. High Courts

The High Court stands at the head of a state's judicial administration and reviews decisions of subordinate courts under its jurisdiction. There are 18 High Courts in the country, with three having jurisdiction over more than one state. Among the union territories, Delhi alone has a High Court of its own, since it has its own government with limited powers. The other six Union Territories come under the jurisdiction of different state High Courts. The High Courts apply state or central government law, as appropriate in each case.

Each High Court is comprised of a Chief Justice and such other judges as the President may, from time to time, appoint. The Chief Justice of a High Court is appointed by the President in consultation with the Chief Justice of India and the Governor of the state. Each High Court has power to issue to any person within its jurisdiction directions, orders, or writs, including writs that are in the nature of habeas corpus, mandamus, prohibition, *quo warranto*, and *certiorari* for enforcement of fundamental rights and for any other purpose. This power also may be exercised by any High Court exercising jurisdiction in relation to territories within which the cause of action, wholly or in part, arises for exercise of such power, notwithstanding that the seat of such government or authority or residence of such person is not within those territories.

Under Article 227 of the Constitution, each High Court has powers of superintendence over all courts and tribunals within its jurisdiction, not only in terms of administrative superintendence, but judicial also. In exercise of this power, the High Courts keep the inferior courts and tribunals within the bounds of their authority and see that they meet their obligations and do so in a legal manner. High courts can call for returns (records of proceedings of the courts) from inferior courts and tribunals, make and issue general rules, and prescribe forms to regulate their practice and proceedings and determine the manner and form in which book entries and accounts are kept.

The Constitution contains detailed provisions for the lower judiciary/courts. These provisions are intended to secure two objectives:

- first, to provide for the appointment of district and subordinate judges and to prescribe their qualifications, and
- second, to place the entire subordinate judiciary under the control of the High Court.

c. *Supreme Court*

At the apex of the entire judicial system is the Supreme Court of India. The Supreme Court of India consists of 26 judges (including the Chief Justice).

The Supreme Court has original, appellate, and advisory jurisdiction, as explained below.

i. *Original Jurisdiction*

The Supreme Court's exclusive original jurisdiction extends to any dispute between the government of India and one or more states, between the government of India and any state or states on one side and one or more states on the other, or between two or more states, if the dispute involves any question (whether of law or of fact) on which the existence or extent of a legal right depends.

In addition, Article 32 of the Constitution gives extensive original jurisdiction to the Supreme Court in regard to enforcement of fundamental rights of citizens as embodied in the Constitution. It is empowered to issue directions, orders, or writs, including writs in the nature of habeas corpus, mandamus, prohibition, *quo warranto*, and *certiorari* to enforce them.

The Supreme Court has been conferred with power to direct transfer of any civil or criminal case from one state High Court to another High Court, or from a state High Court to the Supreme Court. The Supreme Court, if satisfied that cases involving the same or substantially the same questions of law are pending before it and one or more High Courts, or before two or more High Courts, and that such questions are substantial questions of general importance, may withdraw the case from the other courts and dispose of it itself.

ii. Appellate Jurisdiction

The appellate jurisdiction of the Supreme Court can be invoked under Articles 132(1), 133(1), or 134 of the Constitution in respect of any judgment, decree, or final order of a High Court in both civil and criminal cases involving substantial questions of law.

Appeals also go before the Supreme Court in civil matters if the High Court concerned certifies: (a) that the case involves a substantial question of law of general importance, and (b) that, in the opinion of the High Court, the said question needs to be decided by the Supreme Court.

In criminal cases, an appeal goes before the Supreme Court if the High Court (a) has on appeal reversed an order of acquittal of an accused person and sentenced him to death or to imprisonment for life or for a period of 10 years or more, or (b) has withdrawn for trial before itself any case from any court subordinate to its authority and has in such trial convicted the accused and sentenced him to death or to imprisonment for life or for a period of 10 years or more, or (c) certified that the case is a fit one for appeal to the Supreme Court.

Parliament is authorized to confer on the Supreme Court any further powers to entertain and hear appeals from any judgment, final order, or sentence in a criminal proceeding of a High Court.

The Supreme Court has also a very wide appellate jurisdiction over all courts and tribunals in India; it may, in its discretion, grant special leave to appeal under Article 136 of the Constitution from any judgment, decree, determination, sentence, or order in any cause or matter passed or made by any court or tribunal in the territory of India.

iii. Advisory Jurisdiction

The Supreme Court has special advisory jurisdiction in matters that the President of India may specifically refer to the Court under Article 143 of the Constitution, where the issues involve a substantial question of law which in the opinion of the President should be decided by the Supreme Court.

iv. Public Interest Litigation

Although most proceedings of the Supreme Court arise out of the judgments or orders made by the subordinate courts, including the High Courts, of late the Supreme Court has started entertaining matters in which the interest of the public at large is involved. Any individual or group of persons may move the court (petition the court) to accept jurisdiction over a case by either filing a "writ petition" at the filing counter of the Court or addressing a letter to "Hon'ble the Chief Justice of India," highlighting a question of public importance as a rationale for invoking this jurisdiction. Such action is popularly known as "public interest litigation," and several matters of public importance have become landmark cases. This practice is unique to the Supreme Court.

B. The Labor Law Regime

1. Constitution as the Basis for Labor Legislation

The Fundamental Rights and the Directive Principles of State Policy provided in the Indian Constitution and discussed below are of vital importance in directing and influencing labor legislation in the country.

a. Fundamental Rights

The Fundamental Rights cover, *inter alia,*

- equality before the law;
- prohibition of discrimination on the grounds of religion, race, caste, sex, or place of birth;

- equality of opportunity in matters of public employment;
- abolition of the caste of untouchability;
- protection of rights regarding freedom of speech, freedom of assembly and freedom to form associations, freedom to practice any profession, protection of life and personal liberty, and right against exploitation.

Article 16 of the Constitution specifically provides that there shall be equality of opportunity in the matters relating to employment or appointment to any office of the state.

Article 24 provides that no child below the age of 14 years shall be employed to work in any factory or mine or engaged in any other hazardous employment.

b. Directive Principles of State Policy

The Directive Principles lay down the guiding principles that the central government and state governments alike ought to follow both in framing laws and enforcing them. The Directive Principles confer no legal rights and create no legal remedies, but nonetheless provide guidance in charting the path of the government in the governance of the country.

The relevant Directive Principles affecting labor legislation directly or indirectly are as follows:

i. "State to secure a social order for the promotion of welfare of the people"

"The state shall strive to promote the welfare of the people by securing and protecting as effectively as it may a social order in which justice, social, economic and political, shall inform all the institutions of the national life."[4]

ii. "Certain principles of policy to be followed by the state"

"The State shall direct its policy towards securing that

[4]Constitution, Art. 38.

(a) the citizens, men and women equally, have the right to an adequate means of livelihood;

(b) the ownership and control of the material resources of the community are so distributed as best to serve the common good;

(c) the operation of the economic system does not result in concentration of wealth and means of production to the common detriment;

(d) there is equal pay for equal work for both men and women;[5]

(e) the health and strength of workers, men and women, and the tender age of children are not abused and that citizens are not forced by economic necessity to enter avocations unsuited to their age or strength; and

(f) childhood and youth are protected against exploitation and against moral-and material abandonment."[6]

iii. "Right to work, to education, and to public assistance in certain cases"

"The State shall, within the limits of its economic capacity and development, make effective provision for securing the right to work, to education and to public assistance in cases of unemployment, old age, sickness and disablement, and in other cases of undeserved want."[7]

iv. "Conditions of work"

"The State shall make provision for securing just and humane conditions of work and for maternity relief."[8]

v. "Living wage for workers"

"The State shall endeavor to secure, by suitable legislation or economic organization or in any other way, to all workers, agricultural, industrial or otherwise, work, a living wage, conditions of work ensuring a decent standard of life and full enjoyment of leisure and social and cultural opportunities and, in particular, the State shall endeavor to promote cottage industries on an individual or co-operative basis in rural areas."[9]

---

[5]Constitution, Art. 39

[6]Constitution, Art. 39.

[7]Constitution, Art. 41.

[8]Constitution, Art. 42.

[9]Constitution, Art. 43.

vi. "Participation of workers in management of industries"

"The State shall take steps, by suitable legislation or in any other way, to secure the participation of workers in the management of undertakings, establishments or other organizations engaged in any industry."[10]

2. *The Statutory System (Concurrent List)*

As discussed in A. above, under the Constitution of India, labor is a subject in the Concurrent List where both the central and state governments are competent to enact legislation subject to certain matters being reserved for the central government, as listed below.

Table 1. Labor Jurisdiction: Constitutional Status of Various Issues

Union (Central Government) List	Concurrent List
Entry No.55 Regulation of labor and safety in mines and oil fields	Entry No.22 Trade unions; industrial and labor disputes
Entry No.61 Industrial disputes concerning union central government employees	Entry No.23 Social security and insurance, employment and unemployment
Entry No.65 Union agencies and institutions for "Vocational… Training…"	Entry No.25 Welfare of labor, including conditions of work, provident funds, employer-provided invalidity (disability) and old age pensions, and maternity benefit

Thus, on the Concurrent List there are matters relating to:

- employment,
- social security,
- labor welfare,

[10]Constitution, Art. 43-A.

- trade unions,
- industrial and labor disputes,
- conditions of work, and
- provident fund (see VIII.B.3., below).

Specific provisions of legislation are discussed in subsequent sections of this chapter.

3. *Relevant Central Government Labor Agencies and Courts*

The discussion below explains the central government labor system, since labor is in general an area that is regulated concurrently by the central government and state governments, as discussed in B.2., above. State governments have similar administrative systems to implement their labor laws and ensure compliance with those laws.

a. Central Government Ministry of Labour

The Ministry of Labour is the nodal agency entrusted with the task of overall supervision and implementation of matters pertaining to labor and employment. The fundamental duty of the ministry lies in protecting and safeguarding the interests of the working class in general and those who constitute the poor, deprived, and disadvantaged in society in particular. A number of legislative and executive initiatives have been adopted to promote, protect, and preserve their health, safety, and welfare. The ministry, which is committed to the ethos and culture of tripartism (i.e., cooperation among the social partners—labor, management, and government), initiates the process of enacting a new law or bringing about changes in the existing laws only through a process of consultation with the social partners and after obtaining a consensus.

i. Functions of the Ministry of Labour

The ministry performs various important functions with regard to labor and employment laws in the country. These functions pertain to:

- labor policy (including wage policy) and legislation;
- safety, health, and welfare;

- social security;
- policy relating to special target groups such as women and children;
- industrial relations and enforcement of labor laws in the central government sphere;
- adjudication of industrial disputes through central government industrial tribunal-cum-labor courts and national industrial tribunals;
- workers' education;
- labor and employment statistics;
- emigration of labor for employment abroad;
- employment services and vocational training;
- administration of central labor and employment services; and
- international cooperation in labor and employment matters.

ii. Structure of the Ministry of Labour

The Labour Ministry has four "attached offices," 10 "subordinate offices," four "autonomous organizations," 17 "adjudicating bodies" for private-sector labor and employment disputes, and one "arbitration body" for public-sector central government employment disputes, as well as the Central Labour Service.

The attached offices and their functions are as follows:

- *Directorate General of Employment & Training (DGE&T)*: This office is responsible for laying down the policies, standards, norms, and guidelines in the area of vocational training throughout the country and also for coordinating employment services.
- *Office of the Chief Labour Commissioner (Central).* This office is responsible for prevention, investigation, and settlement of industrial disputes in the central sphere; enforcement of awards and settlements; implementation of labor laws in industries and establishments where the central government is the appropriate government entity for oversight; verification of membership of unions affiliated with the central organizations of workers (national trade union centers) giving the unions representation in national and international conferences and committees; and fixing and revi-

sion of the "dearness allowance" component (i.e., regional cost-of-living adjustment) of minimum wages, as authorized under the Minimum Wages Act, 1948 in scheduled employments.

- *Directorate General of Factory Advice Service and Labour Institutes (DGFASLI).* This office is concerned with formulation of policy relating to the safety, health, and welfare of workers in factories and docks; coordinating the implementation of the measures of the Factories Act, 1948 by the state governments and formulation of Model Rules thereunder; administration of the Dock Workers (Safety, Health and Welfare) Act, 1986; undertaking research in industrial safety, occupational health, industrial hygiene, industrial psychology, and industrial physiology. It also is responsible for training—mainly in the field of industrial psychology and industrial safety and health—including a diploma course of one year's duration in industrial safety. The diploma is an essential qualification for appointment of safety officers in factories and regular in-service training of factory inspectors.
- *Labour Bureau.* The bureau is responsible for collection, compilation, and publication of statistical and other information regarding employment, wages, earnings, industrial relations, and working conditions. It also compiles and publishes the Consumer Price Index Numbers for industrial and agricultural/rural workers. The bureau further renders necessary assistance to the states for conducting training programs in labor statistics at state/district/unit levels.

Subordinate offices are as follows:

- *Directorate General of Mines Safety (DGMS).* This office is entrusted with enforcement of provisions of the Mines Act, 1952 and the rules and regulations framed under the Act, and with enforcement of provisions of the Indian Electricity Act, 1910 as applicable to mines and oil fields.
- *Welfare Commissioners.* The nine Offices of Welfare Commissioners are responsible for providing welfare facilities

to the workers employed in mica, limestone and dolomite, iron ore, manganese, and chrome ore mines and in the beedi and cinema industries.

The autonomous organizations are corporations managed by officers of the central government who work for the corporation and who are responsible for implementation of various laws as discussed below.

- *Employees' State Insurance Corporation*. ESIC is responsible for implementing the Employees' State Insurance Act, 1948, which provides for medical care and treatment to insured persons and their families. Assistance is given in terms of benefits during sickness and maternity, compensation for employment injury, pensions for dependents on the death of workers due to employment injury, and other similar circumstances.
- *Employees' Provident Fund Organisation*. EPFO is responsible for administration of the Employees' Provident Funds and Miscellaneous Provisions Act, 1952. Schemes for provident fund, family pension, and deposit-linked insurance (see VIII.B., below) are implemented by the organization for the benefit of workers covered under the scheme. The organization is also responsible for administration of the Employees' Pension Scheme, 1995 which came into existence on November 16, 1995.
- *V.V. Giri National Labour Institute*. VVGNLI, a registered society, conducts action-oriented research and provides training to grassroots-level workers in the trade union movement, both in urban and rural areas, and also to government officers dealing with industrial relations, personnel management, and labor welfare issues.
- *Central Board for Workers' Education*. CBWE is a registered society dealing with schemes for training workers in the techniques of trade unionism and in bringing about consciousness among workers about their rights, duties, and responsibilities. The board also undertakes programs for rural workers' education and functional adult education.

The following adjudicating bodies deal with private-sector employment disputes:

- *Central Government Industrial Tribunal-cum-Labour Courts (CGITs).* Seventeen such courts have been set up under the provisions of the Industrial Disputes Act, 1947 for adjudication of industrial disputes in organizations for which the central government is the appropriate government entity for oversight—i.e., industries or undertakings carried on by or under the authority of the central government. All other disputes come under the jurisdiction of the appropriate state government.

The following arbitration body deals with central government employee disputes:

- *Board of Arbitration (Joint Consultative Machinery).* Established under the Scheme for Joint Consultative Machinery and Compulsory Arbitration, the board is an institution for compulsory arbitration of disputes between the central government and its employees in matters regarding pay and allowances, weekly hours of work, and leave for employees in specific classes or grades. (Government employees, whether of the central government or state governments, are not covered by the labor laws covering the private sector, and are instead covered by rules and enactments framed by the central government or relevant state government for its own employees.) This board is part of the separate system for dealing with grievances of central government employees. Decisions of the board may be appealed to the High Courts.

In addition, there is a specialized labor inspectorate, the Central Labour Service. Under the CLS, labor commissioners are appointed by the central government for the purpose of better industrial relations, labor law enforcement, and labor welfare.

- *Central Labour Service.* CLS was established on February 3, 1987, to ensure better industrial relations, labor law enforcement, and labor welfare. Inspectors working for this service have powers to:

- enter and inspect any area, premises, or compound to confirm compliance with conditions for the safety and welfare of all the employees therein;
- see that employers provide compensation to employees in the event of a breach of any compliance matter by an employer;
- make copies or take extracts from any register, account book, or other document maintained by the employer;
- make the employer, owner, or other responsible party pay the minimum amount that an employee or worker is entitled to get for a particular job or service;
- make rules and regulations, keeping in mind the conditions and interests of the employees (inspectors and labor officers make rules that are applicable to one workplace or more, depending on the nature of work, type of industry involved, and location);
- prosecute the employer in hearings before an administrative judge for any default or noncompliance with regard to any provision under any labor legislation;
- halt work where there is a serious hazard;
- take samples of air, water, or any chemical from any factory, compound, or industry to confirm healthy working conditions and environment; and
- exercise any other power that is in the interest of the employees or in accordance with any of the various pieces of labor legislation.

Assistant labor welfare commissioners (central) and deputy labor welfare commissioners (central) under the supervision of labor welfare commissioners discharge the ministry's statutory functions listed above, and also advise and assist the management of private and public sector establishments in maintaining harmonious industrial relations in the areas of safety, health, and welfare of workers.

In addition, officers appointed as assistant labor commissioners, regional labor commissioners, deputy chief labor commissioner, and joint chief labor commissioner in the Central Industrial Relations Machinery (CIRM) headed by the chief labor commissioner are also entrusted with the task of maintaining good industrial relations in the central government sphere. The officers of the CLS appointed as assistant welfare commissioners and welfare commissioners in the Welfare Organisation of the Ministry of Labour under the director general (labor welfare) administer the welfare funds for workers in the beedi and cinema industries, and certain categories of non-coal mine workers.

In addition to the Central Labour Service, factories and mines employing 500 or more workers and plantations employing 300 or more workers are required to appoint a prescribed number of welfare officers to oversee employer compliance with the various labor welfare statutes enacted by the central government and state governments. These officers are appointed by the employer, but are considered to be government officials charged with enforcement of the provisions of the various labor laws. Their duties, qualifications, and conditions of service are prescribed by the various state governments, although they are paid by the employer and their performance reviews are conducted by the employer. See the additional discussion under "III. Representation by Entities Other than Unions," below.

4. *State Government Ministries of Labor*

State governments may structure their ministries of labor in ways similar to the central government's ministry or in other ways, as they see fit.

5. *Labor Courts and Other Government Dispute Resolution Bodies*

The state governments maintain a system of labor courts as subordinate courts, with appeals to industrial tribunals and then to the High Courts or Supreme Court discussed above. Industrial disputes may go to a conciliation board before going to a labor court.[11] Actions on an employment contract go to the regular civil court system.

---

[11] See II.D., below.

C. International Sources of Labor and Employment Law

India is a founding member of the International Labor Organization (ILO). It has ratified 39 conventions, including four of the core labor standard conventions. (See the chapter on the ILO in Volume I for additional information on the organization.)

The four core conventions that India has ratified are:

- Forced Labor Convention (No. 29);
- Abolition of Forced Labor Convention (No. 105);
- Equal Remuneration Convention (No. 100); and
- Discrimination (Employment Occupation) Convention (No. 111).

The four core conventions that India has not ratified are:

- Freedom of Association and Protection of Right to Organize Convention (No. 87);
- Right to Organize and Collective Bargaining Convention (No. 98);
- Minimum Age Convention (No. 138); and
- Worst forms of Child Labor Convention (No. 182).

India has not ratified conventions number 87 and 98 because of the central government concern about promoting unionization of government employees in light of the highly politicized trade union system of the country. The central government's stance is that guarantees provided for under these two conventions are, by and large, available to workers in both the public and private sectors by means of India's constitutional provisions, laws and regulations, and practices. In particular, the Constitution guarantees job security, social security, and fair working conditions and fair wages to public servants. They have also been provided with alternative grievance redressal mechanisms like the Joint Consultative Machinery and Central Administrative Tribunal.

As regards Convention 138, there is no omnibus provision in Indian labor laws prohibiting children below a certain age from doing any work whatsoever. To ratify Convention 138, India would first need to enact a suitable all-encompassing central legislation prescribing a minimum age of entry into employment. Since there is no omnibus minimum age law and the existing laws prescribe different minimum ages for different sectors, the process is likely to be a long one, requiring adjusting the definition of "child" in all legislation, such as the Child Labour (Prohibition and Regulation) Act, 1986. In addition, an omnibus minimum age law would need to be preceded by creation of a suitable enforcement mechanism and measures that would prevent children from being compelled by circumstances to seek employment. The setting up of such a mechanism, particularly in those sectors of the economy where the workers are not organized (e.g., agriculture, cottage and small-scale industries except for industries covered under the Factories Act) would be a difficult task in a developing country like India. The relevant central government ministries and departments and state governments are cooperating to examine the existing provisions of national laws and practices on the subject vis-à-vis the provisions of the convention.

Regarding Convention 182, concerning the Worst Forms of Child Labor, India is examining the feasibility of ratifying this convention in consultation with the concerned central government ministries and state governments. This is also to be discussed in a tripartite forum with the participation of employers and worker representatives.

I. INDIVIDUAL EMPLOYMENT

Under Indian law, a worker generally has an individual employment contract (also called a service contract) with an employer when beginning employment, regardless of whether he or she is a union member. In many situations, collective bargaining contracts entered into with employers by the union on behalf of workers also exist. No cross-reference from one to the other is necessary in such situations. Part-time, temporary, and other atypical workers normally do not have an employment contract.

A. Contract Formation

The provisions of The Indian Contract Act, 1872 govern employment contracts, which are contracts for services. All of the common law principles of contract law such as offer, acceptance, certainty, consideration, and competence of the parties to enter into the contract should be complied with.

1. Drafting of Service Contract

The following clauses routinely are incorporated into the service contract:

a. *Salary*. The salary to be paid to the employee should be clearly stated. If the employee is entitled to any allowances (e.g., dearness (regional cost of living) allowance, city allowance, housing rental allowance) in addition to salary, the same should be clearly mentioned.
b. *Period of service*. The period of employment should be specified. If the parties contemplate renewal of the service contract extending the period of service, the terms and conditions on which the contract will be renewed should be mentioned.
c. *Leave, bonus, etc*. If the employee is entitled to leave with full pay or half pay, bonus, or commission, the same should be clearly mentioned in the contract.
d. *Scope of work.* The duties of the employee should be clearly defined in the contract. It should be provided that the employee will not be engaged in any other service or business during the tenure of this contract.
e. *Hours of work, rest, and holidays.* The hours of work of an employee, the rest periods, and the number of holidays should be clearly mentioned.
f. *Secrecy/confidentiality clause*. If the employee is working in such a position that the employee comes to know about trade secrets or any information relating to the employer's business, it should be provided that the employee should not divulge such information to a third party. The covenant that the employee will not divulge any confidential information acquired during employment cannot extend beyond employment.
g. *Incentives.* Any incentive that may be given to the employee in the course of employment (e.g., retention bonus to keep key employees) should also be mentioned in the contract.

h. *Termination of contract*. The grounds on which the contract may be terminated before its expiry should be given.
i. *Procedures for resolution of grievances*. These may be specified in the contract or in the employer's employment rules or policies.
j. *Miscellaneous provisions*. Depending upon the nature of the business of the employer or upon the nature of the employment, other miscellaneous provisions may be incorporated into the contract.

2. *Obligations of the Parties*

a. *Employers' obligations*

The following obligations on employers derive from employment contract law and various other labor laws. The employer must:

- provide each employee with a copy of the service rules;
- provide a copy of the appointment letter or employment contract;
- pay the wages or the salary on time;
- communicate in writing any change in the terms of service;
- ensure the payment of bonuses to eligible employees;
- ensure the security of the employees; and
- comply with all other provisions of the service contract it has entered into.

b. *Employees' obligations*

The following employee obligations derive from employment contract law and various other labor laws. The employee must:

a. perform the job with due care and precaution;
b. obey the orders of superiors;
c. safeguard the assets of the employer that are in the employees' possession;
d. notify the employer of any intention to leave the organization following the procedure and requirements specified in the employment contract; and
e. comply with all other provisions of the service contract.

B. Termination

Either the employer or the employee can initiate the termination process. The process should be carried out in accordance with the provisions of the contract of employment entered into between the two parties.

1. *Cases Where the Employer May Legally Initiate Termination*

- If the contract itself comes to an end;
- If the employee's performance is unsatisfactory during probation;
- In cases where the employer wants to terminate by notice;
- If there is a breach of contract by the employee;
- For reasons of retirement by the employee; or
- For purposes of retrenchment (downsizing).[12]

2. *Cases Where the Employee May Legally Initiate Termination*

- In case of breach of contract by the employer;
- If the employee wants to resign during probation;
- If the employee wants to resign by giving notice;
- For medical reasons by giving notice.

3. *Notice and Termination Process*

A termination notice should be given in writing and should also be duly signed by the person initiating the termination, except that the provision for giving notice does not apply to temporary employees, casual workers, probationers, trainees, and the like. A copy of the notice should be supplied to the other party to the employment contract. The process should be carried out in accordance with the provisions of the contract entered into by the employer and employee.

A typical contract of employment provides that an employer can terminate an employee after giving due notice in writing and any outstanding wages. The employer can also ask the employee to continue rendering services during the period of the notice.

---

[12]See the discussion of retrenchment in section IV.A.2., below.

Employment contracts usually stipulate that the employee must provide the employer written notice of his or her intention to discontinue providing services to the employer. In the case of junior-level employees, one month's notice needs to be given, and in the case of senior-level employees, three month's notice, under standard industrial practice in India. If the employer wishes, it can accept the resignation with immediate effect, subject to the payment of wages with respect to the time worked.

No notice is required in case there is misconduct or breach of contract by any of the parties.

C. Dispute Resolution

"Industrial dispute," as defined under the Industrial Disputes Act, 1947[13] means any dispute or differences between two or more employers, between an employer and employee, or between two or more employees pertaining to employment or "non-employment," terms of employment, or work conditions. An industrial dispute can be claimed if the employer or the employee is not following the provisions of the standing orders (written procedures of the company) or the employment contract.

As discussed under II., below, normally unions take up matters of common interest to groups of employees using the dispute resolution mechanisms discussed in II.D.; individual employees with grievances either (a) utilize the grievance cell system (discussed in III., below) or, less frequently, the dispute resolution mechanisms discussed in II.D., or (b) seek a civil remedy. Employees at a higher level—i.e., managers or officers of the company—resort to civil remedies only, since they are employed under more elaborate employment contracts.

Disputes involving individual employees thus may be resolved in the following ways:

- Either the employer or employee, if suffering damages from a breach of the employment contract, can file a claim for compensation from the other party in civil court, under the provisions of the Indian Contract Act, 1872.

[13]See further discussion in II.D., below.

- Individual industrial disputes also may be resolved through the procedures and mechanisms prescribed by the employer or the particular industry; these procedures may involve employee resort to grievance cells provided by the employer in workplaces having more than 50 employees, according to rules established under various pieces of labor legislation. The aggrieved worker files the grievance with the grievance cell, after which the labor authorities take up the matter and make a decision on the merits after a hearing. Alternatively, on occasion an individual employee may utilize the dispute resolution system discussed in II.D., below.

D. Privacy

India has not passed legislation for handling the conflict of interests involved in privacy matters. Most of the systems in place in India are in the form of administrative controls, leaving room for many different kinds of informal arrangements.

Unregulated employee conduct can result in "joint and several liability" for the employer, with damage/liability being personal and corporate, and can invite heavy fines and prosecutions for violations. Employers generally may seek to avoid such liability by:

- Making management policies transparent and firm;
- Reducing employees' expectations of privacy by notice; and
- Ensuring that the policy is not biased and unreasonable.

1. Workplace Surveillance

If a corporate policy expressly warns that all business telephone calls and e-mails will be monitored, then it is absolutely legal to do so. Thus, the employer may conduct surveillance on personal telephone calls and personal e-mails by making the privacy policy known to the employees. The employee cannot plead absolute privacy, because the privacy has essentially been limited contractually, whether expressly or impliedly, based on the inherent right of the employer to conduct surveillance at the workplace of facilities provided by the employer for its own business and purposes. The employer's intrusion or surveillance must match its legitimate business interest, however.

2. *Data Protection*

Imposition of policies to protect data, information, ideas, assets, programs, computers, or work is allowed; the legality of such policies is reinforced by prior notice to employees. Such policies should not be intrusive to the extent of infringing upon the personal sphere of the employee.

A policy not to allow floppy disks or similar data storage devices on information storage equipment in order to prevent the copying and removal of confidential data from the worksite is acceptable, as is a policy of requiring an entry/signature in a book or register for the issuance of materials or books. Employees may be searched before they leave the employer's premises.

E. Employee Duty of Loyalty, Trade Secrets, Covenants Not to Compete

1. *Employee Duty of Loyalty and Trade Secrets*

Any employee under an employment contract is generally barred by the contract from divulging trade secrets or competing with the employer for the employee's personal benefit. For that matter, the employee has an obligation to avoid any fraudulent or dishonest acts, and to avoid disclosing any information that may be useful or important to the organization or the employer, such as a database of customers.

The employee is required to maintain strict confidentiality about the type or nature of his or her work. This stricture is based on the fact that employees are accepted into the employer's establishment, that tools and equipment are entrusted to their care, and that they become party to trade secrets, placing the employee under an obligation to have regard for the employer's interests and in particular to not cause damage to the employer. The implied post-contractual restraint on competition discussed below also derives from the duty of loyalty. Contravention of the duty of loyalty leads to liability for damages. The corresponding obligation on the employer's part is the duty of care.

2. *Covenants Not to Compete*

Covenants not to compete are frequently enforced where an employer's "confidential information" may be used or disclosed by a former employee unless the employee is restrained from competing. The employer must generally demonstrate that it kept the information relatively secret from the public and competitors and that the information gives the employer some competitive advantage, or that it would be useful to competitors. The information must not be readily ascertainable from public sources. It can concern such things as products, marketing and strategic plans, sales data and forecasts, and even customers. Also, confidential information must be distinguished from the former employee's own general skills, knowledge, and experience gained on the job, which the former employee is free to use in competing against the former employer (otherwise, individuals would not be able to advance in their careers). The line between an employer's confidential information and a former employee's general knowledge and experience is often difficult to draw, and it will depend on the specific facts of each case.

Covenants not to compete may be implied from the employee's duty of loyalty, but employers may put covenants in writing in order to enhance the protections they are seeking.

In deciding whether to enforce the covenant, courts will consider whether, based on the specific circumstances, the covenant is reasonably necessary to protect the employer's legitimate business interests, or whether the covenant is too broad and unduly burdensome on the former employee. Courts making this determination will evaluate both the duration and scope of the restraint.[14]

II. COLLECTIVE BARGAINING

Collective bargaining is a subject relating to labor on which both the central government and the state governments are empowered to legislate, as discussed in the Introduction at B.2. In the exercise of this power, the central government formulates the major policy issues relating to labor, while the states implement and operate the labor machinery and legislate on subjects concerning which the central government has not enacted laws. Where the

[14] Niranjan Golikari v. The Century Spinning & Manufacturing Co. Ltd. [(1967) 2 SCR 367]; Deshpande v. Arvind Mills Ltd. [48 Bom. L.R. 90].

central government has passed legislation, the states adopt the same with some modifications.

A. History of Trade Unionism

The trade movement in India can be divided into three phases. The first phase occurred between 1850 and 1900, during which time workers started organizing themselves to protest the prevailing poor working conditions and long hours. Many strikes took place. These strikes reinforced the power of united action, even though workers had yet to form "trade unions" in the true sense of the term.

The second phase of the trade union movement took place between 1900 and 1947. The development of organized trade unions and political movements of the working class characterized this phase. It also witnessed the emergence of militant trade unionism. The period 1900 to 1915 was the preparatory phase for the organized trade union movement.

The third phase began with the emergence of independent India in 1947, when the government sought the cooperation of the unions for planning economic development. The trade union movement was also highly politicized, with many political parties patronizing trade unions. Trade unions are major pressure groups in the modern industrial relations system. India has about 40,000 unions, with a membership of about 17 million workers (about 60 percent of the workforce in the organized sector).

The Trade Unions Act, enacted in 1926, provides for registration of trade unions and, in certain respects, defines legal requirements relating to registered trade unions. The Act is administered by the concerned state governments. The Act also:

(a) incorporates conditions governing the registration of trade unions;
(b) lays down the obligations of a registered trade union; and
(c) fixes the rights and obligations of registered trade unions.

B. Regulation of Unions and Employer Associations

1. Registration

Under the Trade Unions Act, 1926 any seven or more members of a trade union may apply for registration of the union. The application for registration is sent to the registrar of the state where the trade union is located. Within 60 days of a finding that the trade union has complied with all registration requirements of the Act, the registrar records the union's particulars in a register maintained for this purpose and issues a certificate of registration, which is conclusive evidence that the trade union has been duly registered.

In the event that the membership of a union falls below the required minimum membership, it is "derecognized" by the registrar and consequently by the employer. Thus, recognition can be withdrawn if the number of workers who are members falls below seven, after proper verification of numbers by the registrar.

Employer associations are registered under other laws, such as the Societies Act. They are not registered under the Trade Unions Act. Therefore, registration of employer associations will depend on the act they are registered under.

The Trade Unions (Amendment) Act, 2001 amended some of the provisions of the Trade Unions Act, 1926 in order to rationalize the same, as discussed below.

- No trade union shall be registered unless on the date of application for registration at least 10 percent or 100 (whichever is less) of the members are engaged or employed in the establishment or industry with which it is connected, subject to a minimum membership of seven "workmen."[15]
- A registered trade union shall at all times continue to have no fewer than 10 percent or 100 (whichever is less) of the workers as members, subject to a minimum of seven persons engaged or employed in the establishment or industry with which it is connected.
- A provision for filing an appeal before the industrial tribunal-cum-labor court in case of nonregistration or for restoration of registration has been provided.
- All officers of a registered trade union shall be persons actually engaged or employed in the establishment or industry with which the trade union is connected, except that up to one-third of the total number of officers or five individuals (whichever is less) need not be so engaged or employed.

---

[15]See the definition of "workman" in the Introduction at A.3., above.

- The minimum rate of subscription (dues) by members of a trade union is fixed at one rupee per annum for rural workers, three rupees per annum for workers in other unorganized sectors, and 12 rupees per annum in all other cases.
- Unions are authorized to set up separate political funds for the promotion of the civil and political interest of its members.

Where there are multiple unions representing workers in the same plant or plants, the employer has the prerogative to negotiate with the different trade unions, recognized by management as the bargaining agent. Normally, the employer will not refuse to negotiate with any registered trade union having a large number of members in its plant or plants. However, the employer may negotiate with different trade unions to agree on different sets of benefits and promises. The benefits negotiated with one union do not automatically extend to the workers of other unions unless the other unions agree to abide by the conditions of such arrangements. Normally, however, the key terms and conditions of employment accorded to workers at a workplace do not vary among workers in the same class, regardless of which union they belong to or whether they are union members at all, because employers may not treat members of the same class of employees differently as regards matters relating to the common interest or to welfare. (Employees typically are divided into classes or grades, depending on skill and experience.)

The provision that any seven members are able to form and register a union has led to a plethora of unions. In multi-union situations at the plant level, the problem of inter-union rivalry frequently poses a managerial problem. Disagreements among unions as to how to respond to technological change, rationalization (rightsizing), increased automation, or terms and conditions of employment have been known to cause work stoppages. Multiple unionism also may restrain a union's bargaining power during a period of prolonged strife. However, in spite of the potential difficulties, there are organizations where multiple unions exist and the management and unions do effectively negotiate and conclude agreements.

2. *Recognition of Trade Unions*

No union or association, as a general rule, has the fundamental right to be recognized. Recognition of a trade union is, by and large, a matter of agreement between the employer and the union. Only three states—Gujarat, Madhya Pradesh, and Maharashtra—have statutory provisions regarding union recognition.[16] The Bombay Industrial Relations Act is in force in Gujarat, and other acts are in force in Madhya Pradesh and Maharashtra.

The Bombay Industrial Relations Act imposes certain conditions that must be met in order for a union to be recognized by the employer. These conditions include number of members, representative character of unions, etc. The act classifies trade unions into three categories:

1. A *representative union*, which should be able to muster 15 percent of the total number of employees employed in any one industry.
2. A *qualified union*, which should have 5 percent of the employees in an industry enrolled as members.
3. *A primary union*, which should have 15 percent or more employees enrolled in a unit or a plant.

The impetus for employers to recognize unions arises from the fact that recognition helps to establish harmony and peace in the industrial sector. The absence of uniform legislation in all the states and union territories with regard to the recognition issue creates a problem in terms of the process to be employed for verification when a union stakes its claim, either in a new union situation or a multi-union situation.

3. *Employee/Member Rights and Restrictions*

Workers have a legal right under the Constitution to join any association or union. Workers also are free not to belong to a union.

[16]R.B.I. Assn. Reserve Bank 1983-II LLN 872 and M.A. David v. Kerela State Electricity Board, 1974 Lab.IC 637.

Union membership is not a necessary condition for employment. Workers can effectively decertify a union by terminating their membership. In the absence of the minimum number of members required by the Trade Unions Act,[17] for example, the union would be derecognized by the employer.

C. Collective Bargaining Agreements

1. *Subjects for Collective Bargaining*

The usual topics of collective bargaining are as follows:

- wages and hours of work;
- working conditions;
- union recognition and scope of bargaining unit;
- strikes and lockouts;
- union activities and responsibilities;
- union privileges;
- management rights;
- job rights and seniority;
- discipline, suspension, and discharge;
- grievance handling;
- health and safety;
- insurance and benefit programs; and
- other matters.

2. *Types of Collective Bargaining Agreements*

There are four types of collective bargaining agreements:

1. Agreements drawn up after direct negotiations between labor and management and purely voluntary in character. These are bilateral agreements and enforceable in the civil courts like any other bilateral agreements. They may be later sent to the "appropriate governments" and conciliation officer, as discussed in category 2 below, if the parties would like the agreement to be binding in nature. These agreements are binding only on the parties who reached

[17]See discussion under II.B., above.

the agreement (e.g., normally in a multi-union workplace, one union may reach an agreement with an employer and it may not be applicable to nonmembers or to employees who are members of other unions, except on matters relating to common interests/welfare, where the employer cannot discriminate between employees of the same class).

2. Agreements concluded by the parties themselves without reference to a board of conciliation and signed by them. Copies of such agreements are sent to the appropriate governments and to conciliation officers. These agreements are binding on the parties to the agreement by virtue of their being sent to the government and conciliation officers; in lieu of filing a civil suit, if one of the parties files a complaint, the government and a conciliation officer will use persuasion and mediation to resolve the problem. These agreements are binding only on the parties who reached the agreement.
3. Agreements negotiated between the parties during the course of conciliation proceedings at a board of conciliation. A settlement arrived at in the course of conciliation proceedings with a recognized majority union will be binding on all workers of the establishment, not just those who are members of the majority union, irrespective of any objection.[18] A conciliation officer is not competent to impose a decision as regards the various points at issue between the opposing parties. All that he or she can do is to try to persuade the parties to make a fair and amicable settlement. In the event the conciliation officer is unable to mediate a settlement, the matter will be considered by the appropriate government on receipt of a report from the conciliation officer, to be decided in the manner spelled out in the Industrial Disputes Act.[19]
4. Agreements negotiated by the parties on a voluntary basis while the dispute is under consideration before an industrial tribunal, labor court, or arbitrator, and which are later

---

[18]All India Textile Janta Union v. Labour Commissioner, 1994 LLR 203 (P&H) (DB).

[19]Madhavan Kutty v. Union of India, 1982-II LLN 803 (Ker.HC.).

submitted to said industrial tribunal, labor court, or labor arbitrator for incorporation into documents as part of the settlement. These settlements are termed "consent awards" and are enforceable under the Industrial Disputes Act.

D. Deadlocks and Disputes

Industrial disputes generally involve groups of employees and/or employers rather than single individuals. Disputes involving individuals tend to be resolved through contract actions in civil courts, as discussed in I., above, or through the use of grievance cells, as discussed in III., below.

If an industrial dispute exists or is apprehended, the "appropriate government" may at any time, by order in writing, refer the dispute to one of three types of entities: a board of conciliation, a labor court, or an industrial tribunal. (For any industry operating under the authority of the central government,[20] the central government is the appropriate government; for any other industrial dispute, the state government concerned is the appropriate government.) Disputes also may be referred to private arbitrators, provided the parties agree to do so and the dispute has not yet been referred to a government entity.

1. *Private Arbitration*

The collective bargaining agreement defines and prescribes the procedure for settlement of grievances arising out of implementation of the agreement. Under the Industrial Disputes Act, a dispute may be referred to arbitration under the following conditions:

- an industrial dispute exists or is apprehended in an establishment;
- the employer and the workers agree, in writing, to refer the dispute to arbitration;

[20]Industries where the central government is the main stakeholder, involving, e.g., entities such as the Industrial Finance Corporation and the Employees State Insurance Corporation.

- the arbitration agreement is in the prescribed form and signed by the parties in the prescribed manner;
- the agreement is accompanied by the consent, in writing, of the arbitrator or arbitrators;
- the dispute is referred to arbitration before it has been referred to a labor court or tribunal or a national tribunal;
- referral of the dispute that the employer and workers have by written agreement agreed to refer to arbitration must be to the person or persons specified in the arbitration agreement to act as arbitrator/arbitrators; and
- the arbitration agreement must set forth the issue/issues to be decided by the arbitration procedure, with a copy of the agreement forwarded to the appropriate government and to the government conciliation officer.

2. *Government Dispute Resolution Bodies*

There are various authorities under the Industrial Disputes Act to settle and adjudicate industrial disputes. In cases where a dispute cannot be resolved by the parties or by private arbitration, the dispute is referred to industrial tribunals, labor courts, or labor arbitrators, as the case may be.

- *Board of Conciliation*. To encourage settlement of an industrial dispute, the appropriate government may refer the dispute to a board of conciliation.[21]
- *Labor Court*. Labor courts are specialized subordinate courts under state governments that handle all labor issues at the first instance (i.e., not on appeal) whether they relate to subjects under state government jurisdiction or are referred by the central government and pertain to central government undertakings. Issues that labor courts consider include:
  - discharge or dismissal of workers, including reinstatement of, or grant of relief to, those wrongfully dismissed;
  - legality or illegality of a strike or lockout; and
  - all other matters, other than those specified for adjudication by the industrial tribunal.

---

[21]See discussion of conciliation under II.C.2., above.

- *Industrial Tribunal.* Cases decided by labor courts may be appealed to the industrial tribunals, which are appellate courts under the state governments. The industrial tribunals also have original jurisdiction over cases referred to them directly by state governments. Thus, industrial tribunals adjudicate industrial disputes relating to any matter, including those on appeal from the labor courts, and perform such other functions as may be assigned to them. Some matters on which the industrial tribunals adjudicate are:
  – wages, including the period and mode of payment,
  – bonuses, profit sharing, provident funds, and gratuities,
  – retrenchment of workers and closure of establishments,
  – any other matter that may be prescribed.
  Appeals from the industrial tribunal go by means of a "writ petition" to the High Court or the Supreme Court, depending on the subject and importance of the matter.
- *National Tribunal.* For adjudication of industrial disputes that, in the opinion of the central government, involve questions of national importance or are of such a nature that industrial establishments situated in more than one state are likely to be interested in, or affected by, the disputes, the central government may by notification in the *Official Gazette* constitute one or more national industrial tribunals.

E. Strikes and Other Industrial Actions

1. Demonstrations and Meetings

The members and officers of a trade union cannot hold demonstrations or meetings within the work premises; the work premises are owned by the employer and therefore the employees have no right to use them for such purposes. It has been held that the immunity of a trade union from judicial limitations on strikes is not absolute since reasonable restrictions for staging a demonstration can be imposed by the court.[22] The Punjab and Haryana High Court has held that civil courts can bar demonstrations within

[22]Indian Institute of Technology v. Co-ordination Committee & others, 2002 LLR 69 (Del.HC).

a radius of 50 meters of an industrial establishment.[23] Courts can also restrain employees from demonstrating within 100 meters of an employer's premises.[24]

2. *Work Slowdowns*

"Go-slow" actions, or work slowdowns, have been classified as misconduct under the Model Standing Orders appended to the Industrial Employment (Standing Orders) Act 1946. The employer is within its rights to declare a lockout if workers resort to go-slow tactics. It has been held that the declaration of a lockout was justified and the workers concerned were not entitled to any wages for the period of the lockout because it resulted from their own action.[25]

3. *Picketing, Sit-Down Strikes, and Sit-Ins*

Picketing, sit-down strikes, or "stay-in" (sit-in) strikes involve the tort of trespass. Such actions, therefore, constitute a civil conspiracy because employees have a right to enter and remain on the employer's premises only for the purpose of their work or for other purposes as the employer may allow. Thus, in such situations they are usually classified as licensees under common law, and police can be utilized to remove the workers under the rationale that such actions cause undue obstacles to the right of the employer to carry on its business.

4. *Standard Strikes or Lockouts*

The Industrial Disputes Act defines a strike as a cessation of work by a group of persons employed in any industry acting in combination, or a concerted refusal, under a common understanding, by a number of persons who are or have been employed to continue to work or to accept employment. In the case of *Chemical & Fibres of India Ltd. v. D G Bhoir*,[26] the court stated that a

---

[23]Ram Singh & others v. Ashoka Iron Foundry and others, 1993 LLR 327 (P&H HC).

[24]*Ibid.*

[25]Govinda Sheet Metal Work & Foundry v. Their Workmen, (1956) FJR 341.

[26](975) 4 SCC 332.

strike is "a recognized weapon of workmen to be resorted to by them, for asserting their bargaining power and for tacking of their collective demands upon an unwilling employer. It is to be used as a last resort when all other avenues for settlement of industrial disputes as provided for in the statutory machinery [i.e., use of a board of conciliation or other settlement device as discussed above] have proved futile."

The Industrial Disputes Act does not grant an unrestricted right to strikes or lockouts. The appropriate government is empowered to issue orders prohibiting continuance of a strike or lockout. In addition, there are general prohibitions on strikes and lockouts applicable to both utility services and nonutility services when they are classified as illegal, as discussed below. Apart from the general prohibition orders, there are some additional safeguards for the smooth and uninterrupted running of public utility services and to obviate the possibility of inconvenience to the general public and to society.

Under the Industrial Disputes Act, a strike or lockout could be declared illegal if it occurs under the following circumstances:

- In the case of public utility services, (a) if no notice is given to the other party within six weeks before striking, and (b) during conciliation proceedings before a conciliation officer and seven days after the conclusion of such proceedings.
- In the case of any other industrial establishment, (a) during conciliation proceedings before a board and seven days after the conclusion of such proceedings, (b) during a hearing before a labor court, tribunal, or national tribunal and two months after the conclusion of such proceedings, (c) during a hearing by an arbitrator and two months after the conclusion of such proceedings and, (d) during the period in which an award or settlement is in operation.

The Industrial Disputes Act also prohibits any person from knowingly spending or applying money in direct furtherance or support of an illegal strike or lockout or instigating or inciting others to take part in an illegal strike or lockout. The Act further provides that any worker who continues to act in furtherance of an illegal strike could face imprisonment for a term of up to one month, a fine, or both. Similarly, any employer who continues to act in furtherance of an illegal lockout could be imprisoned for up to one month, fined, or both. The remedy indicated here is a designated statutory remedy and no other relief outside the Act can be claimed on general principles of jurisprudence. Therefore, obtaining compensation by proceedings in arbitration is contrary to law.[27]

In the case of *Bank of India v. T S Kelawala*,[28] the court held that both legal as well as illegal strikes invite deduction of wages on the principle that "whoever voluntarily refrains from doing work when it is offered to him, is not entitled to payment for work he has not done." In other words, the court upheld the doctrine of "no work, no pay."

A legal lockout does not give a license to management to act unreasonably.[29] A lockout may be legal inasmuch as it is declared in compliance with statutory requirements. However, management cannot declare a lockout with the ulterior motive of retaliating against workers for their trade union activities or continue the lockout for an unreasonably long time.

III. Representation by Entities Other than Unions

Employees can be represented by organized trade unions (discussed in II. above), by various other entities (discussed below) established under labor laws, or more generally by nongovernmental organizations[30] or societal organizations. There are three major sectors of employees, with varying levels of representation by unions or other entities.

- The private sector, where employees are represented by both organized unions and other entities such as "grievance cells" under various pieces of labor legislation, though usually by only one or the other on a given issue. Normally the union

---

[27]Statesman Ltd. v. Workmen (1976) 2 SCC 82.

[28][1990] II L.L.J. 39 (SC).

[29]Statesman Ltd. v. Workmen (1976) 2 SCC 23.

[30]See the definition of NGOs in a footnote in "I. Historical Antecedents" in the chapter on Corporate Codes of Conduct in Volume 1.

takes up matters of common interest to groups of employees through the industrial disputes process discussed under II.D., above, whereas the grievance cell considers issues involving single employees with individual grievances. Grievance cells are provided by the employer according to rules established under various pieces of labor legislation, in workplaces having more than 50 employees. The aggrieved worker files the grievance with the grievance cell, after which the labor authorities take up the matter and make a decision on the merits after a hearing.

- The public sector, where a smaller percentage of employees are represented by unions and representation mostly takes place through "grievance cells" and consultative machinery established under legislation.
- The unorganized sector (e.g., farmers, artisans, day workers) where worker involvement and representation is through pressure groups formed by each category of worker to air grievances and secure redress at the government level.

A. Government-Mandated Employee Monitoring and Dispute-Resolution Bodies

Under various pieces of labor legislation, the government is required to create administrative networks in all units employing more than 50 employees, as mentioned above, to oversee the implementation of workplace benefits and ensure the representation of employee interests. These networks exist simultaneously with the unions. An employee can file his or her grievance either through the union or through any network that exists in the workplace (although, as noted above, normally the union takes up matters of common interest to groups of employees and the grievance cell represents single employees with individual grievances). Administrative networks can be created through:

- Advisory councils,
- Advisors, officers, inspectors, etc., appointed under various labor laws,
- Medical benefit councils and medical officers,
- Welfare committees and officers,
- Pay boards,

- Conciliation committees and officers,
- Grievance cells,
- Workers committees, or
- Consultation committees.

Individuals acting as representatives of employees under the various "welfare mechanisms" mentioned above have a wide range of powers. These individuals should not be confused with government inspectors and officers affiliated with the Ministry of Labour, who are employed and paid by the appropriate government to implement and enforce the labor laws. In contrast, the welfare officers discussed here are hired and paid by the employer in accordance with rules framed by the government and are essentially semi-official compliance officers, assisting the employer to comply with mandatory welfare and benefit measures established under various labor laws. Although appointed by the employer, these officers are considered government officials charged with proper enforcement of the employee welfare provisions of labor laws. Their duties, qualifications, and conditions of service generally are prescribed by the various state governments, although, as noted above, they are paid by the employer and reviews of their performance are conducted by the employer.

Individuals hired by employers under government requirements and acting as representatives of employees have the following powers:

- They can carry out any inquiry and examination with respect to the interests of the employees.
- They can make and implement schemes for the benefit of the employees, e.g., provident fund schemes and insurance schemes (see VIII.B., below).
- They can provide for any damages suffered by an employee during the course of employment.
- They ensure compliance with provisions of various labor legislation regarding sickness benefits, maternity benefits, disablement benefits, etc.
- They are responsible for promoting health schemes and measures for the benefit of employees.
- They can investigate, or form committees to investigate, complaints filed by employees.

- They have the power to call for adoption of proper safety measures.
- They can call for or require medical examination of employees to check for healthy working conditions and a healthy environment.

As mentioned above, grievance cells are a part of this welfare mechanism for employees. Employees can bring to such cells any matter ranging from the employer's noncompliance with employee welfare provisions to variations in service conditions and health and safety concerns. Because these cells are perceived as helping to solve matters amicably, they are therefore classified as measures for employee welfare and benefit.

Grievances that are not resolved by grievance cells and instead become full-blown disputes are resolved by government officials and machinery through the industrial tribunal-cum-labor courts discussed in the Introduction at B. and in II.D.2., above.

B. Organizations Not Established by the Government

Employees can also be represented by nonstatutory organizations, such as:

- Nongovernmental organizations,
- Social organizations, and
- Various nonunion pressure groups.

These types of representatives have the following powers:

- They can initiate legal proceedings, including public interest suits, against an employer.
- They can pressure employers by getting the public involved in causes involving the welfare of employees.
- They can increase awareness of employee welfare issues through the mass media and newspapers.
- They can create awareness among employees and educate them with respect to their basic rights.

IV. REDUNDANCY AND TRANSFERS OF UNDERTAKINGS

Beginning in 1991, India has instituted economic reforms with the objective of replacing a centrally controlled, protectionist economic regime with a competitive environment where free interaction of market forces would ensure efficient allocation and use of resources, thereby enabling Indian industry to become globally competitive. To this end, measures have been introduced to restructure industry, allow progressive dismantling of state controls and regulatory mechanisms, facilitate establishment of new businesses, clear blocks in the way of foreign capital inflows, open areas for private investment in pockets hitherto reserved for the pubic sector, reduce customs duties, implement tax reforms, move toward full convertibility of the currency, and reform capital markets. These reforms have threatened to substantially increase the rate of unemployment in a situation already burdened with the contradictory impact of stabilization policies, particularly since a sizeable quantity of surplus labor had been carried over from pre-reform days. It is in this context that the notice and payment requirements below should be viewed.

If a workplace has unions in it, the unions' role is to see that workers are not deprived of the rights and benefits available to them under the law. Unions also may seek to negotiate benefits more favorable than those specified by law.

A. Redundancy

Under the Industrial Disputes Act, the right of the employer to retrench "surplus labor" is inherent in its right to manage its business subject to the terms and conditions of the contract of employment and the provisions of the Act. In the absence of any special conditions of service in the contract of employment, the rights of workers are governed by the Act, under which the employer can discharge the surplus labor either temporarily by way of layoff or permanently by way of retrenchment (downsizing) or closure of an undertaking.

The Industrial Disputes Act is the major law dealing with the effect of redundancy in India. Before its enactment, there was no law regulating industrial redundancy and employers had a relatively unfettered prerogative of hiring and firing. The Act initiated restrictions and regulations concerning the industrial redundancy of excess employees, and now contains provisions regarding retrenchments and layoffs and related payment of compensation to workers under certain contingencies.

Currently, provisions relating to the effect of redundancy appear in Chapters V-A and V-B of the Act. These chapters deal with layoffs, retrenchment, closure, and transfer of an undertaking. Industrial establishments that are of a seasonal character or in which work is performed only intermittently are not included in the protections of either chapter.

Protections were expanded when the Act was amended in 1953 to add a new Chapter V-A covering industrial establishments employing 50 to 99 workers employed per work day for the preceding 12 months; for the purpose of layoffs, Chapter V-A does not apply to industrial establishments in which fewer than 50 workers were employed on an average work day in the preceding calendar month. The Act was amended again in 1976 to add a new Chapter V-B covering industrial establishments in which at least 100 workers were employed per work day for the preceding 12 months. For retrenchment, layoff, or closing, prior to that second amendment, employers had an unfettered right to close down establishments after 60 days' notice. The latter amendment was made after large-scale layoffs, retrenchments, and plant closures, particularly by large companies and undertakings. In order to prevent hardship to the employees while still maintaining a higher tempo of production and productivity, the law put some restrictions on the employer's right to retrench and lay off workers. It also restricted the right of the employer to resort to closing its undertaking. The latter amendment also established certain new definitions affecting the discussion in this section.

1. *Layoffs*

a. *Layoffs Under Chapter V-A*

Workers whose names are on the muster-rolls (employment list) of an industrial establishment and who have completed at least one year of continuous service under an employer and who are laid off, whether continuously or intermittently, must be paid by the employer for all days during which they are laid off, except for such weekly holidays as may intervene, subject to the 45-day limitation and the exceptions noted below. Payment is to be 50 percent of the total of the basic wages and "dearness allowance" (regional wage adjustment) that would have been payable had the worker not been laid off.

If during any period of 12 months a worker is laid off for more than 45 days, no compensation shall be payable after the first 45 days if there is an agreement to that effect between the worker and the employer, and after the 45 days the employer is permitted to retrench (see discussion in b., below) the worker at any time in accordance with the provisions of the Act. If the employer does retrench workers after the 45 days, the employer may offset any compensation paid to the workers for having being laid off for the period of 45 days during the preceding 12 months against the compensation payable for retrenchment discussed in b., below.

No compensation shall be paid to a worker who has been laid off:

- if the worker refuses to accept any alternative employment in the same establishment or in any other establishment belonging to the same employer and situated in the same town or village;
- if before the layoff the worker was not present for work at the appointed time during normal working hours at least once a day; and
- if such layoff is due to a strike or slowing down of production on the part of workers in another part of the establishment.

The payment of compensation is not a condition precedent to the layoff of a worker—i.e., the "standing orders" (regulations issued under the Act) read with Chapter V-A create a right in favor of the laid-off worker to claim compensation, but they do not create a right of being paid compensation before a layoff. Workers can claim compensation only after they have been laid off, and the employer may then pay either the actual wages or compensation for the layoff as provided under Chapter V-A.

The Act does not prescribe any notice period for laid-off employees or any payment in lieu of notice. If there are any standing orders or service rules in a particular company with regard to giving of notice, then the same must be observed as regards notice of the layoff. The normal practice under such standing orders or service rules is that the effective date of the layoff and the names of the affected employees are placed on the notice board of the company.

b. Layoffs Under Chapter V-B

No worker whose name is on the muster-roll of an industrial establishment to which this chapter applies may be laid off by the employer, except with the permission of the appropriate government following a request by the establishment to said authority, unless the layoff is due to a shortage of electric power, a natural calamity, or other events that disrupt work and are outside the employer's control. When the employer secures permission and lays off employees, such individuals are entitled to layoff compensation as provided in Chapter V-A of the Industrial Disputes Act.

All the provisions of the Act relating to retrenchment discussed in a., above (Layoffs under Chapter V-A), also apply to cases of layoff under this chapter, except the offset for retrenchment (see discussion in 2., below) following expiration of the first 45 days of layoff. For employees covered under Chapter V-B, the employer can retrench the laid-off employees after the period of 45 days, but it cannot offset the compensation paid for the period of layoff against the compensation payable for retrenchment.

2. *Retrenchment*

Retrenchment is the termination by the employer of the services of an individual worker or groups of workers (excluding mass terminations due to closure discussed in 3., below) for any reason whatsoever except:

(a) as a punishment inflicted by way of disciplinary action,
(b) voluntary retirement of the worker,
(c) involuntary retirement of the worker on reaching the age of superannuation (mandatory retirement), if the contract of

employment between the employer and the worker contains a stipulation specifying same,

(d) termination of a worker as a result of the nonrenewal of the contract of employment between the employer and the worker upon its expiration or as a result of the contract of employment automatically terminating under a stipulation to that effect contained therein,

(e) termination of the service of a worker on the ground of continued ill-health, or

(f) closure of a part or a whole of an undertaking, which is governed by requirements discussed in 3., below.

There are no restrictions on retrenchment of workers whose continuous service with the current employer is of less than a year's duration.

Workers employed in any industry who have been in continuous service with their current employer for a year or more can be retrenched under the following conditions:

(a) the worker
 1) has been given one month's notice in writing indicating the reasons for retrenchment and the period of notice has expired, or
 2) has been paid, in lieu of such notice, wages for the period of the notice;

(b) the worker has been paid, at the time of retrenchment, compensation equivalent to 15 days' average pay for every completed year of continuous service or any part thereof in excess of six months; and

(c) notice in the prescribed manner is served on the appropriate government or such authority as may be specified by the appropriate government in the *Official Gazette*.

3. *Closure of an Undertaking or Place of Employment*

Redundancy may also result in termination of services of employees not on an individual basis but on a mass scale. This form of collective termination takes place in case of permanent closure of an undertaking or place of employment by an employer. Closure can refer to the permanent closing of either the entire place of employment or a part thereof. In view of the fact that the repercussions of termination of services of employees on a large scale are much more severe than terminations of an individual employee, the Industrial Disputes Act provides a detailed procedure to be followed by an employer for closing an undertaking or place of business.

The Act also contains provisions for compensation to the employees whose services have been terminated as a result of the closing. It says that where an undertaking is closed down for any reason whatsoever, every worker who has been in continuous service in that undertaking for a year or more immediately before such a closure is entitled to notice and compensation equivalent to 15 days' average pay for every completed year of continuous service or any part thereof over six months.

B. Transfers of Undertakings

Transfer of ownership and control of a business may in certain cases be prejudicial to the interest of the employees either on an individual or a collective basis due to two possibilities. Either:

- the new employer is not willing to employ them and consequently the transfer results in termination of their employment, or
- the terms and conditions of services offered by the new employer are less favorable than those offered by the previous employer.

Employee protections in this regard are discussed below.

1. Effect of Transfer of Undertaking on Individual Contracts

The Industrial Disputes Act provides that where the ownership or management of an undertaking is transferred, whether by agreement or by operation of law, from one employer to another, every worker who has been in continuous service for at least one year in that undertaking immediately before such transfer shall be entitled to notice and compensation as if the worker had been retrenched. Retrenchment protections are discussed in IV.A.2., above.

2. Effect of Transfer of Undertaking on Collective Bargaining Contracts

Under the Trade Unions Act, in the event of a transfer of an undertaking from one employer to another, the trade union(s) concerned may enter into a tripartite agreement with both the old and the new employers stating that the terms of employment and other service conditions will not be altered in a manner prejudicial to the interests of the employees. Alternatively, the trade union(s) may enter into an agreement with the employer transferring the undertaking to the effect that the new employer will not do any act adversely affecting the interests of the employees; in such an arrangement, the old employer transfers the undertaking to the new employer subject to the agreement the old employer has made with the union(s).

V. Wages, Hours, and Leave

A. Wages

1. Constitutional Directives

The Directive Principles of State Policy in the Constitution of India have various provisions relating to wages. These principles, as noted in the Introduction, confer no legal rights and create no legal remedies.

Article 39 provides that the state shall, in particular, direct its policy toward ensuring:

- (a) That the citizens, men and women equally, have the right to an adequate means of livelihood;
- (b) That the ownership and control of material resources are so distributed as to serve the common good;
- (c) That the operation of the economic system does not result in concentration of wealth and means of production to the common detriment;
- (d) That there is equal pay for equal work for both men and women; and
- (e) That the health and strength of workers, men and women, and the tender age of children are not abused and that citizens are not forced by economic necessity to enter vocation unsuited for their age or strength.[31]

[31] Constitution, Art. 39.

Article 43 provides that the state shall endeavor to secure—by suitable legislation or economic organization or in any other way—work, a living wage, conditions of work ensuring a decent standard of life, and full employment of leisure and social and cultural opportunities to all workers—agricultural, industrial, or otherwise. It also provides that, in particular, the state shall endeavor to promote cottage industries on an individual or co-operative basis in the rural areas.

2. *Statutory Provisions*

In general the term "salary" is used in India to denote compensation to white collar employees, while the term "wage" is used to denote the payment made to blue-collar workers.

a. *The Minimum Wages Act, 1948*

This Act envisages securing the welfare of workers in a competitive market by fixing the minimum rates of wages. This Act applies to all of India. The term "minimum wages" is not at all defined in the Act, since it is literally impossible to pay uniform wages for all the industries throughout the country because of varying conditions of industry in different parts of the country.

The Fifteenth Indian Labour Conference (1957) formally quantified the term minimum wage and laid down the following rules for its determination:

- In calculating the minimum wage, the standard working class family should be taken to comprise three consumption units for each wage earner, the earnings of women, children and adolescents being disregarded;
- Minimum food requirements should be calculated on the basis of a set intake of 2700 calories for an average Indian adult of moderate activity;
- Clothing requirements should be estimated on the basis of per capita consumption of 18 yards of fabric per annum, which would give an average worker's family of four a total of 72 yards;
- In respect of housing, the norm should be the minimum rent charged by the government in any area for houses pro-

vided under the subsidized industrial housing scheme for low-income groups.

- Fuel, lighting, and other miscellaneous items of expenditure should constitute 20 percent of the total minimum wage.

Minimum wages are set through the following process, according to section 3 of the Minimum Wages Act, 1948.

In fixing the minimum rates of wages for the first time or in revising minimum rates of wages, the appropriate government will either: (a) appoint committees to hold enquiries and advise it in respect of such fixation or revision, or (b) by notification in the *Official Gazette,* publish its proposals for the information of persons likely to be affected thereby and specify a date, at least two months from the date of the notification, on which the proposals will be taken into consideration. After considering the advice of the committee or responses to the notice, the appropriate government will by notification in the *Gazette* fix the minimum rates of wages. Such notifications, unless otherwise provided, will come into force three months from the date of issue.

The term "wages" as used in the Minimum Wages Act means all remuneration capable of being expressed in terms of money that would under the terms of the contract of employment, express or implied, be payable to a person employed in respect of his or her employment or of work done in such employment, and includes housing rental allowance, but does not include:

(i) the value of
  (a) any provision of housing, electricity, water, or medical care, or
  (b) any other amenity or any service excluded by general or special order of the appropriate government;
(ii) any contribution paid by the employer to any pension fund or provident fund or under any scheme of social insurance (see VIII.B., below);
(iii) any traveling allowance or the value of any traveling concession;
(iv) any sum paid to the employee to defray special expenses entailed by the nature of his or her employment;
(v) any gratuity[32] payable on discharge.[33]

---

[32]See discussion under VIII.B.7., below.

[33]Minimum Wages Act, 1948 §2(h).

B. Hours

Working hours are set under two laws:

- Under the Factories Act for employees working in a factory.
- Under the Minimum Wages Act for any person who is employed for hire or reward to do any work—skilled or unskilled, manual or clerical—in a scheduled employment in respect of which minimum rates of wages have been fixed.

1. Working Hours Under the Minimum Wages Act, 1948

The normal number of working hours per day for an adult is nine hours, and in the case of a child, four and one-half hours. Overtime must be paid as provided for under the Minimum Wages Act, as discussed in C.2.a., below, if individuals work longer hours.

All employees must receive a day of rest in every period of seven days. The day of rest is ordinarily Sunday, but the employer may fix any other day of the week as the rest day for any employee or class of employees. An employee may not be required or even allowed to work on a scheduled rest day unless he or she has or will have a substitute rest day for a whole day on one of the five days immediately before or after the rest day, provided that no substitution shall be made that will result in the employee working for more than 10 consecutive days without a whole rest day.

These provisions do not operate to the prejudice of more favorable terms, if any, to which an employee may be entitled under any other law (including the Factories Act, 1948 as discussed below) or under the terms of any award, agreement, or contract of service; in such a case, the employee is entitled only to the more favorable terms.

2. Working Hours Under the Factories Act, 1948

Under the Factories Act, no adult worker can be required or allowed to work in a factory for more than 48 hours per week without payment of overtime. As regards daily work hours, no adult worker can be allowed to work in a factory for more than nine hours a day without payment of overtime. Employees may work longer if they are paid overtime as provided for under the Factories Act, as discussed in C.1., below.

Each day, periods of work of adult factory workers must be fixed so that workers receive a rest interval of at least half an hour for every five hours of work.

Women may work in any factory, but only between the hours of 6 a.m. and 7 p.m.

C. Overtime

1. Overtime Pay Under the Factories Act, 1948

If employees are covered under the provisions of the Factories Act, those provisions apply instead of the provisions of the Minimum Wages Act.

If a worker works in a factory for more than nine hours in any day or for more than 48 hours in any week, the worker is entitled to wages at twice the ordinary rate of wages.

According to the Act, state governments may make specific provisions in regard to the maximum hours of overtime permitted, provided the total number of hours in a week, including overtime, do not exceed 60 and the total number of overtime hours for any quarter of the year do not exceed 50.

2. Overtime Pay Under the Minimum Wages Act

According to the provisions of Section 14 of the Minimum Wages Act, if an employee whose minimum rate of wages is fixed under this Act works in excess of the number of hours constituting a normal working day, the employer must pay the employee for every hour or part of an hour so worked at the overtime rate fixed either under this Act or under other any law of the appropriate government, whichever is higher.

The Minimum Wages (Central) Rules, 1950 provides that when a worker works for more than nine hours on any day or for more than 48 hours in any week, the worker shall be entitled to overtime pay as follows:

- in case of employment in agriculture, at one and a half times the ordinary rate of wages, and

- in the case of any other employment, at double the ordinary rate of wage.

For the purposes of this Rule, the term "ordinary wages" means the basic wage plus allowances of food grains and other articles to which the worker is entitled, including cash equivalents of the advantages accruing through the concessional sale of such food grains and other articles to the worker, but does not include any bonus.

There is no specific provision in this Act setting a maximum number of overtime hours that may be worked.

D. Leave

1. Annual Leave

A worker who works for 240 days or more in a factory during a calendar year is allowed annual leave with wages during the subsequent calendar year at the rate of one day for every 20 days of work performed during the previous calendar year.

If a worker does not in any one calendar year take all of the leave accumulated, the unused leave is added to the leave accumulated in the succeeding calendar year; however, annual leave can be accumulated up to a maximum of 30 days only, in the case of an adult worker. Annual leave pay is to be based on the average amount of the worker's daily wage immediately preceding the leave. This includes basic wage and other allowances, but not bonus and overtime.

2. Pregnancy, Childbirth, and Family Leave

See the discussion of leave-related provisions of the Maternity Benefit Act, 1961 and maternity benefit provisions of the Employees State Insurance Act, 1948 under VIII.B.6., below.

3. Sick Leave

Workers can make use of sick leave, or wages in lieu of sick leave, under the Factories Act, 1948. Workers insured under The Employees' State Insurance Act, 1948 can make use of a sickness benefit provided they meet the qualifications and conditions subject to which such benefit may be given. The rates and period of such benefit are prescribed by the central government.

4. Military Service

The Indian Armed forces are governed by an entirely separate set of rules. Broadly, the Indian Army is entitled to 20 days of casual leave for urgent or unforeseen contingencies, limited to no more than 10 days at a time. In exceptional cases, this period may be extended to 14 days at one time, and in very exceptional cases, casual leave may be allowed for up to 20 days at one time. Sixty days of noncumulative annual leave, in addition to casual leave is allowed in each calendar year but must be scheduled in advance.

VI. ANTIDISCRIMINATION

The Constitution of India and the Equal Remuneration Act, 1976 generally prohibit job discrimination based on race, color, caste, sex, religion, disability, and other factors, as outlined below.

- Constitutional provisions
  - Article 15 of the Constitution prohibits discrimination on the grounds of religion, race, caste, sex, or place of birth.
  - Article 16 of the Constitution provides for equal opportunity to all in the matters of public employment.
  - Article 39 (d) of the Constitution provides for equal pay for equal work for both men and women.
- Legislative provisions
  - Equal Remuneration Act, 1976
  - The Persons with Disabilities (Equal Opportunities, Protection of Rights and Full Participation) Act, 1995

A. Discrimination on the Grounds of Religion, Race, Caste, Sex, or Place of Birth

Article 15 of the Constitution specifically bars public and private employers alike from discriminating against any citizen of India on the grounds of religion, race, caste, sex, or place of birth.

The offending ground must be the "immediate and direct" cause of the discrimination.[34]

Also, the Constitution insists on the equality of status and prohibits gender bias; Article 16 guarantees equality of opportunity to all citizens in matters relating to employment or appointment to any office under the state. Thus, no citizen can be discriminated against or deemed ineligible for any employment or office under the state solely on the basis of religion, race, caste, sex, descent, place of birth or residence, or any combination of the aforementioned.

1. Additional Prohibitions Against Sex Discrimination

Article 39 of the Constitution provides that the state shall direct its policy toward ensuring that there is equal pay for equal work for both men and women. The Equal Remuneration Act, 1976 also provides that no employer shall provide remuneration to any worker at rates less favorable than those it pays workers of the opposite sex for performing the same work or work of a similar nature.

The Equal Remuneration Act also provides that no employer shall discriminate against women while recruiting for the same work or work of a similar nature or in any condition of service subsequent to recruitment such as promotions, training, or transfer. However, this provision does not affect any priority or reservation granted to scheduled castes or tribes, ex-servicemen or servicewomen, retrenched employees,[35] or granted to any other class or category of persons in the matter of recruitment.

B. Preferences for Women and Minorities

1. Preferences for Women

While the Indian Constitution insists on the equality of status and prohibits gender bias, nevertheless, by virtue of Article 15(3)

---

[34] *State of Bombay v. Bombay Education Society*, 1955 (1) SCR 568; AIR 1954SC561

[35] See the definition of retrenchment in Section IV.A.2., above.

of the Constitution, the state is permitted to make special provisions for women. This provision recognizes that women in India have been socially and economically disadvantaged for centuries and, as a result, cannot fully participate in the socio-economic activities of the nation on a footing of equality. The basic purpose of this section is to eliminate the socioeconomic disadvantage of women and to empower them in such a manner as to bring about effective equality between men and women.

2. *Preferences for Scheduled Castes and Tribes*

As noted above, Article 16 of the Constitution of India guarantees equality of opportunity to all citizens in matters relating to employment or appointment to any office under the state. However, the state is empowered to make special provision for the advancement of any socially and educationally disadvantaged classes of citizens or for the scheduled (listed) castes and the scheduled (listed) tribes. The state can, for example, make provisions to reserve public appointments or posts for any disadvantaged class of citizens that, in the opinion of the state, is not adequately represented in the government services under the state. Similarly, the state can also make provisions for reservations in matters of promotion to any class or classes of posts in the services under the state in favor of the scheduled castes and tribes. It is pertinent to note that, in making provisions for the disadvantaged classes, the state cannot ignore the fundamental rights of the rest of the citizens of India.

C. Preferences for Disabled Individuals

The Persons with Disabilities (Equal Opportunities, Protection of Rights and Full Participation) Act, 1995 provides for reserving public posts for persons with disabilities. It provides that the various levels of government (central and state) shall identify posts that can be reserved for persons with disabilities in corporations established by or under a central government, provincial government, or state act; an authority or body owned or controlled or aided by the various levels of government; a local authority or a government company; or in the departments of a government.

The Act also provides that the various levels of government shall reserve appointments in every aforesaid establishment where there are vacancies at the rate of not less than 3 percent for persons or classes of persons with disabilities, with 1 percent each being reserved for persons suffering from:

- Blindness or low vision
- Hearing impairment
- Locomotor disability or cerebral palsy.

The various levels of government or local authorities can also by notification formulate schemes for ensuring employment of persons with disabilities, and such schemes may provide for the training and welfare of persons with disabilities, relaxation of upper age limits for work, and issuance of regulations regarding employment, health, and safety measures.

D. Age Discrimination

There is no specific provision governing age discrimination in India; establishments are free to establish age limits for any job according to their requirements. Two exceptions should be noted:

- The Factories Act, 1948 provides that no child under 14 years of age shall be required or allowed to work in any factory.
- No person above the age of 60 is allowed to work in any central government departments—i.e., the mandatory retirement age is 60.

VII. OCCUPATIONAL SAFETY AND HEALTH AND WORKERS' COMPENSATION

A. Occupational Safety and Health

1. *Safety*

The Factories Act, 1948 under Sections 21 to 40 lays down provisions regarding the safety measures to be exercised at the workplace. These measures apply to:

- Fencing of machinery
- Work on or near machinery in motion
- Employment of young persons using dangerous machines
- Striking gear[36] and devices for cutting off power
- Self-acting machines[37]
- Casings of machinery
- Prohibition of employment of women and children near cotton-openers
- Hoists and lifts
- Lifting machines, chains, ropes, and lifting tackles
- Revolving machinery
- Pressurized machinery
- Floors, stairs, and means of access
- Pits, sumps, openings in floors, etc.
- Lifting excessive weight
- Protection of eyes
- Precautions against dangerous fumes, gases, etc.
- Precautions regarding use of portable electric lights
- Explosive or inflammable dust, gas, etc.
- Precautions in case of fire, including safe means of escape for all persons in the event of a fire and the necessary equipment and facilities for extinguishing fire.

The Ministry of Labour ensures compliance with the provisions of this legislation. Under legislation enacted by the central government, state governments must act as enforcement agencies, overseeing compliance with the provisions of this legislation. Further power has been delegated to the state government to frame rules to carry out the purpose of this legislation. Inspectors appointed by the state government carry out inspections. In particular:

- If it appears to the inspector that any building or part of a building or any part of the ways, machinery, or plant in a

[36]A mechanical appliance that moves driving belts and pulleys for conveyor belts, etc.

[37]Automated machines performing various activities in a sequential order.

factory is in such a condition that it may be dangerous to human life or safety, the inspector may serve the occupier[38] or manager, or both, of the factory an order in writing requiring said individual(s) before a specified date (a) to furnish drawings, specifications, and other particulars necessary to determine whether the building, ways, machinery, or plant can be used with safety, or (b) to carry out a test in a manner that may be specified in the order, and to inform the inspector of the results.

- If it appears to an inspector that any building or part of a building or any part of the ways, machinery, or plant in a factory is in such a condition that it is dangerous to human life or safety, the inspector may serve on the occupier or manager, or both, of the factory an order in writing specifying the measures that in the inspector's opinion should be adopted, and may require those measures to be carried out before a specified date or prohibit the building's continued use.
- If it appears to an inspector that any building or part of a building in a factory is in such a state of disrepair as is likely to lead to conditions detrimental to the health and welfare of the workers, the inspector may serve on the occupier or manager, or both, of the factory an order in writing specifying the measures that in the inspector's opinion should be taken and may require compliance before a date specified in the order.

In the event of a violation of any provision of the Factories Act or rules made thereunder, both the occupier and the manager of the factory face imprisonment for up to two years or a fine of up to one lakh[39] rupees, or both. If the violation continues after conviction, a further fine may be imposed of up to 1,000 rupees for each day the violation continues.

---

[38]The "occupier" of a factory is the person who has ultimate control over the affairs of the factory. The occupier may or may not be the actual owner of the factory. The term may include any individual partner in the case of a firm/association of persons and a director in the case of a company.

[39]A "lakh" is a term for one hundred thousand.

In factories in which 1,000 or more workers are ordinarily employed or in which, in the opinion of the government, any manufacturing process or operation is carried on that involves risk of bodily injury, poisoning, disease, or any other health hazard to the workers, the government may require the occupier of the factory to employ safety officers in the number the government specifies.

According to the Apprentices Act, 1961, if any apprentices are undergoing training in a factory, the provisions regarding their safety will be the same as for employees of a factory under the Factories Act.

2. *Health*

Sections 11 to 20 of the Factories Act require various safety provisions, including those relating to:

- Cleanliness
- Disposal of wastes and effluents
- Ventilation and temperature
- Dust and fumes
- Artificial humidification
- Overcrowding
- Lighting
- Drinking water
- Latrines and urinals
- Spittoons.

Health provisions under various other labor laws, such as the Contract Labour (Regulation and Abolition) Act, 1970, and the Apprentices Act, 1961, are similar to those in the Factories Act.

As in the case of safety requirements, inspectors appointed by the state government are authorized to inspect workplace facilities for compliance with safety requirements.

B. Workers' Compensation

The Workmen's Compensation Scheme was established by the Workmen's Compensation Act, 1923 and is administered by the Ministry of Labour. Under this Act, workers in a broad range of industries and economic sectors are eligible for compensation for injury due to an accident. Workers may choose coverage under either this Act or the Employees' State Insurance Act, 1948 (discussed in VIII.B.2, below) where both acts are applicable, depending on whichever scheme will provide them greater benefits.

The Workmen's Compensation Scheme is an employer liability scheme. All employers are required to obtain workers' compensation insurance for all workers in their employ, unless they have been exempted from doing so.

Under the Act, the employer is obligated to:

- Provide a safe place of work, including a safe means of access,
- Employ competent workers,
- Provide and maintain adequate equipment, and
- Provide a safe system of work.

The Act provides for payment of compensation by employers to certain categories of workers and their dependents in case of personal injury caused to workers by an accident arising out of and in the course of employment, or for death or disablement (either total or partial, temporary or permanent). The Act also provides for payment of compensation to workers who contract an occupational disease peculiar to the type of employment concerned, subject to conditions mentioned in the Act.

If personal injury is caused to a worker by an accident arising out of and in the course of the worker's employment, the employer is liable to pay compensation in accordance with the provisions of the legislation, except in cases where the injury is caused by the worker's own fault.

The amount of compensation is established as follows:

- Where death results from the injury, an amount equal to (a) 50 percent of the monthly wages of the deceased worker multiplied by the "relevant factor,"[40] or (b) an amount of

[40]The "relevant factor" is the age of the worker on his or her last birthday before date on which the compensation fell due.

80,000 rupees, whichever is more, plus the payment noted at the end of this section;

- Where permanent total disability results, an amount equal to either (a) 60 percent of the monthly wages of the injured worker multiplied by the "relevant factor,"[41] or (b) an amount of 90,000 rupees, whichever is more.
- Where permanent partial disability results from the injury, (i) In the case of an injury specified in the prescribed list, such percentage of the compensation that would have been payable in the case of permanent total disability and specified as being the percentage of the loss of earning capacity caused by the injury; and
(ii) In the case of an injury not on the prescribed list, such percentage of the compensation payable in the case of permanent total disability as is proportionate to the loss of earning capacity (as assessed by a qualified medical practitioner) permanently caused by the injury;
- Where temporary disability, whether total or partial, results from the injury, a half-monthly payment of the sum equivalent to 25 percent of monthly wages of the worker must be paid.

If the injury of the worker results in his or her death, the employer shall, in addition to the compensation outlined above, deposit a sum of 2,500 rupees for payment (a) to the eldest surviving dependent of the worker to defray funeral expenses, or (b) where the worker did not have a dependent or was not living with a dependent at the time of death, for payment to the person who actually incurred such expenditure.

The Act is administered by the state governments through their commissioners for workers' compensation. The commissioners are entrusted with:

- the settling of disputed claims,
- the disposal of claims arising out of death, and
- the revision of periodic payment schedules.

---

[41] *Id.*

VIII. PENSIONS AND BENEFITS

A. Introduction

In India, the term "social security" is generally used in its broadest sense, to cover all types of measures, whether preventive, proactive, or protective. The term thus encompasses social insurance, social assistance, social protection, the social safety net, and other measures. Social security thus is the protection given by society to its members against contingencies of modern life, such as sickness, unemployment, old age, disability, and industrial accidents.

Social security has been recognized under the Constitution as the basic fundamental right of the citizen of India. Article 41 of the Constitution states that, "the State shall within the limits of its economic capacity and development, make effective provision for securing the right to work, to education and to public assistance in cases of unemployment, old age, sickness and disablement and in other cases of undeserved want."

Social security is offered in the following areas:

- Medical care
- Sickness benefit
- Old age benefits
- Unemployment benefits
- Employment injury benefits
- Family benefit
- Maternity benefit
- Invalidity benefits (benefits to invalids) and
- Survivors' benefits

The following social security schemes (systems) are in operation in India:

1) The Workmen's Compensation Act, 1923
2) The Employees' State Insurance Act, 1948
3) The Employees' Provident Funds Act, 1952
4) The Maternity Benefit Act, 1961
5) The Employees' Pension Scheme, 1995

6) The Payment of Gratuity Act, 1972
7) The Employees Deposit Linked Insurance Scheme, 1976

However, coverage under the schemes is restricted to certain categories of employees in the organized sector[42] of the workforce, to government employees, quasi-government employees, and industrial workers. These benefits are not available to workers in unorganized sectors of the workforce.

Other caveats are in order concerning these schemes:

- The benefits offered under the various schemes are inadequate. In particular, pension benefits under the Employees' State Insurance Act, 1948 and under the Employees' Pension Scheme, 1995 are very inadequate and do not meet the needs of insured persons.
- A multiplicity of schemes targeting the same group of employees has created duplication in organizational set-up and enforcement machinery and has increased the cost of administration.
- Administration of the schemes is corrupt and lethargic.
- There is no comprehensive social security scheme covering all eventualities from birth to death.

B. Laws Implementing Social Security Schemes

The primary provisions of the various laws implementing the schemes are discussed below.

1. The Workmen's Compensation Act, 1923

Workers may choose coverage under either the Workmen's Compensation Act (see VII.B., above) or the Employees' State Insurance Act (discussed in 2., below), depending on whichever scheme will provide them greater benefits.

---

[42]The term "organized sector" refers to the part of the economy involving large establishments carrying on production and manufacturing activities in a systematic manner, where workers generally are represented by unions.

2. *The Employees' State Insurance Act, 1948*

The Employees' State Insurance Act, 1948 (ESI Act) provides medical benefits to employees and unemployment insurance during their illness. It also provides benefits to dependents. Workers may choose coverage under either this Act or the Workmen's Compensation Act (discussed in VIII.B.1., above) where both acts are applicable, depending on whichever scheme will provide them greater benefits.

a. *Benefits*

Employees covered under the ESI Act and their dependents are entitled to the following benefits:

- Sickness
- Maternity
- Disablement
- Dependents
- Funeral

The benefits are in the form of cash payments in the case of sickness, maternity, or employment injury, and in the form of a pension for dependents of workers who die of an employment-related injury. Maternity benefits are similar to those under the Maternity Benefit Act, 1961, discussed under 6., below, which covers a class of working women who are not covered under the ESI Act.

b. *Coverage*

Section 38 of the ESI Act makes it mandatory for all employees in factories and establishments[43] to be insured under the Act.

---

[43]An "Establishment" means any premises, not being the premises of a factory or a shop, wherein any trade, business, manufacture or any incidental work there is carried on for profit and includes a premises wherein journalistic or printing work, banking, insurance, stocks and shares, brokerage or produce exchange is carried on. It also includes premises used as theaters or cinemas or for any other public amusement to which the Factories Act, 1948 does not apply.

The Act covers all employees—manual, clerical, or supervisory, and employees engaged by or through contractors—whose remuneration does not exceed 7,500 rupees a month. A 1966 amendment expanded the definition of covered employees to make it broad enough to include administrative staff and persons engaged in purchase of raw materials or sale or distribution of products and related functions. The Act also applies to the following:

- Nonseasonal factories using power[44] and employing 10 or more persons, and
- Nonseasonal factories not using power and establishments employing 20 or more persons.

The appropriate government entity (state or central) is empowered to extend the provisions of the ESI Act to various classes of establishments—industrial, commercial, agricultural, or otherwise in nature. Under these enabling provisions, most of the state governments have extended the ESI Act to certain specific classes of establishments, such as shops, hotels, restaurants, cinemas, preview theatres, motor transport undertakings, and newspaper and advertising establishments, employing 20 or more persons.

Money in the Employees' State Insurance Fund is to be expended only for the following purposes:

- Payment of benefits and provision of medical treatment and medical attendance to insured persons and, where the medical benefit is extended to their families, provision of such benefit in accordance with the provisions of the ESI Act and defraying the charges and costs in connection therewith;
- Payment of fees and allowances to members of the Employees' State Insurance Corporation (ESIC) set up under the Act, the standing committee constituted to administer the affairs of the ESIC, the medical benefit council, the regional boards, local committees, and regional and local medical benefit councils; and

[44]"Power" is defined as electrical energy or any other form of energy that is mechanically transmitted.

- Payment of salaries, leave allowances and joining time (hiring bonus) allowances, traveling and compensatory allowances, gratuities and compassionate allowances, pensions, and contributions to provident or other benefit funds, for officers and servants of the ESIC, and meeting expenditures for offices and other services set up for the purpose of giving effect to the provisions of this Act.

c. *Funding*

Contributions are made both by the employer and the employee. All contributions paid under the Act and all other money received on behalf of the ESIC are to be paid into the ESI Fund.

Under the ESI Act, contributions to the fund are made by the employer at the rate of 4.75 percent of the total wages paid to the employee, and by the employee at the rate of 1.75 percent of wages for every wage period. Contributions are to be paid into the fund account on or before the 21st of the month following the calendar month in which the wages are due. Interest is payable at 15 percent per annum for each day of default or delay. Advance payments can also be made into the fund.

3. *The Employees' Provident Funds and Miscellaneous Provisions Act, 1952*

The main objective of the Employees' Provident Funds and Miscellaneous Provisions Act, 1952 (EPF Act) is to ensure there is a compulsory provident fund, family pension fund, and deposit-linked insurance scheme in factories and other establishments for the benefit of employees. It is a central Act and extends to all of India except the state of Jammu and Kashmir.

a. *Benefits*

The provident fund makes a payment to the employee at the time of his or her retirement or, in case of death of an employee before retirement, payment is made to members of the employee's family of the amount the employee had accumulated in the fund at the time of death.

b. Coverage

The Act applies to factories that employ 20 or more persons and are engaged in the manufacture of items listed in schedule I of the Act. Apart from factories, the Act also applies to other establishments employing 20 or more persons, and also to such establishments that the central government may specify by notification in the *Official Gazette*. The Act does not apply to individuals with wages above 6,500 rupees per month.

c. Funding

The EPF involves a contributory scheme. The employee has to contribute 10 percent (or 12 percent in the case of establishments or classes of establishments that the central government may specify in the *Official Gazette*) of basic wages plus dearness allowance (regional cost-of-living allowance); excluded from the calculation are other allowances and the cash value of any food concession. The employer has to make an equal contribution.

4. Employees' Deposit-Linked Insurance Scheme, 1976

a. Coverage

This scheme applies to the employees of all factories and other establishments to which the Employees' Provident Funds and Miscellaneous Provisions Act, 1952 (discussed in 3., above) applies.

b. Benefits

On the death, while employed, of an employee who is a member of the Employees' Provident Funds, the claimant will be paid an additional amount equal to the average balance in the provident fund account of the deceased during the preceding 12 months, restricted to a maximum amount of 60,000 rupees.

c. Funding

Employees are not required to contribute to the insurance fund. Employers are required to contribute at the rate of 0.5 percent of the pay of each employee who is a provident fund member. The central government also contributes to the fund an amount equivalent to one-half of the amount of the employers' contribution.

5. *The Employees' Pension Scheme, 1995*

Private and public pension schemes are established for various employees in India under the Employees' Pension Scheme, 1995. The implementing agency for each scheme is different, but most of the schemes are essentially similar in the way they operate.

a. *Benefits*

The schemes provide benefits in the form of monthly retirement pensions, disability pensions, widows' pension, children's pension, and orphans' pension. In some cases, the pension may be paid in installments, called an "uncommuted pension"; in others, it may be paid in a lump sum, called a "commuted pension" (i.e., a pension with a right of commutation). Nominee pensions[45] are allowed.

b. *Coverage*

This scheme applies to employees of all factories and other establishments to which the Employees' Provident Funds and Miscellaneous Provisions Act, 1952 applies.

c. *Funding*

The employer makes a contribution of 8.33 percent of each of its employee's pay (i.e., the basic wages plus dearness allowance and retention allowances,[46] if any). As an exception, the cen-

---

[45]A nominee pension is a mechanism for payment of pensions to a third party (the "nominee") in the event of the death of a member of the scheme who is unmarried or without any eligible family member to receive the pension.

[46]Retention allowances are additional payments made to employees who possess unusually high or unique qualifications, making it essential for the employer to retain the employee.

tral government contributes to the pension fund for its employees at the rate of 1.16 percent of the pay of each employee.

6. The Maternity Benefit Act, 1961

The Maternity Benefit Act, 1961 was passed with a view to providing maternity benefits to women not already covered by the ESI Act discussed in 2., above. There is no statutory provision for paternity leave. The central government (but not state governments) has started to provide 15 days of paternity leave, and some multinational companies have also adopted the practice.

Under the Act, the employer must:

- pay maternity benefits in the form of paid leave and possibly a medical bonus as discussed under a., below;
- allow maternity leave and nursing breaks for female employees;
- refrain from dismissing or discharging a pregnant employee/new mother/woman who has had a miscarriage during her period of maternity leave;
- post the abstract (notice) of the provisions of the Act clearly and conspicuously in the local language in establishments where women are employed;
- prepare and maintain the prescribed registers, records, and muster rolls and submit the prescribed government returns (reports).

Employers also are obligated:

- not to knowingly employ a woman during the six weeks immediately following the day of delivery or miscarriage (women are prohibited from working in any establishment during this period); and
- not to require a pregnant employee to do arduous work involving long hours of standing, nor any work likely to interfere with her pregnancy or to cause miscarriage or to affect her health adversely, for one month preceding the period of six weeks before the expected date of her delivery.

a. Benefits

The Act provides for payment of a cash maternity benefit (paid leave) for a fixed period of absence, of a medical bonus, for nursing breaks, and other benefits.

Paid maternity leave at full salary must be provided for up to 12 weeks. Of this time, six weeks must be taken prior to the date of delivery of the child, and six weeks must be taken immediately following that date. The mother-to-be is not supposed to work anywhere else during this time.

To avail herself of the six weeks of leave before expected delivery, a woman must provide notice in writing stating the date of absence from work, together with a certificate of pregnancy. The employer must pay the maternity benefit (i.e., six weeks' worth of wages) for this period in advance to the worker or to any other person she nominates.

To obtain the six weeks of leave from the date of delivery, the woman must send another notice to the employer, together with a certificate of delivery after the child is born. The employer must pay the employee or her nominee the maternity benefits (i.e., six weeks' worth of wages) within 48 hours of receiving this notice. Failure to give notice concerning the second six-week period does not disqualify a woman from receiving this maternity benefit. In the case of a miscarriage, a woman is entitled to this second six weeks of leave with pay from the day of the miscarriage. In this case too she must give notice to the employer, together with a certificate of miscarriage. If a woman has not used the full six weeks of leave before the expected date of her delivery, she is entitled to use the balance after delivery, provided that the total leave period does not exceed 12 weeks.

Women who do not have prenatal care provided free of charge by the employer are also entitled to a medical bonus of 250 rupees.

b. Coverage

The Act applies to every factory, mine, plantation, shop, or establishment in which 10 or more persons are employed or were employed on any day of the preceding 12 months, except that it does not apply to factories or establishments to which the provisions of the ESI Act apply; this is because the ESI Act contains a similar provision for maternity benefits.

To be entitled to maternity leave, a woman must have actually worked in an establishment for at least 80 days in the 12 months immediately preceding the expected day of her delivery. Only work days (not weekly holidays or paid or unpaid leave days) are taken into account in calculating the work days.

c. Funding

This benefit is paid entirely by the employer, with no employee contribution.

7. The Payment of Gratuity Act, 1972

The Act provides for payment of a gratuity, usually given to employees on retirement, resignation, or death while employed. The Act provides financial support to the employee at the time of retirement and to surviving members of the family in cases of death. This payment plays a significant role in India, where income levels generally are low.

Payment of this gratuity is required of all employers to whom the Gratuity Act is applicable.

To ensure compliance, the employer is required to submit a notice of opening an establishment in the prescribed form to the controlling authority of the area, providing the name and address of the establishment, employer, nature of business, and so forth.

a. Benefits

The employer is required to ensure that the amount of the gratuity to be paid is accurately ascertained. The gratuity is to be calculated at the rate of 15 days' worth of wages (i.e., terminal basic pay plus dearness allowance) for each completed year of service or part thereof in excess of six months. The 15 days' worth salary has to be calculated by dividing the salary earned in the final period by 26 days (not 30 days), then multiplying by 15, and then multiplying by the number of years.

The employer must arrange to pay the amount of the gratuity within 30 days from the date it becomes payable, failing which the employer is required to pay the gratuity along with interest from the date it was payable to the date on which it is paid, calculated at the rate specified by the central government

b. Coverage

The Act applies to every factory, mine, oilfield, plantation, railway company, shop, or establishment employing 10 or more persons on any day of the preceding 12 months, and to other establishments or classes of establishments where 10 or more persons are employed during the same period, when the central government has provided notice in the *Official Gazette* to the establishments of their coverage under the Act.

It covers all employees, whether doing skilled, semi-skilled, unskilled, manual, technical, clerical, supervisory, managerial, or administrative work, irrespective of wage level. It excludes any person who holds a post under the central government or a state government and who is covered under any other gratuity act or by any rules providing for payment of a gratuity.

The gratuity is payable to an employee upon termination of employment after continuous service of at least five years, on superannuation (reaching the age of mandatory retirement as fixed in the terms of service or employment contract), upon retirement under other circumstances, upon resignation, or upon death or disablement due to accident or disease.

In the case of death, an employer is liable to pay the gratuity to the legal heirs/nominees of the deceased employee even if the employee had not completed five years of service.

c. Funding

In order to ensure guaranteed payment of the gratuity, the Act provides for compulsory insurance of the liability with the Life Insurance Corporation. As a result, the cost of this benefit to employers is reduced. In addition, in the event of an employee's death, irrespective of the length of service, the Act provides for insuring the gratuity from the time of death to what would have been the employee's normal retirement age, subject to an overall ceiling of 3.5 lakh (350,000) rupees.

IX. IMMIGRATION

A decade of immigration liberalization has seen a large inflow into India of foreign workers with work contracts. Many of these immigrants are employees of foreign companies or multinational corporations with operations in India. They are either nationals of the country in which the company's home office is located, or they may be from another country in the case of multinationals.

There are no legislative restrictions as such on the type of skills that workers must possess in order to work in India, nor is there any restriction on the number of foreign workers who may be brought into India. However, under central government policy, an employment visa is required of foreign workers, and employment visas are issued only to foreigners who are skilled professionals and are engaged by companies, organizations, and economic undertakings as technicians, technical experts, senior executives, and the like. Applicants are required to submit proof of contract/employment/engagement by the company or organization in India.

In India, there are two principal pieces of legislation governing the use of foreign workers: The Foreigners Act, 1946 and the Registration of Foreigners Act, 1939.

These laws prescribe certain formalities regarding registration, movement, and departure of foreigners in India. Under these laws, the Indian government has unfettered powers to regulate and restrict the movement and presence of foreigners in India. The power to grant or refuse permission to foreigners to enter India, or to restrict employment subsequent to entry into India, are provided in the Foreigners Order, 1948, issued by the central government in the exercise of powers conferred by Section 3 of the Foreigners Act, 1946.

The immigration authority can refuse a foreigner entry into India if he or she does not possess a valid passport, is insane, is suffering from any infectious disease, has been convicted of an offense that would qualify for extradition, or if his or her entry is prejudicial to the interest of the country.

A. Work Sectors Prohibited to Foreigners

No foreigner may, without the permission in writing of the civil authority, either enter any premises relating to or accept employment in, any industry or area that is prohibited to foreigners. This includes military defense industry and areas such as the following: the whole of the union territory of Andaman and Nicobar Islands, the whole of the states of Arunachal Pradesh, Manipur, Mizoram, and Nagaland; and parts of the states of Sikkim, Himachal Pradesh, and Rajasthan. See also G., below, concerning restrictions on the movement of foreigners.

B. Permission Process for Indian Employers

Employers who intend to employ foreign employees must comply with certain legislative requirements. The government authorities dealing with issues relating to expatriate employment in India are the Ministry of Home Affairs and the Reserve Bank of India (RBI).

In general, employers of foreign workers in India must satisfy the following conditions:

- Indian companies may engage the services of foreign nationals without any approval from the government if the period of stay in India is less than three months. However, prior approval of the Ministry of Home Affairs is required for engagements lasting more than three months. The total duration of engagement of foreign nationals by an Indian company should not exceed 12 months.
- When prior approval is required, the employer needs to prepare and send to the prospective employee a contract letter and other documentation to enable the individual to apply for an employment visa.
- The employer must also sponsor the foreign employee and his or her dependents for the required registration.
- Indian companies employing foreigners are required to file returns indicating the number of foreigners and the number of Indians employed in different salary grades.

C. Visa Process for Foreign Workers

Usually, the employer in India who offers an employment opportunity to a foreign worker initiates the visa application process in India. Alternatively, the applicant may apply to the Indian embassy or high commission in the applicant's country of residence. In both cases, the following documents are required:

1. Recent photographs;
2. Proof of employment—i.e., appointment/contract letter, terms and conditions of employment, etc.;
3. Copy of contract with concerned Indian company;
4. Cover/request letter from the company;
5. A form known as an "undertaking" (see Appendix); and
6. A valid passport.

As regards visa requirements for a foreign worker's family and dependents, such individuals planning to join the foreign worker in living in India must apply for entry visas along with the foreign worker. Accompanying spouses must obtain their own employment visas in order to work in India. Children must obtain student visas to attend school in India.

D. Registration of Foreigners

Under the Registration of Foreigners Act, 1939, all foreigners and their dependents (including those of Indian origin) are required to register with the concerned District Foreigners Registration Officer/Foreigners Regional Registration Officer (FRRO), within 14 days of their first arrival in India, if they hold a visa for a period of more than 180 days. Upon registration, they will be issued a residence permit. An exception from the registration requirements is made for foreigners covered under special categories (mentioned below).

The following documents are required of foreign workers at the time of registration with the Foreigners Registration Officers (FROs) in India:

i) Photocopy of the passport and initial visa;
ii) Four photographs of the applicant;
iii) Details of residence in India;
iv) For individuals 15 to 60 years old on a visa for more than one year, an HIV test report from one of the World Health Organization-recognized institutions;
v) For dependents attending school in India on a student visa, bona-fide certificate from the university/college/institution;
vi) For board-level appointees in limited companies, approval of the Department of Company Affairs;
vii) For a joint venture or collaboration, two copies of the approval of the government of India;
viii) For a business/joint venture, etc., a copy of permission from the Reserve Bank of India;
ix) Terms and conditions of appointments and copy of contracts or agreements; and
x) An "undertaking" (see Appendix) from the concerned Indian company.

E. Obtaining a Registration Certificate/Residential Permit

Upon registration, the FRRO issues a foreign national a registration certificate/residential permit. A valid residential permit or certificate is also considered a valid work permit. The residential permit has the same validity as an employment visa. In general, residential permits may be extended upon application, but the permit cannot be extended further once the employment visa has expired.

Registration is required only once during the validity of an employment visa, irrespective of the number of times the foreigner leaves and returns to India, since an employment visa is a multiple-entry visa.

F. Approval of Remuneration of Foreign Nationals

The Reserve Bank of India (RBI) regulates the inflow and outflow of foreign exchange in India. While remitting remuneration to foreign nationals, the RBI, through authorized dealers, verifies with employers their compliance with the following requirements:

- The total duration of engagement of foreign nationals by the applicant firm or company does not exceed 12 months since, as noted under B., above, the total duration of engagement of foreign nationals by an Indian company should not exceed 12 months.
- The amount sought to be paid to the expatriate in foreign currency is in line with the sum specified in the employment contract.
- The services of the foreign national are not covered under any other contract in which such services are required to be rendered free of charge or remuneration.

Salaries for foreign workers may be paid in India or outside India, depending upon the entity with which the foreign worker has the employment contract.

G. Restrictions on Movement of Foreigners

The civil authority has powers to impose restrictions on the movement of any foreigner in India. Military installations and areas, defense organizations, and research organizations are considered protected areas. Foreigners can visit restricted or protected areas only after getting a valid permit for such a purpose; a visa alone is not sufficient to permit access to such places. Permits to visit such areas generally are not given to foreigners.

H. Employment Termination Law Governing Foreigners

As a rule, laws on termination that govern Indian citizens are also applicable to foreign nationals in India, as are all criminal and civil laws governing Indian citizens, except for certain constitutional privileges.

I. Departure from India

All visitors holding a registration certificate must obtain, before departure, an exit endorsement from the registration officer of the district in which they were registered. Prior to their final departure from India, every foreigner must surrender their certificate of registration either to the registration officer of the place where they registered or of the place from which they intend to depart, or to the immigration officer at the port/checkpost of exit from India. If the certificate is surrendered to other than the immigration officer at the port/checkpost of exit, the foreigner should produce for the immigration officer at the port/checkpost of exit the receipt indicating surrender of the document.

All foreign nationals, except nationals of Bhutan and Nepal, leaving India by air, road, or rail must fill out an embarkation card at the time of departure.

Appendix

Undertaking Form for Indian Companies Employing Foreign Workers

On letterhead of the
Indian organization

UNDERTAKING

"We take full responsibility for the activities and conduct of Mr. / Mrs._____________ (Full Name), national of_____________ (Country) during his/her stay in India. If anything adverse against him/her comes to our notice during the period, we undertake to repatriate him/her at our cost."

-/S/-

SINGAPORE*

INTRODUCTION

A. Work Force of Singapore

Originally founded by the British in 1819 and declared independent from Malaysia in 1965, Singapore is a diverse city-state of about 4.2 million people. The citizen and permanent resident population, numbering about 3.4 million, is made up largely of Chinese, Malays, Indians, and Eurasians. English, Mandarin, Malay, and Tamil are the official languages. With a motivated workforce and a high literacy rate of 94 percent, Singapore workers have been highly rated in productivity. Three factors are primarily responsible for the high productivity of the Singapore workforce, as elaborated below: high wages; stable labor-management relations; and a governmental focus on retraining and education. Ultimately, these three factors have helped Singapore make the transition from an imperial colony to an independent economic powerhouse.

- Workers in Singapore are more highly paid than in most other developing and newly industrialized countries in East Asia. This was influenced by Singapore's high economic growth during the 1980s and 1990s, a relatively low unemployment rate (the current unemployment rate is about 4.5 percent), the tripartite National Wages Council that reviews and establishes wage guidelines on an annual basis,[1] and a national policy focused on linking productivity to wages and utilizing variable compensation systems. However, the

---

*Cheong Min Lee, Partner, Rodyk & Davidson, Singapore. This chapter is current through March 15, 2004.

[1]See V.A.1., below.

economic recession since the late 1990s has tempered the growth in wages. The government is encouraging employers to move away from rigid and seniority-based wage systems to a more flexible competitive base wage system. It is recommended that the competitive base wage system comprise a basic wage and a variable component (monthly as well as annual) substantial enough for employers to make quick adjustments according to changes in the business environment. This is designed to save jobs in a downturn and enable employees to benefit from higher wages in good times.[2] The intention of the recommended changes is to give more flexibility to employers to base employee rewards on the value of their jobs, their contribution, productivity, and the performance of the employer.

- Labor-management relations in Singapore are particularly stable. Although workers do have the legal right to strike, Singapore's high wages and job security provide little incentive for disrupting production. There has been only one strike since 1986, and Singapore has a flexible dispute resolution process.
- Singapore's government also provides incentives to enhance workers' skills and knowledge. The Lifelong Learning Endowment Fund, established in 2001,[3] operates in tandem with a network of government-supported programs to foster an environment where workers are encouraged to constantly improve their skills in order to stave off the effects of competition from the cheaper, but less skilled, labor markets available in the rest of Asia. In addition, the Skills Development Fund,[4] which is funded by a levy on employers and other government contributions, is used to subsidize the upgrading of skills by current members of the workforce, as well as those who are preparing to join or rejoin the workforce.

---

[2]See the recommendations contained in the Report of the Tripartite Taskforce on Wage Restructuring, issued in January 2004, available on the website of the Ministry of Manpower at <www.mom.gov.sg>.

[3]See VIII.C., below.

[4]See VIII.C., below.

B. Structure of Singapore's Government

Under its Constitution,[5] Singapore is a republic with a parliamentary system of government, similar to that of the United Kingdom.

1. President

The President of Singapore serves a six-year term and acts as the head of state.[6] Although the President traditionally functioned as a figurehead rather than a policymaker, the Constitution has been amended to provide the President's office with more powers, including some control over budget issues and internal security matters as well as legislative and judicial appointments.[7] Pursuant to these changes in Singapore's constitutional structure, the President of Singapore is now elected by direct election.[8] Unlike most elected heads of state, the President of Singapore is required to be non-partisan.[9] A person who wishes to run for the presidency is required to resign any affiliation with a political party.

2. Parliament

The legislative power of Singapore is vested in the Parliament. The Parliament consists of 84 elected and up to 10 non-elected Members of Parliament (MPs). 84 MPs are elected in direct, constituency-based, "first past the post" elections, on the British model. Of the non-elected MPs, up to six (as the legislature may provide) may be appointed from political parties not forming the government. These are known as non-constituency MPs (NCMPs). The President also may appoint another nine persons to be Nominated Members of Parliament (NMPs). The NCMPs and the NMPs enjoy the same privileges as the popularly elected MPs, but are restricted from voting on matters pertaining to the Constitution or the expenditure of funds.[10]

---

[5]CONSTITUTION OF THE REPUBLIC OF SINGAPORE, promulgated 1963, as amended (CONST.).

[6]*Id.* arts. 17, 20.

[7]*Id.* pt. V, arts. 22, 22A–22P.

[8]*Id.* art. 17.

[9]*Id.* art. 19(2)(f).

[10]*Id.* art. 39.

Elected MPs, NCMPs, and NMPs serve five-year fixed terms; the maximum term of any one session of Parliament also is five years. The Prime Minister is the leader of the political party holding a majority of seats in Parliament. The People's Action Party (PAP) has held the majority of Singapore's Parliament seats since 1966. In the 2001 elections, two members of the Opposition were returned as MPs. Under the NCMP scheme, another member of the Opposition also became an NCMP.

3. *Judicial System*

Singapore's judicial system is similar to that of the United Kingdom. It has a unified judicial system with, in ascending order of authority, the subordinate courts, the High Court, and the Court of Appeal.

- The subordinate courts include the Magistrate's and District Courts. Magistrate's Courts have jurisdiction over disputed claims not exceeding S$60,000.[11] District Courts have jurisdiction over claims not exceeding S$250,000 except in proceedings for probate or administration of the estate of a deceased person, where the claim limit is higher.[12]
- The High Court has jurisdiction over most criminal and civil cases, and appellate jurisdiction over the subordinate courts.[13] The High Court also hears appeals from the Commission of Labour's decisions in employment disputes.[14]
- The Court of Appeal has appellate jurisdiction over the High Court.[15]

In addition, the Industrial Arbitration Courts (IAC), provided for by the Industrial Relations Act, have jurisdiction over all disputes related to trade unions.[16] The IACs are composed of the President of the IAC (appointed by the President of Singapore with

[11]Subordinate Courts Act [Cap 321] (SCA) §2.
[12]*Id.*
[13]Supreme Court of Judicature Act [Cap 322] (SCJA) §§15, 16, 17, 19, 20, 21.
[14]Employment Act [Cap 91] §117.
[15]SJCA §29A.
[16]See I.D. and II.G., below.

advice from the Prime Minister) and one representative from each of two panels, one consisting of 10 employer representatives, the other consisting of 10 employee representatives.

There also are other alternative dispute resolution procedures available to parties in relation to commercial transactions and matters: namely, arbitration by the Singapore International Arbitration Center and other commercial arbitrators, as well as mediation provided by the Singapore Mediation Center, or as agreed between the parties.

C. Singapore's Economy

Although its only significant natural resource is its deepwater harbor, Singapore is a thriving business and financial center. Singapore's economic success is due largely to its business environment. Not only does it possess a strategic geographical location, but it also has an industrious and well-educated workforce and the ability to entice major investments and trade agreements from the United States, Japan, and the European Union countries. Singapore has a well-established double-taxation treaty infrastructure with its major trading partners, with the notable exception of the United States. However, in May 2002, Singapore signed a free trade agreement with the United States[17] (USFTA) that is now effective and makes it attractive for businesses exporting to the United States to locate in Singapore, and for existing exporters to expand their activities in Singapore. It is anticipated that the USFTA, as well as Singapore's other free trade agreements with Japan, New Zealand, Australia, and the European Free Trade Association, will result in economic benefits and create more jobs in Singapore. Singapore is actively pursuing free trade agreements with, among others, the People's Republic of China and the Association of South East Asian Nations (ASEAN), India, Korea, Mexico, Jordan, Sri Lanka, Panama, and Canada, and with New Zealand and Chile to form a Pacific Three (P3) Free Trade Agreement. In addition, Singapore has a distinct lack of foreign ownership restrictions,

---

[17]See the Introduction to the chapter on the United States in Part 2 of Volume I, at H.5.

exchange controls, or tariff barriers. Overall, Singapore has a stable government and the well-developed infrastructure that supports an efficient free enterprise market.

D. Sources of Singapore's Labor and Employment Laws

Labor and employment laws have played a pivotal role in Singapore's industrial and economic success. Singapore's labor and employment laws are based on the English common law relating to employers and employees, and statute. The key statutes include the following:

- the Employment Act,[18] which establishes the basic terms and conditions of employment;
- the Central Provident Fund Act,[19] which establishes a social security system; and
- the Workmen's Compensation Act,[20] which provides compensation for workplace injuries.

Other labor laws, including the Trade Unions Act,[21] the Industrial Relations Act,[22] and the Trade Disputes Act,[23] provide the procedural framework for collective bargaining and for the orderly resolution of union disputes through conciliation and arbitration. The Factories Act regulates conditions in the workplace,[24] while the Retirement Age Act[25] was passed to provide a minimum retirement age for employees. Finally, as noted above, the Lifelong Learning Endowment Fund Act[26] establishes a fund to be used in upgrading the skills of the Singapore labor force.

Singapore is an International Labor Organization (ILO) member.

[18]Employment Act [Cap 91]. See I., below.
[19]Central Provident Fund Act [Cap 36]. See VIII.A., below.
[20]Workmen's Compensation Act [Cap 354]. See VII.B., below.
[21]Trade Unions Act [Cap 333]. See II., below.
[22]Industrial Relations Act [Cap 136]. See II., below.
[23]Trade Disputes Act [Cap 331]. See II., below.
[24]Factories Act [Cap 104]. See VII.A., below.
[25]Retirement Age Act [Cap 274A]. See VI.A., below.
[26]Lifelong Learning Endowment Fund Act [Cap 162A]. See VIII.C., below.

I. INDIVIDUAL EMPLOYMENT

The Employment Act[27] sets out the basic rights of employers and employees. Other rights and obligations may arise under the common law, individual contracts of employment, and, if the employee is a member of a trade union, under a collective bargaining agreement negotiated by the union with the employer.[28]

The Employment Act generally covers all employees—an employee being defined as a person who works under a contract of service with an employer—but excludes from its ambit any seamen, domestic worker, any person employed in a managerial, executive, or confidential position, and any worker whom the Ministry of Manpower has exempted from the Act.[29] Terms of employment for employees not covered by the Employment Act generally are not less favorable than those contained in the Employment Act, although there are instances of employers giving less favorable terms to employees not covered by the Act. As the terms of employment for these employees are determined by contract rather than by statute, this technically is not illegal.

A. Contract Formation

The Employment Act presumes that an employment "contract for service" is at-will, although notice periods for termination are in effect, as discussed below.[30] Evidence of an express or implied contract can rebut the at-will presumption and create a contract that terminates on a specific date. The Employment Act does not require that employment contracts be in writing. Instead, a contract may be oral, express, or implied.[31]

As a general rule, the Employment Act provides employers and employees with considerable leeway in drafting employment agreements. However, any condition of employment that is "less favorable to an employee than any of the conditions of service prescribed by [the Employment] Act shall be illegal, null and void

---

[27]Employment Act [Cap 91].

[28]See II., below.

[29]Employment Act §2.

[30]See I.C., below.

[31]Employment Act §2.

to the extent that it is so less favorable."[32] In other words, the Employment Act sets minimum standards with respect to employees covered by the Act that the parties cannot avoid or circumvent by agreement.

B. Full-Time and Part-Time Workers

Employers and employees may create an employment contract that is either full-time or part-time. The Employment Act defines part-time employees as those workers who are (1) under a contract of service, and (2) required to work fewer than 30 hours per week.[33]

Employers may, of course, apportion wages according to the number of contractual hours worked in a year. In other respects, the Employment Act generally provides part-time employees with the same benefits and protections as full-time employees. However, the Minister of Manpower has the discretion to modify any of all provisions of the Employment Act to exclude part-time employees.[34]

The Employment (Part-Time) Employees Regulations provide formulas for calculating payments for part-time employees for work on a rest-day, overtime pay, and annual, sick, and maternity leave.

C. Termination

1. Termination for Cause

The Employment Act specifically provides that either party may end a contract of service with or without giving notice if there is either a "willful breach" of a contract condition or the employer is willing to pay the employee a sum of money.[35] An employee may stop working without notice if he or his dependent is immediately threatened by danger from violence or disease to which the employee never agreed.

---

[32] *Id.* §8.
[33] *Id.* §66A.
[34] *Id.* §66B.
[35] *Id.* §11.

If the employer alleges that an employee has acted in a manner inconsistent with the express or implied terms of the employment, then the employer must conduct an investigation of the matter prior to dismissal without notice.[36] During the period of investigation, the employer may suspend the employee for up to one week on half pay. Instead of dismissing the employee, the employer may suspend the employee for a period not exceeding one week without salary, or may downgrade the employee instantly. If the employer's inquiry does not disclose any employee misconduct, then the Employment Act allows the employee to recover any withheld wages.[37]

The Employment Act specifically defines certain employee conduct as justifying dismissal. In particular, a willful breach of any express or implied conditions of the employment agreement provides a basis for dismissal.[38] Similarly, a continuous unexcused absence from work for more than two days without prior notice or a reasonable excuse justifies firing an employee.[39] A "for cause" dismissal may occur without the approval of the employee's trade union (if any).

2. *Termination Without Cause*

For employees covered by the Employment Act, both employers and employees must follow the notice procedures outlined in the Act. Where notice is required, it must be in writing.[40] The mandatory minimum length of the notice period depends on how long a worker has been employed. If a contract for service is silent on the length of notice, the Employment Act requires the following minimum notice:

- one day's notice or one day's wages for employment of fewer than 26 weeks;
- one week's notice or one week's wages for employment between 26 weeks up to two years;

---

[36]*Id.* §14(1).
[37]*Id.* §14(9).
[38]*Id.* §11(2).
[39]*Id.* §13(2).
[40]*Id.* §10(5).

- two weeks' notice or two weeks' wages for employment from two to five years; and
- four weeks' notice or four weeks' wages if the employee has worked for more than five years.[41]

If the parties extend these notice periods by agreement, they then must comply with the increased time periods set forth in the contract. Termination procedures for employees outside the Employment Act are determined by the terms of the employment agreement, or, if it is silent, then on the common law, which requires reasonable notice.

D. Third-Party Resolution of Employment Disputes

Under the Employment Act, the Commissioner for Labour is given various powers. For example, the Commissioner may require any employer or class of employers to forward returns with respect to employees, payroll, and deductions,[42] and the Commissioner may enter and inspect any place of employment and make such inquiry into the salary and conditions of employment as he or she considers appropriate. Other powers include inquiring into and determining various types of disputes between an employer and an employee.

Disputes that the Commissioner is empowered to inquire into and determine include:

- salary claims due to the employee under any term in the contract of service or under any provision in the Employment Act (The Commissioner shall not hear any dispute with respect to matters arising more than a year preceding the lodging of the claim or the termination of the contract of service. If the claim arises out of a termination of the contract of service, the employee must lodge the claim with the Commissioner within six months of termination.);
- compliance by the new employer and the old employer in relation to the transfer of the old employer's business to the

[41] *Id.* §10(3).
[42] *Id.* §97–99.

new employer involving a transfer of the old employer's employees;[43]

- deductions that an employer may make from employees' salaries; and
- whether an employee can be compelled to work on a rest day.

The procedure for making and hearing of claims before the Commissioner is summarized below:

1. The claimant must file a memorandum at the Commissioner's office explaining the claim or must make a verbal claim to the Commissioner, who shall cause it to be reduced to writing.
2. Upon receipt of the claim and the appropriate registration fee (S$3 for a claim by an employee; S$20 for a claim by an employer), the Commissioner will summon the party against whom the claim is made, giving particulars of the claim, and summon any other person whose interests will likely be affected by the proceedings.
3. The other party may notify the Commissioner of any counterclaim.
4. Before hearing the claim, the Commissioner may hold a preliminary inquiry for the parties to decide on the terms of the claim, or for the settlement or withdrawal of the claim.
5. If the claim is not settled or withdrawn at the preliminary inquiry, the parties shall attend and state their case before the Commissioner, and may call evidence. The Commissioner will then give his or her decision.

In hearing claims, the Commissioner is not bound to act in a formal manner or be bound by rules of evidence, but shall act according to equity, good conscience, and the merits of the case without regard to technicalities.[44]

---

[43] *Id.* §18A. See IV.B., below.

[44] Employment Act §119.

In proceedings before the Commissioner, an employee may be represented by a trade union of which he or she is a member, and an employer may be represented by one of its employees, but neither party shall be represented by an attorney or paid agent.[45]

The decision or order of the Commissioner may be appealed to the High Court within 14 days. For the purpose of the appeal, the Commissioner's decision or order shall be deemed to be a decision of a District Court.[46] All orders made by the Commissioner shall be enforced by the District Court as if they are judgments of the District Court, notwithstanding that the amount or value of the order may be in excess of the ordinary jurisdiction of the court.[47]

Where an officer of the Ministry of Manpower, including the Commissioner, has reasonable grounds for believing that an offense under the Employment Act has been committed, or wishes to inquire into any matter for which provision is made by the Employment Act or any dispute as to such matter, or whenever any person complains to the Ministry of any breach of any provision of the Employment Act, the officer may compel any person who can give information on the subject matter of the inquiry or complaint to attend and answer truthfully any questions put to him or her with respect to such inquiry or complaint.[48]

If, upon inquiry, an offense appears to have been committed, the Commissioner may institute criminal proceedings in the Subordinate Courts.[49]

It should be noted that where an offense under the Employment Act is committed by a corporate body, and the offense is proved to have been committed with the consent or connivance of or is attributable to any act on the part of, any director, manager, company secretary, or similar officer of the corporate body, he or she as well as the corporate body shall be guilty of that offense and shall be liable to be prosecuted and punished accordingly.[50]

If the circumstances permit, the Commissioner also may institute civil proceedings for and in the name of the employee,

---

[45] *Id.* §120.
[46] *Id.* §117.
[47] *Id.* §118.
[48] *Id.* §124.
[49] *Id.* §129.
[50] *Id.* §113A.

against the employer or person liable for compensation.[51] In case a conviction is had or judgment given against the employer or person liable, the court fees shall be paid by the employer or person liable, along with the general costs of the proceedings.[52]

The Employment Act and the Industrial Relations Act provide employees with the right to challenge their dismissal through an administrative procedure before the Ministry of Manpower.[53] Under the procedure provided in the Employment Act, the employee may complain directly to the Minister of Manpower within one month of dismissal.

Under the Industrial Relations Act, the employee also can make representations to the Minister through his trade union (except with respect to dismissal because of union activities, which may be referred to the Industrial Arbitration Court for decision).

If the Minister determines that the employee was dismissed without just cause or excuse, the Minister can either direct reinstatement of the employee or require the employer to provide the employee with compensation. Employers that fail to comply with the Minister's orders can be liable for a fine not exceeding S$5,000, or for a prison term not greater than 12 months, or both.[54]

Following the amendment to the Industrial Relations Act in September 2002 discussed below, in limited circumstances a recognized rank-and-file trade union can assist a junior executive in making representations to the Minister with respect to his or her dismissal.[55]

Further details regarding the resolution of employment disputes with respect to unionized employees are discussed below.[56]

E. Privacy

There is no statutory right to privacy as such. The Employment Act does not provide for privacy protection for either the

---

[51]*Id.* §125.
[52]*Id.* §126.
[53]*Id.* §14; Industrial Relations Act [Cap 136] §35(3).
[54]Employment Act §14(7); Industrial Relations Act [Cap 136] §35(6), (8) and (10).
[55]See II.G., below.
[56]*Id.*

employer or the employee. The common law also has little to say about the protection of privacy.

However, it appears to be an implied term of the contract of employment that the employer will not, without reasonable and proper cause, conduct itself in such a manner calculated and likely to destroy or seriously damage the relationship of confidence and trust between the employer and employee, for example, the unauthorised disclosure or misuse of confidential information belonging to the employee. Likewise, an employee owes duties of good faith and fidelity to the employer, with an implied duty not to disclose or use the trade secrets or proprietary or confidential information of the employer, except for the employer's benefit.[57]

Some existing laws may be used or be interpreted in such a manner as to forbid employee monitoring in certain circumstances. For example, the Penal Code provides that anyone who, intending to insult the modesty of any woman, utters any word, makes any sound or gesture, or exhibits any object, intending that such word or sound shall be heard, or that such gesture or object shall be seen by such woman, or intrudes upon the privacy of such woman, shall have committed a criminal offense. This may deter an employer from installing surveillance equipment in, for example, women's restrooms.

It is possible that formal privacy legislation will eventually be enacted in Singapore, especially in view of an international trend of individual countries enacting laws to protect privacy and data confidentiality, targeting the collection, storage, and use of such information.[58] These countries may require reciprocal protection in Singapore for their citizens' privacy and data. However to date, there has been no legislation passed concerning protection of personal data.

F. Employee Duty of Loyalty, Trade Secrets, Covenants Not to Compete

The Employment Act does not cover employee's duties in relation to loyalty, trade secrets, or covenants not to compete. Such

---

[57]See I.F., below.

[58]See the discussion of the EU Data Privacy Directive in the chapter on European Union in Part 1 of Volume I, at I.C.

duties may be implied by the common law or must be specifically provided for in the employment contract.

1. Employee Duty of Loyalty

Notwithstanding the absence of specific obligations in the employment contract, the employee still has an implied duty to obey the employer's lawful and reasonable orders, to take care and be competent, and to act in good faith and with fidelity. The extent of the employee's duty of fidelity varies according to the position of the employee and the nature of the employment, and ultimately is a question of construction of the employment contract.

The employee is obliged to act in the best interests of the employer. The employee must not, for instance, abuse his or her position as an employee by making a secret profit (for example, a concealed commission or bribe), and should account to the employer for all benefits or property received from third parties and arising out of the employment. Information that the employee receives in the course of his or her employment that is relevant to the employer's business should be disclosed to the employer.

2. Trade Secrets

The employee's common-law duties of good faith and fidelity include the duty not to disclose the employer's confidential information or use such information except for the employer's benefit. The information can be recognized as confidential either because the employee is told it is confidential or because from its character, the information is obviously or reasonably to be known as confidential. Another test is whether substantial work was done to produce the information. If so, then such information would be valuable, and therefore confidential.

It also should be noted that the Companies Act prohibits an officer of the company (which includes any person employed in an executive capacity) from making improper use of any information acquired by virtue of his or her position as an officer to gain an advantage for himself or herself, or for any other person (other than the company), or to cause detriment to the company.

During employment, disclosure of the employer's confidential information would be a breach of the employee's duty of good faith and fidelity. After termination of employment, the common-law implied term of confidentiality imposed on the ex-employee is more restricted. The general principle is that an ex-employee cannot be prevented from using the general skill and knowledge that he or she has acquired during employment. However, the ex-employee may be restricted from disclosing or using the employer's trade secrets or equivalent.

Trade secrets are generally secret processes, special methods, or other information possessing a high degree of confidentiality, including those even of a non-technical or non-scientific nature. What is a trade secret is a question of fact, and all the circumstances must be considered. There is no conclusive list of trade secrets that the law will protect. Trade secrets may include not just manufacturing processes or secret formulae, but may extend to information relating to the list of names and addresses of the customers and suppliers, specific questions sent to customers, costs, prices, specific needs and requirements of customers, and status of ongoing negotiations with customers. The burden of proof is on the employer, and ultimately it is up to the court to determine whether the information sought to be protected can properly be regarded as a trade secret.

Some guidelines for determining whether certain confidential information can be a trade secret or the equivalent have been adopted by the Singapore courts.[59]

One factor that is relevant is the attitude of the employer toward the information sought to be protected. It is important that the employer show that it had during the employment impressed upon the employee the confidentiality of the information. As a matter of practice, this can be done by expressly and specifically warning the employee of the importance and confidentiality of the information (including imposing a specific confidentiality undertaking in the employment contract specifying the types of confidential information), marking and isolating such information as confidential, and restricting disclosure of and access to such information on a need-to-know basis only to the appropriate level or category of employees and (if necessary) third parties.

---

[59]*Tang Siew Choy v Certact Pte. Ltd.*, [1993] 3 Singapore Law Reports 44.

Another factor is the nature of the individual's employment. An employee habitually handling confidential material will generally have a higher duty of confidence imposed on him or her because that employee can be expected to realize its sensitive nature to a greater extent than if such material only reaches him or her occasionally.

Other factors include the nature of the information and whether the information can be easily isolated from other material that the employee is free to use and disclose. Such information must reasonably be such as can be construed to be of a confidential nature having regard to the employer's business, and the usages and practices of the particular trade or industry concerned.

3. Covenants Not to Compete

Often employers supplement the confidentiality undertaking discussed above with other covenants, to apply both during and after employment. These include imposing non-compete restrictive covenants on the employee:

- not to work for a competitor;
- not to carry on a business or trade similar to that of the employer;
- not to solicit or deal with the employer's customers; and
- not to solicit or employ the employer's staff.

During employment, these restrictive covenants generally are acceptable as part of the employee's agreement (express or implied) to give his or her exclusive services to the employer, and as part of the duty of good faith and fidelity.

However, after the employment terminates, the law is that for such restrictive covenants to be enforceable, they must be no wider than what is reasonably necessary to protect the legitimate interests of the employer. The law will not enforce a covenant merely to restrict competition in business.

The touchstone of what constitutes the employer's legitimate interest is whether the employer has a trade secret that the ex-employee knows, or has special trade/customer connections to protect. Other factors taken into consideration include the nature of the ex-employee's employment: whether the ex-employee, in view of his or her position with the employer, and the connection and access the ex-employee had to the employer's customers and confidential information during his or her employment, would indeed be in a position to entice customers away from the business, or take advantage of these connections; the extent of the area in which the ex-employee's activities would have an effect on the employer's business; and the period the information to be protected is likely to remain secret.

If the validity of the restrictive covenant may be in doubt, the restrictive covenant should be drafted as narrowly as possible, including limiting the time period and the geographical area during which the restrictions are to apply, especially if the secrecy of the information may only be short-lived.

How the employment is terminated is relevant to the employer's right to enforce the employee's covenants. If an employer wrongfully dismisses the employee or breaches the contract of employment so as show that the employer does not intend to be bound by the contract, the employee is entitled to be discharged from any duties under the contract, including the terms of any restrictive covenant, no matter how reasonable.

II. COLLECTIVE BARGAINING

Singapore's labor movement is characterized by an emphasis on national over sectional interests. For example, the Industrial Relations Act states that "[i]n determining a trade dispute, a Court may have regard not only to the interests of the persons immediately concerned but to the interests of the community as a whole and in particular the condition of the economy of Singapore."[60]

The Industrial Relations Act is the primary legal instrument that sets out the methods to prevent or settle trade disputes by collective bargaining, conciliation, and arbitration.

The Employment Act sets out the minimum terms and conditions of service that may be negotiated between unions and management.[61] Prior to the latest amendments to the Industrial Rela-

---

[60]Industrial Relations Act §34.

[61]See II.E.1., below. See additional discussion of the IAC at II.G., below.

tions Act, which came into effect on September 1, 2002, the Act provided that no collective agreement between an employee trade union and the employer shall contain terms and conditions of service that are more favorable to employees than those contained in Part IV of the Employment Act,[62] unless such provisions are approved by the Minister of Manpower.[63] This provision has now been repealed, and any proposed terms more favorable than the Employment Act are now fully negotiable.

A. Unions Defined

The Trade Unions Act[64] defines a union as any temporary or permanent organization of workers or employers whose principal objectives are to promote good industrial relations, improve working conditions of workers or enhance their economic and social status, and increase productivity for the benefit of workers, employers, and Singapore's economy.[65]

B. Union Membership

Generally, any employee in the public or private sector may be represented by a union, unless the Minister of Manpower declares a class of individuals not to be employees under the Industrial Relations Act. The Trade Unions Act permits both associations of employers and associations of workmen to be registered as trade unions. For this purpose, a workman is defined as any person who is hired under a contract of service or apprenticeship to do manual, clerical, or other work. Generally, only persons older than 16 years of age may join a union.[66] Government employees are not allowed to join trade unions, unless the President publishes notification in the *Gazette* that any individual or class of government employees is exempt from this restriction.[67] Currently, gov-

---

[62]Part IV of the Employment Act relates to rest days, hours of work, holidays, sick leave, retrenchment and retirement benefits, and variable payments.

[63]Industrial Relations Act §25.

[64]Trade Unions Act [Cap 333].

[65]*Id.* §2.

[66]*Id.* §28.

[67]*Id.* §28.

ernment employees, other than those serving in the Singapore police force, the Singapore armed forces, the Singapore Civil Defense, and officers in the prisons service and the narcotics service, may form or join trade unions. Employees of a statutory board may join or form trade unions, except that employees of the Housing and Development Board, the Public Utilities Board, and the Urban Redevelopment Authority may only form or join trade unions if membership is confined to employees of their own organization.[68]

The vast majority of unions are affiliated with the National Trades Union Congress (NTUC). The NTUC is the central trade union federation, with 65 affiliated trade unions and more than 300,000 members, and works in close conjunction with government. Many NTUC leaders also are members of Parliament. The NTUC is headed by a Cabinet minister who has no government portfolio and is staffed by various government officials, including Members of Parliament from the ruling political party. Tripartite cooperation between workers, employers, and the government is cited both as cause and justification for government influence in NTUC. This tripartite partnership frequently is noted as a major factor contributing towards Singapore's labor relations stability.

Union membership is not mandatory in a unionized workplace.[69] The terms of a collective agreement do not extend to non-union members,[70] although non-union employees usually enjoy the union-negotiated wage scales. If the employer treats a non-union employee of the same category of employees as that represented by the union less favorably than a union member, this is a strong incentive for the non-union employees to join the union and benefit from the collective agreement.

C. Union Recognition Process

1. *Registration*

The Trade Unions Act provides for the registration, recognition, and supervision of trade unions. Under the Trade Unions Act,

---

[68]*Id.* §29.

[69]See II.H.1.a., below.

[70]See II.E.3., below, regarding extension of collective agreements.

a new trade union may not remain unregistered for more than one month from the date on which it was established. If it is not registered after that time, then it will be considered unlawful and, therefore, ineligible for any of the rights, immunities, or privileges of a registered trade union.[71]

2. Recognition

The Industrial Relations Act provides a detailed discussion of the recognition process. A registered trade union of employees must serve on an employer the prescribed form for claiming recognition. Within seven days of receiving the claim for recognition, the employer either must recognize the union by completing the prescribed form or inform the Commissioner for Labour of its refusal.[72] If an employer refuses to recognize the union on the ground that it does not represent a majority of the employees concerned, or that there is more than one trade union claiming to represent the same group of employees, the Commissioner for Labour then conducts an election by secret ballot. All employees may vote by secret ballot, with the exception of partners, employees employed after the date on which the claim for recognition was served, new or probationary employees, and temporary employees.[73] If an employer refuses to recognize the union on the ground that the employees concerned cannot be members of a particular trade union, the dispute can be settled by making a joint application to the IAC.[74]

3. Jurisdictional Disputes

Jurisdictional disputes are rarely a problem, but in the event of a disagreement, the Ministry of Manpower may supervise a secret ballot election to determine union representation in a particular establishment.

---

[71]Trade Unions Act §§8, 21.

[72]Industrial Relations Act §§16–19; Industrial Relations (Recognition of a Trade Union of Employees) Regulations (Recognition Regulations) §3(2).

[73]Recognition Regulations, reg. 5(2).

[74]Industrial Relations Act §17(4). See II.G., below.

D. Structure of Unions

1. Rights and Privileges of Unions

Unions themselves are provided with rights, privileges, and immunities under the Trade Unions Act, as follows:

- A registered trade union can sue or be sued and prosecuted and can enter into collective agreements;
- A trade union cannot, however, be sued or prosecuted for anything done by or on behalf of the trade union in support of a trade dispute where the trade union does nothing more than to stop its members from working or stop other persons from working or doing business, even if such other persons suffer a loss;
- Officers and members of a trade union are similarly protected for whatever they validly do on behalf of the trade union; and
- A trade union can be held liable for any contracts that it has entered into or that have been entered into on its behalf by an authorized agent unless the contract is void or unenforceable by law.[75]

All unions must have at least three trustees who are citizens of Singapore.[76] All property of a union is invested in the trustees to hold for the benefit of the union and the membership.[77] Rules of the trade union must contain all the matters listed in the Schedule to the Trade Unions Act, including the manner of making, altering, or rescinding any of the rules. Changes in union rules cannot go into effect before due approval by the Registrar of Trade Unions.[78]

2. Funding

Union funding rules are outlined under the Trade Unions Act.[79] Certain unions require membership fees for workers, although there

[75]Trade Unions Act §24.
[76]*Id.* §43.
[77]*Id.* §44.
[78]*Id.* §§7(1), 38.
[79]*Id.* §§47–54.

is no provision regarding mandatory payments of membership fees in the Trade Unions Act. The union may compel payment of fees for specific uses, and members are liable to pay in accordance with the rules. However, the union may not use these fees for purposes other than those that were specified to the members, unless the members agree to such a change.

Under the Trade Unions Act, trade union funds may be used for the following:

- salaries, allowances, and expenses of trade union officers;
- administrative expenses, including auditing fees;
- legal expenses;
- trade dispute support;
- compensation to members for loss arising out of a trade dispute;
- death and other benefits to members or their dependents; and
- any other object approved by the Minister of Manpower, such as fees for affiliation with the NTUC.[80]

The funds of a trade union also may be invested in shares of trade union cooperative enterprises, in interest-earning deposits, in banks or finance companies, or in investments authorized by law for the investment of trust monies.[81]

The treasurer of the union must prepare a statement of receipts and expenditures and a statement of assets and liabilities once each year (or when he or she resigns) and must have them audited. The secretary of the union then must prepare and submit to the Registrar of Trade Unions annual returns consisting of all audited statements, changes of union rules and officers, and a copy of the current union constitution.[82] The penalty on conviction of any secretary of a registered trade union by a Magistrate or District Court for failure to submit returns is a fine not exceeding S$2,000.[83]

---

[80] *Id.* §47.
[81] *Id.* §49.
[82] *Id.* §§52, 53.
[83] *Id.* §53.

On a proven complaint by a trade union member of misuse of union funds, a court can order an officer or other member who has misused union funds to restore or repay to the union the funds or property wrongfully used or kept.[84] In addition, the Minister of Manpower can, by written notice, freeze the funds of a trade union in any financial institution in Singapore to prevent possible misuse. The penalty for failure to comply with the Minister's direction is a fine not exceeding S$3,000 or a jail term not exceeding three years, or both.[85]

3. *Establishment of Registered Union Office*

Under the Trade Unions Act, any premises may be used as a registered office, so long as the address or any change of address is duly reported to the Registrar of Trade Unions, and the registered office is the place of operations.[86]

4. *Dissolution and De-Registration*

Trade unions may be dissolved voluntarily by the members themselves. Notice of dissolution must be signed by at least seven members and the secretary of the trade union, with notification provided to the Registrar of Trade Unions within 14 days. However, the Registrar also can de-register a union under the following circumstances:

- the union was wrongly registered;
- any object or rule, election of executive committee members, or use of union funds is unlawful, improper, unreasonable, or oppressive; or
- the union is likely to be used against the interest of the workers concerned.[87]

As soon as a trade union is voluntarily or compulsorily deregistered, the property of the trade union is vested in the official

---

[84] *Id.* §56.
[85] *Id.* §16.
[86] *Id.* §37.
[87] *Id.* §§14, 15.

assignee in bankruptcy for the purpose of winding up the union's financial affairs. After due payment of debts, liabilities, and costs of winding up, the net assets of the trade union are distributed in accordance with the trade union's rules, unless the Minister of Manpower directs that the net assets be paid into the Workers' Fund,[88] established under the Workmen's Compensation Act.[89]

5. *Amalgamation*

Provisions within the Trade Unions Act allow for the amalgamation of two or more unions into one without dissolution or division of funds.[90] An amalgamation does not prejudice any right of either union or any right of a creditor of either union.[91]

E. Collective Agreements

1. *Negotiating Terms and Conditions of Employment*

The Industrial Relations Act provides that a trade union that has been duly recognized by an employer may invite the employer to negotiate on proposals for a collective agreement.[92] An employer may invite a trade union representing its employees to negotiate as well. Within seven days after receiving an invitation to negotiate, the employer or union should formally accept the invitation. Upon being informed of any refusal to negotiate, the Commissioner for Labour will intervene to persuade the employer or union to negotiate.[93] If a collective agreement is not concluded within 14 days after a notice of invitation, either the trade union or employer may inform the Commissioner, who then may cause conciliation by a conciliation officer, or, if that is unsuccessful or is likely to be unsuccessful, then if the Minister of Manpower so directs a compulsory conciliation may be ordered.[94]

---

[88]See VII.B., below.

[89]Trade Unions Act §20.

[90]*Id.* §34.

[91]*Id.* §36.

[92]Industrial Relations Act §18.

[93]*Id.* §19.

[94]*Id.* §§21, 22, and 23. If conciliation fails, then the dispute is usually submitted to arbitration. See II.G., below.

Most bargaining takes place on a company-by-company basis, but the rules to which each company must adhere are national standards. Bargaining covers those employees in a company who are trade union members. A collective agreement usually provides that non-union employees belonging to the categories of employees for which the trade union is recognized by the employer shall not enjoy better benefits than those enjoyed by union members under the collective agreement.

In negotiations, an employer may be represented only by its employees or by an officer of a trade union of which the employer is a member. A trade union may be represented in negotiations only by an officer of the trade union or an industrial relations officer (who is appointed by the Minister of Manpower for the purposes of the Industrial Relations Act) selected by the trade union.[95] There is no law prohibiting the employer or union from hiring outside counsel or technical experts to advise them, but such individuals are prohibited from being present during the actual negotiations.

A collective agreement is valid where all of the following conditions are met:

- a memorandum of its terms is in writing and is duly signed on behalf of or by all parties to the agreement;
- the duly signed memorandum is deposited with the Registrar of the IAC within one week of signing;
- the memorandum is duly certified by the IAC, which may, on the grounds of public interest or inadequacy of the terms, refuse to certify the agreement and require amendments before certification; and
- the duration of the agreement is set forth.[96]

2. *Effect of the Collective Agreement*

A collective agreement is binding on the trade unions and employers that are named in the agreement or award, and on their successors, assignees, or transferees, and their respective mem-

---

[95]Industrial Relations Act §§27, 64.

[96]*Id.* §25.

bers.[97] A collective agreement also is binding on trade unions and employers if the Minister of Manpower declares that they are bound.[98]

An employer must display the collective agreement in Malay, English, Chinese, and Tamil[99] in a conspicuous position at or near the entrance of and at any other accessible place of work.[100]

If an employee, after the collective agreement is declared valid and binding, believes that the employer's actions are not in compliance with the terms of the agreement, the employee may take the following actions:

- complain to the IAC through his or her union;[101]
- complain to the Parliamentary Secretary, the Minister of Manpower, or the Commissioner for Labour;[102] or
- commence a proceeding in the subordinate courts.[103]

Any failure to comply with an order of the IAC, respecting the terms of a collective agreement or otherwise, is punishable as contempt of court.[104]

3. *Extension of a Collective Agreement*

The Minister of Manpower can ask the IAC to conduct an inquiry as to whether it is in the public interest to extend a collective agreement and make it binding on any person or trade union not already bound.[105] The issues into which the IAC has been requested to inquire must be published in the *Gazette*.[106] Time then is set aside for the IAC to hear employees, employers, and other persons interested in the inquiry.[107] The Minister of Manpower

---

[97]*Id.* §40.
[98]See II.E.3., below.
[99]See the Introduction, at A., above.
[100]Industrial Relations Act §50.
[101]See II.G., below, for a discussion of IAC procedures.
[102]Industrial Relations Act §54.
[103]See the Introduction, at B., above.
[104]Industrial Relations Act §57.
[105]*Id.* §41.
[106]*Id.* §41(3)(a).
[107]*Id.* §41(3)(b).

then makes a final decision,[108] and, if the collective agreement is extended to any person who is not already bound, an official Ministerial Decree is published in the *Gazette*.[109]

4. *Duration of the Collective Agreement*

The term of a collective agreement may not be less than two years or more than three years from its commencement date.[110]

5. *Scope of the Collective Agreement*

Collective agreements generally include provisions covering the following terms and conditions of employment:

- wages,
- salary schedules,
- annual increases,
- bonuses,
- shift premiums,
- severance pay,
- standard workweek,
- overtime,
- vacations,
- sick leave and maternity leave,
- other grounds for leave,
- uniforms,
- medical benefits,
- promotions, and
- transportation.

Certain subjects may not be covered by a collective agreement. Under the Industrial Relations Act, a collective agreement may address all industrial matters, i.e., matters pertaining to the relations of employers and employees and connected with the employment, the terms of employment, or the conditions of work

---

[108] *Id.* §41(5).
[109] *Id.* §41(6).
[110] *Id.* §39.

of any person. However, a trade union may not invite an employer to negotiate under the Act on the following subjects:[111]

- the promotion of an employee;
- the internal transfer of any employee on not less favorable terms and conditions of service;
- the right of an employer to hire any person;
- the layoff by an employer of an employee on any basis due to redundancy or reorganization;[112]
- the dismissal and reinstatement of an employee allegedly dismissed without just cause or excuse, other than dismissal on section 82 grounds;[113] or
- the assignment or allocation of work to an employee, which is consistent or compatible with his or her terms and conditions of service.

F. Strikes and Other Industrial Action

The purpose of the Trade Disputes Act[114] is to control trade disputes, as well as any strikes, lockouts, or other industrial actions. A trade dispute is defined as a dispute between the employer and its employees, or among the employees themselves, regarding work or terms and conditions of service.[115] The right to strike and to take other industrial action is found in Section 2 of the Trade Disputes Act. As noted in the Introduction to this chapter, however, Singapore has been strike free since 1986.

1. *Strikes and Industrial Actions*

A strike is defined as a stoppage of or a refusal to work or to accept work, by a group of workers in any trade, industry, or occupation.[116] An industrial action is defined as an act or omission by employees employed within any trade or industry who have a com-

---

[111]*Id.* §18(2).
[112]See also IV.A., below.
[113]For a discussion of section 82 grounds, see II.H.1.a., below.
[114]Trade Disputes Act [Cap 331].
[115]*Id.* §2.
[116]*Id.*

mon understanding to limit, restrict, or delay the performance of any duties connected with their employment.[117]

Generally, individuals are protected by law for organizing and/or participating in a strike or other industrial action. However, the Trade Disputes Act does not give protection to any person who has committed a criminal offense under the law or who has knowingly endangered the life, health, or property of any person by stopping work. In addition, an industrial action (which includes a strike) becomes illegal under the following circumstances:

- it has any other object than supporting a trade dispute that involves the striking workers;
- it is in support of a trade dispute that has been duly submitted to the IAC; or
- it is intended to put pressure on the government, either directly or indirectly, by inflicting hardship on the community.[118]

Under the Trade Unions Act, a union may order its members either to stop work completely or to reduce their rate of working. However, a strike or other industrial action may not be ordered unless the trade union first has conducted a secret ballot among the affected members, and the majority supports such an action.[119] To be valid, a secret ballot must ensure that the following conditions are satisfied:

- members can vote freely,
- votes are correctly counted and recorded, and
- the secrecy of the voting is properly maintained.

The results of any secret ballot must be provided to the Registrar of Trade Unions within seven days. All ballot papers and other documents used in calculating the results must be safely kept for six months.

The Trade Unions Act has been amended consequential to amendments made to the Industrial Relations Act in September

---

[117] *Id.*
[118] *Id* §3.
[119] Trade Unions Act §27.

2002 (which allow rank-and-file trade unions to represent executive employees in certain circumstances)[120] to prohibit the rank-and-file trade union and its members from participating in or taking any industrial action in connection with any employment dispute between the executive represented by the trade union and the employer. A member of a rank-and-file trade union who is an executive employee is prohibited from participating in or taking any industrial action taken by the trade union.[121]

2. *Lockouts*

The Trade Disputes Act defines a lockout as the closing of a place of work, the suspension of work, or an employer's refusal to allow its employees to continue work, so as to force its own or another employer's employees to accept certain terms or conditions of service.[122]

A lockout becomes illegal when the lockout is:

- for an object other than in support of a trade dispute that involves the employer's locking out,
- in support of a trade dispute that has been submitted to the IAC, or
- intended to put pressure on the government directly or indirectly by inflicting hardship for the community.[123]

A union strike or other industrial action taken after an illegal employer lockout, or an employer lockout established after an illegal union industrial action, is not considered illegal.[124]

3. *Picketing*

Picketing is defined in the Trade Disputes Act as the action of any person who, in support of a trade dispute, places himself or herself at or near the home or place of work of another person so as only to obtain or give information peacefully, or so as only to

[120]See II.G., below.
[121]Trade Unions Act §27.
[122]Trade Disputes Act §2.
[123]*Id.* §3.
[124]*Id.* §4.

peacefully persuade or advise another person to work or not to work.[125] Picketing becomes unlawful when the number of persons picketing is so great or the picketing is conducted in such a manner as to have any of the following effects:

- intimidate a person in the house or place being picketed,
- obstruct the entrance or exit of the house or place that is being picketed, or
- lead to a public disturbance.[126]

4. *Penalties*

It is a violation of the Trade Disputes Act for any person to persuade others to take part in or support an illegal industrial action or lockout.[127] The penalties for violating this provision in connection with a strike or other industrial action are a fine not exceeding S$2,000, or six months in prison, or both.[128] The penalties for a violation in connection with a lockout are a fine not exceeding S$5,000, or six months in prison, or both.[129]

Any offense under the Trade Disputes Act is seizable, which means that the police may arrest on the spot the participants committing any alleged offense under the Act. The consent of the Attorney General is required for any further proceedings to be taken with respect to a charge relating to an illegal industrial action or an illegal lockout. Any offense under the Trade Disputes Act may be prosecuted in a District Court or Magistrate's Court.[130]

G. Third-Party Resolution of Labor Disputes

Arbitration frequently is used to resolve disputes involving unionized employees. The Industrial Relations Act[131] provides the framework for arbitration through the Industrial Arbitration Courts (IACs).

---

[125] *Id.* §10.
[126] *Id.*
[127] *Id.* §§6, 7.
[128] *Id.* §5(1).
[129] *Id.* §5(2).
[130] *Id.* §14.
[131] Industrial Relations Act [Cap 136] (IRA).

Employment disputes are submitted to an IAC in various ways, as follows:

- if the dispute concerns any National Wages Council annual wage supplement, annual bonus, or variable payment,[132] the dispute is submitted to the IAC by written request of either the trade union or the employer;
- if the dispute concerns any matter arising from or connected with the transfer of employment, the dispute is submitted to the IAC by written request of either the trade union or the employer;[133]
- by the Minister of Manpower by notice in the *Gazette*[134] or by the President of Singapore by proclamation of public interest;[135]
- if all the trade unions and employers who are parties to a trade dispute jointly make a request to the IAC for arbitration; or
- if the dispute relates to retrenchment benefits payable to, or a breach of the contract of employment of, an executive employee represented by a recognized trade union, the dispute is submitted to the IAC by written request of either the trade union or the employer.

The IAC consists of the President of the IAC[136] alone when inquiring into disputes concerning the following:[137]

- determination of whether a trade union may represent certain employees or a class of employees, or any executive employees;
- certification of any collective agreement;
- the dismissal or reinstatement of an employee on section 82 grounds;[138]

---

[132]These terms are defined at V.A.1., below.

[133]Industrial Relations Act §31.

[134]*Id.* §31(e).

[135]*Id.* §31(f).

[136]The President of the IAC is appointed by the President of Singapore upon the advice of the Prime Minister.

[137]Industrial Relations Act §§16(6), 30B(5), 24, 35(1A), 39(4), 45(4).

[138]See II.H.1.a., below.

- the continuation or extension to other persons of an award by the IAC;
- the decision of a referee appointed by the IAC to oversee the operation of an award; and
- the interpretation, variation (where the application to vary the award is made with the agreement of all the parties to the award), or noncompliance with an award by the IAC.

In all other matters, the IAC consists of the President and two additional members, one representing the employer and one representing the employees.[139] The Industrial Relations Act also provides for the intervention of the Minister of Manpower, the Parliamentary Secretary of Manpower, and the Commissioner for Labour in cases complaining of noncompliance with an IAC award.[140]

The IAC has the power to decide on the conduct of its proceedings, as long as it acts in accordance with equity, good conscience, and the substantive merits of the case. Thus, the IAC is not bound to follow the provisions set forth in the Evidence Act, and it can make its own rules regarding the production of evidence and the summoning and swearing in of witnesses and other persons.[141] The IAC may seek, and give effect to, the opinion of the Attorney General of Singapore on any question of law.[142] Any offer made during the negotiations may not be admitted into evidence without the consent of the offeror.[143] If the IAC so decides, trade or business secrets may be admitted except that such evidence must be given in private sessions of the IAC and may not be disclosed or published without the permission of the President of the IAC.[144] The IAC also may conduct on-the-spot investigations during working hours of any place relating to the dispute.[145]

In reaching a decision, the IAC takes into consideration not only the interests of the workers (or workers and union where there

[139]Industrial Relations Act §3.
[140]*Id.* §54(7).
[141]*Id.* §60.
[142]*Id.* §65.
[143]*Id.* §62.
[144]*Id.* §72.
[145]*Id.* §67.

is a union) and the employer, but also the impact its decision will have on the Singapore community and economy.

In the collective bargaining context, the role of the IAC may begin even before the parties execute an agreement. As discussed above,[146] if labor and management are unable to conclude an agreement on their own, the Commissioner for Labour and the Minister of Manpower may attempt to settle the parties' disagreement through conciliation.[147] If this conciliation fails, the parties may submit their case to the IAC.[148]

Disputes arising out of the operation of a collective agreement or prior award by the IAC may be submitted by either the trade union or the employer to the IAC in various ways, as follows:

- by an application for the appointment of a referee to hear the dispute, and any party who is dissatisfied with the decision of the referee then may appeal to the IAC;[149]
- by an application for an interpretation of the collective agreement or IAC award in question;[150]
- by an application to vary or set aside a collective agreement or an IAC award only for the purpose of removing ambiguity or uncertainty, unless the President of the IAC is satisfied that there are exceptional circumstances for doing otherwise;[151] or
- by an application for an order to prevent noncompliance with a collective agreement, an award, or a provision of the Industrial Relations Act.

The Industrial Relations Act also provides for the intervention of the Minister of Manpower in cases alleging dismissal without just cause.[152] In addition, the Industrial Relations Act provides for the appointment of a Board of Inquiry by the Minister of Man-

---

[146]See II.E.1., above.

[147]Industrial Relations Act §20, 21, 22, 31.

[148]*Id.* §§31(a).

[149]*Id.* §43.

[150]*Id.* §44.

[151]*Id.* §45.

[152]*Id.* §35(3).

power in special circumstances.[153] The Board may consist of a chairman and one or more members who are appointed through notification in the *Gazette*.[154] The Board's findings are presented in the form of a report to Parliament.[155]

As previously stated, the Employment Act does not currently cover employees in managerial, executive, or confidential positions. These employees therefore do not have recourse to the dispute resolution procedures available under the Employment Act. In the past, their usual legal recourse was civil litigation against the employer. These employees are usually not unionized, although under existing laws executive employees are allowed to form their own unions and engage in collective bargaining with employers. Thus, they were unable to take advantage of the dispute resolution procedures under the Industrial Relations Act.

However, effective September 1, 2002, junior-level executive employees whose employer has recognized any rank-and-file trade union (that is, the majority of whose members are non-managerial, non-executive, and non-confidential workers) may be individually (but not as a class) represented by the recognized rank-and-file trade union to resolve disputes relating to the dismissal, retrenchment, and breach of employment contract of the executive employee. This is now possible because of an amendment to the Industrial Relations Act.[156]

The intention of the amendment is to provide an additional dispute resolution remedy for executives retrenched in the economic recession following the Asian economic crisis and the U.S. recession. Additionally, permitting rank-and-file unions to represent executives would discourage an anticipated trend of executive unions being formed in order to give executives more bargaining power with employers. It was felt that multiple unions would hinder labor-management cooperation and teamwork.[157]

The Industrial Relations Act, however, allows the employer to object to any representation by a rank-and-file trade union of an

---

[153] *Id.* §74.

[154] *Id.* §75.

[155] *Id.* §§74–77.

[156] *Id.* pt. IIIA.

[157] Singapore Parliamentary Reports, Parliament No. 10, Sess. 1, Vol. 75, Sitting 5 (July 23, 2002).

executive, on the ground that the executive performs or exercises a function, duty, or power that may give rise to a real or potential conflict of interest if he or she is represented by the trade union. Therefore, senior executives and executives who are involved in personnel administration, or who have access to confidential information on the employer's finances or employee payrolls, or who represent the employer's union-management matters, cannot be represented by the rank-and-file trade union.

H. Union Security

1. *Protections for Union Members*

a. Right to Join a Union

The Industrial Relations Act, the Trade Unions Act, and the Employment Act all guarantee workers the right to union membership, and it is illegal to discriminate against an employee on the basis of such membership. As discussed above,[158] although workers have a right to union membership, such membership is not mandatory.

The Industrial Relations Act states that a trade union may seek to represent any employee unless the Minister of Manpower has declared that the person is not an employee under the Industrial Relations Act,[159] or unless the person falls within a class of employees who cannot be represented by the trade union under its constitution and rules. As discussed above, with the latest amendment to the Industrial Relations Act, a rank-and-file trade union recognized by an employer may represent a junior executive employee of that employer in limited circumstances.[160]

Section 82 of the Industrial Relations Act prohibits employers from dismissing or discriminating against employees based solely on the following grounds (section 82 grounds):

- the employee benefits from a collective agreement;
- the employee has given evidence in any type of proceeding under the Industrial Relations Act;

[158]See II.B., above.
[159]Industrial Relations Act §2.
[160]See II.G., above.

- the employee is a member of a trade union that is negotiating with the employer;
- the employee, being a member of a trade union seeking to improve working conditions, is dissatisfied with his or her present working conditions;
- the employee intends to become an officer or a member of a union;
- the employee is on leave for the purpose of carrying out union duties; or
- the employee has absented him or herself from work to serve as a duly appointed panel member of the Industrial Arbitration Court and has previously informed his or her employer of this absence.[161]

Furthermore, an employer may not refuse to hire a new employee on the ground that the employee is or intends to be a member or officer of a trade union.[162] The Industrial Relations Act also makes it unlawful for employers to persuade their employees not to become members or officers of a trade union.[163]

In addition to the protections afforded by the Industrial Relations Act, the Employment Act makes it illegal to deprive a worker of rights related to union membership, including the following:

- the right to join a union;
- the right to participate in activities of a union, whether as an officer or otherwise; and
- the right to associate with any persons for the purpose of organizing a trade union.[164]

b. Remedies for Dismissal Due to Union Activities

If an employee alleges dismissal for union activities, the employee may take any of the following actions:

---

[161] *Id.* §82.
[162] *Id.* §80.
[163] *Id.* §79.
[164] Employment Act §17.

- through his or her trade union, apply for a decision of the IAC as to whether he or she should be reinstated to the former job;[165]
- under the Employment Act, directly make representations to the Minister of Manpower (if he or she is not a union member) for reinstatement or compensation on the ground of dismissal without just cause;[166]
- commence civil litigation in the Subordinate or the High Court for compensation and, perhaps, reinstatement to the former job.[167]

Under the Industrial Relations Act, if an employer is found guilty of discrimination based on union status, liability can be imposed by the District Court in the form of a fine not exceeding S$2,000, or imprisonment not exceeding 12 months, or both.[168] The Commissioner for Labour may authorize any investigation of complaints with respect to offenses under the Industrial Relations Act.

2. *Rights and Privileges of Union Officers*

Under the Industrial Relations Act, an employee intending to carry out duties or to exercise rights as a trade union officer must apply in writing for a leave of absence, stating the duration and purposes of the requested leave. An employer, upon the employee's application, shall grant leave, which should not exceed what is reasonably required, for the employee to carry out the union work. If the employee takes leave to represent members of the trade union on industrial matters concerning the employer, then the employer must grant the employee leave with full pay.[169]

Union officers may take time off for union training courses, although the right to payment for such time is at the employer's discretion.

---

[165]Industrial Relations Act §35(3).

[166]Employment Act §14.

[167]This is a general remedy under the common law or to enforce the terms of the employment contract.

[168]Industrial Relations Act §80.

[169]*Id.* §81.

III. Representation by Entities Other Than Unions

At present, only unions represent Singapore's workforce in collective bargaining. The government stresses mutual cooperation and consensus-shaping among the partners of the tripartite labor relations framework. The tripartite committees in which the government, employers' organizations such as the Singapore National Employers' Federation, and employees' unions participate try to formulate employment-related policies that are balanced between workers' and management's interests.

In the area of worker safety, every employer that operates premises subject to the Factories Act must establish a committee of management and worker representatives to promote safe, healthy working conditions.[170]

IV. Redundancy and Transfers of Undertakings

A. Redundancy

As discussed above,[171] the Industrial Relations Act prohibits trade unions from inviting an employer to negotiate regarding employee layoffs or reassignments on the basis of redundancy or reorganization.[172] In other words, the union cannot control the employer's criteria for redundancy or retrenchment, and which employees the employer can make redundant. However, under the Employment Act and generally under common law, an employer may not terminate employees for redundancy without proper warning or notice.[173] In addition to this required notice, if substantial numbers of employees are involved, it is advisable to inform the Ministry of Manpower.

For a non-unionized employee, rights in relation to a redundancy are governed largely by the terms of the employment contract. There is no legal requirement under the Employment Act or

[170]See VII.A., below.
[171]See II.E.5., above.
[172]Industrial Relations Act §18(2)(d).
[173]Employment Act §§9–11. See I.C.2., above.

the common law, as applied in Singapore, for an employer to be obliged to pay the employee any redundancy compensation.

Singapore law does not provide for "retrenchment benefits," except to state that no employee who has been employed with the employer for fewer than three years is entitled to such benefits.[174] This provision appears in a part of the Act applicable to workmen, and other employees earning no more than S$1,600 a month. The Industrial Relations Act previously provided that no collective agreement between an employee trade union and the employer shall contain terms and conditions of service more favorable to employees than those contained in Part IV of the Employment Act, which includes the provision for no retrenchment benefit for employees employed for fewer than three years. The Industrial Relations Act was amended in September 2002 to remove this restriction on collective agreements. Prior to the amendment, collective agreements usually provided that retrenchment benefits would be payable only to employees employed with the employer for more than three years.

Provisions for retrenchment benefits usually are incorporated into collective bargaining agreements or (more rarely) individual employment contracts, and typically allow for one-half to one months' pay for each year of service.

B. Transfers of Undertakings

The Employment Act provides that, before a transfer of the employer's business in which the employees are employed (affected employees), the employer must provide the affected employees with disclosure of the impending action within a reasonable time and before the transfer takes place. Disclosure consists of a notice of transfer provided by the old and new employers to the affected employees and their union (if any). The notice must state the reasons and implications of the transfer, the date of transfer, information about the new employer, and its impact on and plans for the affected employees.[175]

---

[174] *See* Employment Act §45.
[175] *Id.* §18A.

If there is a delay in this process, a union or an affected employee may refer the matter to the Commissioner for Labour to require the current and future employers to comply with the law.

Normally, an employment contract is considered a personal one, and may not be transferred without the employee's consent. However, upon the sale of a business or part of a business as an ongoing concern, the employees are deemed to be transferred with the business, with the transferee as their new employer.[176] Thus, the existing terms and conditions of service remain the same, and the transfer does not break the worker's length of service.

Where, immediately before the transfer of the business, a trade union has been recognized by the old employer with respect to any affected employee, after the transfer the trade union shall be deemed to be recognized by the new employer if, after the transfer, the majority of the employees employed by the new employer are members of the union. In any other case, the trade union can only represent the affected employee in any dispute arising from a collective agreement between the old employer and the trade union, or from the transfer of the employee from the old employer to the new employer.

V. WAGES, HOURS, AND LEAVE

A. Wages

1. *General*

As discussed above,[177] the Employment Act covers all employees, a term defined to exclude seamen, domestic workers, and those employed in managerial, executive, or confidential positions. However, the Employment Act provisions in Part IV of the Act that relate to rest days, hours of work, holidays, leave, wages, retrenchment, and retirement benefits apply only to workmen, and to other employees receiving up to S$1,600 per month (excluding overtime payments, bonuses, annual wage supplements, and pro-

---

[176] *Id.*

[177] See I., above.

ductivity incentive payments).[178] The term "workmen" includes individuals engaged in manual labor (excluding seamen and domestic workers), artisans, apprentices, those involved in operating or maintaining mechanically propelled vehicles, and persons employed by the employer partly to supervise workmen and partly for manual labor. Part IV applies to all workmen regardless of their salary level. (For purposes of this discussion, workmen and other employees covered by Part IV are collectively referred to as "covered employees.")

The Employment Act does not control the rates of salaries, wages, or bonuses; those are set by individual employment contract and by collective agreement. There is no statutory minimum wage in Singapore.

The National Wages Council (NWC), a tripartite council composed of representatives of government, management, and labor, annually recommends wage guidelines acceptable to the three parties. In recent years, the NWC has tried to keep wage increases below increases in productivity.

The NWC has been a strong proponent of "flexible wage" programs; the NWC and the government expound the concept that total wage increases should be tied to company performance, with built-in wage increases lagging behind company productivity growth. Under this concept, firms performing well should reward employees with higher variable bonuses (see below), but are not pressured to increase wages during downturns. Workers thus have a direct interest in the profitability of the firm.

The Minister of Manpower also may make recommendations on wage adjustments for covered employees from time to time.

There are two other general components to wages beyond the basic salary and allowances: the Annual Wage Supplement and the Variable Payment. Salary plus allowances is referred to as the "gross rate of pay."

- The *Annual Wage Supplement* is the lump sum single annual payment made in addition to the basic salary or wages. The maximum amount that may be paid as an annual wage supplement is controlled by the Employment Act. For an

[178] Employment Act §§35–53.

employer that did not pay any annual wage supplement before August 26, 1988, the amount that may be paid or stated in the collective agreement for covered employees may not exceed one month's salary. For contracts of service or collective agreements executed before August 26, 1988, which already contain provisions for payment of an annual wage supplement, annual bonus, or annual wage increase, the contractual payments will continue until and unless an agreement is reached either with the covered employees or unions (if any) to vary the payments.[179]

- The *Variable Payment* is paid annually or at other intervals as an incentive for workers to increase their contribution to the workplace. The amount paid is negotiable between the employer and the employees (or the union) and is based on trading results, productivity, or other agreed-upon criteria.

2. *Salary Period*

For all employees, the Employment Act controls the period at which workers must be paid their basic salary. Specifically, a salary must be paid at least once each month, and within seven days after the end of each month worked.[180] All salaries must be paid on a working day during working hours unless an employee agrees otherwise.[181] Any employer that fails to pay a salary in accordance with the Employment Act is guilty of an offense.[182] The employer's failure to pay salary also would be considered a breach of contract, as a result of which the employee would be free to terminate his or her employment.[183]

3. *Overtime Pay*

For covered employees, the Employment Act limits overtime[184] to 72 hours per month, paid at 150 percent of the normal hourly rate.

---

[179] *Id.* §48.

[180] *Id.* §§20, 20A, 21.

[181] *Id.* §25.

[182] *Id.* §34. For a discussion of the procedures applicable to employee salary claims, see I.D., above.

[183] Employment Act §13. See I.C.1., above, regarding termination of individual employment contracts.

[184] See V.B.1., below, regarding standard working hours.

For work performed on a rest day[185] at the worker's request, the Employment Act provides that the employee will be paid, at the basic rate of pay, half a day's salary for up to one-half the normal hours worked, or one day's salary for work more than one-half the normal hours but not exceeding the normal hours.[186] However, if the employee works in excess of his or her normal hours, the employee is paid one day's salary at the basic rate of pay and any additional hours are paid at 150 percent of the hourly basic rate.

For work performed on a rest day at the employer's request, the worker is compensated, at the basic rate of pay, one day's salary for work up to one-half the normal work hours or two day's salary for work lasting longer than one-half the normal hours. For any time worked in excess of normal work hours, the employee is compensated at two days' salary and any additional hours are paid at 150 percent of the hourly basic rate of pay.[187]

Government employees are covered by a different overtime schedule when they are employed in essential services that require overtime without notice.[188]

4. Deductions

Central Provident Fund deductions[189] are made regularly from an employee's pay, along with any additional disciplinary deductions under provisions spelled out in the individual contract of employment. Such additional disciplinary deductions may be made from pay if an employee is absent from work, damages company goods that are in his or her possession, or loses company monies. The total amount of all deductions made from the salary of an employee by an employer in any one salary period (unless deductions are made for damaged goods, lost monies, etc.) may not exceed 50 percent of the salary payable to the employee during the pay period.[190]

---

[185]See V.B.5., below.

[186]The basic rate of pay excludes the annual wage supplement and variable payment components discussed at V.A.1., above.

[187]Employment Act §37.

[188]*See id.* §37(4).

[189]Both employers and employees (Singapore nationals and permanent residents) contribute to the Central Provident Fund (CPF). A detailed discussion of the CPF is provided at VIII.A., below.

[190]Employment Act §32.

B. Hours

The Employment Act covers hours of work, overtime, rest days, and related conditions of service for covered employees.[191] These various restrictions on working hours are discussed below.

1. *Daily Working Hours and Breaks*

Daily working hours are determined by individual employers. According to the Employment Act, the standard length of a workday is eight hours, but the workday may be up to nine hours a day if the employee is on a five-day week, or is required to work fewer than eight hours on one or more days of the week. An employee is not allowed to work more than six consecutive hours without a break, but, if he or she is engaged in work that must be carried on continuously, this may stretch up to eight hours including at least breaks of not less than 45 minutes to have a meal.[192] An employee may work overtime, but may not work more than 72 hours in one month.[193] Shift workers may be assigned to work more than six consecutive hours without a break, or more than eight hours per day, up to 12 hours in any one day and the average hours worked over a continuous period of three weeks shall not exceed 44 hours a week.[194]

See VI.B., below, regarding daily working hours and break requirements for children.

2. *Duration of Workweek and Overtime Limitations*

Under the Employment Act, a "week" is defined as a continuous period of seven days beginning at midnight on Sunday.[195] Generally, the Employment Act sets the maximum workweek, without overtime, at 44 hours: eight hours on weekdays, four hours on Saturdays. However, this can be adjusted if the employer has a five-day working week.[196] If, by agreement, an employee works

---

[191]For a description of the class of "covered employees," see V.A.l., above.
[192]Employment Act §38.
[193]*Id.*
[194]*Id.* §40.
[195]*Id.* §41.
[196]*Id.* §38.

fewer than 44 hours in a week, he or she may be required to work extra time to make up the hours the following week, but not exceeding 48 hours per week or 88 hours over a two-week period.[197] For working hours in excess of these hours, an employee is entitled to be paid overtime at varying rates depending on the hours worked.[198]

Shift workers may be requested to work more than 44 hours per week, but the average number of hours worked over any continuous period of three weeks may not exceed 44 per week. Any shift worker who, at the request of the employer, works more than an average of 44 hours per week over a three-week period must be compensated at 150 percent of the worker's basic rate of pay.[199]

The Employment Act limits the total amount of overtime work to a maximum of 72 hours per month.[200] The restrictions on work hours do not apply to employees engaged in the fire services or in work that by its nature involves long hours of inactive or stand-by employment.

See VI.B., below, regarding work hours for children.

3. *Flexible Hours*

Flexible hours, also known as "flex time," are encouraged to ease morning rush-hour congestion and to make it easier for mothers to re-enter the workforce.

4. *Night Work*

"Night" is defined as the period between 11:00 p.m. and 6:00 a.m.[201] A pregnant worker may not be required to work at night without her consent and a letter from her doctor certifying her as fit.[202]

---

[197] *Id.*

[198] See V.A.3., above.

[199] Employment Act §40.

[200] *Id.* §38.

[201] *Id.* §139; Employment (Female Workmen) Regulations (Female Work Regulations), cl. 2.

[202] Female Work Regulations, cl. 3. See VI.B. and VI.C., below, regarding additional Employment Act restrictions on child labor and pregnant employees.

5. Rest Days

The Employment Act provides for a rest day without pay, which may be Sunday or another day as determined by the employer. The employer must prepare a schedule before the beginning of the month in which the rest days fall informing the employees of the employer-appointed rest days. No employee is compelled to work on a rest day unless the nature of the work requires it to be carried on continuously by a succession of shifts. Any disputes regarding this matter are brought to the Commissioner for Labour.[203]

C. Leave

1. Annual Leave

According to the Employment Act, a covered employee[204] who has worked for an employer for at least three months is entitled to seven days of paid annual leave from the employer after one full year of service (pro-rated for a part year).[205] Payment for annual leave is calculated at the employee's gross rate of pay.[206] An employee is entitled to one additional day's leave for every subsequent year of service, subject to a maximum of 14 days.[207] Leave for non-covered employees varies according to the individual employment contract or collective agreement.

An employee forfeits annual leave if he or she is absent from work without permission or excuse for more than 20 percent of the working days in the months or year (as the case may be) in which his or her entitlement accrues.[208] Unused leave does not roll over to the next service year; employees lose any unused leave and are not paid for it.[209] Upon termination, an employee is reim-

---

[203]Employment Act §§36, 37. See I.D., above.
[204]For a definition of covered employees, see V.A.1., above.
[205]Employment Act §43.
[206]See the definition of gross pay at V.A.1., above.
[207]Employment Act §43.
[208]*Id.* §43(5).
[209]*Id.* §43(6).

bursed for unused vacation days, unless he or she is dismissed for misconduct.[210]

2. *Holidays*

For covered employees, the Employment Act grants paid time off for public holidays, with such payment calculated at the gross rate of pay.[211] There are 11 public holidays in Singapore, including Christmas, New Year's Day, and Good Friday. If a holiday falls on a scheduled rest day,[212] the employer must set aside the next workday as a paid holiday. If the holiday falls on a non-workday, and the day is not a scheduled rest day, then the employer either may pay for that holiday at the gross rate of pay or give the employee an additional day off. An employee does not receive additional holiday pay where the employee is on leave of absence without pay at the request of the employee.

Private-sector employees required to work on holidays must be paid an extra day's salary at the basic rate of pay in addition to the gross rate of pay for one day.[213] If a government employee must work on a holiday because certain emergency circumstances have arisen, the employee is not entitled to pay, but, rather, to a day off.[214]

3. *Maternity Leave*

For female employees, the Employment Act and the Children Development Co-Savings Act (CDCSA) spell out the terms of maternity leave.[215] The CDCSA was enacted in 2001 to encourage married women to have more than two children. Under the Employment Act, there are no maternity leave benefits for a woman with more than two children at the time of her confinement, thus the enactment of the CDCSA. The CDCSA also covers all employees, unlike the Employment Act, which does not cover man-

---

[210] *Id.* §43(7).

[211] See the definition of gross pay at V.A.1., above.

[212] See V.B.5., above.

[213] Employment Act §42.

[214] *Id.* §42(6).

[215] Employment Act §§76–87. See also VI.C., below; Children Development Co-Savings Act [Cap 38A] Part III (CDCSA).

agement, executive, and confidential employees, as well as self-employed women.

Under the maternity leave provisions in both Acts, a pregnant employee may take leave during the period beginning four weeks before her due date and ending four weeks after her confinement, or during any eight-week period agreed to by her and her employer beginning not earlier than 28 days before the due date. If the employee has been employed for fewer than 180 days immediately preceding her due date, she is not entitled to any maternity leave pay.

To obtain maternity leave, a female employee must give notice of confinement to her employer approximately one week before going on maternity leave and as soon as possible after confinement. Any employee who fails to serve notice of confinement is entitled to only one-half the amount that otherwise would be payable for the period of her maternity leave, unless she provides a reasonable excuse for her failure to notify her employer.[216]

Maternity leave for female employees is paid at the gross rate of pay.[217] If the employee works for any day during the time of her maternity leave, she is entitled to an extra day's pay, or alternatively, may take a day off.

The conditions for claiming paid maternity leave under the CDCSA are:

- the child is a Singapore citizen at birth and born after April 1, 2001;
- the child is the third child born alive to the woman; and
- the woman was lawfully married to the child's natural father when the child was conceived or before the child is born.

Under the CDCSA, an employer may claim reimbursement from the Ministry of Community Development and Sports (MCDS) of the amount of the maternity leave pay, up to a maximum of S$20,000 for each relevant female employee. As for paid maternity leave to self-employed women, a self-employed woman may

---

[216]Employment Act §80; CDCSA §12.

[217]See the definition at V.A.1., above; CDCSA §9(1).

claim from the MCDS the income she would have otherwise derived from her trade, business, or profession, during the aforesaid maternity period, up to a maximum of S$20,000.

4. *Military Service Leave*

The Enlistment Act[218] provides guidelines for employees who are active in the military. An employer must grant a leave of absence for the duration of an enlistment period and must reinstate an employee who has been in continuous employment for at least six months prior to the date on which the employee was to report for or perform either: full-time, operationally ready, national, or mobilized service; or mobilized service under the Police Force Act.[219] An employer must, where practicable, reinstate an employee in the same occupation and under conditions no less favorable than those that would have been applicable to the employee if the employee had not enlisted. It is a violation of the Enlistment Act for an employer to fail to reinstate an employee unless it is proved that the employee failed to apply for reinstatement within three months from the date of termination of national service. An employer is not allowed to dismiss an employee solely or mainly on the ground that he is or is liable to be enlisted (except in limited circumstances).[220] Any disputes between an employer and employee regarding reimbursement of the civilian pay of the enlisted employee are to be finally settled by the Minister of Defense.[221]

5. *Sick Leave*

According to the Employment Act, for covered employees who have served an employer for at least six months, the employer must provide annual paid sick leave in the aggregate of up to 14 days a year,[222] and if hospitalization is required, then up to14 days plus the number of days hospitalized, not exceeding in total 60 days in a year.[223] If no hospitalization is required, the employee is

---

[218]Enlistment Act [Cap 93].
[219]*Id.* §21.
[220]*Id.* §22.
[221]*Id.* §24(3).
[222]Employment Act §44.
[223]*Id.*

entitled to the gross rate of pay,[224] excluding any allowance payable for shift work. If the employee is hospitalized, he or she is entitled to the gross rate of pay in full.[225]

To qualify for sick leave, an employee must be examined by a medical practitioner appointed by the employer or, if no such medical practitioner is appointed, by a doctor employed by the government or an approved hospital, who then must provide medical certification for sick leave.[226] The medical examination must be paid for by the employer.[227] An employee must inform the employer that he or she is sick within 48 hours of failing to report for work, or else the employee is deemed absent without reasonable excuse.[228] Employees who are sick on a rest day, public holiday, or while on annual leave are not entitled to paid sick leave.[229]

VI. ANTIDISCRIMINATION

Singapore's Constitution contains a guarantee of equality before the law.[230] In particular, the position of the minority Malays as the indigenous people of Singapore is recognized, and their language, religion, and culture are accorded special protection.[231]

In terms of legislation, Singapore has no broad-based equal employment or affirmative action provisions similar to those commonly found in the West. The policy of the Singapore government has been to focus on moral persuasion and community self-help instead of relying on legislation to meet the issue of discrimination in the labor market.

The NTUC and the employers' federations (the Singapore National Employers' Federation and the Singapore Business Federation) have jointly issued a Code of Responsible Employment

---

[224]See the definition at V.A.1., above.

[225]Employment Act §44.

[226]*Id.* §44(3).

[227]*Id.* §44(1).

[228]*Id.* §44(3).

[229]*Id.* §44(4A).

[230]CONST. art. 12.

[231]*Id.* art. 152.

Practices that is intended to help employers promote and observe responsible employment practices in the workplace regardless of race, religion, age, gender, marital status, disability, or factors that have no relevance to the requirements of the job, and to encourage self-regulation in relation to recruitment, selection, appraisal, job upgrading, posting, and training, as well as terms and conditions of employment.[232]

However, certain individual groups, including older workers, children, and pregnant women, are protected by specific legislation. This protective legislation is discussed below.

A. Age Discrimination

Protection of older workers is covered in the Retirement Age Act,[233] which provides a prescribed minimum retirement age of 62 for employees in Singapore.[234] The Minister of Manpower has the power to raise this minimum age to a maximum of 67 years, as the government tends to view early retirement as a waste of human resources.

Any collective agreement or contract of service that provides for a retirement age younger than the prescribed minimum retirement age, whether made before or after the Retirement Age Act became effective, is considered void to the extent that it is so less favorable.[235] This means that employees have the right to work until they are 62 years old (which is the current prescribed minimum retirement age), even though their contracts may provide for an earlier retirement age.[236] However, employers may reduce the wages of employees who attain the age of 60 after January 1, 1999, after giving reasonable prior notice of the intent and details of the proposed pay reduction.[237] Employees who disagree with the employer's pay reduction may retire or be retired by the employer after they reach age 60.[238] Workers under fixed-term contracts (doc-

[232]A copy of the Code is available on the Singapore National Employers' Federation website, at <www.sgemployers.com>.

[233]Retirement Age Act [Cap 274A].

[234]*Id.* §4(1); Retirement Age (Prescribed Retirement Age) Regulations 1998.

[235]Retirement Age Act §6.

[236]*Id.* §7.

[237]*Id* §5(3).

[238]*Id* §5(4).

tors, police, etc.) are excluded from these guidelines, as are those working in more physically demanding environments.

It is a violation of the Retirement Age Act for an employer to dismiss an employee younger than 60 years of age or the prescribed minimum retirement age on grounds of age. An employer that does so can be punished by a fine up to S$5,000, or six months in jail for the decisionmaker, or both.[239] If the employer does not comply with the terms of a fine and does not reinstate the employee, it then is liable for an additional fine up to S$5,000, or up to 12 months in jail, or both.

Employees younger than the prescribed minimum retirement age who believe that they have been dismissed unlawfully on account of their age may appeal in writing to the Manpower Minister.[240] Unionized employees may appeal through their union. The Minister can order reinstatement, plus lost wages or compensation (calculated by taking into consideration the loss suffered by the employee, prospects of obtaining another job, age, and length of service).

B. Employment of Children

Guidelines concerning the employment of children are set out in the Employment Act. A child between the ages of 12 and 16 may be employed only in an industrial undertaking in which members of the same family are employed. A child aged 12 or older may be employed in a nonindustrial undertaking in light work suited to his or her capacity. A medical certificate is required to provide proof that the work is suited to the child's capacity.[241] Children younger than age 16 may not work with machinery in motion without written approval of the Minister of Manpower, and they may not work with an improperly insulated electrical apparatus. Children between the ages of 12 and 14 may not work more than six hours per day and may not work for more than three hours without a 30-minute break. Children between the ages of 14 and 16 may

---

[239] *Id.* §4(3).
[240] *Id.* §8.
[241] Employment Act §68.

not work more than seven hours per day, and not more than four hours without a 30-minute break. The Minister of Manpower determines minimum rates of salary for children.

Any person who employs a child in violation of the Employment Act, and any parent or guardian who knowingly or negligently permits such employment, is liable on conviction to a fine not exceeding S$2,000, or to imprisonment for a term not exceeding two years, or both. The prescribed maximum punishments become mandatory when a child suffers serious injury or death as a result of working in violation of the Employment Act.[242]

C. Pregnant Women

The Employment Act and the Children Development Co-Savings Act also protects pregnant employees.[243] As discussed above,[244] a female employee who has worked for at least 180 days, and has no more than three children, is entitled to eight weeks' paid maternity leave. An employer is not allowed to dismiss an employee during her maternity leave unless she works for another employer during the paid leave period. In addition, the employer may not deprive an employee of maternity benefits by dismissing her within three months before her confinement, unless the dismissal is based on just cause.[245]

Under the Employment Act, a woman who feels she has been wrongfully dismissed must appeal within two months from the date of confinement to the Minister of Manpower for reinstatement and compensation. An employer that fails to comply with the direction of the Minister made in response to an appeal is guilty of an offense under the Employment Act and is liable for a fine not exceeding S$5,000, or to imprisonment of not more than 12 months upon conviction, or both.[246]

---

[242]*Id.* §74.

[243]See V.C.3., above.

[244]See V.C.3., above.

[245]For a discussion of just cause, see I.C.1., above.

[246]Employment Act §§81, 83–85.

VII. OCCUPATIONAL SAFETY AND HEALTH AND WORKERS' COMPENSATION

A. Occupational Safety and Health

1. Safety and Health Provisions of the Factories Act

The Factories Act[247] sets out rights and duties of employers regarding the health, safety, and welfare of employees. A factory is defined by the Act as any premises and its surrounding fenced-in area in which persons are hired to do manual work in making, altering, repairing, processing, finishing, cleaning, washing, or breaking up of any article, or adapting any article for sale, for the purpose of trade or business and to which the employer has the right of access or control.[248] A "factory" may include a shipyard, a printshop, premises for bulk storage of toxic or inflammable liquid, and premises for generating electricity or water supply. The President of Singapore has the power to declare any dwelling not a factory on the grounds of emergency or security. The Minister of Manpower also has the power to exempt any factory from the health, safety, and welfare provisions of the Act.[249]

The Factories Act provides guidelines[250] for the following:

- cleanliness,
- overcrowding,[251]
- ventilation,[252]
- lighting,
- drainage, and
- sanitation.[253]

---

[247]Factories Act [Cap 104].

[248]*Id.* §6.

[249]*Id.* §§4, 5.

[250]*Id.* §§12–17.

[251]Every worker must have 11.5 cubic meters of air space, and the height of every room may not be less than three meters.

[252]Every part of the factory where persons are working must have an adequate supply of clean, fresh air.

[253]Toilets must be kept clean, adequately lighted, and separately provided for workers of different sexes.

The Factories Act spells out the specifics of operation, maintenance, and storage of machinery and other items typically used in the workplace. The Act also regulates workers' welfare by providing that workers must be supplied with clean and cold drinking water if exposed to excessive heat, and suitable facilities and water for washing; workplaces that expose workers to toxic or corrosive materials must have suitable facilities for quick drenching and flushing of the eyes or body. Additional provisions of the Act set out guidelines for the control of disease in factories.[254]

The Factories Act also regulates the safety of persons at work through the following provisions:

- requirements to supply a safe working environment for those who are exposed to toxic fumes and dust;
- standards for warning notices and hazard labels;
- requirements for the distribution of safety data sheets regarding the hazards involved in handling toxic, corrosive, or inflammable substances; and
- requirements for the provision of suitable clothing for the protection of eyes and ears.[255]

In addition, if any part of the factory gives rise to harmful dust or fumes, workers must be given separate rooms for meals and/or rest.[256]

The government's Chief Inspector[257] appoints safety officers who must have technical training and acceptable experience in workplace safety. The safety officer is responsible to the employer for ensuring safety in the factory and must be allowed to attend training courses as part of his or her work. Every factory must set up a safety committee on which management and workers are equally represented to promote safe, healthy working conditions.

See VI.B., above, regarding special safety provisions applicable to the employment of children under the Employment Act.

---

[254]Factories Act §§67,69.

[255]*Id.* §§59–72.

[256]*Id.* §61.

[257]See VII.A.3., below, regarding inspections.

2. *Accommodations and Medical Care in the Workplace*

The Employment Act also deals with proper accommodations and medical care to be provided by employers to employees in the workplace. These guidelines are far less exhaustive than those set forth in the Factories Act. Essentially, the Employment Act states that every employer that undertakes to provide quarters for workers must ensure the following:

- sufficient and proper quarters;
- sufficient supply of wholesome water; and
- sufficient and proper sanitary arrangements.[258]

The Employment Act also states that all buildings that house workers must be built in accordance with building codes and titles, and that every place where workers are employed must provide first-aid equipment. Failure to comply with any of these provisions constitutes a violation under the Employment Act and can result in a fine not exceeding S$1,000, or in imprisonment for a term not exceeding six months, or both.[259]

3. *Inspections*

The Department of Industrial Safety undertakes prevention and control of occupational diseases and monitors industrial hygiene in the workplace. Factories are regularly inspected by Department inspectors.

Under the Factories Act, an inspector from the Department of Industrial Safety may enter a factory at any time to inspect the premises, ask questions of employers and employees, take samples of harmful substances, and require hospitals to give information about injured persons receiving treatment. It is considered a violation of the Factories Act to refuse to answer, obstruct the investigation, or refuse to produce documents for the inspector. If an offending employer is a company or cooperative society, any officer, agent, or worker of the employer can be charged with the same

[258]Employment Act §91.
[259]*Id.* §§92–94, 112.

offense. If the employer can prove that it carefully observed provisions of the Factories Act, and the violation was committed without the consent or fault of the employer, only the worker or other person who committed the offense will be charged.[260]

Industrial accidents that result in more than three days of absence or one day of hospitalization must be reported to the Department of Industrial Safety.

B. Workers' Compensation

In Singapore, the Workmen's Compensation Act[261] provides compensation to injured workers or to their dependents in the event that a worker is injured or dies as the result of a work-related accident or illness. The Workmen's Compensation Act's coverage excludes all employees who perform nonmanual work and earn more than S$1,600 a month, domestic servants, police officers, and any additional class of persons excluded by the Minister of Manpower.[262]

For purposes of death benefits, dependents include spouses, children, stepparents, parents, grandparents, stepchildren, brothers, sisters, half-brothers, half-sisters, stepbrothers, and stepsisters.[263] According to the Workmen's Compensation Act, it is not necessary for the dependent to have been actually dependent on the deceased worker for support.[264] If no dependents are found, the money goes into the Worker's Fund to benefit other families whose lives are in distress as a result of a worker's death.[265]

Compensation is payable when a worker is personally injured or dies under the following circumstances:

- in an accident arising out of and in the course of employment, including while traveling to and from work in a transport belonging to or being operated for or by the employer;

---

[260]Factories Act §§84–86, 88(12), 91, 93, 94.
[261]Workmen's Compensation Act [Cap 354].
[262]*Id.* §2.
[263]*Id.*
[264]*Id.*
[265]*Id.* §6(3).

- in an accident that occurs while the worker tries to save a life or property in an emergency while at work; or
- as a result of an occupational disease (defined as an illness or any other abnormal condition resulting from the handling of, contact with, or exposure to, organic/inorganic substances, chemicals, or physical processes).[266]

Compensation is not payable where any of the following occur:

- an injury is shown to have occurred when a worker was drunk or drugged without excuse, unless the worker either dies or is permanently incapacitated and loses at least one-half of his or her earning capacity as a result of the injury;
- the injury is self-inflicted or worsened by the worker; or
- the illness is not listed as an occupational disease, and it cannot be shown to have resulted from an injury or accident arising out of the course of employment.[267]

To claim compensation, the injured worker reports the injury or illness to his or her immediate supervisor as soon as possible, stating the time, date, and place of the accident and the nature of the injury. A claim must be made to the employer within one year of the accident or death.[268] The employer must report to the Commissioner for Labour within a specified period. Any employer who fails to give such notice shall be guilty of an offense liable to a fine not exceeding S$2,000 if convicted.[269] Within five days of being informed of the accident, the employer must provide free medical consultation and treatment.[270]

The amount of compensation is based on the extent of lost earning capacity and is assessed by the Commissioner on the basis of a medical report. If the assessment is not disputed by the employer within two weeks of service of the Commissioner's notice, then the amount of compensation must be paid within 21 days of

[266]*Id.* §§3, 4.
[267]*Id.* §§3(5), 5.
[268]*Id.* §11.
[269]*Id.* §12.
[270]*Id.* §13.

service of the notice.[271] If the assessment is disputed, the Commissioner will conduct a hearing. The order can be enforced as a decision of the District Court. The Commissioner's order also may be appealed to the High Court, provided that the employer deposits the stated amount of compensation with the Commissioner within 21 days.[272]

The Workmen's Compensation Act also provides alternatives to workers' compensation. Specifically, the injured employee has the option of either claiming compensation under the Act or suing for damages at common law. However, an employee may not sue for damages if he or she already has claimed compensation, or if damages already have been obtained from any other person for the same injury or death. If the court finds that no damages are payable, it nonetheless can order payment of compensation under the Workmen's Compensation Act after due deduction for the cost of legal proceedings.[273]

A worker may not be deprived of compensation to which he or she is entitled, and any agreement made by the worker to waive his or her right to compensation is invalid.[274] Employers must obtain insurance to cover their potential liability for workers' compensation.[275]

VIII. PENSIONS AND BENEFITS

A. Central Provident Fund

The Central Provident Fund (CPF) provides retirement benefits from contributions made by both employers and employees. Contributions are held by the CPF Board for payment to workers upon retirement. Employers and employees are free to agree on additional retirement benefits under an individual contract of service or a collective agreement.

---

[271] *Id.* §24.
[272] *Id.* §29.
[273] *Id.* §§18, 33.
[274] *Id.* §21.
[275] *Id.* §23.

The Central Provident Fund Act[276] spells out the terms of the CPF. The CPF is managed by a Board, with the chairman appointed by the Minister of Manpower. Six members sit on the Board, representing employers, employees, and the government. The Minister of Manpower may appoint no more than four others of his or her choosing to the Board.[277] Contributions to the CPF are held by the Board in trust for participating employees and either are deposited in approved banks or authorized investments, or are used for the purchase or construction of properties for the Board's purposes.[278] The Board appoints inspectors to enforce the Central Provident Fund Act. The inspectors may enter any place of work in order to examine and request to speak to, and ask any questions of, any person employed at the workplace.[279] If an employer is found guilty of not abiding by the rules of the CPF, it is liable for a fine not exceeding S$2,500 for the first offense, and a fine up to S$10,000 for second or subsequent offenses. The employer may be asked to pay all arrears of contributions with interest.[280]

All workers who are Singapore citizens or permanent residents are eligible, and are required, to participate in the CPF. From January 2003, non-Singapore citizens who are not permanent residents will not be allowed to contribute to the CPF. The CPF also covers all self-employed persons who earn a net trade income of more than S$6,000 per year.[281] However, such self-employed persons are required to contribute to Medisave only.[282]

CPF contributions are computed based on the employee's wages. For this purpose, wages of employees are divided into "ordinary wages" and "additional wages." Ordinary wages are the basic monthly salary including allowances. Additional wages include annual bonus, leave pay, and incentive pay. Total wages are comprised of both ordinary wages and additional wages.

---

[276]Central Provident Fund Act [Cap 36].
[277]*Id.* §§3–5.
[278]*Id.* §6.
[279]*Id.* §5.
[280]*Id.* §9.
[281]*Id.* §13B.
[282]*Id.* §§13A and 13B.

CPF contributions are payable for all employees (including part-time and casual employees) earning more than S$50 a month, and the contribution rates differ depending on age and the amount of the salary. The maximum ordinary wages on which mandatory CPF contributions are payable is S$5,500 a month.

- Employees in the private sector younger than age 55 and earning more than S$750 a month contribute 20 percent of their ordinary wages to the CPF (up to a maximum of S$1,100 a month).
- For private-sector employees over the age of 55, the rate of contribution is 12.5 percent of their ordinary wages (up to a maximum of S$687.50 a month) until they reach age 60.
- Between ages 60 to 65, the rate falls to 7.5 percent (up to a maximum of $412.50 a month).
- A private-sector employee older than age 65 contributes only 5 percent of his or her ordinary wages (up to a maximum of S$275 a month).
- For employers of private-sector employees aged 55 and younger, the net rate of contribution is 13 percent of the employee's ordinary wages (up to a maximum of S$715 a month).[283]
- For employees older than age 55 but younger than age 60, the employer's net contribution rate falls to 6 percent.
- For employees older than 60 years, the employer's net contribution rate falls to 3.5 percent.

For additional wages, the rates of contribution are the same as for ordinary wages, except that the formula for determining the additional wage ceiling (which is the maximum amount of additional wages for the year subject to mandatory CPF contribution) has been changed effective January 1, 2004. The additional wage ceiling will now be calculated based on the formula: S$93,500 minus the total ordinary wages subject to CPF in the year (which total ordinary wages can go up to a maximum of S$66,000 or

[283]The long term target for CPF rates for employer's contributions for employees age 50 and younger is between 10% to 16%, and for employees older than age 50 but younger than age 55, 6% to 12%.

S$5,500 × 12 months). The respective contribution rates will then be applied on the figure arrived at in order to obtain the mandatory CPF contribution on the additional wages.

In practice, the employer pays both the employee's and the employer's contribution to the CPF Board and deducts the amount of the employee's contribution from the employee's salary.

CPF contributions are channeled in three directions:

- the Ordinary Account, which may be used for housing, approved investments, insurance, and education;
- the Medisave Account, which may be used for hospitalization and medical expenses; and
- the Special Account, which is meant for old age funds and contingency purposes, although it can be used for certain limited investment purposes.[284]

Contributions may be withdrawn:

- at age 55 or upon the death of the employee, or upon the earlier retirement of the employee if the employee is certified by a duly appointed physician to be either physically or mentally unable to continue in any employment or to be of unsound mind, provided that depending on the balance in the CPF member's CPF account, a certain minimum sum (currently S$80,000 and to be increased by S$4,000 each year) must be retained in a CPF retirement account as capital to provide for a regular monthly distribution to the CPF member for his or her old age starting from the legislated retirement age, which is currently 62 years;
- to pay for tuition and fees for the employee, a child, or a relative for courses taken at an approved tertiary institution;
- to buy or upgrade a house or residential property, or as a reimbursement for buying land or building a house, provided that if the employee sells, transfers, or assigns the purchased home or property, the employee must repay the

[284]Central Provident Fund Act §13.

Board the sum of money plus interest accrued; upon an employee's death, the sum credited is paid and shared among the employee's dependents;[285] and
- for approved investments, for hospital and certain other medical expenses, and payment of premiums for CPF Board-approved insurance coverage, including medical and life insurance.

B. Health and Disability Funds

It is customary for employers to provide medical benefits to their employees. If an employee is a member of the CPF, at least 6 percent (increasing progressively with age) of his or her wages (paid from the monthly CPF contribution) goes into a Medisave Account. Self-employed persons—including partners and sole-proprietors who earn in excess of S$6,000 per year—must contribute a percentage of their yearly net trade income (between 6 to 8 percent depending on age) to the Medisave Account.

The current Medisave contribution ceiling (that is, the maximum amount to be retained in the Medisave Account) is S$30,000; any contribution in excess of the ceiling is transferred to the Ordinary Account. All contributions to Medisave must be paid by December 31 of each year. When members reach age 55 and withdraw their CPF savings,[286] they must retain a certain amount in Medisave to cover future medical expenses.

The Medisave Account may be used for medical treatment or services for a member or a member's spouse, child, parent, or grandparent. Grandparents must be either Singapore citizens or permanent residents to qualify for coverage. Medisave Accounts may be used for meeting hospitalization expenses and for buying medical insurance. The Medisave Account may be used at all government and approved private hospitals to pay for ward charges, doctor's fees, fees for surgery and operating theaters, medical treatment and supplies, investigations and rehabilitation services (subject to withdrawal limits), maternity expenses for the first three living children, outpatient treatments including hepatitis-B vaccinations,

---

[285] *Id.* §§15, 24.

[286] See VIII.A., above.

renal dialysis, radiotherapy, chemotherapy, AIDS treatment, and assisted conception procedures.

C. Skills Development and Lifelong Learning Funds

Under the Skills Development Levy Act,[287] employers are assessed monthly for each employee earning S$1,500 or less per month, at the rate of 1 percent of that employee's remuneration or S$2, whichever is higher.[288] The proceeds from this levy are channeled to the Skills Development Fund.[289] Together with other government contributions,[290] the Skills Development Fund is used to subsidize the upgrading of skills by current members of the workforce, as well as persons who are preparing to join or rejoin the workforce.[291]

In 2001, Parliament enacted into law the Lifelong Learning Endowment Fund Act.[292] The Lifelong Learning Endowment Fund stood at S$1 billion in August 2002, with the intent of building the Fund from additional budget surpluses to a target size of S$5 billion.[293] The Fund will be used to promote lifelong learning among workers who are Singaporeans or permanent residents,[294] especially with regard to information technology skills. The Lifelong Learning Endowment Fund is expected to finance the efforts of the Ministry of Manpower, other government agencies, and industry players to help workers upgrade their skills and enhance their employability, including setting up a National Skills Recognition System to develop definitive workplace skills standards and to accord recognition to training that meets these standards. This is very much in character with the prevailing ethos of the government, which sets great emphasis on the upgrading of workers' skills.

---

[287]Skills Development Levy Act [Cap 306].

[288]*Id.* §3.

[289]*Id.* §5.

[290]*See id.* §§5(2), 6.

[291]*Id.* §7.

[292]Lifelong Learning Endowment Fund Act [Cap 162A]. See also the Introduction, above.

[293]LLEFA §§3, 4.

[294]*Id.* §5.

IX. IMMIGRATION

In 2001, the number of foreign workers in Singapore was approximately 450,000. The overwhelming majority of foreign personnel are employed in blue-collar and domestic positions.

In general, the policy followed by the Singapore government is that it prefers employment and training of Singaporean citizens, but it is lenient as to employment of foreigners and foreign workers where there are no qualified local workers.

The Employment of Foreign Workers Act[295] regulates the employment of work permit holders. Work permits must be obtained for foreign unskilled or semi-skilled workers.[296] The Ministry imposes quotas or ceilings on the number of work permit holders an employer may have. These ceilings vary according to the particular industry, for example:

- in the construction industry, the maximum for work permit holders is four foreign workers to one full-time Singapore worker;
- in the marine industry, the maximum is three foreign workers to one full-time Singapore worker;
- in manufacturing, the maximum is one foreign worker to one Singapore worker; and
- in the service industry, the maximum is 30 percent of the total workforce.[297]

The government also imposes a levy on employers for each work permit holder.[298] The amounts levied tend to reflect market conditions and are subject to change. The rates also differ from one industry to another, being highest in the construction industry. To encourage the greater employment of skilled workers, the rate for a skilled worker is much less than that for an unskilled worker. For example:

---

[295]Employment of Foreign Workers Act [Cap 91A] (EFWA).

[296]*Id.* §§2, 5; Cap 91A, Notification 3.

[297]See Ministry of Manpower website at <www.gov.sg/mom>.

[298]EWFA §11(1); Employment of Foreign Workers (Levy) Order (EFWLO).

- S$345 per month for domestic workers (that is, domestic help);[299]
- S$30 per month for skilled construction workers;[300] and S$470 per month for unskilled construction workers;[301]
- S$30 for skilled marine workers;[302] and
- S$295 for unskilled marine workers.[303]

The Immigration Regulations govern the issue of employment passes[304] Professionals, managers, and executives with an acceptable degree, professional qualification, or specialist skill and earning more than S$2,500 per month are eligible for employment passes that may be issued for between one to three years, qualifying them for employment within Singapore if they engage in an approved business, profession, or occupation.[305] As a practical matter, there is little difficulty in obtaining employment passes where the applicants are senior executives of large foreign corporations or are well-qualified specialists. No quota is imposed and no levy is payable by employers on employment pass holders. Generally, employment pass holders may sponsor their dependents for temporary residence in Singapore. Work permit holders have no such dependent privileges.

The Ministry of Manpower has recently announced that it will be introducing a new work pass, called an S pass, which is intended to cover the gap between the employment pass and work permit holders. The S pass is intended for middle-level associate professionals and technicians who earn at least S$1,800 a month. The S pass will come into effect on July 1, 2004. Employers will have to pay a levy (based on a skilled foreign worker levy) on each S pass holder and quotas will be imposed on how many S pass holders an employer may hire. An S pass holder earning at least S$2500 a month will have dependent privileges. The operational

[299]Employment of Foreign Workers (Levy) Order (EFWLO) §5.
[300]*Id.* §6.
[301]*Id.* §7.
[302]*Id.* §9.
[303]*Id.* §10.
[304]Promulgated under the Immigration Act [Cap 133].
[305]Immigration Act [Cap 133] §55(1); Immigration Regs., cl. 9.

and technical details of the S pass are still being worked out by the Ministry.

Concrete measures to lessen dependence on foreign workers include the quotas and imposition of levies and stiff penalties for illegal workers. Workers caught overstaying their work permits are liable for caning and expulsion. The Employment of Foreign Workers Act holds principal contractors responsible for illegal workers found in the workplace and imposes a fine equal to 24 months to 48 months of the worker's levy, or imprisonment not exceeding 12 months, or both.[306] Fines are doubled for corporate repeat offenders. Individuals who are repeat offenders are subject to imprisonment for between one to twelve months and a fine of an amount equivalent to between 24 and 48 months' levy. The burden of proof falls on the employer in these matters.[307] Additionally, the Immigration Act imposes strict liability on landlords who rent their premises out to illegal workers.[308]

Employees who do not have permanent residence status are exempted from the CPF[309] and neither the employer nor the employee is allowed to make contributions to the CPF.

---

[306]EFWA §5.
[307]*Id.* §6.
[308]Immigration Act §§57, 57A.
[309]See VIII.A., above.

SOUTH KOREA*

INTRODUCTION

A. Government Structure

There are three branches, the legislative, the executive, and the judicial, in the Korean government under the Korean Constitution, which was first promulgated in 1948 and last amended in 1987.

1. Legislative Branch

The legislative power is vested in the National Assembly, a unicameral parliament composed of not less than 200 members. As of the 14th National Assembly, commencing on May 30, 2004, there are 299 members. The citizens in small electorates directly elect 243 of these members, and 56 become members from the list of ranked candidates in their party in proportion to the number of seats acquired by their party in the local election. The term of office for members of the National Assembly is four years.

There are various organizations within the National Assembly. Sixteen standing committees and three special committees convene to discuss and deliberate on matters in their field. The standing committees are the House Steering Committee; Legislation & Judiciary; National Policy; Finance & Economy; Unification, Foreign Affairs & Trade; Government Administration & Home Affairs; National Defense; Education; Culture & Tourism; Agriculture, Forestry, Maritime Affairs, & Fisheries; Commerce, Industry & Energy; Science, Technology, Information & Telecommunication; Environment & Labor; Health & Welfare; Construction & Transportation; and Intelligence. The three special

---

*C.W. Hyun, J.C. Jung, and Hye C. Yu, Kim & Chang, Seoul, South Korea.

committees are on Ethics, Women's Affairs, and Budget & Accounts. In addition, the National Assembly is broken up into several bargaining bodies, formed by the members of the same party that has 20 or more seats in the National Assembly. Other legislative organizations within the National Assembly are the Secretariat, the Library, and Budget Office.

The National Assembly has several important powers. First, it has the power to take legislative action. It introduces bills, deliberates on them, passes them, and re-passes them when rejected by the President. It also can propose to amend the Constitution and decide on the proposed amendments. It has the right to consent to the conclusion and ratification of various treaties. Several powers of the National Assembly are related to finance. For instance, it deliberates and decides upon the national tax bill and budget bill, approves a reserve fund and issuance of national bonds, and concludes contracts that may incur financial obligations on the state. The National Assembly also has means to check the power of the executive branch. For instance, it may inspect affairs of the state and give or refuse consent to such actions as the declaration of war or the dispatch of armed forces to foreign states. Another significant power of the National Assembly involves personnel measures. For example, it has the right to consent to appointment of the Prime Minister, Chairman of the Board of Audit and Inspection, Chief Justice of the Supreme Court, Supreme Court Justices, and the President of the Constitutional Court.

2. *Executive Branch*

The executive power is vested in the dual structured Executive Branch. Political executive matters are handled by the President, and administrative matters are handled by the Prime Minister and organizations such as the State Council, 18 Executive Ministries (including the Ministry of Finance & Economy; Unification; Foreign Affairs & Trade; Justice; National Defense; Government Administration & Home Affairs; Education & Human Resource Development; Science & Technology; Culture & Tourism; Agriculture & Forestry; Commerce, Industry & Energy; Information & Communication; Health & Welfare; Environment; Labor; Gender Equality; Construction & Transportation; Maritime Affairs & Fisheries), Board of Audit and Inspection, and four Advisory Councils (Advisory Council of Elder Statesmen; National Security Council; Advisory Council on Democratic and Peaceful Unification; National Economic Advisory Council). However, as the Chairman of the State Council, the President partakes in administrative matters as well. The President is elected directly by Korean citizens for a term of five years and may not be reelected. The Prime Minister is appointed by the President with the consent of the National Assembly. Then the State Council and Executive Ministers are appointed by the President on the recommendation of the Prime Minister.

The President has powers as the head of state and the government. Some of his main powers are as follows. He represents the state vis-à-vis foreign states, concludes and ratifies treaties, and accredits, receives, or dispatches diplomatic envoys. He is the Commander-in-Chief of the Armed Forces and has the power to declare war, dispatch soldiers, and conclude peace. He may submit important policies to a national referendum, propose to amend the Constitution, issue presidential decrees having the effect of law, and proclaim martial law. He also directs and supervises the heads of all central administrative agencies and may suspend or cancel any order or disposition by the Prime Minister or the heads of central administrative agencies as deemed unlawful or unjust. He may grant amnesty, commutation and restoration of rights, and award decorations and other honors.

The Prime Minister deliberates on state affairs, issues Ordinances of the Prime Minister, and directs the Executive Ministries. In addition, there are also several other offices and agencies under the auspice of the Prime Minister. An Office for Government Policy Coordination assists the Prime Minister with respect to the administrative direction and supervision, policy coordination, and the review, evaluation, and regulation reform of each central administrative agency. A Ministry of Planning and Budget takes charge of the duties on budget policies, the management of compilation of budget and execution thereof, financial reforms, and administrative reforms. A Ministry of Legislation takes charge of the review of draft Acts and subordinate statutes, draft treaties, Ordinances of the Prime Minister, draft Ministerial Ordinances to be laid before the State Council, and other affairs on legislation. A Government Information Agency takes charge of the duties on the domestic and foreign public information of state affairs. A Patriots and Veterans Administration Agency takes charge of the affairs on merit reward for persons of distinguished service to the state and their bereaved family members.

3. *Judicial Branch*

The judicial power is vested in courts composed of judges. The Supreme Court, composed of 14 Justices, is the highest court of the state. Under that are found the High Court, Patent Court, District Courts in cities and counties, Family Court, Administrative Court, and a special Martial Court. There is also a separate Constitutional Court. The Chief Justice of the Supreme Court is appointed by the President with the consent of the National Assembly, for a one-term period of six years. Then the Supreme Court Justices are appointed by the President on the recommendation of the Chief Justice and with the consent of the National Assembly. Other judges are appointed by the Chief Justice, for terms of ten years. As for the Constitutional Court, there are nine Justices appointed by the President, three from persons selected by the National Assembly and three from persons nominated by the Chief Justice of the Supreme Court. The President of the Constitutional Court is appointed by the President with the consent of the National Assembly. All Justices on the Constitutional Court serve for terms of six years.

The courts in general are categorized by the type of cases they review, for instance, civil action, criminal action, family matters, administrative matters, and patents. The Constitutional Court decides on the constitutionality of a law upon the request of the courts, impeachment, dissolution of a political party, competence disputes between state agencies, between state agencies and local governments, and between local governments, and constitutional complaints. The Supreme Court has the power to make a final review of the constitutionality or legality of administrative decrees, regulations, or actions, when their constitutionality or legality is at issue in a trial.

B. Overview of South Korean Labor Law

Most aspects of employment and labor relations in the Republic of Korea (South Korea), from minimum terms and conditions of employment to the conduct of collective bargaining, are governed by statute and administrative decrees and regulations. Violations of the mandatory provisions of these laws are criminal offenses punishable by fines (and sometimes, but rarely, by imprisonment).

This perspective may be changing, as employment and labor law violations increasingly expose companies to the risk of criminal complaints during periods of labor unrest or collective bargaining. One proposed explanation for this change is the growth of the domestic labor movement. In fact, the level of labor activism has varied in recent years. From 1987 to 1989, the rate of unionization and the frequency of labor disputes increased substantially. However, since 1990, the frequency of labor disputes has generally declined, although recently, due to hotly debated issues such as job security in light of restructuring and reform of Korean financial institutions and corporations, strike activity has been on the rise. Another explanation, which holds despite the fluctuation of union influence, is that the South Korean government has begun to enforce labor and employment laws more strictly.

C. Characteristics of South Korea's Labor Relations System

1. *Structural Characteristics*

South Korea's labor and employment laws have three main components:

- individual employment law, under which labor contracts must contain certain conditions designed to protect workers;
- collective industrial relations law, which provides a framework for labor unions to seek improved working conditions through independent bargaining with employers; and
- cooperative labor relations law, which establishes a system for developing cooperation between labor and management.

This structure, based on the free enterprise economic system, aims to secure minimum working conditions through autonomous bargaining processes between employers and employees. The South

Korean Constitution gives employees the right to association, collective bargaining, and collective action for these purposes.

The concept of cooperative labor relations is an innovation, and is designed to promote cooperative, rather than adversarial, relations between labor and management. As part of this effort, joint labor and management councils have been established independently from trade unions.

2. *Functional Characteristics*

The main function of the labor relations system is to maintain equivalency between labor and management. However, since the 1960s, trade unions have experienced difficulties in properly carrying out their functions under the current system, which has tended to favor employers. As a result, employees often have been unable to achieve their demands through trade unions.

Increasingly, since the 1970s, the government has involved itself in collective labor relations issues. Contacts between government and management, and between government and labor, have become a notable new feature of South Korean labor relations. In this environment, whether employees' complaints come to light depends in part on the government's willingness to intervene. Acrimonious labor disputes since the so-called 6.29 Declaration can be understood from these viewpoints.[1]

D. Sources of Labor Law

1. *Constitution*

The Constitution, last amended on October 29, 1987, prevails over all other sources of labor law and plays a dominant role in the labor law field. Articles 32 and 33 of the Constitution are regarded as the most fundamental sources of labor law.

Article 32 guides individual employment relationships. Section 1 of Article 32 guarantees the right to work, thus providing a constitutional basis for laws concerning employment security,

---

[1]In 1987, the Korean government, in an effort to meet the demands of the Korean people for political and social democratization, issued the 6.29 Declaration, which led to frequent labor disputes and an increase in the number of trade unions being organized.

minimum wage, unemployment insurance, and vocational training. Sections 4 and 5, which accord special protection to working women and minors, provide a general basis for protective labor laws by requiring minimum standards for working conditions.

Article 33 provides a constitutional basis for legislation in the field of collective labor relations. Section 1 guarantees the right of workers to organize, bargain, and act collectively. However, for public officials or workers employed by important defense industries, these rights are subject to restriction, as prescribed by law.[2]

As with other basic rights, the right to work or to act collectively may legally be restricted when necessary for national security, maintenance of law and order, or the public welfare. However, even when such restrictions are imposed, no essential rights or freedoms are to be violated.[3] An essential right does not only mean the right to work. For example, any laws that would prevent the establishment of a labor union, require government intervention in the internal personnel affairs of the labor union, or involve unfair intervention of the government in collective bargaining, would violate essential rights.

The fact that these constitutional provisions guarantee the rights of workers means not only that workers are protected against restrictions or interference by the state, but also that they have the right to apply to the courts for legal relief when their rights are violated. Moreover, in interpreting and applying labor legislation and other employment regulations, courts must respect the underlying constitutional guarantees.

2. *Legislation*

Rules established by labor legislation are the key source of various labor-related protections. The important labor laws in South Korea were enacted during the Korean War of 1950 to 1952, and have been revised several times since then. Worker protection laws are particularly important, insofar as they set minimum standards for all workers, whether or not they are union members. Labor laws maintain the status of *lex specials* (special laws) to the civil

---

[2]Constitution art. 33, §§2, 3.

[3]*Id.* art. 37.

law, and, in principle, have compulsory power over those within their reach. The labor laws supersede those individual work contracts and collective agreements that provide a lower level of working conditions than the standards established by law. In contrast, in the event that individual contracts, collective agreements, or work rules guarantee better working conditions than those stipulated in the law, the private terms are accepted as valid, under the principle that the labor laws set minimum standards that may be exceeded by agreement between employers and employees.

The primary statutes that regulate labor relations in South Korea are the following:

- The Labor Standards Act of 1953, which prescribes minimum terms and conditions of employment (for merchant seamen and other employees on board ships, the Labor Standards Act is substantially superseded by the Seaman's Act of 1961);
- The Trade Union and Labor Relations Adjustment Act of 1997, which prescribes procedures for the formation and management of unions, rules for collective bargaining, lists of unfair labor practices, procedures for government mediation efforts, and rules on labor disputes;
- The Labor Relations Commission Act of 1997, which provides for the formation and operation of the Labor Relations Commission, the body charged with the mediation of labor disputes, as well as the adjudication of unfair labor practices and wrongful termination cases;
- The Act to Promote Worker Participation and Cooperation of 1997, which requires the formation of labor management councils in companies meeting certain criteria;
- The Minimum Wage Act, which establishes an administrative body to set minimum wage levels for certain employees;
- The Employment Security Act of 1967, which establishes placement services and promulgates rules regarding employee recruitment;
- The Basic Employment Policy Act, which formulates and implements the employment policy of the State and contributes to employment security, improvement in economic and social status of workers, and balanced development of

the national economy and society by helping the individual nationals develop and display their abilities to the maximum and by attaining enhanced efficiency in the labor market and balance in demand and supply of manpower;

- The Gender-Equality Employment Act, which generally requires employers to afford equal employment opportunities and treatment to male and female employees;
- The Handicapped Persons Employment Act of 1990, or The Act for Employment Promotion of the Disabled, which prohibits employment discrimination against the handicapped, and requires employers of a certain size to employ a specified percentage of physically handicapped workers;
- The Aged Employment Promotion Act, which requires certain employers to hire older employees, in numbers proportionate to the employer's total workforce;
- The Act on the Honorable Treatment of Patriots and Veterans, which establishes requirements for hiring eligible patriots, veterans, and members of their families;
- The Industrial Safety and Health Act of 1981, which establishes the basic statutory framework for the regulation of health and safety in the workplace;
- The Act on the Prevention of Pneumoconiosis and Protection of Workers with Pneumoconiosis of 1984, which safeguards employees' health and welfare by providing special protections for employees in dust-generating work situations, and compensates such employees if they develop pneumoconiosis, or their families if they die from the disease;
- The Industrial Accident Compensation Insurance Act of 1963, which prescribes a mandatory employees' compensation program for job-related injuries or death;
- The Employment Insurance Act, which provides unemployment benefits, with features designed to promote employment and job-seeking activities;
- The Basic Vocational Training Act of 1973, which imposes, among other things, a requirement on certain employers to provide vocational training;
- The Wage Claim Guarantee Act, which establishes a pay-guarantee fund that pays pensions and severance pay to employees of bankrupt companies;

- The Act Relating to the Protection for Dispatched Workers, which establishes working conditions for dispatched employees (temporary workers) to allow for flexibility of supply and demand of manpower;[4] and
- The Employee Welfare Fund Act, which grants some tax benefits to a business enterprise making a contribution of five percent of its earnings before tax to its employee welfare fund.[5]

The President may issue presidential decrees concerning matters delegated to him by a particular act with the scope specifically defined and also matters necessary for the enforcement of such acts. In general, these decrees act as addendums to such acts.

3. Court Decisions

Court decisions also play a very important role in labor law. Courts may clarify general provisions of statutes and may fill in the gaps relating to matters left undecided by legislators. Court decisions that provided protection against dismissals (layoffs based on business reasons) before there was any legislation on this subject are a typical example of judicial rulemaking in the face of general statutory clauses. The requirements set forth in the Supreme Court case on layoffs were later codified into law.[6]

Court decisions in the area of labor law can be made by the Constitutional Court or the general courts, and the decision of the Constitutional Court prevails over that of the general courts.

4. Administrative Interpretation

Provision is made for administrative interpretation through the Ministry of Labor (MOL) or the Ministry of Justice that issues,

---

[4]Dispatched employees mean those employees who are employed with a manpower supply company and dispatched to a company requiring their services, and who are under the supervision and control of the company receiving such employees.

[5]An employee welfare fund is a fund that is contributed to by the employees and employer for the benefit of the employees (i.e., emergency funds, housing loans, etc.). Such a fund is not obligatory under the Act, but if such a fund is implemented, the Act provides for certain procedures to be followed. It is not uncommon in Korea for companies to implement employee welfare funds.

[6]Labor Standards Act (LSA), art. 31.

to subordinate offices in the form of notes, official opinions on the interpretation of labor laws. Alternatively, the MOL may issue a ruling on the interpretation of a labor law in response to a question from one of its subordinate offices or an employee or employer. Administrative interpretation has a binding effect on subordinate offices, but it is not the equivalent of a provision in a statute and thus does not have a legally binding effect before the courts. However, even if not legally binding, administrative interpretation certainly has an important effect on labor administration, and an influential effect on court decisions.

5. *Custom*

Custom or established practice may be a source of law favorable to workers. If an employer voluntarily grants a privilege for a certain period of time, workers may claim that they are entitled to have the privilege continue. When such a claim is accepted, the privilege originally established by custom or practice is treated as if it were incorporated in individual employment contracts.

6. *International Sources of Labor Law*

Article 6 of the Constitution provides that treaties duly concluded and promulgated in accordance with the Constitution and generally recognized rules of international law are to have the same effect as domestic laws of South Korea. In labor law, it is generally accepted that ratified conventions of the International Labor Organization (ILO) are legally binding at the national level. Thus, several ILO conventions, such as Nos. 87, 98, and 105, currently are regarded as legal sources of domestic South Korean labor law.[7]

E. Labor Administration

The practical working of government labor policies in any country depends on the nature of its industrial relations. In countries with relatively peaceful industrial relations, the tendency is for decisions to be made by negotiation between labor and management. In other countries, government intervention is more com-

[7]For additional information on ILO Conventions, see the chapter on the ILO in Volume I, Part 4.

mon. In South Korea, the government has a key role in dealing with labor-related matters.

1. *Ministry of Labor*

The government structure for labor matters in South Korea has changed substantially over time. In the early stages, between 1948 and 1962, the responsible central government agency was the Bureau of Labor under the Ministry of Health and Social Affairs. Between 1963 and 1980, this bureau expanded to become the Labor Administration Office. After 1981, the office again enlarged and became the Ministry of Labor (MOL).

The MOL is in charge of government labor policy, and deals with such matters as the status of employment, employment insurance, vocational training, working conditions and workers' welfare, industrial safety and health, and industrial accidents. Other responsibilities of the MOL include general administration of industrial relations and international labor matters.

2. *Labor Relations Commission*

The Labor Relations Commission (LRC), a tripartite body composed of an equal number of representatives of workers, employers, and the public interest sector, plays an important role in the administration of labor laws and policies. The LRC was established in 1953 to enable wider participation in labor matters and to provide a forum for mediation of disputes between labor and management. When labor disputes arise, they may be settled by the courts. However, because of the specialized nature of many labor problems, courts often are not well-equipped to deal with them. A new organization was needed to deal with labor problems more simply and rapidly; hence the LRC.

The composition and function of the LRC are regulated by the Labor Relations Commission Act (LRCA). The LRC is under the jurisdiction of the MOL, but operates as a quasi-autonomous body. The independence of the LRC, combined with the broad basis of representation among LRC members, enables impartial decisions on labor matters.

The LRC consists of the central commission, local LRC offices, and a special LRC established to deal with special labor matters, such as matters involving seamen. The central LRC considers appeals of decisions originally made by local commissions or special commissions, and considers labor disputes that involve the jurisdiction of two or more local commissions. The local offices of the LRC were established to cover large areas of local autonomy such as Seoul, Inchon, Kyunggi Province, etc.

The LRC has two main functions. One is the adjudication of unfair labor practice and wrongful termination cases, and the second is the settlement of labor disputes by mediation or arbitration. The adjudication of unfair labor practices and wrongful termination cases is a quasi-judicial function. Parties can appeal an LRC adjudication in a court of law. Mediation is mandatory for any labor dispute filed with the LRC, while arbitration may be initiated under the terms of an agreement between the parties, at the request of the parties, or by the LRC for a certain essential public interest industry.[8]

In addition to these main functions, the LRC gives advice and suggestions concerning the improvement of labor conditions to other governmental agencies.

3. *Labor Inspector*

The Labor Standards Act (LSA) provides for labor inspectors to implement workers' protection requirements.[9] Under the terms of the statute, the MOL and its subordinate agencies designate labor inspectors to ensure employer compliance with labor and employment laws. To protect their ability to carry out their duties, labor inspectors are given judicial police authority. Judicial police authority means authority given to police officers as permitted by the particular law. As to powers labor inspectors have, please see below.

In addition, the statute requires inspectors to protect secrets acquired during the course of performing their official duties.

Under current law,[10] labor inspectors have the authority to conduct the following functions:

- Inspectors may inspect workplaces, workers' dormitories, and associated buildings, require presentation of documents,

[8]Trade Union and Labor Relations Adjustment Act, arts. 62, 75.
[9]*See* LSA art. 104.
[10]*See* LSA art. 105.

and make inquiries of both employers and employees to ensure that the governmental standard for employment conditions are being maintained.

- Inspectors, or a designated doctor, may conduct a medical examination of workers who appear to be suffering from diseases that may make it impossible for them to continue working.
- With regard to violations of the LSA and other labor-related laws, the labor inspector must perform the duties of judiciary police. Per Article 104 of the LSA, these duties include the duty to inspect, request the submission of documents, and conduct interviews and other aspects of their investigation.
- Inspectors may exercise the powers of the MOL in regard to health and safety violations that are deemed to present immediate dangers to employees.

I. INDIVIDUAL EMPLOYMENT

A. Individual Employment Contracts

Employers must enter into individual employment contracts with their employees, specifying wages, working hours, and other working conditions. Individual employment contracts are an important source of law, even for those employees covered by protective laws, collective agreements,[11] and Rules of Employment.[12] Individual employment contracts serve mainly to ensure working conditions that are better than those guaranteed by the labor laws. Typically, individual contract provisions determine special working conditions or conditions in those matters where the individual contract offers conditions superior to those required by law or by the terms of the Rules of Employment or collective agreement.

[11]See II.C., below.
[12]See I.B.2., below.

B. Individual Employment Law

Individual employment law has its basis in Article 32, Section 3 of the Constitution, which provides that working condition standards must be determined by law at a level guaranteeing human dignity. Individual employment relations are governed generally by the civil law provisions on contracts of employment,[13] but are modified considerably by the employment laws in order to protect and improve the working conditions of employees. Individual employment law consists of the body of rules concerned with the individual relationship between the employer and employee. This includes the following statutes, among others:

- The Labor Standards Act of 1953;
- The Seaman's Act of 1961;
- The Industrial Accident Compensation Insurance Act of 1963;
- The Employment Security Act of 1967; and
- The Vocational Training Act of 1973.

1. *Labor Standards Act: Defining Rights and Responsibilities*

General legal standards for the regulation of individual employment are established by the Labor Standards Act (LSA). A series of presidential and ministerial decrees regulate the implementation of the LSA, and the Ministry of Labor (MOL) is primarily responsible for enforcing the LSA and related decrees. An employer who fails to comply with the LSA usually is subject to criminal punishment.

Consistent with Article 32 of the Constitution, the LSA sets forth minimum working conditions necessary to guarantee every worker's dignity. To this end, the LSA consists of the following 12 chapters:

- General Provisions;
- Labor Contracts;
- Wages;
- Hours of Work and Rest;

[13]Korean Civil Code, ch. 8.

- Women and Minors;
- Safety and Health;
- Apprenticeship;
- Accident Compensation;
- Rules of Employment;
- Dormitories;
- Labor Inspector; and
- Penal Provisions.

The LSA establishes only minimum standards. Employers are free to establish higher standards by means of individual employment contracts; however, any terms of an employment contract not meeting the LSA requirements are null and void, and are deemed automatically replaced with the pertinent LSA provisions.[14]

The most recent amendments (Amendments) to the LSA were passed by the National Assembly on August 29, 2003, and promulgated as of September 15, 2003. The Amendments provide for a gradual schedule for imposing compliance with the new laws on companies, depending on the number of a company's employees and/or the industry involved, starting from July 1, 2004. In the interim, however, companies are permitted to adopt the Amendments with the agreement of the majority of employees or the union (presuming a majority union exists).

The implementation schedule is as follows:

- From July 1, 2004: financial and insurance companies, government-run companies, and companies employing 1,000 or more workers;
- From July 1, 2005: companies employing 300 to 999 workers;
- From July 1, 2006: companies employing 100 to 299 workers;
- From July 1, 2007: companies employing 50 to 99 workers;
- From July 1, 2008: companies employing 20 to 49 workers; and

[14]LSA art. 22.

- Decided pursuant to Presidential Decree of the Korean Labor Standards Act but to be enforced no later than from 2011: companies employing fewer than 20 workers.

Voluntary early implementation is permitted. The primary objective for the Amendments was to adopt the forty-hour workweek, under which the standard working hours for a company in accordance with the LSA would be reduced to 40 hours per week from 44 hours per week.

a. Applicability

Application of the LSA is based primarily on the number of employees at a workplace or within a business. LSA provisions apply in their entirety to all employers with five or more employees. Some of the LSA's provisions apply to those employers with fewer than five employees; the extent of this applicability is outlined by a presidential decree of 1998. The following major provisions of the LSA apply to employers, including those with fewer than five employees, effective January 1, 1999: working conditions for part-time employees; restriction on dismissal during suspension period for work-related disease and injury and/or maternity leave within thirty days and thereafter; prior notice on dismissal; payment of all unpaid wages within 14 days from separation from the company; preferential reimbursement for wage claim; recess periods and weekly days off; maternity leave, etc.

The LSA applies to the workplaces of foreign-owned companies and to South Korean branches of foreign companies, just as it does to domestic enterprises.

The LSA generally does not differentiate between temporary, part-time, and permanent employees. However, in certain instances, the LSA provides different standards for employees who work on a daily basis, for a term of less than three or six months, or on a probationary basis. For example, Article 32 of the LSA requires an employer to give 30-days' advance notice or, in lieu of such notice, 30-days' ordinary wages to a discharged employee. However, this requirement does not apply to probationary or limited-term employees.[15]

---

[15]See I.B.1.d.iii., below.

b. Protection of Minors and Women

Minors under age 15 may not work without MOL approval. This approval is rarely sought or granted. A minor between ages 15 and 18 may work with written parental approval.

The LSA also prohibits women and minors from working in occupations or industries considered dangerous or hazardous to health or morality. The list of occupations and industries concerned is established by presidential decree.[16] Occupations and industries covered by this decree include high-tension electricity, smelting, etc.

c. Regulation of the Employment Process

An employer of five or more persons must enter into employment agreements with each employee, specifying wages, working hours, and certain other working conditions. This requirement applies equally to probationary employees. Covered employers also must prepare a register of employees and a wage ledger in standard legal form, and must retain these, employment agreements, and other specified documents for three years.

d. Employee Dismissal

Generally, it is difficult for an employer to dismiss an employee at will. Thus, care should be taken in hiring to ensure that the right people are chosen from the start. The specific legal restrictions on employee dismissals are discussed below.

i. Protection against dismissal

The LSA provides that an employee may not be dismissed during the period of recuperation from an occupational injury, and for 30 days immediately following such period. Similarly, a pregnant employee may not be dismissed during her maternity leave and for 30 days immediately following such leave.

---

[16]Presidential Decree, art. 37.

ii. Dismissal for just cause

Under the LSA, an employer may not dismiss, suspend, or take other disciplinary action against an employee without "just cause." The LSA does not specifically state what reasons will constitute just cause, but allows employment agreements, Rules of Employment, or collective bargaining agreements to define this standard, provided that an employer is still required to meet this strict just cause requirement.

Applicable precedent has set a fairly high standard for what constitutes "just cause." Generally, "just cause" is considered to include:

- a lack of aptitude;
- continuing unsatisfactory work;
- debilitating disease;
- breach of the employment contract;
- egregiously unacceptable misconduct or behavior on the job;
- misrepresentation of previous school or work experience;
- an improper relationship with another employee; or
- serious criminal violation.

A less strict level of just cause is required in order to terminate probationary employees. In general, the courts or the labor authorities will focus on whether the sanction imposed is commensurate with the reason for the sanction.

iii. Notice for dismissal

An employee terminated for just cause generally must be provided 30 days' advance notice or 30 days' ordinary wages in lieu of notice. This requirement does not apply to the following types of employees:

- employees who are employed on a daily basis and whose consecutive service is no longer than three months;
- employees who are employed for an agreed term of not more than two months;
- employees whose wages are paid monthly and who have been employed not longer than six months;

- employees who are employed for seasonal work for an agreed term of no more than six months; or
- employees who are employed on a probationary basis for a period not exceeding three months.

For probationary employees, despite the fact that the LSA does not limit the period of probation, after three months of probationary employment, an employee is entitled to receive either 30 days' notice or 30 days' ordinary wages in lieu thereof, absent exceptional cases (e.g., where an employee embezzles company funds).

iv. Severance pay

An employer must establish a severance pay plan that provides at least 30 days' average wages to departing employees for each year of continuous service; an employee must serve at least 1 year to be eligible for severance. This should not be confused with the notice period. The severance plan must not discriminate on the basis of gender, nationality, religion, or social status. Severance pay is due on separation for any reason, i.e., death, retirement, resignation, or dismissal within 14 days of separation or a longer period with the agreement of the employee.

A severance payment may take the form of an annuity, and interim severance payments are allowed if the employee and the employer agree to this. Interim severance payments are where an employee can cash out his or her accrued severance while still being employed, with the employer's agreement, provided that upon payment, the employee's service years for purposes of calculating severance shall start anew. As a result, a participating employee's consecutive years of service for severance purposes will start anew after the interim payment is made.

v. Wrongful termination case

An employee who believes that he or she was dismissed without just cause may challenge the dismissal by taking any or all of the following actions:

- requesting an unjust dismissal order from the Labor Relations Commission (where employees may lodge complaints (i.e., unfair dismissal) against the employer; decisions from the LRC generally takes less than three months); and/or

- filing a civil suit with the district court to nullify the dismissal, and to seek injunctive relief and backpay; and/or
- filing a criminal complaint with the District Labor Office (DLO) (the District Labor Office is separate from the LRC and the local subordinate offices of the MOL, as the DLO acts as the police watchdog for labor and employment-related issues) for unjust dismissal (or unfair labor practices, if the dismissal is alleged to be due to the employee's union activities).

Civil litigation generally is troublesome and time-consuming. An employee seeking to use this mechanism would be required to pay legal fees in advance and could not expect a decision of the district court sooner than four to six months after filing. Thus, a dismissed employee normally will complain to the LRC or the DLO before considering court action.

An employee who has been illegally dismissed is entitled to reinstatement to his or her former or a similar position, and to receive backpay and whatever other relief is necessary to restore the employee to his or her prior status. An employer who has dismissed an employee illegally also may be subject to criminal penalties. These include imprisonment for up to five years or a criminal fine of up to South Korean Won (KRW) 30 million. In practice, however, a criminal fine of between KRW two to five million normally would be the sanction for an unjust dismissal.

2. *Rules of Employment (Work Rules)*

Detailed working conditions generally are defined in individual employment contracts, Rules of Employment (ROEs), or collective agreements. The provisions in ROEs typically are formulated unilaterally by employers. To be valid, the rules must be accepted, either explicitly or tacitly, by the employees. Provisions of ROEs that provide worse conditions than those specified by law or in collective agreements are null and void. However, ROEs override any less favorable terms in individual employment contracts.

a. Contents

ROEs must provide for working hours, leave, rest periods, holidays, shift schedules, compensation, promotion, retirement, bonuses, employee expenses, employee education, safety and health rules, accident compensation, commendations and penalties, and other pertinent matters applicable to all employees.

b. Filing Requirements

ROEs must be filed with the MOL by all employers with 10 or more employees. Employers' initial filings of the ROEs must be accompanied by the comments of a majority of the employees or the union (if the union represents the majority of the employees). As the initial ROE, as long as the rules or provisions are in accordance with Korean laws, the employer is not required to make any changes to reflect the employees' comments. However, if disadvantageous changes are made to an ROE thereafter, employee consent is required or such change will be deemed null and void as discussed below.

c. Changes to the Rules

To change the provisions of ROEs, the employer must follow the procedures set out in Articles 96 and 97 of the Labor Standards Act. Advantageous changes (for example, to conform them to the provisions of a collective agreement) must be filed with a local office of the MOL, accompanied by the comments of the employees or the union that represents the majority of the employees. If an employer intends to make any changes in ROEs that may be disadvantageous to existing employees (for example, to reduce employee benefits or increase employees' obligations), the employer must obtain the consent of the majority of employees or the union that represents the majority of the employees, as the case may be. The employer then must file the changes with the MOL.

C. Employee Privacy

Under applicable Korean laws, treatment of employee privacy/information is governed by legal principles that protect employees as well as specific data protection laws, as described below.

As a preliminary note, the interpretation of "third party" under Korean employment and data privacy laws is very strict and embodies any organization or company that is not the specific corporate entity involved, which in this case would mean any affiliate company or parent company that did not directly receive the information from the employee involved.

1. *Legal Principles That Protect Employees*

Korea does not have specific laws or provisions concerning employee privacy that regulate when and how employee information may be collected and/or circulated beyond the employer. Despite the lack of a specific regulation, the use and potential transfer of such information may be subject to a combination of more general laws, depending on the circumstances.

a. Korean Civil Code

An employee may claim a privacy right by instituting a general tort claim against those who invade the employee's privacy based on willful or negligent cause of mental or emotional injury under the Korean Civil Code.[17] If an employee can show that the employer has used or released personal information in a way that caused emotional suffering or mental anguish, the employee could, in principle, sue the company and the responsible individuals for damages. The Korean legal system does not recognize penal damages, and mental damages typically are for a much smaller amount than mental damages awarded in Western countries.

b. Contract

If an employer makes a contractual representation or commitment to an employee or employees to keep certain information secret, an employee may claim damages against the company for any actions taken in breach of such commitment.

---

[17]Article 750 of the Korean Civil Code sets forth the basis for all civil actions by any person claiming that such person has been damaged by the "unlawful" act of another.

c. *Korean Criminal Code*

The Korean Criminal Code[18] prohibits defamation, which is defined as the public allegation of private facts about a person that puts the person in a negative light; truth is not a defense in Korea. Corporations cannot be liable for defamation, which applies only to natural persons; the company's Representative Director or Country Manager would be the party held responsible for the defamation. Although there is no precedent to date, such a charge would be possible depending on the facts of the case.

d. *Korean Labor Standards Act*

No specific provision directly relates to the use of or release of confidential employee information. However, Article 39 of the Korean Labor Standards Act effectively prohibits the use of "blacklists" to oust employees from jobs or to prevent employees from finding new jobs.

e. *Job Security Act*

The Job Security Act (JSA) provides for only duly authorized or registered companies to engage in the business of providing employee services or employment-related information. The JSA would not apply unless employee-related information is given for recruitment purposes and is provided as part of a business.

2. *Data Protection Laws*

a. *Real Name Financial Transaction Law*

The Real Name Financial Transaction Law (RNFTL) prohibits financial institutions from disclosing an individual's financial information (information related to financial assets) without specific, written consent from the concerned individual for each instance of disclosure. The affected entities are limited to financial

---

[18]Article 307 of the Korean Criminal Code provides for two types of defamation: (1) allegations which, although true, are nonetheless defamatory; and (2) false, defamatory allegations. A true allegation may constitute defamation under the Korean Criminal Code to the extent that the allegation is defamatory, but not if the defamatory allegation is made solely in the public interest.

institutions and the information subject to protection is financial information only.

b. Protection and Usage of Credit Information Law

Under the Protection and Usage of Credit Information Law (PUCIL) 2002, an individual's contact information (e.g., name, address, telephone number, etc.) as well as credit information is protected, and a company must have express, written consent to transfer or use such information in ways other than the specific purpose for which it was given.

c. Information and Telecommunication Network Use Promotion and Information Protection Law

The Information and Telecommunication Network Use Promotion and Information Protection Law is intended to protect users of internet service providers or telecommunication companies from unauthorized use of information they provide to said entities.

D. Employee Duty of Loyalty, Trade Secrets, Covenants Not to Compete

1. *Employee Duty of Loyalty*

Korea does not have specific laws or provisions that regulate the employee duty of loyalty. However, it is generally acknowledged that the employee duty of loyalty is a part of the employee's obligation under the employment agreement, including the employee's covenants not to compete or to keep trade secrets as mentioned below.

2. *Trade Secrets*

Under Korean laws, trade secrets or confidential information generally can be protected through a contract between the parties involved and under the Korean Unfair Competition Prevention and Trade Secret Protection Act (the Unfair Competition Act): (1) if the information falls within the meaning of the trade secrets as defined in the Unfair Competition Act; and (2) if an unauthorized disclosure and/or use of the information is prohibited by law, the relevant contract, or otherwise. Under the Unfair Competition Act, trade secrets are defined as confidential information about technology and/or business operations that has been maintained as secret(s) and that also has economic value. In order to be protected under the Unfair Competition Act, the confidential information needs to meet the requirements provided for in the Act.

3. Covenants Not to Compete

Korea does not have specific laws or provisions that regulate the validity of covenants not to compete. According to court precedents, however, the general rule under Korean law is that non-competition agreements, pursuant to which an employee leaving a company is prohibited from being employed by any competitor of the company, are legal and valid, and not violative of the constitutionally guaranteed right of the freedom of choice of employment (and thus not in breach of good public order and customs), where the circumstances and the contents of the agreements are recognized to be valid, and their reasonableness is acknowledged.

In determining "reasonableness" of the restrictions, the courts have taken the following factors into account: (1) the length of the restriction period, (2) the nature of the interest sought to be protected under the non-compete or non-solicit agreement, (3) the availability of compensation to employees for the unavoidable encroachment on the employee's right to work or to engage in a particular line of work, (4) the reason for termination of employment agreement, and (5) the prevailing market practice in the relevant industry.

II. COLLECTIVE BARGAINING

A. Trade Union and Labor Relations Adjustment Act

The main statute governing collective labor relations in South Korea is the Trade Union and Labor Relations Adjustment Act (TULRAA), enacted on March 13, 1997. The TULRAA has its basis in Article 33 of the Constitution, which guarantees all workers the right to organize, bargain, and act collectively.[19]

---

[19]See the Introduction, at C.1., above.

Prior to the enactment of the TULRAA, issues relating to collective agreements and industrial action were governed by separate, poorly coordinated, statutes. These separate statutes were integrated into the TULRAA to prevent the possibility of misunderstanding and to eliminate conflicting legal provisions.

The TULRAA defines and provides for the establishment and operation of trade unions, which are the main body of employee representatives for collective labor relations purposes. The law also addresses the validity of collective bargaining and collective action, and establishes reconciliation procedures that come into play when collective agreements are not achieved peacefully. Finally, the law defines unfair labor practices so as to provide for the protection of basic labor rights.

B. Structure and Organization of Trade Unions

Article 5 of the TULRAA guarantees the free establishment of trade unions. Two or more workers may set up a trade union of any form at an individual company, with the union's scope defined by territory, type of business, or type of occupation. There is no certification procedure like there is in the United States.

Prior to 1987, establishment of a union required the consent of either 30 or more workers, or one-fifth of the company's workforce. Revisions of the law in 1987 lifted these restrictions. Under current law, the procedure by which a trade union is established is quite simple: workers submit a written notice of union establishment to the Ministry of Labor or local government agency in charge of their district and the office is expected to issue a certificate of union establishment within three days.

The law strictly prohibits employers from engaging in unfair labor practices by discharging or in other ways penalizing workers who are engaged in or have control over trade union activities. Furthermore, employers must not intervene in the workers' union activities.[20]

---

[20]TULRAA, art. 81. See the discussion of unfair labor practices at II.G., below.

1. Trade Union Organization

Trade unions in South Korea have various forms. They can be classified by type of business, company, religion, or organizational entity.

Most trade unions in South Korea are organized on a company basis. Trade unions within an individual company join the federation of trade unions at the industrial level; the industrial level federations are affiliated with the federation of trade unions at the national level.

a. National Federations

There are two federations at the national level in South Korea: the Federation of Korean Trade Unions (FKTU) and Korean Confederation of Trade Unions (KCTU), which are comprised of 27 and 19 industrial trade unions, respectively.[21]

FKTU is the only national organization authorized by the labor law since the 1950s, but the KCTU was recently recognized in 1999. After 1987, when the legal restrictions on union formation were lifted, a struggle for power emerged between the existing KFTU and new labor organizations. The new labor organizations developed a political ideology founded on theories of class struggle and labor emancipation. These new organizations were critical of FKTU policies, and claimed to represent a more democratic labor movement. The new organizations also criticized the FKTU as overly collaborative with government labor policies and out of touch with workers' demands at the workplaces. These new organizations, focusing on the more political activities of trade unions, led strikes at some large "chaebol" companies (a chaebol is a large industrial conglomerate), and the strikes occasionally became violent. In addition, they protested strongly against government restrictions on labor movements.

In 1993, when the National Council of Representatives of Trade Unions was formed to investigate cooperation with certain company trade unions, non-mainstream labor power began looking into establishment of a second federation of trade unions. The

[21]Based upon information on their respective websites as of August 5, 2004.

Korean Confederation of Trade Unions (KCTU), the second largest federation of trade unions, was organized in 1995 and legally accepted by the MOL in November 1999. Company trade unions that join KCTU have tended to be interested in setting up broad-based industrial organizations. Thus, in February 1998, the Metalworkers Union, the Union of Automobile and Metal Workers, and the Hyundai Group Trade Union, all of which are associated with KCTU, integrated into one large trade union.

b. Phase-In of Multiple Unions

Amendments to the Trade Union and Labor Relations Adjustment Act (TULRAA), enacted on March 28, 2001, were postponed until January 1, 2007, the date when multiple trade unions will be allowed at one workplace.[22] In principle, multiple trade unions are allowed within an industry under the 1997 TULRAA. At the industrial and national levels, the TULRAA allows immediate establishment of multiple trade unions, which undoubtedly will result in an increase in the number of unions, at least for the time being.

2. Creation of a Union

Under the TULRAA, there is no minimum requirement in terms of the number of employees or proportion of the workforce necessary to establish a labor union. Therefore, as a legal matter, only two employees are needed to organize a union, and employees are not required to provide any advance notice of organization activities. Employees who desire to form a union need only file a report with the MOL or local government agency (the administrative authorities).

The administrative authorities generally are required to issue a certificate of union establishment within three days after an application is filed. When the administrative authorities accept the report and issue the certificate, the union legally comes into existence.[23] It then has the right to engage in collective bargaining on behalf of its members, to engage in collective actions, to file re-

---

[22]TULRAA, addendum, art. 5(1).

[23]TULRAA, art. 12.

ports and petitions with the relevant authorities, to designate labor representatives to the Labor Management Council, and otherwise to act as the members' representative, as permitted by law. It also becomes entitled to immunity from liability for legitimate acts of dispute.[24]

An employer is obligated to recognize and engage in good faith collective bargaining with a duly established labor union.

3. *Civil Servants*

Civil servants are allowed to form consultative bodies beginning in 1999, and gradually to form labor unions at some time in the future. School teachers are permitted to form labor unions as of July 1, 1999.

4. *Dissolution*

Because elections are not required under the TULRAA for a union to be established, there is no procedure for decertification elections. However, a union may be dissolved pursuant to the provisions of its own articles of association, through a merger or division, or by a resolution for dissolution adopted by at least two-thirds vote of the union members present, where a majority of the members are present. If a union has no union officer and does not undertake any union activities for at least one year, it is considered to be dissolved, subject to the decision of the competent LRC.

C. Collective Agreements

In most situations, improved working conditions and the enhanced economic and social status of workers are granted as a result of collective bargaining agreements. Thus, the negotiation of collective agreements plays an important role in South Korean labor relations.

1. *Form*

Under the TULRAA, a collective agreement must be in writing, and both parties must sign and affix their seals thereto. The

---

[24]See II.E.4., below.

parties to a collective agreement must report it to the Ministry of Labor or local government agency within 15 days from the date of execution.

Collective agreements typically have two parts: (a) the normative part, which establishes workplace standards, and thus, directly affects the individual employment relationship; and (b) the obligatory part, which deals with rights and duties between contracting parties. The normative part includes items such as wages, bonus (if any), annual and monthly leaves, working hours, and any other working conditions, while the obligatory part includes union rights such as union office, union activities allowed during working hours, full-time union officers, etc.

2. *Duration*

Article 32 of the TULRAA provides that the maximum period for any collective bargaining agreement may not exceed two years. However, if a new collective agreement has not been executed by the expiration date of a prior collective agreement, and if both parties have no other agreements with each other, the former collective agreement remains valid for three months following its expiration.[25] If the term of a collective agreement is not specified in the agreement, or if it exceeds two years, the agreement is valid for two years.

Some agreements contain an "evergreen" provision, with wording such as "even after the expiration date the Collective Bargaining Agreement shall continue to be effective until the new Agreement is concluded." The enforceability of an evergreen-type provision after two years, such as the above, was a controversial issue. A 1998 amendment to the TULRAA provides that if either party wishes to terminate a collective agreement with an "evergreen" provision, it must give the other party six months' notice (three months under previous laws).[26]

---

[25]TULRAA, art. 32, §3.

[26]TULRAA, amend. no. 5511 (Feb. 20, 1998).

3. *Relation to Labor Laws and Individual Employment Contracts*

The TULRAA provides that all individual employment contracts or Rules of Employment that are less favorable to union members than the workplace standards established by a collective agreement are null and void. Thus, any less favorable rules of employment or individual contract terms for union members automatically are replaced by the standards set in the collective bargaining agreement.

As between legislative standards and the standards in collective agreements, the relationship is as follows: if there is a statute that sets a minimum standard, the collective agreement may not provide less than the minimum, but may provide more. Where there are doubts about whether collective agreements conflict with statutory provisions, courts have the same role as in other areas of the law: they make the necessary interpretations of the conflicting legal provisions.

4. *Scope*

The union has the right to bargain collectively with the company on behalf of its members. In such bargaining, the union represents only its members. In general, this means that the collective agreement covers only union members who are employed by an employer who has signed the collective agreement.

Under certain conditions, however, the TULRAA states that a collective agreement has a legally binding effect on non-union employees, or on those whose employers have not signed the collective agreement, or who do not belong to the employers' association that has signed the agreement. One such example is the extension of a company-level collective agreement to non-union members when the union represents half or more of the employees of a similar occupation in a workplace. This can occur even if the minority group of employees are members of a different union within the company. In this circumstance, the extension occurs and expires automatically, either with the expiration of the collective agreement or if the collective agreement suddenly is not applicable to more than half the employees because union membership or employment levels change.

The other example is extension of a collective agreement on a regional basis. When the coverage of a collective agreement between a regional union and an employer or regional federation of employers applies to more than two-thirds of the total employees in a similar occupation in the same region, the administrative authority may determine that the collective agreement may be extended to non-parties with the consent of the LRC. Any party to the collective agreement may request such an extension, or the administrative authority can decide to implement such an extension on its own initiative.

5. *Breach of Collective Bargaining Agreement*

Amendments to the TULRAA, enacted on March 28, 2001, impose criminal penalties of up to South Korean Won (KRW) 10 million for breaching the following types of provisions in an effective collective bargaining agreement:

- terms on wages, welfare expenses, and severance pay;
- terms related to working hours, recesses, holidays, and leave;
- terms establishing causes and important procedures for disciplinary sanctions and termination;
- terms involving safety and health and accident compensation;
- terms regarding the provision of facilities and other conveniences to the union and union-member participation in meetings during working hours; and
- terms related to collective action.[27]

D. The Bargaining Process

In South Korea, the right to bargain collectively is clearly established in Article 33 of the Constitution. However, the right to bargain, as with other rights, must be exercised fairly within the legal limits discussed below.

---

[27]TULRAA, addendum, art. 92(1).

1. Subjects of Collective Bargaining

While Article 29, Section 1 of the TULRAA explicitly provides that the representative of a trade union shall have the authority to bargain and make a collective agreement with the employer or employer's association for the trade union and its members, it does not clearly enumerate the matters that may be the subject of collective bargaining. However, based on the purpose of the collective bargaining system, subjects of bargaining would include working conditions and matters that relate to the treatment of employees. Such matters must be collective in scope; in other words, they must affect at least some group of the employees who work in a specific environment. Therefore, in principle, a trade union may not request negotiations about matters concerning an individual employee. These matters may only be the subject of a labor-management council (e.g., grievance handling).[28]

The right of private ownership is guaranteed in South Korea by the Constitution. Thus, the employer, as owner of the business, has the right to manage it. Closely associated with this right of management is the legal right to control the factory, the office premises, and the equipment located there, and to maintain free access to and from the production and office sites. In principle, business decisions on such matters of management prerogatives fall outside the scope of collective bargaining, although, as a matter of practice, unions generally try to negotiate union participation in management decisions.

2. Good Faith Bargaining

In the collective bargaining process, all participants must negotiate in good faith, following the rules and procedures established by law.

A trade union has the right to institute collective bargaining, and may demand that an employer meet at reasonable times and confer in good faith about pending issues concerning working conditions.

---

[28]See III., below.

Employers are obliged to respond in good faith to collective bargaining requests of unions, and may not reject a union's reasonable demands.[29] If an employer unjustifiably refuses to bargain with the union, the refusal becomes an unfair labor practice called "refusal or delay to bargain," which is prohibited by the TULRAA.[30]

The TULRAA provides that an employer may refuse to bargain for justifiable reasons. These justifiable reasons exempt the employer from the duty to begin or continue bargaining. To decide whether the reasons are justifiable, the underlying purpose of the law (to facilitate and promote fair collective bargaining) must be taken into consideration. For example, an employer may have justifiable concerns about whether the workers' representatives will engage in *bona fide* collective bargaining, or may have concerns about the subjects of collective bargaining, or about procedural details of the bargaining process.

3. *Mediation*

If, despite the efforts of the union and management, negotiations reach an impasse, either the union or the company then must file a request for mediation with the LRC. At that point the mediation period begins. The mediation period, also referred to as the "cooling-off period," is 10 days for general businesses and 15 days for public interest businesses (such as banking institutions, transportation, and medical facilities), subject to an extension. During the mediation period, employees and management must refrain from industrial action.

Upon the receipt of a request for mediation, the LRC initiates proceedings before a mediation committee. The mediation committee consists of three members representing the employer, the employees, and the public interests. If a mediation proposal is agreed on by both sides, it has the same legal effect as a collective bargaining agreement.

---

[29]TULRAA, art. 30.

[30]*Id.* art. 81, item 3. For a complete discussion of unfair labor practices, see II.G., below.

E. Collective Action

Although the right of workers to act collectively is guaranteed by the Constitution, such collective activities may cause irrecoverable economic loss to the parties engaged in labor disputes and to third parties. For this reason, the right to act collectively has come to be more directly regulated by law than any other labor right, with the objective of preventing labor disputes, and ensuring a fair and speedy settlement of conflicts between labor and management.

The TULRAA is designed to provide procedures to settle labor disputes in a fair and efficient way. To this end, the statute places specific restrictions on collective actions such as strikes and lockouts. These various restrictions are discussed below.

1. Union Actions

After—and only after—mediation,[31] the union may begin collective action, such as a strike. In addition, a trade union may not initiate collective actions without a majority, affirmative vote of union members in a direct, secret ballot.[32]

Once a collective labor action commences, certain basic rules must be honored. First, acts of violence or subversion are not considered acceptable tools in a labor dispute, and are not allowed.[33] The law also bans threatening behavior or violence during picketing, and prohibits attempts to persuade unrelated workers to participate in the strike.

During a strike, labor union members may refuse to work, but they may not occupy the premises or prevent other employees or managers from working or having free access to production and office sites, whether by physical force or by verbal intimidation. The law also provides that maintenance operations to prevent raw materials and products from deteriorating normally must be conducted during a strike, and labor actions may not interrupt the normal operation of security facilities in a workplace. Similarly, no actions that hamper normal maintenance and operation of safety

---

[31]See II.D.3., above.
[32]TULRAA, art. 41, §1.
[33]*Id.* art. 42, §1.

equipment at workplaces are allowed. In light of these rules, union activities conducted within the company's premises that interfere with normal business operations during a collective action are clearly illegal. This is in sharp contrast to prior law, which allowed employees to conduct strikes anywhere on business premises, but prohibited labor actions outside the business premises.

In strike situations the principle is "no work, no pay," and companies have no obligation to pay striking employees. Furthermore, employees may not strike for the purpose of securing wages lost during previous strikes.

2. *Employer Actions*

a. Lockout

The TULRAA recognizes the employer's right of lockout in response to full or partial collective labor action:

> Employers have the freedom to manage their own businesses as they see fit. As a general principle, the lockout is an act in response to a union's collective action. Even during the period of lockout, an employer may continue business operations with those employees who do not participate in the strike. The lockout is allowed only if it is a defensive act. If the employer's business operations reach a level that infringes on employees' rights and affect the balance of power between labor and management, the lockout may no longer be justifiable. Since the lockout can be recognized as a defensive act only, a lockout is not allowed in response to a union's partial strike. If it is impossible to manage the entire business because of a partial strike, lockout of the entire business could be permitted as an exceptional matter.[34]

Under the TULRAA, an employer must seek mediation prior to initiating a lockout.[35] During the period of a lockout, union members are not permitted to enter company premises, with the exception of labor union offices.

---

[34] *Id.* art. 46.

[35] See II.D.3., above.

b. Striker Replacement

The replacement of striking employees, which was not permitted under prior law, is now allowed if employers are replacing strikers with employees transferred from within the same business (company). Such replacements are just temporary transfers for the duration of the strike and are not permanent. However, new subcontracting is not allowed.[36]

3. Defense and Public Service Industries

Collective actions are no longer prohibited for defense industry employees as a whole. However, workers in those defense industries designated under the Special Measure Act may not initiate collective labor actions.[37]

General public service businesses may engage in collective actions. Essential public services are required to take labor disputes to arbitration instead of engaging in collective actions.[38]

4. Union Liability for Collective Actions

If the right to bargain is exercised fairly, trade unions are exempt from civil and criminal liability. When employees strike (or act collectively in other ways), Article 3 of the TULRAA specifically provides that an employer may not make a claim against the union for damages that have arisen as a result of the proper acts of dispute.

However, violent acts and subversive activities in pursuit of labor disputes do not have civil and criminal immunity. The underlying principle is that rights of unionization, as well as the rights of management, are accompanied by responsibilities to respect the legal rights of all concerned. As a result, the normal protections of the labor laws do not apply to actions that violate the law regarding intimidation or damage to property. The failure to follow the legal rules applicable to collective actions may subject the union

[36]TULRAA, art. 43.

[37]*Id.* art. 41, §2.

[38]For a discussion of arbitration procedures in essential public service industries, see II.F.3.b., below.

to criminal prosecution, court injunctions, and disciplinary sanctions. Civil damages also may be awarded by a court to compensate for lost profits or physical damage. Individual union officers and members may be held liable, in addition to the union.

5. Third-Party Intervention

Under the TULRAA, a prior ban on third party intervention in collective bargaining and industrial disputes is eliminated. Current law enumerates the persons and organizations from whom workers and employers can obtain assistance. This includes organizations with which they are affiliated, and anyone about whom the MOL receives advance notice. The purpose of this notice provision is merely to inform the government of those persons or organizations from whom the unions and employers wish to obtain assistance. It does not constitute a ban on third party involvement.

F. Third-Party Dispute Resolution

Because labor and management are autonomous and independent parties, the best way to settle labor disputes is through direct negotiation, without outside interference. In recognition of this, the TULRAA acknowledges a principle of self-regulating resolution between labor and management. Article 47 of the TULRAA definitively prescribes that the legislative provisions for dispute resolution are not to restrict voluntary settlement of a labor dispute by the parties, under terms and conditions in a collective agreement. In this sense, the TULRAA provisions for outside intervention are intended to supplement, rather than supplant, direct negotiations between the parties.

1. Unofficial Procedures

The TULRAA provides that the parties may agree to settle disputes through unofficial dispute resolution procedures, without the involvement of a public authority. These unofficial procedures mean settlement of industrial disputes by other ways of mediation or arbitration pursuant to mutual agreements or collective agreements. In such a case, the parties must report the unofficial dispute adjustment to the relevant LRC.

2. Mediation

If a labor dispute has occurred, either the union or the employer concerned must file a request for mediation with the relevant local administrative authorities (e.g., the city or province) and the LRC. As discussed above, under the TULRAA, mediation is a necessary precondition to any collective action.[39] Only the union and the employer are able to seek mediation, and individual employees have no legal right to do so.

3. Arbitration

a. General Procedures

In a few specified cases, an arbitration committee consisting of three members designated by the chairman of the LRC from among the members representing public interests begins to deal with the dispute. An arbitration committee may arbitrate:

- if both parties concerned request arbitration; or
- if one of the parties concerned requests arbitration, in accordance with the provisions of the collective agreement.

If a labor dispute is referred to arbitration, industrial action must stop for 15 days from the date of referral.

If either of the parties objects to a decision of the arbitration committee of the Local Labor Relations Commission, it can demand that the Central Labor Relations Commission review the case. An award rendered by the Central Labor Committee may be appealed by either party by instituting administrative litigation before the Administrative Court—but only on grounds that the Central Labor Committee's award was beyond the committee's powers or in some other way illegal.

b. Public Service Industries

The TULRAA has introduced certain limited compulsory arbitration provisions for labor disputes in public service industries. For purposes of compulsory arbitration, public services are classi-

---

[39] See II.D.3., above.

fied as those providing either general services or essential services. Only those providing *essential* public services (water, electricity, gas, telecommunications, railroads, hospitals, inner-city bus services, and banking services) are subject to compulsory arbitration. (Current law narrows the earlier definition of essential public services by excluding public hygiene and broadcasting services). Inner-city bus services in Seoul and other metropolitan areas, and banking services except for those involving the Bank of Korea, are no longer regarded as essential public services, and thus, are not subject to compulsory arbitration, as of 2002.

Under prior law, a petition for compulsory arbitration could be filed by an administrative authority or by the LRC *ex officio*. However, the TULRAA now provides that compulsory arbitration can be invoked only if an ad hoc Special Mediation Committee of the LRC, having three public interest representatives, recommends that the LRC refer a case to arbitration.[40] A Special Mediation Committee is an ad hoc mediation panel established within the Labor Relations Commission for the mediation of a certain industrial dispute in public services. This is designed to keep compulsory arbitration cases to a minimum.

G. Unfair Labor Practices

The system of protection against unfair labor practices is aimed at ensuring the constitutionally guaranteed right of employees to organize and act collectively. Certain specified actions of employers towards employees or trade unions are defined in the TULRAA as unfair labor practices. These practices include, for example:

- dismissal or discriminatory treatment of an employee because he or she has joined a trade union or attempted to organize a union;
- refusing to negotiate or conclude a collective bargaining agreement with a union without justifiable reasons; and
- attempts to intervene in the management of a union.

[40]TULRAA, art. 62.

An employee or a union affected by unfair labor practices can file a complaint with and request the relevant LRC to take remedial measures, such as to reinstate a dismissed union member, order payment of money that an employer should have paid if there were no unfair labor practice, post a written apology, order an employer not to do something, etc. There will then be a factfinding investigation and a hearing by a panel composed of five members (three public interest, one employee, one employer). The three public members will issue a decision and a remedy order. An employee who objects to the decision of a local LRC may ask the central LRC for a re-examination. Anyone who objects to the decision of the central LRC can institute administrative litigation before the Administrative Court.

An employee or a union affected by an unfair labor practice also can go to a district court for the issuance of a preliminary injunction or to the MOL's regional labor office for a criminal investigation.

Unfair labor practice disputes are not subject to mediation or arbitration. A strike cannot be initiated as a response to an unfair labor practice, because of the special procedures available to respond to unfair labor practice complaints that must be used instead.

H. Union Security

1. *Right to Join or Refrain From Joining a Union*

As discussed above, workers in South Korea have a constitutional right to organize or join a union.[41] However, until 1987, it was illegal for unions and employers to require eligible employees to join a union as a condition of continued employment. Revisions to the TULRAA changed this: if a union represents at least two-thirds of the eligible employees, the union and the employer may, through collective bargaining, require new employees to join the union, an arrangement known as the "union shop." The union shop, along with the alternative open shop and closed shop systems, are discussed below.

---

[41]See the Introduction, at C.1., above.

a. Open Shop

The open shop is the system primarily utilized in South Korea. Under the open shop system, membership or withdrawal from a union is wholly determined by the discretion of the individual employee. This freedom of choice given to the employee to freely join or withdraw from a union guarantees the employee his or her independence.

b. Union Shop

The fundamental reason for the union shop is to strengthen the power of the employees who are eligible for union membership. Under the union shop system, a newly hired employee is required to join the union within a certain period of the date of his or her employment. If a company and its employees agree to adopt a union shop system, all potential employees who are ineligible for union membership are excluded from employment. However, if a union shop system has been adopted, expulsion from the labor union may not adversely affect the employment situation of the expelled employees.

Under the TULRAA, a union shop system is permitted through collective bargaining with the employer, only if the union represents at least two-thirds of the eligible employees. The MOL has stated that, if the union has the necessary two-thirds representation, it is entitled to use the collective bargaining system to seek the adoption of a union shop. However, if the union does not represent two-thirds of the eligible employees, it is not entitled to make such a demand in collective bargaining.

If despite the fact that the union represents less than two-thirds of the eligible employees, the employer implements a union shop system, the employer's act would be deemed an unfair labor practice. Moreover, if a union initiates collective action because of an employer's refusal to concede to its demand for a union shop, such collective action would not be protected under the TULRAA.

c. Closed Shop

With the exception of the unions for dock employees and the companies that use such unions, the closed shop system is not permitted under the South Korean legal system. Under the closed shop system, a company may hire as an employee only those individuals who are members of a union with which the company has an agreement. Thus, under this system, the employee has to become a member of a union as a precondition of his or her employment. Because this system effectively makes the union the exclusive labor source for the company, the union has considerable leverage in the company's activities.

2. *Eligibility for Union Membership*

Employees whose livelihood is derived from wages, salary, and other like income, irrespective of their occupation, are eligible for union membership.[42] If an individual is part of the management of a business or acts for the business owner with respect to matters concerning the employees in the business, he or she will be deemed an employer (i.e., management), rather than an employee, for TULRAA purposes, and thus, may be ineligible to join a union.[43] This exclusion applies even if the individual is an "employee," within the meaning of the Labor Standards Act. The term "employee" in the Labor Standards Act means a person engaged in whatever occupation offering work to a business or workplace (hereinafter referred to as "business") for the purpose of earning wages.[44]

As was the case under prior law, the TULRAA provides that the unemployed are unable to join labor unions. However, fired employees, who are still engaged in legal disputes with their companies over the legality of their dismissals, are entitled to remain union members until the Central LRC renders a final decision on the issue.

3. *Dues Checkoff*

Employers have no legal obligation to accept checkoff of union dues. However, many employers withhold union dues from the pay of their employees and turn the dues over to the union.

---

[42]TULRAA, art. 2.

[43]*Id.*

[44]LSA, art. 14.

Such matters are determined during collective bargaining between the parties.

4. *Employer Compensation for Union Officials*

Unions in South Korea traditionally have demanded that one or more union leaders be allowed to work full time exclusively on union matters, while being paid by the employer. While this is not required by law, it has not been uncommon for collective bargaining agreements to provide that certain union leaders will continue to receive their normal salaries from the employer, while being excused from some or all of their normal employee responsibilities so that they can devote their time to union matters. The 1997 revision to the TULRAA prohibits the creation of new full- or part-time union officials who are paid by their companies. However, the TULRAA amendments enacted on March 28, 2001, extended the deadline by which companies must stop providing payment for full-time union officers to December 31, 2006.[45] Accordingly, companies will no longer be allowed to pay salaries to full-time union officers from the year 2006. In fact, this arrangement will become an unfair labor practice, and therefore illegal. The original deadline scheduled by the 1997 TULRAA was 2002. However, a heated debate to allow this practice of full-time union officers by deleting this new prohibition clause led to the extension of the original deadline.

5. *Union Activities During Working Hours*

The scope of union activities permissible during business hours is not defined by statute or regulation. The general rule is that employees have no right to engage in union activities during business hours. However, in practice, certain union activities during business hours are often allowed, pursuant to the provisions of the collective bargaining agreement.

[45]TULRAA, addendum, art. 6(1).

6. *Use of Office Facilities*

In principle, a union has no right to use the employer's facilities to conduct its union activities. An employer generally is not obligated to provide the union with an office, a telephone, a secretary, office equipment, or other similar conveniences. However, allowing use of such office or office facilities is not an unfair labor practice, and once such facilities have been provided to a union, it is difficult for the employer to decide unilaterally to remove such facilities unless there is reasonable cause for doing so.

Notwithstanding the foregoing, an employer may not refuse the request of the union to install a bulletin board in a convenient location, although the employer may place reasonable restrictions (size, location, etc.) on the bulletin board.

III. REPRESENTATION BY ENTITIES OTHER THAN UNIONS

A. Introduction—Labor Management Councils

In South Korea, Labor Management Councils (LMCs) have been established at the company level to benefit both employees and companies. LMCs are intended as a mechanism to maintain labor peace and cooperation and to resolve actual or potential labor disputes in a non-adversarial setting. Companies that are not required to establish an LMC may do so voluntarily.

Establishment of an LMC is not intended to affect collective bargaining or other union activities. In practice, however, where there is no labor union, an LMC typically plays a central role in such fundamental collective bargaining issues as wage or benefit negotiations and employee grievances.

The Labor Management Council system was first introduced on April 7, 1963, and on Dec. 31, 1980, the Labor Management Council Act (LMCA) was enacted as an independent act. The LMCA was amended in 1997, and is now known as "The Act to Promote Worker Participation and Cooperation" (the 1997 Act). As discussed in greater detail below, the 1997 Act requires certain companies to establish LMCs for the purpose of "improving the welfare of employees and maintaining the steady development of business enterprises through participation and cooperation between employers and employees."[46] The Ministry of Labor (MOL) is responsible for implementation of the new law.

B. Provisions of the 1997 Act

The 1997 Act made four major changes in the law:

1. The establishment and operation of a Labor Management Council (LMC) at a company or a workplace is now obligatory, with the exception of workplaces employing less than 30 regular employees. Prior law applied only to workplaces with 50 or more employees, and excluded securities and banking businesses. In the case of a minority union, the union represents only the union members. However, under the previous law, the union appointed all of the employee members of the LMC, which represented all the employees.
2. An LMC must be composed of an equal number of representatives of employers and workers.[47] Under the 1997 Act, the employee delegation is composed of individuals recommended by the trade union only when the union has as members more than half the employees of the company. This changed the pre-1997 requirement that an LMC must be established in any company where a labor union existed, regardless of the nature of the industry or the number of employees who were represented by the union. A conflict of duplicity was created between the LMC system and the right of collective bargaining. Collective labor relations were adversely affected, especially because collective bargaining was conducted at the company level.
3. The 1997 Act allows workers to participate in company management in three ways:[48]
   - the LMC must be consulted by the employer on a variety of labor-related matters;

[46]Act to Promote Worker Participation and Cooperation, arts. 1, 4.
[47]LMCA, art. 6.
[48]For additional discussion of the LMC's duties and powers, see III.D., below.

- the LMC must meet on a quarterly basis to hear employer reports on management objectives and the company's financial status, and to answer employee questions on such matters; and
- the LMC has decisionmaking power with respect to certain labor-management matters. The decisions made by the LMC relate to such issues as education and training plans, unresolved workers' grievances, and workplace welfare facilities.

4. The 1997 Act enables the government to supervise the operation of the LMC through a requirement that the bylaws of each council be filed with the MOL, which has the authority to issue an order of correction to the company in case of certain violations of the Act.

C. Structure of Labor Management Councils

1. Employer Obligations

The 1997 Act requires that an LMC must be established by, in principle, any business organization or place of business (e.g., each plant site of a corporation that has several manufacturing and management facilities) that has 30 or more regular employees.

The employer must report the establishment of an LMC to the local office of the MOL within 15 days of establishment. An employer that refuses to establish or hinders the establishment of an LMC is subject to a criminal fine of up to KRW 10 million unless there is just cause for such action.

2. Composition of Labor Management Councils

LMCs consist of an equal number of representatives of the employer and the employees. The employer and the employees each must be represented by not less than three, nor more than 10, members.

The 1997 Act requires that the representative of the company serve as the representative of employer members. The other employer members are appointed by the company representative. Although the qualifications of employer members are not prescribed by statute, the LMC bylaws must contain a provision regarding such qualifications.

If the company has no labor union representing a majority of the employees, the employee members must be elected by a direct secret ballot of the employees. The candidates should have the recommendation of at least 10 employees of the company. If there is a labor union representing a majority of the employees, the chairman of the union automatically will sit as an employee member, and the union will select the other employee members.

There is no restriction on the eligibility of employee members, except that they must be employed by the company. The union may even select non-union members if it wishes. The 1997 Act does not expressly address the issue of whether the LMC bylaws may require that employee members meet certain qualifications. However, because the LMC has an independent status, it appears that the LMC bylaws may establish minimum qualifications.

An employer must not interfere with the election of employee members. In addition, the employer must provide basic facilities such as a place where employee members may meet to discuss their affairs. If an employer interferes with the election of an employee member, the MOL may issue an order overriding the employer interference. An employer who, without just cause, fails to comply with such an order of correction will be subject to a fine of up to KRW 5 million.

3. *Service as Officers and Members of Labor Management Councils*

The LMC must elect a chairperson (or two co-chairpersons), and the employer and the employee members of the LMC must each elect a representative secretary. Members of the LMC serve for three years and may be reappointed or reelected, as appropriate. Although the members serve on the LMC without compensation, attendance at LMC meetings is considered working time. The employer may not discriminate against any employee members of the LMC with respect to the performance of their LMC duties. If an employer commits such discrimination without just cause, the MOL may issue an order overruling the employer's action, and an employer who does not comply with the order will be subject to a fine of up to KRW 5 million.

4. *Operation of Labor Management Councils*

The LMC must hold meetings at least once every three months.[49] A fine of not more than KRW 2 million may be levied against the employer for violating this minimum requirement. Extraordinary meetings may be convened if the LMC wishes. The chairperson is required to respond to requests for a meeting from either the employer or employee representatives. A majority of the employer members and a majority of the employee members constitute a quorum. A two-thirds vote of those present in a properly existing quorum is required for the adoption of resolutions. Because no resolution can be adopted unless both parties agree to it, the proceedings are inherently non-adversarial. LMC meetings are open to all employees unless the LMC resolves that they be closed, but members must not disclose any information that the LMC designates as confidential.

The LMC must keep minutes of its meetings including: information about where and when meetings are held; the members present; and the substance of consultations and agreements. All members present are required to sign and seal the minutes, which must be kept for three years.

5. *Labor Management Council Bylaws*

The LMC must adopt bylaws governing its affairs and furnish a copy to the MOL within 15 days of the date of the LMC's establishment. Bylaws may be amended pursuant to resolution of the LMC. Any amendments to the bylaws also must be submitted to the MOL. A fine of up to KRW 2 million is prescribed for an employer's failure to comply with these provisions.

The bylaws must contain the following provisions:

- the number of members;
- procedures for election of employee members, and registration of candidates for employee members, if there is no union;
- qualifications of employer members;

---

[49]LMCA, art. 12.

- procedures for convening meetings, sessions, and other details pertaining to the operation of the LMC;
- methods and procedures for voluntary arbitration; and
- the number of grievance committee members, and details with respect to the settlement of employee grievances.

D. Duties and Powers of Labor Management Councils

The 1997 Act provides that certain matters are subject to consultation with the LMC, certain matters are subject to report to the LMC, and certain matters may be agreed at the LMC.

1. Consultation Items

The matters subject to consultation are as follows:

- improvement of productivity and profit-sharing;
- recruitment, placement, education, and training of employees;
- prevention of labor disputes;
- employees' grievance handling;
- improvement of occupational safety and health measures and working conditions and promotion of employees' health;
- improvement for the personnel and labor management system;
- general rules of employment adjustment, such as relocation, retraining, dismissal for managerial or technological reasons;
- administration of working hours and break time;
- changes to remuneration system, including job classification and pay scales;
- introduction of new technology and machinery, or improvement of work processes;
- adoption of and changes to work rules;
- employees' stock ownership programs and other ways of helping employees build capital assets;
- improvement of employee welfare; and
- other matters relating to cooperation between employees and the employer.

2. *Report Items*

The 1997 Act requires the employer to report on the following matters at regular LMC meetings:

- general management plans, and the extent to which management objectives are realized;
- quarterly production plans and actual results;
- manpower plans; and
- the economic and financial status of the company.

Employer representatives must answer employees' questions on such matters at the LMC meetings. In cases where the employer does not report on or explain the above matters, the workers' members may request relevant documents, and the employer shall respond in good faith to such requests. If the employer, without just cause, fails to comply with the requirement, a fine of up to KRW 5 million may be imposed.

3. *Agreement Items*

Employer and employee representatives may reach agreement on the following types of items that come before the LMC:[50]

- establishment of a basic training/education plan;
- establishment and operation of welfare facilities;
- establishment of an intra-company welfare fund;
- matters not agreed upon in the grievance committee;[51] and
- establishment of various committees composed of employees and management.

Although the LMC is intended to promote cooperation between labor and management, employee and employer members of the LMC may not reach an agreement on the above items to be agreed upon, in which case such matters may be subject to arbitration by the Labor Relations Commission or by a voluntary arbitra-

[50]*Id.* art. 20.

[51]See III.E., below.

tion committee.[52] An appeal to arbitration is only available by the consensus of the employer and employee members.

The LMC is required to inform employees without delay of all decisions made in committee. The LMC must prepare minutes of the meeting and make them available to the employees. A fine of not more than KRW 10 million may be imposed on those persons (labor or management) who fail, without just cause, to comply with an agreement reached in the LMC, or with a decision by the relevant arbitration panel, Labor Relations Commission, or third-party arbitrator.

E. Management of Employee Grievances: Grievance Committee

Every company that has 30 or more regular employees must have a grievance committee. The LMC must elect the grievance committee from among its members. An employer may be fined up to KRW 2 million if it fails to establish the grievance committee. The grievance committee must have one to three members, as determined by the LMC bylaws.

Employees may bring their complaints to the attention of the grievance committee either orally or in writing. The committee must immediately consider the complaint, and report its findings to the employee within 10 days of receipt. The committee must refer any complaints that are outside its scope (such as complaints involving wages or bonuses) to the LMC for settlement. The grievance committee must keep a record of the receipt and settlement of grievances for one year.

IV. Redundancies and Transfers of Undertakings

A. Redundancy

The term "redundancy" is not used in South Korean labor relations. Business needs to reduce overstaffing are accomplished by means of layoffs (employee dismissals for reasons other than

[52]LMCA, art. 24.

performance or misconduct), or through incentive programs (offers of special employer-provided benefits to encourage voluntary resignations). Each of these methods is discussed below.

1. Layoffs

As part of an International Monetary Fund bailout package, the South Korean Government, on January 15, 1998, formed a Labor-Management-Government Committee (Committee) to discuss ways to resolve the nation's economic crisis. After weeks of tense negotiations, the Committee agreed on legislation to be introduced in the National Assembly that would waive the two-year grace period before the layoff law became effective and allow for layoffs. On February 14, 1998, the National Assembly passed the new layoff legislation, which became effective February 20, 1998. Layoffs were previously allowed by Supreme Court precedent, the criteria of which were later codified by the layoff law—with some exceptions. The criteria for layoffs now in effect are set forth in Article 31 of the Labor Standards Act (LSA). These criteria include not only the Supreme Court judgments, but the following new rules:

- Urgent business reasons are required to dismiss employees based on changes in business conditions.
- Every effort must be made to avoid dismissals.
- Reasonable and fair criteria must be used to select employees to be dismissed. Gender discrimination is strictly prohibited.
- Sixty days' prior notice must be given to the employee representative (in the absence of a union, the employee representative should be elected by the employees) or the union that represents the majority of the employees, and there must be good faith consultation about measures to avoid dismissals and the selection criteria for such dismissals. The union, if one exists, or the employee representative must be consulted. As a matter of practice, the LMC is also consulted.
- When layoffs of 10 percent or more of a company's employees are expected, 30 days' prior notice must be given to the MOL.

- If employers decide to expand their labor force within two years of a layoff, they must make efforts to rehire previously dismissed employees, paying proper regard to the positions of these employees. Employers must exercise their best efforts to return employees to their previous positions, but they are not required to rehire employees in order of seniority.

Previously, because of the absence of clear regulations on layoffs, neither employers nor employees understood exactly when layoffs were permissible. In this regard, by specifying clear requirements and procedures for layoffs, the legislation helps prevent arbitrary dismissals.

2. *Separation Programs*

As a result of the earlier lack of clarity in layoff requirements, as well as the potential adverse effect of layoffs on a company's public image, some firms have tried to encourage voluntary resignations by employees. Several incentive programs have been developed, the best-known being the Early Retirement Program (ERP) developed by the foreign banking community.

The ERP involves the provision of additional severance payments to all employees seeking early retirement. In addition to the severance provided for in either the Rules of Employment[53] or a collective bargaining agreement, a supplementary package was developed to provide additional funds to the employees. These supplementary payments were structured in such a way as to constitute severance for tax purposes, thereby maximizing the benefit to the employees at the least possible cost to the employer.

The severance amount payable under the ERP varies depending upon a number of factors, including the size of the organization, the extent of the layoffs, years of service, and the industry. While the ERP can be effective in inducing employees to resign, it may also be very expensive to the employer.

---

[53]See I.B.2., above.

The principal disadvantage of such incentive programs is the inability to target specific groups of employees other than by years of service with the employer. In order to withstand scrutiny by the tax authorities and avoid any possible infractions of the Labor Standards Act, incentive programs must be generally applicable to the group of employees who meet specified eligibility criteria. This makes it difficult to target specific groups of employees, with the result that in many cases, employers have lost employees who were not the intended target of the incentive program.

B. Transfers of Undertakings

When a business changes ownership through mergers, acquisitions, or other transactions, under the business transfer rule the following implications arise:

- the working conditions of the transferor would transfer to the transferee or new company (newco) without change unless the employees agree otherwise;
- the transferee/newco would be jointly and severally liable for any outstanding employment-related claims of the transferor's employees at the time of transfer, provided that the transferor and transferee/newco may be able to agree on which liabilities would transfer between them (which may not be binding upon the employees) via the contract;
- the transferee/newco would be obligated to accept all those employees working in the transferor who wish to transfer to the transferee/newco; and
- the transferee/newco would assume liability for the transferred employees' severance payments which have accrued during their employment with the transferor.

V. WAGES, HOURS, AND LEAVE

A. Wages

1. Definition of Wage

In South Korea, employee compensation generally consists of a basic monthly wage and periodic guaranteed bonuses, plus any allowances, overtime, or nighttime premiums to which an employee may be entitled.

The terms "average wage" and "ordinary wage," which appear frequently throughout the Labor Standards Act (LSA), are themselves statutorily defined, and are the basis for calculating various payments and allowances to employees as required by the LSA. The average wage defined under Article 19 of the LSA includes all regular and continuous monthly payments, overtime, and compensation for unused leaves over the last three months preceding an employee's separation from the company. Ordinary wage is defined in the LSA Presidential Decree to mean all regular and consistent monthly payments, but excluding payments for overtime, night work, etc. The "basic monthly wage" is included in both the ordinary wage and the average wage.

In addition to wages, in practice many employees receive allowances for meals and transportation. Special housing loan arrangements and allowances for tuition of an employee's child and in connection with a variety of family-related events, such as the birth, death, and marriage of family members, also are common.

2. *Minimum Wage Act*

The purpose of the Minimum Wage Act (MWA) is to provide a safety net and improve the quality of the labor force by guaranteeing a certain minimum level of wages. Workers thereby contribute to the sound development of the national economy through their spending.

The MWA established the Minimum Wage Council (MWC) to consider minimum wage and other related matters. The MWC is composed of nine members with equal representation of workers, employers, and public interest groups.

The Minister of Labor (MOL) determines the minimum wage in light of advice from the MWC. The minimum basic wage is prescribed annually by the MOL no later than August 5th of every year. In November 2000, the Minimum Wage Act (MWA) was amended to expand the minimum wage system to include all industries, based on a fiscal year from September through August.[54] For the period from September 2004 to August 2005, an employer having one or more employees, in all industries, must pay all em-

[54]MWA, arts. 3, 10.

ployees at least KRW 22,720 per eight-hour working day and KRW 2,840 per hour.

3. *Payment of Wages*

Wages must be paid directly, regularly, and in full, one or more times per month on a fixed day. Employees may request advances to meet such events as illness (either of the employee or a dependent), marriage, death, childbirth, or emergency work absences. While not mandated by statute, the prevailing practice is to provide bonuses of approximately one month's wage four or six times per year.

If the business has to shut down temporarily, the employer is required to pay 70 percent of the average wage during the suspension of operations, unless the suspension is for "unavoidable reasons," and verified by the Labor Relations Commission, as provided in the LSA.[55]

B. Working Hours, Overtime, and Rest Periods

1. *Working Hours and Overtime*

Pursuant to the Amendments to the LSA,[56] the 44-hour workweek will be reduced to 40 hours per week depending upon where a company falls under the implementation schedule of the Amendments. The pre-Amendment working hours are eight hours a day, five days a week, with a half-day on Saturday, resulting in a 44-hour workweek.

Working hours may be extended up to 12 hours a week beyond the standard by mutual agreement. For a limited time of three years from the date the company must comply with the Amendments, the statutory maximum overtime hours of 12 hours a week is increased to 16 hours.

For any overtime hours (i.e., hours beyond the 40 or 44 hour week, whichever is applicable), a premium compensation at a rate of 50 percent of ordinary hourly wage must be paid for any work in excess of the standard working hours and any work done on holidays.[57] For a limited time of three years from the date the com-

---

[55]LSA, art. 45 §2.

[56]See I.B.1., above.

[57]LSA, art. 55.

pany must comply with the Amendments, the overtime compensation premium of 50 percent is decreased to 25 percent of the ordinary wages to be applied for the first four hours of overtime.

In addition to any wage or overtime, a premium compensation at the rate of 50 percent of the ordinary hourly wage must be paid for work performed between 10 p.m. and 6 a.m. This is termed the night-time premium.

2. *Alternative Working Hours Systems*

a. *Flexible Working Hours Systems*

In an exception to the standard overtime requirements, an employer is allowed to implement a flexible work hour's system. Under a flexible system, the employer may assign employees to work in excess of the standard 44 or 40 hours, whichever is applicable, during any given week and eight hours on any given day, without incurring an obligation to pay an overtime premium for the excess hours.

Both the pre-Amendment and post-Amendment LSA provides for two alternative flexible work hour's systems.[58] The first system, which is the same under both the pre- and post-Amendment LSA, may be implemented by the employer's initiative in the rules of employment as long as:

- during any two-week period, the hours worked do not exceed an average of 44 or 40, depending upon whether the pre- or post-Amendment is applicable; and
- provided that the working hours for any given week do not exceed 48.

The second system may be implemented only with the written consent of an employee representative. Under the pre-Amendment LSA system:

- during any one-month period, the weekly working hours must not exceed 44 in any given week; and

[58]*Id*. art. 50.

- provided that working hours for any given week and for any specific day shall not exceed 56 and 12 respectively.

Under the post-Amendment LSA system:

- during any three-month period, the weekly working hours must not exceed 40 in any given week; and
- provided that working hours for any given week and for any specific day shall not exceed 52 and 12 respectively.

b. Discretionary and Deemed Working Hour System

In certain situations, as provided for in a presidential decree under the LSA, where employees have substantial discretion in carrying out their jobs, they may be deemed to have worked for a specified number of hours, if this has been agreed to in writing between the company and an employee representative. Regardless of whether a union exists, this arrangement can be included in Rules of Employment or employment contract. Thus, an employee on business travel, whose actual number of working hours would be hard to determine, may be deemed to have worked for a specified number of hours. By agreement between the company and an employee representative, the number of hours worked can be deemed to be the normal day associated with that employee's duties.

In addition, to provide for cases where it is difficult to determine an employee's actual number of working hours, an employer and an employee may agree on a system under which an employee will work a pre-agreed number of hours.

3. Rest Periods

An employer must provide at least 30 minutes of rest for employees working four hours, or one hour of rest for employees working eight hours. It is common practice to allow one hour for lunch and to designate it as the rest period. No other rest period then is required. The rest period is not considered time worked, so the standard working hours of 9 a.m. to 6 p.m., with an hour off for lunch constitutes a standard eight-hour day.

4. *Restrictions on Women and Minors*

The minimum age for working in Korea is 15. However, a younger person may be allowed to work if he or she obtains an employment permit issued by the Ministry of Labor.[59] In addition, workers between the age of 15 and 18 are limited to working a maximum of 7 hours per day and 42 (under the pre-Amendment LSA) or 40 (under the post-Amendment) hours per week. The parties may agree to extend working hours up to one hour per day, or six hours per week.[60]

With regard to working night shifts (i.e., from 10 p.m. to 6 a.m.) or on holidays, if the employee is a female age 18 or older, the employer must obtain consent from the employee. If the employee is a pregnant female or anyone younger than age 18, the employer must obtain permission from the Ministry of Labor in addition to the employee's consent, as well as be in compliance with other procedural requirements.[61]

Also, females within their first year after childbirth are prohibited from working overtime in excess of 2 hours per day, 6 hours per week, and 150 hours per year.[62]

C. Paid Holidays and Leaves

1. *Holidays*

Employees are entitled to paid holidays,[63] which include weekly days off (usually Sunday), and Labor Day and such other additional days off as are designated by the company.

2. *Weekly Day Off*

An employer must allow employees a minimum of one day off with pay per week.[64] The one day need not be Sunday. If an

---

[59] *Id.* art. 62.
[60] *Id.* art. 67.
[61] *Id.* art. 68.
[62] *Id.* art. 69.
[63] *Id.* arts. 54, 57, 59.
[64] *Id.* art. 54.

employee works on the designated day off, the employer must pay 150 percent of the ordinary wage.

The normal practice in South Korea is to set wages and salaries for office employees and certain production employees by the month, not by the hour or day. Under this monthly system, days off are classified as the required days off with pay. The employer will incur additional liability at the rate of 150 percent of the ordinary wage (calculated on an hourly or daily basis) if these monthly employees actually work on the designated days off.

3. *Monthly Leave*

Under the pre-Amendment LSA, an employer must allow one day off with pay each month to employees who worked all workdays during the preceding month. Under the post-Amendment LSA, monthly paid leave was abolished and integrated into paid annual leave.

4. *Annual Leave*

Under the pre-Amendment LSA, an employer must allow 10 working days off with pay to employees who have worked an entire year without an absence, and eight working days off with pay to employees who worked 90 percent or more of the working days during the year. This leave is increased by one day per year for each consecutive year of employment after the first year. Under the post-Amendment LSA, an employer must allow 15 working days off for each year of continuous service and one additional day's paid annual leave for every two years of consecutive service beyond the first year, with a ceiling of 25 days. Under the pre-Amendment LSA, there is no ceiling on the number of days that can be accrued; however, an employer may "buy back" any unused leave in excess of 20 accrued days of annual leave at the rate of 100 percent of the standard wage. Also, if the total number of accumulated annual leave days exceeds 20, the employer may require the employee to work on those days in excess of 20, and pay the standard wage for each leave day workers.

The annual leave accruing during a particular year should be used within one year or the employee will forfeit the unused portion. Under the pre-Amendment LSA, even if the unused portion is forfeited, the employee is still entitled to compensation for the forfeited days, however, under the post-Amendment LSA, unused annual leave days may be forfeited without compensation to the employee if the employer has taken certain steps as set forth in the LSA (i.e., three month's written notice to the employee encouraging and insisting that the employee use his/her accrued paid annual leave). Forfeiture does not apply if the employee is prevented from using the annual leave due to causes attributable to the employer.

An employer must grant the annual leave when requested by an employee. However, the timing of the leave may be adjusted by the employer if the originally requested time off would create significant difficulties in carrying out the employer's business.

5. *Maternity and Other Female Leave*

Female employees who give birth on or after November 1, 2001, are entitled to 90 days' paid maternity leave, of which 45 days must be used after childbirth, with the final 30 days compensated by the Unemployment Insurance Fund. Additionally, an employee who is nursing is allowed two 30-minute nursing periods daily if she has a child younger than one year of age.[65]

As of November 1, 2001, the Gender-Equality Employment Act (GEEA) and presidential decrees issued pursuant to the Employment Insurance Act (EIA) provide that female employees who have children younger than one year of age are entitled to 12 months' child-care leave, compensated at the monthly rate of KRW 400,000 from the Unemployment Insurance Fund.[66] This child-care leave period is inclusive of the 90 days' paid maternity leave.

6. *Sick Leave*

Sick leave is statutorily required only in connection with occupational injuries and diseases.[67] However, the prevailing practice is to grant a certain period of leave to employees suffering from non-occupational injuries and disease, subject to the receipt of proper medical evidence.

---

[65] *Id.* art. 73.
[66] GEEA, art. 19; EIA, Presidential Decree, art. 68-3.
[67] See VII.B.1., below.

7. *Military Leave and Training*

South Korean men are subject to various requirements for compulsory military service and training. They serve on active duty for 26 months and are called back periodically thereafter for training. The amount of time spent in such training may vary depending on the branch of the service, the employee's rank, and his age. Thereafter, some civil defense participation is required.

By law, no employer may penalize an employee in any way because he is called for military training.

8. *Special Leave*

Special leaves must be granted in connection with civic duties, including voting. Though not required by South Korean law, special leaves also are generally given in connection with certain family events such as the birth, death, or marriage of members of an employee's family.

9. *Child-Care Leave*

There is no specific paternity leave in Korea. However, as of November 1, 2001, the Gender-Equality Employment Act (GEEA) and presidential decrees issued pursuant to the Employment Insurance Act (EIA) provide that employees (both male and female) who have children younger than age 1 are entitled to 12 months' child-care leave. This child-care leave period is inclusive of the 90 days' paid maternity leave for female employees.

D. Exempt Employees

Certain types of employees are exempt from the Labor Standards Act requirements on working hours, overtime pay, rest periods, and weekly day off requirements. These employees, known as exempt status employees, include persons who, regardless of specific duties, are engaged in managerial or supervisory work or in handling confidential matters, and who, therefore, sometimes are expected to work beyond normal working hours.

Those employees engaged in "monitoring" (e.g., private security guards) or "intermittent" work (e.g., drivers) also may be exempt from these requirements, as long as the MOL approves the exemption.

VI. ANTIDISCRIMINATION

A. Statutes Establishing a Variety of Protected Classifications

1. Labor Standards Act

Article 5 of the Labor Standards Act (LSA) prohibits discrimination based on sex, nationality, religion, or social status.

2. Employment Security Act

The Employment Security Act of 1967 (ESA) creates placement services and establishes rules on employee recruitment. Article 2 of the ESA provides: "Nobody shall be discriminated against in regard to employment and outsourcing opportunities based upon the individual's sex, religion, social status and marital status."

3. Basic Employment Policy Act

The Basic Employment Policy Act (BEPA) provides for the implementation of employment security policy, promotes employee education, training, employment recruitment, and hiring. It generally applies to all employees, including governmental employees. Article 19 of the BEPA provides: "In the case of hiring and recruitment of an employee, an employer shall not discriminate against the employee on the basis of his/her sex, religion, social status, regional place of birth or school of graduation. Equal employment opportunity must be granted."

B. Gender-Equality Employment Act

In accordance with the constitutional ideal of equality, the Gender-Equality Employment Act (GEEA) is intended to secure equal opportunity and treatment for workers, regardless of gender, to protect the maternal role of women, and to develop the capabilities of women workers and, thus, to enhance the status of women workers and to promote their welfare. Pursuant to the GEEA, a Women Workers' Committee was established to provide leadership in the implementation of the statute, and the political momentum to achieve the statutory objectives.

The GEEA is applicable to the same workplaces as the LSA.[68] However, the GEEA goes far beyond the equal treatment provisions contained in Article 5 of the LSA,[69] because it sets forth specific requirements and prohibitions, and provides for equal employment opportunities as well as equal treatment for workers who are already employed. The important provisions of the GEEA are as follows:

- Discrimination against women in regard to employment, training opportunities, assignments, wages, promotion, retirement, and dismissal is prohibited. In particular, employment agreements may not require retirement in the event of marriage, pregnancy, or childbirth.
- Employers must pay equal wages for work of equal value in the same business. Standards for measuring work of equal value are the following: skill, effort, responsibility, and the working conditions required for the job.
- Employers must grant leaves of absence of one year or less to any employee who has an infant younger than one year of age and who applies for such leave. This leave of absence must be included in the employee's period of continuous service.
- A Committee for Gender Equality has been established to provide an additional channel (i.e., in addition to civil litigation) for resolving disputes related to the GEEA and to develop methods of improving the status and welfare of female employees.
- Punishment of fines up to KRW 10 million and imprisonment for up to two years may be imposed against employers who violate the prohibition against discrimination in regard to wage, retirement age, or dismissal, or who include in their employment agreement provisions listing marriage, pregnancy, or childbirth as grounds for mandatory retirement.

---

[68]GEEA, art. 3.

[69]See VI.A.1., above.

C. Sexual Harassment

All employers are responsible for ensuring that the workplace is free from sexual harassment.[70] Sexual harassment is defined as any unwelcome comment, gesture, request, or physical contact of a sexual nature. The existence of sexual harassment is considered to be dependent on the perceptions of the recipient, rather than the intent or perceptions of the initiator.

D. Handicapped Persons Employment Act

The Handicapped Persons Employment and Rehabilitation Act (HPERA) was enacted in 2000 to provide rehabilitation and occupational stability for handicapped workers. Provisions of the HPERA establish several means to meet this objective. First, Article 4(2) of the HPERA prohibits all discrimination against an employee "in terms of hiring, promotion, transfer, training and other personnel-related matters solely based on the handicapped status of the employee."

Second, the HPERA provides that certain large employers, as well as state and local government agencies, must hire a proportionate number of physically handicapped employees, as prescribed in the relevant presidential decree. Currently, this hiring requirement applies to companies with more than 300 employees.

The HPERA also establishes a fund known as the Employment Promotion Fund for the Handicapped (Handicapped Promotion Fund). Monies from the Handicapped Promotion Fund are used to provide employer hiring incentives, and to finance projects such as vocational training, facilities construction, and transportation.[71]

E. Older Persons Employment Promotion Act

South Korea has no specific age discrimination statute. However, Article 19 of the Older Persons Employment Promotion Act (OPEPA) provides: "In determining a retirement age for employ-

[70]GEEA, art. 8-2.
[71]See VIII.B.2., below.

ees, employers shall use their best efforts to set the retirement age no lower than 60 years of age." In addition, the OPEPA encourages employers with 300 or more employees to hire "older persons," defined as those 55 years of age or older.

F. Act on the Honorable Treatment of Patriots and Veterans

The Act on the Honorable Treatment of Patriots and Veterans applies to businesses that have 20 or more regular employees. Covered employers are required to hire a certain number of eligible patriots, veterans, and members of their families, depending on the type of business involved. This hiring obligation is mandatory; there is no cash buy-out option.

VII. OCCUPATIONAL SAFETY AND HEALTH AND WORKERS' COMPENSATION

The safety and health provisions of the Labor Standards Act (LSA) have been amended by provisions of the Industrial Safety and Health Act (ISHA) and the Industrial Accident Compensation Insurance Act (IACIA). The ISHA establishes the general safety and health standards for South Korean workers, while the IACIA establishes an insurance program to grant workers rapid and fair compensation for occupational accidents. The major provisions of these statutes are discussed below.

A. Safety and Health

Compared to industrial relations or economic growth, the field of industrial safety and health traditionally has attracted relatively less attention. However, the industrialization of the South Korean economy required a reduction in the number of occupational injuries. Therefore, in the early 1980s, specific and practical laws were enacted to prevent industrial injuries and to impose workplace safety regulations. The ISHA, enacted in 1981, and the Law for Prevention of Pneumoconiosis and Protection of Workers With Pneumoconiosis, enacted in 1984 for mining workers, were among the laws created. These laws clearly and specifically state the obligations of employers with regard to workers' safety and health, maintaining proper labor standards and workplace systems, and taking effective measures to prevent hazardous working conditions. Since the ISHA took effect, industrial accidents have decreased. Nevertheless, much remains to be done. In 1987, as part of its effort to improve industrial safety and health, the government established the Industrial Safety Bureau in the headquarters of the Ministry of Labor (MOL), and Industrial Safety Divisions in local MOL offices.

1. *Labor Standards Act*

Article 63 of the LSA prohibits the employment of women or minors under 18 years of age in occupations or industries considered dangerous or hazardous to health or morality. These occupations and industries are enumerated by presidential decree.

2. *Industrial Safety and Health Act*

The purpose of the ISHA is to maintain and promote the safety and health of workers by preventing industrial accidents through establishing safety and health standards, determining the responsible party, and creating a comfortable working environment.

The ISHA applies to all industries except those businesses enumerated in Article 3 of the ISHA Enforcement Decree. The ISHA applies only partially to these industries, or in some cases even leaves them unregulated. For example, only some regulations of the ISHA apply to the banking, insurance, education, health, or social welfare industries (except hospitals), or to industries employing only office workers. Some regulations in the ISHA are limited in application, such as those that are not appropriate for workplaces having less than five workers or lacking the normal characteristics of a workplace.

3. *Employee Health Restrictions*

a. *Restrictions on Harmful or Dangerous Work*

Article 46 of the ISHA prohibits employees from working more than six hours a day or 34 hours a week in a hazardous environment.

For employees engaged in harmful or dangerous work, Articles 45 and 47 of the ISHA require the appropriate certificates, licenses, experience and skills, and also restricts or prohibits employment of workers with infections, mental diseases, etc.

b. Employees' Health Check-up

Article 43 of the ISHA requires employees to undergo a health examination at the time of employment and periodically while employed.

4. Employer Obligations

a. Managing the System of Industrial Safety and Health

For workplaces of more than 100 employees and other workplaces enumerated by MOL decree, Article 13 of the ISHA requires that there be designated personnel responsible for industrial safety and health in the workplace. Article 15 of the ISHA also requires that a person be designated as solely responsible for safety and health in workplaces enumerated by presidential decree. Article 17 of the ISHA requires the presence of medical doctors specializing in industrial safety and health in workplaces where the person responsible for health is not a medical doctor.

Employers also must have written safety and health rules if 100 or more full-time workers are employed. These rules must be considered by a committee of industrial safety and health or by the Labor Management Council (LMC),[72] on which employers and employees are equally represented. The committee of industrial safety and health must be established in the workplace with equal representatives from the management and employees. This committee can be replaced by the Labor Management Council if the total number of employees is less than 1,000.

b. Preventative Measures

Articles 23 and 24 of the ISHA require employers to take adequate measures to protect employee safety and health, and Ar-

[72]For a discussion of LMCs, see III., above.

ticle 25 requires employees to follow safety and health rules established by the company.

Article 28 of the ISHA prohibits subcontracting of work that may cause harm or place workers in danger, without the MOL's prior approval.

c. Protective Devices for Electrically Powered Machines and Tools

The installation or transfer of electrically powered machines and tools used for harmful or dangerous work is not allowed without protective devices for workers. Protective equipment installed for use must be examined and approved for quality.

d. Restrictions on Manufacture of Harmful Materials

Article 37 of the ISHA prohibits the manufacture, import, and use of materials considered to be harmful—for example, yellow-phosphoric matches, benzene, materials containing benzene, etc. Article 38 of the ISHA also requires MOL approval as a condition of manufacturing or using materials listed in the presidential decree as harmful to workers' health, for example, materials containing dechlorobezene or dechlorobezene itself.

5. Safety and Health Education

Article 31 of the ISHA requires employers to provide work-related health and safety education at the beginning of employment, periodically thereafter, and when there is a change to a worker's job.

6. Workplace Inspections

Article 42 of the ISHA requires that any employer operating a hazardous workplace must let a qualified outside expert inspect and appraise the work environment. The results of such inspections must be reported to the MOL and disclosed to employees and, if necessary, working conditions must be improved.

7. Protection From Retaliation

Under Article 52 of the ISHA, employees may inform government agencies of an employer's failure to meet the regulations set forth in the ISHA. Employees who do so must not be subjected to any retaliation by their employers.

B. Workers' Compensation

The LSA requires employers to compensate employees for any work-related injury, disease, or death in amounts set by the statute. To claim this workers' compensation, the employee need not show negligence on the part of the employer, but if the employer was negligent, the employee may also seek tort damages under the civil law. In this situation, the amount of the workers' compensation payment is deducted from the amount of any tort damages awarded to the employee.

The Industrial Accident Compensation Insurance Act (IACIA) was passed to grant rapid and fair compensation for occupational accidents by providing an industrial accident compensation insurance program. The IACIA contributes to the protection of workers by requiring employers to maintain accident compensation insurance at a level adequate to create an incentive for accident-prevention measures. The MOL determines premium rates by classifying businesses according to accident rates over the past three years, and collects premiums from the insured employers to cover the expenses of the insurance program.

In general, any employer with one or more employees must purchase a workers' compensation insurance policy, as administered by the MOL. Employers are insured through this policy against their liability for workers' compensation arising under the LSA. Certain industries are exempted from this workers' compensation insurance requirement by presidential decree.[73]

1. *Specific Components of the Program*

a. *Compensation for Medical Treatment*

Employers must provide necessary medical treatment at their own expense or bear corresponding expenses for an employee who suffers from an occupational injury or disease. The scope of oc-

---

[73]See VII.B.3., below.

cupational disease or medical treatment is determined by presidential decree.

b. Compensation for Suspension of Work

Employers must provide injured employees who are undergoing medical treatment with compensation for any suspension of work due to the occupational injury or disease. This compensation must be equal to 60 percent of the employee's average wage over the last three months, as defined under Article 19 of the LSA, for the period of medical treatment. If the employer is subject to the IACIA, the rate of compensation is increased to 70 percent.

c. Compensation for Permanent Disabilities

If treatment for an occupational injury or disease does not restore an employee to full health, the employer must provide the employee, according to the level of disability, with compensation equal to the product of the employee's average wage multiplied by the number of days specified in Article 83 of the LSA. Disability benefits are to be paid according to disability grades provided for in enacting regulation, to a maximum of 1,474 days' average wages, a ceiling of which is fixed at KRW 151,249, with a minimum of KRW 41,869 per day from September 2004 to August 2005.

d. Compensation for Survivors

If an employee dies during the performance of his or her duties, the employer must provide compensation to the surviving family. Survivors' benefits are paid either in the form of a survivors' compensation annuity or a lump sum compensation of 1,300 days' wages, a ceiling of which is fixed at KRW 151,249, with a minimum of KRW 41,869 per day from September 2004 to August 2005.

e. Funeral Expenses

If an employee dies during the performance of his or her duties, the employer must pay funeral expenses in an amount equal to the employee's average wage for 90 days. If the employer is subject to the IACIA, the compensation is 120 days' average wage.

f. Lump Sum Compensation

If, after two years, an employee receiving medical treatment compensation has not completely recovered from the occupational injury or disease, the employer may be exempted from any further obligation to grant compensation under the LSA by paying a lump sum equal to the employee's average wage for 1,340 days. This lump sum cuts off employer liability for permanent disability.

2. *Exceptions to Employer Liability*

If an employee's gross negligence is the reason for an occupational injury or disease, and the Labor Relations Commission certifies that negligence, the employer need not provide compensation for any suspension of work or disability. In such cases, the employer is still liable for the cost of medical treatments.

3. Exempt Employers

Article 2 of the IACIA's Presidential Decree exempts certain employers, classified according to the South Korean Standard Industrial Classification system, from the requirement to purchase workers' compensation insurance. The exempted businesses are as follows:

- forestry businesses (except for logging businesses over a certain size);
- international or foreign organizations, and membership organizations;
- businesses operated directly by state or local autonomous entities;
- businesses where compensation is paid in accordance with the Seaman's Act;
- businesses with limited life spans (except logging businesses and construction projects over a certain size), and seasonal businesses using an annual total of less than 1,350 man-days; and
- construction projects involving a total amount of less than KRW 40 million.

VIII. PENSIONS AND BENEFITS

A. Pension System

The South Korean pension system has two branches: the Peoples' Pension, which covers most workers; and the Local Pension, which covers public workers, military personnel, and private schoolteachers. The Local Pension system has a 20 to 35 year history. The People's Pension program was introduced in 1988, and, thus, is still in its beginning stages. Initially, the People's Pension was limited to workers employed in a workplace with 10 or more employees. The program has expanded to include workplaces with one or more workers as of July 1, 2003, and small business operators in cities and towns since April 1, 1999.

The People's Pension Act and its presidential decrees govern the South Korean pension system.

1. Contributions and Benefits

a. Basic Requirements

A company with one or more employees must join the government-administered pension program, which is administered by the National Pension Administration Corporation. Both the People's Pension and the Local Pension are part of this program. Currently, the employee and employer each contribute 4.5 percent of the employee's standard monthly salary. The amount transferred to the national pension fund from the employer's contribution for employees' severance pay will be deducted from the final installment of employee severance pay.[74]

Pension participants must contribute to the pension program for at least 20 years (15 in certain cases) to be entitled to receive a retirement benefit, but they may get a refund of their contributions if they die or otherwise are unable to make contributions for the

[74]For a discussion of employee severance pay, see I.B.1.d.iv., above.

minimum period. For purposes of a disability annuity, a participant obtains vested rights after only one year of contributions.

b. Types of Benefits

There are four categories of benefits under the South Korean pension system:

1. *Old Age Annuity*. This is an annuity payable to a subscriber who has contributed to the Fund for at least 20 years or has reached 60 years of age. The old age annuity is classified into several categories such as full annuity, discounted annuity, and special annuity according to the subscription period, age, and existence or non-existence of income.
2. *Disability Pension*. This is a pension payable to a subscriber who has contributed to the Fund for at least one year and has incurred a physical handicap due to a disease or injury during the subscription period.
3. *Survivor's Pension*. This is a pension payable to the dependents of a deceased subscriber who qualifies under certain criteria.
4. *Lump-sum Refund*. This is a lump-sum refund of previous contributions with some interest payable to (dependents of) a subscriber who dies or loses his eligibility as a subscriber and is not entitled to any other benefits under the plan.

2. *Expatriate Employees*

Under prior law, expatriate employees working in South Korea[75] were not required to contribute to the pension program, although they could do so voluntarily. However, under a pension plan amendment effective August 4, 1995,[76] certain expatriate workers in a workplace that has five or more employees may be required to contribute. As a matter of practice, the National Pen-

[75]For a general discussion of expatriate employment, see IX., below.
[76]Law No. 4971.

sion Administration Corporation looks to see whether the particular expatriate worker appears on the income tax report or income tax exemption report of the enterprise at issue. If the worker appears on a report for the South Korean branch or subsidiary, he or she will be deemed an employee of the branch or subsidiary and required to make pension contributions. Companies wishing to challenge this policy may seek a ruling from the Ministry of Health and Welfare, which has the final authority at the administrative level.

There is one notable exception to the mandatory contribution requirement. If the laws of the expatriate's home country exempt South Korean nationals from domestic pension plan contributions when working in that country, then, correspondingly, the expatriate employee will be exempt from South Korean contribution requirements. Theoretically, an expatriate also could be exempt under a pension agreement between South Korea and the expatriate's home country. In the absence of an exemption law or agreement, however, the expatriate will be required to contribute to the South Korean pension program and may, in addition, be required to contribute to a second pension plan at home. South Korea has signed pension agreements with the United Kingdom, Canada, Germany, and the United States. The agreements took effect on May 1, 1999, for Canada; on August 1, 2000, for the United Kingdom; on April 1, 2001, for the United States; and on January 1, 2003, for Germany. Pension agreements also have been signed with Italy, France, Ireland, and Japan but are still awaiting ratification in Korea. Article 102(1) of the National Pension Act now excludes Saudi Arabia as a country with which South Korea has a treaty to provide citizens of both countries reciprocal treatment with respect to pension requirements and obligations.

B. Health and Disability Benefits

1. National Health Insurance

Effective July 1, 2001, employers of all businesses that employ one or more employees under ordinary circumstances (foreign workers are not included for purposes of calculating this threshold) are required to subscribe to the national health insurance plan, pursuant to the National Health Insurance Act (NHIA) and the presidential decree issued pursuant to the NHIA.[77]

The NHIA provides for a premium rate to be set by presidential decree at a maximum of 8 percent of the subscriber's standard monthly salaries.[78] Effective January 1, 2004, a premium rate of 4.21 percent is fixed by the Presidential Decree. The employer and employee share the cost of the premium equally[79] (i.e., each contributes 2.105 percent).

2. *Employment Promotion Fund for the Handicapped*

As discussed above,[80] the Handicapped Persons Employment Act (HPEA) seeks to promote the employment of handicapped workers by prohibiting job-related discrimination, and by establishing hiring quotas for certain large employers and government agencies. In addition, the HPEA establishes the Employment Promotion Fund for the Handicapped (Handicapped Promotion Fund). The various benefits provided by this Fund are described below.

a. *Employer Subsidies and Financial Aid*

Employers that hire handicapped workers in excess of the number required are entitled to monthly financial support for each person employed in the excess of the quota. Employers that are not subject to the employment requirement because they employ less than 300 workers may, nevertheless, be entitled to subsidies if they employ handicapped persons in numbers greater than 2 percent of their total workforce.

Financial aid also is granted to employers when a handicapped worker is newly employed, provided that the worker remains employed for more than six months at minimum wage or higher.

b. *Vocational Training*

Handicapped persons who have finished the second year curriculum provided at special high schools may be eligible for voca-

---

[77]NHIA, arts. 5, 6.

[78]*Id.* art. 65(1).

[79]*Id.* art. 67(1).

[80]See VI.D., above.

tional training. The training period varies from three months to three years, depending on the needs of the employees. This training can be both classroom training and training that takes place on the job.

The cost of training for both the employer and the trainee can be supplemented by the Handicapped Promotion Fund. Trainees also may receive financial aid to cover costs for items such as books and materials in preparing for training. A training allowance in the form of a monthly stipend to cover medical and transportation costs also is granted to the trainees.

c. *Facilities and Transportation Financing*

Grants from the Handicapped Promotion Fund cover up to two-thirds of the costs necessary to provide schools with desks, restrooms, and ramps that are specially designed for the handicapped. Necessary financing for workplaces, dormitories, and shuttle buses also is made available through a loan program for employers. In addition, all registered handicapped workers and handicapped job seekers are entitled to vehicle loans.

C. Unemployment Insurance System

The Employment Insurance Act (EIA) establishes an unemployment insurance system to provide limited compensation and job training to qualified unemployed individuals. The EIA, which became effective in limited form on July 1, 1995, now is applicable to all companies with certain exceptions such as agriculture businesses with less than five employees.

Under the EIA, employers and employees each pay one-half of the unemployment insurance premium. The legal ceiling on insurance premiums is three percent of total wages, although premiums currently are lower than this, as shown in the table below. This ceiling applies not just to premiums for unemployment insurance, but also to the total premiums paid under all EIA components. In addition to unemployment insurance premiums, employers also pay premiums for the Employment Stabilization program, which provides activities for the prevention of layoffs, promotion of re-employment, and new job creation, and the Occupational Competency Development program, which provides opportunities for employees to improve their occupational competency through job training and education. The premium rates for these programs are summarized as follows:

UIA Components	Liability	Premiums
Unemployment Compensation	Employer: ½ Employee: ½	0.45 percent for each
Employment Stabilization	Employer only	0.15 percent
Development of Occupational Competency	Employer only	Less than 150 employees: 0.1 percent 150 employees or more in preferential enterprises: 0.3 percent 150 employees or more, but less than 1000 employees: 0.5 percent Large enterprises (1,000 or more employees): 0.7 percent

Those workers with a paid up insurance policy of six months or more are entitled to receive unemployment benefits. The minimum unemployment benefit period is 90 days. In most cases, employees are eligible to receive 50 percent of their average wage as an unemployment benefit.

If the unemployed are unable to secure new jobs due to mass unemployment, the unemployment benefit period can be extended by the Ministry of Labor for up to 60 days, during which period beneficiaries will receive 70 percent of their previous unemployment benefit.

D. Other Employment-Related Programs

1. *Basic Employment Policy Act and Employment Security Act*

The purpose of these Acts is to supply manpower to manufacturing and other industries by ensuring that workers are able to work in occupations corresponding to their skills, thereby ensuring employment security and promotion, and contributing to the development of the nation's economy.

Under the Basic Employment Policy Act (BEPA), the Minister of Labor is responsible for developing a plan for employment security. Employment trends, prospective supply and demand of manpower, and measures for employment and for employment promotion must be included in this plan.

The Employment Security Act (ESA) creates placement services and promulgates rules regarding employee recruitment. The ESA also establishes the Employment Security Committee to formulate policy on employment security, promotion, and unemployment.

2. *Basic Vocational Training Act*

The purpose of the Basic Vocational Training Act (BVTA) is to improve the national economy and the status of workers by providing vocational training.

Vocational training includes public training, in-plant training, and other authorized training programs. The vocational training provided by these programs can be classified as "basic training," "upgrade training," "job conversion training," or "retraining," depending on the course content.

3. *Wage Claim Guarantee Act*

The Wage Claim Guarantee Act (WCGA) creates a fund to pay deferred wages and severance pay to retired employees on behalf of bankrupt employers. The WCGA became effective on July 1, 1998, and applies to all businesses with one or more employees from July 1, 2000.

The fund guarantees employees their last three months of wages and severance pay for the last three years of service with priority compared to other lien/mortgage holders and general creditors.[81] From January 1, 2001, the WCGA covers the last three months of compensation during a company shutdown due to reasons attributable to the company. Employers must contribute an amount not to exceed 0.03 percent of their total payroll to finance

---

[81]For a discussion of employee severance pay, see I.B.1.d.iv., above.

the fund. However, while the fund is being established, other funds or public money can be used to give "breathing space" to financially troubled companies. Money used in the beginning to pay employees will be made up through later employer contributions.

IX. IMMIGRATION

A. Expatriates

In principle, South Korea restricts the employment of expatriates working in domestic companies to positions for which a qualified citizen is unavailable. For this reason, most expatriates working in South Korean companies are employed at senior levels.

Most foreign nationals working in South Korea are employed as managers in foreign companies, in joint ventures between a foreign company and a South Korean company, and in South Korean companies where certain skills are in short supply.

A growing number of native-born South Koreans who have taken citizenship in another country, particularly the United States, are returning to take up management or professional positions in domestic industry.

B. Foreign Workers Employment

The Employment Permit System (EPS) under the Act on Foreign Workers' Employment came into force as of August 17, 2004. Employers may hire foreign workers after they do their utmost to find a domestic workforce through Employment Stability Centers for one month to no avail. Employers will be informed about foreign job-seekers through the electronic network to manage employment of foreigners, and they may choose themselves the appropriate persons among the candidates.

Industries allowed to employ foreign workers will be decided every January by the Committee on Foreign Workforce Policy attended by representatives of the manufacturing sector experiencing serious workforce shortage and relevant agencies. To prevent foreign workers from being permanently settled here, the government allows foreigners to work for a maximum of three years and afterwards may renew their work contracts to work beyond the maximum period.

When concluding a working contract, parties to the contract must use a standard working contract. Foreign employees have to participate in obtaining insurance to cover their return expenses. They will be forbidden to move to other workplaces, except for in cases of workplace shutdown and suspension of business, reasonable termination of the working contract, and occurrences of diseases and injuries.

C. Entry Requirements for Employment

The entry of expatriate employees is tightly controlled by the South Korean Justice and Labor Ministries. In general, expatriates are admitted on a prearranged employment basis.

Foreign nationals from countries with which South Korea has a visa exemption treaty may enter the country and stay generally for three months without an entry visa (note: for U.S. and Japanese nationals, 30 days only). However, they must obtain permission to work.

A long-term entry visa is obtainable from the Korean embassy/consulate after obtaining a pre-approval certificate from the local immigration office. Once an individual has entered South Korea on a long-term entry visa, he must apply for a residence certificate within 90 days of arrival. Long-term work visas may be extended annually.

The granting of a non-immigrant visa means the granting of similar visas to the spouse and any unmarried children under the age of 21.

It is illegal for expatriates to be employed in any capacity other than the one for which they have been approved. Criminal liability for violations is imposed on both the employee and the employer. The employer must report the termination of a foreign national's employment to the immigration authorities within 15 days.

TAIWAN*

INTRODUCTION

Taiwan is a democracy of approximately 23 million residents, located 100 miles off the southeast coast of China. Its present political form can be traced back to 1950, when the Nationalist government of the Republic of China was forced to retreat to the island after the Communists, led by Mao Zedong, took control of mainland China. Despite being arguably the most diplomatically isolated country in the world due to its conflicts with the People's Republic of China (Communist China), Taiwan has developed into a significant economic power, including becoming the world's third-largest producer of computer products, the 11th largest exporter, and the 25th highest income country in the world.

A. Basic Makeup of the Taiwan Government

The Taiwan Constitution is based on the Constitution promulgated by the Republic of China in 1947. Pursuant to the Constitution, the government of Taiwan consists of five parts: the Executive Yuan, the Legislative Yuan/National Assembly, the Judicial Yuan, the Examination Yuan, and the Control Yuan. As one might expect, the Executive Yuan is the executive branch, the Legislative Yuan and the National Assembly constitute the legislative branch, and the Judicial Yuan is the judicial branch. The responsibilities of the other two branches are perhaps less self-evident: the Examination Yuan is responsible for administering the civil ser-

---

*Baldwin J. Lee, Esq., Allen Matkins Leck Gamble & Mallory LLP, San Francisco, California; Professor Joseph S. Lee, Professor of human resource management, National Central University, and President, Institute of Knowledge-based Economy and Management, Taipei, Taiwan. Baldwin J. Lee may be contacted at blee@allenmatkins.com. Prof. Joseph Lee may be contacted at jslee@mgt.ncu.edu.tw.

vice examinations, and the Control Yuan handles security and auditing matters, as well as discipline of public officials.

Democratic rights in Taiwan have increased since martial law was lifted in 1987, including the commencement of full direct elections for the Legislative Yuan in 1992 and of the President in 1996. The ruling Kuomingtang party also lost the presidential elections for the first time in 2000.

B. General Sources of Taiwan Labor Law

1. Domestic Developments

a. Dormancy of Taiwan Labor Laws Between 1950 and the 1980s

Although a number of Taiwan labor relations and employment laws existed prior to 1984, few of them were enforced. Such laws included the Labor Union Law, the Collective Agreement Law, the Settlement of Labor Disputes Law, the Employee Welfare Fund Law, the Minimum Wage Law, the Factory Law, the Labor Insurance Act, the Rules Governing Employment and Dismissal of Workers by Factories and Mines, and the Labor Safety and Health Law.

Most of the pre-1980s laws fit Taiwan poorly because they were enacted in mainland China during the 1930s to 1940s. For example, the Settlement of Labor Disputes Law was enacted in 1928, amended in 1932, 1943, and 1988; the Labor Union Law was enacted in 1929 and amended in 1949 and 1975; the Factory Law was enacted in 1929; the Collective Agreement Law was enacted in 1930 (but not made effective until 1932); and the Employee Welfare Fund Law was enacted in 1943 and amended in 1948. After the government of the Republic of China retreated to Taiwan in 1950, it found that most of its existing labor and employment laws were outmoded. In particular, the old laws were strongly pro-socialist, which made them unfit for the type of market-oriented economy that the government was promoting at that time. Thus, except for the Labor Insurance Act, which notably was not enacted until 1958, the government has never seriously enforced the pre-1980s laws. This disuse is illustrated by contrasting the frequency with which the various laws were amended. Although the Labor Insurance Act was regularly amended, in 1968, 1973, 1979, and 1988, other labor laws were very rarely amended.

The obsolescence of the labor relations laws is further illustrated by amendments to the Labor Union Law in 1975. In the 1970s, the Taiwan government wanted to encourage workers to form and join unions so that Taiwan labor organizations could develop relationships with trade unions from other countries that had severed diplomatic contacts with Taiwan after it left the United Nations. To promote unions, it had to amend the Labor Union Law because the existing unions had left their officers and constituencies in mainland China and could not hold elections.

b. Seminal Development of Taiwan Labor Law in the 1980s

On August 1, 1984, Taiwan established the foundation of its statutory scheme for workplace regulation by promulgating the Labor Standards Law (LSL).[1] The stated purposes of the LSL are to provide minimum standards of labor conditions, protect workers' rights and interests, strengthen labor-management relationships, and promote social and economic development.[2] The LSL is the most important and comprehensive employment law ever enacted in Taiwan; its enforcement has profoundly affected the operation of the labor market.[3]

c. Legislative Developments in the 2000s

In 2002, two major pieces of employment legislation were passed. First, Taiwan enacted the Gender Equality in Employment Act (GEEA), which became effective March 8, 2002. This law was enacted for the legislative purpose of ensuring equal employ-

---

[1]Although the Taiwan government has translated this Law as the "Labor Standards Law," its name also is translatable into English as the "Basic Labor Standards Law." For the official English translation, *see* Labor Laws and Regulations of the Republic of China, Council of Labor Affairs (CLA) of the Executive Yuan, Republic of China (1999). In case of any discrepancy between the English and Chinese texts, the Chinese text governs. *Id.*, final note.

[2]Labor Standards Law (LSL), art. 1.

[3]*See* Joseph S. Lee, *Changing Employment Relations in Taiwan*, *in* THE CHANGING EMPLOYMENT IN ASIAN PACIFIC COUNTRIES (Greg Bember et al. eds., Business Publishing Inc. 2000).

ment opportunity regardless of gender in the workplace.[4] Taiwan also amended the Employment Services Act of 1992 (ESA). Most substantially, the amendments extended the protections of antidiscrimination law to married persons and to disabled persons,[5] added substantial regulation and duties to public employment agencies,[6] and strengthened the regulations relating to management of foreign workers.[7] These changes are discussed in the appropriate sections below.

The legislature also is turning to substantially revising the Trade Unions Act, the Collective Bargaining Law, and the Labor Dispute Law. Of these intended revisions, the only new law enacted has been the Mass Layoff Law, which became effective on May 7, 2003, and which is discussed in IV., below.

2. *International Influences*

Taiwan's contemporary employment and labor laws have felt little direct influence from international labor law standards or international organizations due to Taiwan's diplomatic isolation since the mid-1970s. Although this isolation formally was marked by the United States' switch of diplomatic recognition from Taiwan to the People's Republic of China in 1979, Taiwan's diplomatic decline dates back to U.S. President Richard Nixon's 1972 visit to Beijing. Indeed, by the time the United States switched its recognition to the People's Republic of China in 1979, Taiwan was recognized diplomatically by fewer than 30 foreign countries and already had given up its founding seat in the United Nations (in response to the admission of the People's Republic of China).

Although Taiwan was a charter member of the International Labor Organization (ILO),[8] it left the ILO in 1972 in the wake of yielding its United Nations membership to Communist China. However, in order to keep its relationships with the many countries that severed diplomatic contacts in the 1970s, Taiwan developed an interest in utilizing international labor organizations. These

[4]Gender Equality in Employment Act (GEEA), art. 1.

[5]*See* Employment Services Act (ESA), arts. 5, 24.

[6]ESA, arts. 6.1–6.6, 10, 25.

[7]*See id.* art. 46 et seq.

[8]For more information about the ILO, see the chapter on the ILO in Volume I, Part 4.

strategic interests fueled the amendments to the Labor Union Law in 1975 to allow unions to develop in Taiwan and become conduits for international diplomatic opportunities. The government became motivated to increase international union involvement because it perceived unions in other countries, such as the AFL-CIO in the United States, as anti-Communist. The government hoped that such anti-Communist unions would help lobby for favorable policies for Taiwan (and accordingly, against the interests of the People's Republic of China).

Such efforts were particularly necessary because since the 1970s, the People's Republic of China has successfully blocked Taiwan's attempts to enter or re-enter international organizations, including multiple attempts by Taiwan to gain separate entry into the United Nations.

In more recent times, the ability of Taiwan and the People's Republic of China to co-exist in diplomatic circles has increased. In 1992, Taiwan was granted observer status in the General Agreement on Tariffs and Trade (GATT) under the entity name "Separate Customs Territory of Taiwan, Penghu, Kinmen, and Matsu." Both Taiwan and the People's Republic of China became World Trade Organization members in 2002.[9]

Although Taiwan's diplomatic status declined in the 1970s, its economy developed rapidly. After developing as a basic manufacturing economy in the 1960s and 1970s, Taiwan has shifted to the technological sector, becoming the world's third largest producer of computer-related products and the world's leading manufacturer of a number of computer peripherals. Taiwan's trading partners have influenced the enactment of a number of labor and employment laws. For example, the 1984 passage of the LSL was strongly influenced by the United States. In the 1980s, Taiwan had a very large trade surplus with the United States. The AFL-CIO, among other organizations, put pressure on the U.S. government to restrict importation of Taiwan-made products, ostensibly because Taiwan lacked adequate legal protection for workers and did not have bona fide trade unions. Taiwan enacted the LSL in part to improve its image regarding worker rights.

---

[9]See the chapter on the World Trade Organization in Volume I, Part 4.

C. Administrative Regulation and Enforcement

1. *Responsible Agencies*

Historically, the Ministry of the Interior was the central government entity responsible for administering labor and employment laws. Pursuant to its authority under the LSL, as established in 1984, the Ministry of the Interior promulgated the LSL Enforcement Rules in 1985.

The Ministry of the Interior's labor and employment duties were transferred in 1987, when the Executive Yuan established the Council of Labor Affairs (CLA). The CLA has taken over central administration of Taiwan's labor and employment laws. Accordingly, it is the most important agency governing labor and employment issues, roughly equivalent to the U.S. Department of Labor.

After a long delay in the process, the CLA will be elevated into the Ministry of Labor and Human Resources in early 2005.

2. *Enforcement*

a. *Labor Standards Law*

The LSL is enforced by the CLA, which has the power to delegate inspection and enforcement duties to local competent authorities.

Businesses are not permitted to reject visits by LSL inspectors.[10] An inspector may demand that necessary documents or explanations be provided.[11] Upon completion of an inspection visit, the inspector is required to report the results of the visit to the business inspected and to submit a report regarding the same to the inspection agency.[12] If the business that was inspected has any objection to the results of the inspection, it may file objections in writing to the inspection agency within 10 days after receipt of the report.[13]

---

[10]LSL, art. 73.
[11]LSL Enforcement Rules, art. 43.
[12]*Id.* art. 44.
[13]*Id.* art. 45.

Workers are permitted to file oral or written complaints of violations of employment laws or regulations to the government.[14] The government is to investigate complaints within seven days after the complaint is received, and the employer is not permitted to retaliate against the employee for raising such a complaint.[15] Workers also may make complaints of violations of employment laws or regulations to their employer.[16] An employer is required to investigate worker complaints, and, in the event a violation is discovered, to correct the violation and notify the complainant of the correction.[17]

b. Gender Equality in Employment Act

For private-sector employers, the Gender Equality in Employment Act (GEEA) is administered on the national level by the Council of Labor Affairs.[18] Enforcement of the GEEA for civil servants, educational employees, and military personnel is the responsibility of the respective agencies that cover those areas.[19] Other levels of government are to establish Gender Equality in Employment Commissions for the purpose of formulating policies to effectuate the GEEA.[20] These commissions must consist of 5 to 11 members, each of whom serves two-year terms.[21] The commissions must consist of at least two representatives from labor organizations and two representatives from women's organizations, with the remainder to be experts in labor and legal issues.[22] Half of the commission members must be women.[23]

---

[14] LSL, art. 74; LSL Enforcement Rules, art. 46.
[15] LSL Enforcement Rules, art. 48; LSL, art. 74.
[16] LSL, art. 74.
[17] LSL Enforcement Rules, art. 47.
[18] GEEA, art. 2.
[19] *Id.*
[20] *Id.* art. 6.
[21] *Id.*
[22] *Id.*
[23] *Id.*

I. INDIVIDUAL EMPLOYMENT

A. Introduction

The Taiwan government historically played little role in regulating the terms of individual employment contracts. As with most other areas of employment law, this changed in 1984 with the enactment of the LSL.

B. General Employment Regulations

1. *Part-Time Versus Full-Time Employment*

Unlike some other nations' laws, Taiwan's LSL broadly extends the same benefits and rights to full-time and part-time employees. This protection of part-time work significantly contributes to employers' disfavor of part-time employees, who comprise only 5 to 6 percent of the Taiwan workforce. Because of these dynamics, the Council of Economic Development and Planning is proposing to amend the LSL so that employees who work fewer than 24 hours per week are entitled to fewer benefits than full-time employees.

2. *Job Vacancy Listings*

Unlike some other countries, Taiwan law does not require employers to list job vacancies with a regional labor bureau. Accordingly, employers do not make such listings.

3. *Recordkeeping*

The LSL requires employers to maintain comprehensive employee records, including name, sex, birthdate and birthplace, address, educational background, identification card number, date of reporting for duty, wage, labor insurance starting date, merits and demerits, injury and disease information, and other significant facts. These records must be maintained by the employer for five years after the employee's termination date.[24]

---

[24]LSL, art. 7.

Employers and job brokers are prohibited from withholding an employee's identification card or work permit against the employee's will.[25]

C. Individual Employment Contracts

1. Mandatory Contract Terms

Under the LSL Enforcement Rules, an employment contract must address the following matters:[26]

- the workplace and the work to be performed in the workplace;
- work start and stop times, rest periods, holidays, public holidays, leave, and any shift changes in a rotation system;
- the methods and schedules for determining, readjusting, calculating, and paying wages;
- formation and termination of the employment contract and retirement;
- overtime work arrangements;
- severance pay, retirement pay, and other allowances and bonuses;
- rules and obligations that the employer and employees must follow;
- safety and health;
- work education and training;
- other fringe benefits;
- compensation in the case of an accident, and subsidies in the case of ordinary injury or sickness;
- rules of conduct and work discipline;[27]
- merits and demerits;
- means through which the employer and employees are to communicate and to work cooperatively; and
- other matters concerning the rights and obligations of workers and management.

---

[25]ESA, art. 5.2.

[26]LSL Enforcement Rules, art. 7.

[27]See I.E., below.

An employment contract must be in writing in most cases, but there are some exceptions, including under the Factory Law.[28]

2. *Fixed-Term Versus Indefinite-Term Employment Contracts*

a. *Initial Characterization*

Regarding terms of employment, the LSL contemplates two categories: fixed-term contracts and indefinite-term contracts (translated into English by the CLA as "non-fixed-term" contracts).

Contracts for continuous work are classified as indefinite-term employment.[29]

Contracts for temporary, short-term, seasonal, or special work are classified as fixed-term employment.[30] Temporary work is defined to mean unexpected work of a noncontinuous nature, not to exceed six months.[31] Short-term work is work that is expected to be completed within a short period of time, of a noncontinuous nature, not to exceed six months.[32] Seasonal work means work of a noncontinuous nature for which the raw materials, source of materials, or market are influenced by seasonal factors, not to exceed nine months.[33] Special work is defined as work that can be completed within a specified period and of a noncontinuous nature, not to exceed one year absent approval by the government.[34]

b. *Conversion of Fixed-Term Contracts to Indefinite-Term Contracts*

Fixed-term contracts become indefinite-term contracts if the employee continues to work past the contract term without objection by the employer, unless the contract is for special or seasonal work.[35] To keep employers from linking short-term contracts together to end-run the regulations on indefinite-term contracts, the

---

[28]*See* Ministry of Interior Administrative Order, Oct. 2, 1984.
[29]LSL, art. 9.
[30]*Id.*
[31]LSL Enforcement Rules, art. 6(1).
[32]*Id.* art. 6(2).
[33]*Id.* art. 6(3).
[34]*Id.* art. 6(4).
[35]LSL, art. 9.

LSL dictates that if two contracts greater than 90 days each are executed within 30 days, the second contract is considered an indefinite-term contract (except for special or seasonal employment contracts).[36]

3. Probationary Periods

Previous requirements limiting the length of a probationary period have been eliminated.

4. Employee Tenure Calculation

If an employee is rehired or the employment contract is renewed within three months after the expiration or termination of the previous contract, the employee's seniority will continue to accrue cumulatively.[37] This seniority is used to calculate an employee's retirement allowance.[38]

D. Minors and Apprentices

1. Minors

Taiwan labor law provides special protections for minors. These protections extend to employees younger than age 16. To employ a worker younger than age 16, the employer must obtain a letter of consent and certificate of age from the child's guardian.[39] In addition, children younger than age 16 may not be employed to do tasks beyond their mental or physical capabilities, or hazardous work enumerated in the Enforcement Rules of the Labor Safety and Health Law.[40]

The law further protects children younger than age 15 by prohibiting their employment unless the child is a graduate of junior high school or the government has confirmed that such work will not harm the child's physical or mental health.[41]

---

[36]*Id.*

[37]*Id.* art. 10.

[38]See VIII., below.

[39]LSL, art. 46.

[40]*Id.* art. 44; LSL Enforcement Rules, art. 25. For additional restrictions on minors' working hours and rest periods, see V.B.4.b., below. For a discussion of the Labor Safety and Health Law (LSHL), see VII.A.2., below.

[41]LSL, art. 45.

2. *Apprentices*

Taiwan law provides special regulation for apprentices, who can be paid lower wages than other employees in equivalent positions.[42]

Apprentices are defined as people whose object is to learn technical skills and receive training from the employer.[43] An employer may not require an apprentice to do household chores, miscellaneous jobs, or other work that is not connected with learning job skills.[44] An apprentice may be required to clean the workplace, including machinery and equipment.[45]

An employer is not permitted to receive training fees from an apprentice.[46] The number of apprentices may not exceed one-fourth of the employer's workforce, except for businesses with fewer than four employees, which are still allowed to hire one apprentice.[47] Apprentices are governed by all other provisions of the labor laws.[48]

a. Special Contract Requirements

An employer must sign a written contract with each apprentice that sets forth the training subjects, training period, board and lodging arrangements, living allowances, relevant teaching subjects, labor insurance, certificate of training completion, the effective date of contract, conditions for termination of the contract, and any other clauses relating to the rights and obligations of the parties.[49] The contract must be executed in triplicate, with one copy kept by the employer, one copy kept by the apprentice, and one copy forwarded to the government for registration.[50] Minors are not permitted to sign apprenticeship training contracts without the prior consent of their guardian.[51]

---

[42]For a discussion of apprenticeship wages, see V.A.2.c., below.
[43]LSL, art. 64.
[44]LSL Enforcement Rules, art. 35.
[45]*Id.*
[46]LSL, art. 66.
[47]*Id.* art. 68.
[48]*Id.* art. 69.
[49]*Id.* art. 65.
[50]*Id.*
[51]*Id.*

b. Retaining Apprentices After the Apprenticeship

An employer may retain an apprentice upon the completion of his apprenticeship training period as long as the employer pays the former apprentice the same wage as other employees doing the same work.[52] If an employment period is specifically written on the apprenticeship contract, then the employment shall not be longer than the specified period.[53]

E. Mandatory Work Rules

Employers with more than 30 workers must establish and display work rules that have been approved by the government.[54] The rules must specify the following items:

- policies regarding work hours, time off, leaves of absence, national holidays, special leaves of absence, and arrangement of shifts for doing continuous work;
- wage rates, the method of calculating wages, and paydays;
- policies regarding overtime work;
- allowance and bonus provisions;
- disciplinary policies;
- rules for attendance, leave taking, commendations or demerits, promotion, and transfer;
- policies for recruitment, discharge, separation, withdrawal of service, and retirement;
- compensation and pension for occupational accidents or diseases;
- welfare measures;
- safety and health regulations; and
- methods for the promotion of communication and cooperation between the employer and the employees.[55]

Employers are permitted to establish different work rules at different work sites.[56]

---

[52]*Id.* art. 67.
[53]*Id.*
[54]*Id.* art. 70.
[55]*Id.*
[56]LSL Enforcement Rules, art. 40.

Employers must report the establishment or revision of their work rules to the government within 30 days of their creation or revision.[57] Copies of the rules must be displayed in the workplace and distributed to each worker.[58]

F. Employee Termination

Taiwan employment law does not presume that employment may be terminated at-will; instead, the LSL lists the specific circumstances under which employment may be terminated.

1. Termination by the Employer

a. Termination With Notice

i. Conditions

An employer may terminate an employment contract, with advance notice, if one of the following five conditions exists:

- the employer's business is suspended or ownership is transferred;
- there is an operating loss or business contraction;
- *force majeure* necessitates business suspension for more than one month;
- a reduction in force is required due to a change in the nature of the business, and the employee cannot be reassigned to another position; or
- an employee is confirmed to be incompetent for his or her job duties.[59]

ii. Notice requirements

For the situations listed above, the following notice requirements apply:

---

[57] *Id.* art. 37.

[58] *Id.* art. 38.

[59] LSL, art. 11. For additional discussion of reductions in force, business suspensions, and transfers of ownership, see IV., below.

- for a worker who has worked continuously for more than three months but less than one year, the employer must either give notice 10 days in advance or pay the equivalent in wages;
- for a worker who has worked continuously for more than one year but fewer than three years, the employer must either give notice 20 days in advance or pay the equivalent in wages; and
- for a worker who has worked continuously for more than three years, the employer must either give notice 30 days in advance or pay the equivalent in wages.[60]

If an employee is given notice of termination, he or she is entitled to request up to two paid workdays per week to search for a new job.[61]

iii. Notification to the government

Amendments to the Employment Service Act have increased notification obligations. Employers are to provide name, age, gender, address, telephone number, and job position information for workers who will be laid off at least 10 days prior to the actual date of layoff.[62] This is intended to allow public service agencies to take timely actions to assist the laid off workers. Upon receiving such notice, government employment agencies are assigned the responsibility of providing placement assistance to the laid-off employees in seeking re-employment.[63]

iv. Severance pay

For employees terminated by the employer with notice, the employer is required to pay severance pay equal to one month's wage for each year that the employee has worked continuously for that employer.[64] Partial years are to be paid pro-rata, and tenure of less than one month is rounded up to one month.[65]

---

[60]LSL, art. 16.
[61]*Id.*
[62]ESA, art. 33.
[63]*Id.* art. 33.
[64]LSL, art. 17.
[65]*Id.*

All severance pay must be paid within 30 days of the termination of the employment contract.[66]

b. *Termination Without Notice*

An employer may dismiss an employee without notice if one of the following six categories of good cause exists:

- material misrepresentations made by the employee at the time of hiring;
- violence or gross insults made by the employee against the employer, the employer's family members or agents, or fellow workers;
- imprisonment of the employee;
- the employee's gross breach of the employment contract or the employer's work rules;
- the employee's deliberate destruction of the employer's property or deliberate disclosure of technological or confidential business information of the employer, with resulting damage; or
- the employee's absence without cause for three days in a row or six days in a month.[67]

For all the above circumstances, except the employee's imprisonment, the employer must terminate the employee within 30 days of learning that such circumstances exist.[68] Unlike other terminations, an employer is not required to pay an employee severance or notice period pay if any of the above six categories of good cause exists.[69]

c. *Involuntary Retirement*

Under Taiwan law, employees may be forced to retire at the age of 60 or if the employee becomes incapacitated.[70]

---

[66] *Id.*
[67] *Id.* art. 12.
[68] *Id.*
[69] *Id.* art. 18.
[70] *Id.* art. 54. See VIII.A.2., below.

d. *Employees Protected From Termination*

In general, an employer may not terminate an employee who is on maternity leave under LSL Article 50,[71] or who is receiving medical treatment for an occupational injury pursuant to Article 59.[72] This prohibition is waived if the employer is discontinuing business as a result of *force majeure*, catastrophe, or other acts of God, and prior approval has been obtained from the government.[73]

2. *Termination by the Employee*

An employee may terminate his or her employment without notice yet still receive statutory severance benefits under the following six circumstances:

- the employer made a material misrepresentation when the employment contract was signed;
- the employer, or the employer's agent or family member, has committed violence or gross insults against the employee, unless the employer discharged the offending agent;
- the work specified in the contract has the risk of ruining the employee's health, and the situation has not been ameliorated after the employer has been advised to make improvements by the employee or a union officer;
- the employer, the employer's agent, or another worker has contracted a contagious infectious disease, unless the employer has discharged the infected parties or sent them to the hospital for medical treatment;
- the employer has failed to pay wages according to the terms of the employment contract, or has failed to provide a piece-rate worker with sufficient work; or
- the employer has violated the provisions of the employment contract or labor laws and regulations in a fashion damaging to the rights and interests of the employee.[74]

---

[71]For a discussion of maternity leave, see V.C.4.f., below.

[72]LSL, art. 13. For a discussion of occupational injuries, see VII., below.

[73]LSL, art. 13.

[74]*Id.* art. 14.

An employee who wishes to terminate employment based upon the employer's misrepresentations or violations of the employment contract or law must do so within 30 days of the date that he or she becomes aware of the relevant circumstance.[75] When an employee terminates employment under such circumstances, he or she is entitled to statutory severance pay, as determined by LSL Article 17.[76]

An employee who terminates his or her employment after the expiration of a fixed-term contract is not entitled to severance pay.[77]

II. COLLECTIVE BARGAINING

A. Introduction

1. *Historical Background*

From 1950 to 1987, Taiwan's labor policies discouraged union activity. Among other things, the government was trying to push the economy forward quickly and was afraid that Chinese Communists would infiltrate labor groups and use them against the government. The government controlled unions in a number of ways. Under the Labor Union Law, unions were (and still are) prohibited from organizing workers across the boundaries of their workplace. Union power also was limited by martial law, which prohibited work stoppages. The ruling political party further controlled unions by nominating only party members to be union officers.

As a result of these anti-union policies, Taiwan faced very few labor disputes between 1960 and 1987 and encountered almost no strikes or work stoppages. Also, although some collective bargaining agreements were created, the content of those agreements was nonsubstantive, consisting only of conditions that already were required by existing laws. By controlling unions during this period, the government was able to pursue its policies of

---

[75]*Id.*

[76]*Id.* See I.F.1.a.iv., above.

[77]LSL, art. 18.

maintaining political stability and maximizing conditions for economic development.

After 1987, when martial law was lifted, unions became more independent. Since that time, bona fide unions have developed and union activity as a whole has increased, especially for unions in public enterprises, such as Taiwan Power Electrical Company and China Petroleum Corporation.

2. *Main Legal Instruments and Authorities Regulating Labor Relations*

The Labor Union Law (LUL) dates back to 1929, with subsequent amendments in 1949 and 1975. Fundamentally, the LUL charges labor unions with the role of protecting workers by upholding their rights and interests, advancing their knowledge and skills, developing productive enterprises, and improving their livelihoods.[78] Unions are further regulated by the Enforcement Rules of the Labor Union Law (LUL Enforcement Rules), established in 1944, and amended in 1948 and 1975. Collective bargaining in Taiwan is regulated by the Collective Agreement Law (CAL), which was enacted in 1930 but only put into effect in 1982.

Historically, labor disputes in Taiwan were subject to the 1947 Measures for Handling Labor Disputes during the Period of National Mobilization for the Suppression of Communists Rebellion, which specifically applied during the "period of national emergency." Labor disputes also were regulated by the Settlement of Labor Disputes Law of 1928 (SLDL), a law of general application that was amended in 1988.

Originally, the primary government authority in charge of labor relations was the Bureau of Labor Affairs in the Ministry of the Interior, with the Council of Labor Affairs (CLA) taking charge of handling enforcement of collective bargaining rights and obligations in 1987.[79]

---

[78]Labor Union Law (LUL), art. 1.

[79]*Id.* art. 3.

3. *Overview of Taiwan's Unions*

a. *The National Federations*

Prior to 2000, the Chinese Federation of Labor (CFL) was the only federation for all unions. It was founded in 1949 in mainland China and was relocated to Taiwan in 1951 after the nationalist government retreated to Taiwan. In 2000, however, a group of industrial unions that were unhappy with the CFL's close relationship with the then-ruling party, KMT, left the CFL. They formed the Taiwan Confederation of Trade Unions (TCTU). Although the Trade Union Law recognizes only one legal federation of unions, the KMT did not take any action to outlaw the TCTU. Since the DDP party became the ruling party in May 2000, it has recognized the TCTU as a legitimate federation. A proposed amendment to the Trade Union Law that would permit multiple federations at the national level was expected to be passed in 2005. Since the government's recognition of the TCTU, additional federations at the national level have been founded and certified by the Council of Labor Affairs as legitimate federations. These new federations are the Chinese Federation of Craft Labor (ROC), the National Trade Union Confederation, the Chinese General Labor League, and the Chinese Federation of Craft Workers Unions. However these five federations generally exist in name only—they lack substantial influence on the labor movement and public issues in Taiwan. Thus, the CFL and the TCTU are the only two major federations with measurable influence on government policy in Taiwan.

b. *Unions at the National Level*

Currently there are eight national unions in Taiwan. They are the Taiwan Power Workers' Union, the Chinese Federation for Railroad Workers Union, the Taiwan Federation of Railroad Workers Union, the Chinese Federation of Telephone and Telegraph Workers Union, the Taiwan Petroleum Workers Union, the Chinese Seamen Union, the China Airline Industrial Workers Union, three Chinese Postal Workers Unions (north, central, and south regions), and the Taiwan Highway Workers Union.

c. Unions at the Regional Level

Currently there are seven unions in Taiwan that are not national unions, but are above the jurisdiction of the Provincial Federation: the Taiwan Telecommunication Workers; the Taiwan Power Workers' Union; the Taiwan Highway Workers' Union; the Taiwan Provincial Federation of Labor; the Federation of Industrial Workers' Unions of Export Processing Zones; the Taipei Municipal Federation of Labor; and the Kaohsiung Municipal Federation of Labor.

Regional unions have lost their effective power due to the change in Taiwan's political environment in recent years. Unions at the city and county level have increasingly grown in independence and authority.

d. Unions at the Provincial Level

As of September 2004, there were 60 unions at the provincial level.

e. Unions at the City and County Level

Industrial unions, at the city and county level, have increased in importance. The central government's control of regional unions has declined, and industrial unions have become more independent. In 2003 there were 51 federations of unions at the industrial level.

As of September 2004, there were 52 unions at the county and municipality level. These federations usually do not participate in collective bargaining or engage in handling grievances. Instead, they tend to emphasize political, social, educational, and recreational activities. Most of these federations have their own office buildings that house offices for themselves and member unions. Recreation halls and other recreational facilities also can be found in these buildings. For example, in 1988, the Hwa Lien County Federation received a 40 million new Taiwan dollar grant (approximately 1.25 million U.S. dollars) from the county government to build a recreational hall for its members.

According to the LUL, workers with no permanent employers, such as barbers, tailors, or taxi drivers, are to organize into craft unions along city or county lines. These craft unions do not bargain for their members. Instead, they pay labor insurance on behalf of their members[80] and provide social, educational, and recreational services.

f. Industrial Unions at the Plant Level

Unions at the plant level are the basic unit of industrial unions. Employees of any plant may petition the appropriate government agency to form a union. When the petition is granted, the union is the sole representative of the employees in the particular plant; plural unionism is banned in Taiwan. However, since 1987, dual unions have emerged in many enterprises to compete with the party-dominated unions (e.g., the Railway Engineers Association), and the government has not yet taken any action against them.

4. International Activities

Although Taiwan diplomatic isolation has prevented it from membership as a nation in the ILO since 1972, the CFL has maintained memberships in many other international labor bodies. The CFL is an original member of the Asian Regional Office (ARO) of the ICFTU (International Confederation of Free Trade Unions), established in 1951. It has participated in all ARO conferences and executive board meetings. Other national unions also have maintained connections with international organizations. For example, the Chinese Railway Workers' Union (now the Taiwan Railway Workers' Union) and the Chinese Seamen Unions have been active members of the International Transport Workers' Federation since 1965, and the Chinese Federation of Postal Workers is a member of Postal, Telephone, Telegraph International.

Because only national unions can be members of international labor organizations, the CFL has organized several committees through which local unions can be members of various international bodies. These committees are as follows:

---

[80]For a discussion of labor insurance, see VIII.B., below.

- the Electric Power Workers' Committee consists of representatives of the Taiwan Electric Power Workers' Union and is a member of ICEF (International Chemical and Energy Federation);
- the Textile Workers' Committee consists of representatives of the Taiwan Provincial Federation of Textile Workers and the Taiwan Municipal Federation of Textile Workers, and is a member of the International Textile, Garment and Leather Workers' Federation;
- the Chemical and Energy Workers' Committee, consisting of representatives of the Taiwan Petroleum Workers Union, the Taiwan Provincial Federation of Paper Workers, the Taiwan Provincial Federation of Plastic Workers, and the Taiwan Alkali Workers' Union, is a member of ICEF;
- the Plantation Workers' Committee consists of representatives the Taiwan Provincial Federation of Sugar Workers and the Taiwan Provincial Federation of Forestry Workers, and is a member of IFPAW (International Federation of Plantation Agricultural Workers); and
- the Machinery Workers' Committee consists of representatives of local machinery workers' unions and is a member of IMF (International Metalworkers' Federation).

However, since the DPP came into power, such international activities have ceased, and the committees exist in name only.

Besides belonging to international labor organizations, the CFL and other unions also have maintained some relationships with foreign labor education institutes, including the University of Philippines Asian Labor Education Center at Manila, labor education programs sponsored by the Griedrich-Ebert Stiftung of Germany in Thailand, the Asian-American Free Labor Institute of the AFL-CIO, and the Afro-Asian Institute of Labor Studies in Israel.

B. Labor Unions

1. Union Organization and Structure

Union organization in Taiwan is rather rigidly structured by the LUL.

a. Formation

LUL article 6 ostensibly requires craft or industrial unions to be established when there are 30 or more workers older than age 20 in a factory or worksite, or in a specific industry or craft within a single administrative area. However, this statute is seldom enforced; only about 38 percent of the workforce in Taiwan belongs to unions. If the requisite number of workers does not exist, establishment of a union is permissive.[81]

b. Internal Organization

Most unions in Taiwan, except for some of the recently formed independent unions (unions independent from the Chinese Federation of Trade Unions), have the same internal organizational structure, which is that prescribed by the LUL. According to the LUL, unions are generally run by the general assembly, which consists of representatives of union members. During the assembly meeting, the delegates elect members to the general council, who then elect standing council members among themselves. The function of the general council is to help the union president formulate policies for administering the union's daily business. A union president is elected by the general council members from the members of the standing committee. Delegates also elect members to the board of supervisors, whose job is to supervise and audit the union's financial affairs. A union normally has one secretary and several staff members who oversee the union's business in five different areas: general affairs, organization, welfare, training and education, and information. However, because most unions lack significant funding, few of them can afford full-time staff members.

c. Groups, Sections, and Branches

If of sufficient size, craft or industrial unions may set up groups, sections, and branches.[82] Groups must consist of 5 to 20 members.[83] A group must have one group leader and one deputy

---

[81]*See* LUL, arts. 6, 8.
[82]*Id.* art. 52.
[83]*Id.*

group leader, elected by union members in the group.[84] A section may be established for three or more groups.[85] Sections must have one secretary and two assistant secretaries.[86] Branches may be established for three or more sections.[87] Branches must have three to nine secretaries, a secretariat, and one to three standing secretaries.[88] A branch may have substitute secretaries numbering up to one-half the number of the secretaries.[89] Group, section, and branch officers are subject to one-year terms, but may be re-elected.[90] Group, section, and branch officers must administer their affairs under the direction of the labor union, except that a branch may act independently regarding external affairs in special circumstances if the union approves.[91]

d. Federations

When a municipality has more than seven industrial or craft unions, and if more than one-third of the unions approve, an application for establishment of a municipal general federation of labor unions may be filed with the government.[92] When a majority of municipalities in a province have established general federations, and if one-third of the municipal federations approve, an application for establishment of a provincial general federation of labor unions may be filed with the government.[93] If seven or more labor unions of the same industry or craft desire, they may apply to the government for registration of a national federation of labor unions for their industry or craft.[94] An application for registration of a national general federation of labor unions may be filed upon approval of 21 or more provincial general federations of labor unions, general federations of labor unions for municipalities under the

[84] *Id.* art. 53.
[85] *Id.* art. 52.
[86] *Id.* art. 53.
[87] *Id.* art. 52.
[88] *Id.* art. 53.
[89] *Id.*
[90] *Id.*
[91] *Id.* art. 54.
[92] *Id.* art. 47.
[93] *Id.* art. 48.
[94] *Id.* art. 49

jurisdiction of the Executive Yuan, or national federations of labor unions for a specific industry or craft.[95]

e. Foreign Affiliation

A Taiwan labor union may associate with a foreign labor union if it receives prior approval of the government, and a resolution approving such an association has been passed at a general union meeting or meeting of members' representatives.[96]

2. Certification, Merger, and Dissolution

a. Certification

To establish a union, the organizers must obtain the signatures of at least 30 workers qualified for the union, each of whom is older than age 20, and must file an application with the government for registration.[97] The organizers also must immediately organize a preparatory committee to address issues such as the soliciting of members and the convocation of the inaugural general meeting of the union.[98]

The inaugural general meeting must be convened within three months after the preparatory committee is established.[99] The preparatory committee may apply for an extension of this deadline for a period of up to three months.[100] The constitution of the union requires approval by more than two-thirds of the members or representatives in attendance at the inaugural general meeting.[101] After the organizers have completed their organization, they must submit to the government for recording a report on their preparatory work, a list of members, a brief personal record of the union's officers, and the constitution of the union.[102] The government is responsible for issuing a certificate of registration after receiving

---

[95]*Id.* art. 50.
[96]*Id.* art. 34.
[97]*Id.* art. 9.
[98]*Id.*
[99]Enforcement Rules of the Labor Union Law (LUL Enforcement Rules), art. 9.
[100]*Id.*
[101]LUL, art. 11.
[102]*Id.* art. 9.

this report.[103] Changes in the union constitution must be reported to the government.[104]

b. Merger, Division, and Dissolution

A union must be merged or divided if there is a change in the classification of its industry or craft or a change in the demarcation of its area of organization.[105] Also, a labor union comprised of workers from another area, who originally joined an existing union because they did not have enough members to create their own union, may divide upon concurrence of more than one-half of its members.[106]

The government is permitted to dissolve a labor union if the union does not meet the requirements for establishment, or if the union disturbs the public peace and order.[107] A union may appeal a dissolution order within 30 days of receipt of the ruling.[108]

A union may voluntarily dissolve if it becomes bankrupt, lacks sufficient membership, or merges or divides.[109] If a union voluntarily dissolves, it must report within 15 days to the government regarding the date and reasons for the dissolution.[110]

3. Single-Union Rule

Only one labor union may be organized by workers in the same factory or worksite, or by workers in the same industry or craft within a single administrative area.[111] If the number of workers in the same industry of a particular administrative area is fewer than the number that triggers mandatory union creation (30), the workers may organize a labor union in combination with workers of the same industry in other areas, factories, or worksites.[112] The

---

[103]*Id.*
[104]*Id.* art. 28.
[105]*Id.* art. 42.
[106]*Id.*
[107]*Id.* art. 40.
[108]*Id.*
[109]*Id.* art. 41.
[110]*Id.* art. 44.
[111]*Id.* art. 8.
[112]*Id.*

LUL also provides that only one national federation of labor unions may be organized for each specific industry or craft.[113]

Up through 2000, many of the unions were controlled by the then-ruling political party, the Kuomingtang (KMT). Dissatisfaction with union performance led workers to form additional unions at some worksites with existing unions. Although these independent unions are illegal, the government has not taken any action against them.

4. *Membership*

a. *Legal Rights and Obligations to Join Unions*

All workers older than age 16 are eligible to form and join unions, except for the following:

- government employees;
- employees of educational institutions;
- employees of munitions industries; and
- managers and assistant managers, who may not belong to the same union that represents their employees.[114]

The LUL requires eligible workers to join the union for their industry or craft, except that workers who already have joined an industrial union are not required to join a craft union.[115] The government has never enforced this compulsory unionism requirement. A proposed amendment to the LUL that would eliminate compulsory union membership is pending in the legislature and is expected to pass in 2005 so that the law is in compliance with international labor standards discussed in the chapter on the International Labor Organization in Part 4 of Volume I.

If a worker refuses to join a labor union, he or she may be suspended from employment for a prescribed period of time by the labor union.[116] A suspended worker may resume work after

---

[113]*Id.* art. 49.

[114]*Id.* arts. 4, 12, and 13; LUL Enforcement Rules, art. 10.

[115]LUL, art. 12.

[116]LUL Enforcement Rules, art. 13.

joining the union.[117] In practice, these mandatory membership provisions historically have not been enforced. Workers seldom join unions and, even more rarely, pay union dues. Accordingly, unions in Taiwan are very poor.

b. Employer Rights to Union Membership Lists

Employers do not have the statutory right to know if a worker belongs to a union. However, management generally has easy access to union lists.

5. *Election and Removal of Officers*

a. Elections

Elections of union officers are supervised by a representative of the higher-level labor union.[118] Officer elections for the national general federation of labor unions are supervised by the CLA.[119]

The LUL provides for the election of union officers, including a board of directors responsible for running the affairs of the union, a board of supervisors responsible for auditing and overseeing operations, and a president.[120] A worker is eligible to be elected as a union director or supervisor if he or she is at least 20 years old, a member of the union, a citizen of the Republic of China, and is not a member of a management organization.[121] For unions organized by a combination of white-collar workers and industrial workers, the industrial workers must compose at least one-half the directors and supervisors.[122]

All officers are subject to three-year terms.[123] Directors and supervisors may be re-elected so long as the number of re-elected officials does not exceed two-thirds of the respective board.[124]

---

[117]*Id.*
[118]LUL, art. 9.
[119]*See id.*
[120]See also II.B.1.b., above.
[121]LUL, art. 16; LUL Enforcement Rules, art. 12.
[122]LUL Enforcement Rules, art. 14.
[123]LUL, art. 17.
[124]*Id.*; LUL Enforcement Rules, art. 15.

Union presidents may serve only two terms.[125] If a union has not elected a president, the standing directors are responsible for overseeing both daily affairs and important matters by rotation. However, external union correspondence must be signed with seals from all the standing directors.[126]

Changes of high-ranking union officers and revisions of union constitutions must be reported to the government.[127]

The government may nullify an election that violates any laws, ordinances, or the union constitution.[128] The union has the right to appeal a nullification within 30 days after it is served with notice of the ruling.[129]

b. Removal

The LUL permits union officers to be removed by resolution at a union general meeting if they have violated a law or ordinance or have been derelict in their duties.[130] Such removals must be reported to the government.[131]

6. Meetings

The LUL dictates when unions are to meet. Regular meetings of national unions must occur once every three years, and regular meetings of unions at the local level (the provincial government was officially abolished in 2000) must be convened annually.[132] Ad hoc meetings may be convened at the discretion of the union or the board of directors, or if more than one-tenth of the union membership requests.[133]

Meetings require attendance by more than one-half the entire membership or union representatives. Resolutions at the meetings require a majority vote for adoption, except for resolutions regard-

---

[125]LUL, art. 17.
[126]LUL Enforcement Rules, art. 18.
[127]LUL, art. 28.
[128]*Id.* art. 30.
[129]*Id.* art. 32.
[130]*Id.* art. 33.
[131]*Id.*; *see also* LUL Enforcement Rules, art. 32.
[132]LUL, art. 19.
[133]*Id.*

ing revision of the union constitution or organization of a federation of unions, which require more than two-thirds of the votes at a meeting.[134] A member's representative may send a proxy if the unions involved approve, if the proxy is limited to one representative, and if the representative unable to attend executes a written authorization.[135]

The government may nullify a union resolution if the resolution violates laws, ordinances, or the union constitution.[136] The government also has the power to require a union to revise its constitution if the constitution violates laws or ordinances.[137] If the government takes either of the above actions, the union has a right to appeal within 30 days after it is served with notice of the ruling.[138]

Union directors and supervisors are required to hold separate meetings at least once every three months.[139] Substitute officers must be permitted to attend these meetings as observers.[140] If the responsible officer fails to call a directors' or supervisors' meeting for more than two sessions without good cause, the officer is deemed by law to have resigned.[141] Also, officers are deemed by law to have resigned if they miss two consecutive officer meetings without good cause.[142]

The groups of a craft or industrial union are to meet once a month.[143] Any decisions made during these meetings must be submitted to the union board of directors for action.[144]

---

[134]*Id.* art. 21.
[135]LUL Enforcement Rules, art. 24.
[136]LUL, art. 30.
[137]*Id.* art. 31.
[138]*Id.* art. 32.
[139]LUL Enforcement Rules, art. 21.
[140]*Id.*
[141]*Id.* art. 22.
[142]*Id.* art. 23.
[143]*Id.* art. 37.
[144]*Id.*

7. *Operations*

a. *Operating Funds*

A labor union's operating funds may come from member initiation fees and membership dues, special funds and special contributions by members or employers, and government subsidies.[145] Unions also derive income from union-owned businesses.

An employee's union initiation fees may not exceed two days' wages at the time the employee is admitted to the union.[146] Regular union dues for individual employees may not exceed 2 percent of the employee's monthly income. A member of an industrial or craft union who is a member of two unions may have membership fees reduced by 50 percent by the unions concerned.[147] Also, unions must reduce or waive membership fees of any unemployed members.[148] If a union member fails to pay membership fees as prescribed by law, the union is entitled, after a warning period, to fine or suspend the member from exercising his or her union rights.[149] As a practical matter, however, unions can do little to compel payment of dues. A general federation of labor unions above the municipal level may establish penalties for affiliated unions that fail to pay their regular membership fees.[150]

A labor union also may collect funds through special contributions or special funds approved by a general meeting resolution and reported to the government. Unions on a municipal or higher level are further entitled to seek government subsidies.[151]

b. *Reporting Requirements*

Labor unions are responsible for auditing the use of their operating funds and making reports to the government regarding the funds.[152] Unions also are responsible for reporting annually to

---

[145]LUL, art. 22.
[146]*Id.*
[147]LUL Enforcement Rules, art. 27.
[148]*Id.* art. 28.
[149]*Id.* art. 29.
[150]*Id.* art. 26.
[151]LUL, art. 22.
[152]*Id.* art. 25.

members regarding union property.[153] Representatives may be elected to check the property of the union upon request, by petition of more than one-tenth of the entire union membership.[154]

Unions must report every December to the government regarding the names and background of their officers, the names of members admitted and withdrawn, union accounts, the operational condition of their enterprises (i.e., whether the enterprises continue to exist), and the status of dispute mediations.[155]

8. *Union Security*

a. *Union Right to an Office on Company Premises*

Unions do not have a statutory right to an office on company premises. However, most unions do negotiate with management to have such a facility on site.

b. *Compensation for Union Duties*

Union officers have the right to request official leaves of absence to handle union affairs.[156] The total leave for each officer may not exceed 50 hours per month.[157] Under special circumstances, the allowable amount of leave may be negotiated by the employer and the union.[158]

Although meetings of union groups of a union are to be held outside of work hours, if any group meetings must be held during office hours, members must be granted leave to attend the meetings.[159]

c. *Union Officer Training*

Union officers do not have an explicit right to time off for union training courses. However, unions can negotiate this issue

[153] *Id.* art. 24.
[154] *Id.*
[155] *Id.* art. 27.
[156] *Id.* art. 35.
[157] *Id.*
[158] *Id.*
[159] LUL Enforcement Rules, art. 37.

with management. Management often has to send union officers to government-sponsored training programs.

9. *Antidiscrimination Provisions*

According to the LUL, employers are prohibited from refusing to employ a worker because he or she is a union officer or conditioning an offer of employment on a worker's promise not to hold office in a labor union.[160] Employers also are banned from dismissing or otherwise unfairly treating employees due to their positions as union officers.[161] In addition, employers may not dismiss employees because of their involvement in a labor dispute.[162]

These antidiscrimination proscriptions do not, however, carry much power in practice.[163]

C. Bargaining Structure

Collective bargaining in Taiwan is subject to regulation under the Collective Agreement Law (CAL). Although the CAL provides the framework for collective bargaining and the Taiwan Constitution provides for freedom of assembly, collective bargaining in its true Western meaning did not exist in Taiwan prior to 1988.

1. *Bargaining Level*

Unlike the United States, where bargaining takes place at the bargaining-unit level, Taiwan law does not dictate at what level bargaining should take place. Bargaining may be conducted at the local, regional, or national level. Negotiations by unions at any particular level (e.g., plant or county) must be conducted with the management association at the same level. In Taiwan, because plant unions exist, negotiations by such unions must be conducted with

---

[160]LUL, arts. 35, 36.

[161]*Id.* art. 35.

[162]*Id.* art. 37.

[163]*See* JOSEPH S. LEE, IS THERE IS BONA FIDE TRADE UNION MOVEMENT IN TAIWAN (Chung Hua Institution for Economic Research, Taipei, Taiwan, 1994) (describing, among other things, the inability of government to obtain reinstatement for a newspaper employee who was discharged after he organized a union).

plant management, which has been the case with the exception of the 1997 and 1998 national negotiations on the minimum wage.

2. *Parties*

a. *Employers*

At the local level, employers negotiate individually. At the regional or national level, agreements must be negotiated by regional or national management associations.

b. *Unions*

Any level of union may negotiate and sign agreements.

c. *Central Union Coordination*

A central union federation may coordinate bargaining, including becoming directly involved in local negotiation.

3. *Subjects of Bargaining*

The CAL does not set forth mandatory, voluntary, or illegal bargaining subjects as U.S. law does. It includes the coverage or jurisdiction of the agreement, negotiation procedures, wages, work hours, overtime work, overtime premiums, rest periods, holidays, and vacations, and also contemplates the negotiation of the following items:

- apprentice relations,
- labor organization within the enterprise,
- utilization of employment agencies, and
- establishment or utilization of labor dispute mediation and arbitration procedures.[164]

D. Collective Bargaining Agreements

Although the CAL suggests that collective bargaining agreements should include a long list of items, few contracts actually

[164]CAL, arts. 1, 2.

do so. Most of the collective bargaining agreements in Taiwan are very simple; they are no longer than a few pages and consist of no more than the minimum conditions required by law. Wages and other financial compensation are seldom set forth in collective agreements, but are determined solely by employers. In recent years the number of collective bargaining agreements has been declining. For example, in 1989 there were 346 agreements signed by employers and their unions, but by the end of 2003 this number dropped to 267.[165] The decline can be attributed to decrease in the number of public enterprises and large-sized factories in Taiwan. Most of Taiwan's union-management contracts cover employers in public enterprises and large-sized factories in the private sector. The decrease of public enterprises in recent years is largely a result of the privatization movement and the drop in the number of large-sized factories, as Taiwan's economy has shifted from a focus on goods production to services.

The CAL gives the government the authority to approve, disapprove, or modify a negotiated contract.

1. Effect of the Agreement

Collective agreements are legally binding. However, the law stipulates that, in order for the agreement to be legally valid, persons negotiating on behalf of their organization must receive authorization for negotiation by their own employer or employee organization. Authorization can be obtained by the constitution of the organization, a decision by the members of a general assembly, or by a special authorization in written form by each member of the organization.[166]

2. Duration of the Agreement

a. Term

A collective agreement can have a fixed or indefinite term.[167] A fixed-term contract may not be longer than three years.[168] If the

[165]Data from Council of Labor Affairs, Department of Labor Management Relations, 2004.

[166]CAL, art. 3.

[167]*Id.* art. 23.

[168]*Id.* art. 25.

stated term is longer than three years, it automatically terminates as a matter of law at the end of the third year.[169] An agreement with no specified duration may be terminated by either party at any time after one year from signing, provided that written notice is given to the other party three months in advance. A contract may specify a written notice period longer than three months.[170]

b. Expiration

Upon expiration of a collective agreement, the provisions of the original agreement continue to constitute the labor contract between the parties until superseded by a new agreement.[171]

3. Scope of the Agreement

Collective agreements are not binding on nonsignatory parties. This was demonstrated recently in a national negotiation between the CFL and two management associations regarding the minimum wage. Traditionally, the Basic Wage Commission meets each year and recommends a minimum wage adjustment to the Executive Yuan. However, in 1997, the CLA decided to ask union and management representatives to negotiate an agreement instead of having the government decide the matter unilaterally. The CFL and the management associations reached an agreement whereby there would be no adjustment of the minimum wage for that year, but each employer would adjust its average wage rate by 3 percent. When this agreement came up for a ratification vote, both union and management association members rejected the agreement. The government had to make its decision without union and management's participation. It decided not to adjust the minimum wage rate that year.

E. Labor Disputes

1. Rights Versus Interests Disputes

The Settlement of Labor Disputes Law (SLDL) distinguishes between rights and interests disputes. Rights disputes are defined

---

[169] *Id.*

[170] *Id.* art. 24.

[171] *Id.* art. 17.

as disputes between workers and employers relating to obligations arising from laws or regulations, collective agreements, or labor contracts.[172] Rights disputes are subject to nonbinding conciliation, pursuant to procedures set forth in Chapter II of the SLDL, and, if necessary, in court.[173] Interest disputes, called "adjustment disputes" under Taiwan law, are defined as disputes between workers and employers that arise when they are unable to agree on whether to continue or change existing working condition or on what the changed working conditions should be (for example, disputes on wage adjustments).[174] Adjustment disputes are subject either to nonbinding conciliation pursuant to the procedures set forth in Chapter II of the SLDL, or to arbitration pursuant to procedures set forth in Chapter III of the SLDL.[175]

a. Conciliation

The parties may request mediation, or the government may initiate mediation if it deems it necessary. A five to seven member mediation board is appointed, one to three of who are government officials, while the others represent union and management, respectively.

After the mediation board is appointed, it has two days to conduct an investigation and come to a conclusion. If both sides agree with the board's decision, the case is settled. Otherwise, the mediation effort fails. If both sides agree to the settlement, the mediation decision becomes an official contract.

b. Arbitration

i. Initiation

When impasse is reached after a conciliation effort, both parties may request arbitration by an arbitration committee on the impasse issue. The government also may order arbitration if it deems the situation warrants such action. However, it must notify the parties of this decision.[176]

[172]Settlement of Labor Disputes Law (SLDL), art. 4.
[173]*Id.* art. 5.
[174]*Id.* art. 4.
[175]*Id.* art. 6.
[176]*Id.* art. 24.

ii. Procedures

The government must appoint an arbitration committee within five days after receiving an application for arbitration by the labor or management party.[177]

The arbitration committee consists of 9 to 13 members. Three to five members are appointed by the government. Three to four members are picked by the union and the management organization from a list of qualified arbitrators provided by the government.[178] This list is compiled from a pool of 12 to 48 impartial and experienced persons recommended by union and management organizations.[179] The chair of the committee is appointed by the government from among the government representatives.

If any of the following situations exist, the person is deemed inappropriate to serve as a member of the arbitration committee:

- the person served as a member of the labor dispute conciliation committee;
- the person, spouse, ex-spouse, or fiancée is a party in the labor dispute;
- the person is closely related to a party in the labor dispute or formerly had such a relationship;
- the person, spouse, ex-spouse, or fiancée has a common creditor or debtor relationship with a party in the labor dispute;
- the person is or was the legal representative, ascendant, or descendant of a party in the dispute; or
- the person is or was the representative of a party in the labor dispute.

A quorum requires over two-thirds attendance of the arbitration committee members. If, in two consecutive meetings, there is still no quorum, the government may appoint substitute arbitrators.[180] A decision is made with the vote of more than three-fourths

---

[177] *Id.* art. 28.
[178] *Id.* art. 29.
[179] *Id.* art. 30.
[180] *Id.* art. 32.

of the attending members. If the committee is unable to reach a decision in the first two meetings, a decision at the third meeting is obtained by a majority vote.[181]

iii. Award

The award rendered by the arbitration committee is final and binding on both parties. The award is considered a contract between the parties to the labor dispute. When one party is a labor union, the award may serve as a collective bargaining agreement.[182]

Should a compromise be reached during arbitration, a written report must be submitted to the government.[183]

iv. Judicial review

Judicial review and enforcement of collective bargaining rights and arbitration awards is available.[184]

F. Strikes and Other Industrial Actions

1. Strikes

The LUL does not permit strikes unless conciliation procedures have failed and the strike is approved by a majority of the entire union membership by secret ballot at a union assembly meeting.[185]

Unions are explicitly prohibited from blockading the factory, taking or damaging goods or other property of the factory without permission, detaining or injuring workers or the employer, carrying weapons at a gathering or in a procession, or engaging in extortion of a worker.[186] Employees who violate any of these can be taken to court, and in serious cases the union can be dissolved by the government.[187]

---

[181]*Id.*
[182]*Id.* art. 35.
[183]*Id.* art. 34.
[184]LUL, art. 20; SLDL art. 37.
[185]LUL, art. 26.
[186]*Id.* art. 29.
[187]*Id.* art. 40.

Pursuant to Article 10 of the Employment Service Act as amended in 2002, public employment agencies are not permitted to refer workers to a struck company during the period of a labor dispute.

2. *Lockouts*

Taiwan law does not regulate employer lockouts. There are no reported cases of employer lockouts.

3. *Picketing*

Peaceful picketing is permitted, with resort to the courts in breaches of the peace.

4. *Slowdowns*

Unions are not permitted by law to engage in slowdowns.[188] However, workers often utilize slowdowns in labor disputes, particularly because of the prohibitions on strikes. In practice, the government has not punished workers for engaging in slowdowns.

5. *Secondary Action*

Taiwan law does not explicitly regulate secondary action, which occurs often.

III. Representation by Entities Other Than Unions

A. Introduction

In addition to trade unions, Taiwan has three other types of employee representatives. First, the LSL mandates that businesses must convene labor-management conferences to coordinate and promote cooperation between management and employees, as well as to increase work efficiency. This requirement is regulated by the Convocation Rules of the Labor-Management Conference (LMC Rules), a set of regulations jointly promulgated by the Min-

---

[188] *Id*. art. 29.

istry of the Interior and the Ministry of Economic Affairs on May 13, 1985.

Second, the Organizational Rules of the Supervisory Committee of Workers' Retirement Fund of the Business Entity (Supervisory Committee Rules), which were enacted by the Ministry of Interior on July 1, 1985, have been established to implement the workers' retirement fund as set forth by the LSL. LSL article 56 requires employers to establish a supervisory committee to monitor the operation of the workers' retirement fund. The committee consists of 3 to 15 members among whom no less than two-thirds are representatives of employees.[189]

Third, the Employee Welfare Fund Law of 1943 (EWFL) requires every public and private factory and mine and many other businesses to set aside an employee welfare fund for promoting employees' welfare and to establish an employee welfare fund committee for each workplace to promote employee welfare. Except for large government enterprises, however, few entities have ever set up committees to comply with the EWFL. For example, in 1997 only 12 percent of covered businesses actually had established employee welfare fund committees.[190]

B. Labor-Management Conferences

1. Mandatory Nature

Article 83 of the LSL mandates that businesses must convene labor-management conferences to coordinate and promote cooperation between management and employees, as well as to increase work efficiency. In principle, these conferences are to convene once a month, with further ad hoc meetings if necessary.[191] If a branch organization of a business exceeds 30 employees, a separate conference may be convened for the branch.[192]

---

[189]Organizational Rules of the Supervisory Committee of the Workers' Retirement Fund of the Business Entity, art. 3.

[190]*See* J.S. LEE, A STUDY OF EMPLOYEES WELFARE FUND LAW IN TAIWAN (Chengchi Univ. Press 1975); J.S. LEE & P.L. HSING, A STUDY OF LSL, EMPLOYEES WELFARE LAW AND UNEMPLOYMENT INSURANCE LAW IN TAIWAN (Chung Hua Institution for Economic Research, Taipei, Taiwan, 1997).

[191]Convocation Rules of the Labor-Management Conference (LMC Rules), art. 18.

[192]*Id.* art. 2.

2. *Composition*

The labor-management conference is to have equal numbers of employer and employee representatives. The conference may range from three to nine representatives from each side, with a minimum of five representatives from each side if the business has more than 100 employees.[193] The conference may have a single chairperson or one co-chair from the employer representatives and one co-chair from the employee representatives.[194]

The composition of the employee representative group is subject to further restrictions. If more than one-half of the employees are women, no less than one-third of the employee representatives must be women.[195] In addition, each of the following groups may not exceed one-third of the employee representatives: members of the union board of directors, members of the union board of supervisors, and employee supervisors who have joined the labor union.

Labor-management conference representatives are subject to three-year terms, with the right to re-election.

3. *Selection of Representatives*

a. *Management Representatives*

The LMC Rules require the employer to select management representatives who are knowledgeable regarding the business and labor affairs of the business.[196] If a representative seat becomes vacant, the employer may appoint a replacement.[197] Representatives must be registered with the government upon their appointment.[198]

b. *Employee Representatives*

If a business operates with a labor union, the union members are responsible for electing the employee representatives to the labor-management conference.[199] If no labor union exists, the em-

---

[193] *Id.* art. 3.
[194] *Id.* art. 16.
[195] *Id.* art. 6.
[196] *Id.* art. 4.
[197] *Id.* art. 10.
[198] *Id.* art. 11.
[199] *Id.* arts. 5, 9.

ployee representatives are selected by the employees through a direct election conducted by persons appointed by the employees.[200] The LMC Rules permit representatives to be selected on a departmental basis if workers are scattered geographically.[201] Employees also select substitute representatives equal to one-half the number of regular employee representatives; the substitutes fill representative seats that become vacant before the end of a term.[202] Workers and the government must be notified five days in advance of an employee representative election.[203] Workers who are age 16 or older have the right to vote for employee representatives.[204]

Workers are eligible to serve as employee representatives if they are at least 20 years of age, a Taiwan national, and have worked for the employer for more than one year.[205] The one-year service requirement does not apply to businesses that have been established for less than one year.[206] Once representatives are seated on the labor-management conference, they must be registered with the government.[207]

All employees are represented by the employee labor-management conference representatives regardless of whether they are union or non-union members.

4. *Operation of the Labor-Management Conference*

Convocation notices of labor-management conferences must be sent by the presiding representative at least seven days before the conference.[208] Conference proposals must reach each representative at least three days before the conference meeting date.[209]

A quorum of the labor-management conference consists of more than one-half of the representatives from each side.[210] A two-

---

[200]*Id.*
[201]LMC Rules, art. 5.
[202]*Id.* arts. 6, 10.
[203]*Id.* art. 9.
[204]*Id.* art. 7.
[205]*Id.* art. 8.
[206]*Id.*
[207]*Id.* art. 11.
[208]*Id.* art. 20.
[209]*Id.*
[210]*Id.* art. 19.

thirds majority of the representatives present is required for the conference to make any decision.[211] Any decisions adopted by the conference must be forwarded by the employer to the labor union or to the business department involved in implementation, and must be reported in writing to the government.[212] If a decision previously taken by the conference cannot be implemented, the decision may be referred back to the next conference for further reconsideration.[213]

The LMC Rules require representatives to do their best to exercise a spirit of harmony and cooperation. At the same time, the LMC Rules make clear that, with respect to opinions expressed at conferences, management representatives are responsible to the employer and employee representatives elected by a labor union are responsible to the union.[214]

The LMC Rules require that the following reports must be presented to the conference:

- reports on the execution of decisions made in the last conference,
- reports on the current labor situation,
- reports on production plans and the condition of the establishment, and
- miscellaneous reports.[215]

Labor-management conferences are charged with discussing the following:

- matters relating to the harmonization of labor relations and labor-management cooperation,
- matters relating to working conditions,
- labor welfare planning, and
- increasing labor productivity.[216]

---

[211] *Id.*
[212] *Id.* art. 22.
[213] *Id.*
[214] *Id.* art. 12.
[215] *Id.* art. 13.
[216] *Id.*

Labor-management conferences also are responsible for generally discussing any suggestions made by either side.[217] The conference may set up committees to deal with particular agenda items or important problems.[218]

The minutes of the labor-management conference are required to record the following matters:

- the number of participants at the meeting,
- the time of the meeting,
- the place of the meeting,
- the names of the participating representatives,
- the names of any observers,
- the names of any representatives absent or on leave,
- the name of the chairperson,
- the name of the person taking minutes,
- the reports to the conference,
- proposals discussed and decisions taken, and
- recommendations.[219]

5. *Employer Obligations*

The employer is in charge of appointing someone to take care of labor-management conference affairs. The employer also is responsible for defraying the expenses incurred by the labor-management conference.[220]

6. *Open Issues*

The law is silent on the issues of information rights, consultation rights, co-determination rights, and the relationship between decisions made by the labor-management conference and issues determined in a collective agreement.

C. Workers' Retirement Fund Supervisory Committees

The Supervisory Committee Rules require businesses to establish committees to monitor workers' retirement funds. The su-

---

[217] *Id.*
[218] *Id.* art. 15.
[219] *Id.* art. 21.
[220] *Id.* arts. 17, 23.

pervisory committees consist of 3 to 15 members, at least two-thirds of whom must be employee representatives.[221]

D. Employee Welfare Fund Committees

The Employee Welfare Fund Law requires certain employers (including governmental entities) to establish employee welfare funds for the purpose of carrying out employee welfare activities, and requires a joint employer-employee employee welfare fund committee to handle these funds.[222] If a union is involved, at least two-thirds of the committee must be union members.[223]

IV. REDUNDANCY AND TRANSFERS OF UNDERTAKINGS

A. Business Dissolution

1. Wage Arrears

a. Worker Priority

If an employer liquidates or dissolves a business or is adjudicated to be bankrupt, the workers are entitled to top priority rights to receive any wages in arrears for the six months prior to the business termination or announcement of the bankruptcy.[224]

b. Wage Arrears Fund

The LSL provides for a Wage Arrears Fund, established through employer contributions, for the purpose of providing workers wages in arrears that their employer has refused to pay after going out of business.[225]

---

[221]Organizational Rules of the Supervisory Committee of Workers' Retirement Funds of Businesses (Supervisory Committee Rules), art. 3. For a complete discussion of retirement fund supervisory committees, see VIII.B.2.b., below.

[222]Employee Welfare Fund Law (EWFL), arts. 1, 2. For a complete discussion of employee welfare funds, see VIII.D., below.

[223]EWFL, art. 5.

[224]LSL, art. 28; LSL Enforcement Rules, art. 15.

[225]LSL, art. 28.

i. Employer contributions

Businesses must contribute .05 percent of their monthly labor insurance payment to the Wage Arrears Fund.[226] The Central Bureau of Labor Insurance (Labor Insurance Bureau) is responsible for calculating and informing a business of the size of its monthly payment.[227] (If a business does not receive the monthly notice from the Labor Insurance Bureau, the business must remit a temporary payment of the same amount paid the previous month.[228])

Employers are permitted to characterize payments to the Wage Arrears Fund as expenses for that year.[229]

ii. Employee payments

If workers do not receive payment for wages due at the time the business is liquidated, adjudicated bankrupt, or otherwise goes out of business, they may apply for payment from the Wage Arrears Fund, provided that the employer was making fund contributions.[230] Application is made to the Labor Insurance Bureau, with the following support:

- documentation verified by the government of the cancellation or withdrawal of the employer's registration, or other proof that production has stopped and the business has been liquidated;
- documentation verified by the government that the liquidation is not limited to a branch organization of the business entity;
- evidence that the worker reported to the supervisors of the liquidation that the debt was owed; and
- evidence that the employer refused to pay the wages allegedly owed.[231]

---

[226]Wage Arrears Repayment Fund Rules, art. 3. For a discussion of the labor insurance system, see VIII.C., below.

[227]Wage Arrears Repayment Fund Rules, arts. 3, 4.

[228]*Id.* art. 4.

[229]*Id.* art. 6.

[230]*Id.* arts. 7, 8.

[231]*Id.* arts. 8, 9.

When multiple workers demand payment for wages owed, they must send the demand letter to the Labor Insurance Bureau with the above documents, along with a list of the workers and wages owed and receipts from payment of wage arrears.[232] Except in special circumstances, the demand letter must be countersigned by the employer and circulated to all involved parties.[233] The Wage Arrears Repayment Fund Rules forbid employers and the Labor Insurance Bureau from charging workers for assistance in claiming wage arrears payments.[234]

As a general rule, the Wage Arrears Rules require the Labor Insurance Bureau to rule on worker demands for payment within 30 days after the demand.[235] In cases where an investigation is required, the ruling may be delayed for an additional 15 days.[236]

If the worker's demand is granted, payment is made directly to the worker.[237] If the worker has died, payment is made to the worker's family in the following order of succession: spouse and children; father and mother; grandfathers and grandmothers; grandsons and granddaughters; brothers and sisters.[238] If no survivors exist, the obligation to pay is cancelled.[239]

Grounds for rejecting a worker's demand include intentional withholding of facts, interference or lack of cooperation with an investigation, or presentation of unsubstantiated facts.[240] If the worker disagrees with the ruling of the Labor Insurance Bureau, he or she may present a letter of disagreement to the Supervisory Committee of the Labor Insurance Bureau within 30 days from receipt of the ruling.[241]

---

[232] *Id.* art. 10.

[233] *Id.*

[234] *Id.* art. 16.

[235] *Id.* art. 12.

[236] *Id.*

[237] *Id.* art. 15.

[238] LSL, art. 59(4); Wage Arrears Repayment Fund Rules, art. 15.

[239] Wage Arrears Repayment Fund Rules, art. 15.

[240] *Id.* art. 11.

[241] *Id.* art. 13.

2. Severance Pay

In the event of a dissolution or bankruptcy, workers are entitled to severance pay.[242] A business that ceases operations may use any surplus from its workers' retirement fund[243] to pay for workers' severance.[244] If a surplus remains after severance payments have been made, the business has the rights to the remaining surplus.[245]

3. Employee Welfare Fund Contributions

In the case of bankruptcy, company officials and the bankruptcy trustee or liquidator must ensure that the business has fully paid its employee welfare fund contributions.[246]

B. Transfers of Undertakings

A business entity that contemplates a transfer in ownership to another business entity or a change in its company structure must, except for the workers to be retained through negotiations between the old and new employers, terminate its labor contracts with the remaining workers on advance notice within the time limit prescribed in Article 16 of the LSL.[247] In addition, the business entity must provide severance payments to the workers in accordance with LSL article 17.[248]

If the business continues following a transfer, the new employer must abide by the terms of any collective agreement then in effect. The new employer also must abide by the terms of individual employment contracts for employees who are retained, and must recognize the seniority of the retained workers.[249]

---

[242]For a discussion of severance pay, see I.F.1.a.iv., above.

[243]See VIII.B.2., below.

[244]Rules for the Allocation and Management of the Workers' Retirement Fund (Retirement Fund Rules), art. 8.

[245]*Id.*

[246]*See* Enforcement Rules of the Employee Welfare Fund Law (EWFL Rules), arts. 8–10. For a discussion of employee welfare fund contributions, see VIII.D.4.a., below.

[247]For a discussion of notice periods, see I.F.1.a., above.

[248]LSL, art. 20. For a discussion of severance payments, see I.F.1.a.iv., above.

[249]LSL, art. 20. For an explanation of worker seniority, see VIII.A.1., below.

C. Notice Requirements for Mass Layoffs

In May 2003, the Labor Protection Under Mass Layoffs Law (LPUML) took effect. The LPUML states that it exists to protect employees' and managements' rights, and to maintain social peace.[250]

1. Mass Layoffs Covered by the LPUML

The LPUML covers "mass layoffs," as defined by article 2:

1. For worksites with fewer than 30 employees, layoffs affecting more than 10 employees within 60 days;
2. For worksites with 30 to 200 employees, layoffs affecting either more than 20 employees within one day or more than one-third of the total number of employees at the worksite within 60 days;
3. For worksites with more than 200 employees, layoffs affecting more than one-third of the employees within 60 days or more than 50 employees in one day;
4. For worksites with more than 500 employees, layoffs affecting more than one-third of the employees within 60 days.

2. Notice Procedures

The LPUML requires notice to be provided 60 days prior to the mass layoffs. To satisfy this requirement, the employer must submit a written report to the government and relevant organizations and persons. The employer also is required to post the announcement in a public place.

In the written report, the employer must provide the reason for the mass layoffs, the name of the affected business unit, the date when the layoffs will occur, the number of affected employees, the selection criteria for the layoffs, and the formula for calculating severance pay and outplacement availability.[251] Based on this report, trade unions or employees can negotiate with the em-

---

[250]Labor Protection Under Mass Layoffs Law, art. 1.
[251]*Id.* art. 4.

ployer the arrangements for carrying out the layoff plan and for compensating affected employees.[252]

This notice is not required if the layoff is caused by natural disaster, accident, or unexpected events.

Notice is to be provided to entities in the following order:

- the union of the affected workers,
- the employee representative of the Labor-Management Conference,[253] and
- all affected employees in the unit.[254]

Any employer who fails to submit a mass layoff plan discussed above as required by this law is subject to a fine of between NT$100,000 to NT$500,000 and an order to submit a plan by a set date. If the employer still fails to comply, the government may fine the employer continuously until the employer complies.[255]

3. Negotiations/Negotiation Committee

The employer and employees are required to engage in negotiations regarding the employer's mass layoff plan within 10 days after the notice of mass layoffs. If either side refuses to negotiate or an impasse is reached, the government is to form a labor management negotiating committee within 10 days for the purpose of negotiating the implementation of the layoff plan or to come up with an alternative plan.[256]

Pursuant to article 5, the negotiation committee must be composed of 5 to 11 persons. One member must be a government representative who serves as the committee chair. The rest of the negotiation committee members must be half from management and half from employee representatives. The negotiation committee chair must call for committee meetings at least once every other week. When an agreement is reached, it must be reduced into a written form and signed by all members.[257] Such a written agree-

---

[252]See the discussion in IV.B.3., below.

[253]See the discussion under III.B., above.

[254]Labor Protection Under Mass Layoffs Law (LPUML), art. 4.

[255]*Id.* art. 17.

[256]*Id.* art. 5.

[257]*Id.*

ment should be submitted to the government office in charge of labor affairs and forwarded to the appropriate court for approval.[258]

After a negotiation committee is formed, the government must assign employment service agency staff to help provide employment service and occupation counseling to the affected workers.[259]

If an employer refuses to negotiate with employees regarding a mass layoff plan or terminates employees without proper cause, the employer is subject to a fine of between NT$100,000 to NT$500,000.[260]

4. *Right to Re-employment*

Under the LPUML, laid-off workers have the first priority to be re-employed. Such requirements are applicable both to the company when it resumes its business and to the same employer and its major partners in the event they start a new business where the nature of the business is similar to the former one.[261]

5. *Enforcement*

The LPUML is enforced by the Council of Labor Affairs in the central government and by the local government agency on the county and city level.[262]

The government may restrict an employer's right to leave the country for employers that implement a mass layoff if the employer owes pension payments, severance pay, and/or wages. This restriction is triggered on the following levels:

- Employers of 10 to fewer than 30 employees: Payment in arrears of NT$3 million or more;
- Employers of 30 to fewer than 100 employees: Payment in arrears of NT$5 million or more;
- Employers of 100 to fewer than 200 employees: Payment in arrears of NT$10 million dollars or more; and

---

[258] *Id.*
[259] *Id.* art. 8.
[260] *Id.* art. 18.
[261] *Id.* art. 9.
[262] *Id.* art. 3.

- Employers of 200 employees or more: Payment in arrears of NT$20 million or more.[263]

6. *Nondiscrimination*

The LPUML also contains a nondiscrimination provision. For covered layoffs, employers may not discriminate against employees on the basis of race, language, class, ideology, religion, place of birth, sex, appearance, disability, age, or union activities.[264]

V. WAGES, HOURS, AND LEAVE

A. Wages

1. *Definition*

Wages are defined as the compensation a worker receives for his work, including wages, salary, premiums, allowances, and other regular payments.[265] The following are excluded from the definition of regular wages:

- dividends;
- bonuses;
- subsidies for medical expenses and educational expenses of workers and their children;
- service charges paid directly to a worker by a customer;
- marriage or celebratory presents from the employer or monetary gifts given for funeral services;
- compensation for occupational accidents;
- premiums for labor insurance and for any business insurance of the employer in which the worker is included as the insured;
- travel and entertainment (in 1999 the CLA changed its definition of wage by including food allowance as part of the wage; thus, employers may pay foreign workers less than

[263] *Id.* art. 12.

[264] *Id.* art. 13.

[265] LSL, art. 2. See Section VI.B.4., below, regarding the Gender Equality in Employment Act's equal pay requirements.

the basic wage by including food and housing in the definition of wages[266]); and
- work uniforms, tools, or funds to purchase the same.[267]

2. *The Basic Wage*

a. *Minimum Wage Standards*

In Taiwan, the minimum wage standards are set by the "basic wage."[268] The basic wage currently applies to workers covered by the LSL. Originally, the LSL covered workers in the agriculture, mining, manufacturing, construction, utility, transportation, and mass communication industries. However, the application of the LSL now has extended to the wholesale, retail, and hotel industries.

Although the Ministry of the Interior is nominally in charge of basic wage issues, the CLA of the Executive Yuan actually handles this area. The CLA promulgated the Rules for the Fixing of the Basic Wage (Basic Wage Rules) in January 1988.[269] Under these Rules, a Basic Wage Commission, consisting of 17 to 23 members who serve two-year terms, is in charge of establishing the basic wage, subject to the Executive Yuan's approval.[270] In 1997, the CLA asked the Chinese Federation of Labor and two management associations to negotiate a wage settlement, instead of allowing the Basic Wage Commission to determine a basic wage adjustment. The parties reached an agreement, but the agreement was not ratified by either union members or association members. Due to this failure, the obligation to determine the basic wage remains with the government.

b. *Minors*

For children younger than age 16, the basic wage is 70 percent of the regular basic wage.[271]

---

[266]CLA Official Letter of Apr. 13, 1998, Doc. No. 87-014421.
[267]LSL Enforcement Rules, art. 10.
[268]LSL, art. 21.
[269]*See* Rules for the Fixing of the Basic Wage (Basic Wage Rules), art. 1.
[270]*Id.* arts. 2, 5.
[271]LSL Enforcement Rules, art. 14.

c. *Apprentices*

There is no sub-minimum wage for apprentices, unlike in other industrialized countries.

d. *Pieceworkers*

The basic wage for piecework laborers is calculated in accordance with the quantity of production in an eight-hour day, or the amount of work performed.[272]

3. *Overtime Pay*

The LSL requires overtime pay based on the following schedule:

- for overtime up to two hours, 1 1/3 the employee's hourly rate;
- for overtime over two hours but under four hours, 1 1/3 the employee's hourly rate; and
- for overtime pursuant to LSL Article 32, paragraph 3 (emergency overtime necessitated by act of God, accident, or unexpected contingency), two times the employee's hourly rate.[273]

If an employer is reallocating hours so that the employee is working a 10-hour regular workday,[274] the employee cannot work more than two additional hours of overtime per day.[275]

4. *In-Kind Wages*

The LSL allows wages to be paid partially in-kind if the arrangement is reasonable, in accordance with the employment contract, and in accordance with custom or business practices.[276]

---

[272] *Id.* art. 12.
[273] LSL, art. 24.
[274] See V.B.2., below.
[275] LSL, art. 30-1.
[276] *Id.* art. 22.

5. *Wages Payable Upon Termination or Death*

Upon termination, the employer must pay workers all wages due.[277] If a worker dies, the employer must pay the wages due to the next of kin in the following order of succession: spouse and children; father and mother; grandfathers and grandmothers; grandsons and granddaughters; brothers and sisters.[278]

6. *Average Wage*

Calculation of the "average wage" is defined by LSL Article 2. Fundamentally, this calculation is made by taking the total amount of wages for the six months preceding the day on which a matter of computation occurs and dividing by the total number of days in the same period.[279] For workers who have worked for fewer than three months, the average wage is calculated by taking the total wages earned during the work period and dividing by the total number of days in that period.[280] For wages computed on a daily, hourly, or piecework basis, the average wage is calculated by taking the total wages for the particular service period and dividing by the actual number of workdays.[281] Wages and the number of days in the following periods are not included in calculating the average wage:

- the day on which the event requiring a calculation occurs;
- any period of medical treatment for an occupational injury;
- maternity leave for workers who have less than six months' tenure;[282] and
- a period where, due to a natural disaster, sudden turn of events, or other *force majeure*, the employer continues business, but there is no work for the employee.[283]

---

[277]*See* LSL Enforcement Rules, art. 9.
[278]LSL, art. 16.
[279]*Id.* art. 2.
[280]*Id.*
[281]*Id.*
[282]For a discussion of maternity leave, see V.C.4.f., below.
[283]LSL Enforcement Rules, art. 2.

7. *Payroll Practices*

a. *Tax Withholding*

The law does not require employer withholding of taxes.

b. *Employer Withholding of Wages*

The LSL prohibits employers from making advance deductions of wages for punitive or indemnification purposes.[284]

c. *Pay Schedules*

Unless otherwise agreed to beforehand, the LSL requires that wages must be paid at least twice per month or in advance on a monthly basis.[285] The CLA is in charge of enforcing the requirement to pay wages on schedule.[286]

d. *Recordkeeping*

The LSL requires employers to keep employee payroll records specifying the amount of wages payable, the items included in the computation of wages (e.g., overtime payment, full attendance awards), and the sum total of wage payments.[287] These records must be kept for at least five years.[288]

B. Hours

1. *Maximum Workdays and Workweeks*

a. *General Rule*

The regular workday is 8 hours per day.[289] Effective January 1, 2001, the law proscribes regular work in excess of 84 hours every two weeks (a change from the previous cap of 48 hours per week).[290] An employer may reallocate regular work hours within

---

[284]LSL, art. 26.
[285]*Id.* art. 23.
[286]*Id.* art. 27.
[287]*Id.* art. 23.
[288]*Id.*
[289]*Id.* art. 30.
[290]*Id.*

an eight-week period such that hours do not exceed 48 per week and 8 per day.[291]

b. Exceptions

With the consent of the government and the employees/union, employees may work overtime, with their consent and that of the union, up to four hours per day, so long as employees do not exceed 46 hours of overtime per month.[292] (The legislature is likely to change this rule so that the maximum is 46 hours for both genders.)

With the consent of the employees/union, an employer may reallocate hours from one day to another, so long as the reallocation does not result in workdays in excess of 10 hours per day or workweeks in excess of 48 hours.[293]

An employer also is allowed to exceed the 8/48 rule if necessitated by acts of God, accidents, or unexpected matters (e.g., machine breakdowns, or unplanned employee absences in the transportation industry), so long as the employer notifies the labor union within 24 hours of such overtime, or, in the absence of a labor union, if the employer notifies the government for approval and registration.[294] After the special period has passed, the LSL requires that employees must be granted suitable time off.[295]

The government also is given discretion to modify the maximum hours requirements for industries other than manufacturing and mining in special circumstances.[296]

c. Limit on Employer Exceptions

The LSL does not permit the employer to compel a worker to work outside of regular hours if the worker cannot do so due to health or other special reasons.[297]

---

[291] *Id.*
[292] *Id.* art. 32.
[293] *Id.* art. 30.
[294] *Id.* art. 32.
[295] *Id.*
[296] *Id.* art. 33.
[297] *Id.* art. 42.

2. *Night Shifts*

If an employer adopts a day and night shift system, the LSL requires workers on such shifts to be rotated on a weekly basis unless the workers consent to a different arrangement.[298]

3. *Apprentices*

Learning time spent by an apprentice is deemed to be working time.[299]

4. *Special Hours Restrictions*

a. Women

Historically, women were not allowed to work from between 10:00 p.m. to 6:00 a.m., unless dormitories or transportation were provided.[300] Currently, however, women are permitted to work during those hours to make the labor market more flexible, according to the amended version of Fair Labor Standards Law.[301]

b. Minors

Children younger than age 16 may not work more than eight hours per day and may not work on regular days off.[302] Children younger than age 16 also are prohibited from working after 8:00 p.m. and before 6:00 a.m.[303]

5. *Breaks*

a. Workday Breaks

As a general rule, the LSL requires employees to be permitted 30 minutes off after every four hours of continuous work.[304] However, an employer may reschedule such breaks to other work

---

[298] *Id.* art. 34.
[299] LSL Enforcement Rules, art. 36.
[300] LSL, art. 49.
[301] *Id.* art. 49.
[302] *Id.* art. 47.
[303] *Id.* art. 48.
[304] *Id.* art. 35.

hours if a shift system is in operation or if the work is of a continuous or urgent nature.[305]

b. Nursing Breaks

If a worker is nursing a newborn child who is younger than age one, the employer must permit her to take two additional breaks per day, beyond the above-described general breaks, for up to 30 minutes per break.[306] Nursing breaks must be deemed working time.[307]

c. Workweek Breaks

The LSL sets forth that workers shall have one regular day off per week.[308] This weekly break may be suspended in instances of *force majeure*, accident, or unexpected matters that require additional work, so long as the employer pays double wages.[309] The employer also must file a report within 24 hours with the government for approval and registration.[310] The suspended leave must be granted after the period of extenuating circumstances has passed.[311]

6. Recordkeeping

The LSL requires employers to keep sign-in books or timecards to record employees' work schedules on a day-to-day basis.[312] These records must use minutes as the unit of measurement.[313] The records are to be maintained for at least one year.[314]

---

[305] *Id.*
[306] *Id.* art. 52.
[307] Gender Equality in Employment Act art. 18.
[308] LSL art. 36.
[309] *Id.* art. 40.
[310] *Id.*
[311] *Id.*
[312] *Id.* art. 30.
[313] LSL Enforcement Rules, art. 21.
[314] LSL, art. 30.

C. Leave

1. Annual Leave

The LSL mandates annual paid leave for workers according to the following schedule:

- 7 days for employees with more than one but fewer than three-years' tenure;
- 10 days for employees with more than three but fewer than five-years' tenure;
- 14 days for employees with more than five but fewer than 10-years' tenure; and
- an additional day for each year of service over 10 years, up to a maximum of 30 days.[315]

The particular days in which annual leave is to be taken are decided by mutual agreement between the employee and the employer.[316] If an employee has not taken annual leave by the end of the calendar year or is terminated, the employer must pay wages for the unused annual leave.[317]

Annual leave may be suspended in instances of *force majeure*, accident, or unexpected matters that require additional work, so long as the employer pays double wages.[318] The employer also must file a report with the government within 24 hours for approval and registration.[319] The suspended leave must be granted after the period of extenuating circumstances has passed.[320] Annual leave also may be suspended for workers employed by public utilities if deemed necessary by the government, and if the employer pays double wages.[321]

The LSL mandates fines of between 2,000 and 20,000 yuan for violations of the annual leave provisions.[322]

---

[315]*Id.* arts. 38, 39.

[316]LSL Enforcement Rules, art. 25.

[317]*Id.* art. 24.

[318]LSL, art. 40.

[319]*Id.*

[320]*Id.*

[321]*Id.* art. 41.

[322]*Id.* art. 79.

2. *Holidays*

The following days are designated paid holidays in Taiwan (the specific dates for some holidays are not noted because they are based on the lunar calendar):[323]

- The Founding Day of the Republic of China (January 1);
- Spring Festival;
- Festival for Visiting Family Graveyards;
- Dragon Boat Festival (the fifth day of the fifth moon in the lunar calendar);
- Mid-Autumn Festival (the fifteenth day of the eighth moon in the lunar calendar);
- Lunar New Year (three days);
- Labor Day (May 1);
- Women's Day/Children's Day (generally in April);
- Revolutionary Martyrs' Day/Youth Day (March 29);
- National Independence Day (October 10);
- Taiwan Restoration Day (October 25);
- President Chiang Kai-Shek's Birthday (October 31);
- Dr. Sun Yat-sen's Birthday (November 12); and
- Constitution Day (December 25).

If an employee consents to work on one of these holidays, the LSL requires payment of double wages.[324] Holidays may be suspended in instances of *force majeure*, accident, or unexpected matters that require additional work, so long as the employer pays double wages.[325] An employer that suspends a holiday must file a report with the government within 24 hours for approval and registration.[326] The suspended holiday must be granted after the period of extenuating circumstances has passed.[327]

---

[323] *Id.* art. 37; LSL Enforcement Rules, art. 23.
[324] LSL, art. 39.
[325] *Id.* art. 40.
[326] *Id.*
[327] *Id.*

3. *Military Service*

An employer must give employees time off without pay for military service. Because of this requirement, employers often do not want to hire male employees who have not completed their two years of mandatory military service.

4. *Other Leave*

Workers are permitted to take marriage leave, bereavement leave, sick leave, occupational sick leave, personal leave, and maternity leave. Workers must personally request such leave either orally or in writing, stating the reasons and time for the leave, except in cases of emergency.[328] The employer may require relevant documentary evidence to support the worker's eligibility for the leave requested.[329]

a. *Marriage Leave*

A worker is entitled to eight days of paid leave for marriage.[330] Marriage leave may not be counted against a worker for purposes of awarding any full-attendance bonuses.[331]

b. *Bereavement Leave*

On the death of a spouse, parent, foster parent, or step-parent, a worker is entitled to eight days of paid bereavement leave.[332] On the death of a child, parent-in-law, foster-parent-in-law, or step-parent-in-law, a worker is entitled to six days of paid bereavement leave.[333] On the death of a brother or sister, a worker is entitled to three days of paid bereavement leave.[334] Bereavement leave may not be counted against a worker for purposes of awarding full-attendance bonuses.[335]

---

[328]Rules On Leave-Taking By Workers (Leave Rules), art. 10.
[329]*Id.*
[330]LSL, art. 40; Leave Rules, art. 2.
[331]Leave Rules, art. 9.
[332]LSL, art. 43; Leave Rules, art. 3(1).
[333]LSL, art. 43; Leave Rules, art. 3(2).
[334]LSL, art. 43; Leave Rules, art. 3(3).
[335]Leave Rules, art. 9.

c. Sick Leave

A worker who is unable to work due to non-occupational injury, sickness, or other physical reasons is entitled to a maximum of 30 days' sick leave per year, to be paid at one-half-pay.[336] If the worker is hospitalized, he or she is entitled to a maximum of one year of unpaid sick leave. However, the total accumulated unpaid sick leave, including hospitalized and nonhospitalized leave, may not exceed one year.[337] After this one-year period, and after other leave has been expended, the employee may be discharged.

An employee whose ability to work is impaired while she is menstruating may take one day of leave per month.[338] The unworked day is counted as a sick day and is to be compensated in the same way as other sick days.[339]

d. Occupational Sick Leave

A worker is entitled to take occupational sick leave while receiving medical treatment for, or recuperating from, an occupational accident.[340] Occupational sick leave may not be counted against a worker for purposes of awarding full-attendance bonuses.[341]

e. Personal Leave

A worker is entitled to take up to 14 days of unpaid leave per year for personal reasons.[342] As part of an employees' right to personal leave, an employee at a workplace with more than 30 employees may take up to seven days of leave per year to take care of a family member who is seriously ill.[343] This leave counts towards the employee's personal leave entitlement.[344]

---

336 LSL, art. 43; Leave Rules, art. 4.
337 LSL, art. 43; Leave Rules, art. 4.
338 Gender Equality in Employment Act, art. 14.
339 *Id.*
340 LSL, art. 43; Leave Rules, art. 6.
341 Leave Rules, art. 9.
342 LSL, art. 43; Leave Rules, art. 7.
343 *Id.* art. 20.
344 *Id.*

f. Maternity Leave

Female workers are permitted up to a total of eight weeks of maternity leave for before and after childbirth.[345] If a female worker miscarries after three or more months of pregnancy, she is entitled to four weeks of maternity leave.[346] Maternity leave is paid at full wages if the worker has been employed for more than six months; for workers employed for fewer than six months, leave is paid at half-pay.[347]

Under a current informal understanding between the CLA and employers, an employer may ask a worker who is on maternity leave to come back to work if her doctor certifies that she has fully recovered from her child delivery. However, in this case, her employer must pay the worker double her full pay plus her regular pay during the remaining period of her maternity leave. This understanding has not been formalized.

g. Child Care Leave

The right to child care leave and family leave is restricted to married employees, except under special circumstances.[348] The Gender Equality in Employment Act (GEEA) provides for new leave rights to care for young children. Pursuant to Article 16, employers with more than 30 employees are obligated to provide child care leave for up to two years or until the child reaches three years of age, whichever is less. When an employee is raising two or more children at the same time, the period of leave is computed aggregately, with a maximum of two years' leave.[349] An employee on child care leave has the right to continue his or her social and medical insurance.[350] The employer is not, however, responsible for the insurance premiums during this period.[351] The employee may defer payment of the insurance premiums for up to three years.[352]

---

[345]LSL, art. 50.
[346]*Id.*
[347]*Id.*
[348]GEEA, art. 22.
[349]*Id.*
[350]*Id.* art. 16.
[351]*Id.*
[352]*Id.*

An employee who has taken child care leave is entitled to return to work, absent special circumstances faced by the employer. An employer may refuse a request to return if it has shut down, contracted out the business, reorganized the company, dissolved or transferred ownership, shut down operations for more than one month due to uncontrollable forces, or changed the nature of the business in a manner that led to a reduction in the workforce which left the employee without a suitable position.[353] An employer who is unable to provide a job to an employee is required to provide 30-days notice and severance pay or retirement benefits.[354]

Under the new GEEA, employees in workplaces with more than 30 employees are also entitled to request reduced hours to care for a child who is younger than three years old.[355] The employee may reduce his or her hours by an hour per day or readjust his or her work hours.[356] The employer is entitled to proportionately adjust the pay consistent with the decreased work hours.[357]

VI. ANTIDISCRIMINATION

A. Introduction

Although the Taiwan Constitution proscribes discrimination against any citizen based on race, sex, religion, or age, Taiwan employment law historically has not addressed discrimination. The LSL articulates a policy promoting equal pay—LSL Article 25 mandates that equal wages shall be paid for equal work of equal efficiency—but there have been few other laws explicitly prohibiting workplace discrimination. In 1992, the new Employment Service Act (ESA) established that employers may not discriminate against job applicants on the basis of race, status, language, ideology, religion, political party, birthplace, sex, appearance, features, physical disability, or past membership in a labor union.[358]

---

[353] *Id.* art. 17.
[354] *Id.*
[355] *Id.* art. 19.
[356] *Id.*
[357] *Id.*
[358] Employment Service Act (ESA), art. 5.

To the extent that Taiwan laws otherwise distinguish between different groups of workers, they tend to specially protect women and permit forced retirement of older workers. In fact, one can see employment ads openly discriminating against older workers by specifying that applicants must be younger than a certain age.

The Gender Equality in Employment Act (GEEA) ushered in substantially more law to prohibit discrimination based upon gender, effective March 8, 2002. For employers who need to alter their policies to remove differential treatment based upon gender, GEEA prohibits employers from reducing their current level of payments or benefits.[359]

See also the discussion on protections against discrimination in carrying out layoffs, established in the LPUML, discussed in IV.C.6., above.

B. Protected Groups

1. Age

The ESA states, as a general public policy, that government agencies should make efforts to assist persons between ages 45 and 65 in finding employment.[360] However, employers are allowed to force workers who are age 60 and older to retire.[361]

2. Disability

Article 5 of the ESA provides that employers may not discriminate against employees based on physical disability. Government agencies are directed to assist disabled persons in their employment efforts, including through the establishment of special training facilities if necessary.[362] If an employer lays off a disabled worker, the ESA requires the employer to notify the local public employment institution so that the worker can receive assistance in finding new employment.[363] However, this specific regu-

---

[359]GEEA, art. 10.
[360]ESA, arts. 24, 25.
[361]See VIII.A.2., below.
[362]ESA, arts. 24, 25, 27.
[363]*Id.* art. 29.

lation for disabled workers does not have significant practical effect, in part due to the requirement that employers notify government authorities 10 days in advance of any layoff.[364]

3. *Pregnancy*

A female employee must be transferred to easier work during her pregnancy if she so requests and if such work is available, without a reduction in her wages.[365] The ESA also states that government authorities should assist women who leave their jobs due to pregnancy, childbirth, or to care for their child, to obtain suitable occupational training.[366]

Work rules, labor contracts, and collective bargaining agreements may not require employees to quit or to take unpaid leave when the employee becomes pregnant, gives birth, or starts to care for a child.[367]

4. *Gender*

a. Prohibited Discrimination

The GEEA prohibits gender discrimination, including in the following:

- recruiting, screening, assigning positions, staffing, performance evaluations, and promotion practices;[368]
- job training opportunities and fringe benefits;[369]
- pay,[370] but the requirement of comparable pay for comparable work may be relaxed in circumstances where the pay difference is based upon seniority, awards for good performance, or other reasons not related to gender;[371] and
- retirement, layoffs, separations, and discharge practices.[372]

---

[364]*Id.* art. 33. See I.F.1.a.iii., above.
[365]LSL, art. 51.
[366]ESA, art. 26.
[367]GEEA, art. 12.
[368]*Id.* art. 7.
[369]*Id.* art. 8.
[370]*Id.* art. 9.
[371]*Id.*
[372]*Id.* art. 11.

b. Prohibited Harassment

The GEEA also sets forth new law banning sexual harassment and placing responsibility upon employers to prevent sexual harassment.[373] Under the GEEA, sexual harassment includes both quid pro quo harassment, such as explicit and implicit requests for sexual favors by an employer, and hostile work environment harassment, where an employee is made uncomfortable in the work environment due to threatening or offensive sexually related conduct.[374]

Employers with more than 30 employees are required to have an antiharassment policy, including a complaint procedure and discipline policy for employees found to have committed sexual harassment.[375]

Employers who learn of sexual harassment in the workplace are obligated to take immediate action to correct the situation and compensate the affected parties.[376] Individual harassers and the employer are jointly liable for injuries from harassment. An employer has an affirmative defense to liability, however, if it can prove that it took all reasonable steps to prevent harassment and has complied with the law.[377] If a victim of harassment is unable to recover from the harasser, however, a court may order the employer to compensate for part or all of the damages, taking into consideration the financial situation of the employer.[378]

5. Marital Status

Work rules, labor contracts, and collective bargaining agreements may not require employees to quit or to take unpaid leave when the employee becomes married.[379] The Employment Service Act also was amended to include an explicit prohibition against employment discrimination based upon marital status.[380]

---

[373] *E.g., id.*
[374] *Id.* art. 12.
[375] *Id.* art. 11.
[376] *Id.*
[377] *Id.* art. 27.
[378] *Id.*
[379] *Id.* art. 12.
[380] ESA, art. 5.

VII. Occupational Safety and Health and Workers' Compensation

A. Occupational Safety and Health

1. Historical Background

The public policy supporting employer responsibility for workplace safety is rooted in the LSL, which provides that employers must take precautions for their employees against occupational hazards and set up proper work environments and welfare facilities.[381]

2. Labor Safety and Health Law

The primary law regarding occupational safety is the Labor Safety and Health Law (LSHL), which was enacted on April 16, 1974. The LSHL covers a broad range of industries, as enumerated in LSHL article 4, including manufacturing, construction, transportation, restaurants, medicine and health, agriculture, communications, utilities, and national defense.[382] The LSHL provisions are further delineated by the Enforcement Rules of the Labor Safety and Health Law (LSHL Enforcement Rules). A summary of pertinent LSHL provisions is set out below.

a. Employer Obligations

The LSHL requires covered employers to perform pre-employment physical examinations of workers and requires workers to submit to such examinations.[383] Workers in designated high-risk industries, such as lead work, high-temperature work, and work involving certain chemicals, are subject to regular periodic health examinations.[384] Employers also must furnish workers with health maintenance booklets, pursuant to guidelines set forth by the CLA.

[381]LSL, art. 8.

[382]Labor Safety and Health Law (LSHL), art. 4.

[383]*Id.* art. 12.

[384]*Id.*; Enforcement Rules of the Labor Safety and Health Law (LSHL Enforcement Rules), art. 21.

The LSHL establishes requirements for employers to regulate occupational safety conditions and mechanisms for coordination of safety between contractors and subcontractors. The LSHL also regulates the work that juveniles, women, and pregnant women may perform.[385] Employers are not permitted to engage female employees in the following work: tunnel-work, work in environments with potentially hazardous substances, work with rock drills or other machinery with extensive or excessive vibration, work with heavy objects, work in environments with harmful levels of radiation (unless the worker is incapable of bearing children), and other hazardous work designated by the CLA.[386]

The LSHL requires employers to prepare, in consultation with worker representatives, appropriate safety and health working rules. These rules must be sent to the government, posted, and enforced by the employer.[387]

b. Accident Reporting

Businesses are required to investigate, analyze, and make a record of occupational accidents.[388]

Businesses also are required to report to their LSHL inspection agency if an occupational accident causes death or injures three or more workers.[389] In these situations, the business is not permitted to alter the accident scene unless rescue or emergency conditions necessitate a disturbance, or if the LSHL inspection agency or a judicial body approves.[390]

Certain businesses with 30 or more employees are further required to file monthly reports of occupational accident statistics with the relevant LSHL inspection agency. These industries include manufacturing; construction; water, electricity, and gas supply; mining and quarrying; shipping; storage; communications; forestry; lumber; and any other industry that has received written notification from the CLA to follow this requirement.[391]

---

[385] *See* LSHL, arts. 20–22.

[386] *Id.* art. 21.

[387] *Id.* art. 25.

[388] *Id.* art. 28.

[389] *Id.*

[390] *Id.*

[391] *Id.* art. 29; LSHL Enforcement Rules, art. 45.

c. Enforcement

The CLA is responsible for administering the LSHL enforcement system. Businesses violating the law are given a period of time to improve any violations. The CLA is permitted to partially or fully shut down businesses that fail to comply with an order to improve within a set period of time, that have had occupational accidents, or that have the potential for occupational accidents.[392] Employers that are shut down for these reasons are responsible for paying workers' wages during the shut-down.[393]

Employees are allowed to report violations of occupational safety and health laws to their employer or to the CLA and the appropriate inspection agency. The LSHL prohibits employers from taking adverse employment actions against employees who have made such reports, absent good cause.[394]

d. Liability

Chapter 5 of the LSHL addresses penalties. Beyond liability for the business, the LSHL provides for punishment of persons directly responsible for violations and the supervisor in charge.[395]

B. Workers' Compensation

Employers should be aware that Taiwan's workers' compensation law is strongly protective of workers and sets forth very high payments that are due on short schedules in the event of a worker's occupational death. These remedies are not exclusive as a matter of law, although as a matter of practice they are the only remedy injured workers typically pursue.

Chapter 7 of the LSL provides for compensating workers injured in occupational accidents, including medical treatment and disability payments. The LSL also establishes joint and several liability for contractor/subcontractor situations.[396]

---

[392]LSHL, art. 27.
[393]*Id.*
[394]*Id.* art. 30.
[395]*Id.* ch. 7.
[396]LSL, arts. 62, 63.

1. Occupational Accident Benefits

A worker who is unable to work due to an occupational accident and is undergoing medical treatment is entitled to be paid his or her original daily wage rate.[397] These payments are due on the worker's regular payday.[398]

Under LSL Article 59(3), if after the termination of medical treatment the hospital definitively finds that the worker is disabled, the employer may pay a lump sum disability payment pursuant to the Labor Insurance Act (LIA).[399] If the worker has not recovered after two years of medical treatment, and the hospital definitively finds that the worker has lost his or her original ability to work but the worker does not qualify as disabled under LSL Article 59(3), the employer may obtain release from further wage liability by paying a lump sum allowance of 40 months' wages within 15 days of the date it is determined that such compensation is due.[400] The payment of regular workers' compensation payments must continue until the lump sum payment is made.[401]

2. Death Benefits

If a worker dies of an occupational injury or disease, the employer must pay a funeral subsidy equal to five months of the worker's average wage[402] within three days after the worker's death.[403] The employer also must pay a lump sum survivorship payment equal to 40 months of average wages.[404] The payment must be made in the following order of succession: spouse and children; father and mother; grandfathers and grandmothers; grandsons and granddaughters; brothers and sisters.[405] The survivorship payment must be made within 15 days after the employee's death.[406]

---

[397]*Id.* art. 59; *see also* LSL Enforcement Rules, art. 31 (pro rata calculation for wages paid on a monthly basis).

[398]LSL Enforcement Rules, art. 30.

[399]See VIII.C.2., below.

[400]LSL, art. 59(3).

[401]LSL Enforcement Rules, art. 32.

[402]For the calculation of a worker's average wage, see V.A.6., above.

[403]LSL, art. 59(4); LSL Enforcement Rules, art. 33.

[404]LSL, art. 59(4).

[405]*Id.* art. 59.

[406]LSL Enforcement Rules, art. 33.

3. *Statute of Limitations*

The right to receive workers' compensation benefits expires if not exercised within two years from the date the worker becomes eligible to receive compensation.[407]

4. *Setoffs*

a. *Labor Insurance Setoff*

An employer is permitted to set off from workers' compensation liability any payments made to an employee for the same accident under other laws, including the LIA.[408] If compensation is made from funds jointly contributed by the employer and employee, the employer is entitled to a setoff in the amount of the employer's contributions.[409]

b. *Tort Liability*

The employer is permitted to set off workers' compensation payments from any damage liability to the employee for the same accident.[410]

VIII. Pensions and Benefits

A. Retirement

1. *Voluntary Retirement*

Workers are entitled to apply for retirement if they have more than 25 years' seniority, or if they are 55 years old and have 15 years' seniority.[411] Seniority is calculated as years worked for the same employer, for a previous company owned by the same employer, or for a company that changed its corporate structure.[412]

---

[407]LSL, art. 60.
[408]LSL Enforcement Rules, art. 34. See VIII.C., below.
[409]LSL Enforcement Rules, art. 34.
[410]LSL, art. 60.
[411]*Id.* art. 53.
[412]*Id.* art. 57; *see also id.* art. 20.

2. *Forced Retirement*

Employers may force employees to retire if they are age 60 or older, or if they have been incapacitated by a physical or mental disability.[413] Employers may petition the government for the right to lower the forced retirement age to as young as age 55 for particularly risky or physically demanding jobs.[414]

3. *Age Disputes*

In disputes over a worker's age, the Ministry of the Interior has dictated that the conclusive determinant of a worker's age is his or her household registration card.[415]

B. Retirement Allowances

1. *Employee's Right to Statutory Allowance*

Article 55 of the LSL establishes retirement allowances that an employer must pay to employees who retire, as described immediately above. The retirement allowance must be paid within 30 days after the worker's retirement.[416] Retirement allowances are not required to be portable.

The retirement allowance is calculated as follows: two units (defined as the average monthly wage[417] at time of approved retirement) per year of service through the fifteenth year of service, plus an additional unit for each year after the fifteenth year, not to exceed 45 units.[418] Any fractions of a year worked are counted as one-half year for up to six months, and as a full year for six months or more.[419] An employee who retires due to a mental defect or physical disability caused by an occupational accident is entitled to an additional 20 percent of the regular retirement payment.[420]

---

[413] *Id.* art. 54.
[414] *Id.*
[415] LSL Enforcement Rules, art. 27.
[416] *Id.* art. 29.
[417] For a definition of average monthly wage, see V.A.6., above.
[418] LSL, art. 55.
[419] *Id.*
[420] *Id.*

These provisions for minimum retirement allowances do not supersede a business's retirement allowance policy that sets forth higher payments.[421]

An employee waives the right to statutory retirement allowances if the right is not exercised within five years from the month following the effective date of retirement.[422] An employer may apply to the government to make statutory allowance payments in installments if the contributions to the workers' retirement fund (described immediately below) are insufficient to pay the allowance or if the management or financial situation of the business is in difficulty.[423]

2. *Workers' Retirement Funds*

To provide for retirement allowances, employers are required to make monthly deductions and deposit these amounts into a special workers' retirement fund.[424] Employers are not required to pay into a state scheme for employee pensions.

a. *Employer Contributions*

An employer's monthly contributions to the workers' retirement fund must be between 2 percent and 15 percent of its total monthly payroll.[425] The employer is allowed to determine the exact allocation amount by considering factors set forth in the Rules for the Allocation and Management of the Workers' Retirement Fund (Retirement Fund Rules), including the seniority of workers, the wage structure, the turnover rate over the past five years, and the number of workers who will retire in the following five years.[426] Changes in the allocation rate must be reported to the government for approval and registration.[427] When the accumulated retirement fund is sufficient to pay workers' retirement al-

---

421 *Id.*

422 *Id.* art. 58.

423 *Id.* art. 55; LSL Enforcement Rules, art. 29.

424 LSL, art. 56.

425 *Id.*; Rules for the Allocation and Management of the Workers' Retirement Fund (Retirement Fund Rules), art. 2.

426 Retirement Fund Rules, art. 3.

427 *Id.* art. 4.

lowances, and the workers' retirement fund supervisory committee approves, the business may request the government to approve temporary suspension of its monthly contributions.[428] If the workers' retirement fund of a business is insufficient to pay workers' retirement allowances, the business must make up the balance.[429]

b. Supervisory Committees

On July 1, 1985, the Ministry of the Interior enacted the Organizational Rules of the Supervisory Committee of Workers' Retirement Funds of Businesses (Supervisory Committee Rules), which require businesses to establish committees to monitor their workers' retirement funds.

The supervisory committees consist of 3 to 15 members, with at least 8 members if the business employs more than 100 workers.[430] At least two-thirds of the representatives must be employee representatives.[431] Employee representatives are elected by the labor union if one exists.[432] If a union does not exist, representatives are elected directly by the workers.[433] Substitute members also may be elected.[434] The membership term for each representative is three years.[435] Worker representatives may be re-elected as long as re-elected members do not exceed one-half of the members.[436] There are no restrictions on reappointment of employer representatives.

If necessary, the business entity may provide staff members to assist the supervisory committee. Reports must be made to the government when supervisory committee members or staff members are seated or in case of changes.[437]

The supervisory committee is to appoint a chairperson chosen from the employer representatives and a vice-chairperson cho-

[428]*Id.* art. 5.

[429]*Id.* art. 7.

[430]Organizational Rules of the Supervisory Committee of Workers' Retirement Funds of Businesses (Supervisory Committee Rules), art. 3.

[431]*Id.*

[432]*Id.* art. 4.

[433]*Id.*

[434]*Id.*

[435]*Id.* art. 5.

[436]*Id.*

[437]*Id.* art. 8.

sen from the employee representatives.[438] If the chairperson is absent, the vice-chairperson assumes the chairperson role.[439]

The supervisory committee meets once every three months, with additional meetings if necessary.[440] The supervisory committee is charged with the following duties:

- examination of proposals for the temporary suspension of employer contributions to the workers' retirement fund;
- verification and auditing of employer contributions to the workers' retirement fund;[441]
- verification and auditing of deposits and disbursements to and from the workers' retirement fund;
- verification and auditing of payments from the workers' retirement fund; and
- other supervisory affairs in connection with the workers' retirement fund.[442]

The government has the authority to notify an inadequately or improperly acting supervisory committee to make improvements or to reconstitute its membership.[443]

c. Control of Funds

The workers' retirement fund must be deposited in a special account in the name of the workers' retirement fund supervisory committee.[444] Funds may not be disbursed without the signatures of the employer and the chairperson and vice-chairperson of the supervisory committee.[445] Within one month after the end of each year, each business must prepare a report of the contributions to and disbursements from the workers' retirement fund, and submit the accounting to the supervisory committee for examination and approval.[446]

---

[438]*Id.* art. 6.
[439]*Id.* art. 9.
[440]*Id.*
[441]See VIII.B.2., above.
[442]Supervisory Committee Rules, art. 2.
[443]*Id.* art. 10.
[444]LSL, art. 56; Retirement Fund Rules, art. 6.
[445]LSL, art. 56; Retirement Fund Rules, art. 6.
[446]Retirement Fund Rules, art. 12.

C. Health and Disability Benefits

Pursuant to the Comprehensive Health Insurance Law of 1996, all employers must subscribe to health insurance for their employees. Under the Labor Insurance Act (LIA), the Central Bureau of Labor Insurance oversees a system that provides benefits for both work-related and non-work-related situations.

1. Coverage

As a general rule, employers with five or more employees are required to insure their employees under the LIA.[447] Certain government employees also are eligible for LIA coverage.[448] If an employer is covered by the LIA because it employs five or more employees, and then later employs fewer than five employees, it must continue to insure the remaining workers who were previously insured.[449]

Certain other government employees, self-employed workers, fishermen, union members, vocational training institute students, and workers who were laid off after more than 15 years of coverage under the LIA also qualify to be insured under the LIA.[450] Individuals older than age 60 are not covered by the LIA unless they are still working.[451]

2. Benefits

Seven types of non-work-related situations are covered under the LIA. These are as follows:

- maternity benefits,
- injury and sickness benefits,
- medical care benefits,
- disability benefits,
- unemployment benefits,

---

[447] Labor Insurance Act (LIA), art. 6.
[448] *Id.* art. 6(4).
[449] *Id.* art. 7.
[450] *Id.* arts. 6, 9(1).
[451] *Id.* arts. 6, 9.

- old-age benefits, and
- death benefits.[452]

Four types of work-related situations are covered, as follows:

- injury and sickness benefits,
- medical care benefits,
- disability benefits, and
- death benefits.[453]

3. *Premiums*

Although the allocation of premium payment responsibility varies, in most cases, the employer/government is responsible for paying 80 percent of the insurance premium, and the employee is responsible for paying 20 percent.[454]

4. *Taxes*

All LIA accounts and payments are tax-exempt.[455]

D. Employee Welfare Funds

The Employee Welfare Fund Law (EWFL) requires certain employers (including government entities) to establish employee welfare funds for the purpose of carrying out employee welfare activities. Regulation of employee welfare funds is supplemented by the Enforcement Rules of the Employee Welfare Fund Law (EWFL Enforcement Rules). Both the EWFL and the EWFL Enforcement Rules originally were promulgated in 1943.

1. *Covered Employers*

The EWFL covers all factories and mines.[456] The EWFL also covers any bank, company, firm, farm, fishery, or pasture that normally employs 50 or more employees.[457]

---

[452]*Id.* art. 2.
[453]*Id.*
[454]*Id.* art. 15.
[455]*Id.* art. 3.
[456]Employee Welfare Fund Law (EWFL), art. 1.
[457]*Id.* art. 1; EWFL Enforcement Rules, art. 1.

2. *Responsible Authorities*

The Ministry of the Interior is the central authority responsible for enforcing the EWFL, with the Department of Social Affairs, Department of Civil Affairs, and Bureau of Social Affairs also charged with responsibility by the EWFL Enforcement Rules.[458]

3. *Employee Welfare Fund Committees*

Employers and employees are jointly charged with the responsibility of forming an employee welfare fund committee that handles the employee welfare fund.[459] If a union is involved, at least two-thirds of the committee must be union members.[460] An accounting of the employee welfare fund must be submitted to the government at the end of every year.[461]

4. *Funding*

a. *Mandatory Employer Contributions*

Under the EWFL, covered businesses must set aside funds for the employee welfare fund in accord with the following schedule:

- 1 to 5 percent of the total amount of capital at the time of entity's establishment;
- from .05 to .15 percent of the entity's monthly income (in the case of government agencies that do not have business income, these allocations may be made proportionately from fees or other income of the agency);
- .5 percent of the monthly wages or salary of each employee; and
- 20 to 40 percent of the proceeds from sales of scrap or waste (e.g., used packing materials, obsolete equipment, defec-

---

[458]EWFL Enforcement Rules, art. 14.
[459]EWFL, art. 5.
[460]*Id.*
[461]*Id.* art. 6.

tive products, remaining industrial supplies) at the time of sale.[462]

The government does not enforce the first and fourth requirements (capital investment contribution and scrap/waste contribution) because they are obsolete and are no longer considered realistic. Although in 1943 factories were small and capital investment was correspondingly small, today the amounts set forth by the EWFL, including the requirements tied to capital investment, would be astronomical amounts for a semiconductor company. Similarly, in 1943, industrial scrap and waste was inexpensive. By the 1990s, however, leftover equipment and industrial materials had become very expensive. Accordingly, the government does not enforce the requirement to contribute proceeds from the sales of scrap and waste.

Contributions must be remitted to the employee welfare fund committee immediately when due.[463] To account for these allocations, the following documentation must be sent to the employee welfare fund:

- monthly salary and allowance reports;
- monthly wage reports;
- monthly reports on business income, fee collection, or other income;
- business reports to the board of directors; and
- financial reports to the supervisors.[464]

b. Mandatory Labor Union Contributions

For workers without fixed employers, the welfare fund contributions are provided by the labor union that covers the workers.[465] The union must allocate 30 percent of its total membership fees to the welfare fund.[466] Unions may apply for government subsidies to cover this requirement.[467]

---

[462] *Id.* art. 2.
[463] EWFL Enforcement Rules, art. 2.
[464] *Id.* art. 3.
[465] EWFL, art. 3.
[466] *Id.*
[467] *Id.*

c. Use of Employee Welfare Funds

All employee welfare funds must be used for the welfare of the employees involved, except that 10 percent of a fund may be given to a municipal, provincial, or national labor union for the purpose of carrying out welfare activities.[468] Funds may not be used for year-end bonuses, severance payments, or allowances for employees engaged in carrying out welfare activities.[469] If a business covered by the EWFL is conducted at different sites under the unified operation of a head office, the fund must be used to promote welfare activities for employees at all sites.[470]

Employee welfare funds must be deposited in a public bank unless the government has given approval for special circumstances.[471]

E. Child Care Facilities

Under the new Gender Equality in Employment Act, workplaces with more than 250 employees are required to establish child care facilities or other similar types of child care services to its employees.[472] Government subsidies are available to assist companies that establish such services.[473]

F. Benefits for Unemployed Workers

Unemployment benefits were covered by the Labor Insurance Law until the Employment Insurance Law (EIL) took effect in 2003. The EIL's stated purpose is to improve the skill level of workers, promote employment, and insure employees' basic living conditions during vocational training or unemployment.[474] The Council of Labor Affairs is the central government agency responsible for administering the EIL. As a general matter, the county

---

[468] *Id.* art. 7.

[469] EWFL Enforcement Rules, arts. 6, 11.

[470] *Id.* art. 5.

[471] *Id.* art. 7.

[472] GEEA, art. 23.

[473] *See id.*

[474] Employment Insurance Law (EIL), art. 1.

governments are responsible for local administration of the law. The city governments in Taipei and Kaohsiung are responsible for administering the law locally.[475]

There are four types of payment under this law: unemployment compensation, early return to work incentive payments, living allowances for vocational training, and health insurance premiums for unemployed workers.[476]

1. General Coverage of the Employment Insurance Law

As a general matter, Republic of China (Taiwanese) citizens between the ages of 15 and 60 are covered by the Employment Insurance Law.[477] The following types of workers are excluded from the EIL's coverage:

- military personnel who are covered by the Military Personnel Insurance Law and civil servants who are covered by the Civil Service Insurance Law;
- retired employees who are receiving pension payments; and
- employees of employers who are exempt from paying taxes to the government.[478]

2. Eligibility

Unemployment insurance is available only in cases of involuntary termination. Involuntary unemployment is defined as loss of employment because the worker's employer has closed, dissolved, declared bankruptcy, or reallocated.[479]

A worker who is covered by the EIL is eligible for unemployment insurance if: (1) the worker has contributed one full year of unemployment insurance premiums during the past three years; (2) the worker is being laid off voluntarily and has the ability and the willingness to work in the labor market; and (3) the worker has registered in a public or a private employment service agency but is unable to locate a job within the last 14 days.[480]

---

[475] *Id.* art. 2.
[476] *Id.* art. 10.
[477] *Id.* art. 5.
[478] *Id.*
[479] *Id.* art. 11.
[480] *Id.* art. 11.

If the worker refuses to accept a job referred to that worker by a public employment agency, the worker is still eligible for unemployment compensation payment if the referred job pays less than 60 percent of the worker's previous salary, or the job referred to the worker is more than 30 kilometers from his or her current residence.[481] An unemployed worker who refuses to participate in vocational training assigned by a public employment agency is still eligible for unemployment compensation if the worker is ill and has a doctor's approval, or if the training institute is too far away from the worker's current residence.[482]

3. *Amount and Duration of Unemployment Benefits*

Unemployment benefits are paid at 60 percent of the unemployed worker's average salary over the previous six months.[483]

The maximum period for unemployment benefit payments is six months.[484] If an unemployed worker returns to work before using six months of unemployment benefits and becomes involuntarily unemployed again before contributing sufficient unemployment premiums, the worker is still eligible to be paid the balance of his or her six-months' entitlement to benefits.[485]

4. *Incentive Payments for Early Return to Work*

If an unemployed worker returns to work before exhausting the six-month maximum entitlement to unemployment benefits, the worker may apply to receive 50 percent of the remaining unclaimed unemployment benefits.[486] The purpose of these benefits is to encourage an unemployed worker to return to work as soon as possible.

5. *Vocation Training Living Allowances*

An involuntarily unemployed worker who has registered at a public employment agency for work and has been assigned by

---

[481] *Id.* art. 13.
[482] *Id.*
[483] *Id.* art. 16.
[484] *Id.*
[485] *Id.*
[486] *Id.*

the agency to full-time vocational training is eligible for training and living allowances. The amount of the living allowance is 60 percent of the worker's average salary over the prior six months. The maximum duration of the vocational training allowance is six months.[487]

IX. Immigration

Chapter Five of the Employment Service Act (ESA), which was promulgated in 1992, regulates the employment of foreign nationals. The central government has the right to limit the number of foreign workers, including the number from any particular country.[488]

Foreign embassies in Taiwan must apply to the Ministry of Foreign Affairs when hiring foreign workers.[489]

A. Qualification

The ESA dictates that the employment of foreign persons cannot interfere with the job opportunities and labor conditions of nationals; thus, an employer may not hire foreign workers if capable Taiwan workers are available.[490] Furthermore, dependents of foreign workers are not entitled to all the same labor insurance benefits as local workers.[491]

B. Employment Limitations

Foreign nationals generally are limited to employment in the following fields:

- special or technical services;
- chief executive positions for enterprises established or financed by overseas Chinese or a foreign person approved by the government;

---

[487]*Id.* art. 19.
[488]ESA, art. 48.
[489]*Id.* art. 49.
[490]Employment Services Act (ESA), art. 41.
[491]*See id.* art. 43. For a discussion of labor insurance benefits, see VIII.C., above.

- teachers at public or registered private colleges or universities or primary schools for foreign residents;
- foreign language teachers at public and private high schools;[492]
- full-time teachers of foreign languages in registered, short-term supplementary schools;
- athletes or athletic coaches;
- work related to religion, the arts, or entertainment;
- family servants, if the employer is unsuccessful in advertisements for local workers;
- work designated by the government as necessary to important economic, social, or other national development strategies, if the employer is unsuccessful in advertisements for local workers;
- other work specifically approved by the government where local talent is lacking, thus necessitating recruitment of foreign nationals, if the employer is unsuccessful in advertisements for local workers;[493] and
- crew members for commercial ships, working ships, ocean fishing vessels, and other government approved ships.[494]

Embassies, consulates, and other institutions of foreign countries in Taiwan are permitted to employ foreign nationals subject to the approval of the Foreign Ministry and CLA.[495]

Foreign students and overseas Chinese post-secondary and high school students who are in Taiwan are permitted to work during summer and winter breaks.[496] During the regular school year, these students' hours are restricted to 16 hours per week.[497]

C. Duration of Employment

Skilled foreign workers generally may work for a maximum term of three years, with extensions permitted, and unskilled for-

---

[492] ESA, art. 46.8.
[493] *Id.* art. 43.
[494] *Id.* art. 46.9.
[495] *Id.* art. 46.
[496] *Id.* art. 50.
[497] *Id.*

eign workers generally may work for a maximum term of two years, with the possibility of an additional one-year extension, along with another six-month extension under special circumstances for major construction projects.[498]

Foreign workers who need to change employers or jobs within the permitted duration of employment generally may apply jointly with the prospective new employer for permission to change.[499] Family servants and foreign workers who are specially approved may not change employers or jobs.[500]

Foreign workers who enter Taiwan as household maids, offshore fishing boat crews, or workers on major construction projects must leave Taiwan for at least 40 days when their contracts expire, before they are permitted to re-enter and work in Taiwan.[501] In addition, such workers may not work in Taiwan for a total of more than six years.[502]

If a foreign worker changes employers, the duration of time the worker is permitted to stay in Taiwan does not change, i.e., the worker is limited to the same period as if he or she had worked for one employer.[503]

D. Work Permits

As a general matter, foreign nationals must apply to the CLA for a work permit before they can work in Taiwan.[504]

A work permit will be partially or totally revoked if the foreign national engages in the following:

- working for an employer not listed on the permit;
- working in a work area not listed in the permit;
- severing the work relationship or leaving work without explanation for three or more days;

[498] *Id.* art. 49.
[499] *Id.* art. 50.
[500] *Id.*
[501] *Id.* art. 52.
[502] *Id.*
[503] ESA, art. 53.
[504] *Id.* art. 42.

- refusing to submit to regular physical examinations;
- failing to meet physical or mental requirements for the work assigned;
- suffering from certain infectious diseases;
- violating restrictions prescribed in conjunction with the permission to work; or
- violating any Taiwan laws or regulations with resulting serious consequences.[505]

If a foreign worker's permit is revoked, the worker must leave Taiwan immediately.[506]

Work permits are not required for the following types of foreign workers:

- spouses of Taiwan citizens who reside in Taiwan;
- refugees with a permit to stay in Taiwan;
- foreign workers who have been working in Taiwan with a work permit for more than 5 years and with good conduct (this provision excludes blue collar workers, who are only allowed to work in Taiwan for a maximum of six years—three years with one extension of three additional years);
- direct relatives of Taiwanese citizens who are living with their relatives; and
- persons with permanent resident permits.[507]

Foreign workers who have completed their employment contracts with good conduct may apply to re-enter Taiwan and work there.[508] Foreign workers who failed their health test the first time but have fully recovered from their illness may also re-apply to enter and work in Taiwan.[509]

Employers are not permitted to employ foreign workers whose authorization is for a different employer.[510] If a foreign worker wishes to change his or her employer during the term of the em-

---

[505] *Id.* art. 54.
[506] *Id.*
[507] *Id.* art. 51.
[508] *Id.* art. 52.
[509] *Id.*
[510] *Id.* art. 57.1.

ployment contract or wants to work for more than one employer to obtain a full-time job, the foreign worker must apply in advance to the government for permission.[511] The new employer must obtain an official document to certify that the employee has terminated his or her old job.[512]

E. Employer Obligations

The prospective employer generally is responsible for preparing the paperwork for foreign worker applicants.[513]

An employer must give written notice to local government authorities and the local police if any of the following events occurs:

- a foreign worker is continuously absent from work without leave for three days and has not contacted the employer;[514]
- a foreign worker has severed employment with the employer; or
- a foreign worker's permitted duration of employment has expired.[515]

Employers are responsible for paying travel and detention expenses for their foreign workers who have been deported by a police agency.[516] The employer also is responsible for paying the funeral expenses of a foreign worker who dies while employed in Taiwan.[517]

Article 5 of the Employment Service Act (ESA) was amended in 2002 to prohibit employers from providing false information or health screening results relating to the recruiting or employment of foreign workers.

---

[511]*Id.* arts. 53, 57.4 (foreign workers may not change workplaces without government approval).

[512]*Id.* art. 53.

[513]*See id.* arts. 44, 45.

[514]*Id.* art. 56.

[515]*Id.* art. 52.

[516]*Id.* art. 52, 60.

[517]*Id.* art. 55.

The health agency of the central government is now responsible for screening foreign worker health.[518] If a foreign worker fails a health test, it is the employer's obligation to effectuate immediate deportation.[519] Employers also are responsible for arranging periodic health check-ups for foreign workers.[520]

If a foreign worker is deported, the employer that brought the worker into Taiwan is responsible for the transportation fees and living allowances of such foreign worker during the deportation proceedings.[521] Such fees may be advanced by the Employment Stabilization Fund Account; in this case, the employer must reimburse the account for such payments.[522]

The 2002 amendments to the ESA further delineate penalties for employers who fail to pay employment stabilization fees to the government for foreign workers. An employer has a grace period of 30 days.[523] After the expiration of the grace period, a 1 percent per day penalty is added, up to twice the unpaid stabilization fees.[524] If an employer persists in failing to pay the fees, the central government may seek relief in court for payment of the fees and the right to terminate the employment of the foreign worker.[525]

If a foreign worker is absent from work for three or more days without notice, the employer may stop paying government stabilization fees.[526]

Employers may not lay off Taiwanese workers in order to employ foreign workers at a lower cost.[527]

Employers may not withhold foreign workers' passports, residency permits, or other things of value.[528] Employers also may not force foreign workers to engage in illicit activity.[529]

---

[518] *Id.* art. 48.
[519] *Id.*
[520] *Id.* art. 57.5.
[521] *Id.* arts. 52, 60.
[522] *Id.*
[523] *Id.* art. 55.
[524] *Id.*
[525] *Id.* art. 55.
[526] *Id.*
[527] *Id.* art. 57.6.
[528] *Id.* art. 57.8; *see also* art. 5.3.
[529] *Id.* art. 5.4.

The ESA sets forth explicit fines for employers who provide false employment advertisements or false information to the government in connection with the hiring of a foreign worker.[530]

[530] *Id.* art. 66.

RUSSIA*

INTRODUCTION

A. Basic Makeup of the Government

The Russian Federation covers one-eighth of the earth's surface, stretches from Eastern Europe to northern Asia, and ranks as the world's largest nation in terms of its geographic size.

Russia Day is celebrated on June 12, the date in 1990 when the "Declaration of State Sovereignty of the Russian Soviet Federative Socialist Republic" was adopted. The attainment of sovereignty by the other Soviet republics in 1990 and 1991 caused the formal dissolution of the Union of Soviet Socialist Republics (USSR). On December 25 of the same year, Mikhail Gorbachev resigned as president of the USSR, and the countries throughout the world, including the United States, recognized Russia and the remaining republics of the former USSR as independent nations. In a letter dated December 24, 1991, Boris Yeltsin, then-President of the Russian Federation, informed the United Nations (UN) that the membership of the Soviet Union in the Security Council and all other United Nations organs was being continued by the Russian Federation with the support of the 12 member countries of the Commonwealth of Independent States.[1]

The current Constitution of the Russian Federation (hereinafter "the Constitution") was approved on December 12, 1993; it replaced the amended constitution that the country had inherited

---

*Evgeny A. Danilov, Pepeliaev, Goltsblat & Partners, Moscow, Russia, with the assistance of Scott T. Adams, Restructuring Associates Inc., Washington, D.C.

[1]The Commonwealth of Independent States, or CIS, is a community of sovereign nations established by treaty. Although there is some legal controversy on the matter, all of the former Soviet republics are generally now considered members, except for the three Baltic states (Estonia, Lithuania, and Latvia).

from the Soviet era. The Constitution declares that Russia[2] is a democratic federative law-governed state with a republican form of government and independent legislative, executive, and judicial branches. The Constitution declares that human rights and liberties are supreme in Russia.[3]

Russian citizens exercise their power directly in the form of referenda and free elections, as well as through national governmental institutions and local self-government bodies.

Russia as a federative state consists of 89 constituent regions (*subyekty*): 21 republics (*respublika*), six areas (*kray*), 49 regions (*oblast*), two cities of federal significance (Moscow and St. Petersburg), one autonomous region (*avtonomnaya oblast*), and 10 autonomous territories (*avtonomniy okrug*).

Powers of state in Russia are vested in the president of the Russian Federation (the head of state), the Federal Assembly (the authority of legislative power), the government of the Russian Federation (the authority of executive power), and the courts of the Russian Federation (the authority of judicial power). The head of state is a popularly elected president whose powers were substantially increased under the new Constitution. The president appoints the prime minister and can dissolve the lower house of the legislature if it three times refuses to approve his choice for that post. The Federal Assembly is divided into an upper house, the Federation Council, and a lower house, the State Duma. The Federation Council has 178 members, consisting of two representatives—one from the legislature and one from the government—of each republic (*respublika*), area (*kray*), region (*oblast*), city of federal significance, autonomous region (*avtonomnaya oblast*), and autonomous territory (*avtonomniy okrug*). The State Duma has 450 members: 225 are elected from districts, and the other remaining 225 seats are distributed proportionally among those parties whose national vote exceeds 5 percent.

In all the constituent regions of the Russian Federation, power is exercised by governmental institutions formed by the constituent regions themselves. Local self-government bodies are inde-

---

[2]Article. 1 states that the names "Russian Federation" and "Russia" are to be considered equivalent.

[3]Constitution of the Russian Federation, art. 2.

pendent within the limits of their competence. They do not form part of the system of state bodies.[4]

B. General Sources of Labor Law (Domestic and International)

The Constitution[5] has the supreme legal force and direct effect and is applicable throughout the entire territory of Russia.[6]

No source of law in Russia may contradict the Constitution,[7] whether federal constitutional laws, federal laws, the Russian president's edicts and directions, the Russian government's resolutions and directions, constituent regions' constitutions (charters) and laws, heads of constituent regions' edicts and directions, constituent region governments' resolutions and directions, or other legal acts.

According to the Constitution, universally recognized principles and rules of international law and international treaties signed by Russia are integral parts of the Russian legal system. If an international treaty signed by Russia establishes rules that differ from those stipulated by law, then the rules of the international treaty are applied.[8]

Russia is a member of the majority of international organizations that develop and adopt draft international treaties, recommendations, resolutions, declarations, and other international documents in the sphere of labor law, such as the United Nations, the International Labor Organization (ILO), the International Maritime Organization, the Council of Europe, and the Commonwealth of Independent States (CIS).

Russia has ratified many of the ILO's 184 conventions, including the following conventions covering fundamental labor standards:

---

[4]*Id.*, art. 12(8).

[5]Constitution of the Russian Federation.

[6]*Id.*, arts. 4 and 15.

[7]*Id.*, art. 15.

[8]*Id.*

- Conventions 29 and 105, adopted in 1930 and 1957, respectively, banning forced labor and slavery;
- Conventions 87 and 98, dating to 1948 and 1998, requiring countries to allow freedom of association and collective bargaining;
- Conventions 100 and 111, from 1951 and 1958, banning workplace discrimination; and
- Conventions 138 and 182, from 1973 and 1999, which set a minimum working age of 15 and ban the worst forms of child labor (e.g., bonded labor, hazardous labor, military conscription, sex trade, etc.).

C. Division of Responsibility for Labor Law Among Federal, Constituent Region, and Local Governments

Since Russia is a federative state, its Constitution names all major issues of federal jurisdiction and of joint (federal and constituent region) jurisdiction. Outside the limits of the jurisdiction of the Russian Federation and its powers under joint jurisdiction, the constituent regions of the Russian Federation enjoy full state authority.

Protection of human and civil rights; protection of family, maternity, fatherhood, and childhood; social protection; and labor legislation are areas of joint competence.[9]

Issues of joint jurisdiction are regulated by federal laws as well as by laws and other normative legal acts of the constituent regions of the Russian Federation, which must be adopted in conformity with those federal laws. In the event of a conflict between a federal law and any other act issued in Russia, the federal law prevails.[10]

Division of powers among federal, constituent region, and local self-government bodies in the sphere of labor relations is established in the Labor Code of the Russian Federation (*Trudovoy*

---

[9]*Id.*, art. 72.
[10]*Id.*, art. 76.

Kodeks Rossiyskoy Federatsii) (hereinafter "the Labor Code"), which entered into force on February 1, 2002.

The Labor Code relegates to federal bodies the adoption of federal laws and other federal legal acts establishing in particular:

- fundamental principles of legal regulation of labor relations and social partnership;
- labor rights, freedoms, and guarantees ensured by the state;
- the system of federal bodies, principles, and procedures for state supervision and control over the observance of labor laws and regulations;
- procedures for settlement of individual and collective labor disputes;
- procedures for concluding, changing, and dissolving labor contracts;
- procedures for conducting collective bargaining and changing collective agreements;
- types of disciplinary sanctions, and procedures for their application;
- systems and procedures for state expert examination of conditions of labor and certification of means of production (plants, machinery, equipment, etc.) with regard to protection of labor;
- procedures for investigating accidents in production and vocation-related diseases.

Federal laws and legal acts are binding throughout the entire territory of Russia. Constituent region laws and legal acts regulating labor relations are effective only in the territory of the respective constituent region. Constituent region bodies legislate and adopt other normative legal acts in the sphere of labor relations with regard to questions not relegated to federal bodies. Where constituent region bodies set a higher level of labor rights and guarantees for workers than the federal standards, the expenses of the increased protections must come from the respective constituent region's budget.

Local self-government bodies also have the right to adopt acts containing norms of labor law within the limits of their jurisdiction. Such acts operate in the respective municipal territory.

D. Major Administrative Bodies Responsible for Overseeing the Labor Law Regulatory System

State supervision and control over compliance with labor laws and other legal acts is carried out by agencies of the federal inspectorate of labor. Regulations pertaining to the federal inspectorate of labor were approved by Resolution of the Government of the Russian Federation No. 78 of January 28, 2000.

Agencies of the federal inspectorate of labor are charged with verifications, inspections, investigations, issuance of binding citations for elimination of violations and restoration of labor rights, and assignment of responsibility to violators in accordance with federal law. The agencies receive workers, consider their applications, letters, appeals, and other recourses, inform and educate employers and workers about labor laws and regulations, and conduct general outreach and extension services concerning the labor rights of workers. The agencies also prepare and publish annual reports on labor legislation compliance, which are submitted to the president of the Russian Federation and to the Russian government.

State inspectors of labor have the right to:

- visit any organization at any time, without obstruction, to conduct an inspection;
- inform the employer of their presence at the organization, unless they believe such notification may prejudice the effectiveness of the inspection;
- take samples of materials for analysis, with written notification to the employer;
- investigate accidents in production;
- present binding orders to employers in case of violations of labor rights;
- suspend the work of organizations, their units, and equipment or apply to courts with a request for an order to shut down organizations or terminate activities of their units in order to protect workers, if the respective violations threaten the life and health of workers;
- file suits in courts;
- file administrative charges against persons suspected of violations of labor laws and regulations, and send to law en-

forcement agencies materials for bringing criminal charges against such persons.

State inspectors of labor are obliged to keep confidential any state, commercial, and other secrets protected by law that become known to them in using their powers. They must consider absolutely confidential the source of any complaint and refrain from communicating to an employer information concerning the individual making a complaint if the latter objects.

Any decisions of state inspectors of labor may be appealed to the respective state inspectors at the next level and/or to a court.

Agencies of the federal inspectorate of labor collaborate with other federal agencies that regulate the following sectors of the economy: mining and industry, electric power and heat, sanitary and epidemiology sanitation, and nuclear and radiation safety. They cooperate with internal labor supervision and control units of federal, constituent region, and local bodies.

State supervision to ensure precise and uniform enforcement of labor laws and regulations is effectuated by the prosecutor general of the Russian Federation and other prosecutors subordinate to him or her.

E. Structure of Dispute Resolution System for Labor Law

1. *Individual Labor Disputes*

The Constitution recognizes the right to individual and collective labor disputes, including the right to strike, with the use of the methods for resolution of disputes provided by federal law.[11]

The Labor Code defines an individual labor dispute as an unresolved disagreement between an employer and a worker (or a former worker, or a person with whom an employer refused to conclude a labor contract) with regard to the application of labor laws and regulations, a collective bargaining contract, or a labor contract.[12]

---

[11] *Id.*, art. 37.

[12] Labor Code of the Russian Federation, art. 381.

Individual labor disputes are considered by commissions for labor disputes, which are formed and operate in accordance with the Labor Code; and by courts, which follow procedures laid down in the Civil Procedural Code of the Russian Federation (hereinafter, "the CPC"), in effect since February 1, 2003. Both entities are guided in their decisions by labor legislation.

a. Disputes Considered by Commissions for Labor Disputes

Formation of a commission for labor disputes is not compulsory. Such commissions are formed in an organization and/or its units at the initiative of workers and/or the employer and are comprised of an equal number of representatives respectively (a) elected by a general meeting of workers and (b) appointed by the employer. The organizational and technical support for the commissions' activity must be provided by the employer.

A worker is initially obliged to try settling an individual labor dispute in direct negotiations with the employer. If the negotiations fail, the worker may file a complaint with a commission for labor disputes within three months from the day he or she knew or should have known about the alleged violation (the commission may extend the period for filing if it believes the circumstances justify such an extension).

A commission for labor disputes must consider an individual labor dispute within 10 calendar days from the day the worker files the complaint. The commission considers the dispute in the presence of the worker, unless he or she agrees to a judgment by default. At the demand of the commission, the chief executive officer of an organization is obliged to submit necessary documents to the commission, which also has the right to summon witnesses to a session and invite specialists. Sessions of the commission are recorded in protocols.

The commission adopts a decision by secret ballot by a simple majority of votes of its members present at the session, provided that at least half of the members from each side are present. A decision is to be handed over to the worker and the employer within three days from its adoption. There is a 10-day appeal period. If no appeal is filed during that period, the decision is to be carried out within three days.

If a decision is not implemented, and provided that neither the worker nor the employer has applied to a court over the labor dispute, a court bailiff enforces the decision by means of a compulsory procedure based on a certificate issued by the commission.

b. Disputes Considered in Court

Individual labor disputes are considered in a court in the following cases:

- refusal to hire a person for work;
- individuals working under a labor contract with other individuals (not organizations);
- workers who believe they have been subjected to discrimination;
- application by a worker choosing to bypass the commission for labor disputes;
- disputes not considered by a commission within the 10-day period;
- application by a worker, an employer, or trade union (defending the interests of a worker) who disagrees with the decision of the commission;
- application by a prosecutor, if the decision of the commission does not correspond to labor laws and regulations;
- application by an employer in a case involving compensation by a worker for harm caused to the organization;
- application by a worker in a case involving transfer to other work, disputes related to dismissal date and cause for dismissal, or reinstatement to work.

A worker has the right to apply to a court for resolution of a dispute within three months of the day the worker knew or should have known about the alleged violation. With regard to dismissal, the period is one month from the day of receipt of the order of dismissal or return of the worker's labor book. A court may extend the periods if circumstances justify such an extension.

Workers' suits arising from employment-related issues are exempt from payment of duties and judicial expenses in court.

The cost of a plaintiff's lawyer in a reasonable amount is paid by the party that loses the case.

According to the CPC, cases involving potential reinstatement must be considered and settled by a court within one month of the day the court receives the application. Other cases arising from employment disputes are to be settled within two months by a court, or within one month by a justice of the peace.[13]

Court decisions and remedies are based on the substance of a suit and circumstances of the case. For example, if a transfer to other work or a dismissal of a worker is deemed illegal, the worker must be reinstated to the previous job and paid the difference in earnings (average earnings) for the entire enforced lower-paid work or idle time, and may demand monetary compensation for moral harm caused by the employer's actions, with the amount of the monetary compensation to be determined by a court.

In general, there are four court levels: the first instance, the appeal, the cassation, and the supervisory. Justices of the peace are considered courts of the first instance. District courts are the courts of second and final instance to which decisions by justices of the peace may be appealed. Decisions of justices of the peace may be appealed to a district court within 10 days of adoption of the decision in final form. On appeal, the district court must consider the case de novo and in accordance with the rules of procedure in a court of the first instance. If the district court does not change the decision of a justice of the peace, nor repeal it and adopt a new decision, the decision of the justice of the peace enters into legal effect immediately. If there is a new decision by the appeals court, that also enters into legal effect immediately.

Decisions by a court of the first instance, except decisions of justices of the peace, may be appealed in the cassation procedure to a court of the next higher level within 10 days of adoption of the decision in final form. A court of this cassation instance checks the legality and substantiation of the lower court's decision as regards the reasons for the cassation appeal and objections to it. If the interests of legality require, a court of the cassation instance has the right to review the decision of the court of the first instance de novo.

---

[13]Civil Procedural Code, art. 154.

A court of the cassation instance may accept the decision of a court of the first instance; alternatively, it may change or repeal the decision and adopt a new one, or it may repeal the decision in full or in part and send the case back to the lower court for reconsideration, with obligatory procedural directions. A cassation decision enters into legal effect from the moment of its adoption.

After a court decision enters into legal force, the parties and other participants in the case may not apply to a court with the same claims on the same ground or challenge in other civil legal proceedings the facts and legal arrangements previously determined by a court.

Within one year of the effective date of a court decision in a labor dispute, participants in the case and other persons whose rights and legal interests were infringed by the decision may lodge complaints against the decision with the court of the supervisory instance. The grounds for repeal or change of a court decision by a court of the supervisory instance are substantial violations of norms of material and procedural law. The appeals process in Russia is complex and is beyond the scope of this chapter. The preceding paragraphs are meant to provide a general summary of employee and employer rights within the context of Russian labor law.

2. *Collective Labor Disputes*

The Labor Code defines a collective labor dispute as an unresolved disagreement between workers and employers with regard to establishing or changing wages and other conditions of labor; concluding, changing, or fulfilling collective contracts and agreements; and refusal of the employer to take into account the opinion of the elected representative body of workers when adopting labor legal norms (the so-called "local normative acts" adopted by an organization itself, e.g., rules of internal labor order) within an organization.[14]

Demands are put forward by workers or their representative body in the organization, approved by a respective meeting of workers, and communicated in writing to the employer, who must notify the representative body about a decision in writing within three days of receiving the demands.

---

[14]Labor Code, art. 398.

A collective labor dispute begins when an employer fails to notify workers of its decision or notifies them that it has rejected all or part of their demands, or on the day the parties draw up a protocol of disagreements in the course of collective bargaining negotiations.

a. Settlement Procedure

The procedure for settlement of a collective labor dispute consists of the following stages: (i) consideration by a conciliation commission, (ii) consideration with the participation of a mediator, (iii) and/or labor arbitration.

i. Conciliation commission

A conciliation commission is comprised of an equal number of representatives of the parties to a collective labor dispute. Neither party has the right to evade participation in conciliation procedures. The employer must create the conditions necessary for the work of the commission.

A collective labor dispute must be considered by the conciliation commission within five days of commencement of the dispute (the parties may extend the period by mutual consent). After the five days, a one-hour warning strike may be conducted once with prior written notification to the employer three days beforehand.

A decision of the conciliation commission adopted by agreement of the parties has binding force upon them. In the event that the parties to a collective labor dispute fail to achieve agreement in the conciliation commission, they must continue conciliation procedures with the participation of a mediator.

ii. Use of a mediator

The procedure for consideration of a collective labor dispute with the participation of a mediator is determined by agreement of the parties and the mediator and must be carried out within seven working days of failure by the conciliation commission to achieve a resolution. At the conclusion of the procedure, the parties must adopt a written agreement or draw up a protocol of disagreements.

In the event that either party refuses to create or participate in a conciliation commission or the parties fail to choose a mediator within three working days or to reach agreement during the mediation process, the dispute is transferred to a labor arbitration body.

iii. Labor arbitration panel

A labor arbitration panel is a temporary entity that is created once the parties have concluded an agreement in writing binding them to adopt an arbitration award. The panel is made up of representatives of each party to the dispute and of the Service for the Settlement of Collective Labor Disputes (a system of agencies from federal, constituent region, and local self-government bodies), and is formed within three working days after failure of the conciliation procedures. A dispute is considered by the panel within five working days after its formation. It is stipulated that the creation, composition, procedure, and competence of a labor arbitration panel are formalized by a joint decision of the employer, the workers' representative, and the Ministry of Labor's Service for the Settlement of Collective Labor Disputes (*Sluzhba razresheniya kollektivnykh trudovykh sporov*).

While they are settling a collective labor dispute, conciliation commission members and labor arbitrators are relieved of their regular duties for up to three months in a year, while retaining their average earnings, and workers' representatives are protected from disciplinary sanctions, transferal to other work, or dismissal at the initiative of the employer without the prior consent of the body that authorized them to act as representatives.

b. Strikes

In the event that an employer refuses to proceed with labor arbitration or to fulfill the recommendations thereof, workers may commence a strike (unless it is prohibited or restricted by law, as it is for some organizations where labor arbitration is compulsory). A strike is announced by a meeting of workers at the proposal of their representative body previously empowered to settle the collective labor dispute. A strike has to be confirmed by the meeting if it is initiated by a trade union. When it is impossible to convene a meeting of workers, the representative body has the right to gather the signatures of the workers, and the strike may be announced if more than half of the workers signify their approval by signing. Participation in a strike is voluntary. A 10-calendar-day written warning to the employer is required prior to commencing the strike.

A representative body of workers must head the strike. It may convene meetings of workers, suspend a strike, and resume it with a three-working-day warning without new recourse to conciliation procedures (i.e., a conciliation commission and a labor arbitration panel). Organizations whose activities are connected with human safety and health must ensure the minimum necessary services and vital interests of society, otherwise a strike may be deemed illegal. While workers are conducting a strike, the parties to a collective labor dispute are obliged to continue trying to settle the dispute.

Participation by a worker in a legal strike is not a violation of labor discipline or grounds for dissolution of a labor contract. The employer must retain the place of work and the post of workers participating in a strike. Employers have the right not to pay workers for the time of their participation in a strike, unless the parties have agreed on a contributory compensation. Workers not participating in a strike and therefore not fulfilling their work through no fault of their own are to be paid downtime in the amount of at least two-thirds of their base pay rates, and may be transferred to other work (i.e., a transfer in the event of a strike for workers who are not participating in the strike does not differ from the usual transfer procedure). Employer-initiated dismissal of workers in connection with their participation in a collective labor dispute or strike is prohibited.

Under special circumstances, the government of the Russian Federation has the right to suspend a strike for a period of up to 10 calendar days. In the event of a direct threat to human life or health, a court may defer a strike that has not begun, or suspend a strike that has begun, for a period of up to 30 days.

If the strike is declared without observance of the established periods, procedures, and requirements, it must be declared illegal by a court upon application by an employer or prosecutor. In such a situation, workers are obliged to terminate the strike and resume work no later than the day after a copy of the court decision is given to the body heading the strike.

In organizations where a strike is prohibited by law, the government of the Russian Federation has 10 days to adopt a decision with regard to the collective labor dispute.

Workers who ignore the legal deferral, suspension, or prohibition of a strike may be subjected to disciplinary sanctions by the employer. A representative body of workers that declares and does not terminate an illegal strike is obliged to compensate the employer for losses caused by the strike at its own expense in the amount determined by a court.

Both employer and worker representatives may be subjected to administrative penalties (primarily administrative fines of a noncriminal nature imposed by the state) established by the Code of the Russian Federation on Administrative Violations (hereinafter the CoAV) for certain violations of the procedure for settlement of collective labor disputes.

I. Individual Employment

A. Statutory Regulation of Employment

Article 37 of the Constitution declares that labor shall be free, and that everyone shall have the right to use labor skills freely and to choose the type of activity and occupation in which he or she wishes to engage. Compulsory labor is forbidden under Article 37.

The Law of the Russian Federation of April 19, 1991, "On Employment of the Population in the Russian Federation" (as amended in 1996 and later) considers the following individuals to be employed. Persons who:

- work under a labor contract;
- are registered as individual entrepreneurs;
- are engaged in "auxiliary" activities (such as picking and gathering of mushrooms, berries, wild honey, various tree saps or syrups, hunting, fishing, etc.) and contractually selling their products;
- perform work or provide services under contracts of civil law (contracts of independent work, compensated services, commission, agency, etc.);

- are members of production cooperatives;
- are elected, appointed, or confirmed to a paid post;
- are in state service (federal civil service, state civil service, federal military service, federal law-enforcement service) or municipal service;
- are taking a full-time course of tuition at an educational establishment;
- are temporarily absent from the workplace to perform state duties or are otherwise legally excused from work;
- are founders or participants of organizations with property rights (such as owners and shareholders).

Thus, labor contracts are a part of all contracts of employment in Russia.

According to Article 25 of the 1991 Law, employers are obliged to submit monthly to state employment agencies information on the existence of vacant jobs in their organizations.

For organizations with more than 30 workers, Article 21 of the Federal Law of November 24, 1995, "On the Social Protection of Invalids in the Russian Federation" establishes quotas for hiring disabled persons that range from 2 percent to 4 percent of the average number of workers. Employers must inform state employment agencies of their progress in meeting the fixed quotas. In the event the quotas have not been fulfilled, employers must make payments to the constituent regions, in amounts determined by the constituent regions.

Implementing Article 37 of the Russian Constitution, which stipulates that everyone shall have the right of protection against unemployment, the Law of the Russian Federation "On Employment of the Population in the Russian Federation" provides for corresponding measures, including payment of unemployment benefits.

B. Individual Labor Contracts

Individual labor contracts are required under the labor law of Russia. Article 56 of the Labor Code stipulates that a labor contract is an agreement between an employer and a worker, with the employer having the duty to provide work to the worker with regard to the agreed labor function, to ensure legally established conditions of labor, and to pay timely and in full earnings to the worker; and with the worker having the duty to fulfill the labor function personally and to comply with the rules of internal labor order in the organization. Under this definition, a labor contract may be only individual, not collective.[15]

The conclusion of a labor contract is permitted with persons who have attained 16 years of age. There are strict legal exceptions from this rule for conclusion of a labor contract with persons 14 or 15 years of age. When concluding a labor contract, persons under 18 years and other persons indicated in federal laws are subject to obligatory preliminary medical certification.

A labor contract covers work under various regimes: normal working hours; part-time work; work beyond normal working hours (nonstandard work hours, overtime, second job); and flexible work hours. It also covers shift work; division of the working day into parts; and summary recording of working time (an employee's work schedule is averaged over an established period—e.g., one month—so that, although it may vary from day to day, the total number of hours worked is the same over the period).

C. Substance of the Labor Contract

A labor contract may be concluded by agreement of both parties. Its conditions may only be changed by mutual agreement as well. A labor contract and changes to it are made in written form.

Pursuant to the Labor Code, the mandatory (material) terms of a labor contract are:

- names of the parties;
- place of work (with specification of the structural division);
- date of commencement of work;
- name of the post, specialty, vocation with specification of qualifications, or specific labor function;
- rights and duties of the worker;
- rights and duties of the employer;
- characteristics of conditions of labor, compensations and privileges for work in arduous, harmful, and/or dangerous and life-threatening conditions;

---

[15] Labor Code, art. 56.

- regime of labor and leisure (if it differs from the general rules in the organization);
- terms of payment (including the amount of the tariff rate or position salary, supplementary payments, increments, and incentive payments);
- types and conditions of social insurance directly connected with labor activity.

Labor contracts may include other conditions, but these conditions must meet or exceed provisions in the Labor Code, other laws and regulations, and collective contracts.

Labor contracts may be concluded either for an indefinite period or for a definite period of up to five years (fixed-term labor contract). A fixed-term labor contract may be concluded only in instances where labor relations cannot be established for an indefinite period, taking into account the character of work or conditions of fulfillment thereof. Some 18 instances of fixed-term labor contracts are listed in the Labor Code, with other possibilities provided in federal laws.

A labor contract not duly formalized is nonetheless considered a contract if a worker begins work with the knowledge of or at the direction of an employer or its representative. In the event of actual admittance of a worker to work, an employer must formalize a labor contract within three days from the day of admittance.

A hiring is also formalized by an order (*prikaz*) of an employer corresponding to the labor contract concluded. The employer must obtain the new hire's signature, verifying his or her familiarity with the order.

An employer who hires a worker is obligated to familiarize that worker with the rules of the organization, other local acts relating to his or her labor function, and the collective contract. An employer is prohibited from demanding that a worker carry out work that is not stipulated by the worker's labor contract, with some exceptions.

Probation may be stipulated in a labor contract by agreement of the parties for the purpose of verifying the worker's suitability for the work assigned. The period of probation may not exceed three months (six months for chief executive officers of an organization and its subdivisions). Probation may not be established for some categories of persons (individuals under 18 years of age, pregnant women, persons who take up work for the first time in the specialty for which they were educated, etc.).

In the event of an unsatisfactory probation, an employer has the right to dissolve the labor contract before the worker's probationary period ends, after having warned the worker of this impending action in writing at least three days in advance of termination of the contract and having specified in the warning the reasons for deeming that the worker has not passed probation. Dissolution of the contract may take place without taking into account the opinion of the respective trade union body and without payment of a severance benefit. A worker may appeal the decision of an employer in court.

If the period of probation has expired, and a worker continues to work, he or she shall be considered to have passed probation. Subsequent dissolution of a labor contract with the worker is permitted only on general grounds.

D. Termination of a Labor Contract

Under the Labor Code, a labor contract may be terminated on the following grounds:

- agreement of the parties (at any time);
- expiration of the period of a fixed-term labor contract (with at least a three-day prior warning to the worker), except for instances when labor relations actually continue;
- dissolution at the initiative of the worker (two weeks' advance notice to the employer is required, and the worker has the right to withdraw his or her dissolution application until the expiration of the notice period);
- dissolution at the initiative of the employer (except that dismissal of a worker shall not be permitted during any period of temporary incapacity on the part of the worker or while the worker is on leave, except when an organization is shut down) in instances of:
  - closure of an organization (for a detailed review of redundancy, see IV below);
  - reduction of the number or personnel posts of the workers (for a detailed review of redundancy, see IV below);

- failure of a worker to conform to the position or fulfill its responsibilities, if it is impossible to transfer the worker (with the worker's consent) to other work, as a consequence of:
  - state of health in accordance with a medical opinion;
  - insufficient qualification confirmed by the results of attestation (review by a special commission in the organization that analyzes the employee's work). Workers who are members of a trade union may be dismissed after the employer takes into account the reasoned opinion of the elected trade union body of the organization; when conducting attestation, a member of the trade union must be included in the attestation commission;
- change of ownership of an organization (with respect to the CEO, deputies, and chief bookkeeper of an organization);
- repeated failure to perform labor duties without justifiable reasons if the worker has incurred disciplinary sanction (workers who are members of a trade union may be dismissed only after taking into account the reasoned opinion of the elected trade union body of the organization);
- a single gross violation of labor duties by a worker:
  - truancy (absence from job without justifiable reasons for more than four successive hours during a working day);
  - appearance at work under the influence of alcohol, a narcotic, or another intoxicant;
  - divulgence of a secret protected by law (state, commercial, official, and other) which became known to worker in connection with duties;
  - stealing (including petty theft), waste, intentional destruction or damage to another's property at place of work (when established by an administrative body/court);
  - violation by a worker of requirements for protection of labor if this violation entailed grave consequences or was known to entail them;
- guilty actions by a worker directly handling monetary goods or valuables that give grounds for a loss of the employer's trust;

  - an amoral offense incompatible with work consisting of nurturing functions;
  - adoption of unsubstantiated decisions by the CEO, deputies, or chief bookkeeper of an organization (or branch, or representative office) that entailed damage to the property of the organization;
  - a single gross violation of labor duties by the CEO or deputies of an organization (or branch, or representative office);
  - submission by a worker to an employer of forged documents or information known to be false when concluding a labor contract;
  - termination of a worker's access to a state secret (classified data) when such access is required for fulfilling work;
  - provisions in a labor contract with the CEO of an organization and members of a collegial executive body of an organization;
  - in other instances established by federal laws;
- transfer of a worker at his or her request or with his or her consent to another employer;
- refusal of a worker to continue work in connection with a change of ownership of an organization or reorganization (for a detailed review of transfers of undertakings, see IV below);
- refusal of a worker to continue work in connection with a change of material conditions of the labor contract;
- refusal of a worker to transfer to other work for health reasons (in accordance with medical opinion);
- refusal of a worker to transfer with the employer (organization) to another locality;
- circumstances beyond the control of the parties:
  - call-up of a worker to military service or assignment to alternative civilian service;
  - reinstatement (by decision of the federal inspectorate of labor or a court) of a worker that results in the ouster of another worker hired in the interim between termination and reinstatement (termination of the interim worker is permitted if it is impossible to transfer the worker with his or her consent to other work);

  - – nonelection for a post;
  - – sentencing of a worker to punishment that excludes continuation of previous work;
  - – a medical opinion acknowledging that a worker is wholly incapable of performing a job;
  - – death;
  - – extraordinary circumstances preventing the continuation of labor relations (if so deemed by the federal government or a state body of a constituent region of the Russian Federation);
- • violation of legal rules for conclusion of a labor contract (in the event that this violation excludes the possibility to continue work; a labor contract may be terminated if it is impossible to transfer a worker with his or her written consent to other work available at the organization):
  - – violation of a court's sentence depriving a person of the right to hold determined posts or to engage in a determined activity;
  - – conclusion of a labor contract for work contraindicated for a person for health reasons, in accordance with a medical opinion;
  - – absence of the respective document on education required for work by federal laws and other legal acts;
  - – in other instances provided by a federal law;
- • other grounds provided by federal laws.

A fixed-term labor contract may be dissolved upon expiration of its term; the worker must be warned of this at least three days before dismissal.

As noted above, a worker may complain to the federal inspectorate of labor about termination of a labor contract on any grounds, or may see the termination as constituting an individual labor dispute, and thus may apply to court for recourse.

E. Privacy

Article 24 of the Constitution stipulates that collecting, keeping, using, and disseminating information about the private life of a person is not permitted without that person's consent. Constituent region and local government agencies and officials are obliged to provide all persons access to documents and materials directly affecting their rights and freedoms, unless otherwise stipulated by law.[16]

Protection of personal data of workers is governed by the Labor Code. The Labor Code defines personal data of a worker as information affecting a specific worker and necessary to an employer in connection with labor relations.[17]

When processing (receiving, keeping, combining, transferring, etc.) personal data of a worker, an employer is obliged to comply with the following general requirements:

- the processing shall be effectuated exclusively for the purposes of fulfilling labor laws and regulations;
- all personal data of a worker should be received from the worker;
- receipt of a worker's personal data from third parties is subject to the worker's written consent;
- an employer must not communicate personal data of a worker to a third party without the worker's written consent (with some exceptions);
- an employer must not communicate a worker's personal data for commercial purposes without the worker's written consent;
- an employer must warn the persons receiving personal data of a worker that the data may be used only for purposes for which the data has been communicated, and must require confirmation from these persons that they have complied with this rule;
- persons receiving personal data of a worker are obliged to maintain the regime of confidentiality of the data (except for cases provided by federal laws);
- an employer should not request information concerning the health of a worker (except in cases where the information pertains to the worker's ability to fulfill his or her work duties);

---

[16]Constitution, art. 24.

[17]Labor Code, art. 85.

- an employer does not have the right to process personal data concerning a worker's political, religious, and other convictions and private life (except in instances directly connected with labor relations, and only with the worker's written consent);
- an employer does not have the right to process personal data concerning a worker's membership in social associations or trade union activity (except for instances provided by federal law);
- decisions affecting the interests of a worker may not be based by an employer exclusively on personal data of the worker received as a result of automated processing of the data—the worker must be communicated with directly;
- an employer should authorize access to personal data of workers only to specially empowered persons, and such persons must have the right to receive only those portions of the data that are necessary for a specific function;
- defense of personal data of a worker against unlawful use or loss must be ensured by an employer at its expense;
- an employer must present documents from the organization concerning processing of personal data of workers and the worker must sign them to verify that he or she is familiar with such documents;
- workers must not renounce their rights to preserve and defend the confidentiality of their personal data.

Under Article 89 of the Labor Code, workers have the right to full information about their personal data and the processing thereof; free access to the data; the right to receive free of charge copies of any entry into the data (with exceptions provided by federal laws); and the right to demand the exclusion or correction of untrue, incomplete, or unlawful personal data. In the event of an employer's refusal to exclude or correct personal data of a worker, the latter has the right to provide notice of his or her disagreement with the information. The worker also may demand that the employer provide a correction to all persons to whom erroneous personal data has been communicated.[18]

[18]Labor Code, art. 89.

A worker has the right to sue an employer in court for unlawful actions or failures to act when processing or defending the worker's personal data. Persons guilty of violating the rules for processing and defense of personal data of a worker face disciplinary, civil, administrative, or criminal penalties in accordance with federal laws.

F. Covenants on Commercial Secrets

A labor contract may include a provision for nondivulgence of a secret (state, commercial, official, or other) protected by law.[19]

Article 139 of the Civil Code of the Russian Federation (*Grazhdanskiy Kodeks Rossiyskoy Federatsii*) (hereinafter the Civil Code, in effect since January 1, 1995) points out that information is regarded as an official or commercial secret if its secrecy presents an actual or a potential commercial value, if there is no free access to it on legal grounds, and if its owner is taking measures to protect its confidentiality.[20]

As mentioned above in I.D., divulgence by a worker of a secret protected by law that became known to the worker in connection with the worker's labor duties is a ground for termination of a labor contract at the initiative of the employer.

Pursuant to the Civil Code, workers who have divulged an official or a commercial secret despite labor contracts are obliged to make recompense for the losses inflicted.

Some employers insist on including in a labor contract requirements that the worker show loyalty to the employer and to the respective organization as well as refrain from competing with the employer during the course of employment and for a period thereafter. However, under Russian labor law, such stipulations are not legally binding. Under civil law, such provisions could instead be a ground for compensating the employer for losses, if both a divulgence by the employee of the employer's official or commercial secrets and the losses are established by a court.

---

[19] *Id.*, art. 57.
[20] Civil Code, art. 139.

As this chapter was being written, the Russian Federation Council (the upper house of the legislature) was reviewing the final draft of a new Federal Law on Commercial Secrets and the draft was expected to become law. This new law would much more closely regulate activities in this area.

II. COLLECTIVE BARGAINING

A. Introduction

1. Statutory Regulation of the Social Partnership and Collective Bargaining

Under the Constitution, the Russian Federation is a social state whose policy is aimed at creating conditions that ensure adequate living standards and free development of individuals.[21] A concept of social partnership, primarily in the field of labor relations, is currently being developed in Russia.

The principal laws regulating social partnership and collective bargaining in Russia include the Labor Code, the Law of the Russian Federation dated March 11, 1992, "On Collective Contracts and Agreements," the Federal Law dated January 12, 1996, "On Trade Unions, Their Rights and Guarantees Related to Their Activities," the Federal Law dated May 1, 1999, "On the Russian Three-Sided Commission for Regulation of Social and Labor Relations," and the Federal Law dated November 27, 2002, "On Employers' Associations."

2. Social Partnership in the Field of Labor Relations

Social partnership is defined in Article 23 of the Labor Code as a system of internal relations between workers (representatives of workers), employers (representatives of employers), and state regulatory authorities and local self-government bodies that serves to ensure observance of mutual interests of workers and employers with regard to regulation of labor and labor-associated rela-

[21]Constitution, art. 7.

tions.[22] The nongovernment social partners are thus defined as the workers and employers as represented by their authorized representatives.

The main principles of social partnership include, in particular, equality of counterparts, freedom of choice of discussed labor matters, voluntary assumption of obligations by the parties, obligatory execution of collective contracts and agreements, overseeing execution of collective contracts and agreements, and liability of the parties for any failure to execute such contracts and agreements.

The system of social partnership includes the following levels: federal, constituent region, sectoral, municipal, and the level of an organization.

The social partnership has a form of collective bargaining with regard to drafting collective contracts and agreements and their conclusion.

- A collective agreement is a legal act concluded by and between workers and employers, through their representatives, which regulates social and labor relations within the organization.
- In turn, an agreement is a legal act concluded by and between authorized representatives of workers and employers at various social partnership levels (federal, constituent region, sectoral, municipal) that sets forth general principles of regulation of social and labor relations, as well as any economic relations associated with these principles at the corresponding level.

The system of social partnership envisages mutual consultations in connection with any matters pertaining to regulation of labor relations, provision of guarantees for workers' labor rights, participation of workers in the management of the organization, and so forth.

[22] Labor Code, art. 23.

3. *Trade Union Membership*

Article 30 of the Constitution declares that anyone has a right to participate in associations, including a right to set up trade unions to protect the interests of certain groups. No one may be forced to join or be a member of any association.

Under Article 4 of the federal law dated May 19, 1995, "On Public Associations" and Article 2 of the federal law "On Trade Unions, Their rights and Guarantees Related to Their Activities," trade unions are deemed to be public associations. Hence, as it has been defined, any individual 14 years of age or older engaged in any labor (professional) activity may at his or her own discretion join a trade union, conduct any trade union activities, and withdraw from trade unions.

The federal law on trade unions applies to all organizations located in the Russian Federation. Other federal laws provide in their respective spheres for variations in the application of the trade union law with regard to individuals in the military, law enforcement officers, federal security officers, customs personnel, judges and prosecutors, and similar categories of public servants.

Under Article 7 of the federal law on trade unions, trade unions may independently draft and approve their charters and regulations on primary trade union organizations.

The legality of a trade union, association of trade unions, and of a primary trade union as a legal entity arises as of the date of their respective state registration through formal notification. Any refusal to follow, or evasion of, a provision of the state registration may be appealed in court.

Trade unions, their associations, and primary (i.e., local) trade union organizations may refrain from the state registration. In such instances, they do not obtain the rights of a legal entity.

Under Article 19 of the Constitution, the state guarantees equal rights and freedoms to individuals regardless of their participation in public associations. Pursuant to Article 3 of the Labor Code, no one's labor rights and freedoms may be limited, and no one may obtain any advantages, due to membership or nonmembership in any public associations. Similarly, Article 9 of the federal law on trade unions prohibits restrictions on a person's social, labor, political, or any other rights and freedoms based on membership or nonmembership in a trade union. In particular, hiring, promotion, or dismissal of any person may not be made contingent upon trade union membership or nonmembership.

Pursuant to Article 86 of the Labor Code, the employer may not receive and process personal information pertaining to a worker's membership in public associations or the worker's trade union activities, unless it has been provided for in the federal legislation.

Persons believing that they have been subjected to discrimination with regard to any labor relations matter may contact agencies of the Federal Labor Inspectorate and/or may go to court to seek restoration of their breached rights, compensation, and reparation for punitive damages.

B. Social Partnership Bodies—Tripartite Entities

The system of social partnership bodies reflects the various levels of government—federal, constituent region, sectoral, municipal—and the level of an organization.

Social partnership bodies are set up to regulate social and labor relations—i.e., conducting collective bargaining, preparation and conclusion of collective contracts—and to oversee their execution.

Under Article 35 of the Labor Code, social partnership bodies are deemed to be commissions established at all levels on the basis of equality, as agreed upon by the parties.

The permanent Russian tripartite commission for the regulation of social and labor relations is set up at the federal level. Its activities are governed by the aforesaid federal law.[23] Members of such a commission include representatives of all Russian trade union associations, all Russian employers' associations, and the Russian government.

Constituent regions of the Russian Federation may set up tripartite commissions for the regulation of social and labor relations; their activities are governed by the laws of such constituent entities.

---

[23]Federal Law "On the Russian Tripartite Commission for Regulation of Social and Labor Relations."

Tripartite commissions for the regulation of social and labor relations may also be set up at the municipal level. Activities of such commissions are regulated by the laws of constituent regions, and regulations governing such commissions must be approved by the representative bodies of the local authorities.

At the sectoral level, commissions may be formed for the purposes of collective bargaining and drafting and conclusion of sectoral (intersectoral) agreements. Sectoral commissions may be formed both at the federal level and at the level of constituent regions.

At the level of a local organization, a bargaining committee is set up in order to conduct collective bargaining and draft and conclude a collective agreement. However, in practice, collective agreements at the individual plant level are rare. Employers and unions typically enter into agreements at a larger territorial or sectoral (industry-wide) level.

C. Representatives of Workers and Employers

On the basis of Article 11 of the federal law on trade unions, in order to exercise the right to represent and protect the interests of workers, trade unions must be assigned certain rights by workers (at the level of an organization) or the legislature (at the federal, constituent region, sectoral, and municipal levels).

Under Article 29 of the Labor Code, representatives of workers may include trade unions and their associations or any other representatives elected by workers under circumstances stipulated in the Labor Code.[24]

---

[24]The previously applied law of the now-defunct USSR dated June 17, 1983, "On Employees and Their Increased Role in the Management of Enterprises, Institutions and Organizations" and the Labor Code of the Russian Soviet Federative Socialist Republic, adopted in 1972 (with changes and amendments thereto) contained provisions on the general meeting (conference) of staff members and the staff members council. These laws assigned certain rights and obligations to the above bodies, in particular a right of representation of workers. However, the new Labor Code and other new laws of Russia do not provide for formation of such bodies. In the future, a federal law to legitimize staff members as a group may be passed.

1. Trade Unions at the Local Level

A primary trade union organization or any other specified representatives may represent a worker in the course of the following:

- Collective bargaining, conclusion and modification of a collective agreement, or overseeing execution of a collective agreement;
- Exercising the right to participate in the management of an organization; and
- Consideration of labor disputes arising between workers and employers.

Trade unions, their local organizations, associations of trade unions, and associations of trade union local organizations represent workers in the course of the following:

- Collective bargaining with regard to the conclusion and modification of agreements, resolution of certain collective labor disputes, or overseeing execution of aforesaid agreements;
- Formation and performance of activities by commissions for the regulation of social and labor relations.

When a trade union is established within a certain organization, usually not every worker becomes a member. In such cases, workers who are not members of the trade union may authorize a body of the primary trade union organization to represent them in their relations with the employer.[25]

It should be noted that after stabilization of the political situation in Russia, the activity of trade unions significantly decreased, some of them fell apart, and many nonstate organizations have no trade unions or very small ones. Article 31 of the Labor Code applies in instances where there is no primary trade union in an organization, or where a trade union unites fewer than half of all work-

[25]Labor Code, art. 30; Law of the Russian Federation "On Collective Contracts and Agreements," art. 2.

ers. In such instances, workers may convene a general conference and assign representation of their interests to the trade union or any other representative. If a company has two or more primary trade union organizations, such organizations should set up a common representative body for collective bargaining and for drafting and concluding a common collective agreement. The representative body is set up on the basis of a pro rata representation principle (based on the number of members in each organization). In such instances, at least one representative should be provided by each trade union organization.

If a common representative body is not set up within five calendar days from the date that collective bargaining commenced, all workers of the organization should be represented by a primary trade union organization that unites over one half of all workers of such organization. When no single trade union organization unites over half of all workers in an organization, a primary trade union organization should be elected at a general meeting of workers through a closed vote by secret ballot. Such organization should be assigned to set up a representative body. In both instances, a right to delegate their representatives to the representative body is retained by other primary trade union organizations until the collective agreement has been signed.

2. *Unions at Higher Levels*

The right to conduct collective bargaining and sign agreements on behalf of workers at the level of the Russian Federation, any constituent region of the Russian Federation, economic sector, or municipality is granted to certain trade or union associations. If there are several trade union associations at a certain level, each of them is granted a right of representation as a member of a common representative body to be set up with a specification of the number of trade union members represented thereby. If no agreement has been reached on setting up a common representative body, the right of collective bargaining is granted to the trade union association that unites the largest number of members.

The employer's representative in the course of collective bargaining and other negotiations to conclude or modify a labor agreement is usually the head of the organization, or any persons authorized by him or her.[26] Executive bodies, self-government authorities authorized to represent the employer as provided for in current legislation or as authorized by employers themselves,[27] may represent employers, including constituent region and municipal enterprises, and organizations financed out of corresponding budgets. When a collective agreement is concluded at a branch, representative office, or any other detached subdivision of the organization, the employer is represented by the head of the subdivision where the bargaining takes place.[28]

During collective bargaining, conclusion or modification of agreements, resolution of certain collective labor disputes, and formation and activities of commissions for the regulation of social and labor relations, employers are represented by employers' associations of a corresponding level. Employers' associations are nonprofit organizations voluntarily set up by employers for representation of their interests and protection of their rights when interacting with trade unions and constituent region and local authorities.

The timetable, location, and manner of collective bargaining are determined by representatives of the parties that participate in the bargaining. Participants in collective bargaining and in the preparation of drafts of collective contracts and agreements are released from their main professional occupation, but their average monthly pay remains at the same level during the term agreed upon by the parties.[29] The term, however, may not exceed three months. Services of experts, specialists, and agents are paid for by the party that engaged such experts, unless otherwise provided for in a collective contract or agreement.

Representatives of workers participating in collective bargaining may not be charged with a disciplinary action, transferred to another position, or dismissed at the initiative of the employer without the prior consent of the body that authorized them while

---

[26]Labor Code, art. 33.

[27]As stipulated in the Labor Code, art. 34.

[28]Labor Code, art. 40.

[29]Labor Code, art. 39, and Law of the Russian Federation "On Collective Contracts and Agreements," art. 9.

the process is under way. An exception is made for instances of termination of an employment contract due to an offense that is grounds for dismissal under the Labor Code or any other federal law.

D. Collective Contracts and Agreements

Since collective contracts and agreements are deemed to be legal acts, they are legally binding upon the parties. Terms and conditions of collective contracts and agreements that do not meet relevant provisions for workers under current legislation are invalid.[30]

A collective agreement may be concluded at the organization, its branches, representative offices, or any other detached subdivisions of the organization.

Article 40 of the Labor Code and Article 7 of the Law of the Russian Federation "On Collective Contracts and Agreements" stipulate that if the parties fail to reach consent on specific provisions of the draft agreement within three months from the commencement of collective bargaining, the parties must draw up a collective agreement on agreed terms and conditions and simultaneously prepare a statement of disagreement. Unresolved differences may be subject to further resolution under the Labor Code and the Federal Law "On Resolution of Collective Labor Disputes."

Under Article 41 of the Labor Code and Article 13 of the Law of the Russian Federation "On Collective Contracts and Agreements," the contents and structure of the collective agreement is to be determined by the parties. The issues may include:

- forms, systems, and size of salaries;
- payment of allowances and other compensation;
- a mechanism for payroll administration that takes into account cost-of-living adjustments, inflation level, and achievement of results as defined in the collective agreement;

[30]Labor Code, art. 50; Law of the Russian Federation "On Collective Contracts and Agreements," art. 3.

- observance of workers' interests during the privatization of a state or municipal organization and certain housing;
- employment, retraining, and terms of workforce release;
- work and rest patterns, including provision and duration of leave;
- improvement of work conditions and protection of workers, including women and young people;
- guarantees and benefits for workers combining work and education;
- occupational safety and health protection;
- compulsory and voluntary social security and health insurance;
- improvement of health and rest of workers and their families;
- social partnership, ensuring adequate work conditions for workers' representatives;
- procedures for incorporating changes and amendments into a collective agreement;
- control over execution of the collective agreement, and refusal from strikes when appropriate conditions of the collective agreement are complied with;
- liability of the parties; or
- any other issues determined by the parties.

A collective agreement must also contain provisions directly prescribed by laws and other regulatory acts for inclusion in such agreements.

A collective agreement covers all workers of a certain organization, its branches, representative offices, and any other detached subdivisions of the organization.[31] The collective agreement is concluded for the term of no longer than three years. The parties may prolong the collective agreement for a term of no longer than three more years. The collective agreement remains in effect even if the name of the organization is changed or an employment contract with the head of the organization is terminated. In the event of reorganization (consolidation, merger, split-up, split-off, trans-

[31]Labor Code, art. 43.

formation) or closure of the organization, the collective agreement remains effective during the entire process of reorganization or closure.

If the ownership of the organization is changed, the collective agreement remains effective for three months from the date of transfer of ownership. In the event of reorganization or change of ownership, either party may send a proposal to the other party requesting negotiations for a new agreement or extension of the term of the existing agreement for up to three years.

Pursuant to Article 45 of the Labor Code and Article 18 and 21 of the Law of the Russian Federation "On Collective Contracts and Agreements," any agreement, whether it be general (concluded at the federal level), state (at the level of a constituent region of the Russian Federation), sectoral and intersectoral (for one or several economic sectors concluded at the federal, constituent region, and municipal levels), local (level of a municipality) or other (at any level for specific types of collective agreements), may contain mutual obligations of the parties pertaining to the following matters:

- payroll;
- working conditions and labor protection;
- work and rest patterns;
- labor discipline improvement;
- assistance in the placement and retraining of workers;
- special measures aimed at social protection of workers and their families;
- observance of interests of workers in the course of privatization of state and municipal organizations;
- prevention of labor disputes and strikes;
- development of social partnership; and
- other matters determined by the parties.

The effective term of a collective agreement is determined by the parties, but it may not exceed a period of three years. For instance, a general agreement is currently in effect among all Russian trade union associations, all Russian employers' associations, and the government of the Russian Federation for 2002–2004. The parties may prolong the term of the agreement for up to three more years.

The agreement is effective for both employers and workers who concluded or joined it, and for constituent region and local authorities. Agreements may include multiple parties, if the parties to collective bargaining agree.

If the agreement was concluded by an employers' association, it is effective for all employers that are members of the association. Termination of membership in the association does not release an employer from the obligation to execute an agreement that was concluded during the membership term. An employer that joined an employers' association during the effective term of the agreement must fulfill the obligations stipulated therein.

Article 48 of the Labor Code and Article 22 of the Law of the Russian Federation "On Collective Contracts and Agreements" set forth that when a sectoral agreement is concluded at the federal level, the top executive officer of the federal executive body for labor relations may urge employers that failed to participate in the conclusion of the agreement to join the agreement. If employers within 30 calendar days from the date of the official publication of such a proposal fail to file in writing with the federal executive body for labor relations a well-grounded refusal to join the agreement, it is deemed effective for such employers from the date of publication of the proposal.

Under Article 50 of the Labor Code and Article 12 of the Law of the Russian Federation "On Collective Contracts and Agreements," within seven days of its execution, a collective contract or agreement must be sent by a representative of the employer(s) to a corresponding labor agency for registration by means of notification. A collective contract or agreement takes effect regardless of the fact of its registration in the form of notification.

Terms and conditions of the collective contracts or agreements may be incorporated in individual employment contracts concluded between the employer and workers and, thus, they may assume an independent meaning. As a part of an individual employment contract, such incorporated terms and conditions remain effective regardless of any change or termination of the collective contract or agreement and may be changed or terminated only under the rules applicable to individual employment contracts.

E. Strikes and Other Actions

As previously mentioned, under Article 37 of the Constitution and Articles 398 and 409 of the Labor Code, workers (or their representatives) have a right to engage in collective labor disputes and utilize various methods for their resolution (reconciliation procedure, mediators, labor arbitration, etc.), including a right to go on strike.[32]

Trade unions may participate in the resolution of collective labor disputes, and may in accordance with the federal law organize and conduct meetings, rallies, street marches, demonstrations, picketing, and other collective actions, using them as a means of protection of social and labor rights and interests of workers.[33]

F. Guarantees of Trade Union Activities

Pursuant to Article 7 of the federal law on trade unions, trade unions independently develop and approve their charters and regulations on primary trade union organizations. The charter of a trade union must contain, in particular, the terms and procedures for acceptance of members and for their exit from the trade union, payment of acceptance and membership fees, sources of generated income and other received property, and management of trade union assets.

Under Article 377 of the Labor Code, in instances provided for in the collective agreement, the employer may allocate to a primary trade union organization funds for social, cultural, and sports events. On the basis of the written authorization of workers that are not trade union members, employers may transfer funds constituting a portion of the pay of such workers to the accounts of a trade union organization.

The Labor Code stipulates that the employer must create adequate conditions for participation of workers' representatives in collective bargaining.[34] Under Article 377 of the Labor Code and Article 28 of the federal law on trade unions, the employer must

---

[32]Constitution, art. 37; Labor Code, arts. 398, 409.

[33]Federal law on trade unions, art. 14.

[34]Labor Code, art. 32.

provide the elected bodies of primary trade union organizations, without charge, premises for meetings and storage of documents, and provide an opportunity to present information at a location to which all workers have access.

In organizations with over 100 workers, the employer must provide to elected trade union bodies for their utilization, without charge, at least one equipped, heated, and electrified room and office equipment, means of telecommunications, and all necessary regulatory documents. Other amenities for trade union activities, in particular, free provision of transport vehicles, may be provided in the collective agreement.

The employer also may provide to an elected trade union body, in compliance with provisions of the collective agreement, buildings, houses, premises, and any other facilities, including holiday centers and sports and recreational centers, for use without charge. In such cases, trade unions may not charge workers who are not members a higher fee for use of such facilities than that paid by members.

Under Article 17 of the federal law on trade unions, trade unions may readily and without charge obtain information pertaining to social and labor matters from employers, employer associations, state authorities, and local self-government authorities for the purpose of conducting their activities as specified in their charters.

Trade unions may establish educational and scientific and research institutions; train, retrain, and improve the qualifications of trade union staff; and educate trade union workers and members. Trade union educational institutions may be partially financed from certain non-union budgets. Members of trade union bodies who are not already released from their main professional duties, such as authorized representatives for labor protection and representatives on commissions for occupational safety, are released for the purposes of fulfilling their trade union responsibilities and during their short-term trade union training. Terms of their release from their main professional occupation and procedures for payment for the time spent on union work or in training are set out in the collective contract or agreement.[35]

---

[35]Federal law on trade unions, arts. 18, 25

III. Representation by Entities Other Than Unions

See section II.C.1., above.

IV. Redundancy and Transfers of Undertakings

A. Redundancy

As mentioned above, pursuant to Article 81 of the Labor Code, an employment contract may be terminated by the employer in the event of closure of an organization, termination of an individual employer's activities, or in the case of layoffs and staff reductions. At least two months prior to their discharge, workers must be personally notified by the employer and must sign a document acknowledging the notification.[36]

In the event of staff reductions or elimination of staff positions, a preemptive right to keep the job is granted to workers with higher levels of productivity and qualifications. Over and above this provision of the Labor Code, categories of workers who may exercise their preemptive right to keep the job when the productivity and qualifications of workers are equal may be set out in the collective agreement.[37]

Workers who agree to be transferred to a different position in the event of staff reductions or elimination of staff positions may not be dismissed. Also, a worker may not be dismissed during a temporary disability or leave.

When a decision is adopted in connection with staff reductions or eliminations and termination of employment is likely, the employer must notify the elected trade union body in writing no later than two months before appropriate procedures are commenced, and if the decision may lead to a mass dismissal of workers, the notice must be delivered at least three months beforehand.

Mass dismissal criteria are defined in sectoral and municipal agreements. A regulation on the organization of work aimed at employment assistance to workers dismissed *en masse* (No. 99,

---

[36] Labor Code, art. 180.

[37] Labor Code, art. 179.

approved by Resolution of the Government of the Russian Federation and dated February 5, 1993) may also apply. This Regulation stipulates that the main criteria for determining a mass dismissal are the number of workers dismissed and the timeframe of the dismissals. In particular:

- closure of an organization of any form of incorporation with a staff of 15 or more;
- the following staff reduction or elimination of staff positions:
  – 50 or more individuals within 30 calendar days;
  – 200 or more individuals within 60 calendar days;
  – 500 or more individuals within 90 calendar days;
- dismissal of 1 percent of the total number of workers due to closure or staff reductions or eliminations within 30 calendar days in regions where the total number of employed individuals is less than 5,000.

Depending on the economic development characteristics and unemployment level in the region, additional criteria strengthening the social security guarantees for workers may be set forth in order to cope with the mass dismissal. Such additional criteria may be provided by state authorities of constituent regions of the Russian Federation and local self-government authorities.

Dismissal of trade union members due to staff reductions or eliminations is performed in conjunction with the "well-grounded" opinion of an elected trade union body of the organization. For such purposes, the employer, as stipulated in Article 373 of the Labor Code, must submit to the trade union body a draft order and copies of documents explaining the grounds for the decision. The union body must consider the matter and, within seven business days, send its written opinion back to the employer. Any opinion that is not presented within seven days or that is not deemed to be "well-grounded" need not be taken into account by the employer.

If the elected trade union body disagrees with the decision of the employer, it may conduct additional consultations with the employer or its representative within three business days. Results of such consultations are documented in the form of a protocol. If a common agreement is not reached as a result of the consultations, the employer, upon expiration of 10 business days from the date of submission of the draft order and documents to the union, may adopt a final decision. The decision may be appealed to a specific constituent region labor inspectorate, which has 10 days from the date it receives the claim to consider the matter. If the inspectorate finds the dismissal unlawful, it may order the worker's reinstatement, with pay for the period of forced absence from work, and the employer must comply. The filing of a claim with the state labor inspectorate does not preclude the right of a worker or union body to appeal the dismissal directly in court. The employer also may appeal in court the order of the state labor inspectorate.

The employer may terminate an employment contract no later than one month from the date of receipt of a well-grounded opinion of an elected trade union body.

A collective agreement may provide for other procedures for compulsory participation of the elected trade union body in matters pertaining to the termination of an employment contract at the initiative of the employer.[38]

Pursuant to Article 178 of the Labor Code, when an employment contract is terminated due to the closure of an organization or to staff reductions or eliminations, the dismissed worker is paid a severance in the amount of his or her average monthly salary and is also paid his or her average monthly salary while looking for another job, for up to two months from the date of dismissal (including the period for which severance pay is provided). An additional one month's salary is paid to the redundant worker during the third month from the date of dismissal under a decision of the state employment service if, during the first two weeks after dismissal, the worker contacted the state employment service and it failed to employ the worker.

An employment contract or collective agreement may provide for an increased amount of severance pay.

Article 180 of the Labor Code stipulates for the first time in Russian law that an employer, with the written consent of a worker, may terminate an employment contract with the worker without a two-month notice and simultaneously pay an additional severance totaling the two-month average monthly pay of the worker.

---

[38]Labor Code, art. 82.

B. Transfers of Undertakings

Under Article 75 of the Labor Code, when the ownership of an organization changes hands, the new owner may, no later than three months from the date of the transfer, terminate an employment contract with the head of the company, his or her deputy, and the organization's chief accountant. In the event that such an employment contract is terminated, the new owner, as provided in Article 181 of the Labor Code, must pay the aforesaid employees compensation in the amount of no less than three months' worth of their average monthly salary.

A transfer of undertakings may not serve as grounds for the termination of any other employment contracts with workers of the organization. If a worker refuses to continue his or her employment due to the transfer of undertakings, his or her employment contract is deemed terminated due to a change in its material conditions.

The transfer itself is not a legal ground for staff reduction. Staff reduction or the elimination of staff positions may be performed only after state registration of the transferred ownership right, and any reduction in the newly-owned undertaking must occur on its own grounds if and when it is deemed necessary. However, there is some legislative confusion on this point.

In case of consolidation, merger, split up, split off, or transformation of the organization, the prior labor arrangements continue if the worker agrees to such continuation.

V. Wages, Hours, and Leave

A. Wages

Under Article 7 and 37 of the Constitution, everyone has a right to remuneration for his or her labor that should at least amount to the minimum monthly wage provided for in the federal law.

Under the Federal Law dated June 19, 2000 (as amended by the Federal Law dated October 1, 2003), the minimum monthly wage (MMW) in the Russian Federation is 600 rubles, as of October 1, 2003. The MMW does not include bonuses, compensation, social payments, and the like.

Article 133 of the Labor Code stipulates that the MMW may not be lower than the minimal subsistence needed by an individual fit for work. However, under Article 421 of the Labor Code, the order and terms of introduction of such MMW is still to be defined in the form of a federal law.

A worker's wages are deemed to be a remuneration for his or her labor and is contingent upon the worker's qualifications and the difficulty, quality, quantity, and conditions of the work performed. It includes compensation and benefit payments. No limitation may be set on the maximum amount of pay.

The terms of pay provided in the employment contract may not be worse than those set out in the Labor Code, other laws and regulatory acts, or pertinent collective contracts and agreements.[39]

Wages are paid in the currency of the Russian Federation (i.e., in rubles). Under Article 131 of the Labor Code, in conformity with the collective agreement and employment contract and on the basis of a written application of the worker, a portion of the worker's wages may be paid in a form other than cash, but such portion may not exceed 20 percent of the total salary.

According to the general rule, wages are paid at least every half-month on a day determined by the internal rules of the organization, as stipulated in the collective agreement or employment contract. Leave should be paid no later than three days before its commencement date. In the event of termination of the employment contract, all amounts due to the worker must be paid on the date of his or her dismissal (his or her last day of work).

Article 142 of the Labor Code stipulates that in the event of any delay of more than 15 days in the payment of salaries, the worker may, after notification to the employer in writing, suspend his or her work completely until the delayed payment is made, except in cases specified in the Labor Code where work may not be suspended.

Under Article 236 of the Labor Code, if the employer delays wage payments and thereby breaches the schedule for payment, the employer must pay such wages with interest in the amount of no less than 1/300 of the refinancing rate of the Central Bank of

---

[39] Labor Code, art. 135.

Russia on the outstanding amount for each day of the delay. The exact amount of such monetary compensation is set forth in the collective agreement or employment contract.

Any delay in the payment of salaries also is deemed to be a violation of labor legislation and may result in imposition of sanctions on the organization's officers, as provided for in Article 5.27 of the Code for Administrative Offenses, in the form of an administrative fine ranging from 500 to 5,000 rubles. In the event of repeated violations, the sanctions can take the form of disqualification from occupying high positions in the management of an organization (e.g., on a board of directors) for a term of one to three years. Article 145.1 of the Criminal Code of the Russian Federation provides for criminal liability for the nonpayment of salaries for over two months, if the nonpayment is the fault of the top executive and is due to his or her mercenary or other personal interest.

Pursuant to the provisions of the Labor Code, the following workers must be paid an increased amount for their work:

- individuals whose working conditions are deemed to be severe, hazardous, dangerous, or special in any other way;
- individuals working in regions with special climatic conditions;
- individuals performing work in conditions that vary from standard working conditions (when work of various qualifications is performed, when there is a combination of professions, working overtime, night shifts, weekend and national holiday shifts, etc.).

For instance, under Article 152 of the Labor Code, payment for overtime work is at least 1.5 times the normal hourly pay rate for the first two hours and at least twice the normal rate for every hour exceeding the first two. A precise pay rate may be set out in the collective agreement or employment contract. At the request of the worker, overtime may be compensated in the form of additional paid leave instead of the increased pay, but the amount of leave may not be less than amount of overtime.

Pursuant to the Tax Code of the Russian Federation, the salary payable to individuals who are deemed to be taxable residents of the Russian Federation receiving income from a source in the Russian Federation is subject to a flat individual income tax rate of 13 percent.

Employers pay a unified social tax (UST) on their workers' income. Funds derived from the UST are designated for state pensions and social security as well as health insurance. The UST is levied, in particular, on salaries and other remuneration provided to workers under their employment contracts. The UST rate is contingent upon the amount of salary earned each year and is regressive—i.e., applied at a steadily lower rate during the year based on the increasing amount of salary earned, dropping from an initial rate of 35.6 percent down to as low as 2 percent of the tax base. The rates applied in each case depend on the total salary earned during the year.

B. Hours

Federal law limits the number of working hours of all persons who work under an employment contract.[40]

Pursuant to Article 91 of the Labor Code, a standard working week may not exceed 40 hours. For a number of categories of workers, the Labor Code and other federal laws set forth a reduced working schedule.

On the basis of an agreement between the worker and the employer, a part-time working schedule may be set. In such an instance, the worker is paid on a pro rata basis for the time worked or based on the amount of work performed.

Under Article 94 of the Labor Code, daily working hours (daily shift) usually may not exceed eight hours.

Under Article 96 of the Labor Code, the night shift is deemed to include working hours from 10 p.m. to 6 a.m. A night shift is usually one hour less than a day shift. Certain categories of workers may not work at night; some may work night shifts only if they have consented to do so in writing and are not prohibited from doing so by a health condition, as evidenced by a medical report.

Overtime work requested by the employer must be performed on the basis of the worker's written consent and, in certain cases,

---

[40]Constitution, art. 37.

taking into account the opinion of the elected trade union body of the organization. Restrictions applied to overtime work are similar to the ones prescribed for night shifts. Overtime work for each worker may not exceed four hours for every two consecutive days and 120 hours annually.

Work may be organized in shifts when the duration of the production process exceeds the allowed duration of a day shift and for the purposes of more efficient utilization of equipment and increased output of manufactured goods or rendered services. Up to four shifts a day are permitted. The opinion of the representative body of workers must be taken into account when work schedules for various shifts are prepared. No one may work two consecutive shifts.[41]

Pursuant to Article 113 of the Labor Code, as a rule, work is prohibited on weekends or national holidays. In a number of cases, work on weekends or national holidays may be allowed on the basis of the written consent of a worker and the approval of the elected trade union body of the organization. Weekend and holiday work requires a written order from the employer summoning the employees to work.

C. Leave

Pursuant to Article 37 of the Constitution, everyone has a right to rest. Anyone working under an employment contract is guaranteed days off leave on weekends and national holidays as provided for in federal law, as well as paid annual leave. Russia has both working and nonworking national holidays; nonworking holidays (which are observed but do not entitle an employee to a day off from work) are determined by the Labor Code.

Types of rest, as stipulated in Article 107 of the Labor Code, include:

- breaks during the working day (shift);
- daily rest (between shifts);
- days off weekends (weekly consecutive rest);
- nonworking national holidays; and
- annual leave (and additional leaves for rest).

---

[41] *Id.*, art. 103.

Under Article 108 of the Labor Code, during a working day (shift) a worker is entitled to a break for rest and a meal. The break may not exceed two hours and may not be less than 30 minutes, and it is not deemed to be part of the working time.

The duration of a weekly consecutive rest may not be less than 42 hours. All workers are entitled to two days off in a five-day work week, and one day off in a six-day work week.

Eleven nonworking days corresponding with nine national holidays are provided under Article 112 of the Labor Code. When a weekend and a nonworking national holiday coincide, the day off rolls over to the next working day after the national holiday.

Workers are entitled to annual paid leaves, during which their position is kept open and they are paid their average wage. The duration of annual primary paid leave equals 28 calendar days.[42] Additional annual paid leave of various durations is granted to persons working under hazardous and/or dangerous/life-threatening conditions, workers performing special types of work, workers with unfixed working hours, persons working in the extreme northern regions of Russia and other regions that have a similar status, and in other instances specified in federal legislation. National holidays that coincide with the leave are not to be included in the number of calendar leave days.

A paid annual leave must be granted at least every two years (annual leave may accumulate and carry over into the second year). In the event of dismissal, the worker must be paid monetary compensation for all unused leave.

Pursuant to Article 126 of the Labor Code, a portion of the leave exceeding 28 calendar days may at the written request of a worker be replaced with monetary compensation.

Federal laws also provide for study leave, maternity leave, child care leave, leave for workers adopting a child, and so forth. These types of leave are usually only partially paid.

Under Article 170 of the Labor Code and other federal rules, the employer must release a worker from work, keeping his or her job open, for the term a worker is required to perform state duties (e.g., military) or public duties, if such duties must be executed

---

[42]*Id.*, art. 115.

during working hours. A specific state body or public association must pay compensation to the worker for his or her execution of such duties in the prescribed amount.

The worker at his or her written request may be granted an unpaid leave for family or other acceptable reasons. The duration of such leave must be agreed upon between the worker and employer, except that for a number of categories of workers employers are required to grant an unpaid leave.[43]

VI. ANTIDISCRIMINATION

A. Introduction

Pursuant to Article 19 of the Constitution, the state guarantees equal rights and freedoms to all people and citizens regardless of gender, race, nationality, language, origin, property owned, office held, place of residence, religion, opinion, membership in a public association, or other circumstances. Any form of restriction on the rights of citizens is forbidden for social, racial, national, language, or religious reasons. Men and women have equal rights and freedoms and equal opportunities for self-realization.

Article 37 of the Constitution underlines that everyone has a right to remuneration for labor without any discrimination. Discrimination in the field of labor relations is forbidden under Articles 2 and 3 of the Labor Code, which state that everyone is entitled to equal opportunities for realization of labor rights. No one may be restricted in labor rights and freedoms or receive any special advantages based on gender, race, skin color, nationality, language, origin, owned property, social and occupational position, age, place of residence, religion, political views, membership or nonmembership in public associations, or any other circumstances that are not related to business characteristics of a worker.

However, it is not considered discriminatory to establish preferences and restrictions due to requirements relevant for a specific type of work, as provided for in federal law, or resulting from the

---

[43] *Id.*, art. 128.

special governmental provisions for persons who, from a social and legal point of view, need particular protection.

Forced labor is prohibited in Russia.[44] Forced labor is defined as an execution of work under a threat of punishment or other compulsory action, including as a means of discrimination on racial, social, national, or religious grounds.

Article 64 of the Labor Code contains antidiscrimination guarantees with regard to concluding an employment contract, including a prohibition on unjustified refusals to conclude an employment contract and a prohibition on any discrimination when an employment contract is concluded. Article 132 of the Labor Code forbids discrimination in connection with the establishment and modification of wages and other remuneration.

Persons believing they have been discriminated against in the field of labor relations may contact agencies of the federal labor inspectorate and/or go to court to make a claim for restoration of breached rights, reimbursement for damages, and reparation for punitive damages.[45]

B. Protection Envisaged for Certain Categories of Workers

Article 7 of the Constitution declares that the Russian state supports families, maternity, fatherhood and childhood, the disabled, and senior citizens. Under Article 38 of the Constitution, maternity, childhood, and families are protected by the government.

As mentioned above, specification by federal law of differences, preferences, or restrictions of workers' rights with regard to various types of work or in connection with special social and legal protections are not deemed to be discrimination.

An example of specifically protected workers would be the disabled, whose legal status from a labor standpoint is mainly prescribed by the Labor Code, the Federal Law dated November 24, 1995, "On Social Protection of the Disabled in the Russian Federation," and the Law of the Russian Federation "On Employment of the Population in the Russian Federation."

---

[44]Constitution, art. 37; Labor Code, art. 4.
[45]Labor Code, art. 3.

Special restrictions with regard to work have been prescribed for women. There are lists of industries, works, occupations, and positions associated with hazardous and/or dangerous working conditions in which women may work on a restricted basis. There is a weight limit for women as regards lifting and relocating of heavy objects without the use of automated mechanisms.

Under Article 254 of the Labor Code, pregnant women—in accordance with a medical report, and at their request—may require a lighter workload or may be transferred to a different job; however, their average pay remains similar to the one that they were paid at their previous job. During absences for compulsory health check-ups at medical institutions, pregnant women retain their average pay at their place of employment.

Under Article 255 of the Labor Code, women, at their request and in accordance with a medical report, are granted paid maternity leave of 70 calendar days before childbirth (in the event of a multiple pregnancy, 84) and 70 calendar days after childbirth (in the event of complicated childbirth, 86, and when two or more children are born, 110). Such maternity leave is paid for out of the state social security fund.

On request, a woman may be given childcare leave until the child turns three years of age, and in such instance she is paid a social security allowance. While on childcare leave, she may work part-time or at home, but she retains a right to receive the above social security allowance. During the term of the childcare leave, the employer maintains a job for the worker.[46]

Working women with children aged 18 months or younger, in addition to their unpaid rest and meal break, may also be granted fully paid breaks for baby feeding at least every three hours. Such baby-feeding breaks are to last at least 30 minutes, and they may be aggregated and rolled over to the beginning or end of the working day (shift), thus reducing the length of the shift.

Pregnant women and women who have children up to three years of age (and in certain cases older children) or children who are disabled, and women who take care of sick children have certain guarantees with regard to their business travel, overtime work, night shifts, and work on weekends and national holidays.

---

[46]Labor Code, art. 256.

Under Article 261 of the Labor Code, an employment contract with a pregnant woman may not be terminated at the initiative of the employer, except in instances of the closure of an organization. There are material restrictions on the termination of women who have children of up to three years of age, single mothers raising a child of up to 14 years of age (a disabled child of up to 18 years of age), and other persons raising the aforesaid children without a mother.

Persons who take care of disabled children are allowed additional days off and unpaid leave.

Under Article 264 of the Labor Code, guarantees and benefits offered to women in connection with their maternity also apply to single fathers and to guardians (custodians) of minors.[47]

VII. OCCUPATIONAL SAFETY AND HEALTH AND WORKERS' COMPENSATION

A. Occupational Safety and Health

People's working conditions and health are protected in the Russian Federation.[48] Under Article 37 of the Constitution, everyone has a right to work in conditions that meet occupational safety and hygiene standards.

Major regulatory acts in the field of occupational safety and health are the Labor Code and the Federal Law of July 17, 1999, "On the Fundamentals of Labor Protection in the Russian Federation."

The goals of government policy in the occupational safety field include ensuring the priority of life and health of workers, adoption and implementation of federal laws and other regulations on occupational safety and health, state monitoring and enforcement of occupational safety requirements, investigation and accounting of all work-related accidents and occupational diseases, compulsory social insurance of workers against on-the-job accidents and occupational diseases, state participation in the financ-

[47] Labor Code, art. 264.
[48] Constitution, art. 7.

ing of measures associated with occupational safety, and implementation of tax policies stimulating the creation of safe working conditions.

The employer must inform workers of occupational safety standards,[49] and workers must comply with such standards.[50] In order to determine the professional fitness of workers, protect their health, prevent diseases, and for public reasons, workers must undergo a compulsory preliminary (at the hiring stage) checkup; periodic and extraordinary health checkups as well as psychiatric examinations are required for certain categories of workers.

The Labor Code and the federal law on the fundamentals of labor protection contain a detailed description of the right of workers to work under conditions that meet occupational safety and hygiene standards.

The government of the Russian Federation is in charge of labor protection matters, as well as the federal executive body for labor relations (now the Ministry of Public Health and Social Development of the Russian Federation), and executive bodies of constituent regions of the Russian Federation that are in charge of labor protection within the framework of their competence.[51]

The Federal Labor Inspectorate is also an important agency, since it is represented by an integral system of bodies overseeing and controlling compliance with labor laws, including labor protection, and has extensive rights.[52]

Article 217 of the Labor Code specifies that, in order to ensure compliance with occupational safety standards, every organization conducting production activities that employs over 100 workers must set up an occupational safety service and hire an occupational safety specialist.

Any organization without an occupational safety department or specialist must enter into an agreement with experts or organizations providing services related to compliance with occupational safety standards.

---

[49]Labor Code, art. 212.

[50]*Id.*, art. 214.

[51]*Id.*, art. 216.

[52]Labor Code, arts. 353-361, 363-365.

Under Article 218 of the Labor Code, committees (commissions) for occupational safety are to be set up in organizations at the initiative of the employer and/or workers or their representative body. The committees must be staffed in accordance with the principle of equality, with equal numbers of representatives of employers and trade unions, or any other representative body authorized by workers.

Occupational safety measures are generally financed by an amount equaling at least 0.1 percent of all costs in an organization related to the direct production of goods (works, services), and at operating companies in the amount of at least 0.7 percent of the total operating expenses.[53] A worker shall not incur any expenses related to the funding of occupational safety measures or measures aimed at improving working conditions.

There exists administrative and criminal liability for occupational safety violations.

B. Workers' Compensation

Article 220 of the Labor Code declares that in the event of any injuries or harm to the life and health of workers during their execution of job responsibilities, federal law provides for compensation for such injuries or harm. Under Article 184 of the Labor Code, in the event of any injuries to a worker due to an on-the-job accident or an occupational disease, the worker must be reimbursed for lost income and repaid any other expenses related to medical, social, and professional rehabilitation. If an on-the-job accident results in a worker's death, the worker's family must be compensated for related expenses in the same manner. The terms and conditions of provision of workers' guarantees and compensation in the above instances are set forth in the Federal Law of July 24, 1998, "On Compulsory Social Insurance Against On-The-Job Accidents and Occupational Diseases." This federal law took effect together with the enactment of the Federal Law of January 2, 2000, "On Insurance Rates for Compulsory Social Insurance Against On-The-Job Accidents and Occupational Diseases for

[53] Labor Code, art. 226.

2000," which (as amended in 2001) prescribed rates that were extended by federal laws adopted for 2002, 2003, and 2004.

Article 1 of the federal law of 1998 on compulsory social insurance does not restrict the right of insured persons to obtain reparation of damages exceeding insurance coverage offered by the federal law.

Compulsory social insurance against on-the-job accidents and occupational diseases is provided to individuals working under an employment contract or appropriate contracts governed by civil law. Organizations employing such persons must provide coverage for them. The right of insured persons to the insurance indemnity becomes effective on/from the date of an insured accident. The insurance indemnity may be in the form of the following: temporary disability due to an insured accident and payable out of the funds allocated to such social insurance; one-time and monthly insurance payments; payment of additional expenses related to the medical, social, and professional rehabilitation of the insured person in the event of direct consequences of an insured accident (health recovery-related expenses, purchase of medicines, medical and household care, professional training, etc.).

The insurer is deemed to be the Social Security Fund of the Russian Federation, which is responsible for making payments to aforesaid persons. However, any mental distress caused to an insured person in connection with an on-the-job accident or occupational disease must be compensated by the party through whose fault such mental distress occurred.

Funds for compulsory social insurance of workers against on-the-job accidents and occupational diseases are funded by the mandatory insurance contributions of employers. Insurance rates differ for various groups of economic sectors, depending on their professional risk category. Insurance contributions must be paid in addition to payment of the unified social tax (UST).

VIII. PENSIONS AND BENEFITS

A. Pensions

Under Articles 7 and 39 of the Constitution, everyone is guaranteed social insurance adequate to his or her age, in the event of disease or disability, as well as survivors' benefits for the upbringing of children and in other instances prescribed by law. Government pensions and social benefits are prescribed by law.

The Federal Law of July 16, 1999, "On the Fundamentals of Compulsory Social Insurance" defines such social insurance as a part of the state social security system, focused on the insurance of employed citizens against a potential change in their material and social position. This federal law essentially establishes compulsory state insurance.

Types of social security pertaining to the compulsory social insurance include, in particular, old age pensions, disability pensions, and survivors' pensions.

The Federal Law of December 15, 2001, "On Government Pensions in the Russian Federation" describes grounds for entitlement to government pensions and specifies types of such pensions for:

- federal government workers (long-service pension);
- servicemen (long-service pension; disability pension);
- disabled participants in the Second World War (disability pension);
- persons suffering from radiation disasters and other disasters of human origin (old age pension; disability pension);
- individuals unfit for labor (social pension).

Government pensions are paid out of the federal budget. Pensions set out in the aforesaid federal law are granted and paid out regardless of the receipt of the accumulated portion of the workers' pension.

Pursuant to the Federal Law of December 15, 2001, "On Compulsory Pension Insurance in the Russian Federation," insured persons include citizens of the Russian Federation as well as aliens and stateless persons residing in the territory of the Russian Federation who are:

- employed under an employment contract or a contract governed by civil law that involves execution of works or provision of services and working under a licensing agreement;
- self-employed (individual entrepreneurs, private investigators, notaries, attorneys);
- farmers;

- individuals working overseas if they pay their insurance contributions;
- members of tribal and family communities of minority peoples of the North engaged in their traditional trades;
- among other categories of citizens who have entered into legal relationships associated with the compulsory pension insurance pursuant to the aforesaid federal law.

An insured event for the purposes of the above federal law is deemed to be: (a) reaching pensionable age, (b) disability, and (c) loss of the breadwinner (not necessarily a family member).

Companies must file with the Pension Fund of the Russian Federation all information required under the Federal Law of April 1, 1996, "On Individual Personal Accountability in the System of Compulsory Pension Insurance."

For each insured person, the pension fund opens an individual personal account with a permanent insurance number. An individual personal account has three parts: general, special, and professional. The general section of the individual personal account specifies:

- duration of work and other activities included in the insurance record for the purposes of the worker's pension;
- a salary or any other income on which insurance contributions are accrued;
- the total of insurance contributions accrued for the insured person;
- information on the estimated pension capital, including its indexation; and
- information on provision of the worker's pension and its indexing.

The special section of the individual personal account specifies the following information:

- insurance contributions received for the accumulation part of the worker's pension;
- information on the choice of investment portfolio by the insured person (management organization);
- information reflecting accounted-for returns on the invested pension savings;

- information on the transfer of pension savings to a nongovernment pension fund (or back to the Pension Fund of the Russian Federation); and
- amounts paid out of the pension savings funds.

The professional section of an individual personal account specifies additional insurance contributions that are made for insured persons who are covered by the professional pension system, and other similar information.

The Federal Law of December 17, 2001, "On Workers' Pensions in the Russian Federation" explains the grounds and procedures for realization of the right of Russian citizens to receive workers' pensions. The right to receive workers' pensions may be exercised by citizens insured in compliance with the Federal Law "On Compulsory Pension Insurance in the Russian Federation" if those citizens meet the requirements listed in the federal law of December 17, 2001.

In instances provided for in the Federal Law "On Government Pension Insurance in the Russian Federation," an individual may simultaneously receive a government pension and a workers' pension.

There exist the following workers' pensions: old age pension; disability pension; and survivors' pension. Workers' pensions may be comprised of the following: basic portion, insurance portion, and accumulated portion (except a survivors' pension):

- The basic portion of a workers' old age pension is 450 rubles per month. The basic portion of a workers' old age pension is paid out of the funds collected by the unified social tax (UST) entered into and allocated to the federal budget.
- The insurance portion of a workers' old age pension is calculated on the basis of a prescribed formula. The basic portion together with the insurance portion of a workers' old age pension must be at least 660 rubles per month.
- The amount of the accumulated portion of a workers' old age pension is calculated in accordance with its own formula.
- For disability pensions, the amount of the basic portion of a workers' disability pension has also been prescribed (depending on the degree of disability), as are the size of the

> insurance and accumulated portions of the pension, which are calculated on the basis of established formulas. The basic portion, together with the insurance portion of a workers' disability pension, must be at least 660 rubles per month.

It should be noted that, under the Federal Law "On Compulsory Pension Insurance in the Russian Federation," pension insurers may be nongovernment pension funds, together with the Pension Fund of the Russian Federation. Federal legislation prescribes the procedure for formation of pension savings at nongovernment pension funds and for investment of such funds, the procedure for the transfer of pension savings from the Pension Fund of the Russian Federation and payment of insurance contributions to nongovernment pension funds, and the extent to which nongovernment pension funds may exercise the authority of an insurer.

Beginning January 1, 2004, insured persons may, as prescribed by federal law, refuse to receive the accumulated portion of their pension in the Pension Fund of the Russian Federation, and may transfer savings from the special section of their individual personal account to a nongovernment pension fund.

It should be noted that pension legislation of Russia is in a transitional period and has been changing substantially.

B. Health and Social Security Funds

Under Article 41 of the Constitution, everyone has a right to health protection and medical assistance.[54] Medical assistance is offered at federal, constituent region, and municipal medical institutions free of charge and is covered by the funds from insurance contributions and other charges.

Currently the Law of the Russian Federation of June 28, 1991, "On Health Insurance of Citizens of the Russian Federation" is in effect. Under this law, health insurance may be compulsory or voluntary.

Employers provide compulsory health insurance for their workers under contracts with health insurance organizations. Funds of the state system of compulsory health insurance are funded by

[54] Constitution, art. 41.

payments from employers. A portion of the unified social tax (UST) payable by organizations has been allocated for such purposes under provision of the Tax Code of the Russian Federation. Federal and municipal funds for compulsory health insurance have been set up in order to implement government policy on the matter. The funds accumulate financial means designated for compulsory health insurance needs.

The Resolution of the Government of the Russian Federation No. 101 of February 12, 1994, approved Regulations on the Social Security Fund of the Russian Federation. The fund manages the state social security funds. The main objectives of the fund include ensuring payments of government-guaranteed temporary disability benefits, maternity allowances, childbirth benefits, adoption benefits, childcare allowances payable until the child turns one a half years of age, health facilities of workers and their children, and social benefits for funerals. The fund also acts in the capacity of insurer with regard to compulsory social insurance for on-the-job accidents and occupational diseases. The fund's finances come from insurance contributions of employers, paid as a portion of the unified social tax (UST).

IX. IMMIGRATION

A. Introduction

Article 17 of the Constitution declares that rights and freedoms of all persons in the Russian Federation are recognized and guaranteed in the Russian Federation in accordance with generally accepted principles and rules of international law and in compliance with the Constitution.[55]

Under Article 62 of the Constitution, foreign citizens and stateless persons exercise rights and bear responsibilities in the Russian Federation that are equal to those of citizens of the Russian Federation, unless otherwise provided for in the federal laws or international treaties of the Russian Federation.[56]

---

[55] *Id.,* art. 17.
[56] *Id.,* art. 62.

B. Employment of Alien Nationals

Under Article 11 of the Labor Code, in the territory of the Russian Federation all rules of the Labor Code and any other labor laws and regulations are applicable to aliens, stateless persons, organizations established by or with the participation of aliens or stateless persons, and employees of foreign legal entities and international organizations, unless otherwise provided in the federal law or any international treaty of the Russian Federation.[57]

Moreover, the recruitment and hiring of workers in the Russian Federation and the legal status of alien workers in Russia are governed by the Federal Law dated July 25, 2002, "On the Legal Status of Foreign Citizens in the Russian Federation," by decrees of the Russian president, resolutions of the government of the Russian Federation, the resolutions of federal executive bodies adopted in order to ensure implementation of the aforesaid federal law, the Tax Code of the Russian Federation, other federal laws, laws and other regulations of constituent regions of the Russian Federation, and regulations of self-governing authorities adopted within the sphere of their competence.

The federal law on the legal status of foreign citizens defines the employment of an alien in the Russian Federation as his or her employment under a labor agreement or a civil contract (for the execution of work or provisions of service). An alien residing in the Russian Federation and undertaking work in compliance with the established procedure is referred to as an alien employee.

An employer or a contractor of work or services may recruit and hire alien nationals only if they hold an alien employment permit. Such a permit is usually granted by a local internal affairs office based on the findings of a local state employment body.

An alien national seeking to be employed in the Russian Federation needs to obtain a letter of invitation from the inviting party. In cases where the inviting party is a prospective employer (a legal entity), such a letter of invitation will normally be issued by the local internal affairs office. In addition to submitting an application form, the prospective employer provides guarantees of the

---

[57] Labor Code, art. 11.

invitee's financial security and medical and housing arrangements for the period of his or her stay in the Russian Federation.

The Russian Federation approves annual quotas for employment invitations to foreign nationals. The quota is developed from proposals submitted by constituent regions based on the principle of giving priority to domestic labor resources and with due regard to the labor market situation, demographic profile of specific constituent regions, and their foreign employment capacity.

In addition to the application for an employment invitation, the employer submits the following to the internal affairs office:

- employer's alien employment permit; and
- documents required for the issuance of work permits to each alien employee.

Such work permits are issued to the employer for each alien employee, together with a letter of invitation. Only foreign nationals holding valid work permits may be employed in the Russian Federation. A work permit is granted to a foreign national subject to the condition that the employer has transferred a deposit to an account opened for this purpose by the federal internal affairs agency. This deposit should be sufficient to ensure that the alien employee may leave Russia by land, water, or air, as appropriate. The deposit is refunded to the employer upon expiration of the contract and departure of the alien employee from the country. A detailed work permit application procedure and a list of documents to be included with a permit application was approved by Russian Federation Governmental Resolution No. 941 of December 30, 2002.

Foreigners may enter and leave Russia if they have a visa and a valid ID recognized by the Russian authorities. A foreign national may obtain a visa on the basis of an official letter of invitation, among other documents. Foreign workers enter and stay in Russia on the basis of a regular working visa valid for the term of the labor agreement, but not longer than a year (see Article 25.6 of the Federal Law of August 15, 1996, "On the Procedure for Entering the Russian Federation and Leaving the Russian Federation").

When entering Russia, an alien completes a migration card to be presented, together with his or her ID, to an official at the

Russian border checkpoint. When leaving the country, an alien must submit his/her migration card to a border guard official. The border guard official stamps the entry and departure dates in the migration card at the border checkpoint.

After entering the Russian Federation, an alien must register with the local authorities within three business days of the date of entry. For this purpose, a migration card bearing an entry stamp made at the border checkpoint and an ID must be presented.

Upon the arrival of an alien in the Russian Federation, the employer or contractor who has either invited the alien for the purpose of employment or signed a new employment agreement or civil contract for work or services with the alien must:

- possess a valid alien employment permit;
- ensure that the alien obtains a work permit;
- lodge the necessary documents for registration of a foreigner at his/her address in Russia;
- notify the local tax office of the recruitment and hire of foreign employees within 10 days of any of the following: submission of an application for an official employment invitation; arrival of the alien at his/her place of work or stay; issuance to the alien of a work permit; signing of a new labor agreement or civil contract for works or services in Russia with the foreign employee; suspension or revocation of the alien employment permit or the foreign national's work permit;
- assist in the alien's departure from Russia upon expiration of his/her labor agreement or civil contract for works or services;
- bear the costs of expulsion or deportation of the alien from Russia if he/she was employed in violation of the procedure for recruitment and hire of alien employees;
- notify the internal affairs office of any breach by the alien employee of the labor agreement or civil contract for works or services or of early termination of such agreement/contract; and
- notify the internal affairs office and the local state security agency of any unauthorized departure of the alien employee from his/her place of work or stay.

In case of breach of the law by the employer or contractor for works or services, the internal affairs office may suspend its alien employment permit until such time as the breach is remedied within time limits stipulated by the office. Should the employer fail to remedy the breach before the deadline, the internal affairs office will revoke its alien employment permit.

Should the alien employment permit be revoked or the employer or contractor for works or services cease to operate, the foreign worker may enter into a new agreement with a new employer or contractor for works or services for the duration of the work permit, provided the work permit is valid for at least another three months and the new employer or contractor for works or services holds a valid alien employment permit.

Should a foreign employee fail to comply with the terms and conditions of the labor agreement or civil contract for works or services, the issuing internal affairs office may revoke his/her work permit if so requested by the employer or contractor for works or services.

Article 18.10 of the Code of Administrative Offenses describes sanctions that could be imposed on employers and foreign citizens for any breach of the rules regarding the recruitment and hire of foreign workers in the Russian Federation.

UKRAINE*

INTRODUCTION

The second largest republic of the former Soviet Union, and the second largest country in Europe, Ukraine emerged as an independent state in August 1991. Steeped in a rich agricultural tradition and with a deep mineral resource base, Ukraine dominated the agricultural and industrial economy of the USSR before its breakup.

Ukraine extends over 603,700 square kilometers in Eastern Europe. Romania, Hungary, the Slovak Republic, Poland, and Belarus surround the country's northern and western borders. The Black Sea lies along its southern border. With its eastern boundaries along the divide between Europe and Asia, the country is strategically positioned at a global commercial crossroads.

Ukraine is one of the most populous countries in Europe, with 50.1 million inhabitants. There are more than 110 different ethnic groups in Ukraine, with the western portion heavily Ukrainian and the eastern more diverse. Ukraine's industrial and agricultural background guarantees a highly skilled workforce of 22.8 million.

A unicameral parliament, the *Verkhovna Rada*, exercises sole legislative authority in Ukraine. Its 450 parliamentarians are elected for four-year terms. The *Verkhovna Rada* appoints the judges of courts of general jurisdiction, as well as one-third of the justices who sit on the Constitutional Court. It also sets the dates for elections of the President and fulfills other important functions specified by the Constitution. In addition, it possesses certain powers of control over the government, known as the Cabinet of Ministers *(Kabinet Ministriv)*.

---

*Helen Kryshtalowych, Squire, Sanders & Dempsey L.L.P., Kyiv, Ukraine, and Ludmila Pavlenko, The Silecky Firm, PC, affiliated with Squire, Sanders & Dempsey L.L.P., Kyiv, Ukraine.

The President is elected for a five-year term and may be re-elected for one additional term. The President may veto bills passed by *Verkhovna Rada*. Upon the recommendation of the Prime Minister, the President appoints the members of the *Kabinet Ministriv*, which is vested with the executive power of the state. The President also appoints one-third of the justices who sit on the Constitutional Court, represents Ukraine in its foreign relations, and is the supreme commander of the armed forces.

Judicial power in Ukraine is vested in courts of law. The Constitutional Court is the sole body of constitutional jurisdiction. As noted above, the *Verkhovna Rada* and the President each appoint one-third of the Constitutional Court's members. The remaining third are appointed by the congress of judges of Ukraine.

Ukraine is divided into 24 administrative regions, known as *oblasts*, and the Autonomous Republic of Crimea. The cities of Kyiv, the capital of Ukraine, and Sevastopol are subordinated directly to the central government.

A. Historical Development of Labor and Employment Law

The first codified labor law applicable to the territory of Ukraine was the Charter of Industrial Labor, which was adopted in 1913 and included in Volume XI of the Code of Laws of the Russian Empire. In general, the Charter of Industrial Labor codified some of what were known as "factory laws." Factory laws were a variety of laws and regulations that the Russian government adopted in the late 19th and early 20th centuries in response to strikes organized by socialist and social democratic political groups.

The Charter of Industrial Labor incorporated few provisions for the protection of individual workers. Standards established by the Charter included: (1) a work day of 11.5 hours (workers between the ages of 12 and 15 were guaranteed a maximum work day of eight hours); (2) the possibility of unlimited overtime work under an agreement between the employer and employee; and (3) the (non-appealable) right of the employer to fine an employee in an amount of up to one-third of the employee's compensation or to dismiss the employee for the employee's "bad behavior." The Charter made no provision for employee vacation time.

Under the Penal Code in effect at the time, a worker could receive a jail sentence of 4 to 16 months for striking. Social insurance for workers covered only industrial accidents and professional diseases. There was no social insurance coverage for illness caused by general disease, unemployment, or retirement. Agricultural workers had even fewer protections. The Regulations on Employment for Agricultural Workers required such workers to follow their employers' instructions on all work matters. There was no minimum wage and no limit on work hours. Agricultural employers were entitled to fine employees in amounts up to three months' salary.

The Russian Revolution of February 1917, which brought to power the first post-tsar Russian government, did not produce any changes in the labor laws. It was only after the October 1917 Revolution, and especially after the creation of the Soviet Union in 1922, that the new Communist regime undertook to reconstruct the labor laws to suit its economic, social, and ideological requirements.

Thus, the Labor Codes of 1918 and 1922 introduced a new system of labor relations under which work was considered both the privilege and the obligation of every citizen. Workers were organized into workers' collectives and required to join trade unions, which in turn represented workers in their relations with the management of the state-owned enterprises. These Labor Codes established minimum legal guarantees for workers, such as eight-hour work days and comprehensive social insurance.

The Labor Code of 1922 was in effect in Ukraine from December 2, 1922 to June 1, 1972, when it was replaced by the new Labor Code of 1971. The Labor Code of Ukraine, dated December 10, 1971, as amended (Labor Code), was based on the rules and principles of the Foundations of Laws of the USSR and Union Republics on Labor, which had been adopted in 1970 (Labor Law Foundations). The Labor Law Foundations accomplished the goal of unifying Soviet labor law, making it essentially the same for each of the constituent republics of the Soviet Union, including Ukraine.

The Labor Code is still in effect in Ukraine. Beginning in 1998, however, Ukraine's Ministry of Labor coordinated the drafting of a new code purportedly designed to suit the market-based economy that the Ukrainian government has proclaimed as a priority. The draft new Labor Code was submitted for consideration to the *Verhovna Rada* of Ukraine (the Parliament) on August 28, 2003, and was passed in the first reading on December 11, 2003. Currently, the draft is being worked out by the Committee on Social Policy and Labor to be submitted to the second reading by the *Verhovna Rada* of Ukraine. The current Labor Code, designed in the Soviet era of a controlled economy, fails in many respects to meet the needs of a market economy. Both employers and employees, therefore, are eagerly awaiting the new code.

Following Ukraine's independence in 1991, labor law has been the subject of continual reform. Though often incomplete and inconsistent, such reform, as described below, is evidenced by a series of newly adopted laws, as well as by numerous amendments to existing laws and regulations, including the Labor Code.

B. Sources of Ukrainian Labor and Employment Law

1. National Sources of Law

a. Constitution

The Constitution of Ukraine, dated June 28, 1996, is the highest source of Ukrainian labor law. The Constitution guarantees each citizen such basic employment rights as the right to safe working conditions and the right to receive a minimum wage. The Constitution also protects workers from illegal layoffs, recognizes the right to strike, provides for a limitation on working time, and establishes that workers shall be entitled to unemployment insurance.

The legal status of the President, the Speaker of the Parliament and other Parliamentary officials, people's deputies, the Prime Minister and members of the Cabinet, the justices of the Constitutional and Supreme Courts, and the Prosecutor General are established and regulated by the Constitution as well as more specific laws.[1]

---

[1]*See, e.g.*, Law on the Constitutional Court of Ukraine (Oct. 16, 1996), as amended; Law on the Status of a People's Deputy of Ukraine (Nov. 17, 1992), as amended; Law on the Prosecutor's Office (Nov. 5, 1991), as amended.

b. Labor Laws and Regulations

While the Constitution's guarantees are stated in general terms, the Labor Code[2] is the more specific primary source of labor law. It remains the basic source of legal regulation of employment relations in Ukraine. The Labor Code is a comprehensive set of rules relating to practically all aspects of relations between employers and employees in Ukraine. It governs employment agreements and employment contracts, working hours, vacations, days off, compensation, social benefits, discipline, employment of women and minors, resolution of employment disputes, and the respective liabilities of employees and employers.

The Labor Code is implemented through or together with other labor laws and regulations, including but not limited to the Pension Law,[3] the Collective Dispute Law,[4] the Compensation Law,[5] the Vacation Law,[6] the Labor Protection Law,[7] the Collective Agreement Law,[8] the Employment Law,[9] the Employment Contract Resolution,[10] and the Labor Book Regulations.[11]

c. State Service Law

The Labor Code is applicable to any employment relationship, including public employment. However, certain of its provisions are superseded by more specific provisions in the State Service Law,[12] which pertains to state servants. State servants are persons employed by state bodies to implement state functions and whose salaries are paid from the state budget.[13] State servants

---

[2]Labor Code of Ukraine (Dec. 10, 1971), as amended.

[3]Law on Pension Security (Nov. 5, 1991), as amended.

[4]Law on the Order of Resolution of Collective Labor Disputes (Conflicts) (Mar. 3, 1998).

[5]Law on Wages (Mar. 24, 1995), as amended.

[6]Law on Vacations (Nov.15, 1996), as amended.

[7]Law on Protection of Labor (Oct. 14, 1992), as amended.

[8]Law on Collective Agreements (July 1, 1993), as amended.

[9]Law on Employment of Population (Mar. 1, 1991), as amended.

[10]Resolution of the Cabinet of Ministers of Ukraine on Application of Contract Form of the Employment Agreement No. 170 (Mar. 19, 1994).

[11]Regulations on Maintaining Labor Books of Employees, approved by the Joint Order of the Ministries of Labor, Justice, and Social Protection of Population No. 58 (July 29, 1993).

[12]Law on State Service (Dec. 16, 1993), as amended (State Service Law).

[13]State Service Law art. 1.

are ranked on a scale from 1 (the highest rank) to 15 (the lowest rank), depending on the category of the position (ranging from 1 (the highest position) to 7 (the lowest position)) that they occupy. State servants' base salaries and employment benefits depend on their ranking and the category of occupied position.

Under the State Service Law, a state servant is entitled, in addition to his or her base salary, to the following:

- additional compensation depending on seniority and performance;
- basic vacation of 30 calendar days and additional vacation of up to 15 days for those serving more than 10 years;
- free housing and interest-free loans for the purchase of a home;
- free medical care in state-owned medical centers; and
- a basic pension in the amount of 80 percent of his or her salary, plus additional pension benefits equal to 1 percent for each year worked after the first 10 years of employment (up to a maximum pension of 90 percent).

State servants are required to disclose their income and financial obligations on an annual basis. In addition to the general disciplinary measures allowed by the Labor Code, the State Service Law provides for official notice of nonfitness and withholding of promotion to the next rank or position as disciplinary measures. State servants also are prohibited from striking. Before taking office, a state servant must take an oath of loyalty in writing. Finally, state servants are not allowed to commit certain actions that are legally defined as "corruption."[14]

d. Civil Code

While the Labor Code applies to employment relationships, labor relations in a broader sense (for example, under agency or contractors' agreements) are regulated by civil law. Thus, effective January 1, 2004, the new Civil Code of Ukraine[15] provides

---

[14]A list of corrupt actions and types of liability are discussed under the Law on the Fight Against Corruption (Oct. 5, 1995), as amended.

[15]Civil Code of Ukraine (Jan. 16, 2003) (Civil Code).

rules regulating the relations of client and contractor, including, but not limited to, their respective rights, duties, and liabilities; the terms for payment; the statute of limitations; and the grounds for invalidating a contractor's agreement.[16]

2. *International Sources of Law*

As a member of the International Labor Organization (ILO), Ukraine has signed and ratified a number of ILO conventions that supersede conflicting provisions of Ukraine's domestic labor laws.[17]

Ukraine also has entered into a number of bilateral and multilateral international agreements that contain provisions on labor, employment, and social protection. Ukraine is party to bilateral agreements of this type with, among others, Armenia, Azerbaijan, Belarus, the Czech Republic, Estonia, Lithuania, the Russian Federation, the Slovak Republic, Spain, and Vietnam, and to multilateral conventions with members of the Commonwealth of Independent States.

3. *Conflicts of Law*

The Labor Code contains a conflict of law rule designed to determine the law applicable to the labor relations of Ukrainian nationals working abroad and foreign nationals working in Ukraine. Under the Labor Code rule, such relations are governed by the law of the country where the employment relations are established.[18] Thus, foreign nationals working in Ukraine are subject to Ukrainian law if their employment contracts are made in Ukraine.

The Labor Code does not provide a conflict of law rule in regard to Ukrainian nationals employed by foreign employers in Ukraine. However, under general choice of law principles, such employment normally would be regulated by Ukrainian law.

International bilateral or multilateral agreements into which Ukraine has entered may provide other conflict of law rules. Generally, under Ukrainian law, such conflict of law rules supersede

---

[16]*See* Civil Code chs. 16, 19, 47, 48, 50–53, 61–63, 68.

[17]Labor Code art. 8-1. For information on ILO conventions, see the chapter on the ILO in Volume I, Part 4.

[18]Labor Code art. 8.

the general rule provided by the Labor Code.[19] Thus, for example, under the agreement between Ukraine and the Czech Republic,[20] labor relations are governed by the law of the country where the services are performed.

C. The State's Powers

Generally, the state has extensive powers in labor relations with regard to, among other matters, the labor market, unemployment, social insurance, labor safety, standard employment conditions, and the resolution of labor disputes. The state's employment policy is set forth in the Employment Program[21] and the Employment Law.[22] The Employment Program contains a detailed analysis of the labor market, outlines the latest trends in employment in Ukraine, and determines the basic principles of Ukraine's employment policy.

Through the Employment Law, Ukraine guarantees to each citizen of working age the following rights:

- freedom to work and to choose a profession;
- protection from unreasonable rejection of an employment application or from illegal termination of employment;
- free assistance in locating a position according to the individual's education and professional training;
- severance pay when a job is lost due to reorganization or the elimination of the position;
- free training while unemployed;
- unemployment compensation; and
- employment in a state-owned entity for at least three years immediately following graduation from a state educational institution.[23]

---

[19]*Id.* art. 8-1.

[20]Agreement Between Ukraine and the Czech Republic on Mutual Employment of Citizens of Ukraine and the Czech Republic (Mar. 21, 1996).

[21]Program for Employment of Population in 1997–2000, approved by the Cabinet of Ministers of Ukraine (Dec. 31, 1996).

[22]Law on Employment of Population (Mar. 1, 1991), as amended (Employment Law).

[23]Employment Law art. 4.

The state provides additional employment guarantees to certain categories of citizens, including women with children younger than the age of six, single mothers with children who are disabled or younger than the age of 14, senior citizens of preretirement age, and persons released from imprisonment.[24]

Primary responsibility for the implementation of state labor and employment policy rests with the Ministry of Labor and Social Policy of Ukraine (Ministry of Labor), the State Center for Employment, the Research Center for Employment of Population and Employment Market of the National Academy of Sciences, and their respective local branches (collectively, State Employment Agencies). Among other functions, the State Employment Agencies accumulate and process statistical and operational information, assist citizens in finding employment, organize professional training, and pay unemployment compensation. The State Employment Agencies are entitled to: (1) receive employment information from any business entity; (2) suggest quotas for employment of persons requiring social protection; (3) collect mandatory payments to the Unemployment Fund from employers and employees; and (4) impose fines for violation of the employment laws and regulations.[25]

D. Resolution of Labor Disputes

Individual labor disputes between an employer and an employee are resolved through a two-tier system that includes: (1) labor dispute committees within companies, and (2) courts of general jurisdiction.

Labor dispute committees are elected by the labor collectives[26] of companies with at least 15 employees. For such companies, labor dispute committees are mandatory bodies of first resort for all labor disputes, with the exception of the following claims:

- by an employee with regard to the termination of an employment agreement,

---

[24]*See id.* art. 5.
[25]*Id.* art. 18.
[26]For an explanation of labor collectives, see III., below.

- by managers and officers with regard to termination and disciplinary measures,
- by the employer with regard to damages caused by an employee, and
- by a citizen whose employment application was rejected.

The above-listed claims must be submitted directly to the people's courts of general jurisdiction (district courts or city courts). These courts also accept appeals from decisions of labor dispute committees.[27]

As discussed below, different procedures govern the resolution of collective labor disputes between an employer and a trade union or other group organized to represent employees.[28]

I. INDIVIDUAL EMPLOYMENT

A. Creation of the Employment Relationship

According to Ukrainian law, certain jobs may be performed either under an employment agreement (or, as discussed below, an employment contract) between an employer and an employee, which is governed by Ukrainian labor law, or under a contractor's agreement between a client and a contractor, which is governed by Ukrainian civil law. As a matter of practice, many issues may arise regarding the application of the Labor Code or the Civil Code to certain labor relations. Therefore, it is important to distinguish an employment agreement or employment contract from a contractor's agreement.

1. The Employment Agreement (and Employment Contract) Distinguished From the Contractor's Agreement

Under Ukrainian law, employment agreements and employment contracts differ from contractors' agreements in the following ways:

- A contractor's agreement, as a rule, must provide for a specific assignment from a client to a contractor defining the

[27]*See* Labor Code arts. 221, 223, 231, and 232.

[28]See II.G. and II.H., below.

scope of work or services to be performed. An employment agreement or employment contract provides for more continuous and systematic work or services to be performed by an employee occupying a specific position within a company.

- A contractor works independently and at his or her own risk. An employee, however, must follow the internal rules and regulations of the employer in the course of fulfilling obligations under an employment agreement or employment contract.
- The performance by a contractor of certain work or services may be recognized as an entrepreneurial activity under Ukrainian law, and, therefore, a contractor may have to register and be licensed as an entrepreneur and as a participant in foreign economic activities (the latter may be required when the client is a foreign entity). Work performed by an employee is not regarded as entrepreneurial.
- A contractor receives payment upon completion of a job or service. An employee receives compensation (which may not be less than a certain minimum rate established by law) on a regular basis during the term of employment.
- To enter into an employment agreement or employment contract, an employee must submit his or her employment record (the so-called "labor book") to the employer, who then is obligated to maintain the labor book during the employment period. A client, in contrast, has no obligations with respect to a contractor's labor book.
- An employer, under an employment agreement or under the Labor Code, may be obligated to provide a two-month termination notice to an employee (if the termination is due to liquidation or reorganization), make severance payments, maintain working hours within established limits, provide vacation time and "rest time," and make payments to the Social Insurance Fund and the Unemployment Fund.[29] A client does not have these obligations.

[29]An employer under an employment contract may have certain additional obligations, such as to provide an employee with a two-week termination notice when the dismissal is due to the employee's breach. The differences between employment agreements and employment contracts are discussed in more detail at I.A.2., below.

Despite the above-noted differences, both an employer and a client are required to make contributions to the Pension Fund of Ukraine.[30]

Although the above comparison illustrates that a contractor's agreement imposes fewer obligations on the client than an employment agreement imposes on the employer, it bears emphasis that a contractor's agreement may be used only where the work to be performed is clearly defined, not subject to the client's supervision, and restricted to the completion of a specific task. Contractors' agreements may not be used for regular labor arrangements where the work is repetitive, continuous, and functional, rather than singular and directed toward a specific result.

2. *The Employment Agreement Distinguished From the Employment Contract*

The Labor Code distinguishes between an employment agreement and an employment contract. An employment contract, according to the Labor Code and the Employment Contract Resolution, is a special form of an employment agreement and may be used only where expressly permitted by law.[31] An employment contract may be entered into only for a definite term or until a specific job is completed. An employment agreement, in contrast, may be concluded in oral form and may be for an indefinite term.

a. Employment Contracts

The law expressly permits the use of employment contracts with certain employees, including, without limitation, the managing director of an enterprise,[32] employees of a commodity exchange,[33] associate attorneys,[34] employees of educational institu-

---

[30]See VIII.A.2., below.

[31]Labor Code art. 21; Resolution of the Cabinet of Ministers of Ukraine on Application of Contract Form of the Employment Agreement No. 170, art. 1 (Mar. 19, 1994) (Employment Contract Resolution).

[32]Commercial Code of Ukraine, art. 65 (Jan. 16, 2003) (Commercial Code).

[33]Law on Commodity Exchange, art. 12 (Dec. 10, 1991), as amended.

[34]Law on Advokatura, art. 8 (Dec. 19, 1992), as amended.

tions,[35] researchers in the area of science and technology,[36] personnel of medical and educational institutions who are employed in contaminated areas due to the Chornobyl accident,[37] professional athletes,[38] and athletes of Ukrainian national teams.[39] For other employees, the restrictive provisions of the regulations and the lack of further clarification in the law "expressly permitting" the contract form[40] create a risk that a court may invalidate a disputed contract for nonconformity with legal requirements. Therefore, if the employment contract is contemplated for positions other than those expressly permitted by law, the more traditional form of an employment agreement will help to avoid these risks and bring more certainty to the employment relationship.

Generally, an employment contract allows the parties more discretion in determining their respective rights and duties, including those as to working conditions, termination, compensation, and benefits. In other words, the parties to an employment contract may include provisions that differ from those prescribed by the Labor Code. A contract usually provides various benefits to an employee as compensation for the contract's limited duration. Such benefits may include, for example, a longer annual vacation and more flexible working hours than the respective standards provided by the Labor Code. Neither a contract nor an agreement may diminish the employment guarantees provided by the Labor Code, other labor laws and regulations, or applicable collective agreements.[41]

An employment contract must be in writing. Either party may terminate an employment contract if the other party defaults, provided that the nondefaulting party provides a two-week termination notice. As discussed in more detail below, under an employ-

---

[35] *E.g.,* Law on Education, arts. 20, 54 (May 23, 1991), as amended.

[36] Law on Scientific and Technical Activity, arts. 1, 24 (Dec. 13, 1991).

[37] Law on the Status and Social Protection of Citizens Affected by Chornobyl Accident, art. 42 (Feb. 28, 1991), as amended.

[38] Law on Physical Culture and Sport, art. 23-3 (Dec. 24, 1993), as amended.

[39] Resolution of the Cabinet of Ministers on Material Support in Sport Activities, art. 4 (Feb. 6, 1992).

[40] *See* Decision of the Constitutional Court of Ukraine on Official Interpretation of Article 21, Chapter III of the Labor Code (July 9, 1998).

[41] Labor Code art. 9; Law on Collective Agreements, art. 5 (July 1, 1993), as amended (Collective Agreement Law).

ment agreement, the employee may terminate the agreement upon two-weeks' notice, while the employer must provide two-months' notice where the termination is due to liquidation, reduction in force, or reorganization.

b. Employment Agreements

The majority of employment relationships are based on employment agreements. An employee may enter into employment agreements with one or more employers, unless otherwise provided by law. An employee may be covered by a collective agreement, as well as an employment agreement. In this circumstance, the collective agreement establishes most terms of the work arrangement,[42] while the employment agreement describes the specifics applicable to the employee's particular position.

In certain cases, when specifically stipulated by law, an employee may be required to comply with minimum requirements concerning age, education, or health.[43] In addition, the Labor Code permits an employer to establish limitations as to employment of close relatives (such as parents, spouses, siblings, children of an employee), if such relatives and an employee are subordinate to each other.[44] Generally, an employee must perform the duties under the employment agreement personally and may not assign it to any other person unless otherwise provided by law.[45]

When entering into an employment agreement, an employee must submit his or her passport or other identification document and labor book. In certain circumstances, the employee also may be required to submit an educational or training diploma, a health certificate, or other documents.

Employment agreements may be either permanent (for an indefinite term) or temporary (for a defined period or until completion of a specific task).[46] If the agreement is temporary, the employer may terminate it at the end of the specified term without cause. If the agreement is permanent, the employer may terminate

---

[42]See II., below.

[43]Labor Code art. 22.

[44]*Id.* art. 25-1.

[45]*Id.* art. 30.

[46]*Id.* art. 23.

it only upon a specific ground set forth in the Labor Code, such as, for example, the employer's liquidation or the employee's absenteeism.[47]

An employment agreement may be written or oral.[48] It must be in writing in the following cases:

- for an organized public recruitment of employees for a specific position or project,
- for a job in regions with extreme climates or with hazardous health conditions,
- upon the employee's request,
- if the employee is a minor, or
- if the employer is a natural person.

Where the employer is a natural person, the employment agreement must be registered with the state employment authority within one week of the job start date.[49]

As a rule, an employer issues an administrative order on the basis of an employment agreement. An administrative order specifies the employee's name, position, salary, and start date.

B. Probation

An employer and employee may agree to a probationary period (which should be specified at the time of hiring) to ascertain that the new employee is fit for the job. As a general rule, the probationary period may not exceed three months. However, in specific cases, with the approval of the trade union committee (if there is one), the law allows a probationary period of up to six months. The probationary period for physical laborers, as defined in the applicable regulations, may not exceed one month.[50] Ukraine's labor laws apply equally to probationary employees.

If, in the course of the probationary period, the employer finds the employee to be unfit for the job, the employment agreement may be terminated. If the probationary period ends and the em-

---

[47]See I.F.3., below.
[48]Labor Code art. 24.
[49]*Id.* art. 24-1.
[50]*Id.* art. 27.

ployee continues to work, the employee is considered to have passed the probationary test. From that period on, termination of the employment agreement may be accomplished only as provided in the Labor Code.[51]

Probationary periods may not be established for:

- persons younger than 18 years of age,
- young employees who have graduated from vocational educational institutions,
- young specialists who have graduated from higher educational institutions, or
- persons discharged from the military or alternative (non-military) service.

In addition, employers may not impose a probationary period on employees who agree to move to a different employment location, and in certain other cases provided by law.[52]

C. Hiring Commitments of the Employer

The Labor Code requires an employer to undertake several actions prior to hiring an employee. In particular, the employer must:

- explain to the employee his or her rights and obligations, provide information about working conditions, detail the presence of potentially hazardous and harmful working conditions and their associated health risks, and describe the employee's benefits and compensation;
- explain all of its internal rules and regulations;
- assign a workplace and provide all required tools; and
- instruct the employee on safety precautions, sanitation, hygiene, and fire protection measures.[53]

---

[51]*Id.* art. 28.
[52]*See id.* art. 26.
[53]*Id.* art. 29.

D. Additional Requirements

The law permits an employer to modify substantially the labor conditions of its employees if it reorganizes its work or production and if employees continue in the same position with the same qualifications. Thus, an employer may, among other things, adjust salaries and wages, benefits, and work schedules, and introduce or eliminate partial working days. Employees must be notified of any changes at least two months prior to their implementation. If employees object to modified labor conditions, the employment agreement may be terminated.[54]

Under Ukrainian labor law, an employer may not require an employee to perform work not specified in the employment agreement.[55] However, an employer may transfer an employee to another position or to another location if the employee consents. (Employee consent is not required for temporary moves that are operational necessities.) In addition, an employer may move an employee to another job in the same office for a period of up to one month, so long as the remuneration for the work to be performed is not less than the average wage that the employee received during the two calendar months (12 calendar months for seasonal workers) immediately preceding the transfer.[56] If the new work is an operational necessity and the employee refuses to perform it without a valid reason, the employer may discipline the employee.[57]

E. Maintaining Labor Books

A labor book, required by the Labor Code,[58] is an employee's primary official employment document. It must be maintained by

[54]*Id.* art. 32.

[55]*Id.* art. 31.

[56]Procedure for Calculation of Average Salary, secs. 2 and 8, approved by Resolution of the Cabinet of Ministers No. 100 (Feb. 8, 1995), as amended (Average Salary Regulations).

[57]See I.H., below.

[58]Labor Code art. 48. Detailed rules for maintaining labor books are contained in Regulations on Maintaining Labor Books of Employees, approved by the Joint Order of the Ministries of Labor, Justice, and Social Protection of Population No. 58 (July 29, 1993) (Labor Book Regulations).

the employer. Labor books contain information on the work performed and on work incentives and awards. Labor books also are used to document employees' entitlement to pensions and other social benefits.[59] The employer must make the required entries in the labor book within five days after hiring a new employee.

Under the Labor Book Regulations,[60] labor books of Ukrainian employees hired by a representative office of foreign entities or other foreign employers in Ukraine (depending on the employer's location) must be processed either by the General Department for Kyiv State Administration for Servicing Foreign Representative Offices (*GDIP* under its Ukrainian acronym), its Yalta branch in the Autonomous Republic of Crimea, foreign relations departments of regional state administrations, or Ukrainian entities selected by the regional state administrations, or the State Administration of the City of Sevastopol. Records in labor books made by a representative office or another foreign employer itself shall be invalid.

F. Termination of Employment

1. General

Under the Labor Code, employment relationships may be terminated upon:

- the agreement of the parties;
- expiration of the term of the employment agreement (except where the employee continues to work and neither party demands termination);
- entry of the employee into military or alternative nonmilitary service;
- the employee's initiative, the employer's initiative, or the initiative of the trade union (if any);
- the transfer of an employee, with his or her consent, to another company or to an elected position;

---

[59]See VIII., below.

[60]See Joint Order of the Ministry of Labor and Social Policy and the Ministry of Justice of Ukraine on Amending Section 2.20 of the Regulations on Maintaining Labor Books of Employees (Sept. 24, 2003).

- the employee's refusal to move to another location or refusal to continue work because of a change in a principal labor condition;
- a court decision sentencing the employee to correctional work away from the workplace or imposing some other punishment that makes further employment impossible; or
- any reason specified in an employment contract.[61]

2. Employee's Termination of the Employment Agreement

As a general rule, an employee has the right to terminate his or her permanent employment agreement without reason upon two-weeks' notice.

An employee may terminate with less than two-weeks' notice for any of the following reasons:

- move to a different location;
- transfer of a spouse to a different work location;
- entrance to an educational institution;
- move for medical reasons;
- pregnancy;
- care of a child who is younger than the age of 14 or disabled;
- care of a sick family member;
- retirement;
- failure of the employer to comply with labor protection laws;
- other employment won on a competitive basis; or
- another reason that prevents the employee from working.

In addition, an employee is entitled to terminate an employment agreement upon less than two weeks' notice if the employer violates the labor laws or the terms of the employment agreement or collective agreement.[62]

If an employee continues to work beyond the termination date set forth in the termination notice and does not insist on termination, the employer may not dismiss the employee on the basis of the expired termination notice except where a new employee has been hired to fill the same position.

[61]Labor Code art. 36.
[62]*Id.* art. 38.

An employee may terminate a temporary employment agreement if an illness or disability impedes his or her work under the agreement, or if the employer violates the labor laws, the employment agreement, or the collective agreement, or for any of the other reasons listed above for the termination of a permanent employment agreement.[63]

A temporary employment agreement is deemed to be renewed for an indefinite period if the employee continues to work after its expiration and neither party demands termination.[64]

3. *Employer's Termination of the Employment Agreement*

An employer may terminate an employment agreement (permanent or temporary) only upon the specific grounds set forth in the Labor Code.[65] These grounds are as follows:

a. the liquidation, reorganization, bankruptcy, or restructuring of the entity, including staff reductions;
b. unsuitable employment qualifications or physical condition of the employee;
c. systematic and inexcusable failure of the employee to observe the requirements of the employment agreement or the employer's internal rules and regulations following prior disciplinary action;
d. unjustified absence from work (including absence for more than three hours during the work day);
e. failure to report to work for more than four months as a result of a temporary disability (not including maternity leave), where the law does not provide an extension for the particular illness;[66]
f. reinstatement of the individual who formerly performed the employee's work;

---

[63] *Id.* art. 39.

[64] *Id.* art. 39-1.

[65] *Id.* arts. 40, 41. *See* Law of Ukraine on Amending Articles 41 and 134 of the Labor Code of Ukraine (Oct. 17, 2002).

[66] For example, a position will be reserved for an employee who is unable to work because of a work-related injury or illness until such time as the employee is able to work again or is diagnosed as permanently disabled. Labor Code art. 40. See also VII.B., below.

g. drunkenness on the job or public intoxication caused by drugs or other intoxicants;
h. conviction for theft by a court of competent jurisdiction;
i. where the employee is a general manager, chief accountant, or the deputy of such, or an officer of a state customs or tax authority, a single severe violation of labor commitments established under labor laws and regulations or an employment agreement;
j. where the employee is responsible for money or other material assets or carries out supervisory functions, dishonest actions that cause the employer to lose confidence in the employee, or
k. in the case of an employee who is a general manager, actions that cause (1) a failure of the timely payment of wages to employees, or (2) payment of wages in an amount that is less than the minimum wage set forth by Ukrainian law.

An employee may be dismissed for the reasons listed under items *a*, *b*, and *f* above only if the employer is unable to transfer the employee, with his or her consent, to another job.

An employee may be dismissed for reasons of reorganization and staff reduction and for the reasons listed under items *b* through *e*, *g*, *i*, and *j* above, only with the prior consent of the trade union committee created within the company unless (1) a trade union committee has not been created, (2) the employee is not a member of the trade union, (3) the termination is due to liquidation of the company, or (4) the law provides otherwise.[67]

An employee may not be dismissed while on vacation or while temporarily disabled (except on the grounds noted under item *e* above). However, this restriction does not apply in case of the full liquidation of the company.[68]

The employer must provide a two-month notice to an employee who is to be terminated for reasons of liquidation, staff reduction, or reorganization. There appear to be no other notice

[67]Labor Code art. 43. See also IV.A., below.

[68]Labor Code art. 40.

requirements for an employer terminating an employment agreement.

4. *Dismissal Order and Return of Labor Book*

An employer is obligated to return the employee's labor book to the dismissed employee, complete with all required registrations. When a dismissal occurs upon the employer's initiative, the employer also must present a copy of the dismissal order. In all other cases, a copy of the dismissal order must be issued upon the employee's demand. At the request of the employee, the employer must prepare a certificate containing information on the employee's profession, position, term of employment, and salary.[69]

G. Severance Payment

The Labor Code requires an employer to make a severance payment under certain circumstances. Specifically, an employee is entitled to a severance payment in an amount not less than one month's average wage[70] in the following cases:

- the employment agreement is terminated due to the employee's refusal to transfer to a different location;
- the employee refuses to continue work after changes in labor conditions, or after liquidation, reorganization, or production restructuring;
- the employee's dismissal is for reasons of unsuitable qualifications or poor health; or
- the employer reinstates the person who formerly performed the job.

If the employment agreement is terminated because the employee enters the military or alternative nonmilitary service, the employee is entitled to severance pay equal to at least two months' average wages. If the employee is terminated because the employer violated the labor laws or regulations, the employment agreement

---

[69] *Id.* art. 49.

[70] For the definition of average wage, see I.D., above.

or the collective agreement, the employee is entitled to severance pay of not less than three months' average wages.[71]

Special rules are established for severance payments in the case of termination due to liquidation, staff reduction, or reorganization.[72]

Under the Labor Code, severance payments must be made on the day of dismissal. If the employee is absent from work on the day of dismissal, then the severance amount must be paid not later than one day from the employee's demand for payment.

H. Disciplinary Measures

Under the Labor Code, only a reprimand and the termination of an employment agreement are allowed as disciplinary measures against an employee, unless otherwise provided by other applicable labor laws and regulations.[73]

I. Employee's Liability to the Employer

An employee may be held liable to the employer for direct actual damage caused by the employee's violation of work duties through a willful or negligent unlawful act or failure to act. This liability, as a rule, is limited to the amount of the damage or the employee's average monthly wage, whichever is smaller. An employee does not bear responsibility for damage related to normal operational and economic risks, for lost profits, or for damage caused while performing work of paramount necessity.

An employee will bear responsibility for the full amount of the damage under certain circumstances, including the following:

- the employee assumes in writing full responsibility for failure to secure property and other valuables;
- property or other valuables are consigned to the employee under a power of attorney;

---

[71]Labor Code art. 44.

[72]See IV., below.

[73]Labor Code art. 147. The State Service Law permits additional disciplinary measures for public employees. See the Introduction, at B.1.c., above.

- the damage is caused by the employee's criminal actions;
- the employee causes the damage while drunk;
- the employee willfully damages raw materials, manufactured products, a work uniform, or any other property received from the employer;
- the employee's full responsibility for the damage is established by law;
- the employee causes the damage when off-duty or during working hours when not performing work required under the employment agreement;
- the employee is the officer responsible for the unlawful dismissal or transfer of a subordinate employee; or
- the employee is a general manager of a company and fails to pay wages to the employees for a period of more than one month, provided that the State and local budgets and state-owned entities did not have arrears to the company.[74]

Once it is proved that the employee's willful or negligent misconduct caused the damage, the employer may deduct the amount of damage from the employee's wages, so long as the amount does not exceed the employee's average monthly wage. If the damage amount exceeds the employee's average monthly wage, or if the employer's deduction thereof is not possible (e.g., when the employment agreement is terminated), the employer may bring a lawsuit against the employee.[75] The statute of limitation for an employer's damage action against an employee is one year from the time the employer learns of the damage.

J. Privacy

When entering into an employment agreement, an employee must submit his or her passport or other identification document and a labor book. In certain cases, the employee also may be required to submit an educational or training diploma, a health cer-

---

[74]*See* Law of Ukraine on Amending Articles 41 and 134 of the Labor Code of Ukraine (Oct. 17, 2002).

[75]Labor Code arts.130, 132–134, 136, and 233. *See also* Resolution of the Supreme Court of Ukraine No. 14 (Dec. 29, 1992); Law of Ukraine on Amending Articles 41 and 134 of the Labor Code of Ukraine (Oct. 17, 2002).

tificate, or other documents.[76] An employee may not be asked information about his or her nationality, origin, or membership in a political party, and may not be requested to present documents the submission of which is not specified by the law.[77]

Generally, medical and psychiatric screening and drug and alcohol testing may not be requested by the employer unless it is required by law for certain professions.[78] Professions that require pre-employment and regular post-employment medical screening are determined by the Ministry of Health Protection of Ukraine.[79] Employers are liable for the timely mandatory medical screening of such employees and for the harmful consequences caused from employees who are allowed to work without passing the mandatory medical testing.[80] An employer also must have employees younger than age 21 take an annual medical screening at the employer's expense.[81] An employer is not allowed to disclose the information about the results of medical testing of its employees.[82]

K. Employee Duty of Loyalty, Trade Secrets, Covenants Not to Compete

1. *Employee Duty of Loyalty*

Employees have an obligation to be loyal to their employer, to look after the employer's interest, and to perform work in a

---

[76]See I.A.2.b., above.

[77]Labor Code art. 25.

[78]Civil Code, art. 286.

[79]*Id.* art. 169; List of Professions and Occupations in which Employees are Subject to the Mandatory Preventive Medical Screening and the Procedure for Taking the Mandatory Preventive Medical Screening and Issuance of Personal Medical Books, approved by Resolution No. 559 of the Cabinet of Ministers of Ukraine (May 23, 2001), as amended; Procedure for Carrying Out of the Mandatory Prior and Regular Psychiatric Screening and the List of Medical Psychiatric Diagnoses Preventing From Performing Certain Types of Activity (Works, Professions, Services), approved by Resolution No. 1465 of the Cabinet of Ministers of Ukraine; Regulation on the Mandatory Preventive Drug and Alcohol Testing, approved by Resolution No. 1238 of the Cabinet of Ministers of Ukraine, as amended.

[80]Law of Ukraine on Fundamentals of Health Protection, art. 31 (Nov. 19, 1992), as amended (Health Protection Law).

[81]Labor Code art. 169.

[82]Health Protection Law, art. 40.

careful, accurate, and diligent way.[83] An employee may refuse to perform the work if manufacturing circumstances appear to be dangerous to his or her health or the health of the other people or the environment.[84]

2. *Trade Secrets*

Trade secrets are defined as information related to the manufacturing, management, finances, and other activity of a company that does not constitute state secrets, the disclosure of which may have harmful consequences for the company. The information that constitutes the trade secrets of the company is defined by the head of the company.[85] Non-authorized disclosure of trade secrets is prohibited.[86]

3. *Covenants Not to Compete*

According to Ukrainian law, jobs are performed either under an employment agreement (or an employment contract) between an employer and an employee, which is governed by Ukrainian labor law, or under a contractor's agreement between a client and a contractor, which is governed by Ukrainian civil law.[87] The majority of employment relationships are based on employment agreements. An employee may enter into employment agreements with more than one employer, unless otherwise provided by the law, a collective agreement, or an employment agreement.[88] A covenant not to compete with an employer is not specifically provided for by Ukrainian law but may be specified in an employment agreement. Upon termination of employment, no obligation concerning competition applies unless specifically contracted.

---

[83]Labor Code art. 139.

[84]Labor Code art. 153.

[85]*See* Commercial Code, art. 36; Civil Code, art. 505.

[86]*See* Law of Ukraine on Protection from Unfair Competition, art. 17 (June 7, 1996), as amended.

[87]See I.A., above.

[88]*See* Labor Code art. 21.

II. Collective Bargaining

The procedure for collective bargaining is established under Chapter II of the Labor Code, the Collective Agreement Law,[89] and the Collective Dispute Law.[90]

Under Ukrainian law, collective agreements may contain provisions relating to production, labor conditions, and employees' social and economic benefits, which are superior to those provided by the labor laws. An employee may be covered both by a collective agreement and an employment agreement. Employment conditions under employment agreements may not be inferior to those granted under collective agreements.

Employees most often are represented by trade unions for purposes of collective bargaining.[91] If there is more than one trade union acting on behalf of the employees in the same workplace, then the several trade unions must agree on joint representation of the employees in the collective bargaining process. If they are not able to agree on joint representation, a collective agreement will be executed by the representatives of those trade unions whose members represent the majority of employees in the respective company, region, economic sector, or, in the case of a general collective agreement, in the nation as a whole.

Any interference with employees' rights regarding collective bargaining by employers or state bodies is prohibited.

A. Union Security

Employee rights arising from membership in trade unions are established under the Constitution, Chapter XVI of the Labor Code, and the Trade Union Law and regulations.[92]

---

[89]Law on Collective Agreements (July 1, 1993), as amended (Collective Agreement Law).

[90]Law on the Order of Resolution of Collective Labor Disputes (Conflicts) (Mar. 3, 1998) (Collective Dispute Law).

[91]For other types of employee representatives, see III., below.

[92]*See* Law on Trade Unions, Their Rights and Guarantees of Their Activity (Sept. 15, 1999) (Trade Union Law); Regulations on a Trade Union Committee of an Enterprise or Organization, approved by the Decree of the Presidium of the Supreme Council of the USSR (Sept. 27, 1971).

Trade unions in Ukraine are public, nonprofit organizations that unite citizens based on their profession or occupation. Creation of a trade union does not require approval of a state authority. All trade unions in Ukraine have equal rights.[93] Employees are free to join any trade union if they meet the membership requirements established by the union's charter. An employee may not be required to join a trade union,[94] and employment discrimination based on membership in a trade union is prohibited.[95]

Membership dues are collected by trade unions according to procedures established under their respective charters. Trade unions are entitled to engage in the following activities, among others:

- representing employees in collective bargaining,
- making legislative proposals and participating in the drafting of labor laws,
- providing employees with advice and protection with respect to their individual employment, and
- monitoring employers' compliance with labor laws and regulations.[96]

A trade union, when properly authorized, may represent employees in collective bargaining irrespective of their union membership.[97] In most cases, a trade union member may not be dismissed on the employer's initiative without the union's consent.[98] An employer is required to consult with the trade union committee when establishing internal work regulations and vacation schedules.[99] A trade union's consent also is required for overtime work, work under a system of aggregate working hours,[100] and work assignments on days off.[101]

---

[93]Constitution art. 36; Trade Union Law art. 10.

[94]Constitution art. 36; Labor Code art. 243.

[95]Trade Union Law art. 5.

[96]Labor Code art. 244; Trade Union Law arts. 19–36.

[97]Collective Agreement Law art. 9; Trade Union Law art. 19. See also II.C., below.

[98]Labor Code art. 43; Trade Union Law art. 39. See also I.F.3., above.

[99]Labor Code arts. 52, 67, and 79.

[100]*Id.* arts. 61, 64. See also V.B.6.b., below.

[101]Labor Code art. 71. See also V.B.3., below.

Trade union committees (union officers) are authorized to represent employees in connection with proceedings before a company's labor dispute committee.[102] Trade union committees also manage all of the cultural, educational, recreational, and sport facilities owned by the company.[103]

A company's trade union committee is entitled to an office on the company's premises and to transportation and communication equipment from the company's management pursuant to the collective agreement.[104] Ukrainian law also provides that members of a trade union committee are entitled to the following protections:

- Officers may not be disciplined or their employment agreements modified without the consent of the trade union committee. The consent of the administratively superior trade union committee, that is, the committee for the district, city, *oblast*, or region, as the case may be, is required for dismissal of officers and for discipline or dismissal of the union committee head.
- Officers may not be dismissed by the employer for two years after the end of their term on the trade union committee, unless the company is liquidated or the dismissal is for one of the reasons listed under items *c*, *d*, or *g* through *k* in I.F.3., above.
- Officers who continue to work in the company are entitled to take time off with pay for collective bargaining and other union business.
- Officers are entitled to take up to six calendar days of additional vacation with pay for participating in union training programs.[105]

---

[102]Labor Code art. 226; Trade Union Law art. 26. For a discussion of labor dispute committees, see the Introduction, at D., above.

[103]Labor Code art. 250.

[104]*Id.* art. 249; Trade Union Law art. 42.

[105]Labor Code art. 252; Trade Union Law art. 41. *See* Law of Ukraine on Amending Certain Legislative Acts of Ukraine Related to the Trade Unions' Activity (July 10, 2003).

B. Types of Collective Agreements

In terms of subject and scope, a collective agreement under Ukrainian law may be one of four types:[106]

- *Corporate collective agreements* are those between the employer and one or more trade union committees (or other employee representatives elected by the collective of employees).[107] To enter into a corporate collective agreement, the employer must be a legal entity.
- *Regional collective agreements* are those between local state executive bodies or authorized regional unions of entrepreneurs and regional trade union associations (or other representatives of collectives of employees within a specific territory or region).
- *Sectoral collective agreements* are those between employers and employees (or their authorized representatives) authorized to conduct collective bargaining and to enter into collective agreements that will bind the companies and employees within a specific industry.
- *General collective agreements* are those between united trade unions and united employers, employing the majority of Ukrainian employees. A general collective agreement is valid only if it purports to bind a majority of Ukrainian companies.

C. Scope

The provisions of a corporate collective agreement are applicable to all employees irrespective their membership in the trade union(s) that signed the collective agreement. The provisions of other collective agreements are binding on all employers and employees within the authority of the respective signatories of the particular agreement.

---

[106] *See* Collective Agreement Law arts. 2, 3.
[107] See III., below.

D. Duration

Unless otherwise provided by the terms of the agreement, a collective agreement becomes effective on the execution date and remains effective, even after expiration of its term, until the parties either revise it or enter into a new agreement.[108] When a company reorganizes, its corporate collective agreement remains in effect through the end of its initial term unless revised by the parties. When a new employer acquires a company, the old employer's corporate collective agreement remains in effect for a period not longer than one year. During this one-year period, a new collective agreement must be negotiated by the employees and the new employer.[109]

E. Registration and Notice of Collective Agreements

Sectoral and regional collective agreements are subject to registration with the Ministry of Labor. Corporate collective agreements are registered with the local state executive bodies.[110]

Employees must receive personal notice of corporate collective agreements. Notice of regional, sectoral, and general collective agreements is accomplished through the mass media.

F. Negotiating Collective Agreements

Generally, in a newly created company, a corporate collective agreement is entered into at the initiative of either the employer or the employees (or their authorized representatives) within three months of the company's registration.

In the case of an existing collective agreement, any party can initiate bargaining by sending written notice to the other party not less than three months prior to the expiration of the effective agreement (or as specified in the agreement).[111] The other party is obligated to start collective bargaining within seven days of its receipt of the notice.

---

[108]Collective Agreement Law art. 9.

[109]*Id.*

[110]*Id.*

[111]*Id.* art. 10.

The parties then will create a working committee for the purpose of negotiating and drafting a new or revised collective bargaining agreement. The parties have discretion to determine the structure of their working committee.

G. Bargaining Disputes

Disputes arising in the course of collective bargaining may be resolved through certain settlement procedures established by law. If the parties fail to reach agreement, they prepare a list of disputed points containing the final proposals of each party and the date for resuming negotiations. Thereafter, within 3 to 10 days (depending on the type of collective agreement), the parties create a settlement committee, which may include an independent mediator appointed by the parties.[112] The settlement committee issues its decision, which is binding on the parties, within 5 to 15 days (depending on the type of collective agreement) after creation of the committee.[113] If the settlement committee fails to issue a decision, the parties may refer their dispute to labor arbitration.[114]

Labor arbitration may be commenced at the initiative of any party or a mediator within three days of the settlement committee's failure to issue its decision. The labor arbitration panel consists of arbitrators appointed by the parties. The arbitration decision is made by a simple majority vote of all the arbitrators.[115] The arbitration will bind the parties to the dispute, if they so agreed. If labor arbitration fails to resolve the dispute, the employees are entitled to strike.

Under the Collective Dispute Law, the President created the National Service of Mediation and Settlement (Mediation Service) for assisting in the prevention and resolution of collective labor disputes. The Mediation Service is financed from the state budget. Its responsibilities include the registration and analysis of collective labor disputes, the preparation of proposals for resolving disputes, the training of mediators and arbitrators, the maintenance

[112]Collective Dispute Law art. 8.
[113]*Id.* art. 9.
[114]*Id.* art. 7.
[115]*Id.* art. 12.

of a list of mediators and arbitrators, and, finally, the mediation of collective labor disputes. Representatives of the Mediation Service are entitled to participate in all stages of dispute resolution.

Parties that have exhausted all other avenues of settlement are entitled to submit their dispute to the Mediation Service. The Mediation Service issues its nonbinding recommendations within 10 days.[116]

H. Execution of Collective Agreements

When the parties agree on a draft collective agreement, it must be submitted to the general meeting of employees or their representatives for approval.[117] If the draft is rejected by the general meeting of employees, collective bargaining procedures must be resumed. However, any additional negotiations may not last longer than 10 days. After approval by the general meeting is received, the collective agreement is signed by the authorized representatives of the parties.[118] Any amendments to the collective agreement may be made only with the mutual consent of the parties.

I. Liability for Refusal to Participate in Collective Bargaining and for Violation of Collective Agreements

Representatives who refuse to participate in collective bargaining may be fined up to 10 nontaxable minimum income units (Ukraine Hryvnia (UAH) 170).[119] Representatives who violate any provision of the collective agreement may be fined up to 100 nontaxable minimum income units (UAH 1700).[120]

J. Disputes Regarding Collective Agreements

The Collective Dispute Law establishes the procedure for resolving collective disputes between organized employees and employers regarding the provisions of collective agreements or

---

[116] *Id.* art. 16.

[117] For an explanation of the general meeting of employees, see III., below.

[118] Collective Agreement Law art. 13.

[119] *Id.* art. 17. For an explanation of nontaxable income units, see V.A.4., below.

[120] Collective Agreement Law art. 18.

violations of the labor laws. Under these procedures, any complaints or demands of employees must be approved at the general meeting of employees[121] or their representatives, or be signed by the majority of employees. The general meeting of employees then appoints a body or a person authorized to represent employees' collective interests in the dispute with the employer. In the case of regional or sectoral collective agreements, such complaints must be approved at the meeting of the respective trade union committee.[122] The employer has up to 30 days to respond to the employees' complaint. If the employer rejects the complaint in full or in part, or if the employer does not respond to the complaint, a labor dispute is deemed to have commenced. The employees' representatives must notify the employer, the local state executive body, and the Mediation Service in writing of the existence of the labor dispute.[123] Labor disputes over collective agreements are resolved by labor arbitration with the participation of the Mediation Service, if necessary.[124]

K. Strikes

1. Legal Strikes

Under Ukrainian law, employees are entitled to strike to protect their economic and social interests.[125] The Collective Dispute Law defines a strike as a temporary, voluntary, collective termination of work by employees with the goal of resolving a collective dispute.[126] A strike is a method of last resort to resolve a collective labor dispute when an employer refuses to satisfy the demands of the employees and when settlement procedures fail or an employer refuses to participate in settlement procedures.[127]

A decision to strike must be approved by a trade union committee, or other body authorized to represent employees in the col-

---

[121]See III., below.
[122]Collective Dispute Law art. 4.
[123]*Id.* art. 6.
[124]*Id.* art. 7. For a discussion of arbitration procedures, see II.G., above.
[125]Constitution art. 44; Collective Dispute Law art. 8.
[126]Collective Dispute Law art. 17.
[127]*See id.* arts. 17, 19.

lective dispute, and by a simple majority vote of the general meeting of employees or by a two-thirds majority vote of the conference of employee representatives,[128] as the case may be. Regional or sectoral meetings may recommend strikes only to employees of companies representing certain regions or sectors of the economy. Employees of the individual companies make their own decisions whether to strike. A strike is considered regional or sectoral if more than half the employees of a certain region or sector of the economy go on strike.[129]

Strikes must be led by a strike committee or by a person appointed by the general meeting of employees. The committee or strike leader must notify the employer in writing at least seven days (15 days for enterprises with nonstop production lines) in advance of the commencement of the strike. An employer must provide notice of an announced strike in the shortest reasonable time to all suppliers, customers, carriers, and other interested parties. The location of the employees during a strike must be determined by the strike committee or strike leader with the consent of the employer.

In the course of the strike, the parties must use their best efforts to resolve the dispute.

2. *Illegal Strikes*

The following strikes are illegal:

- strikes aimed at changing the constitutional system or state boundaries;
- strikes not preceded by mediation or arbitration;
- strikes declared or continued after settlement procedures have commenced; and
- strikes that may endanger human life or the environment or that interfere with responses to accidents, epidemic diseases, or natural disasters.[130]

---

[128]For an explanation of the general meeting of employees and the conference of employee representatives, see III., below.

[129]Collective Dispute Law art. 9.

[130]*Id.* art. 22.

Certain employees, including employees of the prosecutor's office, the courts, the armed forces, any governmental or administrative body, and any security or law enforcement agency, are forbidden from striking. The President or the Parliament may impose a one-month moratorium on strikes during a state of emergency. The moratorium may be extended by a joint decree of the President and the Parliament. Strikes also are prohibited during any military curfew.

If a strike endangers human life or the environment, or if it is conducted by employees forbidden from striking or during a moratorium declared by the President and/or the Parliament, the Mediation Service is required to submit the labor dispute to a court of proper jurisdiction. An employer also may challenge the legality of a strike in court. Once a challenge is filed, the court has seven days to decide the merits of the claim. If the court invalidates the strike, all striking employees must resume work within 24 hours of the strike committee's receipt of the court's decision.[131]

3. *Rights of Strikers*

No employee may be required to participate in or to refrain from participating in a strike. Participation in a lawful strike may not serve as a basis for discipline. Those employees who do not take part in the strike, but who are barred from working because of the strike, are entitled to compensation as established under the law and any collective agreement.

III. REPRESENTATION BY ENTITIES OTHER THAN UNIONS

As a rule, employees are represented by trade unions. However, Ukrainian labor law permits other entities, which are properly authorized by a collective of employees, to represent employees for purposes of collective bargaining. If no trade union or other entity is authorized to represent employees, a collective of employees may elect and authorize individual representatives to act on their behalf in collective bargaining.[132]

---

[131] *Id.* art. 23.

[132] *See* Collective Agreement Law arts. 2, 4.

A collective of employees is an organization that includes all employees of a company. Unless otherwise provided by the charter of the company, a collective of employees acts either through its general meeting (i.e., a meeting of all employees of a company), or through a general conference (i.e., a meeting of employee representatives and a representative board). The general meeting of the collective of employees elects members of the representative board by a secret supermajority vote (at least two-thirds approval required) for a term of two to three years. Members of the representative board of the collective of employees may not be disciplined, dismissed, or transferred by the employer without the representative board's consent.[133]

The authority of the collective of employees includes, *inter alia*, the approval of the collective agreement and decisions on other matters pursuant to the charter of the company.

The law requires employee representation on the supervisory board of a joint-stock company. Such representation is carried out by a trade union or any other authorized entity that signs a collective agreement on behalf of the collective of employees. Employee representatives on the supervisory board are entitled to only an advisory, but not decisive, vote. These employee representatives may not be dismissed by the employer without the consent of the general meeting of employees that elected them.[134]

IV. Redundancy and Transfers of Undertakings

Ukrainian law protects employees during organizational changes, such as mergers, acquisitions, restructurings (including staff reductions), bankruptcies, and liquidations.

A. Redundancy

Generally, in the case of a liquidation, reorganization, bankruptcy, or restructuring, an employee may be dismissed only if the employer is unable to transfer the employee, with his or her con-

---

[133] *See* Commercial Code, art. 65.

[134] Labor Code art. 252.

sent, to another job. Employee dismissal for reasons of reorganization, bankruptcy, or staff reduction also requires the consent of the trade union committee unless: (1) a trade union committee has not been created, (2) the employee is not a member of the trade union, or (3) the law provides otherwise. Consent of the trade union committee is not required if the dismissal is due to liquidation.[135]

Ukrainian employers must give employees two-months' notice of planned terminations due to liquidation, staff reduction, or reorganization. The employer also must inform the state employment authority of the expected terminations not less than two months before they are to occur. The termination notice must list the profession, position, and compensation of each employee scheduled to be terminated. In addition, a list of employees' names must be submitted to the state employment authority within 10 days of the termination date. Employers failing to comply with these requirements face a penalty equal to the sum of the annual salaries of the terminated employees.[136]

The employer must make a severance payment of one month's salary to each employee terminated for reasons of liquidation, staff reduction, or reorganization. Prior to February 22, 2001,[137] the employer was required to pay terminated employees their average wage during their job-search period, although such payments (including the severance payment) did not need to exceed three-months' salary.[138]

Prior to January 1, 2001,[139] employees dismissed due to a liquidation, reorganization, or restructuring of a company also were entitled to job-search payments from the Unemployment Fund according to the following formula:

- for the 4th through 6th months after termination: 75 percent of average salary; and

---

[135]*Id.* art. 43-1.

[136]Law on Employment of Population, art. 20 (Mar. 1, 1991), as amended (Employment Law).

[137]*See* Law on the Amount of Contributions for Certain Types of Mandatory State Social Insurance, art. 6 (Jan. 11, 2001) (Social Contribution Law); Letter of Ministry of Labor No. 03-3/1045-020-6 (Mar. 11, 2001).

[138]Labor Code art. 49-3. For the calculation of average wage, see I.D., above.

[139]*See* Employment Law art. 26; Law on Mandatory State Social Insurance Against Unemployment, Ch. VIII (Mar. 2, 2000), as amended (Unemployment Law).

- for the 7th through 12th months after termination: 50 percent of average salary.

Effective February 22, 2001, the employer is responsible only for a severance payment of one month's salary. All job-search payments are payable as an unemployment benefit by the Unemployment Fund, and not the employer, provided that the dismissed employee personally registers with the state employment authority within seven days of termination, and the employment authority is unable to place the dismissed employee in a new position within seven days of his or her registration. The unemployment payments begin on the day after one month plus seven days following the dismissed employee's registration,[140] and from that day forward are based on the standard formula applicable to unemployment payments.[141]

However, payments to dismissed employees may not exceed the overall average wage calculated by statistical authorities for the respective administrative region at the time of payment, and may not be less than the livelihood minimum established by law.[142]

For 2003, the livelihood minimum is UAH 365.[143] The minimum unemployment benefit is 21 percent of the livelihood minimum.[144]

B. Transfers of Undertakings

Under Ukrainian law, in the event of a merger or acquisition of an enterprise, all rights and obligations of the former owner

---

[140]*See* Unemployment Law arts. 22, 31; Labor Code art. 44.

[141]For general rates of unemployment payments, see VIII.B.2., below.

[142]The livelihood minimum is approved annually by the *Verkhovna Rada*. In 2001, the livelihood minimum is UAH 331.05. However, under the transition rule of the Unemployment Law, the minimum unemployment benefit is currently established at 11 percent of the livelihood minimum. *See* Unemployment Law art. 23, Ch. VIII; Law on Livelihood Minimum, art. 4 (July 15, 1999); Social Contribution Law art. 3.

[143]Law of Ukraine on Livelihood Minimum in 2003, art. 1 (Nov. 28, 2002).

[144]*See* Law of Ukraine on Amending the Law on the Amount of Contributions for Certain Types of Mandatory State Social Insurance (Feb. 6, 2003) (February 2003 Amendment to Social Contribution Law); Law on Mandatory State Social Insurance Against Unemployment, art. 23 (Mar. 2, 2000), as amended (Unemployment Law).

(employer), including those under employment agreements, pass to the new owner (employer).[145]

Based on this rule, employment agreements are not terminated automatically as the result of a merger or acquisition. However, a successor employer is entitled to terminate employment agreements due to reorganization or staff reduction, as discussed immediately above.

When an employer acquires a company that is signatory to a corporate collective agreement, the old employer's agreement remains in effect for a limited period while a new agreement is negotiated by the employees and the new employer.[146]

V. WAGES, HOURS, AND LEAVE

A. Wages

Under Ukrainian law, the wage is defined as compensation that an employer pays to an employee for completed work.[147] The wage may consist of basic compensation, expressed as a fixed amount per working hour or scope of work, as well as additional compensation for work over established standards, additional effort, creativity, or special conditions of work.[148] Such additional compensation may include bonuses, interest, or other payments established by law or provided voluntarily by the employer. Wage amounts are established under employment agreements (or employment contracts) and collective agreements. By law, wages must be paid only in Ukrainian currency; payment of wages in any other form is prohibited.[149]

1. Minimum Wage

The minimum wage is the lowest compensation allowed by law for simple, unskilled work. The minimum wage is established

---

145Labor Code art. 36.

146See II.D., above.

147Law on Wages, art. 1 (Mar. 24, 1995), as amended (Compensation Law); Labor Code art. 94.

148*See* Compensation Law art. 2.

149*Id.* art. 23.

annually by the respective law on the State budget of Ukraine.[150] As of January 1, 2004, the minimum wage in Ukraine is UAH 205.[151] The minimum wage does not include any additional compensation payable to an employee.

2. *Overtime, Holidays, and Night Work*

Overtime work[152] and work on holidays[153] must be compensated at a double rate.[154] Work at night[155] is compensated at an increased rate as provided by corporate, regional, or general collective agreements. Such additional compensation may not be less than 20 percent of the regular hourly rate.[156]

3. *Wage Payment Dates*

Wages must be paid on a regular basis on the dates specified by a corporate collective agreement, but not less than twice a month, with interval(s) not exceeding 16 calendar days.[157]

4. *Taxes*

An employee's income is subject to personal income tax under the Personal Tax Law.[158] Generally, residents of Ukraine (both Ukrainian and foreign nationals residing in Ukraine for more than 183 calendar days per year) must pay the tax on their aggregate income, received both within and outside Ukraine. Tax on income received in connection with employment (provided that the employee's labor book is properly processed and all required pension and social insurance contributions are made) must be calcu-

---

[150] *See* Law of Ukraine on Amending the Budget Code of Ukraine and the Law of Ukraine on Wages, art. 10 (June 10, 2003).

[151] *See* Law of Ukraine on the State Budget of Ukraine for 2004, art. 89 (Nov. 27, 2003).

[152] See V.B.6., below.

[153] See V.B.4., below.

[154] Labor Code arts. 106, 107.

[155] See V.B.5., below.

[156] Labor Code art. 108.

[157] *Id.* art. 115. As a matter of practice, due to the difficult economic situation in Ukraine, wage arrears are common at state-owned companies and institutions.

[158] Decree of the Cabinet of Ministers on Income Tax of Citizens (Dec. 26, 1992), as amended (Personal Tax Law).

lated, withheld, and paid on behalf of an employee by the employer.[159] An employer pays this individual income tax for its employees not later than the date of receiving the payroll funds from its bank. An employer also is obligated to submit certain information related to payment of the personal income tax for each employee to the State Tax Authority before February 15 of each year. If an employee receives income from a second job, his second employer must submit tax information to the State Tax Authority not later than 30 days after the payment of such income.

Revisions to the personal income tax law in Ukraine, effective January 1, 2004, have replaced the progressive income tax.[160] Under the new system, an employee's income is taxed based on a flat rate of 13 percent.[161] An employee is also allowed to claim as a tax credit[162] certain expenses incurred during the taxable period (one year), as discussed below.[163]

Generally, residents of Ukraine must pay the tax on their aggregate income, received both within and outside Ukraine.[164] The Income Tax Law retains the previous 183-day definition for the residency of a taxpayer. However, it also has introduced a number of additional rules for determining a taxpayer's residency. An individual permanently living in Ukraine is considered a resident. If such individual has also a permanent place of residence in another country, residency is defined as the place where the individual has closer personal or economic relations (defined as the "center of his (or her) vital interests"). One of the sufficient but not exclusive reasons in favor of such "center of the taxpayer's vital interests" is the place of residence of the individual's family or the individual's registration as a subject of business activity. In case it is not pos-

[159] *Id.* art. 9. For a discussion of labor books, see I.E., above.

[160] *See* Law of Ukraine on Personal Income Tax (May 22, 2003) (Income Tax Law).

[161] Such rate will be increased to 15 percent as of January 1, 2007. *See* Income Tax Law, arts. 7, 22 (§22.3).

[162] The term "tax credit" is defined as the amount of expenses incurred by a resident from the purchase of goods (works, services) from other residents (individuals and legal entities) within the tax reporting period (except for VAT and excise tax), for which such individual is permitted to decrease his or her annual taxable income. *See id.* art. 1 (§1.16).

[163] *See id.* art. 5.

[164] *See id.* arts. 2, 3.

sible to define the country in which an individual has the "center of his (or her) vital interests," such individual is considered a resident of Ukraine if he (or she) resides in Ukraine for more than 183 calendar days per year.[165]

As under the previous system, currently tax on income received in connection with employment must be calculated, withheld, and paid on behalf of an employee by the employer.[166] An employer must pay this individual income tax for its employees not later than the date of receiving the payroll funds from its bank. An employer also is obligated to submit to the relevant State Tax Authority on a quarterly basis certain information related to payment of the personal income tax for each employee.[167]

As noted above, as of January 1, 2004, an employee is also allowed to claim as a tax credit certain expenses incurred during the year, provided that such expenses are confirmed by the relevant documents. In particular, an employee is able to claim as a tax credit, *inter alia*, the following expenses: (1) interest payments made under a loan secured by a mortgage, provided that the loan is used to finance the purchase or construction of the employee's principal home;[168] (2) charitable contributions of not less than 2 percent but not more than 5 percent of the employee's annual taxable income; (3) a certain amount of expenses from payments to educational institutions for receiving higher education; (4) a certain amount of expenses from payments to medical institutions for personal health care.[169]

An employee is able to claim such tax credit by filing the tax declaration with the relevant State Tax Authority before March 1 of each year. The State Tax Authority is required to recalculate the employee's income tax payments and return the overdue amount to the employee's bank account within 60 days from the date of submission of the tax declaration.[170]

---

[165] *See id.* art. 1 (§1.20.1).

[166] *See id.* arts. 8 (§8.1.1), 17 (§17.1).

[167] *Id.* art. 19 (§19.2).

[168] This provision will be effective from January 1, 2005. *See id.* art. 22 (§22.1.1).

[169] The effectiveness of this provision is conditioned on the adoption of the Law of Ukraine on Obligatory Medical Insurance, which has not been passed yet.

[170] Income Tax Law, art. 18, §18.8.

5. *Foreign Employers*

A foreign employer may find it efficient to engage an outside contractor to perform payroll services, although is not required to do so. The State Department for Foreign Representative Offices (under its Ukrainian acronym, *GDIP*), or similar departments of state regional administrations, also may be engaged to process payrolls.

B. Hours

1. *Normal Working Hours*

Under the Labor Code, normal working hours may not exceed 40 hours per week.[171] The workweek is 36 hours for employees between the ages of 16 and 18, and for employees in certain other categories, for example, employees working in hazardous occupations.[172] The workweek for persons between the ages of 14 and 16 is 24 hours. For high school students working after school the workweek is established at one-half the normally allowed limits. Some other categories of employees, such as teachers and physicians, also may have shortened normal working hours.[173]

Daily working time is reduced by one hour on the eve of holidays and "non-working days."[174] Similarly, under the six-day workweek arrangement discussed immediately below, daily working time is reduced on the day preceding the scheduled day off.

The Labor Code requires employers to allow a reduced workday or a reduced workweek upon the request of a pregnant woman, a woman with a child who is younger than age 14 or disabled, or a woman who takes care of an ill family member. The law also permits an employee and employer to agree to a reduced workday or a reduced workweek (either at the time of or subsequent to hire). Wages in these cases are for hours worked.[175]

---

[171]Labor Code art. 50.

[172]The list of such professions and positions is approved by the Cabinet of Ministers of Ukraine.

[173]*See* Labor Code art. 51.

[174]For an explanation of holidays and nonworking days, see V.B.4., below.

[175]Labor Code art. 56.

2. *Five-Day and Six-Day Workweeks*

The Labor Code establishes a five-day workweek with two days off. Subject to the limits discussed above, the duration of the workday is determined by the rules and regulations approved by the employer and agreed to with the trade union committee, if any exist. Normally, a five-day workweek consists of eight-hour workdays.

An employer also may establish a six-day workweek with one day off. With a six-day workweek, the workday preceding a day off may not exceed five hours, and no workday may exceed seven hours.[176]

3. *Days Off*

Under a five-day workweek, the days off are Sunday and, as a rule, either Saturday or Monday. Under a six-day workweek, Sunday is the day off. The Labor Code also requires that the duration of a continuous rest from work should be not less than 42 hours every week.

When a holiday or a nonworking day falls on a weekend, the day off is shifted to the day after the holiday or weekend.

The law generally prohibits work on days off. An employer may assign employees to work on days off only with the consent of the trade union committee, if any, and then only to perform urgent, unforeseen work that affects regular operations, to avert a natural disaster, or to respond to an operational accident or other emergency.

An employer assigns employees to work on days off through a written order. For working on a day off, an employee is granted either another day off or double pay, as agreed to by the parties.

4. *Holidays and Nonworking Days*

The Labor Code defines "holidays" as days of celebration by all citizens of significant political, religious, and other events. "Nonworking" days are defined as days of celebration by believers and other citizens of significant religious and other events. An em-

---

[176] *Id.* art. 52.

ployer may grant certain employees days off to celebrate their significant non-Orthodox religious events.

The Labor Code establishes the following holidays: New Year's Day (January 1); Orthodox Christmas (January 7); International Women's Day (March 8); Days of International Workers' Solidarity (May 1 and 2); Victory Day (May 9); Constitution Day (June 28); and Ukrainian Independence Day (August 24). Easter and Trinity also are holidays of one Sunday each.[177]

With certain exceptions, work is not permitted on holidays and nonworking days.

5. *Night Work*

Night work is defined as work performed between 10 p.m. and 6 a.m.[178] Generally, normal working hours for night shifts are one hour less than the normal daytime working hours.

6. *Overtime*

a. *Overtime Provisions in the Labor Code*

Employment agreements must comply fully with the requirements of the Labor Code regarding overtime. As a general rule, Ukrainian labor law prohibits employers from requiring employees to work overtime[179] (i.e., to work longer than the established normal working hours).[180] Permissible exceptions from the prohibition on overtime include work performed in response to an emergency, a natural disaster, or an operational accident, or to replace an absent employee. Even under these circumstances, overtime work is allowed only with the consent of the company's trade union.[181] When permitted, overtime work may not exceed four hours per two consecutive days or 120 hours per year.[182] Overtime work must be compensated at a double rate.[183]

---

[177]*Id.* art. 73.
[178]*Id.* art. 54.
[179]*Id.* art. 63.
[180]See V.B.1. and V.B.2., above.
[181]Labor Code art. 64.
[182]*Id.* art. 65.
[183]*Id.* art. 106.

b. Aggregate Working Hours

If an employer needs to assign employees to work more than normal working hours, it may introduce a system of "aggregate working hours."[184] Under this system, the limit on working hours applies to periods longer than a week (for example, one month or several months). The duration of such periods (record periods) may be set forth in the employment agreement. The total number of working hours during a record period may not exceed the maximum number of working hours allowed for the same period based on a ratio of 40 working hours (or fewer, if applicable) per week. For example, if a calendar month is considered the record period, then an employee's total working hours, given a 40-hour work week, must not exceed 160 to 184 hours a month, depending on the number of days in the month.

Under the Labor Code, a system of aggregate working hours may be introduced only if: (1) the work cannot be performed according to daily or weekly standards of working hours for the particular category of employee; and (2) the enterprise's trade union consents to the aggregate working hours system.

c. Unlimited Workdays

Ukrainian labor law also provides for the possibility of a more flexible work schedule for certain employees.[185] These flexible schedules, known as "unlimited workdays," are permissible when it is not possible to establish definite working hours. To qualify for unlimited workdays status, the employment agreement must describe the scope of work and the functions to be performed. Under an unlimited work days arrangement, the overtime provisions of the Labor Code do not apply, with the result that extra working hours are not considered overtime. However, unlimited workdays employees are entitled to as many as seven additional vacation days as compensation.[186]

---

[184] *See id.* art. 61.

[185] *See* Decree of the Ministry of Labor and Social Policy of Ukraine No. 7 (Oct. 10, 1997), as amended (Unlimited Work Day Decree).

[186] Law on Vacations, art. 8 (Nov. 15, 1996), as amended (Vacation Law); Unlimited Work Day Decree §3. For a general discussion of vacation leave, see V.C.1., below.

The list of professions and positions to which unlimited workdays may apply is determined by a collective agreement. The standard for working hours established within an enterprise generally applies to employees working under an unlimited workdays arrangement. Therefore, an employer may not require such employees to work longer than established working hours on a systematic basis.

C. Leave

1. Vacations

Ukrainian labor law provides for a basic annual vacation of at least 24 calendar days.[187] Of these 24 calendar days, a minimum of 14 are consecutive calendar days to be used for the employee's main annual vacation.[188] The employee may use the remaining 10 days of vacation in any combination, provided that each unused part of vacation starts on the day of the week that immediately follows the last day of the most recent used part of vacation. Certain categories of employees are entitled to longer basic vacations and/or additional annual vacations, as follows:

- for disabled employees, 26 or 30 days;
- for employees younger than age 18, 31 calendar days;
- for employees in the coal, metallurgic, and electric energy industries, 24, 26, or 28 days, depending on the length of employment;
- for employees working in mines of at least 150 meters depth, 28 days;
- for employees of scientific and educational institutions, up to 56 calendar days;[189]
- for employees working in hazardous occupations, up to 35 calendar days in addition to the basic 24 days;[190]

---

[187] Vacation Law art. 6.

[188] *Id.* art. 12; Labor Code art. 79.

[189] Vacation Law art. 6.

[190] *Id.* arts. 7, 8. For the list of such hazardous occupations, see Order of the Ministry of Labor No. 16 (Jan. 30, 1998); Resolution of the Cabinet of Ministers No. 1290 (Nov. 17, 1997).

- for unlimited workdays employees,[191] up to 7 calendar days in addition to the basic 24 days;[192] and
- for state employees, 30 calendar days basic vacation plus up to 15 additional days.[193]

In general, aggregate annual paid vacation time (including the basic annual vacation and any additional vacations) may not exceed 59 days (69 days for those working in mines).

Certain vacations are available, over and above the general limits, for special purposes. These include vacation periods of 10 days to four months for educational purposes.[194] Under special regulations, longer vacations also may be allowed for certain creative activities such as completing a thesis or writing a book. In addition, an employee may be eligible to take unpaid vacation, ranging from 3 to 60 days, depending on the legal reason.[195]

After six months on the job, an employee is entitled to take annual vacation for the first year of employment. Annual vacations for the second and following years may be taken at any time during the respective year.

2. *Maternity and Child-Care Leave*

Ukrainian labor laws grant female employees a right to leave, known as "social vacation," for purposes of pregnancy, childbirth, and child care. These social vacation allowances are as follows:

- prior to giving birth, 70 days;
- after giving birth, 56 days (70 days if there is more than one child or complications arise);[196]
- for child care, until the child reaches three years of age;[197] and

---

[191]See V.B.6.c., above.

[192]Vacation Law art. 8.

[193]See the Introduction, at B.1.c., above.

[194]Vacation Law arts. 13–15.

[195]*Id.* arts. 25, 26.

[196]*Id.* art. 17.

[197]*Id.* art. 18. Alternatively, child-care leave until the child reaches three years of age can be provided in full or in part to the child's father, grandparent, or any relative who takes care of the child.

• for child care where there is more than one child younger than 15 years of age or a disabled child, 5 days annually.[198]

The laws regulating payments during maternity and child-care leave include the Family Law[199] and the Social Insurance Law.[200] Payments for maternity and child-care leaves are made from the Social Insurance Fund operated by the state.[201] Under Ukrainian Law,[202] employed women are entitled to an average wage payment[203] during their maternity leave, and a minimum wage payment during child-care leave.[204]

For purposes of maternity leave, average wage payments are based on the wage received by the employee during the six months immediately preceding the leave, and are calculated by multiplying the average daily wage by the number of days in the maternity leave period.[205] During child-care leave, women are entitled to the livelihood minimum.[206]

After exhausting paid child-care leave, a woman may be entitled to additional unpaid leave until a child reaches the age of six. This additional unpaid leave may be provided if the child, according to a medical certificate, requires special care at home.[207]

---

[198]*Id.* art. 19.

[199]Law on State Aid to Families with Children, arts. 3, 15 (Nov. 21, 1992), as amended (Family Law).

[200]Law on Mandatory State Social Insurance for Temporary Disability and Expenses for the Birth of a Child and Funeral, arts. 39, 43 (Jan. 18, 2001), as amended (Social Insurance Law).

[201]See VIII.B.1., below.

[202]Family Law, arts. 11, 23 (Nov. 21, 1992), as amended.

[203]For the calculation of average wage, see I.D., above.

[204]For the minimum wage amount, see V.A.1., above.

[205]Procedure for Calculation of the Average Wage for the Purpose of the Mandatory State Social Insurance Payments, approved by Resolution of the Cabinet of Ministers No. 1266, §§4, 20 (Sept. 26, 2001) (Resolution No. 1266).

[206]For a discussion of the livelihood minimum and the current livelihood minimum amount, see IV.A., above. Pursuant to February 2003 Amendment to Social Contribution Law, the child-care minimum is established at 15 percent of the livelihood minimum.

[207]Labor Code art. 179.

VI. ANTIDISCRIMINATION

Under the Constitution and the Labor Code, all citizens of Ukraine have equal employment and labor rights regardless of race, color, political, religious or other beliefs, gender, national or social background, wealth, language, residence, or other differences.[208] The Labor Code and other laws also provide certain additional protection and special employment and labor rights for working women, minors, students, senior citizens, and disabled individuals. These various protections are discussed below.

A. Women

1. Restrictions on Employment

The Labor Code imposes several restrictions on the employment of women. Women may not undertake hard physical labor or work involving harmful or hazardous labor conditions. Women may not work underground, except when performing nonphysical work or sanitary and service work. Women may not be required to work at night, except in those economic sectors where there exists a special need for such work, and even then only temporarily.[209]

Pregnant women and women with children younger than three years of age may not be required to work at night, to work overtime, to work on days off, or to travel on business trips. Women with children between the ages of 3 and 14 may not be required to work overtime and may not be sent on a business trip without their consent.

Pregnant women, upon presentation of a medical certificate, and women with children under three years of age are entitled, upon their request, to be transferred to a position requiring lighter work. In the event of a transfer, the employee's average wage[210] in her previous position must be preserved in her new position. A pregnant woman also has the right to be relieved from her job until a transfer decision is made and, during the relief period, is entitled

[208]Constitution art. 24; Labor Code art. 2-1.

[209]Labor Code arts. 174, 175. For an explanation of night work, see V.B.5., above.

[210]For the calculation of average wage, see I.D., above.

to receive her average wage from her previous job for all days missed.[211]

2. *Hiring and Dismissal*

An employer may not decrease the wages of an employee simply because she is pregnant or has a child younger than the age of three and may not refuse to hire a woman solely because she is pregnant or nursing. Single mothers with children younger than the age of 14 and mothers of disabled children are similarly protected. If an employer refuses to employ a woman in these categories, the employer must inform her in writing of the reasons for the refusal. An improper refusal may be the basis for legal action against the employer. Dismissal of women in these categories is not permitted, except due to the full liquidation of the company.[212]

B. Minors

Minors (i.e., persons younger than 18 years of age), generally have the same employment rights as adults. However, in some areas, such as occupational safety, working time, vacations, and working conditions, they are entitled to certain additional benefits.[213] As a rule, a child younger than age 16 may not be hired as an employee unless he or she receives parental consent. Children who are 14 years of age may be hired for simple after-school jobs, again with parental consent.[214] Minors may not be employed for hard labor, including dangerous or unhealthy work, work underground, overtime work, or work at night or on holidays. The list of positions that may not be occupied by minors is approved by the Ministry of Health and the State Committee on Labor Protection.[215] Minors may be employed only after prior medical examination, and are subject to re-examination each year until age 21. Although normal working hours for minors are less than normal working

---

[211]Labor Code arts. 176–178.
[212]*Id.* art. 184.
[213]*See id.* art.187. See also I.A.2.b. and I.B., above.
[214]Labor Code art. 188.
[215]*Id.* art. 190.

hours for adults,[216] minors' wages are equivalent to those for full working hours.[217]

Minor employees are entitled to vacations at any time of their choice. The first employment position held by employees between ages 15 and 28, who are graduates of educational institutions or military veterans, may not be for less than two years.[218] An employer may terminate a minor employee only with the consent of the local state committee for juveniles.[219]

C. Student Employees

The Labor Code creates certain employer obligations with respect to student employees, a group defined to include practical trainees and students of educational institutions.[220] Student employees attending secondary or technical schools may not be requested to work overtime on days when they have classes. In addition, such student employees are entitled to shortened paid work hours. All student employees are entitled to a different number of days off or additional vacation days (for exams, laboratory work, etc.), ranging from four calendar days to four months annually. An employer also is obligated to reimburse student employees for 50 percent of expenses incurred in traveling to and from the higher educational institution once a year.[221]

D. Senior Citizens

Age discrimination against senior citizens is prohibited.[222] Senior citizens are defined as men of at least 60 years of age, women of at least 55 years of age, and persons who are within 1.5 years of the retirement age.[223]

---

[216]See V.B.1., above.

[217]Labor Code art. 194.

[218]*Id.* art. 197.

[219]*Id.* art. 198.

[220]*Id.* art. 202.

[221]*Id.* art. 219.

[222]Law on Foundations of Social Protection of Labor Veterans and Other Senior Citizens in Ukraine, art. 2 (Dec. 16, 1993), as amended (Senior Citizen Law).

[223]Senior Citizen Law art. 10. For a definition of the retirement age, see VIII.A.1., below.

An employer may not reject an employment application or dismiss a senior employee for reasons related to the applicant or employee's age. Senior employees are entitled to shortened workdays or workweeks, with wages prorated to time actually worked. Night work and overtime are allowed only with the senior employee's consent. Similarly, a senior employee must consent to being transferred to a new position with different labor conditions.

Collective agreements may establish special retirement programs intended to help senior employees prepare for retirement. These programs may provide for beneficial labor conditions, shortened working hours, professional training, or additional financial support for health and recreation purposes.[224]

E. Disabled Individuals

Discrimination against disabled individuals is prohibited. An employer may not refuse to hire a person based on his or her disability unless the disability prevents the person from performing the work duties, as determined by a special medical committee, known by its Ukrainian acronym, *MSEK*.[225]

Employers having 15 to 25 employees are required by law to establish an employment position for one disabled person. Employers with more than 25 employees are required to hire disabled persons in a number that amounts to 4 percent of the total number of its employees.[226]

Employers that do not comply with the hiring requirement must pay a penalty to the Social Protection Fund of Disabled Individuals equal to the average annual salary paid to its employees, for each disabled person that was not employed.[227] Employers also are required to submit an annual report to the Social Protection Fund of Disabled Individuals identifying the number of their em-

---

[224]*See* Senior Citizen Law art. 15.

[225]Law on Fundamentals of Social Protection of Disabled Individuals in Ukraine, art. 17 (Mar. 21, 1991), as amended (Disabled Social Protection Law).

[226]*Id.* art. 19.

[227]*Id.* art. 20.

ployees, the average annual salary, and the number of disabled persons employed.[228]

VII. Occupational Safety and Health and Workers' Compensation

A. Occupational Safety and Health

Both the Labor Protection Law[229] and the Labor Code contain provisions relating to occupational safety and health protection. Additionally, these provisions are complemented by the Labor Safety Regulations as follows:

- Regulation on Investigation of Accidents and Occupational Diseases;[230]
- Regulation on the Procedure for Imposing Fines on Enterprises, Institutions, and Organizations for Violation of Normative Acts on Labor Protection;[231]
- Regulation on National Council for Secured Existence of Population;[232] and
- Standard Regulation on Labor Protection Service.[233]

Labor protection is defined as the system of legal, social, economic, organizational, sanitary, and medical procedures designed to preserve the health and working capacity of employees in the course of their employment.[234]

---

[228]Regulation on Establishment of Employment Positions for Disabled Individuals §14, approved by Resolution of the Cabinet of Ministers No. 314 (May 3, 1995), as amended.

[229]Law on Protection of Labor (Oct. 14, 1992), as amended (Labor Protection Law).

[230]Approved by Resolution of the Cabinet of Ministers No. 1094 (Aug. 21, 2001), as amended (Resolution No. 1094).

[231]Approved by Resolution of the Cabinet of Ministers No. 754 (Sept. 17, 1993), as amended.

[232]Approved by Resolution of the Cabinet of Ministers No. 733 (Sept. 15, 1993), as amended.

[233]Approved by Decree of the State Committee of Ukraine on Labor Protection No. 73 (Aug. 3, 1993), as amended.

[234]Labor Protection Law, art. 1.

Pursuant to the Labor Protection Law approved in a new edition on November 21, 2002, state supervision of labor protection is carried out by the following agencies:

- State Committee for Supervision of Labor Protection;
- State Committee for Nuclear and Radiation Safety;
- Fire Department of the Ministry of Internal Affairs; and
- Sanitary Service of the Ministry of Health.[235]

State labor protection inspectors are appointed by these authorized labor protection agencies and are entitled to:

- inspect any company for compliance with the Labor Safety Regulations;
- receive any labor protection information and documents from employers; and
- send warning notices, suspend operations, and impose fines for violations of the Labor Safety Regulations.[236]

Trade union committees also have authority to control and supervise labor protection measures within a particular company. They are authorized to conduct inspections and expertise of working conditions, to demand that an employer stop operations if the working conditions are dangerous to the life or health of the employees, to participate in investigation of work accidents and professional diseases, and to submit proposals to the employer and relevant labor protection agencies regarding labor protection issues.[237]

If there is no trade union committee, control and supervision of labor protection measures within a specific company may be performed by representatives of collectives of employees. Such representatives are authorized to conduct inspections and to submit proposals to the employer regarding labor protection issues that the employer is obligated to consider. They also may apply to relevant labor protection agencies if the employer does not take

[235] *Id.* art. 38.
[236] *Id.* art. 45.
[237] *Id.* art. 41.

sufficient labor protection measures in response to their proposals.[238]

Employers are obligated to create labor protection departments that are responsible for daily labor protection work. Of course, employees always must be concerned for their own safety at work and should be aware of the Labor Safety Regulations and the safety rules established by the employer.

Under the Labor Protection Law, any employee in Ukraine is entitled to:

- refuse a work assignment if the working conditions will endanger the life or health of the employee or others, or threaten the environment;
- terminate his or her employment if the employer violates the Labor Safety Regulations or labor protection provisions of the collective agreement (in this case an employee is entitled to severance pay of at least three months' wages); or
- transfer to another position, if his or her medical condition so requires.[239]

Employees occupying positions with hazardous working conditions are entitled to free nutritional products (food, milk, mineral water), free uniforms and protective clothing, additional breaks during working hours, shortened working hours, additional vacation, additional pension, and other benefits specified by law.[240]

The State Committee for Labor Protection publishes a list of positions requiring special labor safety training and testing as a precondition of employment. Employees occupying positions with hazardous working conditions also must undergo regular medical examinations at the employer's expense. Employees avoiding such medical examinations may be disciplined by the employer.[241]

---

[238] *Id.* arts. 41, 42.
[239] *Id.* art. 7.
[240] *Id.* arts. 9, 10.
[241] *Id.* art. 39.

B. Workers' Compensation

A new workers' compensation system went into effect in Ukraine on April 1, 2001. As under the previous system, employers are required to investigate each employment-related accident or occupational disease and to prepare a report explaining its cause and identifying any associated violations of law. However, the employee's compensation no longer depends on the employer's fault.[242]

Under the new system, employers contribute to a special social insurance fund, known as the Social Insurance Fund for Workplace Accidents and Occupational Diseases (Social Insurance Disability Fund), from which workers' compensation claims are paid.[243] Employers' contributions to the Social Insurance Disability Fund are established by law based on their payroll and the level of risk assigned to the employer's business.[244]

Payments from the Social Insurance Disability Fund cover the entire range of workers' compensation, from temporary disabilities, as confirmed by a doctor's certificate, to permanent loss of working capacity, as confirmed by the special medical committee, *MSEK*. The Social Insurance Disability Fund provides the following types of financial aid as workers' compensation:

- compensation for temporary disability (until recovery or proof of permanent disability);
- one-time financial support (in case of permanent disability or death);

[242] Law on Mandatory State Social Insurance Against Workplace Accidents and Occupational Diseases That Result in Working Disability, art. 13 (Sept. 23, 1999), as amended (Working Disability Law); Resolution No. 1094.

[243] Working Disability Law, arts. 10, 46; Labor Protection Law, art. 9; Fundamentals of Legislation of Ukraine on Mandatory State Social Insurance, art. 4 (Jan. 14, 1998) (Social Insurance Fundamentals).

[244] Working Disability Law, art. 47; Law on Insurance Tariffs for Mandatory State Social Insurance Against Workplace Accidents and Occupational Diseases That Result in Working Disability (Feb. 22, 2001), as amended (Insurance Tariff Law); Procedure to Determine Insurance Tariffs for Enterprises and Organizations Regarding Mandatory State Social Insurance Against Workplace Accidents and Occupational Diseases, approved by Resolution of the Cabinet of Ministers No. 1423 (Sept. 13, 2000), as amended (Insurance Tariff Procedure). See also VIII.B.3., below.

- compensation of lost wages (in case of partial or total permanent disability);
- pension due to permanent disability;
- pension to a dependent of a deceased employee;
- compensation for pain and suffering; and
- medical and social rehabilitation expenses.[245]

For temporary disability during periods that an employee is absent from work to receive medical treatment or to recover from work-related injuries or an occupational disease, but before permanent disability is established by *MSEK*, workers' compensation is paid by the employer for the first five days and by the Social Insurance Disability Fund until recovery or until permanent disability is established.[246] The temporary disability payment is based on the average wage that the employee received during the six calendar months immediately preceding the disability, and is calculated by multiplying the employee's average daily wage by the number of days of the temporary disability period.[247]

Lost wages paid in the event of a partial or total permanent disability are based on the employee's disability level, established by *MSEK* as a percentage of his or her lost working capacity, and the employee's average wage.[248] For this purpose, the employee's average wage is calculated by multiplying the average daily wage by the average number of working days per month.[249]

An employee who suffers a partial or total permanent loss of working capacity is paid a one-time financial support fee. This one-time fee is calculated by multiplying the employee's average wage by the percentage of permanent loss; however, the amount of a one-time financial support fee may not exceed four maximum wages.[250] If the employee contributed to the injury, as determined

---

[245]Working Disability Law, arts. 21, 28.

[246]*Id.* art. 34.

[247]Resolution No. 1266, §§4, 14, 20.

[248]Working Disability Law, arts. 30, 34; Resolution No. 1266.

[249]Regulation on Calculation of the Average Wage for the Mandatory State Insurance Payments Due to Workplace Accidents and Occupational Diseases That Result in Working Disability, approved by Resolution of the Social Insurance Disability Fund No. 43 (Nov. 1, 2001), as amended; Resolution No. 1266.

[250]Working Disability Law, art. 34. As of June 1, 2003, for the purpose of the Social Insurance Disability Fund, the maximum wage is defined as UAH 2,660.

by a relevant investigation commission,[251] the amount of the one-time financial support fee is reduced to no more than 50 percent of the legally established amount.[252]

In case of an employee's death, the one-time financial support fee is paid to the employee's family and may not be less than five times the employee's annual salary, plus the equivalent of one year's salary for each of the employee's dependents. In addition, each eligible dependent is entitled to an equal share of the deceased's lost wages. Under Ukrainian law, a dependent is a person for whom the deceased's financial support was a permanent and principal source of income and who falls within any of the following categories:

- a child until age 16, or 18 if not employed, or if a student, age 23 or until graduation, whichever is earlier;
- a woman at least 55 years old, or a man at least 60, if not employed;
- a disabled person; or
- a parent or family member, irrespective of age or working capacity, provided that the person is not employed and cares for the children, siblings, or grandchildren of the deceased (until the age of eight).[253]

The Social Insurance Disability Fund also pays all funeral expenses for deceased employees.[254]

Employees also are compensated for medical and other expenses resulting from an occupational injury or disease, including for example, expenses for special meals, nursing and artificial limbs, as well as any pain and suffering.[255] The employee's com-

---

[251] *MSEK* does not investigate work accidents. Pursuant to Regulation 1094, work accidents are investigated by a commission created by the employer that consists of a head of the labor safety department or an employee responsible for the labor safety, other than the employee responsible for the labor safety of the injured person, a representative of a trade union or a representative of a labor collective, if the injured employee is not a member of a trade union. Depending on the injury, the commission may include a representative of the Social Insurance Disability Fund, State Sanitary and Epidemiological Service, etc.

[252] Working Disability Law, art. 34.

[253] *Id.* art. 33.

[254] *Id.*

[255] *Id.* art. 34.

pensation for work-related pain and suffering is provided by the Social Insurance Disability Fund as a one-time payment, the amount of which is established by a court but is not to exceed 200 times the minimum wage, as determined on the date of payment.[256]

As a separate benefit, employees disabled as the result of work-related injuries or occupational diseases are entitled to disability pensions under the Pension Law.[257]

VIII. Pensions and Benefits

A. Pensions

1. Benefits

At present in Ukraine, all employees participate in the mandatory Pension Fund, to which both employers and employees contribute.[258] Contributions to the Pension Fund provide retirement benefits to qualified employees, as well as pensions to disabled persons and dependents of deceased providers, and child-care benefits until a dependent child reaches age three.

The retirement age is 60 years for men (provided that the employment period is not less than 25 years) and 55 years for women (provided that the employment period is not less than 20 years).[259] Employees in certain occupations (such as air traffic controllers, pilots, flight attendants, truck drivers, geologists, actors, etc.) may retire before the standard retirement age after their employment periods exceed limits specified for the particular occupation.

The standard pension amount is 55 percent of the average salary received by the employee, but not less than the minimum

[256]For the current amount of the minimum wage, see V.A.1., above.

[257]Law on Pension Security, arts. 19, 64–67 (Nov. 5, 1991), as amended (Pension Law). See VIII.A.1., below.

[258]Law on Pension Security (Nov. 5, 1991), as amended (Pension Law). Separate pension benefits are provided for state employees under the State Service Law. See Introduction, at B.1.c., above.

[259]Pension Law art. 12.

pension.[260] For total employment periods shorter than the established minimum, the pension amount is determined on a pro rata basis. For each employment year above the minimum period, the pension is increased by 1 percent of the average salary or 1 percent of the minimum pension, whichever is greater.

The minimum retirement pension is UAH 50, effective July 1, 2003.[261] The pension amount is determined under the Pension Law based on the average salary received by the employee during any 60 consecutive employment months and the employment period from July 1, 2003, until the retirement date. At the request of the employee, the pension amount may be calculated based on the average salary received by the employee during the 24 months immediately preceding the retirement date. Such employment period will be extended to 36 months in 2004 and 48 months in 2005. The amount of the employee's salary paid prior to July 1, 2003, must be confirmed by the relevant documentation. Salaries paid after July 1, 2003, will be verified from the computer data for each individual employee's account.[262]

As a rule, the total monthly pension may not exceed three times the minimum (four times the minimum for some categories of employees, such as those working underground or in other difficult labor conditions).[263] For certain occupations, the maximum monthly pension is established at 75 percent (civil flight crew members) or 85 percent (test pilots) of average salary.[264]

The following categories of citizens are entitled to social pensions that are not based on employment:

- men of 60 years of age,
- women of 55 years of age,
- disabled persons, and
- dependent children of a deceased.

---

[260] *Id.* arts. 19, 64–67.

[261] Resolution of the Cabinet of Ministers of Ukraine No. 544 (Apr. 15, 2003). As a matter of practice, the minimum pension is increased by payment of certain compensations and amounts to UAH 92.

[262] Law of Ukraine on Amending the Law of Ukraine on Pension Security (May 22, 2003).

[263] Pension Law art. 19.

[264] *Id.* art. 53.

The social pension amount varies from 30 to 200 percent of the minimum pension, depending on the category[265] of recipient. For disabled persons, pensions range from 40 to 70 percent of average salary, depending on the type of disability.[266]

Effective January 1, 2004, the new Law of Ukraine "On Mandatory State Retirement Insurance" introduced a new structure of pension system of Ukraine, which comprises three levels: (1) solitary pension system—a mandatory state retirement insurance, based on payment of pensions from the Pension Fund of Ukraine; (2) saving pension system—a mandatory state retirement insurance, based on saving funds with the Saving Fund of Ukraine that are subject to finance life pension insurance agreements and/or one-time payments for definite categories of people; and (3) nongovernmental pension system—a voluntary retirement insurance based on voluntary participation of citizens and employers in pension savings. Notwithstanding the effectiveness of the foregoing Law since January 1, 2004, most of its provisions will come into effect beginning the year 2005 and/or upon adoption of other applicable legislative acts required for its implementation.

2. *Contributions*

An employer is obligated to contribute 32 percent of its monthly payroll to the Pension Fund, based on a maximum monthly gross wage per employee for employment contracts or employment agreements. A client under a contractor's agreement also must contribute 32 percent of the sum payable to the contractor.[267] An employer's or an employee's respective contributions to the Pension Fund, effective June 1, 2003, is based on a maximum monthly gross wage per employee of UAH 2,660.[268]

Employees and individual contractors are required to contribute to the Pension Fund 1 percent of their monthly gross taxable income, up to a maximum income of UAH 150, and 2 percent

---

[265]Pension Law arts. 93, 94.

[266]*Id.* art. 29.

[267]Law on Payment for Mandatory Pension Insurance, arts. 1, 4 (June 26, 1997), as amended (Pension Insurance Law). For a discussion of contractor's agreements, see I.A.1., above.

[268]Resolution of the Cabinet of Ministers No. 605 (Apr. 26, 2003) (Resolution No. 605).

of their monthly gross taxable income for amounts exceeding UAH 150 (from 2 to 5 percent, under a set scale, for civil servants and civil flight crew members), up to a maximum income of UAH 2,660.[269] Normally, employees' contributions are withheld by the employer.

In addition, certain business transactions are subject to a Pension Fund contribution. These transactions include sales of goods made of gold, platinum, or gems (taxed at 5 percent of the purchase price); sales of passenger cars (3 percent of the purchase price); production and importation of tobacco products (taxed at 5 percent of the price); purchases of real estate (1 percent of the purchase price); and, with certain exceptions, use of cellular phone services (6 percent of the service fee).[270] Effective January 1, 2004, the one percent contribution to a Pension Fund from foreign currency purchase is suspended for 2004.[271]

3. *Recordkeeping*

The Pension Law states that employees are entitled to pensions provided that their employers make the required contributions to the Pension Fund.[272] In addition to its own contributions, the employer must withhold the contributions of its employees via a withholding mechanism similar to tax withholding.

For purposes of determining pension benefits, the employee's labor book evidences the employment period, and the employer's certificate evidences wages.[273] As a matter of practice, the proper registration of an employee's labor book presently is sufficient for preserving the pension rights of the employee.

According to a 1998 Presidential Decree,[274] the Pension Fund, together with the Ministry of Labor and Social Policy, the Minis-

---

[269]Pension Insurance Law art. 4; Resolution of the Cabinet of Ministers No. 225 (Mar. 7, 2001), as amended (Resolution No. 225).

[270]Pension Insurance Law art. 4.

[271]Law of Ukraine on the State Budget of Ukraine in 2004 (Nov. 27, 2003).

[272]Pension Law art. 3.

[273]For a discussion of labor books, see I.E. and I.F.4., above.

[274]Decree of the President on the Personal Data Bases in the System of Mandatory State Pension Insurance (May 4, 1998). *See also* Resolutions of the Cabinet of Ministers No. 1902 (Oct. 15, 1999), and No. 794 (June 4, 1998).

try of Finance, and the State Tax Authority, created computerized personal employees' accounts in the mandatory pension system that took effect on July 1, 2002. Unlike the former system, which provided employees with pensions based on the employment period recorded in their labor books, the new system makes it possible to electronically record mandatory contributions to the Pension Fund and other relevant information with respect to each employee. Under the new system, the right to a pension is linked to contributions made to the Pension Fund on behalf of each employee. Thus, it is important for each employee to demonstrate not only that he or she has been employed over a certain period, but that the required Pension Fund contributions have been made.

B. Other Benefits

In addition to pension benefits, other social benefits are available to employees through the Social Insurance Fund for Temporary Disability (Social Insurance Fund), the Mandatory State Social Insurance Fund for Unemployment Fund), and the Social Insurance Disability Fund. Each of these funds is discussed below.

1. Social Insurance Fund

An employer is obligated to pay to the Social Insurance Fund each month an amount equal to 2.9 percent of its payroll.[275] All employees are required to make contributions to the Social Insurance Fund in the amount of 0.5 percent of their monthly salary if such amount is less than the livelihood minimum, and in the amount of 1.0 percent of their monthly salary if such amount exceeds the livelihood minimum.[276] An employer's or an employee's respective contributions to the Social Insurance Fund is based on a maximum monthly gross wage per employee of UAH 2,660.[277] These contributions provide the following types of mandatory financial aid to employees:

---

[275]Law of Ukraine on Amending Certain Laws of Ukraine on Mandatory State Social Insurance, §3 (Jan. 17, 2002) (Amendment to Social Contribution Law).

[276]April 9, 2004, Amendment to Social Contribution Law, effective January 11, 2001, as amended.

[277]Resolution No. 225, as amended.

- payment upon the birth of a child;[278]
- wage payments to employees on maternity leave and child-care leave;[279]
- financial aid for a funeral (except for a funeral of a pensioner, an unemployed person, or an employee whose death is the result of a work accident);[280]
- compensation for temporary disability (including pregnancy and child-care) (the amount may be 60, 80, or 100 percent of the average wage,[281] depending on the length of employment and other benefits available to the employee);[282] and
- payment for sanatorium/resort vacations.[283]

Trade union committees are entitled to grant a rest period in an employer-owned sanatorium to any employee certified as requiring special medical treatment.[284] In addition, certain categories of employees, such as war veterans and senior citizens retired after 35 years (for women) or 40 years (for men) of employment, are entitled every two years (every year for retirees with state awards and war veterans) to sanatorium/resort vacations paid from the state budget or the Social Insurance Fund.[285]

Under collective agreements and employment agreements, employees may be entitled to additional payments and benefits.

---

[278]Law on Mandatory State Social Insurance for Temporary Disability and Expenses for the Birth of a Child and Funeral, arts. 34, 38, 39, 42, and 44 (Jan. 18, 2001) (Social Insurance Law); Law on State Aid to Families with Children, arts. 16 and 17 (Nov. 21, 1992), as amended (Family Law); Resolution of the Cabinet of Ministers No. 1751 (Dec. 27, 2001).

[279]Social Insurance Law arts. 34, 38, 39, 42, and 44; Family Law arts. 10 and 22; Law on Vacations, art. 23 (Nov. 15, 1996) (Vacation Law). See also V.C.2., above.

[280]Social Insurance Law arts. 34, 45, and 46; Resolution of the Cabinet of Ministers No. 1753 (Dec. 27, 2001).

[281]For the calculation of average wage, see I.D., above.

[282]Resolution of the Cabinet of Ministers No. 571 (Apr. 27, 1998).

[283]Social Insurance Law arts. 34, 47, and 48.

[284]Regulations on Financing Sanatoriums and Improvement of Health on the Account of the Social Insurance Fund of Ukraine, §5, approved by Resolution of the Social Insurance Fund No. 46 (Dec. 28, 1994).

[285]Law on the Principles of Social Protection of Retired Veterans and Other Senior Citizens in Ukraine (Dec. 16, 1993), as amended, arts. 7, 9; Law on Status of War Veterans and Guarantees of Their Social Status, arts. 12–14 (Oct. 22, 1993), as amended; Resolution of the Cabinet of Ministers No. 236 (Apr. 3, 1995), as amended.

However, such payments and benefits are provided by employers from their own funds, and not through the Social Insurance Fund.

2. *Unemployment Fund*

Under the Social Contribution Law, an employer is obligated to pay to the Unemployment Fund each month an amount equal to 1.9 percent of its payroll.[286] Employees also are obligated to make contributions to the Unemployment Fund in the amount of 0.5 percent of their monthly salary.[287] An employer's or an employee's respective contributions to the Unemployment Fund is based on a maximum monthly gross wage per employee of UAH 2,660.[288] The Unemployment Fund's resources assist terminated employees in finding new jobs.

Unemployment payments are based on the average wage that the employee received during the six calendar months immediately preceding the period of unemployment. For this purpose, the average wage is calculated by multiplying the average daily wage by the number of days that the employee is unemployed.[289]

The amount and the duration of payments to unemployed persons depend on the person's unemployment insurance status, employment period, and the reason for their dismissal. Payments begin on the eighth day after the unemployed's registration with the local state unemployment office, but this start date may be extended for up to three months, depending on the amount of the severance payment received by a dismissed employee.[290] Payments are made according to the following formula:

- Unemployed persons who were employed at least 26 calendar weeks during the 12 months immediately preceding unemployment receive unemployment benefits depending on the insurance term, i.e., the period, during which an employee was covered by unemployment insurance. An unemployment payment to a person with an insurance term

---

[286]February 2003 Amendment to Social Contribution Law.

[287]Social Contribution Law art. 1; Resolution No. 225.

[288]Resolution No. 605.

[289]Regulation 1266.

[290]Unemployment Law arts. 22, 31.

of up to two years is established at 50 percent of such person's average wage;[291] a person with an insurance term from two to six years receives 55 percent of the average wage; a person with an insurance term from 6 to 10 years receives 60 percent of the average wage; and a person with an insurance term of longer than 10 years receives 70 percent of the average wage. The unemployment payment is paid in full for the first 90 calendar days of unemployment. Only 80 percent of the unemployment payment is paid during calendar days 91 to 180 of unemployment. Thereafter, an unemployed person is entitled to only 70 percent of the unemployment payment.[292] The unemployment payment may not exceed the average statistical wage approved for the respective administrative region for the immediately preceding month and may not be less than the livelihood minimum.[293]

- Unemployed persons who were employed for less than 26 calendar weeks during the 12 months immediately preceding employment, persons who did not work for more than six months immediately prior to unemployment, and persons dismissed for reasons such as
  - systematic failure to observe the requirements of the employment agreement,
  - unjustified absence from work,
  - drunkenness on the job,
  - conviction for theft,
  - single severe violation of labor commitments by a company's officer, or
  - dishonest actions by employees responsible for money or for carrying out supervisory functions,

  are entitled to unemployment payments in the amount of the livelihood minimum, irrespective of the insurance term.
- Unemployed persons who were not subject to unemployment insurance and persons seeking jobs for the first time

---

[291]For the calculation of average wage, see I.D., above.
[292]Unemployment Law art. 23.
[293]For a discussion of the livelihood minimum, see IV.A., above.

are entitled to unemployment payments in the amount of the livelihood minimum.

Unemployment payments are made until the unemployed person finds a job, but generally may not last longer than 360 calendar days during two years. This period is increased to 720 calendar days for senior citizens (i.e., men at least 58 years of age and women at least 53 years of age), and is decreased to 180 calendar days for unemployed citizens who are registered for the first time or were not otherwise covered by unemployment insurance. After the initial payment period, an unemployed person is entitled to a payment in the amount of 75 percent of the minimum wage for a period of 180 calendar days,[294] provided that the average monthly income per family member does not exceed the livelihood minimum, as established by law.[295]

Unemployment payments may be terminated for up to 90 calendar days if the unemployed person refuses two job offers from the state unemployment authority, violates the registration procedure, or for certain other reasons.[296]

3. *Social Insurance Disability Fund*

Effective April 1, 2001, employers are required to contribute to the Social Insurance Disability Fund. The amounts of such contributions, ranging from 0.2 percent to 13.8 percent of total payroll, depend on the type of business and the established level of risk assigned to the employer's business, ranging from level 1 (low risk) to level 67 (high risk).[297] Employees will not be required to contribute to the Social Insurance Disability Fund.[298] The Social Insurance Disability Fund will provide financial aid to employees in connection with employment-related injuries or diseases.[299]

[294] Unemployment Law art. 28.

[295] For a discussion of the livelihood minimum, see IV.A., above.

[296] Unemployment Law art. 31.

[297] See Law of Ukraine on Amending the Law on Insurance Tariffs for Mandatory State Social Insurance Against Accidents at a Work Place and Occupational Diseases Which Result in Working Disability (Insurance Tariff Law) (Apr. 3, 2003).

[298] Working Disability Law; Social Insurance Fundamentals art. 4; Insurance Tariff Law arts. 1–4; Insurance Tariff Procedure arts. 1–23.

[299] See VII.B., above.

IX. IMMIGRATION

Foreign nationals in Ukraine have the same employment and labor rights as Ukrainian citizens unless otherwise provided by Ukrainian law or international agreement. Ukrainian law does restrict employment in certain positions to Ukrainian citizens.[300] For example, the captain of a vessel used for business, scientific, or cultural purposes,[301] a notary,[302] a state servant,[303] a judge,[304] a licensed attorney,[305] an auditor,[306] a prosecutor, or an investigator[307] must be a Ukrainian citizen.

Foreign citizens immigrating to Ukraine to work for a definite period of time must receive an employment permit. An employment permit may be issued to a foreign national only if: (1) there are no Ukrainian nationals in the region (or, in certain cases, in the entire country) capable of performing the work for which the employment permit is requested; or (2) there are sufficient other grounds for using foreign labor.[308]

Any employer in Ukraine, whether Ukrainian or foreign, may employ foreign nationals only if they have valid employment permits, unless otherwise provided by international treaties of the Ukraine,[309] or if such noncitizens are employed by investors under production-sharing agreements.[310]

An employment permit is issued by the State Employment Center of the Ministry of Labor (Employment Center) or, upon

---

[300]*See* Law on Legal Status of Foreigners, art. 8 (Feb. 4, 1998), as amended (Foreign Status Law).

[301]Maritime Code, art. 53 (May 23, 1995), as amended.

[302]Law on Notaries, art. 3 (Sept. 2, 1993), as amended; *see* Foreign Status Law art. 8.

[303]Law on State Service, art. 4 (Dec. 16, 1993), as amended (State Service Law).

[304]Constitution art. 127.

[305]Law on Advokatura, art. 2 (Dec. 19, 1992), as amended.

[306]Law on Auditing Activities, art. 5 (Apr. 22, 1993), as amended.

[307]Law on the Office of the Prosecutor, art. 46 (Nov. 5, 1991), as amended.

[308]Regulations on the Procedure of Issuing Employment Permits to Foreign Citizens in Ukraine §1, approved by the Resolution of the Cabinet of Ministers of Ukraine No. 2028 (Sept. 1, 1999) (Foreign Permit Regulations).

[309]*Id.* §2.

[310]Law on Production-Sharing Agreements, art. 35 (Sept. 14, 1999).

consent of the Employment Center by the regional employment centers, for a period of up to one year. The one-year period may be extended.[311]

An employer must submit the following documents to the Employment Center when applying for an employment permit:

- an application stating the reasons for employing foreigners and demonstrating the employer's readiness to provide all necessary working and living conditions;
- notarized copies of the company's charter and certificate of registration;
- a list of foreigners, stating the full name, year of birth, sex, passport number, and profession of each;
- a copy of the agreement, if any, between the foreign company and the Ukrainian legal entity providing for employment of foreigners;
- a copy of the draft employment agreement between the employer and the foreign employee;
- copies of the documents that evidence the foreigners' education or profession;
- the employer's good standing certificate from the state tax administration;
- a power of attorney for the employer's representative; and
- evidence of payment of the required application fee (equal to 10 nontaxable income units (UAH 170)).[312]

The Employment Center is required to issue its decision regarding an employment permit within 30 days of submission of a completed application.

The employer must inform the Employment Center of the commencement or termination of work by a foreign national within three days. The employer also is required to report the foreign employee's income and withheld taxes to the state tax administration on a quarterly basis.

---

[311]Effective June 7, 2002, the four-years' restriction of the maximum term of continuous stay in Ukraine for employment purposes became void. The six-month delay for submission of a new application after the expiration of the prior employment permit was also abolished. Resolution of the Cabinet of Ministers No. 649 (May 17, 2002).

[312]Foreign Permit Regulations §§5, 9. For an explanation of nontaxable income units, see V.A.4., above.

ISRAEL*

Introduction

A. General

The state of Israel was founded on May 14, 1948, following the United Nations' resolution of November 29, 1947, ending the British mandate and forming a Jewish state. The United Nations' resolution was the culmination of an eventful 70-year period in which the Zionist movement sought to found an independent state for the Jewish people. This pre-state period included many interconnected processes, events, and characteristics, which had an important impact on Israel's modern-day political, economic, and legal systems, including the character of Israeli labor law and relations. For example, the Histadrut Federation of Labour (Histadrut), which is discussed in more detail below,[1] was founded in 1920 as a multifunctional institution, acting in the role of the not-yet-founded branches of government. The presence of the Histadrut was a determining factor in forming the character of Israel's trade union structure.

In its 56-year existence, Israel has fought five major wars and has been at the center of countless armed conflicts. As a result, army service in Israel is compulsory for most men and women and plays a dominant role, among other things, as a factor influencing the workforce. An example is the late entrance of young Israeli

---

*Frances Raday, Professor of Law, Elias Lieberman Chair in Labour Law, Hebrew University of Jerusalem, Israel; Israeli advocate and barrister-at-law, acting as consultant practitioner and litigator in labor law; independent expert to the United Nations CEDAW Committee. The author wishes to warmly thank Advs. Rachel Barag-Hirshberg and Ariel Avgar for their most helpful research assistance.

[1]See the Introduction, at B. and II.A.1., below.

men and women into the workforce due to their two- to four-year army service and annual absences for reserve service for many adult males. The constant state of conflict, as well as the aftermath of the Holocaust trauma, helps to explain the emphasis placed on the family unit in Israel, which, in turn, has influenced protective labor legislation.

Israel is a parliamentary democracy based on legislative, executive, and judicial branches. In 1995, the election method was reformed with the creation of a two-ballot system in which the voter casts a separate ballot for a party and directly for a Prime Minister candidate. This reform resulted in an increased number of small sectarian parties in the Knesset, the Israeli legislature. As a result of this fragmentation, the 1999 elections witnessed the two-seat election of a political party representing workers as such. In 2002, direct election for the prime minister was reversed and the previous system readopted, in which the voter casts a single ballot for a party and prime minister, rather than a separate ballot for each.

Israel has a population of 6,748,100. The majority of this population, approximately 79 percent, is Jewish. The minority Arab and Druze populations number 1,300,800 and constitute approximately 19 percent of the population. Within the Arab population are both Christians and Muslims. Israel has two official languages: Hebrew and Arabic. The birthrate in the Israeli population as a whole is 2.98 children per family. However, among the Arab Muslim population, this rate is considerably greater, approximately 4.76. The birthrate in the Jewish Ultra-Orthodox population, which constitutes a small minority of the Jewish population, also is extremely high and stands at approximately 7.6 children.

The civilian labor force in Israel totals approximately 2,645,900. This number represents 53 percent of the population 15 years or older. However, each of the many sub-groups within the Israeli population, as defined by ethnic characteristics and religious affiliation, has different workforce participation rates.

The Jewish Ultra-Orthodox community, which is a small but vocal minority of the population, does not serve in the army because of religious convictions. They have an extremely low percentage of workforce participation because men spend their time in religious studies. In recent years, however, there has been a rise in workforce participation among women in this group.

The minority Arab and Druze populations also are characterized as traditional communities. Despite recent improvements resulting from a move away from agricultural occupations, the Arab population still is mostly situated in the lower socio-economic bracket. In addition, the Arab women's workforce participation falls well below the general average.

Due to Israel's unique nature, throughout its years the state has been subject to a number of large immigration waves. In the 1950s, large numbers of immigrants arrived in Israel from North Africa and Eastern countries. In its first 20 years, Israel's population grew from approximately 650,000 to 2,600,000. In the 1990s, approximately one million immigrants entered the state of Israel from the former Soviet Union. In addition, in the 1980s and 1990s, there was a large immigration from Ethiopia. These large waves of immigration have had a strong impact on the Israeli economy and have provided both a benefit and a challenge regarding integration into the labor force.

Israel's economy can be divided into two main parts, referred to as small and large economies. The small economy is comprised of thousands of small- and medium-sized businesses. Although the number of such businesses was approximately 18,056 and employed close to 350,000 workers in 1995, the contribution of the small economy is relatively minor. The large economy is made up of approximately 150 large corporations, which employ the majority of the educated workforce and produce most of the gross domestic product.

A major characteristic of the Israeli economy is the relatively dominant role played by several family-owned corporations, which have a substantial influence on the entire economy, particularly in the area of communications.

An additional characteristic of the Israeli economy, which has a significant impact on labor law, is the relatively large role played by the government. Until the early 1990s, the public sector owned and operated a majority of traditional industries, such as food, chemicals, and the military. Due to the government's dominant role in the Israeli economy, government is one of the country's major employers. During the 1990s, Israel went through an extensive privatization process. Today, attempts are being made to introduce the free market to a number of monopolies still controlled by the government, such as the national airline.

2003 was the third year of *intifada* (armed hostilities) and world recession in which:

- unemployment reached 291,000, approximately 11 percent;
- GNP per capita dropped to $16,400; and
- the number of persons living in poverty increased.

The average monthly wage per employee in Israel is equal to approximately 6,800 NIS,[2] although there is wide disparity among various groups of Israeli workers. Israel began its statehood on the basis of socialist and egalitarian ideologies. In the early 1950s, the gap between rich and poor was one of the lowest in the world. Over the years, however, socioeconomic gaps within the population have grown considerably. Today, among Western democracies, Israel has one of the highest rates of income disparity. In addition, Israel has a significant gap between the status of men and women in the workplace. In both the public and private sectors, there is a gap in salaries and promotions of men and women.

Ironically, one of the factors contributing to income disparities is Israel's successful development of a high-technology industry. Although the growth of this industry has created a large boost for the economy as a whole, it also has led to a growing income and wealth gap between populations employed in the new economy and those employed in the traditional manual labor industries.

2003 was the year of Israel's Economic Recovery Plan. This Plan had sweeping implications for labor law and relations as regards both content and method. It introduced reduction of wages of public sector employees, reduction of pension rights, structural changes in pension fund ownership and management (nationalization) all of which had been established in collective agreements, and restructuring (privatization). The Plan was, from the start, introduced by the Finance Ministry under threat of legislation. After failed negotiations with the New Histadrut, many of the measures proposed in the Plan were imposed on employees by legislation:

[2]The Israeli currency is the New Israel Shekel (NIS), which has been in use since 1985. The NIS strength vis-à-vis the U.S. dollar is approximately 4.5 shekels for each dollar. Thus, the average wage in shekels is approximately 6,000 NIS.

the Law for the Recovery of the Israeli Economy. The passage of the Law resulted in an application to the National Labour Court by the New Histadrut to cancel the Law on the grounds that this was legislative intervention in collective bargaining and violated the fundamental right to freedom of organization and collective bargaining. The New Histadrut held a public sector strike for nearly 100 days. A collective agreement was subsequently reached in concession bargaining with the New Histadrut, which lessened the severity of the wage reduction and pension reduction measures. The Law was amended and remained the sole source of reduction of conditions as regards non-Histadrut unions, such as University faculty, doctors, and teachers, who had not reached agreement with the government. These groups petitioned the High Court of Justice or applied to the National Labour Court to oppose the legislative intervention in their labor conditions. The doctors and teachers reached out-of-court compromise agreements, and only the University Faculty's Association retains its application in court.

The method the government employed of achieving the imposition of the Economic Plan by means of legislative power and intervention marks a watershed in Israel's labor relations. The extent and aggressiveness of the state's overpowering of the unions is unprecedented and signals future structural weakening of trade union power and of the collective bargaining system. The impact of the government's unilateral changing of the rules of the game in labor relations on labor law and relations and the decisions of the courts on the matter is discussed at II.C., below, because it was in the context of strike orders that judicial rulings regarding the Law for the Recovery of the Israeli Economy were given.

B. Status of Labor and Employer Unions

Unionism in Israel developed on the infrastructure of the Histadrut, which was formed in 1920, 28 years before the State of Israel was created. Indeed, the Histadrut formed the nucleus of the developing pre-state entity. As such, the Histadrut formed a number of separate corporate entities, which operated as key players in the areas of economic and commercial entrepreneurship, pension insurance, and health insurance. Indeed, until the 1990s, the Histadrut remained the largest single employer and the largest supplier of health fund and occupational pension insurance in Israel.

Since the mid-1990s, there has been a dramatic change in the centrality of the Histadrut's role in these diverse areas, and most of the Histadrut's economic activities were sold. In 1994, after a leadership policy change, the Histadrut was renamed the New Histadrut. In 1995, the National Health Insurance Law was passed, severing Histadrut membership from health fund membership. The result has been a drastic fall in Histadrut membership from approximately 80 percent of the workforce before the mid-1990s to between 20 and 30 percent in the year 2000. The Histadrut traditionally has been a political union at the central level, with internal elections based on political party lists. In the 1999 elections, the Histadrut chairperson headed a parliamentary list that won two seats in the 120-seat Knesset.

Employers in Israel are divided into three main sectors: private, state, and labor (Histadrut). Organizations of employers exist only in the private sector. The Histadrut, although functioning as a major employer, has not created an employer association for its employing enterprises. The private sector is organized by an umbrella organization, known as the Coordinative Chamber of Economic Organizations (Chamber), which, in 1990, encompassed 80 percent of Israeli private industry. The Chamber represents a number of specific employer unions such as the Farmers' Association and the Manufacturers' Association. The Chamber is responsible for negotiating framework collective agreements[3] with the trade union department of the Histadrut and with the government. In addition to its role in the collective negotiating process, the Chamber acts as a lobby, promoting different economic policies, tariffs, and tax legislation.

The Chamber and the Histadrut, in its capacity as the central union organization, conduct a number of joint activities. There is an extensive history of cooperation between them with regard to reaching framework agreements. Cooperation between the Histadrut and the Chamber also exists in the labor courts,[4] where publicly appointed officials sit on the bench as representatives of each.

---

[3]For a discussion of framework agreements, see II.B.1., below.

[4]See the Introduction, at C.2.c., below.

C. Sources of Israeli Labor Law

1. *General*

Israeli labor law is derived from a number of different sources: constitutional principles established through the enactment of Basic Laws, which guide the courts' interpretation of labor laws and agreements; specific labor legislation, which usually is of a mandatory, protective nature; and international labor treaties used by the labor courts in the interpretation of existing laws. Other sources include individual employment contracts,[5] collective agreements and arrangements,[6] employer regulations, and custom and case law.

2. *National Labor Law Sources*

a. *Basic Laws*

Constitutional drafting and development in Israel has been by legislation of separate Basic Laws, which serve as chapters of the yet-to-be-completed constitution. In 1992, the Basic Law: Human Dignity and Freedom and the Basic Law: Freedom of Occupation were enacted. These Basic Laws are considered to have full constitutional effect. They empower the courts to declare legislation, subsequent to its enactment, void if it is not in accordance with their principles.

In their opening statements, the Basic Laws declare that their principal objective is to preserve human dignity according to the spirit of the state as expressed in the Declaration of Independence. The rights to human dignity, life, property, freedom of movement, freedom of occupation, and privacy all receive specific mention and protection in the Basic Laws; however, for reasons unconnected to labor law,[7] the Basic Laws are silent on the right to equality. Some, but not all, of the Justices of the Supreme Court have

---

[5]See I.B., below.

[6]See II.B., below.

[7]The Basic Laws' silence on the issue of equality is the result of opposition of the religious parliamentary parties to the inclusion of a right that would threaten religious hegemony over marriage and divorce status.

declared that equality is, nevertheless, protected under the rubric of "human dignity."[8]

The Basic Laws have had a strong influence on most areas of Israeli law, not least of which is the area of labor law. The Basic Laws have affected the interpretation of labor law principles. They have been utilized by the courts to introduce constitutional factors into the resolution of both collective and individual labor disputes. For example, the firing of employees for union-related activity was prohibited and the right to picket recognized, at least in part, on the basis of the Basic Law: Human Dignity and Freedom. Other rights, such as employees' right to strike, the prohibition of employment discrimination, and employers' right to restrict the use of trade secrets have been reinforced by reliance on the fundamental rights guaranteed in the Basic Laws. The rights to property and freedom of occupation under the Basic Laws also have served, in many instances, as values that enhanced employer prerogatives, such as the right to transfer an enterprise and to transfer employees without their consent, or the right to control the expression of journalists in the employ of a newspaper.

b. Labor Legislation

In the state's early years, intensive legislation in the labor sphere established a comprehensive infrastructure of minimum standards for the individual employment relationship and facilitative norms for collective bargaining and dispute settlement. Most of these laws were of a protective nature.

These protective laws, for the most part legislated in the 1950s and 1960s include:

- The Hours of Work and Rest Law, 5711-1951;[9]
- The Employment of Women Law, 5714-1954;
- The Sick Pay Law, 5736-1976;
- The Annual Leave Law, 5711-1951;
- The Wage Protection Law, 5718-1958;
- The Severance Pay Law, 5723-1963;

---

[8]Alice Miller v. Minister of Defence (1995) (IV) P.D. 49, 94.

[9]The first number at the end of the law's title stands for the date according to the Jewish calendar.

- Male and Female Workers (Equal Pay) Law, 5724-1964; and
- The Minimum Wage Law, 5747-1987.

In addition to these protective laws, labor legislation includes additional specific laws such as:

- The Collective Agreement Law, 5717-1957;
- The Settlement of Labor Disputes Law, 5717-1957;
- The Labor Courts Law, 5729-1969;
- The Employment (Equal Opportunities) Law, 5748-1988;
- The Work Safety Ordinance (New Version) 5730-1970; and
- The Labor Inspection (Organization) Law, 5714-1954.

c. *Labor Law Courts*

In 1969, the labor law court system was founded. The labor courts were established as a separate court system to deal with the specific requirements of settling both individual and collective labor disputes. This separate court system was established due to the legislature's perception that a specialized court system similar to the one existing in continental legal schemes would help reduce the growing number of serious labor disputes in the 1960s. The unique character of the labor courts is due to its combined makeup. In addition to the professional judges who preside over each case, there are also public representatives, of both the employers and employees, who preside in all cases with the exception of criminal cases. There are two court levels, regional and national.

There are five regional labor courts, which have jurisdiction over:

- disputes between individual employees and employers;
- legal disputes concerning the formation of an employment contract;
- labor disputes, in a specific workplace or of a specific employer, between a representative union and an employer or an employers' organization representing the employer;
- labor disputes between an employee and a union; and
- lawsuits concerning social security benefits and the National Insurance Institute.

Cases in the regional labor courts are heard by a panel of one professional judge and two public representatives.

The National Labour Court, situated in Jerusalem, has both original jurisdiction and appellate jurisdiction. The National Labour Court's original jurisdiction includes:

- disputes between parties to a general collective agreement, i.e., between a representative union and an employers' organization; and
- disputes between unions or between employers' organizations.

In sum, the National Labour Court presides over appeals from the district labor courts and over major labor disputes. Cases in the National Labour Court are usually heard by three professional judges and two to four public representatives.

There is a distinction in Israeli labor law between legal and economic disputes. Legal disputes are disputes concerning the implementation of rights whereas economic disputes are those concerning the creation of new rights. The labor courts only adjudicate legal disputes.

The National Labour Court overturned the decision of a Regional Labour Court judge not to disqualify himself when the proposed compromise agreement of the mediators was included, by mistake, in the court file and the judge had seen it. The National Labour Court held that the disqualification was required in order to avoid breach of privacy in the mediation process and to preserve the impartiality of the judicial process.[10]

The Supreme Court, in its function as the High Court of Justice, sits as an *ex certiorari* court over the National Labour Court's decisions.

3. *International Labor Law Sources*

International conventional law is not self-executing in Israel; however, international labor standards have been adhered to as a basic minimum, through their inclusion by legislative incorporation or by their application in judicial decisions.

---

[10]Zika Elecs. Ltd. v. Judith Yakobovitch (2002) 37 P.D.A . 796.

In many instances, the protective legislation listed above was based on International Labor Organization (ILO) Conventions, for example, the Hours of Work and Rest Law, 5711-1951; the Annual Leave Law, 5711-1951; the Wage Protection Law, 5718-1958; and the Male and Female Workers (Equal Pay) Law, 5724-1964. In other instances, the Israeli legislature went beyond the protective requirements of ILO legislation, as was the case in the Severance Pay Law, 5723-1963, and the Minimum Wage Law, 5747-1987.

The labor courts have expressly applied the principles of freedom to organize and collectively bargain, in reliance on ILO Conventions 89 and 98.[11] They also applied the principles of ILO Convention 111 to strike down discrimination in promotions against women employees; the labor courts held that discrimination of this kind was contrary to the norms of the international conventional law and hence contrary to Israeli public policy.[12]

I. Individual Employment

A. The Employment Relationship

1. *General*

Israeli law recognizes a number of frameworks for the implementation of work: employment relationships, freelance contracts, independent contracting, and predetermined status. The task of delineating these categories for the purpose of applying the labor laws, individual and collective, is assigned to the labor courts. An express provision by the parties that the implementation of work is not in the context of an employment relationship acts to transfer the burden of proof to the party claiming otherwise, but is not dispositive; the court is the final arbiter. However, in the event that a court finds an employment relationship despite an express

[11] *See, e.g.*, Markovich Leon v. Histadrut (1974) 6 P.D.A. 197; Horn et Laybovich v. Histadrut (2000) 35 P.D.A. 145.

[12] El-Al Flight Crew v. Edna Hazin (1972/3) 4 P.D.A. 365.

contractual provision to the contrary, the parties may provide for restitution of any payments made in reliance on the expressly agreed non-employment status.

2. *Tests for Employment Relationship*

Judicial tests for determining the existence of an employment relationship have been developed in labor court and High Court of Justice jurisprudence. In developing these tests, there has been a progressive move toward greater flexibility. The original test was the control test, under which the courts examined merely whether the relationship was based on the complete control and supervision of the employer over the employee. In early labor court jurisprudence, the control test was subsumed into the integration test. According to the integration test, all the circumstances of the relationship under which work is implemented are taken into account in determining whether the work is being performed as an integral part of the user's enterprise or as part of an enterprise of the person performing the work. Further flexibility purportedly was added to this test by the High Court of Justice. The Court accepted dicta of the National Labour Court to the effect that the proper test is a mixed one in which not only the integration test, but also all other tests, are taken into account in order to account for the increasing complexity of employment relationships.[13] The distinction between the integration test and the mixed test seems to be rhetorical rather than substantive; however, under the auspices of the mixed test, the High Court of Justice extended recognition of an employment relationship to an elected post in which there clearly had been no contract of employment.[14]

The Supreme Court has held, following its own previous decisions, that the existence of an employment contract was not essential to the finding of an employment relationship.[15] This approach was accepted in *obiter dicta* by the National Labour Court.[16]

---

[13]Moor v. National Labour Court (1996) (IV) 50 P.D. 628.

[14]Sarosi v. National Labour Court (1998) (IV) 52 P.D. 817.

[15]Ofer Sadot v. Prison Auth. (2001) 55 (IV) P.D. 817.

[16]Moshe Asulin v. National Broad. Auth. (2001) 36 P.D.A. 689.

Thus, elected officials may be considered entitled to some employee rights. In the *Sarosi* case,[17] a member of a local council was held entitled to unemployment benefits under the National Insurance Law. Although confirming that an employment contract is not essential for finding an employment relationship, the Supreme Court nevertheless held that a prisoner who was required to work by the Prison Service was not considered an employee for the purposes of the Minimum Wage Law. Applying similar reasoning, the National Labour Court held that the elected assistant chairperson of a Religious Council was not entitled to statutory severance pay.[18] Each of these decisions was reached on the basis of a purposive reading of the statutory entitlements to discover whether they were intended to apply to these non-contractual relationships.

In some recent judgments handed down by the National Labour Court, the criteria for establishing an employment relationship, in cases of freelancers and independent contractors, were further expanded. The *Zadka* case,[19] decided on October 16, 2001, held that a journalist, reporting from abroad, who was characterized as a "freelancer" under the parties' contract, was actually an employee. In a minority opinion, the President of the National Labour Court recognized the existence of a category of "freelancer-employees," who are the product of a changing labor market where new work relationships exist and new employment tests are needed. Thus, he asserted, the journalist was not an employee, due to characteristics of the relationship that existed between the two parties, but was, nonetheless, entitled to some of the protection granted by the protective labor statutes, specifically severance pay and early notice compensation.

In another case, the National Labour Court held that technicians and cameramen at the National Broadcasting Authority (NBA) who provided services via independent companies founded and encouraged by the NBA for the purpose of circumventing

---

[17]Sarosi v. National Labour Court (1998) (IV) 52 P.D. 817.

[18]Joseph Vaaknin v. Religious Council Ofekim (Nat'l Lab. Ct., Dec. 31, 2003, not yet published).

[19]Shaul Zadka v. State of Israel–Gali Zahal (IDF radio) (2001) 36 P.D.A. 625.

employment relationships were, in fact, employees.[20] However, in further cases, the line followed by the National Labour Court was less clearly an expansion of the employment status.

In two cases, after the decision in *Zadka*, the National Labour Court considered the status of "freelancers." Regarding a tourist guide,[21] the National Labour Court held by a majority that there was an employment relationship, while, regarding the legal adviser of a political party for 25 years, who had his own law office,[22] the Court found by a majority no employment relationship; however, in 2003, the Court, distinguishing its previous decision, held that the legal adviser of a town council was in an employment relationship even though he had his own law office.[23] A volunteer working in a theater as an administrator and assistant stage manager was held not to be an employee.[24]

In three cases concerning the boundary between independent contractor and employee status, although the contracts of service included clauses that provided that the service-giver would not be considered an employee, an employment relationship was found to exist: thus, a welder,[25] a diver,[26] and an academic coordinator[27] who also provided the same service in his own business, were all found to be employees. In two of these cases, it was held that the employers were entitled to restitution of payments made in reliance on the expressly agreed non-employment status. In this matter, the National Labour Court held that although employers cannot demand restitution as a rule, they may do so either where the right to restitution was expressly included in the contract or where it was the employee who requested to be employed as an indepen-

[20]Moshe Asulin v. National Broad. Auth. (2001) 36 P.D.A. 689.

[21]Ami Cohen v. "Dan"—The Cooperative Ass'n for Public Transportation Ltd. (2002) 37 P.D.A. 817.

[22]Z'eav Trainin, Adv. v. Micha Charish and The Labor Party (2002) 37 P.D.A. 433.

[23]AG v. Advocat Raphael Shtubb. (Nat'l Lab. Ct., Mar. 24, 2003, not yet published).

[24]Ahuva (Agi) Friedman v. Eliezer Houz (2003) 38 P.D.A. 39.

[25]Joseph Tuito v. Cooling for Airconditioners Eng'g (1965) Ltd. (2002) 37 P.D.A. 354.

[26]Uri Izik v. T.H.L (Water Planning for Israel) Ltd. (2001) 36 P.D.A. 817.

[27]Sami Ben-Chamo v. The Institute for Productivity and Production (2003) 38 P.D.A. 433.

dent contractor. However, even in such cases the Court may exercise its discretion in deciding whether restitution is warranted. Indeed, in a 2003 case, the Court awarded a welder, who had been defined in his contract as an independent contractor, employee status and gave him his employee rights calculated on the basis of his considerably higher independent contractor's salary.[28] Furthermore, the Court indicated that this policy was intended to act as a deterrent against the flawed practice of signing employees on contracts that negate their employee status.

In the case of state employees, a special problem arises with regard to retroactive change in status from independent contractor to employee because appointment as a state employee has to be in accordance with statutory procedures. The National Labour Court has held that, in these circumstances, recognition of entitlement to employee status only gives eligibility to participate in internal appointment tenders and does not automatically confer the status of state employee.[29]

3. *Labor-Only Contracting*

There is a growing trend toward diversification of the labor force in nontraditional employment relationships. A major form of such employment is labor-only contracting, which has grown to about 5 percent of the labor force. Labor-only contracting produces a triangular set of relationships, among a labor contractor, a contract worker, and an end user of the worker's services. Originally, it fell to the labor courts to determine whether the contractor or the user was to be viewed as the employer. The labor courts initially adopted a facilitative approach to such relationships and, later, a more restrictive approach.

In 1996, the Employment by Labour-Only Contractors' Law (Contractors' Law) was passed. The Contractors' Law legitimized the triangular relationship, although apparently leaving it to the courts to determine the identity of the employer. The Contractors'

---

[28] Marja Elias Rafik v. Sdom Metal Indus. (1989) Ltd. (2003) 38 P.D.A. 223.

[29] Yaakov Hasson v. State of Israel, Ministry of Housing & Constr. (Nat'l Lab. Ct., Sept. 9, 2003, not yet published).

Law also established a licensing system for labor contractors and a supervisory system for enforcement of the Law's requirements. As regards the contractor's employees, the Contractors' Law gives precedence to collective agreements of the contractor over collective agreements in the user establishment and provides that, in the absence of a collective agreement with the contractor, the contractor's employee will, after three years of work, become entitled to the terms and conditions prevailing in the user establishment, not including protection against dismissal without cause.

As originally enacted, the Contractors' Law was the subject of severe criticism and, in 2000, was amended. According to the Amendment, labor-only contracting was to be limited to nine months of employment. After nine months of employment, the employee would be considered the employee of the user. The implementation of this provision has been postponed from year to year in the Annual Budget Laws. The Amendment additionally provided that, even before the nine months have elapsed, employees are entitled to employment conditions equal to those under the collective agreement of the user or under that of the contractor, whichever is to the employee's benefit. The only exception to this is where the contractors' employment conditions have been established by a sectoral collective agreement[30] that has been authorized for extension by the Minister of Labour. This provision is in effect.

The District Labor Court of Tel Aviv addressed the complexity of the triangular relationship involved in labor-only contracting.[31] The Court held that stenographers of the Israeli courts who were employed via labor contractors, and yet had a longstanding, permanent relationship with the user (the state), were recognized as state employees and entitled to employment conditions equal to those of state employees. This decision was handed down prior to the date of coming into force of the Amendment to the Employment of Employees by Labour Contractors' Law. The Court held that the labor-contractors were used as a means to circumvent the

---

[30]See II.B.1., below.

[31]Hani Avni Cohen v. State of Israel (Dist. Lab. Ct. Tel Aviv, July 29, 2001) (unpublished).

requirement to provide the stenographers with employment rights and conditions of full-fledged state employees. The Court based this conclusion, among other things, on the fact that over the years, many different contractors were used while, for the most part, the actual employees remained the same.

4. Multiple Employers

The National Labour Court continued with a policy of recognizing multiple employer status for the purpose of guaranteeing employee rights. Thus, in a case of a holding company and its component subsidiary companies, the Court held that both also would be considered employers where negation of such recognition would allow either company, in bad faith, to deprive the employee of collective or individual employment rights. In the case at hand, the conditions for recognizing the holding company as employer were not established to the satisfaction of the Court.[32]

B. The Employment Contract

The employment relationship is a based on contract. There is no special statutory regulation of the employment contract. Two employment contract bills, which were presented by the government to the Knesset in 1968 and 1985, failed to pass into law.

1. Contract Formation

Israeli labor law does not impose any general restrictions on the mode of forming an employment contract. The contract may be written or oral, and there are no requirements for giving written evidence of the terms of contract to the employee after the contract has been entered. The only exceptions to this lack of regulation are those concerning labor-only contracting and employment of workers from foreign countries.[33]

The General Contract Law, 1973, applies to employment contracts and imposes a good-faith obligation in both the negotiation and implementation of contract terms. Beyond this, the labor courts

---

[32]Amiel Cohen v. Israel Chems. Ltd. (Nat'l Lab. Ct., June 8, 2003) (not yet published).

[33]See I.A.3., above, and IX., below.

have held that the employment relationship is fiduciary in nature; hence, the parties are bound to a higher level of good faith and disclosure than that prevailing with respect to general contracts.

2. *Content of the Contract*

The parties are free to determine contractually terms and conditions of employment above the statutory or collective agreement minimums. Additionally, the contents of the contract are supplied by judicial implication of employer and employee rights and obligations, such as the employer's obligations to take care of the employee's welfare, pay wages, and, in certain situations, provide actual work tasks, and the employee's obligations of loyalty, obedience to instructions, and duty of care.

3. *Employer Prerogatives and Contract Variation*

Employers are considered to have a prerogative to manage the enterprise as they see fit. This prerogative includes disciplinary powers, the right to dismiss, and the right to determine the organizational infrastructure of the business. This prerogative is considered by the labor courts to be derived from the employer's property rights in the enterprise and also to constitute an implied term of the employment contract.

One of the crucial problems arising in the context of employer prerogatives is the extent of the employer's right to vary, unilaterally, the terms and conditions of the contract. The rule established by the High Court of Justice is that employers have neither the right nor the power to unilaterally change any of the terms and conditions of the employment contract; they may only terminate the contract and offer the employee a new contract.[34] The approach of the labor courts has been, in practice, somewhat different. Despite the High Court of Justice ruling, the labor courts have tended toward recognizing unilateral employer changes in a variety of situations, such as public service employment or the changing of conditions that are not considered fundamental and immutable terms of the contract.

---

[34]Milfelder v. National Labour Court (1987) (II) 41 P.D. 210.

4. Trial Period

Provisions regarding trial periods are to be found in collective agreements and may vary between 6 to 24 months. According to the labor courts, the employer has a good-faith obligation not to dismiss an employee during the trial period without giving suitable opportunity for proof of ability to do the job.

C. Termination of Employment

There is no comprehensive statutory regulation of termination, and the underlying principle is that the employer is free to dismiss the employee at any time, for any reason, or for no reason at all. However, as discussed in further detail below, there are extensive restrictions on this freedom. Extensive collective bargaining regulation of dismissal provides a considerable level of job security in the collective bargaining sector.[35] There also is protection, under contract law principles, against dismissal that is not in good faith, there are statutory restrictions on dismissal in specific circumstances, and there is protection against dismissal for exercise of human rights.

1. Modes of Termination

a. Termination of a Fixed-Term Contract

At the date of termination, nonrenewal of a fixed term contract normally is not considered to constitute a dismissal. However, where the contract is renewed time and again, nonrenewal may be considered a bad-faith dismissal.

In 2003, there was a trilogy of National Labour Court decisions dealing with employers' claims to the right to terminate fixed-term contracts unilaterally without any termination procedure.[36] The Court held that where the nature of the fixed-term contract is such as to establish a legitimate expectation of continuity, the con-

---

[35]See I.C.3.b., below.

[36]Dr. Yossi Gutterman v. The Academic College of Emek Israel (2003) 38 P.D.A. 448; General Health Servs. v. Dr. Shmuel Friedlander (Nat'l Lab. Ct., May 20, 2003) (not yet published); State of Israel v. Eli Sadeh (Nat'l Lab. Ct., Mar. 3, 2003).

tract cannot be considered as summarily terminated at the end of its term but, rather, employers must give advance notice of their intention not to renew the contract and give their reasons for that decision and employees have the right to contest the termination. In one of these cases, in order to allow proper procedures to be followed, the Court enforced the continuation of the employment relationship after the end of the fixed-term contract.[37]

b. Dismissal by the Employer

Dismissal is defined as a unilateral act of termination on the part of the employer during the period of a fixed-term contract or a contract for an indefinite period. The employer has a prerogative to dismiss, but this prerogative is restricted in various circumstances: by collective agreement provisions, specific statutory prohibitions, and the contractual good-faith doctrine.

c. Resignation

Resignation is defined as a termination of employment at the initiative of the employee. The employee has a right to resign unless restricted by contractual provision.

d. By Mutual Agreement

An example of termination by mutual agreement is retirement. Where there is an agreed pension plan, termination of employment at the pensionable age is not considered as either dismissal or resignation.

e. Frustration

The doctrine of frustration is given very limited application, but can be applied in cases of illness or death. It has been held that the closing of a firm in case of bankruptcy is not a cause of frustration.[38]

---

[37]General Health Servs. v. Dr. Shmuel Friedlander (Nat'l Lab. Ct., May 20, 2003) (not yet published).

[38]See IV.A.2., below.

2. *Termination Procedures*

a. Notice

As a general procedural restriction on dismissal, prior notice is required. This requirement has been recognized as binding custom by the labor courts and has been incorporated in a collective agreement, which has been given general application in an extension order issued by the Minister of Labour.[39] The period of notice depends on the length of employment; after one year, the required notice is one month. In the case of teaching staff, notice must be given before the end of May to enable them to find an alternative placement for the following academic year. The notice period may be dispensed with in case of a fundamental breach of contract by the employee.

The employee also is required to give notice of resignation. The notice period corresponds to the period of employer notice.

In May 2001, the custom that requires a notice of termination of the employment contract was given legislative force by the Law of Early Notice for Termination of Employment and Resignation. Among other things, the Early Notice Law established a mutual duty on the part of both the employer and employee to give proper notice. According to the Law, salaried employees are entitled to up to 15 days notice during the first year of employment. Following the first year, the length of the required notice is progressively increased up to a maximum of 30 days.

---

[39]Section 25 of the Collective Agreements Law grants the Minister of Labour and Welfare the power to extend provisions of a general collective agreement by extension order. When he or she issues an extension order, the Minister extends the collective agreement provision to cover employees and employers who were not originally a party to the agreement. The Minister can extend the provision to an entire labor sector or to the entire workforce. An extension order may be granted either upon request or upon the Minister's initiative, after consultation with collective labor partners. Extension orders are considered to be secondary legislation and are intended to secure certain basic rights for all employees. Examples of provisions extended in this way are the rights to reimbursement for costs of public transport to work and cost-of-living increments in times of inflation.

b. Good Faith

The good-faith obligation inherent in employment contracts requires the employer to inform the employee of the reason for dismissal and give the employee an opportunity to be heard.

3. Substantive Restrictions on Dismissal

a. Principles of Contract Law

Under general principles of interpretation, the employment contract may restrict the employer's prerogative of dismissal. Fixed-term contracts are interpreted as restricting the employer's right to dismiss during the term of the contract unless the employee commits a fundamental breach.

The employer's right to dismiss also is restricted by the contractual doctrine of good faith. In addition to the procedural instances of bad-faith dismissal discussed immediately above, a dismissal will be deemed to be in bad faith if it is for reasons other than those stated by the employer.

b. Collective Agreement Provisions

Collective agreements and collective arrangements, including employer regulations, provide a measure of job security for covered employees.

Collective agreements may provide procedural protection against dismissal by imbuing the union with a right of veto, in which case lack of union agreement to a dismissal will usually activate arbitration. Alternatively, the union may have only a right of consultation, in which case after the consultation the employer will usually have the power to dismiss the employee, provided it is done in good faith and without contravention of any specific statutory protection.

In addition to procedural protections, collective agreements also provide substantive protection against a dismissal that is not for good cause. The employee will have an individual right of action derived from the agreement if the dismissal is not for good cause, whether or not consultation took place.

c. Statutory Protections

Various statutes prohibit employee dismissals in specific situations. These statutory prohibitions include the following:

- The Equal Employment Opportunity Law prohibits discriminatory dismissal on grounds of race, sex, parenthood, sexual orientation, age, or nationality.[40]
- The Employment of Women Law, 1953, prohibits dismissal of a woman during pregnancy, unless authorized by the Minister of Labour as based on a reason unrelated to the pregnancy. The Employment of Women Law also prohibits dismissal during a 90-day statutory maternity leave and a 12-month child care leave, for 45 days subsequent to the employee's return to work, during periods of absence due to a stay in a battered women's shelter, and for 30 days subsequent to the woman's return to work.[41]
- The Released Soldiers' Law, 1949, prohibits dismissal of a soldier on reserve service.
- The State Comptroller's Law and the Employees' Protection (Disclosure of Offenses, Improprieties and Administrative Irregularities) Law, 1997, both prohibit the dismissal of whistleblowers.

Applying the provisions of the Amendment to the Collective Agreements Law, which gave statutory force to prior judicial protections for employees engaged in union activities, the National Court, in two cases, reinstated employees, who had been dismissed on account of their union activities or because the employer intended to reduce the number of organized employees.[42] The Court shifted the burden of proof to the employer to rebut prima facie

[40]See VI.C.2.a.iv., below.

[41]For additional discussion of maternity leave, see V.D.3. and VI.C.3., below.

[42]The Israel Center for Congresses and Exhibitions v. The New New Histadrut (2004) 39 P.D.A. 106; The New New Histadrut v. Community Ctr. of Kiryat Melachi (Nat'l Lab. Ct., Nov. 25, 2003) (not yet published).

evidence that the dismissal was on account of the employee's union activities.

d. Protection for Exercise of Human Rights

There is protection against dismissal based on the employee's exercise of fundamental human rights. Thus, for instance, the labor court invalidated dismissal of employees on grounds of their union activism. The Court regarded the employees' right to organize as overriding the employer's prerogative of dismissal.[43]

4. State Employees

A ministerial prerogative of dismissal applies to state employees under the King's Order in Council, a statute originating during the time of the British Mandate in Palestine. However, dismissal of state employees for disciplinary reasons is regulated under the State Employees (Discipline) Law, 1970. The State Employees' Law establishes a special tribunal to determine whether any state employee is to be dismissed on disciplinary grounds. An employee may not be dismissed for disciplinary reasons except by order of the tribunal.

Where the tribunal decides on dismissal of an employee, if it also finds the employee to be unfit for future state service, then the employee's right to a budgetary pension from the state will be forfeited.[44]

5. Remedies for Wrongful Dismissal

If a dismissal is contrary to one of the restrictions discussed above, the employee is entitled to either an enforcement remedy, such as reinstatement, or damages.

Reinstatement is not the primary remedy for wrongful dismissal because it is restricted by a provision of the Contracts (Remedies for Breach) Law, 1970, which explicitly excludes an enforcement remedy under a contract for personal service. An express statutory right to an enforcement remedy was introduced under

---

[43]*See, e.g.*, Mifali Tahanot v. Histadrut (1999) 33 P.D.A. 289.

[44]For a discussion of budgetary pensions, see VIII.A.3.b., below.

the Equal Employment Opportunity Law in 1988, although that law still provides that damages, and not enforcement, are the primary remedy. Since then, case law has established that, for wrongful dismissals in general, reinstatement may be ordered where the employment relationship is, in reality, not personal or where the employee was dismissed for the exercise of a fundamental human right.[45] Furthermore, reinstatement will be ordered, as a matter of course, where the dismissal is contrary to a specific statutory protection or is in breach of a dismissal procedure set forth in a collective bargaining agreement.

Damages are awarded for economic loss resulting from a wrongful dismissal. Damage awards include future loss of earnings, usually limited to one year, and are subject to the employee's duty to mitigate damages. Aggravated damages may be awarded on rare occasions, and punitive damages may be awarded under the Equal Employment Opportunity Law.[46]

In a recent judgment, the National Labour Court refused to reinstate an employee who had been dismissed on grounds of suspected theft from the employer. The employee had ultimately been acquitted in the criminal proceedings, on the basis of a technicality.[47] Although there was a provision in a collective agreement mandating reinstatement after acquittal, the Court was of the opinion that in a situation where mistrust still exists on the part of the employer, reinstatement should not be the legal remedy. The Deputy President of the Court, Judge Elisheva Barak, wrote a dissenting opinion, arguing that reinstatement should be awarded on the basis of the collective agreement and of an employee's quasi-property right in the job.

6. *Severance Pay*

The Severance Pay Law, 1963, confers the right to severance pay, upon termination of employment, in a wide variety of situations, without reference to the status of termination as lawful or unlawful. The situations in which the employee is entitled to severance pay are discussed below.

---

45 "Tsari" Indus. Pharm. Co. v. Dr. Rix (1972/3) 4 P.D.A. 477.

46 See VI.D.2.c., below.

47 David Bivas v. Supersol, Inc. (2001) 36 P.D.A. 481.

a. Dismissals

Employees are entitled to severance pay in the event of a dismissal after, or approaching the end of, one year of employment, upon nonrenewal of a fixed-term contract by the employer, or upon the death or insolvency of the employer.

b. Resignation

Employees are entitled to severance pay if a resignation is on grounds of defective health of the employee or a close family member, in order for a mother or father to take care of a newborn, because of residential changes pursuant to marriage or a move to work in development areas, in case of the employee's enlistment in the police force, or where the resignation is due to a substantial worsening of employment conditions or circumstances of the employment relationship in which the employee cannot be required to continue working.

c. Exclusions

The Severance Pay Law provides that where, either under the terms of a collective agreement that binds the employee or under a sectoral collective agreement's provisions, the grounds for dismissal are such as to negate or reduce the employee's right to severance pay, severance pay is not payable or is only payable in part. Where there is no collective agreement directly applicable, the Severance Pay Law grants the labor courts discretion in deciding, in accordance with the principles of the most widely applicable collective agreement, whether the circumstances of the dismissal are such as to justify the complete or partial negation of severance pay. Usually, in accordance with collective agreement provisions, severance pay is negated only where the employee commits an especially severe disciplinary offence. Even then, the labor courts will tend to reduce, rather than negate, the severance pay.

d. Amount

The amount of severance pay is one month's salary per year of employment for salaried and non-salaried employees. This amount may be set off against pension entitlements if so provided in a collective agreement or by statutory provision. There is no ceiling on the amount of severance pay that the employer is required to pay.

D. Competition and Trade Secrets

1. *Sources of Law*

In 1992, the Basic Law: Freedom of Occupation was passed. This Basic Law bestowed constitutional status on the right to freedom of occupation, which had already been recognized as a basic right in the case law. However, the right to freedom of occupation is not absolute; under the limitations clause of the Basic Law, restrictions may be allowed if they are in accordance with the values of the State of Israel as a democratic and Jewish state, and if they are for a fit purpose and meet the test of proportionality. The National Labour Court has held that the Basic Law applies to private labor relations.[48] The right to freedom of occupation has been of great importance in formulating principles applicable to restricting competition by employees.

Additionally, under the Basic Law: Human Dignity and Liberty, the right to property is protected as a constitutional right. This Basic Law, confirming previous case law, has consolidated the protection against the employee transfer of trade secrets.

In addition to these constitutional rights, issues of noncompetition and trade secrets are regulated by statutory provisions on restrictive practices and commercial torts, by judicial rules of public policy, and by an implied contractual duty of the employee to show loyalty to the employer during the term of the contract.

2. *Employee Obligations*

Under applicable law, restrictions on competition and the transfer of trade secrets by employees are imposed under certain conditions, both during the period of employment and after termination. During the period of employment, two restrictions apply: first, the employee has an obligation to refrain from competing

[48]Toni Toama v. Techno-Gami, Inc. (1993/4) 25 P.D.A. 227.

with the employer in any way; and, second, the employee is bound not to divulge trade secrets, whether these were generated by the employee or not, and to refrain from transferring them to any third party or using them for his or her own business purposes.

After termination of the employment relationship, the employee's obligation regarding trade secrets continues on the same basis. However, the obligation to refrain from competition with the former employer continues in force only in defined circumstances.

a. Noncompetition

The employee's obligation to refrain from competition during the period of employment derives primarily from a duty of loyalty implied in the contract. Subsequent to termination of employment, no such obligation is imposed automatically. However, express noncompetition clauses often are incorporated in the employment contract in order to bind the employee after termination. Noncompetition clauses have been subjected to scrutiny by the courts for consistency with public policy. Traditionally, the obligation not to compete subsequent to termination had to be restricted to a reasonable period of time and to a reasonable scope of occupation and of geographical area, in the light of custom in the industry concerned. However, in a transformative 2000 decision, the Supreme Court held that an employee is not bound automatically by a noncompetition clause.[49] The Court was of the opinion that such clauses are signed in the context of the employee's inherent lack of power in negotiating the employment contract and, thus, a clause would be held void as contrary to public policy if the only reason for its inclusion was to prevent the employee from competing. However, where a noncompetition clause protects a legitimate right of the employer, the courts must weigh the competing rights and make a decision on a case-by-case basis. Hence, if the purpose of a noncompetition clause is to prevent the use of trade secrets or customer lists of the previous employer or to protect the good will of the enterprise, the provision will be enforced.

---

[49] AES Sys. v. Saar and The State of Israel (2000) (III) 54 P.D. 850.

These judicial restrictions are reinforced by the Law on Restrictive Trade Practices, 1988, which authorizes the courts to limit the impact of noncompetition clauses where they will damage the public interest.

Thus, the courts have developed legal principles that go beyond the express terms of noncompetition clauses, and the regulation of post-termination competition is no longer left entirely to the discretion of the contracting parties. On the one hand, as discussed above, the Supreme Court has held that an express clause will not preclude competition by the employee where the employee did not sign the contract freely and where no legitimate employer interest is at stake. On the other hand, the National Labour Court has held that the obligation not to compete may apply even in the absence of a contractual clause, where there is a danger of the transfer of trade secrets by the employee.[50]

In a recent case, the National Labour Court refused to enforce a noncompetition clause against an employee who opened two shops in competition with his previous employer.[51] The Court emphasized the importance of free competition and took a lenient approach in allowing the employee to sell merchandise purchased from the former employer's exclusive suppliers.

b. Trade Secrets

The employee's obligation not to divulge or to transfer trade secrets derives, both during and after employment, from the employer's right of property and the employee's duty of loyalty. This obligation has been incorporated in the Commercial Torts Law, 1999, which defines the prohibited behavior to include any unauthorized use of trade secrets. Trade secrets are defined by the courts as scientific or production processes or collated information, such as customer lists, that have been established by the employer and to which the employee has become privy during the course of employment. Trade secrets are defined, under the Commercial Torts Law, as "any business information which is not com-

---

[50]*Toni Toama,* 25 P.D.A. 227.

[51]Euroka Int'l, Inc. v. Antony Kori (Nat'l Lab. Ct., Mar. 16, 2001) (not yet published).

mon property and which cannot easily be discovered by others, legally and whose secrecy imbues a business advantage over competitors and on condition that the owner takes reasonable precautions to ensure secrecy."[52]

The Commercial Torts Law provides some exceptions to the employee's obligation not to transfer trade secrets or make unauthorized use of the employer's trade secrets. Specifically, no liability is imposed where the information embodied in the trade secret was acquired by a person in the course of employment and has become an integral part of that person's general professional skills. The Commercial Torts Law also creates a public policy exception for the justified transfer or use of trade secrets but provides that, where this exception applies, the courts have jurisdiction to order restitution of any profit derived from such transfer or usage.

In a recent case, the National Labour Court overturned a Regional Labour Court judgment that had prohibited the use of a list of customers of a raw chocolate dealer by a former employee.[53] The Court held that the list should not be considered secret, in accordance with the following tests: the general accessibility of customer identities and details, the extent of competition between the former and the subsequent employer, the characteristics of the branch of business, and the inclusion of customer details. The Court also held that injunctions should, as a rule, be issued only against the employee and not against the subsequent employer.

c. *Remedies*

The remedies available for breach of the obligations regarding competition and trade secrets are, variously, an injunction against the employee, damages for proved injury to the employer, and, in certain circumstances, an injunction and/or damages against a third party for causing a breach of contract. Furthermore, as regards trade secrets, the Commercial Torts Law provides an additional remedy of up to 100,000 NIS, which is approximately $25,000, without proof of actual damage.

---

[52]Commercial Tort Law, 1999, §5.

[53]H'ar Zahav Food Servs. Ltd. v. Micha Nechushtan (2003) 38 P.D.A. 72.

II. Collective Bargaining

A. Unions

1. General

A central characteristic of the law regarding unions in Israel is the absence of an overall statutory framework to regulate their formation, registration, and management. Regulation of this area, therefore, is left largely to the courts. Judicial regulation is based on support for the trade unions' collective bargaining role, which is ensconced in statutory provisions.

The Histadrut (now renamed the New Histadrut) Federation of Labour (Histadrut),[54] the primary trade union organization in Israel, is not a federation of unions but is a direct membership union, which incorporates independent unions or local units, divided according to industrial sector, professional classification, or plant organization. Although the Histadrut is, as has been mentioned previously, a political union at the central level, at the industrial, professional, and plant levels it functions on the basis of economic, and not political, unionism. The industrial and professional organizations are recognized as independent unions within the Histadrut and are authorized to conduct collective bargaining and strikes autonomously.

A limited number of unions operate outside the Histadrut. Three other political unions were established by political parties (two of them religious) that stood in opposition to the Labour Party at the time of the creation of the state. These unions have not played a significant role in labor relations. In addition, there are some independent unions based on professional affiliation: doctors, academic staff, teachers, and journalists.

2. Freedom of Association

The right of employees to freedom of association, although not expressly guaranteed in constitutional or statutory sources, is recognized as a fundamental right under the jurisprudence of both the labor courts and the Supreme Court. The right of freedom of

[54] See the Introduction, at B., above.

association is a collective, rather than an individual, right. Both the positive and the negative aspects of freedom of association are recognized; that is, employees have the right to join the union of their choice or not to join a union at all.

Unions are free to establish their own regulations and institutional framework. Union security arrangements—the closed shop and the union shop—have been held void as contrary to the right of freedom of association. However, by statute, the union may collect agency fees.

The labor courts have held that employees may not belong to more than one union and that, in the case of dual membership, the later membership will be void as a breach of the prior membership obligation. Employees' freedom to belong to a union other than the representative union at their workplace is specially protected by the statutory agency fee provisions: an employee belonging to another union is not obliged to pay agency fees to the representative union.

Union activists are protected against employer discrimination and, if dismissed on grounds of their union activities, are entitled to reinstatement. This protection originated in labor court jurisprudence and was included in a statutory amendment to the Collective Agreements Law in 2001.

3. *Union Recognition*

After the passage of the National Health Insurance Law in 1995,[55] the Histadrut's quasi-monopoly over trade union membership was broken. In the wake of this, an attempt was made by a non-union organization, which emphasized representation of employees on an individual contract basis, to attract employee-members. The organization held out that its members would pay membership fees at a lower rate than that payable to the Histadrut, whether as membership or agency fees, and that they would save payment of agency fees to the Histadrut as their representative union, hence enjoying a net financial benefit.

The attempt failed as the High Court of Justice held that the primary function of a union is collective bargaining, and that the organization in question did not satisfy this and other necessary

[55]See the Introduction, at B., above.

criteria for recognition as a union.[56] The Court's restriction on acquisition of trade union status was not a denial of freedom of association but of entitlement to privileges granted to trade unions under the law. Foremost among the criteria imposed by the Court is the requirement that the union be independent of employer influence and conflict of interest, whether with regard to the specific company employer or to employers in general. Additional criteria for recognition as a trade union include the following: permanency of the organization, personal and voluntary membership of employees, the promulgation of regulations, democratic election of officials, and authenticity in the role of representing employee interests.

4. *Union Representation*

The representative union, which is exclusively entitled to represent employees for the purpose of concluding an enforceable collective bargaining agreement, is defined by union membership. In accordance with the Collective Agreements Law, 1957, for the purpose of a sectoral collective agreement, a simple majority of organized employees is required; for an enterprise-level agreement, there is an additional requirement of a one-third membership of the employees in the enterprise.[57]

Representative trade unions represent both members and nonmembers in the bargaining process. The union is autonomous as regards collective bargaining policy and determination of the contents of the collective agreement. The courts will refrain from interfering in the policymaking decisions of unions except where intervention is justified on grounds of public policy, as in instances of group discrimination.

The National Labour Court has developed standards for union conduct in collective bargaining and in the administration of the collective agreement, as regards both member and nonmember employees. As regards members, the basis for supervision of union conduct is the membership contract. As regards all employees, members or nonmembers, the representative union is required, by

---

[56]New Histadrut v. National Labour Court (1997) (II) 51 P.D. 63.

[57]For a discussion of sectoral and enterprise-level agreements, see II.B.1., below.

general principles of contract and by virtue of its privileged legal status, to behave in accordance with the following standards: good-faith negotiation and implementation of the collective agreement; fulfillment of a fiduciary obligation to employees; and the duty of fairness required under principles of administrative law, which are analogous to the duty of fair representation.

The National Labour Court held that, in the case of a union complaint regarding the behavior of one employee towards another, the employer is obliged to hold an investigation and take reasonable measures to redress the complaint.[58]

Where an air steward and a ground stewardess attempted to bring a class action for payment of wages and social benefits for participation in a required preparatory course, the National Labour Court rejected their request, holding that, where there is a representative union, there is no place for class actions.[59]

The National Labour Court clarified the conditions in which a claim of unfair representation against a union will be allowed. The President held that there would be a right of action where the union acted in an arbitrary way on the basis of the employee's membership of another union, sex, nationality, citizenship, or residence.[60]

B. Collective Regulation of Employment Conditions

1. *General*

Collective regulation of employment conditions may be by agreement between employers and employees or by unilateral employer regulation. Where regulation is by agreement between employers and employees, the employees may be represented by the Histadrut, by an industrial or professional union, or by the local union unit at the enterprise level.

Collective regulation takes place at three levels. At the first level are framework agreements reached among the state, the ma-

---

[58]The Mizrachi United Bank Workers Union v. Mizrachi United Bank (2003) 38 P.D.A. 206.

[59]Amir Bibering & Michal Yung v. El-Al Israel Airlines (2003) 38 P.D.A. 115.

[60]Dov Vinkler v. The New New Histadrut (2004) 39 P.D.A. 153.

jor economic organizations, represented by an employer's federation, and the Histadrut. These are collective agreements that have, in the past, regulated central employment policy issues, such as minimum wage, inflation linkage of wages, payments for transportation to work, vacation allowances, the transition to a five-day working week, and notice requirements for dismissal and resignation. Contemporaneous with the decline in the power of the Histadrut, framework agreements have played a less central role.

At the second level are sectoral agreements, reached between the industrial or professional unions with employer federations representing an industrial sector, such as the hotel industry, food production, the metal industry, etc. These are collective agreements that set sectorwide conditions for a wide range of matters, including wages, employment conditions, discipline, pensions, and social security rights.

The third level is comprised of agreements at the enterprise level, reached between the employer and the local branch of the Histadrut, an industrial or professional union, or the local union unit. Agreements with the state as employer are considered to be enterprise-level agreements. Enterprise-level agreements may be collective agreements or may be collective arrangements, and they cover the full range of matters covered by sectoral agreements.

Under the Collective Agreements Law, where more than one collective agreement is applicable to any particular employee, the provision that is to the employee's benefit will take effect. This way of solving clashes between different collective agreements does not establish a hierarchy of sources, but rather provides maximum benefits to the individual employee. The employee may, in the result, accumulate rights in excess of those intended under any one of the applicable agreements.

2. *Good-Faith Bargaining*

The employer has no statutory duty to recognize a representative trade union or to bargain with it. However, the National Labour Court has developed a doctrine of the duty to bargain in good faith. For this purpose, the Court has classified subjects into three categories. First are subjects on which bargaining is prohibited, such as bargaining for terms that are illegal or contrary to public policy. Second are subjects on which there is a duty to bargain, such as renewal of a collective agreement regulating those topics deemed suitable under the Collective Bargaining Law.[61] Third are subjects over which the employer has a managerial prerogative, and on which bargaining is optional, such as the determination of production policy, marketing, management, and financing.

Both parties must conduct collective bargaining in good faith. This obligation derives from general statutory principles of contract law. Good-faith bargaining requires, among other things, disclosure of relevant information and a preparedness to participate in genuine negotiation.

The National Labour Court recently ordered that an employer must consult with the trade union at the place of work prior to dismissal of an employee, even where such a duty was not established by law or by collective agreement.[62] Furthermore, the Court ruled that, where such a consultation did not take place, the proper remedy was reinstatement of the dismissed employee.

In 2003, the National Labour Court held that where wage incentives had become contractual conditions of employment, the employer cannot, in accordance with the *Milfelder* precedent in the High Court of Justice, unilaterally cancel them. The employer must engage in collective bargaining. The Court left open the question of what the legal situation would be if bargaining were to reach an impasse.[63]

3. *Collective Agreements*

Collective agreements are regulated by the Collective Agreements Law.

a. *Required Conditions*

The Collective Agreements Law requires that covered agreements fulfill three basic conditions. First is a formal condition, according to which the agreement must be in writing and signed

[61]See II.B.3.b.ii., below.

[62]Levin v. National Broad. Auth. (2001) 36 P.D.A. 400. See also IV.A.1., below.

[63]Israel Teachers' Union v. State of Israel and The Center for Local Gov. (Nat'l Lab. Ct., Dec. 12, 2003) (not yet published).

and submitted to the Ministry of Labour for registration. The purpose of this requirement is to guarantee publication of the agreement and its availability to the employees governed by it. Nonregistration by the Ministry does not affect the validity of the agreement.

Second is a condition *in persona*, according to which the parties to the agreement must be an employer or an employers' association and a representative trade union. This requirement makes an organization's recognition as a trade union[64] crucial to its ability to function in labor relations.

The third condition is substantive, according to which the subjects covered by the agreement must relate only to the following:

- hiring of employees;
- termination of employment;
- employment conditions; or
- the rights and obligations of the parties to the collective agreement.

The courts have held that subjects such as employment quotas and acquired rights are not, per se, suitable subjects for collective agreements.

b. Legal Status

The legal status of collective agreements under the Collective Agreements Law has a dual character. On one hand, the collective agreement constitutes an enforceable contractual obligation between the signatory parties. Under the Law, the collective agreement continues to bind the parties after the designated date of termination unless one of the parties gives notice of an intention to terminate. The statutory notice period is 60 days. The National Labour Court has indicated that it will scrutinize notice of termination to ensure good faith, and there is dicta to the effect that notice to terminate with a view to nonrenewal of collective bargaining may not stand the test of good faith.[65]

---

[64]See II.A.3., above.

[65]"Tsari" Indus. Pharm. Co. v. National Labour Court (1974) (I) 28 P.D. 372.

On the other hand, as regards the governance of employees, collective agreements are characterized by three special aspects of enforceability under the Collective Agreements Law: normative effect, mandatory application, and continuity of binding force of collective agreement provisions in employment contracts under their auspices.

i. Normative effect

Collective agreements have normative effect in that they are binding on all employees in the categories designated by the agreement, whether or not the employees are members of the signatory union. The personal provisions of the collective agreement, dealing with employment conditions, termination of employment, and personal obligations of the employer or employee relating to such, take effect automatically as part of the individual employment contract of the employee. On this basis, the labor courts have termed collective agreements "autonomous legislation."[66]

ii. Mandatory application

The application of collective agreement provisions is mandatory, and individual employees may not waive their rights under the personal provisions of the agreement. Furthermore, where there is a discrepancy between the collective agreement provisions and an individual employment contract, the provision that is to the benefit of the employee will take effect unless a sectoral collective agreement expressly provides otherwise. Although employees may not waive rights, they may, retroactively, reach a compromise with the employer on rights that are in dispute.

The National Court, in a 2003 case, modified its prior interpretation of the Collective Agreements Law, according to which where there was a discrepancy between a collective agreement provision and an individual employment contract provision, the provision to the benefit of the employee would take effect, unless a sectoral collective agreement expressly provided otherwise. In its new decision, the Court decided that a purposive interpretation

[66]Dr. Nevo v. Israeli Jewish Agency (1987/8) 18 P.D.A. 197; El-Al Airlines v. Herut (1976/7) 8 P.D.A. 197.

of the Law required comparison between the collective agreement and the contract on the basis of an entire subject matter rather than per individual provision. The employee must then choose the more beneficial regulation of the subject matter in question.[67]

iii. Continuity

The personal provisions of the agreement, which become part of an employee's individual employment contract, continue in effect even after the collective agreement is no longer in force. Such provisions remain in effect until they are lawfully cancelled or varied. Under the case law, it seems that lawful cancellation or variation must be by mutual agreement. In case of a failure to agree, the only course of action open to the employer is termination and the offer of a new contract.

4. *Collective Arrangements*

As an alternative to collective agreements, which, by statute, have special normative and mandatory force, regulation of employment conditions may be by means of collective arrangements, which may be agreed on between employers and employee representatives or may be issued by the employer unilaterally. Classification as a collective agreement depends on fulfillment of the statutory conditions discussed immediately above; in the case of collective arrangements, one or more of such conditions have not been met.

The legal status of collective arrangements is inferior to that of collective agreements under the Collective Agreements Law. The labor courts have held that collective arrangements are not usually legally enforceable.[68] Where the collective arrangement is bilateral, it usually will be regarded only as a "gentleman's agreement" and not enforceable by law. However, exceptions have been recognized where the parties have exhibited a clear intent to enter into contractual relations, or where the employer party is a public

[67]The New New Histadrut and the Bezek Employees' Union v. Bezek, Israel Co. for Telecomms. (Nat'l Lab. Ct., Dec. 10, 2003) (not yet published).

[68]Histadrut v. "Loubit" Ins. Co., Inc. (1980) 12 P.D.A. 169.

agency.[69] The collective arrangement does not have the statutory features of a collective agreement as regards normative, mandatory, and continuing force over the individual employees to whom it applies. However, the provisions of a collective arrangement may be enforceable as implied terms in the individual employment contract.

The National Labour Court continued its policy of creating exceptions to the general non-enforeability of collective arrangements. In prior cases the Court had held that, where the employee representative signing the collective arrangement was eligible to be a party to a collective agreement, the collective arrangement could in certain circumstances be enforced.[70] In its 2003 decision, the Court extended this exception to circumstances in which there is a long established tradition of collective labor relations and the parties regarded their collective arrangements as binding even where the party signing was not eligible to sign a collective agreement.[71]

C. Settlement of Labor Disputes and Strikes

In 2003, there were severe labor disputes and strikes in reaction to the Law for the Recovery of the Israeli Economy and its legislative intervention in labor relations and in collective agreement conditions of employment. These labor disputes and strikes fell into three categories, each of which led to proceedings in court and judicial rulings: the first was a general strike; the second was with regard to the restructuring of the Ports Authority; and the third was a dispute with regard to the legislative intervention in pension rights, which is discussed at VIII.A., below.

In September 2003, the New Histadrut gave statutory notice of a labor dispute and intended general strike by all employees against all employers. The notice enumerated the grounds in dis-

---

[69]Histadrut v. Senior Employee Org. at Paz (1982) 14 P.D.A. 367; Histadrut v. Council for the Marketing of Citrus Fruits (1990) 22 P.D.A. 445.

[70]Israel Bank of Industrial Dev. v. Hava Koslovsky (2000) 35 P.D.A. 536.

[71]Yaakov Punis v. Israel Housing & Dev. Co. (Nat'l Lab. Ct., Dec. 10, 2003) (not yet published).

pute: the changes to the pension system; restructuring (privatization); and unilateral change of the rules of the game and violation of the essence of labor relations, as a result of intervention by legislation in the collective bargaining framework. This resulted in a marathon of court proceedings and decisions:

- The major employers' associations applied to the National Labour Court for temporary strike injunctions to prevent the strike altogether or, alternately, to preserve essential services. The government was not a party to these or any other legal proceedings and the Court called the Attorney-General to present the government's position. The Court gave an injunction against the general strike but allowed the New Histadrut to conduct a four-hour demonstration strike on the grounds that the strike was a quasi-political strike, because the government policy directly affected labor relations and collective bargaining.
- In a second decision some days later, with the dispute continuing, the Court cancelled the strike injunction and recommended, with the force of a judgment, that the New Histadrut uphold its voluntary undertaking not to strike and that the parties conduct negotiations on the basis of detailed position papers.
- In a third decision, in view of the failure of negotiations, the Court said that the proper balance between the right of public employees to hold a demonstration strike, on one hand, and injury to the public, on the other, can best be achieved by allowing a virtual strike, in which the employees continue to work but all income from their work will be held in a joint bank account belonging to the State and the New Histadrut; this would allow the employees to apply economic pressure but avoid serious damage to the public. On the basis of this decision, there was a virtual strike for one week and then it was terminated by the Court and the monies collected in the joint account were transferred to the relevant State agencies.
- In a fourth decision, the Court held that the New Histadrut is not prohibited from holding a general strike. However, in conduct of the strike, it is subject to the limits of proportionality. These limits include the requirement of 24 hours'

> notice of any public services to be withheld, non-endangerment of life or health, non-interference with the regular functioning of the security forces, and maintenance of essential services. It seems that in this decision, the Court was treating the strike as an economic strike of unrestricted duration, against the direct intervention by the government in labor relations.

Subsequent to this decision, no general strike was actually held.

The government decided in September 2003, in the context of the Economic Plan, to restructure the Ports Authority and took two measures to achieve this goal: the first was the licensing of loading rights to a private company, the Israel Shipping Co., and the second was introduction of a legislative proposal for privatization of the ports. The New Histadrut called a strike in Haifa and Ashdod ports on the 10th of October. Before commencement of the strike, the Ports Authority, joined by third parties who would be injured by the strike, sought temporary strike injunctions. The National Labour Court gave the requested temporary strike injunctions; it also issued an order for good-faith bargaining, and gave an order to the government to suspend legislation and to do all in its power to prevent the Knesset from proceeding with legislation, until the parties reported back to the Court as regards progress in reaching an agreed solution. On November 13th, while these orders were still in force, the Ports Authority employed the Israel Shipping Co. to unload a ship, the *Shelley*, and, in response, the New Histadrut brought the port workers out on strike for four days. The Ports Authority renewed its request for temporary strike injunctions; the Court held that the unloading of the *Shelley* by the Israel Shipping Co. was an uncalled-for provocation and gave an order that the Ports Authority should not use the services of the Israel Shipping Co. and its previous orders would continue in force, until December 2nd. The High Court of Justice rejected a petition by the Ports Authority to cancel the orders of the National Labour Court, which limited its freedom of action. After the lapse of the Court's orders on December 2nd, the parties extended them by agreement; however, the dispute as to the substance of the dispute continued and has not been settled to date.

1. Settlement of Labor Disputes

Labor disputes may be referred to settlement procedures of mediation, conciliation, or arbitration by statute, by collective agreement, or by other specific agreement.

The Settlement of Labour Disputes Law, 1957 (Labour Disputes Law), provides settlement facilities for collective labor disputes, where the disputes are disputes of interests, that is, disputes regarding the creation of new rights rather than the implementation of existing rights. Under the Labour Disputes Law, disputes reported by the parties under their obligation to give notice of strike and lockout are subject to mediation. The Labour Disputes Law also provides for arbitration wherever a dispute is designated for arbitration under a collective agreement. Where the dispute involves a public service,[72] there is a default arbitral jurisdiction even though the parties have not provided for it in their collective agreement. An arbitral decision under the Labour Disputes Law is enforced as a collective agreement between the parties.

Apart from the Labour Disputes Law, the labor courts frequently advise the parties in litigation to refer their dispute to conciliation or mediation. Such mediation is subject to the specific agreement of the parties.

Where the parties agree to arbitration, other than arbitration under the Labour Disputes Law, the matter is governed by the Arbitration Law, and the arbitral decision, on authorization by the court, is enforced as a judgment.

There are different arbitration mechanisms for the various arbitration routes that may be selected by the parties. Where arbitration is under the Labour Disputes Law, it is administered under the auspices of the Ministry of Labour. Where the parties choose arbitration under the Arbitration Law, they generally choose their arbitrators ad hoc. There is, however, also a standing voluntary arbitration tribunal for the resolution of economic or mixed disputes, which was established under a central collective agreement between the government and the Histadrut.

---

[72]See II.C.2.b.iii., below.

2. *Strikes and Lockouts*

a. The Right to Strike

The right to strike is not, as such, guaranteed by specific statutory provision. However, it is partially protected by immunities set out in the Collective Agreements Law, which provides that a strike will not constitute a breach of employment obligation, and under the Torts Ordinance [New Version], 1968 (Torts Ordinance), which provides protection for strikers against tortious liability for causing breach of contract. Furthermore, the right to strike has been accorded recognition as a fundamental right in the case law,[73] and some judges have accorded it the status of a full constitutional right under the Basic Law: Human Dignity and Liberty.[74] The right to picket has also been accorded protection, as derived from the fundamental rights to freedom of expression and demonstration.[75]

In a recent judgment, the National Labour Court reiterated the importance of the right to strike.[76] The court was asked by the Mekorot Water Company to issue an injunction against a strike by its employees on the grounds that the supply of water was an essential public service. Although the Court refrained from making a final decision, because the issue had become theoretical, it said that it would not automatically forbid striking in such cases. Instead, the Court stated that, where essential services are concerned, the right to strike should be determined on a case-by-case basis after weighing issues such as the potential damage to the public, the scope of the strike, and available alternative services.

With regard to payment of wages during strikes, the National Labour Court recently upheld longstanding case law pertaining to the employer's right to withhold payment.[77] However, the Court held that the principle of good faith and the duty of loyalty require

---

[73]Finstein v. High School Teachers Union (1971) (I) 25 P.D. 129; Histadrut v. Airports' Auth. (1988) 19 P.D.A. 449; Ramat-Gan and Givatim Labor Council v. Elko, Inc. (1977) 9 P.D.A. 113; "Katza" Employee Comm. v. "Katza" Co. (1976) 8 P.D.A. 421.

[74]Ashdod Auto Factories, Inc. v. Tsizuk (1987) (I) 41 P.D. 129; Government Legal Advisor v. National Labour Court (1995) (II) 49 P.D. 485.

[75]The New Histadrut v. Machteshim Chem. Works, Inc. (1997) 30 P.D.A. 449.

[76]Mekorot Water Co. v. New Histadrut (2001) 36 P.D.A. 560.

[77]New Histadrut v. Center for Local Authorities (2001) 36 P.D.A. 418.

the employer to negotiate the reduction in pay and to take proper measures in order to minimize damage to the employees.

The National Labour Court has held that unions have the right to strike in disputes over the pension rights of retired employees and may do so even where this is the only dispute over which strike action is taken.[78]

b. Limitations on the Right to Strike

Limits on the right to strike are derived from three different sources: case law, collective agreements, and specific statutory provisions. These limits are piecemeal, and their application is cumulative. Hence, in each strike situation, the legality of the strike action must be check-listed as against each separate provision, doctrine, or decision.

i. Case law

There is no right to strike for the implementation of rights. The right to strike is a collective bargaining right intended for the purpose of furthering disputes of interests, and not disputes of rights. This doctrine derives from the case law of the labor courts.[79]

Unofficial strikes are unlawful. Where there is a union, only the union can declare a lawful strike. This doctrine derives from the case law of the High Court of Justice and the labor courts.[80]

Secondary strike action against an employer other than the striker's own employer is usually unlawful. However, sympathy (solidarity) strikes are lawful.[81]

Strikes that infringe the fundamental rights of others may be considered unlawful. Thus, the labor court issued a strike injunction against a strike of Interior Ministry employees that prevented the issue of passports and violated the public's right of movement.

A catch-all limit on the right to strike was developed by the Supreme Court when it held that strikers would be liable for vari-

---

[78]University of Bar-Ilan Senior Academic Staff Org. v. Bar Ilan Univ. (2002) 37 P.D.A. 769.

[79]Workers Comm. of the Elec. Wire & Cable Co. v. Electric Wire & Cable Co., Inc. (1973/4) 4 P.D.A. 122.

[80]Koka v. Broadcasting Auth. (1991) (II) 40 P.D. 408.

[81]Chatib v. National Labour Court (1984) (I) 40 P.D. 673.

ous torts where no specific immunity had been provided by the Torts Ordinance.[82] Because the Torts Ordinance specifically provides immunity only for the tort of causing breach of contract, under this decision the torts of negligence and nuisance became potential traps for all strikers, irrespective of the labor relations context of the strike.

Political, as opposed to economic, strikes do not fall within the ambit of the right to strike at all. However, not all strikes against state action are considered political. If the disputed action is taken by the state as employer, the strike may be considered an economic strike subject to the rules applicable to economic strikes directed against private employers. Furthermore, even where the action is taken by the state as sovereign, and not as employer, if it directly affects employees' interests, then the employees have the right to a short demonstration strike.

ii. Collective agreements

Industrial peace clauses in collective agreements limit the right to strike. Such clauses may be comprehensive, precluding all strike action for the duration of the agreement, or they may be partial, precluding strike action only with regard to matters regulated in the agreement.

iii. Statutes

A cooling off period is imposed on all strikes and lockouts under the Labour Disputes Law, as amended in 1969.

The right to strike in public services is further restricted by the Labour Disputes Law, as amended in 1972. Public services are defined broadly to include the civil service, state agencies, statutory bodies, air transport, hospitals, oil supply, and educational institutions. Public service employees may not strike lawfully over wages or social benefits during the course of a collective agreement. They may strike on other matters during the term of the collective agreement or on any matter after termination of the collective agreement, provided there is authorization by the union party to the agreement.

---

[82] Ashdod Auto Factories, Inc. v. Tsizuk (1987) (III) 41 P.D. 129.

c. *Employer Lockouts*

There is no statutory right of employers to lock out their employees. Although the immunity granted under the Torts Ordinance extends to lockouts as well as strikes, this provision is of marginal significance.

The labor courts have recognized the right of the employer to engage in a defensive lockout only. Defensive lockouts are restricted to cases in which employees are engaged in partial strike action, and the employer is forced by business necessity to lock them out.[83] Alternatively, the employer simply may refuse to allow the employees participating in the lockout to work on terms different than those agreed in the employment contract; in this case, the employer may suspend the employees or accept partial work on a noncontractual basis for which reasonable compensation must be paid.

III. REPRESENTATION BY ENTITIES OTHER THAN UNIONS

Employee representation is by unions. There is no requirement under Israeli law for work councils or other non-union representation in the workplace.

IV. REDUNDANCY AND TRANSFERS OF UNDERTAKINGS

No Israeli legislation deals with redundancy or transfers of undertakings in a comprehensive way. Indeed, only one statutory provision relates specifically to these issues, that is, a clause in the Collective Agreements Law, 1957, which bestows continuity on collective agreements in case of a transfer of undertaking. The principles underlying case law decisions on these issues consist of general principles of company law, contract law, and severance pay law. The courts have regarded ownership as bestowing on the employer a managerial prerogative deriving from the right of prop-

---

[83]Histadrut v. "Elko," Inc. (1976) 8 P.D.A. 57; Kozolovich v. Ordan (1980) 12 P.D.A. 200; BeerSheva Labor Council v. Dead Sea Factories, Inc. (1982) 14 P.D.A. 225.

erty, within which the employer has the right to dismiss and the right to transfer the enterprise. The legislature and the courts have perceived the employee's relationship with the undertaking as being a connection with the workplace itself and not necessarily limited to a specific owner. Hence, in a transfer of undertakings, the employee's accumulated statutory rights continue as against the new employer. If the employee does not wish to transfer, he or she must resign. However, the employee is not protected from dismissal in the course of a transfer of an undertaking, unless so provided in a collective agreement. In the event of dismissal or resignation resulting from a transfer of an undertaking, the employee will, as a rule, be entitled to severance pay.

A. Redundancy

1. Collective Dismissals

As discussed above,[84] the protection against dismissal under Israeli law generally is derived from the contractual good faith principle and collective agreement job security provisions. The same applies to redundancy dismissals.

Existing collective agreements, as a rule, have specified that redundancy dismissal is dismissal for good reason and, therefore, legitimate under the job security provisions of the agreement. Employers have no obligation under collective agreements to bargain collectively with employee representatives as regards a decision to carry out collective dismissals or the scope of such dismissals. One limited exception to this rule exists with respect to public services, where there is an obligation to bargain for 80 days, after which the employer's prerogative to dismiss is restored. Collective agreements generally require the employer to bargain collectively only as regards the names of employees to be included in the redundancy list. In case of failure to agree regarding the names on the list, the issue usually will be referred to arbitration.

Interpretation of collective agreement provisions by the courts resulted in the making of a legal distinction among workforce reduction, outsourcing, and closure of an undertaking. The National Labour Court, affirmed by the High Court of Justice, held that

[84]See II.C., above.

collective agreement redundancy provisions, requiring the employer to bargain collectively with employees, apply only to a workforce reduction.[85] In the other two situations, the employer's prerogative to dismiss is not restricted by the bargaining requirements of the collective agreement. However, more recent case law may perhaps be regarded as imposing a duty to bargain in these situations, too.[86] Furthermore, in a later decision, the National Labour Court held that employees were entitled to strike against an employer's decision to outsource jobs without bargaining collectively with the union.[87]

In a recent ruling, the National Labour Court held that where dismissals are collective, resulting from the employer's economic needs and difficulties, rather than the suitability of the employees, the employer had a duty to consult with the trade union.[88] Based on the collective agreement, the Court held that, although the obligation to consult does not include the actual decision to cut back, it does include the obligation to consult with regard to the number of employees who are to be dismissed as well as with regard to the names of the employees on the list and with regard to the benefits that are to be granted to the employees upon dismissal. The Court stated that this obligation stemmed from the proper balance between the employer's managerial prerogative and property rights in the workplace and the employees' employment protection and quasi-property rights in the workplace.

The National Labour Court has clarified that individual employees have no standing as regards the collective negotiations regarding the names on the list; however, after the list has been finalized, the employee will have a right to be heard regarding his or her inclusion on the list.[89] The Court also has held that the employer must conduct the process with maximum transparency.[90]

---

[85]Histadrut of State Employees v. National Labour Court (1986) (III) 40 P.D. 318.

[86]See II.B.1., above.

[87]Tel- Aviv Municipality Workers Org. v. Tel- Aviv Municipality (1998) 31 P.D.A. 109.

[88]New Histadrut v. E.C.I Telecom, Inc. (2001) 36 P.D.A 289.

[89]Government Co. Medals & Coins v. Rachel Cohen (Nat'l Lab. Ct., July 18, 2003) (not yet published).

[90]State of Israel v. Eli Sadeh (Nat'l Lab. Ct., Mar. 3, 2003) (not yet published).

2. *Closure of Undertakings and Bankruptcy*

There is no comprehensive regulation of the impact on the employment relationship of closure of undertakings and resultant redundancy. However, in the case of fixed-term employment contracts, it has been held that interruption of the contract as a result of closure constitutes an employer breach that cannot be regarded as frustration.[91] Hence, in this particular case, the employer is required to pay damages for loss of wages.

In the case of bankruptcy, provisions in the Bankruptcy Ordinance and the Companies Law bestow priority in the payment of company debts for employee salaries and redundancy pay, up to a fixed ceiling. Where the employee is unable to recover unpaid wages or severance pay from a bankrupt employer, the National Insurance Institute will make the payment up to a fixed ceiling and then seek to recover the debt directly from the employer.

3. *Severance Pay*

In case of redundancy dismissal, employees are entitled to severance pay under the Severance Pay Law.[92] Entitlement to severance pay in case of redundancy is not treated differently from entitlement to severance pay in the case of an individual dismissal.

B. Transfers of Undertakings

Recently, there has been an increase in litigation regarding transfers of undertakings. This has transpired against a background of a more flexible marketplace with greater employer mobility. It also has occurred as a result of the trend to privatize public undertakings, which, before the process of privatization, are frequently divided into separate units with a new legal personality and employer.

At the level of the individual employee, no specific legislative provision determines the legal consequences of a transfer of undertakings. The General Contracts Law and the Assignment of

[91]M.D.T v. Shoshi (1993) 25 P.D.A. 255.

[92]See I.C.6., above.

Obligations Law regulate transfers of contractual obligations. According to the Assignment of Obligations Law, it is possible to assign a contract, but only if the party entitled to a right consents to its assignment or if the party obliged to perform a duty of a personal nature consents to assignment of the obligation. Although this provision would appear to preclude the transfer of an employee without his or her consent, the National Labour Court has held in the *RAMTA* case that the Assignment of Obligations Law does not apply to labor relations.[93]

By majority decision, the National Labour Court also held that the prospective rule under the Proposed Employment Contract, 1985, which has not yet been passed by the Knesset, is the law applicable to a transfer of undertakings. Under this rule, the new employer replaces the previous employer as a party to the contract of employment. According to the Court, this means that where an employee is offered employment with a new owner, he or she is automatically transferred to the new employer. Hence, an employee who does not wish to work for the new owner must resign, thus forfeiting dismissal entitlements, such as early pension rights, due from the previous employer. However, as a general rule, those employees who prefer to resign rather than continue working with the new owner would be entitled to statutory severance pay.

The union presented a petition to the High Court of Justice to overturn the National Labour Court's findings regarding the rights of an employee who refuses to continue working with a new owner, claiming that, in such a case, the previous employer must continue employing the employee until dismissal. The employer counter-petitioned to overrule the finding of entitlement to severance pay for employees who resign. The case is still pending.

In the *RAMTA* case, the Court also implied that the new owner would be obliged to accept the employees of the previous owner and offer them contractual continuity. However, in a later case, it was made apparent that no such legal obligation has yet been established.[94]

---

[93]New Eistadrut v. Israel Aviation Indus. & RAMTA (1996) 29 P.D.A. 601.

[94]Moadim v. Ministry of Defence (Nat'l Lab. Ct., Dec. 2, 1998) (unpublished).

On the collective level, by decision of the National Labour Court, the employer is obliged to consult with the employee representative before a transfer of undertaking or a transfer of the controlling shareholding.[95] Upon transfer of an undertaking from one employer to another, the Collective Agreement Law provides that the new employer will be regarded as party to the collective agreement. The significance of this provision is somewhat limited because the new employer may cancel the agreement, with a notice of 60 days, as soon as the contractual date of termination has been reached. Because the employer has no duty to recognize the union as collective bargaining representative,[96] a transfer of undertaking may facilitate the employer's exit from the collective bargaining framework.

V. WAGES, HOURS, AND LEAVE

A. General

Statutes that regulate the minimum terms and conditions of employment, including wages, hours, and leave, are termed protective labor laws in the Israeli system. The guiding principle of these laws is that they establish minimums, which may be added to in favor of the employee but must not be derogated from in the individual employment contract or, as a rule, in the collective agreement. There is an extensive array of protective labor laws and, in this area, the Israeli legislature was very active during the first 30 years of the state. Many of the laws were based on standards promulgated in ILO Conventions.[97] However, in some cases, the Knesset went beyond the requirements of the ILO.

The labor courts have held that the individual employee may not waive rights under the protective labor laws, although it is possible to compromise, retroactively, rights in dispute, on grounds of legal or factual uncertainty. However, some decisions hold that an employee who has de facto waived rights may be precluded

[95]New Histadrut v. Cor Indus. (1999) 34 P.D.A. 510.

[96]See II.B., above.

[97]See the Introduction, at C.3., above. For a general discussion of ILO Conventions, see the chapter on the ILO in Volume I, Part 4.

from later claiming those rights if the employer relied on the waiver; in such a case, the employee may be considered to have acted in bad faith.[98]

Most of the protective labor laws provide both a civil and criminal remedy. Violation of the protective laws is a criminal offense for the employer, but not for the employee. Furthermore, under the case law, the fact that work has been carried out illegally, in violation of statutory standards, does not preclude enforcement by the employee of his or her right to minimum statutory benefits. An obligation is imposed on the employer to keep records for the purpose of proving compliance with the requirements of the protective labor laws, and the burden of proof is placed on the employer.

Some academics have claimed that the system of protective labor laws is called into question by the Basic Law: Human Dignity and Liberty and the Basic Law: Freedom of Occupation.[99] According to this argument, the protective labor laws may be considered to infringe the basic rights to property and freedom of occupation under the constitutional provisions of the Basic Laws. The High Court of Justice has rejected an employer's claim to this effect with regard to restrictions on labor-only contracting, holding that the legislation in question stood the tests of proper purpose and proportionality, as required of statutes that infringe basic rights under the Basic Laws.[100]

In a recent decision, the National Labour Court refused to award National Broadcasting Authority employees compensation, under the Hours of Work and Rest Law, for overtime hours they had worked. The Court held that they were not entitled to statutory compensation because their overtime work arrangement had been in accordance with their collective agreement that had been adhered to for many years, and that the employees were well compensated for this arrangement. Thus, the Court held, the employees' lawsuit for statutory compensation was in breach of their obligation to act in good faith.[101]

---

[98]The State of Israel v. Bochris (Nat'l Lab. Ct., Mar. 3, 1997) (unpublished).

[99]See the Introduction, at C.2.a., above.

[100]Tnufa Personnel & Maint. Servs., Inc. v. Negev and The Minister of Labour and Welfare (High Court of Justice, May 27, 1998) (unpublished).

[101]Ezra Shmueli v. State of Israel (2001) 36 P.D.A. 577.

B. Wages

1. Mode and Time of Payment

The Protection of Wages Law, 1958 (Wage Law), regulates the mode of payment and the time of payment.

The Supreme Court recently ruled that prison inmates who carry out work as an integral part of their sentence are not entitled to the minimum wage.[102] The Court held that the underlying objective of the Minimum Wages Law, such as ensuring the employees' ability to maintain a decent standard of living for themselves and their families, did not pertain to prison labor.

In three cases in which apprentices were employed on contracts that denied their right to any wages in return for their training—in law,[103] in tax consultation,[104] and in private investigations,[105] respectively—the National Labour Court held that the contract was illegal and that the apprentices were entitled to the minimum wage under the Minimum Wages Law.

a. Mode of Payment

Under the Wage Law, wages must be paid in full at the place of work, in cash or by check, or by payment into the employee's bank account. The employer may not pay the employee in-kind, except as agreed by collective agreement. Furthermore, the employer is prohibited from requiring the employee to purchase commodities or services from the employer. The Wage Law also prohibits the fixing of a global salary, which includes overtime pay or holiday pay, except if allowed in a collective agreement that has received the authorization of the Minister of Labour. A global salary that does not meet the requirements of the Wage Law will be regarded as the base salary.

---

[102] Ofer Sadot v. Prison Auth. (2001) 55 (IV) P.D. 817.
[103] Adv. Chaim Kazis v. Taufik Ariyat (2003) 38 P.D.A. 394.
[104] Asher Twily v. Yitzhak Dhary (2002) 38 P.D.A. 746.
[105] Nazy Shary v. Yakov Rogel (2003) 38 P.D.A. 481.

The employer may not make deductions from the employee's wages except for those deductions permitted in an exhaustive list set out in the Wage Law. This list includes the following:

- income tax;
- union membership or agency fees, up to the maximum amount fixed in regulations (currently 0.8 percent), if the deduction is agreed to by the employee or in a collective agreement;
- disciplinary fines under a collective agreement; and
- any outstanding fixed-amount debt owed by the employee to the employer, up to the amount of 25 percent of salary, or 100 percent of salary on termination of employment.

b. Time of Payment

A monthly salary must be paid at the end of the month for which it is due, and an hourly wage after two weeks of work. The Wage Law provides punitive damages for late payment, at the high level of 5 percent for the first week of nonpayment and 10 percent for each subsequent week. A shortened limitation period of one year (or 30 days after payment is made) applies to a claim for damages under the Wage Law.

2. *Minimum Wage*

The Minimum Wages Law, 1987, establishes a minimum wage, which is set at 45 percent of the average monthly wage for a full-time job, with a proportionate adjustment for part-time work. Calculation of the minimum wage is without reference to additional payments such as seniority and family supplements; these additional payments are added to the minimum wage. Currently, there is a political lobby for increasing the minimum wage from the present level of 3,000 NIS, which is approximately $750, to the level of 4,000 NIS, which is approximately $1,000.

Every employee older than age 18 is entitled to the minimum wage, and the duty to pay the minimum wage is imposed on the employer. Failure to pay the minimum wage results in both civil and criminal liability, punishable by fine.

C. Hours

The Hours of Work and Rest Law, 1951 (Hours of Work Law), was intended to protect employees' social and physical well-being by fixing maximum working hours. In addition, the Hours of Work Law guarantees a day of rest to be taken by the employee on the weekly religious day of rest in his or her community, whether Jewish, Muslim, or Christian. The law does not apply to certain categories of employment, such as the following:

- employment requiring a special level of personal trust or a managerial role;
- work of a kind that does not allow for supervision of work and rest hours; and
- police and civil service employment, which requires work outside regular hours.

1. *Regular Working Time*

The Hours of Work Law fixes regular working time as a 45-hour working week and, for youths younger than age 18, 40 hours. The law originally fixed regular daily working time as eight hours per day for a six-day week, but the alternative of nine hours per day for a five-day week has been introduced by a framework collective agreement. Employment beyond the regular hours must be authorized by the Minister of Labour or a collective agreement.

2. *Overtime*

All hours worked beyond regular working hours are overtime hours. Currently, there is a general authorization by the Minister of Labour permitting overtime work of 4 hours per day and 12 hours per week. For overtime work, the employer is required to pay 125 percent of regular wages for the first two hours in a day, and 150 percent for any additional overtime hours. As discussed above,[106] statutory overtime pay may not be included as part of a global salary.

[106] See V.B.1.a., above.

3. *Weekly Rest Day*

Employment on the day of rest is prohibited, unless approved by the Minister of Labour on the basis that cessation of work might damage national security or the safety of person or property, or might cause great damage to the economy, work process, or the supply of essential services.

The hours of rest to be taken on the weekly rest day are fixed at a minimum of 36 consecutive hours, unless the Minister of Labour authorizes a shorter rest day, of not less than 25 hours, in certain sectors such as transport or postal services.

D. Leave

1. *Annual Leave*

The Annual Leave Law, 1951, provides for a minimum of 14 to 28 days annual leave, depending on length of employment. Employees are entitled to the full 28-day leave after 14 years of employment with the same employer. Annual leave must be paid at the employee's full regular salary.

According to the case law, the employer is obliged to provide annual leave. The employer may determine the timing of the leave in accordance with the needs of the workplace but must, as far as possible, do so in coordination with the employee. The employee may, with the employer's consent, take only seven consecutive leave days and accumulate the remaining days of annual leave for a period of up to two additional years. The employee's failure to take annual leave, or silence on the part of the employee regarding failure of the employer to allow leave, will not be considered a waiver of the employee's leave rights. However, the employee must not take paid work in an alternative workplace during the annual leave period; in case this requirement is violated, the employee will forfeit the right to leave pay.

The employee is entitled, on termination of employment, to compensation for any annual leave not taken during the course of his or her employment. A shortened limitation period of three years applies to actions to recover annual leave compensation.

2. *Sick Leave*

The Sick Leave Law, 1976, provides residual rights to sick leave for employees who have no guaranteed sick leave under a collective agreement or individual employment contract. The Sick Leave Law does not determine a mandatory minimum for employer-provided sick leave. Where the provisions of a collective agreement grant fewer days of leave, it will prevail. Sick leave provided by the Sick Leave Law depends on the length of employment with the same employer, with a maximum of 90 days' leave after five years. The level of sick pay is 37.5 percent of regular salary after one day's absence, and 75 percent after three days' absence. An Amendment to the Sick Leave Law gives the employee a right to take up to eight days' sick leave to care for a sick parent or minor child.

3. *Maternity and Paternity Leave*

The Employment of Women Law, 1954, as amended, establishes a right to leave for pregnancy-related illness or forced rest, birth, breastfeeding, and childcare, as maternal or, where relevant, parental rights.[107] Under the Employment of Women Law, the length of regular maternity leave is 12 weeks, and this leave can be shared between the parents at their request, provided the mother takes a minimum of six weeks.[108] In certain circumstances, such as hospitalization of the newborn, there is an additional four weeks of entitlement. The National Insurance Agency is responsible for the employee's pay during this leave. In addition, the Law allows for up to six months of sick leave after the maternity leave ends, if authorized by a doctor.[109] It also grants an hour's leave per day for up to four months after the maternity leave ends, without a reduction in pay.[110] The Law entitles a mother to take further unpaid leave of up to a maximum of 12 months starting from the seventh week after the birth; this leave may alternatively be taken by the father.[111]

---

[107]See also VI.C.3., below.
[108]Employment of Women Law §6.
[109]*Id.* §7.
[110]*Id.*
[111]*Id.*

The Employment of Women Law provides women with entitlement to periods of sick leave for fertility treatment or leave without pay in cases of stay in a battered women's shelter. The law prohibits dismissal during the authorized leaves and for a period after the employee's return to work.[112] An amendment to the Employment of Women Law, enacted March 2001, prohibits the dismissal of an employee undergoing fertility treatments for a period of 150 days after treatment. However, an employer may receive special permission from the Ministry of Labour to dismiss such an employee.

VI. ANTIDISCRIMINATION

A. General

Since the late 1980s, Israeli statutes and case law have prohibited a wide range of employment discrimination—on grounds of race, religion, sex, family status (parental and marital), national origin, sexual orientation, age, disability, or political opinion or party affiliation. Until the mid-1990s, however, statutory prohibitions against employment discrimination were concerned almost exclusively with the issue of gender discrimination; other forms of discrimination were prohibited only by a general judicial principle of the right to equality. Statutory prohibitions against the remaining forms of discrimination were added between 1992 and 1996. In addition, in 1988, the legislature extended maternal protections to include paternal rights as well, thereby facilitating the integration of family and work.

B. Historical Development of the Right to Equality

The issue of equality between the sexes first was treated as a basic and guiding principle in the Declaration of Independence and in the Women's Equal Rights Law, 1951, as amended in the year 2000. Although these enactments have no binding constitutional impact and do not limit the legislature's ability to legislate

[112]See I.C.3.c., above.

contradictory norms, they do establish a guideline for the interpretation of statutes.

The general principle of equality, under the Declaration of Independence and the Women's Equal Rights Law, was used by the labor courts in 1973 to develop the concept of public policy as a tool to cancel discriminatory provisions in contracts. In the case law, a collective agreement that limited women's opportunities for promotion was deemed to be contrary to public policy and, therefore, void.[113] In reaching this result, the National Labour Court relied on ILO Convention 111,[114] which prohibits sex discrimination in employment conditions, holding that the ILO Convention represented the normative policy prevailing in the world and was applicable in Israeli law as a matter of public policy.

Subsequent development of the principle of equality took place on the statutory level in the Equal Employment Opportunity Law, 1988; on the constitutional level, under the Basic Law: Human Dignity and Freedom;[115] and through case law in the labor courts and the Supreme Court, sitting as the High Court of Justice.

C. Equal Employment Opportunity Laws

1. *General*

Israeli legislation dealing with equal employment opportunity can be divided into three categories. The first category consists of rules prohibiting specific kinds of employment discrimination. In the second category is legislation providing protective and accommodating standards for the integration of persons with group differences—such as women, parents, and the handicapped—in employment. A third category of legislation addresses affirmative action.

---

[113]El-Al Flight Crew v. Edna Hazin (1972/3) 4 P.D.A. 365.

[114]For a discussion of ILO Conventions, see the chapter on the ILO in Volume I, Part 4. See also the Introduction, at C.3., above.

[115]See the Introduction, at C.2.a., above.

2. *Rules Prohibiting Discrimination*

a. Statutes

Statutory law expressly prohibits various types of employment discrimination by employers and others, in both the public and private sectors. These statutory provisions are discussed below.

i. Employment Service Law

The Employment Service Law, 1959, prohibits discrimination on the grounds of age, gender, race, religion, nationality, country of origin, political viewpoint, or party affiliation. This legislation was directed mainly at referral to work by employment service bureaus.

ii. Hours of Work and Rest Law

A 1981 amendment to the Hours of Work and Rest Law, 1951, prohibits discrimination on grounds of religion. According to this provision, employers may not refuse to hire candidates solely for the reason that they will not work on their weekly religious rest day.

iii. Equal Retirement Age Law

The Equal Retirement Age Law, 1987 (Equal Retirement Law), forbids gender discrimination with regard to mandatory retirement. According to the Equal Retirement Law, female employees, who previously were required by collective agreements to retire earlier than their male counterparts, are no longer required to do so. The Equal Retirement Law leaves them an option, so long as the collective agreement continues to fix different ages for men and women, to retire at any time between the earlier age fixed for women and that fixed for men under the agreement.

iv. Equal Employment Opportunities Law

The Equal Employment Opportunities, 1988 (Equal Opportunities Law), provides comprehensive protection against various types of employment discrimination and establishes much more effective remedies than had existed previously.

The Equal Opportunities Law originally banned discrimination on grounds of gender and marital and parental status. In 1992, sexual orientation was added as a forbidden ground for discrimination, and, as recently as 1995, the criteria of age, race, religion, country of origin, political viewpoint, and party affiliation were added. The Equal Opportunities Law prohibits discrimination in any of the following areas:

- hiring,
- employment conditions,
- promotions,
- professional training,
- dismissal,
- severance pay,
- retirement benefits,
- sexual harassment, and
- job advertising.

By an Amendment enacted in March 2001, the legislature extended the protection of the Equal Employment Opportunities Law to workers of labor contractors.[116] The Amendment also prohibits the user from encouraging or demanding discriminatory behavior on the part of the labor contractor.

Under the Equal Opportunities in Employment Law, a male employee is entitled to the same parental rights as are granted to female employees in his place of work. His entitlement is conditional, however, upon his spouse "being employed" and not taking absence on the same grounds. The National Labour Court has held that the expression "being employed" includes the self-employed.[117] Purposive interpretation of the Law also led the Court to include situations in which the spouse works in a workplace that does not give the same parental rights.[118]

---

[116]For a discussion of contract workers, see I.A.3., above.

[117]State of Israel and The Israel Police Force v. Menachem Yahav (2003) 38 P.D.A 26.

[118]State of Israel v. Alexander Muskelenko (Nat'l Lab. Ct., Aug. 31, 2003) (not yet published).

The Equal Opportunities Law clarifies that bona fide occupational qualifications are not considered discriminatory; conversely, conditions laid down by the employer that are not relevant qualifications for performance of the job will be considered discriminatory.

With respect to remedies, the Equal Opportunities Law provides for enforcement remedies[119] and gives the courts the discretion to award damages without proof of economic injury.

v. Equal Pay to Female and Male Employees Law

The Equal Pay to Female and Male Employees Law, 1996 (Equal Pay Law), amending an earlier 1964 statute, prohibits gender discrimination in regard to employees' pay by declaring that female and male employees employed by the same employer are entitled to equal pay, including all extra benefits and payments, in return for equal or equivalent labor. The Equal Pay Law also requires equal pay for comparable work, which is defined to mean positions that are comparable with respect to qualifications, effort, skill, responsibility, and workplace conditions. The Equal Pay Law provides the labor courts with authority to appoint an expert in occupational analysis to assist in determining the equivalence of positions; in certain circumstances, this analysis may be conducted at the state's expense.

vi. Prevention of Sexual Harassment Law

The Prevention of Sexual Harassment Law, 1998 (Sexual Harassment Law) established prohibitions against sexual harassment in the workplace. The Sexual Harassment Law prohibits all forms of sexual harassment by physical or verbal actions, which give rise either to a hostile environment or loss of employment benefits for the harassed employee. Employers are required to publish regulations for prevention of sexual harassment in the workplace.

Sexual harassment in the workplace is actionable, whether or not the harassed employee has shown his or her opposition to the sexual proposal, and is punishable by up to three years' imprison-

---

[119]See I.C.5., above.

ment. The employer is liable for harassment committed by himself or herself, by a supervisor of the employee, or by other employees, where the employer has not taken reasonable measures to prevent the harassment and, in the case of an employer of more than 25 employees, where the employer has not published standards and procedures for that purpose. In order to establish liability, two stages of proof must be met. First, the employee must prove that he or she was sexually harassed by the employer, a supervisor, or another employee. The second stage shifts the burden to the employer to prove that it did not violate the requirements stated.[120] There have been virtually no court cases based on this law; thus, it is hard to predict the evidentiary requirements that will be imposed by the courts in the future. Employees who have been harassed are entitled, in addition to compensatory damages, to a damage award of up to 50,000 NIS, which is approximately $12,000, without proof of actual injury.

Recently, the Supreme Court handed down a judgment that dealt with the definition and notion of sexual harassment.[121] The Court ruled that there should be no distinction between sexual statements made directly to a person and statements made in the presence of people who might be offended. The Court stated that expressions of a sexual nature, which are degrading and offensive, are by definition expressions made toward anyone present at the time of the statement and who is of the gender referred to in or by the statement.

The National Labour Court recently upheld a District Labour Court judgment that awarded 50,000 NIS in punitive damages to an employee harassed by her employer.[122]

Overturning the judgment of a Regional Labour Court, the National Labour Court held that the plaintiff in a civil sexual harassment case was not required to bring a higher level of evidence than that required in ordinary civil proceedings.[123]

---

[120]Prevention of Sexual Harassment Law, 1998, §7.

[121]Podlinski v. State of Israel (Sup. Ct., Oct. 24, 2001) (not yet published)

[122]Doe Co. v. Roe (Nat'l Lab. Ct., Dec. 19, 2001) (not yet published).

[123]Nazy Shary v. Yakov Rogel (2003) 38 P.D.A. 481.

vii. Equal Rights for Handicapped Persons Law

In 1998, the Equal Rights for Handicapped Persons Law (Handicapped Persons Law) was passed, applying pertinent provisions of the Equal Opportunities Law to persons with physical or mental handicaps who are capable of performing the work in question.

b. Judicial Enforcement

The labor courts, both at the regional and national levels, have a checkered record with regard to implementing the antidiscrimination laws. On the issues of sexual orientation and age, they have found for discrimination plaintiffs, but in gender discrimination cases, they have been more reluctant. Although empowered by statute to order reinstatement, in only one gender discrimination case have the courts done so.[124] Furthermore, the labor courts have hesitated to find the employer guilty of discrimination against women where the employer has not expressly articulated the gender basis for his or her actions. However, in recent cases, the Regional Court has accepted more gender discrimination claims and, in one recent case, the National Labour Court has taken a sharper stand and has imposed heavy punitive damages for gender discrimination.[125]

The Supreme Court has a consistent record of strong equality rhetoric in regard to all forms of discrimination. On one occasion, the Supreme Court reversed the decision of the National Labour Court in order to invalidate employment practices that were discriminatory on the basis of sex.[126]

The High Court of Justice held that an employer is not allowed to offer female employees a bridging pension that is lower than that offered to their male colleagues and that this amounted to illegal discrimination. The rationale given by the employer that female employees may exercise their right to an early retirement option five years earlier than men and, hence, qualify for an occupational pension under the regular pension plan, does not justify discrimination in the number of years of the bridging pension given

---

[124]Blitz v. Hebrew Univ. (Feb. 26, 1993) (unpublished).

[125]Plotkin v. Izenberg Bros. (Sept. 8, 1997) (unpublished).

[126]Dr. Nevo v. Israeli Jewish Agency (1987/8) 18 P.D.A. 197.

by the employer. Such an arrangement would result in reduction of the female employees' income and pension rights. Furthermore, the written agreement of the female employees to the discriminatory terms is not evidence of free choice and their waiver of equal terms is invalid. Overruling the decision of the National Labour Court, Justice Cheshin stated that this discriminatory practice projects a concept of the inferiority of women in working life.[127]

3. *Protective Rules and Accommodation Standards*

Since the 1950s, Israeli statutes have included protective measures for working mothers. These measures were enacted in accordance with ILO standards. The statutory arrangements were generous for their time, providing women with protection against dismissal during pregnancy and maternity leave, with compulsory 12 weeks of paid maternity leave, and an option of 72 weeks of unpaid childcare leave with preservation of job security rights.[128] The paternalistic characteristics of these laws made them controversial. Hence, in 1988, Israel introduced sweeping reforms to convert maternal childcare leave rights into parental rights, thereby removing the stereotypical stigma inherent in restricting such rights to mothers.

Necessary accommodation measures, which remain exclusively maternal rights, allow women to integrate their family and working lives. Strict maternity accommodation rules include fertility treatment, a minimum of six weeks of statutory leave for birth, and other rights to absence for breastfeeding and pregnancy-related illness or enforced rest.[129]

These provisions are based on biological differences between men and women and should be regarded as promoting equality by enabling women to better integrate into the labor force.

Employees are required to take necessary measures to accommodate persons with handicaps, including adaptation of the workplace, equipment, job requirements, hours of work, etc., all provided that this does not impose an unreasonable burden on the

---

[127]Eitana Niv v. The National Labour Court (2002) 36 (VI) P.D. 663.

[128]Employment of Women Law, 5734-1954, §§ 6, 7, 8, and 9.

[129]*Id.* See discussion in V.D.3., above.

employer considering the cost of the adaptation and the size of the enterprise.[130]

The National Labour Court held that, where a pregnant employee was dismissed on grounds of pregnancy, she would be entitled to damages, even where the Equal Employment Opportunities Law did not apply because the workplace had fewer than six employees, which is the minimum for application of the Law, and the Women's Work Law did not apply because the employee had not worked six months, as required for the Law's protection against dismissal. In the case at hand, on acceptance of employment an employee had undertaken not to become pregnant. Immediately after commencing her employment, she became pregnant and was dismissed. The employee recorded a conversation in which the employer had explicitly explained that she was not prepared to employee a pregnant woman. The Court awarded damages for loss of wages and national insurance payments up until the end of the maternity leave.

4. *Affirmative Action*

A number of affirmative action measures have been introduced by the executive and the legislature. In 1985, the government decided that government authorities should make an effort to ensure a balanced representation of men and women in key positions, and that women should be included on every nominating committee, unless there were reasons to prevent it. In 1993, an amendment to the Government Companies Law introduced a provision requiring that there must be fair representation of both sexes on the boards of directors of government companies, and that until fair representation is achieved, government ministers should appoint board members of the underrepresented sex, as far as this is possible in the circumstances. This policy was given recognition and legitimacy by the Supreme Court both in strong affirmative action rhetoric and in an enforcement remedy.[131]

In 1996, a law similar in principle and technique to the Government Companies Law was passed, introducing affirmative action to civil service appointments and requiring the Civil Service

---

[130]Handicapped Persons Law, 5748-1998, §8.

[131]Israeli Women's Lobby v. The State of Israel (1994) (V) 48 P.D. 749.

Commissioner to take appropriate measures to achieve fair representation of both sexes at various levels of the civil service staff hierarchy.[132]

In 2000, an amendment to the Women's Equal Rights Law, 1951, provided that affirmative action is a legitimate element of gender equality in all spheres.

In 2001, the affirmative action provisions in the Government Companies Law and in the Civil Service (Appointments) Law were extended to include members of the Arab minority.

D. Procedural Aspects

Two alternative procedures exist for enforcing the employment discrimination statutes: criminal claims and civil claims.

1. *Criminal Claims*

Criminal claims are prosecuted by the Ministry of Labour. However, to date the Ministry has prosecuted only technical claims for discriminatory job advertising.

2. *Civil Claims*

a. *Initiating a Claim*

Under the Equal Opportunities Law, either the employee victim of discrimination or the representative labor union or an organization involved in promoting human rights may initiate legal proceedings. However, except in precedent-setting cases, responsibility for taking action against employment discrimination rests, in practice, on the victim. The result is very low-key litigation and only partial enforcement of equal opportunity rights.

b. *Burden of Proof*

One of the main innovations of the Equal Opportunities Law is that it provides procedures to deal with the difficulty of proving discrimination. Specifically, the law transfers the burden of proof to the employer and expressly provides that requirements that are

---

[132]Equal Pay to Female and Male Employees Law, 5756-1996.

irrelevant to job performance will be regarded as discriminatory if they adversely affect one sex.

The Equal Pay Law uses a similar technique by creating an assumption that any discrepancy between salaries (or other payments) in equal positions is illegal, and by placing the burden on the employer to prove that the difference in pay is a result of the character or essence of the job.

Under the case law, intent does not have to be proved to succeed in a civil claim for discrimination.

c. *Remedies*

Once discrimination has been proved, there are two possible remedies: (1) canceling the discriminatory provision, or (2) enforcing the nondiscriminatory solution and providing the victim with the benefit or right he or she deserves. The Equal Employment Law provides that where discrimination has been proved, the remedy must level the employment conditions and not derogate from them.

The Equal Opportunities Law also provides that the court may award damages to a discrimination victim even where there has been no economic loss.[133] This is an unusual provision that allows the victim to claim damages for the distress caused by discrimination. It has been interpreted by the labor court to empower the court to award punitive damages.[134] The Equal Opportunities Law further departs from the general rule of contract law by allowing enforcement of the victim's right to promotion, reinstatement, or other enforcement remedies.[135]

The National Labour Court has held that where an employer dismisses a pregnant employee without authorization by the Minister of Labour, as required under the Employment of Women Law, the proper remedy is reinstatement and the employee must continue to be employed until authorization has been given. In this decision, the court reversed previous judicial policy according to which authorization by the Minister of Labour may be retroactive

---

[133]Equal Employment Opportunity Law §10(1).

[134]Plotkin v. Izenberg Bros. (Sept. 8, 1997) (unpublished).

[135]See also I.C.5., above.

and, if it is not given after the dismissal of the employee, the proper remedy is compensation.[136]

Where a prospective employer reversed its decision to employ a bio-tech research worker after she revealed that she was pregnant, the Regional Labour Court awarded heavy damages. The damages were for loss of salary until the date of birth, loss of maternity benefits during the mandatory maternity leave, and statutory (punitive) damages for discrimination on grounds of sex or parental status.[137]

d. Limitations Period

Under section 14 of the Equal Opportunities Law, the limitation period is only 12 months. This poses difficulties for discrimination victims, especially in view of the fact that there are no official agencies to prosecute claims on their behalf.

VII. OCCUPATIONAL SAFETY AND HEALTH AND WORKERS' COMPENSATION

A. Occupational Safety and Health

Israeli law protects employees' health and safety at work under various statutory arrangements, and these are supervised by a number of different agencies.

1. Statutes

a. Work Safety Ordinance

The Work Safety Ordinance [New Version] 1970 (Safety Ordinance) is the central statutory arrangement, which lays out the criteria and requirements for safety standards in a wide range of specific situations. Numerous regulations under the Safety Ordinance have been promulgated by the Ministry of Labour.[138] As

---

[136]Dana Shany v. Start-Net Entrepreneurship and Constr. Ltd. (Nat'l Lab. Ct., Apr. 30, 2002) (not yet published).

[137]Dr. Alma Levy v. Rad Ramot-High Tech Co. Incubator (Dist. Lab. Ct., Oct. 24, 2002) (not yet published).

[138]These regulations are published in the Ordinance cited above.

regards safety, the Safety Ordinance establishes specific rules for the use of machinery, equipment, and substances, for example, the need for guard fences, protective clothing, etc. In the field of health, the Safety Ordinance requires that plants be maintained in proper sanitary conditions, for example, with regard to lighting, heating, ventilation, etc. In the field of workers' welfare, the Safety Ordinance requires the provision of drink, food, and hygienic facilities.

Application of the Safety Ordinance primarily is limited to plants in which manual labor is used in the process of producing or maintaining goods. There is some criticism of this limited scope of application. Provisions of the Safety Ordinance may be enforced by means of a civil action for damages. In addition, the Safety Ordinance establishes criminal penalties for employer violations. The employer's criminal liability is absolute; there is no requirement of *mens rea*, and liability is not contingent on a resulting injury. Criminal enforcement of the Safety Ordinance is entrusted to the Ministry of Labour. However, there is evidence of a low rate of prosecutions, and of ineffective enforcement by means of criminal sanctions.

b. Employment of Women Law

The Employment of Women Law, 1953, prohibits the employment of women in tasks or processes that will specially endanger their health. Regulations have been promulgated under the Employment of Women Law to prohibit women from working in tasks or processes that would endanger their reproductive health or the health of a fetus during pregnancy.[139]

c. Labor Inspection (Organization) Law

The Labor Inspection (Organization) Law, 1954, established the Work Safety Supervisory (WSS) Service, with safety supervision functions, and the Institute for Safety and Hygiene, with training and information functions. The Labor Inspection Law obliges employers to provide training and guidance to employees with re-

---

[139]Employment of Women Regulations (Prohibited Occupations and Restricted Occupations), 5740-1979.

gard to prevention of accidents or work-related diseases. Employees are obliged to attend all such training programs. Employers also are required to formulate and update a work safety plan for the plant, which must be submitted to the WSS Service's safety supervisors. Regulations under the Labor Inspection Law require employers to disclose work-related risks to employees, for example, those deriving from equipment, substances, or processes in the plant.

d. Occupational Accidents and Diseases Law

The Occupational Accidents and Diseases Ordinance, 1945, requires employers to report all occupational accidents and diseases that result in death or work incapacity for more than three days to the WSS Service's safety supervisors.

e. Supervision of Workplaces Law

Under the Supervision of Workplaces Law, in plants where there are more than 25 employees, the employer must appoint a safety committee of employer and worker representatives and, where there are more than 500 employees (150 where there is a highly dangerous work process), the employer also must appoint a safety supervisor. These plant safety officials are authorized to report on safety problems to the WSS Service's safety supervisors, who should take appropriate action.

2. Regulation by Collective Agreement

The collective bargaining partners are involved in the regulation of occupational health and safety. In 1979, the major collective bargaining partners—the Histadrut and the major employer federations—signed a Collective Agreement for Promotion of Quality of Workplace Conditions, which is still in force. In this agreement, the parties undertook various commitments to promote occupational health and safety beyond the statutory minimum requirements.

B. Workers' Compensation

The National Insurance Law, 1954, provides coverage for work injuries and occupational diseases. Coverage for work injuries and occupational diseases includes not only employees, but also self-employed persons, other persons injured through involvement in the work process, and prisoners.

Benefits under the National Insurance Law are funded through employer and employee dues. The employer's National Insurance dues are graduated in accordance with the plant's accident rate.

The National Insurance stipend for work injuries and occupational diseases is paid at the level of 75 percent of the employee's wage, but where the disability is less than 20 percent, the benefit is limited to 182 days. There also are provisions for rehabilitation and for the payment of medical costs. Occupational diseases are defined in accordance with a list drawn up under the National Insurance Law; diseases not included in the list are not covered.

In 1999, 55,000 work injury and occupational disease stipends were awarded under the National Insurance Law.

VIII. Pensions and Benefits

A. Pensions

1. Pension Reform

Beginning in 1995, Israel initiated a significant reform of pension arrangements. This reform was motivated by demographic changes in the ratio between employed and retired persons, which resulted in a serious deficit in pre-reform pension funds. Investigation into the status of the funds revealed that, without reform, there was a high risk of pension fund collapse. A review of pension arrangements was undertaken, and a government commission submitted its recommendations to raise the retirement and pension eligibility ages and to remove existing distinctions between men and women in this respect.

The pension system in Israel is divided into three layers, each of which is discussed in more detail below: (1) National Insurance (mandatory state pension insurance); (2) occupational pensions (divided into budgetary pensions and contributory pensions); and (3) private pension-saving schemes. The recent pension reform was concentrated on the second layer of pension coverage.

2. *National Insurance*

The Institute for National Insurance (Institute) is an independent statutory corporation, founded in 1954, which is subject to supervision by the Knesset and the State Comptroller. The Institute is funded by dues of all individual Israeli residents who are eligible for general benefits, as well as by employer and employee dues as benefits deriving from employment. The primary purpose of the Institute is to develop an infrastructure of financial protection for individuals and families in a variety of situations. In addition to pension insurance, the Institute provides insurance for income maintenance, loss of work ability, disability, child allowances, unemployment benefits, nonpayment of spousal maintenance, bankruptcy, army reserve service, and more. Eligibility for compulsory insurance extends to all residents older than age 18, other than housewives, who are entitled to voluntary insurance.

The first layer of pension insurance from the Institute provides a basic old age and survivors' pension. Its purpose is to secure for all Israeli residents a fixed monthly income during old age and to protect the elderly population from falling below the poverty line. This layer of pension insurance is universal both in scope of coverage and payment of a fixed pension, irrespective of the insured person's level of earnings or income during the qualification period.

The age of eligibility has been 65 for men and 60 for women. However, beginning July 1, 2004, the age of eligibility will be gradually raised to 67 for men and 64 for women. Between the age of eligibility and the age of 70 for men and 65 for women, the pension is not payable to those who have an income over 57 percent of the average wage.

The minimum qualifying period for pension entitlement is 60 months' payment of insurance dues during the 10 years prior to pension age. The amount of the basic individual pension was fixed at 16 percent of the average wage, which as of January 2000, amounted to 1,000 NIS per month, which is approximately $250. However, since July 1, 2002, it has been reduced to 12 percent on a temporary basis, which has been extended annually. The basic pension can reach 29 percent of the average wage, depending on family status and the number of dependents. There is a 2 percent increase in pension benefits for every additional year of dues payments beyond the 10-year minimum, up to an additional 50 percent. Recipients of National Insurance pensions who have a very low level of additional income also are entitled to an additional income supplement.

The Institute also provides survivors' pensions for insured persons' widows and widowers who are older than the age of 50. The amount of survivors' pensions is fixed at 16 percent of the average wage but is reduced by one-half if the survivor is himself or herself a recipient of pension benefits.

3. *Occupational Pensions*

a. General

Occupational pensions traditionally have been provided for employee members of pension funds. This second layer of pension insurance is intended to provide an income after retirement that is commensurate with salary earned prior to retirement and can reach up to 70 percent of the insured person's qualifying salary.

Occupational pensions are of two types: budgetary and contributory. Budgetary schemes, which are funded by employer contributions, apply to all employees who are employed by designated government employers. Contributory pension schemes are voluntary and are funded by combined employer-employee contributions.

This second layer of pension insurance is not comprehensive. In 1995, prior to the pension reform, one of the major pension funds estimated that roughly 80 percent of the workforce was insured by occupational pension schemes, including both contributory and budgetary pension insurance. However, some human rights associations have claimed that as many as 1.15 million members of the workforce (50 percent) have no occupational pension insurance; to solve this problem, these associations are lobbying for legislation of comprehensive compulsory pension insurance.

b. Budgetary Pensions

Budgetary pensions are funded solely by the employer without employee contributions. State employees are entitled to budgetary pensions under the State Service (Pensions) Law [Consolidated Version], 1970 (State Pension Law). The State Pension Law applies to government employees, municipal workers, and employees of government agencies and authorities. State budgetary pensions provide for old age, disability, and survivors' pensions, and are funded from the state budget. The basis for determining the pension level under the State Pension Law is the final salary earned by the employee in the employing institution, which is defined to include the basic salary plus fixed increments to salary. The employee's actual pension benefit is calculated on the basis of length of service, with an accumulation of 2 percent per year of employment. The age of eligibility is 65 for both men and women, although the Civil Service Commissioner has discretion to allow earlier retirement, with pension eligibility.

There also are budgetary pension schemes in some large institutions such as major universities. These schemes are funded from the universities' current budgets. The terms of these pensions are fixed in collective pension agreements between the universities and the unions of university employees.

c. *Contributory Pensions*

Contributory pension schemes are voluntary, and employees may decide whether to join them. Until the pension reform of 1995, the decision to participate was made solely at the collective agreement level. However, following the 1995 reform, the decision to join may be made at the collective agreement or the individual contract level. However, if a decision to join is made at the collective agreement level, the individual employee is not able to opt out. Contributory pension funds operate as defined benefit funds; that is, they provide a definite level of benefits according to a set formula.

Contributory pensions are provided by independent funds. Until 1995, there were seven contributory pension funds, all of which were established by the Histadrut. The financial arrangements of contributory pension funds are subject to supervision under the Supervision of Insurance Transactions Law and the Income Tax Ordinance Regulations. In general, contributory pension schemes are funded by combined employer-employee contributions. However, the funds have been supported by public subsidy, both through tax benefits and preferential terms for saving in government bonds. Furthermore, in case of budgetary deficits, the funds have enjoyed various forms of government guarantees.

Pension coverage in contributory pension funds is almost exclusively by means of collective agreements and by extension orders of the Ministry of Labour that have extended the provisions of these agreements to some unorganized work sectors.[140] The terms of membership in contributory pension funds are fixed by collective agreements and, under the agreements, employers and employees are required to join and contribute to specific funds. The funds are required to admit employees covered by the agreements to membership, irrespective of personal data.

The agreements generally establish the age of eligibility at 65 for men and 60 for women. Most of the agreements provide comprehensive insurance including old age, disability, and survivors' pensions, although some agreements provide comprehensive insurance on an optional basis, and some provide only basic old age insurance. Payments to contributory pension funds are made by employers and employees at a ratio of two-thirds to one-third, respectively. Employees are entitled to a defined benefit on the basis of their membership in these funds: the benefit is accumulated at the rate of 2 percent per year up to a maximum of 70 percent. The amount of benefit is calculated on the basis of either the average salary for the entire period of contribution or the average salary for the last three years of contribution.

The issue of vesting of pension rights came before the National Labour Court in two cases. In the first case, the Court reiterated prior judicial decisions, including decisions of the Supreme Court, according to which pension rights vest only at the time of occurrence of the event that confers entitlement. Hence, the pension conditions may be changed by the pension fund at any time before the employee's date of entitlement to payment of the pension. This is the case whether or not the change derogates from the rights established at the time of the employee's joining the fund.[141]

---

[140] As regards the use of extension orders, see I.C.2.a., above.

[141] Abrham Leibovitch v. The New Histadrut Worker's Cent. Pension Fund Ltd. (Nat'l Lab. Ct., May 30, 2002) (not yet published).

In the second case, the court applied this principle to override an express agreement made between the employee and the pension fund, which had stated that the pension conditions would be determined solely in accordance with the agreement.[142]

d. The 1995 Reform

As noted above, in 1995, the government decided to introduce a sweeping pension reform. An agreement was reached with the Histadrut that, in exchange for future government guarantees of existing fund deficits, comprehensive structural changes would be made for future occupational pension insurance.

The reform involved a gradual phase-out of the old Histadrut funds by closing the old pension funds to all new employee entrants. For future entrants to the labor force, new funds would be provided in the form of limited shareholder companies. The market for the new pension funds was, in addition to the Histadrut (which created new funds to take up from the old funds), opened up to newcomers. This opening of competition answered both liberal economic policy preferences of the government and, in the view of some legal observers, answered the constitutional requirements of the Basic Law: Freedom of Occupation.[143]

The new funds must be actuarially independent. In order to launch and/or maintain a new fund, the fund must have independent capital of at least 5 million NIS, which is approximately $1.25 million. Management of the new funds is subject to more stringent supervision than either the old occupational pension funds or the private pension-savings schemes, discussed immediately below. In case of an actuarial imbalance, the fund is required to raise dues and/or reduce benefits. The government no longer holds itself responsible to subsidize budgetary deficits in the new funds. However, the new funds, like the old ones, enjoy certain tax and investment privileges granted by the government.

---

[142]Moshe Eliav v. Makefet Cent. Pension and Benefit Fund, Coop. Soc'y Ltd. (2001) 36 P.D.A. 721.

[143]See I.C.2.a., above.

Unlike the defined benefits policy of the old funds, the new funds function on the basis of defined contributions; that is, benefits are calculated based on the amount of accumulated contributions allocated to the employee. The amount of benefits payable from the new funds is limited to twice the average wage. The new funds are required to provide comprehensive insurance for old age, disability, and survivors' pensions. They also are required to give equal benefits to men and women as regards age of eligibility and widows' and widowers' pensions.

As part of the reform process, it was decided that the budgetary pension scheme for state employees would be eliminated for new employees. All new state employees are required to join one of the new contributory pension funds. Implementation of this aspect of the reform requires amendment of the State Pension Law, which, at the time of writing, still remains to be done.

Even after the 1995 reform, occupational pension coverage has remained voluntary and not comprehensive. There still is no government policy commitment to impose compulsory occupational pension insurance. The consequences of this policy are important for two major reasons. First, the National Insurance pension provides too low a level of income to be adequate as a pension without additional occupational pension rights. Second, the vulnerability of significant sectors of the labor market to loss of occupational pension coverage potentially is growing as the coverage of collective agreements shrinks, both because of the reduced power of the Histadrut and the expansion of contingent labor.

e. Reform in 2003 and 2004

Under the Law for the Recovery of the Israeli Economy, 2003, a number of measures were taken to transform the pension system and to reduce pension rights. The target of the government's attack was the pension fund system established by the Histadrut prior to 1995. The Histadrut pension funds were trade union-owned and the right of employees to a pension from one of the various funds was established in collective agreements with employers in both the public and the private sectors. The 2003 law removed the pension funds from Histadrut control and transferred them to control by state-appointed managers, under the direct control of the Supervisor of the Financial Market in Israel; the law established that there would be unified articles of association for all the funds. In essence, this was a move to nationalize these pension funds, in stark contrast to the general policy of privatization, which was the theme of the government's economic policy. The law also cancelled the guarantee of minimum interest rates on government bonds, which it had previously, in 1995, promised the New Histadrut for its pre-1995 pension funds, thus requiring the fund managers to invest the funds holdings in the Israeli stock market. Furthermore, it reduced the rights of members of the funds, increasing the amount of the premiums to be paid by employees who are members of the funds and imposing an additional management fee on pensioners drawing pensions from the funds. Finally, it postponed pensionable age from 60 for women and 65 for men to 67 for both, conditional upon legislation to enforce the change.

The New Histadrut applied to the National Labour Court to cancel the law's intervention in the collectively agreed pension arrangements. It asked the court to declare the existing collective agreements valid and binding and to require the employers to continue to abide by their provisions. The state argued that the National Labour Court did not have jurisdiction over what was in essence a constitutional petition to cancel legislation. The Court rejected this argument and held that it did have jurisdiction. The High Court of Justice upheld the National Labour Court's jurisdiction to hear the case.

In subsequent concession bargaining, the New Histadrut reached agreement with the government on the changes in the pension funds, achieving some modification of the severity of the law's reduction of members' rights. Among other things, it was agreed that the pensionable age of women would be fixed at 62 and not 67.

However, in the Pension Age Law, 2004, the pensionable age of men was fixed at 67, as agreed, but the pensionable age for women who were born after 1953 was fixed at 64 (with a graduated increase from 62 to 64 for women born between 1950 and 1953) and, in addition, a committee was established to examine the issue of women's pension age in accordance with the recommendations of a public committee, which had advised equalization of men and women's retirement ages at age 67. Furthermore, the National Insurance Law was amended: men's age of eligibility was raised from 65 to 67 and age of entitlement to a full pension independent of other sources of income (more than $1,000 per month) remained 70. As regards women, the age of eligibility was raised from 60 to 64 and the age of entitlement to a full pension independent of other sources of income (more than $1,000 per month) was raised from 65 to 70.

4. *Private Pension-Savings Schemes*

The third layer of pension insurance consists of managerial insurance policies and provident funds. These forms of insurance are provided by financial institutions, private insurance companies, and banks. The financial arrangements of these funds are subject to supervision under the Supervision of Insurance Transactions Law and under the Income Tax Ordinance Regulations. Private pension funds provide a combination of savings and insurance, and may provide either a lump sum or an annuity at retirement age. The terms of the plans are determined on the basis of individual agreements and are subject to individual variation in accordance with age, sex, family status, medical situation, etc. The general trend of such individual agreements is to provide similar coverage to that provided by occupational pension schemes, thus insuring old age income, disability, and survivors' benefits. As a result of the legislative changes regarding occupational pension schemes and of the reduction in the scope of collective agreements, insurance through managerial insurance policies is on the increase.

B. Unemployment Benefits

Unemployment benefits are provided under the National Insurance Law. The cumulative requirements for eligibility are as follows:

- residency;
- an age of 18 to 65 years;
- prior payment of National Insurance dues by an employer on behalf of the employee;
- dismissal from the previous place of employment, or in case of voluntary resignation, unemployment for 90 days; and

- absence of refusal to work in suitable employment or, in case of such refusal, unemployment for longer than 90 days.

Unemployed persons younger than age 35 must agree to take any work, not only suitable work, offered by the employment agency.

Unemployment benefits are paid up to a maximum of 175 working days in any one year; however, for unemployed persons younger than age 45 with fewer than three dependents (one of whom may be a spouse), the maximum is 138 days. For the first five months of a benefit period, payment is at the rate of the average wage and, after that, at a reduced rate. Unemployed persons who attend special Ministry of Labour training courses are entitled to unemployment benefits for the period of the course.

In the third quarter of 2001, unemployment in Israel stood at 262,000, which represents 10.3 percent of the civilian workforce. During this period, an average of 118,000 unemployed persons per month received unemployment benefits.

IX. IMMIGRATION

According to a 2002 poll of the Central Bureau of Statistics, workers from foreign countries made up 13 percent of the workforce in Israel. Approximately 81,000 were legally employed, and some 150,000 illegally employed. In 2003, there was a police campaign to crack down on illegal employment of foreign workers: 17,000 illegal foreign workers were deported and 753 prosecutions were brought against employers, in contrast with 300 the previous year.

A regulation enacted by the Minister of Health in April 2001 established that employers must provide medical insurance for foreign workers. This statute guarantees the right to basic medical services, hospitalization, and medication.

There is a growing volume of case law on issues concerning foreign workers. The National Labour Court has held that the employer must on no account hold a foreign worker's passport since this would be an infringement of the worker's rights to human dignity and freedom of movement.[144] The Court also has held that

[144] Dan Buchiman v. Best Ltd. (2003) 38 P.D.A. 824.

an *au pair,* who was employed without a work permit, was entitled to all employment rights including minimum wage, thus overriding the contract for services that provided that she would work in return for board and lodgings only.[145] The Court also held that an action brought by a foreign worker would not be dismissed on the grounds that the plaintiff could not be cross-examined as a result of being compelled to leave Israel; the Court should weigh the evidence before it.[146] Furthermore, where a foreign worker is under a deportation order, the Court will take early evidence and hold the hearing on the case as soon as possible.[147]

Under the Foreign Workers' Law, the employment of foreign workers must be in accordance with conditions established by the Law. In a 2003 case, the National Labour Court held that the employer's obligations under this law cannot be avoided by indirect employment through a foreign labor-only contractor. Furthermore, the Court held that the local user of the foreign worker's services cannot avoid the obligations of Israeli labor law, such as minimum wages, by transferring the responsibility for payment of these rights to a labor-only contractor from the employee's country of origin. In the case at hand, the local employer's ruse of paying the Chinese employees' wages into a bank account, ostensibly in the employees' names, from which they were to be immediately withdrawn by a Chinese labor-only contractor (who then paid the employees a minimal subsistence payment) was in bad faith and did not absolve the local employer of full responsibility for payment of the wages to which the employees were legally entitled under Israeli law.[148]

The phenomenon of employment of workers from foreign countries started in the 1990s, when the number of Palestinian workers declined dramatically. The number of foreign workers now employed in Israel is extremely high, and the ratio of illegal to legal employees is six-to-four. Illegality stems from the absence of an entrance permit to work in Israel or a valid work permit.

---

[145] Aliza & Abraham Cohen v. Ramona Kaverra (Nat'l Lab. Ct., Dec. 8, 2002) (not yet published).

[146] Avian Orsez v. Denya Sybos Ltd. (2002) 37 P.D.A. 305.

[147] Rauman Chito Anterada v. Ada Shanun (Nat'l Lab. Ct., Aug. 26, 2003) (not yet published).

[148] Xue Bin v. Aleph Dori Co. (2003) 38 P.D.A. 615.

Work permits are granted, under the Employment Agency Law, 1959, and the Entrance to Israel Law, 1952, on the basis of a designated employment relationship and, hence, the permit expires if the employee leaves the designated employer. Indeed, the employment relationship must be secured by employer bond. The permits are limited to short periods, up to three years, and do not confer rights to personal or family residency beyond the terms of the initial permit. The criteria for admission of foreign workers are on an ad hoc basis, depending on labor market requirements.

The general employment laws, including protective labor legislation and collective agreements, apply to foreign workers, whether or not the employee is legal. Hence foreign workers are entitled to minimum wages, holidays, hours of work regulation, protection of wages and severance pay as are Israeli workers. The Foreign Workers Law (Unlawful Employment and the Guarantee of Decent Conditions), 1991, which was amended comprehensively in 2000, provides some special protective measures for foreign workers. Employers are required to give the employees a written contract, setting out terms and conditions of employment, and such contracts are subject to the general provisions of Israeli labor law. In addition, the employer is obliged to provide the foreign worker with adequate dwelling conditions and is required to arrange health insurance. The Law explicitly requires employers to include foreign workers in social benefit or pension funds provided under relevant collective agreements or extension orders and to make the required employer payments and employee deductions to these funds.[149]

Foreign workers are presently covered by National Insurance for only three risks: work injuries and occupational diseases, maternity, and bankruptcy.[150] However, in 2001, the Amendment to the Foreign Workers Law (Unlawful Employment and the Guarantee of Decent Conditions), 1991, established a Special Fund to supplement National Insurance provisions,[151] into which employers are required to pay up to $175 (700 shekels) per month into the

---

[149]For a discussion of occupational pensions, see VIII.A.3., above.

[150]See VII.B.2. (work injuries and occupational diseases), V.D.3. and VI.C.3. (maternity), and IV.A.2., (bankruptcy), above.

[151]Foreign Workers Law (Unlawful Employment and the Guarantee of Decent Conditions) 1991, as amended in 2000, §1(11).

Special Fund, of which up to a third is deductible from the employee's wages. The proceeds are to be paid to the employee three months after leaving Israel. The purpose of the law was to ensure that both the gross remuneration to foreign workers and the costs to employers of employing foreign workers would not be less than in the case of Israeli workers. Israel is a party to the ILO Convention 97, Migration for Employment Convention (Revised), 1949, and the Special Fund is intended as a "special arrangement" under section 6(b)(ii), which will meet the requirement set forth in section 6(b) of the Convention that all benefits covered by national social security benefits must be provided for foreign workers.

SAUDI ARABIA*

INTRODUCTION**

The Kingdom of Saudi Arabia is an Islamic state. Arabic is the official language, and the Holy Qur'an, or Koran, is the constitution.[1] Saudi Arabia recognizes both the Hijra and Gregorian Calendar.[2]

---

*Douglas M. Nabhan, Williams, Mullen, Clark & Dobbins, Richmond, Virginia. The author owes a debt of gratitude to Andra Jade Zavoy for her excellent work on this chapter. He also wishes to thank Ronald E. Pump, Esq., of the Mohamed Al-Sharif Law Firm, Riyadh, Saudi Arabia, and Chris Johnson, Johnson and Pump, Washington, D.C.

**The terms "worker" and "employee" are used to indicate that the law applies to both sexes; however, there is no commingling of the sexes in the workplace in Saudi Arabia. See I.A., below.

[1]Profile of Saudi Arabia: History,<http://www.saudi.net/profile/ history/ hist_intro.html> (July 29, 1997), at 1.

[2]The Islamic era dates from the Prophet Mohammed's flight or *hijra* from Mecca to Medina in 622G. There are 12 lunar months in the Hijra calendar, each having either 29 or 30 days. Accordingly, the Hijra calendar advances approximately 11 days annually relative to the Gregorian calendar (see below), completing a cycle roughly every 33 years. Saudi laws, procedures, and contracts generally refer to Hijra rather than Gregorian dates. Hijra and Gregorian calendar conversions are shown in the following table:

GREGORIAN (A.D.)	HIJRA (A.H.)	GREGORIAN (A.D.)	HIJRA (A.H.)
07/24/1990	01/01/1411	04/05/2000	01/01/1421
07/12/1991	01/01/1412	03/25/2001	01/01/1422
07/01/1992	01/01/1413	03/15/2002	01/01/1423
06/20/1993	01/01/1414	03/04/2003	01/01/1424
06/09/1994	01/01/1415	02/21/2004	01/01/1425
05/30/1995	01/01/1416	02/10/2005	01/01/1426
05/18/1996	01/01/1417	01/31/2006	01/01/1427
05/07/1997	01/01/1418	01/20/2007	01/01/1428
04/27/1998	01/01/1419	01/10/2008	01/01/1429
04/16/1999	01/01/1420	12/29/2008	01/01/1430

This Chart was prepared by the U.S.–Saudi Arabian Business Council, <http://www.us-saudi-business.org/Basic%20Facts.html> (last visited July 27, 2004).

From its austere origins, Saudi Arabia has developed into one of the world's 20 largest economies. It is the leader of the Gulf Cooperation Council, a regional economic and security organization, and is involved in accession negotiations to join the World Trade Organization (WTO). As of 1997, it is a member of more than 40 international organizations, including the International Labor Organization (ILO).[3]

Foreign investment is strongly encouraged. The Saudi Offset Program, established in 1984, is designed to help form profitable business partnerships in the Kingdom between foreign investors and Saudis by offering substantial incentives with respect to finances, infrastructure, and ease in regulatory compliance.[4] Although the Saudi Arabian Investment Law passed in 2001 allows 100 percent foreign owned business in many sectors to be licensed, foreign investors often secure the cooperation of a Saudi business or sponsor and must employ Saudis in skilled and well-paying positions whenever possible. Although the Saudi economic climate is inviting to global investors, it is imperative that potential foreign investors recognize the objectives, customs, and regulations of the Saudi people and government. Violations of any of these will not be tolerated, particularly those that result in injury or insult to Saudi citizens. The successful foreign businessperson will thus be the one that consults experts proficient in the morals and mores of the Kingdom.

Likewise, foreign businesses seeking to employ persons in the Kingdom of Saudi Arabia must understand the conditions and requirements of employment. A review of these regulations reveals a sophisticated and orderly process that is in some ways con-

---

[3]*See* U.S.–Saudi Arabian Business Council, *Saudi Arabia's Membership in International Organizations and Agreements*, <http://www.us-saudi-business.org/Business%20Regulations.html> (last visited July 27, 2004).

[4]Financial incentives include low-cost loans from the Saudi Industrial Development Fund (SIDF), corporate tax holidays for 10 years, unrestricted repatriation of funds, and a stable and freely convertible currency.

Infrastructure incentives include low-cost utilities, fuels, and rents, and the availability of modern ground, air, and sea transportation and related facilities.

Regulatory incentives include tariff exemption on imported materials and equipment, government procurement preferences, and exemption from export tariffs in neighboring states. <http://www.saudinf.com/main/e32.htm> (last visited Aug. 23, 2004).

sistent with and comparable to the laws of many Western countries. Because Saudi Arabia is unique in its political organization and governmental structure, however, a brief overview of those topics follows prior to a discussion of employment matters. Under the Saudization program, priority employment is given to Saudi nationals.[5] Saudis recently have imposed restrictions on residence permits for professional and skilled occupations in an effort to find employment for its large youth population and workforce and to combat high levels of unemployment.

A. Government

1. The Monarchy

Saudi Arabia is an Islamic Monarchy headed by King Fahd Bin Abdul Aziz, who assumed power on June 13, 1982. The royal family selects the King; their choice is subject only to the approval of the religious elders, or *Ulema*, and the principal tribal leaders. The King is commonly addressed as the Custodian of the Two Holy Mosques, in reference to the mosques at Mecca (*Makkah*) and Medina (*Madinah*), which are regarded as the holiest sites in Islam. The King also serves as the Prime Minister and recognized Head of State, and thus assumes the role of both chief executive and, as Prime Minister, the legislative head. The King has a judicial role as well. Final appeals from many of the courts and specialized tribunals also may be made to the King.[6]

Assisting the King in his duties are the Crown Prince (Abdullah Bin Abdul Aziz) as the Deputy Premier, or Deputy Prime Minister; he serves on the Council of Ministers and functions as the Commander of the National Guard. The King also relies on the advice of the Prince (Sultan Bin Abdul Aziz), who serves as the Second Deputy Premier of the Kingdom. The Prince further holds office as the Minister of Defense and Aviation and as the Inspector General.

---

[5]For more detailed information about the Saudization program, see VI.D., below.

[6]See the discussion in the Introduction, at C.2., below.

2. *The Council of Ministers*

The King governs through the Council of Ministers, each of whom heads one of 21 government ministries.[7] The Council was first established by King Abdul Aziz Bin Abdul Al-Saud in 1953. According to the Council bylaws pronounced by King Fahd in September 1993, "the Council is responsible for drafting and overseeing implementation of the internal, external, financial, economic, educational and defense policies, and general affairs of the state."[8] It meets every Monday except on two national holidays each year. As necessary, the Council may seek the assistance and advice of a Bureau of Experts or of other government agencies. Independent agencies of the Saudi government include the Saudi Arabian Monetary Agency (SAMA), the Saudi Seaports Authority (SEAPA), and the General Organization for Social Insurance (GOSI).[9]

3. *Provincial Government*

The Kingdom is divided into several provinces called governorates. Overseeing the administration of local affairs for most governorates is a governor (*Emir*) appointed by the King. Assisting the governor is a vice governor. Experts differ as to the number of actual provinces. There are many small political subdivisions of the Kingdom, some of which are recognized as provinces while others are not. Depending on the definition of province applied by the source, the number of provinces ranges from 13 to 18.

---

[7]The government ministries are: Agriculture; Civil Service; Commerce and Industry; Communications and Information Technology; Culture and Information; Defense and Aviation; Education; Economy and Planning; Finance; Foreign Affairs; Health; Higher Education; Interior; Islamic Affairs, Endowments, Mission and Guidance; Justice; Labor and Social Affairs; Municipal and Rural Affairs; Petroleum and Mineral Resources; Pilgrimage; Transportation; and Water and Electricity.

[8]Saudi Arabia Government Profile, available at <http://www.saudiembassy.net/Country/Government/GovDetail2.asp>.

[9]Other independent agencies are the Saudi Consulting House (SCH), affiliated with the Ministry of Commerce and Industry, which prepares economic, industrial, and marketing studies; Saudi Arabian Standards Organization (SASO), with responsibility for standards and measurements; Royal Commission for Jubail and Yanbu (RCJY), concerned with development and maintenance of public works in the cities of Jubail and Yanbu; General Organization for Technical Education and Vocational Training (GOTEVT); and Saudi Industrial Development Fund (SIDF).

4. *Municipal Government*

By order of the Crown Prince, elections for 178 municipal councils in Riyadh have been announced for November 2004. One-half of the members will be appointed by the King. The announcement said election organizers were planning to hold voting for 178 municipalities in 13 districts across Saudi Arabia over three stages. The first stage would be held in the region of Riyadh, the capital, and would begin in November. The second stage would cover the Eastern Province and southern regions. The third stage, occurring after the annual pilgrimage in January, would be held in the western regions of Mecca and Medina and the northern regions.

5. *Royal Decrees Establishing the Structure of the Government*

Under King Fahd, the Saudi government has undergone considerable reform and revision. On August 2, 1995, the King issued a Royal Decree abruptly dissolving the Council of Ministers, reassigning three current ministers, and appointing several new members to the Cabinet under his direction.

Earlier, on March 1, 1992, King Fahd issued three Royal Decrees of similar significance and impact.

- Royal Decree A/90 introduced a new Basic Law for the System of Government. A comprehensive document, it addressed such fundamental issues as the monarchy and the succession of power, the essential organs of government, social welfare, basic civil rights, defense, foreign affairs, and the international economy. In short, it outlined the government's goals and responsibilities while redefining the King's relationship with the citizenry.
- Royal Decree E/92 addressed the regional system of government. The Royal Decree of 1992 established provincial councils to further aid the provincial governor in his duties. Chaired by the governor, the councils are composed of the heads of the province's government departments and a 10-member council of local prominent individuals, each of whom is appointed to four-year renewable terms. These councils aid in the administration of the provinces, facili-

tate continued regional development, and recommend priorities to the King.

- Royal Decree A/92 established a revised, national Consultative Council (*Majlis Al-Shura*). Rooted in Islam, the first Majlis Al-Shura had convened in the 1920s. The first session of the newly restructured Council, consisting of 60 members and a chairman, was inaugurated by King Fahd on December 29, 1993. The members of the Shura are all appointed by the King for a four-year renewable term. Because the Shura is intended to represent "the spectrum of Saudi society,"[10] all members must be native-born Saudi nationals, at least 30 years of age, of good reputation, and well educated.[11] Except by royal waiver, Shura members may not be government employees or officers of companies.[12] More than half of the Council members hold Ph.D.s. Officially, they advise the King on issues of importance to the nation and make recommendations. The Shura Council was expanded to include 120 members serving four-year terms in 2003.

A decree issued May 1, 2001, further refined the composition and mission of the Consultative Council, which was chaired in August 2004 by Dr. Salih Bin Abdullah Bin Hemaid. Membership was increased, and members of the second term (1997–2001) were divided into the following eleven committees (as of August 2004):

1. Organization and Administration (10 members);
2. Education, Culture, and Information Affairs (12 members);
3. Islamic Affairs (11 members);
4. Services and Public Utilities (11 members);
5. Health and Social Affairs (8 members);
6. Foreign Affairs (12 members);
7. Security Affairs (9 members);
8. Economic and Financial Affairs (16 members);

---

[10]Shura Council, <http://www.saudiembassy.net/Country/Government/Council.asp> (last visited Aug. 20, 2004).

[11]*See* Royal Decree A/91, arts. 3, 4.

[12]*Id.* art. 9.

9. Transport, Communication and Information Technology (9 members);
10. Educational and Scientific Research Affairs (13 members); and
11. Energy (12 members).

B. Sources of Law in Saudi Arabia

1. *In General*

The Saudi legal system is founded on the Islamic Shari'a law. The Shari'a is derived from the Sunna, or teachings and traditions of the Prophet Mohammed; the Koran; the writings of legal and religious scholars; and by legal analogy to other Islamic precedent (*Ijtihad*). Royal Decree A/90, issued in 1992 and discussed above, confirmed that the Koran functions as the constitution of Saudi Arabia.

Because Saudi Arabia is an Islamic monarchy, law is developed differently there than in the West. As there is no division between church and state, the Saudi legal system does not distinguish between religious and secular law. The Shari'a is thus accorded a paramount role in the formulation and determination of the law—whether by the executive and legislative authority, with the King assuming both the role of the chief executive and, as the Prime Minister, the legislative head, or by the courts. As discussed immediately below, legislation is by royal decree and takes the form of "regulations" rather than "laws."[13]

Proposed legislation is initially drafted by one of the Saudi government ministries, or by one of the specialized bureaus of the Council of Ministers. Since the 1992 Decrees, the Consultative Council may also propose legislation and is expected to review regulations prior to their being presented to the King and Council by the appropriate Minister.[14] If found acceptable to the King and the Council, the regulations are issued by Royal Decree. These regulations are not made effective until they are published in the official gazette (*Umm Al-Qura*).

---

[13]The court system is discussed in the Introduction, at C.2., below.

[14]Royal Decree A/91, art. 17.

Legislation by Royal Decree typically serves to delegate the responsibility for implementation to the competent ministry, which issues more detailed "implementing rules." These implementing rules (ministerial "decrees," "resolutions," or "circulars") issued by government agencies or departments further elaborate on a Decree and provide for more specific requirements.[15] Given the

[15]Significant government regulations issued as Royal Decrees to be administered by the appropriate ministries include the following:

(1) Commercial Agency Regulations, reserving an absolute monopoly for Saudi nationals and wholly owned Saudi entities on the import or local purchase of goods for resale. Regarding joint ventures, the Commercial Agency Regulations permits such companies to import products and materials necessary to perform the licensed projects or activities free of customs or other duties. These regulations are administered by the Ministry of Commerce.

(2) Commercial Fraud Regulations, providing consumer protection, are administered by the Ministry of Commerce. Violators are subject to fines up to SR 100,000 for each infraction. (The official currency of Saudi Arabia is the Saudi Arabian Riyal (SR). Since June 1, 1986, SR3.75 is equal to US$1.)

(3) Companies Regulations, providing extensive regulation from start-up formalities to reports to the government to capital management, also are administered by the Ministry of Commerce.

(4) Foreign Investment Act and Executive Rules.

(5) Income Tax Regulations. Saudi Arabia does not have a personal income tax per se, but does impose a religious tax (on Saudis and other Gulf Cooperation Council Nationals only), known as Zakat. Any income from business conducted in Saudi Arabia is subject to general income tax and the investor should seek consultation regarding the tax implications of various transactions. These regulations are administered by the Department of Zakat and Income Taxation (DZIT) and Income Department of the Ministry of Finance and National Economy.

(6) Labor and Workmen's Regulations, discussed at I.B.3 in the text below.

(7) Protection of National Industries Regulation, implementing the Saudi priority of Saudization, discussed in the text at VI.D., below. These regulations are administered primarily by the Ministry of Finance.

(8) Service Agency Regulations, regulating service agents. A service agent is a Saudi citizen or company that represents the foreign entity throughout the bidding and contracting process. These regulations are primarily administered by the Ministry of Commerce.

(9) Social Insurance Regulations, discussed in the text at VIII.A., below.

(10) Trademark Regulations, in effect since 1984, enforced by the Ministry of Commerce.

(11) Patent Regulations, adopted in 1989. The regulations are administered in part by the King Abdulaziz City for Science and Technology, KACST, to which all patent applications must be submitted for approval.

(12) Tenders Regulations includes the procurement preference program. Public procurement preference is normally 10%. These regulations are administered primarily by the Ministry of Finance and National Economy.

generality of most Saudi legislation, many important legal issues are resolved through administrative policies and interpretation.[16]

2. *Labor and Employment Laws*

Overall employment relations in the Kingdom are heavily controlled by Saudi law. The obligations of the employer to the employee are many and must be strictly complied with.[17] Labor and employment laws in Saudi Arabia develop as do other types of law described above: the legislation is proposed, revised, and later approved by the Council and the King. It is then issued in the form of Royal Decrees containing the applicable regulations. Such Decrees present the objectives of the law, which are later implemented by more detailed Ministerial regulations. A new labor law is expected to be promulgated sometime in 2004, although a specific date is unknown. Unions and organized labor activities are prohibited in Saudi Arabia. Visa regulations related to labor and employment are currently changing because of the recent emphasis on Saudization.

a. *Saudi Labor Regulations*

The Ministry of Labor and Social Affairs is the primary originator of regulations (issued as Royal Decrees) in the area of labor and employment law. These regulations are generally collected in the Saudi Labor Regulations (hereinafter Labor Regulations). Originally enacted in November 1969 as the Labor and Workmen's Regulations,[18] the requirements are obligatory both for Saudi and for foreign employers. (The Labor Regulations, however, are not binding on persons working in solely family-owned businesses, or on herdsmen, nonindustrial farmers, or domestic servants.[19])

(Information provided in part by Christopher H. Johnson, *Saudi Arabia*, LEGAL ASPECTS OF DOING BUSINESS IN THE MIDDLE EAST—SUPPL. 1 (Dec. 1995), at 5–6; and "Doing Business in Saudi Arabia," prepared by the U.S.–Saudi Arabian Business Council, <http://www.us-saudi-business.org/Business%20Regulations.html> (last visited July 27, 2004).

[16]Christopher H. Johnson, *Saudi Arabia*, LEGAL ASPECTS OF DOING BUSINESS IN THE MIDDLE EAST—SUPPL. 1 (Dec. 1995) [hereinafter Johnson]. See the Introduction, at B.2.a., below.

[17]See I.B., below.

[18]Royal Decree Number M/21 of 6 Ramadhan 1389H. See I., below.

[19]Saudi Arabia Labor Regulations (hereinafter SALR), Ch. 11, art. 3.

Amended and expanded since their creation, the Labor Regulations in their present form are extensive. Among other things, they govern who a company may hire and the terms of the employment. The Labor Regulations establish guidelines concerning employment hours, compensation, benefits, and training. The Labor Regulations "provide for enforcement of employees' rights, record keeping and reporting, protection of women and children, inspection of places of work, provision of medical and other facilities, and resolution of employment disputes."[20]

The Labor Regulations are enforced by the regional Labor and Settlement of Disputes Commissions: the Primary Commissions for Settlement of Disputes and the Supreme Commission for Settlement of Disputes,[21] which sits in Riyadh. The Council of Ministers issues rules of procedure, conciliation, and applicable settlement proceedings before the Primary Commissions and the Supreme Commission.[22]

If an employee believes that his or her rights[23] have been infringed upon, the employee may seek the direct assistance of the local Ministry of Labor office. The Commissions are authorized by the Saudi Labor Regulations[24] to inspect and investigate places of employment when deemed necessary. If it is determined that there is basis for complaint, then further action will be taken by the Commissions to resolve the problems by an adjudicatory proceeding. The Commissions' role in dispute resolution is discussed below.

Employment contracts are regulated; even if such a contract establishes that employment is to be "at will," the company may not terminate an employee unfairly. If an employee believes that his or her rights have been unlawfully restricted, the Labor Regulations further provide that he or she may bring action through the Labor and Settlement of Disputes Commissions.[25]

---

[20]Johnson, *supra* note 14, at 28.
[21]See discussion of Specialized Tribunals in the Introduction, at C.2.c., below.
[22]SALR, ch. 11, art. 177.
[23]See the discussion of mutual rights and responsibilities at I.B., below.
[24]See I., below.
[25]See the Introduction, at C.2.c.v., below.

b. International Sources of Labor and Employment Law

Saudi Arabia is a member of the ILO, but does not fully comply with all the Conventions and Recommendations of the ILO.[26] Saudi Arabia has ratified four of the ILO's eight "fundamental" conventions and, in total, only 13 ILO conventions have been ratified and are in force.

C. Dispute Resolution

1. Arbitration

It is preferred in Saudi Arabia that disputes of all types be resolved between the parties without resort to litigation. Where the parties are at an impasse, arbitration presents a viable and acceptable alternative to resolving disputes through the Saudi judicial system. The parties must be cognizant of and adhere to the particular regulations and limitations unique to the arbitration process in Saudi Arabia.[27] (Note, however, that all disputes involving a government agency must proceed through the Grievance Board[28] and may not be arbitrated except with the permission of the Council of Ministers.) There are a detailed set of requirements that govern the selection of arbitrators, the length of the arbitration, and review of the arbitrator's decision. The arbitrator, or the chair of an arbitration committee, must be an expert in Shari'a or the topical Saudi law. The arbitration takes place under the aegis of the local Chamber of Commerce.

Once an arbitration decision is reached, it is not uncommon for the award to be effectively unenforceable if careful steps were not taken to ensure conformity with Saudi regulations. The reason for this is that, unlike most other countries, such as the United States, Saudi Arabia requires a Saudi court to approve the arbitration award and the Saudi decisions of some arbitration services headquartered outside Saudi Arabia will simply not be enforced by Saudi courts; therefore, foreign companies should take care to avoid their use. With respect to arbitrations occurring in Saudi

---

[26]The International Labor Organization is discussed in Part 4 of Volume I.

[27]Note that the 1983 Arbitration Regulations established the procedures for implementation of arbitration agreements and for the enforcement of arbitral awards.

[28]See the Introduction, at C.2.c.i., below.

Arabia, the Saudi Civil Rights Directorate enforces all awards. Regarding those outside the country, methods of enforcement are determined by applicable treaties, if any. This situation is similar for decisions by foreign courts.[29]

In summary, the Grievance Board will only enforce arbitration conducted in strict accordance with Saudi regulations. As for foreign arbitration, despite the discussion below, the award must be in line with the Shari'a, the principles of which are not always consistent with modern commercial practices.

On April 19, 1994, Saudi Arabia acceded to the New York Convention on Foreign Arbitral Awards. Nonetheless, a Saudi court may still decline to enforce such an award under Royal Decree No. M 11/1994, issued January 21, 1994. The court may decline to enforce an award if it is "contrary to public policy." (See below.) Saudi Arabia also chose the reciprocity reservation that limits recognition of awards under the Convention to those rendered in the territory of another contracting state. The Convention, as ratified by the Kingdom, further permits Saudi Arabia to deny the recognition and enforcement of an award on certain substantive and procedural grounds, including the ground that a particular award would, if enforced, operate in ways contrary to Saudi public policy.[30] Additionally, the Saudi courts are in no way bound to enforce agreements resolving disputes initiated prior to the ratification of the Convention.

With some reservation, in 1979, Saudi Arabia ratified the Convention on the Settlement of Investment Disputes Between States and Nationals of Other States and is a member of the associated International Center for Settlement of Investment Disputes (ICSID). As of 1995, however, the ICSID had yet to address any dispute involving Saudi Arabia. In July 1995, the Saudi government signed the Agreement on Legal Protection for Guaranteed Foreign Investment Between the Multilateral Investment Guarantee Agency (MIGA) and the Kingdom of Saudi Arabia. Arbitra-

[29]See the Introduction, at C.2.e., below.

[30]New York Convention, art. V, paras. 1–2.

tions under this Agreement are subject to a specific set of MIGA rules, consistent with those of the ICSID.[31]

2. *Judicial Forums*

When the parties are unable to come to an agreement either between themselves, or through the services of an arbitrator, a dispute will proceed to the appropriate judicial forum:

- for general issues, the Shari'a courts; and
- for certain issues (to be discussed), one of the specialized tribunals with limited subject jurisdiction.[32]

a. *Shari'a Courts*

Since 1928, the Saudi government has required all Saudi courts to apply the Hanbali School of Islamic, or Shari'a, law, one of four major schools of this type of law. This approach includes principles comparable to equity in common law jurisdictions, and to the general clauses of civil codes. Unlike most Western legal systems, however, there are no statutes of limitations within which suit must be brought. Additionally, all Saudi courts are guided by Shari'a rules of evidence and procedure. Generally, wide latitude is extended to contracting parties regarding the terms of the agreement. Unless contrary to Shari'a norms, principles of good faith, or relevant regulation, the contract (and its terms) becomes the law between the parties and will be upheld as such. With this in mind, although Saudis often prefer to do business by "gentleman's agreement," it is recommended that the contract specifically provide for term and termination, termination damages, and dispute resolution procedures.[33]

---

[31]Information on arbitration in Saudi Arabia was provided in part by "Doing Business in Saudi Arabia," prepared by the U.S.–Saudi Arabian Business Council, available at <http://www.us-saudi-business.org/Doing%20Business%20in%20the%20Kingdom.html> (last visited July 27, 2004).

[32]Procedures for labor dispute resolution are discussed at I.G., below.

[33]Christopher H. Johnson, *Saudi Arabia*, LEGAL ASPECTS OF DOING BUSINESS IN THE MIDDLE EAST—SUPP. 1 (Dec. 1995).

b. Jurisdiction and Rules of Procedure

Shari'a courts, established in 1928 under the Ministry of Justice, exercise general jurisdiction over all matters including personal status, domestic law, real property, inheritance, and criminal offenses. Shari'a courts usually render a decision within a few months. All decisions may be appealed to appellate Shari'a courts. A final appeal to the King is available to the losing party. Essentially religious courts, as the name implies, Shari'a courts apply the Shari'a without exception. The regulations issued as Royal Decrees and implementing rules issued by other government ministries on various matters supplement the Shari'a, but do not supersede it. New procedures were issued for the Shari'a courts in 1991. Some Shari'a judges, trained in the Shari'a rather than Western legal systems, disregard the new procedures on the theory that the Shari'a cannot be codified, either in substance or procedure. As is the case with all Saudi courts, the Shari'a courts do not recognize Western concepts of conflicts of law, and will apply the Shari'a even if the parties have agreed otherwise.

c. Specialized Tribunals

Certain issues have been assigned to specialized tribunals, such as

- the Grievance Board (*Diwan Al-Mazal'im*);
- the Civil Rights Directorate;
- the Tax Courts;
- the Commercial Papers Committee (CPC);
- the Saudi Arabian Monetary Agency Banking Disputes Committee (SBDC); and
- the Labor and Settlement of Disputes Commissions, comprised of the Primary and Supreme Commissions for Settlement of Disputes.

These are discussed in greater detail immediately below.

Decisions of these more specialized forums are not necessarily appealable; the Shari'a courts have been directed to refrain from accepting claims within the jurisdiction of these specialized tribunals. There is some question, however, as to whether the jurisdiction of the Shari'a courts can be limited in this manner, and not all

Shari'a judges have fully accepted this limitation on their authority. In 2004, new procedures require all litigation involving any commercial entity as a party be referred to the Board of Grievances.

i. Grievance Board

Established in 1955, the Grievance Board has exclusive jurisdiction over all disputes regarding Saudi government contracts; appeals from decisions of government ministries, departments, and agencies; civil service and pension claims; official corruption offenses; trademark claims; and enforcement of foreign judgments (including arbitral awards).[34] The Grievance Board has limited appellate jurisdiction, and, as of 1987, may also hear some types of commercial disputes. The Grievance Board operates on a circuit system, with most matters being heard by three-judge panels. When confronted by a particularly minor case, the Board President has the authority to appoint sub-circuits (a single judge) to hear the case. As with decisions of Shari'a courts, decisions of the Grievance Board may be appealed to the Council of Ministers and then to the King. The Board differs, however, from the Shari'a courts in two respects: (1) the Board often uses technical experts to decide cases that are particularly complex, and (2) the Board observes a system of precedent.

ii. Civil Rights Directorate

The Civil Rights Directorate decides certain commercial disputes between private parties. It also is charged with the duty of enforcing the judgments of other Saudi courts or tribunals.

iii. Commercial Papers Committee

The Commercial Papers Committee (CPC) decides cases involving bills of exchange, promissory notes, and checks. The Conciliation Committee settles problems arising out of an attempt by a foreign company to change commercial agents.

---

[34]Grievance Board Regulations, Royal Decree No. M/51 (May 28, 1983).

iv. Monetary Agency Banking Disputes Committee

Created in 1986, the Monetary Agency Banking Disputes Committee (SBDC) resolves certain disputes between banks and their customers. Members of this Committee are trained in Western rather than Shari'a law; however, they are not inclined to entirely dismiss the Shari'a, and members will generally choose not to enforce interest claims, for example, on grounds that they are prohibited by Shari'a law.

v. Labor and Settlement of Disputes Commissions

The Labor and Settlement of Disputes Commissions consist of the Primary Commission for Settlement of Disputes and the Supreme Commission for Settlement of Disputes.[35] As is the situation with the Shari'a courts,[36] these tribunals do not recognize precedent.

There is a Primary Commission for Settlement of Disputes in every labor office. Each Primary Commission is composed of three members experienced in legal matters. The Chair holds a degree in Shari'a, and another member must have a degree in law or Shari'a.[37] The Primary Commission has exclusive jurisdiction to render *final* decisions on

- labor disputes valued at less than SR3,000;
- disputes relating to the stay of execution of decisions to terminate workers; and
- disputes relating to the imposition of fines.

The Primary Commission may render decisions of first instance on

- labor disputes valued at less than SR3,000;
- disputes pertaining to labor injuries; and
- disputes pertaining to termination of service.[38]

---

[35]SALR, Ch. 11, art. 172. The procedures of the Primary and Supreme Commissions are discussed at I.G., below, regarding responding to employee complaints.

[36]See the Introduction, at C.2.a., above.

[37]SALR, ch. 11, art. 173.

[38]*Id.* art. 174.

There is one Supreme Commission for Settlement of Disputes in the country, which sits in Riyadh. It consists of five members—three from the Ministry of Labor, one from the Ministry of Commerce and Industry, and one from the Ministry of Petroleum. All members are required to be experienced in legal matters.[39] The Supreme Commission has exclusive jurisdiction to render final decisions in all disputes on appeal, including arbitral awards, and to impose penalties.[40] In theory, as is the case generally in the Saudi judicial system, all decisions may be further appealed to the King. This option, however, is never taken.

vi. Insurance disputes

The Ministry of Commerce has jurisdiction over all insurance cases. Any case involving a claim of more than SAR 1 million must be submitted to arbitration under the Chamber of Commerce. A dependant legal officer hears cases brought before a committee established to hear the case.

d. Effect of Precedent

With respect to the effect of precedent, Islamic law does not impose a strict obligation of *stare decisis*. Whereas courts in the U.S. system are bound to respect and apply the decisions of superior courts (and strongly encouraged to uphold decisions of parallel courts), Shari'a courts maintain that it is better to correct one's mistakes than to persevere in error. Accordingly, excepting those of the Grievance Board, decisions issued by the Saudi courts have no absolute precedential value and are rarely reported. In order to adequately understand how the laws will be interpreted, it therefore is necessary to consider customs, religion, and the fact-specific issues of each case.

Nonetheless, although Saudi judges are theoretically free to rule as each sees fit, wholly arbitrary rulings are not common. Both practitioners and judges alike recognize that the Shari'a has been developed over the centuries through the traditions of the community of the faithful (the *Ijma*) and by scholarly interpretation (such

---

[39]*Id.* art. 175.
[40]*Id.* art. 176.

as *Qiyas*). These interpretations are generally accepted and applied with consistency.

e. Foreign Judgments

For reasons relating to the strict application of the Shari'a by Saudi courts, foreign judgments typically are not enforced in the Kingdom.[41] This is of particular importance to a foreigner who wishes to bring suit against a Saudi in another country. If a foreign company successfully sues a Saudi in another country and then attempts to enforce a judgment in Saudi Arabia, the Saudi Foreign Ministry must first review that judgment. Moreover, in order for a Saudi court to even consider whether to enforce the judgment of a foreign court, that country must have signed a reciprocal enforcement treaty with Saudi Arabia. No such agreement exists between the United States and Saudi Arabia. In most cases, any claims arising from a foreign proceeding will usually be considered *de novo* by the Saudi courts, though the Saudi judge may credit the foreign decision with some evidentiary weight.[42] Assuming proper personal and subject matter jurisdiction, Saudi courts normally hear any matter brought before them.

I. INDIVIDUAL EMPLOYMENT*

Unions and organized labor activities are prohibited in Saudi Arabia.[43] To compensate for any resulting imbalance in power between the employer and its workers, the Saudi Labor Regulations have been drafted with a decidedly pro-worker bias. Because labor unions are prohibited in the Kingdom, the labor offices of the Ministry of Labor are charged with the responsibility of ensur-

---

[41]See related discussion regarding arbitration awards in the Introduction, at C.1., above.

[42]In 1989, it looked as though the Saudi courts might begin to defer to foreign decisions when the Grievance Board in Jeddah issued a judgment confirming a judgment issued by a UK court. However, true to tradition, this judgment was promptly overturned on appeal.

*The terms "worker" and "employee" are used to indicate that the law applies to both sexes; however, there is no commingling of the sexes in the workplace in Saudi Arabia. See I.A., below.

[43]See II., below.

ing that workers are treated fairly and with respect. They oversee, implement, and enforce the regulations handed down by Royal or Ministerial Decrees.[44]

Reflecting its Islamic origins, underlying the Saudi Labor Regulations are the moral requirements that the employer:

1. treat its workers with due respect and refrain from any word or deed that may affect their dignity or religion;
2. cooperate with the labor authorities to comply with all of the labor laws; and
3. grant workers time off so they can exercise their rights under the labor laws unless it would disrupt the progress of work.[45]

The Labor Regulations apply to "[a]ny contract under which any person undertakes to work for the account of an employer under the latter's direction or control in consideration of a wage."[46] An "employer" is defined as "any natural or juristic person employing one workman or more in consideration of a wage."[47] Interestingly, "workman" is defined as "*any person* working for the account of an employer under the latter's direction and control."[48] The Labor Regulations thereinafter use the term "workman" when referring to what U.S. employers generally call an "employee." For this reason, a "workman" can be a person of either sex. Although the Labor Regulations use the term "workwoman," the term is never specifically defined. Thus, the term "workman" is used in a gender-neutral sense by the Saudi Labor Regulations, and the requirements established therein should in no way be construed to apply only to male employees, although as noted below, there is a general prohibition on women working in traditional businesses or working with men.[49]

---

[44]Regulation by Royal Decree and Ministerial Decree are discussed above in the Introduction, at A.4. and B., respectively.

[45]SALR, ch. 2, art. 91.

[46]*Id.* ch. 4, §1, art. 70.

[47]*Id.* ch. 1, art. 7(8).

[48]*Id.* art. 7(7) (emphasis added).

[49]For further information on women in the workplace, see V.C.3., below, discussing maternity leave; for a discussion of restrictions on hours of work for women, adolescents, and juveniles, see V.B.2.

A. Special Considerations Regarding Employment of Women and Children

Women are permitted to work in Saudi Arabia, but only in a limited fashion. Employment opportunities for women are "concentrated in those areas where they can be of direct assistance to other women, as doctors and nurses in female hospital wards, as teachers and support staff in girls' schools and colleges, and in all-female establishments such as the women's banks and retail stores set up in recent years."[50] In such sectors not affected by the general prohibition against women working in traditional business, women who are employed seem to avail themselves of the complete range of protections afforded by the Labor Regulations. Additionally, in no case may men and women commingle in the place of work, the accessory facilities, or other appurtenances thereto.[51]

The provisions prohibiting or restricting the employment of adolescents, juveniles, and women do not apply to charitable or official institutions of vocational or professional training, provided that the bylaws of such institutions are approved by the Minister of Labor.[52]

Restrictions on night work and, in the case of young workers, on the age of the worker and the number of hours worked per day are discussed in V., below. Prohibitions regarding work in hazardous operations or harmful industries are discussed in VII.A., below.

B. Mutual Rights and Responsibilities

Saudi Arabian law places a responsibility on both the employer and the worker to know all the contents of Saudi employment laws, "so that each shall know where he stands and be aware of his rights and obligations."[53]

---

[50] *Monthly Newsletter of the Royal Embassy of Saudi Arabia*, Washington, D.C. (Jan. 1996).

[51] SALR, ch. 10, §1, art. 160.

[52] *Id.* §3, art. 170.

[53] *Id.* ch. 1, art. 9.

1. Employer Obligation to Post Work Rules

In order to assist the employee in becoming aware of his responsibilities and to ensure consistency in the application of the rules, every establishment that employs 20 or more persons must prepare a list of work rules. Subject to the approval of the Ministry of Labor and Social Affairs, this list must be displayed in a conspicuous location and contain the following information:

1. classification of workers according to their occupational categories;
2. work periods and hours, official holidays, weekly day of rest (typically Friday), and pay days for various categories of workers;
3. work shifts;
4. rules governing attendance, tardiness, absence, entry into and exit from the places of work, and inspection;
5 vacation and relevant eligibility schedules;
6. any other details required by the nature of work in the establishment; and
7. a set of disciplinary rules.[54]

This last requirement, the requirement to post disciplinary rules, specifically obligates the employer to list the acts, offenses, acts of insubordination, and the workers' obligations and the corresponding cash penalties or disciplinary standards.[55]

2. Obligations of Concessionaires

With particular respect to the obligations of "concessionary companies" (i.e., companies that contract out work), they are expected to observe all rights and obligations generally established, (i.e., to treat contract employees the same as their own employees).[56] The workers of such contractors are subject to the company's work rules and receive company benefits.[57] Concessionary com-

[54]*Id.*
[55]*Id.* See discussion at I.E.5., below.
[56]SALR, ch. 7, art. 138.
[57]*Id.* art. 139.

panies assume legal liability toward the employees of their contractors, and they may withhold amounts from the price of contracted work to guarantee such liability.[58] If the contractors fail to comply with regulatory provisions concerning benefits, the Minister of Labor has the right to cancel such contracts.[59]

3. *Employer Rights and Restrictions on Those Rights*

As mentioned, the Saudi Labor Regulations are extensive and require many things of the employer. Notwithstanding this fact, it is notable that many of the specific terms and conditions of employment may ultimately be determined by the employer. The Saudi Labor Regulations mandate only that the employer not diminish any rights otherwise provided by law. Where there are no detailed provisions, wide latitude is thus afforded to the employer. Where the law is specific, however, strict compliance is strongly advised.

Accordingly, the potential employer should be aware that Saudi Labor Regulations establish with particularity the calculation of overtime pay,[60] termination awards,[61] and benefits.[62] Employee benefits are mandatory and may not be waived, even in exchange for other benefits.[63] Any attempt to evade the Labor Regulations will not be tolerated. Even if a labor agreement has been entered into outside of the Kingdom and relies on foreign law, the Labor Regulations will nonetheless be controlling and will be applied to all employment relationships in Saudi Arabia. For this reason, foreign employers should adapt their standard labor agreements to reflect the unique requirements and rights embodied in Saudi law.

4. *Employee Obligations*

The Saudi Labor Regulations also obligate the worker to some extent. The Labor Regulations establish the legal subordination of

---

[58]*Id.* art. 140.

[59]*Id.* art. 141. For more information on benefits, see VIII., below.

[60]See V.A.3., below.

[61]See I.F., below.

[62]See VIII., below.

[63]SALR, ch. 1, art. 6

Saudi employees; accordingly, workers must acquiesce to the control and direction of their employer.[64] Each employee must perform the required work pursuant to his or her employment contract. All work must be performed in accordance with given instructions, the contract, the law, or public morals. The worker must return to the employer all unconsumed materials and take adequate care of machines and tools. All workers must observe good conduct and behavior, extend assistance in case of disasters and dangers without demanding additional pay, submit to medical examinations requested by the employer, and keep confidential the technical, commercial, and industrial secrets of the employer and its products.[65]

5. *Right to Work Product*

If a worker develops an invention while in the service of the employer, the employer has no right to such invention. An exception within the Saudi Labor Regulations establishes that any invention belongs to the employer if the worker devotes all his efforts to its development, or if so provided for in the employment contract. If the invention has a significant economic value, the employee may claim a special consideration.[66]

C. Prior to Employment: Considerations and Contracts

The law provides for a number of regulations that affect the hiring phase of the employment relationship. A person acting as an employment agent or as a contractor to supply workers must receive permission to function in that capacity from the Deputy Minister for Labor and must be in possession of an annual license.[67] The employment agent receives compensation for its services from the employer for whom it refers workers. Accordingly, the agent may not demand or accept from any worker, either prior to or after being hired, any money or material reward for the referral.[68]

---

[64] *Id.* arts. 7(7), 70, and 96(a).
[65] *Id.* ch. 4, §3, art. 96.
[66] *Id.* §3, art. 97.
[67] *Id.* ch. 3, §1, art. 40.
[68] *Id.* art. 41.

An employer has an obligation to inform the labor office, by registered letter or by any other means proving receipt, of any vacancies or newly created jobs and must state the type of available employment and location of each opening. In the report, the company must include the job requirements, the wage allotted, and the date fixed for filling the opening. The notice must be given within 10 days from the date on which the job becomes vacant or is created.[69]

In addition to the above requirements, each employer must file an annual report during the month of Dhu al Hijjah. That statement must include:

- the number of workers, their names, jobs, occupation, rate of pay, age, nationality, and the number and date of the work permit issued for each employee;
- the vacant and newly created jobs and positions, including the position, rate of pay, and reasons for not filling a job during the year preceding the statement; and
- the condition, circumstances, and nature of the work done by the company and the expected decrease or increase in work during the year following the date of the report.[70]

Establishments employing 10 or more workers are further obligated to provide each employee with a service card bearing the signature of the employer or its agent and the stamp of the establishment. The card should bear the worker's name, surname, occupation, date of birth, nationality, and date of employment. At termination of employment, the ending date should be added to this card, a copy of which is to be retained in the employee's personnel file.[71]

[69]*Id.* art. 42.
[70]*Id.* art. 43.
[71]*Id.* ch. 4, §2, art. 95.

D. The Employment Contract

1. Duration

In Saudi Arabia, the employment contract serves to establish the terms and conditions of employment.[72] Although generally drafted for a specified term of employment, contracts in the Kingdom may provide that the employment is to be at will. Employment contracts for a specified term automatically terminate upon the expiration of the specified term. If the parties continue the relationship past the expiration of the term, the contract is considered to have been renewed for an unspecified period and not for a like term.[73] If the contract is for an unspecified amount of time, either party may cancel it for a valid reason as long as proper notice is given. Proper notice is 30 days with respect to workers paid at a monthly rate and 15 days with respect to other workers. Failure to give proper notice entitles the employee to an "indemnity" equal to the worker's pay for the notice period. Calculation of this amount is based on the worker's last wage payment, or if the work is on a piecework basis, then the amount is determined on the basis of the average pay received during the last three months.[74]

2. Part-Time Employment

With respect to what are called in European terms atypical employment relationships, employers and employees in the Kingdom are afforded broad discretion in their freedom to contract for labor and its compensation. The establishment of applicable terms and conditions of employment is at the discretion of the contracting parties and must be included in the agreement. Accordingly, Saudi labor law does not recognize a distinction between so-called part-time and full-time workers. Nor do the Labor Regulations treat such workers disparately.

---

[72] *Id.* §1, art. 70.
[73] *Id.* art. 72.
[74] *Id.* art. 73.

3. *Written Contract*

The contract for a state-employed worker is the appointment decision or order.[75] Private employers in Saudi Arabia customarily use different employment agreements for each of the three basic employee groups that work in Saudi Arabia: one for employees from the company's home country, one for so-called "local hires" (either of Saudi or of another nationality), and one for Third Country Nationals, or TCNs (typically, laborers from third-world countries). The foreign employer is strongly encouraged to adapt its usual agreement to these forms, because Saudi labor law requires various unique provisions.

Saudi law entitles every worker to a written employment contract. Thus, technically, a labor agreement must be in writing, although it is not uncommon for such a contract to be an oral one. If the agreement is oral, a worker can appeal to the labor office to compel an employer to document the agreement in written form. Such an appeal, however, is rarely made. If the contract remains unwritten and a dispute later arises concerning the specific terms thereof, the burden is always on the claimant to prove (1) the existence of the agreement, and (2) its terms. Typically used as proof are payment stubs and benefit receipts. Manifestations of mere intent made during the negotiations stage, even if proven, will not suffice to support an action.

It is generally the case that any subsequent changes to the terms contained in the contract must be in writing and with the approval of the worker.[76] Because extraneous evidence is admissible to prove the existence of a contract, however, additional oral agreements or documents modifying the terms of a contract may be found to have been incorporated into the original labor agreement. As before, the burden to prove incorporation lies with the claimant.

The written employment contract must be prepared in Arabic and in duplicate. Each party is to receive a copy. The contract must state the terms and conditions of employment,[77] including:

---

[75] *Id.* art. 77.

[76] For more information on specific terms and conditions of employment, see I.E., below. Regulation of wages, hours, and leave is discussed at V., below.

[77] SALR, ch. 4, §1, art. 77.

- compensation,
- work classification,
- hours, and
- benefits.

Although compensation ideally should be noted in the contract, the Labor Regulations provide that it is not essential.[78]

4. *Marine Employment Contract*

There is a special section of the Saudi Labor Regulations for ships and marine workers. Any company anticipating an employment relationship of this variety is advised to refer to the relevant section in the Labor Regulations for specific obligations arising therefrom.[79]

E. Terms and Conditions of Employment

1. *Probationary Period*

Saudi labor law provides that new employees may be hired in a probationary status. The contract must state that the worker is under probation and must specifically define the probationary period. The determination of whether or not an employee has performed adequately while under probation is solely at the discretion of the employer. During this period, the employer may discharge the worker without benefits and for any cause.

The total length of probation may not exceed three months for workers employed on a monthly rate, or one month for other types of employees. Once an employee has successfully served an employer in a probationary capacity (for the maximum period permitted), the worker may not, even if rehired at a later date, be employed under probation again by that same employer.[80]

---

[78]For more information on the determination of an appropriate wage when one is not identified in the contract, see V.A. and VIII., below.

[79]SALR, ch. 1, art. 4(b).

[80]*Id.* ch. 4, §1, art. 71.

2. *Recordkeeping Requirements*

Companies doing business in the Kingdom are well advised to keep detailed personnel files as required by law. The Labor Regulations require that the following be recorded:

1. full name;
2. nationality;
3. trade or occupation;
4. date of birth or age;
5. place of residence;
6. family status;
7. date of commencement of service;
8. wage and/or wage supplements;
9. any change in the employee's status;
10. any penalties imposed on the worker and any related investigative reports;[81]
11. regular hours and overtime;
12. vacations and benefits in cash or in kind; and
13. date of termination and reasons for such termination.

The employer also is charged with retaining any further information sufficiently relevant to the worker's employment history. Additionally, all information regarding the employment of women and juveniles, labor injuries, and occupational diseases must be recorded.[82]

Under no circumstances will an employee be permitted access to the contents of his or her personnel file, consistent with the private and secretive culture that pervades public and private sectors alike in this highly opaque society, so different from the U.S.-style transparency that informs our sunshine and freedom of information principles. Saudi Arabia does not recognize the right to discovery in litigation as broadly as does the Western system of

[81]With respect to disciplinary action, although noted in each employee's personnel file, each employer is bound to maintain a separate Registry of Fines. Here the employer must record fines imposed on workers pursuant to its Disciplinary Rules. Information to be recorded includes the name of the affected employee, the amount of the worker's wage, reason for the fine, and imposition date. SALR, art. 127.

[82]SALR, ch. 1, art. 10.

law. Thus, even when an employee undertakes legal action against the employer, the courts rarely if ever compel disclosure of personnel documents.

3. *Working Conditions*

The employer is responsible for ensuring that the work site is free of prohibited items. Contraband includes alcohol, narcotics, pornographic material, and pork products.[83] The health and safety requirements of the Labor Regulations are discussed below in VII.

4. *Place of Work*

Unless the labor agreement states otherwise, it is presumed only to require work in the original workplace. Accordingly, an employee may not be transferred from the initial site to another location requiring a change in residence if this causes a "serious prejudice" and is not properly justified.[84] For similar reasons, an employee has the right to refuse such transfers and may not be discharged for this refusal unless the contract stipulated the employee's acceptance of possible relocation.[85]

Thus, contracts may include a provision expressly confirming the company's right to transfer employees to any place of work within the Kingdom. Inclusion of this language precludes future refusals by workers to relocate. Potential employers must be aware of this at the outset of the employment relationship and adapt their labor agreements appropriately.

5. *Disciplinary Provisions*

Establishments with 20 or more workers must post a set of rules addressing penalties and rewards. These rules must be posted by the employer in a conspicuous location and must be approved by the Minister of Labor. The Minister may issue standard rules. The Saudi Labor Regulations specifically provide that an employer (employing more than 20 workers) may not impose a fine exceed-

---

[83] *Id.* ch. 4, §2, art. 94.
[84] *Id.* art. 78.
[85] *Id.* art. 75.

ing five-days' wages upon a worker for a single offense, nor may it suspend a worker without pay as a disciplinary measure for a period exceeding five days for a single offense. Additionally, an employee may not be subjected to more than one penalty for the same offense.[86]

Before a penalty can be imposed, there must be a hearing allowing for the worker's remarks in his or her defense.[87] An employee may not be accused of any offense discovered more than 15 days prior to the accusation. Penalties may not be imposed more than 30 days after the offense is proven, in the case of workers paid monthly, or more than 15 days after the offense is proven in the case of other workers.[88] All fines imposed must be recorded in a special register that is made available to the government for inspection.[89]

F. Termination of Employment

1. Obligations Upon Termination

Generally, the employment relationship is considered to have been concluded once the terms and obligations of the contract are fully satisfied by both parties. Premature termination occurs when the worker either quits or is discharged by the employer prior to the full satisfaction of the terms and conditions of the employment contract.[90]

The contract is never terminated by the death of the employer unless the parties agreed to the contrary. The contract does, however, come to an end with the death of the worker; his or her total disability, as established by a medical certificate; or an illness resulting in prolonged absences.[91] Qualifying disability or illness must be established by a competent physician accredited by the employer or by a physician appointed by the appropriate government agency.[92]

---

[86]*Id.* ch. 6, art. 125.
[87]*Id.*
[88]*Id.* art. 126.
[89]*Id.* art. 127.
[90]Discharge is discussed in I.F.3., below.
[91]See discussion in V., below.
[92]SALR ch. 4, §1, art. 82.

If the worker's employment terminates, his or her wages must be paid immediately unless the worker resigns, in which case the money is due within seven days of the resignation.[93] The employer is relieved of the obligation to pay if the worker refuses to acknowledge receipt of the wages by signing a special register.[94]

By statute, employees are entitled to severance pay. Known as the "end of service award" or "termination award," this payment is not punitive and may be imposed upon the employer even when it is not responsible for terminating the contract. This requirement is discussed in greater detail in the next subsection. Occasionally, an employer will be absolved of the obligation to pay an end of service award to a departing employee.

Assuming the employee is not at fault, at the conclusion of the employment relationship, the employer is obligated to return a transferred worker to the place from which the worker was brought. However, the employer is relieved of this obligation if the employee takes another job in his or her present location, has prematurely ceased working for no valid reason, or has expressed in writing that he or she does not wish to return to the place where the contract was concluded or the place of hiring. If the employer does not fulfill this obligation, the government will, in certain circumstances, assume the responsibility of returning the worker, and will later seek to recover its costs from the employer.[95]

The same regulations require that foreign workers must be similarly repatriated by the employer at the conclusion of the employment relationship.

Additionally, when the employment relationship is concluded, every employer must provide a parting worker with a service certificate specifying the period of the employee's service and the salary and benefits received. The employer also must return to the worker all funds deposited on the worker's behalf with the employer.[96] This payout may include proceeds from savings and profit sharing plans in which the employee participated.

[93] *Id.* ch. 6, art. 117.
[94] *Id.* art. 118.
[95] *Id.* ch. 4, §1, art. 85.
[96] *Id.* art. 86.

2. *End of Service Awards Explained*

Upon termination of the employment relationship, workers generally are entitled to end of service, or termination, awards. This is one of the most controversial and poorly understood areas of Saudi labor law. It is not uncommon for foreign employers to seek to manage their overall tax burden by attempting to "pre-pay" termination awards on an incremental and annual basis. This strategy, however, cannot be reconciled with the well-settled principle that end of service awards must and may only be paid at termination. Consequently, many a well-intentioned employer discovers to its dismay that it is required to pay a full termination award, even after paying the same amount incrementally over the full employment period.

a. *Types of Awards*

Regarding the end of service award, there are principally two categories of such awards. Both categories are computed using the last rate of pay, and the worker receives a proportionate amount of money for fractions of a year.

The first category is for contracts of a specified term when they reach their natural conclusion, or for a situation where an employer cancels a contract of unspecified duration. In these cases, the employee is entitled to one-half month's pay for each of the first five years and to one month's pay for each year subsequent. A worker is entitled to an end of service award if called to military service or if the worker leaves as a result of *force majeure*.[97] A working woman is entitled to an end of service award if she resigns because of marriage or the birth of a child.

The second category pertains to contracts of an unspecified term where the employee resigns. In these cases, if his or her service period is not less than two consecutive years, a worker is entitled to one-third of the award provided for in the previous calculation. If his or her service period is more than five consecutive years but fewer than 10 years, the worker is entitled to receive two-thirds of the award. If a worker resigns and gives the 30-days'

---

[97] *Id.* art. 87.

required notice of resignation, however, the worker is entitled to the full end of service award.[98]

b. Basis of Calculation

Although the regulations specify that "wage" is all that is given to an employee in consideration of his services,[99] there is a substantial disagreement of what components other than the base salary are to be included in computing the end of service award.

c. Tax Liability

When computing tax liability, termination awards may only be deducted from an employer's income upon actual payment to a departing employee. No deductions are permitted for reserves for such accrued liabilities.[100]

d. Right to End of Service Award

An employer may cancel the employment contract without payment of an end of service award in certain limited circumstances. The worker, however, has a right to object to the uncompensated termination. In order to prevail against such a challenge, the employer must show that one or more of the following conditions or commissions of acts apply:

- The employee committed an assault against the employer or against any of his supervisors.
- The employee failed to fulfill the essential obligations arising under the contract, failed to obey legitimate orders, or, despite being warned in writing, deliberately failed to observe safety instructions posted by the employer in a conspicuous place.
- The employee demonstrated bad conduct or committed an act affecting honesty or honor.
- The employee deliberately committed an act of negligence with the intent to cause a loss to the employer. (An em-

---

[98] *Id.* art. 88.
[99] *Id.* ch. 1, art. 7(6).
[100] Cir. No. 6902/2 dated 4/8/1398H, at 373.

ployer is obligated to report such a loss to the local labor office of the Ministry of Labor and Social Affairs within 24 hours of acquiring knowledge of the incident.)
- The employee resorted to forgery to obtain the job.
- The employee was fired while on probation.
- The employee was absent without reason for an unreasonable length of time or number of times. Regarding absence, the discharge must be preceded by a written warning.
- The employee left without first obtaining permission from the treating physician or the hospital where he was receiving treatment.
- The employee divulged the industrial and/or commercial secrets of the employer.[101]

Conversely, a worker may resign from work without loss of salary, benefits, or an end of service award:

- in the event of the employer's substantial breach;
- if compelled to perform work beyond the original terms of the agreement;
- for the employer's, or its agent's, assault or immoral act against the employee or his or her family;
- for serious workplace health or safety hazards;
- for material misrepresentation of work conditions; or
- if the employer, through its own actions and by unfair treatment, caused the worker to appear as the party terminating the agreement.[102]

It is noteworthy that the last two circumstances mirror the concepts in U.S. jurisprudence of fraudulent inducement and constructive discharge, respectively. Accordingly, these are obligations already incumbent upon and thus familiar to the U.S. employer. By contrast, the other four situations may not be sufficient to terminate the contractual obligations of an employee to his or

[101]SALR, ch. 4, §1, art. 83.
[102]*Id.* art. 84.

her employer under U.S. law. Consequently, the U.S. employer should take special heed of them and the resulting increase in responsibilities it must assume in order to do business in the Kingdom.

3. *Discharge*

The Saudi Labor Regulations provide different levels of protection for employees depending on whether the contract term is (a) "indefinite" (or "unspecified") or (b) "definite" (or "specified").

- If the employment relationship is for a specified period, the employee may be discharged only "for cause" as defined in the Labor Regulations. "Cause" includes the failure to fulfill essential obligations, dishonesty, misconduct, prolonged unexcused absences, and divulgence of trade secrets.[103]
- Where no specific term is provided, then discharge may be effectuated only for a "valid reason." A valid reason need not rise to the level of "cause" and may include, for example, well-documented unsatisfactory performance or inadequate completion of an employer's assignments.[104]

Under either type of contract, employees must be given a requisite statutory termination notice of not less than one month.

A worker who is discharged without sufficient reason may apply to the appropriate local labor office of the Ministry of Labor and Social Affairs for a stay of the actual discharge. This must be done by written application to be filed no later than 15 days from the delivery date of the discharge. The labor office will first try to settle the matter and, if it cannot, the matter will be forwarded to the Labor and Settlement of Disputes Commission.[105] A hearing will be scheduled within two weeks of receipt of the unsettled matter by the Primary Commission. If the Commission orders a stay of the discharge, the employer is required to pay back wages from the date of discharge and may (if the contract was for a speci-

---

[103] *Id.* art. 83.

[104] *See generally* Christopher H. Johnson, *Saudi Arabia*, LEGAL ASPECTS OF DOING BUSINESS IN THE MIDDLE EAST—SUPPL. 1 (Dec. 1995), at 29.

[105] See the Introduction, at C.2.c.v., above.

fied term) reinstate the worker to his or her former position, and may be required to pay further damages. If the employer complies, the dispute is considered settled. If during this period the dispute is not resolved, the Commission will issue a binding decision within 15 days.[106]

In the resolution of such matters, the employer has the burden of proving that there was a sufficient reason for discharge.

a. Invalid Terminations

Examples of a discharge without valid reason[107] are those following a worker's legitimate demand for rights due him by the employer or a worker's refusal to comply with an order transferring him that is not based on an adequately valid reason. Although valid reason for termination or other action has been held to include convenience of the employer, it must be remembered that, although similar issues tend to be decided similarly in different cases, precedent is not formally recognized by the Saudi Primary or Supreme Commissions.[108] Accordingly, an employer cannot depend on such prior favorable findings as a matter of right. Assessment by the Primary Commission will take into account the nature of the work, the family burdens of the worker, and the degree of arbitrariness involved in the decision to discharge.[109] (This is somewhat similar to the "arbitrary and capricious" standard occasionally applied in the United States.)

If the Primary or Supreme Commission finds that the termination was unreasonable (i.e., was a discharge without valid reason), back pay and reinstatement are common remedies. The Commission is further empowered to award the worker damages based on the nature of the work, the period of service, age, salary, family obligations, arbitrariness, effect on reputation, and "any other con-

---

[106]See I.G., below, for further details about this process.

[107]The discussion of discharge without valid reason applies only to contracts for a definite term; contracts for an indefinite term are always month to month, and thus an employer may effectively "discharge" an employee with a month-to-month contract by giving the requisite 30-day notice.

[108]See the Introduction, at C.2.c.v., above.

[109]SALR, ch. 4, §1, art. 75.

ditions and concomitant circumstances in accordance with the rules of equity and current generally accepted practice."[110]

b. Valid Terminations

In the event of proper termination for cause, an employer is absolved of the responsibility to pay an end of service award[111] and may withhold the worker's wages as is necessary to pay for loss, damage, or destruction that is caused by the worker or that occurred in contravention of the employer's instructions. The amount withheld cannot exceed an amount equivalent to five days' wages per month. The employee has a right to appeal the withholding to the local labor office of the Ministry of Labor and Social Affairs. If the employer is found to have wrongfully withheld such sums, it must refund the money within seven days of a ruling in the employee's favor.[112]

G. Responding to Employee Complaints

Every employer must adhere to the applicable regulations and guidelines established by the Ministry of Labor and Social Affairs. To assist in this task, each company must appoint one person "who is a resident of the place of work" to represent the employer and be responsible for any violation of the regulations. Because this representative will be the person served with the notice of a complaint, the local labor office must be notified of the name of the company's representative. In the event the representative is terminated or otherwise reassigned, the company has an affirmative obligation to inform the local labor office of the Ministry of Labor and Social Affairs of the name of that person's replacement.[113]

1. Labor and Settlement of Disputes Commissions

A complaint may be brought by any worker who feels that his or her employment rights were violated or otherwise restricted.

---

[110]*Id.* art. 74.
[111]See discussion at I.F.2., above.
[112]SALR, ch. 6, art. 116.
[113]*Id.* ch. 1, art. 11.

Complaints of violations of the labor and employment regulations are to be submitted to the local labor office of the Ministry of Labor and Social Affairs, which is then responsible for notifying the company's representative and conducting an investigation. Filing a false complaint may result in a fine, which can be substantial.[114] The statute of limitations for the filing of a complaint is 12 months from the date of the occurrence of such violation.[115]

A complaint also may be brought by an attorney or any Saudi citizen on behalf of the affected employee.

Arabic is the language used during the labor office complaint procedure. Even if two languages have been used by the employer, Arabic prevails at all times in interpreting the dispute. Notice of the complaint and the time of the hearing is stated in terms of the Arabic calendar (*Hijra*[116]), unless another calendar is agreed upon. The deadlines require expeditious handling of complaints.[117] The Hijra notice should be translated by the expatriate employer to the Western calendar immediately upon receipt in order to avoid missing deadlines.

Complaints to the labor office are investigated by a specialized tribunal of three individuals, termed a Primary Commission for the Settlement of Disputes.[118] The Chairman is required to have a degree in Islamic law, and at least one of the other two members is required to have a degree in law, either Islamic or decree law.[119]

The Primary Commission renders its decision by majority vote.[120] It has the exclusive right to examine all disputes relating to employment contracts.[121] In the course of carrying out its judi-

---

[114]*Id.* art. 12.

[115]*Id.* art. 13.

[116]See note 2, *supra*, for an explanation of the Hijra calendar and its translation to the Western Gregorian calendar.

[117]SALR, ch. 1, arts. 16–17.

[118]As noted in the Introduction, Primary Commission members are experienced in Shari'a and law. The Chair must have a degree in Shari'a, and another member must have a degree in Shari'a or law.

[119]SALR, ch. 11, art. 173.

[120]*Id.* art. 178.

[121]The Primary Commission's decisions are final in labor disputes valued at less than SR3,000, disputes relating to termination, and disputes relating to the imposition of fines; its decisions may be appealed to the Supreme Commission in cases involving labor disputes valued at more than SR3,000, injuries, and termination of services.

cial responsibilities, Commission officials may summon any person for interrogation, require the production of documents, or visit the work premises.[122]

If the decision of the Primary Commission is not appealed properly, the decision becomes final.

Decisions of the Primary Commission may be appealed to the Supreme Commission for Settlement of Disputes within 30 days after having received a copy of the Primary Commission's decision.[123] The Chairman of the Supreme Commission is authorized to set a date for hearing the appealed case within 15 days of the registration of the appeal petition. The Supreme Commission renders its decision within 30 days from the date of the first hearing.[124]

All decisions of the Supreme Commission are deemed enforceable and binding immediately upon the notification of the parties.[125]

Neither of the Commissions provided for in the Labor Regulations may abstain from rendering a decision on the pretext that there are no applicable provisions in the law. When confronted by such a situation, the Commission is charged with applying the Shari'a law, local rules, established judicial precedents, principles of justice, usage, and the rules of equity.[126] Neither party to a dispute may raise an issue that has been decided previously by one of the Commissions.[127]

The Primary or Supreme Commission may order the losing party to pay the winning party all or part of the expenses incurred by the winner.[128] When the worker is the winner, such amounts are considered "first-class privileged debts such that the workman or his heirs shall have a priority right over all of the employer's property."[129] Furthermore, an employer who delays implementation of an award issued by the Labor Commission may be subject to double

---

[122]SALR, ch. 11, art. 179.
[123]*Id.* art. 180.
[124]*Id.* art. 181.
[125]*Id.* art. 182.
[126]*Id.* art. 185.
[127]*Id.* art. 186.
[128]*Id.* ch. 1, art. 14.
[129]*Id.* art. 15.

penalties, a fine of SR500 to 1,000, or imprisonment for up to three months, pursuant to Articles 172 to 188 of the Saudi Labor Regulations.[130]

2. *Procedures for Arbitration in Lieu of Resort to the Labor Commissions*

Subject to the considerations discussed in the Introduction,[131] labor disputes may be resolved by arbitration in lieu of resorting to the Commissions. The parties to a dispute may, by mutual agreement, appoint a single arbitrator, or, formally or otherwise, the parties may each appoint one arbitrator and instruct the two so appointed to agree on a third to serve as umpire. If an arbitrator or umpire is not selected, the chair of the local Primary Commission may appoint one. The arbitration agreement sets out the rules of procedure, a copy of which is to be deposited at the local Primary Commission.[132] The arbitrator's award may be appealed to the Supreme Commission unless the arbitration agreement provides otherwise.

If there is no appeal or the decision is sustained on appeal, the arbitrator's award is executed following its registration with the Primary Commission and after receiving the endorsement of the Commission's Chair. Once registered and approved, the settlement is binding.[133]

In the midst of conciliation and arbitration proceedings (before the labor office or Primary Commission becomes involved), the employer may not change the terms of employment to cause prejudice to the employee. During such proceedings the employer also may not dismiss or penalize any worker without written permission from the appropriate Commission.[134]

3. *Employer Reprisals*

No matter what the outcome, once the labor office complaint proceedings are concluded, the employee is not ensured specific

---

[130]*Id.* ch. 12, art. 205.

[131]See the Introduction, at C.1., above.

[132]SALR, ch. 11, art. 183.

[133]*Id.* art. 182.

[134]*Id.* art. 187.

protection from reprisal by the employer for filing a complaint. A worker is protected only to the extent that the law may otherwise provide. For instance, if a worker, employed at will, successfully brings a complaint for unlawful labor practices and obtains a remedy, and the worker is then terminated, the law will not permit further action based on that "coincidental" discharge, except for further actions based on lack of cause or a valid reason, as discussed above.[135]

H. Privacy

See information on recordkeeping requirements under I.E.2., above. The Labor Regulations are silent on the issue of employer surveillance or monitoring of employees, no doubt in part due to the fact they were promulgated in 1969 (1389 H). There is no other Royal Decree with accompanying regulations on this matter that would establish limitations on or liability for employer surveillance or monitoring of employees. In practice, drug testing is rare—the penalty for using drugs in Saudi Arabia is death. Testing or monitoring of Saudi national employees in particular would raise Shari'a concerns, because "spying" is anathema to Islam.

I. Employee Duty of Loyalty, Trade Secrets, Covenants Not to Compete

1. *Employee Duty of Loyalty*

There exists a duty of loyalty; however, there are few effective remedies for enforcing this.

2. *Trade Secrets*

An employee is required to "keep the technical, commercial and industrial secrets of the products which the workman produces or in the production of which he directly or indirectly participates, and in general, keep all the trade secrets relating to the work which, if divulged, are apt to prejudice the interests of the employer."[136]

---

[135]See I.F.3.a. and b., above.

[136]Labor and Workmen's Regulations art. 96.F.

An employee can be discharged for cause "if it is proved that the workman has divulged the industrial and commercial secrets of the work in which he is engaged."[137]

3. *Covenants Not to Compete*

Non-compete considerations as regards expatriates in the Kingdom are effectively handled by the structure of Saudi employment law. An expatriate employee under normal circumstances is blocked from returning to accept new employment in the Kingdom for a period of one year, or, on special request by his employer to the Saudi immigration authorities, for three years if the employee is deemed to know the commercial secrets of the company. The latter normally applies only to high-level expatriate employees.

This same restriction does not apply to Saudi nationals, who have no similar restrictions placed on them. There is no proscription that would stop an employer from imposing a non-compete agreement on a Saudi; however, it would be almost impossible to enforce such an agreement. A court would be unlikely to stop a Saudi national from competing because the effect would be to deprive that individual and the family of their means of sustenance. In addition, there is no injunctive relief in the Saudi legal system; while recent Shari'a court regulations for the first time provide for some injunction-type remedies, this mechanism remains untested.

II. COLLECTIVE BARGAINING

Unions and other organized labor activities are strictly forbidden in the Kingdom. Accordingly, any involvement in work stoppages or interference will subject the participants to certain and severe penalty, including deportation as well as criminal prosecution and incarceration, not to mention other more severe remedies that are claimed by some international human rights organizations to be applied to political prisoners, which could include labor organizers.[138]

---

[137] *Id.* art. 83.9.

[138] SALR, ch. 12, arts. 189–91.

III. Representation by Entities Other Than Unions

Due to the prohibition on formal unions and workers' councils, individual employers are free to make their own arrangements for consultation with employees. Generally, there is not a strong labor presence or participation by employees in management of the enterprise. Nor has there been significant movement in this direction.

IV. Redundancy and Transfers of Undertakings*

A. Redundancy

Adverse business conditions may necessitate reductions in salaries and benefits despite the prohibition on such action in the Saudi Labor Regulations.[139] (Such a business climate was prevalent during the mid-1980s, for example.) When compelled by business necessity, an employer may achieve this result by terminating an employment agreement in a manner consistent with its terms and offering to rehire the recently discharged employee under a new, less generous agreement. The former worker is free at this point to accept the new terms or reject the entire offer of employment. Though technically lawful, this plan is precarious in its implementation and competent legal assistance should be sought whenever such action is contemplated by the employer.

B. Transfers of Undertakings

Under Saudi Labor Regulations regarding the survivability of a contract entered into by a preceding employer, it is generally accepted that both a successor to an employment contract and the original employer are jointly and severally responsible for the ful-

---

*The terms "worker" and "employee" are used to indicate that the law applies to both sexes; however, there is no commingling of the sexes in the workplace in Saudi Arabia. See I.A., above.

[139]SALR, ch. 12, art. 208.

fillment of the contract's obligations.[140] This article of the Saudi Labor Regulations must be read with a later article that states that while both the original and new employer are responsible for the discharge of obligations arising from the contract that were due prior to the transfer of ownership, obligations arising after transfer are to be assumed solely by the new owner.[141] To be safe, the employer should heed the stricter of the two provisions. The law has supported a finding of continued obligation upon the new owner in the event of an establishment's dissolution, merger, or subdivision, or if the business is conveyed by inheritance, legacy, donation, sale, or assignment. In all these events, the employment contract and all obligations incumbent upon the original owner survive and must be assumed by the new owner and operator of the establishment. In the event of liquidation, bankruptcy, or authorized final shutdown, obligations will continue only to the extent that the impoverished owner can meet them.[142]

V. WAGES, HOURS, AND LEAVE*

A. Wages

Service is presumed rendered for pay if it consists of work that is not customarily performed gratuitously or that is in the worker's occupational line.[143] Wages are considered by Saudi law to be the most important right of the worker, and the relevant regulatory provisions should be strictly complied with by employers. Terms of compensation are generally provided for in the labor

---

[140]*Id.* ch. 4, §1, art. 76. Continuity of service of the expatriate worker is similarly maintained in the event of a legal successor to the employer or a change in the corporate sponsor. *See* ALISON LERRICK & Q. JAVED MIAN, SAUDI BUSINESS AND LABOR LAW: ITS INTERPRETATIONS AND APPLICATIONS 282–83 (Alden Press 2d ed. 1987); SALR, arts. 82, 89.

[141]SALR, ch. 4, §1, art. 90.

[142]*Id.* art. 89.

*The terms "worker" and "employee" are used to indicate that the law applies to both sexes; however, there is no commingling of the sexes in the workplace in Saudi Arabia. See I.A., above.

[143]SALR, ch. 6, art. 122.

agreement. If wages are not stipulated in the contract, by law, or in the basic work rules, the wages determined for similar work are adopted; if this reference cannot be utilized, the generally accepted practice of the trade and for the area determines the wage amount. If no such practice exists, the appropriate Primary Commission for the Settlement of Disputes determines the wage.[144]

By international standards, Saudi salaries are considered high. Though this is the case overall, actual compensation amounts vary greatly within the Kingdom and depend on such factors as the nature and location of the job, available amenities, and the nationality of the employee. For instance, although salaries for Saudis are generous, it is not uncommon for Bangladeshi or Nepalese laborers to work for the equivalent of U.S. $100 a month, plus room, board, transportation, and minimal health care. Regarding foreign workers, it is typical for *skilled* non-Saudi workers to receive a location bonus in addition to their usual foreign base pay.

The following amounts are considered an integral part of wages:

- commissions;
- percentages of sales generated paid to employees;
- cost of living allowances; and
- any grant made to the worker, in addition to his or her salary, as a reward for honesty or for increased family obligations.[145]

In addition, as noted below, it is important to understand that "wages" in Saudi Arabia may include forms of compensation typically grouped under "benefits" in the United States.

1. *No Minimum Wage*

With the assistance of a committee comprised of various deputy ministers, the Council of Ministers is charged with the responsibility to ultimately establish a minimum wage either in gen-

[144]*Id.* art. 123. See discussion of Primary Commissions in the Introduction and at I.G.1., above.

[145]SALR, ch. 6, art. 124. *See also* SALR ch. 1, art. 7(6).

eral or with respect to a given occupation.[146] Despite such regulations, as of August 2004 there was no minimum wage rate. It is unknown what the new labor regulations will state, but there remains widespread opposition to enacting a minimum wage.

Employers should be aware that although most wages are expressly provided for by a contract, wages represent not only statutory rights but also contractual, customary, and acquired rights of an employee. Generally, Saudi courts will uphold any contractually established wage that is not repugnant to Saudi law, traditions, or morals.[147] If in practice an employee receives greater compensation than that provided for by custom or contract, he or she may later assert a judicially enforceable acquired right to the higher wage.[148]

2. *Frequency of Payment*

Workers may either be paid monthly, weekly, daily, or by piecework. This determination is generally stipulated in the employment contract. Once a monthly rated worker has been placed into one of these categories, the worker retains the right to remain in the original classification unless he or she agrees to a reclassification in writing and without prejudice to rights acquired during the period spent as a monthly rated worker. The employer must pay each worker his or her wages at the time and place specified in the contract or as accepted in general practice.[149] Daily rated workers must be paid at least once per week. Piece workers must be paid at least once per week if they work as such for a period exceeding two weeks. Monthly rated employees, as the classification implies, are to be paid once per month. All other workers are to be paid at least once per week.[150] If the employee's service terminates, his or her wages must be paid immediately. If the employee leaves of his or her own accord, the employee must be paid within seven days. In order to obtain such wages, the former employee must acknowledge their receipt by signing a special register.[151]

---

[146] *Id.* ch. 6, art. 115.
[147] Note generally LERRICK & MIAN, supra note 140, at 261; SALR, ch. 6, art. 123.
[148] LERRICK & MIAN, *supra* note 140, at 259–260.
[149] SALR, ch. 4, §2, art. 92.
[150] *Id.* ch. 6, art. 116.
[151] *Id.* art. 117.

3. *Overtime and Reporting Pay*

Overtime is earned by any employee working in excess of the maximum number of hours specified by the contract or the statute (whichever is fewer). The overtime wage is equal to the worker's usual wage per hour plus half that amount again.[152] On designated holidays and rest days, an employee is due his or her full pay.[153] If an employee opts to work on such days, the employee is entitled to double his or her normal rate of pay.

If an employee reports to work ready and able to perform but is prevented from doing so by the employer, the worker is entitled to receive pay for the entire day.[154]

4. *Deductions and Outstanding Wages*

No amount may be deducted from a worker's wages except in the following cases:

- payment of advances or any amounts paid in excess of the worker's normal rights to his or her usual wages (not to exceed 10 percent of such wages);
- social insurance premiums;[155]
- contributions to the savings funds;
- installments pertaining to any plan for the construction of houses to be owned by the worker;
- fines for disciplinary offenses or for damage to the employer's goods; and
- any debt to be recovered in the execution of a judiciary judgment that does not exceed one-fourth of the wages due the worker (alimony or debt for food, clothing, and lodging may be satisfied before all other debts).[156]

The percentage of the amounts deducted cannot exceed one-half of the wages due the worker unless the Primary Commission for the Settlement of Disputes approves.[157] If any amount is de-

[152]*Id.* ch. 9, art. 151.
[153]*Id.* art. 155.
[154]*Id.* ch. 4, §2, art. 93.
[155]See VIII.A., below.
[156]SALR, ch. 6, art. 119.
[157]*Id.* art. 120.

ducted or if the employer delays payment of wages without justification, the employee, his or her representative, or the head of the appropriate labor office may submit an application to the applicable Primary Commission. The Primary Commission may order the employer to pay the worker any wrongfully deducted amounts or any outstanding wages. The Commission also may impose a fine, not to exceed double the amount deducted from the worker's wages or double the outstanding wages.[158]

5. *Salary or Grade Reductions*

A worker's grade or salary may not be lowered;[159] violators of this prohibition are subject to penalties. Salary or grade reductions based on economic necessity are discussed above in IV.A.

B. Hours

1. *Limits on Working Hours*

The Saudi Labor Regulations provide that no worker may work for more than eight actual working hours in any one day or more than 48 hours per week, except as noted in V.B.1.c., below. In the month of Ramadan only six hours of work per day, or a maximum of 36 hours a week, is permitted. The number of working hours may be reduced for certain categories of workers by the Minister of Labor.[160] Generally, and especially in commercial centers, a workweek of five and one-half days is the norm.

No employee may work more than five consecutive hours without an interval of rest, prayer, and meals of at least half an hour. Even with the consent of both parties, this right may not be forfeited by the employee and will be upheld even where a worker receives additional breaks. Rest periods must total at least one and a half hours during full working hours. The worker may not remain at the place of work more than 11 hours in one day.[161]

[158] *Id.* art. 121.
[159] *Id.* ch. 12, art. 208.
[160] *Id.* ch. 8, art. 147.
[161] *Id.* art. 148.

It should be noted that an employer may not violate the statutory obligations by means of the employment contract. For example, in the event a contract provides for a 55-hour workweek in consideration of a specified wage, the contract will be upheld only with respect to the promised wage; the worker will not be similarly bound to perform the excess work. In addition, the employment contract may not provide for any work period otherwise inconsistent with the regulatory language noted above. Employers have little success in upholding practices that violate the Labor Regulations, and employers are better advised to apply the regulations strictly so as to avoid possible penalties of SR500 to 1,000, which may be assessed for each violation.[162]

a. Rest Days and Holidays

The Labor Regulations direct that Friday is to be a day of rest for which workers receive full pay. Another day may be established as the rest day, but only with the approval of the local labor office of the Ministry of Labor and Social Affairs. In requesting an exception, the employer must demonstrate that the number of actual workdays will not exceed six and that its workers are nonetheless able to perform their religious duties.[163]

The employer is not required to adhere to the preceding provision on working hours, weekly rest, and vacations

- during annual inventory, balance sheet preparation, liquidation, closing of accounts, or preparation for sales or festive seasons, provided that the number of excess days does not exceed 30 in one year;
- when the work is intended to prevent a dangerous accident, or to repair damage resulting from an accident;
- when the work is necessitated by unusual work pressure (in the case of accidents and in claims of work pressure, a report must be submitted within 24 hours to the appropriate local labor office for official approval); or
- on holidays, festive seasons, or other exceptional occasions so noted by the Minister of Labor.

---

[162] *Id.* ch. 12, art. 203.
[163] *Id.* ch. 8, art. 149.

In these four specific areas, the number of actual working hours may not exceed 10 in one day.[164]

Although employees in Saudi Arabia are not endowed with an absolute right not to work on official holidays and rest days, the employer's right to compel work on such days is limited to the above exceptional circumstances.[165] In reviewing these Labor Regulations, the employer should note that the Labor Regulations treat days of rest the same as holidays both with regard to requiring employees to work and with regard to the compensation offered for such work.

b. Preparatory and Supplementary Time

Work hours and interval requirements do not apply to preparatory and supplementary operations before or after the end of work. (Note, however, that the Labor Regulations allow only for 30 additional minutes of work time for preparing and "winding up" operations.[166])

c. Excluded Occupations

The following occupations are excluded from the strict working hours provisions: work that is necessarily intermittent (such as technicians or mechanics employed for the purpose of repairing or operating machinery), watch and janitorial duties, or drilling or exploration for petroleum and minerals in remote areas. Custodial employees are subject to special provisions and may not work for more than six hours at a time. Both janitors and watchmen may be required to work up to 12 hours within a day without an interval for rest, prayer, and meals, but must be permitted to pray when appropriate.[167]

Work in drilling or exploration for petroleum and minerals in remote areas may in no case exceed the standard limit of 48 hours per week. There are, however, ways in which companies may exceed 48 hours per week, such as characterization of drilling work

---

[164] *Id.* ch. 9, art. 150.

[165] *Id.*

[166] *Id.* art. 152(a).

[167] Resolution No. 16, arts. 1(c)(2) and 4, interpreting art. 152 of the SALR.

as hardship duty with appropriate time off.[168] Furthermore, as noted in B.1., above, contractual language requiring the employee to work in excess of the maximum number of permitted hours, even for a higher wage, will not be binding on the nonexcepted worker, because such provisions violate the regulatory limits.

d. *Overtime*

Saudi courts have been consistent and clear in their conviction that additional work may not be imposed on workers continuously and regularly. This was tested by a 1979 case brought before a Primary Commission for the Settlement of Disputes. In this case, an employment contract for a term of two years provided that the employee was to "work overtime from time to time whenever so required." When the worker refused, he was discharged for breach of contract. The Primary Commission overturned the dismissal, holding that employers may continuously impose added work only in cases of emergency or danger, or as may be explicitly provided for in the Labor Regulations. In the same way, just as the law prohibits an employer from demanding overtime, the right to work overtime may never be acquired by the employee, even by virtue of recurrent overtime.[169]

2. *Limits on Working Hours for Women and Children*

Adolescents, juveniles, and women may not be employed in night work except in cases determined by the Ministry of Labor and Social Affairs and in cases of *force majeure*.[170] An "adolescent" is a person who is older than 15 years old, but who is younger than 18 years of age. A "juvenile" is a person who is younger than 15 years of age. Juveniles and adolescents may not be employed for a period exceeding six hours a day, without exception.[171]

Any juvenile younger than age 13 may not be employed or allowed into any workplace. The employer must set up a personnel file of every juvenile, aged 13 to 15, with an official birth cer-

[168]SALR, ch. 9, art. 152.
[169]LERRICK & MIAN, *supra* note 140, at 279.
[170]SALR, ch. 10, §1, art. 161.
[171]*Id.* art. 162.

tificate or age estimation certificate, a certificate of physical fitness for the required work, and the consent of the juvenile's guardian. The employer must notify the local labor office of the Ministry of Labor and Social Affairs of all employment of juveniles, as well as keep a special register for juvenile workers.[172]

C. Leave

1. Vacations, Leave, and Holidays

After one year of service, a worker is entitled to an annual vacation of 15 days at full wages; vacation time increases to 21 days after 10 continuous years of service.[173] The employee may, with the employer's consent, defer the vacation to the following year but the worker may not forgo his or her annual vacation altogether. The employer has the right to choose the dates of such vacations.[174] If the worker leaves the job, he or she is entitled to payment for all unused vacation days.[175]

With the employer's approval, a worker may obtain leave without pay for not more than 10 days per year.[176] While on vacation or leave, an employee may not work for another employer; if an employee does this, an employer may recover any vacation pay given to the employee.[177]

An employee is entitled to a three-days' marriage leave. Workers are further entitled to one day of leave with full pay for the birth of a child and the death of a spouse or any relatives.[178]

---

[172]*Id.* §2, art. 163.

[173]It is noteworthy that continuity of service is primarily based on the employment relationship. Accordingly, any alteration of the terms of employment, the place of work, or the nature of the services rendered does not disrupt the continuity of employment. Even if contracts for a term are successive and not self-renewed, the relationship is not considered to be disturbed.

Continuity of service is similarly maintained in the event of a legal successor to the employer or a change in corporate sponsor (regarding the expatriate worker). *See* LERRICK & MIAN, *supra* note 140, at 282–83; SALR, arts. 82, 89.

[174]SALR, ch. 9, art. 153.

[175]*Id.* art. 154.

[176]*Id.* art. 156.

[177]*Id.* art. 157.

[178]*Id.* art. 159.

On designated holidays, each worker is entitled to the specified days off with full pay.[179] There are two official holiday periods per year, during which business activity essentially ceases for about one week. The first is the *Eid Al-Fitr* holiday. This is customarily a 10-day holiday occurring between the end of the ninth month (of the Hijra calendar), Ramadan, and the start of the tenth month, Shawal. This holiday, observed by both government and businesses, celebrates the end of the month of fasting. The second major holiday is *Eid Al-Adha* (Feast of Sacrifice). It lasts from the fifth to the fifteenth of the twelfth month (*Thul-Hijja*) and is likewise observed by both the government and the private sector. It is during this period that the performance of the *Hajj* (the Islamic religious pilgrimage to the holy city of Mecca) occurs. Employers should also note that Saudi National Day falls on the twenty-third of September each year.

2. *Sick Leave*

If an illness is confirmed by a medical certificate, an employer must grant a worker sick leave with full pay for the first 30 days and three-quarters pay for the next 60 days in any one year.[180] An employee cannot be discharged during illness until he or she misses 90 consecutive days, or 120 days in any year. Even in such an extreme instance, the worker may be entitled to pay for sick leave as noted above and to his or her full end of service award upon termination.[181]

3. *Maternity Leave*

A female worker is entitled to maternity leave for four weeks before the expected delivery date and six weeks following delivery. During maternity leave, she is entitled to half pay if she has worked for the employer for longer than one year, and to full pay if she has been working for longer than three years. If she receives full pay during her maternity leave, she cannot be paid any wages

[179] *Id.* art. 155.
[180] *Id.* ch. 9, art. 158.
[181] *Id.* ch. 4, art. 82.

during her regular annual vacation. Similarly, if she received half pay during maternity leave, she is entitled only to half wages during her annual leave.[182] Following maternity leave, upon her return to work, a woman is entitled to not more than one hour's rest daily to feed her newborn child, in addition to regular rest periods.[183] Expenses for related medical examinations and treatment are to be borne by the employer.[184]

The employer is not permitted to terminate a female employee's employment while she is on maternity leave.[185] Similarly, the employer may not terminate a female employee during illness caused by work or caused by the delivery if her absence does not exceed six months. Nor may a woman be discharged during the six months preceding the expected date of delivery. If such provisions are violated, prompt reinstatement is required.[186] It is important to note that a woman forfeits her entitlements if she works for another employer during her authorized leave. In such a case, the original employer is permitted to recover any wages it paid to her during that same period.[187]

VI. ANTIDISCRIMINATION*

Unlike other countries that follow nondiscrimination principles regarding the employment of women and other protected categories, Saudi Arabia prides itself on its faithfulness to local religious and social custom in aggressively protecting and enforcing traditional gender and other roles and stereotypes, as embodied in local law.

---

[182] *Id.* ch. 10, §2, art. 164.

[183] *Id.* art. 165.

[184] *Id.* art. 166.

[185] *Id.* art. 167.

[186] *Id.* art. 168.

[187] *Id.* art. 169.

*The terms "worker" and "employee" are used to indicate that the law applies to both sexes; however, there is no commingling of the sexes in the workplace in Saudi Arabia. See I.A., above.

A. Women and Juveniles

Special rules relate to the employment of women and juveniles in Saudi Arabia. These are discussed above in V., Wages, Hours, and Leave, as they apply to restrictions on types of employment, hours of work, and maternity benefits and leave for working women. Other special considerations regarding the employment of women and juveniles are discussed in the Introduction and in VII., Occupational Safety and Health. The provisions prohibiting or restricting the employment of adolescents, juveniles, and women do not apply to charitable or official institutions of vocational or professional training, provided that the bylaws of such institutions are approved by the Minister of Labor.[188]

B. Foreign Workers

Except for the social insurance pension plan, foreign workers are entitled to the same substantial consideration in kind that may be given to Saudi workers.[189]

C. Disabled Individuals

Circumstances permitting, companies employing 50 or more workers are obligated to employ a workforce consisting of up to 2 percent disabled and vocationally rehabilitated workers. Such workers may be recruited either independently or with the assistance of the local labor office.[190] Although regulations providing for the employment of disabled workers have not been aggressively enforced, voluntary compliance appears to be the general trend.

D. Saudization

"Saudization" is a term that refers to the concerted effort being made by Saudi Arabia to train, educate, and prepare Saudis to

[188]SALR, ch. 10, §3, art. 170.
[189]See VIII., below.
[190]SALR, ch. 3, art. 54.

be more employable and qualified for better paying professional and skilled positions.

In the private sector and regarding joint ventures, the government has instituted economic and administrative incentive programs to encourage businesses to employ primarily Saudis. Compliance with the terms of these programs and related laws is an important aspect of successfully doing business in the Kingdom. Saudi law requires every employer in the Kingdom, employing more than 100 workers, to train no less than 5 percent of its Saudi employees in technical jobs. Moreover, the number of Saudi workers cannot be less than 75 percent of the total number of employees. Most important is the requirement that the total wages paid to the Saudi workers may not be less than 51 percent of the total wages paid to the employer's workforce.[191]

In the past, enforcement of these requirements has at times been lax in tacit recognition of the relative shortage of qualified Saudi candidates. In recent years, however, Saudization efforts have been given top priority.[192] The government has concentrated its efforts on two levels: first, educating and training young Saudis to assume technical and skilled positions; and second, encouraging employers to employ more Saudis in such jobs. To this end, a register must be kept of the names of Saudis who have replaced non-Saudi employees.[193] This and all relevant records will be periodically reviewed by the labor office to monitor compliance with the above requirements.

"Saudization" regulations have begun to establish reserved business sectors in the economy. For a list of professions where jobs should be granted only to Saudi nationals, see IX.B., below.

In an effort to eliminate "trading in visas," the Ministry of Labor has banned all recruitment of manpower by small and medium enterprises effective August 23, 2004. Businessmen have urged the Ministry to review the ban due to its negative effect on labor requirements.

---

[191]*Id.* §1, art. 45.

[192]The Protection of National Industries Regulation is in effect to implement the Saudization program. It is administered primarily by the Ministry of Finance.

[193]SALR, ch. 3, §2, art. 50.

VII. Occupational Safety and Health*

A. Protection of Workers' Safety and Health

Every employer is required to take necessary health and safety precautions to protect workers from potential workplace hazards and diseases. An employer may not charge the workers for providing such protection. The rules require every employer to maintain an establishment that is

- clean and sanitary;
- adequately ventilated;
- not overcrowded;
- adequately lit; and
- provided with an adequate supply of potable water and sufficient wash facilities, including accessible toilets, at the rate of one for every 15 workers.[194]

Moreover, precautions must be taken to protect employees from injuries that may result from exposure to gas, dust, smoke, or other waste. It is further incumbent upon all employers to take all necessary fire precautions.[195]

In all places and in all occupations where women are employed, they must be provided with seats to ensure their comfort.[196]

Adolescents, juveniles, and women may not be employed in hazardous operations or harmful industries, such as those involving power-operated machinery, mines, quarries, and the like. The Minister of Labor is charged with the designation of such occupations.

The Ministry of Labor and Social Affairs may issue decisions on any special actions that the employer must take to protect workers in especially hazardous jobs. The employer, or its agent, must inform workers of the hazards of the job and of the necessary pre-

---

*The terms "worker" and "employee" are used to indicate that the law applies to both sexes; however, there is no commingling of the sexes in the workplace in Saudi Arabia. See I.A., above.

194 SALR, ch. 7, arts. 128–29.

195 *Id.* art. 133.

196 *Id.* ch. 10, §2, art. 171.

cautionary measures to be taken to avoid injury. The employer must enclose dangerous parts of machines and fence dangerous manholes and obstructions. Employees must use the safety equipment designated for each operation and must preserve such equipment. A worker must abide by health and safety instructions, and refrain from any act or negligence that would result in a failure to abide by the safety instructions or in misusing or impairing the safety equipment.[197] If an accident is due to employer negligence, the employer must compensate workers for the resulting injuries.[198]

The employer is responsible for accidents causing injury to nonemployees who enter the workplace in connection with official duties, or with the employer's consent. If the accident is due to employer negligence, the employer also must compensate the victim for the resulting injuries.[199]

Occupational illness and injury benefits are included as part of the Saudi Social Insurance Regulations.[200]

B. Maintenance of Business Establishments

The Ministry of Labor and Social Affairs oversees the health and safety aspects of business establishments. If the labor office finds that any building, roads, machines, or equipment in any establishment constitutes a danger to human life or safety, then it may issue a written order requesting the necessary repairs be done within a specified period. The employer may appeal to the Minister of Labor and Social Affairs who will uphold, modify, or cancel the order.[201]

C. Permits for New Business Establishments

Any person employing at least 20 workers who wishes to construct buildings for a new project, to increase the mechanical power used in running the project, or to convert existing buildings into a mechanically operated project, must apply for a necessary

---

[197] *Id.* ch. 7, arts. 130–31.
[198] *Id.* art. 132.
[199] *Id.*
[200] See discussion in VIII.A., below
[201] SALR ch. 8, art. 146.

license with the Ministry of Commerce and Industry. Attached to this application must be a map of the site, the design of the building, a layout showing the locations of machines and equipment and their specifications, and drawings or photographs of the machines. The maps must be detailed and other information may be required. Only when the Ministry is satisfied with the arrangements will it issue the license.[202]

VIII. PENSIONS AND BENEFITS*

Prior to discussing specific benefits, it is necessary to explain the wage/benefit distinction mentioned in V.A., above. Forms of compensation typically grouped under "benefits" in the United States may in fact be treated as wage remunerations in Saudi Arabia. Whether consideration in kind is considered to be a wage or benefit becomes important on four occasions:

1. when determining an employee's specific tax liability;
2. at the time of termination (regarding the calculation of the end of service award[203]);
3. when determining the amount of monthly social insurance contributions; and
4. in the event of a grievance, because compensatory judgments are typically based on the wages earned by the wronged employee.

Employers are thus advised to be aware of the distinction and plan accordingly.

Although this text refers to many such wages as benefits for the purpose of lexical convenience, care has been taken to note the actual status of the various forms of consideration. A reliable rule of thumb for the employer struggling with the wage/benefit dis-

---

[202] *Id.* ch. 8, art. 145.

*The terms "worker" and "employee" are used to indicate that the law applies to both sexes; however, there is no commingling of the sexes in the workplace in Saudi Arabia. See I.A., above.

[203] End of service awards are discussed at I.F.2., above.

tinction is that any "extras" that are not compulsory under the Labor Regulations will generally be considered as a part of wages. Accordingly, all of the following are typically considered wage earnings and are not to be treated as benefits:

- foreign service premiums;
- hardship allowances;
- extended work week bonuses; and
- insurance premiums paid on the worker's behalf and not deducted from the worker's compensation.[204]

Saudi Labor Regulations establish that workers may be given substantial "consideration in kind," i.e., benefits. Except for the social insurance pension plan, all such "benefits" are to be provided without prejudice to Saudi and foreigner alike. What follows is a brief overview of some of the major benefits to be extended to workers in the Kingdom. Additional benefits are discussed in greater detail in the succeeding sections.

A. Social Insurance

The Saudi Social Insurance Regulations (Royal Decree Number M/21 of 6 Ramadhan 1389H, 15 November 1969) established the framework for a comprehensive social insurance system. The growth of the program and application of these Regulations is overseen by the Ministry of Labor and Social Affairs. Designed to be directly administered by the General Organization of Social Insurance (GOSI), the Social Insurance Regulations contemplate the system's development through a process of phased implementation. Ultimately it is to provide for compensation or benefits in the event of

- occupational injury or illness;
- incapacity, old age, and death;
- maternity and temporary disability;
- family hardship; and
- unemployment.

[204]*See generally* LERRICK & MIAN, *supra* note 140, at 263–64.

Presently only the portions providing for pensions (the "annuities branch") and for compensation in the event of occupational injury (the "occupational hazards branch") have been partially implemented. Each portion is discussed below.

All companies must register with GOSI, to which they are thereafter required to make monthly payments.

In 2003, employees who are Saudi nationals must contribute 9 percent of their wages, deducted by the employer and remitted to GOSI. The employer's contribution for Saudi nationals is 9 percent as well, plus 2 percent for occupational hazard insurance for all employees, including expatriates as well as Saudi nationals.

Employer contributions to GOSI are deductible for tax purposes. However, similar payments for employees' social security taxes in a foreign jurisdiction are not deductible as business expenses.[205]

1. Annuity Provisions

Monthly contributions to the annuities branch must equal 9 percent of each of the employer's Saudi employees' gross compensation (including cost of living, overtime pay, and expatriation and housing allowances—if paid in cash).[206] Theoretically, contributions are to be calculated on the "total" compensation. In practice, many companies figure contributions on a base consisting of only the salary plus the cash value of the housing allowance. (If housing is provided by the employer, its value is generally estimated to be equal to two months' salary.) The monthly social contribution is typically figured at the beginning of the year. This amount remains stable throughout the year, regardless of subsequent increases or decreases in employees' compensation. Additionally, every Saudi employee must personally contribute 9 percent of his or her gross compensation to the annuities branch.[207] Employers customarily withhold a worker's contribution from pay.

The annuity provisions guarantee a generous pension to qualifying workers. To be eligible to collect under the Social Insurance

---

[205] Cir. No. 4863/5181 dated 8/4/1395H.

[206] Social Insurance Regulations, art XIX, Cir. No. 3252/2 dated 19/3/1393H, at 309.

[207] *Id.* art. XVII, para. 2.

Regulations, an employee need only to have submitted contributions for a certain total number of years and to have begun participation a certain number of years younger than the age of 60, at which age the account is available for disbursal. As initially conceived, the pension benefits were to be made available to all workers regardless of nationality. As of 1987, however, pension benefits are limited to Saudi nationals.

2. *Occupational Illness and Injury Provisions*

For the occupational hazards (or disability) branch, employers are required to make a further monthly contribution to GOSI in the amount of 2 percent of all of their employees' gross compensation. An exception is permitted with respect to foreign employees with contracts for a term of less than one year; although employers are not initially subject to a contribution for such workers, employers may find that later renewals of the contract trigger retroactive liability.

B. Benefits to Be Provided by Employers of 50 or More Workers

1. *Savings and Thrift Plan*

Every employer who employs 50 or more workers must set up a savings and thrift plan. The worker's participation must be voluntary.

2. *Rest and Recreation Facilities*

The company must also provide, at its own expense, suitable rest and recreational facilities.

3. *Day Care*

It is further established by the Labor Regulations that any employer employing 50 or more women must provide a suitable place for child supervision for children younger than the age of six. This "day care" is to be entrusted to a female nurse qualified to care for children younger than six years of age.[208]

[208]SALR, ch. 7, art. 144.

4. *Medical Services*

The employer must provide first aid services for its employees. (In establishments with fewer than 50 employees, the employer must provide only a medical aid cabinet.[209]) Saudi Arabia provides universal health care to its own nationals, but no longer provides such benefits to foreign workers and their dependents.[210] Companies with more than 50 workers, however, must provide basic health care to their employees, and every company employing 50 or more workers is obligated to employ a nurse, assign a physician, and provide necessary medicines. Such services are free of charge.

Every employer with more than 50 employees must inform the appropriate local labor office of the Ministry of Labor and Social Affairs of the name of the appointed physician and the minimum number of days fixed for the examination of workers.[211] Additionally, every employer must prepare a medical file for each employee.[212]

If the employer employs more than 100 workers, it must provide them with treatment by a specialist. When an operation is necessary, it is paid for by the social insurance fund. Cost of treatment, as well as the party who is to assume such cost, is ultimately determined by the Minister of Labor and Social Affairs.

C. Benefits to Be Provided by Employers of 500 or More Workers

If an employer employs 500 or more workers, the Ministry of Labor and Social Affairs may require the employer, at its own expense, to provide all or part of the following:

---

[209] *Id.* art. 134.

[210] The Saudi Government is preparing draft regulations requiring all employers to obtain health insurance for their foreign workers. The Health Insurance Regulations have been finalized and have been implemented at least with respect to companies having more than 500 workers. However, due to the problems with insurance generally under Shari'a law and the delayed issuance of new Insurance Regulations, which was only recently promulgated, it is not yet clear that the program has been extended to smaller companies in the timeframe that originally was envisioned.

[211] SALR, ch. 7, art. 135.

[212] *Id.* art. 136.

- shops for the sale of food, clothes, and other necessary commodities to the extent that such shops are not ordinarily available;
- parks, athletic fields, and cultural libraries;
- medical arrangements for the employees' legal dependants;
- schools for the education of the employees' children, to the extent that no adequate schools are available;
- mosques in the place of work;
- programs to combat illiteracy among workers; and
- rules agreeable to the Ministry of Labor and Social Affairs for the hiring and promotion of workers, and for their allowances and benefits.[213]

D. Housing and Other Support Provisions for Workers in Remote Areas

Generally, housing allowances are not compulsory and, if given, are considered to be part of wages. Housing and related provisions will not be considered part of wages, however, with regard to workers who work in places distant from inhabited areas. In such an instance, the employer is obligated to provide the workers with:

- adequate living quarters;
- suitable camps for living, if workers are employed in exploration areas and in certain occupations;
- three meals per day with food deemed appropriate by the Minister of Labor and Social Affairs;
- special food, as needed; and
- medical, social, and cultural services.[214]

E. Transportation

Cash allowances for transportation are considered to be part of wages and not a benefit per se. However, as with housing, if the

[213]*Id.* art. 137.
[214]*Id.* art. 143.

work site is remote and no public transportation facilities are available to the employee, the Labor Regulations direct the employer to provide transportation. Such provisions are then considered to be a benefit.[215]

With respect to foreign workers, employers are required to provide them with return transportation once the terms of the employment contract have been fully satisfied. And, though not required, it is common for employers to provide skilled and valued foreign workers with return airfare home for themselves (and their families) at least once each year.

F. Benefits to Be Provided by Employers of All Workers

The Saudi Arabian government is phasing in the requirement that all employers provide mandatory health insurance coverage for their workers. Large companies (those having 500 or more employees) were required to have insurance as of September 2002, with smaller companies having a compliance date in 2003–2004. Because the Insurance Regulations have only been promulgated recently, the timeframe for their implementation remains uncertain. Over time all expatriate employees are likely to be covered, and eventually all employees who are Saudi nationals as well. Because government regulations promulgated each year generally do not have effective dates, employers that want to be completely safe should acquire health insurance before the compliance date.

IX. IMMIGRATION*

A. Visas and Work Permits

Visas are required for all foreign visitors to Saudi Arabia. No tourist visas are issued and the interested foreigner must procure one of the three types that are available: (1) business visit visa, (2) an employment block visa, (3) a family visit visa. Each type is

---

[215] *Id.*

*The terms "worker" and "employee" are used to indicate that the law applies to both sexes; however, there is no commingling of the sexes in the workplace in Saudi Arabia. See I.A., above.

discussed further below. In the United States, entry visas may be obtained through application to the Royal Embassy of Saudi Arabia in Washington, D.C., or from one of the Saudi consulates.

It is notable that employees and their dependents must surrender their passports to their sponsors upon entry except when needed for travel. The potential visitor should be further aware that Saudi Arabia is one of the only countries in the world that requires an exit visa. Exit/reentry visas may be issued to employees and dependents who are traveling. However, multiple exit/reentry visas (which are valid for 6 or 12 months) are generally available only for senior executives.[216]

1. Business Visas

All business visitors to the Kingdom must be invited by a Saudi company or organization. Typically, the Saudi sponsor will send a letter of invitation, certified by the Chamber of Commerce in Saudi Arabia, to the Saudi Embassy or consulate. The letter must be in Arabic, on company letterhead, and should include the name of the visa applicant, his or her passport number, company name and address, approximate dates of the visit, and the reason for the visit. On rare occasion the Saudi Embassy or consulate may grant, at its discretion, a sponsorless business visa to employees of prominent U.S. firms. It is, however, recommended, that parties seek Saudi sponsorship.

Additionally, business visa applicants are required to have a letter from the U.S. company indicating the name of the Saudi sponsoring company, the nature of the applicant's visit, the length of stay, and financial responsibility. The letter must include the corporate stamp or seal.

Business visas are valid for up to three months and are good for only one entry. Under exceptional circumstances, the Embassy or consulates may permit two entries. Likewise, if necessary, the period for which the visa is valid may be extended for a like term.

---

[216]The visa requirements portions of this section are taken from U.S. Saudi Arabian Business Council, <http://www.us-saudi-business.org/Traveling%20to%20Saudi%20Arabia.html> (last visited July 26, 2004).

2. *Employment Block Visas*

An employment block visa (*iqama*) is available only to applicants older than age 22. Akin to a residence visa, the employment block visa enables foreigners to stay and work in the Kingdom for an extended period. Once the foreigner arrives in Saudi Arabia, he or she must obtain a work permit[217] from the Ministry of Labor and Social Affairs. The employment block visa applicant must supply a letter from the Saudi employer on company letterhead, certified by the Saudi Chamber of Commerce, and indicating the employment block number and date. Other requirements include a certified and notarized copy of the applicant's university degree, which must be validated by the Saudi Arabian Educational Mission at the Saudi Embassy, and an official transcript or a certified and notarized copy of the diploma, validated, in the case of U.S. citizens, by the U.S. State Department. Police clearance reports and medical forms are among other requirements.

In order to qualify for a work permit, non-Saudis must meet the following conditions:

- They must have entered the country legally and satisfied the conditions and residence requirements;
- They must possess the vocational skills and educational requirements of which the country is in need; and
- They must be under contract to, and guaranteed by, either a Saudi employer or a non-Saudi employer authorized to conduct business in the Kingdom under the Regulations for the Investment of Foreign Capital.[218]

Work permits may be issued for employment by one employer only. A foreign employee may have a work permit transferred from one employer to another only if the worker has a college degree or technical certificate. The worker must receive the written approval of the original employer in the form of a "letter of no objection," without which the employee will be repatriated. If all these requirements are satisfied for the transfer, an additional corresponding employment block visa is not necessary.

---

[217]See discussion at IX.B., immediately below.

[218]SALR, ch. 3, §2, art. 49.

3. Family Visas

Family visit visas may be issued to the foreign worker's spouse and minor children. Entry visas will only be issued to the dependents of higher-skilled employees. In addition to visa applications and valid passports, passport-sized photos and a letter on company letterhead from a Saudi company sponsoring the applicant is required. If the family visit visa applicant is a wife visiting her husband, she must supply a copy of their marriage certificate. If the applicant is a child visiting a parent, a birth certificate is required.

4. Tourist Visas

Passengers on cruise liners visiting Jeddah on Port Calls are allowed to visit. Given the priority of developing tourism, tourist visa applications procedures are under review by the Supreme Commission on Tourism.

B. Employment of Foreigners

Non-Saudis are eligible for work permits, which must be obtained in conjunction with employment block visas,[219] only if they have special skills that will contribute to the country's economic growth and development.[220] They must be sponsored and their skills attested to by a Saudi company. Foreigners may not take jobs away from qualified Saudis. The Ministry of Labor and Social Affairs and the Ministry of the Interior will review the application and confirm the scarcity of such Saudis for the proposed position.[221]

Mindful of market realities, the Labor Regulations state that "within the limits dictated by the need to attract foreign workmen, an employer who employs foreign workmen may not pay them wages and remunerations in excess of what he pays Saudi workmen of equal competence, technical proficiency and academic qualifications."[222]

---

[219]See IX.A.2., above.
[220]*Id.*
[221]*Id.* art. 48.
[222]*Id.* ch. 4, §1, art. 80.

Noncompliance with the strict requirements and conditions for the employment of foreigners will subject the violator to fines of SR500 to 1,000.[223]

"Saudization" regulations have begun to establish reserved business sectors in the economy. Currently, all taxi drivers and any persons operating businesses selling gold or vegetables must be Saudi citizens, although it is uncertain when expatriates will be ultimately phased out. The Kingdom has recently expanded the lists of professions where jobs should be granted only to Saudi nationals as follows:

a) Ministerial Resolution of 21/4/1415 AH.
   1) Recruitment communities (department)
   2) Recruitment heads
   3) Receptionist
   4) Expediters (following up applications with governmental departments)
   5) Treasurers (cashiers)
   6) Security guard jobs

b) Ministerial Resolution No. 6733 dated 21/4/1423 A.H.
   1) Administrative manager
   2) Training manager
   3) Public relations jobs
   4) Clerical works
   5) Administrative assistant
   6) Purchases manager
   7) Purchases official
   8) Secretary
   9) Telephone operator
   10) Storekeeper
   11) Credits collector
   12) Customer's clearing officer (bookkeeper)
   13) Tellers
   14) Mailman
   15) Information recorder
   16) Librarian
   17) Bookseller

---

[223] *Id.* ch. 12, art. 196.

18) Ticket seller
19) Car dealers
20) Housing caretaker
21) Tourist guide
22) Delivery person

As always in the Kingdom, the extent to which these resolutions are being enforced is open to question.

The Ministry of Labor, Undersecretary for Work Affairs, in its *Guide of Professions Restricted to Saudi Arabians*, lists some 231 positions reserved to Saudis.

AUSTRALIA*

Introduction

A. Government

European settlement of Australia began on January 18, 1788, when a British fleet commanded by Captain Arthur Phillip established a penal colony in what is now Sydney. The British government's Australian Colonies Government Act of 1850 empowered the colonies to establish legislatures and frame constitutions. On January 1, 1901, the Constitution was approved by the Australian people, and the Commonwealth of Australia came into being. Today, Australia is a democratic nation with a population of more than 18 million.

Australia's government functions on a three-tier system of federal (Commonwealth), state, and local representation. The Australian Parliament and federal government are responsible for all matters of national interest. The governments of the six states[1] and their legislatures, and the Northern Territory (NT) and Australian Capital Territory (ACT), complement the functions of the federal government. The federal government retains exclusive power over defense, foreign affairs, trade and commerce, taxation, customs, pensions, immigration, and postal services. Other powers are shared

---

*Jordan W. Cowman, Partner, Akin Gump Strauss Hauer & Feld, Dallas, Texas; Kimberly F. Rich, Associate, Baker & McKenzie, Dallas, Texas; Ian M. Dixon, Partner, Baker & McKenzie, Melbourne, Australia; Tim Dixon, Consultant, Baker & McKenzie, Sydney, Australia.

[1]The six Australian states are New South Wales (NSW), Queensland (Qld), Western Australia (WA), Victoria (Vic), South Australia (SA), and Tasmania (Tas). There are 10 territories. The six states have a large measure of autonomy. The two main territories, the Northern Territory (NT) and the Australian Capital Territory (ACT), are more directly subject to Commonwealth lawmaking powers, but they do have their own legislative bodies. The other smaller island territories have their own administrators.

with the states, but federal law prevails where there is a conflict over concurrent powers.

The Australian government is based on a composite of Western democratic systems, including executive, legislative, and judicial branches. The legislative branch is based on the English Westminsterial system. Australia's House of Representatives (the lower house) is similar to the British House of Commons in that representatives are elected directly to represent defined areas (electorates) throughout Australia. The upper house, the Senate, is similar to the U.S. Senate, in that it is a "states house." Regardless of population, 12 senators are elected from each State, and two senators are elected in each of the two main territories, the NT and the ACT. There also is a symbolic reminder of the past British system. Legislation that passes both houses receives a formal "Royal Assent," which occurs when any new statute is signed by the Queen's representative, the Governor General federally, and the governor in each state.

The executive branch—the Ministry—consists of 28 members. The 15 most senior ministers are members of the Cabinet, with the Prime Minister as chair.

The judicial branch is based on the British common law tradition, with judges appointed for life. Although there is an underlying Australian Constitution, it does not have the same role or effect as the American Constitution, particularly insofar as the courts are concerned. The courts do not interpret a set of constitutional guarantees, but draw on the common law as codified, amended, or supplemented by statute.

The Australian Constitution provides that the judicial power of the Australian government is vested in the High Court of Australia and other courts created by the federal parliament. The High Court has concurrent federal and state jurisdiction and original jurisdiction in interpreting the Constitution and determining legal disputes between federal and state courts. The High Court also is the final court of appeal from federal and state courts. All six states, and the two main territories, have their own court systems. State courts are vested with federal jurisdiction in some matters.

B. Sources of Labor and Employment Law

1. Employment Contracts, Agreements, and Awards

In Australia, each state and the Commonwealth have different employment regulations and industrial tribunals. There also are two types of employees: "award" and "nonaward" employees.

As a general matter, the employee–employer relationship is governed by a contract for services (employment contract or agreement). Employment contracts, in turn, are affected by federal and state statutes and regulations, as well as the awards of industrial tribunals.[2] Statutes are the enactments of a parliament—federal or state. An award is an industrial agreement. It consists of a collection of employment-related rules or employment benefits as set forth by an industrial tribunal, usually in settlement of workplace disputes between employers and unions.[3]

An award typically would confirm a detailed set of minimum conditions, such as hours of work and minimum salary; employment categories, such as probationary, full-time, casual, and part-time; salary ranges; consultative mechanisms and dispute resolution procedures; hours of work and overtime arrangements; redundancy; training; termination and severance pay; rostering arrangements; and annual leave, public holidays, jury service, etc. For nonaward employees, these matters usually are set out in individual contracts of employment. Some minimum conditions are prescribed by legislation and apply to both award and nonaward employees, for example, annual leave and long-service leave. Where an employee's services are covered by an award, the provisions of the award prevail over the contract of employment, to the extent that the award provisions are more beneficial.

There are two types of industrial awards—state and federal—each created by the relevant industrial tribunals. State awards apply to all employers with employees in that state who do the type

---

[2]See the Introduction, at E., below.

[3]MACKEN, O'GRADY & SAPPIDEEN, THE LAW OF EMPLOYMENT 562–63 (4th ed. 1997).

of work covered by the particular award. For instance, most clerical employees are covered by state clerical awards. Federal awards apply only to the specific employers named as respondents to the award or belonging to an employer representative body named as a respondent to the award. The federal award provisions prevail if there is both federal and state award coverage in a particular area.

About 50 percent of all Australian workers are employed under awards made by the Australian Industrial Relations Commission (AIRC), the federal industrial tribunal.[4] Many other workers are employed under state awards. The remaining, nonaward, employees work under individually negotiated employment contracts.

The complex interplay[5] of Australian common law, statutes, and awards on the employment contract has been explained as follows:

> The significance of the common law can be recognized if contracts of employment are seen to be stratified. First there is a foundation strata [sic] being the common law. Superimposed on this are State Acts, regulations and State industrial determinations; in places such State law cuts through and replaces the common law foundational strata. Above this again are Commonwealth Acts, regulations and awards of the Arbitration Commission. Federal law cuts through state law in places, sometimes at the point where State law has already cut through common law, sometimes direct into common law.[6]

This complexity of jurisdictions and regulations caused the Australian government to pass new legislation, discussed immediately below, to simplify the award process, ensure the fairness of employment agreements, provide simplified court procedures for enforcing entitlements, and foster harmonization of federal and state handling of employment agreements.

With increasing frequency, industrial agreements determine the terms and conditions of employment. State and federal legislation permits registration of various forms of workplace agreements

---

[4]*Id.* at 22. See also the Introduction, at E., below.

[5]Due to the complexity of Australian labor and employment law, foreign labor and employment law practitioners are strongly encouraged to seek local Australian counsel or associate with an international law firm with offices in Australia.

[6]J.L. WEBB, INDUSTRIAL RELATIONS AND THE CONTRACT OF EMPLOYMENT 21 (1974).

including Australian Work Agreements (AWAs) and Certified Agreements (CAs).[7] Legislation also prescribes the role of trade unions in the bargaining process, union right of entry into the workplace, and the circumstances in which parties taking industrial action are protected from penalty. The Workplace Relations and Other Legislation Amendment Act 1996 has facilitated a greater range of options for bargaining at the workplace between employers and employees, with varying roles for unions.

2. *The Workplace Relations and Other Legislation Amendment Act 1996*

The Workplace Relations and Other Legislation Amendment Act 1996, amending the former Industrial Relations Act 1988, was passed by the Commonwealth Parliament on November 21, 1996, and received Royal Assent on November 25, 1996. Under the 1996 Amendments, the title of the former Industrial Relations Act was changed to the Workplace Relations Act 1996 (WR Act). The purpose of the WR Act is to provide a framework for cooperative workplace relations that promotes the economic prosperity and welfare of the Australian people. The WR Act is intended to open the way for employees and employers in Australian enterprises and workplaces to work together to make their workplaces more flexible, competitive, and fair to both employee and employers.

As amended, the WR Act focuses on the following objectives:

- giving primary responsibility for industrial relations and agreement-making to employers and employees at the enterprise and workplace levels, with the role of the award system focused on providing a safety net of fair and enforceable minimum wages and conditions;
- ensuring freedom of association;
- avoiding discrimination;
- assisting employees to balance their work and family responsibilities effectively; and

[7]For a discussion of AWAs, see I.B., below. For a discussion of CAs, see II.D., below.

- assisting in giving effect to Australia's obligations with respect to international labor standards.[8]

The government's stated goal in reforming Australia's labor laws was to establish a workplace relations system based on the following principles:

- a more direct relationship between employers and employees, with a reduced role for third-party intervention;
- a fair deal for all sides—so that the system is appropriately balanced and delivers benefits for both employees and employer;
- genuine freedom of association and a greater choice of union representation; and
- a more accessible system.[9]

Industrial relations have always been heavily influenced by the politics of the government of the day, both at federal and state levels. The WR Act is often amended over a government's tenure, ostensibly for industrial relations purposes, but clearly reflecting the underlying philosophy of the government or in turn the opposition when it becomes the government. The federal government in 2002 was the Liberal Government, usually viewed as being aligned with business and employers. The major opposition party, the Labour Party, has a clear historical and current close relationship and links with the trade union movement, with many of its parliamentary personnel (including past Prime Ministers) having had positions of office within the trade union movement.

During 2002, for example, at least 10 bills to amend the WR Act, on topics such as paid maternity leave, the prohibition of compulsory union fees, simplifying agreement making, and dealing with the transmission of business, were presented to Parliament. Depending on the government's parliamentary majority, many such bills may not become law. However, it is imperative, on any par-

[8]DEPARTMENT OF WORKPLACE RELATIONS, CHANGES IN FEDERAL WORKPLACE RELATIONS LAW—LEGISLATION GUIDE (Dec. 1996).

[9]COMMONWEALTH DEP'T OF EMPLOYMENT, WORKPLACE RELATIONS AND SMALL BUSINESS, WORKPLACE RELATIONS ACT USER GUIDES NO. 1, PRINCIPAL OBJECT OF THE ACT (Jan. 1998).

ticular issue, to ascertain whether there are any new legislative provisions that may be applicable.

Some of these bills became law during 2003, as set out below. Others, however, were rejected by the Parliament where the current conservative federal government does not have a majority. Nevertheless, they remain in the parliamentary process and further laws are put forward both with genuine intention to change working conditions but also for political purposes (such as forcing a double dissolution of Parliament). As before, it is necessary to ascertain the current legislative framework.

The Federal (conservative) Liberal Government was returned with a slightly increased majority in October 2004. It has indicated that Industrial Relations is a priority. Accordingly, much of the proposed legislation dealing with a wide range of topics that has been held up in the Upper House of Parliament may be represented with every chance of becoming law. It is likely these changes, if any, will only come into effect from mid-2005.

3. *International Laws*

Australia is a member of the International Labor Organization (ILO). Various governments, particularly Labor governments, pay more deference to ILO conventions[10] than other governments. Australia has ratified a number of conventions and has codified in the WR Act conventions concerning termination of employment, equal opportunities and equal treatment for men and women workers, and workers with family responsibilities (or paternity or maternity leave). Other legislation includes conventions relating to discrimination, including Convention 158 on termination and conventions on racial discrimination.

C. Harmonization of Federal and State Industrial Relations Systems

The WR Act seeks to harmonize the delivery of industrial relations services between the states and territories and the Com-

---

[10]For a discussion of ILO Conventions, see the chapter on the ILO in Volume I, Part 4.

monwealth. In the past, the delivery of efficient services was adversely affected by the interplay of jurisdictional issues, duplication, and overlap. Cooperation has been sought from the states in passing complementary legislation to enable all employers to utilize federal agreements (particularly AWAs).

Under the WR Act, parties to a federal award are able to enter into agreements also recognized under state legislation, provided that the state law under which the employment agreement is made specifies that the agreement must be approved by a state industrial authority. The agreement also must meet the following requirements:

- employees covered by the agreement must not be disadvantaged in comparison to their entitlement under the relevant award;
- the agreement must be genuinely made (i.e., the result of good-faith bargaining) or made in the absence of duress or coercion; and
- the agreement must cover all employees who reasonably could be covered.

In June 2003, the federal government sought to extend greater protection to Victorian workers. In the mid-1990s, the Victorian government had ceded its industrial relations power to the federal government, leaving behind only bare minimum conditions within the *Workplace Relations Act* Schedule 1A dealing with five basic terms and conditions. Those terms and conditions applied to all Victorian workers, but in many cases were overshadowed by federal award coverage. A significant number, however, effectively remained with the five basic conditions as their statutory minimum.

The federal government passed the Workplace Relations Amendment (Improved Protection for Victorian Workers) Act 2003 (WRAA). The WRAA increased the number of conditions such as an hourly rate beyond the standard 38-hour week and allowed for sick leave, carers' leave and bereavement leave, and provided for out-workers. Out-workers are individuals who work similar to independent contractors in the textile clothing or footwear industry under conditions that some allege are substandard and approach "sweated labour." The Act seeks to give minimum rates and some statutory protection.

In addition, the WRAA set out the statutory framework under which a relevant federal award already in existence could, through a process to be established, come into existence within Victoria as a "common rule." That is, it would apply to any business that came within its definitions and classifications so that it applied as a matter of law and provided a statutory minimum. The WRAA also set out a process that would be followed in applying for a common rule and the position of individual companies under that rule. This process would take place in the Australian Industrial Relations Commission. Complementary legislation, the Federal Awards (Uniform System) Act 2003, was passed by the Victorian government. The processes are being re-undertaken, but the application of common rule will not take place until January 1, 2005, to give the parties time to debate which award is relevant, what provisions should become common rules, and assess the consequences on the previously largely deregulated Victorian businesses and employees.

D. Major Administrative Bodies Under the WR Act

The major administrative bodies responsible for effectuating the goals of the WR Act are the federal AIRC[11] and the newly created Office of the Employment Advocate (EA). The EA is established as a distinct entity in the federal Department of Industrial Relations to facilitate the operation of AWAs between employers and employees. The EA is not an industrial tribunal, but it is similar to an employer and employee ombudsman. It is an independent statutory body designed to assist all parties, particularly with respect to AWAs and other specific powers granted under the WR Act. The broad functions of the EA are to:

- provide assistance and advice to employees and employers, especially small businesses, on the WR Act, AWAs, the "no-disadvantage test,"[12] and the freedom of association[13] provisions;
- approve AWAs, ensuring that they meet the "no-disadvantage" test and other statutory requirements; and

[11]See the Introduction, at E., below.
[12]See I.B., below.
[13]See II.A., below.

- handle alleged breaches of AWAs or the freedom of association provisions, and to assist employees in prosecuting breaches where appropriate.

The EA has the power to do the following:

- ascertain AWA observance through inspection activities (for example, entering premises, inspecting work machinery, interviewing employees, and requiring the production of documents) and to facilitate voluntary compliance where there have been breaches;
- assist an individual party to an AWA in seeking court intervention for the recovery of an outstanding entitlement, interests costs, and penalties against a party for breaching an AWA or the WR Act and its regulations; and
- assist claimants in using a quick, inexpensive, and simplified procedure to recover small claims of less than AUD 10,000 in magistrate's courts.

In all cases, using the services of the EA is a matter of choice, as a party is able to pursue matters in court independently, if preferred.

E. Dispute Resolution System

1. *Industrial Relations Tribunals*

The AIRC is the specific tribunal for labor disputes. Although the AIRC has powers of conciliation and arbitration and limited order-making powers, it does not exercise a judicial function under the Australian Constitution. Such judicial powers are expressly reserved for the courts. One of the states, Victoria, has ceded its industrial relations powers to the Commonwealth, but all other states and territories have their own industrial relations tribunals, known as commissions. Under the Constitution, the states have the right to vest these tribunals as courts. The awards they make, which are a comprehensive set of terms and conditions governing employment (for example, covering clerical and administrative occupations, or the hospitality, metal trades, racing, or other industries), have the force of law and apply to the occupation or industry named in the award.

State commissions typically utilize conciliation as a first approach and may move on to a degree of formality with hearings and then arbitration. Some labor disputes may go through this process and then move to the federal court or to any particular state (common law) supreme court, for example, to obtain common law injunctions to prevent industrial action or to sue for damages or for other remedies.

The AIRC is empowered under the Australian Constitution to only "prevent and settle industrial disputes." Disputes subject to AIRC jurisdiction must be interstate by nature. As a result, considerable technicality and symbolic effort goes to creating a real or "paper" dispute that extends beyond one state so as to attract the federal jurisdiction. The awards and CAs made by the AIRC can be enforced by the legal system. The power to prevent and settle interstate industrial disputes comes from one subsection of the Australian Constitution. More recently, the Australian government has endeavored to regulate industrial relations by reliance upon other subsections of the Constitution, which, for example, gives the government the right to regulate corporations. It is possible that the new Australian government may seek to impose an Australia-wide federal system dealing with unfair dismissals over the state jurisdictions in this manner.

The AIRC consists of a president, a number of deputy presidents, and commissioners who can be, but who are not required to be, lawyers; usually, they are men and women of experience and standing in the industrial relations area. They are assigned to various panels of industry.

Matters notified to the AIRC usually are heard by a single member of the commission in the first instance. There is an appeal right in certain circumstances to a full bench, which consists of three to five members of the commission, but leave to appeal first must be obtained by showing at least a demonstrable case, and that the matter is of such importance that it is in the public interest to allow the appeal.

The Australian Industrial Relations Commission (AIRC) may periodically undertake a "test case." These test cases are really matters of universal interest where the AIRC decides that a national common minimum should be established.[14] In such cases,

---

[14]For an example of such a "test case," see the discussion of the Termination Change & Redundancy case in 1984 at IV.A., below.

submissions are invited from interested parties. The ultimate ruling has no force of itself. However, following a decision the unions (and sometimes employers) often apply to amend the federal awards to which they are a party to include that provision. It does result in a long process to spread the result throughout the community throughout the thousands of awards, but the standards are generally applied for and granted without much debate, given that the issues have been reviewed in the test case. However, an individual company can take the opportunity to seek to oppose the application of the standard in the test case to its operation if there is good reason.

2. *New Role of the Australian Industrial Relations Commission*

The emphasis in the WR Act is on the parties taking responsibility for their own industrial relations outcomes. The AIRC merely facilitates the agreement-making functions of the parties by setting minimum standards in key areas. The AIRC also can arbitrate and render an award, but only as a last resort.[15] Furthermore, the jurisdiction of the AIRC to make an award in settlement of an industrial dispute is now statutorily limited to 20 "allowable award matters."[16] The allowable matters are as follows:

(a) classifications of employees and skill-based career paths;
(b) ordinary time hours of work and the times within which the work is performed,[17] rest breaks, notice periods, and variations in working hours;
(c) rates of pay generally (such as hourly rates and annual salaries), rates of pay for juniors, trainees, or apprentices, and rates of pay for employees under the supported wage system;
(d) piece rates, tallies, and bonuses;
(e) annual leave and leave loadings;[18]
(f) long-service leave;

---

[15]Workplace Relations Act 1996 (WR Act) §89.
[16]*Id.* §89A(2)(a)–(t).
[17]For a discussion of working hours, see V.B., below.
[18]For a discussion of leave loading, see V.A.4., below.

(g) personal/carer's leave, including sick leave, family leave, bereavement leave, compassionate leave, cultural leave, and other like forms leave;
(h) parental leave, including maternity and adoption leave;
(i) public holidays;
(j) allowances;
(k) loadings [premiums] for working overtime or for casual or shift work;
(l) penalty rates;
(m) redundancy pay;
(n) notice of termination;
(o) stand-down provisions;[19]
(p) dispute settling procedures;
(q) jury service;
(r) type of employment, such as full-time employment, casual employment, regular part-time employment, and shift work;
(s) superannuation;[20]
(t) pay and conditions for outworkers,[21] but only to the extent necessary to ensure that their overall pay and conditions of employment are fair and reasonable in comparison with the pay and conditions of employment specified in a relevant award or awards for employees who perform the same kind of work at an employer's business or commercial premises.

In addition, the WR Act provides that the AIRC may include in an award provisions incidental to the allowable matters and necessary for the effective operation of the award.[22]

The AIRC prescribes minimum pay rates and handles all manners of disputes involving pay and remuneration. However, the AIRC no longer is permitted to make awards that prescribe the actual rate of pay to be received by an employee. This restriction

---

[19]See V.A.5., below.

[20]See VIII.A., below.

[21]An "outworker" is defined as "an employee who, for the purposes of the business of the employer, performs work at private residential premises or at other premises that are not business or commercial premises of the employer." WR Act §89A(9).

[22]*Id.* §89A(6).

only precludes the AIRC from making awards or CAs that prescribe actual rates of pay.

The AIRC also reviews awards to ensure that provisions do not include matters of detail more appropriately dealt with by agreement at the workplace or enterprise level, or do not prescribe work practices or procedures that restrict efficiency or productivity.

3. *Federal Court of Australia*

See the discussions at I.C.5.c., II.A.4., and II.F., below.

I. INDIVIDUAL EMPLOYMENT

A. Individual Contract of Employment

At the most basic level, the relationship of employer and employee arises from a contract for services, which can be written or oral. Much of Australian employment law is based on the English common law of contracts. Under Australian law, an employment contract is no different than any other contract in that it is a legally binding promise to do (or refrain from doing) something in the future.[23] The common law holds that every simple contract must meet the following elements: (1) the parties must intend to enter into a contract; (2) there must be an offer by one party and acceptance by another; (3) the contract must be supported by valuable consideration; (4) the parties must be legally capable of entering into a contract; (5) there must be genuine consent to the contract terms; and (6) the contract cannot be for an illegal purpose.[24]

In addition to the fundamental requirements set forth in the common law, individual contracts are subject to minimum standards set forth in federal or state awards or statutes.

1. *Outsourcing and Co-employment*

There has been increasing outsourcing of some company functions as companies restructure to meet international competitive-

---

[23]MACKEN, O'GRADY & SAPPIDEEN, THE LAW OF EMPLOYMENT 71 (4th ed. 1997).
[24]*Id.* at 74.

ness and globalization. Allied with this trend is a growing use of temporary employment companies to provide labor when required during peak or seasonal times, or simply to supply skills when needed.

As part of this phenomenon, the first indications have appeared that Australian industrial tribunals and Australian courts may be moving toward an acceptance or development of a doctrine of "co-employer." The temporary employment companies are the subject of considerable union agitation unless they provide the labor on the same terms and conditions as the hiring company, whereas the hiring company seeks to reduce its labor costs by the provision of a more economical labor force. Arising out of this agitation is the question as to who is the actual employer and therefore properly a party to any awards or certified agreements sought by the unions to establish the terms and conditions of employment. During 2002, there has been the first indication of a doctrine or concept that there may be "joint venturers" as employers or "co-employers." The trend is only just beginning and is contrary to the conventional wisdom and acceptance of there being a single employer in most cases.

Part of this debate develops through continued leading cases seeking to determine the difference between an employee who has certain rights under the WR Act and an independent contractor who may have other rights. Recent cases, for example, include bicycle couriers and whether each courier is an independent contractor or an employee of the courier company.[25] Such differentiation is important, not only as to whether there are union or award and certified agreement obligations but also as to the question of whether there is vicarious liability on the part of an employer for the acts of the bicycle courier and, for example, as to the question of workers' compensation insurance.

To decide whether an individual is an employee or independent contractor, the standard test at common law—whether the company has "control" of not only *what* the worker does but *how* he or she does it—is at times under severe challenge or subject to rephrasing by the courts. The differentiation is not helped by legislation regarding matters such as workers' compensation and taxa-

[25] Hollis v. Vabu Pty. Ltd. (2001) 181 ALR 263.

tion laws, which may by legislation consider a person to be an employee or an independent contractor for the purposes of a particular law, causing some confusion concerning their status for purposes of other laws. The new Australian Government has indicated that legislation may be passed to endeavor to clarify the distinction.

The government moved to clarify circumstances regarding employees who can access the unfair dismissal claims in the federal jurisdiction. The Workplace Relations Amendment (Fair Termination) Act 2003 came into being largely as a response to the numerous cases arising in the unfair dismissal jurisdiction dealing with probationary and casual employees. The period of probation must be three months or less or, if it is more than three months, must be reasonable regarding the nature and circumstances of the employment.

A casual employee is someone who is engaged for a short period unless they are engaged by a particular employer on a regular and systematic basis for a sequence of periods of employment in excess of 12 months and there is a reasonable expectation of continuing employment. Other exemptions continue to apply. In all cases if the exemption was in some way being used to avoid the obligations of the legislation it would be struck down. The cut-off point for the federal jurisdiction was raised to $A90,400. Any employee not able to access the federal jurisdiction may have rights under various state jurisdictions, but they generally reflect the federal standard.

B. Australian Workplace Agreements

To provide more effective choice and flexibility for parties in reaching agreements, the WR Act now provides for AWAs. The AWA is intended to enable employers and employees at the workplace to take responsibility for their own industrial relations. AWAs are a new type of agreement that can be made between a corporate employer and individual employees or groups of employees.[26]

---

[26]AWAs are to be distinguished from Certified Agreements (CAs), which are made between employers and unions with certified majorities only. See discussion at II.D., below.

AWAs are intended to be negotiated individually and are signed individually by the employee and the employer. As a practical matter, AWAs are likely to be extremely similar, if not identical, in terms save perhaps job position, job description, job responsibilities, and remuneration arrangements. Employees may appoint a bargaining agent (including a union) to negotiate an AWA on their behalf, though there can be no unsolicited union involvement. If a collective, non-union agreement is negotiated, a majority voting procedure would be required, and the majority would rule.

AWAs must be in writing and must deal with matters pertaining to the employment relationship. AWAs have no legal effect until approved by the EA.[27] The EA must carefully scrutinize an AWA to ensure that it meets the "no disadvantage test," that is, that when considered as a whole, the agreement is no less favorable to the employee than any prior relevant award or applicable laws. If the EA is unable to determine whether the AWA meets the "no disadvantage" test, the AIRC resolves the question by determining whether the agreement violates public policy.

To approve an AWA, the EA also must be satisfied of the following:

- the agreement contains an antidiscrimination clause and a dispute resolution procedure;
- the agreement does not contain any clause that would prohibit one of the parties from disclosing the terms of the AWA to another person;
- the employer provided the employee(s) with a copy of the AWA 14 days prior to signing for existing employees, and 5 days prior to signing for new employees;
- the employer explained the effect of the agreement to the employee(s);
- the employee(s) genuinely consented to the making of the AWA; and
- where an employer enters into a AWA with another employee on different terms, the employer did not act unfairly in doing so.

[27] See the Introduction, at D., above.

AWAs still have legal effect as a common law contract of employment until they are approved by the EA. However, as common law contracts of employment, AWAs will not override a CA, nor will they override any state or federal award that otherwise might apply to the employer. Accordingly, the value of an AWA is realized only upon EA approval, which then removes the application of any CAs or state or federal awards.

Employees and employers have the right to take industrial action such as a strike or a lockout during the negotiation of an AWA. However, immunity from civil liability for industrial action during the bargaining period is conditioned on the initiating party giving three working days' notice to the other party. Strikes and lockouts are prohibited during the period in which an AWA is in operation.

AWAs may be terminated by the employer or employee in writing at any time. After the agreement has been in operation for a nominal period fixed in the agreement, an AWA continues in force unless replaced by a new agreement, terminated by the parties, or upon application, terminated by the AIRC.

C. Termination of Employment

1. Policy Considerations

Provisions governing termination of employment are contained in Division 3, Part VIA, of the WR Act. The main policy considerations behind the termination provisions are as follows:

- to provide employees access to a fair and simple process of appeal against dismissals, based on the principle of "a fair go all around," that is, a process fair to both employers and employees;
- to ensure that all unfair dismissal applications are dealt with in the first instance by conciliation conducted by the AIRC;
- to minimize legal costs;
- to discourage frivolous and malicious claims; and
- to ensure that the federal system is consistent with the states' unfair dismissal systems and with Australia's international

obligations under the ILO's Termination of Employment Convention 1982 (ILO Convention 158).[28]

2. *Exempt Employee*

The following types of employees are not covered by the termination provisions of the WR Act:

- an employee engaged under a contract of employment for a specified period of time or for a specific task;
- probationary employees;
- a casual employee engaged for 12 months or less;
- a trainee whose employment under a traineeship agreement or an approved apprenticeship is for a specified period; and
- a nonaward employee whose annual rate of remuneration is AUD 69,200 per year (the annual rate of remuneration is indexed each June).

3. *Types of Termination*

In keeping with ILO Convention 158, the WR Act defines termination of employment as termination at the initiative of the employer. The WR Act covers two types of termination: "harsh, unjust, or unreasonable" termination, known as "unfair dismissal," and "unlawful" termination.

a. *Harsh, Unjust, or Unreasonable Termination (Unfair Dismissal)*

Although the WR Act does not specifically define the phrase "harsh, unjust, or unreasonable termination," it does set forth certain factors for the AIRC to consider when addressing a claim falling under this category.[29] These factors are as follows:

---

[28]COMMONWEALTH DEP'T OF INDUS. RELATIONS, USER GUIDE NO. 8 TERMINATION OF EMPLOYMENT AND UNFAIR DISMISSAL (Jan. 1997). For a discussion of ILO Conventions, see the Introduction, at B.3., above, and the chapter on the ILO in Volume I, Part 4.

[29]For a discussion of AIRC dispute resolution procedures, see the Introduction, at E., above, and I.C.5., below.

- whether there was a valid reason for the termination that was related to the capacity or conduct of the employee or to the operational requirements of the employer;
- whether the employee was notified of the reason for termination;
- whether the employee was given an opportunity to respond to any reason related to his or her capacity or conduct;
- whether the employee was warned of any unsatisfactory performance before termination; or
- any other matters that the AIRC considers relevant.[30]

These factors demonstrate that with regard to allegations of "harsh, unjust, or unreasonable termination," the AIRC focuses upon procedural due process.

Only employees falling into the categories listed below are covered by the unfair dismissal provisions of the WR Act. All other employees are covered by state laws and tribunals. This scheme allows the individual states to pass complementary legislation and thereby protect their jurisdiction over certain unfair dismissal claims. Thus, as a general matter, "unfair dismissal" jurisdiction under the WR Act applies in the following circumstances:

- to the dismissal of an employee covered by a federal award or agreement who was employed by a constitutional corporation, or in relation to interstate or overseas trade or commerce, or as a waterside worker, maritime employee, or flight crew officer;
- when the relevant state has passed complementary legislation;
- to the dismissal of Commonwealth public sector employee;
- to the dismissal of an employee in a territory;[31] or
- to the dismissal of an employee in Victoria.

---

[30]WR Act §170.

[31]*Id.* §170CB(1).

b. Unlawful Termination

The WR Act provides several instances in which a termination will be considered "unlawful."[32] Statutorily proscribed reasons for termination include:

- temporary absence from work due to illness or injury;
- trade union membership or participation in lawful union activities;[33]
- nonmembership in a trade union;
- seeking office as, or acting in the capacity of, an employee representative;
- filing a complaint or participating in a proceeding against an employer involving alleged violation of labor laws or regulations;
- discrimination on the basis of race, color, sex, sexual preference, age, physical or mental disability, marital status, family responsibilities, pregnancy, religion, political opinion, national extraction, or social origin;[34] or
- absence from work during maternity leave or other parental leave.[35]

The following unlawful termination provisions apply to all employees nationally:

- the requirement of minimum notice of termination or pay in lieu of notice, except in cases of serious misconduct;[36]
- the prohibition against dismissal on discriminatory grounds; and
- the requirement to notify the Commonwealth Employment Service (CES) of the decision to terminate 15 or more employees on redundancy grounds.[37]

---

[32]*See, e.g., id.* §170CK (discrimination), §170MU (protected industrial action).

[33]See II.A., below, regarding an employee's right to join or refrain from joining a union.

[34]See VI., below.

[35]See V.C.4., below.

[36]See I.C.4., below.

[37]WR Act §170CB(3). See also IV.A., below.

4. *Notice*

The WR Act requires employers to give employees a minimum period of termination notice or pay in lieu of notice.[38] Although the minimum period of notice is for employees within the jurisdiction of the WR Act, it effectively applies to most employees nationally (as noted immediately above), subject to the monetary limit. The statutory period of minimum notice is as follows:

PERIOD OF SERVICE WITH THE EMPLOYER	PERIOD OF NOTICE
Not more than 1 year	At least 1 week
More than 1 year but not more than 3 years	At least 2 weeks
More than 3 years but not more than 5 years	At least 3 weeks
More than 5 years	At least 4 weeks

The period of notice is increased by one week if the employee is older than 45 years and has completed at least two years of continuous service with the employer.[39]

If no notice period is specified in the employment contract, the employee should be provided with reasonable notice or payment in lieu of such notice that is commensurate with the employee's length of service, age, and responsibilities. If the employer provides payment in lieu of notice, the amount of the payment must be at least equal to the amount that would have been paid to the employee had his or her employment continued during the notice period. Notice or payment in lieu thereof is not required in cases of serious misconduct such as stealing from the employer.[40]

5. *Dispute Resolution Procedures*

An aggrieved employee or a union (the applicant) may apply to the AIRC for relief with respect to a termination of employment if the termination was either harsh, unjust, or unreasonable or unlawful under the WR Act; if the employer failed to give notice of termination or payment in lieu thereof; or if the employer breached an order of the AIRC in relation to termination of employment.[41]

---

[38]WR Act §170CM.

[39]*Id.*

[40]*Id.* §170CM(7).

[41]*Id.* §170CE(3).

a. Conciliation

The AIRC attempts to settle all termination cases by conciliation.[42] Where the AIRC determines that conciliation has failed, it issues a written certificate stating the grounds on which conciliation failed and assessing the merits of the case. The AIRC also may suggest that the applicant elect not to pursue a particular ground or grounds.[43]

If conciliation fails, an applicant must make a decision whether to arbitrate, litigate, or dismiss the matter. If the AIRC's certificate indicates that conciliation was unsuccessful and involved an unjust dismissal, the applicant may elect to proceed to arbitration or may elect to discontinue the matter. If the AIRC's certificate indicates that conciliation was unsuccessful and involved unlawful discrimination, the applicant may begin proceedings in a regular court or may discontinue the matter. If the AIRC finds that conciliation was unsuccessful and involved mixed grounds, including both unlawful termination and unfair dismissal, the applicant must choose which claim he or she will pursue, after which jurisdiction lies with the appropriate body, as discussed above. This restriction on the choices available reflects the government's policy that an employee should not pursue an application in respect of unfair dismissal and unlawful termination simultaneously or one after the other.[44] Accordingly, the employee must make an election of remedies.

b. Arbitration

As noted above, in cases involving allegations of unfair dismissal, arbitration is available if a certificate has been issued by the AIRC and if the applicant has elected to pursue arbitration.[45] Arbitration before the AIRC is binding on the parties. The AIRC may make orders for remedies including reinstatement or payment in lieu of reinstatement. The maximum amount of payment in lieu of reinstatement is the total remuneration received by the employee in the six-month period before termination; for a nonaward em-

[42] *Id.* §170CF(1).
[43] *Id.* §170CF(2).
[44] *Id.* §170HB (dual application relating to a single dismissal is not allowed).
[45] *Id.* §170CG(1).

ployee,[46] the payment may not exceed a pre-set, indexed monetary amount. For example, in July 1999, the amount was AUD 34,600. The amount usually is equivalent to one-half the jurisdictional limit, which currently is set at an annual salary of AUD 69,200.[47]

Cases for unfair dismissal are heard by individual commissioners. AIRC orders are appealable, with leave, before the full bench of the AIRC, which usually is made up of one or two deputy presidents plus another commissioner.[48] The AIRC also may make an order for costs against a person or organization when it is satisfied of the following:

- the application was made vexatiously or without reasonable cause;
- a party to an arbitration proceeding has acted unreasonably in failing to discontinue a matter or to agree to terms of settlement that could lead to the discontinuance of the matter; or
- a person or organization discontinues the matter but the AIRC determines the matter could have been discontinued sooner.[49]

The AIRC also may make orders of general application for the payment of severance pay or other separation allowances and for consultations with employees in redundancy situations involving 15 or more employees,[50] but only where there is no alternative mechanism giving effect to the relevant provisions of ILO Convention 158.[51]

c. Court Intervention

Application to a court may be made only if the applicant has received a certificate from the AIRC. An applicant may apply to the federal court for an order in respect to the following situations:

---

[46]See the Introduction, at B., above, regarding award and nonaward employees.
[47]WR Act §§170CH(8), (9).
[48]*Id.* §170CI. See also the Introduction, at E.1., above.
[49]WR Act §170CJ(3).
[50]Redundancy is discussed at IV.A., below.
[51]See the Introduction, at B.3. and I.C.1., above.

- an unlawful termination;
- a termination based on an employer's failure to notify the CES of the redundancy of 15 or more employees;[52] or
- an employer's breach of an AIRC order.[53]

An applicant also may apply to the federal court or to a court of competent jurisdiction (such as, a district, county, local, or magistrate's court) in case of an employer's failure to give notice of termination or pay in lieu of notice.[54] The courts may issue orders including reinstatement, compensation, and penalties as set forth in the WR Act.[55]

D. Privacy

Like many other countries, the legal obligations relating to employee privacy have grown more complex in Australia during recent years. In 2001, the Federal Privacy Act 1988 (Privacy Act) was extended to cover business, and while it purports to exempt records on employees from its coverage, in reality the law has complex effects on how employers manage personal information about their staff. In addition, several states have passed laws regulating specific workplace privacy practices, such as the use of video surveillance and the handling of health information relating to employees.

Workplace privacy issues often highlight tensions between the interests of employees and employers. Employers have an interest in protecting their property, maximizing the productivity of employees, minimizing exposure to liability, and detecting fraud and misconduct. This creates a general pressure to collect information about the work patterns of employees. At the same time, employees have an interest in maintaining a sense of autonomy and freedom in the workplace. As a result, debate about workplace privacy issues often centers on the loss of dignity and privacy caused by extensive employee surveillance.

---

[52] See IV.A.1., below.
[53] WR Act §17CP(1).
[54] *Id.* §17CP(2).
[55] *Id.* §17CP(4).

In Australia, several laws regulate surveillance of employees directly or indirectly and influence the way that information collected through surveillance practices is handled. Additional changes to laws relating to workplace privacy also can be expected in coming years. A study of privacy law by the Victorian Law Reform Commission recently recommended that laws relating to workplace surveillance be extended, and the New South Wales state government has also indicated its intention to provide greater protections for employees from workplace surveillance.

1. Employee Data

Privacy laws in Australia have only limited application to employees in the private sector. The amended Privacy Act provides a limited exemption for the handling of employee information by private sector employers. At the time it amended the Act, the government's stated policy was to leave the regulation of workplace privacy to the employment relations legal framework.

In addition, at the time of the passage of the Privacy Amendment (Private Sector) Act in December 2000, the government announced that the Attorney-General's Department and the Department of Employment, Workplace Relations and Small Business would conduct a review of the extent of privacy protection for employee records under existing commonwealth, state and territory laws to determine whether there was a need for further regulation. The employment records review was completed and a Discussion Paper released in February 2004 asking for comment by April 2004. Since that time there has been little movement because the review is a part of the general review of the operation of the Act. The Privacy Commissioner is to deliver her report of the overall review to the Attorney-General by May 31, 2005.

The industrial relations system provides little protection for the collection or use of employee information. Specifically, Section 353A of the Workplace Relations Act allows the government to make regulations relating to employee records. The regulations under this provision mainly require employers to maintain records about the conditions under which an employee is hired and information concerning their working hours. Regulation 131L(1) also provides that an employer must make a copy of a record available on request to the employee or former employee to whom the record relates. Failure to do so can result in a fine of up to AUD 1,000. Regulation 131M provides that an employer must inform the employee of the location of the record the employee is requesting and make the record available within a maximum of 14 days after the request.[56]

Employee records are given a limited exemption from coverage under the Privacy Act. This exemption effectively allows employers to use information concerning their employees for appropriate internal purposes. Three requirements need to be satisfied for the exemption to apply:

1. the organization is acting in its capacity as a current or former employer of an individual;
2. the use of employee information is directly related to a current or former employment relationship between the employer organization and the individual; and
3. the use of employee information is directly related to an employee record held by the employer organization and relating to the individual.

These requirements are discussed individually below, followed by a discussion of what happens when the exemption does not apply.

a. Existence of an Employment Relationship

For the exemption to apply, the individual and the organization must be or have been in an employment relationship. The Privacy Act does not define the scope of "employment," but it appears that this exemption does not extend to contractors and subcontractors. Future or prospective employment relationships also do not fall within the exemption, which means that prospective employers and recruitment agencies must comply with the Act. The exclusion of both recruitment processes and contractors is an important limitation on the employee records exemption, which will have the practical effect of requiring human resources professionals to implement privacy principles in at least some areas of their responsibilities.

---

[56] *Id.* §353A, Reg. 131L(3).

b. Direct Relationship Between the Employment Relationship and Employee Record

The use of employee information must be *directly* related to the employment relationship and also must be directly related to employee records held by the employer. This is intended to prevent employers from using employee records for commercial purposes unrelated to the employment relationship or exploiting the employee records exemption for commercial purposes. For example, the sale of personal information from employee records by an employer to a direct marketer would not be within the exemption. However, it is unclear how "direct" the relationship must be. It is likely that the exemption would not extend to information that is not directly related to a person's employment, such as personal e-mail sent using the employer's equipment from an e-mail address supplied by the employer.

c. Protection After Employer Discloses an Employee Record to Another Organization

This exemption only applies to employee records held by the employer and does not continue if the employee records are disclosed by the employer to another organization. For example, if records containing personal information about an employee are disclosed to the employer's insurer for the purposes of workers' compensation, then those records do not retain their exempt status in the hands of the insurance company. That is, in the hands of the insurance company, the personal information is subject to the coverage of the Privacy Act.

d. Effect of Privacy Act Coverage

To the extent that employment data does come within the coverage of the Privacy Act, the National Privacy Principles apply minimum standards for handling personal information. The main features of the Principles are:

- *Collection of personal information*: Collection must be necessary for an organization's activities; information must be collected lawfully and fairly, and must be collected with the individual's awareness.

- *Use and disclosure of personal information*: Information can only be used or disclosed for its original purpose unless the person has consented to its use or disclosure for another purpose. Exemptions apply in situations such as when there are issues of law enforcement, public safety, or protecting the company from fraud.
- *Accuracy of personal information*: Organizations must take reasonable steps to ensure that they keep personal information accurate, complete, and up to date.
- *Security of personal information*: Organizations must take reasonable steps to protect the personal information that they hold from misuse, loss, unauthorized access, modification, or disclosure.
- *Openness in relation to the organization's practices*: Organizations that collect personal information must be able to document their practices and must make this information available on request.
- *Access and correction rights*: Organizations must give individuals access to their personal information and must allow them to correct it or explain something with which they disagree, unless disclosing this would have an unreasonable impact on someone else's privacy. This principle is subject to exemptions, such as if this disclosure would compromise a fraud investigation.
- *Use of government identifiers*: Organizations cannot use a government agency's identification number as its main method of identifying an individual on its database.
- *Restrictions on transborder data flows*: Organizations can only transfer personal information about an individual to a foreign country if the individual consents or they believe that the information will be protected by a law or a contract in that foreign country that upholds similar privacy principles.
- *Special provisions for sensitive personal information*: A higher level of privacy protection applies to sensitive personal information, which includes information about a person's health, political or religious beliefs or affiliation, and sexual preference. This information must only be collected with the individual's consent.

The Privacy Commissioner has released a set of guidelines on the National Privacy Principles, which form the basis of the Privacy Act, spelling out some of the factors taken into account in the interpretation of the principles.

2. *Criminal Record Information*

Criminal record checks are a common means of obtaining background information to identify any major risks in hiring or promoting an employee. However, such checks are subject to laws that regulate the manner in which old criminal record information can be used in the context of employment decisions.

The use and disclosure of certain criminal records of employees is regulated by "spent convictions" legislation in a number of jurisdictions, which disallow consideration of old transgressions. Spent convictions are convictions that have not occurred within a recent time period (such as five or ten years) and did not involve a lengthy prison sentence. Different spent convictions systems operate at a commonwealth and state level.

3. *Tax File Numbers*

Special provisions govern the handling of individuals' personal Tax File Numbers in Australia, a reflection of concerns at the time of the Tax File Number's introduction that it should not be permitted to become a national identification number in the way that the Social Security Number has in the United States. Section 18 of the Privacy Act obliges recipients of information about others' Tax File Numbers not to perform acts that breach guidelines issued by the Commissioner. Affected individuals may complain to the Privacy Commissioner. Where appropriate, the individual may seek compensation. Unauthorized use or disclosure of Tax File Numbers is also an offense under the Taxation Administration Act 1953, subject to a fine of up to AUD 10,000, two years imprisonment, or both.

4. *Employee Use of E-mail and the Internet*

As a general principle, employers can view all employee movements on the work e-mail system (including e-mail addresses to which messages are sent, web sites visited, times of access, and transmissions) and gain access to the content of e-mails (even if deleted). An employer does not have to seek the *consent* of its employees to be able to monitor and access such communications and transactions, because the employer's computers and computer systems are recognized as their property over which they can consequently exert control. However, employers are strongly advised to *notify* individuals of their monitoring of e-mail and Internet usage. This is particularly important for those individuals who are not classified as employees (and who therefore are not within the limited employee records exemption in the Privacy Act), but it also applies to employees' non-work related e-mail communications from the workplace, since it is generally understood that the Privacy Act covers this area of employee records.

A workplace computer usage policy plays an important role in clearly setting out to employees the appropriate limits on the usage of personal computers in the workplace. It establishes the boundaries between personal usage and work usage, in relation to both access to the Internet and use of e-mail. In a general sense, a policy also can establish constraints on the monitoring of employees, by establishing a clear policy on the circumstances in which surveillance may occur and the way in which information gathered from surveillance will be used. By setting this out clearly in the policy, employers can avoid potential disputes and the weakening of the trust relationship with employees that may occur if surveillance is conducted without appropriate notification being given to employees. For the purposes of the privacy legislation, requiring employees to sign an agreement to a computer usage policy may satisfy the requirement to notify individuals of the collection of their personal information and to explain how it will be used.

A clearly communicated workplace computer usage policy is also critical if an employer in the future wishes to take disciplinary action against employees for the breach of that policy. The clarity of that policy, and the extent to which it has been communicated to employees and implemented fairly, will be significant factors in whether a company can lawfully terminate an employee for breach of its computer usage policy. Evidence gathered from surveillance of e-mail and Internet usage is more likely to be accepted in an unfair dismissal case if the employer can show that employees had been made aware of the company's policy of monitoring computer usage. Misuse then will constitute a clear breach of a company policy.

5. *Other Surveillance of Employees*

A growing range of technologies is being utilized at low cost in workplaces as means of monitoring employee conduct and protecting the interests of employers. These surveillance technologies include video surveillance, telephone monitoring, location monitoring, access cards, and keystroke monitoring.

Some state laws restrict the use of technologies that monitor employees in the workplace, including technologies that record phone calls and video surveillance equipment. In most instances, the requirements of these laws are that employees must be clearly informed of the fact that surveillance is conducted and of the purposes for which information obtained through surveillance will be used. Certain types of surveillance are, in some instances, prohibited altogether if they involve particular privacy sensitivities. For example, in New South Wales video surveillance of employees is subject to the Workplace Video Surveillance Act 1998 (NSW). The Act establishes specific conditions that must be met for covert surveillance to be conducted legally, including obtaining a warrant from a magistrate. Section 4(1) of this Act specifies that video surveillance is covert unless:

- the employees are advised in writing of the surveillance at least 14 days before the surveillance;
- the cameras are visible; and
- there are signs at the entrance of the workplace which inform employees that there are video cameras in operation.

Video surveillance will not be covert if an employee has agreed to surveillance for purposes other than surveillance of employee activities.[57]

Victoria also has specific legislation relating to the use of surveillance devices, although it is not specific to video surveillance.

---

[57]Workplace Video Surveillance Act §4(2).

In general, both the Telecommunications (Interception) Act 1979 (Cth) (the TIA) and legislation relating to listening devices in most states prohibit listening to or recording a communication or conversation without the consent or knowledge of both parties to the communication or conversation. The TIA applies in circumstances where a communication is in passage over a telecommunications system. When a communication has ceased passage over a telecommunications system, listening or recording of that communication is not an "interception" under the TIA, and the state listening devices regime applies.

E. Employee Duty of Loyalty, Trade Secrets, Covenants Not to Compete

1. *Employee Duty of Loyalty*

At common law in Australia an employee has a general duty of good faith and loyalty to the employer. Specific behaviors such as theft, working for a competitor, misuse of trade secrets, etc., give rise to the relevant causes of action. However, this general duty underpins those particular instances. There is usually an expression of that duty in a contract of employment, often aimed at covering an employee to ensure he does not undertake any activity or make any statements or behave in a way that causes prejudice or damage to the employing company.

While it is not a major factor in Australia at the moment, there also is growing evidence of a similar duty (or at least claims that such a duty exists) owed by the company to its employees—that is, to act in good faith and in their interests. However, this has not been the subject of widespread litigation.

2. *Trade Secrets*

There is in Australian common law a general obligation to maintain confidentiality which includes trade secrets but which may go beyond that description. The general duty at law of an employee is often reinforced with specific provisions within a contract, particularly defining what is regarded as "confidential information."

In court the usual difficulty is proving first that the information was confidential or is a trade secret and second that it is being used. As a general rule there is a fine line between enforcing the protection of trade secrets and other confidential information and prohibiting (which is not allowed) an ex-employee from using general knowledge and information that he has acquired in the course of his employment history with the first employer.

If this general knowledge of information includes what clearly is a trade secret or a protected process or confidential information which ought to be protected, then it will still be protected. However, if an employee has not gone out of his way to make photocopies of client lists, pricing policies, design processes, financial information, etc., but is simply an astute and experienced person in the field, it becomes more difficult to prove a breach of confidentiality or misuse of trade secrets.

3. *Covenants Not to Compete*

Covenants not to compete usually have been written into an employee's contract if the employee's work is regarded as significant or particularly confidential or if the employee is in a position to cause "trade harm" to the company if he or she were to work for a competitor. There are a number of difficulties, however, with enforcement of such covenants. The common law in Australia generally supports freedom of trade and the courts traditionally have taken a critical approach to such provisions. Fundamentally, the covenants have to be "reasonable" in all the circumstances.

Covenants should be clearly demonstrable as being for the protection of the business of the existing employer rather than there being any suggestion that they are a penalty or a prejudice against the departing employee. They are not a general part of the common law but are contractual, and accordingly the written provisions will be carefully analyzed to see if they are sufficiently certain and capable of comprehension and enforcement. They will be tested to see if they are too wide geographically or across industry, or for too long a period. They will not be enforced if they completely prohibit an employee from earning a living (unless there has been some form of major payment or other benefit which would support the period of inactivity).

Such covenants were once written in a cascading form; for example a restraint for three years, two years, or one year, either around the world, the Asia Pacific, or in Australia or an Australian state, with a view that a court would at any hearing rule out those provisions that were inappropriate and unreasonable and ultimately leave the necessary restrictions in place. This has fallen out of favor with the courts.

The most effective restraint is carefully focused, for example, on particular clients of the existing employer, or a particular market, or product. It is necessary to demonstrate that the restraint was understood by the employee at the time of entering the contract of employment and clearly relates to potential prejudice to the existing employer's business. If reasonable and properly constructed, the covenant or restraint can be supported by injunction or the seeking of damages for harm to the existing employer's business.

II. COLLECTIVE BARGAINING

An industrial organization (union) is defined as an association registered or recognized under an industrial law. The WR Act has radically changed the manner in which unions become registered and attract new members, the circumstances under which unions may enter the workplace, and the circumstances for dissolution. The new federal scheme addresses the main issues facing unions and employers and attempts to strike a fair balance between the parties.

Under the WR Act, rather than amalgamating into super unions, as happened during the 1980s, the unions are able, if they go through the appropriate process, to disamalgamate if it is in the interests of the union divisions or previously amalgamated unions and their members. Not many unions have done this, however.

There is recognition in the WR Act that collective bargaining is the intended mainstream for any agreement in the workplace.[58] There are two forms of collective bargaining, one with the unions on behalf of its members and employees and the other with the employees directly. In addition, there is the third stream of direct employer/employee agreement, the Australian Workplace Agreement.

---

[58]See the discussion in the Introduction, at B.2., above.

Additionally, provisions were introduced to set up a fair and reasonable way in which unions could have a guaranteed right of access to speak to their members or discuss various issues while not causing difficulty or interfering with the business. The WR Act also made it easier to register new unions and encouraged "enterprise-based unions" rather than unions that exist across a particular industry. Further, protection from discrimination against individuals based on union or non-union membership was enhanced. Overall, agreement-making at the workplace became a major underlying part of Australia's workplace relations.

For some time concern had been expressed regarding the collective bargaining tactics of the unions involved in the building and construction industry. There were allegations that the unions had enforced the "no union ticket—no start" behavior. The federal government had established a Royal Commission under Mr. Justice Cole and it released its findings in 2003. In summary, the commission found considerable behavior and conduct that it regarded as unlawful or inappropriate and recommended the creation of a national task force, the Australian Building and Construction Commission, to monitor conduct in the industry, allow free and equal collective bargaining, and prosecute unlawful industrial action and breaches of freedom of association laws. An Interim Building Force (IBF) was set up to investigate and refer for prosecution any alleged breaches of commonwealth industrial, civil, and criminal laws on building and construction sites. A small number of prosecutions were launched against union officials and some action also was taken against employers. Although it provides an avenue of investigation and potential redress, the IBF's success at the outset is only limited and time will tell whether it can alleviate coercion and intimidation in this industry.

As a further step by the federal government to legislate in the collective bargaining area, it passed the Union (Workplace Relations Amendment (Prohibition of Compulsory Union Fees)) Act 2003 to ban provisions from being included in certified agreements that required employers to deduct "bargaining agents' fees" from the pay of non-union members. That is not to say that an employee cannot appoint a bargaining agent or that the union cannot be appointed a bargaining agent, but it is simply to avoid the "compulsory" payment of such fees by a non-union member through deduction from the employee's wages by an employer on the basis, as the unions argue, that that employee receives the benefit of the higher wages and conditions negotiated by the union. That union argument has not found sufficient favor to be allowed as yet.

A. Freedom of Association and Organization

The freedom of association provisions of the WR Act give effect to the principles that employers, employees, and independent contractors have the right to choose whether or not to join an employee or employer association or union, and that discrimination on the basis of membership or nonmembership in a union is unlawful.[59] The freedom of association provisions in the WR Act have the following features:

- application beyond the usual boundaries of federal industrial jurisdiction;
- abolition of preference in employment based on union or non-union membership and compulsory union membership; and
- prohibition of victimization or discrimination on the grounds of a person's membership or nonmembership in a union,[60] or the exercise of a person's rights under industrial laws.[61]

1. Federal Jurisdiction

Usually federal industrial jurisdiction is founded on Section 51, subparagraph 35, of the Constitution, which gives the federal government power to "prevent and settle industrial disputes" of an interstate nature. Otherwise the matter is one for state law. However, the freedom of association provisions in the WR Act rely on a separate subparagraph of Section 51 that enables the federal government to deal with corporations or companies. Accordingly, the freedom of association provisions apply to conduct by a constitutional corporation or conduct that adversely affects a constitutional corporation.

---

[59] WR Act pt. XA.
[60] *Id.* §298A(a).
[61] *Id.* §298A(b).

2. *Abolition of Employment Preference*

The employment preference abolished by the WR Act normally applies to a union's demand that the employer give hiring preference to union members. However, in fairness, the statute abolishes any preference between union or non-union applicants; that is, union membership or nonmembership are prohibited reasons on which to base an offer of work (which should be based on an applicant's capabilities, experience, skills, competencies, etc.).

3. *Antidiscrimination Provisions*

a. *Prohibited Employer Conduct*

Under the WR Act, an employer may not dismiss, retaliate, refuse to employ, or discriminate in the terms and conditions of an employee's employment or an independent contractor's contract because the employee or independent contractor falls within any of the following categories:

- is, or is not, a member of an industrial organization (union), or proposes or does not propose to become a member;
- is, or proposes to become, an officer or delegate of an industrial association;
- has refused or failed to join in industrial action (i.e., a strike, boycott, walkout, etc.);
- has refused to vote on or agree to the making of an agreement to which the employee-member's industrial association would be a party;
- has made, or proposes to make, application to an industrial body for a secret ballot to be held under an industrial law;
- has made, or proposes to make, an inquiry or complaint to a body under an industrial law to seek compliance with that law;
- seeks to better industrial conditions;
- has been absent from work without leave to carry out duties as an officer of an industrial association, and leave was unreasonably refused; or

- as a member of an industrial association, has attempted to promote or protect the industrial interests of the association.[62]

Termination for any of the above reasons is considered an unlawful termination.[63]

b. Prohibited Union Conduct

A federally registered industrial organization, or an officer or member of a federally registered organization, must not engage in any of the following acts:

- take, or threaten to take, industrial action against an employer because the employer is a member of an industrial association;[64]
- take, or threaten to take, action against an employee or a person in order to coerce that employee or person to become a member of an industrial association;[65]
- advise, encourage, or incite an employer, or organize an industrial action, in order to coerce the employer to take action in relation to a person that would amount to unlawful conduct under the WR Act;[66] or
- coerce an employer to prejudice a member of the organization in his or her employment because the member refused or failed to comply with a direction given by the organization.[67]

The prohibitions against unlawful union conduct in the WR Act apply if the employer is a corporation or if the conduct occurs

[62] *Id.* §298L(1).
[63] See I.C.3.b., above.
[64] WR Act §298P(1).
[65] *Id.* §298P(2).
[66] *Id.* §298P(3).
[67] *Id.* §298P(4).

in a territory. The prohibited conduct provisions also apply to the conduct of any union or industrial association (whether federally registered or not) if the reason for the conduct is that the employer is not a member of a federally registered industrial association Although unions may be considered industrial associations, the industrial association referred to in these provisions is an employer association such as the Metal Trade Industry Association, the Master Builders Association, or the Civil Contractors Federation. Thus, the restrictions are intended to prevent a union from taking action because the employer belongs to an employer association.

4. Federal Court Remedies

Issues regarding the freedom of association provisions may be the subject of conciliation proceedings before the AIRC. However, given the structure of the WR Act, it is likely that after discussions between the parties, formally or informally, action will be taken in federal court. The federal court may issue orders to remedy breaches of the freedom of association provisions, including the following:

- assessing a penalty of not more than AUD 10,000 in case of a corporation, or AUD 2,000 in any other case;
- ordering the reinstatement of an employee or the reengagement of an independent contractor;
- ordering the payment of compensation;
- ordering a person or an industrial association not to carry out a threat or not to make any further threat;
- issuing interim and permanent injunctions or any other order to stop the conduct or remedy its effects; or
- issuing any other consequential orders.[68]

When a complaint alleges that the conduct or threat was motivated by a "prohibited reason," the respondent has the burden to prove, on balance of probabilities, that the conduct was not carried out for a prohibited reason. However, the complainant bears the burden of proof on all other matters.

[68]*Id.* §298U.

B. Australian Workplace Agreements

As discussed above,[69] the WR Act introduced a new kind of agreement, the AWA. Because AWAs are individual agreements, politically and philosophically, they are treated by the union movement as being directly opposed to collective agreements. For this reason, an attempt to introduce AWAs often can meet with considerable resistance from the unions.

C. Awards

As discussed above, many of Australia's workers are covered by federal or state industrial awards.[70] An award usually is negotiated collectively, that is, by a union acting on behalf of a large number of member-employees. An award can have one or two union parties and usually applies to a large number of employers within a particular industry. A union, for example, the Transport Workers Union, may be respondent to a wide range of awards covering a number of different industries. Alternatively, a union may be respondent or party to only a limited number of awards, depending on the nature of the organization and its membership.

D. Certified Agreements

The CA also is a form of collective agreement. A CA is negotiated between a single employer and one or more unions that have members in the employer's workforce. The CA is intended to be enterprise-specific and to give greater efficiency and flexibility than multiemployer or industrywide awards. Pursuant to the WR Act, CAs require the approval of a "valid majority" of the employees covered by the agreement.

Where multiple unions negotiate with the employer, they can form single bargaining units or can negotiate directly with the employer who then must assess conflicting or "leap-frogging" demands. Usually, the unions present a reasonably common front

---

[69]See I.B., above.

[70]See the Introduction, at B.1., above.

but watch the progress of other unions in the negotiation. The resulting CA will then cover the employer and all unions participating in the negotiations. In most cases, the conditions negotiated by each union will be similar, or there may be specific benefits or conditions that relate to only one union.

A CA does not have effect until certified by the AIRC. The AIRC must certify the agreement if it is satisfied that the agreement passes the "no disadvantage test."[71] The AIRC may certify a CA even if it does not pass the "no disadvantage" test if the agreement is not contrary to public policy and if the following conditions are satisfied:

- the CA has the genuine approval of a valid majority of the employees;
- the employees have been given an explanation of the terms of the agreement, having regard to the employees' particular circumstances and needs;
- the agreement contains dispute resolution procedures in relation to matters in the agreement;
- the employer has not coerced its employees into not having their union represent them in negotiations; and
- the agreement has a nominal expiration date of no more than three years after the agreement comes into operation.

The AIRC must refuse to certify a CA unless it is satisfied that the agreement will settle, further settle, or maintain a settlement of an industrial dispute, or that it will prevent further industrial disputes, or prevent an industrial situation from giving rise to an industrial dispute. The AIRC also must refuse to certify a CA if the agreement discriminates against employees on the basis of union membership, or on the basis of race, color, sex, sexual preference, age, physical or mental disability, marital status, family responsibilities, pregnancy, religion, political opinion, national extraction, or social origin.

Any variations to a CA generally must be approved by a valid majority of employees. The AIRC also may vary a CA for the purpose of removing an ambiguity or uncertainty or for the pur-

---

[71]See I.B., above.

pose of including, omitting, or varying a term that authorizes an employer to "stand down" an employee.[72]

A CA ceases to be in operation after its nominal expiration date if it is replaced by another CA or on application by a party, or if the AIRC considers that it is not contrary to the public interest to permit cessation.

The CA can be negotiated directly with the majority of the employees under Section 170LK of the WR Act or with a union or unions under Section 170LJ of the WR Act. Both methods of obtaining a CA follow the same procedure in dissemination of information, voting procedure, registration with the AIRC, and certification after passing the "no disadvantage" test against an underpinning award.

Tactically, if it has not been possible to reach a CA with a union involved in the workplace under Section 170LJ, employers then attempt to have the agreement approved directly by a majority of the employees in the workplace under Section 170LK, since it will then bind all employees. Even if the attempt to have the Section 170LK agreement approved fails, the attempt is often useful to employers in looking for more successful negotiations with the unions, since the unions in a Section 170LK proceeding run the risk of being put to one side in the agreement-making process and having a CA made without their involvement.

E. Strikes and Industrial Actions

During the collective bargaining period, certain industrial actions such as strikes or lockouts are permitted without penalty so long as the requisite statutory notice is given.

For decades, industrial action was often taken at any time and without notice or the necessity for any voting or other procedure. Often matters would be referred to the AIRC only after action had been taken. The strike or stoppages could affect a particular employer or be industrywide, and involve only one union or all of the unions. They could be for any length of time, for example, either continuously or on a stop and start basis.

---

[72]For an explanation of stand-downs, see V.A.5., below.

An employer's only remedy was usually to contact the AIRC to attempt conciliation/arbitration. However, the AIRC, while it has arbitral power, has no judicial power to make an enforceable award. That power resided in the common law courts of the states and the Federal Court of Australia. If the industrial action was causing sufficient damage, reference was occasionally used to the old economic torts of "interference with trade" or "interference with contract" as a means of seeking an injunction to prevent the action from continuing and/or to recover damages lost due to the action. These proceedings rarely, if ever, were pressed to the recovery of damages stage.

During the 1990s, the WR Act moved toward the American collective bargaining approach. Industrial action is largely but not entirely prohibited during the life of a collective agreement certified by the Commission. The exception may be over issues not already covered by the agreement.

At the conclusion of the CA, a Bargaining Notice can be delivered by either side. Within the bargaining period established by the Bargaining Notice, a Notice of Intent to Take Industrial Action can be given by the union or by the employer. The Notice gives three days' warning of the industrial action and sets out the type of action that will be taken, such as continuous stoppage, a stop and start stoppage, partial refusal to work as directed, or other form. The employer is essentially limited to a lockout of its employees, which has little appeal due to the severe economic consequences. The common law right not to pay a person who refuses to work as directed is preserved, which means the employers often take striking employees off the payroll. There also is a direct prohibition against paying people at the time they are taking industrial action, or paying them for that time later.

Industrial action taken pursuant to the appropriate notices and process is "protected" and civil action cannot be taken by employers against the union or the union members due to these actions. The response is to ultimately apply to the AIRC to bring the bargaining period to an end on a number of grounds that are statutorily set out, for example, because the union is not genuinely seeking to negotiate an agreement, or on national safety grounds that the health and welfare of the community or a part of the economy is likely to be threatened by this action.

Any other industrial action that is "unprotected" can be the subject of the common law action or a new federal court injunction to cause it to come to an end.[73]

Once a new CA has been made, no further claims are expected nor is any further industrial action anticipated during the life of the agreement. As outlined below, however, there is some judicial thought that if the agreement does not cover all topics (which is almost certain), then protected bargaining must be able to take place over those topics "outside" the existing agreement. It should be noted that the well-known "picket line" for some time has not been considered protected action. This has caused community protests to develop at the gates of employer businesses that are in dispute. However, recent judicial comment has led to speculation that a picket line in some circumstances may constitute industrial action, at least where it constitutes a restraint or limitation on work by employees on the picket line who would otherwise be working. This is to be contrasted with the position of fellow unionists who are not employees, who may join the picket line.

Not surprisingly, the ability to take protected industrial action (i.e., without penalty) in the negotiation of and during a collective agreement has received considerable attention. Each step in the process giving that protection as set out in the WR Act is being tested carefully by unions and employees.

The intention of the government was to allow for a certain amount of industrial action in support of negotiation toward a collective agreement. Such action would be "protected"; that is, an employer could not take civil or tort action against a union or its members who engage in that action. Once a CA had been signed and certified, any further grievances were to be dealt with by the dispute resolution procedure inside the agreement and not result in industrial action.

Whether the Notice initiating the bargaining period and its details comply with the WR Act, whether the Notice of Industrial Action which must be given at least 3 days before action is taken complies with the WR Act, and whether the action itself can be

---

[73]WR Act §127.

said to be "protected" action are all the areas being subjected to considerable examination, up to and including litigation.

In addition, the provisions under the WR Act, Section 170MW, giving the power to suspend or terminate the bargaining period, are the subject of an increasing number of applications.

The ultimate outcome if a bargaining period is suspended or is terminated is that the parties are forced into compulsory arbitration. Such cases are extremely rare, but a leading case involving the power industry proved a setback to the unions in the outcome of the arbitration. Accordingly, they resorted to the tactic of withdrawing their bargaining period notices, which meant that the process to compulsory arbitration came to an end before such arbitration took place. Legislation was passed in late 2003 to enable the other party (usually the employer) to obtain on order preventing the union from re-instituting a new bargaining period that would otherwise have enabled further industrial action to be taken under legal immunity (amendment to the Workplace Relations Act commenced February 7, 2003).

In *Emwest Products*,[74] Justice Kenny decided that there is no prohibition against protected industrial action for the purpose of advancing further claims with respect to matters *not agreed on initially* in a CA.[75] Given that CAs have never been regarded as the complete code of all matters in the contract of employment and are limited to 20 approved topics[76] that can be covered in them, this has caused some consternation, as it may allow industrial action during the life of the CA. Employers are calling for legislation to overturn the effect of this federal court decision.

It also was thought initially that, given that awards are limited to 20 allowable matters, it would not be possible for the purposes of negotiation of a CA to take industrial action over matters that did not formally pertain to the relationship between employer and employees (i.e., outside those allowable matters). However, a decision of the federal court in *Electrolux*[77] indicated that this view

---

[74]Emwest Prods. Pty. Ltd. v. Automotive, Food, Metals, Eng'g, Printing & Kindred Indus. Union [2002] FCA 61.

[75]See the discussion in II.D., above.

[76]See the discussion in the Introduction, at E.2., above.

[77]Automotive, Food, Metals, Eng'g, Printing & Kindred Indus. Union v. Electrolux Home Prods. Pty. Ltd. [2002] FCAFC 1999.

may not be correct and that such action can be protected, provided it was for the purpose of genuinely supporting and advancing claims made in respect of the proposed agreement.

In September 2004, though, the High Court overruled *Electrolux* (*Electrolux Home Products Pty. Ltd. v. Australia Workers' Union* [2004] HCA 40). Taking a narrow view, the High Court ruled that the AIRC has the power to certify only agreements that are about matters "pertaining to the relationship to employer and employees as such." The Court excluded from the list of items that could be certified matters of a philosophical, political or management nature. If any agreement including such matters had already been certified, the court said, it was an invalid act of certification. Further, the fault could not be corrected simply by striking out the offending clauses of an existing or proposed agreement, the court said. Rather, an amended agreement had to restart the process of voting and lodgment in the Commission to obtain fresh certification.

Not surprisingly, the decision has caused some consternation. Already some AIRC members are seeking to implement more expansive views of what is allowed and not allowed. In addition, government legislation may be called upon to preserve existing agreements at least insofar as the provisions within them that are not inappropriate are concerned. Some clauses initially considered inappropriate were trade union training leave, the restriction on the engagement of contractors, union notice boards and a requirement that "Australia Made" products would be used wherever possible.

F. The Role of the Federal Court

Over the past years, recourse to the Federal Court of Australia has increasingly been made as either a tactic in negotiation or dispute, or as a means of resolving disputes. The Federal Court is the appropriate court to apply for injunctions against proceedings in the AIRC and/or by way of appeal from the AIRC. It also has jurisdiction over matters arising in this area (although not exclusively).

This recourse to the Federal Court has always been available, but this practice was given significant impetus by the major stevedoring dispute between the wharf union, the Maritime Union of Australia (MUA), and one of the two stevedoring companies, Patricks, in 1998.[78] Due to the significant corporate and commercial factors present in that dispute, both parties used the Federal Court for injunctions, preliminary hearings, and causes of action.

The Federal Court's ability to give quick injunctions on a holding or interim basis, together with its longer-term willingness to issue judgments outside of long understood industrial relations results by applying corporate or commercial litigation practices and approaches, have added to its attraction. In addition, the increasing complexity of the WR Act and the increase in use of legal procedure under the WR Act encourage greater resort to the Federal Court.

In any dispute or negotiation of some significance there is now almost as much likelihood that either the unions or the employing company will resort to the Federal Court as there is a likelihood that they will resort to the AIRC.

For a discussion of the role of the Federal Court in freedom of association issues, see II.A.4., above.

G. Outsourcing

A recent development, confirmed in 2002 by a decision of the Full Bench of the Federal Court, has the potential to cause considerable difficulty with the practice of outsourcing. Universally recognized as a method of corporate restructuring and of having corporate services and functions carried out more efficiently by third parties, outsourcing was undertaken widely during the 1990s to cope with international competitiveness and globalization. Outsourcing also occurred in the public sector, as various functions and services were hired out to private tenderers, who usually are regarded as more efficient and economic and who may have their own awards and CAs, but not all of the costs and conditions arising out of public-sector employment.

---

[78]Maritime Union of Austl. v. Patrick Stevedores No. 1 Pty. Ltd. (1998) 77 FCR 456.

In the *Greater Dandenong Council* case,[79] the Council sought to outsource its home health services. The successful tenderer had its own CA. There were considerable savings to the Council as a result of the new service provider, but when the contract was outsourced the employees of the Council were made redundant.

The reason for the outsourcing was the Council's high labor cost arising from the Council's CA, which had more generous conditions than that of the successful tenderer. Accordingly, the Court found that the employees were being injured in their employment and terminated because they were entitled to the benefit of the CA and that this was a prohibited and discriminatory reason. Almost two years after the employees had been made redundant, the Court ordered that they be reinstated. The Council was found in breach of the WR Act and a nominal fine was imposed.

Under one interpretation, this decision establishes a severe barrier to most, if not all, outsourcing, which is usually based on cost and is often a reflection of the existing terms and conditions of any award or CA that regulates the labor costs of the primary employer. However, there has been a decision by another judge in the Federal Court that may help this difficulty.

Justice Branson, in the *MUA v. CSL Yarra* case,[80] held that while dismissing the Australian crew from a Canadian owned ship and replacing it with another crew of a different nationality—and therefore with different terms and conditions of employment—may have had the cost effectiveness of the ship as one of its purposes, it was not a prime or main motivator and therefore was not a breach of the WR Act.

The potential conflict between the two interpretations has not yet been resolved, neither has the actual effect on outsourcing as a practice.[81]

---

[79]Greater Dandenong City Council v. Australian Mun., Clerical & Servs. Union (2001) 184 ALR 641.

[80]Maritime Union of Austl. v. CSL Austl. Pty. Ltd. [2002] FCA 513.

[81]See also the discussion of outsourcing under I.A.1., above.

III. Representation by Entities Other Than Unions

In most cases, workers are represented by unions. In any collective negotiation of either an award or a collective agreement, representation in any other way is extremely rare. In those workplaces that have undertaken a collective non-union agreement, employee representatives either are appointed, nominated, or elected from among the workforce to undertake a role, usually in the form of a committee, to represent the employees. These negotiations vary in their degree of formality and structure, but often are informal and established only for the period of the negotiation.

A. Bargaining Agents

The introduction of AWAs led to the introduction of formal "bargaining agents," though their use is still extremely limited. These bargaining agents are appointed by individual employees who are negotiating their individual AWAs with their employer. There is no real limit on who may act as a bargaining agent. Unions may be appointed as bargaining agents, and often they seek such appointments with a view to becoming involved in negotiations from which they otherwise would be excluded.

B. Consultative Committees

In day-to-day affairs, most awards and CAs allow for the establishment of a consultative committee consisting of an equal number of employer and employee representatives, one of whom invariably is a union official. The consultative committee usually is given a wide charter, though its effectiveness depends on the commitment of all parties to using this structure.

C. Other Specialists

In disputes, unions come to the forefront, and they often engage lawyers or other experts who may need to be involved on the employee side. In unfair dismissals, however, employees frequently are represented by their own lawyers. Although unions will take up potential terminations concerning either individuals or large groups at the workplace as an industrial matter, if formal unfair termination proceedings are instituted, they will not be keen to be involved. Nevertheless, they frequently appear, at least in the initial conciliation proceedings, to see if a resolution can be achieved.

Employers use their own management or human resource officers to represent them in the workplace and in hearings before the AIRC. In addition, they frequently use the employer industry association to which they belong for industrial relations advice and representation. Many employers are not slow to engage lawyers who are specialists in the area. As well, there are growing numbers of industrial relations consultants who offer their services in the negotiation of awards, CAs, or AWAs, or in the handling of industrial disputes or human resource strategies generally.

A court decision[82] has caused some concern in the use of employer industry associations to represent employers. Under the Australian system, membership in a registered employer organization meant that the individual company members were bound by, and parties to, any federal awards that named the industry association as a respondent party.

To avoid this automatic respondency, some employer associations developed associate or other forms of limited membership with the view that the arrangement meant the employers could enjoy the benefits and advantages of association membership without being bound by the federal awards. However, the AIRC has held that an employer who was not a full member of the Victorian Employers Chamber of Commerce and Industry (VECCI) but rather a nonvoting "subscriber member" was nevertheless a respondent to a federal commercial sales award. This may mean that employers who believe they are award-free are inadvertently not complying with terms of relevant awards.

IV. REDUNDANCY AND TRANSFERS OF UNDERTAKINGS

A. Redundancy

Redundancy is defined as a situation where an employer no longer desires to have a particular job performed by anyone or

---

[82]Carpenter & Corona Mfg. Pty. Ltd., Comm'r Whelan AIRC PR924136.

performed at a particular location by anyone. A dismissal for redundancy is not on account of any personal fault of the employee.[83] Redundancies may arise as a result of closing a business, the introduction of technological or organizational changes, the sale of a business, or privatization.[84]

The standard termination, change, and redundancy (TCR) case of first impression was in 1984. Since that time, many unions have sought to increase redundancy payments, particularly following the years 1989 to 1991, when a recession in Australia resulted in large-scale restructuring, redundancies, and outsourcing, as well as simply increasing claims over the passage of time.

Commencing with the TCR maximum of eight-weeks' pay after a person had been employed for more than four years, unions calculated an allowance of two-weeks' pay per year of service and then attempted to apply that allowance to each year of service beyond four (that is, a person with 15-years' service would get 30-weeks' pay). As a result, whenever any significant redundancies have been proposed, negotiations must be undertaken with the unions, which seek to impose higher standards. At present, community standards range from two-weeks' pay per year of service to four-weeks pay per year of service, with the potential average of around two to three weeks. Redundancy pay usually is capped at the time of retirement, and, increasingly, has been scaled back from a cap of 104 weeks to a negotiated cap of 52 to 104 weeks.

Redundancy payments based on years of service are in addition to the period of notice contained in an applicable award or CA, which usually reflects the notice required by the WR Act (a maximum of four weeks after five years of service, or an extra week if the employee is older than 45 years).[85]

The accumulated entitlement for redundancy payments in the event of a company closure can often be substantial. Redundancy entitlements negotiated at three or four weeks' pay for each year of service for long standing employees in a large company can amount to millions of dollars. Such entitlements are jeopardized if the company collapses financially. Increased attention is being

---

[83] *Ex parte* Adelaide Milk Supply Co-Op, Ltd., 16 S.A.S.R. 6, 8 (1977).

[84] MACKEN, O'GRADY & SAPPIDEEN, THE LAW OF EMPLOYMENT 183 (4th ed. 1997).

[85] For a discussion of notice requirements, see I.C.4., above.

given by the unions, the workforce, and the community on two fronts to protect those entitlements:

- Unions are seeking to establish industry trust funds or schemes into which payments of such entitlements can be made by employees and/or employers, to protect them from a particular company collapse. The move is being strongly resisted as being expensive "on cost" (or overhead) for companies.
- Pressure is being brought on the political parties in Australia to legislate statutory protection and priority in any bankruptcy or corporate liquidation to employees' claims for accrued annual leave, long service leave, or redundancy entitlements.

These two proposals are often accompanied by direct industrial action against companies or by political campaigns and protests. These proposals will become an increasingly important element whenever CAs are renegotiated.

1. Federal Award Employees

The majority of federal awards have incorporated a standard TCR clause. Under the standard TCR clause, employers are subject to the following restrictions:

- the employer may not dismiss an employee without union discussion;
- the employer must meet minimum severance pay requirements;
- the employer must notify the CES of all terminations of 15 or more employees; and
- the employer must provide the employee with time off during the notice period to search for new work.

Severance payments under federal awards are determined under a fixed scale that ranges from no severance pay for persons employed for less than one year to up to eight-weeks' pay for persons employed more than four years.

With the spate of corporate failures, company transfers, relocations, and restructuring leading to employment terminations and redundancies, entitlements to payments upon severance of employment have become a major focus. The top union council, the Australian Council of Trade Unions, has undertaken a test case to revisit the minimum Federal Award redundancy payments with a view of the 1984 termination change and redundancy (TCR case). The decision of the Australian Industrial Relations Commission was given in June 2004 (Redundancy Case–Supplementary Decision, PR062004). It provides for two scales of redundancy payments, depending on whether there are fewer than 15 employees, and other rights and obligations. For the larger employers, severance commences after one year of continuous service with a payment of four-weeks' ordinary pay and rises incrementally to a maximum of twelve-weeks' pay after 10 or more years of continuous service. For the smaller employer, severance commences with four weeks' ordinary pay, rising to a maximum of eight-weeks' pay for four or more years of continuous service. It should be noted that this award minimum is usually exceeded by negotiations contained in a CA for any company or by negotiations undertaken among the unions and the company in the event of a company closure. It should be noted that this award minimum is usually exceeded by negotiations contained in a CA for any company or by negotiations undertaken among the unions and the company in the event of a company closure.

2. *State Award Employees*

State award employees also may have specific legal entitlements to severance payments in the event of a redundancy. For example, in New South Wales, workers covered by a state award are entitled to severance payments ranging from four-weeks' pay for one or two years of service to 16-weeks' pay for more than six years of service. The range in severance payments increases if the terminated employee is age 45 or older. This is the highest scale approved by an industrial tribunal in Australia. The federal severance pay scale has been followed by a majority of states.

Various states that have previously adhered to the federal standard are independently seeking to upgrade their minimum scale along the same lines.

3. *Nonaward Employees*

There is no obligation to make any redundancy payment to nonaward employees unless it is a condition of their contract of employment. This position, however, must be considered in the context that in some circumstances, if all other employees are receiving redundancy pay, for example, on a closure of a factory, it may be an element of a harsh and unfair dismissal if a severance payment is not made. There is an increasing tendency to make redundancy payments to employees engaged under contracts.

B. Transfers of Undertakings

Under the WR Act, awards, CAs and AWAs are binding on a company and "any successor, assignee or transmittee (whether immediate or not) to or of the business or part of the business of an employer who was a party to the industrial dispute, including a corporation that has acquired or taken over the business or part of the business of the employer."[86]

During the 1990s, there was considerable restructuring and outsourcing, which meant that these sucessorship provisions received considerable judicial interpretation. Although subject to a High Court decision, it is fair to say that the terms "successor, assignee, or transmittee" are read as broadly as possible and do not have any technical or legal meaning. The term "business or part of the business" also is broadly defined and does not mean, for example, an independent profit center or identifiable enterprise of its own, but rather a "bundle of activities" or "the character of the business in the hands of the transferor when compared with the character of the business in the hands of the transferee," which was the nature of the test applied by the latest High Court decision.

The debate is easily demonstrated when government privatizations are considered. If government enterprises, which

---

[86]WR Act §149(1)(d) (awards). *See also id.* §170MB (CAs), §170US (AWAs).

typically contain generous terms and conditions, are sold or transferred to private enterprise, the acquirer often seeks to have private-sector terms and conditions govern the acquired workforce. Unions, to maintain their influence and to protect their members, have sought to maintain the pre-existing terms and conditions. In broad terms, any person who acquires a business or part of a business through tender or private sale must face the almost certain likelihood that there will be a claim that they will take over the terms and conditions of the workforce that exist at the time.

As a theoretical matter, the successorship provisions may cause an employer to be respondent to a number of awards and CAs. This might occur, for example, if a call center takes over activities that have been outsourced from a bank, as well as from an airline and an insurance company. However, the response from both the federal court and the AIRC is that systems are in place to seek alternative orders to sort out an appropriate industrial relations labor regulation and create a new award or CA that would override any of those that the employer inherited. In these situations, however, it must be appreciated that the affected unions likely would seek to apply the most favorable of the applicable awards or agreements.

The legal interpretations that are asserted when there is a "transmission" of a business, and the effect that transmission may have on the existing awards and CAs of the original business, continue to be a major topic of debate and judicial decision in Australia. Frequently, these claims of successorship and transmission are made by unions in an effort to continue union coverage of the employees of the successor company and to maintain and protect the existing terms and conditions. Since 1994 the trend, particularly supported by the Federal Court, was to protect the employees' terms and conditions by finding that there had been a transmission of the underlying award or any applicable CA to a successor, transmittee, or assignee of the business or part of the business of the original company. The jurisprudence developed to the extent that if it was found that the same "bundle of activities"[87] was carried on in both undertakings, there would be a likelihood a

[87]Stellar Call Centres Pty. Ltd. v. CEPU (Communications, Elec., Elec., Energy, Info., Postal, Plumbing & Allied Servs. Union) (2001) 106 FCR 302.

transmission would be found, and the original awards and agreements would be applied to the successor company.

The trend reached its high point when a pharmacy in a coastal resort took over some of the counter and automatic teller functions of a branch of a bank that was closing its own office. The Federal Court found that banking terms and conditions that had previously applied to the bank should apply to the pharmacy. Ultimately, the High Court said that, although some banking functions were being undertaken by the pharmacy, it clearly was not part of the banking industry and did not undertake banking business.[88]

The High Court's approach is still a subject of much debate. The characterization of the business in the first company when compared with the character of the business in the hands of the second company is still difficult to predict with any certainty.

In 2002, the Federal Court extended the transmission doctrine further when it found that award terms and conditions may occur in certain circumstances even where there is no commercial or direct relationship between two employers other than that they, for example, might be sequential contractors providing services to the same business.

In *HSU v. Gribbles Radiology*,[89] MDIG provided a particular health clinic with radiology services. Subsequently, the health clinic awarded the contract to Gribbles Radiology, which replaced MDIG, and the Federal Court found that the award that was binding on MDIG also bound Gribbles Radiology by way of transmission of business. Facts such as the same employees undertaking the same services were present.

A similar case may be, for example, a company which takes over the management of a commercial carpark for the carpark owner and leaves the existing staff in place undertaking the same functions. It may well be that such companies will "inherit" the award employment terms and conditions of the previous management company. This case is under appeal to the High Court.

The question of employees' redundancy entitlements, which are often negotiated in CAs in excess of any minimum and which

---

[88]PP Consultants Pty. Ltd. v. Finance Sector Union of Austl. (2000) 201 CLR 648.
[89][2003] FCAFC 56.

can represent substantial sums, continues to receive attention with considerable activity in the political and practical sphere. Collapses such as that of Ansett (one of Australian's domestic aircraft carriers) left claims for accumulated redundancy entitlements in the hundreds of millions of dollars. (For example, if the redundancy scale is four weeks per year of service per employee at the current and therefore usually the highest rate of pay, a person employed for 30 years is entitled to 120 weeks, or in excess of two-years' pay. If that is multiplied for several thousand employees, the figure becomes significant.) Union and employee endeavors to secure the payment of this benefit in the case of corporate collapses or on restructuring include litigation, negotiating appropriate award or CA provisions, and/or promoting legislation making such payments a priority in the event of company insolvency.

Another leading case, *Construction Forestry Mining and Engineering Union v. Amcor Ltd.*,[90] demonstrates other difficulties in this area. In an intercompany group structure, there was a transfer of business and employees from one company to another. In the circumstances, although accumulated entitlements were transferred to the receiving company and employee service and existing terms and conditions were continued as with the first company, there was found to be a termination at law by the first company and an offer of new employment by the second company. The termination triggered a right of the employees and union to claim redundancy payments from the first company despite the continuing employment. The claim has been upheld with the first appeal, but it is possible there will be a further appeal to the High Court.

V. WAGES, HOURS, AND LEAVE

A. Wages

Entitlement to wages is found in employment contracts, statutes, or awards. The right to be paid wages pursuant to an award creates a statutory debt that may be enforced in industrial or civil courts.

[90][2002] FCA 610.

1. *Minimum Wage Rates*

Minimum rates of pay typically are established by the AIRC in the context of an award or CA. These minimum rates can be adjusted by individual members of the commission or usually are adjusted nationally after national "safety net reviews" designed to lift the minimum rates in each award. Above the minimum rates, employees are paid whatever is necessary to attract their labor, with rates negotiated individually or through their unions. It may be, however, that the rate employees are paid are the minimum rates set out in the award. This depends on bargaining strength and market conditions. The AIRC's awards provide only a safety net of minimum wages.[91]

2. *Overtime Pay Rates*

It is necessary to examine the applicable award to determine overtime pay provisions.[92] Overtime pay rates generally are based on a percentage system. For example, a common award provision requires an overtime rate of time and one-half for the first three hours of overtime and double-time thereafter.

3. *Penalty Rates for Work on Saturdays, Sundays, and Public Holidays*

Special penalties are commonly fixed for work on Saturdays, Sundays, and public holidays; these are not overtime payments.[93] The usual rate for Sundays and public holidays is double-time or double-time and one-half. Attempts to overcome overtime and penalty rates may be made through the use of CAs and AWAs, subject to the watchful eye of the AIRC and the EA.

4. *Leave Loadings*

Leave loadings are a percentage payable for time taken on annual leave.[94] For example, the common standard is a premium of 17.5 percent above employees' ordinary salary for each week

---

[91]WR Act §89A(3).

[92]For a discussion of overtime hours, see V.B.2., below.

[93]For a discussion of Saturday, Sunday, and holiday hours, see V.B.3., below.

[94]For a discussion of annual leave, see V.C.2., below.

they are on holiday. This leads to the interesting result that employees may be paid more while they are on holiday than while they are at work. The practice of leave loading initially arose out of a claim by strongly unionized workers to the effect that by going on holiday they were deprived of the opportunity to work overtime as they normally would do in their ordinary working week. At their highpoint in some industries, leave loadings reached as much as 25 percent.

5. *Stand-Down Provisions*

Generally, to "stand down" is to put an employee on unpaid status. A stand-down provision is a clause included in an award or CA that allows the employer to stand down (and therefore not pay) employees who cannot usefully be employed due to an industrial dispute in which they may or may not be taking part, a breakdown of machinery, or some other cause for which the employer cannot reasonably be held responsible.

B. Hours

1. *Ordinary Hours*

Awards and agreements set the spread of hours within which ordinary work hours may be assigned. Employees covered by industrial awards generally work a 38-hour week. It is usual for an award also to prescribe a minimum period of rest, often 10 hours, between ceasing work one day and commencing work the next day.

2. *Overtime Hours*

For employees covered by an award, any work in excess of ordinary work is paid at overtime rates of pay specified in the award. The award also may limit the number of overtime hours that may be worked by an employee on a single day or over a single week.

Employees not covered by awards may be employed to work in excess of ordinary work hours without payment of overtime. Salaried employees are paid on the basis that their salary covers all duties, hours, and work required to adequately perform their functions.

3. *Saturday, Sunday, and Holiday Hours*

The number of public holidays varies from state to state. Generally, employees are entitled to 10 to 12 paid holidays annually.

Award provisions usually set maximum periods for work on Saturdays, Sundays, and public holidays.

C. Leave

1. *Sick Leave*

Employees are entitled to paid sick leave either as a matter of contract or under appropriate statutes, awards, or agreements. The standard award entitlement is five-days' sick leave during the first year of employment and eight-days' sick leave for every year thereafter. Sick days, if not taken, accumulate. In each case, it is necessary to consult the relevant award or agreement to find the precise terms of the leave clause.

2. *Annual Leave*

Employees are entitled to annual leave under state legislation, awards, or agreements. The standard annual leave is four-weeks' leave at the end of every year of service. As a general rule, annual leave must be taken within six months of accrual.

3. *Long-Service Leave*

Employees are entitled to long-service leave under state legislation, awards, or agreements. Entitlement to long-service leave accrues after a prescribed period of continuous service or employment with a particular employer. The periods of entitlement differ with the relevant legislation. In New South Wales, for example, employees are entitled to two-months' leave after the completion of 10-years' service, and there is pro rata payment entitlement where employment is terminated by the employer after five years.

4. *Parental Leave*

Federal legislation provides a minimum entitlement to unpaid parental leave. Parental leave (maternity or paternity) is restricted to permanent employees who have been employed by their current employer for at least 12 months prior to the leave. An application is necessary for parental leave.

Maternity leave entitlement is for a period between 6 and 52 weeks. Paternity leave entitlement is up to one-week's leave at the time of the birth and up to 51 weeks if the employee is taking leave for the specific purpose of becoming the primary caregiver to the child. The maximum amount of paternity leave is reduced by the maternity leave taken by the employee's spouse and, with the exception of the one-week's leave at the time of the birth, paternity leave may not be taken concurrently with the spouse's maternity leave.

However, the general standard of 12-months unpaid leave in Australia is rapidly changing. Periods of up to 12-weeks' paid maternity leave and one week paid paternity leave (and the same with adoption leave) are becoming common in CAs with a number of companies or government undertakings. In 2002, there was a general push in Australia by the Federal Anti-Discrimination Commissioner to implement up to 14-weeks paid leave as a community standard applicable to all employees by the establishment of a test case in the AIRC. If successful, it could be anticipated that the paid leave would be written into all underpinning industry and other awards or reflected in CAs. This 14 weeks of leave is a paid part of the 12 months of unpaid leave allowed, and is not an additional/separate period of leave.

VI. ANTIDISCRIMINATION

Australia passed its first antidiscrimination statutes in the mid-1970s. Since then, this area of the law has developed dramatically. There are numerous state and federal antidiscrimination statutes that seek to address new cases of discrimination, as well as to remedy past discrimination.[95] Australia also is party to several interna-

---

[95]*See, e.g.*, Affirmative Action (Equal Employment Opportunity for Women) Act 1986 (Commonwealth [Cth]); Racial Discrimination Act 1975 (Cth); Sex Discrimination Act 1984 (Cth); Disability Discrimination Act 1992 (New South Wales [NSW]); Anti-Discrimination Act 1977 (NSW); Equal Employment Opportunity Act 1995 (Victoria); Anti-Discrimination Act 1991 (Queensland); Employment Opportunity Act 1984 (South Australia [SA]); Employment Opportunity Act 1984 (Western Australia); Sex Discrimination Act 1994 (Tasmania); Discrimination Act 1994 (Australian Capital Territory [ACT]); Anti-Discrimination Act 1992 (Northern Territory [NT]).

tional antidiscrimination treaties, including ILO Conventions on the Elimination of all Forms of Racial Discrimination and the Elimination of all Forms of Discrimination Against Women.[96]

A. Sexual Harassment

The federal Sexual Discrimination Act (SD Act) provides that a person sexually harasses another if he or she makes an unwelcome sexual advance or request for sexual favors, or engages in other, unwelcome conduct of a sexual nature. The WR Act, as well as several state statutes, also prohibits sexual harassment as a form of unlawful discrimination against a person with regard to the terms of his or her employment.

B. Sexual Preference

The WR Act makes it unlawful to discriminate against an employee on the basis of sexual preference. Australian states have defined discrimination on the basis of sexual preference to include heterosexuality, homosexuality, bisexuality, and transexuality.[97]

C. Marital Status

Australian federal and state statutes prohibit discrimination against individuals due to their marital status. The prohibition of discrimination against individuals due to their marital status is interesting because unlike race or sex, marital status is not an immutable characteristic. Australian laws prohibit discrimination on the basis of a person's marital status whether a person falls within any of the following categories:

- single;
- married;
- married, but separated from his or her spouse;
- divorced;

---

[96]See the Introduction, at B.3., above. For a discussion of ILO Conventions, see the chapter on the ILO in Volume I, Part 4.

[97]*See, e.g.*, Employment Opportunity Act 1984 (SA) §29(1)(b); Discrimination Act 1994 (ACT) §7(1)(b); Anti-Discrimination Act 1992 (NT) §19(1)(c).

- widowed; or
- the *de facto* spouse of another person.

Notwithstanding prohibitions against discrimination based on sexual preference (discussed immediately above), the prohibition against marital status discrimination applies only to heterosexual relationships.[98]

D. Pregnancy or Potential Pregnancy

Another type of prohibited discrimination is that related to pregnancy or potential pregnancy.[99] Dismissal from employment when a woman either informs her employer that she is pregnant or her pregnancy begins to "show" is a typical basis for a complaint.[100]

E. Family Responsibilities

An employer may not dismiss an employee due to the employee's responsibilities to care for or support a dependent child or any other immediate family member who is in need of care and support.[101]

F. Race and Racial Hatred

The first federal discrimination law enacted in Australia was the Racial Discrimination Act 1975 (RD Act). Ironically, of all the antidiscrimination laws based on immutable characteristics, the RD Act is the most underutilized. Under the RD Act, it is unlawful to make "a distinction, exclusion, restriction or preference based on race, color, descent or national or ethnic origin."[102] The RD Act further provides as follows:

It is unlawful for a person to do an act, otherwise than in private, if:

---

[98]MACKEN, O'GRADY & SAPPIDEEN, THE LAW OF EMPLOYMENT 599 (4th ed. 1997).
[99]Sexual Discrimination Act (SD Act) §7.
[100]MACKEN, O'GRADY & SAPPIDEEN, *supra* note 98, at 600.
[101]SD Act §4A.
[102]Racial Discrimination Act (RD Act) §9.

(a) the act is reasonably likely in all the circumstances, to offend, insult, humiliate or intimidate another person or a group of people; and
(b) the act is done because of the race, color or national or ethnic origin of the other person or of some or all of the people in the group.[103]

The prohibition against racial discrimination also is included in the WR Act, as well as in various state statutes.

G. Disability

Adopted in 1992, the federal Disability Discrimination Act (DD Act) makes it unlawful to discriminate against an employee on the ground of the employee's disability by, among other things, dismissing or demoting the employee. The DD Act is very broad and defines "disability" to include the following:

- a total or partial loss of the person's bodily functions or mental functions;
- the presence in the body of organisms capable of causing disease or illness;
- a malformation, malfunction, or disfigurement of a part of a person's body; or
- a disorder or malfunction that results in a person learning in ways different from learning practices of most individuals.

The DD Act reflects the realities of disabling conditions such as the human immunodeficiency virus/acquired immune deficiency syndrome (HIV/AIDS) and learning or attention deficit disorders. Additionally, the DD Act includes a disability that presently exists, previously existed, or may exist in the future, or one that is imputed to a person.

In addition to the prohibition on discriminating against an employee on the basis of an employee's disability by, among other

[103]RD Act pt. 2A. *See also id.* §18c(2) (defining when an act is not performed in private) and §18c(3) (defining public place).

things, dismissing or demoting the employee, the employer is prohibited from altering the employee's work circumstances to the employee's prejudice or injuring the employee in his or her employment for that reason.

Discrimination is considered to occur where a person is treated less favorably than others without the disability in circumstances that are the same or are not materially different. Discrimination also may be indirect, i.e., when on its face a requirement may be neutral but applies prejudicially to those with a disability. There are grounds for exceptions from these prohibitions based on the inherent requirements of the particular job, profession, or occupation, or due to unjustifiable hardship of compliance, and there are other specific exceptions that may be applicable.

H. Age

Federal law and all state laws, except the laws of Tasmania, prohibit age discrimination. Some states also prohibit mandatory retirement based on age.[104] Direct or indirect attempts by employers to force employees to retire upon attaining a specific age are illegal and leave the employer open to damages and injunctions against such conduct.

Employees of any age are protected regarding the actions of an employer based on age. Age can only be a legitimate factor in an employer's decision concerning retirement, recruitment, or promotion if it is justified with reference to the work. Age cannot of itself be a determinant, since that would be discriminatory.

I. Union Activity

Under the WR Act, an employer may not terminate a person for membership in a union or for taking part in union activities.[105]

---

[104] *See* MACKEN, O'GRADY & SAPPIDEEN, *supra* note 98, at 604 (detailing all the states that prohibit age discrimination).

[105] WR Act §170CK(209b). See also II.A.3., above.

VII. Occupational Safety and Health and Workers' Compensation

A. Occupational Safety and Health

1. Employee Duties

Employees are held to specific standards of care with regard to safety in the course of their employment so that they do not pose a danger to themselves, others, or the property of the employer. In this regard, employers should ensure that employees receive training in proper safety precautions, including the use of appropriate safety devices where necessary. Employees also form an important part of an employer's compliance with health, safety, and welfare requirements. For example, in New South Wales, the Occupational Health and Safety Act 1983 provides that employees must take reasonable care for the health and safety of persons in the workplace who may be affected by the employee's acts or omissions at work.[106]

2. Employer Obligations

In addition to various state occupational safety regulations, employers are subject to a common law duty of care to their employees. An employer must provide adequate safety training and take action to discipline employees who engage in unsafe practices. The employer also must provide employees with a safe place to work, including safe appliances and tools. Inspections should be made by the employer of all tools, machinery, and work spaces to prevent accidents. All accidents should be investigated by the employer and documented, and adequate remedial measures taken.

B. Workers' Compensation

Most states, through workers' compensation acts, limit the right of employees to sue their employers for work-related injuries. The federal government also has limited the rights of its employees to sue for personal injuries in the Workers' Rehabilitation and Compensation Act.

---

[106]Occupational Health and Safety Act 1983 (New South Wales) §19(a).

As a general matter, workers or their surviving dependents may recover limited compensation for injuries arising out of, or in the course of, employment, for accidents occurring in work-related travel, or for work-related diseases. An exception to coverage occurs when the employee's injury is the result of his or her own willful misconduct.

All employers must maintain workers' compensation insurance, although qualified employers may act as self-insurers. By maintaining workers' compensation insurance, employers limit their liability for accidental, work-related injuries suffered by their employees. Employees benefit from the workers' compensation regime because they do not have to expend time and resources to prove an employer's liability. Nor do they have to face the possibility that their employer will become insolvent.

VIII. PENSIONS AND BENEFITS

A. Superannuation, Pensions, and Retirement Funds

In Australia, the normal retirement age is 65; however, employees in some industries may retire as early as age 55. Retirement benefits are provided through superannuation, pension, and other retirement funds. The majority of large companies in Australia have established pension plans and lump-sum superannuation for salaried employees. Normally, both the employer and employee contribute to these funds.

The Australian government has imposed a mandatory superannuation guarantee levy payable by employers. Under this mandate, employers must contribute a minimum amount to an employee's superannuation fund, which can be a personal, union, industry, or commercial fund. The minimum contribution currently is set at 9 percent of employees' salary, as of July 1, 2002. Employers must pay a superannuation guarantee charge for failure to provide a minimum level of superannuation contributions.

A "superannuation" is a form of retirement fund. In the past, funds were often established by a particular company only for its employees and the company would make contributions to that fund. The employee also was entitled to make a contribution to that fund that would be held and invested until the employee retired. The funds now are also industrywide and independent, being offered by insurers and other financial institutions. They often can be contributed to by a wide variety of employers as an employee moves from company to company during his or her working life. The ultimate payments are through lump sum payments or are converted into a weekly "pension," and are subject to regulated limits to preserve the tax status.

Currently, in a move to prepare Australia for its "growing old," superannuation funds receive a favorable tax treatment. However, they are subjected to considerable regulation and scrutiny by the Australian Taxation Office and other corporate regulators. Employees may continue to make their own contributions; however, there are restrictive regulations as to when the employee can draw on this fund, due to its favorable tax treatment.

Legislation regulates not only the contribution to the funds by the employer and the employee, but it also regulates the administration and operation of the funds and the activities of the trustees or administrators of those funds, for example, the investments they may make, the information to be distributed to fund participants, when the funds can pay out to an employee, and in what form and in what circumstances such payments can be made.

The superannuation industry is a private industry when compared with, for example, pensions, which are largely the product of government payment.[107]

B. Benefits

Employee fringe benefits given at the employer's option, industrial agreement, or by law include the following:

- health insurance;
- termination pay including annual leave, sick pay, long-service leave, and severance pay;
- overtime allowance;
- superannuation;
- bonuses;
- share schemes (stock option programs);

---

[107] See the discussion in VIII.C., below.

- meals or meal allowance;
- living away from home allowance;
- interest-free or low-interest loans;
- motor vehicles; and
- uniform allowance.

The employer must consider various tax consequences when providing fringe benefits. Fringe benefits tax may be payable by the employer, even though many benefits are not tax deductible.

C. Social Security

All permanent residents of Australia may be eligible for social security payments. The social security system is noncontributory, and payments are made from consolidated revenue. The benefits include the following types of pensions:

- *Age Pension*: Age pensions are paid to persons who have lived in Australia for 10 years. The benefits are available to men at age 65 and to women at age 60 and older.
- *Carer's Pension*: The carer's pension is paid to persons who are caring at home on a long-term basis for a severely handicapped aged or invalid pensioner or recipient of the rehabilitation allowance.
- *Child Disability Allowance*: The child allowance is paid for a disabled child who needs substantial extra care.
- *Family Allowance*: The family allowance is paid to parents or guardians of children younger than age 16 who are subject to their parents' care and control. The allowance also is paid to parents or guardians of dependent student children who are ineligible for Austudy, a benefit paid for full-time dependent students ages 18 to 24.
- *Invalid Pension*: The invalid pension is paid to persons at least 16 years of age who are certified to be at least 85 percent incapacitated for work or permanently blind. At least 50 percent of the incapacity must be caused by a permanent physical or mental impairment.
- *Job Search Allowance*: The job search allowance is paid to persons ages 16 to 17 who are unemployed but capable of working, available to work, and actively seeking work.

Recipients must register with the CES.

- *Orphan's Pension*: The orphan's pension is paid if both parents are dead or if one parent is dead and the other is unavailable to care for the child.
- *Rehabilitation Allowance*: The rehabilitation allowance is paid to persons undergoing a Department of Health and Community Services rehabilitation program who would otherwise be receiving a pension or a benefit.
- *Sheltered Employment Allowance*: The employment allowance is paid to women ages 16 to 59 and men ages 16 to 64 who are employed in a sheltered workshop or in supported employment and who otherwise would be eligible for a pension or a benefit.
- *Sickness Benefit*: The sickness benefit is paid to women ages 16 to 59 and men ages 16 to 64 who are temporarily unable to work as a result of illness or injury. A medical certificate must be supplied, and if the illness or injury is work-related, a compensation claim must have been filed.
- *Sole Parent Pension*: The sole parent pension is paid to persons who are alone or are living apart from their partner and have at least one dependent child.
- *Special Benefit*: The special benefit is paid to persons in financial hardship who are unable to earn sufficient money to support themselves and their dependents.
- *Unemployment Allowance*: Unemployment allowance is paid to women ages 18 to 59 and men ages 18 to 64 who are unemployed but are capable of working, available to work, and actively seeking work. Recipients must register with the CES.
- *Widowed Person's Allowance*: The widowed person's allowance is paid to a person whose spouse has died and who does not qualify for the sole parent pension. It is paid for a maximum of 12 weeks from the date of death, but can be extended if the recipient is pregnant.

IX. IMMIGRATION

A person may travel to Australia as a non-immigrant or an immigrant. Under the non-immigrant category, a person may apply for a visitor visa or a visa for temporary residence. An immigrant visa may be issued for family migration, skilled migration, or humanitarian migration.

A. Non-immigrant Visas

Non-immigrant visas are divided into the following three types:

- visitor,
- business, and
- temporary resident.

The visitor visa generally is appropriate for tourists, and a person may not take up employment under this visa category. A business visa or a temporary residence visa is available to a person wishing to remain in Australia for a certain amount of time to perform business, professional, or employment functions.

1. Business Visas

a. Temporary Business Visa (Short Stay)

A temporary business entry visa (short stay) is permitted for persons seeking a short-term stay in Australia for business purposes. This visa may be granted for multiple visits to Australia for a period of up to three months on each visit. The visa is valid for five years or the life of a passport, whichever is longer, up to 10 years.

b. Temporary Business Visa (Long Stay)

A temporary business visa (long stay) allows the holder to remain in Australia for a period of more than three months, but not more than four years, with multiple re-entry privileges. Applicants can be any of the following:

- personnel for Australian-based companies;
- personnel (executives and specialists) from offshore companies seeking to establish a branch of the company in Australia, participate in joint ventures, or undertake employ-

ment in relation to a contract between an offshore company and an Australian company;
- independent executives seeking to establish new business or joining existing businesses in Australia;
- personnel coming under a labor agreement;
- service sellers; or
- persons accorded diplomatic privileges and immunities.

To apply for a temporary business visa for long stay, the employer first must complete a sponsorship application. On approval of the sponsorship, the employer lodges a nomination application. Once the sponsorship and nomination are approved, the applicant then may apply for the visa at an Australian government agency overseas.

2. Temporary Residence

A temporary residence visa allows persons to enter Australia temporarily, for either a short- or long-term period, to engage in employment or other activities. A visa for temporary residence should be sought for the following types of activities or reasons:

- business/employment (e.g., professional staff, company directors);
- cultural/social (e.g., media and film, entertainment, sport, religious worker);
- educational (e.g., foreign government agency, visiting academic, occupational trainee);
- domestic worker;
- family relationship;
- retirement;
- supported dependent;
- expatriate; and
- working holiday.

Spouses and dependent children may accompany the applicant for the same period of time as the applicant is permitted to remain in Australia. However, the applicant must provide proof that he or she can financially support the dependents during their stay. Generally, spouses and dependents of temporary resident visa holders are not entitled to work in Australia unless they qualify independently to do so.

Application for a temporary residence visa generally requires submission of the following documents:

- application;
- one passport-sized photograph;
- health check certificate (normally required if the stay is for more than 12 months);
- police certificate (normally required if the stay is for more than 12 months);
- sponsorship, if applicable;
- passport; and
- application fee.

The required documents for this visa will vary depending on the type of activity the applicant will perform in Australia.

B. Immigrant Visas

The Australian immigration program is divided into three categories: (1) family migration including immediate family members (not required to be point-tested) and extended family members (subject to point test); (2) skilled migration comprised of an "employment" element, a "business/investment" element, and an "independent" element; and (3) humanitarian migration comprised of refugees.

1. *Family Immigration*

a. *Immediate Family*

The immediate family subcategory applies to applicants with close family members in Australia. It covers people sponsored by relatives already living in Australia and allows for the consideration of the following individuals:

- spouses;
- dependent unmarried children;
- children younger than age 18 coming to Australia to be adopted;

- orphaned unmarried relatives younger than age 18;
- a relative of the sponsor to assist with a serious family crisis brought about by death, disability, prolonged illness, or some other serious circumstance;
- fiancé(e)s;
- parents with the balance of their families in Australia; and
- the last remaining brother, sister, or nondependent child if he or she has no parent, brother, sister, or nondependent child outside Australia.

There is a two-year probationary period for the spouse and fiancé(e) categories.

b. Extended Family

The extended family category is also known as the "skilled Australian-linked concessional" category. Concessions are given to the following relatives who are sponsored by relatives in Australia:

- parents who do not have the balance of their families in Australia;
- nondependent children sponsored by a parent resident;
- brothers and sisters sponsored by a sibling resident; or
- nephews and nieces sponsored by an uncle or aunt resident.

A "floating" pass mark has been introduced to control the inflow of immigrants in this category. Only applicants scoring the pass mark or higher will be selected. The factors under the points test include the following:

- employability, including the applicant's qualifications, skills, work experience, and the current demand for the relevant skills in Australia;
- age (the younger the applicant, the higher the points);
- English language ability; and
- relationship factors and the attributes of the sponsors.

If the applicant secures a priority mark, he or she may be approved automatically, subject to satisfactory health and character checks. These individuals are given fast-track processing and, subject to visa availability, may immigrate to Australia. Applicants with a score just below the pass mark qualify to enter a "pool" of applicants. The Australian government, from time to time, may raise or lower the pass mark. Those pooled may qualify should the pass mark drop during the course of the year. Applicants remaining in the pool after one year are automatically rejected. However, they may re-apply as often as they wish.

If the applicant applies in the skilled Australian-linked concessional category, he or she also will be considered under the "regional-linked" subcategory. This subcategory enhances the prospects of some applicants whose sponsors have lived in a designated area of Australia for one year or more. The application criteria for the regional-linked visa are as follows:

- the sponsor must have lived in a designated area for one year before the sponsorship;
- the sponsor must not have received defined social security benefits for more than two weeks in the year before sponsorship is lodged;
- the applicant must be younger than 45 years old at the time the application is lodged;
- the applicant must have recognized skills relevant to his or her usual occupation that are the equivalent of an Australian diploma (or higher) qualification; and
- the applicant must have functional English language ability.

c. *Assurance of Support*

A sponsor must make a legal commitment to repay the Australian government any special benefit or job search paid by the Department of Social Security to the person covered by the assurance within the first two years of arrival in Australia or upon approval to remain permanently in Australia. The assurance of support covers parents who meet the balance of family test (i.e., have the balance of their families in Australia), adult dependents, relatives with special needs, last remaining overseas relatives, and dependent children. The government intends to extend the assurance of support to the spouse and fiancé categories.

For each principal immigrant, the sponsor must deposit a bond of AUD 3,500 with the Australian government. In addition, the sponsor must deposit AUD 1,500 for each adult (i.e., age 18 or older) dependent child of the immigrant. The bond must be paid prior to issuance of the immigrant visa. It is refunded with interest two years after the immigrant arrives in Australia if no claims are made by the Australian government in relation to welfare benefits paid to the immigrants during their first two years of settlement. In addition, a nonrefundable levy of AUD 924 per sponsored immigrant (including children of any age) has been introduced. The levy aims to recover a portion of the health costs that most immigrants in the family category are likely to incur.

2. *Skilled Immigration*

a. *Employment Immigration*

i. *Employer Nomination Scheme*

The Employer Nomination Scheme is designed to enable Australian employers to sponsor highly skilled workers from overseas when they have been unable to fill their needs from the Australian labor market or through their own training efforts. The Employer Nomination Scheme has the following requirements:

- Nominated workers must be younger than age 55 at the time of application. However, officers have discretion to determine, in exceptional circumstances, whether to accept applications from persons older than 55 years of age.
- Employers must lodge nominations with the Australian Immigration Department.
- Nomination must be supported by documentary evidence that the employer has tested the Australian labor market without success (e.g., newspaper advertisements, employment agencies, etc.). Employers are required to provide details of local applicants and the reasons why the employers have not accepted the local applicants. Nominations may not be approved where the Australian labor market has not been adequately tested or where the employer cannot satis-

factorily explain why local applicants have not been selected.

- Terms and conditions of the employment offered must meet minimum Australian awards and conditions for the occupation concerned.
- The nominees must be highly skilled, having formal training or extensive work experience. The nominee's qualifications and experience also must match the requirements of the vacancy. In addition, the nominee must fill the vacancy on a permanent, full-time basis.

ii. Labor agreements

Employers, trade unions, and government industries may enter into labor agreements where a shortage of skilled workers is identified and where all parties agree that some immigration of a larger group of skilled workers is warranted until long-term training arrangements are put into place.

This scheme is similar to the Employer Nomination Scheme. An employer still is required to lodge a nomination, but there is no requirement to test the labor market. Instead, the endorsement of the industrial association that negotiated the agreement must accompany the nomination.

b. Business/Investment Immigration

The business/investment subcategory of skilled immigration is aimed at promoting the establishment of new business, employment creation, and increased exports from Australia. Despite lower intake levels for other immigration categories, the present Australian government continues to promote this category. The following five classes of people may qualify under the business/investment category:

- owners/part-owners of businesses;
- state/territory-sponsored owners/part-owners of businesses;
- senior executive employees of major businesses;
- state/territory-sponsored senior executive employees of major businesses; and
- owners/part-owners of eligible investments and/or qualifying businesses.

i. Business owners

Owners/part-owners of businesses and state/territory-sponsored business owners must show successful business careers, net assets of AUD 300,000 in their business for two of the last four years (AUD 200,000 if state/territory-sponsored), and active participation in the management of a business (in which he or she owns at least 10 percent equity) for two of the last four years.

The applicant also must demonstrate a genuine and realistic commitment to establishing a new business in Australia or purchasing equity in an existing business, be registered with a state or territory government business development agency, and obtain at least 105 points under the business skills points test.

The largest single factor in the points tests is the applicant's business attributes. Owners/part-owners are awarded between 35 to 60 points if their business has AUD 500,000 to AUD 5,000,000 in annual sales turnover. Additional points are awarded for the amount of annual labor costs and total assets of the business. Other factors in the point test include the following:

- age and language ability, which are worth 0 to 30 points each;
- net assets of the applicant and spouse together, worth up to 15 points; and
- in some cases, sponsorship by the state/territory governments, worth another 15 points.

ii. Senior executives

Senior executives and state/territory-sponsored senior executives must have been employed in the top three levels of management by a major business with an annual turnover of at least AUD 50 million for two of the last four years (AUD 10 million if state/territory sponsored).

Applicants in this category also must demonstrate a genuine and realistic commitment to establishing a new business in Australia or purchasing equity in an existing business, be registered with a state or territory government business development agency, and obtain at least 105 points under the business skills points test.

Senior executives are awarded 65 points for working for a major business with an annual turnover of more than AUD 50 million, and state/territory-sponsored senior executives are awarded 65 points for working for a major business with an annual turnover of more than AUD 10 million. Points also are awarded for other factors such as age, language ability, net assets, and state/territory sponsorship.

Business owners and senior executive applicants are subject to an annual reporting requirement during their first three years of immigration. As part of this requirement, they must demonstrate that they have made a genuine and realistic commitment to their business plans. Failure to do so may lead to revocation of their immigrant status.

iii. Owners of eligible investments or qualifying businesses

This new subcategory, known as investment-linked immigration, was introduced in April 1995. A successful applicant under the investment-linked immigration subcategory must satisfy the following requirements:

- demonstrate at least three-years' experience in actively and successfully managing a "qualifying business" or an "eligible investment," as defined by the governing regulations;
- during at least one of the last five years, have had at least a 10 percent interest in the qualifying business, or have managed an eligible investment worth at least AUD 1,000,000;
- make an investment in a state-issued security for a minimum period of three years (there are four investment levels ranging from a minimum of AUD 750,000 to a maximum of AUD 2,000,000);
- demonstrate that he or she has a net worth of at least 50 percent more than the amount of capital he or she intends to invest in the state issued investment;
- show that funds used to finance the designated investment are personally owned and unencumbered and were legally accumulated as a result of the qualifying business and/or eligible investment activities;
- immigrate with the intent to maintain investment or business activities in Australia; and
- meet other standard immigration requirements and pass the investment-linked points test.

The pass mark for this subcategory is 105 points. Points are awarded for the amount of money to be deposited into a designated investment by the applicant. Between 60 and 80 points are awarded for investments of AUD 750,000 to AUD 2,000,000. Other factors in the points tests include age and language ability, which are worth between 0 to 30 points, and 0 to 35 points, respectively.

c. Independent Immigration

This subcategory is aimed at attracting young, skilled, and educated immigrants with a wide range of abilities. In addition to meeting the standard processing requirements, independent applicants also are subject to a points assessment.

Under the points test, independent applicants are assessed on their employability, taking into account their qualifications, skills and experience, age, and English language abilities. At present, the priority mark is 115. If an applicant scores above the priority mark, he or she is accepted automatically, subject to satisfactory health and character checks. These people are given fast-track processing. At present, a score of 100 will entitle the applicant to enter a "pool." Pool applicants who are not selected after one year are automatically rejected. However, they may reapply as often as they wish.

3. Immigrant Visa and Resident Return Visa

a. Issuance

Australia provides great flexibility for immigrants to travel during their early years in Australia. Upon approval of the immigration application, an immigrant visa and a five-year multiple resident return visa will be issued. Anyone who is not a citizen of Australia or New Zealand must have a valid resident return visa if he or she intends to return to Australia after a period overseas.

b. Renewing the Resident Return Visa

Immigration regulations provide that subsequent resident return visas may be issued in certain circumstances. An applicant may be granted a five-year resident return visa if he or she has been a permanent Australian for a total of two years or more in the five years immediately before making the application, and if the applicant (1) is employed outside Australia by the Australian government or an organization that has its principal office in Australia, or (2) has established a business in Australia and is required to travel outside Australia in the interests of that business and also has personal ties with Australia.

An applicant may be granted a three-month resident return visa if he or she was a permanent Australian resident for a period of fewer than two years during the period of five years immediately preceding the application, and if the applicant establishes substantial reasons for leaving and reentering Australia in the next three months.

The spouse and dependent children also may be granted resident return visas to accompany the applicant in the above cases. Other rules apply if the applicant seeks to accompany an Australian citizen spouse overseas. Generally in those cases, the applicant will receive a five-year resident return visa.

4. *Humanitarian Immigration*

Humanitarian immigration covers persons seeking immigrant status after being forced to flee due to circumstances in their country of citizenship, which can involve physical or political oppression or dire economic circumstances. Australia has a detailed investigation and assessment process regarding those seeking migration as refugees, and there are general guidelines as to the number that would be admitted in those circumstances. The process is currently under criticism as being too lengthy, too difficult, and causing distress, but it is defended by the government as being necessary to allow proper investigation and processing of those claiming refugee status.

C. Citizenship

Australian citizenship is a broad and complex field. The most common ways to become an Australian citizen are as follows:

- birth in Australia (either to Australian citizens or permanent residents);
- application for the grant of Australian citizenship (formerly called naturalization);

- birth overseas to an Australian citizen parent;
- legal adoption in Australia by an Australian citizen; or
- resumption of Australian citizenship.

1. General Criteria

Australian citizenship cannot be acquired simply by having lived in Australia for a certain time or by marriage to an Australian citizen. Application must be made for citizenship. Basically, before an applicant can apply successfully for Australian citizenship, he or she must be of good character, have a basic knowledge of English, understand the privileges and responsibilities of Australian citizenship, and fulfill residency requirements.

Australia requires citizens to be able to speak and understand basic English (but does not require them to be able to read or write in English), although exemptions from this rule exist for the following individuals:

- the spouse of an Australian citizen;
- anyone older than 50 years of age; and
- either a husband or wife, if both apply for citizenship together (only one spouse need satisfy the requirement).

2. Residency Criteria

Generally, if a permanent resident has resided physically in Australia for a total of two years in the five years immediately preceding the date of application, and if one of those two years was accumulated within the two-year period immediately preceding the date of application, he or she will be eligible to apply for the grant of Australian citizenship. This means that the shortest period in which Australian citizenship can be obtained is two years, through continuous physical presence in Australia following arrival as an immigrant.

The Australian Citizenship Act does provide for the Ministry to consider days outside Australia as days in for the purpose of calculating the two-year physical presence requirement. In these situations, the applicant must be able to prove that the time absent from Australia was for the benefit of Australia. To date, the Australian government has been quite liberal in defining "benefit."

ARGENTINA*

INTRODUCTION

A. Basic Composition of the Government

Argentina is a democratic republic with a federal system of government very similar to that of the United States. The Argentine National Constitution of 1853, patterned after the U.S. Constitution, provides for a tripartite federal government consisting of executive, legislative, and judicial branches. The Argentine National Constitution was amended in 1994.

The executive branch of the national government is headed by a President elected by direct vote every four years. The President is limited to two consecutive terms. The executive branch historically has been the dominant branch in national politics.

The bicameral legislative body is comprised of a 72-member Senate and a 257-member Chamber of Deputies. Deputies are elected directly to four-year terms; they represent the people and the number of deputies appointed in each province is directly proportional to its population. Senators also are elected directly and serve for six years; they represent the provinces and each province appoints three senators (two belong to the political party of the majority and the other one to the political party of the first minority).

The Constitution grants exclusive legislative power to the federal legislature with respect to areas of federal concern such as international affairs, inter-provincial trade, immigration, and citizenship. The federal legislature also has power to enact uniform

---

*Jordan W. Cowman Partner, Akin Gump Strauss Hauer & Feld LLP, Dallas, Texas; Carlos A. Dodds, Partner, and Jorge Daniel Orlansky, Partner, Baker & McKenzie, Buenos Aires, Argentina.

codes and laws in certain areas, including commercial, criminal, mineral, labor, and social security matters. These codes are enforced nationwide.

The project of law requires approval by both chambers of the legislature and promulgation by the President, who may reject it partially or totally. The Presidential veto can, however, be overturned by a qualified majority of two thirds of the votes in each Chamber.

The judicial power is vested in a Supreme Court (nine Judges appointed by the President with the approval of the Senate) and in lower courts. Depending on the substance of the dispute at stake, or the nature of the parties to a judicial procedure, legal cases may be heard either by federal or by provincial jurisdictions.

Labor courts in the district of the city of Buenos Aires are integrated with ten appellate courts (each with three judges) and 80 lower instance courts.

The Supreme Court of Justice has original jurisdiction in cases in which a foreign country representatives or a province is involved.[1] The Supreme Court of Justice intervenes as the final appellate court in cases in which there is an issue that is addressed directly or indirectly by the National Constitution ("Federal Issue"). Legal commentators have classified cases in which there are Federal Issues, into three categories: (i) cases involving "Simple Federal Issues," (ii) cases involving "Complex and Direct Federal Issues" and (iii) cases involving "Complex and Indirect Federal Issues."

(i) Simple Federal Issues involve disputes of interpretation of issues addressed by the National Constitution, by international treaties and by the laws of the National Congress. The National Constitution sets forth that civil, commercial, criminal, mining, and employment codes or laws have a special status. These laws are defined as "Common Laws," as opposed to "Federal Laws."[2] Be-

---

[1]National Constitution §117.

[2]National Constitution §75 (12).

cause of the special status of Common Laws, the interpretation of Common Law issues is not a Simple Federal Issue.

(ii) Complex and Direct Federal Issues involve conflicts between the National Constitution and an international treaty, a National law (including both Federal Law and Common Law), a provincial law, an executive order, or any other resolution from National or provincial authorities.

(iii) Finally, Complex and Indirect Federal Issues involve conflicts between a federal law and an executive order or resolution from federal authorities, and also between a law, executive order or resolution from a federal authority and a law, executive order or resolution from a local authority. As a rule, the Supreme Court of Justice intervenes in such a situation when the appellate court's ruling is contrary to the alleged federal issue.

In principle, the Supreme Court of Justice does not intervene in a controversy over an interpretation of a Common Law, such as an employment law, that does not deal with a Federal issue. Nor does the Supreme Court intervene when the appeal relates to facts or evidence presented in a lawsuit. However, the Supreme Court has admitted an exception to said rule when there is an arbitrary ruling. The Supreme Court of Justice has identified many arbitrary rulings that need revision.

In addition to the central government, each province elects its own governor and legislature. Each province maintains a judicial system parallel to the federal courts. The lower provincial courts are divided according to subject matter jurisdiction. Labor courts in the province of Buenos Aires are integrated with three judges and their decision can be appealed to the Supreme Court of the Buenos Aires province.

B. General Sources of Labor and Employment Law

The relationship between employees and employers is subject to stricter regulation in Argentina than in the United States.

1. *National Constitution*

Many labor rights that govern Argentina stem from the National Constitution. Among its provisions, Section 14 *bis* of the Constitution establishes a number of workers' rights, including dignified and equitable working conditions; limited working hours; paid rest and vacations; fair remuneration; minimum vital and adjustable wage; equal pay for equal work; participation in the profits of enterprises, with control of production and collaboration in management; protection against arbitrary dismissal; stability of the public worker; and free and democratic labor union organization. The Constitution also guarantees trade unions the right to enter into collective bargaining, the right to resort to settlement and arbitration, the right to strike, and protection of union representatives. This list of workers' rights requires further development by law, as the wording of the constitutional provision does not allow for direct implementation. Some of the above rights have been actually implemented by laws, while others (for example, profit sharing and co-determination) have not.

2. *International Agreements*

Another source of labor and employment law in Argentina is international treaties approved by Congress, such as the social security treaties with certain countries, as well as the Conventions of the International Labor Organization (ILO) (currently 62 conventions are in force).[3]

Among the 1994 amendments to the National Constitution was an extremely unusual provision that purported to incorporate a number of ratified human rights treaties and other human rights instruments into the Argentine Constitution. This provision, in Article 75(22), specified 10 instruments and a procedure for elevation of other instruments to constitutional status. These are:

- American Declaration of the Rights and Duties of Man;
- Universal Declaration of Human Rights;
- American Convention on Human Rights;

[3]For more information about the ILO, see the chapter on the ILO in Volume I, Part 4.

- International Covenant on Economic, Social and Cultural Rights;
- International Covenant on Civil and Political Rights and its Optional Protocol;
- Convention on the Prevention and Punishment of the Crime of Genocide;
- International Convention on the Elimination of all Forms of Racial Discrimination;
- Convention on the Elimination of all Forms of Discrimination against Woman;
- Convention Against Torture and other Cruel, Inhuman or Degrading Treatment or Punishment; and
- Convention on the Rights of the Child.

3. *Statutory and Executive Sources*

Legislative and executive actions are two important sources of Argentine labor and employment law. There are many federal laws passed by Congress that address certain employment or labor law issues, such as the Employment Contract Law,[4] Work Hours Law,[5] Union Law,[6] and Collective Bargaining Agreement Law.[7] In addition, there are specific statutes that regulate work for certain activities, like agrarian workers,[8] traveling salespersons,[9] and construction workers.[10]

The Employment Contract Law recognizes the following principles that serve as guides for the parties and to the judges:

- protection of the employee, which includes requirements to: (1) rule in favor of employee in case of doubt about the terms of the law (*in dubio pro operario*), or (2) rule in favor of employee when there are two laws that conflict;
- prohibition against waiver of minimum labor rights, except when there is a formal settlement of a claim or when the

[4]Law 20,744, as amended.
[5]Law 11,544.
[6]Law 23,551.
[7]Law 14,250 as amended.
[8]Law 22,248.
[9]Law 14,546.
[10]Law 22,250.

two-year term set forth in the statute of limitations applies;
- preservation of the employment contract;
- supremacy of reality over formalities (substance over form);
- acting in good faith;
- nondiscrimination; and
- gratuity of labor procedures.

Executive Orders of the Executive Branch complement and regulate many laws. Under the Constitution, the government is empowered to issue any instructions and rules necessary for the enforcement of the laws approved by Congress, without altering their spirit with regulatory exceptions.[11] Only in exceptional circumstances can the President issue Executive Orders on grounds of necessity and urgency, provided they are decided by a general agreement of ministers who countersigns them together with the Chief of the Ministerial Cabinet.[12] It should be noted, however, that as the constitutional order was interrupted not less than six times between 1930 and 1983, it became customary that in the absence of Congress, the President assumed lawmaking powers and regulated substantial issues by Executive Orders-Laws. According to judicial interpretation, said Executive Orders-Laws have the same force as laws, and do not need to be confirmed by Congress once the constitutional order is reestablished.

4. *Collective Bargaining Agreements and Other Sources of Law*

In addition to the minimum standards set by statutes, Argentina has a strong organized labor presence, which through collective bargaining agreements has been able to secure concessions that play an important role in labor regulation, particularly because they are legally binding and usually cover a wide range of industries or branches of industries. Most workers in Argentina are covered by a collective agreement. The actual impact of the collective agreements varies widely from one industry to another, and in most cases, apart from fixing wages, they are not a meaningful source of labor regulation.

[11]National Constitution §28.
[12]National Constitution §99(3).

Employment rights also can be derived from employers' policies and practices.

Case law plays a certain role, albeit limited, in actual labor regulation, to the extent that leading judicial decisions may clarify the actual bearing of the numerous law provisions.

C. Division of Responsibility Between Federal and Provincial Governments

The federal government of Argentina has responsibility for enacting employment and labor laws.[13] The Argentine National Constitution grants power to the federal government to enact uniform employment and labor laws applicable to all provinces. Under this authority, the federal government has enacted comprehensive statutory regulation of employment and labor matters.

Provincial governments have responsibility for enforcing employment laws and hygiene and safety laws within their jurisdictions.

D. Major Administrative Bodies Responsible for Regulating Labor and Employment Law

The National Ministry of Labor (Labor Ministry) acts as a supervisor, with the authority to inspect when the provincial authority fails to enforce the employment and hygiene and safety laws.[14] In addition, the Labor Ministry enforces collective bargaining laws and union laws nationwide. Ultimately, when a party challenges the enforceability of a law, executive order, or resolution from the Labor Ministry or any other competent authority, the final ruling is reserved to the labor courts. Among its functions, the Labor Ministry analyzes national employment rates and develops programs for the promotion of employment, requests parties in dispute to appear at settlement hearings, etc. The labor authority of each province can appoint certain union members as inspectors, with powers to inspect for compliance with proper registration of workers and employees.

---

[13]National Constitution §75(12).

[14]Law 25,877.

The federal tax authority has powers to inspect compliance with social security contributions and income tax withholdings.

The health and medical organizations managed by the unions have specific powers to inspect contributions that are due to them.[15]

All administrative offices, including labor and tax authorities, are charged with conducting on-site inspections and auditing employers to ensure full compliance with the respective laws. In the event that a violation is found, an employer is entitled to present its defense. The administrative office then has the discretion to impose a fine against the employer. The amount of the fine that may be levied varies upon the nature of the infraction. Infractions of employment, labor, hygiene, and safety laws range from ARP 80 to ARP 5,000 per employee.[16] Infractions of social security contribution requirements, including the ones to health and medical organizations, also result in fines that depend upon the nature of the infraction, with the maximum fine being 200 percent of the social security contributions that were omitted.[17] In addition to the fines, extremely high interest rates are also imposed.

I. INDIVIDUAL EMPLOYMENT

A. Individual Contract of Employment

The Employment Contract Law sets forth a presumption of an employment relationship whenever there is an individual rendering paid services, unless the hiring party proves otherwise. The law puts on the hiring party the burden of proof about the different nature of those services. In addition, the law also sets forth the rule "substance over form," whereby judges have the power to analyze the nature of the services and eventually confirm whether the paid services should have been governed by the Employment Contract Law, regardless of any agreement or covenant of the parties.[18]

Generally, a written contract of employment is not required to create an employment relationship. Written contracts or job of-

[15]Law 23,660.
[16]Law 25,212.
[17]Law 17,250 and Resolution 1566/03 from the Tax Authority.
[18]Law 20,744 §23, as amended.

fer letters are not customary. However, special hiring alternatives, such as fixed-term contracts, contingent-term contracts, and apprenticeships, do require a written agreement, because they are special exceptions to the general rule of indefinite-term employment. In addition, particular agreements are convenient for certain matters such as definition of clientele and commission structure of traveling salespersons, entitlement to bonus pay, etc.

Employers' policies and usual practices are incorporated into the employment relationship. It is preferred that they be in writing and duly accepted by employees.

Employers legally are entitled to terminate any employment relationship, at any time and without cause. However, as per recent employment emergency regulations,[19] employers must comply with the reporting procedure of the labor authority, which depends upon the number of affected employees. In addition, employers must pay severance to the terminated employees. In certain cases, an employee also may be entitled to additional compensation or penalties.

B. Statutory Regulation of Employment

Employees in Argentina are entitled to numerous statutory protections. All aspects of the relationship from hire to discharge are regulated by statute.

The Employment Contract Law[20] is a consolidated text that contains detailed regulations dealing with subjects such as contract of employment; rights and obligations of employers and employees; special contracts of employment (e.g., as part-time, fixed-term contracts, seasonal employment); remuneration and protection of wages, hours of work, public holidays, and paid leave; maternity protection; minimum age and protection of young workers; suspension and termination of the contract of employment; and transfer of enterprises.

Special statutes have been enacted to regulate employment relations in specific occupations, such as agrarian workers, construction workers, salespersons, journalists, home workers, and domestic helpers.

---

[19]Executive Order 264/02.

[20]Law 20,744, as amended.

Collective or individual agreements can only improve employees' rights that are set forth in the laws.

1. *Hiring*

According to the Employment Contract Law,[21] no legal formality is required to create an employment relationship. However, once created, the relationship is endowed with legal significance and the expectation of certain rights.

The Employment Contract Law establishes a number of special hiring alternatives, including probationary periods, fixed-term contracts, contingent-term contracts, apprenticeships, and scholarships. Each of these arrangements is discussed below.

a. *Probationary Period*

Unless otherwise agreed by parties (i.e., waiver of trial period), all indefinite-term employment contracts are subject to a trial or test period of three months.[22] Employers must record the trial period in the labor book. During this period, the employer may dismiss the employee without just cause with 15 days of notice, and without any other severance. An employee may not be subject to more than one trial period with the same employer.

b. *Fixed-Term Contracts*

Fixed-term contracts are available and applicable only when the end of the contract term is fixed and certain and the employer has an extraordinary and temporary need for personnel.[23] A fixed-term contract is subject to a minimum term of one month and a maximum term of five years. The fixed-term employment contract may be renewed, but the total length of the relationship may not exceed five years. If the contract or its renewal is unreasonable, it will be deemed a contract for an indefinite term.

If a fixed-term contract is terminated without just cause before the lapse of the term, the employee is entitled to receive the regular severance pay of an indefinite-term employee,[24] plus a spe-

[21]Law 20,744 §21, as amended.

[22]Employment Contract Law §92 *bis*, as amended by Law 25,877.

[23]Law 20,744 §§93–95, as amended.

[24]See I.C.3., below.

cial indemnification equal to his or her remaining salary for the balance of the contract term. Upon normal termination of a fixed-term contract with a term of one year or less, the employee is not entitled to any additional payment or severance. In case of normal termination of a fixed-term contract exceeding a one-year term, the employee is entitled to receive 50 percent of the regular severance payable to employees who are terminated without just cause under an indefinite-term contract.

c. *Contingent-Term Contracts*

Contingent-term contracts are available and applicable only when the employer has an extraordinary and temporary need for personnel and the end of the contract is uncertain, but subject to the completion of a service or a specific job.[25]

Upon normal termination of the contract at completion of the service or job, the employee is not entitled to further payment or severance indemnity. However, in case of early termination without just cause, the employee is entitled to receive the regular severance of an indefinite-term employee, plus a special indemnification equal to his or her remaining salary through the end of the term of the contract.

d. *Apprenticeship*

The apprenticeship is an employment contract available only for individuals younger than age 28.[26] Employers and apprentices must comply with a training program. The minimum term of an apprenticeship contract is three months, and the maximum term is 12 months. Apprentices are subject to a working limit of 40 hours per week, including those for learning. In all cases, the employer must give one-month's prior termination notice. Upon normal expiration of the contract, the apprentice is not entitled to receive any severance payment. In case of early termination without just cause, apprentices may make a claim for severance payments. There are certain limits as to the number of apprentices that can be hired.

---

[25]Law 20,744 §§99–100, as amended.

[26]Law 25,013.

e. Scholarships

The scholarship is a special alternative for training purposes. Scholarships are not considered employment and are therefore exempt from social security contributions. These contracts are only available for students. There are three alternatives and each one has different rules and proceedings: (1) Executive Order 340/92; (2) Law 25,165 and Executive Orders 1200/99 and 487/00; and (3) Law 25,013 and Executive Order 1,227/01. Under alternatives (1) and (2), employers must enter into an agreement with an educational institution or organization (for example, university), setting out a training program to be performed at the employers' premises. The term of the scholarship varies in each alternative, as well as the work schedule.

2. Suspensions

The employment relationship can be suspended on various grounds, such as the employee's sickness, maternity, or holding of public or trade union office. Other grounds for suspension are lack of work because of a downturn in demand or disciplinary reasons, in which cases the suspension cannot be for more than 30 days within a 12-month period.

3. Employers' Obligations

Employers are obligated to register employees with governmental authorities, provide active and adequate work to employees, pay employees their salary and other compensation, as well as pay social security contributions to the government, provide equal employment opportunities to their employees, respect their dignity, provide a safe and hygienic workplace and provide workers' compensation insurance. Failure to fulfill these obligations entitles an employee to terminate the relationship and to consider himself or herself dismissed without just cause (constructive termination).

4. Employer Recordkeeping

To ensure compliance with the myriad regulations imposed on employers, the payroll and general employment information regarding each employee must be recorded and maintained by the employer in a special book. The book must be registered with and certified by the labor authority. Failure to keep the book or to properly record an employee's data results in a presumption against the employer and in favor of the employee regarding the information, plus severe penalties.

5. Joint and Several Liability

Argentine law sets forth joint and several liability between companies vis-à-vis affected employees. The principal company is jointly and severally liable with the contractor when it hires a work or service related to its ordinary and specific activity, to be executed within or outside its premises.[27] The law places on the principal company a duty of supervision over the contractor, whereby the principal company must audit the contractor's adequate fulfillment of its employment and social security liabilities. Failure to comply with the provisions of the law makes the principal company jointly and severally liable for the contractor's obligations with the personnel employed for those works or services related to the employment relationship, including its termination and social security obligations.

The law does not define when a work or a service is related to the ordinary and specific activity of the hiring party. The labor courts are very erratic on the interpretation of this issue, although the trend is a) that the concept of a normal and specific activity relates to the activity actually entertained by the principal company in its facility; b) that the works or services must complement or complete the principal company's normal activity, thus forming a technical unity for the core of the business; and c) that the segmentation of the activity by concession, distribution, and franchise, by which one party assigns to another certain tasks or products and excludes itself from doing the work related to those tasks or products, is a perfectly legal agreement, and no joint liability arises from it.

However, the nature of certain works or services (i.e., cleaning services, security, food vendors with concessions inside the facility, etc.) is still debated because it is not clear whether and to

[27]Law 20,744 §30, as amended.

what extent these works and services are connected with the principal company's normal and specific activity. The Supreme Court of Justice has not analyzed and ruled on this issue as regards such works or services yet (because it has a very restrictive procedure for accepting cases), and the first- and second-degree courts, as well as the legal commentators, are divided.

C. Termination of Employment

1. Causes of Termination

In general, an employee may be terminated by mutual agreement, resignation, dismissal with or without just cause, retirement, total disability, death of the employee, bankruptcy of the employer, or expiration of an agreed term of employment.

During the first three months of employment, an employee is considered a probationary employee and may be dismissed at will, with 15 days of notice and without other severance pay. After the probationary period is completed, an employee may be dismissed with or without cause, but the employee is entitled to notice and severance pay based on seniority.

The employer may terminate employment with just cause when the employee has engaged in certain activities that are offensive or prejudicial to the employer. Activities that may be considered offensive or prejudicial to the employer are determined according to the general principles of law and legal precedent. Under Argentine legal precedent, just cause includes insubordination as regards the employer's instructions, fighting or insults to fellow workers or superiors, work for a competitor, criminal offense toward the employer, and any other serious offense that does not permit the continuance of the relationship. The employer must provide the employee with a written explanation of the cause for termination. The employee can challenge the reason for termination in a judicial proceeding in which the employer bears the burden of proof. The labor courts are very restrictive when evaluating employers' arguments asserting just cause because dismissal should be the last resource of employers, to be used when no other sanction or remedy is available to them.

2. *Notice*

The employee and employer must give prior notice of termination.[28] This notice must be given in writing.

Employees must give their employers a termination notice of 15 days in advance. Employers have the obligation to give prior notice of termination to employees who are dismissed without just cause per the following guidelines: (1) employees whose seniority is less than three months must receive a prior termination notice at least 15 days prior to their dismissal; (2) employees whose seniority ranges from three months to five years must receive the termination notice one month prior to their dismissal; and (3) employees whose seniority exceeds five years must receive the termination notice two months prior to their dismissal. The abovementioned terms are to be computed as of the first day of the subsequent month to which formal notice is delivered.

If employers provide said notice, employees are entitled during the aforementioned term to receive a paid daily license of two working hours that may be accumulated in one or more working days in order to look for another job.

Employees of small and medium-sized companies, as defined in Small and Mid-Size Companies Law,[29] who are hired after April 6, 1995, are only entitled to a one-month notice.

---

[28]Law 20,744 §§231–239, as amended.

[29]Law 24,467 defines companies as small and medium-sized if they (1) do not have more than 40 employees, and (2) have annual billing inferior to: Annual Billing amounts in ARP (not including VAT) for the rural sector: $2,500,000; for the industrial sector: $5,000,000; for the commercial sector: $3,000,000; and the services sector: $4,000,000. Regarding companies existing prior to the effective date of this law, the estimation of employees shall be based on the staff existing as of January 1, 1995. Companies going beyond one or both above-mentioned conditions may remain under the special regime of this law for a term of three years, provided they do not double their staff (number of employees in their headcount/payroll) or billing mentioned in the second paragraph.

3. *Severance Payments*

As a general rule, employees are entitled to severance pay at the time of termination.

If the termination is without just cause, or due to the employee's total disability, the employer must make the following severance payments:

a. termination salary,
b. severance indemnity salary,
c. payment in lieu of prior termination notice (if applicable),
d. termination indemnity for seniority,
e. payment of accrued proportional vacation,
f. payment of accrued proportional 13th salary,
g. payment of the 13th salary on the payment in lieu of prior termination notice,
h. payment of the 13th salary on vacation,
i. indemnity for clientele, and
j. indemnity for maternity.

When employment is terminated with just cause or by mutual agreement; or through expiration of an agreed term; or by resignation, retirement, death or total disability of the employee; or by the employer's death or bankruptcy, the employer must make only the severance payments listed under *a*, *e*, *f*, and *h*, above.

When employment is terminated due to *force majeure*, or a reduction in the employer's business activities (not attributable to the employer), the employer must also make the severance payments listed under *g* and *h* above. In addition, in such cases, the employer must pay a termination indemnity for seniority (item *d* above), although at a reduced rate of 50 percent.

Due to the economic crisis, the National Congress and the Executive Branch passed a set of emergency provisions, including an additional aggregate severance pay provision when employers terminate without just cause, as well as a special reporting procedure for said terminations.[30] For the period July 1 through Decem-

[30]See I.C.5., below.

ber 31, 2004, the additional aggregate severance pay is 80 percent of the ordinary severance package.

Each component of severance pay is described below. For purposes of these payments, fringe benefits of a permanent or repeated nature must be taken into account (except as otherwise provided by law).

a. Termination Salary

The employer must pay the terminated employee's salary for the days worked in the month in which the termination occurs (accrued salaries).

b. Severance Indemnity Salary

The employer must pay a severance indemnity salary for the days remaining in the month in which the employee's termination occurs.[31] Under emergency regulations in force described under 3. above, an additional aggregate payment also is required. This payment is subject to income tax but is exempt from social security contributions.

Employees who work in small and medium-sized companies, as defined in the Law for Small and Mid-Size Companies,[32] and who are hired after April 6, 1995, are not entitled to this payment.

c. Payment in Lieu of Prior Termination Notice

If no prior notice of termination is given, employers must pay the terminated employee compensation in lieu of such omitted notice. Under emergency regulations in force described under 3. above, employers terminating an employment contract without just cause must also pay an additional aggregate payment. This payment is subject to income tax but is exempt from social security contributions.

d. Termination Indemnity for Seniority

Employers terminating an employment contract without cause must pay a termination indemnity for seniority, equivalent to the

[31] Law 20,744 §233, as amended.
[32] Law 24,467.

best gross monthly, normal and habitual salary in the last year of employment for each year of service or fraction thereof (in excess of three months). For purposes of this calculation, neither tax nor social security withholding is made.

The best gross monthly normal and habitual salary used in this calculation is subject to a statutory ceiling. Specifically, it may not exceed three times the average remuneration contemplated in the pertinent collective bargaining agreement. If more than one collective bargaining agreement is applicable to the activity of the employer, the one most favorable to the employee applies. This ceiling is applicable to both unionized and nonunionized employees. As per the law, the minimum amount payable as a termination indemnity for seniority is two actual gross monthly salaries.[33] However, as per a ruling of the Supreme Court of Justice, the statutory ceiling set forth in the law is unconstitutional when that cap exceeds 33 percent of employees' best gross monthly, normal and habitual salary; the court held that the termination indemnity for seniority should never be less than 67 percent of an employees' best gross monthly, normal and habitual salary.[34]

Under emergency regulations in force described under 3. above, this payment is subject to an additional aggregate payment. The employer is obliged to pay 50 percent of the termination indemnity for seniority when the termination of the employment contract is the result of employer's bankruptcy or reorganization procedures due to causes not attributed to employer, employee's death or total disability, and expiration of a fixed term contract for more than one year of term. The employer may also be able to reduce the termination indemnity for seniority by proving that a dismissal is the result of circumstances beyond the employer's control, such as decrease in available work or force majeure, such as a natural disaster.[35] Courts have recognized that only unforeseeable and unavoidable cases may diminish the employee's indemnity, and have also interpreted the provision in such a way

[33]Law 20,744 §245, as amended.

[34]Vizzoti, Carlos Alberto vs. AMSA S.A. (Supreme Court of Justice, Sept. 14, 2004).

[35]Law 20,744 §247, as amended.

that almost all of these events fall into the category of entrepreneurial risk. Layoffs must be in order of seniority.

e. Proportional Vacation Payment

Employees are entitled to a minimum amount of paid vacation, ranging from 14 to 35 days.[36] At termination, employees are entitled to payment for the proportional vacation accrued during the year. This payment is subject to income tax but is exempt from social security contributions. The following formula is applied to calculate the proportional vacation payment:

(monthly salary (net of social security withholding) / 25 days) × (days worked in the year / 365 days) × days of vacation according to seniority

Under emergency regulations in force described under 3. above, employers terminating an employment contract without just cause must also pay an additional aggregate payment.

f. Thirteenth Salary

In addition to the hourly wage, each employee is entitled to an annual bonus (13th salary) equal to one month's salary.[37] The bonus is paid in semi-annual installments in June and December, and the accrued portion of the bonus is payable to the employee at the time of termination. This payment is subject to social security and income tax.

g. Proportional 13th Salary in Lieu of Termination Notice

If the employee has not received prior termination notice, then the employer must pay 1/12 of the amount of the payment in lieu of prior notice as the 13th salary discussed in f. above.

h. Payment of Proportional 13th Salary on Vacation

The employer must pay, as 13th salary on the vacation accrued during the year, 1/12 of the amount payable as proportional vacation.

---

[36]See V.C.1., below.

[37]See V.A.2., below.

i. Indemnity for Clientele

In case of termination of the employment contract with traveling salespeople with more than one year of seniority, an additional severance item, known as the indemnity for clientele, must be paid by the employer.[38] This indemnity is equal to 25 percent of the statutory severance pay described above.

j. Indemnity for Maternity

A recent mother who has enjoyed maternity leave has the right to resign after her leave expires and will be entitled to 25 percent of the statutory severance pay based on seniority.[39]

4. Penalties

Employers must pay severe penalties to employees if the employer violates statutory requirements in any of the following ways:

a. failure to pay statutory severance;
b. improper registration;
c. failure to deliver employment certificates;
d. lack of payment of social security contributions withheld to employee;
e. dismissal without just cause of women during pregnancy, maternity, or the wedding period; and
f. dismissal of union representatives without just cause.

Each case is analyzed below.

a. Failure to Pay Statutory Severance

Employers must make severance payments within four working days of the termination date. Employers that fail to make severance payments in due course, causing the terminated employees to file a legal action to pursue payment, are subject to a penalty[40]

[38]Law 14,546.
[39]Law 20,744 §183, as amended.
[40]Law 25,322 §2.

equal to 50 percent of the amount of the statutory severance indemnities for notice and seniority.

b. Improper Registration

Employers who fail to register the employment relationship in the mandatory labor books are subject to a number of penalties.

When the employee demands the registration prior to termination, sending a copy of this demand to the AFIP (National Tax Authority) within 24 business hours after having requested it from the employer, the employee is entitled to receive the fines set forth in sections 8, 9, or 10 of National Employment Law[41] if the employer refuses to modify its records within 30 days.

According to Section 8, employers who fail to register the existence of the employment relationship shall pay 25 percent of all remuneration accrued during the employment relationship but under no circumstance for remuneration accrued before December 25, 1989. Under no circumstance may this compensation be lower than three times the employee's best regular and habitual monthly salary.

According to Section 9, employers who fail to register the real date of hiring and register a later one shall pay 25 percent of all accrued remuneration within the hiring date and the actual registration date, but under no circumstance for remuneration accrued before December 25, 1989. According to Section 10, employers who fail to register the actual salary and register a lower one shall pay 25 percent of all non-registered and accrued remuneration during the employment relationship, but under no circumstance for remuneration accrued before December 25, 1989.

In addition, Section 15 requires that if the employee is terminated for any reason for two years after his demand of registration, the employer also must pay to the terminated employee an additional 100 percent of the regular mandatory severance pay based on seniority paid to employees upon their dismissal without just cause.

---

[41]Law 24,013, as amended by Law 25,345.

Finally, those terminated employees who had not demanded proper registration during the employment relationship are entitled[42] to a special fine equivalent to an additional 100 percent of the statutory severance pay.

c. Failure to Deliver Employment Certificates

Upon termination of the employment relationship, the employer has 30 calendar days to provide the employee with two certificates: the Work Certificate and the Certificate of Services and Remuneration. The purpose of these certificates is to attest to the nature and length of service and to the remuneration paid and social security contributions made. The latter also is used for obtaining the retirement benefits.

If the employer fails to provide the certificates within the 30-day period, then the employee has two working days thereafter to request their delivery. An employer that fails to comply with a timely employee request is liable for three times the employee's highest monthly normal salary of the last year or, if lower, during the term of the employee's services.[43] This indemnity is payable without prejudice to any other penalty that may be imposed by the competent judicial authority.

d. Failure to Pay Social Security Contributions Withheld for the Employee

When the employer, acting as withholding agent, withholds social security or union contributions and fails to deposit such amounts at the time of termination of the employment contract, it is liable from that time to pay the employee a fine equivalent to his or her monthly salary until said deposit is completed.[44]

e. Dismissal Without Just Cause of Women During Pregnancy, Maternity, or the Wedding Period

The law provides for an additional indemnity where the employer dismisses an employee without just cause during her preg-

---

[42]Law 25,322 §1.

[43]Law 20,744 §80, as amended.

[44]Law 20,744 §132 *bis*, as amended.

nancy or maternity period. The Employment Contract Law sets forth a presumption that termination is due to pregnancy or maternity reasons where the dismissal is without just cause during the 7½ months before or after birth, so long as the woman provides the employer with effective notice of the pregnancy or birth.[45]

The Employment Contract Law also provides a special indemnity for a dismissal based on marriage. In this case, the law sets forth a presumption that termination is due to marriage where the dismissal is without just cause during a term of three months before or six months after the marriage, so long as the employee provides the employer with effective notice of the wedding date. Most courts have ruled that this presumption applies only to women, although men are entitled to protection if they provide conclusive evidence that they were dismissed for this reason.[46]

For a dismissal based on pregnancy, maternity, or marriage, the special indemnity is 13 months' salary.[47]

f. Dismissal of Union Representatives Without Just Cause

Employers cannot discharge workers council representatives, nor can they change these working conditions without their consent.[48]

A special judicial procedure must be followed to sanction or terminate a representative with just cause. The law grants the workers council representative the choice, when employers sanction them or dismiss them without following the special judicial procedure, to request reinstatement by means of interim measures or to request a special compensation for damages, equal to the salaries corresponding to the remaining term of representation, plus one year of salaries.

5. Emergency Provisions

Emergency Law 25,561, enacted on January 6, 2002, suspended the employers' right to dismiss employees without just cause for a period of 180 days from the Law's date of enactment.

---

[45]Law 20,744 §178, as amended.
[46]Law 20,744 §181, as amended.
[47]Law 20,744 §182, as amended.
[48]Law 23,551.

Subsequent Executive Orders extended this term.[49] Employers who terminate contracts without just cause during the protected period must pay an aggregate additional amount as penalty, at the rate specified under I.C.3. above. The rate applies to the severance items described in I.C.3.b, c, d, e, g, and h, above. As an exception, employees hired beginning January 1, 2003, who increase the payroll as compared to the count on December 31, 2002, are not subject to the suspension and aggregate pay rules.[50] The courts are erratic when applying the additional payment to any special protection, such as for pregnancy, maternity, or marriage leave,[51] as well as indemnities for lack of registration pursuant to Section 15 of Laws 24,013 or 25,323.[52]

Pursuant to Executive Order No. 264/02, the employer must give prior notice of the dismissal without just cause to the labor authority, by complying with a reporting procedure.[53]

D. Privacy

The right to privacy is a constitutional right,[54] which declares that those private actions that do not offend in any way public order or public morals and do not damage others are only reserved to God and exceed judges' authority.

One issue that concerns employers is related to general screening of candidates. Section 16 of the National Constitution sets forth that all men and women are equal before the law and qualified for work, with the sole condition being their natural ability or skill. The issue is to what extent an employer can measure the candidate's natural ability without invading his or her privacy.

Regarding medical screening, the regulations in force rule that medical screening and testing can be done only to evaluate the natural ability of the candidate or monitor the current

---

[49]The protected period was originally set in the Emergency Law 25,561 in 180 days and during such period severance items were to be doubled. Emergency Executive Orders 883/02, 662/03, 256/03, 1351/03, 369/04 and 823/04 have extended such period.

[50]Emergency Executive Order No. 2639/02.

[51]See I.C.4.e., above.

[52]See I.C.4.b., above.

[53]See IV.A.1., below.

[54]National Constitution §19.

employee's qualification for the job. The regulations set forth the minimum medical tests to be taken by candidates and employees. The employer can require additional specific tests whenever the nature of the industry or services so requires them. The regulations specifically mention that the results of these tests cannot be used for discriminating against the candidate or employee. In many cases, the invasion of privacy claim is basically related to an employer's discriminatory decision.

Drug and alcohol testing are not provided for in the regulations and the ordinary set of screening tests does not reveal them. Although there is no provision for this, it is advisable to obtain employees' consent when performing these tests. Employees under the effects of drug or alcohol during working hours create a risk and employers must separate them from their job. Application of sanctions is cumbersome because they require conclusive evidence. Unless the effect is clearly evident and confirmed by witnesses, it could be difficult to prove because employees could refuse to take the test and also could argue that a physician hired by the employer administered the test and the employee had no opportunity to supervise the conducting of the test. In many cases where there are incidents at work, such as fighting or property damage, employers end up sanctioning employees for the outcome rather than attempting to test them for drug or alcohol use.

As regards AIDS testing, the specific law does not authorize the test without individual's consent.

Psychological screening during the hiring process is permissible to determine the candidate's qualifications and capabilities. Screening during the relationship would be acceptable only if a condition is somehow likely related to stress or other psychological cause.

Checking prior criminal, credit, and commercial references is permissible, as long as these records are related to the position. Prior employment screening is permissible.

As regards employers' right to control their employees' work and personal belongings, Section 70 of the Employment Contract Law sets forth that control systems for protecting company's property must always protect the worker's dignity, must be made with discretion, must apply to all workers, and must be applied through automatic selection mechanisms. This section also requires that only women can check other women's bodies.

Employers are entitled to monitor the appropriate use of work tools such as e-mail, the Internet, and phones. Using today's technology, employers can extract detailed listings from main servers and can require employees to explain whether e-mails, web pages, or calls were work-related. Employers would not violate an employee's privacy through this activity. It is advisable that employees be informed of this practice and that a control mechanism be applied to all employees, however.

Under data privacy law, employers cannot transfer or provide information about their employees to third parties, unless authorized by the employees or by the law.

A violation of privacy entitles the adversely affected employee to terminate the employment relationship with just cause (constructive termination). However, the employee is required to formally request that the employer cease such offensive conduct before the employee may terminate the relationship.

Additionally, a violation of privacy and the subsequent compensation for damages would be adjudicated under Civil Code provisions for torts.

E. Employee Duty of Loyalty, Trade Secrets, Covenants Not to Compete

1. *Employee Duty of Loyalty*

Section 63 of the Employment Contract Law states that "the parties have the duty to act in good faith, fitting their acts and doings to those typical of a good employer and employee, when executing, performing or terminating the employment contract or the labor relationship." Both the employer and the employee must act in good faith. Many other contractual obligations derive from the duty to act in good faith. Thus, the employer must comply with certain obligations (e.g., not to discriminate, avoid any abuse of rights, pay the salaries and wages, provide for employees' safety, entrust to them the performance of certain tasks, and the like), and the employee must act as a good worker, undertaking the duties of loyalty and confidentiality. Section 85 of the Employment Contract Law, in turn, establishes that "the worker must comply with all those fidelity or loyalty duties deriving from the nature of the tasks entrusted to them, keeping all kind of information available to them in the strictest confidence or in secret."

A set of labor rights and duties arises from these legal provisions. Some of them are positive (diligence in performing the work, duty to report to the employer any difficulty preventing the regular performance of the work, duty to give notice of the dangers and hazards that may adversely affect the assets, property, and individuals of the company, duty to preserve labor tools, duty to prevent thefts and other irregularities, etc.), and others are negative (not to cause any damage, not to disclose secrets, not to engage in unfair competition, not to accept bribes or gifts from customers or suppliers, etc.).

The higher an employee's position and function and the more reliance placed on the employee, the higher the employee's duty of loyalty to protect the company's interest is. Similarly, the more serious the breach, the greater the loss of confidence will be. An employee does not breach his or her duty of loyalty merely by looking for another job, provided the employee does not engage in unfair or disloyal acts such as working for a competitor simultaneously and without the employer's consent, engaging in unfair competition, or breaching the confidentiality duty.

The employer is authorized to apply punitive measures to an employee who breaches the duty of loyalty. These measures may consist of a warning, a suspension, or a justified dismissal, depending upon each case. Before dismissing an employee, the employer must assess the seriousness of the default as well as the employee's background (seniority, etc.). The employer must always make sure that the punitive measure is proportional to the default committed. Judges are empowered to assess the reasonableness of the punitive measures, but they usually seek to preserve employment and consider dismissal only as a last resort. However, unless there is a fixed- or contingent-term contract, or some specific reason for preserving employment (e.g., employee is a trade union delegate, or is pregnant or a newlywed, etc.), the employer may dismiss an employee at any time by paying the employee the pertinent severance compensation made up of seniority pay and any compensation for lack of the prior termination notice required by law.

In general terms, the duty of loyalty is extinguished by the termination of the labor relationship. In principle, former employers do not have an absolute right to keep their clients, because competitors may obtain the clients by lawful means. However, Argentine courts have pronounced judgment in some unfair competition cases in which employees acted in bad faith or unfaithfully abandoned their employer for the purpose of competing with the employer. When the employee leaves a job to join or create a competitive company and begins a disloyal struggle for clientele, by taking advantage of deceitful maneuvers to harm or cause a serious detriment to a former employer, courts have upheld the duty of loyalty.

2. *Trade Secrets*

Section 85 of the Employment Contract Law establishes that the employee must not disclose any kind of information available to the employee that is to be treated as confidential and secret.

The "confidentiality duty" is part of the duty of loyalty discussed in 1., above. In general, to enjoy trade secret protection, information must be generally unknown in the industry, must give the employer a competitive advantage by virtue of its secrecy, and must be subject to reasonable secrecy measures. Both technical and non-technical information may be deemed a trade secret; thus, computer source codes, chemical formulae, inventions, specialized machinery, manufacturing processes, overseas customer or supplier identities, payroll data, and compilations of information may merit protection. Customer lists, in some instances, may also meet this standard if they contain information that cannot be easily compiled from memory or public sources. If information is readily ascertainable through non-confidential means, such as telephone directories or trade publications, trade secret status will be denied.

For the duty of confidentiality to arise, the information must be available to the employee and be kept in the strictest secrecy by the employee. The purpose of the duty of confidentiality is to protect the employer from competitors, because the employees are forbidden to disclose any information belonging to the employer.

Section 1 of the Confidentiality Law 24,766 sets forth that all individuals or corporations may prevent the information kept by them from being disclosed to, or being acquired or used by, third parties without their consent in a way contrary to honest commercial usage, provided said information meets the following conditions: (1) is secret, in the sense that it is neither generally known nor may it be easily obtained by the individuals regularly using said kind of information; and (2) has a trade value for being secret; and (3) has been subject to reasonable measures, under the circumstances, to be kept secret by the person lawfully holding it. Any non-fulfillment of contracts, abuse of confidence, inducement to commit a breach, and acquisition of information not disclosed by third parties having knowledge or ignoring, on account of their serious negligence, such acquisition implies that said acts shall be deemed contrary to honest trade usage.

Section 3 sets forth that any individual who as a result of his or her employment, work, position, office, performance of profession, or business relationship has access to information complying with the conditions mentioned in Section 1, the disclosure of which was forbidden, shall refrain from using and disclosing it without a justified reason, or without the consent of the individual keeping said information or of its authorized user.

Law 24,766 also provides that the following measures may be taken as a result of third parties' access to confidential information:

- provisional remedies or injunctions intended to cause the infringement to cease;
- civil actions filed to forbid the use of the undisclosed information and obtain the recovery of damages suffered; and
- criminal actions for infringement of trade secrets.

Section 156 of the Criminal Code establishes that those who, on account of their status or craft, employment, profession, occupation, or art, become acquainted with a trade secret, the disclosure of which may cause a harm, and disclose it without a fair cause, shall be punished by a fine of $1,500 to $90,000 and a special deprivation of their right to work for a period of six months to three years. Moreover, depending on the case the employer may dismiss with just cause the employee who breached the duty of confidentiality.

3. Covenants Not to Compete

The duty not to compete or engage in any unfair competition during the course of the employment is part of the duty of loyalty discussed in 1., above. The duty not to engage in unfair competition is the obligation that best defines the duty of loyalty to the company's interests, by virtue of which the employee may not devote himself or herself to a similar activity that currently impairs or may adversely affect the employer's interests.

Under Section 88 of the Employment Contract Law, the worker must refrain from performing any transactions on his or her own account or on account of third parties that may adversely affect the employer's interests, unless otherwise expressly authorized by the latter.

The following three requirements must be met for an unfair competition to exist:

> (1) *Negotiation on the employee's own account or on account of third parties.* The employee's performance of activities identical or analogous to those performed by the employer belonging to the same industry or trade, or consisting of the same services, gives rise to a conflict of interest with the company. The duty to refrain from doing so includes both acts performed on the employee's own account and those performed in cooperation with third parties, competing with the employer, when the employee is under a duty of fidelity towards the latter. Moreover, legal textbooks and opinions of legal authors as well as case law express the view that the duty not to compete is not restricted to the tasks but includes all effective terms of the labor relationship.
>
> (2) *Actual or potential detriment to the company's interests.* It is not necessary that the damage shall have effectively been suffered. The mere possibility or threat of suffering damage will suffice (potential damage). This is so because, if employees compete unfairly, although not having caused any damage, they have nonetheless breached their loyalty duty towards the company.
>
> (3) *Lack of employer's authorization.* The employer may authorize the employee to exercise a certain competitive activity; this is the only situation in which the employee's conduct would not be a violation of the duty of loyalty.

In general, the duty not to compete is extinguished by the termination of the labor relationship. Notwithstanding this fact, the confidentiality duty continues indefinitely, even after the termination of the labor relationship, without any express agreement being necessary.

The validity of agreements not to compete with the employer after the termination of the labor relationship must be assessed on the basis of the right of freedom to work set forth in the Argentine Constitution, which affirms the right of any individual to perform any kind of commercial or industrial act or activity freely. Under this general principle, the employee may not be compelled to stay inactive or to perform any other kind of activity different from the one related to the employee's own skills and knowledge, because it is logical that the employee is more valuable working within the same branch or field of expertise in which the employee was trained from the very beginning and in which the employee specializes.

Some legal textbooks and opinions state that non-compete agreements covering a brief period after the termination of the labor relationship and for a valuable consideration are valid. Usually such restrictive covenants prohibit joining competitors or restrict post-employment activities, such as customer solicitation or solicitation of former fellow employees.

There are not enough judicial precedents to set out a trend. Legal commentators believe violation of such post-termination agreements would give rise to an injunction (a negative covenant) that, in case of default, would trigger the legal consequences typical of a violation of loyalty, according to Argentine civil law. Section 634 of the Civil Code states that "should it be impossible to reverse the performed act, the creditor may file a claim to recover all damages suffered as a result thereof." Therefore, the employer could resort to certain provisional remedies, such as injunctions, intended to avoid the damage, as well as to a claim for damages.

The duty of loyalty to be fulfilled during the labor relationship has been repeatedly dealt with by the legal textbooks, opinions, and case law. However, after the termination of the labor relationship, the duty of loyalty (including the duty not to compete) has not been significantly treated, except in some cases concerning unfair competition.

An employment agreement establishing the duty not to compete for a brief period and in consideration of the payment of a fair compensation, plus a covenant setting forth the confidential nature of certain information, would highly protect the employer's interests and could be enforced later on. However, employers may find it difficult to enforce confidentiality covenants, since it is not easy for them to find conclusive evidence to prove the breach of the confidentiality duty by their former employees, as well as the actual damage effectively suffered by them. Similar considerations apply to cases of unfair competition.

II. Collective Bargaining

A. Introduction

Organized labor has played an important role in Argentina's turbulent political history. Unions were the backbone of the populist state created by Juan Peron, who served as chief of labor relations in the regime of General Pedro Ramirez prior to making a successful bid for the national presidency in 1946.

Peron's success came largely from his ability to draw rural and agricultural workers and the industrial working class into his political Labor Party, the *Partido Justicialista* (Labor Peronist Party), which, now divided among several factions, continues to play a dominant role in national politics.

At the high point of Argentine organized labor—in the mid-1950s—about 50 percent of workers belonged to unions. At the present time, the rate of participation has fallen considerably. Carlos Menem's administration (1989–1999) was widely seen as a major turning point in the history of the labor movement. Although backed by the unions and partly dependent on them for executing his policies, Menem's administration carried out reforms that weakened union power. Menem's government replaced industry-wide collective bargaining with labor-management negotiations at the individual company level.

Former President Fernando De la Rua (1999–2001), under pressure from the International Monetary Fund (IMF) to further reform Argentina's labor laws, managed to obtain from Congress a Labor Reform Law (No. 25,250, effective June 2000). The aim of the proposed reforms was to give companies more flexibility in hiring and firing workers, expecting to spur growth among small-to-medium-sized companies and, in turn, help to reduce unemployment (a major problem in Argentina since 1995, with rates that fluctuated between 16 and 20 percent).

Following De la Rua's abrupt exit, the political and economic situation became extremely turbulent. Emergency regulations were approved in January 2002, during Eduardo Duhalde's provisional presidency; many of them have direct relation with labor and employment matters and are still in effect today (e.g., duplication of mandatory severance payments, special procedures to execute dismissals without just cause).

Nestor Kirchner, elected president in April 2003, declared his intention to reverse many of the reforms in labor and employment matters that were carried out during Menem and De la Rua's administrations. By enacting labor regulations that favor unions and workers to the detriment of the employers, Kirchner has managed to obtain support from the three union confederations: the CGT, the MTA, and the CTA. Although the three confederations coexist, only the CGT has official recognition from the Labor Ministry to represent the organized union force, and it is the most important one in terms of affiliated unions.

Recently, a new Labor Reform Law[55] abrogated Law No. 25,250. The new law reestablished industry-wide collective bargaining (to the detriment of the labor-management negotiations at the individual company level) and, unless parties agree to the contrary, established the continuous effect of the collective agreement after its expiration, until a new collective agreement replaces the one in force.

B. Union Recognition

The Argentine National Constitution[56] guarantees workers the right to organize themselves under worker associations. In Argentina, trade unions are organized as civil legal entities. Workers and employees may freely become members or opt-out of trade unions.

Law 23,351 regulates trade unions. Under this law, all workers have the right to establish and to join trade union associations

---

[55]Law 25,877.

[56]National Constitution §14 *bis*.

of their choice. Workers also have the right not to join a union and to withdraw from a union. Workers are free to set up industry or branch-level unions, craft unions, or company-level unions.

Any trade union is granted the right to represent their individual members. However, for a union to be granted collective representation rights it is indispensable that it be certified as a *trade union with union recognition*, upon fulfillment of the following requirements: (1) the union is officially registered and has been acting for at least six months; (2) the union's membership covers no less than 20 percent of the workers it intends to represent; and (3) it is the most representative trade union in the respective industry or branch, within a given territorial scope (frequently a city or a province, but may also be the national territory). To obtain recognition, unions must submit a copy of their bylaws to the Labor Ministry for approval. The bylaws must clearly state the union's territory and level of representation, such as workers industry wide, with a specific craft, specific company, or a combination.

Apart from very few exceptions, only one union in each branch or industry, and within a given geographical area, is granted trade union recognition. This means that in practice the country has a single-union structure, because a union that is merely registered does not enjoy collective representation rights. Only those trade unions that are officially recognized as most representative of a particular group of workers have the monopoly of the representation vis-à-vis the employers and can negotiate a collective agreement.

The Labor Ministry is the competent authority to register unions and to grant *trade union recognition.* It also determines which union represents a particular group of workers in the event that two or more unions compete for the representation of the same workers. Its decisions may be challenged before the National Labor Court of Appeal.

Two or more trade unions may establish a federation, and two or more federations may establish a confederation.

Collection of union dues by check off is mandatory under the trade union law. This includes ordinary and extraordinary union dues that are due by all union members, as well as special contributions that may be due by all workers, including nonunion members.

Recognized unions are entitled to manage health and medical organizations that provide medical attention to non-exempt employees. These organizations receive their funds from a portion of mandatory social security contributions

Therefore, once a union obtains the official recognition, it becomes economically powerful and is almost impossible for a new union to replace it.

Today, very few new unions are recognized because most workers are already under the representation of an existing recognized union. Consistently, almost all activities or industries have recognized unions, making it impossible for companies to be "union free," even when their employees are not affiliated with a union.

The system is criticized because it concentrates the power on unions with official recognition, violating the spirit of the ILO agreements.

If a dispute arises between two recognized unions, the matter should be mediated by the federation that they have in common. If they do not have a common federation, or if the issue is between two federations, the issue should be addressed by the common confederation. However, if there are internal disputes or if there is no common confederation, unions will force the ruling of the Labor Ministry. The decision of the Labor Ministry is legally binding, but may be appealed to the National Labor Appellate Court.

C. Collective Bargaining Agreements

Collective Bargaining Agreements' Law 14,250, as amended,[57] and its Executive Order 199/88, establishes the legal framework for collective bargaining agreements. Collective bargaining agreements can only create better work conditions than the ones set forth in the laws.

Only recognized unions or union federations can be parties to a collective bargaining agreement. As regards chambers of employers, the Labor Ministry has powers to define whether such entity has sufficient representation of the sector.

[57] Law 25,877.

The same parties to a collective bargaining agreement may renegotiate the terms of their prior agreement entirely, or only a portion thereof. However, when the level of negotiation is not the same, the terms of the collective bargaining agreement may only be more favorable to employees. This analysis shall be made comparing each institution (for example, leaves, salaries, work hours, etc.) separately.

Once approved, collective bargaining agreements are binding, not only on the members of the unions and chamber of employers that are parties to the agreement, but on all workers and employers in the particular activity or industry involved.

High-level employees and managers are not usually subject to collective bargaining agreements.

Parties to a collective bargaining agreement may negotiate the scope and applicability of the agreement, including workers within the following alternatives: (1) employer's industry (for example, metallurgic); (2) particular jobs within an industry (for example, supervisors); (3) job duties regardless of the industry (for example, traveling salesperson); and (4) a particular company.

Through collective bargaining agreements, recognized unions can agree with employers concerning special contributions that will be mandatory for all employers or employees that are ruled by the agreement, regardless of their affiliation to the union.

The Labor Ministry coordinates the negotiation of collective bargaining agreements, regardless of the territory where they will apply. This process begins when either the employer (i.e., a company, group of companies, or a chamber) or a recognized union notifies the Labor Ministry of its intention to negotiate a collective bargaining agreement. The Labor Ministry then sets a time period during which the parties must meet to negotiate. Labor Ministry officials attend the negotiations. Once an agreement is reached, the parties must submit the agreement to the Labor Ministry for approval. However, when the agreement is limited to a specific company, the Labor Ministry does not have to approve it unless one of the parties requests it.

The Labor Ministry's approval means that an agreement does not violate any law or public interest. Approval is necessary for a collective bargaining agreement to become enforceable against all employers and employees.

Generally, collective bargaining agreements state a term of validity. However, unless parties agree to the contrary, the law sets forth that after the expiration of the initial term, the existing collective bargaining agreement remains in effect until a new agreement is negotiated and approved by the Labor Ministry. Under this scenario, many collective bargaining agreements dating from 1975 and 1989 still remain in effect, although salary scales and specific issues may be periodically revised.

Most of the collective bargaining agreements in force are enforceable on a national level and relate to specific industries (for example, metallurgic, plastic, food).

Negotiation during recent years was mostly on a company level and related to special issues or agreements that integrate with one of the activities. The clauses usually included in the agreements are salary adjustments, flexibility on assignment of work, work time, and commitment of labor peace.

Individual conflicts related to enforcement of collective bargaining agreements are resolved within each jurisdiction, while collective (union) conflicts are resolved at the national level.

D. Strikes

The Argentine National Constitution[58] guarantees the right of workers and employees to strike. Only recognized trade unions can call for strikes.

For a strike to be legal, it is indispensable that a settlement period of not more than 15 days be observed,[59] during which period a settlement must be tried before the Labor Ministry. The conciliator may extend the settlement period for five additional days, after which, if no agreement is reached, the parties are left free to engage into action.

The Labor Ministry can declare a strike illegal if the trade union fails to comply with the settlement procedures, or if the strike does not respond to a labor cause, or if there is strike-related violence either on or off the employer's property. Illegal strikes en-

[58] National Constitution §14 *bis*.

[59] Law 14,786.

title employers to request workers and employees to withdraw, and eventually to dismiss employees with just cause due to such offense. In addition, the union that called the illegal strike could be suspended or lose their official recognition.

Workers and employees are not obliged to adhere to a strike, but if they do, they are not entitled to their wages. Employers cannot suspend employees on grounds of the strike but can ordinarily dismiss without just cause. However, due to emergency regulations in force, an employer would be required to comply with the procedure set forth for an employment crisis.

III. Representation by Entities Other Than Unions

Only trade unions with official recognition from the Labor Ministry have the right to legally represent workers, so trade unions without said recognition are only legal entities, without effective power to negotiate or call on strikes, and without economic power.

Workers' representation at the enterprise level is held by workers' delegates, who can integrate internal committees. Workers' delegates and members of internal committees are elected by all the workers in the enterprise, but they must be union members and should have been working in the enterprise for at least one year before the election is held. Workers' delegates hold office for two years and can be re-elected.

Workers' delegates are protected against dismissal except in the case of serious misconduct. This protection starts as from the moment they put forward their candidature and lasts until 12 months after their mandate has come to an end. During this period, the delegates cannot be suspended from employment, transferred to another job or position, or otherwise prejudiced in their conditions of work.

These workers' delegates represent both the workers of the enterprise and the union vis-à-vis the employer. They are entitled to verify the compliance of their employer with employment laws and with the collective bargaining agreement. Workers' delegates may submit grievances to the employer, and they may accompany labor inspectors when the latter undertake inspections in the enterprise.

When negotiating a collective bargaining agreement that will apply for a specific company, workers' delegates should be included at the discussion table, along with union representatives.[60]

Under the Labor Union Law No. 23,551, there can only be one workers' delegate when a company has between 10 and 50 workers; two delegates when a company has between 51 and 100 workers; and one additional delegate for every 100 workers, when a company has more than 101 workers. Collective bargaining agreements can increase the number of delegates.

Collective bargaining agreements stipulate the number of work hours that delegates have in order to fulfill their function. Delegates are entitled to meet with fellow workers on company premises and also meet with a representative of the employer.

IV. Redundancy and Transfers of Undertakings

A. Redundancy

Due to the economic and employment crisis, Emergency Law No. 25,561 (effective January 7, 2002) suspended the employer's right to dismiss employees without just cause for 180 days and increased the penalty for infringement of such suspension with an additional aggregate pay of the severance items as discussed under I.C.3. above.

The regulations impose the same procedure for dismissals without just cause (including ordinary redundancies) and redundancies based on economic or other grounds not attributed to the employer. However, the amount of severance differs.

Executive Order No. 264/02, enacted February 11, 2002, expressly prohibits employers from dismissing employees without first filing a report with the Labor Ministry. The content of the report and the proceedings depend on the number of employees to be terminated.

[60] Law 25,877 §22.

1. *Layoffs*

a. *Massive Layoffs*

Under the National Employment Law,[61] a massive layoff is where 15 percent or more of a company's headcount is terminated when the company has fewer than 400 employees, 10 percent of the headcount is terminated when the company has more than 400 and fewer than 1,000 employees, and 5 percent of the headcount is terminated when the company has more than 1,000 employees.

In such cases, the employer must comply with a Crisis Prevention Proceeding,[62] filing a report with the requirements set forth in Executive Orders 265/02 or 2072/94, depending on the number of employees in the payroll. The Ministry of Labor will notify the union and call for hearings so that the parties may discuss alternatives to minimize the impact and reach an agreement. Unions are reluctant to accept dismissals in such situations and will negotiate for full payment of severance plus extended medical coverage for employees; this can be an extremely complex and time-consuming procedure.

b. *Other Dismissals and Redundancies*

When dismissals do not reach the percentages necessary to qualify as a massive layoff, including individual contract terminations, the employer must file a report complying with the requirements of Executive Order 328/88 and file the special form therein. Employers must file this report with the Ministry of Labor at least 10 days prior to the actual dismissal date.

When the employee is included in or should be within a given category of the collective bargaining agreement, a copy of this report also must be filed with the union.

If the employer fails to file this report or fails to comply with the Ministry's potential call to a settlement hearing, the Labor Ministry may (1) reinstate the dismissed employees in their job positions with a right to back wages, and (2) impose fines.

Nevertheless, the employee's receipt of severance entitlements and silence thereof for a period of more than 30 days would prob-

---

[61]Law 24,013.
[62]Law 24,013, ch. VI.

ably create a serious presumption of the employee's acceptance of the termination.

B. Transfers of Undertakings

According to the Employment Contract Law, in case of transfer of an ongoing concern, transferees must acknowledge employees' seniority and all rights related to such seniority. Both transferor and transferee shall be jointly and severally responsible for all obligations as from the transfer date and all obligations after that date shall rely on the transferee. Employees can only oppose the transfer of their relationship when some type of damage is caused. Additionally, the transferred employees may oppose the transfer if the buyer's solvency is substantially lower than that of the seller.

The Employment Contract Law provides that the parties of an acquisition of an ongoing concern are jointly and severally liable for all labor obligations existing at the time of the transfer. The statute of limitations is two years from the day the credit is borne. Case law has decided as a rule of law that the buyer of an ongoing concern is also liable for the seller's labor obligations deriving from relationships terminated prior to the transfer. Therefore, the buyer of the business is equally responsible for all debts to former employees who were terminated prior to the transfer.

From a social security standpoint, any non-assessed liabilities of the seller would not pass onto the buyer if the Social Security Authority is notified of the proposed ongoing concern transfer at least 15 working days before its consummation and does not object to it three months thereafter, respectively. Normally, but not always, this notice would trigger a social security audit of the seller. If the notice is not given, the ongoing concern transfer may still be consummated, but the seller and buyer shall be jointly and severally liable for non-assessed social security obligations that the seller may owe, for the period of the statute of limitations for social security debts, which is 10 years. If (1) the audit is not conducted during those three months, or (2) the audit is conducted and either the seller is not assessed any social security payments or, if assessed, the seller pays them, the joint and several liability between the seller and buyer with respect to non-assessed liabilities will disappear and the buyer would not be liable for such liabilities that the seller may owe. In the case of assessed social security, buyer and seller will be jointly and severally liable, therefore, the corresponding due diligence should be made.

V. WAGES, HOURS, AND LEAVE

A. Wages

1. Minimum Wage

The minimum hourly wage is ARP 2.25 and the minimum monthly salary for salaried workers is ARP 450.[63]

Collective bargaining agreements set forth minimum salary wages, in accordance with each category of workers (i.e., salary scales). In addition to the minimum wages, the collective bargaining agreements also include additional payments, of a fixed or variable amount.

In many cases, companies pay additional compensation on top of the salary scales of the collective bargaining agreements.

2. Thirteenth Salary

Employees are entitled to receive, each calendar year, a 13th salary, consisting of 1/12 of the total amount received by the employee during the calendar year. The 13th salary is payable in two semi-annual installments, due on June 30 and December 31. The amount of each installment is equal to one-half of the highest remuneration paid to the employee (including all benefits) during the corresponding semester, and is considered additional remuneration for services rendered during such period. The employee must receive the prorata of this payment at the time of termination.

3. Salary Increases

During the years 2002 and 2004, under the argument that after devaluation salaries were not adequately compensating the in-

---

[63]Resolution 2/04, in force since September 1, 2004 .

crease of the cost of living, the government imposed on employers payments that were originally non-remunerative and later on became of a remunerative nature. As of May 2004, the amount of ARP 224 was added to the basic pay of the salary scales of the collective bargaining agreements. In addition, since January of 2004, ARP 50 was to be paid as a non-remunerative payment.[64]

4. *Bonuses and Other Variable Compensation*

There is no legal restriction on employers paying, at any time, any amounts as bonuses to their employees. Repetitive bonuses generate an acquired right in favor of the employee.

Under Argentine law, there is no legal obligation on employers to offer to their employees stock purchase, stock option, or profit-sharing plans. The benefits employees receive through such plans would be, in principle, of a remunerative nature and should be recorded in the statutory payroll book.

5. *Fringe Benefits*

In principle, all benefits are considered part of the salary and subject to social security contributions.

However, Law 24,700 provides that certain fringe benefits are not considered salary and therefore are not subject to such contributions. The law creates two groups of fringe benefits: (1) benefits of a non-remunerative nature, not subject to social security taxes; and (2) benefits of a non-remunerative nature that are subject to a special social security contribution of 14 percent. These two groups of fringe benefits are not salary and therefore should not be taken into account when estimating severance payments.

As regards the provision of housing, education assistance, or a car for personal use of the employees or their families, employers must treat the economic value of such benefits as remuneration, subject to social security contributions.

[64]Executive Order 1347/03.

a. Non-Remunerative Benefits

The non-remunerative fringe benefits listed below cannot be granted to employees in substitution for, or to account as, their remuneration:

- employers' cafeteria services;
- lunch coupons issued by special authorized companies up to a daily limit of $15, granted for those days actually worked;
- reimbursement for medical and dental services and medicine expenses, duly evidenced by receipts issued by licensed physicians and pharmacies;
- provision of work clothes and of any other item related to the clothing and to the equipment of the worker, to be used exclusively at the workplace;
- reimbursement for child-care and nursery expenses, evidenced by receipts, incurred by workers with children younger than six years old;
- provision of school supplies, school uniforms, and toys for the employee's children;
- training or specialization courses;
- payments for properly documented funeral expenses to funeral homes or insurance companies;
- withdrawals made by managing partners of limited partnerships from the tax year's earnings that are properly accounted for in the balance sheets;
- reimbursements for expenses, without receipts, related to the use of a vehicle owned by the company or by the employee, calculated and based on distance traveled, within a set range, or those reimbursements that are declared deductible, in the future, by the General Tax Authority;
- travel expenses of salesmen, evidenced by receipts and the reimbursements for car expenses under the same conditions as set out above; and
- use of housing owned by the employer, located in neighborhoods or premises surrounding the workplace, or leases in those cases where access to housing is very difficult.

b. Non-Remunerative Benefits Subject to a Special Social Security Contribution

Food coupons and groceries delivered through specialized companies[65] cannot exceed 20 percent of the salary of a regular employee and 10 percent of the salary of a top employee or manager. Employers must pay a special social security contribution of 14 percent over the amount of this benefit.

c. Increase in Food Coupons and Groceries

From July 1, 2001, up to March 31, 2005, employers may increase up to the sum of $150 per month the food coupons and groceries granted to their employees, when employees' gross monthly salaries are equal or inferior to $1,500.[66] This increase shall not be computed in order to calculate the maximum caps admitted to grant these benefits (10 percent of the monthly gross salary earned for employees not comprised in the collective bargaining agreements and 20 percent for the employees falling within its scope). Moreover, this increase shall be exempted from the payment of the special contribution of 14 percent on the amounts paid by the employers to their employees in food coupons.

In addition, transportation cards are also a non-remunerative social security benefit up to a maximum cap per working day.

B. Hours

1. Working Time Limits

Laws 20,744 and 11,544 provide for a working limit of 8 hours per day or 48 hours per week.[67] Therefore, a regular working schedule would consist of eight-hour days, six days per week (Monday through Saturday). Neither limit is mutually exclusive.

---

[65]Executive Orders Nos. 1477 and 1478/89.

[66]Executive Orders No 815/01 and 510/03.

[67]Special working time limits apply to apprenticeships and scholarships.

Under regulatory Decree 16,115/33, the employer may set forth a schedule with unequal distribution of the 48 working hours, provided that the workday does not extend for more than nine hours.

Night work (performed between 9 p.m. and 6 a.m.) cannot exceed seven hours. Mixed day and night work should be computed by reducing eight minutes per each night hour of work (or pay these eight minutes as overtime).

Work under fixed or rotated shifts can exceed the legal limit, as long as the average of the hours worked in a three-week period does not exceed the 8 hours per day or 48 hours per week limit; thus, the limit would be 144 hours in 18 working days. In addition, under no circumstance can these employees work more than 56 hours per week. Overtime will only be paid when they exceed the 144-hours limit within 18 days of work. Employees are not entitled to overtime when they work in night shifts and exceed the 7 hours, but are entitled to a day of rest every 7 days of night work, besides the weekly rest of Saturday evening and Sunday. Only when this additional day of rest cannot be granted will the employee be entitled to overtime pay at a rate of 8 minutes for every night hour worked.

The working time limits established by Argentine law are of a public policy nature, which means that individual or collective contracts may allow a more convenient schedule for the worker (e.g., a weekly schedule of 36 hours), but may not provide for a regular work schedule in excess of the legal limits.

2. *Overtime*

When an employee works beyond the working time limits and their exceptions, the extra hours are considered overtime. According to Executive Order 484/2000, under no event may the employee work overtime in excess of 30 hours per month or 300 hours per year. Exceeding these limits could trigger the imposition of a fine by the labor authorities.

Overtime during ordinary days must be compensated with an additional 50 percent of the employee's regular hourly salary. An additional 100 percent of the regular hourly salary must be paid for overtime work on Saturdays after 1 p.m., or on Sundays or holidays.

3. *Rest Periods*

Employees are entitled to a rest period of not less than 12 hours between the end of one working day and the beginning of another.[68]

An employee also is entitled to a weekly rest from 1 p.m. on Saturdays until 12 p.m. on Sundays, or a rest period during the week of the same duration. If an employer fails to grant an employee an appropriate rest period, when an employee has worked Saturday and Sunday, the employee may, with 24-hours' notice, take the first working day of the next week off. In such a case, the employer must pay the employee all of the day's wages. However, the employee is not compensated as though the time were overtime, unless the employee has worked more than 48 hours in the preceding week.

4. *Exempt Employees*

Top employees are exempted from working time limits and overtime.[69] Top employees include the chief, manager, director, top administrators or technicians with personnel under their command, assistant managers, private secretaries of directors and managers, section chiefs, and department chiefs.

5. *Employer Penalties*

Should an employer be found liable of violating the regulations described above, the labor authorities may levy fines. The fines range between ARP 250 and ARP 1,000 per employee.[70]

C. Leave

1. *Vacation*

Employees are entitled by statute to a minimum and continued period of paid annual vacation of 14 calendar days when se-

---

[68]Law 20,744 §97.
[69]Law 11,544 §3.
[70]Law 25,212.

niority does not exceed 5 years; 21 calendar days when seniority is between 5 and 10 years; 28 calendar days when seniority is between 10 and 20 years; and 35 calendar days when seniority exceeds 20 years.[71] The employee must be paid at the beginning of his or her vacation for all days, not just those he or she would have worked. At termination, employees are entitled to payment for accrued vacation.[72]

2. *Sick Leave*

Each employee is granted the right to sick leave.[73] Employees with less than five years' seniority are entitled to three-months' paid leave for injury or illness. Employees with more than five years' seniority are entitled to six months of sick leave. The leave period automatically is doubled for employees with dependents.

Upon the expiration of the paid leave, if the employee is not in physical or mental condition to return to his or her position, then the employer must keep the position open for the employee for at least one year without further compensation. An employee may be entitled to reinstatement for up to one year after paid sick leave is exhausted.

Upon the expiration of the one-year waiting period, if the employment relationship is not reestablished, either of the parties may terminate the relationship, without any right of the employee to claim severance indemnity.

If a total disability of the work capacity is certified, the employee shall be entitled to a severance payment as if the employee were dismissed without just cause. If the disability is not absolute, the employer must provide the employee with a task in accordance with his or her work capacity, or pay a severance payment as dismissed without just cause.

---

[71]Law 20,744 §§150–157, as amended.

[72]For a discussion of vacation payments at the time of termination, see I.C.3.a., above.

[73]Law 20,744 §208, as amended.

3. *Maternity Leave*

Female employees are entitled by statute to maternity leave of 45 days before and 45 days after childbirth.[74] Upon the worker's request, prenatal leave may be reduced to 30 days, in which case postnatal leave would be extended to 60 days. During maternity leave the female worker is entitled to cash benefits paid out of social security funds.

During the period of maternity leave, employees are entitled to allowances. These allowances are basically the payment of an amount equal to the basic salary, without perks or other compensation, and are paid by a mutual governmental fund. Women on maternity leave also are entitled (at their discretion) to an additional non-paid leave of up to six months, beginning at the expiration of the mandatory leave.

A female worker is entitled to two daily breaks, of 30 minutes each, to breastfeed her child. This entitlement lasts for one year after childbirth, but it may be extended upon submission of a medical certificate.

4. *Other Paid Leaves*

All employees are entitled to additional short leaves of absence for special occasions,[75] such as:

- birth of employee's child: two calendar days;
- marriage: 10 calendar days;
- death of the spouse, or the person to whom employee was in apparent marriage, or children or parents: three calendar days;
- death of a brother/sister: one calendar day; and
- in order to sit for an examination at a high school or university level: two calendar days per examination, with a maximum of 10 calendar days per year.

Collective bargaining agreements may grant additional days of leave.

---

[74]Law 20,744 §§177–179, as amended.

[75]Law 20,744 §158, as amended.

5. *Holidays*

Argentina has 11 national holidays: January 1, April 2, Good Friday, May 1, May 25, June 20, July 9, August 17, October 12, December 8, and December 25.

Employees are paid for national holidays, even if they do not work on them. However, if employees do work on national holidays, they are entitled to overtime pay at the rate of 100 percent, based on the regular hourly rate.

In addition, certain holidays are optional, which means that employers may grant them at their sole discretion (for example, Good Thursday or December 24).

VI. ANTIDISCRIMINATION

The Employment Contract Law prohibits any kind of discrimination among workers, based on sex, race, nationality, religion, political affiliation, union affiliation or age.[76] Additionally, it states that the employer must treat all employees equally under identical situations. Unequal treatment is defined as involving arbitrary discrimination based on sex, religion or race, but not as involving treating individuals differently in response to reasonable principles, such as more efficiency, dedication, or reduction of work.[77]

There are specific laws that prohibit discrimination based on diabetes,[78] epilepsy,[79] or genetic factors.[80]

An employee who suffers workplace discrimination also may seek relief under the Employment Contract Law 20,744 (ECL). Under the ECL, the employee may bring suit to recover the salary that would have been earned absent the discrimination, or may treat the discrimination as an offense terminating his or her em-

[76]Law 20,744 §17.

[77]Law 20,744 §81.

[78]Law 23,573.

[79]Law 25,404.

[80]Law 421 of Buenos Aires City.

ployment due to a constructive dismissal and claim regular severance from the employer.[81]

In addition, according to the Antidiscrimination Law 23,592, those who on arbitrary grounds impede, obstruct, restrict, or in any way reduce the equal exercise of the rights and guarantees set forth in the National Constitution, shall be obliged to take back the effects of the discriminatory act or to cease in such conduct. Under the law, the cases based on race, religion, nationality, ideology, political or union opinion, gender, economic position, social condition and/or physical characteristics are in particular considered discriminatory acts. Through this law, employees discriminated against on said grounds may request reinstatement or any other remedial action to end discriminatory conduct or mitigate its effect. The affected employee may file a petition for relief from discrimination under Section 43 of the National Constitution, which provides for a summary proceeding to guarantee constitutional rights. The adversely affected employee also may seek indemnity for pain and suffering and emotional distress and for lost wages under the provisions of Law 23,592. There is no statutory ceiling to such damages, although Argentina's current legislation does not provide for punitive damages.

There are not a significant number of judicial cases of discrimination brought in the Argentine labor courts. Rather, most such claims are associated with wrongful dismissals, where the employer claims to have discharged the employee for cause and the employee claims discrimination on the part of the employer.[82] There is little significant precedent regarding discrimination in the hiring process. In one case, the Civil Court of Appeals[83] decided that the arguments of the employer were insufficient and therefore ordered it to hire women in future.

---

[81]For a discussion of severance pay, see I.C.4.a., above.

[82]See I.C.1., above.

[83]Civil Court of Appeals, Chamber H, Dec.16, 2002 - Fundacion Mujeres en Igualdad y otro vs. Freddo S.A.

VII. Occupational Safety and Health and Workers' Compensation

A. Occupational Safety and Health

The Hygiene and Safety Law[84] provides the general legal framework for hygiene and safety in the workplace.

Specifically, the Law establishes a number of employer obligations, requiring employers to:

- conduct a pre-hiring medical examination for each employee;
- maintain machinery and other working elements in good condition;
- install the necessary equipment for elimination of gases, vapors, and other harmful particles in suspension;
- maintain the electrical supply system and water supply in good condition;
- eliminate, isolate, or reduce harmful noises and/or vibrations;
- install equipment for fire protection;
- make available adequate first aid services;
- comply with hazardous material regulations;
- install safety signs in visible places;
- teach safety and hygiene regulations and practices to company personnel;
- report any and all accidents or on-the-job sickness; and
- hire physicians and hygiene and safety experts specializing in work-related accidents and their prevention, who must comply with a series of duties within the company's premises.

Executive Order 351/79 completes the regulations of Law 19,587 with 233 articles that deal with the following topics:

- employers' internal and external medical services, scope and implementation of the services, medical examinations, and employer liabilities;

[84] Law 19,587.

- employers' internal and external hygiene and safety services, scope and implementation of the services, and employer liabilities;
- employers' facility building characteristics and water supply;
- hygiene facilities' condition, environmental pollution, lighting and colors, ventilation, noises and vibrations, electric supply, machinery and tools, elevators and lifts, workplaces with special risks (e.g., explosive materials, dusts, gases), and fire protection;
- individual workers' protection elements;
- training of personnel;
- accidents and on-the job sickness statistics; and
- penalties.

B. Workers' Compensation

The Workers Compensation Law[85] provides a general framework of compensation payable to employees who suffer an accident or illness related to the job. Accidents on the way to or back from the workplace are also covered.

According to the Workers Compensation Law, employers must hire workers compensation insurance with companies specially created for this purpose, named "ART." Employers may freely choose any ART duly registered.

ART must counsel their insured about prevention of labor risks, supervise their insured prevention policy and compliance with occupation safety regulations, provide medical attention to employees who suffer an accident or illness related to the job, and pay special compensation due to a job-related accident or illness. The employers' obligations are to pay the premium and comply with the Hygiene and Safety Law 19,587.

The Law provides for compensation in money and in services or goods:

- Employment risks to be compensated by ARTs in money are: temporary disability, partial permanent disability (up

---

[85]Law 24,557 and Executive Order No. 1278/00.

to 66 percent disability), total disability (66 percent or more disability), and death. The maximum compensation in money amounts to ARP 230,000.

- Employment risks to be compensated with services or goods are: medical and pharmaceutical assistance, prosthesis, rehabilitation, employment training for relocation, and burial services.

As per the law, no civil action is admitted against employers or their ART based on a labor accident. However, many injured employees have contested in the labor courts the validity of this "shield system" whereby employers are exempted from civil liability. A Supreme Court decision has declared that the shield was not reasonable and therefore was unconstitutional.[86] The Court in that decision not only ordered the ART concerned to comply with its limited obligations, but also authorized the claimant to seek further damages. This decision created direct exposure for employers, since supplemental insurance for civil liability has not been permitted, on the grounds that Law 24,557 did not authorize such civil actions.

VIII. Pensions and Benefits

A. Introduction

The Argentine government provides a comprehensive public welfare and retirement system. Payment to this system is mandatory and rates are based on a percentage of the worker's earnings.

After devaluation of the currency, there are almost no private pension plans. Due to the heavy burden placed on employers by the mandatory state scheme, few offer additional benefits, unless granted as part of the collective bargaining process.

---

[86] Aquino, Isacio vs. Cargo Servicios Industriales S.A., (Supreme Court of Justice, Sept. 21, 2004).

B. Retirement and Pensions

Argentina maintains a mandatory retirement and pension system.[87] According to the Retirement and Pension Law, all employees working in Argentina must be covered by the Argentine social security system. The Law provides that employees should be duly registered with the social security authorities.

Both employees and employers are required to pay into the system. The contribution is figured as a percentage of the employee's gross wages.

Workers qualify for retirement at age 65 for men and age 60 for women. To qualify, the worker must show 30 years of contributions into the system. When an employee qualifies for the ordinary benefit under the state retirement plan, the employer may request that the employee retire. The employer must provide the employee with all necessary paperwork and information to obtain the pension. The employer must retain the employee until the pension benefits begin, but not for longer than one year from the request for retirement. The employment relationship is terminated at that time, and the employee is entitled to receive limited severance pay.

As regards their future retirement and pension benefits, employees can choose between: (1) an exclusive public scheme, or (2) a combination of a public and capital-based scheme. This last alternative consists of enrolling in competing, privately managed companies named A.F.J.P., instead of with the state pension agency.

---

[87] Law 24,241.

1. Social Security Contribution Rates

Contribution to the social security system is per the following chart:

Concept	Law	Employee's Contribution (Decree 1387/2001; Decree 1676/2001; Decree 2203/2002 and Decree 390/2003)		Employers' Contribution (Decree 814/2001, modified. by Law 25,453)	
		Public System (in %)	Capitalization (in %)	Services that invoice more than 48 million (in %)	Remaining activities- (in %)
Retirement and Pension	24,241	From 3/1/2002: 11.00	From 3/1/2002: 5.00 From 3/1/2003: 7.00 From 7/1/2005: 9.00 From 10/1/2005: 11.00	12.71	10.17
Family Allowances	24,714			5.56	4.44
Unemployment Fund	24,013			1.11	0.89
Health and Medical for Retired Employees	19,032	3.00	3.00	1.62	1.50
Health and Medical for Employees	23,660	3.00	3.00	6.00	6.00
TOTAL		17.00	13.00	27.00	23.00

Employers' contributions shall depend upon their activity and amount of invoicing. The contribution is higher when an employer's activity is a provision of services or commerce and the amount invoiced exceeds ARP 48,000,000.[88]

Employers with a maximum payroll of 80 employees and annual net invoicing does not exceed ARP 10,800,000 for agricul-

[88]Executive Order 814/01 and Law 25,453.

tural activities, ARP 43,200,000 for industry and mining activities; ARP 86,400,000 for commercial activities, and ARP 21,600,000 for service activities,[89] are granted an exemption (for the term of 12 months) equivalent to 1/3 of the employers' contributions in force, in relation to each new employee that they hire before December 31, 2004. This exemption shall be raised to half of the employers' contributions if the employee hired to hold the new position was a beneficiary of the Head of Household Program (*Plan Jefes de Hogar*).[90]

Employees' contributions also depend upon the retirement benefit they have chosen. The system that includes capitalization through private retirement funds has a lower rate of contribution, but this reduction should be eliminated in October 2005. Employers must withhold employees' contributions and pay them to the tax authorities together with their contribution as employers.[91]

Both contributions to the social security system have currently a cap. Employees' contributions are based on actual gross salary, up to a gross amount of ARP 4,800. The portion of the monthly salary exceeding ARP 4,800 is not subject to social security contributions.

Employers' contributions also have a cap, which is to gradually increase, and by October 1, 2005, it will disappear.[92] Contributions from October 1, 2004, to March 31, 2005, have a cap of ARP 8,000; and from April 1, 2005, until September 30, 2005, have a cap of ARP 10,000.

Employers also must pay the premium for workers' compensation insurance as a social security contribution.[93] This premium is fixed by the ART concerned and depends upon the activity of the employer. It is usually an average of 3 percent of the payroll.

Employers also must pay a contribution of 14 percent of the amount of food coupons and groceries delivered through specialized companies to its employees, when they are delivered.[94]

---

[89]Executive Order 817/04.

[90]Law 25,877.

[91]Law 24,241, Executive Orders 1387/01, 1676/01, 2203/02 and 390/03.

[92]Executive Order 491/04.

[93]Law 24,557.

[94]Law 24,700.

C. Health Care

Employee health insurance is mandated by statute.[95] The cost of health insurance is financed by a 3 percent employee contribution and a 6 percent employer contribution, based on the employee's gross monthly salary.

Workers and employees under a collective bargaining agreement can elect from one of the institutions controlled by labor unions.

Exempt employees can elect from another list of institutions that provides better services.

D. Life Insurance

Employers must hire and pay the premium for a collective life insurance policy in favor of their employees. The mandatory coverage amounts to $6,480[96] per life or total disability of employee.

Collective bargaining agreements may also request additional life insurance for employees.

E. Family Allowances

Employees receiving a salary lower than ARP 1,725 are entitled to receive from the government a payment of a specific amount to aid them with regard to certain special events (e.g., pregnancy, birth of a child, adoption, marriage, per child, child with disability, and school help). A maternity allowance is paid to all women during their maternity leave, even for those having salaries exceeding ARP 1,725.

F. Unemployment

The Argentine government also pays an unemployment subsidy when individuals have more than one year of seniority and are dismissed without just cause, or as a result of force majeure or

[95]Law 23,660.

[96]As of March 1, 2004, pursuant to Resolution SSN 29734/2004.

lack of work, as a result of a constructive discharge, or as a result of the employer's bankruptcy or reorganization procedure or expiration of the agreed term. The amount of the aid ranges between ARP 150 and ARP 300, and between 4, 8, or 12 installments.

Individuals older than age 45 who have children attending school or children less than 5 years old or older than 18 with a disability and who continue to be unemployed, are entitled to receive additional six months of aid, with a subsidy equivalent to 70 percent of the one already paid.[97]

The government has also designed a complimentary plan for certain groups of unemployed individuals.[98] This aid, in the amount of ARP 150, is aimed at unemployed individuals who are the head of a family with children under 18 years of age or with disabled children of any age, or when the woman is pregnant.

IX. IMMIGRATION

Argentina's immigration policy correlates to the need for, or excess of, available labor. Foreigners desiring employment in Argentina must have an entry permit as well as a work visa. Executive Order No. 1117/98 establishes the procedure to obtain an entry permit and a visa, provided always that the applicant be employed by a local entity that requests his or her entry permit.

In the first stage, the procedure requires that the applicant file an application with the Argentine Migration Authority requesting an entry permit. In addition, the requiring entity must also file certain documentation with the Migration Authority. After filing the application along with the required documentation in due course, the entry permit usually is granted during the following 20 to 45 days.

In the second stage, the Argentine Consulate with jurisdiction over the place of residence or country of origin of the applicant receives the entry permit issued by the Migration Authority, along with certain documents of the applicant, and collects the

---

[97]Resolution MTEySS 858/02.

[98]Executive Order 565/02.

visa fees. The Consulate then should grant the visa within the following two or three days.

In addition, before the expiration of the term for which the visa was granted, the requiring entity should request its extension before the Migration Authority, filing certain documents and paying the visa extension fee.

Once the visa has been obtained, the applicant needs to obtain the "D.N.I." from the Registry of Civil Status. The D.N.I. is the local identification document, which is necessary to open a bank account and to obtain a social security number, as well as the local driving license. The D.N.I. is granted to the applicant for the same term of the visa and can only be renewed after the visa has been extended.

With respect to customs, once the applicant has the corresponding visa stamped on the passport, he or she will be entitled to enter Argentina without paying any import duty on personal belongings, including furniture, personal effects, electronic devices, etc. A custom's agent should distinguish these exempt personal belongings from those items that are not exempt.

CHILE*

Introduction

The Republic of Chile, a country of more than 14 million residents, has experienced substantial economic growth in recent years while undergoing significant political changes. In 1990, Chile returned to a normal democratic system of government after 17 years of military rule. During its years in power, the military regime implemented dramatic changes in the country's employment laws to give employers greater flexibility and encourage economic growth. With the return of a democratically elected government in 1990, it was believed that Chile's employment laws would quickly become much more protective of workers than those adopted by the military government. However, although the new government did, indeed, undertake a gradual reform of Chile's employment laws and continues to move in that direction, changes have come slowly and have not departed dramatically from the earlier legal framework. This appears to be due both to the fact that conservative forces controlling the Chilean Senate have resisted broad changes in the country's employment laws and to the now well-established model of an open and competitive economy shared—with more or less emphasis—by almost all political forces in the country. Notwithstanding legislation passed by the Chilean Congress on September 11, 2001, implementing new protections for workers,[1] the country's employment laws remain among the most employer-friendly bodies of labor law in Latin America.

---

*Laurence E. Stuart, Legge, Farrow, Kimmit, McGrath & Brown, L.L.P., Houston, Texas, with Ignacio García and Diego Ferrada, Cruzat, Ortuzar & Mackenna Ltda., members of Baker & McKenzie, Santiago, Chile.

[1]See discussion in the Introduction, at B.2., below.

A. Basic Organization of Chile's Government

The government of Chile is divided into three branches: the Executive Branch, the Legislative Branch, and the Judicial Branch.

- The Executive Branch is headed by the President of the Republic, who serves a single six-year term. In 2000, Ricardo Lagos Escobar, the socialist candidate of the *Concertación de Partidos por la Democracia* or Coalition of Parties for Democracy, was elected president. Enforcement agencies within the Executive Branch are discussed in C., below.
- The Legislative Branch consists of the National Congress, which has two houses: the Senate, whose members are elected for eight-year terms; and the Chamber of Deputies, whose members are elected for four-year terms.
- The Judicial Branch consists of various courts, the highest of which is the Supreme Court. A special group of courts, the Labor Courts, are devoted to employment-related claims.[2]

B. Sources of Labor and Employment Law

The rights and obligations of employers and employees in Chile arise from a number of sources, including the National Constitution, statutes and decrees, Executive Branch regulations, judicial and administrative jurisprudence, employers' internal regulations, and both individual and collective employment contracts. Each is discussed below.

1. National Constitution

The Constitution of 1980, as amended, establishes certain social rights relating to employment and social security.

- The Constitution establishes a right of all people to work in the profession of their choice and prohibits employment

[2]The Labor Courts are further discussed in the Introduction, at B.4., below.

discrimination based on factors other than personal ability.[3]

- The Constitution states that a law or public authority may not require that individuals be affiliated with or not affiliated with a particular organization or entity as a condition of carrying out any task or performing any employment.[4] The Constitution permits, however, legally established qualifications for certain professions, including the requirement of a university degree.[5]
- The Constitution establishes certain norms relating to unions, collective bargaining, strikes, and social security.[6]

These constitutional rights and norms bind private as well as public employers.

2. *Legislated Laws*

Most of the laws currently governing the employment relationship in Chile originated as legislated statutes or executive decrees issued under legislative authority.

In Chile, the Legislative Branch of the state can delegate legislative power to the Executive Branch to issue what are known as "Decrees with the Force of Law," and this delegation of authority has occurred frequently in the area of labor and employment legislation. Moreover, during the military regime, the Executive Branch assumed legislative power and issued decree laws, many of which remain in effect in the labor and employment area.

In 1987, the then-existing statutes and decree laws dealing with labor and employment were compiled into one unified body of law called the Labor Code. With revisions and additions, this 1987 Labor Code remained in effect until 1994, when a new Labor Code was issued. The 1994 Labor Code deals primarily with employee rights, individual employment contracts, unions, collective bargaining, and administrative and judicial procedures relating to

---

[3]*Constitución Política de la República* (Chilean Constitution), art. 19, §16, para. 2.

[4]*Id.* art. 19, §16, para. 3.

[5]*Id.*

[6]These are discussed in II. and VIII., respectively, below.

employment. Other statutes and regulations outside the Labor Code deal with pensions, health insurance, and workers' compensation insurance.[7]

On September 11, 2001, the Chilean Congress passed legislation implementing significant labor reforms.[8] Revisions to the Chilean Labor Code include expansion of reporting requirements to cover employers with as few as 11 employees, imposition of penalties when an employer improperly designates its official reason for terminating an employee, and imposition of penalties for failure to comply with the terms of a negotiated severance agreement. The 2001 amendments also expand union organizing rights and require employers to pay a replacement bonus as a pre-condition to replacing strikers after a work stoppage. Additional changes include increased statutory overtime premiums, changes to the standard workweek to take effect in 2005, and creation of a claim for unlawful retaliation for union support or involvement. These items are discussed under the appropriate topic entries below.

3. *Executive Guidelines*

The Executive Branch has the power to issue guidelines that may take the form of administrative regulations, decrees, or instructions.

- Administrative regulations, comparable to those issued by federal agencies in the United States, are a systematic collection of legal standards for the execution of a law or for the exercise of powers vested in the Executive Branch by the Constitution.[9]
- A decree is a more specific guideline that applies general legal norms to a particular situation.[10]

---

[7]These are discussed in VIII. and VII., respectively, below.

[8]Law No. 19,759, published in "Official Gazette" on Oct. 5, 2001, effective Dec. 1, 2001.

[9]An example of an administrative regulation relating to labor and employment is Supreme Decree No. 745 of the Ministry of Health (*Ministerio de Salud*), which established basic health and environmental conditions in the workplace.

[10]Among the decrees in the labor and employment area is one containing the annual national list of labor arbitrators.

- Instructions are orders issued by the Executive Branch for the purpose of carrying out tasks pursuant to the laws or regulations.[11]

All three types of Executive guidelines are important in the labor and employment area.

4. Judicial and Administrative Jurisprudence

Jurisprudence on labor and employment matters may come from either the courts or administrative agencies. Although both types of jurisprudence can provide guidance for employers, only rulings by the courts ultimately govern and enforce the rights of parties. Administrative agencies do, however, have authority to impose fines and other sanctions on employers that they find are not in compliance with labor laws and regulations, and they have developed a large body of administrative jurisprudence on this subject.

Absent an agreement to the contrary, disputes under a labor contract, whether collective or individual, may be referred to the appropriate Labor Court and then to a civil Court of Appeal. If an employee brings a claim in the Labor Court, that employee is barred from asserting the same claim before the Labor Directorate (*Dirección del Trabajo*).[12] An employee may, however, raise the claim with the Labor Directorate before initiating a lawsuit in the Labor Court, and many employees do follow this course of action.

Courts and administrative agencies have the authority to interpret the law, but where the law is clear, a judge or administrative authority may not ignore the letter of the law and issue a ruling based on its "spirit" instead. If no law exists on a particular issue, however, a judge is free to issue a judgment based on general principles.

Because Chilean labor statutes are often complex in form, jurisprudence plays an important role in determining rights and

---

[11]For example, the Labor Inspectorate's (*Inspección del Trabajo*) Instruction No. 4 (May 15, 1987) defines the procedure for calculating overtime pay for employees with a monthly, weekly, daily, or hourly wage.

[12]See the Introduction, at C., below, regarding disputes brought before administrative agencies.

obligations in employment relationships, but the jurisprudence itself is sometimes contradictory, thereby contributing to the difficulty of applying the labor statutes. Complicating matters further is the fact that the rulings of the Supreme Court, the highest court in Chile, can provide guidance for lower courts deciding similar cases, but they are not binding on the lower courts.

5. *Employers' Internal Regulations*

The Labor Code requires employers with more than 10 employees to establish internal regulations containing certain employment practices.[13] At a minimum, these policies must address the following matters:

- working hours;
- rest periods;
- types of remuneration;
- the place, day, and time of remuneration payments;
- employees' obligations;
- prohibited employee conduct;
- the identity of the employer's representative responsible for handling employee grievances;
- the means of ensuring compliance with the laws and regulations relating to social security and military service;
- the norms and directives on risk prevention, safety, and hygiene in the workplace;
- special provisions excusing women, minors, and older workers from heavy-labor jobs;
- sanctions for violations of the employer's internal regulations; and
- procedures for imposing those sanctions.[14]

An employer's internal regulations may not be less favorable than employment standards established by statute or contract. Apart from the above internal regulations required by the Labor Code, an employer may establish whatever policies it wishes to manage its

---

[13] Labor Code art. 153, as amended by Law No. 19,759 (Oct. 5, 2001).
[14] *Id.* art. 154.

business, provided those policies do not violate legal standards or those established by individual or collective labor contracts.

6. *Employment Contracts*

Individual and collectively bargained employment contracts can create rights in excess of those provided by law. In such cases, employers must comply with the greater benefits provided by the employment contract.

7. *Other Sources of Law*

Chile has been a member of the International Labor Organization (ILO) since 1919. It has ratified 48 ILO conventions, although it subsequently denounced three of those conventions.[15]

In 1996, Chile entered into a bilateral free trade agreement with Canada. This agreement, which includes a bilateral labor side agreement,[16] is intended to serve as a bridge to Chile's eventual entry into the North American Free Trade Agreement (NAFTA) and its labor side agreement, the North American Agreement on Labor Cooperation (NAALC).[17] Unlike the NAALC, which authorizes monetary fines and trade sanctions[18] for violations of health and safety, child labor, and minimum wage laws, the labor side agreement between Chile and Canada provides only for fines in such instances. Under both agreements, the only remedy available for possible violations of other labor laws is consultations.

---

[15]Chile has denounced ILO Convention 3 (Maternity Protection Convention, 1919), Convention 4 (Night Work (Women) Convention, 1919), and Convention 45 (Underground Work (Women) Convention, 1935). See the chapter on the ILO in Volume I, Part 4, for information on ILO conventions.

[16]This labor side agreement, formally called the Agreement on Labour Cooperation Between the Government of Canada and the Government of the Republic of Chile, is available at the web site of the Labour Program, Human Resources Development Canada, <www.labour-travail.hrdc-drhc.gc.ca>.

[17]See the chapter on NAFTA/NAALC in Volume I, Part 2.

[18]Trade sanctions, in the form of suspension of NAFTA benefits, can be applied if a party fails to pay a monetary fine within 180 days. Trade sanctions cannot be applied against Canada, however, because Canada has undertaken to render monetary fines directly enforceable in Canadian courts. See the discussion in section III.E.2.c. of the chapter on NAFTA/NAALC in Part 2 of Volume I.

A U.S.-Chile Free Trade Agreement (FTA) was ratified by the United States in 2003, to take effect at the start of 2004.[19] As noted above, Chile already has an FTA with Canada that includes labor standards provisions, and an FTA with Mexico. Chile was to have been added to NAFTA, but this was prevented by failure in the United States Congress to renew fast-track negotiating authority for trade agreements from 1997 to 2002.[20] The U.S.-Chile FTA was negotiated on the U.S. side under the U.S. Trade Promotion Authority Act of 2002, which requires incorporation of labor standards provisions in free trade agreements.[21] Thus, the U.S.-Chile FTA includes a chapter on labor issues in which each party agrees not to fail to effectively enforce labor laws in a manner affecting trade and not to depart from labor laws recognizing certain internationally recognized worker rights as an encouragement for trade or investment, subject to dispute settlement procedures and possible remedies for noncompliance, including monetary assessments.[22]

C. Enforcement Agencies

Two agencies in the Executive Branch are primarily responsible for enforcement of the labor and employment laws in Chile.

The Ministry of Labor and Social Security (*Ministerio del Trabajo y Prevision Social*) is the primary source of regulations implementing labor and social policies drafted by the Executive Branch.

The Labor Directorate (*Dirección del Trabajo)* is primarily responsible for ensuring that employers comply with the labor laws. To this end, the Labor Directorate conducts compliance inspections on its own initiative or upon the receipt of a complaint by workers or their representatives. The Labor Directorate has the

---

[19]171 DAILY LAB. REP. (BNA) A-11 (Thurs., Sept. 4, 2003); 149 DAILY LAB. REP. (BNA) A-6 (Mon., Aug. 4, 2003).

[20]See the Introduction, at H.5., in the chapter on the United States in Volume I, Part 2.

[21]See the Introduction, at H.3., in the chapter on the United States in Volume I, Part 2.

[22]For further information, see the chapter on Labor Provisions in U.S. Free Trade Agreements Under the Trade Promotion Authority Act of 2002 in Volume I, Part 5.

authority to issue fines against violators. It is also authorized to interpret the labor laws and has developed a large body of administrative jurisprudence on this subject. The Labor Directorate maintains a registry of unions and oversees union activities, including compliance with the collective bargaining laws. The Labor Directorate maintains offices called Labor Inspectorates (*Inspecciones del Trabajo*) throughout Chile.

An employee or union having a labor dispute with an employer may assert a claim before the Labor Inspectorate, which has the authority to act in connection with labor disputes that involve an apparent violation of the labor laws and, in exercising that authority, has the power to impose fines.[23] Alternatively, appeals may be taken before the Labor Courts and then to the civil Court of Appeals, and an employee who initiates a claim before a Labor Court has no further recourse before the Labor Inspectorate. If an employee asserts a claim initially before the Labor Inspectorate, that agency normally provides some basic legal assistance to the employee and conducts a hearing with the parties in an attempt to conciliate the dispute. If conciliation fails, the Labor Inspectorate generally directs the employee to the appropriate Labor Court to file a legal action.

I. INDIVIDUAL EMPLOYMENT

A. Hiring and the Employment Relationship

1. Types of Employees

The Chilean Labor Code recognizes two broad classes of employees: dependent workers and independent workers.[24] This distinction is analogous to the United States distinction between an employee and an independent contractor. The Labor Code regulates the employment contracts of dependent workers but does not regulate those of independent workers.

---

[23]Other dispute resolution procedures are discussed in II.F.4.a. (mediation and arbitration during regulated bargaining negotiations), and II.G. (economic labor disputes), below.

[24]Labor Code art. 3.

One group of workers that is expressly excluded from the "dependent worker" classification is the class of individuals performing services in their own home or in some other place freely chosen by them. These "homeworkers" are not covered by the Labor Code and are not entitled to pensions and other social security benefits available to dependent workers. They may, however, enroll in and contribute to the government-sponsored social security programs as independent workers.

Throughout this chapter, the terms "employee" and "worker" standing alone will be synonymous with "dependent worker."

2. *Dependent Worker Contracts (Individual Labor Contracts)*

A written labor contract is required for all dependent workers.[25] The employment contract for a dependent worker, also known as an "individual labor contract" (*contrato individual de trabajo*), is defined by the Labor Code as "an agreement by which employer and worker commit themselves reciprocally, the latter to render personal services under dependence upon and subordination to the former, the former to pay a determined remuneration for these services."[26] The condition of "subordination" exists when the employer supervises the employee and controls such aspects of employment as the working hours and the methods of performing the work.

a. *Duration of Contracts*

Individual labor contracts for dependent workers are classified as to duration. The law recognizes three durational categories: (i) contracts of indefinite duration, (ii) contracts with a definite duration, and (iii) contracts for a particular task or service. Each is discussed below.

i. *Contract of indefinite duration*

A contract of indefinite duration, which is the most common form in Chile, does not specify a termination date. Such a contract

---

[25]In the absence of a written contract, the contract is presumed to exist. Labor Code art. 8.

[26]*Id.* art. 7.

may be terminated by either party, although termination by the employer is subject to legal restrictions described in the next section, including possible payment of a statutory indemnity based on length of service.[27]

ii. Contract of definite duration

A contract of definite duration, by contrast, specifies a termination date and may not be unilaterally terminated without statutorily recognized just cause. Chilean law does not permit the parties to stipulate to a term of employment for longer than one year, except in the case of managers and professionals, who may contract for up to two years. An employee who is terminated upon the expiration of a contract of definite duration is not entitled to a statutory severance indemnity based on length of service. An employee who is terminated without just cause before expiration of the contractual term is entitled to the balance of the full salary under the contract from the time of termination to the expiration of the specified term.[28] If an employee under a contract of definite duration continues working after the expiration date with the employer's knowledge, the contract then becomes one of indefinite duration. Such an indefinite contract is also created upon the second renewal of a contract of definite duration.

iii. Contract for a specific task or service

A contract for a specific task or service ends upon the termination of the specific work covered by the contract. Under this type of contract, the employee is not entitled to any indemnity or compensation once the contract expires.[29] Moreover, unlike em-

---

[27]See I.B., below.

[28]See I.B.1., below, regarding severance indemnity.

[29]If an employer terminates a contract of employment for a specific task or service before the employee completes the task or service, the employee's entitlement to a statutory severance indemnity depends upon the length of the employment. If the employee was employed for fewer than 12 months, the employee has no statutory entitlement to a severance indemnity. If the employment lasted for 12 months or more, the employee would be entitled to a severance indemnity unless the employer terminated the employment contract for good cause, as that term is defined in the Labor Code. The statutory severance indemnity is discussed in I.B.1., below.

ployees hired under contracts in categories (i) and (ii), employees hired for a specific task or service are not entitled to engage in formal collective bargaining.

b. Form of Contract

The form of an individual labor contract is prescribed by the Labor Code, which requires that such a contract contain the following items:

- the date and place of the contract;
- the identities of the parties, including the worker's nationality and date of birth;
- a description of the nature of the services to be rendered and the place in which the work is to be performed (for traveling employees this should include the entire territory covered);
- a description of the amount, frequency, and form of payment to the employee;
- the duration of the workday, except where the work is to be performed in shifts, in which case the employer's own internal regulations will govern;
- the term of the contract; and
- any other items agreed to by the parties.[30]

If the employment requires the worker to relocate, the worker's place of origin also must be included in the written contract.

Like a union contract, a dependent labor contract may not waive any of the employee's minimum legal rights. The lack of a required item in the contract does not invalidate the contract, but can lead to the imposition of fines in certain circumstances. The absence of a required item can also make it difficult to establish the actual terms of employment in case of a dispute.

c. Contract Procedure

Generally, the contract must be reduced to writing within 15 days after the employee begins rendering services for the em-

---

[30]Labor Code art. 10.

ployer. If the employment contract is for a fixed duration of fewer than 30 days or is for the completion of a particular task or service, however, it must be executed in writing within five days of the time the employee begins rendering services for the employer. An employer's failure to put the employment contract in writing within the applicable time limit does not invalidate the contract,[31] but it can result in a fine, and, if a legal proceeding arises over the employment, Chilean courts and administrative agencies will presume that the contract is whatever the employee declares it to be.

Two signed copies must be made of the contract, one of which is kept by each party to the contract. The employer must keep its copy at the place of employment. If an employee refuses to sign the contract, the employer must send the contract to the local Labor Inspectorate to request the worker's signature. If the employee still refuses to sign, the employer may dismiss the employee without paying any statutory indemnity that otherwise might be required, unless the employee can prove that he or she was hired under conditions different from those contained in the contract. If the employer does not dismiss the worker and the contract remains unsigned, the law will presume that the terms of the contract are whatever the employee declares them to be.[32]

d. Failure to Put Contract in Writing

Although the Labor Code states that an individual labor contract must be in writing, the failure to put the contract in writing does not invalidate the contract or make it unenforceable. All that the law requires for an enforceable individual labor contract between an employer and an employee is a meeting of the minds on the terms and conditions of the employment. The requirement that the contract be reduced to writing is intended to protect the employee and to preserve a record of the agreement in the event that a labor dispute arises between the employer and the employee.

e. Modification of Contracts

Because individual labor contracts are bilateral, they normally can be modified only in writing and with the consent of both par-

---

[31]See I.A.2.d., immediately below.

[32]Labor Code art. 9.

ties. Any modifications to the written labor contract mutually agreed upon by the parties should be set forth in writing on the back of both copies of the written contract or affixed on a separate sheet to both copies and signed by both parties. Amendments to the contractual terms and conditions of employment that have been agreed upon by the parties are, however, valid and enforceable in the absence of a signed, written document recording the changes, but proof of the amendments in a legal proceeding would be difficult in the absence of written documentation.[33] Some unilateral changes are permitted, as noted in (i) and (ii), below, and well-established past practices also may modify the contract, as discussed in (iii), below.

i. Nature of services or place of employment

Although mutual consent is ordinarily required for a modification to a labor contract, the Labor Code provides that an employer may unilaterally modify either the nature of the services or the place at which the services are to be rendered, provided that the new services are similar to those previously agreed to under the contract or that the new place of work is within the same locality or city. In either case, the change must not cause any damage or detriment to the employee.[34]

ii. Starting and stopping time

An employer may also unilaterally change the time an employee starts or ends work by a maximum of 60 minutes, provided that the employee is notified at least 30 days in advance. The legality of such unilateral changes may be adjudicated by the Labor Inspectorate and appealed to the appropriate Labor Court.[35]

iii. Benefits or privileges

Any benefits or privileges that an employer grants to employees on a fairly regular basis[36] may be deemed to become part of the

[33] *Id.* art. 11.

[34] *Id.* art. 12, para. 1.

[35] *Id.* art. 12, para. 2.

[36] As noted in II.H., below, the "past practice doctrine" does not apply to the interpretation of collective contracts in Chile because of the requirement that collective contracts be in writing.

employment contract, even though not expressly stated in the contract. When this occurs, the benefits or privileges may not be unilaterally terminated or modified by the employer.

3. *Independent Worker Contracts*

Labor contracts for independent workers are considered to be outside the coverage of the Labor Code, as they involve independent workers rather than a dependent employment relationship. Independent worker contracts typically involve the performance of technical or professional services, services performed sporadically at the domicile of the person paying for the service, or services habitually performed in the home of the individual rendering the services or at some other place freely chosen by the individual.[37] The key elements of an independent worker contract are the absence of dependence or subordination on the part of the individual performing services and the payment of a fee instead of a wage or salary.

4. *Apprenticeship*

Chile also recognizes an apprenticeship system based on apprenticeship contracts between employers and employees. These contracts are restricted to workers younger than age 21 and must conform generally to the requirements for regular labor contracts. In addition, the contract must specify the plan agreed to for the apprentice's development. The parties to an apprenticeship contract may agree to a wage below the minimum wage, and an apprentice may not engage in collective bargaining. The term of an apprenticeship contract is limited to two years.[38]

Apprentices may not constitute more than 10 percent of the total number of employees on a shift.[39] Moreover, an employer must provide the apprentice's tools, must appoint a mentor for the apprentice, and must employ the apprentice for only the work specified in the contract. The apprenticeship program is subject to government oversight.[40] Up to 60 percent of an apprentice's wages

---

[37]Labor Code art. 8.
[38]*Id.* arts. 78–86.
[39]*Id.* art. 85.
[40]*Id.* art. 83.

may be counted as part of the employer's training costs for purposes of the training-cost tax deduction.[41]

5. *Capacity to Contract and Child Labor*

Individuals older than age 18 are deemed capable of freely entering into labor contracts. At ages 16 and 17, individuals may enter labor contracts with the permission of their parent or guardian. Likewise, individuals who are 14 or 15 years old are permitted to enter labor contracts provided that they have the permission of their parent or guardian, have fulfilled school attendance requirements, and will perform only light work that does not endanger their health or prevent them from attending educational or training programs. A married woman younger than age 18 may enter into a labor contract without her parents' permission.

Children younger than age 18 generally are not allowed to work more than eight hours per day, nor are they permitted to work in industrial settings between 11 p.m. and 7 a.m., or in certain dangerous or strenuous jobs.[42]

B. Termination of Employment

The termination of employees is governed by the Labor Code. Each termination must be justified on one of the bases provided in the law, except that employees having authority to represent the employer (for example, managers, attorneys, and agents) and employees working in confidential capacities may be dismissed without cause. To the extent just cause is necessary for termination, an employee may not be terminated based on conduct not related to work or the workplace.[43] In addition to the general statutory provisions regulating employment terminations, several classes of employees, including union officials, pregnant women, and new mothers, enjoy special job-security protections.

As discussed below, depending on the circumstances of the termination, the terms of the labor contract, and the employee's

---

[41]See generally VIII.F., below, regarding employer- and state-provided training programs.

[42]Labor Code arts. 13–18. See generally V.B., below, regarding hours of work under Chilean law.

[43]Labor Code art. 160.

length of service, an employer may or may not have to pay a severance indemnity to the terminated worker.

1. *Termination With Indemnity*

Except in certain circumstances identified in the Labor Code,[44] a terminated employee is generally entitled to receive a sum of money, called a severance indemnity, from the employer.

If an employee working under an employment contract of definite duration is terminated without just cause before the expiration of the contractual term, the employee is entitled to payment of an amount equal to the full salary under the contract from the time of termination to the expiration of the contractual term.

For employees working under a contract of indefinite duration, the amount of the indemnity depends on the length of service.

The right to a severance indemnity arises if the employer terminates an individual labor contract that has been in place for more than one year based on (1) the economic or other needs of the enterprise, or (2) the employee's lack of ability.[45] Indemnity is also available to terminated employees who had authority to represent the employer or who served in confidential positions, even though such employees may be terminated without the employer having to state a cause.

In all of these cases, the employer must pay an indemnity equal to one month's salary for each year of service, up to a maximum indemnity of 11-months' pay. For purposes of calculating the indemnity, a fractional year of service greater than six months is counted as a full year. Employees hired before August 14, 1981, are entitled to an indemnity of one month's pay per year of service with no 11-month cap. The monthly salary on which the indemnity is based is limited to 90UF[46] by law, but may be increased by contract. Employees who may be entitled to a different indemnity

---

[44]See I.B.3., below.

[45]Labor Code art. 161, para. 1.

[46]The UF, or *Unidad de Fomento* (Development Unit) is a monetary unit indexed daily to inflation by the Chilean government. As of April 30, 2004, 1UF was equivalent to Ch$16,868. The Chilean Peso (Ch$) is the fundamental Chilean monetary unit. As of April 30, 2004, Ch$625 was equivalent to one U.S. dollar. Thus 1UF is approximately US$27.00.

under the terms of their contracts must choose between the contractual indemnity and the legal indemnity; double recovery is not permitted.[47] Employers may negotiate payment of severance on an installment basis, including interest and adjustments, with the approval of the Labor Inspectorate. Breach of the agreement will entitle the employee to accelerate full payment of the severance.

Additional financial liabilities may be created based on the reasons behind an individual termination, and as in many jurisdictions, certain kinds of terminations are proscribed under Chilean law.[48]

a. Disputes

An employee who feels that his or her termination was not justified (i.e., not based on (1) the economic or other needs of the enterprise or (2) the employee's lack of ability, as discussed above) may sue the employer in the Labor Court. If the employee prevails, the employer must pay a surcharge of 30 to 100 percent over the normal indemnity as a penalty.[49]

The 2001 amendments to the Chilean Labor Code[50] significantly changed employer obligations in the context of employee terminations, including increasing the severance penalties imposed when an employer's dismissal of an employee is unjustified, undue, or incorrectly characterized.[51] Key changes include the following:

- When an employer unjustly invokes "corporate needs" pursuant to Article 161 of the Labor Code as the basis for the employee's termination, the Labor Court may increase the employee's severance by 30 percent as a penalty.
- When an employer improperly invokes Article 159 (completion of work or service, act of God, or *force majeure*) or does not invoke any legal cause as the basis for an

[47] Labor Code art. 168, para. 2.

[48] See, for example, the discussion concerning wrongful dismissal based on union animus at II.A.7.c., below.

[49] *Id.* art. 168, paras. 1 and 2.

[50] Law No. 19,759 (Oct. 5, 2001).

[51] As noted at I.B., above, the employer must specify its reasons for termination.

employee's termination, the Labor Court may increase the employee's severance by 50 percent.

- If an employer unjustly relies on Article 160 of the Labor Code to terminate an employee for misconduct or gross breach of contractual obligations, the employer may now be ordered to pay a penalty equivalent to 80 percent of the employee's severance.
- When an employer unjustly invokes section 1, 5, or 6 or Article 160 of the Labor Code (serious misconduct, imprudent dangerous acts, or damage to company properly) and a Labor Court determines that an employer lacked any plausible motive for terminating an employee, a penalty of 100 percent of severance may be ordered.

Under the 2001 amendments to the Labor Code, the employer also may be ordered to pay an additional 150 percent of severance as a penalty if it breaches an employment agreement.

Before filing a claim for wrongful dismissal in the Labor Court, the discharged employee may bring the claim before the Labor Directorate, which ordinarily will attempt to conciliate the dispute. If the Labor Directorate finds a clear violation of law, it can fine the employer, but it has no jurisdiction to determine whether the employer breached the employment contract or to award damages to the discharged employee.

b. Notice

Employees terminated in situations requiring indemnity are entitled to 30-days' advance written notice of termination or to an extra 30-days' pay in lieu thereof, in addition to any indemnity. Pay in lieu of notice is limited to an amount equal to 90UF, however. If notice of termination is provided, a copy must be sent to the Labor Directorate.[52]

*c. Termination Settlement (*Finiquito*)*

The termination settlement, or *finiquito*, is a document providing notice of termination, the conditions of same, the reasons

---

[52]Labor Code art. 163, para. 3; art. 164, para. 4.

for the termination, and itemization of the social benefits to be received by the employee as part of the termination (certain compensation, indemnification for unjustified firing without prior notice, payment of proportional vacations, etc.). Although not a mandatory document, the *finiquito* is the only legally binding way for the employer to prove the termination of the employment and the conditions under which the contract was terminated. If the *finiquito* is duly signed and ratified by both parties before a notary public or before the labor authority, it constitutes irrefutable evidence of the parties' obligations, preventing subsequent claims before the Labor Courts for something different from that contained in the *finiquito*.[53]

2. *Substitute Indemnity*

Through the AFP[54] system detailed in the discussion of the Chilean social security system in VIII., below, Chilean law has developed a system of substitute indemnity, which is effectively a form of indemnity insurance. This indemnity is financed by monthly employer allocations of at least 4.11 percent of the employee's monthly wage or salary, with the salary to which this percentage applies limited to 90UF. Contributions to this fund can be made only by mutual, written agreement of employer and employee, and only between the employee's sixth and eleventh years of service. This indemnity is payable regardless of the reason for termination.[55]

3. *Termination Without Indemnity*

Except as otherwise provided by contract, employment contracts terminate without indemnity by (1) mutual agreement, (2) the conclusion of the particular task covered by the contract, (3) *force majeure* (i.e., an unexpected and uncontrollable event, such as a natural disaster), (4) the employee's death, (5) the expiration of an agreed-upon term, or (6) resignation.

Contracts may also be terminated by the employer without a right of indemnity when employees engage in the following mis-

---

[53]*Id.* art. 177.

[54]*Administradoras de Fondos de Pensiones*, or Administrators of Pension Funds.

[55]Labor Code art. 164.

conduct: (1) immoral conduct, (2) destruction of the employer's property, (3) illegal strikes, (4) material noncompliance with contractual terms, (5) desertion of work, (6) unjustified absence, or (7) other serious misbehavior.[56] When the contract is terminated because of the employee's alleged misbehavior, the employee may claim in court that this reason is false. If the employee prevails, the employer must pay the indemnity mentioned above plus a surcharge of 30 to 100 percent, depending on the existence of some reasonable grounds for termination and some level of fault by the employee.[57]

4. *Protection From Termination Under the* Fuero

A legal doctrine called the "*fuero,*" or "immunity privilege," protects some union members and officers from termination of employment in certain circumstances. The classes of employees protected and the specific restrictions on the employer's right to terminate such employees are discussed below.[58]

The *fuero* also applies to pregnant employees and employees returning from maternity leave.[59]

5. *Restrictions on Modification of Contracts Under the* Fuero

An employer may not unilaterally modify the employment contract of any worker protected by the *fuero*, except in case of accident or *force majeure*.

6. *Job Security for Employees Performing Military Services*

Employees who are performing duties in the military service, including employees who are part of mobilized national reserve forces and employees who have been called for instruction in the fighting services, are entitled to retain their jobs while performing their military service and for one month thereafter (or up to four

---

[56] *Id*. art. 160.

[57] *Id*. art. 171. See discussion under I.B.1.a., above, for penalty amounts applicable in specific circumstances.

[58] See II.A.7.a., below. See also the discussion of the claim for wrongful dismissal based on union animus at II.A.7.c., below.

[59] See VI.B.1., below.

months thereafter if they become ill or disabled while performing military service). Although an employer may not terminate an employee during the prescribed period of military service or post-military service, the employer has no duty to pay the employee for time away from the job due to military service.[60]

C. Privacy

Although Chile was the first Latin American country to enact a comprehensive data protection law, Chilean privacy law is still developing as it relates to employers, and it remains a mix of conflicting (and often confusing) rights and obligations.

1. Conflicting Rights in the Employment Relationship Reconciled

The Chilean Constitution contains two conflicting provisions relating to employee privacy. Article 19(5) guarantees the inviolability of all forms of private communication except as provided by law.[61] However, Article 19(24), which guarantees certain property rights, grants the employer the right to organize, direct, and manage its enterprise as it sees fit.[62] These two provisions are reconciled by Article 5(1) of the Chilean Labor Code, which provides that the exercise of the employer's legal rights is limited by the employee's constitutional guarantees, particularly when they may affect the private life or good name (*honorabilidad*) of the employee.[63]

2. Employer Monitoring of Employee E-Mail or Internet Use

Employer monitoring of employees' use of company e-mail and Internet systems implicates the competing privacy and business needs discussed in 1., above, whenever such monitoring is carried out. Under Chilean law, if an employer seeks to monitor or otherwise limit an employee's use of company-provided e-mail or Internet access, it ordinarily will not conflict with an employee's

---

[60]Labor Code art. 138.
[61]Chilean Constitution, art. 19, no. 5.
[62]*Id.* art. 19, no. 24.
[63]Labor Code art. 5, no. 1.

constitutional rights unless the monitoring is done in such a way as to affect his or her private life and/or good name (*honorabilidad*). As in most jurisdictions where such monitoring is permitted, prudent companies that monitor employee e-mail or Internet usage provide employees clear notice of the monitoring, either through written handbook provisions, pop-up notices on the company's computers, or in a written document signed or otherwise acknowledged by the employee.

3. *Protection of Personal Data*

Chile was the first Latin American country to enact a data protection law along the lines of the European Data Protection Directive.[64] However, the Chilean law does not meet the requirements of the European Directive. The Chilean Act on the Protection of Personal Data (CAPPD)[65] took effect on August 28, 1999, and it provides extensive restrictions on the use and processing of personal data. Unlike its European counterpart, the CAPPD did not create a separate regulatory and adjudicatory structure to ensure compliance with the law. Private individuals or entities that handle protected personal data are covered by the law but need not register with any government body; only government data banks must be registered, and there are specific rules governing government agency use of information. Individual complaints about the mishandling or misuse of personal data are resolved through Chile's regular court system, with final appeals made to Chile's Supreme Court.

a. Data Subjects' Rights

Data subjects must be informed about what information will be collected about them, who will collect the information, why the information is collected, and to which third parties the information may be transferred. Individuals have the right to request a free copy of any personal data collected about them from any public or private entity, every six months. Public agencies can only refuse to disclose information if disclosure would violate Chilean law or

---

[64] See the chapter on the European Union in Volume I, Part 1, at I.C.

[65] Law No. 19,628 (Aug. 28, 1999).

threaten national security interests. Data subjects have the right to require corrections to the information collected about them, and they may request that information collected about them be destroyed or its disclosure limited if (1) the data subject voluntarily provided the information at issue, (2) the data has become obsolete or outdated, or (3) the data is being used for commercial purposes. Data controllers or processors have a duty to correct inaccurate, false, or incomplete data on an ongoing basis and to protect the security of any data collected or maintained. Data subjects who believe their rights have been violated must file a complaint in court and may recover money damages and penalties if successful.

b. Processing and Use of Personal Data

Personal data may generally be collected and processed as long as it is done in a manner consistent with internationally recognized standards, but processing of certain types of personal data is restricted under CAPPD. For example, information concerning an individual's sexual activities, personal habits, race, ethnic origin, political opinions, religious or other philosophical beliefs, or physical or mental health are considered "sensitive data." Sensitive data may only be processed if (1) such processing is authorized by law, (2) the data subject expressly consented after being fully informed, or (3) processing is necessary in connection with the individual's receiving medical treatment and health benefits. Information related to medical diagnosis, analysis, testing, or prescription usage may only be disclosed pursuant to the data subject's express, written consent. Consent is not required if the data at issue (1) is available from public sources; (2) is only used for internal purposes, including by corporate affiliates or associated companies; or (3) is used only for statistical purposes. To the extent data is transferred lawfully to a third party, the third party may only use the information for the purpose for which it was transferred.

4. Electronic Surveillance of Employees

Chilean law prohibits collection of information about individuals through unauthorized tape recording or wiretapping, or other such means, except in narcotics-related cases pursuant to a judicial order.[66]

D. Employee Duty of Loyalty, Trade Secrets, Covenants Not to Compete

1. Employee Duty of Loyalty

a. In General

Under Chilean law, employees do not have an express statutory duty of loyalty and fidelity to their employers that would require the employees to treat as confidential and privileged any information gained by them as a result of their employment, including the internal policies, procedures, production methods, customer listings, and any other data or information about which employees become aware due to the delivery of services under their employment agreements.

Despite the lack of specific regulations governing these topics, however, loyalty, secrecy, and confidentiality obligations are implicit in all employment agreements governed by Chilean law, and any breach thereof is grounds for immediate termination, with ensuing negative consequences for the employee. An essential requirement of any employment agreement is the employee's duty to behave loyally and faithfully toward his or her employer, which necessarily entails the employee's obligations of confidentiality and secrecy. This is based on the principle of good faith and transparency that must be present in all employment relationships. Any breach of this duty will be considered justified grounds for termination of the employment agreement by the employer as a "gross breach of [an] employee's obligations under the employment agreement."[67] In this circumstance, the employer would be entitled to terminate the employee's employment without having to make otherwise mandatory severance payments.

[66]Law No. 19,423 (Oct. 11, 1995).

[67]Labor Code art. 160, no. 7.

b. Employee Penalties for Breach of Duty

An employee owes his or her employer a duty of loyalty for the duration of the employment agreement, and sometimes beyond the employee's termination. Employers may claim indemnity for damages if their employees breach their confidentiality and secrecy obligations during the term of their contract. When an employee's obligations of loyalty, secrecy, and confidentiality are breached after the labor relationship has ended, the employee's breach will be actionable only if the employer incurs actual damages. The damages must stem from a breach of confidence or secrecy as to information known by the employee and secured through the delivery of his or her personal services to the company.[68] In this circumstance, the employer can make a claim for damages actually caused by the employee's improper conduct. This liability is regulated by Chilean civil law and is therefore more expansive than the scope of labor legislation (because the employment relationship no longer exists).

2. *Trade Secrets*

Chilean law does not specifically address protection of corporate trade secrets other than registered intellectual property. However, as discussed below, the criminal statutory regime's protections provide for concomitant civil remedies.

a. Civil Claims

Chilean law does not contemplate a purely civil claim for the theft of trade secrets or other such property. Generally, the legal description of theft requires the taking of a tangible item (Chilean law uses the word "moveables"). When physical objects are stolen, the plaintiff may demand indemnification for damages suffered in connection with the criminal offense. However, information and ideas ordinarily do not fit within the statutory definition, so their theft would not ordinarily be considered theft for Chilean criminal law purposes. Nevertheless, in some cases, trade secret "theft" may constitute a type of criminal fraud, depending on how

---

[68]See the discussion of Articles 246 and 284 of the Chilean Criminal Code under I.D.2.b.i., below.

the "theft" is carried out, for which civil indemnity may be ordered as punishment. It also may be possible to recover damages pursuant to Chilean tort law. In this case, it would be necessary to establish (1) the negligence of the employee, (2) the damage caused, and (3) the connection between the negligence and the damage. Additionally, if the individual's employment agreement includes a confidentiality clause, it may be possible to enforce the contract in equity or to claim damages for a contractual breach.

b. Criminal Penalties

i. Secrets learned during professional services

Article 246 of the Chilean Criminal Code makes it a crime for a civil servant or public entity's employee to reveal a secret learned in the context of his or her professional services.[69] Likewise, Article 284 of the Chilean Criminal Code applies to employees of privately owned or publicly traded companies.[70]

Chilean criminal procedure allows the aggrieved party to demand indemnification for damages suffered in connection with the offense, thus effectively establishing civil penalties.

ii. Information in computerized form

If the information is contained in a computerized system, any appropriation, damage, or non-authorized disclosure constitutes a crime under Law No. 19,223 (Computing Crimes).[71] If the offense falls under this law, the aggrieved party may obtain appropriate civil remedies, including money damages and injunctive relief.

3. Covenants Not to Compete

a. In General

Chilean statutory law does not expressly address non-competition agreements. The Chilean courts typically enforce covenants not to compete during the term of an employment relationship, but

---

[69]Criminal Code, art. 246.
[70]*Id.* art. 284.
[71]Law No. 19,223.

constitutional rights guaranteeing freedom of work and freedom to engage in any lawful economic activity make these covenants difficult to enforce once the employment relationship has ended. Article 19(16) of the Chilean Constitution guarantees the freedom of work and its protection to all persons.[72] It states that all persons have the right to freely choose their workplace of preference, and it forbids discrimination on the basis of anything except the personal capability of the employee. Furthermore, no type of work can be prohibited, unless it is contrary to the public's morals, security, or health, or it is declared by law to be against the national interest.[73] Consistent with the Chilean Constitution, Article 2 of the Chilean Labor Code imposes an obligation on the state to guarantee the employees' right to freely choose where to work.[74] Article 20 of the Chilean Constitution includes freedom of work within the rights protected by the *Recurso de Protección*, violations of which can be submitted to the Chilean courts by any person who feels that his or her rights have been injured.[75]

b. Specific Exceptions to the General Rule

Notwithstanding these constitutional and statutory protections, administrative rulings in the antitrust context reflect that post-employment covenants not to compete can be enforceable. For example, where a company has been purchased or transferred, a covenant not to compete may be enforced if included within the purchase/transfer agreement, but not if the covenant is for more than two years in duration. In this context, it is important to note that these covenants have only been enforced in certain cases, and there is no guarantee they will be enforceable in any particular situation.

[72] Chilean Constitution, art. 19, no. 16.

[73] *Id.*

[74] Labor Code art. 2.

[75] Chilean Constitution, art. 20.

II. Collective Bargaining

A. Labor Unions and Industrial Relations

The National Constitution and the Labor Code guarantee the right to form labor organizations without employer or government interference.[76] Membership in labor unions is voluntary. More than one union is permitted in the same workplace. Employees may belong to only one labor union for each job that they hold. Employees may not be required to join a union as a condition of employment.[77] Laws enacted during the military regime in Chile somewhat diluted the power of labor unions by restricting their ability to bargain collectively on an industrywide or areawide basis, but the trend of labor legislation in the 1990s has been to strengthen union bargaining power. Collective bargaining on an areawide basis is an issue prompting bitter debate in the National Congress. As a practical matter, however, union power remains limited, and, as of 2004, the percentage of nonagricultural workers represented by unions was a relatively small 13.5 percent.[78] Union-represented employees are found primarily in midsized to large companies. In small companies, union representation is rare. Labor unions and labor relations are overseen by the Ministry of Labor and Social Security through the local Labor Inspectorates.[79]

1. *Purposes of Unions*

Under Chilean law, the purposes of labor unions include the following:

- to provide mutual assistance to union members and to represent workers in collective bargaining;

[76]*Id.* art. 19, §19, para. 1; Labor Code art. 212.

[77]Labor Code arts. 212–215.

[78]By way of comparison, the percentage of unionized workers in the nonagricultural work force was approximately 15.83% in Brazil in 2002. In the United States, the percentage of unionized workers in the total workforce was 12.9% in 2003.

[79]See the Introduction, at C., above.

- to promote education and workplace security;
- to monitor employer compliance with employment legislation and social security;
- to provide various nonprofit services, including humanitarian services, for union members; and
- to represent workers in the exercise of their contractual rights.[80]

2. *Types of Unions*

Chilean law recognizes seven types of unions:

1. enterprise unions (all members are employees of the same employer);
2. inter-enterprise unions (members are employees of two or more employers);
3. unions of self-employed workers;
4. unions of temporary workers;
5. federations;
6. confederations; and
7. workers' centrals.[81]

Selected categories are discussed below.

a. *Enterprise and Inter-Enterprise Unions and Unions of Self-Employed Workers*

Employees in enterprise and inter-enterprise unions must each be employed under individual employment contracts.

- Enterprise unions may be formed by employees across different facilities of the same employer and must have a minimum of 8 to 25 members, depending on the size of the employer.
- Inter-enterprise unions must have at least 25 members, and these members may include employees under contracts for a definite period or a particular service.

[80]Labor Code art. 220.

[81]*Id.* art. 216.

- A union of self-employed workers must also have at least 25 members.

Any of these unions may join together to form federations, confederations, and workers' centrals.

b. Federations and Confederations

Federations are groups of three or more unions,[82] while confederations are groups of five or more federations or 20 or more unions.[83] Federations and confederations support the activities of their member unions by providing technical support and assistance in carrying out the unions' functions, by providing social security and mutual-aid programs, and by advising member unions on collective bargaining matters. They also represent the interests of their member labor organization before legislative, executive, and administrative bodies in the promotion of legislative or regulatory changes or the promotion of particular international treaties. Federations and confederations may themselves act as the bargaining representatives of their member unions, provided that both the

---

[82]Major labor federations in Chile include the following: Federación Nacional de los Trabajadores de la Salud Fenats, the National Federation of Health Workers' Unions; Federación de Sindicatos de Trabajadores de la Cia Minera Disputada de Las Condes, the Federation of Unions of the Disputada de Las Condes Mining Company; Federación Nacional de Sindicatos Industriales de Endesa, the National Federation of Unions of the Electric Company, Endesa; Federación Nacional Sindicato Empresas de Trabajadores Canales Televisión Chilena, the National Federation of Unions of the Chilean Television Broadcasting System; and Federación Nacional de Sindicatos Petroleros y Afines de Chile, the National Federation of Petroleum Workers' Unions.

[83]Major labor confederations in Chile include the following: Confederación de Federaciones y Sindicatos de Trabajadores del Sector Privado CEPCH, the Confederation of Private-Sector Workers' Unions; Confederación de Sindicatos de Empleados de la Industria Molinera y Fideera de Chile, the Confederation of Mill and Wheat Industry Workers' Unions; Confederación de Sindicatos de Trabajadores de Empresas Bancarias y Afines, the Confederation of Bank Workers' Unions; Confederación Nacional de Trabajadores de Cobre, the National Confederation of Copper Workers' Unions; Confederación Nacional de Trabajadores del Plástico, the National Confederation of Plastics Workers' Unions; Confederación Nacional de Sindicatos de Telecommunicaciones, the National Confederation of Telecommunication Workers' Unions; Confederación Nacional de Sindicatos de Trabajadores de la Construcción, the National Confederation of Construction Workers' Unions; and Confederación Nacional de Sindicatos de la Siderurgia, the National Confederation of Steel Workers' Unions.

employers and a majority of the union members at each employer's facility agree.[84]

c. Workers' Centrals

Workers' centrals are defined by the Labor Code as "any national organization set up to represent the interests of its worker members who belong to different fields of production or of services."[85] Thus, workers' centrals may include unions, federations, and confederations. These organizations may each belong to only one workers' central. The legal functions of a workers' central include representing its member organizations to public authorities and national employer associations and representing its members to international trade and labor organizations. The workers' centrals also perform the same educational, enforcement, and humanitarian functions as labor unions.[86]

3. Formation of Unions

The unionization of employees in Chile is quite different from the process of unionization in the United States. Unlike unions in the United States, where a union is certified to represent all employees in a defined bargaining unit regardless of whether they are members of the union, in Chile, unions represent only those employees who are members.[87] Thus, more than one union is permitted in the same workplace.[88]

When a sufficient number of employees become members of a union at a particular company, a union is "formed" in that workplace and may negotiate with the employer for a collective labor contract covering its members. The following numerical restrictions apply to the formation of an enterprise union:

---

[84]Labor Code arts. 266–268.

[85]Law No. 19,049 (Feb. 19, 1991). The largest workers' central in Chile is the *Central Unitaria de Trabajadores*, the Central Workers Union.

[86]Labor Code art. 277.

[87]*Id.* arts. 221–223. But see II.A.4.b., below, regarding extension of union benefits to nonunion members.

[88]See II.F., below, regarding collective bargaining when multiple unions are present in one workplace.

- In companies with 50 or fewer employees, a union may be formed with a minimum of eight employees, regardless of the percentage of employees represented.
- In companies with more than 50 workers, a union may be formed with at least 25 workers joining within one year of its creation, provided that this represents at least 10 percent of the employer's workforce.
- If an employer has several places of business, a union may be formed with at least 25 workers at each site, provided the number of workers totals at least 30 percent of the employees at each location.
- In companies with 250 or more employees, a union may be formed regardless of the percentage of employees represented.[89]

These numerical restrictions do not apply to inter-enterprise unions and unions of self-employed workers, which are formed when they have at least 25 members, regardless of where those employees are employed.

The required number of employees must assemble before a "Minister of Faith" (*Ministro de Fé*) (a labor inspector, a notary, an official of the Civil Register, or a civil servant designated as a Minister of Faith by the General Director of Labor).[90] The Minister polls the assembled employees to verify that the required degree of support for the union exists, and the employees vote their approval of the union's bylaws and board members.[91] The Minister must certify the minutes of the assembly; the minutes must name the attending employees and state that the members have approved the union's bylaws and elected its directors.[92] The names of the members and directors must also be included in the minutes. The union must inform management of these proceedings

---

[89]Labor Code arts. 227–228, as amended by Pub. L. 19,759 (Oct. 5, 2001).

[90]Such an assembly is not required if the employer has fewer than 25 employees. In such cases, the union must furnish written proof of the assembly to the employer and file one copy with the Labor Inspectorate.

[91]Labor Code art. 221, para. 2.

[92]See II.A.5., below, regarding union directors. Employees who do not wish to form a union may elect a "staff delegate." See III., below.

within three working days of their occurrence and must give management the list of union directors. The union's board of directors must file the minutes and two certified copies of the bylaws with the Labor Inspectorate within 15 days of the proceeding, and the Labor Inspectorate will enter the documents in the official union register, thereby certifying the union.

The formation of a union is a matter left entirely to the discretion of employees. An employer may neither interfere with its employees' right to form and join a union nor require employees to form or join a particular union. Chilean law establishes a right on the part of each employee[93] to join, refrain from joining, or withdraw membership from any union or labor organization, and membership in a union cannot be required as a condition of employment. A union may not engage in a strike or other economic pressure against an employer while organizing the employer's employees. If organizing efforts fail, neither the union nor the employees must wait any prescribed period of time before again attempting to organize employees at the establishment.[94]

The Labor Code does not provide a specific procedure by which an employer, an employee, or another union may challenge the formation of a union. The Labor Code does, however, authorize the Labor Inspectorate to object to the formation of a union during a 90-day period following the purported creation of the union.[95] The objection would be based on noncompliance with the legal requirements for forming a union, and there is nothing in the Labor Code that would bar an employer, an employee, or another union from bringing alleged instances of noncompliance to the attention of the Labor Inspectorate. If the Labor Inspectorate does object to the formation of a union, the union may either both cure the deficiency and bring itself into compliance with the law, or it may challenge the Labor Inspectorate's ruling in the Labor Courts.

---

[93]Although managers, supervisors, and policymaking officials may form and join a union, their employment contracts with their employers may prohibit them from engaging in collective bargaining through their union. Certain classes of employee apprentices, employees hired for a particular task, and temporary employees are forbidden by law from engaging in collective bargaining through a union, although they are also free to form and join a union.

[94]Labor Code art. 214.

[95]*Id.* art. 223, para. 2.

If an employer, an employee, or another union becomes involved in a legal proceeding against a union in the Labor Courts, it may assert the union's nullity under general principles of law.

4. Union Dues

a. Members

Union dues are established by the union members' adoption of a resolution approving the amount of the dues. Once the amount of the dues is established, the union members' employer must deduct the monthly dues amount from the members' wages when asked to do so by the president or treasurer of the union or at the written request of an employee who is affiliated with the union. Unions can compel the payment of dues through legal actions, and employees who are delinquent in their dues payments must pay penalties on late dues payments.

b. Nonmembers

An employer may not extend benefits conferred by a union contract to employees not covered by that contract unless it also deducts an amount equal to 75 percent of monthly union dues from the paychecks of such employees and pays this amount to the union. If the contract in question covers more than one union, the employee may choose which union receives the payments for deductions relating to nonmembers.[96]

5. Union Officers

Union officers, known as "directors," represent and run the union. A union with fewer than 25 members must have at least one director. Other unions must maintain the minimum number of directors set forth in their bylaws. Union directors must fulfill all requirements provided in the union's bylaws. Union directors serve terms of between two and four years.[97] Union directors must be

---

[96] *Id.* art. 289(f).

[97] *Id.* art. 235, as amended by Pub. L. 19,759 (Oct. 5, 2001).

Chileans older than age 18 who have worked for the employer for at least six months, who are literate, and who have not been convicted of a crime subject to corporal punishment.[98]

6. *Time for Performance of Union Business*

a. *Weekly Leave*

Union directors are entitled to six hours of leave per week to perform union business. If the union has 250 or more members, the leave may be increased to eight hours per week. The director's leave may accumulate within a calendar month.[99]

b. *Annual Leave*

Union directors receive an additional week of leave each year for necessary union business. A director also may go on leave for anywhere between six months and the term of the contract if the union so decides in accordance with the union bylaws. A director of an inter-enterprise union may receive leave of one month for collective bargaining. Directors of federations and confederations may receive leave for the entire term of their mandate and for one month after its expiration.[100]

c. *Payment for Leave*

Time spent on leave is considered hours worked, but the wages for these hours are paid by the union. While the employer must preserve the union director's job during leave, it may fulfill this obligation by giving the director an equivalent job upon return from leave.[101]

---

[98]Crimes subject to corporal punishment are those crimes for which the punishment can last longer than three years.

[99]Labor Code art. 249.

[100]*Id.* art. 250.

[101]*Id.* art. 250, para. 6.

7. *Employment Security for Union Members and Officers*

a. *Employees Protected*

The legal doctrine called the *fuero* protects some union members from termination of employment in certain circumstances. The *fuero* extends to the following:

- candidates for a union director position, beginning from the time the election date is set until the election is completed, but not to exceed 15 days;
- union directors and directors of federations, confederations, and workers' centrals during their terms of office and for six months thereafter;
- employees involved in collective bargaining during the period starting 10 days before bargaining begins and ending 30 days after bargaining is completed; and
- staff delegates during their terms of office and for six months thereafter.[102]

b. *Restrictions on Termination of Employees*

An employee subject to the *fuero* may be terminated only by court order, based on one or more of the following:

- expiration of the employee's fixed-term employment contract;
- conclusion of the work, if the employee's contract is for the performance of a definite task;
- dishonesty or immoral behavior;
- engaging in business activities forbidden by the labor contract;
- unjustified absences of two consecutive days, two Mondays, or three days in a month;

---

[102] *Id.* art. 174, para. 1; art. 238; and art. 243. See III., below, regarding staff delegates.

- unjustified absence if the employee is a supervisor and the absence disrupts service or production;
- abandonment of work, defined as leaving the workplace during the work day without permission;
- reckless or negligent acts or omissions affecting other employees' safety, health, or work performance;
- intentional damage to the employer's equipment or merchandise; and
- serious noncompliance with the terms of the labor contract.[103]

An employer may not unilaterally modify the employment contract of any worker protected by the *fuero*, except in case of accident or *force majeure*.

c. Wrongful Dismissal Based on Union Animus

In addition to increasing penalties for unjustified dismissal generally, the 2001 amendments to the Labor Code also created a new legal claim for wrongful dismissal based on antiunion animus. Pursuant to these provisions, the worker may have the option of reinstatement or receiving an expanded severance payment. In the event a Labor Court determines that an employer unlawfully terminated an employee based on union animus, the employer may be ordered to pay the employee between 3 and 11 times his or her salary in addition to any severance otherwise due.

B. Employer Organizations

Employers may form their own organizations, also known as "craft associations" (*Asociaciones Gremiales*), for the purposes of undertaking common activities and providing mutual aid within the area of the employers' commercial activity. Craft associations do not represent their members in collective bargaining with unions. Craft associations also may not engage in political or religious activity, but they do represent their members in discussions with governmental agencies and the National Congress to promote eco-

[103]Labor Code art. 174, para. 2.

nomic and labor policies favorable to their members' interests. Matters that a craft association may address include tax policies, import and export regulations, foreign currency policies, and labor laws. These organizations must register with the Ministry of Economy, Development, and Reconstruction (*Ministerio de Economía, Fomento y Reconstrucción*) and also may form federations and confederations.

C. Unfair Labor Practices

Chilean law identifies certain unlawful acts constituting unfair labor practices. Unfair labor practices include acts committed by unions and employees as well as those committed by employers. Charges of unfair labor practices are heard by the Labor Courts, which have the power to punish violators by imposing a fine. The Labor Directorate maintains a register of unfair labor practice violators and periodically publishes a list of repeat offenders.

1. Unfair Labor Practices Committed by Employers

An employer commits an unfair labor practice if it:

- offers special payments or benefits to employees or exerts other pressure to prevent their joining a union;[104]
- discriminates among workers for the purpose of discouraging union membership or requires an employee to join a union as a condition of employment;[105]
- uses moral or physical coercion to induce an employee to join or resign from a labor union or if it interferes with free speech among union members;[106]
- refuses to bargain with a certified union;
- refuses to provide necessary information to a union, including failure to provide certain financial information to the union to facilitate bargaining;[107]

---

[104]*Id.* art. 289(b).
[105]*Id.* art. 289(c).
[106]*Id.* art. 289(e).
[107]*Id.* art. 289(b), as amended by Law No. 19,759 (Oct. 5, 2001).

- interferes with the establishment of a union by threatening to reduce wages or benefits or to close the facility, or to manipulate the number of employees in the workforce to prevent or interfere with the formation or maintenance of a union;[108] or
- interferes in a union's affairs, arbitrarily discriminates between labor unions, or requires an employee to join a union or to authorize wage deductions for union dues as a condition of employment.[109]

2. *Unfair Labor Practices by Unions and Employees*

Unions or employees commit an unfair labor practice if they:

- conspire with an employer to help the employer commit an unfair practice;
- conspire with the employer to terminate or discriminate against an employee for nonpayment of union dues or fines, or if they exert pressure on an employer to perform any of these actions;[110]
- use moral or physical coercion to induce an employee to join or resign from a labor union or if they interfere with free speech among union members;[111]
- disclose an employer's confidential information to third parties; or
- interfere with an employer's right to choose its representatives for collective bargaining.[112]

It is an unfair labor practice for a union to fine a union member for not obeying an unlawful union decision or for bringing charges against or testifying against the union. A union officer who ignores a member's complaint or claim also commits an unfair labor practice.[113]

---

[108] *Id.* art. 289(a).
[109] *Id.* art. 289(d).
[110] *Id.* art. 290(a), (b).
[111] *Id.* arts. 290, 291(a).
[112] *Id.* art. 290(d), (e).
[113] *Id.* art. 290(c).

D. Challenging Employer Internal Regulations

As noted earlier in this chapter, each employer with more than 10 employees, whether unionized or not, must promulgate internal regulations establishing certain practices and procedures in the workplace.[114] Unions and staff delegates[115] have certain rights relating to these regulations. The internal regulations must be published 30 days before their effective date, and, within five days following their effective date, copies must be sent to each employee, to all unions and staff delegates representing employees, to the employee safety committees, and to the Labor Inspectorate and Ministry of Health (*Ministerio de Salud*).[116] Among other things, the internal regulations must name the employer representative who will handle grievances or proposals from the employees.[117] The internal regulations may be challenged by the staff delegates, the unions, the employees, the Labor Inspectorate, or the Ministry of Health. Staff delegates, unions, and employees may file objections to an employer's internal regulations with the Labor Inspectorate or the Ministry of Health, depending on the subject of the challenged regulation, and the Labor Inspectorate and the Ministry of Health, acting either on the basis of filed objections or on their own initiative, may request that an employer change its internal regulations.[118] If the employer fails to comply with such a request, it may be found in violation of the Labor Code and fined by the Labor Inspectorate or Ministry of Health. Regulations promulgated by those agencies establish a procedure by which the employer may appeal such a fine.

E. Termination of Unionized Employees

An employee under a collective contract may be terminated in the same manner as an employee with an individual contract, unless he or she is entitled to the protections of the *fuero* as explained above,[119] or unless further protections are provided by the

---

[114]*Id.* art. 153, para. 1.
[115]See III., below.
[116]Labor Code arts. 156 and 153, para. 2.
[117]*Id.* art. 154.
[118]*Id.* art. 153.
[119]See II.A.7.b., above.

applicable labor agreement. Similarly, union members are on an equal footing with nonmembers with respect to termination, unless they are entitled to the protections of the *fuero*. It is unlawful for an employer to terminate a worker based on antiunion animus.[120]

F. Collective Bargaining

1. The Duty to Bargain

Generally, an employer has a duty to bargain with any union of its employees that has met the legal requirements for establishing a union. However, employers who have been in operation for less than one year and employers with fewer than eight employees are exempted from collective bargaining.[121] In addition, the following classes of employees are not entitled by law to engage in collective bargaining, although they may form or join a union:

- apprentices,
- employees hired for a particular task, and
- temporary employees.

An employment contract may also exempt the following employees from bargaining, although they, too, may join or establish a union:

- managerial employees,
- employees authorized to hire or fire employees, and
- upper-level employees with decisionmaking authority as to policies or processes of production or commercialization.

If the employment contract of an individual employed in one of these categories does not expressly exclude the individual from collective bargaining, the individual is presumed to be eligible to participate in and benefit from collective bargaining.[122]

---

[120]See II.A.7.c., above.
[121]Labor Code art. 308, as amended by Law No. 19,759 (Oct. 5, 2001).
[122]*Id*. art. 305.

2. *Subjects of Bargaining*

In general, collective bargaining covers matters concerning compensation and working conditions. The parties may not negotiate any waiver or modification of the employees' minimum legal rights, nor may the parties negotiate limits on the hiring of non-union workers. The parties may not negotiate limits on management's right to administer and organize the company, including the use of machinery and the various forms of production, nor may the parties negotiate any matters that are unrelated to the company.[123] Union security clauses, such as provisions requiring union membership as a condition of employment or requiring employees to join the union within a certain time period after being hired, are not permitted.

3. *Level of Bargaining*

Although Chilean law generally restricts the scope of collective bargaining to a single employer and its unions, collective bargaining may take place on a multi-employer or multi-union level as agreed to by the parties.[124] Collective bargaining negotiations between an employer and all of the unions or bargaining groups representing its employees take place at one time, unless the parties agree to separate negotiations. When multiple unions represent various groups of employees at an employer's establishment, the unions may choose to present a common proposal for a collective bargaining agreement to the employer, or they may present multiple proposals, each covering one or more of the unions or bargaining groups.[125]

4. *Bargaining Procedure*

a. *Regulated Bargaining and Collective Contracts*

Formal collective bargaining, which may be carried out at the enterprise level or at multi-enterprise levels, is called regulated bargaining (*negocìaciòn reglada*) and is a highly detailed

---

[123] *Id*. art. 306.
[124] *Id*. art. 303, para. 2.
[125] *Id*. art. 315.

procedure established by statute. The collective bargaining process begins with the submission of a proposal for a collective contract (*contrato colectivo*)—as opposed to a collective agreement discussed in b., below—by a union or bargaining group.[126] The Labor Code establishes a 45-day period for collective bargaining, and during this period the employer is expected to respond to the initial proposal.[127] If the employer does not respond at all within 20 days, it is deemed to have accepted the proposal.[128] Any agreement that the parties reach becomes the exclusive contract between the parties and must remain in effect for at least two years.[129]

If the employer does respond but the parties have not reached an agreement by the end of the 45-day period, the parties may agree to continue negotiations. If the parties do not continue negotiations beyond the 45-day period, the union must vote to decide whether to accept the employer's last offer or go on strike. When an employer does not expect to reach a final agreement within the 45-day period, it normally presents a final proposal that must be delivered at least seven days before the end of the collective bargaining period.[130] The employer may inform employees of the advantages and benefits of its final proposal, but it may not coerce the employees to accept the offer. The timely submission of a final offer that, at a minimum, grants employees their existing benefits and existing wages enhanced by the increase in the cost of living according to the consumer price index, gives the employer the right to hire strike replacements immediately upon the commencement of a strike if the employees reject the final offer.[131] However, under Labor Code amendments[132] the employer also must pay a replacement bonus to all striking employees equivalent to UF4 (approximately $100) for each employee hired as a replacement. If the employer does not submit a timely final offer, it must wait for 15 days after the commencement of a strike before it may hire strike replacements,[133] and it also must pay the replacement bo-

[126]*Id.* art. 315, para. 1.
[127]*Id.* art. 322.
[128]*Id.* art. 332, para. 3.
[129]*Id.* art. 347, para. 1.
[130]*Id.* art. 328.
[131]*Id.* art. 381, paras. 1, 2.
[132]*Id.* art. 381, as amended by Law No. 19,759 (Oct. 5, 2001).
[133]*Id.* art. 381, para. 4.

nus. Strikers may return to work 30 days after the strike commences.[134]

An agreement reached between a union or bargaining group and an employer must remain in effect for at least two years and may be in effect for no more than four years.

i. Mediation during regulated bargaining negotiations

At any time during collective bargaining negotiations, the parties may agree to appoint a mediator to aid the negotiation process. The mediator can be any person the parties choose to designate. In Chile, there is no government agency like the Federal Mediation and Conciliation Service in the United States that furnishes mediators for labor disputes. Also, there are no laws in Chile establishing minimum qualification standards for mediators. The parties may agree to procedural rules for the mediator to follow, but, in the absence of such agreement, the mediator must adhere to procedural rules established by statute. Unless the parties agree otherwise, the mediator has 10 days in which to try to bring the parties to agreement. If no agreement is reached during that period, the mediator convenes the parties for a meeting at which they will formalize their final proposals for a collective bargaining agreement. The mediator then submits to the parties a proposed solution to their differences, and the parties must respond to the proposal within three days. If either party rejects the mediator's proposal or does not respond within three days, the mediator concludes the mediation efforts and prepares a report describing the mediator's proposal and the final proposal of each party that made one. This report is submitted to the parties in the hope that it will help them reach an agreement.[135]

ii. Arbitration during regulated bargaining negotiations

Arbitration is also available as a means by which parties to collective bargaining negotiations can resolve their differences and

---

[134]See II.G.3., below.

[135]Labor Code arts. 352–354.

reach an agreement. The parties may submit their negotiations to arbitration at any time, regardless of whether the 45-day negotiation period has ended or whether a strike or lockout is in progress. An arbitrator chosen by the parties acts pursuant to procedures agreed on by the parties. If the parties cannot agree on arbitration procedures, the arbitrator follows procedures established by law.[136]

b. Nonregulated Bargaining and Collective Agreements

Informal or nonregulated bargaining may be initiated at any time by the parties and is not regulated by Chile's formal bargaining statutes. Employees who are precluded from regulated collective bargaining (for example, temporary employees) can engage in nonregulated collective bargaining, but this process is also available to all employees. When nonregulated collective bargaining fails to result in an agreement, however, the employees may not lawfully engage in a strike. When nonregulated collective bargaining is successful, the resulting agreement is called a "collective agreement" (*convenio colectivo*) and is governed by the same norms and formal requirements that apply to collective contracts established through regulated bargaining.[137]

G. Strikes and Lockouts

When the parties to regulated collective bargaining negotiations are unable to reach an agreement, the only economic weapon available to the employees is the strike. Any other activities the employees may undertake to pressure the employer into accepting their proposal (for example, picketing, work slowdowns, or secondary boycott activity) would be illegal. In nonregulated bargaining, strikes are illegal.

A strike may not be called during the term of a collective contract. Consequently, a no-strike clause is superfluous in a collective contract. Even when no collective contract is in effect, a strike is legal only when it is called in furtherance of lawful regu-

---

[136]*Id.* arts. 355–368.
[137]*Id.* art. 369.

lated collective bargaining demands. Strikes in protest of unfair labor practices are unlawful at all times.[138]

1. *Commencement of a Strike*

A strike may be called only upon a majority vote of the union members or bargaining group, as the case may be.

2. *Effects of a Strike*

A strike suspends the individual employment contracts of strikers and suspends both the striker's duty to work and the employer's duty to pay the strikers. Once a strike begins, the employer may hire temporary replacement employees, provided that the employer's final offer to the union was timely made (that is, presented to the union at least seven days before the end of the 45-day negotiating period), was at least equal to the prior working conditions, and included a pay raise equal to at least 100 percent of the increase in the cost of living with future pay tied to increases in the Consumer Price Index.[139] If the employer's offer does not meet these conditions, then the employer can hire temporary replacements only after the strike has gone on for 15 days. The parties to a strike may appoint an arbitrator at any time to settle their differences.[140]

3. *Return to Work*

Once employees go on strike, they do not have an unfettered right to return to work at will. Instead, the law imposes restrictions on their individual ability to abandon the strike and return to work. If the employer complies with the rules governing replacement employees, the strikers may return to work 15 days after the strike begins. If the employer does not so comply, the strikers may return to work 30 days after the strike begins or 15 days after the submission of the employer's final offer, whichever comes first.[141]

---

[138] *Id.* art. 373.
[139] *Id.* art. 381.
[140] *Id.* arts. 377–378. See also the discussion under II.F.4.a., above.
[141] Labor Code, art. 381, as amended by Law No. 19,759 (Oct. 5, 2001).

Strikers who return to work must do so under the terms of the employer's last offer. If more than 50 percent of the strikers return to work, the strike is terminated, and the remaining employees also must return within two days.[142] If the remaining strikers fail to return to work within that time period, the employer may terminate them for abandoning their jobs, which will disqualify the employees from receiving the statutorily required severance indemnity.[143]

4. *Lockouts*

A lockout is defined as the employer's right to prohibit employee access to its premises in case of a strike. A lockout bars plant access not only to striking employees, but to all employees in the plant other than management, persons with the power to hire and discharge employees, and high-ranking personnel with decisionmaking authority over company policies and procedures. A lockout may be declared only if more than 50 percent of the employees at the affected location are on strike or if the strike threatens to endanger activities that are essential to safeguard the functioning of the business. A lockout suspends the collective or individual labor contract of the affected employees, but the employer must pay the pension and social security payments[144] of all employees not on strike who are affected by the lockout. When a lockout occurs, it must terminate at the same time as the strike or on the thirtieth day after the strike began, whichever occurs first.[145] Thus, if the strike continues after 30 days of lockout, the employer must terminate the lockout at the end of the 30-day period and reopen the plant. This situation rarely arises, however, because private-sector strikes in Chile seldom last more than 15 days.

H. Third Party Resolution of Disputes

The parties to an economic labor dispute related to collective bargaining may agree to voluntary arbitration or mediation. Arbitration is compulsory in certain public industries (for example,

---

[142]*Id.* art. 381.

[143]Severance indemnity is discussed at I.B.1., above

[144]See VIII., below, regarding pension benefits and the social security system.

public utilities) where strikes are forbidden.[146] In compulsory arbitration, the arbitrator is authorized to award only the full terms and conditions of employment proposed by one of the parties and is not free to make his or her own proposal, even if it incorporates parts of the proposals made by the parties.[147] By thus limiting the authority of the arbitrator, Chilean law encourages the parties to compulsory economic arbitration to submit realistic and reasonable proposals, because the failure of one party to do so would be likely to cause the arbitrator to adopt the proposal of the other party.

The parties to a collective contract may include in the contract a provision stating that future disputes between the parties over the terms of the collective contract will be resolved by arbitration. This type of arbitration is called "arbitration of law" (*arbitraje legal*). Arbitration of law is never available, however, to resolve disputes relating to individual employment contracts.[148]

In arbitration of law, the arbitrator acts as a judge whose power is limited to interpreting the language of the collective contract. Although an arbitrator is not free to supply missing terms that the arbitrator feels are important, the arbitrator can interpret the contract in light of terms that, according to law or custom, are understood by the parties to be part of the contract, even though they are not expressly stated in the document.

The "past practice doctrine," a theory of contract interpretation in U.S. labor law that allows well-established and consistently applied workplace practices to be deemed binding obligations, does not apply to the interpretation of collective contracts in Chile because of the requirement that collective contracts be in writing. A well-established past practice can, however, become an implied term of an individual contract. Because individual labor contracts run concurrently with collective contracts,[149] an employer cannot

---

[145]Labor Code art. 376.

[146]*Id.* art. 355.

[147]*Id.* art. 363.

[148]*Id.* art. 345, para. 2. See the Introduction, at C., above, regarding the role of the administrative agencies, and at B.4., regarding role of the courts in dispute resolution.

[149]Unlike collective bargaining agreements in the United States, a collective contract in Chile is not the sole contract governing the terms and conditions of employment for unionized employees. In Chile, a collective contract does not displace the individual employment contracts entered into by the employer and each employee.

escape obligations incurred through past practices simply by negotiating a collective contract that does not expressly refer to those practices.

1. Economic Arbitration Procedures

An agreement to arbitrate must be in writing and must contain either the name of an arbitrator or the procedure agreed upon to select one. This agreement must be submitted to the Labor Inspectorate within five days of signing. The procedure of the arbitration itself is largely within the discretion of the parties and the arbitrator.[150] However, when arbitration is compulsory, the following requirements must be met:

- the dispute must be arbitrated by a single arbitrator;
- the procedural formalities of the Code of Civil Procedure for arbitrators must be followed;
- the arbitrator must be free to weigh evidence without the constraints of formal evidentiary rules; and
- the award must be entirely in favor of one party's position. A middle-ground approach or split decision is not permitted.[151]

2. Appeals in Economic Arbitration

The parties may appeal an arbitration award to an Arbitration Court, which is composed of three arbitrators. Petitions must be submitted within five days of the arbitrator's award. The losing party bears the costs of appeal.[152]

3. Effects of Arbitration Awards

An arbitrator's award is effective for at least two years from the date the dispute is submitted to arbitration, and its effects are

---

Those individual contracts remain in effect during the term of a collective contract and after the expiration of a collective contract. Throughout the term of a collective contract, an employee remains free to assert and seek enforcement of rights established by the individual employment contract, including those that have impliedly become a part of the individual contract as a result of past practice.

[150] Labor Code art. 355.

[151] *Id.* arts. 358–359.

[152] *Id.* art. 364.

the same as the provisions of a bargained agreement. Employees who are not involved in arbitration, but to whom the applicability of the award is extended, must pay the arbitrating union 75 percent of the monthly union dues during the period that the award is effective.[153]

III. Representation by Entities Other Than Unions

Employees who do not wish to form a union may nonetheless elect a representative, known as a "staff delegate." The employees who wish to be represented by a staff delegate must fulfill the representational requirements applied to enterprise unions (i.e., numerosity and representative status[154]) and must not be affiliated with any union. Like union directors, staff delegates serve two-year terms and are the means of communication and negotiation between the represented employees and the employer. Staff delegates also may represent their workers before government labor authorities. Employees who elect a staff delegate must submit the delegate's name to the employer, along with the names and signatures of all represented employees.

During their term of office, staff delegates receive the same employment protections afforded to union directors,[155] including protection under the *fuero*.[156] The *fuero* covers staff delegates during their terms of office and for six months thereafter.[157]

A staff delegate subject to the *fuero* may be terminated only by court order, based on one or more of the reasons set out above.[158] An employer may not unilaterally modify the employment contract of any worker protected by the *fuero*, except in case of accident or *force majeure*.

The 2001 Labor Code amendments dictate that staff delegates serve no less than two-year and no more than four-year terms, and

[153] *Id.* art. 347.
[154] See II.A.2., above.
[155] Labor Code art. 302.
[156] See the discussion of the *fuero* in II.A.7., above.
[157] Labor Code art. 174, para. 1; arts. 238 and 243.
[158] *Id.* art. 174, para. 2. See II.A.7.b., above.

the delegates must communicate for and negotiate on behalf of the employer's represented employees.

IV. REDUNDANCY AND TRANSFERS OF UNDERTAKINGS

Chile does not have any special laws or regulations regarding group terminations. However, in certain cases of group layoff for just cause, the employer must serve the laid-off employees with a termination notice within three days of their last day of active service (or within six days if the layoff was due to *force majeure* or an act of God). The employer may not substitute pay in lieu of this notice. The failure to serve the termination notices in a timely fashion is punishable by a fine, but does not affect the validity of the layoffs.[159]

V. WAGES, HOURS, AND LEAVE

A. Wages and Other Forms of Remuneration

1. Wages

Wages are defined as a fixed remuneration payable in equal periods in exchange for a worker's services. Thus, in Chile the term "wage" includes what is commonly thought of as "salary" in the United States. Wages may include not only money, but also payment in kind, such as housing, food, or fuel. The amount of in-kind payment is restricted, however. The value of such in-kind payments must be added to the regularly paid cash payments to determine an employee's total wage for purposes of social security contributions and other payments based on wages. Employees who are paid a daily wage (as opposed to those whose wages are stated in terms of weekly, monthly, or annual pay) are entitled to pay, known as *semana corrida,* for Sundays and holidays[160] if they have worked their full shifts during the preceding week.[161]

---

[159] *Id.* art. 162.

[160] This special benefit also applies to employees working on commission, as discussed in V.A.3., below. See also V.B.2., below, discussing Sunday and holiday work.

[161] Labor Code art. 38.

2. *Overtime*

Any work in excess of normal working hours done with the employer's knowledge is considered overtime.[162] The concept of "normal working hours" and the limitations on the amount of overtime work that an employer may require are discussed below.[163] Overtime must be paid at the rate of 50 percent over the agreed-upon wage for normal working time.[164] Employers and employees may agree to a higher rate of overtime compensation and often do so, particularly with respect to overtime work performed at night or on Sundays or holidays. The definition of overtime and restrictions on overtime work are discussed below.

a. *Temporary Needs Overtime*

"Temporary needs" overtime must be performed pursuant to a written agreement that is in effect for no more than three months. The contract may be renewed by agreement. A temporary needs overtime is permitted pursuant to mutual agreement of employer and employee. Temporary needs overtime does have its limits, however. Employees may not work more than two hours of overtime per day, and overtime must be spent performing work that will not harm the employee's health.[165] By law, overtime is payable at 150 percent of the ordinary working rate and must be paid at the same time as the employee's normal compensation.[166] Overtime worked during night hours requires payment of at least a 100 percent premium over the employee's regular hourly wage. Individual and collective labor contracts, however, often provide for a higher overtime rate, particularly when the overtime work is performed at night or on a Sunday or holiday.

b. *Mandatory Overtime*

Mandatory overtime is permitted only in the following circumstances:

---

[162] *Id.* art. 32.
[163] See V.B.1., below.
[164] Labor Code art. 32.
[165] *Id.* art. 31, para. 1.
[166] *Id.* art. 32, para. 3.

- to avoid harm to the normal functioning of the employer,
- in case of *force majeure*,
- to prevent accidents, or
- as necessary to effect emergency repairs to machinery or equipment.

Any work done pursuant to these requirements must be paid at 150 percent of the normal rate. There are no time limits on this type of overtime.[167]

Under the Labor Code amendments in 2001, the Labor Bureau is authorized to approve special working hours on the basis of objective and reasonably assessable criteria, with the consent of the workers involved, for up to four years, subject to regular oversight of health and safety conditions at the company.

3. *Commissions*

Payment in the form of commissions—that is, a variable remuneration based on a percentage of sales or some other aspect of business operations—is common for salespeople in Chile. Chile recognizes commissions as a means of remuneration and also permits combinations of commissions and fixed wages.[168] Employees paid solely on a commission basis are entitled to an additional payment for Sundays and holidays, based on their daily average earnings from commissions. This special benefit (*semana corrida*) is not applicable when employees are paid a monthly fixed wage plus commissions.[169]

4. *Mandatory Profit Sharing and Bonuses*

Under the Labor Code, employers are required to distribute 30 percent of their net profits to employees each fiscal year, divided among employees according to each employee's remuneration for the year. The net profit subject to distribution is calculated by figuring actual net profit and then deducting an amount equal to 10 percent of the employer's capital. Alternatively, an employer

[167] *Id.* art. 29.
[168] *Id.* art. 42.
[169] *Id.* art. 41.

may fulfill the profit-sharing requirement by giving each employee a bonus of 25 percent of the employee's earnings for the fiscal year, adjusted for inflation and with a maximum annual payment of 4.75 times the monthly minimum wage. The parties may contract for a higher level of profit-sharing.

The parties also may contract for other annual bonuses based on the company's profits that may be offset against the mandatory profit-sharing bonus. Such agreements may not result in a bonus below the legal minimum, and a productivity bonus may not be substituted for the profit-sharing bonus. The profit-sharing bonus must be paid during the first 10 days of May each year and is based on the balance sheet that the employer submits to the Revenue Tax Service. That balance sheet must be submitted by April of each year and covers the preceding calendar year.[170]

All bonuses should be recorded in the labor contract.

5. *Other Forms of Compensation*

Employers may pay periodic allowances, such as holiday bonuses, not expressly provided for by law. For example, it is customary for an employer to pay 13 months of wages per year, with the extra month paid either one-half in September and one-half in December, or entirely in December.

6. *Compensation That Is Not Remuneration*

Certain other forms of compensation are not considered payment for services, and thus are not taxable or subject to social security contributions. These include travel allowances corresponding to actual work-related travel expenses incurred by employees, cash-deficit allowances (granted to cashiers, bank tellers, and other employees in possession of money or securities to make up for small cash shortfalls), tool depreciation allowances for employees who use their own tools in the performance of their work, meal allowances, per diem expense allowances for work performed away from the employee's regular workplace, and family allowances.[171]

---

[170] *Id.* arts. 46–50.

[171] *Id.* art. 41, para. 2.

7. *Payment of Wages*

The frequency and time of wage payment should be stipulated in an employee's labor contract, but, by statute, remuneration must be paid at least once per month.[172] In the absence of a contractual stipulation on the subject, wages must be paid on a weekday, at the place where the employee's service is rendered, and no later than one hour after the end of the employee's working hours.[173] The parties may, however, agree on a different method of payment. Monetary wages must be paid in cash or, at the employee's request, by check or direct deposit.[174]

8. *Payroll Deductions and Attachments*

a. *Mandatory Deductions*

Employers must deduct from an employee's paycheck any income taxes, employee social security payments, and union dues that are required by law.[175] A 2003 amendment to the Chilean Labor Code[176] increased the formalities that must be honored by employers before ratification of an employment termination settlement, or *finiquito*, by requiring the submission of a Certificate of Paid Social Security Contributions. The Certificate, which must be issued by the competent social security entity, acknowledges that payment of all social security contributions for the corresponding employee has been made up to the last day of employment. The appropriate Public Notary must request this certificate from an employer before the *finiquito* can be finalized.

Additionally, as of May 14, 2001, Law 19,728[177] established mandatory unemployment insurance benefiting employees regulated by the Labor Code. Unemployment insurance is mandatory in all labor agreements executed after October 1, 2002, and employers must pay additional amounts to finance these benefits. This additional payment will generally be 2.4 percent of the employee's

---

[172] *Id.* art. 55.
[173] *Id.* art. 56.
[174] *Id.* art. 54, para. 2.
[175] *Id.* art. 58.
[176] Law No. 19,844 (Jan. 2003).
[177] Law No. 19,728 (May 2001).

taxable remuneration; in cases of labor agreements on a fixed-term basis and piece-work contracts, the additional payment will be 3 percent of the taxable remuneration. The employer is responsible for withholding and paying these amounts. The employee is responsible for payments equivalent to 0.6 percent of his or her taxable remuneration. Companies that employ workers whose labor contracts were executed before October 1, 2002, may elect to provide the benefits. Many collective agreements require employers to provide benefits made available by law after execution of the agreements, so companies should check their agreements to determine whether they may be required to provide unemployment benefits for all of their employees (regardless of hire or contract date) going forward.

b. Voluntary Deductions

An employee may elect to have other deductions made, provided that the employer and employee consent in writing, the deductions do not exceed 15 percent of the worker's total pay for the period, the deductions are in a predetermined amount or percentage, and the deductions will be used to effect payments on behalf of the worker.[178] Voluntary deductions may include mortgage credit payments relating to the purchase of a home. Deductions for such mortgage credit payments may be in an amount up to 30 percent of the employee's wages for the pay period instead of the 15 percent limit that normally applies to voluntary deductions.[179]

c. Forbidden Deductions

Employers may not deduct rentals for housing or utilities provided by the employer, charges for the use of tools, charges for in-kind contributions, charges for medical services (not including the appropriate social security deductions),[180] or fines not authorized by the employer's internal regulations.[181]

---

[178]Labor Code art. 58, para. 2.

[179]*Id.* art. 58, para. 1.

[180]See VIII.B., below.

[181]Labor Code art. 58, para. 3.

d. Garnishments

Generally, wages and social security payments under 60UF[182] are not attachable for the payment of an employee's debt. However, up to 50 percent of remuneration may be attached to pay alimony, to compensate an employer for an employee's theft or fraud, or to pay wages owed by an employee to his or her own dependent employees.[183]

9. *Minimum Wage*

The Chilean Labor Code establishes a monthly minimum wage.[184] As of May 2004, the minimum wage was Ch$105,000 per month.[185] Employees who are younger than age 21 and who are employed under an apprenticeship contract may agree to work for a lower rate of pay for up to two years. The statutory monthly minimum wage assumes full-time employment. For part-time employees, the applicable minimum wage is proportional to the statutory minimum wage, calculated by comparing the number of hours worked by the part-time employee per month to the ordinary working time per month authorized by law. Most employees in Chile earn considerably more than the statutory minimum wage.

B. Hours

The Labor Code defines working time as "the period during which the worker is effectively rendering his or her services pursuant to the contract."[186] Working time is also defined as "time during which the worker is at the employer's disposal without actually carrying out any work, for reasons not attributable to the former."[187] An example of the latter category might be time in which

---

[182]As noted in I.B.1., above, as of April 30, 2004, 1UF was equivalent to Ch$16,868. As of April 30, 2004, Ch$625 was equivalent to one U.S. dollar. Thus, 1UF is approximately US$27.00.

[183]Labor Code art. 57. For the definition of a "dependent employee," see I.A.1., above.

[184]Labor Code art. 44, para. 3.

[185]As noted in I.B.1., above, as of April 30, 2004, Ch$625 was equivalent to one U.S. dollar.

[186]Labor Code art. 21, para. 1.

[187]*Id.* art. 21, para. 2.

an employee is at the worksite but cannot work because of equipment failure. To ensure that employees are properly paid for all hours worked, employers must maintain a record of employee working hours through the use of an attendance book or a control clock with registration cards. Other means of recording working hours can be used with the prior authorization of the Labor Directorate.

1. Limits on Work Hours

Starting January 2005, the standard workweek in Chile will change from 48 hours per week to 45 hours per week (over five or six days), and the working day will be a maximum of 10 hours.[188] Prior to that time, the ordinary Chilean workweek was limited to 48 hours and the working day to 10 hours. Employers and employees may agree to a shorter workweek, and commonly do so. In such a case, working time in excess of the agreed-upon workweek must be paid as overtime. Under the Labor Code, the working day is divided into two parts separated by a period of at least half an hour for lunch or another meal. This meal period is not considered part of the normal working hours.[189]

a. Partial Exemptions: 12-Hour Limit

Certain employees are partially exempted from the workweek limit, including employees who work intermittently, employees whose jobs require only their presence, and other employees designated by government authorities. These employees still may not work more than 12 hours in a day, however, and must receive a break of at least one continuous hour during the workday. This one-hour break is considered part of the working time, thus effectively limiting such employees to 11 hours of actual work.[190]

b. Complete Exemptions

There is no statutory workday or workweek limit for managerial employees and certain administrative employees, for attor-

---

[188] *Id.* art. 22, as amended by Law No. 19,759 (Oct. 5, 2001).
[189] *Id.* art. 22.
[190] *Id.* art. 27.

neys, for employees who work without immediate supervision, for certain employees such as collection agents who work outside the employer's premises, for employees working on fishing boats, or for commissioned agents. There is also no statutory limit on total working hours for employees who work for more than one employer. In all of these instances, however, if regular working hours are set forth in the worker's labor contract, employment in excess of the contractually stated working hours will constitute overtime.[191]

2. Sundays and Holidays

Work on Sundays and holidays is generally prohibited, although certain exceptions are permitted as discussed below. The occupational exceptions discussed above (attorneys, etc.) apply to limitations on daily and weekly working hours only.

If an employer illegally requires its employees to work on a Sunday, the employer must pay them at the overtime rate. The right to Sunday rest may not be waived.

In certain situations an employer may require work on Sundays or holidays, provided that the employees are given an additional free day during the week as compensation for each Sunday or holiday worked. These situations include:

- work to repair damage caused by *force majeure* or acts of God, provided the repairs cannot be postponed;
- work requiring continuity in order to avoid damage to industry or the public interest;
- seasonal work;
- work that is immediately necessary for the good of the company;
- work on vessels or in ports; and
- work involving public services.

When work is performed on a Sunday or holiday pursuant to one of these exceptions, the work time is considered part of the ordinary workweek of the employee. It is paid at the employee's ordi-

[191] *Id.* art. 22, para. 2.

nary wage, unless it causes the hours of work to exceed the maximum ordinary workweek established by law or contract. An employer that requires an employee to work on a Sunday or holiday pursuant to one of these exceptions must grant the employee a rest day during the week to make up for the work required on a Sunday or holiday. When work on both a Sunday and a holiday results in the accumulation of more than one rest day during a week, the parties may agree on monetary compensation equal to 150 percent of the daily wage or salary in lieu of a second day off.[192]

Sunday and holiday work also may be performed pursuant to special dispensation from the government. Under certain circumstances, not covered by the exceptions listed above, the Labor Directorate may allow employers to implement special systems for the distribution of working time and rest days. The Labor Code also provides that where work must be performed in places distant from urban areas, the parties may agree on working periods of up to two continuous weeks, after which the employee must receive one free day to compensate for each Sunday or holiday worked, plus one extra free day.[193] This exception often applies to the following industries: agriculture, mining, fishing, and essential services.

Law 19,220, which was recently enacted, allows employers to reach agreements with their employees concerning "sandwich holidays," those which fall on a weekday between two holidays (other than Monday or Friday), that cause many employees to take the "sandwich" day off. In exchange for being permitted to take the sandwich day off, employees may agree to work extra hours before or after the holidays, which will not be considered as overtime for labor purposes.

C. Leave

1. Standard Requirements

Employees who have worked for more than one year for an employer are entitled to 15 working days of vacation with pay,

---

[192] *Id.* art. 38, para. 1.
[193] *Id.* art. 39.

called "annual holidays." The law suggests, but does not require, that the annual vacation be granted in the spring or summer.[194] In addition, an employee who has worked a total of 10 or more years for one or more employers, whether continuously or not, is entitled to one additional day of vacation for every three years of additional service over 10 years. Pursuant to mutual agreement, these additional days can be exchanged for monetary compensation equal to at least the normal day's pay for each day exchanged.[195] Employees who take vacation time must be given at least 10 consecutive working days off; only the remaining five (or more) days may be broken up by the agreement of the parties.[196] For purposes of paid vacations, Saturdays are always considered to be nonworking days, even if an employee normally works a six-day week including Saturdays.[197] Therefore, the 15-day vacation guaranteed by statute effectively ensures the employee three full weeks of vacation each year.

An employee is entitled to receive his or her regular wage while on vacation. If the employee's remuneration varies from week to week, as is the case with employees paid on a piecework or commission basis, the vacation pay is based on the average pay during the three months preceding the vacation.[198]

An employee who terminates his or her employment must be paid for any unused vacation days. Apart from the employment termination situation, monetary compensation may not be substituted for the 15 days of basic vacation time provided by statute, although, as noted above, an employee can agree to substitute monetary compensation for any additional vacation days beyond the basic vacation allotment.[199]

2. *"Forced" Vacation*

An employer may force all of its employees to take their vacation at the same time by closing all or part of its business for a

---

[194]*Id.* art. 67.
[195]*Id.* art. 68.
[196]*Id.* art. 70.
[197]*Id.* art. 69.
[198]*Id.* art. 71.
[199]*Id.* art. 73.

minimum of 15 working days. If an employee has not yet earned 15 days of vacation,[200] this vacation must be credited against his or her future vacation entitlement.[201] In addition, in businesses that close for certain portions of the year, employees will not be entitled to a vacation at a time other than during the closing, provided that the period of closure is not shorter than the vacation to which the employees would otherwise have been entitled and provided that, during the period of closure, the employees receive the normal compensation established in their contracts.[202]

3. *Family Leave*

An employee is entitled to one day of paid leave for the birth or death of a child and for the death of a spouse. The day of paid leave is in addition to any paid vacation to which the employee may be entitled and is available regardless of the length of the employee's service with the employer. The day of paid leave must be provided within three days of the event triggering the leave.[203]

Chilean law also grants employees a right to a leave of absence to care for a seriously ill infant younger than one year of age. When an appropriate health care institution certifies that a small child's health requires the attention of the parents at home and both parents work, either the father or the mother (at the option of the parents) is entitled to a leave of absence for the period of time determined by the health care institution. The leave is paid by the worker health insurance agency used by the employee taking leave.[204]

A 1997 amendment to the Labor Code permits an employee to take a leave of absence because of serious illness of a child younger than age 18. Under this provision, the employer must deduct the leave time from the employee's next annual vacation or from the employee's regular wages and overtime. Thus, the employee may either effectively substitute paid vacation time for the child-care leave or take the leave without pay.

---

[200] As noted in V.C.1., above, employees who have worked for more than one year are entitled to 15-days' vacation.

[201] Labor Code art. 76.

[202] *Id.* art. 74.

[203] *Id.* art. 66.

[204] See VIII.B., below.

4. *Maternity Leave*

Female employees are entitled to six weeks of paid leave before childbirth and 12 weeks of paid leave after childbirth. The employee's pay during the maternity leave, calculated pursuant to a rather complex formula, comes from the government or private health insurance fund in which the employee participates and is generally close to her regular wage (subject to a ceiling of approximately 60UF per month),[205] less deductions for social security contributions.[206] In the case of prenatal illness, the prenatal leave may be extended. If the mother does not give birth within six weeks of taking leave, the prenatal leave is extended to the date of birth, and the 12 weeks of postnatal leave begins upon birth. Postnatal leave also may be extended in the case of birth-related illness. Additional supplementary postnatal leave may be granted for up to a year if the child's health requires the mother's attention at home. If this type of leave is necessary and both parents work, the mother may choose to let the father take the leave while she returns to work. Parents on supplementary leave receive an allowance equal to their normal wage less deductions for social security. This allowance is paid by the government or private health insurance fund in which the parent participates. The right to maternity leave may not be waived, and Chilean law effectively prohibits an employer from employing a woman in active service during the periods specified by statute for maternity leave.[207]

5. *Leave to Feed Children*

Mothers of children younger than age two are entitled to two paid feeding periods during the workday, not to exceed one hour total.[208]

---

[205]As noted in I.B.1., above, as of April 30, 2004, 1UF was equivalent to Ch$16,868. As of April 30, 2004, Ch$625 was equivalent to one U.S. dollar. Thus, 1UF is approximately US$27.00.

[206]Social security and health insurance are discussed in VIII.A. and B., below.

[207]Labor Code art. 195.

[208]*Id.* art. 206.

6. *Medical Leave*

Employees are entitled to medical leave in case of illness, provided the leave is authorized by a doctor and approved by the employee's health insurance agency of choice. Both the *Fondo Nacional de Salud* (FONASA)[209] and the *Institución de Salud Previsional* (ISAPRE)[210] provide illness benefits beginning from the fourth day of absence from work if the leave is for fewer than 10 days. If the leave is for longer than 10 days, benefits accrue from the first day of leave. Benefits are available only if the affected employee has been a participant in the health insurance agency's program for at least six months and has made at least three months' worth of contributions. The affected employee receives salary continuation benefits for the duration of the illness or until disability is established, but the salary continuation is capped at approximately 60UF per month. Some employers finance and provide their own sickness benefits in addition to the government-mandated benefits, but typically do not provide disability benefits. Moreover, as discussed below, different benefits are available if the medical leave is caused by an occupational illness or injury.[211]

7. *Military Leave*

Employees are entitled to retain their jobs when called up for military service or training.[212] This requirement can be fulfilled if the employee is given an equivalent job upon his return to work. Employees are not entitled to be paid during service, except that reserves called to active duty for fewer than 30 days are entitled to their full wages for the period of military service. Military service

---

[209]FONASA is the popular name for the *Fondo Nacional de Salud,* the national health care system.

[210]ISAPRE is the popular name for the *Institución de Salud Previsional,* a private health system.

[211]See VII., below.

[212]Men are generally subject to military service of one year when they are 18 years old, but the mandatory military service can be deferred to enable young men to complete their high school or university studies. Although all young men are required to register for mandatory military service, not all of them are called to active service. Women serve in the Chilean armed forces on a voluntary basis. Chile has military reserve forces, but those forces are not required to undergo periodic training.

does not interrupt an employee's accrual of seniority. An employer's obligation to reinstate or reemploy an employee following completion of military service continues for one month after the employee is dismissed from military duty, but this period is extended for up to four months in the event of the employee's medically verified illness.[213]

VI. ANTIDISCRIMINATION

A. In General

The Chilean constitution guarantees the right to contract for one's labor and prohibits any discrimination for reasons other than personal ability.[214] A constitutional remedy (the "*recurso de protección*") for unlawful discrimination is available before the courts of appeals. The purpose of the *recurso de protección* is to restore the legal order created by the constitutional mandate and to ensure full protection for the victims of discrimination, notwithstanding any other rights and remedies the victim may have. If the court finds that the employer has violated the constitutional prohibition against discrimination, it has broad authority to issue an order ending the discriminatory situation. The *recurso de protección* does not authorize the award of damages, however.

The Labor Code also prohibits discrimination based on sex, race, color, religion, political views, national origin, or union membership. Discrimination in violation of the Labor Code constitutes either a breach of the labor contract (in the case of lawful discrimination against an existing employee) or a civil-law tort (in the case of a discriminatory refusal to hire an individual). In both situations, the victim may sue the employer for damages in a Labor Court. Moreover, the Labor Directorate may fine an employer for violating the statutory prohibition against discrimination.[215]

Although the Labor Code imposes a blanket prohibition against discrimination based on certain protected factors and does

---

[213]Labor Code art. 209.
[214]Chilean Constitution, art. 19, no. 16.
[215]Labor Code arts. 2, 477.

not recognize the concept of bona fide occupational qualifications[216] based on any of the protected factors, it is common and accepted practice in Chile for employers to adopt certain age- or sex-based qualifications for a particular job. Moreover, the Labor Code requires that at least 85 percent of the work force of an employer with 25 or more employees be Chilean nationals.[217] This requirement effectively mandates that employers give some consideration to national origin in their hiring decisions.

B. Pregnant Woman and New Mothers

1. *Job Security for New Mothers*

Female employees are entitled to protection from termination of employment under the *fuero,* the legal doctrine described above.[218] These protections begin during pregnancy and end one year after the expiration of maternity leave. If an employee is terminated in violation of these provisions because the employer did not know of the pregnancy, the employee may be reinstated upon the presentation of a doctor's or midwife's certificate confirming her pregnancy.[219]

An employer may not unilaterally modify the employment contract of any worker protected by the *fuero,* except in case of accident or *force majeure.*

2. *Working Conditions for Pregnant Women*

Pregnant women may not be required to work overtime, work at night, do work requiring physical effort (including prolonged standing), move heavy weights, or perform certain other tasks.[220]

Additional provisions are made for maternity leave,[221] paid time off for feeding a child younger than age two,[222] and employer-provided day care.[223]

---

[216]See VI.B.1.b.ii., in the chapter on the United States in Volume I, Part 2.
[217]Labor Code art. 19.
[218]See II.A.7.a., above.
[219]Labor Code art. 201.
[220]*Id.* art. 202.
[221]See V.C.4., above.
[222]See V.C.5., above.
[223]See VIII.D., below.

VII. OCCUPATIONAL SAFETY AND HEALTH AND WORKERS' COMPENSATION

A. Occupational Safety

The Ministry of Health regulates workplace health and safety. Employers with more than 25 employees must have written internal regulations dealing with order, hygiene, and safety in the workplace. They also must have at least one joint employer-employee committee for health and safety, which must implement the government standards, investigate accidents and diseases, and engage in activities related to accident and disease prevention. These committees are composed of three representatives each from the employer and the employees. Mining, industrial, or commercial companies with more than 100 employees must also have an Occupational Hazard Prevention Department headed by a health and safety expert.

B. Occupational Injury and Disease and Workers' Compensation

Benefits for on-the-job injuries and occupational illnesses are most commonly provided through Employers Mutualities (*Mutualidades de Empleadores*). These institutions manage a workers' compensation fund pursuant to the Work Accidents Statute.[224] Employers are required to make a basic contribution to cover these risks at the rate of 0.9 percent of payroll, plus an additional 1.7 percent to 3.4 percent of payroll, depending on the risk level of the industry. In a minority of cases, such coverage is carried through the government's Social Security Standardization Institute (*Instituto de Normalización Previsional*). Further, companies with at least 2,000 employees may self-insure against occupational injury if they meet certain requirements, including the maintenance of medical staff and services, the maintenance of preventive activities, and the maintenance of a joint employer-employee safety board.[225] Few companies pursue this option.

---

[224]Law No. 16,744 (Feb. 4, 1968).

[225]Labor Code art. 158.

1. *Accrual of Benefits*

The concept of "occupational injury" is interpreted very broadly in Chile. Employees are entitled to benefits for injuries sustained either at work or en route to or from work. Moreover, employees who serve on the governing body of a labor union and who are injured in the course of union business are also considered to have been injured on the job. Both accidental injuries and those inflicted intentionally by co-workers or third parties in the workplace or en route to or from work constitute occupational injuries. Employees are not considered to have sustained occupational injuries, however, when they intentionally injure themselves or participate in a fight with a co-worker.

Benefits also are available for occupational diseases that cause disability or death. An occupational disease is an illness contracted through the employee's profession or work. The government periodically issues a regulation identifying illnesses that are classified as occupational diseases. This is not an exclusive list, however, and employees may file claims based on illnesses that are not named in the regulation. If an employee's disabling illness is found not to be an occupational illness by the public or private entity providing occupational disease coverage, the employee may nevertheless be entitled to disability benefits from the common disease insurance program managed by the government or by a private entity (AFP or ISAPRE[226]), but these benefits are often less than those available for occupational diseases.

2. *Compensation*

Occupational injuries and diseases are compensated by both medical and cash benefits.

- Medical benefits for work-related injuries and diseases are extensive and include hospitalization, medical and dental care, pharmaceuticals, prostheses, travel expenses, and rehabilitation. These benefits are provided without charge to

[226]See VIII., below. AFPs (*Administradoras de Fondos de Pensiones*) are private government-regulated pension fund administrators. ISAPRE is the popular name for the *Institución de Salud Previsional*, a private health system.

the individual by the applicable carrier (an Employer Mutuality, the Social Security Standardization Institute, or a self-insuring employer) until the individual is completely cured or otherwise free of the residual effects of the occupational injury or disease.

- Cash benefits depend upon the degree of disability, as measured by the decline in the victim's earning capacity. Employees with a temporary disability caused by an occupational injury or accident are entitled to a sickness benefit for up to one year, and this benefit may be extended for an additional year if necessary to provide the employee with better treatment or rehabilitation. Benefits for permanent disabilities range from lump-sum payouts in the case of lesser disabilities to a pension equal to 70 percent of base salary for more serious cases (and even 100 percent if the employee requires another person's assistance to carry out the essential functions of living). Certain additional increases are granted if the employee has dependents, but pensions are capped according to the level of disability.

VIII. PENSIONS AND BENEFITS

A. Social Security

Chile's mandatory social security system is financed by employee contributions that the employer must withhold from the employee's pay and remit to the social security entity providing coverage for the employee. Employers do not contribute to the coverage except as discussed below. Employees are required to contribute a total of 20 percent of their monthly earnings (up to a ceiling of 60UF)[227] to purchase medical coverage and the three forms of "pension" coverage:

---

[227]As noted in I.B.1., above, as of April 30, 2004, 1UF was equivalent to Ch$16,868. As of April 30, 2004, Ch$625 was equivalent to one U.S. dollar. Thus, 1UF is approximately US$27.00.

- old age,
- survivors', and
- disability pensions.

Although some employees have elected to remain covered under the old state-run pension system, most pension benefits today are provided and administered through AFPs (*Administradoras de Fondos de Pensiones*, or Administrators of Pension Funds), which are private companies regulated by the government. Employees may choose the fund in which they wish to participate and may transfer their account balances from fund to fund on 30-days' notice. Employees may also make additional voluntary contributions to their funds. As of 1997, Chile had 13 AFPs with a total membership of approximately 5.5 million employees. Independent workers are not automatically covered by this system, but may voluntarily purchase coverage. At the employee's option, mandatory medical coverage is provided either through the public health system or by a privately managed health system.[228]

1. *Old-Age Pensions*

Ten percent of an employee's salary (which is half of his or her social security contribution) goes into the employee's old-age pension fund managed by an AFP. Once a participant in an AFP has reached retirement age or achieved a certain level of capitalization, the participant may either draw on the capital or buy insurance equal to the value of his or her funds. The normal retirement age in Chile is 65 for men and 60 for women, but employees are not required to retire when they reach these ages. The government provides a minimum pension to employees who have contributed for at least 20 years and whose AFP funds produce less than a certain minimum amount.

2. *Survivors' and Disability Pensions*

a. *Survivorship Benefits*

Three percent of an employee's salary goes toward survivors' and disability insurance, which is also carried through the AFP.

[228]Law Decree 3.500 (1980). See discussion in VIII.B., below.

Survivors' pension benefits for the spouse of a deceased employee are 60 percent of the employee's retirement pension if there are no children, or, if there are children, 50 percent plus an additional 15 percent for each child. If the employee dies before retirement, the survivors' pensions are based on the greater of (1) the accumulated pension fund, or (2) 70 percent of the employee's average earnings over the past 10 years. Some employers also provide group life insurance, typically in an amount between 24 and 36 times the employee's monthly salary, and typically at the employer's expense. Additional accident benefits are sometimes also provided by employers.

b. Disability Benefits

If an employee is more than 66 percent disabled (considered total disability), the AFP provides a pension equal to 70 percent of average earnings over the last 10 years; if an employee is 50 percent to 66 percent disabled (partial disability), the pension equals 50 percent of average earnings over the past 10 years. Although individual employers often will provide their own compensation for illness, they typically do not provide coverage for long-term disabilities.

3. Taxation of Benefit Contributions

Chileans in general are subject to a progressive tax on all income, with rates varying from 0 to 45 percent.[229] Employee contributions to social security are entirely tax-deductible. In addition, employer contributions toward benefits that complement social security, such as life insurance, health insurance, and pensions, are deductible for the employer and under certain circumstances may be considered as nontaxable income to the employee.

B. Medical Coverage

Seven percent of an employee's monthly earnings are used for mandatory medical coverage. The employee has the option of being covered by FONASA, the public health system, or by an

[229]Labor Code art. 58.

ISAPRE, which is a private health system. The ISAPRE system covers approximately 27 percent of the country's employees. The required medical coverage under either system is typically inadequate; consequently, many large companies provide supplementary health coverage, including hospitalization, maternity, and cancer coverage. The cost of this increased coverage is generally shared 60/40 between employer and employee, respectively. Individuals covered by an ISAPRE may also make additional voluntary contributions in exchange for enhanced benefits. Large companies sometimes take out group ISAPRE coverage. Such coverage continues the 7 percent mandatory contribution but usually provides a higher level of coverage than an individual ISAPRE account. Employees covered by FONASA or an ISAPRE lose their coverage upon the termination of their employment. If the employee remains unemployed, he or she will receive medical benefits from the National Health Fund as an unemployed person.

C. Family Allowances

Family allowances are payments made to certain classes of individuals with dependents for the benefit of these dependents. Family allowances are payable to dependent workers, independent workers who are members of the social security system, recipients of widowhood pensions, and the mothers of illegitimate children of persons receiving a pension as a result of an occupational accident or disease. The allowance is paid for the benefit of the following persons:

- disabled spouses;
- children younger than age 18;
- unmarried children between the ages of 18 and 24 who are studying at an educational institution;
- orphaned or abandoned children, grandchildren, or great-grandchildren younger than age 18 or between ages 18 and 24 and studying at school;
- widowed mothers; and
- parents older than age 65.

Generally, these persons must be living with the employee and must not earn any income over 50 percent of the minimum monthly income. The family allowance is limited to Ch$1,800 per month for workers with salaries up to Ch$120,000 per month, and Ch$640 per month for employees with salaries up to Ch$250,000 per month. Employees who earn more than Ch$250,000 per month are not eligible. These allowances are paid with the employee's salary and are deducted from the money transferred by the employer to the social security system on the employee's behalf, thereby reducing the employee's contribution into the social security system.

D. Day Care

Employers employing 20 or more women of any age and any marital status must provide and pay for day care, either on the employer's premises or in a separate location, for all employees' children younger than age two. This obligation may be fulfilled by joining with other nearby companies to provide collective day care or by paying day-care expenses directly to an independent provider. The employer has the right to choose the independent nursery to which payments are made.[230]

E. Unemployment Compensation

Unemployment benefits are state-provided and quite small. As noted above,[231] medical benefits are provided to unemployed persons through the National Health Fund.

F. Occupational Training

1. *Employer-Provided Training*

Chilean law establishes a system of private occupational training that offers certain tax incentives to employers. Under this system, occupational training meeting certain requirements as to faculty and quality of instruction may be carried out in-house or through an independent contractor or educational institution. Employees in training are paid as if they were normally employed,

---

[230]*Id.* art. 203. Issues relating to pregnancy and childbirth are covered in V.C.4. amd 5., above, and VI.B., above.

[231]See VIII.B., above.

except that overtime used for training does not confer a right to overtime pay. For tax purposes, compliance with the legal training standards enables the employer to deduct training expenses equal to up to 1 percent of payroll per year.[232]

2. *State-Provided Training*

The Chilean government also sponsors training for low-income persons, first-time employees, and the unemployed. The programs and their eligibility requirements vary from place to place and from year to year. Employers are forbidden to interfere with their employees' right to participate in these programs, and in certain cases must permit an employee to work reduced hours (with a corresponding reduction in pay) to attend training.

IX. Immigration

A. Employment of Foreign Personnel

Generally, Chile's employment laws apply equally to Chilean citizens and foreign nationals working in Chile, but certain special requirements do apply to foreign workers. By law, no more than 15 percent of a Chilean company's employees may be non-Chilean personnel.[233] In calculating whether an employer has exceeded the permitted percentage of non-Chilean workers, foreign specialized technicians who cannot be replaced by Chilean personnel are excluded, as are foreign employees who have lived for more than five years in Chile and foreign employees who are married to Chileans.[234]

1. *Documentation for Foreign Personnel*

To work in Chile, a foreign employee must have a valid passport, a labor contract visa, a notarized employment contract containing certain special provisions, a health certificate stating that

---

[232]Labor Code arts. 179–183. Training must comply with Decree No. 1446 (1976).

[233]Labor Code art. 19.

[234]*Id.* art. 20.

the employee has no contagious diseases, and a certificate issued by local police.

a. Labor Contract Visa

The labor contract visa is granted to foreigners and their families and is valid for up to two years. As long as they live at the expense of the foreign worker, the worker's family members are entitled to reside in Chile pursuant to the foreign worker's labor contract visa. They may not perform services for remuneration in Chile, however. The visa can be renewed in Chile, but after a foreign worker has resided in Chile for two years under a labor contract visa, the worker may seek a permanent residence visa instead of a renewal of the labor contract visa.

An individual must have two years of uninterrupted residency in Chile to qualify for a permanent residence visa. For this purpose, residence in Chile is considered uninterrupted if the individual's absences from the country amount to fewer than 180 days in a year. Permanent residence visas are denied to individuals who are forbidden from entering Chile (for example, arms and illegal drug dealers, persons suffering from certain illnesses, and persons who have engaged in violent criminal or terrorist activities); individuals who have been convicted of a crime in Chile; violators of Chilean law, including the tax laws; and persons who have entered Chile using falsified documents or false statements.

b. Obtaining a Labor Contract Visa

There are currently three ways in which a foreign national may obtain a labor contract visa to work in Chile.

1. A foreign worker who has not yet entered Chile or an employer of such an individual may submit a request for a labor contract visa to the Ministry of Foreign Affairs (MFA or *Ministerio de Relaciones Exteriores*) in Chile. A copy of the worker's individual labor contract, signed either by both parties or by the employer only, must be filed with the visa request. If the Ministry determines that the visa should be granted, it sends a telex to the Chilean consulate in the country where the foreign worker resides, authorizing the consulate to issue the visa. If the labor con-

tract visa is denied, the foreign worker may request reconsideration by the MFA. If the MFA's denial of a labor contract visa is arbitrary or illegal, a foreign worker may pursue a legal action against the agency on the ground that the denial violated the worker's constitutional right to equal treatment under the law regardless of nationality.

The process of issuing the visa ordinarily takes approximately five days. Before the consulate issues the visa, the worker must provide it with a health certificate,[235] a police certificate, six identification photographs of the worker, and additional documents (for example, proof of marital status, proof of economic situation, and proof of education and training) as appropriate.

2. A foreign worker who has not yet entered Chile may apply for a labor contract visa at the Chilean consulate in the worker's country of residence. The worker must provide the same documentation that is required for a visa request initiated through the MFA, but the process takes slightly longer (usually up to two weeks) when it is initiated through a Chilean consulate.
3. A foreign national who has entered Chile as a tourist or on some other nonworking basis and who wishes to remain in the country for the purpose of employment may apply for a labor contract visa through the Ministry of the Interior, Department of Immigration (*Ministerio del Interior, Departmento de Extranjeria*). This process is considerably more complicated than the issuance of a visa to a worker who has not yet entered Chile, and the applicant must supply additional documentation. The additional documentation includes a tourist card, a statement of expenses for the individual (and his or her family, if applicable), and a letter from the potential employer setting forth reasons justifying the hiring of the foreign worker. It of-

[235]The health certificate must be issued by a physician and must certify that the worker is in good health and does not suffer from a serious and contagious illness. The certificate must specifically state that the worker is not infected with human immunodeficiency virus (HIV), the virus that causes acquired immune deficiency syndrome (AIDS).

ten takes up to three months to obtain a labor contract visa in this manner, and the foreign national may not work in Chile until the visa has been issued.

2. *Registration of Foreign Personnel*

After a foreign worker has entered Chile under a labor contract visa, the worker and family members older than age 18 must obtain national identity cards and register in the special registry for foreigners maintained by the police department. If the worker changes domicile or work activity while in Chile, the worker must personally notify the police of the change within 30 days.

3. *Individual Labor Contracts for Foreign Personnel*

Certain special formalities and substantive requirements apply to the individual labor contracts of foreign personnel working in Chile under a labor contract visa. The contract must be entered into between an employer domiciled in Chile and a non-Chilean national. If the contract is executed outside Chile, the parties must sign the contract before an authorized Chilean diplomatic agent or consulate, and the contract must be submitted to the Ministry of Foreign Affairs in Chile for approval. If the contract is executed in Chile, the parties must sign it before a notary public. If the employee is a specialized professional or technician, the employee must provide evidence of that special status. In addition to the elements required in any individual labor contract in Chile, an individual labor contract with a foreign national entering Chile under a labor contract visa must contain the following elements:

- the date and place of the contract's execution;
- the name, citizenship, and domicile of the parties;
- the marital status, profession, and place of origin of the employee;
- a statement of the employer's obligation to pay the employee's labor tax, social security, and health care contributions;
- the date on which the employee will begin working in Chile (or a statement that the employee will start performing services in Chile after the employee's visa becomes effective); and

- a statement that the employer will pay the cost of returning the foreign employee and the employee's family to their country of origin.

B. Foreign Personnel and Social Security

In general, both the employer and the foreign employee must pay social security contributions in accordance with Chilean law, and these contributions are withheld from the wages of the foreign employee, just as they are from the wages of Chilean nationals.[236] However, Law Number 18,156 of 1982 creates an exemption from certain social security contributions for foreign technicians under the following conditions:

- the employee must have social security outside Chile covering illness, retirement pension, disability, and death; and
- the employee must expressly declare in his or her individual labor contract that the employee will remain a member of the foreign social security system.

These requirements should be satisfied by participation in the U.S. social security system. To qualify for an exemption, the foreign employee must present a certificate from the social security agency of the country where the employee is covered and must present evidence of his or her technical degree. This exemption does not apply to employee contributions to mandatory health insurance and does not relieve the employer from its duty to make contributions on behalf of the foreign employee to the Chilean labor accident fund managed by Employers Mutualities.

C. Income Taxation of Foreign Personnel

1. Income Tax

Foreign employees working in Chile under a labor contract visa are subject to a "Second Category" tax withheld from their wages by their employer. A "Second Category" tax is a month-to-

---

[236]See VIII.A., above.

month tax based on a progressive rate ranging between 0 and 45 percent.

2. Taxation of Resident Aliens' Foreign Income

During the first three years that a foreign employee resides in Chile, the employee is required to pay Chilean income tax only on the employee's Chilean income. This three-year period may be extended by the Regional Director of the Chilean Internal Revenue Service (*Servicio de Impuestos Internas*) in certain cases. After the initial three-year period (and any extension thereof) has ended, the foreign employee must pay Chilean taxes on all of his or her income, regardless of whether it originates in Chile or abroad. With respect to non-Chilean income, however, the foreign employee is taxed only on the net foreign income—that is, the total foreign income less any taxes the employee has paid on that income outside Chile. A foreign employee's income is considered non-Chilean when the goods or activities generating the income are located or developed outside Chile. All income derived from services an employee performs in Chile is considered Chilean income.

VENEZUELA*

INTRODUCTION

A. System of Government

The Republic of Venezuela is a country of approximately 25 million people, located in the northern extremity of South America. It has had a democratically elected government since 1958. The Constitution, enacted in 1999, sets forth the division of power among the executive, legislative, and judicial branches of government.

The Venezuelan executive branch is headed by a President, who is elected by direct, compulsory, and universal suffrage for a term of six years. Ministers, who head the various executive departments, are appointed by the President.

The Venezuelan legislative power is exercised by the National Assembly. Members of the National Assembly also are elected by direct, compulsory, and universal suffrage for six-year terms. The National Assembly has legislative powers. For a bill to become law, it must be approved by a majority of the Assembly. The President has the constitutional power to reject bills passed by the Assembly.

The judicial branch is governed by the Supreme Court of Justice and other lower courts. The Justices who comprise the Supreme Court of Justice are appointed by the Assembly for 12 years. The Supreme Court of Justice is the final court of appeal; it also functions as a constitutional tribunal because it has the power to declare null and void any laws, regulations, or other acts of the executive or legislative branch that conflict with the Constitution.

---

*Miguel A. Zaldívar, Jr., Hogan & Hartson, L.L.P., Miami, Florida; Ramón A. Azpúrua, Steel Hector & Davis, S.C., Caracas, Venezuela.

B. Sources of Labor Law

1. Constitution

The Constitution establishes the fundamental rights that rule employment law in Venezuela. The Constitution expressly provides the following rights: (1) the right to work, (2) freedom of work, (3) the right of the employees to be part of a union, and (4) the right of employees to negotiate collective bargaining agreements with their employers. These rights are developed by the Venezuelan Labor Law, as explained below.

2. The Labor Law

The first statute governing employment relationships in Venezuela was enacted in 1917. Over time, many other statutes followed. By the end of the 1980s, labor regulations could be found in at least nine different instruments, making labor law a complex and diverse set of rules. The longest-lived labor statute was the Labor Law of 1936, which, with several subsequent amendments, remained in effect until December 2, 1990, the date on which the President signed into law the Organic Labor Law.

The Organic Labor Law consisted of 665 articles, which merged, and expressly superseded, the Labor Law of 1936, as amended, along with a number of other employment-related statutes and regulations.[1]

On June 19, 1997, the Organic Labor Law was amended.[2] Eleven articles were changed, one was expressly superseded, and nine new articles were added. The primary effect of these amendments was to change the system of calculating seniority payments owed to a worker at the time of termination.[3] The Organic Labor

[1]The provisions displaced by the Organic Labor Law included the following: the Law Against Unjustified Dismissals; the Law of Privilege for Employee Social Benefits; the Law on Immunity of Workers' Profits from Attachment or Execution; the Law on Representation of Workers in the Institutions, Companies and Development Agencies of the State; Decree No. 125 on Review of Accounts and Financial Records for the Determination of Profits; Articles 8 and 9 of Decree No. 247 on the Control of Usury; Statutory Decree No. 440 on Collective Contracts by Branches of Industry; and Statutory Decree No. 540 on Penalties for Employers Who Exceed the Percentage of Foreign Workers Permitted by the Labor Law.

[2]Published in the Special Official Gazette No. 5,152 (June 19, 1997).

[3]See I.F.5.a.i., below.

Law, as amended (the Labor Law), currently is the central legislative source of employment regulation in Venezuela. The Labor Law expressly recognizes the right of all persons to employment.[4] The freedom of each person to pursue his or her preferred activity is guaranteed, so long as the activity is not otherwise prohibited by law. It is forbidden to impede the work of others or compel them to work against their will.[5]

Under the Labor Law, employment is not only a right but also is a duty. All capable persons are charged with a duty to work in order to maintain themselves,[6] and the law reiterates and explains the constitutional duty of the State to maintain high levels of employment.[7]

3. *International Sources*

Venezuela is a member of the International Labor Organization (ILO), an organization that is part of the United Nations.[8] The ILO drafts recommendations to its members with regard to different areas of labor law. All of the ILO's recommendations have become law in Venezuela and have been included in the Labor Law. Venezuela has adopted ILO recommendations regarding maternity rights, union rights, free association rights, salaries, and profit sharing.

C. National Preemption

Under Article 136 of the Constitution, labor, welfare, and social security matters are reserved to the national government. Similarly, the Labor Law provides that the national authorities have exclusive power to establish labor rules and regulations of national scope.[9] Thus, the states and municipalities are prohibited from legislating on labor matters.

---

[4]Labor Law, art. 24.

[5]*Id.* arts. 31, 32.

[6]*Id.* art. 23.

[7]*Id.* arts. 24, 25.

[8]For additional information about the ILO, see the chapter on the ILO in Volume I, Part 4.

[9]Labor Law, art. 12.

D. Application of the Labor Law

1. Territorial Reach

The Venezuelan Labor Law applies to work performed in Venezuela or to work performed outside of Venezuela, provided that the contract was executed in Venezuela.[10]

2. Employers

a. Enterprises Covered

For purposes of its application, the Labor Law defines company, commercial establishment, other business enterprises not having a separate legal personality, and other employment ventures (*faena*), all of which are subject to the Labor Law.[11] No types of enterprises are exempt from the Labor Law.

b. Employer Representatives

The Labor Law considers "employer representatives" to include all workers who exercise powers of management or administration on behalf of the employer, even though they are not expressly authorized to do so. For example, the following are considered employer representatives: directors, managers,[12] officers, industrial relations chiefs, personnel managers, ship or airplane captains, and "liquidators" or "depositories."[13] The terms "liquidator" and "depositor" are defined as the officials in charge in a liquidation of assets procedure. A liquidator is a person empowered to distribute the assets of a company among its creditors. A depository is a person that guards the assets and goods before they are distributed.

c. Intermediaries and Contractors

The Labor Law defines an intermediary as a person who utilizes the services of one or more workers in his or her own name

[10]*Id.* art. 10.

[11]*Id.* arts. 15, 16.

[12]For a definition of management employees, see the Introduction, at D.3.c., below.

[13]Labor Law, arts. 50, 51.

and for the benefit of another.[14] The intermediary, therefore, is a person who contracts, compensates, or manages the services of certain workers, and later delivers the project or service completed by them to a third party (beneficiary), pursuant to a civil or commercial agreement. When the services of an intermediary are utilized, the beneficiary is jointly responsible with the intermediary for labor liabilities to the workers, provided that he or she has expressly agreed to accept liability, when he or she receives completed work from the intermediary. In addition, the intermediary's workers enjoy the same terms and conditions of employment as those of the beneficiary.

A contractor is defined by the Labor Law as a person who is obligated by contract to perform work or services using his or her own equipment and personnel.[15] As opposed to an intermediary, the use of a contractor generally does not create labor liabilities for the beneficiary or the owner of the project with respect to the contractor's workers. However, if the activity of the contractor is inherent or related to the activity of the beneficiary, the latter will be liable in labor matters to the contractor's workers, or to the workers utilized by subcontractors. Furthermore, these workers will enjoy the same rights and terms of employment that the beneficiary's workers enjoy. The following activities are presumed to be inherent or related to the activity of a beneficiary: (1) the works and services performed by contractors for mining and hydrocarbon companies; and (2) the works and services performed for a company to such an extent that they constitute the largest source of income for the contractor.

3. *Covered Workers*

The Labor Law defines the terms worker (*trabajador*), independent worker, management employee, laborer (*obrero*), qualified laborer, employee of confidence, and inspection or guard employees.[16] These various categories are discussed below.

---

[14] *Id.* art. 54.
[15] *Id.* arts. 55, 57.
[16] *Id.* arts. 39–58.

a. Worker Defined

Article 39 of the Labor Law defines a worker as a person who does any kind of work on behalf of and dependent upon another. This provision contrasts with the original definition contained in the Labor Law of 1936 whereby a worker was anyone economically subordinated to another.

b. Independent Workers

An independent worker is defined as a person who supports him- or herself with his or her work without depending on any employer.[17] This category of workers (known as the "informal economy") has the rights to:

- Organize unions. In this regard, the Labor Law permits independent workers to join established professional, sectoral, or industrial unions, and to form their own unions with a minimum of 100 members dedicated to the same activity.[18]
- Enter into contracts similar to collective labor contracts.[19]
- Incorporate themselves progressively into the social security system and the system of rules that protect workers. There is a special procedure established for these workers, so they only have to register themselves in the Social Security Office as independent workers.
- Retain the name and ownership rights, and receive equitable compensation, for inventions, improvements, and intellectual or artistic works that are utilized by a third party, but which the independent worker owns according to the laws of intellectual property.[20]

c. Management Employees

Management employees are defined as those who take part in the decisions and direction of the company, as well as anyone

[17] *Id.* art. 40.
[18] *Id.* art. 418. See also II.A.1., below.
[19] See II.C., below.
[20] Labor Law, art. 90. See also I.D., below.

who is able to represent and substitute for the employer in any or all employer functions.[21] The classification of management employees depends on the actual character of the services performed, regardless of the title agreed to by the parties or established by the employer for the position.[22]

d. Laborers

Laborers are defined as those employees for whom manual labor dominates the material effort. Employees who prepare or supervise the work of other laborers, such as guards, forepersons, and the like, are also considered to be laborers.

e. Qualified Laborers

Qualified laborers are defined as those employees who require special training in order to perform their duties.

f. Confidential Employees

A confidential employee is defined as an employee whose duties involve the personal knowledge of industrial or commercial secrets of the employer, participation in the administration of the business, or supervision of other employees.

g. Inspection or Guard Employees

Inspection or guard employees are defined as those employees in charge of the supervision and revision of the duties of other employees or the supervision and security of the goods of the employer.

4. Public Officials

All public officials and workers are entitled to the benefits provided by the Labor Law in all matters not already provided for in the regulation of public employment.[23] For example, the statutes applicable to public workers govern all matters related to their

---

[21]Labor Law, art. 42.
[22]*Id.* art. 47.
[23]*Id.* art. 8.

income, promotion, transfer, suspension, retirement, compensation systems, employment stability, and the jurisdictional system.[24] However, the Labor Law recognizes the rights of public workers to collective bargaining and dispute resolution, including the right to strike, to the extent the exercise of these rights is compatible with the nature of the service they perform and the necessities of public administration.

E. Administrative Regulation

1. Administrative Agencies

The Labor Ministry and the Labor Inspector's Office are the agencies with principal responsibility for administering the Labor Law.[25] The Labor Law prohibits labor officials from having a direct or indirect interest in enterprises under their jurisdiction.

Labor Inspector Offices are headed by an inspector with the authority to visit work premises without prior notice in order to verify employer compliance with the Labor Law. The Labor Inspector's authority to enter and inspect work premises is quite broad, and includes the power to review the books, records, and documents that an employer is required by law to maintain.

2. Regulation of Employment Agencies

The Labor Law authorizes the operation of private employment agencies, subject to certain requirements.[26] Among other things, employment agencies must register with the Ministry of Labor. The Labor Ministry also is authorized to regulate the fees charged by such agencies. The Labor Law expressly forbids the deduction of any amount from a worker's wages in order to pay the fees or commission of an employment agency.

3. Penalties

Violations of any provision of the Labor Law by employers, labor officials, or other persons, are subject to various minimum

---

[24]G.O. Ext. No. 1,745 (May 23, 1975).

[25]Labor Law, arts. 586, 596.

[26]*Id.* arts. 597, 609.

and maximum fines.[27] The amount of these fines is linked to the minimum monthly wage[28] in effect at the time so that, in theory, when the cost of living and minimum wage increase, the amount of the fine should increase in the same proportion. Fines provided in the Labor Law vary from one-fourth to four times the monthly minimum wage. For repeated violations the fine may be increased by 50 percent.

Fines may be imposed by the Labor Ministry, the Labor Inspector, or by delegated officials, although any person may report violations of the Labor Law to the government labor agencies.

The Labor Law provides a series of specific procedural rules for penalties and fines that should be applied in preference to Labor Law's general rules on administrative procedures. Under these specific procedures, a penalized party need not request reconsideration from the official who imposed the penalty, but may appeal directly to the superior official. For example, if a penalty is imposed by a Labor Inspector, an appeal can be taken directly to the Labor Ministry. The Labor Law procedures also require that the penalized party must post a bond for the amount of the fine before an appeal may proceed.

F. Resolution of Labor Disputes

On August 13, 2003, the Organic Law on Labor Procedures (OLLP) became effective. It incorporates a number of general principles such as the following: the autonomy and specialization of the labor courts; cost-free access to the system; oral presentation of evidence; open proceedings; rapid, simple procedures; the primacy of judges in the process; and an emphasis of substance over form. The OLLP has been designed to alleviate the economic burdens that the current legislation imposes on workers and to accelerate the administration of justice in labor matters. Some commentators believe, however, that the OLLP has sacrificed fairness in favor of the speediness of the process; the burdens placed in the way of litigating employers seem excessive in many of the OLLP's provisions.

---

[27]*See id.* arts. 625–652.

[28]For a discussion of the minimum wage, see V.A.1.d., below.

1. Jurisdiction

Conflicts between employers and workers are resolved in special labor courts, which—at least in theory—are expressly required to administer justice rapidly, simply, and free of cost.[29]

The Judges of First Instance for Labor Cases have jurisdiction to hear claims for violations of constitutional rights and guarantees of a labor nature,[30] in conformity with the provisions of the current Law of Protection for Constitutional Rights and Guarantees.[31] (The Courts of First Instance for Labor Cases are the same as the Courts of Labor Stability.)

2. Procedures

The Labor Law provides that administrative or judicial notices to the employer for judicial or administrative labor actions will be effective when served personally on the employer representative, even when express authority has not been conferred on him or her to receive such notice or appear in judicial proceedings.[32] (Administrative officials are in charge of violations of union rights or bars against dismissal.) However, the labor official must confirm the service of notice by affixing a letter to the company door and personally delivering a copy to the employer, or leaving it with the secretarial office that receives company correspondence. The time limit for the employer's response begins to run on the date the letter is affixed to the door and delivered.

The employer may authorize a representative to give legal testimony in labor actions on the employer's behalf.[33]

The proceedings conducted before judicial or administrative labor officials are free of cost and exempt from taxes and any other government fees.[34]

---

[29]Labor Law, art. 4.

[30]*Id.* art. 11.

[31]G.O. No. 34,060 (Sept. 27, 1988).

[32]Labor Law, art. 52. For a definition of employer representatives, see the Introduction, at D.2.b., above.

[33]Labor Law, art. 53.

[34]*Id.* art. 14.

3. *Applicable Law*

The Labor Law expressly establishes the protective principle of *Dubio Pro Operario*,[35] which provides that when there is doubt as to the application of the various rules in effect or as to the interpretation of a given rule, the determination most favorable to the worker must be applied. Additionally, in cases of conflicting laws, the labor laws take precedence, whether they are substantive or procedural. In addition to the Constitution, the laws of Venezuela, and the treaties ratified by Venezuela, the following are applied in order to resolve a given case:[36]

- the applicable collective contract or arbitral decision;
- the employment contract;
- the principles upon which labor laws are founded, such as the agreements and recommendations adopted by the ILO that have not been ratified yet by Venezuela, and principles of Venezuelan jurisprudence;
- custom or practice when it does not contravene the laws in effect or the principles that inspired the labor legislation;
- universally accepted principles of labor law;
- rules and general principles of law; and
- equity.

4. *Statute of Limitations*[37]

The statute of limitations for labor actions is one year, and runs from the date of termination of the performance of services. However, the one-year statute of limitations on claims for statutory profit sharing[38] begins to run two months after the day the fiscal year closes.

In practice, the statute of limitations for labor actions may be extended to 14 months, as the running of the statute is considered to be tolled as of the date on which the legal summons or the administrative notice is served on the other party, so long as service

---

[35] *Id.* art. 54.
[36] *Id.* art. 60.
[37] *Id.* arts. 61–64.
[38] See V.A.2., below.

is effected before the expiration of the 12-month limitation period or within the two months following such period.

The statute of limitations for claims of compensation for employment accidents or work-related illnesses[39] is two years.

5. *Settlement*

In general, the rules favoring workers may not be waived.[40] Nevertheless, in the event of a dispute there remains the possibility that workers may waive their rights by means of a settlement, provided that the waiver is in writing and describes both the circumstances that motivate the waiver and the rights involved. A settlement can only occur after termination of the employment relationship and, if effected in the presence of a competent labor official, will have res judicata effect.

I. INDIVIDUAL EMPLOYMENT

A. The Employment Relationship

The Labor Law provides for a presumption of the existence of an employment relationship between a person who performs a service and a person who receives the service.[41] However, certain cases are excepted in which, for ethical reasons or reasons of public interest, the service is performed for purposes distinct from those of an employment relationship. These cases include, for example, religious workers or persons who voluntarily lend their services to institutions such as the Red Cross, League Against Cancer, or other similar organizations. It is further provided that the performance of services in an employment relationship must be compensated. Therefore, if an employment relationship exists, services must be compensated.

---

[39]See VII.B., below.
[40]Labor Law, art. 3.
[41]*Id.* arts. 65, 66.

B. Effect of the Labor Law on Individual Terms of Employment

The Labor Law expressly permits employers and workers to negotiate terms and conditions of employment, so long as the negotiated terms are not below the standards set by law and in collective contracts.[42] The provisions of the Labor Law are characterized as essential to public welfare. Therefore, their waiver in individual agreements is prohibited, except for those provisions that, by their context, may be deemed nonimperative.[43]

C. The Employment Contract

1. Definition

The employment contract is defined as that which creates the duty of one person (the worker) to render services to another (the employer) under the latter's control (subordination) and with compensation (wages).[44]

2. Formalities

Preferably, the employment contract should be in writing, be signed in two originals, and contain the following specifications:

- name, nationality, age, marital status, and domicile or residence of the contracting parties;
- the service to be performed, described as fully as possible;
- the duration of the contract (when it is for a fixed duration) or an indication that it is for an indefinite duration, as the case may be;
- the project or labor to be performed, when specific work is contracted for;
- the duration of the normal workday, whether defined by units of time or production;

[42] *Id.* arts. 185, 186.
[43] *Id.* art. 10.
[44] *Id.* art. 67.

- the agreed wages, or the manner of calculating them, and the manner and place of payment;
- the place where the work is to be performed; and
- any other lawful provision agreed to by the parties.[45]

3. Performance of Services Outside Venezuela

When a contract is made under which a Venezuelan is to perform services outside the country, the following requirements apply:

- it must be in writing;
- it must be notarized at the place of signing; and
- it must be legalized in the Venezuelan consulate of the country where the services will be performed.[46]

The employer must guarantee the costs of the worker's return trip to the Labor Inspector's satisfaction. In addition, the transportation, meals, and immigration costs of the worker must be borne directly by the employer. Venezuelan labor laws apply during the performance of service outside the country.

4. Duration

Under the Labor Law, an employment contract may be for an indefinite or fixed duration.[47]

a. Indefinite Duration

This is the typical kind of contract entered into in Venezuela, in which the parties do not specifically limit the relationship to a definite time period or a specific task.

b. Fixed Duration

An employment contract that establishes a fixed duration is the exception in Venezuela. The Labor Law does not require that

---

[45]*Id.* arts. 70, 71.
[46]*Id.* art. 78.
[47]*Id.* arts. 72–77.

these kinds of contracts be in writing or that administrative labor officials participate in their execution in order that they be enforceable.[48] Notwithstanding this legislative omission, it is advisable that an employment contract of fixed duration be in writing.

Contracts for a fixed duration are subject to certain limitations. First, the maximum term of a contract of fixed duration is one year for laborers and three years for employees and qualified laborers.[49] Second, the nature of the service must justify the stipulated term, or the contract must have the purpose of substituting provisionally for another worker or contracting for services to be performed outside Venezuela by a Venezuelan worker.[50] Substituting provisionally means that contracts for a fixed term can be executed only for purposes of substituting an employee for a limited period of time, and once the term is concluded, the substituted employee shall return to his or her work. It is important to spell out such circumstances in the text of the contract.

Employment contracts of a fixed duration terminate at the close of the agreed term, although they may be extended.[51] In the event of two or more extensions, the contract will be considered to be of indefinite duration, unless reasons exist that justify the extension and that exclude the possible intention of creating an indefinite relationship. Additionally, if a new contract is signed within one month after the expiration of the prior contract, it is presumed that the parties have contracted for an indefinite term unless the will of the parties to establish a fixed term is demonstrated. Thus, when less than one month has lapsed between the first and the second contracts, two distinct relationships are considered to exist.

c. *Specific Projects*

A contract may describe a specific project or task to be completed by the worker, thus allowing the employer to retain the worker until the project is completed.[52] This type of contract ter-

---

48 *Id.* art. 74.

49 *Id.* art. 76. For definitions of laborers and qualified laborers, see the Introduction, at D.3.d. and e., above.

50 Labor Law, art. 77.

51 *Id.* art. 74.

52 *Id.* art. 75.

minates on completion of the worker's defined project or task, independent of whether the larger project of which it is part is completed. If a new contract is signed during the month following termination of the initial contract, the relationship becomes one of indefinite duration, with the exception of construction contracts.

D. Inventions and Improvements

Inventions and improvements are divided into categories of service, company, or chance (*ocasionales*), and extend to all kinds of inventions, including industrial, commercial, financial, or any other kind.[53]

In general, the Labor Law adheres to the principle of "transference of work performed," on the basis of which all economic benefits derived from worker inventions and improvements in service or in the company inure exclusively to the employer. However, when the profits derived from an invention are obviously disproportionate to the compensation of the worker-inventor, in addition to his or her wages, the worker will be entitled to an equitable share of profits, to be established by mutual agreement of the parties and subject to the approval of the Labor Inspector. In the absence of a mutual agreement, a judge will determine the worker's share.

E. Suspension of the Employment Relationship

The Labor Law lists the following causes for suspension of the employment relationship:[54]

- an accident or work-related illness that disables the worker for up to 12 months;
- illnesses not related to work;
- compulsory military service;
- maternity leave;[55]
- a collective dispute (declared as such pursuant to the law);[56]

---

[53]*Id.* arts. 80–87.
[54]*Id.* art. 94.
[55]See V.C.2., below.
[56]See II.D., below.

- preventive detention of the worker during a judicial or police investigation, when the worker has not committed an act that justifies such detention;
- permission given to the worker by the employer for studies or other activities; and
- chance events or acts of God that result in an immediate suspension of work.

Suspension does not end the employment relationship.[57] However, during a suspension the employer is not required to pay wages, and the worker is not required to work. The time during which a suspension of the employment relationship is in effect is not computed for purposes of determining the seniority of the worker, except in the case of maternity leave,[58] and collective dispute procedures.[59]

The worker whose employment contract has been suspended is protected by law against dismissal.[60]

F. Termination of the Employment Relationship

1. Causes

The employment relationship may be terminated by dismissal, resignation, mutual agreement, of the parties, or intervening causes.[61]

Dismissal and resignation may be justified or unjustified. Dismissal is justified only if based on good cause described in the Labor Law and previously verified by the Labor Inspector.[62] Examples are when the worker commits a serious misdeed (*falta grave*), when the employee seriously compromises the security and hygiene of the workplace, or in the case of three unjustified absences during a month. When a resignation or dismissal occurs without good cause, it is considered unjustified. The rights of a worker in the case of a justified resignation (e.g., a constructive

---

[57]Labor Law arts. 93, 95, and 96.
[58]*Id.* art. 389.
[59]*Id.* art. 505.
[60]*Id.* arts. 96, 453.
[61]*Id.* arts. 98–103.
[62]*Id.* art. 102.

dismissal) are the same as those resulting from an unjustified dismissal. As discussed further below,[63] this permits the dismissed worker to claim termination benefits.

2. *Termination Notice*

The employer must give written notice to the worker, setting forth the reasons, if any, for the dismissal. Once notice is given, the employer may not rely on other causes to justify the dismissal.[64]

a. Unjustified Dismissal or Resignation

i. Notice period

In the case of unjustified dismissal or resignation, the other party must be given prior notice of the termination, according to the following rules:

- after one month of interrupted work, one-week's notice;
- after six months of uninterrupted work, 15-days' notice; or
- after one year of uninterrupted work, one-month's notice.[65]

The Labor Law adds that if the employment relation terminates as a result of an unjustified dismissal or based on technical or economic reasons, and the worker has completed more than five years of service, the following notice periods apply:

- with 5 to 10 years of uninterrupted service, two-months' notice; or
- after 10 years of service, three-months' notice.

ii. Employee indemnity in lieu of notice

In lieu of the required notice, an employer may pay an indemnity to the worker. This indemnity is calculated in accordance with the following rules:

---

[63]See I.F.2.b. and I.F.6.c., below.
[64]Labor Law, arts. 105–116.
[65]*Id.* arts 104, 107.

- 15-days' wages, when the worker has rendered services for one to six months;
- 30-days' wages, when the worker has served for six months to one year;
- 45-days' wages, when the worker has served for one to two years;
- 60-days' wages, when the worker has served for 2 to 10 years; and
- 90-days' wages, when the worker has served for more than 10 years.

The base wage used in calculating the indemnity in lieu of notice may not exceed 10 times the monthly minimum wage.[66]

iii. Employer indemnity in lieu of notice

When a worker resigns without justification, the termination notice may be omitted, but the worker must pay the employer an indemnity equal to the wages the worker would have earned during the notice period.[67]

b. Justified Dismissal or Resignation

The employment relationship may be terminated by dismissal or resignation without any prior notice to the other party when a cause exists that justifies the dismissal or resignation, and so long as 30 days have not passed since the cause was known or should have been known.[68] Additionally, a subsequent written notice of dismissal must be given to the worker, explaining the reason for the dismissal. Once this notification has been given, the employer may not cite other causes to justify the dismissal. The Labor Law does not indicate how an employer is to provide notice of dismissal to a worker who has abandoned his or her position and cannot be located.

---

[66]For an explanation of the minimum wage, see V.A.1.d., below.

[67]Labor Law, art. 107.

[68]*Id.* arts. 101, 105, and 109.

In the case of a justified dismissal or resignation of a worker contracted for an indefinite duration, the party who initiated the termination must pay to the other an indemnity corresponding to the termination notice period that would have applied.

3. *Judicial Notice*

When an employer unjustifiably dismisses a worker, the employer must notify the Judge of Labor Stability (a Court of Law is the same as the Judge of First Instance for labor cases) for the particular jurisdiction within five working days, specifying the reasons that justify the dismissal.[69] If timely notice is not provided, the employer will be deemed to have admitted that the dismissal was unjustified. As discussed immediately above, if the worker was provided with written notice of dismissal, no reasons other than those given in the worker's notice may be cited to justify the dismissal before the Judge of Labor Stability.

4. *Employment Certificate*

If a worker requests a certificate of employment upon termination of the employment relationship, the employer must issue a certificate containing the following information:

- term of the employment relationship,
- last wages earned, and
- position held.[70]

5. *Employee Termination Benefits*

a. *Seniority Payments*

i. *Calculation*

Seniority payments[71] are earned by all workers in accordance with the following schedule:

---

[69] *Id.* art. 116.
[70] *Id.* art. 111.
[71] *Id.* art. 108.

- five-days' wages[72] for each month of service, which begin to accrue as soon as the employee reaches three uninterrupted months of employment; and
- after the first year of service (or fraction of six or more months), two additional days' wages for each subsequent year, cumulative up to 30-days' wages.

ii. Accounting

Seniority payments must be deposited or credited to the worker's account monthly. For this purpose, the worker must inform the employer in writing of where to deposit or credit the seniority payments, whether to (1) an individual trust, (2) a Seniority Payments Fund (*Fondo de Prestaciones de Antiguedad*), or (3) an independent account in the employer's accounting records.

Seniority payments yield interest based on where they are deposited or credited. In general, the rates of return are those produced by the trusts or Seniority Payments Funds. If the worker directs deposits to an individual trust or to a Seniority Payments Fund, and the employer does not comply with the worker's instructions, the applicable interest rate is determined by the Central Bank, which uses as a reference the active interest rate paid by the six most important commercial banks in the country. If the worker directs deposits to an individual account in the employer's accounting records, the applicable interest rate is the average of the active and passive interest rate, as determined by the Central Bank.

Interest on seniority payments is exempt from income tax, must be deposited or credited monthly, and must be paid after each year of employment unless the worker decides that the interest should be reinvested.

A financial institution or Seniority Payments Fund must provide the worker with detailed information regarding the amount of deposits and accrued interest. Similarly, if seniority payments are credited to an individual account in the employer's accounting records, the employer must provide detailed annual information to the worker.

---

[72] For additional information on the calculation of seniority payments, see V.A.1.i.v., below.

iii. Payment at termination

Seniority payments credited to a worker's account are payable to the worker at the time of termination.[73] These payments are calculated in accordance with the following schedule:

- 15-days' wages when the worker has rendered services for three to six months, or the difference between such amount and the amount deposited or credited monthly;
- 45-days' wages when the worker has rendered services for six months to one year, or the difference between such amount and the amount deposited or credited monthly; or
- 60-days' wages when the worker has rendered services for more than a year, or the difference between such amount and the amount deposited or credited monthly, provided that the worker rendered services for at least six months during the year in which the employment relationship terminates.

These are minimum payments, to be supplemented by the employer, if the worker's account contains less than these amounts.

iv. Advances

The worker has the right to receive seniority payment advances of up to 75 percent of credited or deposited amounts for the following purposes:

- to build, acquire, improve, or maintain a residence for the worker and the worker's family;
- to discharge debt relating to the residence of the worker and the worker's family;

[73]This system, which was enacted by the Organic Labor Law of 1997, amounts to a radical change in the method of calculating seniority payments owed to the worker at termination of the employment relationship. Under prior law, seniority payments were calculated by taking into account the years of service rendered by the worker and the amount of the worker's last wage. In practice, this gave retroactive effect to the last wage and increased considerably the amounts paid to workers at termination. Under current law, seniority payments are deposited or credited every month and then paid to the worker upon termination. This system effectively eliminates the retroactive effects of wage increases.

- to pay educational tuition for the worker, spouse (or significant other), or children; and
- to pay medical bills for the worker, spouse (or significant other), or children.

If seniority payments have been credited to an independent account in the employer's accounting records, the employer can either loan or guarantee the debt of the worker. If the employer chooses to provide a guarantee instead of a loan, it must pay any excess of the commercial interest charged over the rate that would be obtained for direct employer loans. If the seniority payments have been deposited in a financial institution or a Seniority Payments Fund, the worker may guarantee with the amount of the seniority payments any obligations incurred for the purposes set forth above.

v. Death of a worker

In the event that the employment relationship is terminated by death of a worker,[74] the following persons are entitled to receive the seniority payment:

- children of the worker younger than 18 years of age, or any children who are disabled to such an extent that they cannot earn a living;
- a surviving spouse who has not requested or obtained a legal separation, or a concubine;
- other direct ascending relatives who had the worker in their care at the time of his or her death; and
- orphaned grandchildren younger than 18 years old, or grandchildren with parents who are not otherwise entitled to the seniority payment and who cannot provide for the subsistence of their children.

The above-listed persons are not given any relative preferences to the seniority payment, so that if it is solicited by two or more of them, it will be distributed equally among them. The em-

[74]Labor Law, arts. 108, 568–570.

ployer is free of liability for any claims based on the seniority payment once payment has been made to all relatives who duly claim a share within the three months following the death. Thereafter, other relatives may claim a share only from those relatives who already received payment. Accordingly, in the event of a worker's death, employers are advised to make the seniority payment at the close of the three-month period.

b. *Additional Payments for Unjustified Dismissals*

i. *Contracts for an indefinite duration*

In the event that an employer unjustifiably dismisses a worker who is employed for an indefinite duration, the employer must pay the worker, in addition to the seniority payments described immediately above and the wages that the worker failed to receive during the required notice period,[75] an amount that is calculated as follows:

- 10-days' wages for each year of service (including fractions of six or more months), when the worker has rendered services to the employer for three to six months; and
- 30-days' wages for each year of service (including fractions of six or more months), when the worker has rendered services to the employer for more than six months, with a maximum limit of 150-days' wages.[76]

ii. *Contracts for a fixed duration or a specific project*

In the event of an unjustified dismissal or a justified resignation before the conclusion of a contract for a fixed duration or a specified project, the employer must pay, in addition to the seniority payment described above, an indemnity equal to the amount of wages the worker would have earned through the conclusion of the fixed term or project.[77] If, on the other hand, the contract is

---

[75]For a discussion of termination notice periods, see I.F.2.a.i., above.
[76]Labor Law, arts. 104, 106, and 125.
[77]*Id.* art. 110.

terminated prematurely by the worker without good cause, the worker must pay an indemnity to the employer in an amount calculated by a judge, but which may not exceed one-half the amount the worker would have earned through the conclusion of the time period or project. In this situation, the employer still must pay the seniority payment accrued by the worker up to the date of termination.

6. *Judicial Proceedings*

A worker declared to have been dismissed unjustifiably is entitled to seek reinstatement to his or her position and payment of the wages not received during the claim procedure.[78]

a. Jurisdiction

The procedure for evaluating dismissals is carried out in Special Courts of Labor Stability.[79] The procedure is brief and is initiated by a petition submitted by the worker within a period of five working days following the date of dismissal. The worker may appear on his or her own behalf, or be assisted or represented by a union executive or delegate. The employer also may appear on his or her own behalf, or may be assisted or represented by a person in his or her confidence, such as an employer representative or an attorney possessing power of attorney.[80] If the worker allows five days to elapse without requesting a ruling on the dismissal, he or she will lose any right to reinstatement. However, the worker still may pursue other rights in the Labor Courts.

Either party may petition the Court to appoint a special panel of judges to hear a case. The decision of the Court of Labor Stability may be appealed in the Superior Labor Courts, and the final decision of these Superior Courts will end the procedure, with no further appeal.

---

[78] *Id.* arts. 112–128.

[79] *Id.* arts. 116–124.

[80] For a definition of employer representatives, see the Introduction, at D.2.b., above.

b. Excluded Workers

The Labor Law expressly excludes the following categories of workers from the right to reinstatement:

- permanent workers who have completed fewer than three months of uninterrupted service;
- management employees;
- seasonal, occasional, sporadic, and domestic workers; and
- workers contracted for a fixed term or a specific project, when the term has not come to a close or the project is not complete.[81]

Confidential employees may seek reinstatement and payment of lost wages in cases of unjustified dismissal.[82] Those who work for establishments employing fewer than 10 workers may not seek reinstatement if unjustifiably dismissed, but will be entitled to seniority payments and other termination benefits.[83]

c. Justified Resignation

When a worker resigns for a good cause (claiming, for example, a constructive dismissal), then he or she is entitled to the same benefits as would apply to a dismissal without justification.[84] However, the worker may not seek reinstatement to his or her former position.

d. Premature Termination of the Procedure

The procedure will not be allowed if, at the moment of dismissal, the worker is paid all termination benefits due.[85] The procedure also may be dismissed at any time if, in addition to termination benefits, the wages that would have been earned up to that time are paid to the worker.

---

[81]Labor Law, arts. 112–115.

[82]For a definition of confidential employees, see the Introduction, at D.3.f., above.

[83]See I.F.5., above.

[84]See I.F.5.b., above.

[85]Labor Law, arts. 125, 126. See also I.F.5.b., above.

G. Special Cases

1. Minors

The age of majority under the Civil Code is 18. The Labor Law contains a series of provisions regulating the employment of minors.[86] Specifically, minors may not work in mines and smelters, positions that involve risks to their lives or health, positions requiring strength or endurance beyond their physical development, or in any positions that impede or retard their normal physical development.[87] In addition, minors may not perform work that is prejudicial to their intellectual or moral development, such as work in retail liquor establishments. Hotels, restaurants, diners, aircraft, and similar places are not retail liquor establishments for this purpose.[88]

In order to enter into employment agreements or perform any work, minors must be furnished with a special permit by the Labor Ministry.[89] In addition, they may not work without a certificate issued by the Labor Ministry's medical service, or alternatively, by the medical service of the Ministry of Health and Social Welfare.[90] They also must undergo periodic medical examinations. If the work they perform impairs their health or their normal development, they may not continue, and the employer must provide them with a more appropriate position, in addition to paying the medical expenses associated with their recovery.[91] Minors between 14 and 16 years of age must have written authorization to work from their parents or guardians, or from the appropriate government authorities.[92] Minors between 12 and 14 years of age may be authorized to work by the Council for the Protection of Children and Adolescents (or the Labor Inspector), provided that they perform tasks appropriate to their physical development, and that their

---

[86]Labor Law, arts. 247–255. For additional restrictions on the working conditions of minors, see V.D.1., below.

[87]Labor Law, art. 249.

[88]*Id.* art. 250.

[89]*Id.* art. 263.

[90]*Id.* art. 252.

[91]*Id.* art. 253.

[92]*Id.* art. 248.

education is guaranteed.[93] Apart from this exception, it is strictly forbidden to employ any minor younger than 14 years of age.

Any employer that hires minors has a duty to maintain a registry of certain personal and employment data.[94]

2. *Apprentices*

Apprentices[95] are minors who undergo systematic professional training in the skills of their work, and who have not completed any such training prior to their employment.[96] Apprenticeships generally are regulated by the Organic Law for the Protection of Children and Adolescents and the Law and Regulations of the National Institute of Cooperative Education (INCE). The provisions contained in the Labor Law do not diminish the duties, restrictions, or protections of the INCE.[97]

If an employer is under a legal duty to hire minor apprentices, then the employment relationship must be described as the full term of the apprenticeship.[98] This contract is similar to a contract for a specified project in that it terminates on completion of the apprenticeship. If the parties agree, either expressly or implicitly, to continue the employment relationship beyond the apprenticeship period, it is considered to be an employment for an indefinite duration, as of the date on which the apprenticeship began.

Employers that hire apprentices must notify the Labor Inspector's Office.[99]

3. *Domestic Workers*

Domestic workers are those who work in a house or residence in the personal service of a specific person or one of his or her relatives.[100] Examples are private drivers, butlers and maids, cooks, nursemaids, laundry workers, pressers, and persons who

---

[93] *Id.* art. 247.

[94] *Id.* art. 265.

[95] *Id.* arts. 266–273. For additional Labor Law provisions applicable to apprentices, see V.D.2., below.

[96] Labor Law, art. 267.

[97] *Id.* art. 272.

[98] *Id.* art. 268.

[99] *Id.* art. 270.

[100] *Id.* art. 274. For additional Labor Law provisions applicable to domestic workers, see V.D.3., below.

perform similar work. If a domestic worker works both in the employer's home and in a company, business, or other enterprise managed by the employer, the worker is considered to be employed by the business entity.

For domestic workers, the termination notice period is always 15 days, regardless of their length of employment.[101] Domestic workers also are entitled to a termination indemnity equal to 15-days' wages for each year of service if their employment contract or relationship is terminated by an unjustified dismissal or justified resignation, or due to lapse of the employment term (if hired for a fixed duration), or other causes beyond their control.[102] Thus, if domestic workers resign or are dismissed for good cause, they are not entitled to this indemnity.

II. Collective Bargaining

In Venezuela, collective bargaining rights are established in the National Constitution, as well as in the Organic Labor Law.

Collective bargaining rights were established in Venezuela to offer employees the opportunity to negotiate better working conditions than those set forth in the law. Once a collective bargaining agreement has been agreed upon and executed, its provisions constitute mandatory clauses that must be incorporated in all labor agreements, including the labor agreements of employees who are not members of the union that signed the collective bargaining agreement. Therefore, collective bargaining benefits a large number of employees.

Specifically, collective bargaining agreements are established in article 96 of the Constitution. According to this article, all public and private employees are entitled to negotiate collective bargaining agreements in order to negotiate better working conditions. This article also establishes that the law shall protect, develop, and promote collective bargaining.

---

[101] Labor Law, art. 279.

[102] *Id.* art. 284.

Regarding the Organic Labor Law, collective bargaining agreements are established and defined in Title VII. Basically, the Organic Labor Law develops the principles set forth in the Constitution.

A. Unions

Under Venezuelan law, unions may be composed either of workers or employers.[103]

1. Labor Unions

Labor unions[104] may be organized in a variety of ways, based on a common employer, occupation, industry, or economic sector.

- *Company Unions* are composed of the workers of a single enterprise, including operations located in different towns and regions.[105] Twenty or more workers are required to form a company union.[106]
- *Trade Unions* are composed of workers in the same profession or trade, or who have similar or related professions or skills, whether they are employed by one or several companies.[107] Forty or more workers are required to form a trade union.[108]
- *Industrial Unions* are composed of workers who are employed by several employers in the same industrial field, even though they work in different professions or trades.[109] Forty or more workers are required to form an industrial union.[110]
- *Sectorial Unions* are composed of the workers of several employers in the same commercial, agricultural, production, or service branch, even though their professions and

[103] *Id.* arts. 410–468.
[104] *Id.* art. 411.
[105] *Id.* art. 412.
[106] *Id.* art. 417.
[107] *Id.* art. 443.
[108] *Id.* art. 418.
[109] *Id.* art. 414.
[110] *Id.* art. 418.

trades differ.[111] Again, 40 or more workers are required to form a sectorial union.[112]

Unions also may be organized by independent workers, that is, those persons who are not bonded to any employer by an individual employment agreement or relationship.[113] Formation of such a union requires 100 or more persons.[114] Professional associations, provided they are legally established, also may be registered as unions with the Labor Ministry.[115] In order to register a union, the founding members must present before the Labor Inspector the registration request, accompanied by the articles of incorporation, a copy of the by-laws, and a list of the founding members.[116] All of these documents must be signed by the members of the Board of Directors.

Once the required documents have been presented, the Labor Inspector has 30 days to register the union. If the documents presented have any mistakes or omissions, the members must amend such mistakes within 30 days following the labor inspector's notice of such mistakes or omissions.

The decision of the labor inspector may be challenged before the Labor Ministry, and the Labor Ministry's decision may be challenged before the Administrative (*Contencioso-administrativo*) Courts, within 10 days following notification to the union's board of directors of the decision.

Labor unions may be local, state, regional, or national in their geographic scope.[117] If they are regional or national, 150 or more workers are required for a union's formation.[118]

---

[111] *Id.* art. 415.

[112] *Id.* art. 418.

[113] See the Introduction, at D.3.b., above.

[114] Labor Law, art. 418.

[115] *Id.* art. 405.

[116] The required content of these documents is established in articles 422, 423, and 424 of the Labor Law.

[117] Labor Law, art. 416.

[118] *Id.* art. 418.

2. *Employer Unions*

Employers' unions may be composed of 10 or more employers in the same industry or activity, or other related activities.[119] A duly established employers' association also may be registered as a union with the Labor Ministry.[120] The registration requirements and procedures are the same as those for labor unions, discussed immediately above.

3. *Union Dissolution*

When there are sufficient reasons, interested parties may petition for the dissolution of a union before a Judge of First Instance for Labor Cases in the appropriate jurisdiction. Article 462 does not specify what constitutes "sufficient reason," therefore, the judge shall decide if the reason given constitutes a sufficient reason. However, the courts have decided that the lack of union members constitutes sufficient reason for dissolution.

B. Union Recognition

Once a union has been registered before the Labor Inspector, according to the procedure set forth in A.1., above, the union becomes recognized for all legal effects.

The board of directors shall be appointed in accordance with the procedure set forth in the union's bylaws.[121] The board of directors will perform its duties for the period of time set forth in the bylaws, however, it may not be for a period of time greater than three years.[122]

In order to demand bargaining, the union must present to its employer, through the labor inspector, a "*Pliego Conflictivo*" in order to negotiate a collective bargaining agreement, request the application of better working conditions, or eliminate certain working measures adopted by the employer. Within 24 hours after the *Pliego Conflictivo* has been presented, the labor inspector must send it to the employer.

---

[119] *Id.* art. 419.
[120] *Id.* art. 405.
[121] *Id.* art. 433.
[122] *Id.* art. 434.

Forty-eight hours after the employer's notice, both the union and the employer shall notify the labor inspector of the members appointed to the conciliation board (there are two representatives and two substitutes for each party). The members of the conciliation board then meet before the labor inspector to reach an agreement or a solution. After the meetings are concluded, the conciliation board prepares a decision establishing either the impossibility of conciliation between the parties or a recommendation to reach an agreement. This recommendation may adopt specific measures and agreements or submit the conflict or negotiation to arbitration.

Once the conciliation procedure is exhausted, if the parties do not agree to submit the conflict to arbitration, the conciliation board must prepare a report stating the reason for such decision, as well as a summary of the causes of the conflict, the meetings, and a summary of the parties statements.

C. Collective Bargaining Agreements

1. Definition

Collective contracts[123] are those entered into between one or more labor unions, federations, or confederations, on the one hand, and one or more employers, employers' unions, or associations, on the other hand, to establish the general terms and conditions of employment, and the rights and duties of both parties. Five or more unions may constitute a federation, and three or more federations may constitute a confederation. Both must register before the Labor Ministry.

2. Signatory Parties

In order to compel a company to enter into a collective agreement, a labor union must represent an absolute majority of the company's workers. If the workers are engaged in different occupations or trades, the trade union must represent a majority of the

[123]*Id.* arts. 469–559.

workers in each respective occupation,[124] excluding management and confidential employees.[125]

Under current law, the possibility of a collective employment agreement entered into directly with a group of workers has been eliminated. Thus, what formerly was known as an Employer-Worker Collective Contract, or notarized contract, has disappeared.

3. *Industrywide Bargaining*[126]

The Labor Law makes clear that collective contracts may be negotiated on an industrywide or sectorwide basis.[127]

Employers that are summoned to industrywide bargaining may present arguments that they should be excluded from the corresponding rulemaking or negotiation meetings.[128] The labor officer will summon the parties by a simple notification process. Employers that attend more than 50 percent of the rulemaking meetings are entitled to abstain from executing the agreement, and thereby are not bound, just as employers not summoned to the meetings are not bound.[129] However, employers that are summoned but fail to attend more than 50 percent of the meetings are nevertheless bound by the resulting agreement.[130]

Workers of companies summoned to rulemaking meetings may not be dismissed by their employers.[131]

4. *Scope of the Collective Contract*

The collective contract's provisions are mandatory clauses, which form an integral part of any individual employment contract entered into while the collective agreement is in force. This means that a collective contract applies to all workers in a company, even if they are hired after the execution of the agreement.[132]

---

[124] *Id.* art. 514.

[125] *Id.* art. 515. For definitions of management and confidential employees, see the Introduction, at D.3.c. and f., above.

[126] Labor Law, arts. 528–559.

[127] *Id.* art. 528.

[128] *Id.* art. 536.

[129] *Id.* art. 534.

[130] *Id.* art. 535.

[131] *Id.* art. 533(f). See also II.E.2., below.

[132] Labor Law, art. 509.

The contract applies as well to workers who are not members of the labor union that executed the agreement.[133] If a company has departments or branches in different jurisdictions, a contract entered into with a majority labor union may apply to all workers in the various departments or branches.[134]

The employer's representatives who participate in the negotiation of the contract and who authorize its execution are excluded as beneficiaries of the agreement.[135] Management employees and workers of confidence also may be excluded from coverage.[136]

5. *Filing Requirements*

A collective contract must be filed with the Labor Inspector's Office of the respective jurisdiction in order to be valid. If entered into by a worker's federation or confederation, the contract must be filed with the National Labor Inspector's Office.[137]

From the day and hour on which the draft collective contract is submitted to the Labor Inspector's Office, the workers are protected by a bar against dismissal.[138]

6. *Duration*

A collective agreement may have a duration of not more than three years, nor less than two years. However, the Labor Law provides that some clauses of the contract (in particular, those related to economic matters) may be negotiated by the parties for shorter periods of time or for shorter terms (fewer than two years).

7. *Modification*

The Labor Law preserves the principle of "non-revocability of the collective agreement." By virtue of this principle (1) a new collective contract may not be entered into if it contains terms and conditions less favorable to the workers than those contained in

[133] *Id.* art. 508.
[134] *Id.* art. 513.
[135] *Id.* art. 510.
[136] *Id.* art. 509.
[137] *Id.* art. 521.
[138] See II.E.2., below.

the labor agreements already in force between the parties; and (2) the provisions in force may be modified only when such modification is favorable to the workers.[139] In both cases, the contract should specify the benefits of the new provisions in relation to the old.

If economic circumstances threaten a company's activity or existence, the employer is allowed to negotiate modifications of the terms of employment before the Labor Inspector's Office. These modifications would be in effect only for the remaining term of the agreement. During this term, all workers are protected against dismissal.[140]

D. Collective Disputes

1. *Parties*

The collective dispute procedure[141] is available only to labor unions.[142] This means that the union is the only party that is able to demand arbitration, and employers may not engage in industrial actions such as lockouts.

2. *Strikes*

a. *Public Services Strikes*

The Labor Law recognizes the right to strike for workers in public services, provided the strike does not cause irreparable harm to the public, or to affected public service institutions.[143]

b. *Workers Compelled to Work During a Strike*

Workers who perform services essential to public health, or essential to the care and maintenance of machinery that, if allowed to stop, would impair the renewal of work or risk serious damage to the machinery, must continue working during strikes.[144] Those

---

[139]Labor Law, art. 511.
[140]*Id.* arts. 520, 526. See also II.E.2., below.
[141]Labor Law, arts. 475–506.
[142]*Id.* art. 476.
[143]*Id.* art. 474.
[144]*Id.* art. 498.

workers charged with the care and safekeeping of the work premises are under the same obligation. The number of workers who are compelled to continue working during strikes should be established by mutual agreement of the employer and the labor union.

c. Industrywide Strikes

Generalized strikes in an industry are permitted when agreement cannot be reached at the labor rulemaking meeting.[145]

d. Notification

Both workers and employers must notify the First Civil Authority (*Jefatura Civil* or Civil Police headquarters)[146] having jurisdiction over them of the declaration and termination of a strike.[147] The notification is simple and informal, and there is no set time frame for providing this notice.

In order to initiate the strike procedure, the strike must be based on the demand made to the employer in order to take, modify, or stop applying measures regarding the labor conditions; to execute a collective bargaining agreement; or to comply with a collective bargaining agreement. Additionally, the union, federation, or confederation involved must represent the majority of the employees of the company involved in the conflict. Prior to any strike, the parties must exhaust the conciliation procedure set forth in the Organic Labor Law and in the corresponding collective bargaining agreement.

e. Accumulation of Seniority During Strikes

For purposes of calculating worker benefits, a strike does not suspend the term of services of participating workers, provided that the strike has been carried out in accordance with the Labor Law.[148]

---

[145] *Id.* art. 549. Under derogated Decree 440, if agreement was not reached, the matter is subject to mandatory arbitration and strikes are not permitted

[146] The First Civil Authority is part of the Judicial Ministry. It is in charge of administrative civil issues such as family disputes, marriages, and declarations of good conduct.

[147] Labor Law, art. 501.

[148] *Id.* art. 505.

f. Bar Against Dismissal

Workers involved in a collective labor dispute may not be dismissed during the duration of the dispute.[149]

3. *Arbitration*[150]

Arbitration is used to resolve collective conflicts that arise from the causes mentioned above. The parties may request arbitration by mutual agreement. Once the parties decide to submit the conflict to arbitration, the arbitrators shall then be appointed.

The arbitration panel is composed of three members. These are designated as follows: one arbitrator for the employees, elected from among three candidates nominated by the workers; one arbitrator elected from three candidates nominated by the employers; and a third arbitrator appointed by the first two designated arbitrators. If the parties cannot agree on the elected arbitrator, the labor ministry will appoint the third one. The third arbitrator presides over the panel in lieu of the Labor Inspector, and rules are established for solving objections made by one party concerning the three nominees of the other party.

Arbitral awards have a minimum effective term of two years and a maximum term of three years.

E. Protection Against Dismissal

1. *Union Officers*

Members of a union's board of directors are protected against dismissal from the date on which they are elected until three months after their term ends.[151] This prohibition is limited to protecting directors in the following proportions: up to seven directors when the company employs fewer than 500 workers; up to nine directors when the company employs between 500 and 1,000 workers; and up to 12 directors when the company employs more than 1,000 workers.

---

[149]*Id.* art. 506. See also II.E.2., below.

[150]Labor Law, arts. 490–493.

[151]*Id.* art. 451.

When a national union has local branches corresponding to the states of Venezuela, up to five members of the local branch's board of directors in each state can benefit from the prohibition against dismissal, from the date of their election until three months after expiration of their term.[152]

2. Workers

The Labor Law protects unionized workers against dismissal in a variety of circumstances:

- While a union is being formed, the workers who are signatories or who join the union are protected from dismissal. The total duration of this prohibition may not exceed three months.[153]
- During a union election, workers participating in the election may not be dismissed from the moment the election is called until after the election. This prohibition may not exceed a total of two months over a two-year period.[154]
- Workers of companies summoned to rulemaking meetings[155] may not be dismissed by their employers.[156] This prohibition applies as of the date the Labor Ministry is petitioned to authorize the summons until the rulemaking meetings conclude.
- From the time a draft collective contract is submitted to the Labor Inspector's Office,[157] workers may not be removed, transferred, suspended, or demoted without prior authorization.[158] This prohibition remains in effect for 180 days and may be extended by the Inspector for up to 90 additional days.
- If an employer is permitted by the Labor Inspector's Office to modify the terms of an existing agreement due to eco-

---

[152] *Id.* arts. 418, 451.
[153] *Id.* art. 450.
[154] *Id.* art. 452.
[155] See II.C.3., above.
[156] Labor Law, art. 533(f).
[157] See II.C.5., above.
[158] Labor Law, art. 520.

nomic circumstances,[159] all workers are protected against dismissal during the remaining term of the agreement.[160]
- Workers involved in a collective labor dispute[161] may not be dismissed during the duration of the dispute.[162]

3. *Authorization for Dismissal and Reinstatement*

These procedures apply only to those employees protected against dismissal.

a. Authorization for Dismissal

An employer who for good cause intends to dismiss, transfer, or demote a worker must seek prior authorization from the Labor Inspector of the jurisdiction where the worker's union is located. The Labor Inspector must call the employee for a meeting to respond to the dismissal request. The employer must also attend this meeting. If the employer fails to attend the meeting, then it is presumed that the employer has withdrawn the solicitation for dismissal. However, the worker's failure to appear is deemed a rejection of the solicitation. If the employee does not appear it is considered that he or she has denied all of the employer's statement. The decision of the Labor Inspector is not subject to administrative appeal, but it may be challenged by means of a petition in court to nullify the administrative action.

b. Reinstatement

Any worker who is dismissed, transferred, or demoted may petition the Labor Inspector for reinstatement to his or her position within 30 days.[163] There is no administrative recourse against the Labor Inspector's final decision, although the parties have the right to request review in the courts.

---

[159] See II.C.7., above.
[160] Labor Law, arts. 520, 526.
[161] See II.D., above.
[162] Labor Law, art. 506.
[163] *Id.* arts. 449, 458.

III. Representation by Entities Other Than Unions

The Labor Law contains provisions concerning the representation of workers in company management (co-management). The following is a summary of the significant provisions.

A. Enterprises Where Co-Management Applies

Worker participation in management is mandatory for autonomous institutes and economic and social development agencies in the public sector, and for enterprises (and their majority-owned subsidiaries) in which the State, or an entity of the State, holds more than 50 percent of the equity.[164]

Mandatory co-management consists of the appointment of two worker directors to the board of directors, administration, or administrative council of the enterprises subject to the co-management duty.[165] One of the worker directors is elected by the labor confederation representing the majority of workers of the enterprise, and the other is elected directly by the workers.

Private sector enterprises are not obligated to provide for worker representation. However, the Labor Law provides that enterprises in the private sector that voluntarily establish co-management programs will enjoy special protection under regulations to be issued by the National Executive (the President and executive ministries).[166]

B. Powers of Worker Directors

The powers of worker directors[167] are broader than those of other directors, as they may not be dismissed and may be removed only by those who elected them. However, worker directors may be dismissed if a Labor Judge rules that a serious misdeed has been committed.

Worker directors have access to all types of information related to the enterprise's management, and any resolution of a meet-

---

[164] *Id.* art. 610.
[165] *Id.* arts. 610–615.
[166] *Id.* art. 623.
[167] *Id.* arts. 616–624.

ing of the board of directors to which they have not been summoned is void. Worker directors otherwise have all the powers of other board members and remain in office for the same term. Workers who serve as worker directors retain all the rights of active workers, as well as the benefits contained in the collective contract of their respective enterprise.

IV. Redundancy and Transfers of Undertakings

A. Redundancy

When an employer wishes to lay off a substantial number of employees, the matter must be treated as a collective dispute[168] even though the employer cites technical or economic reasons to support such a layoff.[169] The existence of a collective dispute means that the employer can apply the procedures established for the resolution of disputes that arise between employers and workers.[170] Notice of the employer's request for such a procedure must be provided to the respective labor union, or in the absence of a union, to the workers themselves. If the parties do not reach agreement through the collective dispute procedure, the matter will be submitted for arbitration.[171]

As with any other collective dispute, employees are protected by a bar against dismissal.[172] Also, it should be emphasized that a request to reduce personnel will not be allowed while the employees are exercising their rights to organize and negotiate collectively.

In the case of a mass layoff, the Labor Ministry is authorized to stop or suspend the action by means of a special resolution in order to uphold the principle of freedom of work. Under current law, a layoff is considered en masse if, within a three-month period (or longer, if circumstances indicate a critical situation), it affects a number of workers equal to or greater than:

---

[168]See II.D., above.

[169]Labor Law, arts. 33, 34.

[170]*Id.* arts. 469, 506. See also II.D.3., above.

[171]Labor Law, arts. 490, 493. See also II.D.3., above.

[172]Labor Law, art. 506. See also II.E.2., above.

- 10 percent of the workers of a company that employs more than 100 persons;
- 20 percent of the workers of a company that employs more than 50 persons; or
- 10 workers of a company that employs fewer than 50 persons.

B. Transfers of Undertakings

Under Venezuelan law, a transfer of undertaking is referred to as a "substitution of employers." The Labor Law provisions applicable to a substitution of employers are summarized below.

1. Definition

The Labor Law defines the substitution of employers as the transfer of the property, ownership, or business of an establishment from one person to another for any reason, with the continued operation of the business.[173]

2. Presumption of Substitution

A substitution of employers is considered to have occurred even though ownership of the company is not transferred. The rule is that if a new employer continues to carry out the activities of a prior entity with the same personnel and installations, there is a substitution of employers regardless of whether ownership of the company has changed.[174]

3. Effects

A substitution of employers does not alter existing employment relationships. The new employer must recognize the seniority, as well as other benefits and terms of employment, of all workers who continue to work in the company.

In addition, for up to one year, the former employer will be jointly liable with the new employer for all of the labor obliga-

---

[173]Labor Law, art. 88.
[174]*Id.* art. 89.

tions that arose before the substitution. In the event that there are pending labor actions at the moment of substitution, the former employer's responsibility for such cases will continue for a period of one year from the date of a final decision on the labor action.[175]

4. *Notification*

In order for a substitution of employers to be valid, it is necessary that written notification be given to the workers. Written notice of the substitution also should be provided to the Labor Inspector and the union to which the workers belong.[176] Evidently, the required notification may be given by either of the employers involved.

5. *Worker Rejection of the Substitution*

If a worker does not accept the substitution for being counter to his or her interests, the employment relationship may be terminated at the worker's request, and the worker will be entitled to the amount of employee benefits and indemnities as if it were a case of unjustified dismissal.[177]

6. *Payments to the Worker*

If, with the purpose of substitution, an employer pays termination benefits and indemnities to a worker who nevertheless continues performing services for the company, the payment is considered an advance on the amount that would be owed the worker on termination of the employment relationship.[178]

---

[175] *Id.* art. 90.
[176] *Id.* art. 91.
[177] *Id.* See also I.F.5., above.
[178] Labor Law, art. 92. See also I.F., above.

V. WAGES, HOURS, AND LEAVE

A. Compensation

1. *Wages*

a. Definition of Wages

Wages are broadly defined to include any compensation a worker receives for rendering his or her services, regardless of form.[179] Thus, wages include, but are not limited to, the following:

- commissions,
- premiums,
- expense allowances,
- statutory and contractual profit sharing,[180]
- bonuses,
- vacation bonuses,
- holiday pay, and
- overtime or night work pay.

Also characterized as wages are meals and housing, allowances therefor, and any other kind of income, benefit, or perquisite that the worker receives in consideration for his or her services. The Labor Law presumes that fees paid to professionals who perform services in an employment relationship constitute wages received from the employer, unless otherwise expressly agreed.[181]

The following are expressly excluded from wages:

- dining services, food, and food stock given by the employer;
- day care centers;[182]
- reimbursement of medical, pharmaceutical, and dental expenses;
- provision of work attire;

---

[179] Labor Law, art. 133.
[180] See V.A.2., below.
[181] Labor Law, art. 9.
[182] See VIII.B.2., below.

- provision of school supplies and toys;
- the grant of scholarships and the payment of specialized courses; and
- the payment of funerary expenses.

b. Ordinary Wages

The term "ordinary wages" is defined by the Labor Law as the compensation regularly and permanently earned by the worker during the period immediately prior to the date of calculation. Therefore, the concept of ordinary wages is more restrictive than wages. When the worker receives a fixed salary, ordinary wages are calculated on the basis of the salary (which is earned regularly and permanently) of the previous month. If, on the other hand, the worker is compensated by work units, piecework, or commission, the ordinary wage is the average of the wages earned (again, in a regular and permanent manner) during the year preceding the day on which the calculation is made. Consequently, the following items, among others, are not included in ordinary wages: incentives, gifts, and sporadic bonuses. On the other hand, a subsidy established by the employer so that workers can obtain goods and services at reduced cost, or any subsidy created to allow an improvement in workers' quality of life, is considered to constitute part of the worker's ordinary wage. For example, if an employer offers its employees the opportunity to purchase a computer in installments at a reduced cost rather than its actual market value, the difference between the price offered by the employer and the market value of the good, in this case the computer, its considered to be part of the employee's salary.

The Labor Law provides that any kind of tax or fee payable to a public agency will be based on the ordinary wage corresponding to the month immediately prior to the payment of the tax or fee, and not on the broader concept of wages. The Labor Law also provides that ordinary wages shall be the basis for calculating vacation pay, seniority payments, and other worker entitlements.[183]

[183]Labor Law, arts. 145, 146. For more detail on these calculations, see V.A.1.i., below.

Collective contracts or individual employment agreements (if employees are not unionized) may provide that up to 20 percent of ordinary wages be excluded for the calculation of any statutory or contractual benefit, compensation, or indemnity that may arise from the employment relationship. However, the whole amount of the minimum wage[184] must be taken into account in calculating such benefits, compensation, or indemnities.

c. Percentage of Consumption and Tips

When a business establishment charges an additional percentage of consumption to its customers (such as a compulsory 10 percent service charge), which is passed on to workers pursuant to an agreement or established practice, amounts so received are considered part of the worker's ordinary wages.[185] In addition, the right to receive voluntary tips from customers is included in wages according to the value such right is given in a collective labor contract or individual employment agreement, or as otherwise estimated by the Labor Inspector or a judge. To this extent, the value of the right to receive voluntary tips is appraised by taking into account the quality of the service rendered, the professional level and productivity of the employee, the reputation of the establishment, and any other element that is deemed relevant.

d. Minimum Wage

Wages may be freely negotiated by the parties, but in no case can they be less than the minimum wage set by the National Executive.[186] When wages are not expressly stipulated, they must not only be at least equal to the minimum wage, but also to the wages paid to workers in the same type of position in the geographic area, or in the same company.[187]

The minimum wage is reviewed annually by a Commission comprised of representatives of the most important employers' association, the most important union, and the government.[188] The

---

[184]See V.A.1.d., below.
[185]Labor Law, art. 134.
[186]*Id.* art. 129.
[187]*Id.* art. 69.
[188]*Id.* arts. 167–173.

Commission is installed during January of each year, and must submit a recommendation to the National Executive within 30 days of its installation. This recommendation must take into account, among other factors, variations in the cost of basic food stock. The National Executive then establishes the amount of the minimum wage after reviewing the Commission's recommendation. Normally, the minimum wage is increased every year by a governmental decree. As of October 1, 2004, the minimum wage was set at Venezuela Bolivar (VEB) 321,235.20 per month for urban workers and VEB 298,111.70 per month for rural workers. The Presidential Decree through which the minimum wage was adjusted also provided that the minimum wage for workers of companies or enterprises with fewer than 20 employees was VEB 294,465.60 per month.

e. *Equality of Wages*

The Labor Law establishes the principle that for equal work performed under equal conditions and with equal efficiency, equivalent wages should be paid.[189] For this purpose, the skills of the worker in relation to the kind of work he or she performs may be taken into account.

Without violating the principle of equality, and in order that varied wages may exist, the employer may establish bonuses based on workers' seniority, diligence, family responsibilities, basic economic needs, and other similar circumstances, so long as such bonuses are applicable to all workers in similar circumstances. Under the Labor Law, such bonuses would be characterized as wages.[190]

f. *Increases in Productivity*

The Labor Law provides that a company's improved productivity or increased production is to result in increased compensation for workers.[191] To this end, the company and workers are to

---

[189] *Id.* arts. 135, 136.

[190] See V.A.1.a., above.

[191] Labor Law, art. 137.

agree on an incentive program according to the contribution of the worker.

This provision does not specify the duties of the employer and the rights of the worker in case the company and workers have not reached any agreement on this matter, and the employer has not adopted an incentive program to improve productivity. Additionally, the law does not specify the cycle or time period in which productivity improvements should be made, or what period of comparison or reference should be used to determine whether production has increased. Neither does the text mention the possibility of diminished productivity or production levels. Given these ambiguities, if an agreement is reached on productivity incentives, employers would be well advised to establish specific goals or parameters and arrange for any incentive payments to be made separately from the fixed or basic wages of the worker.

g. *Cost of Living Increases*

The National Executive is authorized to decree wage increases, based on prior consultation with worker and employer representatives, the National Economic Council, and the Central Bank of Venezuela, when the cost of living increases disproportionately to workers' wages and the buying power of workers is affected.[192]

A wage increase decree may establish nonwaivable clauses in favor of workers, which must be included in labor contracts.[193] Wage increase decrees may encompass all workers, certain categories of workers (by wages or activity), certain geographic regions, or a combination of the above. A wage increase decree also may specify whether wage increases received by the worker during the three months prior to a decree, or which will become effective by agreement with the employer during the three months following a decree, should be imputed to the decreed increase.[194]

Wage increase decrees must be submitted to Congress for consideration within five days of publication in the Official Gazette.[195] However, the statute does not specify whether the decree

---

[192] *Id.* arts. 13, 22, and 138.
[193] *Id.* art. 13.
[194] *Id.* art. 138.
[195] *Id.* art. 22.

takes effect pending its approval or rejection by the Congress. An argument could be made that the wage increase becomes effective upon publication of the decree, with the option that Congress may later suspend or reduce it. The more logical position is that the decree does not take effect until approved by Congress.

Should Congress fail to make a pronouncement with respect to a wage increase decree within 10 days of submittal, it will be considered tacitly approved. When Congress decides to suspend a decree, it may recommend that the President issue a new decree that makes certain modifications to the previous one. The new decree need not be submitted to Congress.

h. Wage Calculations

i. Fixed wages

Workers may be paid a fixed monthly wage or salary. In this case, the worker's daily wage is calculated as 1/30 of the wage earned in a month. The hourly wage is determined by dividing the daily wage by the number of hours in a normal workday.[196]

ii. Wages based on units of time

Wages commonly are calculated based on work performed during a fixed period such as an hour or work shift, regardless of the results of such work.[197] In this case, the hourly wage is the amount earned per hour during a normal workday.

iii. Variable wages

Variable wages are those calculated on the basis of units of production (piecework), performance of a specific job, or commissions:

- *Wages by unit of production, piecework, or task* are calculated based on work actually performed, without regard to the time required to do so.[198] Wages based on units of pro-

[196] *Id.* art. 140.
[197] *Id.*
[198] *Id.* art. 141.

duction must not result in lesser wages than would be earned on an hourly basis for the same work.

- *Wages by job* are calculated based on the duration of the job as well as the results, with the worker being responsible for a certain defined performance within the daily working period.[199] This is a combination of wages calculated by units of time and units of production.
- *Commissions*[200] are not specifically defined. However, the Labor Law equates commissions to piecework wages for the purpose of calculating entitlements to vacation pay, seniority payments, and pay in lieu of notice at termination.[201] Commissions also have been interpreted in jurisprudence as equivalent to piecework pay for purposes of calculating rest and holiday pay.

If wages are calculated on the basis of units of production, jobs, or commissions, the employer must post an explanation of the calculation method in visible locations within the work premises.[202]

i. Calculation of Special Wages and Other Benefits

i. Overtime pay

An additional 50 percent of the hourly wage agreed to for a normal workday must be paid for overtime work.[203] This also applies to workers who are paid on a piecework or commission basis.

ii. Night work

An additional 30 percent of the hourly wage agreed to for a normal workday must be paid for night work.[204] This also applies to workers who are paid on a piecework or commission basis.

---

[199] *Id.* art. 142.
[200] *Id.* art. 216.
[201] *Id.* art. 145, 146.
[202] *Id.* art. 143.
[203] *Id.* arts. 154–156. For an explanation of overtime work, see V.B.2., below.
[204] Labor Law, art. 156. For an explanation of night work, see V.B.1.b., below.

iii. Work during the weekly rest day or on holidays

When a worker works four or more hours on a weekly rest day or holiday, he or she is entitled to compensation for that day, plus one and one-half times the wages payable for an additional full day.[205] The basis for calculation is the ordinary wages earned during that week. This provision applies equally to those workers whose payment is based on units of production, jobs completed, or commissions.[206]

iv. Paid vacation

The base wage for calculating vacation pay[207] is the ordinary wage earned during the month of work ended just prior to the day in which annual vacation is earned. For workers paid by units of production, job, or commission, the base wage is the average of the ordinary wages earned during the year of work ended just prior to the day in which the vacation is earned.[208]

v. Seniority payments

The base wage used in calculating seniority payments[209] is the ordinary wage plus the monthly impact of the vacation bonus and profit sharing payment earned by the employee in the corresponding month. Monthly calculations of seniority payments are final; consequently, such payments may not be adjusted or recalculated during the employment relationship or at its termination.[210]

vi. Payments for unjustified dismissal

The base wage used for calculating payments due to a worker for an unjustified dismissal or justified resignation[211] is the ordi-

[205]Labor Law, arts. 154, 217, and 218. For an explanation of rest days and holidays, see V.B.3., below.

[206]Labor Law, art. 144.

[207]For a discussion of vacations, see V.C.1., below.

[208]Labor Law, art. 145.

[209]See I.F.5.a., above.

[210]Seniority payments may be affected by subsequent profit sharing distributions. See V.A.2.d., below.

[211]See I.F.5.b., above.

nary wage plus the monthly impact of the vacation bonus and profit sharing payment earned by the worker in the month preceding termination. If the worker is compensated by units, job, or commission, the base for the calculation is the average of the ordinary wage earned by the worker in the year preceding the day on which calculation is made.[212]

j. Protection of Wages

Under Venezuelan law, workers are free to dispose of their wages as they wish, and any limitation on this right that is not contemplated by law is void.[213]

i. Waiver or assignment

The right to payment of wages may not be waived. Neither may it be assigned, except to the spouse (or the person with whom a married life is maintained), or children of the worker. However, wages may be used to guarantee obligations within the limitations imposed by law.[214]

In companies of 50 or more workers, a worker may request the employer to deduct one-time or periodic dues for unions, charitable, social and civic associations, and nonprofit foundations. The worker also is entitled to revoke such authorization.

ii. Attachment

A worker's compensation that does not exceed the minimum wage is immune from attachment.[215] When a worker's compensation exceeds, but is less than twice, the minimum wage, no more than one-fifth of the excess may be attached. Only one-third of any compensation in excess of twice the minimum wage may be attached.

Termination benefits, indemnities, and other liabilities may not be attached if they amount to less than 50 times the minimum wage.[216] Up to one-fifth of the amount between 50 and 100 times

---

[212]Labor Law, art. 146.
[213]*Id.* art. 129.
[214]*Id.* art. 132.
[215]*Id.* art. 162. For an explanation of the minimum wage, see V.A.1.d., above.
[216]Labor Law, art. 163.

the minimum wage may be attached. Up to one-third of any further amount in excess of 100 times the minimum wage may be attached. However, immunity from attachment does not apply to worker liabilities of a family nature (e.g., alimony) or to employer loans or guarantees made pursuant to the Labor Law.

iii. Worker debts to the employer

A worker's debts to an employer, such as those incurred to purchase or improve a residence or to pay a mortgage, may be paid in weekly or monthly installments which may not exceed one-third of the worker's weekly or monthly wages.[217] Upon termination of the employment relationship, the employer may set off only 50 percent of the employer's liabilities to the worker against the worker's debts.

iv. Prohibition against employer selling in the workplace

The Labor Law prohibits employers from establishing eateries, supply stores, or other businesses in the workplace to sell goods or provisions to the workers, except under the following circumstances:

- access of workers to commercial establishments is difficult;
- the workers are free to choose where they make their purchases; and
- the terms of sale by the employer's establishment are publicized, and the union receives a list of prices for its review.

A further exception is that collective contracts may authorize these kinds of goods and provisions establishments where they are financially accountable to the workers and the proper governmental authority.[218]

---

[217] *Id.* art. 165.
[218] *Id.* art. 166.

k. Wage Preferences

Any employer liabilities to workers for an amount up to their total wages for the prior six months, and any amounts owed as worker termination benefits up to the 90 days of workers' ordinary wages, must be paid in preference to any other employer liabilities.[219] If any amounts of the workers' claims remain unsatisfied after application of this preference, the remaining claims are entitled to high priority with respect to the employer's real and personal property.[220]

Under the Civil Code, liabilities to domestic workers for amounts up to three months of wages also constitute preferred claims against the employer.[221]

In the event of a transfer of goods, delay (a declaration made by a court when an individual or company has no assets to meet its immediate obligations), or bankruptcy, the judge in the matter may order summary payment of liabilities to workers from available employer funds at the time the transfer of goods, delay, or bankruptcy is declared. If the liabilities to the workers have already been liquidated, the judge must verify the liquidation prior to moving forward in the corresponding process.

2. *Profit Sharing*

Venezuelan law requires employers to distribute to their workers 15 percent of net liquid profits accrued for each fiscal year.[222] Net liquid profits are the net profits subject to tax,[223] as well as profits that are tax-free pursuant to the Income Tax Law.

a. Covered Employers

Statutory profit sharing generally applies to all corporations, business establishments, and other enterprises that operate for profit.

---

[219]*Id.* arts. 158–160.

[220]*Id.*

[221]Civil Code, art. 1870.

[222]Labor Law, art. 174.

[223]For the purposes of calculation and payment of the income tax, profit sharing is considered a business expense, and therefore is deductible from net taxable income to the extent that profits are statutorily required to be distributed to workers.

Companies that are divided into different enterprises, or are composed of various legal entities, divisions, agencies, or branches with separate books and accounting have their profits consolidated as one economic unit for purposes of calculating statutory profit sharing.[224] However, detailed rules for consolidation are not provided in the Labor Law.

Small companies and not-for-profit employers are excluded from statutory profit sharing.[225] Nevertheless, these entities are required to pay a year-end bonus (instead of distributing profits) that is equivalent to at least 15 days' wages. For this purpose, small companies are defined as follows:

- commercial companies whose invested capital is no greater than 60 times the monthly minimum wage;[226]
- industrial companies whose invested capital is no greater than 135 times the monthly minimum wage; or
- agricultural or livestock companies whose invested capital is no greater than 250 times the monthly minimum wage.

b. Calculating the Distributable Amount

i. Mandatory minimum

The minimum amount of profits to be distributed to each worker is equivalent to 15 days' wages for each fiscal year. When an employer does not realize profits, or the profits realized are insufficient to meet the mandatory minimum, the employer nevertheless must pay a bonus to each worker equivalent to 15 days' wages.

ii. Maximum amount

For companies whose capital is less than VEB one million, or that employ fewer than 50 workers, the maximum profit sharing is two months' wages for each worker.[227] For companies whose

---

[224]Labor Law, art. 177.
[225]*Id.* arts. 183, 184.
[226]For an explanation of the minimum wage, see V.A.1.d., above.
[227]Labor Law, art. 174.

capital is more than VEB one million, and that employ 50 or more workers, the maximum profit sharing for each worker is four months' wages.[228]

iii. Basis for calculation

The basis for calculating the distributable amount is the income tax statement filed by the employer with the Income Tax Administration.[229] If the amount of profits turns out to be greater than the amount declared on the income tax statement, the company is required to make an additional distribution within the month following the date on which the additional profits are determined.[230]

Losses suffered in prior fiscal years by an employer may not be applied to reduce the profits of the last fiscal year subject to statutory profit sharing.[231]

c. Calculation for Each Worker

The total of all distributable profits is divided by the wages earned by all workers during the respective fiscal year. The share of a worker is obtained by multiplying the figure obtained from the above calculation and the amount of wages earned by the worker in the same fiscal year.[232] Although the Labor Law does not expressly indicate what wages are to be used in calculating statutory profit sharing, it is generally agreed that the calculation should be based on the concept of "wages" as defined in Article 133 of the Labor Law.[233]

When the worker has not worked for the entire year (which should be taken to mean the company's fiscal year), the profit sharing distribution is reduced in proportion to the months not worked during that fiscal year.[234]

---

[228] *Id.* art. 644.
[229] *Id.* art. 176.
[230] *Id.*
[231] *Id.* art. 178.
[232] *Id.* art. 179.
[233] See V.A.1.a., above.
[234] Labor Law, art. 174.

d. Effect on Seniority Payments

The Labor Law expressly provides that amounts distributable to workers from statutory profit sharing must be allocated among the number of months in which the worker has effectively rendered services.[235] Thus, if the employer's profits have not been determined as of the time seniority payments are calculated[236] due to the fact that the fiscal year has not ended, the employer is obligated to recalculate seniority payments once the profits are determined, and to pay the corresponding amount within 30 days.[237]

e. Contractual Profit Sharing

When it has been contractually agreed that the worker will share in profits and this share exceeds the statutory profit sharing, statutory profit sharing will be deemed satisfied by the contractually shared profits, unless otherwise expressly agreed by the parties. The reverse is true when statutory profit sharing exceeds contractual profit sharing.[238]

f. Date of Distribution

Shared profits must be distributed within two months after the close of the company's fiscal year.[239] However, workers are entitled to an advance, to be paid during the first 15 days of December, or at the time established in a collective labor contract.[240] The advance payable to each worker is equal to 15 days' wages or the amount of profit sharing corresponding to the months actually worked during the fiscal year, with such amount being imputed to the payment to be made at the close of the fiscal year.

g. Review of Accounts and Financial Records

The Labor Law establishes workers' rights to review their company's accounts and financial records for the purpose of veri-

---

[235]*Id.*

[236]For a discussion of seniority payments, see I.F.5.a. and V.A.1.i.v., above.

[237]Labor Law, art. 146.

[238]*Id.* art. 182.

[239]*Id.* art. 180.

[240]*Id.* art. 175.

fying the company's income in one or more fiscal years.[241] Review may be requested by an absolute majority of a company's workers or by a union in which more than 25 percent of the company's workers are members. In both cases, management employees and employees of confidence are excluded from the calculation.

Requests for review of accounts and financial records are directed to the Income Tax Administration. A review consists of examination and verification of the company's accounts and financial records. The review is conducted by experts in the Income Tax Administration.

B. Hours

1. The Workday

a. Computation

The workday is computed[242] from the moment workers arrive at the place where they are to perform their work or receive orders or instructions, until they are free to do what they wish with their time.

If the employer is legally or contractually required to provide transportation to the workplace,[243] half of the time typically required for transportation is included as part of the workday, unless the union and the employer agree not to include such time, and the workers are otherwise compensated.

Time allowed for meals and rest in cafeterias set up by the employer is generally not computed into the workday as actual working time. However, if the worker is unable to leave the workplace due to the nature of the particular job, the time for meals and rest is counted as working time. The Labor Law defines these positions as those whose performance requires the worker's presence in the workplace (i.e., a specific area of the company where work is performed), or which require that the worker be on call

[241] *Id.* art. 181.
[242] *Id.* arts. 189–193.
[243] See VIII.B.3., below.

to comply with the employer's instructions or respond to emergencies.

b. Maximum Limits

The workday for both laborers and employees[244] is subject to the following limits:

- day positions (5:00 a.m. to 7:00 p.m.), 8 hours daily and 44 weekly;
- night positions (7:00 p.m. to 5:00 a.m.), 7 hours daily and 40 weekly;[245] and
- mixed positions (with fewer than four hours of night work), 7½ hours daily and 42 weekly.

In positions that do not require continuous work, the worker may not be required to work more than five consecutive hours, and must be allowed at least one-half hour of rest.[246]

A daily limit of 11 hours, with the right to a minimum of one hour of rest per work session,[247] applies to management employees, confidential employees, inspectors, guards, workers who perform discontinuous or intermittent tasks (or jobs that require the sole presence of the worker, or jobs with periods of inactivity in which the worker is on call), as well as workers who perform jobs that by nature are not subject to working days (e.g., watchmen).

c. Partial Workdays

When a workday shorter than the legally permitted workday is agreed to (i.e., part-time work), wages may be based on the hours actually worked.[248]

---

[244]Laborers and employees are defined in the Introduction, at D.3.a. and D.3.d., above.

[245]Workers who are assigned to night work are entitled to extra compensation. See V.A.1.i.ii., above.

[246]Labor Law, art. 205.

[247]*Id.* art. 198.

[248]*Id.* art. 194.

d. Extension of the Workday

The normal workday may be extended in the following exceptional situations described in the Labor Law:

- preparatory or complementary tasks;
- coordination of the work of two teams that relieve each other;
- special tasks such as repairs, modifications, or installation of new machines;
- responses to increased demand at certain times of the year; and
- accidents or emergencies in the company.[249]

Time worked in excess of the normal workday must be compensated as overtime.[250]

e. Shift Work

When a continuous job is performed by rotating work shifts, the daily and weekly limits on working hours may be extended so long as the total hours of each worker do not exceed the total limit for a period of eight weeks.[251] If a system of compensatory time for hours worked in excess of these limits is established, the total number of hours worked each week may be limited to an average of 44 hours per worker.

f. Additional Day of Rest

To provide workers with two full days of rest during each week,[252] the workday may be extended to nine hours, subject to a maximum of 44 hours per week.[253]

---

[249] *Id.* arts. 199, 200, 202, and 203.
[250] See V.A.1.i.i., above, and V.B.2., below.
[251] Labor Law, arts. 201, 206.
[252] See V.B.3., below.
[253] Labor Law, art. 196.

g. Required Notice of Rest Days and Hours

The employer must post notices in visible locations within the work premises regarding company rules on days and hours of rest.[254] Alternatively, the employer may provide this information to the workers in any other manner approved by the Labor Inspector.

2. Overtime

a. Limitations

The Labor Inspector may authorize the performance of overtime work,[255] subject to the following limitations:

- the duration of the workday must be limited to 10 hours, including overtime, so that if a worker's normal workday is eight hours, he or she would be limited to two hours of overtime per day; and
- no one may work more than 10 hours of overtime weekly, or more than 100 hours in a year.

In unforeseeable and urgent circumstances, overtime may be worked without the prior permission of the Labor Inspector, so long as the Inspector is notified on the following working day and the reasons for the overtime are explained.[256]

b. Compensation

Overtime work is compensated at one and one-half times the hourly wage agreed to for a normal workday.[257]

c. Recordkeeping

All employers must maintain a record of the overtime worked, the type of work performed during overtime, the workers who

---

[254] *Id.* art. 190.
[255] *Id.* art. 207.
[256] *Id.* art. 210.
[257] See also V.A.1.i., above.

worked during overtime, and the compensation paid for the overtime.[258]

3. *Rest Days and Holidays*[259]

The Labor Law establishes Sunday as a weekly day of rest. In addition, the following days are designated as holidays:

- January 1, Good Friday and the Thursday preceding it, May 1, and December 25;
- the dates listed in the Law of National Holidays, including April 19, June 24, July 5, July 24, and October 12; and
- those days declared holidays by the National Government, the States, or the Municipalities, up to a limit of three days per year.

a. Prohibition Against Working

No work of any kind may be performed during the weekly day of rest or on holidays,[260] apart from the exceptions permitted by the Labor Law and the Regulations. The exceptions include, for example, work that must not be interrupted for reasons of public interest, or other technical or special reasons.

b. Compensation

The weekly day of rest and holidays are compensated by the payment of one day's wages.[261] The right to this compensation is not lost when the worker misses one day of the workweek. Note that this dilutes the computation of an ordinary day's wages (the employee will still receive his or her monthly salary, therefore, if he or she has worked five days instead of six days, the daily salary of that month will be higher), which is used as the base figure for other calculations in the Labor Law.

When a monthly salary has been agreed upon, the payment of holidays and the required weekly rest day are included in the salary.

---

[258] Labor Law, art. 208.
[259] *Id.* art. 212.
[260] *Id.*
[261] *Id.* arts. 216, 217. See also V.A.1.i., above.

c. Compensation for Work Performed on Rest Days or Holidays

If a worker works on a weekly rest day or holiday for four hours or more, he or she is entitled to be paid for that day, plus one and one-half times the wages payable for a normal workday.[262] Additionally, the worker is entitled to a compensatory rest day in the following week. If the work is for fewer than four hours, the worker is entitled to the wages corresponding to the work performed on that day, plus one and one-half times the wages payable for an additional half day of work, plus one-half day of compensatory rest in the following week.

C. Leave

1. Vacations

a. Entitlement

Upon completion of one year of uninterrupted service with an employer, the worker is entitled to 15 paid days of vacation. For each additional year of service, the worker is entitled to an additional paid day of vacation, up to a maximum of 15 additional days.[263] For purposes of determining entitlement to additional paid days of vacation, the period of service begins on May 1, 1991.

b. Scheduling Vacation Time

Annual vacations generally must be taken within the six months following the period in which the time was earned.[264] However, at the request of the worker, up to two years of vacation may be postponed, allowing for the accumulation of up to three vacation periods.[265]

Vacation time should be taken at a time agreed to by the worker and the employer. If no agreement is reached, the Labor

---

[262]Labor Law, arts. 217, 218. See also V.A.1.i., above.
[263]Labor Law, art. 219.
[264]*Id.* arts. 227, 230.
[265]*Id.* art. 229.

Inspector will set the time for taking the vacation. Note that vacation time taken is counted only against days on which the worker otherwise would be required to work, and not rest days or holidays, for example.

Workers with family responsibilities enjoy a preference in scheduling a vacation so that their vacation period can coincide with the vacation of their children. Workers who work for two or more employers are entitled to take vacation upon completing years of service for the employer with whom they have worked longest. In this case, the secondary employer(s) should allow the vacation and pay wages corresponding to the worker's respective service with them.

Although the text of the Labor Law neither prohibits nor regulates the division of vacation time into fractional periods, it may be possible to do so, provided that one of the periods consists of at least two uninterrupted weeks.[266]

c. Collective Vacations

The Labor Law permits employers and workers to agree to a rotating or collective vacation system for all workers.[267] When a collective vacation system is established, the days all workers are on vacation are imputed to the annual vacation time of each worker. If the worker is entitled to additional vacation days, they may be taken annually at the time provided by law. However, if the worker has not completed one year of service at the time of the collective vacation, the additional days are considered to be compensatory rest days, which may be subtracted from future vacation time.

d. Compensation

The payment of wages corresponding to vacation time should be made at the start of the vacation period.[268]

---

[266]*See id.* art. 60(c). Dividing vacation time in this manner is consistent with Agreement No. 132 of the International Labor Organization (ILO). However, this Agreement has not been ratified by Venezuela.

[267]Labor Law, art. 220.

[268]*Id.* arts. 145, 221, and 222. See also V.A.1.i., above.

Workers who receive meals and/or lodging as part of their ordinary compensation are entitled to receive them during their vacation or receive their monetary equivalent at the start of the vacation period. The value of meals and lodging is set by agreement of the parties or, in the absence of such an agreement, by the Labor Inspector.

In addition to the payment for vacation days, when workers begin their vacation period, they are entitled to receive a special vacation bonus equivalent to seven days of wages for the first year of service, plus one additional day for each year of seniority, up to a maximum of 21 days.[269]

e. *Work During Vacation Time*

The Legislature's intent is that workers should actually enjoy their annual vacation time. Consequently, with respect to the first 15 days of vacation, if the worker and employer agree that the employer will pay compensation corresponding to vacation time without giving the worker the time necessary to enjoy it, the employer will remain obligated to grant the vacation time and pay it fully.[270] In cases where workers have brought claims after their employment contracts terminate, the courts have required employers to pay the vacation time again.

During the 15 additional working days of vacation that a worker may acquire with seniority, the worker is able to perform services for the employer. In this case, the worker is entitled to vacation pay in addition to the wages that correspond to the work performed on those days.

If a worker performs services compensated by someone other than the employer during his vacation time, he or she loses the right to be paid the wages corresponding to that vacation period.

f. *Effect of Absences*

Justified absences (such as illness) are treated as actual service time for the purposes of annual vacation. However, the sched-

---

[269] Labor Law, art. 223.

[270] *Id.* arts. 219, 226, and 234.

uling of vacation time may be postponed for a period equivalent to the days of absence.[271]

When a worker has been absent without good reason for seven or more days in a year, but was paid the wages corresponding to those days, the unjustified absence days may be deducted from annual vacation.

g. Termination of Employment

i. Fractional vacations

When the employment relationship terminates for any reason (except a justified dismissal) before the completion of one year of service, the worker is entitled to receive an indemnity commonly called "fractional vacation," which is equal to the proportional part of the annual payment of vacation wages and the vacation bonus corresponding to the months of service actually completed in that year.[272] The minimum amount of fractional vacation is approximately two days' wages for one complete month of service.

ii. Vacations earned but not taken when employment ends

When the employment relationship terminates for any reason, and the worker has not taken accrued vacation days, the employer must pay in full the compensation corresponding to the accrued vacation time and the respective vacation bonus.[273]

iii. Termination notice period

Vacation time may not be taken during the termination notice period.[274]

---

[271] *Id.* arts. 232, 233.

[272] *Id.* art. 225.

[273] *Id.* art. 224.

[274] *Id.* art. 231. For a discussion of termination notice periods, see I.F.2., above.

2. *Maternity Leave*

Female workers are entitled to maternity leave consisting of 12 weeks prior to birth and 12 weeks after, for a total of 24 weeks.[275] Maternity leave is counted as actual service for the purposes of determining the worker's seniority.[276]

If the prenatal leave is not fully utilized, the remaining portion is added to the postnatal leave.[277] If a birth occurs after the expected date, the prenatal leave period is extended to the date of birth, but the postnatal leave is not reduced.[278] Additionally, if a worker seeks to take her accrued vacation time immediately after maternity leave, the employer must allow it.[279]

Female workers who adopt a child younger than three years of age are entitled to 10 weeks of maternity leave.[280] The employer does not pay the employee's wages during the maternity leave; wages during maternity leave are paid by the social security system. The social security system only pays 2/3 of the employee's ordinary salary. Although the Social Security Law does not provide any indemnities in the event of adoption, it is possible to request that the employer continue paying the worker her ordinary wage during the 10-week leave period.

D. Special Cases

1. *Minors*

The employment of minors younger than 18 years of age is subject to the following wage and hour restrictions:[281]

- they may work only during the hours between 6:00 a.m. and 7 p.m.;[282]

---

[275] Labor Law, art. 385.
[276] *Id.* art. 389.
[277] *Id.* art. 386.
[278] *Id.* art. 388.
[279] *Id.* art. 389.
[280] *Id.* art. 387.
[281] For additional restrictions on the employment of minors, see I.G.1., above.
[282] Labor Law, art. 257.

- their compensation may not be based on units of production, tasks, piecework, or commission;[283]
- they must be allowed to take their employment vacation during school vacation periods;[284] and
- they are entitled to such job flexibility as the employer can allow, in order to enable them to pursue their primary education, or attend professional or technical schools.

Minors younger than 16 years of age are limited to a maximum workday of six hours, divided into two periods of no more than four hours. There must be a mandatory rest period of at least two hours between the two periods, during which time the minor must leave the work premises. Minors younger than age 16 may not work more than 30 hours per week.[285]

2. *Apprentices*

The Labor Law provides that the time required for an apprenticeship is to be considered part of the workday.[286]

3. *Domestic Workers*

a. *Christmas Bonus*

Domestic workers are entitled to a Christmas bonus,[287] which must be paid during the first 15 days of December. The bonus is calculated on the basis of a calendar year and is payable in the following amounts:

- after three months of service, five days' wages;
- after six months of service, 10 days' wages; and
- after nine months of service, 15 days' wages.

---

[283]*Id.* art. 259.

[284]*Id.* art. 260.

[285]*Id.* art. 254.

[286]*Id.* art. 271. For a definition and additional discussion of apprenticeships, see I.G.2., above.

[287]Labor Law, art. 278. For a definition and additional discussion of domestic worker employment, see I.G.3., above.

b. Rest Days

Domestic workers are entitled to at least one day of rest per week.[288]

c. Vacations

The annual paid vacation for domestic workers is 15 consecutive days.[289] Unlike paid vacation for other types of workers, consecutive vacation days for domestic workers include weekly rest days and holidays. Also, none of the Labor Law's provisions on fractional vacations apply to domestic workers.

4. Motorcycle Messengers

Motorcycle messengers are defined as those who perform services as errand boys, messengers, or other similar activities, regardless of whether they own the vehicles with which they conduct their activities.[290] Motorcycle messengers are entitled to receive the following benefits from their employers:

- *Vehicle Maintenance Expenses*: When the parties are unable to agree on vehicle maintenance expenses, the amount is established by the Labor Ministry and the Ministry of Transport and Communications.
- *Fuel Expenses Incurred in the Performance of the Work*: In the absence of agreement between the parties, the amount is established by the appropriate authorities.
- *Casualty and Civil Liability Insurance*: This insurance must cover both the operator and the vehicle (in amounts established by the appropriate authorities).
- *Uniforms and Equipment*: The employer must supply uniforms, helmets, and other safety gear required for performance of their work.

---

[288]Labor Law, art. 276.
[289]*Id.* art. 277.
[290]*Id.* arts. 371–373.

VI. ANTIDISCRIMINATION

Venezuelan law prohibits all employment discrimination based on age, sex, race, marital status, religion, political affiliation, social status, or criminal record.[291] Unlawful employment discrimination includes offers of employment, which are expressly prohibited from containing discriminatory job descriptions.

The Labor Law also provides special preferences and protections for heads of family, disabled workers, and women. These provisions are summarized below.

A. Heads of Family

Employers are obliged to give preference in hiring to heads of family for up to a total of 75 percent of their workers, with other qualifications being equal.[292]

B. Handicapped Workers

The Labor Law expressly recognizes the right of the handicapped to be employed in order to provide for their basic subsistence.[293]

Provisions specifying the terms and conditions for hiring the handicapped will be issued at a later date by the National Executive. In order to promote the employment of handicapped persons, the Labor Law requires the state to give tax and financing incentives (without specifying their type) to:

- companies of handicapped persons;
- companies that have established departments composed of handicapped workers; and
- enterprises that encourage in any fashion the employment, training, rehabilitation, and readjustment of the handicapped.

There are no incentives currently in place.

[291] *Id.* art. 26. The Labor Law does not expressly prohibit employment discrimination based on the nationality of the worker.

[292] Labor Law, art. 29.

[293] *Id.* arts. 375–378.

C. Women

The Labor Law contains a special Chapter devoted to the protection of maternity and family that essentially governs the status of pregnant women.[294] In addition, the law provides that female workers are entitled to all of the same rights as male workers, and may not be subject to discrimination or differences in regard to wages or other employment conditions. The law further provides that regulations or special resolutions may establish rules tending to protect maternity and the family where work is hazardous, unhealthy, or strenuous. No such regulations have been implemented yet.

1. *Pregnancy Test*

The Labor Law prohibits employers from requiring female job applicants to undergo medical or laboratory exams, or to require medical certificates that they are not pregnant.[295] However, women may demand a pregnancy test whenever they wish to be protected by provisions of the Labor Law relating to pregnancy.

2. *Protection for Women Who Work While Pregnant*

A pregnant woman may not be transferred from her position unless the business requires such a transfer, and the transfer does not impair her pregnancy.[296] In addition, a pregnant woman's wages may not be reduced, nor may other terms of her employment be altered to her disadvantage.

Pregnant women may be excused from performing tasks that require significant physical effort or that might otherwise produce an abortion or impair the normal development of the fetus. A woman's exercise of her right to be excused from such work may not affect the terms of her employment in any way.

---

[294] *Id.* arts. 379, 380.
[295] *Id.*
[296] *Id.* arts. 382, 383.

3. *Bar Against Dismissal*

A prohibition against dismissal applies to female workers during their entire pregnancy and until one year after giving birth.[297]

If a woman adopts a child younger than three years of age, the prohibition will apply during the year following the adoption.

4. *Maternity Leave*

Female workers are entitled to prenatal and postnatal maternity leave, up to a total of 24 weeks.[298] Female workers who adopt a child are entitled to 10-weeks' leave.

5. *Rest During the Nursing Period*

If the employer has established a day care center for workers,[299] female workers are entitled to two rest periods per day of one-half hour each, for breastfeeding their children at the center.[300] In the absence of a day care center, breastfeeding mothers are entitled to two rest periods per day, of one hour each.

VII. OCCUPATIONAL SAFETY AND HEALTH AND WORKERS' COMPENSATION

A. Occupational Safety and Health

Safety and health in the workplace are governed primarily by the Labor Law of Occupational Health and Safety. The Labor Law also contains provisions relating to worker hygiene and safety.

1. *The Labor Law of Occupational Health and Safety*

The Labor Law of Occupational Health and Safety (Health and Safety Law)[301] protects the physical and mental health of workers and regulates the prevention of work-related accidents and ill-

---

[297] *Id.* arts. 384, 387.

[298] *Id.* arts. 385, 390. For a detailed discussion of maternity leave, see V.C.2., above.

[299] See VIII.B.2. below.

[300] Labor Law, art. 393.

[301] Published in the Official Gazette No. 3,850 Extraordinary (July 18, 1986).

nesses. The Health and Safety Law essentially is an employer's liability act, the chief characteristics of which are to impose considerable regulation and, more importantly, to establish severe criminal and civil penalties, including imprisonment, for employers and company officials who are found responsible for the work-related death or injury of workers.

a. Scope and Enforcement

The Health and Safety Law applies to all public and private sector employers and to all full and part-time workers, with the exception of members of the Armed Forces and other State Security Forces such as the police. Although the Law extends to commercial and service establishments, it is aimed principally at regulating industrial, agricultural, and livestock workplaces.

Enforcement of the Health and Safety Law generally is accorded to the National Prevention Institute, Health and Job Safety (Health and Safety Institute). However, prison terms contemplated by the Law may be imposed only by the criminal courts, and labor courts have jurisdiction over death and disability benefits.

The Health and Safety Law requires every industrial, agricultural, and livestock business to establish a Health and Safety Committee composed of industrial safety technicians and representatives of management and labor. The purpose of the Health and Safety Committee is to monitor the working conditions and environment in each establishment in order to ensure compliance with the Health and Safety Law, and to assist and advise both employers and workers on occupational accident and illness prevention programs.

b. Administrative Regulation

The Health and Safety Institute has the authority to approve all projects involving new work methods and stations, or the redesign thereof. If the Institute requires extensive changes to plans submitted, the employer may take an administrative appeal from the decision.

The operating condition and safety features of machinery and equipment intended for use in the industrial, agricultural, or service sectors also are subject to Institute approval and control, whether manufactured locally or imported. Moreover, manufacturers and importers of machinery must guarantee easy access to sufficient supplies of spare parts for the maintenance of safety features.

The Health and Safety Law also authorizes the Institute to establish a National Registry of Toxic Substances, and requires employers to notify the Institute of the introduction into production and service processes of any new substances that, due to their chemical nature, toxicity, or physical condition, could damage workers' health. Importers of substances that represent a potential health hazard to workers must obtain a certificate of unrestricted sale in the country of origin.

c. *Employer Obligations*

No worker may be exposed to the action of physical agents, ergonomic conditions (i.e., the adaptation of the work environment to the worker), psychosocial risks, or the presence of chemical, biological, or other agents without first being alerted by the employer in writing and by any other necessary means, of the nature of the risk and the potential health damage, and being instructed on the means to prevent any damage. Warning by "other necessary means" probably is intended to ensure that all workers receive adequate information of the risks involved.

Any person conspiring or attempting to minimize the danger of any of the mentioned risks, thereby creating a false sense of security in the mind of a worker, is deemed guilty of intentionally violating the Health and Safety Law for profit purposes.

It is not clear whether the obligation to alert extends to uncertain and controversial risks, the extent and nature of which are not yet fully known, such as the much-debated risk to pregnant women working exposed to video screens. This could become an important issue in determining the liability of employers for progressive illnesses caused by exposure to elements in the workplace that are not detected or otherwise detectable at the time of exposure.

The Health and Safety Law imposes a number of additional obligations on the employer, the most significant of which are the following:

- reporting work-related illnesses and accidents to the Health and Safety Institute;[302]
- educating workers on occupational health and safety;
- ensuring that workers in industrial, agricultural, and live-stock establishments have access to medical attention; and
- receiving written suggestions and complaints of infractions of the Health and Safety Law from workers and taking appropriate action where required.

Workers who exercise their right to make safety-related suggestions or complaints may not be dismissed or otherwise penalized for having done so. Although the employer's duty to take action is clear in the case of infractions, there would not appear to be any corresponding duty to implement suggestions that are neither reasonable nor cost effective.

d. Employer Sanctions

i. Prison terms

Employers that violate the Health and Safety Law with full knowledge that the safety of workers will be affected, may be held criminally liable for their conduct and sentenced to prison if a worker's death or injury is attributed to the violation. Where the employer is a corporation, the legal representative, administrator, agent, or manager deemed responsible for the violation will be tried and, if found guilty, sentenced to prison. The length of prison terms range from two years for the partial temporary disability of a worker to six years for complete permanent disability. In the event of a worker's death, the penalty is seven to eight years' imprisonment.

Although the purpose of these criminal penalties may be worthy of praise, the provisions are seriously flawed by the inflexibility of their application. The Health and Safety Law does not distinguish between injuries or deaths caused by work-related accidents and those produced directly or indirectly by exposure to

[302]For additional reporting requirements, see VII.A.2.c., below.

toxic substances. As a result, a worker's death or injury from occupational illness potentially could expose an employer to the sanction of imprisonment.

ii. Death and disability benefits

In addition to prison terms, the Health and Safety Law also requires at-fault employers to pay death and disability benefits, the amount of which correspond to the severity of the case. For example, should a worker be killed in an industrial accident as a result of the willful failure of his or her employer to comply with the Health and Safety Law, the employer, in addition to any criminal penalty, is required to pay to the worker's beneficiaries an amount equal to five years' wages. Because the Health and Safety Law does not repeal the Labor Law or the Social Security Law, it is arguable that a worker (or his or her lawful beneficiaries, in the case of the worker's death) would be entitled to receive both the benefits under the Health and Safety Law as well as those available from the government under the Social Security Law, and from the employer, under the Labor Law.[303]

iii. Penalties for mental and emotional disturbance

If an occupational accident or illness results in disfigurement or disease, which, in turn, causes mental or emotional disturbance beyond the simple loss of the worker's ability to earn a living, the employer may be sentenced to five years' imprisonment and required to pay the employee an indemnity equal to five years' wages.

iv. Exoneration from liability

If the death or injury of a worker is caused by an employment-related accident, as opposed to an occupational illness, the employer (or corporate officials), may be exonerated from liability if the accident (a) resulted from an act of God, or (b) was caused knowingly by the worker's own conduct.

---

[303]See VII.B., below.

v. Fines and plant closures

In the event that the Health and Safety Institute becomes aware of an imminent danger or a prejudicial situation in the workplace that requires correction, it may, independent of the penalties discussed above, take the following actions:

- close the business establishment permanently or temporarily;
- levy a fine on the employer ranging from VEB 5,000 to VEB 500,000; and/or
- suspend the activity or production of the business establishment partially or totally, and order the employer to pay workers' salaries during the suspension period.

e. Worker Obligations and Sanctions for Noncompliance

The Health and Safety Law requires workers to use and maintain in good condition the safety devices provided by the employer, report any loss or damage to safety devices, and observe the health and safety notices posted in the workplace. The only sanction provided in the Health and Safety Law for failure to comply with these obligations is an admonishment from the Health and Safety Committee. However, under the Labor Law, omissions and carelessness of a worker, which affect industrial health and safety in the workplace, constitute just cause for dismissal. In addition, the Health and Safety Law expressly provides for the lawful dismissal of a worker who intentionally destroys safety devices or removes them from the workplace.

2. Labor Law Regulation of Hygiene and Safety in the Workplace

a. Regulatory Powers

The National Executive may establish specific standards of hygiene and safety for all kinds of work.[304] The President has not established any such standards yet.

[304]Labor Law, art. 236.

b. Warning of Workplace Hazards

As with the Health and Safety Law, the Labor Law requires employers to warn workers who are exposed to physical hazards, ergonomic conditions, psychosocial risks, or chemical, biological, or other agents.[305] Preferably, the warning should be in writing and must address the following topics:

- the nature of the hazards, risks, or agents to which the worker is subjected;
- the harm that such hazards, conditions, or agents may cause to the worker's health; and
- measures that will protect the workers' health.

c. Notice of Work-Related Accidents and Illnesses

The employer is obligated to notify the Labor Inspector's Office of any employment accident or work-related illness within four calendar days of the date on which the accident occurred or the illness was diagnosed.[306]

d. Meals

Workers are not permitted to eat in their workplace (i.e., a specific area of the company where work is performed), except in those cases where it is not possible for them to leave.[307]

e. Chairs for Workers

In retail establishments open to the public (i.e., stores, shops, or markets), the employer must maintain a sufficient number of chairs to be used by workers during work breaks. Industrial establishments also must comply with this obligation where it is compatible with the nature of the work performed.[308]

---

[305] *Id.* art. 237.
[306] *Id.* art. 565. See also VII.A.1.c., above.
[307] Labor Law, art. 238.
[308] *Id.* art. 239.

B. Workers' Compensation

The provisions discussed in this section apply only to employment accidents and work-related illnesses of workers who are not governed by the Law of Mandatory Social Security.[309]

1. Benefits

The Labor Law provides benefits in the form of medical services and disability compensation to covered workers who suffer an employment accident or work-related illness. In the event of a worker's death, the law requires the employer to pay funeral expenses and compensation to the worker's relatives.

a. Medical Services

Workers must be reimbursed by the employer for medical attention and surgical or pharmaceutical services, in amounts up to five times the monthly minimum wage,[310] in all cases of employment accidents or occupational illnesses.

b. Disability Benefits

i. Permanent total disability

A worker who suffers total and permanent disability is entitled to a one-time compensation payment equal to two years' wages, subject to a maximum limit of 25 times the monthly minimum wage.[311]

ii. Temporary total disability

The compensation for temporary total disability is a single payment equal to the wages for the period of the disability, with a maximum limit of one year's wages.[312]

---

[309] For a discussion of the social security program, see VIII.A.1., below.

[310] For an explanation of the minimum wage, see V.A.1.d., above.

[311] Labor Law, art. 571.

[312] *Id.* art. 573.

iii. Permanent partial disability

Compensation for a permanent partial disability is based on the reduction in the worker's earning capacity, subject to a maximum limit equal to the lesser of one year's wages, or 15 times the monthly minimum wage.[313]

iv. Temporary partial disability

Compensation for a temporary partial disability is based on the worker's wages, the degree of disability, and the duration of the disability.[314]

c. Death Benefits[315]

If a worker's death is caused by an employment accident or work-related illness, the employer must pay funeral expenses, up to a maximum of five times the minimum wage. In addition, the employer must pay a death benefit to the relatives of the deceased worker.[316]

2. Basis for Calculation

Any compensation owed to a worker as a result of an employment accident or work-related illness is calculated on the basis of the ordinary wage[317] he or she would have been entitled to on the date that the accident occurred or the illness was diagnosed. For workers whose wages are based on units of production or tasks,[318] the basis for calculation is the average wage earned by the worker in the three months immediately preceding the accident or the date of the worker's inability to work due to illness.[319]

---

[313]*Id.*

[314]*Id.* art. 574.

[315]*Id.* arts. 567–570.

[316]The amount and conditions for payment of this benefit are the same as those applicable to benefits paid at the death of a worker under other circumstances. See I.F.5.a.v., above.

[317]See V.A.1.b., above.

[318]See V.A.1.h.iii., above.

[319]Labor Law, arts. 566, 575, and 576.

VIII. PENSIONS AND BENEFITS

A. Pensions, Health, and Disability Benefits

There is a public pension, health, and disability program administered by the National Government and funded by social security contributions.

1. Social Security System

The Law of Mandatory Social Security provides employees with an indemnity in case of accidents, illness, maternity, temporary and partial disability, marriage, age, death, and other protected circumstances. In the event that any of these circumstances occur, the social security system will pay an indemnity in accordance with the provisions set forth therein. The Law of Mandatory Social Security covers the vast majority of workers subject to the Labor Law.

2. Social Security Contributions

Both employers and employees must contribute monthly to the Venezuelan Social Security Institute (IVSS). The employer is required to withhold and pay the employee's contributions. All contributions are computed as a percentage of the employee's normal salary.

Companies must register with the IVSS within three working days of beginning activities. Companies must also register all their employees with the IVSS within three working days of the employee's hiring.

B. Other Benefits

1. Unemployment Insurance

Under applicable regulations, the social unemployment insurance is funded by mandatory contributions paid by the employer and the worker, which are calculated based upon the employee's compensation. Employers must contribute an amount equal to 2 percent of the employee's normal salary to unemployment insurance and must withhold and pay 0.5 percent of the employee's salary for these purposes. The maximum taxable base is 20 minimum monthly salaries.

This contribution must be made by the employer within the first three days of each month.

2. *Day Care Centers*

Employers with more than 20 workers are required to maintain day care centers staffed by qualified and specialized personnel.[320] Day care centers are established so that workers (both men and women) can leave their children during the workday. Employers must agree with the Labor Ministry on the installation and operation of a day care center in a location near to the workplace, or must pay outside institutions to provide day care services for the company's workers.[321]

The Labor Law does not indicate at what age children are entitled to use the centers, or whether a minimum number of children are necessary to establish a center. However, the Regulations to the Labor Law set forth minimum requirements for the establishment and operation of day care centers.

The Labor Law expressly provides that day care benefits are not considered part of ordinary wages.

3. *Transportation*

Employers must furnish free transportation to their workers where the work premises are located 30 kilometers or more from the nearest populated area.[322] As a general rule, where employers are required to provide transportation, one-half of the normal transportation time is taken into account as part of the workday.[323]

---

[320]*Id.* arts. 391–393.
[321]*Id.* art. 392.
[322]*Id.* art. 240.
[323]See V.B.1.a., above.

4. *Housing, Education, and Medical Care*

a. Housing Policy Law

As provided under applicable regulations, mandatory contributions made to housing funds are deposited in a saving fund, which, in turn, offers low-interest housing loans to employees.

The employer must contribute an amount equal to 2 percent of the employee's normal salary and is required to withhold and pay an amount equal to 1 percent of the employee's salary.

b. Employers With More Than 200 Workers

Any employer that employs more than 200 workers has a duty to grant a scholarship to one out of each 200 workers (or to a child of the worker) for technical, industrial, or practical studies related to his or her trade.[324]

c. Employers With More Than 500 Workers

Employers that typically maintain more than 500 workers at work sites more than 50 kilometers from the nearest populated area must do the following:

- provide the workers and their immediate family with clean housing of at least 10 square meters per person;
- maintain a first aid station at the employer's expense; and
- provide, at the employer's expense, one physician and one pharmacist for each 400 workers, or fraction greater than 200.[325]

d. Employers With More Than 1,000 Workers

Employers that hire more than 1,000 workers must do the following:

- maintain facilities for the basic education of the children of their workers, where none exist in the vicinity of the work premises; and

[324] Labor Law, art. 245.
[325] *Id.* arts. 241, 242.

- maintain a health clinic equipped with everything necessary for medical, surgical, or pharmaceutical care, as determined by the health authorities, where the workers are located more than 100 kilometers from a town with hospital services, or between 50 and 100 kilometers from a town with hospital services, but no adequate and reliable means of transportation.

IX. IMMIGRATION

A. Language and Nationality

1. Spanish Language

The Labor Law requires employers to give all orders and instructions in the Spanish language.[326]

2. Positions Reserved to Venezuelans

The following positions are reserved to Venezuelans: industrial relations managers; personnel managers; ship and airplane captains; foremen and analogous positions.[327] In this regard, workers who are naturalized Venezuelans have the same rights as other Venezuelans.[328]

3. Number and Compensation of Foreign Workers

Under the Labor Law, at least 90 percent of employees and 90 percent of laborers must be Venezuelan.[329] Furthermore, the total compensation paid to foreign employees and laborers is limited to a maximum of 20 percent of the total paid to each category of workers. These limits apply on a company basis.

The Labor Law authorizes the Labor Ministry to create temporary exceptions to the limits on foreign workers in the following cases:

---

[326] *Id.* art. 19.
[327] *Id.* art. 20.
[328] Labor Law Statement of Purposes.
[329] Labor Law, arts. 27, 28.

- the activity requires special technical knowledge and Venezuelans are not available;
- the Minister verifies that there is insufficient Venezuelan personnel to meet the demand for a particular kind of work;
- the foreign persons are immigrants under the control of or contracted by the National Government;
- the foreign persons are refugees; or
- the employer is a small- or medium-sized company.

If foreign personnel are employed, preference must be given to the following individuals:

- those who have children born in Venezuela,
- those who are married to Venezuelans,
- those who are domiciled in Venezuela, or
- those who have been resident in Venezuela the longest.[330]

B. Visas[331]

Among the types of visas available to foreigners are business and labor visas, which can be obtained at any Venezuelan Consulate.[332]

1. Business Visas

Business visas are issued to foreigners who travel to Venezuela to engage in commercial activities or to those who will render services as technical, cultural, or scientific advisors. A business visa is valid for one year from the date of issuance and allows multiple entries into the country.

---

[330]*Id.* art. 30.

[331]A new Immigration Law, providing for new categorization of migrating foreigners, was enacted on May 4, 2004. However, the regulations defining the requirements and processes for admission, entry, permanence, exit, and re-entry applicable to each category, as well as the establishment of subcategories, have not been issued by the National Executive to the date of preparation of this chapter. Thus, the information herein contained is consistent with prior law and current practice but likely will change in the near future.

[332]Regulations pertaining to the issuance of visas to foreigners are found in Joint Resolutions Nos. 072 and 62 of the Ministries of Internal Affairs and Foreign Affairs (Apr. 28, 1989), published in the Official Gazette No. 34,211 (May 3, 1989).

2. *Labor Visas*

Labor visas are issued to foreign employees who are hired by companies or individuals domiciled in Venezuela to render services in the country. To this extent, a company hiring a foreigner must submit an application to the appropriate administrative agency (Labor Ministry and the ONI-DEX (Judicial Ministry, Immigration department)), which must be accompanied by a notarized statement guaranteeing payment of any expense associated with the employee's permanence in and departure from the country. The consular authority also may require the presentation of other documents, including criminal records. A labor visa is valid for one year from the date of issuance; it is renewable and allows multiple entries.

Part 4

International Organizations

PART 5

Multinational Corporations